THE HOLOCAUST

STUDIES IN JEWISH HISTORY
Jehuda Reinharz, General Editor

The Holocaust

The Fate of European Jewry, 1932-1945

LENI YAHIL

Translated from the Hebrew by
Ina Friedman and Haya Galai

New York · Oxford
OXFORD UNIVERSITY PRESS
1990

Oxford University Press

Oxford   New York   Toronto
Delhi   Bombay   Calcutta   Madras   Karachi
Petaling Jaya   Singapore   Hong Kong   Tokyo
Nairobi   Dar es Salaam   Cape Town
Melbourne   Auckland

and associated companies in
Berlin   Ibadan

Originally published in Hebrew by Schocken Publishing House Ltd.
Copyright © 1987 by Schocken Publishing House Ltd., Tel Aviv,
and Yad Vashem, Jerusalem

English edition copyright © 1990 by Oxford University Press, Inc.

Published by Oxford University Press, Inc.,
200 Madison Avenue, New York, New York, 10016

Oxford is a registered trademark of Oxford University Press

Library of Congress Cataloging-in-Publication Data
Yahil, Leni.
[Sho 'ah. English]
The Holocaust : the fate of European Jewry, 1932–1945 / Leni Yahil;
translated from the Hebrew by Ina Friedman and Haya Galai.
p.   cm. — (Studies in Jewish history)
Translation of: ha-Sho 'ah.
Includes bibliographical references.
ISBN 0-19-504522-X
1. Holocaust, Jewish (1939–1945)   2. Jews—Germany—
History—1933–1945.   3. Germany—Ethnic relations.
I. Title.   II. Series.
D804.3.Y3413   1990
940.53'18—dc20   89-37750

9 8 7 6 5 4 3 2 1

Printed in the United States of America
on acid-free paper

IN MEMORIAM

My husband, Chaim Yahil
Valašské Meziříčí, 1905–Jerusalem, 1974
Our son, Jonathan, first lieutenant in IDF
Tel Aviv, 1945–fell in Jerusalem, June 1967

Preface

This book represents the English version of the original Hebrew edition published in Israel jointly by Schocken Publishing House and Yad Vashem. To render the book in translation it was necessary to abridge to some extent the text of the original two volumes by deleting occasionally illuminating details and shortening extensive descriptions without, however, sacrificing specific information or affecting the overall meaning. I have attempted to correct errors that crept into the Hebrew edition, to include important new results of recent research and, in particular, to update the bibliography. I am grateful to Oxford University Press for showing so much understanding of the difficulties involved in this time-consuming process.

To the Jacob and Clara Egit Foundation for Holocaust and Jewish Resistance Literature (Canada) and The Lucius N. L. Littauer Foundation (New York) I am indebted for financial support permitting the translation of the book into English. For the difficult task of translating the multifaceted and emotionally taxing text, I thank Ina Friedman (Jerusalem) and Haya Galai (Beer Sheva).

Dina Cohen (Jerusalem) diligently copied the revised English version of the notes and Elisheva Shaul (Yad Vashem) organized the bibliography, including the transliteration of titles from Hebrew and Yiddish sources, and helped with proofreading. The index was compiled by Hillel Wiseberg. My sincere gratitude goes to all of them. I also wish to repeat my thanks to my friend Israel Gutman, who supported my work on the book since its inception and contributed the chapter on the armed struggle of the Jews in Nazi-occupied countries.

I am very grateful for the useful cooperation and friendly relations with my freelance copy editor, Andrew Yockers, and Oxford's Associate Editor Henry Krawitz, who worked so patiently and conscientiously in preparing the book for production, adapting the text to American stylistic conventions. With the completion of this task, I wish to express my heartfelt thanks to my friend Jehuda Reinharz, General Editor of the series Studies in Jewish History, whose firm support was a source of constant encouragement through all the stages of the English edition, and to Nancy Lane, Senior Editor at Oxford, for her sympathetic and constant interest, from the initial decision to publish an English-language version of the book to its actual appearance.

My work on this book started about twenty years ago. During this period, Holocaust research and interpretation have undergone many changes, which have been expressed in many different ways. I do hope that my somewhat audacious undertaking—to provide a kind of historical overview—will be of interest to those in the English-speaking world who feel, as I do, that it is our duty to confront this cataclysmic event of our time.

Jerusalem   L. Y.
February 1990

Contents

THE HOLOCAUST

Only the ones who remember always grow as living plants.
Only the ones who remember live: grow almost forever.

רק הזוכרים צומחים תמיד צמיחה חיה.
רק הזוכרים חיים: צומחים כמעט לעד.

Simon Halkin

Introduction

The events and experiences of the Holocaust have been portrayed in thousands of memoirs and testimonies. Countless diaries, letters, newspapers, and other documents have been collected and are piled up in the institutions of research and remembrance as well as in the courts that have tried war criminals—the shelves of all these archives comprise miles of documentation. Historical research has broadened in scope, divided into specializations, and delved deeper into the subject. The publication of sources and documents has burgeoned, and countless books and articles about general and specific aspects of the Holocaust have been written in any number of languages. The psychological and physical effects of the suffering on Holocaust survivors and their offspring are even a subject of health research, and the period is also being dealt with from the standpoint of sociology and economics. Fiction, poetry, and art from the Holocaust and post-Holocaust periods have expressed the impact of the experience—for many these were the only way that they could confront and convey the terrors of the time. And in terms of confronting the Holocaust, theater and films have, of course, played a signal role. Ever since World War II, clerics, philosophers, and other intellectuals—both Jewish and Christian—have continuously been trying to articulate the meaning of the Holocaust and the conclusions to be drawn from it. It seems the farther away we get from that war, the greater the urge to deal with the Holocaust and inquire into its implications. This cataclysm stands out among the revolutionary events of the twentieth century as a focal phenomenon from both the broad human and the specifically Jewish point of view. Hitler's aim of annihilating the Jewish people was the point of departure for defining the crime of genocide—a concept that some hold to be the moral and political epitome of World War II. *Auschwitz* has become a widely known symbol, but like any symbol that has gained political currency, this one, too, is liable to be counterfeited. Thus, parties who—for whatever reason—wish to deny the Holocaust ever took place invoke the concept summed up in the word *Auschwitz* to argue that no such thing ever happened, that millions of people were never killed in gas chambers or incinerated in crematoria, that all this is a fabrication conceived by the Jews to force the world to acquiesce in the establishment of the "Zionist state." These claims ring like a contemporary variation on the medieval blood libel, with a political charge replacing the original accusations that were based on deprecation of the Jewish faith.

When World War II ended, we believed that anti-Semitism had run its course—both as theory and practice—and that the absurdity of its claims had been proved. But in the years that followed, we came to realize that this was far from so. The disparity that had existed for centuries between the Jews and other peoples began to take on a new form: with the emergence of the Jewish national and political entity in the State of Israel, the disparity was now expressed in the national and political clash between that sovereign framework and the surrounding Arab world. Borrowing elements from Soviet Communist rhetoric, the new formula denounced Zionism and the State of Israel as vehicles of racism and capitalist imperialism.

In the years after this book was first written, from 1971 to 1980, debate broke out—mainly with, and among, German historians—about how the Nazis came to pursue the Final Solution. Was it a premeditated action or did the general circumstances of the war act as a catalyst in bringing it about? It is as a consequence of this debate between the "intentionalists" and the "functionalists" that the place of the Holocaust in contemporary history, especially contemporary German history, has been put forward for scrutiny.[1] The other controversial question that has recently been raised is whether the Holocaust should be viewed as a unique and pivotal event or should be depicted and explained as one of the more brutal phenomena engendered by Nazi rule and the war.[2] There is no explicit reference to these debates herein; nevertheless, readers will readily find answers to the questions raised.

Another debate that has been going on since World War II is about the degree to which racist anti-Semitism was born out of the hatred of Jews in the Middle Ages; it is being pursued by the Christian churches themselves as part of the examination of anti-Semitism as a social, psychological, and historical phenomenon. For the first time hatred of the Jews, in its various forms, has become the subject of inquiry by Jews and non-Jews alike, for it has become clear that such hatred not only imperils Jews but also corrupts those who bear them enmity.

Persecution and pogroms have been long-standing phenomena in the annals of the Jews, and their scope has often accorded Jewish history the flavor of martyrology. The historian Shimon Bernfeld, author of *Sefer ha-Dimaot* (The Book of Tears), who catalogued the history of Jewish suffering as passed down in legends, prayers, and other Jewish testimonies, wrote:

> When I was working on *The Book of Tears*, I sometimes cried like a child. My whole body quaked. And occasionally I had to stop in the middle of work out of sheer anger. —Think about it: an entire great and ancient nation that has so enriched mankind's

treasury of science and spirit has all the torments in the world inflicted upon it, torments of the flesh and of the soul. And all because the nation is devoted to the Torah of its God and refuses to renounce its truths.[3]

It was not for their faith that the Jews were persecuted in Hitler's day—that is precisely why the extermination campaign astounded the Jews and the rest of the world. It was as if forces of hatred and destruction unparalleled in recent history—forces whose potency was unsuspected by the peoples of the so-called enlightened world—had burst forth from the depths of the human soul.

In light of the facts uncovered after World War II, attempts were made to argue that the Holocaust was a new phenomenon in no way related to the recent past. After all, following their struggle for emancipation, hadn't the Jews been granted almost full equal rights? It was further argued that the religious motives that had prompted the violent persecution of the Jews in the Middle Ages had meanwhile been subverted. Thus, not only was the Holocaust incongruent with any acceptable rational standard but it was not perceived as a product of historical continuity.[4] How, then, is a Jew—or anyone else, for that matter—to relate to this historical aberration?

Historical continuity manifests itself in men's lives on two planes: as experience and as perception. Under conditions not particularly marked by turmoil, the transfer from past to present is a natural process, an experience of continuity to which we give little or no thought. But perception manifests itself as the historical awareness through which man comprehends and interprets his present condition. Neither of these approaches was applicable to the Holocaust, which descended on the Jews of Europe like the burning lava of a volcano and swamped their world to the point where it could no longer sustain normal continuity. In vain that generation turned to the past to find meaning in the present. Even the Zionists—who were conscious of the crisis threatening Diaspora Jewry—did not think in terms of the extermination of European Jewry.

After World War II researchers slowly began to uncover the historical roots of the tragedy. So, too, historians slowly began to reweave the skein of thought that had been spun in Europe since the French Revolution but had become, after World War I, snarled in the political and economic imbroglio out of which Hitler rose to power. Jews and non-Jews began to admit that they had failed to read the signs of the times or to construe their overt and latent implications.

Once the shock had subsided, it gave way to a need to contend with the Holocaust and its outcome. The initial reaction of the Jews, like that of other peoples, was to take action, namely, the historic action of establishing the State of Israel. Thus, destruction unparalleled in history was contrasted with a creation unparalleled in history. The Jewish philosopher Emil L. Fackenheim, whose thinking centers on the philosophical and theological facets of the Holocaust, has argued that one cannot prove a cause-and-effect relationship between these two signal events:

Why were the survivors not desperate to stay away from Palestine rather than reach it—the one place on earth which would tie them inescapably to a Jewish destiny? . . .

Why did the Zionist leadership rise from vacillation to resoluteness rather than simply disintegrate? . . . The State of Israel after the Holocaust may be viewed as a near-necessity, yet, with equal justice, as a near-impossibility.

. . . To seek a *cause* or a *meaning* is one thing, to give a *response* is another. . . . The heart of every *authentic* response to the Holocaust . . . is a commitment to the autonomy and security of the State of Israel.[5]

From the outset Zionism was by its very nature a revolutionary movement. Its visionaries, espousers, and executors rejected the historical reality of Diaspora life, void as it was of political independence, and laid the foundations of an independent political future for the Jewish people in their own land. The establishment of the State of Israel was the consummate achievement of this revolutionary process. Since 1948 a new historical reality with a continuity of its own has been evolving, and it is distinguished from the pre-Holocaust life of European Jewry by a new experience and consciousness. A sense of continuity with the past exists only in the lives of the generation of founding fathers who came to Palestine before or after the Hitler era, whereas the generation that has come of age in Israel has difficulty in seeking its roots in the past. For this generation, the tie with the Diaspora is not one of actual continuity; at most, it is a tie built on tradition. Thus, young Israelis who do not shrink from confronting the Holocaust are faced with a twofold difficulty: (1) they must comprehend a situation that is unfamiliar to them from their own experience, one that is radically different from the circumstances of their own lives and that has no direct bearing on their own reality in the present; and (2) they must contend with the aberrant and abysmal nature of the component events of the Holocaust. It is this multiple foreignness that creates for Israeli youth their difficulty in confronting the Holocaust and identifying with its victims.

Living beside one another in the State of Israel are fathers and sons, immigrants, young and old, many of whom did not come from Europe and did not live through its terrors. To the natural tension between the generations we must therefore add the difference in the formative experience of those who left the Diaspora for Palestine (or, later, Israel) and those who grew up in the country. Even in the older generation, a barrier exists between those who came from Europe prior to the Holocaust and those who came after it. In a certain sense both are survivors. Even those who did not personally experience the crucible of blood lost, however, family and friends and saw their communities destroyed; how much more deeply are the scars of those days etched on the souls of those who personally experienced the events. The generation that knew the Diaspora at firsthand is also burdened by a sense of guilt for not having been able to rescue the doomed.

The major question facing all—fathers and sons—is: Why were the Jews of Europe abandoned to their fate? The search for an answer has led in various directions, and responsibility has been placed on a number of parties, above all the Nazis and their minions. Yet charges have also been laid against the peoples of the free world for not lending a hand in rescue actions. And Jews have even cast blame on the Jews themselves—those who enjoyed freedom and those trapped under Hitler's rule—arguing that their conduct contributed to the tragedy. Every accusation, the self-blame included, has been attended by an apologia; all have tried to explain away their actions and failings.

Questions have been asked not only in Israel but also, perhaps primarily, in the Diaspora, for the condition of Diaspora Jewry today is closer to that of European Jewry prior to the Holocaust than to the situation in Israel. The sense of continuity is also stronger in the Diaspora than in Israel, and the dangers inherent to Diaspora life are more patent. Perhaps these are the reasons why the public controversy surrounding the Holocaust has expressed itself there—notably in the United States—more sharply than in Israel. To the degree that it has concerned itself with the Holocaust, the generation that has grown up in Israel has asked two questions that stem from its own experience:

Why didn't the Jews of Europe defend themselves, fight back, or try to save themselves?

Why didn't the Jews in the rest of the world, including Palestine, take action to save them?

If the Jews are a single people and, whether living in their homeland or the Diaspora, share a common fate and mutuality of responsibility, how come this shared destiny did not engender a united act of rescue?

Much has been said and written to elucidate these points, but essentially it is events and reactions that have occurred in Israel itself that have heightened an understanding of, and generated a greater identification with, the events of the past.

The State of Israel has undergone a process of identification with the memory of the Holocaust in four main phases that represent the levels of confrontation in the minds of both the generation of the founders and the generation of the sons.

During the first phase—that of shock upon discovery of what had happened and the response in the form of action—the population in Israel was immersed in a struggle for its political existence and for the immigration of the surviving Jews of Europe. After the establishment of the state and the War of Independence, most attention was focused on the problems of absorbing the mass influx of immigrants and of securing the state's economic viability and physical security. However, in 1954 the Yad Vashem Remembrance Authority was established on the basis of a law brought before the Knesset by the minister of education and culture, Professor Benzion Dinur.[6]

The second phase opened with the capture of Adolf Eichmann and his trial in Jerusalem. The sovereign Jewish State regarded itself as entitled to try the man who was among the leading perpetrators of the extermination of the Jews. Bringing Nazi murderers to justice and punishing war criminals were among the ambitions of the nations that had defeated Hitler. The trials held between 1949 and 1954 by the Four Powers in Nuremberg gave both a public and a legal seal of approval to the civilized world's outrage at the crime of genocide. Although the crimes the Nazis had perpetrated against the Jews were uncovered in these legal proceedings, the Jewish people—not recognized as a partner in the war—were represented neither by a prosecutor nor by a judge on the panel that made up the court. Eichmann's trial in Jerusalem, his conviction by the judges of the Jewish State, and the implementation of the death sentence passed on him were, therefore, a sovereign act that made up for what had been missing at Nuremberg. The Eichmann trial had many other implications for the Jewish people in both Israel and the Diaspora. It publicly unfolded the terrifying story from beginning to end; thus Jews and non-Jews were presented with the facts and their inevitable conclusions. Not everyone responded positively to the trial, but from then on it was no longer possible to ignore the decisive historic significance of the Holocaust. After the Eichmann trial a new stage opened in the research on the Holocaust by Jewish institutions and other parties in Israel and abroad.

This identification found expression during the third phase, at the time of the Six-Day War in 1967. The memory of the millions who had been wiped out now sharpened the sense of danger and spurred the nation to defend itself by fighting back. In a discussion by young members of kibbutzim a few days after the war, one participant commented;

> It's true that people believed that there we would be exterminated if we lost the war. They were afraid. We got this idea—or inherited it—from the concentration camps. It's a concrete idea for anyone who has grown up in Israel, even if he personally didn't experience Hitler's persecution, but only heard or read about it. Genocide—it's a feasible notion. There are the means to do it. This is the lesson of the gas chambers.[7]

The fourth phase began during the Yom Kippur War of 1973, which created a new level of identification. The danger of annihilation was more concrete and stronger then; here is one observation, made after the war, concerning its effect on the Jewish people, "Even more intense and sober was the Diaspora reaction to the Yom Kippur War. It is clear that the Yom Kippur War has heightened the sense of interdependence among all parts of the Jewish people. The events of May 1967 had revived the memory of the Holocaust. But the Yom Kippur War gave that prospect even greater focus."[8] Now the threat to the State of Israel was more tangible in contrast to the experience during the Six-Day War. This time the Jews of Israel and the Diaspora encountered a negative attitude toward the State of Israel on the part of groups or nations, some of which had until then been regarded as its supporters. These negative manifestations expressed themselves on different levels: indifference, silence, passivity, or overt hostility. Jews in the Diaspora were gripped by a sense of helplessness, as if a sentence had been passed despite Israel's victory on the battlefield. This feeling in some ways resembled the sense of impotence that gripped the Jews during World War II.

Another factor played a role in intensifying the identification with the past. The Israeli people, especially the young, realized—perhaps for the first time—that a large population, even if arrayed to defend itself, may not be sufficiently aware of the danger facing it or adequately prepared to cope with it from the start. Errors of judgment, shallow-mindedness, and the application of outmoded concepts became a tangible and very painful experience for all Israelis, and it also opened eyes to the far more perilous and desperate situation in which the Jews were caught up under Hitler's rule.

The Holocaust was a tragedy, and every tragedy inevitably implies failure. There is no denying that during the period of the exterminations, the Jewish people suffered a crushing defeat, and there is no evading the painful question of why this tragic defeat occurred. We have to face it. But the failure was not only ours; the catastrophe was not of the Jews alone. It was a general human catastrophe: Europe's culture and civilization, forged through centuries, was ravaged during the days of Hitler's rule, and the human condition in the modern, technological world was illuminated by the fires of the crematoria at Auschwitz. The Jew, not for the first time in his history, epitomized man's fate in a time fraught with peril. No historical event can ever be eradicated; once it has happened the possibility of its occurrence is proven. The history of the world since World War II shows that Hitler created a fissure in the moral dam of religion and culture through which a flood of violence and cruelty, stemming from man's most sinister impulses, burst forth. Thus, our period has been dubbed the *Age of Violence*,[9] and its most prominent and shocking manifestation was the extermination camp, where violence was raised as a banner and became the emblem of the age.

In this book we shall deal with the fate of the Jews of Europe to its bitter end. This history cannot be presented as usual historiography, that is, surveying a series of events, actions, and developments in society and in the relations among peoples and social groups. Usually, a history portrays ways of life with death as an attendant. Herein, we shall describe ways of death with life a backdrop, and we shall deal with the murder of masses of people against the background of their struggle for life. Our subject is tragedy and suffering, the suffering of millions of living beings with millions of distinct faces—it is only death that has but a single aspect. The suffering of living beings is individual; only death eradicates individuality. The words of the historian Shimon Bernfeld on the persecutions of the past seem appropriate in our time as well, "No poet could express the forcefulness of the pain as it is so sincerely expressed in the original writings of the ancients. And what they have left us in their prayers and lamentations is not poetry nor a description of things, but the natural voices that emerge from the heart when it contracts and prays out of great sorrow."[10]

We also have lamentations from the days of the Holocaust (e.g., the poems of Yitzhak Katzenelson), although most of the testimonies are in the form of diaries, letters, newspapers, various narratives, and documents from Jewish sources. To these we must add the memoirs and the writings perpetuating the memory of others lest they be forgotten, lest their faces be erased by the anonymity of death. The novels, stories, plays, and films about the Holocaust period are also based, for the most part, on these sources. They are able to serve novelist and historian alike because many were written expressly to tell the Jews, and the rest of the world, what was done to "the murdered Jewish people" (in the words of Katzenelson's great poem).[11] The most comprehensive original historiographic effort was that of Emmanuel Ringelblum, who put a special team together in the Warsaw ghetto to collect historical material for the institution known by the underground name *Oneg Shabbat* (Delight of the Sabbath). Only a portion of this archive was saved from the flames and has reached our hands. But Ringelblum was not the only one engaged in this effort. In the midst of the struggle for life—even in the preparation for the final, armed struggle before death—others also took pains to leave behind testimony of the deeds of their oppressors and their own counterefforts. Some of the writings and documents that had been hidden in walls, under floors, or in the ground were uncovered and collected in the ghettos of Bialystok, Lublin, and Łódź; in Auschwitz (Oświęcim), Treblinka, and Theresienstadt; and in many other places. Others have been lost.

The need to preserve the historic testimony was also shared by many of the survivors who returned to their native cities and villages in Poland and elsewhere only to find that their homes had been destroyed and their communities devastated. Among the most prominent of these survivors is the historian Philip Friedman, who established the Historishe Kommissie (Historical Commission) in liberated Poland. The commission was dedicated to the collection and cataloguing of Holocaust material; subsequently, it continued its work in the DP camps in Germany. Friedman was one of those special people who found the strength to submit the events of the Holocaust to rigorous examination immediately after they had occurred; to this day his articles serve as an eminent source for understanding the period.[12]

Alongside the Jewish sources are archives containing a wealth of German and other documents that have served as the basis for trials and research. The earliest scholars of the period who have given us a comprehensive description of the extermination of the Jews by the apparatus of the Final Solution based their studies mainly on German documentation. The work of Gerald Reitlinger and Raul Hilberg is among the enduring contributions to such Holocaust research.[13] Yet consonant with their leanings and the material available to them, their main interest was in the Nazis' deeds and their results. Thus, the disposition of the Jews, their response and actions, for better or worse, were treated only marginally, often in a one-sided fashion.

Meanwhile, research based on Jewish sources that completes and corrects the picture has been steadily developing. This research has now made it possible to draw a more comprehensive and balanced picture. In this book I have tried to interweave the broad circumstances created by the times; the intentions and actions of the Nazis toward the Jews; the condition, fortunes, and behavior of the Jewish communities from the eve of the period of persecution until its end; the nature of the relations between the Jews and the peoples among whom they lived; the attitude of the world's nations to the Jewish problem before and during World War II; and the response and endeavors of the Jews in the free world.

As far as possible, I have summarized the facts, attempted to get to the root of events, to comprehend their significance, and to analyze situations and motives. Research into the Holocaust continues apace. It is unquestionably beyond the power of any single person to cover all of the events that compose it or to interpret and elucidate all its meanings and implications. Nevertheless, an attempt has been made to present as inclusive a picture as possible of that fateful period in the history of the Jewish people; it has been done owing to the conviction that what is needed—particularly by the younger generation—is a comprehensive presentation of the subject based on a historical analysis of the evolution of the period's events. This book does not intend to present the final analysis; rather, it is meant to be something like an interim account.

The theoretical objective adopted has two aspects, one oriented toward the nature of the Holocaust, the other toward the stages of its historical development. This approach is predicated on the belief that these two main facets—essence and evolution—are interrelated and that one can speak of the character of the Holocaust only in terms of the stages in which it manifested itself. This dictum is equally true of its perpetrators, the Nazis, and their victims, the Jews. To underscore the character and development of each I have tried to separate the discussions of the Nazis and the Jews, describing each subject on its own in addition to their influence on each other. I do not believe there was a clear-cut division of roles, that is, that the Germans were acting and the Jews were acted on. One of the aims in writing this work was to liberate historians and our readers from the view that the Jews went to their deaths "like sheep to the slaughter." The adoption of this stereotypical approach was itself one of the aims of those who wrought the Holocaust as well as one of its results.

In order to highlight the various stages of this historical development, I have drawn a distinction between three main periods in time. The first runs from 1932, the year of Hitler's takeover, reaching up to 1939; the second covers the war's first stage until 1941. The beginning of the third period is marked by preparations for the attack on Russia. It opens on the eve of the campaign, in the spring of 1941, and runs until the end of the war in 1945. The nature of the persecutions differed during these three phases, and this difference finds expression in the structure of the book's three parts. In Parts I and II, I have tried to separate the description of the aims and actions of the Germans from those of the Jews, allocating separate chapters or divisions to each. Part III (1941–1945) is devoted to a description of the preparation and execution of the systematic extermination; in this section events unfold at a rapid pace, creating a swift dynamic of action and reaction to the point where there is no longer any justification for dealing with German and Jewish topics separately. Since it is impossible to include all the events of the Holocaust or to narrate most of them in detail, I have tried to concentrate on the basic and the characteristic so that often a specific detail is meant to be indicative of a broader phenomenon. Here and there it has likewise proved impossible to shape the narrative to cohere with the time limits set for any one chapter.

I have intended to write a book that serves all who are prepared to struggle with the problems and enigmas of the Holocaust. It was necessary to build the historical structure layer by layer, subjecting each successive level to rigorous scientific scrutiny. The challenge was thus to be self-disciplined in examining the content while easing the way for the reader by the manner in which the material was conveyed.

During the years of writing this book, the State of Israel continued its struggle for existence and a secure future. The fortunes of the Jewish people in the twentieth century have been forged by two events: the destruction of the Jews' basis of existence in Europe and the establishment in Israel of a new political basis for Jews. Both are revolutionary events that occurred in the space of a single generation. Both unfolded before our very eyes; our generation experienced them personally.

So, we are called to examine the meaning of these vicissitudes of history even if it is beyond our power to explain them in full. There are various ways of confronting and responding to the events of the time; one of them is the writing of history. The work of historians is based on research; it is a rational act that obliges one to strive for objectivity and maintain detachment. Confronting the terrors of the Holocaust likewise demands restraint, yet it is impossible to convey the message without identifying with those who walked in the valley of the shadow of death. I have tried to make their voices heard, the voices of those who were trapped by events over which they had no control; frightened people who struggled, erred, despaired, surrendered, and prevailed. Hence, this book, the product of research and thought, has been written with trepidation.

Part I

The Jews of Germany During the Rise and Under the Rule of the National Socialists, 1932–September 1939

German Jewry is today rather like a
laboratory of the Jewish question.
Jüdische Rundschau (August 11, 1933)

1

1932: The Year of Decision

Nineteen thirty-two will be the year of the decision that determines whether the German Reich will defeat the forces of injustice and oppression threatening the safety of the homeland from without and within. It will be a year of decision that determines whether the demands of the enemies of the Jews, who are calling for the abrogation of the administrative and legislative rights of the Jewish component of the German people, will be partially or wholly fulfilled. And it will likewise determine whether we German Jews will indeed be relegated to the status of second-class citizens.

These words were spoken in mid-January 1932 by Ludwig Holländer, the director of the Central Union of German Citizens of the Jewish Faith (Central Verein deutscher Staatsbürger Jüdischen Glaubens, or CV), which had been founded in 1893 to fight for full equal rights for the Jews of Germany and to combat anti-Semitism.[1] With a membership of sixty thousand, out of a total Jewish population of about half a million (or 12 percent of the Jews of Germany), the CV was the largest Jewish organization in the Weimar Republic and justly claimed to represent the overwhelming majority of German Jews.

What was the decision that the leaders of the Liberal camp of German Jewry foresaw at the beginning of 1932? According to the quote, it had two aspects: one general, the other Jewish. Today we know that what lay in the balance for the enfeebled democratic state of Germany was not just stability at home and peaceful relations abroad, but the fate of all Europe, which was the key to the fate of the world. The threat that loomed in 1932 was not to the Jews of Germany alone but also to the rights gained during the emancipation; it was a threat both to the very existence of European Jewry—constituting more than half the world's Jewish population—and to the abiding source of the Jewish people's vital and creative forces. We know the outcome of the decisions taken in 1932. In the words of the prophet, "storm and tempest, and the flame of devouring fire"[2] ravaged Europe for the twelve years of Hitler's rule: Thirty-eight million people lost their lives; a third of the Jewish people and its nucleus in Europe were wiped off the face of the earth. The "devouring fire" of the crematoria at Auschwitz became the emblem of the era.

But the gap between what the Jewish leaders knew then and what we know now is as abysmal as the hell into which the Jews were cast during the Hitlerite era. Today it is recognized also by the German-Jewish leaders who managed to escape that they—the first to be attacked—failed to protect the status of the Jews as a constituency and failed even to save the lives of many individual Jews. German Jewry as a whole—Liberal, Zionist, and Orthodox—was also the first to founder. How did this come about? This question has been asked about each successive stage of the course that led to the bitter conclusion of the extermination process. It is a complicated question. To the degree that it can be answered at all, the answer also will be complex, for it must take into accout German, Jewish, and worldwide circumstances and forces, each in itself a tangled weave of expectations and reality. How were all of these factors reflected in the "year of decision" that preceded Hitler's rise to power?

Germany in Crisis

As the fate of the Weimar Republic is well known and has been the subject of extensive research, I shall confine my discussion to some events that were decisive to its collapse and the rise of the Nazis.

The year 1932 was still shadowed by the world crisis that had begun on October 24, 1929 ("Black Thursday"), with the crash of the New York stock market. Germany had just recently begun to recover from the economic recession resulting from its defeat in World War I. All strata of the population were affected. By January 1932 unemployment had reached a high of 6,141,010.[3] The country's crippled industries sank into debt: The workers, who had been fired in droves, loitered about the streets and crowded into the beer halls; unemployment benefits were insufficient to sustain families. The lower middle class of craftsmen and small businessmen was on the brink of ruin, and the financial difficulties pressed especially on small farmers; the job shortage dashed the hopes of youngsters, those from the working class as as well as those at universities. The only people who were able to maintain their standard of living were the moneyed upper middle classes, particularly owners of large commercial enterprises, department stores, and chain stores.

Economic insecurity only exacerbated existing class and political antagonisms, which undermined Germany's parliamentary system starting in 1931. It became impossible to gather a majority in the Reichstag on which to base a government. In the spring of 1930 the country's aging president, Field Marshal Paul von Hindenburg, invited Heinrich Brüning of the Catholic party Zentrum to form a government. The party did not rest on a coalition and therefore did not require a parliamentary vote of confidence. Brüning's so-called presidential government promulgated its laws through emergency decrees signed by the president. This arrangement was made possible by a clause (Article 48) of the Weimar constitution that was designed to protect the republic from subversion, but it now served as an instrument for neutralizing the parliamentary system and paving the way for the transition toward a dictatorship.[4] When the Social Democrats opposed these regulations, Brüning dispersed the Reichstag in the summer of 1930. His move led to the disastrous election of September 14 that increased the number of National Socialist delegates from 12 to 107 and made the Nazis the second largest party in the Reichstag after the Social Democrats.

Germany was not the only country in Europe racked by political turmoil during this period. Alongside the Fascist takeover in Italy, the forces of Fascism had grown stronger in Rumania, Hungary, Poland, and the Baltic states in the 1920s; eventually dictatorial regimes developed in all of these countries. The Social Democratic regime in Austria was centered in Vienna. Only Czechoslovakia remained a stable democracy thanks to the foundations laid by Tomáš Masaryk. In light of the unrest in southern and eastern Europe, the League of Nations tried to promote compromise, to maneuver between the opposing positions and interests of the East and West, and to deal with the complex problem of the national minorities that remained or had been created in these areas after the war.[5] The political crises had a great impact on the large Jewish concentrations of eastern and southeastern Europe even though the process of democratization and recognition of the rights of minorities had initially accorded them a new and improved status.

The severe political and social crisis that had overtaken Germany, fed by the harsh economic situation, was neither sudden nor incidental. The period from November 9, 1918, the day on which the German Empire fell, to January 30, 1933, when Hitler became chancellor, was marked by a succession of struggles within Germany and with forces beyond. The new democratic government had to withstand attacks from the Communists on the left and the old ruling classes on the right. Insurrections by these groups at the two poles of the political spectrum occurred in almost every one of the states that composed the republic; political terrorism and murder were commonplace during the first years of the Weimar era. The prime and strongest force sustaining the republic was the Social Democratic party, whose stronghold was in Prussia—the largest, wealthiest, and strongest of the German states. Yet the Social Democrats never won a majority in the national parliament, the Reichstag, and thus always had to find coalition partners. For this reason the center parties—such as Zentrum and the Democratic party, which had been founded on the establishment of the republic—carried great weight. On the right, the conservative owners of large estates, senior officials, army officers, and the owners of major industries wielded the greatest influence. These circles, smarting from the loss of their social prestige, regarded the republic not as their political home but merely as a way station on the road back to monarchy.[6]

In 1932 the ground was cut out from under the democratic center as the conservative bourgeoisie began to flock to the National Socialists. One reason for this shift in allegiance was a fear of the rising power of the Communist party, which was competing with the Social Democrats on the Left. The Nazis received their greatest support from the lower middle class, which had been hardest hit by the inflation of the early 1920s and was the first victim of the economic crisis at the start of the 1930s. Lacking the support of a strong political base like the Social Democrats and their labor organizations, young people from this strata eagerly turned to National Socialism and even joined the SA storm troopers as a way out of their forced idleness.

But economic advantage alone does not explain why these young people streamed into Hitler's ranks. They found in him two things they needed no less than bread: an outlet for their frustration and a sense of purpose. The outlet was to vent their hatred on the people who were blamed for all their ills, the Jews. The anti-Semitic canard was taken by this disintegrating social class as the key to why they were being crushed between two major blocs: the capitalists and the so-called Marxists. At the same time, Hitler offered them a positive role by calling on them to save the German fatherland. They were told that they would rescue not just themselves, but the whole of the German people, who had been humiliated by the despicable Versailles treaty. They were proffered the vision of being chosen to restore Germany to a ruling position in the world. This was how National Socialism imbued those looked upon as the dregs of humanity with a sense of security and self-respect. Now they were organized into a mass movement, marching together in the streets, attending huge public rallies, cheering their leader, Hitler. Most of the leaders and organizers came from the intellectual strata of school teachers, students, and academicians, to whom the Jews could easily be portrayed as their worst enemies for having usurped and corrupted German culture.[7] Their proof for this contention was the relatively large number of Jews in the free professions, the press, literature, and the theater, which was in any event a cause of envy.

What happened in Germany was not an overt civil war. Hitler reached power as the result of a three-pronged action that undermined law and order by sowing fear and creating an atmosphere of impending civil war, by mounting a campaign of terrorism against the Jews, and most of all by inciting violent clashes between the Communists and the National Socialist SA. Hitler's second move was "the legal takeover of power." As far back as 1930 he had explained, "We will penetrate the legal institutions and thus turn our party into a decisive force. Once the constitutional rights are in our hands, naturally we will reshape the state in the form we think is correct."[8] Meanwhile, his deputies held demonstrations in the Reichstag and systematically disrupted the orderly conduct of its sessions, thereby paralyzing the country's parliamentary life and the legislative work of the legitimate representatives of the people. The third prong of Hitler's assault on the seat of power was the vicious oral and written propaganda with which the Nazis flooded Germany, especially during the successive election campaigns of 1932.

In the spring of 1932 it took two elections to extend the tenure of President Hindenburg, who was then almost eighty-five years old. Though renowned as a national hero since World War I, Hindenburg did not easily defeat his rivals on the Left and the Right. In the second election Hitler received 36.8 percent of the vote; two weeks later, in the elections to the Prussian Parliament (Landtag), the National Socialist party became the largest in Prussia, with 38.3 percent of the vote, whereas the Social Democratic party lost about one-third of its seats and the middle-class parties supporting the republic were wiped out altogether.[9]

The Collapse of the Republic

At the end of May 1932 Hindenburg abruptly dismissed the leader of the Zentrum party and appointed a Conservative, Franz von Papen, as the prime minister. The minority Social Democratic government led by Otto Braun was toppled by force of arms on July 20, 1932, and Papen was appointed commissar of Prussia by emergency decree.[10] Despite the ensuing furor within the Social Democratic party and the willingness of members of the Reichsbanner, its paramilitary organiza-tion, to take up arms, the party's leaders feared the prospect of a civil war and placed their hopes on the upcoming Reichstag elections scheduled to be held eleven days later on July 31. In executing the coup, Papen was unwittingly advancing the interests of the National Socialists; indeed, the next day, July 21, Goebbels wrote in his diary: "The Reds have missed their great chance, and it will never return."[11] In that he was right. Though the Social Democrats had lost about a million votes (some 3 percent) in the July election, the workers remained loyal to the party and their leaders believed that they had made the right decision and would ultimately defeat their opponents by legal means. This view appeared to be vindicated when the National Socialists lost 4.1 percent of their votes in another election held on November 6, 1932, after the fall of the Papen government. But Papen's successor, General Kurt von Schleicher, was likewise forced to resign on January 28, 1933, whereupon the president's Conservative party advisers per-suaded the reluctant Hindenburg to invite "the Austrian corporal," Adolf Hitler, to form a coalition government with the conservative German National Party (Deutschnationale Partei). On January 30 the new chancellor took Germany's fate into his hands.[12]

Hitler rose to power not only because he was able to sense when the time was ripe to act but primarily because, blinded by their ambition to rule, the leaders of other parties—left, right, and center—failed to gauge the severity of the crisis. All the parties scoffed at the power of the National Socialists and assured themselves that before long the people would see that Hitler did not hold the key to salvation. The Conservatives, headed by Alfred Hugenberg, deluded themselves that they would be able to shape the regime and determine its policy.[13] They thought they would outsmart Hitler and that once he assumed the burden of rule he would be forced to moderate his views and take his direction from them. But Hitler would soon show them how badly they had misjudged him.

Emancipation: German Jewry's Asset

> Whoever denies me the right to my German homeland denies me the right to my thoughts, my feelings, the language I speak, the air I breathe. Hence I must protect myself from him as if he were a murderer.

Penned by Gabriel Riesser, a champion of emancipation, who began his struggle in the early half of the nineteenth century, these words appeared as the epigraph to a pamphlet entitled *The Obligation of Self-defense,* a report presented at the close of 1893 by Martin Mendelsohn, the first president of the CV and chairman of its first annual meeting.[14] The Jewish struggle for equal rights in Germany appeared to have reached its goal with the founding of the Weimar Republic. For a brief historic moment, the Jews believed that out of the ruins of World War I had arisen a democratic Germany that accorded genuine freedom and equality to all, a country with which they could fully identify, one whose laws they would defend and whose laws would protect them in return. The identity of interests and aspirations of Germany's young republic and its Jewish community found expression, *inter alia,* in the fact that it was a Jew, the lawyer and politician Hugo Preuss, who as minister of the interior chaired the committee that framed the Weimar constitution. However, it soon emerged that only a portion of the German people accepted the Jews as having a legitimate place in their nation and its political system—and even then not wholeheartedly.

Most of the Jews of Germany would have echoed Riesser's quoted statement. Their identification with Germany as their homeland was based first and foremost on a cultural foundation that combined both psychological and rational elements into a special and very powerful bond.[15] Its most concrete expression was their devotion to the German language as a vehicle of their spirit and ethos—a development that traced back to the venerated figure of Moses Mendelssohn. To this covenant with Germany's culture we must add the Jews' integration into the developing economy, which was undergoing an accelerated industrialization.[16]

Nevertheless, the Jews remained a distinct and defined group. Even though their emancipation in Germany—as everywhere else in Western Europe—was conditional on forfeiting their internal Jewish autonomy, in a sense they continued to exist as a covert minority. On the one hand, they were responsible for this ambiguity because consciously or otherwise they were loath to abandon their Jewish identity; on the other hand, to a large degree this ambiguity was caused by a host society that accorded them civil, cultural, and economic equality but not social acceptance.[17] The kehillah (communal body) was the one comprehensive Jewish organization that remained. In addition to providing services related to religious ritual and personal status (such as marriage and burial rites), the kehillah continued to function in only two spheres: Jewish education and social services.

Indeed, the Jews in Germany found themselves in the grip of a sharp paradox: by law they were citizens with equal rights, but most of German society, even the authorities, thwarted the full manifestation of this equality, making it necessary to wage a constant battle to protect these rights. For the most part, the Jews remained within the framework of their community, though its spiritual and psychological complexion had been superseded by the German cultural experience (the exception was the Orthodox sector of the community, which tried to combine "Torah with the ways of the land"). Their political life had no orientation than the collective defense of their rights.

The majority, under the leadership of the CV, wished "to unite all German citizens of the Jewish faith, regardless of religious and political orientation, in order to help them maintain their civil and social equality as well as help them to cultivate their German mindedness."[18] Its defense campaign (called *Abwehr*) against anti-Semitism was conducted on the legal and public-relations plane.

Since I have discussed this subject elsewhere, I shall confine the treatment of it here to a brief overview.[19] The members of the CV addressed themselves mainly to the non-Jewish population in an attempt both to defend the Jews against attack and to demonstrate their involvement in German society. As the power of the National Socialists increased at the end of the 1920s, this defensive action also grew more intense, as we shall see later.

In contrast to the CV, the Zionist camp was so small as to be almost negligible, with the Zionistische Vereinigung für Deutschland (ZVfD) accounting for only 2 percent of the country's Jewish population. The Zionists' point of departure was identical to that of the CV. They, too, regarded themselves as Germans in every way and were deeply rooted in German culture; they, too, found themselves in the paradoxical situation of feeling a sense of belonging to a nation that did not reciprocate by accepting them. But they reached the opposite conclusion from the CV in acknowledging the barrier that divided them from German society. The Zionists regarded Germany as the Diaspora, but they imagined that it was precisely this approach that would enable them to live there, for they posited, "A good Zionist concerned about the fate of the Jewish people who wishes to make his contribution toward providing it with a home secured under public law can serve the country to which he belongs as a loyal patriot."[20]

German Jewry During the Crisis Years

To better understand the Jewish predicament we must first clarify who the Jews of Germany were in 1932. The 1925 census established that there were 564,379 Jews in Germany at that time, composing 0.9 percent of the country's population. The exact number of Jews on the eve of Hitler's rise to power is not known, and we must rely on estimates that range from 510,000 to 525,000 in the winter of 1932/1933.[21] How did the complexion of this populace—composing less than 1 percent of the total German population of 65 million—make it possible to portray the Jews of Germany as the "root of all evil" and "a cancer in the body of the nation" that must be cut out of that body in order to restore its health?

Two-thirds of the Jews were concentrated in cities of over 100,000 inhabitants, with over 50 percent divided among seven large communities. The remaining third lived in settlements ranging from middle-sized cities down to villages. For example, the Jewish population of thirty-six villages was affiliated with the kehillah in the northern city of Stettin (Szczecin).[22] On the whole, the number of Jews living in towns and villages was small and sometimes consisted of no more than a family or two, though taken together they constituted some 20 percent of Germany's Jewish population. They were employed mostly in the traditional crafts, petty trade, and in providing services to local farmers. More characteristic and prominent, however, was the concentration of the Jews in the large cities, where they tended to cluster in specific neighborhoods. In Berlin the Jewish population was divided on a class basis between the wealthy western sectors and the poor neighborhoods on the eastern side of the city. In 1933, when the Jews' places of residence were still unchanged, 69.5 percent of all Berlin's Jews lived in five neighborhoods (compared with 31.6 percent of the overall German population residing in the same areas) where they made up an average not of 3.8 percent of the population (which was their ratio of the city's population) but of 8.7 percent; in one section they even reached 13.5 percent of the population.[23] Thus the Jewish presence was strongly felt in these neighborhoods.

To this we must add that the Jews tended to be concentrated in certain professions and occupations—a phenomenon that went hand in hand with the process of urbanization, the influx to the cities as a by-product of industrialization, the concentration of capital, and the organization of businesses. The Jews in Germany (as in various other countries) had preceded the general population in this trend.

The Jews were involved mainly in brokerage, finance, and commerce, though toward the end of the Weimar period their influence in a number of branches of commerce—such as metals, where they had enjoyed a strong foothold—began to decline. The same was true of their share in the wholesale grain trade, which increasingly passed into the hands of the German cooperatives. For a while the Jews also played a pioneering role in various branches of the electrical industry and in the modernization of the textile industry, though their main contribution to the growth of the economy was in the establishment of the department and chain stores. Still, most of all they were employed in workshops and small and medium-sized stores connected with the food and clothing trades.

It is well known that there was a substantial rise in the number of Jews who practiced the free professions or were employed in academe—even to the point where in some of these professions the ratio of Jews was several times that of the population at large. Laborers composed 46.3 percent of the German work force in Germany, whereas 46 percent of the Jews were self-employed. The other striking statistic about the Jewish population was the number of people employed in the white-collar professions: 33.5 percent as opposed to 12.5 percent of the population at large. On the other hand, the number of Jews in the upper social, political, or military echelons was very small.[24] Similarly, certain spheres of the economy were categorically closed to Jews—notably heavy industry and the mining and chemical industries—and this, in turn, influenced Jewish banking.[25]

Hence, the Jews lacked representation in Germany's two main centers of economic power: heavy industry and the working class.[26] The overwhelming majority of them belonged to the middle class. As a rule the Jewish craftsmen and tradesmen were better off than their German counterparts. What is more, their German neighbors saw that it was the Jews who introduced the "abominable" innovation of the department store or the large retail store that was able to mobilize credit and sell a greater selection of items at lower prices, thereby ruining the petty tradesmen.

As far back as 1911 demographic data had indicated that the Jewish population of Germany was aging at a rapid pace; the forecast was that it would decrease to the point of extinction even without being subjected to persecution. The reasons for this trend were the low birthrate, the high ratio of deaths over births, and the high rate of intermarriage, which reached 60 percent by 1932. Also noted was the rising incidence of Jews leaving the framework of the kehillah (on which there are no statistics).[27] This, then, was the Jewish community that the Nazis' anti-Semitic doctrine portrayed as a threat to the biological vitality of the German people.

The community had to grapple with many problems caused by the influx of Jews from Eastern Europe who wished to settle in Germany. This was not a new phenomenon. It could be traced back to the massive wave of emigration that had moved westward at the end of the nineteenth century and left a trail of *Ostjuden* as it passed through Germany.[28] In 1933 close to 99,000 of the Jews in Germany—19.8 percent of the country's Jewish population—were East European nationals. The demographic structure of this element was more positive than that of the veteran German-Jewish community and had an ameliorating effect on the projections. Most of these Jews settled in the cities, primarily the large cities, where they assumed a prominent role in the textile and leather industries and were involved in the development of the clothing industry, especially its marketing side. Their activities in the fur trade were a boon to the Germany economy. In the free professions they made the greatest impact in the arts, primarily the plastic arts, the theater, and music. Hence, the widespread negative image of this population as backward "ghetto Jews" is quite exaggerated. Still, not all their activities had beneficial results. Thus, the dealings of the Jewish land speculators among this populace created a problem of real estate owned by foreign nationals, especially in Berlin. However, most of the emigrants from Eastern Europe belonged to the middle and lower classes, and not a few of them lived in the poorer sections of town.[29]

Though variegated in terms of its cultural background, occupations, and social standing, the Jewish population nonetheless made up a distinct community that was easy to assail and depict before the bourgeoisie as the main cause of its present suffering and a menace to the future. The anti-Semitic ideology countenanced the envy felt toward the Jews, and the Nazi party channeled the frustration into the "people's rage," while the maligned Jewish population—divided as it was socially and ideologically—had no political base of its own.

Jewish Activities in Weimar Germany

In 1925 Jews were living in 3,000 locations in Germany organized in, or associated with, 1,800 independent kehillot.[30] Officially, the kehillah was defined as "a Body Corporate under Public Law"; in cooperation with the treasury, it had the right to collect taxes, which were fixed in proportion to the general tax rate. Each kehillah was headed by a board of deputies; the larger ones also had councils that were chosen in general elections, the size of the administration being determined by the size of the community's membership. The communities were subordinate to the governments of Germany's constituent states, and the greatest number of them were in Prussia: 720 communities encompassing four hundred thousand Jews. During the Weimar period the communities affiliated into statewide unions, with the Prussian union recognized as the leading organization of German Jewry as a whole. These unions represented the communities vis-à-vis the authorities, negotiated the amount of financial support they would receive, and tended to the educational and welfare needs of their constituent communities in addition to providing them with administrative and financial support.

In 1933 the jurist, historian, and Jewish official Dr. Ismar Freund, who had been the secretary of the union of communities in Prussia from its establishment in 1922, wrote a report summarizing the organization's activities.[31] It reflected the communities' weak standing and lack of political influence, despite the great strides forward they had made during the Weimar period. In the report Dr. Freund described his endeavors to establish that the rights of the kehillot should be equal to those of the Christian churches with which he compared their status. "The churches do not have to fight for their rights," he wrote, "since these have long been ensured and are no longer disputed by anyone." However, Judaism was like a beggar at the gates of the German establishment, "It must fight for its rightful place and conduct this struggle in the face of the most vehement opposition; the government circles authorized [to deal with such matters] adamantly reject any notion of concessions to a religion they consider inferior and historically and universally impugning their religion." He went on to explain that the Jews had no parliamentary representation of their own, the few Jewish deputies were usually wary of drawing attention to themselves as Jews; sometimes it was easier to enlist the support of a gentile deputy to the Jewish cause than a Jewish one.

Dr. Freund's criticism was directed internally as well. He deplored the fact that the institutions dealing with Jewish affairs were headed by amateurs who, rather than regard this work as their primary occupation, treated their position as an honorary office. He also complained of the naïveté that enabled the authorities to manipulate them. Finally, he bemoaned the lack of a national organization that would represent Jewish interests vis-á-vis the government. Actually, a national Jewish umbrella organization called the Reichsvertretung der jüdischen Landesverbände (Reich Representation of the Jewish Federative Associations in Germany) had been founded in 1932, but it proved ineffectual. The Jews of Germany participated in a nationwide enterprise in only one sphere: the community's social services were handled by a national organization that enjoyed the cooperation of all the relevant parties. The Zentralwohlfahrtsstelle der deutschen Juden (Central Welfare Organization of German Jews), with headquarters in Berlin, operated throughout Germany under the aegis of local organizations and institutions, thus making it possible to provide the Jews with a network of social services run by highly professional personnel. Morever, in 1926 the government of the Reich recognized the Zentralwohlfahrsstelle as the authorized representative of German Jewry regarding all welfare activities. Thus, it represented the Jewish aid organizations in Germany, responsible for the social services of the kehillot and private societies, and acted on behalf of international Jewish welfare organizations.[32]

Dozens of institutions affiliated with this social-action network tended to the elderly, the sick and convalescent, teenagers, children, and infants. Special emphasis was placed on occupational needs and vocational training, and credit societies were formed to help craftsmen and small businessmen establish themselves. The welfare institutions, especially the homes for the aged, were far more numerous than schools and other educational enterprises, as the number of Jewish public schools in the rural communities had decreased with the decline in these communities during the 1920s. However, thanks to the private Jewish schools, one child out of three was still receiving an education in a Jewish school at the time.[33]

Most of the Jews rightly felt at home in the halls of German culture. The Jews imagined that the intellectual province they had created was the intellectual world of Germany, and they failed to observe that a wholly different worldview was evolving right beside them. When the Weimar era is discussed today and its cultural-intellectual activity is appraised, it is common either to applaud or censure the Jews for their achievements. Either way, this endeavor is cited as one of the reasons for the anti-Jewish feeling in Germany. From an internal Jewish standpoint, however, most prominent figures in the arts, sciences, and jurisprudence had already transcended the Jewish realm even if they had not yet severed their formal ties with the organized community.[34]

Meanwhile, the rabbinical seminaries and other institutions of Jewish studies—the pride of German-Jewish creativity—continued their work. In addition, the modern seminaries and other schools for adults and children established throughout Germany cultivated the study of the Hebrew language and were especially popular with the members of the youth movements. The outstanding leaders of this revival movement were Martin Buber and Franz Rosenzweig.

The Jewish cultural renaissance was hampered by the sharp ideological and political division between the Liberals and the Zionists. The tension was particularly evident in the political struggles within the kehillot. The Zionists, or at least some of them, ascribed supreme importance to the community's internal life and invested great energy in developing Jewish educational institutions. Dr. Freund, from the opposing camp, warned against ceding the community's institutions to the Zionists lest they create a distorted picture of the Jewish public and lead the authorities to believe that it supported Zionism—an image that, Freund believed, would prejudice the status of the Jewish community in Germany. Thus, even internal Jewish issues were judged according to the likely response of the state and society.[35]

Rather than being grounded in social, economic, or cultural differences, which are usually the background to political struggles, the rivalry within the Jewish community stemmed from the opposing ideological conclusions that the Liberals and the Zionists had drawn from the Jewish position within German society.[36] The Jews lacked the option of contending with their precarious situation through conventional political means: true to the principles of the emancipation, they had refrained from forming an independent political body, though they failed to find a place for themselves among the existing parties. Dr. Alfred Wiener, one of the architects of the CV's ideological and operative program, described this problem in the union's newspaper on January 22, 1932, "Unlike the English Jews, for instance, German Jews have never been able to make an independent political decision. Despite their strong inclination toward conservatism, they have not joined the pertinent political parties, as a natural course, since these parties have rejected them because of their Jewishness."[37] The fact that the Jews lacked a political base of their own within the German parliamentary system blunted their political acumen somewhat and left them more susceptible to harboring illusions.[38]

As the National Socialist propaganda intensified in 1932, the position of the Jews deteriorated as vociferous calls to boycott them led to attacks of their shops; the desecration of graves and synagogues became a daily occurrence; and Jews were increasingly driven out of villages and small towns.[39] Considering the prevailing atmosphere, even moderate middle-class circles dared not defend the Jews; the Social Democrats tried to belittle the significance of the anti-Semitism by depicting it as marginal and, in line with Marxist ideology, as a by-product of fascistic activities and the class struggle that would disappear once they were overcome.[40]

The Jewish leaders did not underestimate the gravity of the situation. Neither can they be accused of failing to search for a solution. But the means of defense they adopted were ineffective.[41] They invested great effort in persuading the authorities to come to their defense, but this approach was, for the most part, futile and even counterproductive. In the spring of 1931, the leaders of the CV and president of the ZVfD, Kurt Blumenfeld, tried unsuccessfully to get Prime Minister Heinrich Brüning publicly to affirm the rights of the Jews.[42] These attempts to prevail upon leading government figures to speak out in behalf of the Jews climaxed in the summer of 1932 when the CV submitted a comprehensive memorandum to President Hindenburg in the form of a white paper—a folder containing hundreds of documents that cited the Nazis' acts of anti-Jewish terrorism and incitement. Such evidence, it was hoped, would move the government to make some sort of categorical statement about the need to protect the safety of the state's Jewish citizens.

The reply was noncommittal, saying that the president expressly denounced and deplored the assault on German citizens and their political and religious rights. It was published prominently in the CV's newspaper as proof that law and justice were being maintained in Germany and that the rights of the Jews were being faithfully protected.[43] Even though the facts revealed by the white paper were appalling, no action was taken, and the Jews' position continued to deteriorate. In these contacts with the government, the Jews pointed out the negative impact of the violence against them on Germany's image abroad. But this intercession was worse than fruitless: by attempting to apply the leverage of world Jewry to Germany's foreign relations, it appeared to substantiate the anti-Semitic charge of a "world Jewish conspiracy."

The Defense Campaign in Action

The collection of facts presented in the white paper was composed as a result of one of the CV's most important actions in its defense campaign against anti-Semitism and, increasingly, against the National Socialist movement. This campaign, the CV's prime political endeavor, was carried out in three spheres.

The first sphere was the involvement of the Jews in the foundering republic's successive election campaigns. Special funds were established, assemblies were held, gatherings were hosted in homes, and the CV even tried to oblige members to take an active part in the campaigns. Its propaganda in articles and circulars essentially took a negative approach: against Hitler, National Socialism, and anti-Semitism. This offensive, which the CV waged in the name of the "Decent Peoples' Front," was conceived as an effort to save the state from the perils confronting it from the extremist parties on the Left and especially on the Right. Its appeals were addressed to the middle classes, which had, in fact, deserted the Liberal camp by then. This situation had not escaped the Jews, but they hoped to reverse it.

The second sphere was comprehensive legal action. The CV's representatives waged a relentless struggle at all levels of the legal system in the Reich's constituent states. Legal defense (*Rechtsschutz*), one of the union's first and most substantive activities, was also an area in which it had accumulated decades of experience. Seasoned lawyers defended Jews' property and professional standing, their civil and human rights, and their dignity. By taking recourse to the civil and criminal courts, the CV combated boycotts, acts of terror, and anti-Semitic incitement while trying to persuade the Reichstag to toughen the laws protecting the rights of the Jewish citizen. Often, it scored success in this endeavor. In 1932 over two hundred verdicts were issued against incitement to boycott,[44] and some of the National Socialists' leading propagandists—such as Goebbels, Theodor Fritsch, and Julius Streicher—were sentenced to brief prison terms and nominal fines for anti-Semitic agitation. The CV's staff took pride in these achievements[45] even though they occasionally created more problems than they solved or had a boomerang effect.

One of the Nazis' strategies was to turn the courtroom into a platform for disseminating their propaganda. The fiery orations declaimed by the Nazi defendants and their attorneys obscured the real purpose of the trial, and their rhetorical takeover of the courtroom made a greater impression on the public than the verdict at the trial's end. The lawyers who subsequently became leading figures in the Third Reich's legal system—Ronald Freisler and Hans Frank—turned the courts into a showcase for their cause. Thus, with the witnesses, jurors, and often the judges themselves disposed toward National Socialism, most of these trials ended in the payment of token fines, which had the effect of being more a prize than a punishment. Such results forced the CV to abandon the strategy of utilizing the judicial system for political ends. Even quarters in the German judiciary supportive of the Jews advised them to stop pressing criminal charges, and in 1932 such trials were halted altogether—to say nothing of the fact that the claims regarding the desecration of cemeteries and synagogues usually led nowhere. Ultimately, legal action, which had been one of the cornerstones of the CV's defense campaign, became pointless, for the rule of law utterly collapsed.

The third aspect of the defense campaign was educational or public relations work, which was based on the premise that the future of German Jewry was intimately bound up with the fate of the Weimar Republic. This identity of interests was noted by the chairman of the union, the prominent jurist Dr. Julius Brodnitz, in a speech delivered at one of the CV's public gatherings in Berlin on January 16, 1932, "Our fate is bound insolubly to the German fatherland's fate."[46]

The CV's information endeavor was conducted on two levels, one official and public, the other camouflaged and clandestine. In their public appearances at assemblies and the like, the leaders of the CV tried to reach Germans of goodwill.

Their appeals were predicated on their faith in the eternal values of liberty and justice, which they held to be consonant with the philosophy underlying the Weimar constitution. In this they differed in principle from the views of right-wing circles—conservative and radical alike—which regarded the republic as the epitome of the forces responsible for Germany's decline. The Jews based their demands and protests against the violation of the law on universal values and identified these values with Germany's welfare both domestically and in the international area. The tragedy of their position was that although their analysis was correct in principle and history vindicated their premise, in practical political terms they were operating in a vacuum.[47] Their defense of the republic and their claim that the touchstone of its principles was the manifestation of equal rights for its Jewish citizens had the effect of turning the Jews into a negative political symbol. Thus, their vilification and the call to revoke their equality became a symbol of the desire to bring down the hated republic. Virulent anti-Semitism naturally added weight to this symbolic equation.

In its search for allies, the CV spent millions of marks on distributing tens of thousands of leaflets and information pamphlets.[48] Because this action was not conducted within a defined or concrete political framework, it failed to yield the desired results, despite the dedication and enormous, systematic effort invested in it. The people running the information program were cut off from reality. The CV's leaders naïvely believed, for example, that the problem lay in the fact that leading government figures were insufficiently informed about what the Jews were suffering. However, it did dawn on some of the CV members that the hatred of Jews could not necessarily be overcome by better information.[49] The Jews were mistaken to persist in their faith in morality, spiritual values, and the power of rational persuasion in a contest with unbridled hatred. It was a faith born of both the covenant they had made with German civilization and their indigenous heritage. The Jews' intensive involvement in all fields of cultural endeavor enhanced this faith and created the illusion that it would stand them in good stead in their struggle to maintain their status and to defend the state. Hence,they ascribed great importance to the conduct of an ideological debate with the intellectuals in the opposing camp, treating it as a historic duty for the sake of the Germany with which they wished to be identified.

During the crisis years, especially in 1932, the Jewish problem was discussed in the daily press, public debates, assemblies, and on the radio. These discussions were joined by both Liberal Jews and Zionists, and particularly active among the latter was Robert Weltsch, the editor of the ZVfD organ, *Jüdische Rundschau (JR)*. These deliberations created the impression that there were some among the German people who shared the Jews' faith in universal values. In alliance with those referred to as "men of prudence," the ideologues of the CV hoped to effect a change for the better.[50] In the Zionist camp, Robert Weltsch sincerely believed— as he admitted after the war—that an intellectual affinity existed between Jewish nationalism and the German *völkisch* movement of national renaissance that pursued positive goals.[51]

In the shadow of this major information effort, the CV conducted another, secret operation. It was run by a special bureau established in 1929 for the purpose of waging a political war against National Socialism in collaboration with a few of the department store owners who had particularly suffered from anti-Semitic incitement. The bureau was kept completely separate from the union's official office and had its own staff, funding, and premises. It is ironic, in a way, that its headquarters were located on Wilhelmstrasse, the same street as the government's ministries in Berlin, and that the office took its name—the Büro Wilhelmstrasse—from that address. In essence the bureau was an archive of information systematically collected on the National Socialist movement. In addition to collecting Nazi newspapers and other publications, it sent observers and stenographers to rallies, held by the National Socialists, to take down every word. The bureau was headed by a non-Jewish member of the Democratic party and worked in concert with a number of German newspapers to keep a surveillance on National Socialist activities. It also maintained ties with all the forces that supported the republic. The bureau's archive was the largest and most efficient of its kind in Germany as no other group or political party had made an effort to establish a similar monitoring agency. It served the press and members of parliament as well as a growing circle of people with an interest in utilizing the information it collected. All the material presented in the white paper was drawn from this source, and the archive even prepared propaganda material during the election campaigns. Hans Reichmann, one of the leading personalities in the CV, was the director of the bureau on the CV's behalf and acted as a liaison with the various quarters that supported the republic, including senior officials in the administration. He took part in the consultations of representatives of the Democratic party, the trade unions, and defense organizations such as the Reichsbanner who met once a month, but these discussions never produced any concrete results. Surprisingly, until their rise to power the Nazis never discovered the location of the Büro Wilhelmstrasse, although they were aware of its activities. In 1933 the organizers of the bureau tried to transfer its more than two hundred thousand files to southern Germany, but when they realized that they would not be able to conceal them, they destroyed the files instead.[52] Alfred Wiener renewed the bureau's activities in Amsterdam; later the archive was reestablished in London as the Wiener Library; today it is housed at Tel Aviv University and continues to serve research on National Socialism.

All of this clandestine activity was carried out by members of the CV. The Zionists, who were opposed on principle to any intervention in Germany's affairs, did not cooperate in this effort, though not all the members of the ZVfD accepted this approach and some Zionists acted as supporters of the *Abwehr* activities.[53]

Toward Decision

The rise in political tension in 1932 was clearly reflected in the Jewish press and the debates conducted among the Jews and with the society around them. During the summer of that year, the changes that began to affect the political structure of the German Reich were accompanied by incidents that gave ample cause for alarm, particularly to the Jews. At the beginning of June, the National Socialist faction in the Prussian Parliament proposed a number of demonstrative laws that were a sign of things to come. They demanded the dismissal of actors and other artists "not of German descent" *(nicht deutschstämmig)* and the prohibition of "plays whose purpose is anti-national, pacifistic, or morally destructive." They also called for a ban on the Jewish ritual method of slaughtering animals and the expropriation of property belonging to East European Jews residing in Germany. A similar demand was made in regard to officials who were "card-carrying members of the Marxist parties."[54] The laws relating to the Jews were passed through the addition of the votes of the Conservatives and the Communists; the Social Democrats abstained. Essentially these laws lacked all force because they contravened the constitution of the republic and thus could have been nullified by an appeal to the Reich's Supreme Court. However, the Jews well understood the real threat conveyed by this formal ratification of the Nazis' intentions. The CV's newspaper discussed the problem at length and analyzed the implications of the laws based on the racial principle. It also delved into the political significance of the Social Democrats' abstention, emphasizing, "Of course one cannot ignore the fact that what is today still within the bounds of demagoguery may some day become *brutal reality* if the ratio of forces continues to change." But the author of this piece immediately consoled himself with the conviction that if they ever did come to power, the National Socialists would be more concerned with subduing the forces of organized labor than with confiscating the property of a few East European Jews. The concept of "German descent" was another matter that occupied the attention of Jewish jurists, who determined that no such definition existed in legal terms. Moreover, to show how absurd it was, they asked how many generations one had to go back to establish that a man was of German extraction.[55]

Among the slanderous statements assembled in the white paper was an interview granted by Hermann Göring to the Italian journalist Solari in which he declared that since National Socialist rule would have to "defend itself against Jewry," it would not permit marriages between Germans and other races, to say nothing of Germans and Jews. The Jews from the East would be expelled from Germany and barred from entering it in the future. Local Jews would be dismissed from any job, honorary position, or capacity in which they might exert their destructive, antinational, or international influence. At the same time, he promised that "the decent Jewish merchant" would be allowed to carry on his business without interference, regarded as a foreigner living under the aegis of the Alien Law.[56] The white paper also included a statement predicting that life would be made so intolerable for the Jews that they would consider it impossible to go on living in Germany and would emigrate; others threatened that on the day of vengeance, they would set the synagogues aflame,[57] close the "murderous band" of Jews up in ghettos and prisons, and hang them from trees.[58] In March 1932 the Gauleiter and SA commander in East Prussia, Gillgasch, urged his subordinates, "Please wait, comrades of the SA. In a few weeks you will be able to lock up the Jews in the garages of the Fire Brigade, jammed in like salted fish. Then a few hundred kilos of animal salt will be sprinkled over them and nobody will open up. They will be pickled [like fish] until the blood and sweat that has been sucked out of you is restored."[59]

After their gains in the July 31 election, however, the National Socialists were no longer satisfied with mere talk. Goebbels's articles in the newspaper *Der Angriff* openly called for a pogrom, and a wave of anti-Jewish violence spread through Germany. The CV newspaper gave the assaults prominent coverage and interpreted them as an expression of "the Nazis' helplessness against the power of the state" and "as deflecting the 'people's rage' against the Jews."[60]

The director of the CV, Ludwig Holländer, summed up his views on "German Jews in Crisis," saying, "The new nationalism means an end to law and justice and the victory of the violent regime based on power. . . . People become drilled factors of the will for power." Nor did he relent in his dispute with the Zionists "who claim that we have adopted a concept of [what it means to be] German that no longer exists." He went on to express his credo, "Only strong inner courage, only the strength of our spiritual and moral principles, without compromising with the mood of the day—these [principles] alone will let us overcome the harsh times and extract the Jews from the crisis together with the whole German people to which they belong as a part."[61] This was a posture of noncompliance, a refusal to capitulate to the circumstances of the day, to forsake any emotional and spiritual qualities, or to forfeit the gains of the emancipation that had been achieved through the struggle of generations past.

There were many expressions of this staunch position during the summer of 1932. On July 1, 1932, the CV paper proclaimed in a bold front-page headline, "War All the Way Down the Line." After describing attacks on the Jews, it went on to state:

> We German Jews will not be frightened by vain threats. We have strong nerves. With clenched teeth we will defend every patch of land and fight courageously for equal rights down to the last detail. A handful of people with justice on their side are determined to fight, are prepared to make sacrifices, are proud of their glorious history and their timeless religion, are Germans living on the soil of the German fatherland. We shall endure and we shall prevail.

The most comprehensive and sober analysis offered by the Zionists was Blumenfeld's address at the ZVfD congress in September 1932.[62] He spoke of a fundamental change that had occurred, one leading to a new concept of state and nationality. He then defined the nature of the totalitarian state, described its characteristics, and concluded that one of the main objectives of the new German movement was the annihilation of Jewry, "They extol the murder of members of other races, especially the Jews; they think that the best way to serve the national renewal is to stir up feelings of hatred against anyone who is different." Yet he, too, thought that it was possible to conduct a dialogue with those nationalists who did not identify with National Socialism, that is, the Conservatives. He also made the fatal error of believing that the Conservatives would be able to preserve a renewed Germany (in the sense that he meant it). Blumenfeld read all the signs, but he failed to draw far-reaching conclusions.

In his autobiography Blumenfeld described how the audience responded to his "prophecy of doom": his speech was received with a "chilled silence" and he was asked "why [he felt] the need to tempt fate." In contrast, he relates, the other, reassuring speech given by Naḥum Goldmann was received with "thunderous applause and a general sense of relief," for Goldmann claimed that he had reported the world political mood and that it was pointless to arouse alarm.[63]

In Blumenfeld's view it was the Zionists who were in a prime position to insist on equal rights for the Jews. Yet he stressed their deep attachment to the German spirit from which the emancipation of the Jews had derived,"But let it be said here that we feel very deeply how many of the values that fill our lives are traceable to Germanism. It is above all we Jews with a nationalist outlook who are trying to comprehend this world and the country in which we live and in which a substantial portion of our people will continue to live for the foreseeable future."[64]

The fact is that the Zionists and Liberals harked back to the same sources and attempted to solve the same problem. Both became snarled in inherent contradictions, and it was precisely their resemblance that exacerbated the dispute between them. Both possessed a resolve to dig in and continue to fight.[65] In the face of attacks from without, they both wished to close and reinforce their ranks so that they could withstand the pressure; however, attempts at cooperation did not bear fruit. Together with the great majority of the German people, they failed to see that Germany's fate was already a foregone conclusion. This was one instance of a phenomenon that we shall confront repeatedly in the history of the Holocaust: the strange paradox of a sober approach to reality coexisting with demands and deeds that bespoke a desperate clinging to illusion.

A year after Ludwig Holländer had defined the looming peril, the decision that he had feared came to pass: on January 30, 1933, Hitler was appointed the chancellor of Germany. That same day three events took place in Berlin that were to prove symbolic, though their occurrence together was merely coincidence.

All the principals of the city's Jewish elementary schools were invited to attend a meeting held in the offices of the Berlin kehillah. The number of Jewish schools had grown during the period in which the Zionists had controlled the kehillah, but in 1930 the Liberals had won a majority on the community board, and now they decided to cut back on the number of schools. On that day the principals were informed that for reasons of economy the school system would have to be gradually pared down, and the first to go was the largest and most developed of the schools. The warnings sounded at that meeting were by Joseph Gutmann, director of the education department. He feared that there would soon be a need for these Jewish schools to absorb the children expelled from the state-run system. His warnings went unheeded. Shortly after the meeting ended, Hitler's appointment as chancellor was announced.[66]

That evening another meeting was held in a café on Berlin's main boulevard, the Kurfürstendamm, to discuss the problems plaguing the country's Jewish craftsmen. In addition to representatives of the craftsmen union, it was attended by one Liberal and one Zionist. Hitler's appointment became known shortly before the meeting began. The first speaker was the Liberal, who confined his remarks to the matter at hand, taking sharp issue with the Zionist approach. He was followed by the Zionist representative, who held that there was no point squabbling over their differences now because history had outstripped them, and they had now reached a critical turning point. The other participants treated such remarks as alarmist hyperbole and did not respond.[67]

The third event occurred outside the framework of the Jewish establishment. That evening at the home of a notary public, Recha Freier together with a group of Jewish youngsters who could not see a future for themselves in Germany, established the Aid to Jewish Youth Society, which was later to become Youth Aliyah. When the meeting ended, as Freier and the youngsters made their way through the streets of Berlin, they were passed by a torchlight procession—the victory parade of the SA.[68]

Hitler Implements
Twentieth-Century Anti-Semitism

Racism and Anti-Semitism: The Antitype

Vain to adjure the nation of poets and thinkers in the name of its poets and thinkers. Every prejudice one thinks disposed of breeds a thousand others, as carrion breeds maggots.

Vain to interject words of reason into their crazy shrieking. They say: He dares to open his mouth? Gag him.

Vain to act in exemplary fashion. They say: We know nothing, we have seen nothing, we have heard nothing.

Vain to seek obscurity. They say: The coward. He is creeping into hiding, driven by his evil conscience.

Vain to go among them and offer them one's hand. They say: Why does he take such liberties, with his Jewish obtrusiveness?

Vain to help them strip off the chains of slavery. They say: No doubt he found it profitable.

Vain to counter the poison. They brew fresh venom.

Vain to live for them and die for them. They say: He is a Jew.

These harsh words were how the German writer Jakob Wassermann characterized anti-Semitism after World War I in his autobiography *My Life as German and Jew.*[1] Together with Stefan Zweig, a fellow Viennese, Wassermann was regarded as the most popular German-Jewish writer of his day, and his books were translated into a number of languages.[2] His bitter words highlight some of the basic properties of modern anti-Semitism. Hatred of the Jews is not a function of their behavior or deeds; it is an entirely irrational phenomenon and, thus, not given to explication or rectification by means of reason. Neither is it amenable to moral critique. Anti-Semitism's divorcement from the accepted norms of human society and its disregard of logic enable it to make contradictory claims. The hatred of Jews is all-encompassing in its scope and implications; thus it is almost inevitably a by-product of totalitarian regimes.

As to its scope, anti-Semitism is predicated on the imputation of contradictory traits: the Jew is a braggart and a coward, arrogant and obsequious, shrewd and maladroit. He is omniscient and noncreative, sterile, racially pure and a mongrel. These are a few examples of the contrary traits ascribed to the Jews according to the needs and views of the indicter. This Jew is not flesh and blood, not a vital, palpable creature; he is an abstract creation, a ghost whose appearance in any one place need not be related to the presence of living, breathing Jews.

Just as the characterization of the Jew is all-embracing, the actions of which he is thought capable affect all strata of society, all walks of life, and all points of view. Thus, anti-Semitism makes it possible to identify the Jew with every conceivable foe and direct every kind of hostility against him. Historians, sociologists, and psychologists have written countless books and articles in an attempt to get to the root of modern anti-Semitism. But all the studies and explanations of this visceral hatred seem somehow unsatisfactory and fail to illuminate its essential nature. The most far-reaching definition may be found in the ideology of one of the Nazi professors who dubbed the Jew the antitype *(der Gegentypus)*.[3] This adversary is not defined as a political opponent, an economic competitor, or a national enemy; he is *the* antithesis, just as death is the antithesis of life, failure the antithesis of success, sorrow the antithesis of joy, hatred the antithesis of love.

Uriel Tal elaborated on this idea, which became the underlying concept of the Nazis' racist ideology:

> The Jewish character was not only corrupt and evil; it was the essence of corruption and the principle of evil. . . . Conversely, the German character was not only deep, upright, diligent, and enterprising but the essence of profundity, probity, industry. and courage. This mode of thinking hypostasized traits of character and symbols into empirical realities and ontological categories.[4]

Conjuring up the antitype liberates man from his existential fears and enables him to identify with the ideal, indomitable, independent figure. Hatred of the Jew fulfilled a similar function in the Middle Ages as well. According to the dogma, the Jew epitomized the static antithesis of the process of redemption over which the church held sole prerogative. In the first half of the twentieth century, racism superseded religion in this context. Race is now a fixed and immutable property of universal Nature; it can, however, be corrupted and purified—just as a religious man is corrupted by sin but is given the opportunity to purify himself. But in the eyes of the anti-Semite, the corrupt nature of the Jews is static and in no way given to change, whether they are regarded as a race whose purity has been preserved since its genesis or a racial mixture.

The racial doctrine was a product of modern biological and anthropological research whose results were interpreted by Comte Joseph-Arthur de Gobineau[5] and Ernest Renan[6] as basic elements in the evolution of human society and culture. However, it was primarily German exponents who applied these doctrines

into the realm of practical politics and social problems. The most sweeping interpretation of this new doctrine was offered by the writer Houston Stewart Chamberlain in his book *The Foundations of the Nineteenth Century,* published in German in 1899. This work was an attempt to review the history of Europe from
antiquity until the modern era through the instrument of racialist principles. Born
in England, Chamberlain became a German by choice and found his spiritual
mentor in Richard Wagner. It was he who stated that modern man lives in the
"Jewish age" as the Jews had taken over Europe; and paraphrasing Renan, he
pronounced that the Semitic race, "compared with the Indo-European race, con-
stitutes an inferior hybrid of humankind."[7]

Chamberlain's contention denotes the basic factor that generated anti-Semitism, namely, the paradoxical existence of the Jewish people. Throughout history
peoples had come and gone, states had risen and fallen, but the Jews—who were
neither specifically a nation nor a religious sect—continued to endure. They displayed almost an immortal power denied to other nations. This despised and persecuted community, bereft of a home, excelled not only in its perseverance but
also in its creative abilities. Indeed, "the Jew" remained a constant in the cycle of
life and death of nations. This immortality was declared, however, to be a punishment, as he was doomed to roam like the murderer Cain; he had no place of his
own and lived off the natural lives of others as a parasite.[8] He was the legendary
Ahasuerus, the eternal wanderer, and from the sixteenth century onward became
the symbol of the fears of modern man, whose faith in the cosmic order had been
undermined.

No age could match the nineteenth century for optimism and pessimism, for
its combination of arrogance and abysmal fear. And it was then, too, that the
Jewish collective suddenly reawoke, as if from a deep slumber, and began a dizzying ascent, participating in all spheres of life and culture while continuing to
maintain its distinct identity. Thus, the Jews symbolized both the prospects and
the perils of the age.[9] Resistance to Jewish progress and gains, which was first
expressed at the beginning of the century, had evolved by its end into a tide of
hatred that has been known ever since as anti-Semitism. As a catchword for
enmity toward the Jews, the term was coined in 1879, when Wilhelm Marr established the Anti-Semitic League as the first organization devoted to putting political
anti-Semitism into practice.[10] The word derived from the study of linguistics,
which started in the eighteenth century and at some point determined that the
Indo-Germanic (also known as Aryan) languages were superior in their structures,
variety, and vocabulary to the Semitic languages that had evolved in the Near
East. This judgment led to a certain conjecture about the character of the peoples
who spoke these languages; the conclusion was that the "Aryan" peoples were
likewise superior to the "Semitic" ones, thus creating the basis for a racist outlook.

Just as he appraised his languages, the Germanic as well as the Romanic, as
most highly developed, the European regarded himself as the elect of peoples. We
have already noted that such views were originally developed primarily by Gobineau and Renan, and they found theoretical and artistic expression in Germany
in the works of Wagner. In the course of time, however, they were joined by the-

ories based on Charles Darwin's doctrine of the survival of the fittest, following which Herbert Spencer argued that those better adapted to the conditions of life prevailed not only in nature but in human society as well.[11] Thus, from Darwin's doctrine, the racists concluded that the strong and victorious were also in the right, since nature determined the ways of the world. According to Gobineau, only racially "pure" people are worthy and capable of ruling, whereas peoples tainted by racial adulteration are doomed to extinction. Chamberlain, in contrast, held that just as it was possible to raise excellent breeds of horses and dogs, so it would be possible to enhance the human race by attaining a fine breed of "Aryans." Social Darwinism was soon repudiated in France and England, but in Germany these theories led to a new school of racialism.

According to this ideology race was the factor that governed men's lives. It was because of their race that they acted for good or bad and tended toward survival or extinction. When citizens were corrupted by the rule of an inferior race, government was corrupted. When they were governed by a positive and lofty race— endowed with the right, the will, and the ability to rule—they enhanced humankind, its society, and its culture. Hence, the reform of government was possible only by improving the race. Since the ideal race was a fictitious abstraction, an antitype was needed to solidify this concept, and it was found in the figure of "the Jew."

By basing itself on racism, political anti-Semitism transcended the normative framework of the state and became, by its very nature, a revolutionary instrument. It strove to topple the existing social order and political regime without taking recourse to its component organizations and institutions. According to Hermann Rauschning, Hitler said, "I know perfectly well . . . that in the scientific sense there is not such a thing as race. . . . I as a politician need a conception which enables the order which has hitherto existed on historic bases to be abolished and an entirely new and antihistoric order enforced and given an intellectual basis."[12] Thus the issue of rule was at the heart of the racist doctrine.

Racism as political doctrine rests on three propositions: (1) race is a biological given, a determining factor, like the forces of nature themselves; (2) race is a generic factor that finds expression in all aspects of life; (3) race is the prime element of any form of rule. This triple nature makes the racist doctrine a revolutionary and deterministic one devoid of all the ethical norms that human society has set for itself. It is amoral, just as nature is amoral.

It follows that the Nazis' hatred of the Jews was not directed solely at the Jews active in the economy, culture, or politics; its deepest source may well have been an enmity toward the Jews for having brought God's Ten Commandments into the world. Hence, the one way to engender a racial revolution in social, cultural, and political mores was by destroying all the elements that had evolved under the influence of the Jews. "This revolution of ours," Hitler told Rauschning, "is the exact counterpart of the great French Revolution. And no Jewish God will save the democracies from it."[13] Moreover, since the traits of the antitype are anchored in its biological structure, "the only way to wage a thorough war against it is by biological means."[14]

Anti-Semitism in Political Praxis

Political anti-Semitism in Germany went through three stages: the first ended at the close of the nineteenth century; the second began after World War I; and the third served Hitler as both an ideological basis and a tactical political instrument. The first stage has been described at length in a number of works examining the political, social, economic, and even cultural and intellectual circumstances that prompted the development of modern anti-Semitism in Germany. That the second stage occurred just after World War I, during the years that also witnessed the height of the Jews' achievement of legal emancipation in Germany, is one of the paradoxes of Jewish history. The third stage began with Hitler's rise to power and climaxed with the destruction of European Jewry, which we have come to call the Holocaust.

The first stage did not end in any solid political achievements, though it did prove that the doctrine of racial anti-Semitism was politically explosive. With the decline of the parties that had rallied around the anti-Semitic slogans, racial anti-Semitism disappeared from the political arena as an overt force. However, it continued to canker beneath the surface, permeating the country's social life and becoming a propaganda element for the conservative parties until the profound crisis that followed World War I laid the ground for its revival as a revolutionary political force. Nevertheless, modern anti-Semitism was never a specifically German phenomenon. Anti-Semitic parties and organizations arose under the leadership of prominent figures throughout Europe and were supported by an anti-Semitic press. Although this political movement tried to enter into an alliance with the nationalists and the conservatives in each of the countries involved, its self-image from the outset was of an international movement. Subsequently, Hitler coined the slogan "Workers of all classes and of all nations, recognize your common enemy!"[15]

France was no less important than Germany in developing the movement's ideological and tactical methods. Testing new political tactics, it provided practical information on ways of inciting the masses and threatening the government. The impact of deceptive propaganda and the effectiveness of using hooligans in a political struggle were first proven during the Dreyfus affair, notwithstanding that the reactionary forces who provoked the affair by resorting to anti-Semitism failed to achieve their aim of toppling France's republican regime. Russia, on the other hand, showed how a despotic regime could use hatred of the Jews to deflect social tension and political unrest into a channel that posed no threat to the central government. The pogroms in Russia were the first examples in modern European history of a regime inciting its subjects to murder Jews. In Rumania the Jews suffered from both official discrimination and from pogroms perpetrated by the populace. The doctrine of Zionist anti-Semitism, which advocated expelling the Jews to Palestine, was developed by the Hungarian Victor Istóczy. Thus, during the period in which the National Socialists were struggling for power, innovations were no longer necessary; it was sufficient for the movement to compile ready-made elements and reinterpret what had already been proposed or effected in the recent or distant past. Still, by striving to turn theory into practice, National Socialism as a regime sought new forms of implementation.

Considering the long-standing anti-Jewish tradition of the Christian churches and the more modern tradition of political and social anti-Semitism that had taken root among the masses, it was not difficult in the electrified atmosphere following the war to portray the Jew as the epitome of the forces that had brought about the defeat of the Second Reich. Many Germans felt a strong urge to punish the party they had branded as responsible for the disaster. As early as 1918 a *Jewish Order* was proposed. It contained demands and suggestions aired by anti-Semites over the previous decades; as we shall see, the Nazi regime forged its Jewish policy around these provisions. They are as follows:

— Jews living in Germany have to be subject to the Alien Law and those from abroad are to be forbidden to enter or be expelled

— Jews have to be barred from holding public or administrative offices and be forbidden to become lawyers; Jewish doctors shall treat Jews alone

— The right to vote is to be accorded to Jews only within their communities

— Jews shall not serve in the army

— Jews are not to study in German educational institutions and Jewish teachers will not teach German children; German teachers who teach Jewish children will have their licenses revoked

— Jewish journalists will be able to publish only in Jewish newspapers and all their publications have to be approved by the censor

— Jews have to sell their holdings in agricultural land within a year; Jewish businesses have to be marked prominently by the Star of David

— Jews are forbidden to bear German personal or family names

— Jews cannot be members in German societies; for the protection they enjoy, they have to pay the same dues paid by Germans

— Jews who have been expelled and returned to the Reich will be executed by hanging; those who were sentenced to over a year in prison have to leave the Reich together with their families, within a month of their release.[16]

These proposals were published as an appendix to the scurrilous document that poisoned the minds of millions of people and was to be distributed by anti-Semites throughout the world: *The Protocols of the Elders of Zion.* Its successful dissemination began in Germany in 1918. This forgery had a highly intricate literary and political history.[17] Composed at the end of the nineteenth century in France—on the instigation of the Russian secret police—the *Protocols* is a fictional account of the proceedings of an allegedly secret Jewish organization that was planning to take over and rule the world. The original purpose of this "document" was to aid the struggle against the liberal forces in Russia, but it had little effect in that context. The *Protocols* was distributed again during the Russian Revolution, this time by the White Army in an attempt to invoke anti-Semitism as part of its war against the Red Army. White Army officers brought the *Protocols* with them when they fled to Germany, where they charged that the tragedy of World War I was the result of a worldwide conspiracy of Jews hungry for power and destruction. Following this line of thinking, the Jews were also held responsible for the "stab in the back" that had allegedly led to the defeat of the army, the collapse of the regime, and the founding of the Weimar Republic. The *Protocols* also contributed to the Nazi ideology the identification of the Freemasons with the Jews, depicting them both as bitter enemies of Germany.[18]

The aura of secrecy and mysticism that surrounded the *Protocols* helped it to play on the imagination of frightened people the world over. Within a short time it had been translated into dozens of languages and surpassed only the Bible in distribution. Whoever reads this libel will try in vain to find a logical line in it; however, a more thorough examination reveals three tiers of argument. The first decries liberalism and calls for strengthening the central, absolutist government (the original reference was to the czarist regime in Russia). The second tier describes ways of instituting a dictatorial regime by exploiting the latest technical inventions available to modern society and relies heavily on psychological manipulation. Although the original point was to expose the ambitions of liberalism, this section is, in fact, a master plan for a totalitarian revolution. On the third level all the threats looming over humanity are ascribed to the intentions and actions of the Jews. As a result, in the words of one of the many writers and scholars who have analyzed the phenomenon of German anti-Semitism during the Weimar era, "the effects of anti-Semitism gripped millions of hearts like an inexorable plague."[19]

Innumerable books, pamphlets, circulars, newspapers, and debates in private salons and public assemblies spread the anti-Semitic argument, always in relation to the actual political conflicts of the Weimar Republic. The results were not long in coming: three Jews—Rosa Luxemburg, Kurt Eisner, and Gustav Landauer, all leaders of the socialist movement and revolution in Germany—were murdered in 1919 by the anti-Semitic counterrevolutionary movement. Among its leaders, as well as among the organizers and perpetrators of the mounting wave of terrorism, were many officers of the defeated German army. Three years later on June 24, 1922, the German foreign minister, Walter Rathenau, of Jewish extraction, was murdered by members of two radical nationalist organizations. The interrogation and trials of some of the conspirators revealed that they had been profoundly influenced by the *Protocols* and were convinced that Rathenau belonged to a secret Jewish organization that strove to dominate the world. Concluding the trial of Rathenau's murderers, the judge declared:

> Behind the murderers and their accomplices the chief culprit, irresponsible, fanatical antisemitism lifts its face . . . reviling the Jews as such, irrespective of the individual, with all those means of calumny of which that vulgar libel, *The Protocols of the Elders of Zion,* is an example; and in this way sows in confused and immature minds the urge to murder. . . . May the insight which this trial has brought concerning the consequences of unscrupulous incitement . . . serve to purify the infected air of Germany and to lead Germany, now sinking in mortal sickness in this moral barbarism, towards its cure.[20]

The Political Myth

The legend of a secret Jewish organization that aspired to control the world by means of war, revolution, and economic ruin merged with the nationalistic and racist doctrine—Rathenau's murder being one of the first results. More than anyone else, the purveyors of this doctrine were Houston Stewart Chamberlain and Alfred Rosenberg. The latter had been born in Estonia and came to Germany after World War I; thus neither man was a native German.

During the war years Chamberlain stepped up his literary activity, writing a spate of articles, circulars, and leaflets that were later collected into small anthologies. In these pieces he explained the point of the war to the Germans, arguing that Germany was the elect of nations and should therefore rule the world and bring it peace, whereas all the other nations—none more than England—aspired to dominate the world for the sole purpose of plundering it. Hence, before Germany could fulfill its own lofty mission, it would have to defeat them in war. Moreover, to accomplish its mission Germany would have to free itself of the democratic rule that distorted its character. Militant Germany, being a young state, must organize itself into a regime of discipline and obedience, he wrote, for that alone would ensure its citizens true freedom and equality. Many of the ideas and even the idioms that Hitler was to use in his talks, writings, and speeches were drawn from Chamberlain's articles. Chamberlain also stressed the great threat that Germany faced from barbarian Russia. "If the necessary steps are not taken now," he wrote in 1916, "in another hundred years, perhaps another fifty years, Germany will be lost beyond salvation." When asked by a friend which German statesman would be capable of taking this task upon himself, Chamberlain replied by quoting Martin Luther, "It takes a man of valor with the heart of a lion to write the truth." But the leader of Germany would also have to turn the truth into reality.[21] The Jew, Chamberlain wrote in 1918, always has been and always will be a disintegrative factor. "Even the 'noble Jew' will be of no benefit to the developing young nation; even he cannot help but harm it."[22] Though he had not yet been introduced to the *Protocols* at that time, Chamberlain likewise determined that the Jew aspired to dominate the world.

The anti-Jewish and racist-Aryan myths coalesced particularly in the writings of Alfred Rosenberg. He had been familiar with the *Protocols* (from his stay in Russia at the time of the 1917 revolution), and the work had made an indelible impression on him. Rosenberg was working on his book *Die Spur des Juden im Wandel der Zeiten* (The Footsteps of the Jew Throughout Time) even then, and he found support for his approach to the events of the day in the *Protocols.* The Russian edition of the *Protocols* already associated the "Elders of Zion" with the Zionist leadership, portraying the First Zionist Congress in 1897 as a gathering of the Jewish conspirators, and this connotation was passed on to the German edition and later extensively exploited by Rosenberg.[23] That Rosenberg had always been a racist anti-Semite is attested to by the Israeli historian Benzion Dinur, who as minister of education and culture founded Yad Vashem. Dinur related in his memoirs that during the early days of World War I, while traveling by train from

Germany to Copenhagen on his way back to Russia, he met Alfred Rosenberg, then a student of architecture, and heard him hold forth on his racist anti-Semitic views.[24] However, Rosenberg's principal development as an anti-Semitic propagandist and the chief ideologue of National Socialism did not begin until he arrived in Munich after the armistice of November 1918. There he soon gravitated toward the circle that became the nucleus of the National Socialist party. The leading figure in this group was Dietrich Eckart, who published an anti-Semitic nationalist newspaper that was later to become the *Völkische Beobachter (VB).* Rosenberg subsequently related that at their first meeting he turned to Eckart and asked, "'Can you use a fighter against Jerusalem?' Eckhard laughed: 'Certainly!' "[25] In *Die Spur des Juden im Wandel der Zeiten,* published in Munich in 1920, Rosenberg pointed to "Bolshevik Jewry" as the moving force behind the Russian Revolution. Over the next two years he published no fewer than four other books in which he denounced the Jews as wanting in morals (following the dictates of the Talmud), as the founders and perpetuators of the criminal Freemason societies, and as a people of decisive influence in Russia who were plotting to overthrow governments throughout the world by means of Zionism. In 1922 he published the program of the party that was making strides under Hitler's leadership and appended a commentary on "The Essence, Principles, and Aims of the National-Socialist Workers' Party."[26] A year later he reissued the *Protocols;* he continued to occupy himself with these subjects until 1943. His best remembered book, *The Myth of the Twentieth Century,* came out in 1930; a number of his pieces were published even after he had been sentenced to death by the Nuremberg court.

The Myth of the Twentieth Century was apparently conceived as a sequel, so to speak, to Chamberlain's book *The Foundations of the Nineteenth Century.* Both writers were familiar with a broad range of world literature, and both utilized the information they had imbibed in an eclectic and even erratic way. Among other things, Rosenberg denounced the churches—primarily the Catholic church but the Protestant denominations as well—as the heirs to the materialistic Jewish spirit that was alienated from nature and inimical to the Germans' Nordic soul. The German spirit was striving to return to its mythical source and crying out for a renewal of Aryan blood. He also decried the "naïve humanism" that was the religion of the Freemasons. But the antitype incarnate was the Jew, whose soul was governed by rationalism and was devoid of all creativity, artistic or functional. The Jews dreamed of the world domination of parasites and, therefore, propounded the counterracist doctrine embodied in the Zionist movement. Zionism was in no way a political movement, he held, for the Jews were wholly incapable of political creativity; its purpose was rather to use Jerusalem as a means to exploit the entire world. But the emergent German Reich would sweep them out like an iron broom.

Rosenberg was not without influence on Hitler, but the latter rejected his mystical bent—he even claimed that he never managed to read Rosenberg's book through to the end! Still, Rosenberg's main contribution was political. He branded the Jews as *political opponents* who were the purveyors of communism and the Russian Revolution, and he directed Hitler's glance toward the east, thus helping to fashion his basic outlook. For a long while Rosenberg was regarded as the chief expert on Russian affairs, and as the editor of *VB* he had an enormous impact on public opinion. But the more that Nazi policy took shape, especially after the abortive 1923 putsch, the more his influence declined.

The Swedish-Jewish historian Hugo Valentin has summed up the character of German anti-Semitism in the years after World War I:

> Anti-Semitism, which now struck the German people as a means of discharging aggression, was no longer the same hatred of Jews as in days past. . . . Anti-Semitism was the great store of heterogeneous aggressions and heterogeneous interests. The anti-Jewish mythology had a magnetic effect on the reactionaries, who despised the Weimar Republic; on the unemployed intellectuals; on the classes that had been worst hit by inflation and industrialization, namely, the middle class and the farmers; and on the conservatives, who were full of contempt for secularization, the disintegration of ethics, and modernization in art and literature.[27]

Hitler

The Shaping of His Personality

> Actually the reasons for anti-Semitism should be sought first and foremost not among the objects of hatred, to whom—contrary to fact and logic—the anti-Semite has ascribed practically everything he wished to find, but among the haters.[28]

If this statement by Hugo Valentin is applicable to anyone, it is Adolf Hitler. Ever since his debut on the stage of history at the beginning of the 1920s, attempts have been made to analyze his personality, fathom the secret of his success, and elucidate his downfall. But no less difficult than analyzing the führer's personality is explaining the fact that masses of people in Germany fell under the spell of his demagogy and the propaganda of the fascistic National Socialist movement that he inspired and led. Notwithstanding all the political, economic, social, and psychological explications—including the considerable research devoted after World War II to Germany's romantic, reactionary, and religious heritage—it is impossible to understand the success of National Socialism, its campaign of conquest, and the harrowing events of the war without Hitler as the focal figure and prime mover. Among the thirty-eight million people who died because of his tyrannical rule and unchecked ambitions were six million Jews—two-thirds of European Jewry. Hitler's campaign to annihilate the Jews was not a sudden whim. From the inception of his political career, the struggle against the Jews had been a prominent component of his Weltanschauung and political method. In his conversations with Rauschning, he once defined it as "a merciless struggle for world domination." Anti-Semitism was for Hitler both an ideological principal and a political and propaganda tactic that he used in a calculated manner. When asked by Rauschning if he believed it was necessary to destroy the Jew, Hitler demurred, "We should have then to invent him. It is essential to have a tangible enemy, not merely an abstract one."[29] Later he identified the Jew with all of his most hated enemies—the Marxists, the Russians, even the Western leaders who made war on him. Moreover, his entire historical and political outlook was based on his perception of the Jews as they were depicted in the *Protocols*. As the biographer Joachim C. Fest put it, "Certainly the thesis that the Jews were striving for world domination made good propaganda; but . . . he really believed this thesis, saw it as the key to all sorts of phenomena. He clung more and more to this 'redeeming formula,' convinced that through it he understood the nature of the great crisis of the age that he alone could cure."[30]

The first formulation of Hitler's anti-Semitic outlook is found in a letter he wrote in 1919:

> Antisemitism as a political movement may not and cannot be moulded by emotional factors but only by recognition of facts. To begin with, the Jews are unquestionably a race, not a religious community. . . . Through inbreeding for thousands of years, often in very small circles, the Jew has been able to preserve his race and his racial characteristics much more successfully than most of the numerous people among whom he lives. As a result we have living in our midst a non-German, alien race, unwilling and indeed unable to shed its racial characteristics. . . .
>
> Everything that makes the people strive for greater things, be it religion, socialism, or democracy, merely serves the Jew as a means to the satisfaction of his greed and thirst for power. The result of his works is racial tuberculosis of the nation. . . .
>
> Rational antisemitism, by contrast [to emotional antisemitism] must lead to a systematic and legal struggle against, and eradication of, what privileges the Jews enjoy over other foreigners living among us (Alien Laws). Its final objective, however, must be the total removal of all Jews from our midst.[31]

Hitler fused all the thoughts, impulses, and influences that anti-Semitism ascribed to the Jew into a comprehensive ideology on which he attempted to base not only his movement but also his personal career. He denied the Jews the designation of "human beings," for he believed they were created not in God's image but in Satan's, "The Jew is the creature of another god, the anti-man. . . . He is a creature outside nature and alien to nature."[32]

More than twenty years after writing this letter, on February 22, 1942, in one of his dinner-table monologues, Hitler reiterated the pronouncement that the Jew was the tuberculosis germ of humankind and compared his war against the Jews to the work of Louis Pasteur and Heinrich Koch against bacteria in the previous century. Diseases were caused by the Jewish germ, he continued, but "We shall be cured if we dispose of the Jew. . . . The cause of those diseases is the racial germ that corrupts the mixture of the blood."[33] This statement was made a month after the Wannsee Conference, by which time the extermination program was already in progress in Eastern Europe and the comprehensive plan for the "Final Solution" had already been completed. It can be assumed that Hitler's companions at that dinner knew that this was not idle talk but rather his explanation and justification of the extermination.

How did Hitler arrive at this anti-Semitic approach? He was born in the town of Braunau, Austria, on April 20, 1889, and his path from the provincial city of Linz—where he spent his youth—to Vienna has been described many times.[34] At first these accounts were based primarily on Hitler's own description of his development in his autobiographical–ideological work *Mein Kampf.* Combining his views and political aspirations with this narration of his life was characteristic of the way in which he chose to present himself and his mission. Napoleon was but a human being, Hitler once said, not a "world event."[35] Today it is clear that he fabricated and distorted facts in order to build an image that would be attractive to his followers and the millions of others he aspired to lead.

Failing to advance at school, Hitler abandoned his studies and lived aimlessly for a while in his mother's home (his father, a customs officer, had died by then). At the age of eighteen he went to Vienna to study architecture, but as his drawing ability proved insufficient, he failed to win a place at the Academy of Art. From then on he avoided any course that involved steady work and provided a fixed income; he lived a rather abstemious life, steeped in his dreams of grandeur for the future. Contrary to what he wrote in *Mein Kampf,* initially he did not suffer want and even came into a small inheritance after his mother's death at the end of 1907. Later, he lived on the fringe of society, lodging in a "men's hostel" (1910) where homeless and usually unskilled transients found shelter. Through the help of a partner, he was able to sell postcards and miniature pictures he had drawn, but eventually they fell out over money. In May 1913 Hitler moved to Munich, a change of venue designed to help him evade the draft (which he was certainly not interested in having revealed).[36] The Austrian police traced him to Munich and forced him to return to Linz for a clarification of the matter, but he managed to have himself classified as unfit for military service. (In 1938 he attempted to have the papers relating to this episode destroyed but failed to locate them.[37]) Yet when World War I broke out, he felt quite differently about the matter, immediately—even enthusiastically—volunteering for the German army. The war gave him a sense of purpose, cured his restlessness, and saved him from his inability to provide direction to his life.

From his youth onward Hitler had tried to build a life according to his own conception of things; thus he had had difficulty adjusting to existing frameworks and a steady job. This was also probably the reason for his failure in school. His interest in politics developed alongside his artistic ambitions, which were nurtured by a love for music, especially for operas—above all those of Wagner.[38] Reading was also one of his avid pastimes. But he read haphazardly, storing in his excellent memory data and impressions that were consistent with his beliefs and dreams. Hitler expanded on his method of reading in *Mein Kampf.*[39] He fed his imagination with stories of fantasy and adventure, with which German literature was generously endowed. Together with literature and art he also imbibed the prevailing prejudices of the day; Wagner's music conveyed to him the Aryan ideal and the composer's mythical-heroic conception of life and death. After the death of his deeply loved mother, Hitler at the age of twenty remained alone in Vienna, increasingly withdrawing into the world of his imagination.[40]

We can believe his statement that his Viennese period was a time of learning. Observing the political and social struggles going on around him, Hitler appreciated the potentially explosive situation inherent in the German rule of the Hapsburg Empire because of its diverse nationalities: Hungarians, Czechs, Poles, Serbs, Croats, and Italians. He was attracted to the pan-German ideology of the nationalist faction that went under the name of the Pan-German party, led by Georg Ritter von Schönerer. No less noteworthy at that time in Vienna was the Social Democratic party's struggle for supremacy, entailing as it did confrontations with both the Catholic church and the lower middle class. The bourgeoisie backed the leader of the Christian Socialist party, Karl Lueger, and with its help he succeeded in being elected mayor of Vienna. The rabid anti-Semitism common to Lueger and Schönerer was inflamed by the relatively large number of Jews in Vienna, many of whom had immigrated from Eastern Europe. But whereas Schönerer's anti-Semitic doctrine was primarily racist and nationalistic in character, Lueger attacked the Jew on economic grounds as being competitive, a successful merchant, and an exploiter. It was here that Hitler learned how great was the bourgeoisie's latent store of hatred and how effectively this enmity could be turned against the Jews. But he also learned from these two men that the Catholic church was the most powerful of the country's traditional institutions. Schönerer was at loggerheads with the church, whereas Lueger was clever enough to exploit the opposing interests of the prelates and the low-level clergy. In *Mein Kampf* Hitler summarized his view of the two anti-Semitic parties:

> If in addition to its shrewd knowledge of the broad masses the Christian Socialist party had adequately understood the importance of the race problem as the Pan-German movement had grasped it, and if finally the party had been nationalistic; or if the Pan-German movement besides its true insight into the goal of the Jewish question and the meaning of the nationalist idea had adopted also the shrewdness of the Christian Socialist party, and particularly the latter's attitude toward Socialism, the result would have been the one movement which in my opinion might successfully have changed the German fate.[41]

Along with observing these political struggles, Hitler studied the use of propaganda and demagoguery, especially the employment of anti-Semitism. He also learned a lesson from the people he hated most: the Social Democrats (he consistently referred to them as Marxists). He abhorred their doctrine of the inevitable class conflict and detested them just as he detested most members of the class from which he himself had come: the petite bourgeoisie. But he admired the Social Democrats' ability to organize the masses and get them out onto the streets. In *Mein Kampf* he related that on May Day he had stood for hours and watched the great parade of workers marching through the streets of Vienna with their red flags unfurled.[42] Hitler was sufficiently astute to learn from friend and foe alike, from those who conformed to his ideas and those who attacked them. But rather than conceive of his ideas as his personal opinion he held them to be absolute truths. Descriptions that have come down from his Viennese period make Hitler out to be an aloof man who had a way of lecturing when he spoke about his views. He loved a political debate but could not tolerate opinions that differed from his own. Even then there was already talk of his outbursts of rage and hysterical ranting when someone disagreed with him.

Hitler spent the war years with a regiment in France as a runner liaising between his battalion's units, so that he came into contact with all the companies and their officers. He is usually described as having been a disciplined and courageous soldier who earned a number of decorations. These included one of the German army's highest medals—the Iron Cross, First Class—which was usually only awarded to officers. Hitler related the circumstances in which he earned his other medals, but he never went into the background of this one, which at one point led to rumors that he had not received it rightfully or honestly. However, it appears that there was another reason for his silence on the subject: he wished to conceal the fact that the decoration had been awarded to him on the recommendation of the regiment's adjutant, who was a Jew. In any event he was never promoted any higher than corporal and apparently never wished to be. Toward the end of the war he was wounded in a gas attack that caused him temporary blindness, and this experience remained with him as a profound trauma.

Early Political Career

News of the armistice, the kaiser's abdication, and the founding of a republic found Hitler in the hospital recuperating from the effects of the gas attack. The tidings were a great shock to him—this was not the Germany for which he had gone to war—and he later recalled that on hearing the news he wept.[43] After being released from the hospital, he returned to Munich, remained in the army, and began to associate with the many soldiers in the Bavarian army—officers and enlisted men alike—who were opposed to the new regime. The Division of Information and Intelligence systematically worked to undermine the socialist regime that had been established in Bavaria; in May 1919 the socialist government was toppled with the aid of the Freikorps, paramilitary units dedicated to fighting against socialism in general and communism in particular. Hitler underwent a training course in political science at the University of Munich and was assigned to the staff of army lecturers whose task was to monitor the views of the soldiers who had been POWs and to indoctrinate them with nationalistic and anti-Marxist ideas. Thus Hitler began to hone the skill that was later to become his greatest political asset: oratory. Even then he often spoke of the threat that the Jews posed to the German people. It was also during this period, for example, that he wrote the letter quoted earlier. A few days afterward, on September 12, 1919, on orders from his commander, he attended the assembly of a small political party calling itself the German Workers Party (Deutsche Arbeiter Partie, or DAP) and participated in a debate. The party's members were so impressed by his speaking ability that they later tried to recruit him into their ranks. Hitler joined this small group as Member Number 555 and soon began to prepare the party for the great role he envisioned for it: a revolutionary party that would wrest unto itself the rule of Germany.

At first the party grew slowly, the most conspicuous element to join being active and demobilized soldiers referred to the new nationalist nucleus mainly by Major Ernst Röhm of the Division of Information and Intelligence. Before long, however, Hitler embarked on a systematic effort to bring the party to the public's attention. Meetings were organized in the beer cellars of Munich, demonstrations were held, and Hitler did not refrain from deliberately disturbing the peace and disrupting the public in order to attract attention. Within half a year he found himself speaking at a rally before two thousand people. He was not yet listed as the main speaker, but on that day, February 24, 1920, he introduced the new party's platform, and it is assumed that he also played a part in framing it.[44] The platform defined the aims of the National Socialist movement in twenty-five points that were divided among nationalist and anti-Semitic principles and social objectives (the Nazis made no attempt to realize these once they were in power). The thinking behind it was, for the most part, borrowed from systems and doctrines that had evolved during the nineteenth century. Generally speaking, it promised to satisfy the demands of most of the disaffected citizens of Germany and stressed its positive attitude to Christianity without committing itself to any specific church. But between the lines one could discern its far-reaching political goals and even a call for totalitarian rule. A week after the assembly at which the program was announced, the party changed its name and was known thereafter as the Nationalsozialistische Deutsche Arbeiter Partei, or NSDAP (National Socialist German Workers' Party). The new appelation was chosen in collaboration with similar organizations that had come into being prior to the war in the Sudeten district of Czechoslovakia (then still part of the Hapsburg Empire) as well as other groups in Germany and Austria.[45]

A few days later an insurrection broke out in Berlin. Mounted by an extreme right-wing group that was led by Max Kapp—thus subsequently known as the Kapp putsch—it was swiftly quelled by the army. But not before Hitler reached Berlin to follow the events at close hand. On returning to Munich he decided to devote his life to politics. From his demobilization on April 1, 1920, he lived as a politician, evidently receiving financial support from circles in Bavaria that were interested in reinforcing the opposition to the German Reich's central Social Democratic regime. His supporters included distinguished members of society; it was Dietrich Eckart who gained Hitler access to the salons of the aristocracy and financiers, schooling him in the etiquette necessary to circulate in this society. Hitler called attention to himself by both his long silences and his eruptions into extemporaneous discourse, and he succeeded in exciting his audiences—particularly its female members—in this circle as well.

Hitler regarded propaganda as the primary instrument for advancing his political aims and disseminating his ideas among the masses. His chief propaganda tool was the oration, and oratory skill may have been the one thing he learned thoroughly and systematically.[46] Unquestionably, he had a natural talent as a speaker, and his instincts led him to focus on issues that perturbed his listeners, promising them what they wanted to hear. That was how he earned their confidence. But beyond following his instincts, he planned his appearances carefully: coordinating appropriate gestures, studying the halls in which he was scheduled to appear, testing the acoustics, and so on. At the same time he took pains to give his orations the ceremonial character of a show in which every detail was worked out in advance, and the military and ritual aspects of his appearances became increasingly pronounced and sophisticated.

Hitler himself noted the power of "mass suggestion" and its "spellbinding effect" in *Mein Kampf,* "The will, the longing, and likewise the power of thousands are accumulated in every individual. The man who enters such a meeting doubting and wavering leaves it inwardly reinforced; he has become a link in the community."[47] His rapport with the masses has often been described in erotic terms; he himself referred to the masses as a woman, with his objective being to overpower them and eradicate their independent thought and will. He viewed the rally as an arena of struggle from which he must emerge the victor. While speaking at these assemblies, he abandoned all restraint and worked himself into a state of ecstasy that usually left him drained. Hitler needed the oration and the uninhibited devotion of the masses no less than they were in need of the assurance and inner reinforcement that he provided them. Perhaps oration was the means through which he achieved the sense of power that was the basic aspiration of his being. As the biographer Joachim Fest has noted:

> Anyone who thought the entire secret of Hitler's success as an orator lay in [his] use of speech as a sexual surrogate would be making a serious mistake. Rather, once again it was the curious coupling of delirium and rationality that characterized his oratory. Gesticulating in the glare of spotlights, pale, his voice hoarse as he hurled charges, tirades, and outbursts of hatred, he remained always the alert master of his emotions. For all his seeming abandon, he never lost control. We are dealing here with the same ambiguity that governed his entire behavior and was one of the basic facts of his character.[48]

Although Hitler regarded the spoken word as his main means of influence, he also worked on developing symbols and other means of captivating the masses. Though he was not the one who discovered the swastika, as he claimed (it had earlier been used by other nationalist groups), he made it the symbol of his party. Similarly, he copied the use of the color red on the flag from the Socialists but went beyond it by posting huge red placards to announce his rallies. In December 1921, with the generous aid of donors, he purchased *VB* and turned it into the party's main organ. But he also regarded terror as a vital means of gaining attention. As early as the summer of 1921, Hitler began organizing a violent unit that was initially called a defense force and was officially introduced under the guise of the Division for Propaganda and Sports but soon received the name Sturmabteilung, or SA (storm troopers). The members of the paramilitary organizations were recruited to this militia, as were people who had earlier been active in perpetrating the right-wing terror that spread through Bavaria.

Hitler evidently acquired some of his knowledge of mass psychology from Chamberlain, who had noted that mass rallies blunt the individual's judgment and intensify his zeal and that the effect is similar to hypnosis, which is why there is special importance to the speeches of people of brutal strength, who win out over sharper and subtler minds.[49]

The Abortive Putsch

The tension in Germany, meanwhile, was rising as a result of rampant inflation, unemployment, and political unrest. The friction between the central government in Berlin and the reactionary and separatist forces in Bavaria soared. In the belief that he could exploit the situation to his movement's advantage, Hitler tried to incite an armed insurrection on May 1, 1923. Although he failed and was forced to retire from the political arena for a few months, the Bavarian authorities preferred not to place him on trial. This hiatus was spent in a house placed at his disposal in the alpine resort of Berchtesgaden. By the end of that summer, it appeared that new conditions had emerged for collaboration between the army and the National Socialist party. Having acquired the support of General Erich Ludendorff together with a number of other nationalists, Hitler established a militant alliance that set as its goal a revolution to dissolve the Weimar Republic and abrogate the Versailles treaty. He expected to gain backing for his aims among the ruling circles in Bavaria and thus began making preparations for a putsch to be executed on the anniversary of the Second Reich's downfall, November 9, 1923. Following Mussolini's example, he dreamed not only of wresting power in the Bavarian capital of Munich but of marching on Berlin. The putsch was immediately quashed by the army, which failed to collaborate as Hitler had expected. The shots fired at the insurrectionist marchers killed a number of Hitler's supporters, including the man with whom he was walking arm in arm. Hitler himself was slightly wounded and fled the scene.

Surprisingly, however, the movement recovered quickly, and Hitler succeeded in turning his trial into a political spectacle that spread his fame throughout Germany. In the course of the proceedings, he publicly declared his intention to topple the regime but rejected the charge that this was an act of treason. Sentenced to five years' imprisonment, he was released after nine months, and the efforts of the police and the state prosecutor to have him deported proved fruitless.

Hitler's prison term more closely resembled house arrest in the company of his followers than internment behind bars. He used it for two ends: to draw the necessary conclusions from the abortive putsch and to plan his next move. He also started writing *Mein Kampf* during this period. Hitler's conclusions can be summed up in three points: (1) the rule of Germany must be attained by legal means, not by a violent coup; (2) rule cannot be wrested against the will of the army; and (3) it will be necessary to exacerbate the unrest in the country and employ methods appropriate to a civil war without violating the first two principles. The Nazis conducted their struggle along these lines in the years to come, which were the first years of stability for the Weimar Republic. From a propaganda and organizational standpoint, they laid the foundations that enabled them to begin their countdown toward assuming power once the grave economic crisis set in at the end of the 1920s.

Forging an Ideology

Considering their circumstances, Hitler and his movement ascribed supreme importance to the task of fashioning an ideology. In subsequent years he would repeatedly stress that Weltanschauung was even more important than military strength, political influence, or organizational ability, and the focus of his own outlook was racial anti-Semitism.

A vehicle for conveying this Weltanschauung, *Mein Kampf* is a poorly organized work, full of repetition and written in an unpolished and often abstruse

style. Only occasionally does the writing move along on a wave of Hitlerite rhetoric; rarely does it develop a subject systematically. Initially, the book did not sell
well, and most readers found it difficult to take its superficial and distorted views,
demagogy, and anti-Semitic threats seriously. It was only after World War II that
people began to analyze the book's contents and found that it contained almost
everything that Hitler ultimately brought to pass as head of the Third Reich. *Mein
Kampf* addressed itself to many issues: Germany's standing after World War I;
political strategy and Germany's political objectives on both the domestic and
foreign fronts; ways of influencing the masses (the issue of propaganda was one of
the few developed systematically); and, of course, Hitler's personal career and the
principles that directed his actions. Again and again, the subject of the Jews came
up, their destructive influence being depicted as the primary obstacle to redressing
Germany's condition, ensuring its recuperation, and returning the country to the
standing it deserved in the world. The book gave expression to the total fusion of
Hitler's personal ambitions and what he understood as Germany's fate. Only with
Hitler at its head, *Mein Kampf* implied, would Germany fulfill its destiny.

Hitler roundly condemned the two main classes in German society—the bourgeoisie and the proletariat—accusing the middle class of treason and the working
class of the crime of Marxism. But essentially he saw them both as victims of the
Jew. His depiction of the Jews reflects all the traits ascribed to them by the various
anti-Semitic doctrines, and his explanation of their behavior runs in the spirit of
the *Protocols.* In *Mein Kampf,* however, this "historical" exegesis and "political"
analysis were joined by a new element: the denunciation of the Jew for his alleged
sexual tendencies and his aspiration to corrupt pure Aryan blood through sexual
relations, "For hours the black-haired Jew-boy, diabolic joy in his face, waits in
ambush for the unsuspecting girl whom he defiles with his blood, and thus robs
her from her people. With the aid of all means he tries to ruin the racial foundations of the people to be enslaved . . . a racially pure people, conscious of its blood,
can never be enslaved by the Jew."[50]

Hitler reiterated here the contention so popular among the anti-Semites that
the Jews were responsible for the outbreak of World War I, for Germany's defeat,
and for the fall of the Wilhelmine government. To his statements on World
War I Hitler added expressions of slander and hatred against the Jews that, in light
of his subsequent actions during World War II, foreshadowed a real threat. Thus
he deplored the fact that the national frenzy inspired by the outbreak of World
War I was not used to do away with "the whole fraudulent brotherhood of Jewish
poisoners of the people." Hitler continued, "It [is] the duty of a prudent government . . . to mercilessly root out [*ausrotten*] the instigators against this nationality.
If the best were killed on the front, then one could at least destroy the vermin at
home."[51] And toward the end of *Mein Kampf,* he reiterated this approach in an
even more explicit form:

> If at the beginning of the war and during the war, twelve or fifteen thousand of these
> Hebraic corruptors of the nation had been subjected to poison gas, such as had to be
> endured in the field by hundreds of thousands of our very best German workers of all
> classes and professions, then the sacrifice of millions at the front would not have been

in vain. On the contrary; twelve thousand scoundrels, opportunely eliminated, and perhaps a million orderly, worthwhile Germans had been saved for the future. But it is also part of the bourgeois "statecraft" to deliver millions to a bloody end on the battlefield without blinking an eyelash while regarding ten or twelve thousand traitors, tricksters, userers and swindlers as a priceless national shrine and hence publicly to proclaim their inviolability. Indeed, one cannot tell whether this bourgeois world is richer in blockheadedness, feebleness, and cowardice, or through dissipated principles. It is truly a class doomed by Fate to decline but which, unfortunately, is dragging the whole nation along with it into the abyss.[52]

When the time came, however, Hitler was very adept at using the bourgeoisie to ascend to power. To this end he used terror, political tactics, and propaganda based on the racist ideology. Undermining the foundations of the German state, he would eventually drag it to the brink of the abyss.

Jews in Germany During the Early Days of Nazi Rule (Through the End of 1935)

The National Socialist Revolution (1933–1934)

The Creation of a Totalitarian Government

> By appointing Hilter chancellor you have delivered our sacred German homeland into the hands of the worst demagogue of all times. I foresee that this evil man will lead our country into the abyss and will inflict boundless trouble on our people. Future generations will curse you in your grave for this deed.[1]

On February 1, 1933, General Erich Ludendorff, Hilter's cohort in the aborted coup of 1923, wired these ominous words to Field Marshal Paul von Hindenburg, who had been his comrade-in-arms during World War I. But this was not the way the majority of the Conservatives, headed by Franz von Papen and Alfred Hugenberg, envisioned the future. They cooperated with Hilter in the hope that they would be the ones to gain control of the dictatorship that would rise in Germany with the help of the "drummer" Hilter, whose demagogy would arouse the masses to his banner. Their concept seemed reasonable because there were eight Conservatives in the government headed by Hilter and only two National Socialists, who ran seemingly unimportant ministries: Hermann Göring, a commissar of the Prussian Ministry of the Interior and Reichskommissar of the Air Force, and Wilhelm Frick, head of the Reich Ministry of the Interior. The ministries of Foreign Affairs, Finance, Defense, Labor, Postal Service, and Transport would all be headed by Conservatives. Hugenberg, as minister of industry and agriculture and economic commissar of Prussia, visualized himself as the Reich's economic dictator.

At Hilter's request the Reichstag was dissolved and new elections were called. He even promised that the composition of the government would remain unchanged regardless of the outcome of the elections. Hence, he pledged, in effect, not to abolish Germany's parliamentary regime; in point of fact it was the Conservatives who planned to abolish the democratic government. At the very first meeting of the new government, on January 31, 1933, Papen, the deputy chancellor, proposed the immediate enactment of an enabling law that would paralyze the Reichstag. However, aware that he was not yet strong enough to overthrow the existing regime, Hilter rejected the proposal as being "contrary to the constitution."[2] Neither did the opposition consider Hitler as the essential source of peril then; as far as the Social Democrats and even the Communists were concerned, it was the Conservatives who had emerged as the victors. On February 6, 1933, Papen, in his capacity as commissar for Prussia, abolished that state's Social Democratic government, but the heads of the Social Democratic party, fearing a civil war, were reluctant to activate the power inherent within their organizations.[3] Meanwhile, Hitler saw to it that responsibility for the police was transferred to his own people. His fellow ministers agreed to appoint Göring as commissar of the Prussian police (there was no nationwide police force, each secondary state was responsible for its own force), and Göring soon demonstrated that this key position was more important than all the offices held by the Conservatives.

At the height of the election campaign, an event took place that rightly became the symbol of the Nazi revolution in Germany: the burning of the Reichstag on the night of February 27. Scholars are still debating the question of who set fire to that grand edifice. The building was consumed in a matter of minutes, and it was as if the entire parliamentary regime had gone up in flames with it. A young, unstable Dutch drifter named Marinus van der Lubbe was caught red-handed, but although he stubbornly insisted that he had acted on his own, the widespread assumption both in Germany and abroad was that the Nazis had set fire to the building.[4] This, then, is the first outstanding example we have of the means used by Hitler and his companions to hasten the realization of their designs and steer developments in the direction they desired. Whether the National Socialist leaders simply exploited whatever opportunities happened to come their way as they struggled for political power or whether they organized and, when necessary, staged such opportunities, their intent and objectives were clear from the outset. In fact, their plans were often prepared in advance, down to the last detail, and they were put into effect when an opportune moment presented itself.[5]

This unique combination of methodical planning and opportunism, of tight control and improvisation, of rational preparation and intuitive action was characteristic not only of Hitler himself but of the way in which the Nazis rose to power, exercised power, and then fell from power. In the context of this political technique, which we shall encounter time and again in our discussion, it is not particularly important whether van der Lubbe was the Nazis' unwitting accomplice or whether he acted entirely on his own; what counted was the decisive step the Nazis took the next day toward establishing a dictatorship. The Emergency Regulation in Defense of the People and the State, passed by the government and signed by Hindenburg on February 28, abolished the basic rights and legal protection enjoyed by the citizens of a democratic state. On the pretense of acting against the Communists, this regulation abrogated the legal protection of the citizen's personal freedom, the right of free expression and freedom of the press, and the right of free assembly and organization. It permitted violation of the right to secrecy in the mails, telegraph, and telephone; the search of homes; and the confiscation of property. Anyone found violating the new regulations was liable to severe punishment, with harsh prison terms or the death sentence being stipulated for insurrection, attempts on the lives of cabinet members, arson against public buildings, and so on.[6]

This legislative groundwork for the institution of a dictatorship was accompanied by a campaign of propaganda and terror, two methods that the Nazis had employed very effectively during their rise to power and that they would now be able to exploit even more extensively. The elections gave them a pretext to cover the entire country with a barrage of propaganda. Hitler was flown from place to place in a special plane, and his speeches were broadcast over all the radio stations.

No less important was the terror practiced by the police under the command of Göring as Prussia's commissar of internal affairs. He operated on three levels, firing officials loyal to the republic (including many police officers), legalizing the SA and SS as "guardians of law and order in the country," and introducing state-generated terror by means of the police. The change in the nature and activity of the police was no less crucial. For example, the force received an explicit order to use arms liberally, and Göring's shooting order *(Schiessbefehl)* not only authorized the use of firearms but obliged the police to kill.[7] Göring also revised the structure of the police force. Rudolph Diels, who had proven himself during the uprising against the government in Prussia in July 1932, was assigned to head the Political Department now staffed almost entirely with new personnel. Once it was securely established and began to expand, this department became the Secret State Police, known by the acronym Gestapo, the powerful instrument of dictatorial rule that extended throughout the Reich and all the territories conquered and annexed thereto.

By February all the elements necessary for the foundation of a totalitarian state were in place. The Reichstag fire accelerated the process and helped to give it a public and widespread effect. In a sense the regulations promulgated on February 28 can be viewed as the declaration of the establishment of the Third Reich.[8]

Meeting with army commanders on February 1, Hitler declared that the objective of his domestic policy was "to overturn completely the present political situation in Germany." At that first meeting with the heads of the military, he explained the basic points of the regulations issued afterward at the end of February.[9] He also outlined his prime political aspirations in terms of both domestic and foreign affairs—aspirations he later realized.

After dealing this initial blow, primarily to the Communists, the Nazis expected to win a clear-cut victory in the elections on March 5. But rather than achieve the absolute majority they had hoped for, they received only a slim majority of 51.7 percent, including the 8 percent gleaned by the Conservatives. The resultant political and parliamentary situation made other extreme measures necessary to ensure the establishment of a totalitarian government by the Nazis.

Forging the Regime

With the establishment (on March 13) of the Ministry of Information and Pro-paganda under Goebbels—meaning that another Nazi minister was added to the government—the first step was taken toward the effective and institutional iden-tification of the National Socialist Party with the German Reich, for now the ide-ology of the Nazi party assumed an official nature. The identity of the party and the Reich was formally recognized on December 1, 1933, when Hitler announced the law granting the party the status of a body recognized by law and establishing the "unity of the state and the party."[10] Nevertheless, in March of that year Ger-many still retained many of the independent public bodies that characterize free societies. The government addressed this situation by enacting what the Nazis called *Gleichschaltung* (coordination). This is one of many examples of phrases coined or imbued with special content by the National Socialists. The changes they introduced in the vocabulary, syntax, and even the grammar of the German language were among the most prominent expressions of the revolution they engendered not only in politics and society but in German culture as well. To the Nazis language was a tool for issuing orders, conveying propaganda, and creating deception. Hence, they designated what they called a *Sprachregelung* (language regulation) to serve the administrative and propaganda purposes of the totalitarian regime. Goebbels, for instance, used this regulation to issue his orders to the newspapers.[11]

Gleichschaltung was the means by which the Nazi apparatus gained control over the German people. Opponents who did not flee the country in time were purged, some were murdered, others were tortured in bunkers of the SA or incar-cerated in concentration camps. From March 1933 to the end of the year, fifty such camps were established in various parts of Germany.[12] Many people joined the ranks of the Nazis out of fear, indifference, or because they had secretly sym-pathized with them. As a result German society was torn asunder and the tottering democratic regime was shattered completely. This trend was particularly wide-spread among officials serving in the state governments and the judiciary. At the end of 1932, for example, the Society of National Socialist Jurists numbered 1,347 members; a year later its membership had reached 80,000.[13]

Göring's achievements in Prussia were duplicated in Bavaria, where Heinrich Himmler laid the foundations of the "SS State" by means of which he would subsequently extend his supervision and control throughout Germany. He built the Dachau concentration camp in Bavaria, thereby inaugurating the system of institutionalized terror. In April 1934 he also succeeded in encroaching on Göring's territory in Prussia when he was appointed deputy commissioner of the police and his loyal follower, Reinhard Heydrich, replaced Diels.[14]

The "Enabling Act," passed by the Reichstag on March 23, 1933, provided Hitler with a legal instrument to sanction the existing situation and empowered him to continue developing it further. Called the Law for Removing the Distress of People and Reich *(Gesetz zur Behebung der Not von Volk und Reich)*, the "Enabling Act" invested Chancellor Hitler with legislative authority.[15] Immediately after its passage, on March 31 and April 7, Hitler signed laws making *Gleichschaltung* mandatory (the term being used here for the first time). Effectively these laws abolished the parliamentary regime in Germany's secondary states and replaced it with commissars called Reichsstatthalter (Reich Governors). On April 7 Papen had to resign from the post of Reichskommissar of Prussia and Göring was appointed its prime minister. Thus, the government of the largest and most powerful of the German secondary states passed into the hands of the National Socialists. All these acts were accompanied by grandiose public ceremonies at which Hitler portrayed himself to the German people as the redeemer who would restore Germany to its past glory.[16]

After triumphing over the republican state governments, Hitler turned his attention to the Social Democratic labor organizations and the church, which offered strong resistance to *Gleichschaltung*. The struggle between the Nazis and the church was the most bitter and protracted of all, though eventually the Nazis succeeded in weakening the religious groups from within and eliciting their support for the government. A fairly significant number of the clergy, particularly of the Protestant church, even supported National Socialism enthusiastically. However, the Nazis never acquired complete control over the churches, as evidenced by thousands of clergymen who were sent to concentration camps.

After gaining control of the government, the Nazis focused their energies against the labor unions and the large Labor party. In the spring of 1933 these bodies still appeared to be a solid, organized bloc in which the Nazis had failed to make any inroads as compared with the foothold they had gained within the bourgeoisie. Early in May, however, the National Socialists landed a crushing blow that broke the labor front in short order. For the first time the Nazis made use of deception on a large scale, a technique they were eventually to perfect as a means of psychological warfare against their victims. May Day (May 1), the workers' holiday, was declared a national holiday under the official name National Labor Day. In a nationwide broadcast of a long speech delivered at a mass meeting in Berlin, Hitler announced that the slogan for the day would be "Honor labor and honor the laborer!" He proclaimed an end to the class war that had impaired the national spirit, so that from then on all Germans, "brain workers and fist workers," would be united in their labor under the leadership of National Socialism for the good of the people and the state. The following morning the meaning of these words became clear: units of the SA and the SS seized the offices, homes, clubs, and banks owned by the socialist trade unions and most of their leaders and many of their active members were arrested, disappearing into prisons and concentration camps. The unions, with their 4.5 million members, were disbanded.[17]

A week later, on May 10, Hitler mounted his assault on the Social Democratic party. Throughout Germany the Nazi rulers seized the party's offices, funds, and more than a hundred of its newspapers. That same day, with all the important government figures in attendance, Hitler held the first open-air rally of the new German Labor Front, which was placed under the leadership of Robert Ley. Within a few days all independent organizations and free societies were purged and disbanded. On June 22 the Social Democratic party itself was officially banned. It was not necessary for Hitler to move against the bourgeois parties, which included his Conservative partners; they disintegrated and folded on their own initiative. At the end of June, Hugenberg, the head of the Conservative party, resigned from the coalition government, and on July 7 Hitler announced to the Reich deputies that the "revolutionary period" had ended. The fact that the parliamentary republic had ceased to exist was officially recognized on July 14 with the promulgation of the law forbidding the establishment of any new political parties. Thus the National Socialist Party became the only recognized party in Germany.[18] As early as April 22 Goebbels had noted in his diary that developments had unfolded far more quickly than they had dared to hope.[19]

Of all the bases of power in the Weimar Republic, only two still retained their independence: industrialists and the army. From the standpoint of the German economy, Hitler inherited a painful legacy of some six million unemployed, and his much-touted promise to assure the livelihood of every worker was an important factor in his swift victory over the Social Democrats. It was Hitler's good fortune that the world economy began to recover in the spring of 1933, but the relative speed with which the German economy was overcoming the depression was also due to a number of measures introduced by the "economic wizard" Hjalmar Schacht. Schacht had been president of the Reichsbank during the 1920s but left it in 1930. He supported Hitler even before the Nazis rose to power, and he acted as his mediator with the country's industrialists and leading capitalists. Hence, it was only natural in March 1933 that he would be called on to resume management of Germany's central financial institution; in July 1934 he was also appointed minister of economics.

Germany's main economic problems were the need to revitalize industry and reduce the number of unemployed, improve the trade balance, supervise the means of payment, and above all acquire foreign currency. The workers were forced to become members of a new organization called the Nationalsozialistische Betriebszellenorganization, or NSBO, under the control of "leaders." Employers also had to join a new organization under Nazi leadership, and their roles and rights were defined by special regulations. But they effectively remained independent in their economic activities and were accorded broader powers vis-à-vis their employees. The same cannot be said of the middle class, however, The petite bourgeoisie, which had played an important role in bringing Hitler to power, waited for the rewards he had promised. Instead, their organizations were swamped by the *Gleichschaltung,* losing their independence and being forbidden to engage in any activity outside the framework of the all-embracing labor organization.[20] Moreover, as we shall see later, the whole process had a strong, perhaps decisive, influence on the attitude toward the Jews during that period.

Hitler's Totalitarian Methods of Rule

Did Hilter exert unified, centralized, systematic control over Germany? Did his totalitarian system mean that his wishes were the moving spirit behind everything that happened in the complex entity known as the Third Reich? That the answer to this question is unequivocally negative is now confirmed by all scholars of the period.[21] At the same time, there is also no doubt that until his death in the bunker beneath his Berlin chancellery, Hitler was absolute master of Germany. He held both legislative and executive power; after the slaughter of the leaders of the SA on June 30, 1934, he also assumed the mantle of supreme judge, with the authority to pass the death sentence. Time and again in the course of the years, his absolute authority was reaffirmed by his party—the only party that functioned in the Reich. Thus the Reichstag was composed of members of the Nazi party only: in later years it was convened at the will of the führer for the sole purpose of hearing his speeches and approving his laws.

Probably never in all of history did the Roman motto *divide et impera* (divide and rule) have had a more conscientious follower than Adolf Hitler. Nazi Germany was ruled not by a systematic division of powers, but by a chaotic profusion of authorities. No field of action was concentrated under a single jurisdiction, institution, or bureaucratic apparatus; two or more bodies always competed for control of any given geographical region, sphere of activity, power base, or government post. The Reich authorites and ministries functioned alongside, and in competition with, those of the secondary states. The administrative regions and their local institutions worked alongside the party's civic district managers and against the party's Gauleiter, who was usually an old warrior now looking forward to enjoying the power for which he had struggled. Party members recently appointed to administrative posts worked alongside officials from the Weimar days, who were retained because their professional experience was needed to run the government. Within the Nazi movement the Gauleiter competed with the commander of the SA, who, in turn, competed with the commander of the SS; the head of the Hitlerjugend, the National Socialist youth organization, established his province somewhere between them. There were no clearly delineated spheres of influence; all of them seemed to overlap and infringe on one another. The result was constant bickering between one institution and the next, one authority and another. The bureaucracy was awash with jealousy and disgruntlement, fear and raw ambition. Hitler called this relentless struggle, engaged in at all levels of the regime, "noble competition," thereby confirming that it was an integral part of his dictatorship.[22]

The main antagonism arose between the body broadly regarded as the state, which represented a defined, static political entity that was striving to establish norms (in the form of laws), and the revolutionary party, which was bent on destroying those very norms in demanding for itself absolute rule. The party's objective was not the establishment of norms, that is, a new political structure, but rather constant, dynamic movement. Such incessant dynamism needed an arena of relentless struggle. But struggle implies enemies, and now that Germany had been vanquished in one fell swoop, where were these enemies to be found?

Domestically, there were still Marxists, clergy, Jews, and when necessary, bureaucrats and intellectuals; but most of the enemies were beyond Germany's borders. Martial aggression was among the inherent needs of the regime, so that Hitler's system was not perfected until the outbreak of World War II. This need also explains the special status he ascribed to the army from the outset and why in June 1934 he was even ready to sacrifice the leaders of the SA to ensure its primacy. Hindenburg's death two months later enabled Hitler to place himself at the head of the army, so that henceforward the military swore allegiance to, and took orders directly from, him.

Each of the high-ranking Nazis fortified his own position to the best of his ability, but in the final analysis each man's power depended on his closeness to the führer—a situation that prompted fierce jockeying for power within the hierarchy. As one of the chief organizers of the slaughter of the SA on June 30, 1934, Himmler learned his lesson well and attempted to transform the SS into Hitler's instrument of state terror. Hitler, for his part, exercised his power with unmatched virtuosity by means of three instruments used individually or in combination— terror, legislation or administrative decree, and propaganda—his skill arising from a blend of blind impulse, instinctive initiative, and cold, sober calculation.

April 1, 1933: The Anti-Jewish Boycott and Legislation— Significance and Results

The Attack on the Jews in View of Gleichschaltung

> In every local branch and organizational section of the National Socialist German Workers' Party, Action Committees are to be formed immediately for the practical systematic implementation of a boycott of Jewish shops, Jewish goods, Jewish doctors and Jewish lawyers. The Action Committees are responsible for making sure that the boycott will not affect innocent persons, but will hit the guilty all the harder.

This is the first of eleven points included in an order published on the front page of the official Nazi newspaper, *Völkischer Beobachter (VB)*, dated March 29, 1933.[23] The entire page was devoted to the subject. The main headline set in large, bold type read, "Let Jewry Know Against Whom It Has Declared War." The official decree of the Nazi party leadership had been decided on the day before, March 28, between Goebbels and Hitler. On Saturday morning, April 1, at exactly ten o'clock, at a "single stroke," a general boycott was to go into effect against the Jews throughout Germany. As the boycott was meant to "hit the Jews in their most sensitive spot," meaning their commercial activities, the SA and SS were to station guards at the entrance to Jewish establishments "to warn the public against entering the premises." Most of the points in the order dealt not with ways of effectuating the boycott, but with preliminary propaganda measures. The Action Committees were to explain the campaign to the people as "a defensive measure that has been forced upon us" because of "Jewish atrocity propaganda abroad." Newspapers were to be carefully scrutinized to make sure they were fulfilling their duty; if not, "they must be subjected to public scorn" by no longer being read or having advertisements placed in them. The committees were also to visit industrial plants and "explain to the workers the need for a national boycott as a defensive measure to protect German labor." The farmers, on the other hand, were to be made aware of the need to "strike particularly at Jewish traders in the countryside," making it necessary for the propagandists to reach "into the smallest peasant villages." All this was not enough, however, so that signs and placards were distributed and thousands of mass meetings were organized to "demand the imposition of a limited quota of Jews in all professions, according to their ratio to the German population."

Two restrictions were placed on all these actions: maximum protection was to be ensured "for all foreigners, without regard to their religion, origin or race. The boycott is . . . directed exclusively against the German Jews"; and "the entire struggle is [to be] carried out with strict discipline," and no harm was to be done to any Jew. The Action Committees were charged with carrying out these two orders. Additional explanations to the party members stressed that "More than ever before, it is necessary for the whole party to stand in blind obedience, as one man, behind the leadership." Moreover, the entire operation was portrayed as a continuation of the "realization of the miracle" of the overthrow of the "November Government," a "second task" to be accomplished by the National Socialists to prove that "the national revolutionary government is not floating in a vacuum" and that the entire nation stands behind it. While the overt threat was directed at "international world Jewry," a sort of editorial emphasis was placed on the Marxists, who were accused, after having been overcome in Germany, of "continuing their criminal traitorous actions against our people abroad." The claim that the Socialist forces had been overcome was unfounded at the time, as was the bragging declaration that in their vote on March 5 the large majority of Germans had "expressed their faith in the new government."[24] In fact, the decisive struggle against the Social Democrats and their powerful organizations still lay ahead for the new rulers of Germany.

Moreover, the Nazi regime was then deeply involved in striving to impose *Gleichschaltung,* whose first law was scheduled to be published on April 1, the very day of the boycott. In preparation for this fateful struggle, it was necessary to mobilize all the National Socialist forces and place them under the strictest control, because ever since the elections terror ("the party revolution from below," as Martin Broszat had put it) had been rampant, and the Nazi leadership seemed to be in danger of losing control of the rank and file. For several months terror had been directed against individual Jews, Jewish organizations, and Jewish institutions and businesses as well as other "enemies of the regime." These activities aroused strong reaction abroad, and there were growing indications that they might affect Germany's foreign relations and exacerbate its economic problems. The Nazi leaders needed a period of domestic tranquility to secure their control of the country; hence, they were eager to put a stop to the uncontrolled terror and the so-called atrocity propaganda it provoked.[25] One clause of the boycott program instructed Germans with contacts abroad to explain, orally and in writing, that "calm and order reign in Germany, that the German nation has no more ardent a desire than to go about its work in peace and to live in peace with the rest of the world." Within the country, the Nazis wanted to spread their message and introduce their organizational apparatus into industrial concerns, most of which were still controlled by the socialist trade unions. They also strove to establish themselves in even the "most remote villages," particularly in the Catholic areas of the south where overall organizational authority had yet to be imposed. It was no coincidence that on the same April 1 Himmler was appointed commander of the Bavarian police. There were still newspapers in Germany that dared to write critical articles; they, too, had to be silenced.

In the same way that the Emergency Regulation in Defense of the People and the State of February 28 had been introduced together with struggle against the Communists, the April action against the Jews also served the tactical struggle for *Gleichschaltung* and was a sort of dress rehearsal for the blow that would be dealt the Social Democrats. Just as the deception practiced in February had not been grasped, now, too, people believed that the boycott and accompanying laws were directed against the Jews alone. This time the Nazis took pains to have this perception prevail abroad as well as in Germany. Of course, they really did regard the Jews as their enemies, just as they knew that the Marxists—including the Communists—were their implacable foes.

The anti-Semitic ideology was a focal tenet of Nazism, and Hitler himself undoubtedly believed that the Jew was a subhuman creature *(Untermensch)* who possessed dangerous international influence. The first signs of the danger implied in this influence was expressed (as the Nazis then saw it) in the protest meetings held abroad, the calls for boycotts of German goods, and the diplomatic approaches by foreign governments.[26] But the Nazi policy toward the Jews during that period should be viewed from another perspective as well. Ideologically, the Nazis were able to incorporate into their totalitarian regime every group and class that accepted their dominance, but their very conception of *Gleichschaltung* excluded the Jews; no place could be found for them in their totalitarian system. Now that *Gleichschaltung* was being put into practice throughout the country, the Nazis intended to exclude the Jews from the process being imposed on all the rest of German society and accord them a special status that would be manifested on three main levels: social, cultural, and economic. On each of these levels, the isolation and ostracism of the Jews were effected gradually, at varying rates. The exclusion of the Jews from the economic, cultural, and social life of Germany was not accomplished according to a definite, preconceived plan, but steadily expanded and became more rigorous in the wake of broader developments within the country. The Nazis used three methods to achieve their objective of oppressing the Jews: terror, propaganda, and legislation.

All three were combined in the April action. The ferment within the ranks of the Nazi party, instigating acts of terror not controlled by the central government, traced primarily to dissatisfaction within the petite bourgeoisie and other circles that took the party's socialist slogans seriously. As noted, these elements not only failed to enjoy any gain from Hitler's rise to power, but found themselves trapped in organizations that afforded them absolutely no influence. Attacking Jewish-owned shops and businesses was a way of rebelling. Jews were also kidnapped as they walked along the street or were snatched out of homes and offices, held in bunkers, beaten, injured, and sometimes shot—usually, "while trying to escape." With the institution of an organized boycott, however, the feelings of frustration found an outlet that simultaneously demanded strict discipline. Ironically, the man responsible for this disciplined action was, of all people, the most rabid anti-Semite and agitator, Julius Streicher, the editor of the anti-Semitic weekly *Der Stürmer*.[27] The boycott, then, was designed both to control the unruly forces and permit them to vent their feelings. It was also meant to frighten Jews and non-Jews opposed to the regime and convey the party's message to workers and farmers' groups. Toward this end, on the afternoon of April 1, industrial workers (described in the press as workers in Jewish concerns) were called to a protest meeting in Berlin's central square, where Goebbels addressed them.[28]

The April 1 action had to begin exactly at ten o'clock in the morning throughout the country. It was designed to show the outside world who the real rulers of Germany were and prove that they were strong enough "to maintain quiet." (The same pattern was used on May 2 against the Social Democrats.[29]) Indeed, it accomplished these goals, but with one unforeseen result: it caused a great uproar abroad, prompting more negative reaction than any other move undertaken by the Nazis. This also explains why the government quickly brought the action to a halt. Although the initial intention was apparently to prolong it, an official declaration on April 4 informed the public that the "boycott has achieved its purpose and is over."[30]

Anti-Jewish Legislation: Its Nature and Significance

The anti-Jewish propaganda and the April 1 boycott were accompanied by certain legislative measures. Before the "Enabling Act" was passed in the Reichstag, the Nazi legislators' legal experts in the Interior and Justice ministries of the various states—particularly Prussia—and the Reich government discussed the changes they wished to make in the Weimar constitution regarding the status and social benefits due to government officials. They wanted to hire and fire officials as they saw fit, their primary target being the irksome presence of Jews. By March 16 Hitler had already appointed an interministerial committee to examine the legal aspects of legislation regarding civil servants, and in Prussia the Nazis did not even wait for the outcome of its deliberations but set about drafting proposals for new laws pertaining to employees in the state administration and judiciary.

After the publication of the "Enabling Act," the focus of deliberations shifted to the Reich Ministry of Interior. But Hitler seems to have intervened personally, summoning Goebbels on March 26 and making him responsible for organizing the boycott of Jewish enterprises.[31] The party manifesto prepared for April 1 included a special demand that the number of Jewish officials, jurists, and physicians be made proportionate to the number of Jews in the population as a whole, with the imposition of similar restrictions on Jews studying in institutions of higher learning. What we have before us, then, is a full program to dispossess the Jews by ousting them from all spheres of intellectual and public life together with the threat to their economic status.

With the publication of this manifesto, all restraint was thrown to the winds. The homes of Jewish doctors and the offices of Jewish lawyers, marked with a special sign, were included among the places at which SA guards were stationed on the day of the boycott. The actual acts of terror also increased. Many people were arrested at their places of work; lawyers were blocked from entering the courts or were forceably removed from them. On March 31 Hanns Kerrl, commissar of the Prussian Ministry of Justice (and later minister of justice), and his friend Hans Frank, the commissar (later minister) of the Ministry of Justice in Bavaria, announced on their own initiative, and probably after mutual consultation, that all Jewish judges and prosecutors were to take immediate leave; and Jewish lawyers and notaries would no longer be permitted to work and could appear in court only if their relative number did not exceed the ratio of Jews to the population at large. Other states followed the example of Prussia and Bavaria; early in April Kerrl and Frank added further restrictions and prohibitions.[32]

On April 3 Hitler approved the proposals of the director-general of the Reich Ministry of Justice, Franz Schlegelberger, who suggested "accelerating and unifying the judicial arrangements in the Reich" so as to bring a halt to improvised actions.[33] Legislation was hastily prepared and brought before the government; laws were passed one after another without thorough examination or, indeed, without logic. The first basic statute was the Law for the Restoration of the Professional Civil Service, promulgated on April 7, 1933.[34] On the same day the second law of *Gleichschaltung* was also passed; it restricted the independence of the secondary states in favor of the central government.[35] The civil service law must be understood both in name and in content: its primary purpose was to remove Jews from important posts in government service. Although ostensibly part of the *Gleichschaltung* legislation, its true aim was to achieve precisely the opposite of "coordination," that is, not to integrate the Jews but to isolate them.[36]

After the lawyers came the doctors. On March 24 Dr. Gerhard Wagner, chairman of the League of German National Socialist Doctors, issued a proclamation to the effect that "as a gesture of goodwill, he had assumed the position of commissar of the leading doctors' organizations." The prime objective of this move was to abrogate the rights of "Jewish and Marxist doctors in the Health Service."[37] The next legal act of the Reich government was the Decree Licensing Physicians for the National Health Service (April 22, 1933),[38] which merely confirmed the exclusion of Jewish doctors from the service. The pharmacists followed suit, with the administrative committee of their society declaring on March 29 that "with representatives of the new Germany," they were participating in *Gleichschaltung* with "exultation" and "consider[ed] it the only sure way of protecting the affairs and status of the pharmacists."[39]

Teachers in all the country's educational institutions, from primary schools to universities, had already been affected by this wave of legislation. Many were fired upon publication of the Law for the Restoration of the Professional Civil Service. Instances of harassment of Jewish professors and students that occurred at the universities, in particular, were no less savage than the atrocities perpetrated on the streets. The students demanded the ouster of instructors and professors of whose opinions or origins they disapproved. Generally speaking, the strongest pressure was exerted in the large cities, but even in places such as Kiel, the student body demanded that no fewer than twenty-eight professors be fired.[40] This was the background for the promulgation of the Law Against Crowding in Schools and Institutions of Higher Learning (published on April 25), which limited the number of Jewish pupils—particularly in secondary schools and universities—to 1.5 percent of the student body (at one school a maximum of 5 percent was allowed). But the Nazi students demanded more than this law stipulated, and twelve theses were published in universities calling for the "preservation of the German spirit" and demanding, *inter alia,* that in the future professors of Jewish origin be forced to publish their work only in Hebrew.[41] In view of these manifestations of the "revolution from below," Goebbels proceeded to act in the universities in a manner similar to the enterprise he had mounted on April 1.

For university students, May 10 was the equivalent of what April 1 had been to the small businessman. Goebbels methodically organized public ceremonies at all the country's universities on that day for the burning of books by banned authors. In Berlin the ritual was carried out by torchlight a few hundred yards from the square where, that same morning, Hitler had proclaimed the constitution of the German Labor Front. It would seem that just as the declaration of the *Gleichschaltung* laws on April 1 and 7 was timed to coincide with anti-Jewish actions, so the coincidence of time and place between these two ceremonies was not fortuitous.

Of all the laws and decrees, only two dealt specifically with the Jews and made no pretense of being concerned with general issues. The first, published on April 21, prohibited the practice of ritual slaughter.[42] Issued in the wake of a series of similar prohibitions enacted in many parts of the Reich, the purpose of this law was to furnish the imprimatur of centralized legislation. A more important article of legislation, and one affecting not only observant Jews, was the first "implementation order" to the Law for the Restoration of the Professional Civil Service, which defined a non-Aryan (April 11). For the first time, there was an official definition of who was a Jew:

1. A person is to be considered non-Aryan if he is descended from non-Aryan, particularly Jewish parents or grandparents. It is sufficient if one parent or grandparent is non-Aryan. This is to be assumed in particular where one parent or grandparent was of the Jewish religion.
2. Any civil servant who was not already serving on August 1, 1914, must bring proof that he is of Aryan descent or fought at the Front, or is the son or father of a soldier who fell in the World War. Such proof is to be supplied by presenting documents (birth certificates or marriage license of the parents, military documents).
3. In the event that Aryan descent is questionable, an opinion must be obtained from the expert on racial research attached to the Ministry of Interior [Bernard Lösener].[43]

Two facts stand out here: under Point 1 the concept of non-Aryan is not clearly defined and is used interchangeably with the concept of Jew. We shall see later that the people who framed this legislation were unable to extricate themselves from this complication, even when promulgating the all-encompassing Nuremberg Laws, because they could not avoid defining a Jew according to his own or his parents' affiliation with the Jewish religion or community. Under Point 2, on the other hand, the conditions that exempt a civil servant from the obligation of proving his Aryan origin are defined. This paragraph was added at the intervention of President Hindenburg, who wrote Hitler a letter recommending that he make an exception for those Jews who had served at the front in World

War I. Hindenburg explained his thinking thusly, "As far as my own feelings are concerned, officials, judges, teachers and lawyers who are war invalids, fought at the front, are sons of war dead, or themselves lost sons in the war should remain in their positions unless an individual case gives reason for special treatment."[44]

This is the first instance of the expression *Sonderbehandlung* (special treatment) being used in relation to the Jews—a number of years before it acquired the very different connotation of annihilation. The reasoning behind this qualification, as formulated by Hindenburg, is included almost verbatim in the law. Although it helped to secure the position and livelihood of thousands of Jews, this exemption was honored only until Hindenburg's death. Moreover, in places where people were classified as Jews before these exceptions were made public, the situation was never reversed.

The first period of arbitrary actions "from below" and of anti-Jewish legislation "from above" came to a close when Hitler declared that the revolution had ended. At the same time (July 14, 1933) a series of laws was promulgated—some general, some directed against the Jews. Among them was a law making sterilization mandatory in cases of people with hereditary diseases (see chap. 12 on euthanasia).[45] Two other laws passed at that time were directed primarily against East European Jews. One cited the grounds for revoking German citizenship acquired during the Weimar period or granted to immigrants who had subsequently left Germany; the second provided for the confiscation of the property of Jewish or political émigrés.[46] When this issue was discussed by the government Hitler stressed that "he was constantly being told there was no sympathy for the measures taken against Jews as a whole, but there was indeed understanding [for the steps taken against] the Jews of the East." Minister of Interior Frick regarded these laws as "essentially the inception and genesis of German racial legislation" (on the later use of these laws, see chap. 11).

Developments during the first months of Nazi rule undermined the status of the Jews by giving free sway to the outpouring of hatred and jealousy that had swept the National Socialists into power. Nevertheless, the new rulers of Germany learned that it was not easy to turn rabble-rousing slogans into concrete action. This lesson was particularly true in the sphere of economics, where the Nazis soon began to backpedal on their declared policy. On July 14 when the government established its Guidelines for the Allocation of Public Works Projects, the demand that Jews not be invited to participate was actually rejected.[47] Just as the anti-Jewish laws reflected the public attitude that made the Jews vulnerable to attack during the first revolutionary wave, this decision now suggested that the Jews might still find some source of support.

At the end of the summer of 1933, there appeared to be an abatement of the zeal to evict Jews from their position in the economy. Although the boycott continued in smaller communities and outlying towns, it was rather haphazard. Nevertheless, many Jews in these areas were forced to leave their homes and abandon their sources of livelihood; those who could not or would not emigrate from Germany moved to the larger cities—primarily to Berlin—where it was easier to find lodging, work, and assistance.[48] To some degree the implementation orders of the discriminatory laws against lawyers and doctors corrected their shortcomings, which, as it turned out, were disrupting the orderly conduct of the administration and services.[49]

The authorities encountered particular difficulty in enforcing the Law for the Restoration of the Professional Civil Service. One set of implementation orders followed another, but none were able to simplify the cumbersome procedures. It became evident that the law was too extreme: affiliation with a "non-Aryan race" could not be determined on the basis of the identity of only one of four grandparents. Nor was the same procedure followed in all cases, so that the resulting situation was rife with contradictions.[50]

Only in the cultural sphere were clear and uniform measures adopted. Goebbels was adamant about driving the Jews out of Germany's cultural life and dealt with the Jewish question on two planes: (1) cultural and intellectual life and (2) the communications media (press and radio). July 14, the fateful day on which so much legislation was enacted, also saw the publication of the Law Establishing the Cinema Office; this authorized Goebbels to choose the personnel who would henceforth make films in Germany.[51] Contrary to what might be expected, it was, however, to his advantage to permit some Jews to continue working, whereas general artistic and scientific institutions usually hastily disposed of Jews. The seventy-five-year-old Max Liebermann, one of the most famous artists of the day, was expelled from the Academy of Arts over which he had presided since 1922.[52] Albert Einstein, who had been a member of the Prussian Academy of Sciences for almost twenty years, sent a letter from abroad informing the academy of his resignation. These are but two examples of leading Jewish intellectuals who were driven out of Germany; hundreds, if not thousands of others—doctors, chemists, physicists, mathematicians, philosophers, philologists, historians, writers, stage directors, and so on—were exiled or left the country of their own volition. With the establishment of the Reich Office of Culture, the Aryan proviso was officially introduced in all spheres of cultural life, thereby incorporating them into the cycle of *Gleichschaltung* (September 22, 1933). Shortly thereafter Goebbels capped this process with the Newspaper Editors' Law (October 4, 1933), which made Aryan origin a prerequisite for anyone to edit a German newspaper.[53]

At the same time, Schacht, as head of the Ministry of the Economy, to some extent safeguarded the economic status of the Jews and asserted that Hitler had promised him "the Jews could continue working exactly as they had before 1933."[54] Jewish businesses with clients abroad were particularly important in the eyes of the economists, who hoped to overcome the severe shortage of foreign currency by stepping up foreign trade. Official declarations were made against the boycott, and government and party bureaus assured the public that "there are no laws providing a special status for Jews in the economic sphere."[55]

The Nuremberg Laws

The Deterioration of the Jews' Condition (1935)

From the standpoint of the Jews, 1934 was a relatively quiet year, although there was no dearth of anti-Jewish vilification and physical attacks against Jewish individuals, businesses, synagogues, and the like. Moreover, the May 1934 issue of *Der Stürmer* was devoted entirely to a vicious libel headlined "Revelation of a Jewish Plot to Perpetrate Murderous Acts Against Non-Jewish Humanity." The government was even constrained to confiscate the issue.[56] In 1933 German Jewry founded its own organization, the Reichsvertretung der dentschen Juden (National Representation of German Jews), giving its public life a new internally independent character and according it an autonomous status within the rising totalitarian state (discussed later). Yet this status, in turn, became the subject of ideological and practical discussions in Nazi circles and served as the background to the racial legislation known as the Nuremberg Laws. They established the inferior status of the Jewish community in two respects: (1) the civic equality granted the Jews by the emancipation was officially abolished and (2) the racial principle became law, segregating the Jews as individuals and as a community from the rest of the population.

Unlike most of the thousands of laws enacted by the Third Reich, the Nuremberg Laws were not issued by virtue of the "Enabling Act" and validated by Hitler's signature alone. Instead, they were passed by the Reichstag at the annual demonstrative public gathering of the party leadership in Nuremberg, this time held as the Congress of Freedom (September 8–14, 1935). Three laws were promulgated on this occasion. The first ruled that the party's red flag emblazoned with the swastika in the center would become Germany's flag. The other two, the Reich Citizenship Law and the Law for the Protection of German Blood and German Honor, were framed in speciously generalized terms but were unmistakably designed to fix the status of the Jews in the Third Reich.

For the first time since April 1933, Hitler dealt openly with the Jewish problem. What motivated him at that point to initiate legislation that not only surpassed any previous action taken vis-à-vis the Jews but also went beyond most of the steps taken to forge the National Socialist regime?

Prior to the promulgation of the Nuremberg Laws, 1935 witnessed a series of events reminiscent of the developments that culminated in the boycott of April 1, 1933. Once again, the highly problematic relationship between the state and the party came to the fore; anti-Jewish action was one expression of the tensions prevailing among the various centers of power in the Reich. The propagandists led by Goebbels and drawn to Julius Streicher, the ideological circles identified with Alfred Rosenberg, the various arms of Himmler's Security Police, the administrative branches of the party, many Gauleiters, and the labor organizations led by Robert Ley all adopted a harsher attitude toward the Jews. Waves of poisonous anti-Semitic propaganda as well as acts of 1933-style violence steadily spread through Germany. Local and regional administrative orders restricted freedom of movement and action of the Jews as nationwide laws imposed yet other limitations. Jews were forbidden to enter movie houses, restaurants, swimming pools, and other recreation sites. More and more signs appeared declaring that Jews were not wanted *(Juden unerwünscht)*. On July 15, 1935, violence reached a peak with the outbreak of anti-Jewish riots on Berlin's main boulevard, the Kurfürstendamm. Inflammatory pronouncements became the order of the day, for example, the observation by Gauleiter and Reichskommissar Jakob Sprenger of Hesse,

"Everywhere one can again sense that the Jews are coming back, emerging from their hiding places and trying to interfere. We must renew the struggle in our campaign against Jewry."[57]

German economists attributed the decline in exports in 1934 to the boycott of German goods declared by Jews and other parties, particularly in the United States. On February 26, 1935, the Reichskommissar of Berlin, Dr. Julius Lippert, stated at a meeting held at the American Chamber of Commerce, "It is claimed that we have destroyed the economic prospects for Jews to exist in Germany, and even if this has not been accomplished, that we are striving for such total destruction." He then tried to prove that the claim was unjustified, stressing that restrictions on the professional activities of Jews pertained solely to the political and cultural spheres and that Jews were free to engage in economic activity as long as it was consonant with the public good.[58] In May 1935 when members of the SA in Munich were destroying Jewish-owned shops, giving rise to tension between them and the police, who tried to stop the wanton destruction, Adolph Wagner, the Bavarian minister of interior and Gauleiter of Munich, issued a statement decrying the "criminal" elements and "anti-Semitic trespassing."[59]

The most important person to come out against the terror, however, was Economic Minister Hjalmar Schacht, who appealed to party and national institutions to check the assaults on Jewish economic enterprises. In a speech delivered at Königsberg (Kaliningrad, USSR) in East Prussia on August 18, he stressed the importance of allowing the Jews to engage in free economic activity, intimating that special legislation then under consideration would soon settle the questions concerning the Jews. At the same time, he declared that Jews must resign themselves to the fact that their influence had come to an end once and for all. Indicative of the tension that existed among the leading figures in the Reich is Goebbels's refusal to allow publication of this speech in the press, whereupon Schacht saw to it that the printing press of the Reichsbank distributed it through its own channels. Two days later, on August 20, at Schacht's initiative, the government's top-ranking officials met to discuss the position of the Jews in the economy. Schacht warned that unless illegal actions against Jews came to a halt, he would not be able to acquire the raw materials for armaments or the foreign currency needed to run the public works program, for which the führer and chancellor of the Reich had made him responsible. Minister of Interior Frick also favored solving the Jewish problem gradually and by legal means, but Goebbels's representative insisted on the confiscation of Jewish shops. Finally, a compromise was reached whereby a limited number of actions would be undertaken.[60]

During that period, conflicting influences were brought to bear on Hitler himself. The heads of the party's Racial Bureau, Dr. Gerhard Wagner and Walter Gross, tried to convince him of the need for a law to protect "German blood." However, at about the same time—just a few days before the party conference convened—Schacht also paid Hitler a visit. We have no record of their conversation, but it may be assumed that the economic minister explained to, and even convinced, the führer that harsh anti-Jewish action would cause the country severe economic damage and have an adverse effect on the armament program.

Several new laws had implied what the future held in store for the Jews. The official decision to exclude Jews from military service was of principal importance (the Conscription Law was announced on March 16; the Defense Law was enacted on May 21). In June the same restriction was applied to the Employment Service when it was made compulsory for all Germans.[61]

Hitler's Initiative

In 1935 Hitler enjoyed his first breakthrough in foreign policy. He wanted to make Germany independent of the Great Powers by lifting the restrictions of the Versailles treaty so as to restore the government's freedom of action, make it possible to expand Germany's territory, and prepare for a campaign of military conquest. His first success came on January 13, 1935, when the Saar region voted in favor of annexation to the Reich, thereby expanding Germany's industrial potential. His next achievement came when the Law of Compulsory Military Service was passed and the world accepted the fact that, in clear contravention of the Versailles treaty, Germany was again an armed power. The following day Hitler also divulged the fact that Germany already had an air force. When the final statute providing for the reorganization of the army likewise failed to elicit a particularly sharp reaction from the Great Powers, he went a step further and secured conditions for building a navy by signing a maritime agreement with Great Britain on June 18, 1935. At the same time, the very fact that the Olympic Games were to be held in Germany in 1936 implied international recognition of the new order. Just as Hitler had wanted to avoid negative world reaction to the oppression of Jews in the spring of 1933, when he needed time to set his regime on a firm footing, so was he now in need of a neutral, even sympathetic attitude abroad to pursue his rearmament plans. He certainly did not want new atrocity stories to begin circulating during this period of sensitive political developments. To avoid them he was prepared to contain, if not entirely quash, the ferment in the lower ranks of his movement. He could not and would not renounce anti-Semitism as the single immutable and focal feature of Nazi ideology. However, he had come to see that the world accepted discriminatory laws and statutes more readily than it acquiesced to acts of violence. Thus at Nuremberg Hitler declared, "The only way to deal with the problem which remains open is that of legislative action."[62]

Although maintaining that he sought a solution to the Jewish problem through law and justice, Hitler, nevertheless, hinted to his more impatient followers that another option existed and that the situation might be reconsidered in the future. If the present attempt failed, he would turn the problem over to the National Socialist Party "for a final solution."[63]

Ideological Assumptions and Practical Motives for the Racial Laws

From its inception the National Socialist Party openly declared its approach to the Jewish question and its intentions concerning the Jews. The twenty-five points of the platform of the German Workers party, accepted on February 24,1920, included the statement, "Only Nationals [*Volksgenossen*] can be Citizens of the

State. Only persons of German blood can be Nationals—regardless of religious affiliation. No Jew can therefore be a German National. A person who is not a Citizen will be able to live in Germany only as a guest, and must be subject to legislation for Aliens."[64]

Programs following this or similar formulas were put forward throughout the years of "the struggle," that is, before the National Socialists rose to power, and pragmatic recommendations were prepared. It was, therefore, quite natural that in the spring of 1933, a number of programs of this sort were brought before the party and government institutions in the belief that the Jewish problem would be quickly solved along the lines of these long-standing principles.[65] It may also be assumed that the specialists on racial problems in the Ministry of Interior were well acquainted with these proposals. On September 13 Dr. Bernard Lösener was called to Nuremberg and given less than twenty-four hours to draft the proposed laws.[66] It is quite likely that in the course of the two and a half years after the spring of 1933, he and Dr. Wilhelm Stuckart, the director of the ministry, had frequently discussed these matters. Addressing diplomats in 1934, the minister of interior, Wilhelm Frick, had stated, "In the law-abiding state of Germany, only by means of the law is it possible [to remove the Jews from their positions]." He emphasized that the Germans had no intention whatsoever of regarding peoples of another race as inferior, contrary to "fears that have been expressed, particularly in the Far East."[67] Apparently, protests on the part of countries populated by other races (i.e., Japan) were among the pressures that forced the Nazis to differentiate semantically between Jews and other non-Germanic races. This is clearly the major reason why the term *Jew* rather than *non-Aryan* (as in April 1933) was used in the Nuremberg Laws.

The Nuremberg Laws were designed to achieve two purposes: to separate the races and to define the rights of a citizen of the Reich. The first proposal forwarded for legislation was the Reich Citizenship Law, which distinguished between a subject of the state *(Staatsangehöriger)* and a citizen of the Reich *(Reichsbürger)*. A subject of the state was "a person who enjoys the protection of the German Reich and who in consequence has specific obligations towards it" (Clause 1). A citizen of the Reich, on the other hand, was "a subject of the State who is of German or related blood, who proves by his conduct that he is willing and fit faithfully to serve the German people and Reich" (Clause 2).

The law stipulated that the right to citizenship in the Reich depended on the acquisition of a Reich citizenship certificate by those entitled to it—one of the far-reaching Nazi concepts that was never realized. More important was Section 3 of Clause 2, which stated, "The Reich citizen is the sole bearer of full political rights in accordance with the Law."

The second piece of legislation, the Law for the Protection of German Blood and German Honor, contained a preamble explaining the motivation behind it, "Moved by the understanding that the purity of German blood is the essential condition for the continued existence of the German people and inspired by the inexorable determination to ensure [the existence of] the German nation for all time, the Reichstag has unanimously adopted the following law, which is promulgated herewith." The body of the law forbade marriages between Jews and "sub-jects of the state of German or related blood" and also prohibited sexual relations between these two categories of people out of wedlock. Jews were forbidden to employ German female domestics under the age of forty-five and were forbidden to fly the Reich flag, though they were permitted to display the "Jewish colors"—a right that, somewhat ironically, was guaranteed under state protection. About half the law's seven clauses were devoted to enumerating the dire penalties await-ing anyone violating its provisions.[68]

After the passage of this law, Hitler told the delegates, "You have now agreed to a law whose full significance will only be recognized hundred of years from now."[69] We may conclude from this vision that he considered the Nuremberg Laws a milestone on the road to achieving his objective: "purging" Germany of Jews as an essential prerequisite to the establishment of the Reich that would last for a thousand years.

Explanations and Conclusions

This, however, was not the public explanation given for the new laws. Instead, they were officially explicated as follows:

> After years of struggle the new Laws passed by the Reichstag at the Party Congress of Freedom . . . establish *absolutely clear relations between the German nation (Deutsch-tum) and Jewry.* Unmistakably clear expression has been given to the fact that the Ger-man people has no objection to the Jew as long as he wishes to be a member of the Jewish people and acts accordingly, but that, on the other hand, he declines to look on the Jew as a national of the German Nation *(Volksgenosse)* and to accord him the same rights and duties as a German. . . . Germany has given the Jewish minority the oppor-tunity to live for itself and is offering State protection for this separate life of the Jewish minority.[70]

From then on, the Nuremberg Laws were the primary sanction for further anti-Jewish legislation. Most of the important orders and decrees abrogating the Jews' civil rights and imposing restrictions on them were issued as Implementa-tion Orders to the Reich Citizenship Law. The overwhelming majority of these decrees were published in 1938, the "Fateful Year," and the final one came on July 1, 1943, marking the final liquidation of German Jewry.

As the Nuremberg Laws used the term *Jew* without defining it, in the suc-ceeding months the problem of formulating a precise definition all but preoccu-pied the German experts. On November 14, 1935, after a long internal debate, they finally published a definition of the concept as part of the First Implemen-tation Order to the Reich Citizenship Law. Once again, it was explicitly stated that a Jew could not be a citizen of the Reich, had no right to vote on political issues, and could not hold public office. Clause 5, containing the definition of a Jew, was the most important:

> 1. A Jew is a person descended from at least three grandparents who were full Jews by race. . . .

2. A *Mischling* who is a subject of the state and descended from two full Jewish grandparents is also considered a Jew if:

   a) he was a member of the Jewish religious community at the time of the promulgation of this law, or was admitted to it subsequently;

   b) he was married to a Jew at the time of the promulgation of this law, or subsequently married a Jew;

   c) he is the offspring from a marriage with a Jew in accordance with Paragraph 1, contracted subsequently to the promulgation of the law for the protection of German blood and German honor of September 15, 1935;

   d) he is the offspring of extramarital intercourse with a Jew in accordance with Paragraph 1, and will be born illegitimately after July 31, 1936....[71]

These provisions also served as guidelines for the implementation of laws enacted in most of the European countries under the sway of the Third Reich.

During that period, the authorities deliberated a problem that they would be forced to confront as long as the Nazis remained in power: the offspring of mixed marriages *(Mischlinge)* and converted Jews—referred to collectively by the Nazis as Jewish offspring (*Judenstämmlinge,* literally "of Jewish extraction," but carrying a derogatory connotation in German). Only people with three Jewish grandparents were defined as full Jews, but there were additional gradations such as half-Jews and quarter-Jews. These loose definitions and the absence of statistical data prevent us from citing definitive information on how many people were considered full or partial Jews even if they no longer subscribed to the Jewish religion. It is estimated that there were between 160,000 and 260,000 offspring of mixed marriages. These estimates are based on the known number of mixed marriages and the average number of children of such marriages (which was known to be lower than that of Jewish marriages). The number of converts is estimated at 50,000. Usually, they were not affiliated with Jewish organizations and were represented by Christian groups, both Protestant and Catholic.

The German Jews' Struggle for Existence
(Through the End of 1935)

First Reactions

In March 1933 only the Jews of Germany realized they were involved in a struggle for which they were not prepared. For the first time we see a phenomenon we shall encounter again and again throughout Hitler's rule and his campaign against the Jews: the contradiction between the Jews' intellectual grasp of what lay ahead for them and their inability to draw far-reaching pragmatic conclusions from this understanding. The first severe test for the Jews of Germany was, of course, the April 1 boycott. The most significant reaction—and one that had repercussions within and beyond the German-Jewish community—was articulated by Robert Weltsch, the editor of *Jüdische Rundschau (JR),* the official organ of the Zionistische Vereinigung für Deutschland (ZVfD). On April 4 Weltsch published a front-page article under the headline that was becoming something of a slogan:

"Wear It with Pride, the Yellow Badge." The piece laid stress on the moral and emotional significance of what was taking place in Germany and called on the Jews to recognize the great change being wrought by the "national revolution of the German people." April 1, wrote Weltsch, must become the day of Jewish awakening and revival, and the mark of shame must be transformed into a badge of self-respect. The journal of the Central Verein *(CVZtg)*, which had previously expressed the conviction that the Jews' equal civil rights would not be revoked, now gave prominent coverage to the call issued by Professor Ismar Elbogen, a well-known Jewish historian and one of the leaders of Liberal Judaism, "The order of the day is: work and help!" Elbogen went on to predict, "They may doom us to starvation but not to die of starvation." One must not succumb to despair because "no society goes under unless it annuls itself."[72] Both Weltsch and Elbogen felt the need to stress that the day of the boycott had passed quietly, and they argued against the "defamation of Germany." But they added that it was not the "atrocity stories" that alarmed those concerned for the welfare of the Jewish public, but the official measures taken by the Reich.[73] Some writers expressed the hope that the facts of life and the needs of running a large country in the throes of economic difficulties would give rise to a balanced policy toward the Jews. This hope was not vindicated by the laws enacted after April 1, though from the end of 1933 to the end of 1934 it may have appeared that the opportunistic outlook had something to it.

The overwhelming majority of Jews considered it their primary duty to preserve whatever possible and were convinced that in spite of what the future might bring, the Jews must persevere in Germany. The idea of emigrating was not ruled out, particularly not for young people; but mass emigration was regarded as unrealistic. This view was advanced by the Liberal leaders, who wanted the Jews to fight for their status in Germany and opposed the voluntary abandonment of any position. The other extreme was advocated by Georg Kareski, a member of the executive of the Revisionist Organization of State Zionists. He, too, believed that hundreds of thousands of Jews would go on living in Germany, but he called on them to adapt themselves to the new basic concepts, arguing that "a member of a minority within a large nation can also be a useful and respectable citizen." Rabbi Menachem Cohen of Agudat Yisrael adopted a special stance in advocating the traditional ruling of the Jewish sages over the centuries, "The law of the government stands."[74]

Responding to the Needs of the Hour

In the meantime the situation was taking its toll since thousands of people lost their source of livelihood or were forced to leave their places of residence. German Jewry's welfare organization, which had been one of the community's most comprehensive and effective organs during the Weimar period, now developed into the base for self-help and mutual aid. The Central Jewish Bureau for Economic Assistance met in Berlin and together with all the major Jewish economic organizations founded the Central Committee of German Jews for Relief and Reconstruction (April 13, 1933), calling on the Jewish public to contribute generously.[75]

Initially the committee regarded itself as an advisory body equipped to extend legal protection, but its work soon expanded to encompass: (1) general economic assistance in the form of advice, loans, mediation, and aid, particularly to academicians and people in the free professions; (2) a center for loan funds; (3) vocational training and rehabilitation; (4) agricultural training; and (5) an employment agency. In 1935 the Committee for Relief and Reconstruction had fifty-five branches throughout Germany, most of them functioning as departments within the local community organizations.[76]

German Jewry based its struggle for economic survival on its involvement in the German economy, which Schacht was trying to revive. In this respect great importance was ascribed to the connections Jews maintained around the world with commercial, industrial, and financial centers as well as with sources of raw materials. Moreover, it was still possible to defend Jews by legal means against physical assault or professional harassment; the CV was active in this sphere, utilizing the experience it had acquired during the Weimar period (see chap. 1, The Defense Campaign in Action). Of particular importance was its defense in labor courts of Jewish employees who had been fired from their jobs, especially as the courts' rulings were repeatedly favorable to the Jews. The various branches of the employment agency introduced unemployed Jews to Jewish businessmen, thereby helping thousands of people to find new jobs. Efforts were made to protect the social welfare benefits that Jews were entitled to receive from the state, and in the early years of the Nazi regime they were successful, for example, by ensuring that the Winter Aid Project extended to needy Jews as recipients of clothing, coal for heating, and extra food. However, most social welfare assistance was supplied by the independent Jewish framework, to which the Jews made large contributions. In 1935 alone the Jews of Germany collected RM (Reichsmark) 25 million.[77]* The assumption was that the Jews' economic status would determine their future in Germany. Thus, the 1934 report of the Central Committee for Relief and Reconstruction stated, "The German policy toward the Jews has made the economy the crucial objective for German Jews."[78]

If the Jews were still able to struggle for their rights and defend themselves against exclusion in the economic sphere, in the cultural sphere they were forced to accept the verdict of almost total dissimilation. It was in this field, however, that the Jewish public demonstrated great initiative and within a relatively short time had established a framework for independent cultural activity known as the Culture Association (Kulturbund). Within this framework the Jews were able to maintain their affinity for German culture while cultivating the new trend of intensifying their affinity with Jewish culture. Cultural associations were formed throughout Germany, and in the summer of 1935 the government merged them into a comprehensive association headed by Hans Hinkel, a special appointee of Goebbels's office.[79] The authorities then strove to restrict the Jews' freedom of cultural action and to increase their supervision of these activities. However, notwithstanding that programs were reviewed by the Gestapo and that in time more and more prohibitions were placed on the use of German literary and artistic

*See Wartime Currencies table in Appendix.

material, Jewish cultural activities included the presentation of plays, films, lectures, public readings, art exhibits, concerts, and even operas.

The people behind the establishment of the Culture Association intended that it fulfill two functions: to answer the cultural needs of Germany's Jews and to create jobs and other opportunities for Jewish artists, writers, and intellectuals both to express and to support themselves. In 1933 more than two thousand people applied to work under the auspices of the association, but it proved impossible to employ so many people; initially no more than two hundred, including technical and administrative personnel, were accepted. By 1938, however, seventeen hundred artists were employed. In 1935 seventy thousand people were members of thirty-six cultural associations functioning in forty-nine communities. Those without means were allowed to participate in the associations' activities without paying dues, this in order to keep up morale.[80]

No less important a function was filled by the institutions for adult education that flourished in Germany. The courses and lectures held in special study centers focused on Jewish subjects; often this was the first time the participants had been exposed to the rudiments of a Jewish education. Martin Buber was particularly active in this project, establishing the Center for Jewish Adult Education in the summer of 1934. Teachers and instructors worked under the direction of Ernst Akiba Simon, who came from Palestine specially to work in this program. The number of people studying Hebrew increased steadily, as did the number of students attending the traditional seminaries.[81]

The Jewish press in Germany, above all *JR,* made a substantial contribution to bolstering the community's emotional ability to withstand the persecution, assaults, and insults. The paper tried to shore up its readers' self-respect by imbuing them with a Jewish and Zionist consciousness. The CV journal as well as most of the other Jewish papers devoted considerable space to Zionist settlement activities in Palestine and information on developments within Jewish communities around the world. The press took care to convey useful information and practical advice and often came out in defense of the Jews. In the summer of 1935, for example, two leading papers, *JR* and the *CVZtg,* spoke out strongly against the mounting wave of riots and carried reliable reports of the boycott activities and the assaults on Jewish businesses, for which they were consequently banned for quite a while. In 1935 sixty-three Jewish publications existed in Germany. The Berlin community's paper had a distribution of 52,000 copies that year; *CVZtg* and *JR* had a circulation of about 40,000 each.[82]

The activities of Jewish publishers, led by the Schocken Publishing House, were equally as impressive during that period. From 1933 to 1938 there were 92 books published by Schocken's "Little Library," which made the greatest treasures of the Jewish heritage available in the German language. During the same period, the works of 148 authors were published—28 of them by Martin Buber alone—alongside children's books and textbooks. A total of twenty-five publishing houses continued to function, issuing over 1,000 publications. At the end of 1934, the Philo Publishing House brought out a *Jewish Lexicon,* of which 26,000 copies were sold in one year.[83]

The National Representation of German Jews

I have discussed some of the ways in which the Jews of Germany reacted and some of the new initiatives undertaken in an attempt to create a framework that would enable them to stand fast and endure the new conditions of life. The high point of their organizational and intellectual effort was the formation of a comprehensive, nationwide representative organization that assumed a twofold task: to lead the community through this perilous period and to represent it before the hostile authorities. Even though prior to the establishment of the Nazi regime, attempts had been made to form a comprehensive representation of German Jews, now it became obvious that the most pressing need was the formation of a new organization with broad authority. Owing to the evolving situation, the ZVfD had grown steadily stronger and made every effort to increase its influence in the communities and unite all Jewish organizations under its aegis. At the same time, influential members of the CV in the Jewish community of Essen, in the Rhine district, attempted to encourage other organizations and community leaders to join in a similar initiative.

Max Grünewald, the Liberal rabbi of Mannheim, made two basic demands: first, that the new national representation accept a program that takes into consideration the total and fundamental change in intellectual and political concepts; second, that in principle the new body should not be composed of representatives of communities and organizations but rather of well-known personalities who enjoyed the public's confidence and were capable of leading it.[84] On September 17, 1933, the Reichsvertretung der deutschen Juden (National Representation of the German Jews) was established, and on September 20 Justizrat D. Julins Brodnitz, president of the CV, wrote a lead article in *CVZtg.* announcing its formation and noting that the intent behind it was "to come to grips with the troubled times and form an organization that, notwithstanding ideological and sectoral differences, would be capable of functioning in the *common* interests of the German Jews." He also announced that Rabbi Leo Baeck, one of the most respected figures in German Jewry, would serve as president of the new body and would be responsible for directing its affairs in collaboration with a board headed by Otto Hirsch, who had been a consultant in a government ministry in the state of Württemberg and was well-known to the Jewish public. Although Brodnitz emphasized that "the board is composed solely of individuals who do not consider themselves dependent upon the organization in any way," its constituency generally represented a cross-section of the major Jewish organizations, all of which expressed their readiness to work in close cooperation with the new body. On September 21 a proclamation was issued in which the Reichsvertretung presented itself to the public for the first time. It opened with the following statement:

At a time that is as hard and difficult and trying as any in Jewish history, but also significant as few times have been, we have been entrusted with the leadership and representation of the German Jews by a joint decision of the State association of the Jewish Communities [Landesverbände], the major Jewish organizations and the large Jewish communities of Germany.... We must understand [the new regime in

Germany] and not deceive ourselves. Only then will we be able to discover every honorable opportunity, and to struggle for every right, for every place, for every opportunity to continue to exist. . . . There is only one area in which we are permitted to carry out our own ideas, our own aims, but it is a decisive area, that of our Jewish life and Jewish future. This is where the most clearly defined tasks exist.[85]

The Reichsvertretung was to fulfill the following functions: provide for education and the establishment of Jewish schools; guide youth toward vocational training; strengthen the religious base of Judaism; protect the Jews' economic status and right to work; prepare—especially the youth—for building a new life in Palestine or any other place. Finally, it expressed "hope for the understanding assistance of the Authorities, and the respect of our gentile fellow citizens whom we join in love and loyalty to Germany."[86]

The formation of the Reichsvertretung in the summer of 1933 was both the result and the expression of a new awareness on the part of German Jewry. The community's leading thinkers were convinced that the era of emancipation had ended—a foreboding conclusion they arrived at unwillingly. This realization was especially difficult for the members of the CV. On August 10, 1933, the CV's newspaper ran a lead article headlined "Changing the Soul" ("Seelische Umschichtung") proposing what it defined as "collective emancipation." This approach stemmed from the illusion that even under the totalitarian regime of the Jew-hater Hitler, it was possible to carve out an independent realm with equal rights for Jews. Such ideas also grew out of the new organizational activity and were one of the motives behind it.

The authorities were interested in isolating the Jews in order to achieve their total dissimilation. This approach was tantamount to social and cultural ghettoization, but it did not yet include official economic displacement. This civil ghettoization was sealed by the Nuremberg Laws. The interpretation of the laws by an authority such as "the leader of the German Legal Front" and Minister of Justice Hans Frank and by the author of the legislation, Bernard Lösener, underscored this intent. Frank stated, "I can only reiterate that the Jews of Germany will be able to live and support themselves undisturbed; however, as soon as possible we must establish a legal protection against creating any ties with these people of a foreign race." Lösener had a more positive approach, arguing that the laws transforming dissimilation into an established fact would minimize racial hatred and create a healthier, more serene atmosphere that would make life in the same political milieu tolerable for both peoples. He also stressed that legal segregation meant legal protection. Nevertheless, he, too, was of the opinion that the Jews would not be recognized as a national minority *(nationale Minderheit)* according to international law and defined them instead as a "folk minority" *(völkische Minderheit).*[87]

The way in which the Jews themselves interpreted the Nuremberg Laws was not very different from these explanations. They tended to feel that after the chaotic flood of regulations, counterregulations, and erratic actions, they finally found themselves in a situation that, degrading as it might be, was at least clear. This is how we are to understand the statement issued by the Reichsvertretung a few days after the enactment of the Nuremberg Laws:

> The Laws decided upon by the Reichstag in Nuremberg have come as the heaviest of blows for the Jews in Germany. But they must create a basis on which a tolerable relationship becomes possible between the German and the Jewish people. The Reichsvertretung der Juden in Deutschland is willing to contribute to this end with all its powers. A precondition for such a tolerable relationship is the hope that the Jews and Jewish communities of Germany will be enabled to keep a moral and economic means of existence by the halting of defamation and boycott.[88]

The statement went on to outline the functions assumed by the Reichsvertretung. In contrast to the proclamation published when the Reichsvertretung was founded two years earlier, this statement stressed the "increased need for emigration," which should be planned on a large scale. Moreover, this time there was no mention of cooperation with the citizens of the Nazi state. Twenty-five community organizations—some ideological in character, others devoted to practical objectives—signed the statement.[89]

Jewish Organizations and Their Relations with the Authorities

The community groups that signed the Reichsvertretung statement represented almost the entire range of organized Jewry. Among the organizations that excluded themselves were the Independent Orthodoxy and two strongly assimilationist groups: the National German Jews led by Dr. Max Naumann and the German Vanguard (Deutscher Vortrupp) led by Hans-Joachim Schoeps. The members of Agudat Yisrael, who were organized in separate communities, did not agree to participate in a secular organization headed by the Liberal Rabbi Leo Baeck; in a special memorandum submitted to Hitler in October 1933, they demanded the right to exist independently, following Jewish tradition.

The Naumann group, on the other hand, hoped to secure a preferred status because of its nationalist German outlook. In memoranda addressed to Hitler's chancellery as early as April and May 1933, Naumann proposed that those German Jews who represented (in his words) the true nationalist Jews be assured equal rights and that such rights be revoked from the Zionists and from Jews who had immigrated to Germany from the East. Unsparing in his defamation of all other currents within Jewry, Naumann went so far as to maintain that anti-Semitism in Germany was justified: the Jews were responsible for the situation in which they found themselves because they had not identified with, and sufficiently assimilated into, Germany.[90] He also suggested forming a liaison group of Jews and non-Jews to deal with all matters pertaining to the Jewish community and proposed that the community's constituent groups be ranked by their degree of loyalty to Germany. In words that could not possibly be misconstrued, he proposed himself as "a Jewish commissar for the Jews." In the spring of 1935 Naumann asked that his group alone be granted the privilege of serving in the army. At the end of 1935 his organization was banned.

The members of the German Vanguard were mostly young academics led by Hans-Joachim Schoeps, whose theories were a mixture of German youth movement traditions and Jewish theology, this supplemented by protestations of the German character of the organization's members. Schoeps hoped to salvage the Jews' right to participate in German life and be partners in Germany's future. He opposed the assimilationists and the Zionists alike and declared, "We are fighting to preserve the condition of German Jewry and the right of the German Jew to a German future." The Vanguard, too, was disbanded in December 1935.[91]

The behavior of these dissident groups was exceptional, indeed, but their perseverance attests to the fact that, initially, the multiplicity of Jewish organizations and communities continued even under the new conditions. Even the groups that joined the Reichsvertretung held to their different viewpoints. The authorities were not averse to this complex situation and were even interested in perpetuating it. As a result, each of the various organizations attempted to find channels of communication with the regime. The complex and cumbersome structure of the Third Reich, rife as it was with administrative contrarieties, made it possible for most of the groups to find some way of exercising influence on one authority or another. Moreover, on the state government level it was still possible to find officials who did not condone the anti-Semitic policies of the new leadership. Even though many of the channels that had opened to the Jews during the Weimar era were blocked after Hitler's rise to power, various groups kept on trying to gain access to the powers that be. Apparently, many of them believed that it was possible to enter into pragmatic negotiations even with Hitler—of course, this proved to be a vain hope. In contrast, approaches made by the Reich Union of Jewish Veterans (Reichsbund jüdischer Frontsoldaten) to their erstwhile commander, Hindenburg, met with success, at least for a while. Thus, when the organization approached President Hindenburg on April 4, 1933, asking that he intervene to defend their rights as German citizens who had fulfilled their duty to their country in wartime, he complied with their request (see pp. 65–66). The union's members tried to convince the authorities of their desire to be an integral part of the country and serve its people. They even offered to volunteer for work at segregated labor camps and received usually polite but evasive replies from the Reich's officialdom.

The attitude of the Nazi leadership toward Jews seeking recognition of their German nature was expressed in an article published by Heydrich in the SS journal, *Das Schwarze Korps,* in the spring of 1935, "The assimilationists deny their Jewish race, based on their many years of life in Germany claim to be Germans, and after baptism claim to be Christians. Those assimilationists are the very ones who are trying to subvert and abrogate the principles of National Socialism by means of various declarations of loyalty typical of this race, protestations that make them despicable in the eyes of others."[92] This assessment was often expressed regarding the CV as well, and it led to both prohibitions and the demand that the Jews stop calling themselves German Jews. Indeed, from then onward all the Jewish organizations were obliged to change their names to follow the formula, Jews in Germany, so that instead of being called the Reichsvertretung der deutschen Juden (National Representation of the German Jews), for example, the name of the organization was changed to the Reichsvertretung der Juden in Deutschland (National Representation of the Jews *in* Germany).[93]

Radical assimilationists were not the only people who sought personal contact with the new rulers of Germany. In the early days of the Nazi regime, leading public figures, including Zionist leaders, took steps toward instituting active cooperation with the authorities. In February 1933, for example, the chairman of the Keren Hayesod in Germany, Oskar Wassermann, incurred the anger of the ZVfD by appending his name to an election poster of the German National Party (Deutschnationale Partei). Together with Hitler, the banker Max Warburg, president of the Hilfsverein der deutschen Juden, signed Schacht's appointment as president of the Reichsbank.[94] Some of these matters transpired during the early transition period when confusion and uncertainty reigned. Yet even as time went on, attempts to establish a dialogue continued at various levels. Of prime practical importance was the contact between Jewish representatives and officials in the low and middle echelons of government who not only provided valuable information but sometimes even managed to bring about beneficial changes.

Most surprising was the attitude of the authorities regarding the status and rights of the kehillot. Until the spring of 1938, the authorities took no steps that prejudiced their status, and the role of the kehillot constantly expanded in response to current needs. As already noted the Central Committee for Relief and Reconstruction operated in most places under the aegis of the kehillot, which obviously necessitated the expansion of their staffs and budgets. Indeed, social welfare, vocational training, aid in securing jobs, and legal advice were now joined by educational endeavors as their primary fields of activity. In their efforts to meet the new organizational and financial demands, the kehillot found the authorities not only understanding but willing to help. They were allowed to collect taxes and prepare their budgets freely, in some respects with greater freedom than they had enjoyed during the Weimar period.[95] We do not know what motives prompted the Nazis to act as they did; however, at least during the initial period of National Socialist rule, the authorities apparently believed it best to let the Jews conduct their own affairs. They were also very interested in having the Jews finance their projects with their own funds, thereby freeing the national and local governments of financial responsibility. This economic segregation increased after the promulgation of the Nuremberg Laws, at which time the Jews' lost the right to be included in the Winter Aid Project. As a result Jewish institutions had to fund this project on their own; again, however, the authorities did not interfere.[96]

Less consistent was the official attitude toward Jewish organizations and public activities of various kinds. In 1933, the first year of Nazi rule, the authorities in Bavaria took a jaundiced view of the Jewish organizations, arresting most of their activists and keeping them imprisoned for long periods. Beginning in 1934 the Security Service (Sicherheitsdienst, or SD) and the Gestapo began to keep tabs on Jewish activities in the framework of monitoring popular opinion for its situation reports *(Lageberichte),* which assessed the prevailing mood and general disposition of the German public.[97] These reports noted the lively activities going on in the Jewish sphere, which the Nazi monitors failed to assess properly. For example, in March 1935 they wrote from Berlin, "Consonant with the increase in Jewish activity in all fields, the number of meetings is also on the rise. In the month covered in this report [February], 3,001 meetings took place, compared with 2,500 in January; observers were present at 72 of them. This yields an average of 100 meetings a day."[98] Even if the reporters were deliberately exaggerating, the SD and the Gestapo still did not succeed in covering or reporting on all activities going on in the Jewish sphere.

One of the more popular Jewish activities was sports. Together with many other young people, those youths who had been expelled from the German sports organizations now turned to their Jewish counterparts, the most outstanding of which was Maccabi. In its desire to supervise these activities, the government created umbrella organizations under the supervision of the Gestapo, which demanded precise information on their constituent organizations and memberships. This wealth of information was used in the summer of 1935 to start the Jewish card file *(Judenkartei)* in order to register every single Jew—a measure that had been recommended in the earliest anti-Semitic programs. Registration took place throughout the Reich up to the planned deadline of October 1, 1935, with a further directive instructing the authorities to update the file every three months.[99]

Unlike any other organization, the Reichsvertretung was not subject to direct government supervision; neither was it officially recognized by the authorities. Nevertheless, it considered itself the spokesperson of the Jewish public, thereby causing a degree of tension with the larger Jewish organizations and kehillot, which laid claim to being the truly authorized representatives of the Jewish public and reiterated this point in the negotiations that each conducted separately with the authorities. The Reichsvertretung did not hesitate to bring protests and petitions before the authorities, deploring, for instance, the exclusion of Jews from military service.[100] (On this issue, at least, it took the same stand as Naumann, except that the latter demanded exclusive rights for the members of his group.) While protests of this sort generally did not lead to any change in policy, they did attest to the readiness of the leading figures in the Reichsvertretung to defend what they considered their rights and obligations as citizens, without concern for their own safety. In the course of time, the functions of the Reichsvertretung expanded, and the struggle for survival steadily assumed a more important place in its activities.

Jewish Children and Youth Under the National Socialist Regime

The problem of education became one of the major concerns of the Jews during this period. Although elementary-school children were not expelled from schools by law, as were the secondary-school pupils and university students, the hostility of their teachers and classmates was oppressive enough to constitute a threat to their emotional stability. Particularly distressing was the state of the children of the so-called *Ostjuden,* as in most cases their parents were not German citizens. Educational opportunities varied in different places, depending on size and character of the community. In the large cities, where a certain anonymity could be maintained, the children enjoyed relatively better conditions than they did in smaller communities. Similarly, the larger Jewish communities were better equipped to carry the burden of supporting a Jewish school. While the situation in the outlying towns was uncomfortable, in the rural areas, where only the very smallest of Jewish communities remained, the state of affairs became insufferable. We have already noted that the network of Jewish schools had been considerably reduced before the National Socialists rose to power. There had been a tendency to close the Jewish schools in the large, heterogeneous Berlin Jewish community for ideological reasons—albeit under pretense of financial difficulties (see p. 32). As Joseph Gutmann had already then predicted, by the beginning of 1933 it became apparent that the existing Jewish schools had to be expanded and new ones established. A growing number of the Jewish teachers who had been forced to leave their jobs in the general school system were now absorbed into the Jewish educational network after undergoing brief courses to supplement their knowledge of Jewish subjects. According to its reports, the Reichsvertretung employed 766 teachers in 1934, 813 by the end of 1934, 1,057 in 1935, and 1,237 in 1936.[101]

There were two types of Jewish schools: public and private. The public schools were maintained by the local authority or the kehillah, the latter enjoying the financial support of the local or state authorities and being subject to supervision by the government's educational authorities. The private schools, which were supported by the parents of their pupils as well as by Jewish organizations in Germany and abroad, were also usually subject to the supervision of the Ministry of Education. Surprisingly, during the first years of the National Socialist regime, this situation did not change. No legal means were found to free the authorities of responsibility for the education of the Jewish child, who was included under the compulsory education law. The right of parents and communities to demand parochial schools, which was secured by state laws, applied to Jews as well as to Protestants and Catholics. In essence, the authorities supported Jewish schools in the hope that they would eventually absorb all the Jewish children, thereby achieving segregation in the educational sphere. In places without any Jewish school or where the existing schools were unable to absorb all the children, attempts were made to concentrate Jewish children in special classes within the state public schools. In 1934 forty-four of the sixty-nine Jewish elementary schools in Prussia were public schools, twenty-five of them being run by municipalities and nineteen by kehillot.[102] Bernhard Rust, the Reich minister of education, tried for years to have a comprehensive law enacted to standardize the curriculum of Jewish schools throughout the country. However, Hitler refrained from establishing rules and regulations regarding matters on which there was no consensus—a fact that makes the enactment of the Nuremberg Laws an even more exceptional phenomenon.

Three arms functioned in the field of education: the kehillot, the Committee for Relief and Reconstruction, and the Reichsvertretung. The kehillot were usually involved in solving organizational problems, whereas the Committee for Relief and Reconstruction and the Reichsvertretung participated in planning, training teachers, and, of course, in supporting the burgeoning budget. The

Reichsvertretung was particularly concerned about maintaining working relations with the authorities. Professor Ismar Elbogen was head of its Educational Committee and Dr. Adolf Leschnitzer headed its Education Department.

In 1933/1934 there were 58,000 Jewish pupils in Germany, 12,700 (21.7 percent) of whom attended Jewish schools. In 1934/1935 the number attending Jewish schools had reached 18,500 (43.2 percent). In 1935/1936 this number again rose, to 20,000. However, the total number of Jewish pupils had in the meantime decreased to 44,000, so that 46.1 percent of the children were attending Jewish schools, whereas 24,000 (or 54 percent) were in general schools. Even in the peak year of 1936/1937, when 23,670 pupils were studying in Jewish schools, they represented only 61.3 percent of all the pupils, and almost 39 percent (15,230) continued to attend general schools. These figures pertain to primary schools (eight grades), secondary schools (of which there were few), and vocational schools.[103] Occasionally a ninth grade was added to the primary school to extend the schooling of children for whom no other educational opportunities were available.

The authorities recognized the special needs of Jewish schools and permitted them a certain degree of autonomy in determining their curricula. The functions of the Jewish schools during this frightening period were multifaceted. Not only did Jewish children have to master the curriculum of the general school, they also had to be taught Jewish subjects, with special emphasis on Hebrew. Moreover, the school had to create the atmosphere of a protected island where the child could live his life safe from the dangers lurking for Jews throughout Germany.[104]

A teacher from Königsberg in East Prussia described the difficulties as follows:

> The terrifying loneliness of the Jewish child in the provinces, the daily struggle of the recently founded Jewish school with hostile governmental authorities, the enormous difficulty of finding appropriate teachers, the isolation from larger Jewish centers—but despite it all, the "we shall overcome" spirit of Jewish education [that manifests itself] in a cruel environment. What's more, he is also [caught] in between the "struggles" and "ideologies" of the small communities that their leaders and functionaries conduct among themselves.[105]

As noted before, not all the children found their way to Jewish schools: some because there was no opportunity to do so, others because their parents were unwilling to send them. Nevertheless, this independent educational enterprise was without question among the most ambitious and important tasks undertaken by German Jewry during this period. Following the pogroms of Kristallnacht in November 1938, Jewish children were forbidden to attend general schools; and although attendance at Jewish schools was permitted in December 1938, these schools could only be operated to a limited extent, primarily because of a lack of teachers.

Jewish Youth Movements Put to the Test

Since the fate of its youth was of great concern to the German-Jewish community, special importance was ascribed to the activities of the independent Jewish youth movements. During the 1930s there was a wide variety of such movements, and outside the marginal, radically assimilationist groups—such as those of Naumann and Schoeps or the Communists—all these movements took Judaism to be a basic tenet and aspired to enhance their members' attachment to it through the study of traditional sources, Jewish history, and above all the Hebrew language. This was the background for the establishment of the School of Jewish Youth in Berlin. With the exception of the Revisionists, who created a separate association, all the Zionist youth movements belonged to the pioneering framework of Heḥalutz, saw their goal as joining one of the kibbutzim in Palestine, and fostered a socialist worldview in the spirit of the movements that belonged to the Palestine Labor Federation. The Revisionists created their own framework. The religious youth formed a movement whose goals included labor and pioneering. Called Torah and Labor (Torah v'Avodah), it forged a new archetype of religious youngster—a pioneer—and its members laid the foundations for the religious kibbutzim in Palestine.[106]

The tight, disciplined organization of the youth groups and the strength they fostered through the sharing of experiences endowed them all with far greater moral weight than their actual size would otherwise have merited. It was particularly during the crisis of 1933 that the importance of this influence became manifest. At that time the ranks of the youth movements were swelling, and they displayed a dynamism whose potential they themselves may not have suspected before. Their members became the prime movers behind the organization of activities to further vocational training and settlement in Palestine, and they imbued their peers with the strength to withstand the threats all around them. Because they appreciated how fateful were the times and how heavy the responsibility borne by the Jewish public, these youngsters resolved to help their people. More than once, their devotion made rescue possible, but their very refusal to desert their posts turned many of them into victims. These same qualities prevailed during the period of total liquidation.

Even before the establishment of the National Socialist regime, a National Committee of Jewish Youth Organizations was functioning in Germany. The moving spirit behind its foundation was Ludwig Tietz, who, together with Georg Lubinski (Giora Lotan), was one of the most prominent figures involved in internal Jewish organization during the first year of Nazi rule—both men were instrumental in the establishment of the Central Committee for Relief and Reconstruction. The new regime obliged all youth organizations to register with the Reich Youth Movement Department, and the almost one hundred organizations that complied even received fairly favorable treatment from the authorities. As a result of negotiations with the relevant authority, the National Committee of Jewish Youth Organizations became the first Jewish umbrella organization. It came under the control of the Reich Youth Directorate, headed by Baldur von Schirach, and received a letter from the Directorate dated November 2, 1933, recognizing it as "the central organization solely responsible for the Jewish youth societies." As time went on, the strongly assimilationist Reich Union of Jewish Veterans and the Revisionist youth organization Herzliyah were also forced to join, the latter despite its denunciation of any kind of negotiations with the National Socialists, as demanded by Vladimir Jabotinsky. In the manifesto Tietz drafted and that after his sudden death was to become his last will and testament, he expressed the belief that owing to this recognition, the youth movements would be able to continue functioning, "Thus the Jewish youth movements can now devote all their energies to the great task placed upon them—the education of Jewish youth—and give themselves wholly to the work that the demands of the times have imposed upon the young generation of Jews in Germany."[107]

The practical directives stressed that from then on all questions concerning Jewish youth were to be brought to the National Committee of Jewish Youth Organizations, and the Reich Youth Directorate was not to be contacted directly. Thereafter, the youth movements throughout Germany were organized into national, regional, and local committees. On the whole they enjoyed relative freedom of action (except in Bavaria), but they were forbidden to display emblems, uniforms, or flags. They had to inform the authorities of their meetings and outings, and Gestapo men often attended their activities. The National Committee worked closely with the Reichsvertretung, whereas the rest of the cultural organizations, particularly the Liaison Office for Adult Education, helped the youth movements in their work, which included the running of special courses for training youth leaders. Moreover, the movements played an especially important role in the organization of Youth Aliyah and joined in the establishment of training farms that prepared pioneers for life in Palestine.

Hitler and his people effected the National Socialist revolution stage by stage, turning Germany into a totalitarian state preparing for a war of conquest. This new situation engendered considerable tension both within Germany and beyond. The ideology that had been developed before the National Socialists rose to power was not always manageable in the reality that emerged after they became the rulers of Germany. This dissonance had special relevance for the Jews, for the situation did not allow for the immediate solution of the "Jewish problem" in accordance with the ideological principles fundamental to National Socialist theory. On the other hand, on several occasions anti-Jewish actions served to distract attention from tensions that existed within the new Nazi regime. This situation, so fraught with contradictions and conflicting messages, consistently worked against the interests of Germany's Jews, who continued to subscribe to a variety of ideologies anchored in the period prior to the advent of the National Socialists. Considering that the entire political and social structure of the Weimar Republic had collapsed in a matter of weeks, it is not surprising that, exposed to the brunt of Nazi terror, the Jews fell into disarray. They found themselves in a situation whereby they had to do opposing things: adapt themselves to the new reality, yet maintain their dignity and independence; preserve the community's internal unity in the face of a concerted assault, yet utilize divergent means of influencing the separate branches of government; maintain the cultural, social, and economic strength and solidarity of the community, yet encourage and organize for emigration.

The Nuremberg Laws transformed the Nazis' racial ideology into political–legal reality, sweeping away the last traces of the emancipation. From that point onward, the struggle of German Jewry became a stark fight for survival. The

Nuremberg Laws were also a milestone in the reinforcement and spread of anti-Semitism to the rest of the countries of Europe. Today we know that the Jews of Germany were only Hitler's first victims. As the Third Reich built up its power and extended its borders and as the danger of war approached, the Jews' struggle for survival became increasingly desperate, and the threats facing them loomed constantly larger wherever they turned.

Emigration: The Dilemma of the Jews
(Through September 1, 1939)

Hitler's Foreign Policy and Its Impact on the Jews

> Today there is in each and every one, young and old, high rank and low, rich and poor, the crazed will gradually to turn the German people into a world power. We are all convinced: we must take part in ruling the world and educate our people to be a master *Volk.*

With those words Josef Goebbels addressed an audience of thousands in Berlin's largest hall early in 1936.[1] The dream of Germany ascending to the zenith of world rule was one of the strongest and most pronounced drives of many members of the Nazi movement, and none more than Hitler himself. Time and again, beginning with his book, *Mein Kampf,* he referred to his political objective as Germany's expansion not only beyond the borders laid down in the Treaty of Versailles but beyond even the country's 1914 boundaries. In his scheme of things, Germany's future status was to be achieved by a *Blitzkrieg* in which everything was to be risked on a single card. This approach admitted only two possibilities: victory or defeat; all or nothing. These alternatives were not of Hitler's invention, nor did they reflect an outlook peculiar to him. Rather, they were a feature that had been deeply ingrained in Germany's political and military tradition.[2] Right-wing circles in Germany had always been convinced that political power in the international arena could only be ensured by military might. That same might would likewise make economic expansion possible once the bounds of German rule had been extended by force of arms. Alongside the extreme Right was another political current called "liberal imperialism," one that sought to reinforce Germany's status and enhance its strength by economic means.

By World War I the champions of the militant position had gained the upper hand. Even then they had pressed for military conquests in Eastern Europe so as to create *Grossraum* (expanded space) within which Germany could fortify and prepare for the fateful struggle for world domination. A memorandum written in March 1926 advocated the following steps to be taken in sequence:

1. Liberation of the Rhineland and the Saar;
2. Abolition of the Polish corridor and the recovery of Polish Upper Silesia;
3. Annexation *(Anschluss)* of Austria;
4. Abrogation of the demilitarized zone.[3]

In the autumn of 1933 Germany withdrew from the League of Nations as the first public expression of the new regime's desire to nullify the conditions of the Versailles treaty. In 1936 Hitler entered the demilitarized Ruhr region and the Rhineland, in violation of the treaty, and officially annulled the Locarno Pact. The gambit had a twofold result: Britain and France did not react militarily as the German military had feared they would, and this demonstration of Hitler's audacity and power brought Mussolini closer to him. With the subsequent dispatch of German units to fight on Franco's side in the Spanish civil war, the Reich began to intervene directly in the affairs of Europe at large.

Hitler's attempt to induce a National Socialist revolution in Austria in July 1934 was unsuccessful. But what he failed to accomplish in the second year of his rule, he effected in a matter of days in March 1938. What is more, the European powers, especially France and England, which had pursued the policy of nonintervention during the Spanish civil war, now acquiesced in Hitler's demands—a trend that culminated in the abandonment of Czechoslovakia to Hitler's designs in Munich on September 29, 1938. The annexation of the Sudetenland, which the führer had demanded and obtained at Munich, led to the annexation of the entire Czech portion of Czechoslovakia (Bohemia and Moravia), whereas Slovakia, though proclaimed an independent country, essentially became a German satellite. There was no longer any doubt that Poland would be the next object of German aggression. "If Italy's friendship was a key to Austria," the historian Alan Bullock wrote, "Poland's was one of the keys to Czechoslovakia."[4]

Each of these aggressive actions was accompanied by a declaration that "this is the last demand"; or "I will not sign any document knowing that it will never be possible to fulfill its terms";[5] or, as he proclaimed at the signing of the nonaggression pact with Poland on January 26, 1934, "Germans and Poles will have to learn to accept the fact of each other's existence."[6] At home, however, the führer ventured, "When they hear me speak of universal peace, disarmament, and mutual security pacts, my party comrades will not fail to understand me correctly."[7]

Just as the Jewish question was a part of Germany's domestic problems, it also left its mark on the country's foreign policy. Hitler regarded the purge of the Jews as a prerequisite for preparing the German people for the struggles ahead. Indeed, as we have seen, forces were eager to bring about the purge, but they were prevented from doing so by outside interference, as the experience of April 1, 1933, demonstrated. Yet opposition to the notion of ousting the Jews came not only from abroad. As long as Germany's economy continued to suffer from the worldwide Great Depression and as long as the armament program had yet to materialize, Hitler was bound to cooperate with the economic forces represented by Hjalmar Schacht, which were essentially an extension of traditional liberal imperialism. The armament program, moreover, was highly dependent on the import of raw materials; in turn, that was closely tied to two troubling problems: exports and foreign currency. This is why Schacht argued for fostering proper relations and opposed the use of terror against the Jews.[8] Consequently, the Nazi policy toward the Jews had two contradictory aims: to undermine their social, political, and cultural status and to dispossess them economically while ensuring that the measures taken toward these ends would not disrupt Germany's foreign relations.

At his first meeting with his generals in February 1933, Hitler had already noted that his aim was "the conquest of new living space [*Lebensraum*] in the East and its ruthless Germanization."[9] He dubbed this approach *Raumpolitik* (space politics), as opposed to *Grenzpolitik* (border politics) of the nationalist bourgeoisie from which he sought to distinguish himself by his political, economic, and military methods.[10]

Hence in the autumn of 1936, Hitler called for what he termed *economic armament* along with military and political preparations "at the same pace, with the same decisiveness, and if necessary with the same ruthlessness." As an example of what he meant, he referred to the operation of the Soviet economy and added that if the German economy did not properly understand its tasks, "not Germany but just a few businessmen will go under."[11]

To spur the economy into making a maximal effort Hitler proposed two laws: (1) enact the death penalty for causing damage to the economy and (2) hold the Jews as a group responsible for damage caused to the German economy or the German people "by any individuals from that gang of criminals."[12] It was not Schacht, the spokesperson of the traditional economy, who was appointed to carry out the new Four-Year Plan but Göring, who proceeded systematically to undermine Schacht's standing until finally, a year later, the latter was compelled to resign as minister of the economy. Thus the way was open for a definite change in the economic policy toward the Jews.

Hitler's rise to power and the vigorous legal, social, and economic persecution of the Jews of Germany forced world Jewry to face up to a new situation for which it, like German Jewry itself, was sorely unprepared. Facing the Jewish people was the most aggressive country of the day in the process of amassing vast political and military might to mount a campaign of conquest and domination. Hitler portrayed the Jews as a demonic power, the quintessence of all his adversaries. Having almost no practical or even spiritual common ground or unified leadership, the Jewish people reacted with limited, often haphazard, and counterproductive measures.

The world's sovereign states were just then beginning to recover from the most severe economic crisis the world had known in decades. Historically, the masses of Jews had always been the first to suffer from any kind of crisis in their host countries—spiritual, economic, social, or political. In the 1930s all four such crises were combined: the spiritual crisis opened the floodgates of anti-Semitism; the economic and social crises led to the closing of borders to immigration; and the political crisis gave rise to the policy of appeasement, which forestalled effective political action on behalf of the persecuted Jews in Germany, Austria, and Czechoslovakia.

It is against this complex and tragic background that we must review the actions taken on behalf of the Jews and by the Jews themselves. The efforts mounted by Jews in the Diaspora outside Germany were of two kinds: (1) to provide relief and assistance to groups under attack, especially refugees, and (2) to activate political and economic deterrents by public protests, by boycott of German goods, and by cooperation with national and international political institutions and agencies.

Emigration in the 1930s

Opportunities and Obstacles

Years later it became clear that the only sure way to save the Jews of Europe was through emigration to Palestine or countries overseas. But that was not evident to the Jews in Germany—or anywhere else for that matter—in the early days of the Nazi regime; even the imaginings of the Nazis themselves had probably not reached that far at the time. Nevertheless, there can be no doubt that in the 1930s, the German authorities were interested in Jewish emigration and to some extent were even prepared to promote it. However, there was no unanimity on this issue. Some officials believed that the presence of Jewish emigrants might stir up opposition to Germany abroad, whereas others hoped that the virus of anti-Semitism would spread once the world was flooded with Jewish immigrants. Similarly, some deemed it best to encourage emigration by establishing suitable arrangements, including permission for the emigrants to take along most of their property and capital, whereas others saw an opportunity to boost the German economy by appropriating the assets of the fleeing Jews.

Although the Jewish community did not deny the importance of emigration, it saw its primary task as the struggle to ensure the community's continued existence within Germany. The approach of most Jewish groups throughout the world, Zionist and non-Zionist alike, was essentially identical: one reason was that from the start of this period, the limited prospects to find countries ready to absorb immigrants stood as a major obstacle to mass emigration. For the most part, the Jewish refugees did not meet the economic needs of the countries they sought to enter and were, thus, regarded as either dangerous competitors or as a potential economic and social burden. Indeed, it can be said that the three parties to the emigration problem—the Nazi authorities in Germany, the nations of the world, and the Jews—were equally confounded by the inherent contradictions in their attitudes toward the emigration of Jews from Germany, and this necessarily precluded the formulation of a clear and solid policy on an issue that ultimately became a matter of life and death. Here, then, is the genesis and crux of one of the most acute problems of the Holocaust period: the rescue of Jews.

The first wave of frantic emigration came in the wake of the terror perpetrated during the early months of Nazi rule. France was the leading haven then, but many emigrants also made their way to Holland and Czechoslovakia; in smaller numbers they also found their way to Belgium, England, the Scandinavian countries, and Switzerland. About fifty thousand Jews are estimated to have emigrated between the beginning of 1933 and the spring of 1934.[13] They included a large number of Jews from Eastern Europe who had recently arrived in Germany, some of whom now returned to the countries from which they had just come—particularly Poland.[14] The Jews in these countries of refuge formed aid committees or tried to solve the problem by recourse to existing Jewish relief organizations; in most places the authorities also came to their aid.[15] Nevertheless, many of the refugees failed to achieve even the most minimal footing and were forced to roam from one country to another. And when it seemed to them that the storm had passed in Germany, a movement of return set in. The extent to which the organized Jewish community in Germany took a jaundiced view of panicky emigration can be seen from the first statement issued by the Central Committee of German Jews for Relief and Reconstruction, which warned against undirected emigration, "It will not help anybody to go abroad aimlessly, with no prospect of making a living, but only increase the numbers there who are without work and means." On the other hand, help was promised to "those who no longer have any hope of earning a living in the German Fatherland to find some means of settling abroad."[16]

When the movement back to Germany gathered momentum, especially in the course of 1934, the authorities set up special camps or simply incarcerated the returnees in concentration camps for "re-education." It is likely that this wave of returning Jews was one of the factors leading to the deterioration that began to be felt in early 1935. It was also at that time that the Gestapo first published instructions specifically calculated to discourage Jews from continuing to reside in Germany.[17]

Vocational Rehabilitation

One way of reshaping the future of German Jews was by retraining them in occupations more in line with the opportunities still open to Jews in Germany or making it possible for them to earn a living elsewhere. Vocational training was one of the spheres in which the problem of the Jews' continued existence in Germany overlapped with the issue of emigration. Agricultural training could have been of benefit only to those planning to emigrate, particularly to Palestine; but at least in the early years, training in the crafts, trades, and technical occupations was also regarded as the basis for building a life in Germany itself. A special committee to organize vocational rehabilitation was established within the framework of the Central Committee for Relief and Reconstruction, and in the spring of 1934 attempts were made to formulate a systematic vocational policy. It distinguished between three spheres: Germany, Palestine, and other countries. At that time 6,069 people were undergoing occupational retraining, 3,331 of them studying crafts and 2,738 agriculture, with 900 of the latter training abroad.[18] Centers for agricultural training were also established in the neighboring countries of France, Holland, Czechoslovakia, Denmark, Sweden, Italy, and Yugoslavia; the ORT schools in Lithuania, Latvia, and Poland were likewise utilized for this purpose.

Training centers were even established in Germany proper, while Jewish youth were also able to gain experience from their work alongside German farmers and in German workshops.

Closed Doors

The struggle to emigrate had to contend with one especially critical problem: Germany's willingness to allow the transfer of some of the emigrants' assets. As far back as 1931 (i.e., before Hitler's rise to power) Germany had instituted an emigration tax to impede the drain of foreign currency.

Apart from the Palestine Office, it was mainly the Hilfsverein der deutschen Juden that handled emigration and helped individuals overcome the thorny administrative problems that had to be settled before they could leave the country.[19]

The wave of immigration that had brought millions of Jews to the United States, mostly from Eastern Europe, was gradually halted after World War I. Isolationism thrived and the rise in animosity toward "foreigners" stimulated anti-Semitism. The Jews were highly sensitive to the change in the climate of public opinion and, fearing that refugees might become a burden on the American economy, denied any possibility of revising the extant immigration laws. Wishing to assist the persecuted, however, U.S. Jews tried to gain entry for "nonlaborers and some exceptional persons."[20] Their efforts to improve the situation and raise the problem before the public led to the Evian Conference (see later discussion) and to a certain rise in the number of entry visas granted from 1937 onward; however, public opinion polls continued to show that over 80 percent of the population was opposed to any change in immigration policy.[21]

The difficulty in gaining entry to overseas countries meant that prospective immigrants sometimes had to wait months for a visa. As a result, thousands of Jews who had left the Reich in haste remained in the bordering countries in transit while waiting for the redeeming visa. These transmigrants created a problem in places such as Czechoslovakia, France, Holland, Denmark, and Sweden, all of which treated them rather liberally. Moreover, they often required considerable assistance, which was provided by international Jewish organizations and local committees.

While it appeared that the sojourn of these transmigrants would be relatively brief, other refugees were in need of long-term assistance. As most countries refused them work permits, they were dependent on continuous aid. This was the case in Switzerland, Czechoslovakia, and the Scandinavian countries; in Holland a relatively large number of refugees were absorbed into the economy. When the country was overrun in 1940, some 15,000 refugees—out of a total of close to 34,000 who had entered Holland—remained, whereas the other 18,500 left the country after a short or long stay. The vast majority of these remaining refugees were settled, and only about 900 "illegals" were still being accommodated in the Westerbork absorption camp.[22]

After World War I responsibility for refugees had been turned over to the League of Nations. Now France, Holland, and Belgium pressed for the establishment of a special institution, under league auspices, to deal with the refugee problem created by Germany. Concomitant pressure was applied by the large Jewish philanthropic organizations in the United States, which sustained most of the costs for the migration and were interested in consolidating the refugee-aid activities on the international level. In the autumn of 1933 the league did, in fact, agree to establish the Office of the High Commissioner for (Jewish and other) Refugees from Germany; on the initiative of the American-Jewish organizations, James G. McDonald was appointed as high commissioner. Thus, for the first time in the history of the League of Nations, an official personage from the United States headed a league institution. As it was clear that most of the refugees would be Jews, a special Department for Jewish Affairs was opened in McDonald's office, with Norman Bentwich, a well-known British Zionist, as its director and with the principal Jewish organizations represented on its executive board. McDonald defined his tasks as coordinating aid activities, negotiating with the governments concerned, designing a plan for integrating immigrants into the economies of the countries involved, and handling the problem of refugees' documentation. He addressed the questions of property and the right of settlement besides examining the prospect of immigration to various countries, particularly Palestine.[23]

As time went on, however, it became apparent that the high commissioner's latitude was highly limited. His mandate did not permit him to act in the name of the League of Nations, which left him bereft of political authority at a time when the league's power was on the decline anyway. In the autumn of 1935, when McDonald saw that he was unable to solve the problems created by the surge in emigration following the Nuremberg Laws, he resigned his post, and in February 1936 Sir Neil Malcolm was appointed in his place.[24]

After the annexation of Austria and the Gestapo's recourse to the method of forced emigration (see later discussion), it became evident that the existing arrangements for dealing with the refugee problem were sorely inadequate. It was then that Roosevelt took a step ostensibly designed to resolve the impasse: he called for an international conference to chart solutions to the pressing refugee problem.

On July 6, 1938, in response to an invitation from the president of the United States, representatives of thirty-two countries gathered in the French resort town of Evian on Lake Geneva, with three countries (Poland, Rumania, and Germany) sending observers. In addition, thirty-nine refugee-aid organizations were represented at the conference—twenty of them Jewish organizations—and with Gestapo approval representatives of the Jews of Germany and Austria were allowed to attend.[25] The conference lasted for seven days and heard a plethora of speeches. Yet rarely, it seems, has a special, comprehensive international effort of this sort and scope yielded such meager, even detrimental, results. For above all, the Evian Conference made it clear to all concerned that there was no haven for Jewish refugees from Germany. Of all the countries represented at Evian, only the Dominican Republic was prepared to offer anything concrete by declaring its willingness to permit the settlement of one hundred thousand Jews on the island. But even that generous offer was not acted upon until after a substantial delay—and then on only a much reduced scale of five hundred people. The only practical

result of the conference was the decision to establish a permanent intergovernmental committee charged with investigating the possibilities of settling refugees
and striving to reach a general agreement with Germany about organizing the
systematic emigration of the Jews.[26]

Much has been written about Roosevelt's real motive in calling this conference.[27] The president's chief advisers, including Secretary of State Cordell Hull
and Assistant Secretary Sumner Welles, recommended that he "get out in front
and attempt to guide,"[28] that is, create the impression of genuinely seeking a solution to the problem without committing the United States to any far-reaching
measures. What remained of the conference was the distinct impression that the
countries involved were unwilling to admit Jews, and Hitler could draw the conclusion that the Jews were, in fact, defenseless and had no way out of their
predicament.

Attempts to Place Pressure on Germany

It was not always possible to draw a sharp distinction between philanthropic aid
and political–diplomatic activities undertaken on behalf of the Jews of Germany—as attested by the attempts to involve the League of Nations in the aid
effort and even more so by Roosevelt's initiative to involve other countries in the
search for a solution. Some governments even tried to apply direct diplomatic
pressure on Germany, though most of these diplomatic protests were in response
to measures taken against Jews who were foreign nationals residing in Germany.
In March 1933, for example, the Polish legation submitted no fewer than four lists
of citizens who had suffered abuse.[29] Hitler occasionally discussed this matter with
one ambassador or another, but in such instances the führer usually launched into
one of his tirades, and nothing came of the audience. In effect, only two efforts—
one economic, the other political—left any mark on life in Germany or on the
Jewish population there: the movement to boycott German goods, organized
mainly in Britain and the United States, and an action executed within the framework of the League of Nations known as the Bernheim Petition.

The Anti-German Boycott Movement

In Britain the boycott movement began as a spontaneous response by Jews and
non-Jews that subsequently coalesced into an organized effort, even though
the conservative Board of Deputies of British Jews withheld its support from the
movement. In the United States the American Jewish Congress took part in the
establishment of a boycott committee in March 1933, with the American Jewish
Committee and B'nai B'rith abstaining. The movement was accompanied by public protests, the most prominent being the mass rally at Madison Square Garden
on March 27, 1933, under the leadership of Stephen Wise.[30] At the beginning of
that month, a boycott movement was also formed in Poland and took hold in a
number of other East European countries.

The debate going on in Jewish circles at that time reflects some of the fundamental problems that preoccupied the Jews during the early phase of the Nazi regime. On the one hand, it seemed that the world had to be aroused to forthright opposition and forceful action against the Nazi regime; on the other hand, it was feared that denunciations of, and sanctions against, Germany might provoke reprisals that would endanger the Jews by serving as "proof" of the diabolical world Jewish conspiracy.

Just as the Jews were divided over how to react, so were governments and public opinion in the free world desirous of denouncing the Nazi persecutions and dictatorial regime but, at the same time, concerned about maintaining serviceable relations with Germany. These competing needs, in turn, influenced the position taken by Jewish officials, who were careful not to contradict their governments' policies or provoke the antagonism of the public at a time when Jewish refugees from Germany were knocking at the gates of their respective countries. Owing to this ambivalence, actions were sometimes neutralized by counteractions or were only partially executed. Typical was the behavior of the three members of the Jewish delegation from Germany (two Zionists and one member of the CV) whom Göring sent to London to call off the Madison Square Garden meeting and put a stop to so-called atrocity propaganda. Reporting behind closed doors, they tried to convey to the leaders of British Jewry and the Zionist movement an accurate picture of the situation in Germany and convince them of the great peril looming over German Jewry. According to one member of the delegation, Martin Rosenblüth, they also intimated in a phone conversation with Stephen Wise that he should go ahead with the Madison Square Garden rally. At the same time, frightened by the announcement of the April 1 boycott, they rushed to get public statements—even from the Jewish Agency Executive in Jerusalem—to the effect that "no official Jewish institution had declared a boycott against Germany."[21]

A favorable view of the boycott was expressed by the veteran Zionist Leo Motzkin in a comprehensive report about the precarious situation of the Jews in Germany, stressing the boycott's impact on German trade.[32] The rift in the American-Jewish public deepened when the American Jewish Committee and B'nai B'rith tried to muffle the public protest and quash the boycott movement, advocating instead "quiet diplomacy," in line with the approach favored by the U.S. State Department. Although the authorities tried to mute the public protest and bridle the boycott, the movement was successful enough to prompt Schacht, on a visit to the United States in May 1933, to meet with a number of Jewish leaders and urge them not to carry out the boycott threat.[33]

The boycott intensified in 1936, especially after the American Jewish Congress joined with the Jewish Labor Committee (founded in 1934) in forming the Joint Boycott Council. This partnership also led to greater support from American trade unions, and on March 15, 1937, another mass rally was held at Madison Square Garden, this time with the participation of prominent non-Jewish figures. Stephen Wise, identifying as an American, rather than as a Jew, declared, "The boycott, moral and economic, is a warless war against the war makers."[34] The Jews in Germany, he stressed, were but one element of the civilization that Nazism had sworn to destroy.

Although Germany's economic condition and foreign trade prospects remained difficult, in time, the Germans stopped viewing a boycott of their goods and services as the most serious threat. However, since Germany could not provide for all its needs by itself, the materials it lacked would have to be obtained by conquest and the coercion of willing and unwilling allies. (On the conflict between the Zionist movement and the boycott, see later discussion.)

The Bernheim Petition

Altogether different was the campaign known as the Bernheim Petition.[35] After World War I, Upper Silesia, a region bordering on Germany on one side and Poland on the other, was divided between the two. The 1922 Geneva agreement stipulated that minorities in the sector that had been incorporated by Germany would enjoy a special status for a period of fifteen years under the protection of the League of Nations. Since the Reich's government treated the Jewish minority in the district as it did all the other Jews in Germany, the Committee of Jewish Delegations—originally established to represent Jewish interests at the Paris Peace Conference—decided to try to activate the protection of the League of Nations under the clause of the 1922 agreement that entitled any citizen in that district whose minority rights were infringed to lodge a complaint with the league.

Franz Bernheim, a Jewish resident of Upper Silesia who had been fired from his job and subsequently had emigrated to Czechoslovakia, addressed a complaint to the League of Nations, to which a petition by the Committee of Jewish Delegations, the American Jewish Congress, and a number of other Jewish organizations was attached. Overruling the German representative's efforts to block discussion of the petition, the league's council took up the matter in two public sessions on May 30 and June 6, 1933, with all the speakers denouncing the violation of the Geneva agreement and even focusing their remarks specifically on the disaster that had befallen Germany Jewry as a whole. Meanwhile, the Jews of Upper Silesia themselves approached the Reich authorities and demanded that the Geneva agreement be honored, threatening to take the matter before the league. Indeed, despite German threats, a memo was sent to the League of Nations on September 16, 1933. But the struggle continued. Until the tenure of the agreement expired in 1937, Upper Silesia remained something of an enclave within the Third Reich in which the Jews retained their status and the Nuremberg Laws did not apply. Hitler expressly consented to this policy, as he had also agreed to exclude Upper Silesia from the various clauses applied to institutions of higher learning because he was conscious of the presence of ethnic German minorities in other European countries, including Poland. But by 1937 the situation had changed, for the Third Reich felt strong enough to deter acts of reprisal against these German minorities.

The Zionist Movement Vis-à-Vis the National Socialist Regime

Discussion about what Jews did or should have done during the period of the Third Reich, especially in the 1930s, often focus on the Zionist movement and the role it played or should have played considering the looming disaster. At that time—in contrast to our own when the State of Israel has become the focus of Jewish policy—there was a striking gap between the Zionist movement's objectives and the reality it had created. On the evening of July 29, 1934, and the following morning, toward the end of lengthy discussions with Sir Arthur Wauchope, British high commissioner for Palestine, Ben-Gurion (who had stayed at Government House as a guest) indicated:

> I am not concerned about the existing Jewish population. We did not come to Palestine for our own sake but for the purpose of fulfilling the historic aspirations of the Jewish people. . . . A very heavy responsibility rests upon us. All the generations that preceded us anxiously waited for this hour. What happens in our generation in this country will seal the fate of all the coming generations.[36]

However, the Zionist movement and the Yishuv did not yet have the tools or resources to meet that responsibility at a critical time for the Jewish people. The Yishuv numbered only 450,000 souls. Its incipient political power was limited and its economic strength, though developing during the first half of the 1930s, still rested on a frail base; nonetheless, it served the Mandatory government as the yardstick for fixing the schedule of Jewish immigration. Moreover, the Jewish communities in almost all the East European countries were also in the throes of political, social, and economic crises. A third of the nearly 3.5 million Jews of Poland were threatened by hunger, and Jewish welfare organizations—primarily the American Jewish Joint Distribution Committee (JDC)—were making great efforts to assist them. The problem of emigration, as pressing in Poland as in Germany after Hitler's rise to power, was so acute that the leaders of the Polish government were eager to institute talks with other countries, even with the Zionist movement, in order to find a way out of the predicament.[37] Given these circumstances, the problem of German Jewry seemed to be but one of many severe problems confronting the movement.

Before Hitler's ascension to power, no special importance was attached to the small Zionist movement in Germany, whose supply of immigrants to Palestine was barely a trickle. Moreover, the economic and social structure of the assimilationist German-Jewish community did not seem congruent with the needs of the mostly agricultural economy in Palestine. The broader significance of the abolishment of the emancipation in Germany was not fully grasped by the Yishuv.

A number of German Zionists who had already emigrated to Palestine in the 1920s were the first to conceive the idea of conferring with the German authorities to facilitate emigration to Palestine. They were supported by the young, broadminded head of the Jewish Agency's Political Department, Chaim Arlosoroff, who with great determination and powers of persuasion overcame the misgivings and opposition voice in the Zionist Executive and at the end of April 1933 went to Germany to examine the situation firsthand. Disregarding the regime's character and outrageous behavior, Arlosoroff hoped to engage the German authorities in negotiations on the organized emigration of Jews to Palestine while taking their assets with them, stating that "a solution must be based on concessions from, and advantages for, both sides."[38] Thus, he posited a principle diametrically opposed to the boycott movement.

Over the years these two approaches became the two poles of the Jewish response in the hour of trial: combat or negotiation. They composed the two faces of European Jewry's struggle for existence. The choice of one method over the other was not related to association with a particular political outlook. Whereas the American Zionist Stephen Wise was one of the leading organizers of the boycott movement, Chaim Arlosoroff chose to enter into talks with the Nazi authorities. Similarly, although two German Zionists went to London—on Hermann Göring's orders—to try to contain the boycott movement, behind closed doors members of the CV who attended the 1933 Prague Zionist Congress as guests urged their hosts not to abandon the boycott movement and in other secret contacts supported the action of the Committee of Jewish Delegations at the League of Nations.[39]

The Zionists in Germany—and to a certain extent the Zionist Executive—were of two minds: on the one hand, they acknowledged the need to fight for the right of the Jews to remain in Germany; on the other, they recognized the urgency of emigration to Palestine that led over forty thousand people to apply to the Palestine Office for entry visas in the first few months of 1933. However, even Chaim Weizmann thought that the masses of European Jews were doomed, not at the hands of systematic murderers—to foresee that was beyond anyone's ken—but because of the economic situation and the inability to emigrate.[40] Weizmann concluded that above all it was young people who should be rescued and brought to Palestine, where they could be channeled into occupations that the Zionist leadership deemed crucial for laying a healthy foundation for the state-in-the-making. "Let us be frank with each other, . . ." Weizmann said in an address. "You cannot flood Palestine indefinitely with a population recruited from all over the world without running a grave risk of endangering the very structure which we are trying to create."[41]

Zionist leaders in Germany and elsewhere tried to act on three fronts: (1) to fight for the Jews' right to live in equality within Germany; (2) to organize the emigration to Palestine of *halutzim* (pioneers) and other youth who would be educated in the agricultural settlements as well as young families capable of being integrated primarily into agriculture but also into industry and the crafts; and (3) to organize systematic emigration from Germany, mainly to countries overseas, in cooperation with the Jewish philanthropic organizations. Three organizational bodies were established to implement this program, two of them within the framework of the Jewish Agency and the third as a worldwide Jewish aid organization. The 1933 Zionist Congress, accepting a proposal originally advanced by Arlosoroff, decided to establish a body under the aegis of the Zionist Executive to be headed by Weizmann. This body came to be known as the German Department, officially called the Central Office of the Jewish Agency for the Settlement of the Jews of Germany in Palestine. But the work of the department, which operated simultaneously out of London and Jerusalem, suffered considerably from internal difficulties.[42] The second body was Youth Aliyah, which grew out of the initiative of Recha Freier, with Henrietta Szold becoming its director in Palestine.

The third executive arm was envisioned as uniting the forces of the Jewish organizations that provided assistance to refugees and immigrants, but except for the efforts made within the framework of the League of Nations, it never became operational.

Notwithstanding the esteem that Weizmann personally enjoyed in the world at large, the Zionist movement had not yet achieved an influential status and was certainly not the accepted leadership of world Jewry. What is more, the Zionist leaders differed among themselves on basic political issues. Nevertheless, even liberal Jewish circles such as the CV could not disregard the prominent place that Palestine took among the countries open to Jewish immigration, and the columns of its newspaper began to fill up with items about the economic, cultural, and political situation there.

Initially, Nazi propaganda organs attacked the Zionist movement for its cosmopolitan character, which presumably confirmed the stereotyped image of the Jews. However, this approach changed following the 1933 Zionist Congress held in Prague from August 21 to September 4. The *Völkische Beobachter (VB)*, which carried detailed reports of the congress, actually welcomed its program for immigration to Palestine, hailing it as a chance to reach an agreement with the Jews on emigration.[43]

As was true of all other matters relating to the Jews, the attitude of the German authorities toward Zionism was marked by a lack of uniformity. The ascendant tendency, however, was to take a somewhat more favorable view of the Zionists and discriminate against the assimilationist circles. On more than one occasion, Revisionist quarters were favored in particular, even to the point where the members of Betar, the Revisionist youth movement, received permission to wear uniforms.

Especially conspicuous in his activities at that time was Georg Kareski (one of the leaders of the Revisionists in Germany), who headed the Organization of State Zionists. Although in the first two years of the Nazi regime he stressed the demand that the Jews be granted the status of a recognized minority, in 1935 he shifted the focus to emigration, which he hoped to regulate by the establishment of a bureaucratic apparatus under his direction as "Kommissar of emigration." The Jewish public distrusted Kareski because of his good relations with the Gestapo (see p. 74).[44]

The Transfer Agreement: An Attempt at a Practical Solution

The complexity of the Jewish predicament became evident during the major operation to promote immigration of German Jews to Palestine—the Transfer *(Haavara)* Agreement became an object of controversy throughout the Jewish world. We have already noted that Arlosoroff tackled the problem to safeguard the capital of German Jews while procuring their immigration to Palestine. One type of immigrant allowed free entry to Palestine by the Mandatory government was the so-called capitalist, that is, one who, on entering the country, could produce a sum of £1,000 (U.S. $4,000)—an amount deemed sufficient to guarantee that the immigrant would be able to establish himself in the country.[45] In 1933 many German Jews were able to put together that sum (the equivalent of about RM 12,500 (U.S. $3,676), despite the 25 percent emigration tax levied by the German government. (During the years from April 1, 1936, to September 2, 1939, the cost of £1,000 increased from RM 17,500 [U.S. $7,000] to RM 40,000 [U.S. $16,000].)[46] The wealth of many Jews exceeded these figures, and they were not prepared to forfeit their holdings or have them frozen in special accounts in Germany for the sake of getting out of the country. Arlosoroff was the first who proposed the establishment of a special bank to enable the gradual liquidation of the property and capital of Germany Jewry, hoping at the same time to turn this financial instrument into a means of stimulating the economic development of Palestine. His basic idea was to transfer blocked capital in the form of goods. Arlosoroff's murder on the Tel Aviv shore in June 1933 put an end to this endeavor, but in the meantime private schemes were being developed. One such undertaking began on the initiative of Sam Cohen, director of the Hanotea (Planter's) Company in Netanya, Palestine, in cooperation with the German consul in Jerusalem.[47] Eventually, it assumed a more official standing when the director of the Anglo-Palestine Bank, Eliezer Hoofein, took over the conduct of the negotiations with the German authorities in coordination with ZVfD.The agreement he concluded with the Germans in August 1933 provided for two special accounts in which prospective immigrants could deposit their money in order to receive it in local currency in Palestine. The overall scope of the transfer noted in the agreement was originally RM 3 million (U.S. $888,353), but once that figure had been reached the sum was raised, and the final sum amounted to £8.1 million (U.S. $32.4 million). However, the amount of foreign currency provided by the Reichsbank dwindled considerably during the years, as shown in Figure 1.

Figure 1. Transfer Transmissions of the Reichsbank and Haavara, 1933–1939

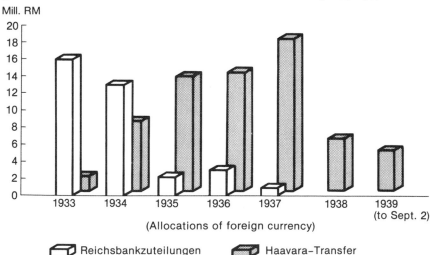

(Allocations of foreign currency)

Reichsbankzuteilungen   Haavara–Transfer

Source: W. Feilchenfeld et al., *Haavara-Transfer nach Palästina und Einwanderung deutscher Juden 1933–1939* (Tübingen, 1972), p. 45.

After Arlosoroff's murder, the director of the Jewish Agency's Immigration Department, Werner Senator, assumed responsibility for the plan. He spent considerable time in Germany, became a member of the executive board of the Central Committee for Relief and Reconstruction, and participated in the negotiations on the Transfer Agreement.

The main problem the Transfer Agreement posed for the Jewish public at large was not an economic issue but a political one. The agreement was concluded by the Germans because it promoted emigration and accorded them the opportunity to improve the trade balance and provide employment. Thus, it flew directly in the face of the boycott movement's efforts. The debate on this problem raged throughout the life span of the agreement and has continued into our own day.[48] It was raised primarily at the Zionist Congress in Prague, with supporters of the boycott arguing that the prospect of saving German Jewry through the boycott was neutralized by the readiness of the Zionists to enter into an economic agreement with Germany. The argument was that this meant capitulation to the organized onslaught on Jews and implied a threat to Jewry everywhere while making self-defense through the boycott imperative. A movement opposed to the Transfer Agreement and favoring the boycott even arose in Palestine, where its main supporters were among the youth.[49]

The debate over the agreement developed into a sharp clash at the World Jewish Conference held after the Congress in Geneva in September 1933, with Stephen Wise coming out vigorously against it and the non-Zionists demanding that it be denounced, accusing the Yishuv of abandoning moral and political principles for the sake of economic gain. The conference did not reach any decision, however, and the conflict raged on, especially in the United States and Poland, where the agreement was decried as "the disgraceful deal of Zionist and Palestinian politicians with Hitler."[50] For some time the Jewish Agency Executive tried to avoid taking a clear public stand on the issue because of opposition within the Zionist Executive and the movement's ranks. After a heated debate, however, the 1935 Zionist Congress in Lucerne decided that the Jewish Agency would recognize the Transfer Agreement.

Since the quantity of goods that the Yishuv was capable of absorbing from Germany was limited, it was necessary to find other ways to compensate the Reich for the foreign currency it would allocate for the transfer program. Various means of expanding the scope of trade and financial activity were tried, including the export of citrus to Germany and the export of German goods to neighboring countries in the Middle East. In some cases other international transactions were financed by Transfer funds, and an agreement was reached on the use of funds for welfare payments to the Jews in Germany. But this expansion of German transactions under the aegis of the Transfer Agreement only heightened the opposition to the arrangement in the proboycott circles.

Neither was the German stand on the agreement uniform. Over the years, some of the difficulties that arose were overcome with the aid of officials in the Foreign Ministry and the Ministry of the Economy who regarded the agreement favorably.[51] But when the Four-Year Plan went into effect, the Germans' interest in the agreement diminished; it was linked to Schacht's economic approach but had no place in the autarkic economy guided by Göring and gearing up for war.[52] A substantial shift in outlook began with the change in personnel at the German consulate in Jerusalem.[53] The new consul, Wilhelm Döhle, was opposed to the agreement and tried to prove that it neither brought benefit to Germany nor was necessary as a means of countering the economic boycott, which was in any event of meager consequence.[54]

Political considerations assumed greater importance in 1937 when the Peel Commission, hoping to find a way out of the situation created by the violent turn of events in Palestine, proposed the partition of the country into a Jewish state and an Arab state. Until then, the Nazi authorities had viewed Palestine mainly as a place to dispose of the Jews. But when they began to realize that the Jewish community there differed substantially from its counterparts in the Diaspora and was striving for political independence, their attitude changed radically, for the establishment of an independent Jewish commonwealth was regarded as highly undesirable. This point was stressed particularly by the Foreign Department of the Nazi party, which had opposed the Transfer Agreement from the start. In 1937 the matter appeared important enough even for the foreign minister to warn the British government that Germany would view the establishment of a Jewish state in Palestine unfavorably. These views were recorded in a classified circular issued by the German Foreign Ministry in June 1937:

> Germany is in fact more interested in maintaining the dispersion of Jewry [than in easing immigration to Palestine]. Even if not a single member of the Jewish race is on German soil, the Jewish question will not have been solved as far as Germany is concerned.... A Palestine state will not absorb world Jewry, but—like the effect of the Vatican state—will provide it with an enhanced status under the aegis of international law, and that is liable to have fateful consequences for German foreign policy.[55]

The internal German debate about the emigration of Jews to Palestine and the Transfer Agreement, from the economic and political point of view, went on until the beginning of 1938 when it was decided by Hitler himself. Apparently he pondered two opposing considerations: to keep the Jews in Germany as hostages and as a means of pressuring world Jewry or to rid Germany of its Jews and extract maximal economic gain in the process. Both approaches had been reported in his name at an interministerial meeting on November 17, 1935; eventually he decided in favor of promoting emigration.[56] In 1937, however, Hitler halted the

Table 1. The Impact of the Transfer Agreement on Immigration to Palestine

Years	Total Immigration	From Germany	Special Categories from Germany		Percentage	In Numbers	Percentage of Total
1933–39	204,000	51,700 25.3%	A-1 capitalists £P 1,000 A-2 professionals £P 500 A-3 artisans £P 250	36.0 0.2 0.9 } 37.1		19,181	9.4

Note: In the years 1933–1939 about 250,000 Jews left Germany; a fifth emigrated to Palestine and 37.1% of them made use of the Transfer Agreement, which was also instrumental in financing other emigration.

Source: Based on Werner Feilchenfeld, et al., *Haavara Transfer nach Palästina und Einwanderung deutscher Juden 1933–1939* (Tübingen, 1972), passim; Herbert A. Strauss "Jewish Emigration from Germany: Nazi Policies and Jewish Responses," *YLB*, 26 (1981), pp. 343–47.

Transfer operation for a period of several months because he shared the misgivings evoked by the Peel Commission's proposal on Palestine, and it was not until the spring of 1938 that he reinstated his approval of the Transfer undertaking.[57] As war approached, however, the Transfer activities inevitably faded out.

1938: The Fateful Year

Adolf Eichmann and the System of Forced Emigration

At the same time that doubts were raised about the necessity and efficacy of the Transfer Agreement, the Gestapo and the SD were pressing for the acceleration of Jewish emigration. Their treatment of the Jewish problem is associated with Adolf Eichmann, who was to become a symbol of the mass murder of the Jews, figuring as the loyal henchman of the master butchers of the Third Reich and as the moving spirit behind the bureaucratic organization of the "Final Solution." Ever since Eichmann's trial in Jerusalem and the death sentence of the Israeli court, his character has been a point of contention among historians and commentators. Some regard him as the personification of the evil spirit of National Socialism, a man impelled by an insatiable hatred who not only put the teachings of anti-Semitism into practice but also took them to their most extreme form in calculated, daily practice. Others contend that Eichmann was merely a small cog in an enormous wheel, an ordinary man who merely wished to please his superiors. According to Hannah Arendt, he was not even motivated by any special anti-Semitic impulse. What has caused this major discrepancy in the assessments of the man when there is no disagreement about the horrendous consequences of his actions? Eichmann was instrumental in adding a new dimension to the experience not only of the Jewish people but of all humankind: genocide. The very dispute about his nature reflects the Janus-faced character of the Nazi regime, which could dress the most destructive of man's irrational drives in the guise of routine activities.

Adolf Eichmann was born in 1906 to a bookkeeper in Solingen, a German industrial city in the Rhineland. When he was eight, his family moved to Linz, Austria, where Eichmann lived until 1933. He did not complete high school or the course in mechanics that he pursued for two years in a vocational school. After trying his hand at various jobs, he worked for a few years as a traveling salesman for the Vacuum Oil Company, crisscrossing the country on a red motorcycle; at one point he suffered an accident that resulted in severe skull fractures. In 1932 Eichmann joined the Austrian National Socialist party and later the SS, under the influence of Dr. Ernst Kaltenbrunner (who in 1942 succeeded Reinhard Heydrich as head of the Reichssicherheitshauptamt, or RSHA [Reich Main Security Office]. After losing his job in 1933, he moved to Germany and enlisted in an Austrian unit of the SS (then outlawed in Austria) that was training in exile in Germany. He received his military training in SS camps and did his first tour of duty in Dachau. In 1934 when Himmler shifted his headquarters to Berlin, Eichmann volunteered for the head office of the SD; later he claimed that he did not know what that institution engaged in and that he had found his way there almost by chance.[58] In his book on the early development of the SD, Shlomo Aronson explained Eichmann's adjustment to the Nazi hierarchy in these words, "He turned into a mass murderer because he could develop his future actions from latent personality traits compatible with the atmosphere in the SD."[59]

Eichmann was initially employed in the section that investigated the Freemasons, but early in 1935 he was transferred to a new SD Intelligence Department that dealt with the Jews. At that time the Gestapo and the SD intended to coordinate their activities related to the Jews, pooling information and systematizing their handling of affairs. They also moved to extend the scope of their activities to Jewry abroad and to establish direct contact with Jewish leaders in order to speed up emigration.[60]

Serving in the SD's Jewish Department (II–112), Eichmann became the leading expert on all things Jewish. He even claimed that he tried to learn some Hebrew and Yiddish and that he took a special interest in Zionism. In the autumn of 1937, together with the director of his department, Herbert Hagen, he traveled to Palestine and Egypt to examine the political situation there. At the end of his detailed report on that journey, Eichmann concluded that the Third Reich should not step up the emigration of Jews to Palestine, for "as far as the Reich is concerned, the creation of an independent state by the Jews in Palestine should be impeded."[61]

As early as January 1937 the SD called for concentrating the management of Jewish emigration in the framework of a special office of the Gestapo and the SD, one that would deal with all matters related to accelerating emigration, including immigration opportunities abroad, negotiating economic arrangements, and even the transfer of capital.[62] To induce the many Jews who still seemed unwilling to emigrate, two courses of action were recommended in January 1938: destroying the Jews' economic base and frightening them by terror.[63]

After the annexation of Austria these directives were put into practice, with the pogroms instigated against Austria's nearly two hundred thousand Jews being more extreme than the acts of terror perpetrated in Germany during the early months of 1933. Great numbers of Jews were arrested, humiliated, tortured, and sent to the Dachau concentration camp.[64] On March 18 the community's institutions were closed down and its leaders arrested.

Several days after the Germans entered Austria, Eichmann showed up in Vienna to organize the emigration of the Jews and introduce a new system conducted according to the following principles:

1. Emigration was no longer to be an act of choice organized by the Jews but an operation conducted under the supervision of the Security Police.
2. This forced emigration was to be effected by requiring existing Jewish organizations to carry out the instructions of the SD.
3. The economic power of Jewry would be destroyed and the property of the emigrants would be confiscated, leaving them only the sum required to enter their proposed countries of immigration.

In Vienna Eichmann demonstrated for the first time that he was capable not only of analyzing and assessing the Jewish situation in Germany and elsewhere but of acting on the conclusions drawn from his inquiry. He also evinced organizational abilities that his superiors were quick to praise.[65] At the beginning of May, he saw to it that the institutions of the Jewish community headed by Dr. Joseph Löwenherz as well as the Palestine Office would resume functioning by having their directors released from internment.[66] Under the constant threat of incarceration in a concentration camp, the Jews were forced to collaborate, and the pressure to emigrate was so strong that Löwenherz suggested consolidating the organizational and technical procedures for obtaining emigration permits because the fragmentation of administrative bodies was delaying departure. Eichmann, however, established the Central Office for Jewish Emigration in August 1938, which operated as a coercive apparatus.[67] One of the witnesses at the Eichmann trial compared it to "a flour mill tied in with a bakery. You put a Jew in at one end . . . [and] he comes out at the other with no money, no rights, only a passport saying: You must leave the country within two weeks; otherwise you will go to a concentration camp."[68] Thus, the foundation was laid for the method that would henceforth be used to handle Jewish emigration.

Revocation of the Communities' Public Status

The SD was not the only arm of the German regime interested in making life intolerable for the Jews. The desire to dispose of them as quickly as possible, a wish shared by all the arms of the Nazi regime, gave rise to different proposals.[69] In the spring of 1938 the Reich minister for church affairs persuaded the interior minister to set about changing the legal status of the Jewish communities. On March 28 the status of the Jewish communities as corporate bodies under public law was abrogated by statute; henceforth these communities became private associations, with all their activities subject to government supervision. The law marked a new stage in the process of stripping the Jews of their rights. While the Nuremberg Laws deprived the Jews as individuals of the rights attained by the emancipation, this new law nullified the rights of the Jewish collective as a public body. The communities could no longer receive financial benefits from the state or levy taxes on their members. During the summer decrees and regulations eroded the Jews' status further and limited their freedom of movement. Even before, on November 16, 1937, the Ministry of Interior in Prussia had issued a secret circular prohibiting the issuance of passports to Jews.[70] Jews were also forbidden to change their names and were required to carry special identity cards. In August 1938 another regulation required Jews who did not have their "Jewish names" appearing in a special list of first names to add to their given name the word Israel, if male, or Sarah, if female.[71]

Aryanization: The Destruction of the Economic Base

These isolating actions were accompanied by a wide-ranging and systematic program to undermine the Jews' economic base, officially called the Aryanization of Jewish property. As long as Schacht was piloting the German economy, he tried to prevent interference with the economic activity of the large Jewish businesses, although medium and small establishments suffered considerably. Especially affected by the boycott were Jewish-owned businesses in small towns and rural regions and small clothing, footwear, and food enterprises in the cities. Of about 100,000 Jewish-owned businesses, 39,552 were left by April 1, 1938.[72] In January 1938 discussions had been instituted to define the term *Jewish businesses,* and a law was eventually promulgated on June 14 as the Third Implementation Order to the Reich Citizenship Law, that is, to the Nuremberg Laws.[73]

The annexation of Austria, which imbued the Nazi leadership with a bouyant sense of confidence, accelerated the process. On March 26 Göring—as head of the autarkic Four-Year Plan—stated in Vienna that Aryanization must be implemented in an "absolutely systematic manner,"[74] intimating that the arrogation of Jewish property by the Nazis would be effected by the state and not through isolated and arbitrary actions (as had happened more than once, particularly in Austria). To prevent the Jews from saving their property by fictitious sales and token registration under the names of non-Jewish associates, Göring issued the Order Against the Support of the Camouflage of Jewish Businesses on April 22. Four days later, in conjunction with the Ministry of the Interior, he published the Order Requiring the Declaration of Jewish Property,[75] whereby all Jews—including those married to non-Jews—were enjoined to declare their holdings in Germany and abroad. The term *property* included assets of all kinds: works of art, jewelry, even all types of commercial and social benefits. Property amounting to less than RM 5,000 (U.S. $2,000) did not have to be declared, but any change—such as a sale, rental, or opening of a business or a branch—would henceforth require authorization. From then on Aryanization was carried out under the supervision, and with the participation, of party institutions. Many foreign countries adamantly protested the application of the order to their Jewish nationals residing in Germany. As a result Jews who were foreign nationals holding property in Germany but living abroad were exempted only in cases where there was a special obligation to the countries involved in accordance with the principle set down by Hitler personally.[76]

Within the framework of these provisions, the so-called voluntary Aryanization proceeded apace; as a consequence businesses were sold at 60 to 75 percent of their value. The real amount decreased even further as a result of taxes and harsh payment terms; in the best of circumstances the Jewish seller received from 30 to 60 percent of the value of his property. The party's involvement in this process was conspicuous. Under the banner of conducting "a healthy middle-class policy," it demanded that buyers take care not to pay Jews "an unseemingly high price, so that Jewry will compensate for some of the damage it caused the German people."[77]

The situation for the Jews was especially grave in Austria, where major and minor party leaders tried to take over as many businesses as possible. Many Nazis installed themselves as commissars in Jewish businesses or simply attempted to confiscate Jewish property on a variety of pretexts. Beginning in April the Property Traffic Office (Vermögensverkehrstelle) handled close to 25,000 cases of Aryanization and liquidation, resulting in the closing of more than 80 percent of Jewish businesses.[78] As Helmut Genschel observed, "Aryanization in Austria during the first months [after the *Anschluss*] gave the impression of a massive robbery campaign. . . . Much of what had been done in Germany over a number of years was compressed into a period of half a year [in Austria]."[79]

In Germany more and more occupations were closed to Jews, and the free professions were totally banned to them. However, during the drafting of a general law designed to completely displace the Jews from their positions in the economy, it became evident that the problem could not be solved without simultaneously clearing the way for increased emigration; for once dispossessed, the Jews were liable to become a burden on the German economy. In June Martin Bormann, acting on behalf of the führer's deputy, Rudolf Hess, sent party activists a secret directive about "the removal of the Jews from the economy." Its purpose was to prevent arbitrary Aryanization, and in August he assured a meeting of Nazi Gauleiters, "Göring intends to have a fundamental cleaning up of the Jewish question."[80] In a meeting held on October 14, 1938, Göring declared that Aryanization was the state's, and only the state's concern, adding that he was not prepared to allocate foreign currency to dispose of the Jews. He also dropped the remark that "if the need arises we will have to establish ghettos in the big cities,"[81] and for the first time mention was made of the plan to set up Jewish work brigades.

The Jewish Question at an Impasse

These considerations were aired about two weeks after Hitler's great political victory at Munich. If Neville Chamberlain—and the majority of the British people along with him—believed he had saved the peace, Hitler drew the very opposite conclusion, namely, that he should step up preparations for the war he wanted and launch it soon while his adversaries were rearming.[82] However, Hitler also had reasons for concern. It turned out that the German public did not fully share his evaluation or ambitions and, in fact, welcomed Chamberlain with overt enthusiasm as the man who had, indeed, saved the peace. Since that was not the response Hitler had hoped for in the people he wished to turn into a master *Volk,* the question now was how to imbue the German people with the necessary militant spirit.

Meanwhile, the Jewish question persisted in Germany, even though the various arms of the regime were working to eradicate it. In the summer of 1938 there were twenty-two hundred "asocial" Jews arrested by the Gestapo and incarcerated in Dachau, Buchenwald, and Sachsenhausen concentration camps. In many cases the crimes for which they were arrested were administrative infractions, such as illegal parking, failure to make payments on time, and the like; unemployed people were arrested on the charge of dodging the obligation to work. Their release was made conditional on their immediate departure from Germany.[83] However, emigration became more and more restricted, for the gates of Palestine were being closed by the Mandatory government and the outcome of the Evian Conference showed how poor the chances were of finding refuge in other countries.

At that conference the head of the Swiss Federal Police, Dr. Heinrich Rothmund, had complained about a new wave of Jewish refugees, three to four thousand in number, fleeing from Austria after the *Anschluss*. In reaction, the Swiss government required an entry visa for bearers of Austrian passports. The subject was first mooted between the Swiss and German governments in April 1938.[84] In August 1938 the Swiss authorities went a step further by threatening to rescind the right of free entry to bearers of German passports as well; eventually Rothmund hinted to the German consul in Bern that Switzerland would drop its visa requirement "if there were a distinct mark on the passports borne by Jews." When Rothmund arrived in Berlin toward the end of September 1938, an agreement to that effect was signed within a few days. On October 5 all passports held by Jews were declared invalid and had to be returned; the new ones issued in their place bore a red *J*.[85] Thus, in addition to the special identity card that Jews had to carry within Germany, they were now stigmatized in all foreign countries as well. The Germans had actually been compelled to introduce a measure contrary to their aim to accelerate Jewish emigration.

By the autumn of 1938, despite new laws, restrictions, and humiliation, only 150,000 to 170,000 Jews had left Germany—about a third of the approximately 500,000 who had been counted in May 1933. Yet by the methods he employed, including simply driving Jews over the Austrian border, Eichmann forced more than 50,000 Jews—about one-fourth of the country's Jewish population—to leave within six months.[86]

The Turnabout: Kristallnacht

Soon expulsions became almost the order of the day. After the Munich Pact and the territorial changes concerning the Sudetenland, Slovakia, and Hungary, about three thousand Jews were expelled and left destitute in the new border areas.[87] Heinrich Himmler had decreed the first official expulsion from Germany proper, ordering Russian Jews and their families who had entered the country before World War I but had never become German citizens to leave within ten days. After the deadline was extended several times, these "citizens of Soviet Russia" (as they were called) were sent to concentration camps from which they would be released only upon emigrating[88]—a practice that had become standard. Moreover, in reply to a query from the Foreign Ministry, Himmler asserted in May 1938 that by forcing people over borders into countries denying them entry, the Gestapo had acted "according to a general instruction."[89]

The occasion that served as the catalyst for the Kristallnacht pogrom is well known. The German authorities had long wanted to dispose of the Polish Jews residing in Germany, at least 20,000 of whom had already returned to Poland more or less voluntarily. Now the Foreign Ministry and the Gestapo were handed an opportunity to take action by an administrative ploy used by the Polish government. The Poles decreed a renewal of the passports of their citizens abroad but deliberately delayed processing the papers of the Jews to deprive them of their citizenship and prevent their return, especially from annexed Austria. The German Foreign Ministry, not wishing to be left with tens of thousands of stateless Jews, negotiated with the Poles, but to no avail. Before the deadline fixed for the renewal, October 31, 1938, the Gestapo, acting as "Alien Police," rounded up whole families of Polish Jews (for a total of about 17,000 people), transported them in sealed railway cars to the Polish border, and expelled them into no-man's-land. The plight of these people, whom the Poles tried to drive back over the border, was appalling. Eventually about 8,000 of them found shelter in warehouses, stables, a railway station, and the like, near the small border town of Zbanszyn. The Polish government, under pressure from the Jewish communities and organizations of Poland that were sustaining the refugees with food, blankets, and the like, finally admitted most of the deportees.[90] Though it had not been planned in advance, this deportation operation was typical of the Nazis' mode of operation: given their practice of coercing emigration and expelling individual Jews by force, they ushered in organized mass deportations by improvisation, setting the precedent for the next stage of their Jewish policy.

In reprisal for the expulsion of his family, seventeen-year-old Hershel Grynszpan, then living in Paris, entered the German Embassy there on November 7 and shot the third secretary, Ernst vom Rath, who died two days later.[91] By the day after the shooting *VB* had already carried an inflammatory editorial reminding its readers of the 1936 killing of the head of the Swiss Nazi party, Wilhelm Gustloff, by a Jewish medical student from Yugoslavia named David Frankfurter. That evening, November 8, violence and rioting were instigated by some local party leaders in Germany. But the signal for a countrywide pogrom was given by Goebbels—apparently with Hitler's consent—on the evening of November 9, after vom Rath's death. Haranguing the party's "old fighters" at their annual commemoration of the so-called Beer Hall Putsch of November 1923, he made it clear that the hour had come for "revenge," meaning action against the Jews they had so longed to execute.[92]

The Gauleiters and party heads present rushed to the phone to transmit instructions, Goebbels's ministry sent its directives by teleprinter, and orders were issued to the SA. The move caught Himmler, Heydrich, and Göring by surprise. It was not until late at night that Heydrich, not wishing to leave Goebbels as the sole author and beneficiary of the action and trying to avert irreparable damage, issued orders to the State Police and the SD.

It can be assumed that the Gestapo and the SD had already made some preparations for a major action against the Jews, for Heinrich Müller, the head of the Gestapo, had already issued orders almost identical to Heydrich's about an hour and a half before the instructions reached him.[93] Lists of wealthy and influential Jews marked for arrest in Heydrich's directives had been prepared in advance. Moreover, late in the summer of 1938 the Dachau, Buchenwald, and Sachsenhausen concentration camps had been enlarged and readied to absorb a greater number of people, and some of the Jewish prisoners there were told by SS men that these new inmates would be Jews.[94] Another indication of a premeditated action are the recollections (related after the war) that some well-connected Germans had suddenly urged Jewish friends to leave the country as quickly as possible.[95]

Himmler and Heydrich may have planned an action similar to the measures taken against the Russian Jews, probably to be coordinated with Göring's Aryanization program. Goebbels's coup was apparently designed to outwit his rivals by activating the SA and the party, just as he had on April 1, 1933. He failed in the end, as he had then, but in the meantime, on November 9 and 10, a pogrom that burgeoned into a mass frenzy of destruction spread throughout the country.

According to figures that Heydrich issued on November 11 in a preliminary report to Göring, 191 synagogues were set ablaze and another 76 were completely destroyed. Actually, the number of ravaged synagogues was about double those figures.[96] The next day Heydrich reported that seventy-five hundred Jewish businesses had been demolished. The debris of the shattered shop windows gave the pogrom its name, their value coming to RM 10 million (U.S. $4 million). In his first report Heydrich related that thirty-six Jews were killed and another thirty-six severely injured; eventually the number of murdered reported was ninety-one.[97]

Thirty thousand Jews or more were arrested and incarcerated in Dachau, Buchenwald, and Sachsenhausen[98] as planned in advance, and hundreds of Jewish-owned apartments were looted and ruined. Jewish institutions were damaged and closed, but care was taken not to destroy the communities' archives, which were subject to confiscation. Among the arrested was Otto Hirsch, the chairman of the Reichsvertretung, while its president, Rabbi Leo Baeck, was told not to leave his apartment. The Jewish leaders who escaped arrest proceeded to live a sort of double life by going into hiding at night and spending their days trying to run the Jewish community's affairs and influence the authorities to restore life to normal on the grounds that only under such circumstances could emigration be organized.[99]

As already noted, violent methods had been used in Austria after its annexation. The instructions to carry out a pogrom on November 9 and 10 reached Vienna a bit later than in Germany, so that the main action did not begin until the morning of November 10. According to the report of that date issued by the SD headquarters in Berlin, forty-two synagogues were destroyed in Vienna. At the same time an arrest operation got under way, accompanied by extensive searches and the confiscation of property in apartments and businesses. Some 7,800 Jews were arrested in Vienna alone, and 4,600 men from all parts of Austria were sent to the Dachau concentration camp (4,000 of them, who were able to guarantee their emigration, were subsequently released). In addition, 4,083 shops in Vienna were closed, and 1,950 apartments were forcibly vacated in one section of the city alone. The official report spoke of 680 cases of suicide; brutality reigned at the places where people were concentrated. There is testimony that at one such place, 27 people were killed and 88 seriously wounded.[100] Many Jews had already undergone similar experiences in Vienna. One letter from that period related:

> I've already noted that we had a visit like the one on Yom Kippur and, like then, the outcome was tragic and bloody. . . . Not a single dress, coat, piece of underwear [remained]. . . . When the doctor came to bandage Father, Rosa, and Berta—all three of them with blood gushing from their heads—we couldn't give him a towel or any other piece of cloth to wipe off the blood. . . . All the glasses, windows, mirrors [were] shattered. . . . We are left destitute. . . . But that was not enough; two days later we were told to accommodate two more families in our apartment immediately.[101]

The Austrian population did not intervene, except to participate in the looting. Whoever spoke out on behalf of the Jews risked arrest. However, the mood soon changed with the confiscations and pointless destruction arousing the public's disapproval. A report from Vienna dated November 18 stated, "the attitude toward the action, which was initially sympathetic, has now been spoiled." Reaction was especially sharp in business circles. Basing itself on the report from Vienna, the SD's summary analysis stated that in commercial quarters the events were viewed from a narrow capitalistic point of view "and an appreciation of the larger goals remains beyond them."[102] The reason for the "intellectual stratum's" inadequate understanding of the National Socialist outlook was explained as a lack of proper indoctrination.

As noted earlier, the weakness of popular support for the regime was of particular concern to the Nazi leadership just then as they were planning to lead the nation into war. Hitler delivered two speeches during those critical days, the first on the evening of November 8 to the "old fighters" in the beer hall; the second on the evening of November 10 to newspaper editors in Berlin. In neither of these speeches did he mention the Jewish problem by so much as a word; both addresses were aimed at rousing his supporters to vigorous action for what he called the "education of the people." While the November 8 speech was devoted mainly to debating his opponents outside Germany, the address on November 10 called on the press to amplify the propaganda for what lay ahead, by which he meant war. He had been forced to speak of nothing but peace, he said, for only by stressing the desire for peace was he able to prepare the nation step by step for war. Nevertheless, he added, "It is obvious that such peace propaganda, conducted for tens of years, also has its harmful sides." It was necessary "to make it plain [to the nation], slowly, that there were some things that may not be achievable by peaceful means and must be achieved by force." He then launched into a vicious attack on "degenerate intellectuals" whose allegiance could not be relied on. Along with such aspersions he expressed a threat: "Seeing the intellectual strata among us— unfortunately we need them—otherwise it would be possible one day, yes, I don't know, to exterminate them or something like that. [Movement in the audience.] But unfortunately, they're needed."[103] Since everyone at that gathering, including Hitler, was certainly aware of the current events, it may be assumed that the lesson of the day was not lost on the men of the press. The assault on the Jews was born of a conglomeration of divergent motives, one of them being an interest in evoking "educational" fright in the public at large.

The violent onslaught on the Jews was followed by measures designed to fulfill three premeditated objectives: (1) to deprive the Jews of their economic footing, to the benefit of the government's empty coffers; (2) to expedite their emigration by resorting to outright terror; and (3) to isolate them completely from the general population, while abolishing their ostensibly autonomous organization. Thus, as in the spring of 1933 in Germany and later on in Austria, three modes of action were employed in concert: terror, propaganda, and legislation. On November 12 Göring took the lead by presiding over a very large meeting called to decide the future course of action in light of the radically changed situation. In a series of talks he had persuaded Hitler to place him in charge of executing the Reich's Jewish policy, which would thus come under the jurisdiction of the Four-Year Plan. This decision blocked Goebbels's bid to control the Jewish sphere; never again was he able to play a decisive role in the affairs and decisions concerning the Jews. From then on the chief rivals in such policy-making decisions were Göring and Himmler.

Opening the November 12 meeting, Göring announced his latest authorization and then defined the meeting's agenda as a continuation of the October 14 discussion on Aryanization, stressing that this time definitive decisions must be taken. The first item on the agenda was the extensive damage caused by the destruction of merchandise, looting, and the devastation to shops on Kristallnacht, for which insurance estimated at RM 25 million (U.S. $10 million at the time) had to be paid. After an extended discussion it was decided to honor these obligations; however, the state would then confiscate these payments, and the Jewish shopowners would be held responsible for repairing their enterprises. Moreover, a fine of RM 1 billion (U.S. $400 million) would be imposed on the Jewish community as "expiation" for the murder of vom Rath.

The major item on the agenda, however, was the Aryanization procedures. Here the system instituted by Dr. Hans Fischböck, the Austrian minister of commerce, was accepted as yielding the best results. Göring summed up the plan's objective, "The basic idea of Aryanization of the economy is this: The Jew is removed from the economy and transfers his economic property to the state, he gets compensation. The compensation is registered in the debit registry, and he gets a certain interest on it [later set at 3.5 percent]. That is what he is to live on."[104] As the discussion continued, it turned out that some of the economic regulations had already been drafted for promulgation that very day along with the regulation on the expiation fine.[105]

Two other problems taken up at the meeting were the isolation and emigration of the Jews. Here Goebbels and Heydrich competed in advancing proposals for making things worse for the Jews. When the discussion turned to emigration, Heydrich cited the Austrian model, proposing that an emigration center like the one established by Eichmann in Vienna be set up in the *Altreich* (Old Reich). Once this suggestion was accepted, he ventured that it would take from eight to ten years for the Jews to emigrate from Germany, since he could not conceive of organizing the departure of more than eight thousand to ten thousand Jews per year. But he did raise the question of what would become of the Jews who remained in Germany with no means of their own and no economic base. Göring again proposed setting up ghettos or special areas of residence for the Jews—along the lines of ghetto–cities—but Heydrich, who saw a large concentration of Jews as a danger, rejected the idea. The question of how the Jews would survive in the ghettos was not clarified. "You cannot let them [the Jews] die of starvation," Heydrich declared in this context. On the other hand, if they were allowed to maintain shops that would necessitate commercial ties with Aryans outside the ghetto. The question was left open, but mention was again made of employing the Jews in labor units.

As to isolating the Jews, Goebbels's and Heydrich's proposals essentially overlapped. Both wanted not only to cut the Jews off completely but also to deprive them of their individual rights, including the right to own a car or hold a driver's license, avail themselves of public transport, or enter places of recreation and amusement. All Jewish children would be excluded from public schools, and Jews would no longer be treated in general hospitals. Heydrich even suggested that all Jews—apart from those who were foreign citizens—be required to wear a special emblem, arguing that the combination of these measures would "automatically lead to the creation of a ghetto."

Most of the ideas and proposals relating to the economic and social spheres were acted on a few weeks later in a spate of legislation and regulations.[106] The authorities not only exacerbated the segregation of the Jews but sharply curtailed their independent activities by heightening surveillance, cutting back institutional budgets, banning the Jewish press, and closing communal institutions. The shock that came over the Jewish public was related both to the pogrom (which in some places continued for days after it had been officially halted) and to the fact that for the first time thousands of people were sent off to concentration camps and exposed to all the methods of torture and humiliation employed there. Worse yet, hundreds of them died in the process. As a rule prisoners were released on one of two conditions: either emigration or the Aryanization of their businesses—and frequently both.

On the day Göring was holding his meeting, the Jewish Cultural Association in Berlin was forced by order of Commissar Hans Hinkel to reopen its theater. Herbert Freeden, at that time an associate stage manager, called that performance "ghost theater."[107]

The response abroad to the anti-Jewish violence in Germany was sharp—to the point that the United States recalled its ambassador from Berlin—and the boycott movement concomitantly intensified in both the United States and England. But unlike the effect that the protests had had in 1933, this time they failed to faze the Nazi leaders. In the interim they had discovered just how empty were the threats of the foreign governments, and they anticipated nothing more than a verbal reaction.

1939: The Approaching War

On October 21, 1938, Hitler notified his military chiefs that they were to prepare for these following short-range goals: (1) securing Germany's borders, (2) dismantling Czechoslovakia by the rapid conquest of Bohemia and Moravia, (3) seizing the Memel Territory (Klaipeda). At Berlin's instigation, the priest Josef Tiso declared an independent Slovakian government on March 14, and on that same night Hitler confronted Czechoslovakia's aging president, Dr. Emil Hácha, with the choice of capitulation to the Germans or the ruthless conquest of his country by force. Hácha and his government gave up as the German army had already begun to stream across their borders. On the morning of March 15 the Germans entered Prague; less than a week later, on March 21, they also appeared in the Memel Territory, a region that had been attached to Lithuania by the Treaty of Versailles but that Hitler claimed as a German realm.

These moves finally convinced even Chamberlain that Hitler could not be trusted to honor peace treaties. Clearly Poland stood to be his next target, with the Free City of Danzig (Gdańsk) a long-time bone of contention between Germany and Poland. On March 31 Chamberlain informed the House of Commons that in the event of any act threatening Poland's independence, the British government would consider itself bound to take practical measures in support of the government in Warsaw. The announcement that the British would support Poland came as a surprise to Hitler and kindled his ire—as did any and all opposition—but it did not prompt him to alter his intentions in the least. By May 1 plans for a German attack on Poland were ready.

Hitler had long made it understood that the fate of the Jews in the territories under his rule was intimately related to broader political developments—or, more precisely, to the war he was then planning. The paragraph worked into the speech he made to the Reichstag on January 30, 1939—the anniversary of his rise to power—has been widely quoted, for in it he stated:

> One thing I should like to say on this day which may be memorable for others as well as for us Germans. In the course of my life I have very often been a prophet and have usually been ridiculed for it. During the time of my struggle for power, it was in the first instance the Jewish race which only received my prophecies with laughter when I said that I would one day take over the leadership of the state—and with it that of the whole nation, and that then, among other things, I would settle the Jewish problem. Their laughter was uproarious, but I think that for some time now they have been laughing out of the other side of their face. Today I will once again be a prophet: If the international Jewish financiers in and outside Europe should again succeed in plunging the nations into a world war, the result will be not the Bolshevization of the globe and thus victory for Jewry but the annihilation of the Jewish race in Europe.[108]

This paragraph came at the end of a broad discussion of the Jewish problem built on two premises: (1) while the democratic world expressed sympathy for the Jews, it was not willing to receive or settle them, and (2) a new European order would be achieved only after the Jewish problem was solved. Hitler concluded by rephrasing the famous Marxist slogan, "Workers of the world unite!" as "Workers of all classes and of all nations, recognize your common enemy!"

As conceived at the November 12 meeting, the status of German Jewry underwent a significant change during this period. Two weeks after the Kristallnacht pogrom, Heydrich began to establish a new emigration center in Germany following the Austrian model. Göring, however, was trying to keep up a more regular process and prevent rash action, and he attained the führer's consent to this course. Thus on December 5, for example, Hitler notified the Gauleiters all over Germany that he had rescinded Heydrich's order requiring the Jews to wear an identifying emblem. Invoking Hitler's decision, Göring by the end of December had published new orders easing some of the harsh regulations that had been promulgated after Kristallnacht. As Uwe D. Adam has observed, this was a tactic typical of Hitler's policy toward the Jews (though not only of that policy). He mitigated harsh regulations after they had been enacted and then awaited the "organic development" of the next phase.[109] On the other hand, Göring issued an order to have unemployed Jews put to work as soon as possible, so that work brigades were later established in a number of places throughout the Reich, and on Hitler's initiative new regulations concerning the leasing of Jewish-owned apartments paved the way for concentrating the Jews in certain buildings and streets. Thus the first steps were taken toward the formation of ghettos.[110]

On January 24, 1939, Göring put his signature to Heydrich's appointment as the head of the new Reich Central Office for Jewish Emigration. Heydrich was charged with "[appointing] the director-general and [regulating] the administration of the Reich Center," and his task was defined as "promoting emigration of the Jews from Germany by all means."[111] With that, the struggle between the various arms of the regime over the implementation of the policy against the Jews was decided in favor of the SS. Hitler's menacing remarks of January 30 served as implicit approval of this arrangement.

Decisive changes were imposed on the internal administration of the Jewish community. Early Nazi schemes had posited the establishment of a compulsory organization—called Judenrat—that would execute the regime's orders (see chap. 2), and the implementation of this idea began with the elimination of the representative Jewish body, the Reichsvertretung. In 1938, after the legal status of the Jewish communities had been abrogated, attempts were made by various sectors of the Jewish public to form a new umbrella organization. But even in the face of the rapidly deteriorating situation, they were unable to unite into a single organizational body. Already in December the SS planned to impose unity in the form of a compulsory national association that would encompass all the Jewish communities, community associations, and secular organizations.[112] Word of this new union reached the Jews at the beginning of February and on February 17 the news was published in the *Jüdisches Nachrichtenblatt* (Jewish Newsletter), the only organ authorized by the authorities. For several months the new organization operated more or less according to the old format of the Reichsvertretung, with the same people filling the same posts. Though increasingly dependent on orders from the regime, in negotiations with the authorities the organization strove to retain a certain freedom of action in financial matters and in the handling of welfare, education, and emigration. The decree establishing a new national body was promulgated as the Tenth Regulation to the Reich Citizenship Law of July 4, 1939.[113] It defined the new organization as the Reichsvereinigung der Juden in Deutschland (Reich Association of Jews in Germany) and specified its tasks as promotion of the Jews' emigration from Germany, the provision of schooling for Jewish children, and social welfare—but the emphasis was on emigration. Apart from restricting the organizational independence of the Jews, the regulation required everyone defined as a Jew by the Nuremberg Laws—including Christian "non-Aryans"—to belong to the organization.

The conquest of Bohemia and Moravia brought an additional 120,000 Jews under National Socialist rule (including some 17,000 who had fled from the Sudetenland after the Munich Pact). These provinces, which now became known as the Protectorate, also contained thousands of refugees from Germany and Austria. Soon thereafter, Eichmann turned up in Prague, but his Central Office for Emigration was not officially established until July 22, 1939. During the half year before the outbreak of war, about 25,000 Jews left Czechoslovakia, some in the framework of Youth Aliyah groups.[114]

Attempts at Rescue

The end of 1938 marked the onset of what one Nazi ideologue called "the third phase of the National Socialist victory over Jewry."[115] At that time the League of Nations representatives for the refugees were winding up their activities; thus the only international body still dealing with the refugee problem was the intergovernment committee set up at the Evian Conference—and it was headed by the British representative, Earl Winterton, who was known for his negative attitude toward the Jews and his pro-Arab stand on the Palestine issue. The director of Winterton's office was the American attorney George Rublee, who tried to institute negotiations with Germany on the emigration problem in October 1938 but met forceful opposition to what his interlocutors called "interference in an internal German problem." After Kristallnacht, however, the Germans became more concerned about easing the increasingly tense relations with the protesting nations of the world, especially the United States. They also wanted to improve their foreign currency balance. Thus Schacht (then still president of the Reichsbank) initiated contacts with the heads of the intergovernment committee and presented them with his proposal, thereafter known as the Schacht Plan, during a visit to London. Like the Transfer scheme, the Schacht Plan was based on the idea of allowing Jews to leave the country in return for granting preferences to German exports and, in addition, boosting the Reich's foreign currency reserves. World Jewry was to establish a fund of RM 1.5 billion (then the equivalent of U.S. $600 million) to finance the resettlement of 150,000 able-bodied Jews from the Reich and Austria in an as yet unspecified place to which they would emigrate within three years and where they would be joined by 250,000 dependents. Each family would receive a loan of RM 10,000 (U.S. $4,000) from the fund. Schacht valued the emigrants' property in Germany somewhat exaggeratedly at RM 6 billion (U.S. $2.4 billion). This sum was to be invested in a "trust fund" that would remain in the Reich.[116] Of this fund, 25 percent was to be considered collateral for the loan and would go toward financing German exports, which would be in payment of the loan. The remaining 75 percent was ostensibly to be used for maintaining those Jews who would be unable to emigrate. In this way Jews would leave the country without Germany losing any of its foreign currency. To reinforce his argument Schacht described the existing situation faced by any Jew who emigrated on his own: he lost 25 percent of the value of his holdings upon selling them, 25 percent in the form of a flight tax, and 90 percent of the remainder by foreign exchange rates.

Like the transfer scheme, Schacht's plan clashed with the principles of the boycott movement, which was beginning to revive at just that time. Moreover, the Jews feared that their consent to it would be construed as confirmation of the anti-Semitic libel about a Jewish-controlled worldwide financial network. Hence, they sought to shift the implementation of the plan onto the governments represented on the intergovernment committee. These governments were, in turn, reluctant to do anything that would advance Germany's foreign trade. Moreover, according to the terms of the proposal, they would be required to pay the loan money in goldmarks, which were worth more than reichsmarks, and the loan to the emigrants was to be paid within three years but repaid by the Germans over a period of twenty years. What the plan came down to, then, was an ill-disguised plunder of Jewish property in Germany by which the Germans would earn the difference between the two types of marks and even receive a long-term international loan, with the Jews of the world footing the bill. Apart from that, it was not at all clear where the Jewish emigrants could settle.[117]

Views of this scheme were sharply divided among the Jews as well as the Germans themselves. Initially Schacht had managed to obtain Hitler's and even Göring's support, overriding the vigorous opposition of Foreign Minister Joachim von Ribbentrop.[118] But on January 20, 1939, Schacht was removed from his post as president of the Reichsbank, and Göring subsequently withdrew his support of the plan. Then, however, he reversed himself and let Helmut Wohlthat, one of the directors of the Four-Year Plan, continue negotiating with Rublee. In the course of these protracted negotiations, a compromise was reached whereby German goods exported at the expense of the Jews would be used solely for Jewish settlement. This agreement was never implemented, however. After Rublee resigned in February 1939, the new high commissioner for refugees, Sir Herbert Emerson, worked out the required international cooperation, whose charter was published on July 20, 1939. It never went into effect, however, as the war broke out on September 1. The efforts to bring about the large-scale settlement of Jews in overseas countries had come to naught.

Between the signing of the Munich Pact and the outbreak of World War II, the gates of most countries definitely began to close to Jews. In the autumn of 1938 France and Holland refused to accept any additional refugees. Sweden and Denmark tightened the restrictions they had imposed on the issue of entry visas and even forcibly returned to Germany refugees who arrived without the proper papers. After Kristallnacht, however, a stream of refugees surged across the borders despite these restrictions.[119]

Surprisingly, it was Great Britain that agreed to admit a large number of refugees at that time. The British Committee for the Jews of Germany, in cooperation with the World Movement for the Care of Children from Germany, persuaded the government to accept more than nine thousand children, of whom only two thousand were non-Jews. About the same number of adults were admitted by Britain, having been released from concentration camps on that condition. A special reception center was set up for them at the beginning of 1939, and most of the children were taken in by British families. The British government acted less out of a humanitarian impulse than a desire to avoid pressures to admit more Jews to Palestine. On December 14, 1938, the cabinet was told that "it might be necessary to make some further concessions [to the Jewish Agency] in order to avoid a violent conflict with the Jews in Palestine."[120]

After Czechoslovakia was overrun, Britain also agreed to renew an earlier-granted loan of £500,000 (U.S. $2 million) for Jewish emigration, because the former loan could no longer be utilized since the Germans now controlled the banks. Thus, a few thousand Jews managed to escape to Britain.

The Jews of Great Britain had made some attempts to rescue German Jews after Kristallnacht. A delegation of distinguished Jewish figures met with Prime Minister Chamberlain and explained that they were not seeking diplomatic intervention with the Germans or asking Great Britain to open its gates to great numbers of refugees: all they were asking was a loan for refugee assistance and entry visas for a limited number of children and teenagers who would undergo agricultural training and eventually settle elsewhere. They also stressed that the Jews of the world had already raised £5 million (U.S. $20 million) for that purpose, £1.5 million (U.S. $6 million) in Britain alone. Chamberlain replied that he saw no possibility of influencing Germany. On the contrary, he feared that any attempt at intervention would only aggravate the plight of the Jews there. The same excusatory reply recurred time and again during the war whenever intervention on behalf of the Jews was sought. As to the matter of the children and teenagers, Chamberlain promised to give the proposal sympathetic consideration.[121]

Generally speaking, the Jews, with their passports brandishing the letter *J*, had a difficult time finding refuge in overseas countries. Pressed as they were to escape Germany quickly, they became easy prey to all kinds of deceit. Quite a few consuls, especially from South American countries, lined their pockets by selling entry visas that turned out to be worthless. Many of the people who arrived at the shores of those countries were not permitted to enter and were by then stripped of all their means. The Germans, too, had a hand in these activities. One of the most notorious and heinous instances was that of the ship *Saint Louis,* onto which the Germans loaded more than nine hundred Jews in May 1939 with the assurance that their entry into Cuba was guaranteed, even though the Cuban government had already invalidated all the entry permits. The *Saint Louis* sailed from one country to the next, but its passengers were never allowed to disembark. Eventually, it had no choice but to return to Hamburg, where, it was feared, the returning emigrants would probably be sent directly to a concentration camp. Through great efforts, Jewish organizations finally persuaded Belgium, Holland, England, and France to divide the major part of the stranded refugees among them. The JDC paid these four governments $500,000 for the maintenance of the refugees; the rest of the refugees met the dreaded fate at Hamburg.[122]

Beyond encouraging such bogus emigration schemes, the Germans also forcibly loaded people onto boats and made them set sail. Eichmann was particularly proficient at this tactic in Austria and sent people wandering from country to country in small boats on the Danube. Others were driven over borders into no-man's-land or infiltrated into Western countries.

Ever since the formation of the new Jewish community in Palestine (the Yishuv), Jews had tried to get around the entry restrictions imposed first by the Turks and later by the British; thus they reached Palestine by means of illegal immigration. An unending stream of people, either as individuals or in organized groups, were brought into the country surreptitiously, overland and by sea. In the 1930s the Jewish Agency tried to increase the number of immigrants by all possible legal means and was somewhat successful; it utilized to the full all available types of entry permits (e.g., for "capitalists" and craftsmen, Youth Aliyah, students, and tourists.) It was, therefore, opposed to the illegal immigration of organized groups, fearing that such activity would severely prejudice its understanding with the British Mandatory authorities. In 1937 when the Peel Commission proposed the establishment of a Jewish state in part of Palestine, the Jewish Agency was anxious to avoid an open clash with the Mandatory government—though the Revisionists, who had seceded from the World Zionist Organization, proceeded to organize illegal immigration on their own. The Jewish Agency also withheld its support of the venture because of the appalling conditions on the dangerously overloaded ships provided by merchants and speculators exploiting the Jews' distress. With pressure mounting on the Jews in Europe—not only in Germany and the annexed territories but in Poland and Rumania as well—and with worsening relations between the British government and the Jewish Agency, this opposition gradually relented. Early in 1938 the Heḥalutz movement began to organize illegal immigration, with the Yishuv sending special emissaries to Europe for this purpose. The trend intensified during 1939, especially after the British white paper of May 1939 announced a "final" schedule of ten thousand immigration certificates and banned acquisition of land by Jews, which sparked a political struggle. The Mossad l'Aliyah Bet (Institute for Illegal Immigration), which ran the operation in collaboration with the Haganah from late 1938 onward, tried to assure elementary safety and sanitary conditions on the small boats that were carrying people in numbers much greater than their listed capacity. As they approached the country's shores, the boats faced the danger of being stopped by the British. Since the Gestapo was interested in the departure of the Jews by whatever means, it negotiated and cooperated with all kinds of illegal immigration operations, especially within Eichmann's domain in Austria. Several hundred people left for Palestine directly from Germany, for after Kristallnacht the Jewish institutions decided to activate even this hazardous rescue channel for German Jews.[123]

On January 25, 1939, a day after Reinhard Heydrich's appointment, the German Foreign Ministry issued a memorandum on the Jewish question as a factor in foreign policy in 1938 and distributed it to the major agencies of the regime and to all German diplomatic missions abroad. Summarizing the "achievements" in isolating the Jews from the mainstream of life in Germany and Austria, the paper established the emigration of all the Jews as the major goal of the Jewish policy in Germany. It also noted with satisfaction the rise in anti-Semitic feeling and the measures taken against Jews in Italy, Rumania, Hungary, and Poland. The memorandum went on to describe the evolution of the emigration issue and the change that had occurred in Germany's attitude toward Jewish emigration to Palestine because (as noted earlier) even a small Jewish state would constitute a danger. Germany was, therefore, interested in having the Jews dispersed throughout the world, especially because poor immigrants would be particularly effective in spreading anti-Semitism.[124]

National Socialism viewed the Jewish question as a worldwide problem that would have to be solved on a global framework. Thus emigration became the focal point of the Nazi domestic and foreign policy toward the Jews. In contrast to this eminently political concept, the attitude of other governments toward the Nazi persecution of the Jews was a contradictory mixture of political interests and humanitarian impulses that seldom blended into any clear-cut rescue action. That this inherent contradiction remained unsolved proved to be the undoing of the Jews; one of its consequences was that Jewish refugees were denied the right of asylum that most countries granted to fugitives from political oppression.

The Jews lacked the necessary leverage to overcome these political obstacles. The paradox of the Jewish condition was that the anti-Semites were accusing Jewry of the very thing it lacked: the power to control world politics. Struggling to persevere, the Jews sought political forces, within Germany and abroad, with which they could conclude an alliance. To this end they used every contact and pursued every glimmer of support. Mostly, however, their endeavor was limited to the humanitarian realm, in which their own organizations could engage in self-help even though these operations also depended on local or international political circumstances.

The Jewish people's political impulse manifested itself in Palestine, and the state-in-the-making demonstrated its potential political impact in the instance when the British government agreed to open its own borders to thousands of Jewish refugees from Germany to divert pressure from the gates of Palestine. Yet neither the Yishuv nor the Zionist movement had the wherewithal to mount a broad-scale rescue program. Soon after being appointed high commissioner for refugees from Germany, James McDonald met Chaim Weizmann and subsequently related in his memoirs the latter's dark vision, "He foresaw the extermination of millions of his fellow Jews and the persecution and displacement of other millions. Only in Palestine did he foresee a secure haven. 'If before I die,' he said, 'there are half a million Jews in Palestine, I shall be content because I shall know that this "saving remnant" will survive.' "[125]

Despite the obstacles in the path of emigration, the shock of Kristallnacht and its consequences had the intended effect: fear seized the Jews and induced them to leave Germany, whatever the circumstances. In the first eight months of 1939, until the outbreak of war, 78,000 Jews left the Old Reich, marking the largest number in a single year since 1933. The number of emigrants from Austria in 1939 was close to 55,000.[126] Some people realized what lay in store for the Jews of Europe; even before Kristallnacht one American-Jewish author wrote:

> Should present trends continue, the German refugee problem may be dwarfed by the magnitude of those now appearing on the horizon. Foremost among these is the prospect of disaster confronting the 5,500,000 Jews dwelling in that portion of Europe bounded by the Baltic Sea, the Mediterranean and the Adriatic, and the dictatorships of the Soviet Union, Germany and Italy. In this area the Jews constitute about 5 percent of the total population, and are only one of a large number of minority groups which make up over 23 percent of the total. The lot of most of the non-Jewish minorities is eased by the existence of closely related national states which may intercede for them, or to which they may hope to migrate, or by the fact that they constitute a solid territorial or ethnic bloc. For the highly scattered Jewish communities, torn by factional strife and composed of individuals of highly diverse degrees of assimilation, these protective factors do not operate.

And after discussing the problems and failures of the international assistance offered the refugees, he concluded:

> It is apparent that the technical obstacles to emigration, great as they are, are not the principal factor preventing adequate treatment of the refugee problem. Given a real determination to assist the refugees, these obstacles could be quickly overcome. . . . Fugitives must continue to be trapped in Central and Eastern Europe because of the political and financial difficulties of emigration—unless they are goaded to mass suicide, or unless the outbreak of a general war still further aggravates their condition.[127]

Part II

Prologue to the "Final Solution": The First Phase of World War II, September 1939–1941

And yet it is good that we comfort ourselves
even with false hope. It does not let us collapse
under the suffering of the persecution.

The Warsaw Diary of Chaim A. Kaplan
(November 14, 1940)

5

Toward the Struggle for World Domination (1939–1941)

The Outbreak of the War

On August 23, 1939, a nonaggression pact was signed between National Socialist Germany and the Soviet Union. It established that "if one of the signatories of the pact were to be the object of military aggression by a third power, the other signatory would not aid this third power in any way."[1] Appended to the pact was a secret protocol predetermining the spheres of influence that would fall to each side "in the event of political-territorial changes" in the countries of Eastern Europe, meaning Poland, the Baltic states, and Finland. The conclusion of this agreement (subsequently referred to as the Molotov–Ribbentrop Pact) took the world by surprise. The Western Powers did not expect it because Stalin, while negotiating with the Germans, was conducting parallel negotiations with them. Socialist elements throughout the world were taken aback by it because they regarded the National Socialists as their bitterest enemies and believed that Hitler's regime was ideologically irreconcilable with that of Stalin. Only the Communist parties toed the line by duly justifying the move.

Albert Speer noted in his memoirs that after the Soviets agreed to receive Joachim von Ribbentrop for negotiations, Hitler was heard to exclaim at a dinner held in Berchtesgaden, his Alpine retreat, "I have them! I have them!" When the meal had ended, the diners retired to the veranda to observe the rare phenomenon of the Northern Lights, which cast a red light over the surrounding mountains and even bathed the hands and faces of the observers as the rainbow-colored sky glistened and gleamed. "The last act of *Götterdämmerung* could not have been more effectively staged," Speer wrote and then quoted Hitler's comment on that occasion, "It is a sign of much blood. This time it will not be achieved without the use of force."[2]

Europe under Nazi occupation (before 22 June 1941). (After C. E. Black and E. C. Helmreich, *Twentieth Century Europe: A History,* New York, 1966)

In signing a nonaggression pact, both Stalin and Hitler violated all the political principles and repudiated all the views they had been publicly professing for years. Yet even then Hitler remained true to his fundamental goal of eventually obtaining *Lebensraum* (living space) for Germany in the East. On August 11, 1939, he had told a group of close associates, "Everything I do is directed against Russia. If the West is too stupid and blind to understand that, I shall be forced to reach an agreement with the Russians and strike at the West. Once [the West] is defeated, [I shall] turn my concentrated forces against the Soviet Union."[3]

Hitler's ultimate objective was to rule the world, and in this respect he regarded the United States as his main adversary. In accordance with his racial theories, he believed the Slavs to be inferior beings and therefore did not take Russia's strength seriously.[4] Neither did he regard England as a threat. In a conversation with Alfred Rosenberg on November 1, 1939, the führer claimed that even if England won a war with Germany, the United States, Japan, and Russia would be the ones to benefit from its victory because "England would be laid waste by the war."[5] Hitler's attitude toward Britain was essentially ambivalent, for he both scorned and admired the British; although he doubted they would work up the resolution to fight, he was impressed with the empire they had succeeded in building.

Hitler's ambition to dominate the world was closely bound up with his conception of the Jews as his implacable enemies. The war he was to wage against this imaginary foe was an integral part of his overall military and political campaign. Millions of Jews were living in Eastern Europe, the very region he looked to as *Lebensraum* for the German people. Hence, their annihilation was one of the war's objectives. Moreover, Hitler regarded the countries of Eastern Europe, particularly Poland and Rumania, as a storehouse of international Jewish power, much as the entire population of Eastern Europe was in his eyes the biological foundation of the Bolshevik regime.[6]

Occupied Poland

Following the staged attack of the Germans, purportedly mounted by Poles on a German broadcasting station near the Polish border, Hitler's mechanized forces swept into Poland along most of its frontier, from the Baltic Sea in the north to the Slovakian border in the south, crushing the Polish army in a massive pincer movement. Polish cavalry units were torn to shreds by the tanks advancing under the cover of the German air force, which sent in wave after wave of planes to bomb not only the army units but Poland's cities and fleeing civilian population as well. The Polish army fought valiantly but never had a chance. Despite the heavy aerial and relentless artillery bombardments, Warsaw held out until September 27, while Lwów, in eastern Galicia, had fallen by September 12. Faced with this rapid advance, the Russians feared that the German troops might overrun the sector of Poland allotted to them by the protocol to the August 1939 nonaggression pact; therefore, on September 17 Soviet forces likewise crossed the Polish frontier and moved westward into the Polish heartland.

The secret protocol to the Molotov–Ribbentrop Pact had fixed the border between the German- and Soviet-occupied zones as the Vistula River (because it cuts through Warsaw, the suburb of Praga was included in the Soviet zone). When the Russians began to penetrate into the eastern half of Poland, the German troops pulled back. In the meanwhile, however, Stalin had had a change of heart and proposed to the Germans that he would relinquish the eastern part of the Warsaw district in exchange for control over Lithuania. Hitler agreed, and it was along these lines that the final frontier was drawn on September 28, 1939.

These military movements profoundly affected the fate of the Jews in the conquered areas. Germany now occupied 188,000 square kilometers (72,600 square miles) of territory with a population of over 20 million people, of whom 675,000 were Germans. The Russian zone comprised 201,000 square kilometers (77,600 square miles), with fewer than 12 million inhabitants, of whom only 4.7 million were Poles, the rest being Ukrainians, Russians, and Jews.

What type of regime was established to govern the German-occupied zone inhabited by a majority of Poles? In talks with the journalist Eduard Breiting, Hitler had remarked that it was necessary to develop a policy in stages and adapt it to the needs of the hour.[7] He regarded the occupation of Poland as a stage that would last for quite a while, until he was ready (after his presumed victory over the West) to turn his forces against Russia. Accordingly, Poland would have to forfeit its status as an independent state, and Hitler planned ruthlessly to destroy it in order to obtain the necessary *Lebensraum* for the German people. This process was dubbed a political purge *(politische Flurbereinigung)* in the summary of a discussion between the chief of the Intelligence Services *(Abwehr),* Admiral Wilhelm Canaris, and the head of the High Command, Field Marshal Wilhelm Keitel, on September 12, 1939. In this talk Keitel observed that the purge planned for Poland—primarily of the aristocracy and the clergy—had been decided on by the führer; if the army was unwilling to assume the task, it would have to consent to have the SS and the Gestapo work alongside it. Thus, civilian commissioners would be appointed alongside the military commander in every military zone to see to the "destruction of national elements [*Volkstümliche Ausrottung*]."[8]

These plans took shape in discussions held by a limited circle—consisting of Hitler and a coterie of faithful followers—as the battle for Poland was drawing to its close. The final meeting of this forum was apparently held on September 20, 1939. On the following day Reinhard Heydrich briefed the chiefs of the RSHA and the commanders of the Einsatzgruppen (Special Operations Squads), which accompanied the conquering German army. He reported that Poland would be divided into two principal regions: one to be annexed to the Reich; the other to be placed under the control of the occupation forces and to be known as the Generalgouvernement. The territory annexed to the Reich would be further divided into four areas called Eastern districts *(Ostgaue),* each of which came under the control of a Reichskommissar. Some of these districts were tacked onto areas of the Reich (East Prussia and West Prussia-Danzig). In the center was the large district of Warthegau (named after the Warthe [Warta] River), and in the south a broad territory known as Eastern Upper Silesia *(Ost Oberschlesien)* was joined onto Upper Silesia. It was decided that the Jews and the Polish elite and intelligentsia living in the areas annexed to the Reich would be liquidated, impris-oned, or expelled to the Generalgouvernement. "The primitive Poles are to be used as migrant laborers in the work process. . . . The Jews are to be concentrated in ghettos within the cities to facilitate their surveillance and eventual deportation."[9]

By then it had already been decided to appoint Heinrich Himmler Reich Com-missioner for the Consolidation of German Nationhood (Reichskommissar für die Festigung des deutschen Volkstums, or RKFDV), whose task was threefold: the liquidation of foreign cultural and biological elements; the selection and reha-bilitation of Aryan racial elements from the Polish population; and the transfer of Germans into areas that had been purged of their indigenous populations. This process of bringing in *Volksdeutsche* (German nationals), hundreds of thousands of whom were scattered throughout the eastern territory, was called *resettlement (Umsiedlung).*[10] The German-Polish frontier was finally fixed in a meeting on October 17, 1939, at which Hitler made clear the policy that should be pursued in the Generalgouvernement. The region would serve the Reich by enabling it to cleanse its old and new territories by getting rid of Jews, Poles, and riffraff: mean-ing deporting them to the Generalgouvernement. The development of a leading group of Polish intelligentsia would have to be thwarted by wiping it out. The standard of living would have to remain low, and the country should provide Ger-many with cheap labor.[11] Here Hitler was trying to bring to fruition plans and ideas that had occupied his thoughts for over a decade. The implementation of these programs was placed in the hands of the police, Himmler's SS, and a civilian administration headed by veteran party members personally appointed by Hitler. It consisted of Hans Frank, the head of the Generalgouvernement; Erich Koch, the ruler of East Prussia; Albert Forster in charge of West Prussia; and Artur Greiser, ex-chairman of the Danzig Senate, ruler in Warthegau—all of whom acted as Reich or regional commissars. (The administration in Upper Silesia, in contrast, was headed by a so-called supreme governor [Oberpräsident].)

At a meeting held on October 23, 1939—to which only the directors of gov-ernment ministries were invited because the subject on the agenda was top secret—Wilhelm Stuckart, the director of the Interior Ministry, explained the führer's instructions regarding the treatment of the Poles in the Generalgouverne-ment and the territories that had been "restored to the homeland." Even the filed notes of this meeting do not make explicit reference to the subject discussed;[12] apparently the Nazis still feared the public reaction should their murderous plans become known. The manner in which their decision was relayed to the various arms of the Reich's political administration in order to secure their cooperation was typical. The party was dependent on the government bureaucracy to carry out actions that radically departed from customary administrative procedure. It, therefore, found ways to force the governing bodies to participate in such actions—a phenomenon that was to recur throughout the process of the Final Solution and found its most flagrant expression in the Wannsee Conference, which ratified the program for the implementation of the *Final Solution of the Jewish question* in January 1942 (see chap. 12). The German historian Martin Broszat has compared the situation that came into being in occupied Poland with the state of affairs in Germany at the beginning of 1933 (see chap. 3) and termed Hitler's intentions "almost like a second stage of the National Socialist revolution."[13]

While the general policy line was set down by Hitler personally, its implementation was turned over to various organizations and pressure groups that jockeyed for control over the territory placed in their hands. The SS units that followed in the wake of the German army competed with the so-called civilian authorities, staffed by party functionaries, and both employed terror tactics to whatever degree they saw fit. Here and there, voices were raised in concern or protest; some even reached Hitler's ears. For example, the commander of the army in the East, Marshal Johannes von Blaskowitz, wrote a memorandum enumerating thirty-three cases of shooting, robbery, vandalism, and the like, expressing his fear that such incidents would affect the discipline of the soldiers who had witnessed them. He also noted that discussions with the Security Police (Sicherheitspolizei, or Sipo) and local Gestapo had been fruitless, since the latter was acting on instructions from the national command of the SS. He therefore asked that the rule of law be restored.

On November 18, 1939, Hitler's adjutant reported the führer's reaction that a war cannot be conducted by the methods of the Salvation Army. Blaskowitz's continuing complaints were of no avail.[14] The events of September, when an estimated 4,000 to 5,000 Germans were killed by Poles, were cited as justification for the German terror. Apparently on Hitler's instructions, the number of German casualties was exaggerated tenfold in the Reich's official propaganda, which spoke of 58,000 Germans missing or known to have been murdered.[15] Moreover, Hitler issued a special amnesty on October 4, 1939, whose opening paragraph stated, "Actions carried out in the occupied Polish territories from September 1 until now, to express resentment of atrocities committed by the Poles, are not to be investigated as criminal acts." This amnesty was declared "to commemorate the victory concluding the battle imposed on us by Poland."[16]

Himmler's SS State

The Security Apparatus

Following the conquest of Poland, the state and party police—already instrumental in establishing the National Socialist state—were considerably expanded and reinforced. Within this domain, the SS State, Himmler—like his führer—took pains to maintain absolute control by delegating only partial and rarely exclusive authority to his subordinates. Ever since the 1920s, when he began cultivating the small force responsible for Hitler's personal safety into a large and comprehensive unit, he had based the Schutzstaffel (guard corps), known by its initials as the SS, on a creed that combined a racist worldview with elements borrowed from the experience of long-standing religious orders.

An SS candidate had first to meet strict standards of racial purity and physical appearance. He also had to pledge to uphold the principles of the organization's constitution. Its tenets included discipline and blind obedience, which Himmler had evidently copied from the Jesuits. Racial theories replaced the religious faith that was at the heart of the order founded by Ignatius Loyola, yet like the latter Himmler regarded himself as the commander of each and every one of the members of his organization and entitled to do with them as he pleased. The officers of the SS were often men who for one reason or another failed to find their place in the upper ranks of society but satisfied their desire for social status by joining an organization that professed to represent the nation's elite. Included in this category were members of the German aristocracy (many of whom had suffered great frustration during the Weimar period), dissatisfied academics, former army officers, and young people associated with nationalist organizations—all of whom derided the vulgarity of the SA and believed that the SS would enable them to realize their national and social aspirations alike. In the course of time, they were joined by people with a history of misconduct (to a greater or lesser degree) in their previous jobs as well as by government officials who were eager to establish a place for themselves in the new Nazi hierarchy. Heydrich, for example, a naval officer who had been forced to relinquish his post as the result of a scandal, was Himmler's choice to head the intelligence service he began developing in 1931.

At first the Security Service (SD) operated primarily within the party. Himmler saw his great opportunity when he prepared the purge of the SA's leadership in the summer of 1934 and used the occasion to extend his authority over the network of detention camps in Germany. From 1934 to 1936 he concentrated on expanding and diversifying the SS. Its newly established administrative section, headed by Oswald Pohl, began to establish contacts with German economic factors. At the same time, new units were added to the SS, the most important being the Death Heads, who took their name from the emblem worn on their caps.

Placed in charge of the concentration camps, the Death Heads were commanded by Theodor Eicke, who was the prime commander of the Dachau camp. Also formed and given rigorous professional military training was the Unit for Special Tasks (SS Verfügungstruppe), which was the nucleus of the later Armed SS (Waffen SS).

On June 17, 1936, Himmler was appointed chief of the German police in the Ministry of Interior. For the first time, the German police was organized into a nationwide framework that was henceforth under the command of a single man: Himmler. As Reichsführer-SS (RFSS) Himmler thus concentrated in his hands unlimited control over all matters having to do with security and the police. There was only one authority above him: the führer himself.

The police force was now composed of a number of units. The Order Police (Ordnungspolizei, or Orpo), commanded by Kurt Daluege, was responsible for maintaining order and the usual policing duties. Working alongside it was the Criminal Police (Kriminalpolizei, or Kripo) and the Border Guards (Grenzschutz). Finally, there was the Security Police (Sicherheitspolizei, or Sipo), which dealt with intelligence. Reinhard Heydrich headed the Security Police as well as the Security Service (SD), which was the intelligence arm of the SS. The Security Police—comprising the Political Police, known as the Gestapo (Geheime Staatspolizei), and the Criminal Police—supposedly functioned only as state agencies and did not intervene in party affairs. However, the duplication of the two bodies, the SS and the police force, was truer in organizational terms than in practice because SS men filled most of the posts in both these forces. Nevertheless, there was considerable trespassing and infighting among the various arms and organizational frameworks over spheres of authority.

Over the years the ranks of the SS swelled to hundreds of thousands of people, with millions more working alongside them in auxiliary capacities. Under such circumstances the principle of elitism could be maintained in theory only. At the outbreak of the war, Himmler created yet another echelon of senior commanders charged with supervising both the SS and the police force and with handling special operations. They were known as Higher SS and Police Leaders (Höhere SS-und Polizeiführer, or HSSPF); one rank below them were the SS and Police Leaders (SS- und Polizeiführer). Their status was distinguished from that of the other commanders of the SS and the police force in that they were not subordinate to the central administrations of these two forces; instead, they were responsible for a specific geographical area and took their orders directly from Himmler.[17]

At the same time Himmler established an organizational framework that embraced all the security services and the police. Called the Reich's Security Main Office (RSHA) and officially established on September 27, 1939, it was headed by Heydrich. The RSHA was divided into branches and departments to deal with problems of domestic and foreign security,[18] and over the years its internal organization underwent a number of changes. Working parallel to the RSHA was the administration in charge of the concentration camps and the Race and Settlement Main Office (Rasse und Siedlungshauptamt, or RUSHA), before which a broad new field of activity opened with the inception of the resettlement program. Altogether the SS bureaucracy consisted of twelve main offices, but the RSHA took pride of place among them. These huge bureaucracies swallowed up all the smaller organizations that had once functioned independently and concentrated under their auspices both the state's agencies, the Gestapo and Security Police, and the armed SS corps and their offices. It is quite likely that this organizational and administrative centralization was prompted by Himmler's anticipation that new tasks would fall to him after the army's conquests. He was clearly interested in expanding his control over the new territories and could do so only by virtue of the authority vested in the SS and the police.

Special police units had been fielded during the *Anschluss* to ensure the security of the new rulers, and the SS had prepared to take similar action prior to the conquest of Czechoslovakia. On October 10, 1938, immediately after the annexation of the Sudetenland, the *VB* had announced that "in cooperation with the vanguard of the army, men from the Gestapo immediately began to purge the liberated territories of traitors, Marxists, and other enemies of the state." Six Special Operations Squads (Einsatzgruppen), totaling two thousand men, had been prepared for the war against Poland and were attached to various army groups.[19]

Himmler's appointment as Reich Commissioner for the Consolidation of German Nationhood made it possible for him to establish additional institutions of his own in the occupied territories beside the SS and the police force, which were already under his command. If we add to this the bureaucracy of the so-called civilian administration, headed by veteran party members, we get an idea of the German polyhierarchy. As the spheres of authority were never sharply defined, the upshot of this plethora of offices and agencies was the administrative chaos that prevailed in conquered Poland.

The Concentration Camps

The concentration camp was the instrument by which Hitler terrorized the population—first in Germany and later in every territory subjugated by the Nazi regime. As early as March 1933, Himmler established the first camp near Dachau, a town not far from Munich. Theodor Eicke, Dachau's commander since the fall of 1933, created the general framework that became the archetype for all the subsequently established camps. The SS had exclusive and unrestricted control over these camps. Their organization evolved from 1934 to 1936 alongside Himmler's growing power as Reichsführer-SS. Detained in these camps was anyone considered an opponent of the regime: socialists, clergy of various faiths, and to an increasing extent Jews and members of other "inferior races." From 1938 onward the Nazis also imprisoned common criminals in the camps as well as such "asocial" elements as homosexuals, prostitutes, and beggars.

Arrests were made by special orders known as protective-custody warrants *(Schutzhaftbefehl)*. The Weimar laws had allowed for such custody without a court order to protect people against harassment, but now the Nazis used the same term to camouflage actions that were diametrically opposed to the spirit of the original law, namely, the arrest of people they deemed their enemies. The judiciary protested this illegal detention and in April 1934 the Gestapo issued a regulation ostensibly substantiating its right to make such arrests. In May 1935 the independent authority of the Gestapo was officially recognized in Prussia, and the right to appeal its actions was restricted to the highest ranks of its own administration. On February 10, 1936, the Gestapo Law was enacted in Prussia, giving that body the exclusive right to make arrests. From then on the Gestapo was entitled to investigate all activities considered hostile to the state: the same law established the Gestapo's complete independence of the courts. Hitler appended his official approval by recognizing the Gestapo as a police force whose power extended throughout the country.[20] Thus, a division of authority came about whereby the Gestapo alone had the power to arrest people and send them to concentration camps, whereas the SS remained responsible for running the camps. However, the Gestapo managed to retain a foothold in the camps through so-called political departments and by conducting the registration of the prisoners.[21]

Beginning in 1936 one new camp was established after another: Sachsenhausen in September 1936, Buchenwald in August 1937, Flossenbürg and Mauthausen in Austria in 1938. In May 1939 the women's camp of Ravensbrück was added to the list. As the number of camps rose, the composition of their inmates was broadened and they were henceforth called State Camps for Education and Labor (Staatliche Besserungs-und Arbeitslager). At the same time, the Germans began to use the prisoners as a labor force, primarily in the enterprise known as the Deutsche Erd-und Steinwerke (DEST), which was created to further Hitler's construction projects and was directed by Albert Speer. Particularly notorious was the quarry at Mauthausen, where thousands met their death, though other new camps were also built in the vicinity of quarries. This exploitation of prisoners as forced laborers led to the formation of special labor camps, many of which were attached to, and run by the staff of, the larger concentration camps.[22]

Masses of Jews were first arrested in 1938, initially in Austria in the wake of the *Anschluss* and then in Germany on Kristallnacht. Thus, the overall number of prisoners in camps rose that year from 24,000 to 60,000. Owing to the forced emigration of the Jews, the figure was later reduced (see chap. 4). At the outbreak of the war, the concentration camps within the boundaries of the Reich contained 25,000 inmates, and by September 2, 1939, the Stutthof camp near Danzig was already prepared to take prisoners from the conquered territories.[23]

The camps were run by a command hierarchy based on the tenets of leadership and discipline fostered in the SS. The deputies subordinate to the camp commander were responsible for the tasks of guarding the camp, running its offices, supervising the prisoners, overseeing the work program, and the like. The camp's administrative structure provided for prisoner self-management, whereby certain inmates were placed in charge of their fellow prisoners as a means of fomenting tension and discord. Poor nutrition, appalling sanitary conditions, iron discipline, the humiliation of prisoners, and the imposition of unspeakably brutal corporal and other punishments for even the slightest transgression—all made the concentration camp "educational system" into a hell with few parallels in the history of humankind.

Dachau, the first concentration camp, established the pattern that would be followed by all the rest. The camps were built in easily accessible places, that is, near a railroad and not too far from a city, for the supply of various services. Nevertheless, the Nazis were careful to conceal them from prying eyes by situating them either in a forest or some other isolated spot. They were divided into sections that were very different from each other in nature and appearance. The staff areas and living quarters of the commanders and lower ranks of the SS were built outside the camp and were well-tended and clean. They served as a pleasant facade for the camp proper, which was surrounded by a high electrified barbed wire fence and was guarded from watchtowers. Within the compound a large courtyard served as the area for the prisoners' roll call every morning and evening. Their living quarters were wooden barracks and their beds consisted of boards fixed to the walls in tiers. The inmates were classified according to type, which determined their status in the camp hierarchy. Each had a triangular patch of a given color sewn on his uniform: political prisoners had a red patch; criminals, green; socialists, black; homosexuals, pink; Jehovah's Witnesses, purple; emigrants, blue. The Jews had a second yellow triangle superimposed above the first to create a Star of David.[24]

The guard units in the camps numbered between a thousand and fifteen hundred men, with another hundred or so people in attendance as service personnel, including a doctor and his staff. These numbers changed, of course, as the camps grew in size. Qualified prisoners were also used for technical work in the camps' offices and as help in the hospitals. Under Eicke, moreover, Dachau became a school for concentration camp guards and commanders; once these SS men were trained to command and punish the prisoners, by means ranging from beatings to executions, he assigned them to other camps. Hence, the uniform style of contempt and cruelty that prevailed in all the camps.[25]

Even before the establishment of the special extermination camps, a vast number of people died or were killed in detention. The camp inmates succumbed to exhaustion or illness as a result of malnutrition, debilitating labor, and harsh punitive measures. Some were shot while purportedly attempting to escape; others rotted away or were murdered in bunkers. These deaths were often reported as suicides rather than ascribed to illness. As a result the concentration camps—referred to by the initials KZ for *Konzentrationslager*—cast a pall of terror over the entire population and were an effective deterrent to disobedience of the government's orders, to resistance of any kind, and even to criticism.

The Polyhierarchy in Occupied Poland

Conditions in occupied Poland made it possible for Himmler to take another step toward extending his power in the Third Reich. Originally conceived as an instrument for *executing policy,* the huge policing mechanism under his control developed into *a source of policy,* a policymaker in its own right. A circular issued by Himmler on November 7, 1939, addressing itself to the organization of the Gestapo in the Eastern territories stated, "The directors of the State Police Offices [Stapoleitstellen] are authorized to deal with political affairs, alongside the Reich commissioners and the civil administration in their districts."[26] They acted in combination with the Einsatzgruppen, who, when the combat stage drew to an end, were stationed in various regions as permanent garrisons and now fulfilled the functions of the SD. Both these forces came under the authority of the HSSPF; together, they established the concentration camps that became important instruments of terror and control in the occupied territories, just as they were in the Reich proper.

In contrast to the areas that were officially, though not always effectively, annexed to the Reich, the Generalgouvernement was looked on as occupied territory and on Hitler's orders no orderly and independent administration was established there. Instead, the area was deliberately left in a state of near-anarchy in order to exploit the human potential as a work force and forestall any possibility of organizing cells of resistance.

Beyond the administrative disarray that traced to the absence of orderly and fruitful cooperation between the Polish and German agencies, the chaos was exacerbated by the relentless competition among the various German authorities: the army, as the occupying force; the civilian administration headed by Frank; and the various branches of the RSHA were all working parallel to, and against, one another. The profusion of administrative bodies that characterized the administrative system of the Reich was carried even further in the occupied territory, to the point of creating an inextricable jumble of authorities in which the Poles, and above all the Jews, became trapped. Moreover, as time went on, the civilian administration became increasingly dependent on the police arm, without whose help it could not have exploited the country's economic and manpower potential.[27]

Although Frank had been invested with his sovereign rank by none other than the führer himself, it turned out (as Broszat has observed) that his authority existed on paper only. This situation came out most clearly in the tense relationship that developed between Frank and Higher SS and Police Leader Friedrich-Wilhelm Krüger, who was essentially a minister in Frank's government and thus subordinate to him. A similar relationship prevailed between the civilian governor of the Lublin District, E. Zörner, who was Frank's deputy, and Odilo Globocnik, who from the beginning of November 1939 commanded the SS and the police force in that area. As to the Gauleiters who governed the territories annexed to the Reich, Hitler stressed that "in the Eastern territories [they] had to be given the necessary freedom of action." As Martin Bormann, the director of Hitler's chancellery, explained, the führer expected only one thing of them: a statement that the entire territory had become German![28]

Resettlement: The First Deportations

Himmler's appointment as Reich Commissioner for the Consolidation of German Nationhood marked the opening of a chapter that became one of the hallmarks of the Third Reich's policy throughout Europe: the transfer of masses of people for the purpose either of resettling or eliminating them. In the course of time, these deportations were to cause death or unspeakable suffering to millions of people. Hitler first tried the system in the summer of 1939 following an agreement with Mussolini on an exchange of populations between Germany and Italy in the southern Tyrol. But the method was used most extensively against the Poles and the Jews in evacuating them from territory that was to be permanently annexed to the Reich to make room for the resettlement of people of German origin *(Volksdeutsche)* from the Baltic states and other areas under Soviet control. One of the intentions was probably to evacuate them from border regions that were destined to become battlefields in the campaign to be launched against the Soviet Union. Perhaps out of similar considerations, the Russians signed an agreement with Germany permitting the transfer of Germans from Soviet territory to the areas controlled by the Reich.[29] According to his instructions issued on October 30, 1939, Himmler planned to have about a million people from the Old Reich and the annexed territories deported by the end of the following February.[30] About half of these deportees would be Jews; the other half, Poles.

Before the war more than 600,000 Jews had been living in the "Eastern districts" subsequently annexed to the Reich. Their distribution was: 14,400 in the Danzig district (western Prussia); 79,000 in East and South Prussia; 384,000 in Warthegau; and 125,000 in Eastern Upper Silesia, for a total of 602,400 people.[31] Of the 3.5 million Jews to be found in Poland before the German conquest, 2,350,000 were living in the area that came under German control and 1,150,000 were in the Soviet-controlled sector. When the war began, some 60,000 Jews fled from the western districts of Poland into the area that was to become the General-gouvernement; about 300,000 managed to cross the border from the General-gouvernement into the Soviet zone. During the first weeks of the fighting, some 30,000 managed to escape the area of German occupation and leave Poland alto-gether, going primarily to the Baltic states and via Slovakia to Hungary and Rumania.

On November 28, 1939, Heydrich instructed the HSSPL and the commanders of the SD that the deportation of Jews and Poles was to be carried out by the SD in a two-phase operation. In the first stage, instituted immediately, 80,000 Jews and Poles were to be deported by December 17, 1939. The problem of absorbing them in the Generalgouvernement was left to the Poles heading the local councils and municipalities there; it was deemed sufficient to inform them of how many people to expect and when they would arrive. The second stage, a longer-range program, was to be based on a population census scheduled for December 17, 1939. To prevent deportees from filtering back to their places of origin the census questionnaires were taken away from them and orders were issued that anyone found in the area without a questionnaire would be shot.[32] On December 18 the results of the first stage were summed up in a comprehensive report that classified all those marked for deportation on the basis of three factors: biological, meaning Jews; political, meaning Poles who had belonged to organizations hostile to the Germans and the Reich; and social, meaning Poles who belonged to the intellec-tual or political elite.[33]

With the institution of long-range planning, the focus of responsibility for the deportation program was transferred to the RSHA in Berlin, and Heydrich was officially charged with centralizing its implementation. On December 19, 1939, he created a special department of the RSHA (IV B IV) for this purpose; two days later he charged Adolf Eichmann, until then the special agent for Jewish emigra-tion, with the responsibility for the evacuation of Poles and Jews, appointing him "special agent in behalf of the RSHA."[34] He worked in collaboration with the ministries of Economy, Finance, and Transport and with the staff of the local Center for Resettlement, reinforcing them with special teams. Polish farms were confiscated as part of the action; their owners were loaded onto trucks and driven to trains that carried them to the Generalgouvernement, where no provisions had been made to accommodate them. The brutality that characterized these depor-tations knew no bounds. By December 17 close to ninety thousand Poles and Jews had been deported to the Generalgouvernement in eighty transports. This depor-tation was regarded as only the beginning of the project, but the problems it entailed immediately became apparent. As no preparations had been made to absorb the deportees, they were held in the trains for days at a stretch and shifted from one place to another without being given food or water. The following note appears in the RSHA record of January 8, 1940, "The people had to remain locked in the railroad cars for as long as a full week without being able to relieve themselves. Moreover, in one transport one hundred people froze because of the fierce cold."[35]

Himmler's instructions for proceeding with the action stipulated that "first and foremost the Jews must be evacuated from all areas formerly administered by the Poles."[36] In the meantime Frank and the other Germans involved in running the Generalgouvernement, including army people, began to intervene. Even Hermann Göring was prepared to support the opponents of the action when he saw that there was a danger of epidemics breaking out in the deportees' temporary quarters, especially as the general food situation in the Generalgouvernement was so poor that foodstuffs had to be shipped in from the Reich at a time when there was also a shortage of trains. At a February 12 meeting chaired by Göring and attended by Himmler and most of the commissioners of the Eastern districts, Frank was granted the right to determine the size of the transports he was willing to receive. On March 23 Göring ordered the deportations stopped. Before that, however, on Heydrich's orders, Eichmann and his staff had managed to carry out an interim plan whereby over 40,000 people were deported, mainly from Łódź and Posen (Poznań), in February and March.[37] At the end of April the transports were resumed, albeit on a more limited scale. From then until October 1940, an average of 10,000 to 15,000 people were deported each month, with a total of some 430,000 Germans brought in to replace them. By the end of 1940, a total of 325,000 inhabitants had been moved out in organized deportations. A third of them—some 100,000 people—were Jews. Owing to irregular actions, the actual number of deported Jews was much higher (this point will be discussed in chap. 6). Toward the end of 1940, with the backing of the army—which commandeered the railroad cars for its own use—Frank managed to halt the influx.[38]

It was not by chance that Göring issued instructions to halt the deportations in March 1940. On February 12, while Frank was pleading his case before Göring, Himmler, and others assembled at Göring's retreat, Karinhall, close by a fateful operation was about to take place: the deportation of people from the original territory of the Reich. On January 30, 1940, Heydrich had convened the senior staff handling the resettlement in the Eastern districts and the responsible parties in the RSHA (a total of forty-four people) to present his overall program. This meeting, which lasted less than two hours, undertook to decide the fate of all the Jews as well as that of tens of thousands of Poles and 30,000 Gypsies in the territory under discussion. It was also decided to deport 1,000 Jews from Stettin (Szczecin), a port town on the Baltic Sea in northeastern Germany.[39] The measure was effected with extreme cruelty on the night of February 12–13, when 1,300 Jews—men and women, from children to the aged—were loaded onto the trains that would carry them to Lublin in the Generalgouvernement. Some of these deportees died during the journey—they had not been permitted to take any food along—and many more succumbed as they were forced to march in temperatures of −22 degrees centigrade (−3 degrees Fahrenheit) through heavy snow from Lublin to the distant villages in which they were to be resettled. By March 12, a total of 230 of the deportees had perished. News of these atrocities was published in the world press, and at that time adverse public opinion still had something of a deterrent effect—at least on some of the leading figures in the regime. Hence Göring issued the order that tied Heydrich's hands for the time being. The latter was forced to slow down the rate of deportations and could not carry out his program to the full.

Himmler and Heydrich had chosen the Lublin area, where the Stettin deportees were sent, back at the beginning of the winter, conceiving of it as a reserve in which they would concentrate the Jews. They planned to move the Jews first out of the areas of Poland annexed to the Reich and then out of the rest of the occupied territories in accordance with Hitler's design. Thus thirty thousand Germans living in the Lublin area were evacuated to Warthegau to make room for these Jews. There, in the expanse between the San and Bug rivers, they planned to establish the "Land of the Jews" and, at the appropriate time, send whoever survived their sojourn there on to an as yet undetermined destination. This plan was drawn up with Frank's approval. It did not work, however, and in the spring of 1940 as the pace of deportations was decreasing, it was scrapped altogether (see chap. 6).

The Lublin area did serve as a testing ground for another project, however: the first of its kind in which Jews from the West were deported to the occupied territory in the East. This plan was devised by Eichmann and his superior, Franz Walter Stahlecker, but was carried out under the supervision of the heads of the RSHA. Eichmann, who understood that there was less likelihood of Jews emigrating in wartime, may have been loath to relinquish his job of ridding the *Ostmark* and the Czech Protectorate of their Jews. The resettlement program for the Czech and Austrian Jews is known as the Nisko Operation, after the place near the San River to which Eichmann sent them.

At the beginning of October 1939, the heads of the Jewish community in Vienna and Moravská Ostrava (Mährisch-Ostrau) were summoned before agents of the Jewish Department of the RSHA and were told that about one thousand people were to be sent to a new place of settlement in Poland. They would have to pack their personal belongings as well as building materials, tools, food, and medicine; each person would be permitted to take along a certain sum of money and 50 kilograms (110 pounds) of luggage. Their homes, businesses, valuables, and all other property would be left in the hands of a proxy to be appointed by the Gestapo. On October 17 all the members of the Czech community were assembled, and after a cursory medical examination one thousand people were selected, placed on trucks, and driven to the railway station. They left the following day, locked in regular passenger cars after their money and documents were confiscated, and they were forbidden to drink water. Some of the community leaders from Vienna and Prague accompanied this transport and subsequently returned. In Nisko they were met by Eichmann accompanied by SS officers. He delivered a speech that was later recalled by one of the witnesses testifying at his trial in Jerusalem. Here the Jews were to build their new home, he said. The camp would be surrounded by barbed wire, and since all the water in the vicinity was polluted, wells would have to be dug to ensure a supply of drinking water. Then the Jews were taken to a barren hillside with two wooden shacks and left there. It rained that night, and the next day about a quarter of the deportees were sent marching eastward. SS men stood looking on, laughing as they discarded their luggage along the way, since it proved too heavy to carry along. The Jews walked some 150 kilometers (90 miles) until they reached Lublin, where the local Jewish community came to their assistance.

Jews who arrived on later transports were sent directly over the Russian border. Those who remained in Nisko tried to negotiate with the authorities; eventually their efforts bore fruit: in April the survivors were sent home. But until that juncture, transports continued to come in from Vienna and other places in Austria and in Bohemia-Moravia, with the treatment of the deportees growing increasingly harsh.[40] After a while the Jews realized what this resettlement plan actually held in store for them. At the end of November, the leaders of the Jewish community in the Czech town of Teschen (Český Těšin), who were told to report for deportation together with the members of their community, relayed the instructions to their people verbatim but presented the Gestapo with a long list of requests and suggestions. As their list makes clear, they knew:

> Most of the people who had been sent away [were] not where they were supposedly destined for, and rather than find their relatives, the members of their families who [were] now about to join them [would] be lost. According to various reports, it appear[ed] that gangs of Poles and Ukrainians [were] robbing all the property of the evacuees [the thieving done by the SS was not mentioned]. The transports often [made] long stops en route, and the people [had] no way of obtaining food.[41]

Jacob Edelstein, one of the Socialist-Zionist leaders in Czechoslovakia, was among the men ordered to accompany the first transport, so that he witnessed the terrible fate awaiting the Jews when they reached Poland. His conclusion was that anything was better than being sent to the East—in most cases it meant certain death—and that everything possible should be done to hold out in Bohemia-Moravia until the storm had passed.

Europe Under German Domination

On May 10, 1940, the war entered a new stage as units of the German army launched their *Blitzkrieg* against the West, the same day that Winston Churchill became prime minister of Great Britain. Before moving westward, however, Hitler had decided to invade the north, thereby securing his flank there and preventing the British from moving into Norway. He also wanted to ensure the supply of iron ore that was shipped from Sweden via the Norwegian port of Narvik. Denmark was conquered in a single day, April 9, with the Danish government choosing to surrender to preserve its internal independence and protect its land and population. In contrast, the battle for Norway lasted twenty-eight days. At first, with the help of the British, the Norwegians successfully withstood the German assault on the northernmost reaches of the country, with Narvik changing hands twice. The Norwegian king and government were forced to flee Oslo. When Sweden refused to grant them asylum, they managed to escape to Britain at the end of April, where the government-in-exile carried on.

According to the terms of Denmark's surrender to the German conquest, the traditional diplomatic relations between the two countries were maintained and the Germans did not impose any administration of their own. Thus, the German presence at first had only a minor impact on the population or on political and social affairs. The country's small Jewish community comprised about six thousand local Jews and about fifteen hundred refugees of the four thousand or so who had reached Denmark over the previous years. Concentrated mostly in Copenhagen, these Jews enjoyed the prevailing relative freedom together with the bulk of the population.

The situation in Norway was radically different. A small fifth column, operating there under the leadership of Vidkun A. L. Quisling, became the symbol of collaboration with the Nazis. Yet the Quisling government did not actually come into being until the spring of 1942, and even then it did not fulfill decisive functions. Instead, the civilian government was run by a former Gauleiter and one of Hitler's close associates, Reichskommissar Josef Terboven, who established police rule in Norway. Nevertheless, during the first two years of the occupation, the country's eighteen hundred Jews, including some three hundred refugees, were no more severely oppressed than the rest of the population.

A month after the fall of Norway, the onslaught against the West began with the invasion of Holland and Belgium on May 10, 1940. Holland was forced to surrender after five days; here, too, the government and royal family fled to Britain. Belgium continued to fight for eighteen days, with the king remaining in the country while a Belgian government-in-exile was formed in London. Paris fell on June 14, about a month after Hitler mounted his *Blitzkrieg,* and on June 22 the government headed by the eighty-four-year-old Marshal Henri-Philippe Pétain and the collaborator Pierre Laval was forced to sign a cease-fire agreement in the same railroad car and at the same place (Compiègne) where the cease-fire between victorious France and defeated Germany had been signed in 1918. Charles de Gaulle, who had reached London before the surrender and was to become the leader of the Free French, summarized the reasons for France's defeat, "France lost the war for very definite reasons. First, our military system did not develop any mechanized strength in the air and on the ground; second, the panic paralyzed our civilian population when the German mechanized units advanced; third, the tangible effect the fifth column had on the minds of many of our leaders; and fourth, lack of coordination between us and our Allies."[42]

As masses of Frenchmen fled south in the wake of the fighting, the Germans deliberately heightened their panic by sending in planes to bomb them, thus clogging the roads and impeding the movements of the French army. Among these refugees were some 50,000 Jews. Before the German invasion there had been over 300,000 Jews in France. This figure included the tens of thousands of refugees who had come mostly from Eastern Europe between the wars, mainly from Germany, Austria, and Czechoslovakia during the 1930s, the last alone estimated at 55,000 people.[43]

Defeated France was divided into two zones: the northern occupied territory, under direct German control, and the southern region, ruled by the Pétain–Laval government or Vichy government, named after the place in which it was installed. In addition to the Jews escaping from northern France, during the first weeks of the occupation Jewish refugees—mainly from Belgium but also from Holland and Luxembourg—poured into southern France by the thousands.

Germany's control of these newly occupied territories was manifested in a variety of ways. The areas closest to its borders, namely, Alsace-Lorraine and the Duchy of Luxembourg, were annexed to the Reich following the precedent set in the East. Holland was placed under a regime similar to that in Norway, and Dr. Artur Seyss-Inquart—who had taken an active role in the annexation of Austria and had served as Frank's deputy in the Generalgouvernement after the conquest of Poland—was appointed Reichskommissar. He had to share his rule with a strong contingent of the SS. Hence, there could be no doubt about the threat looming for the 140,000 Jews then living in Holland. This figure included 15,000 Jewish refugees, about half the number who had fled to Holland during the 1930s; the remainder had in the meantime emigrated overseas.[44]

Belgium, like northern France, was ruled by a military government. Its Jewish community, numbering some 65,700 people at the time of the occupation, was very different in nature from the neighboring Dutch community, as most of the Jews in Belgium were immigrants and refugees. Many of the wealthy Belgian Jews, who constituted the leadership of the community, fled in time, leaving the defenseless behind. At first the refugees tried to get away to southern France in droves, but after a while most of them returned to Belgium.[45]

Marking Hitler's successes on the battlefield, Benito Mussolini was quick to enter the war on June 10. On June 18, even before the fall of France, he met with Hitler in Munich to join in planning the coming moves and reap whatever benefits he could from the German victories, but Hitler allotted him only a small piece of southern France.

As far back as November 1939, when the Germans began discussing an attack on the West, plans were also reviewed for an assault on Britain. The subject arose again after the fall of France. At first Hitler seemed to believe that Britain, not willing or not daring to pursue the fight against him, would be prepared to conclude an agreement. But when he saw that Churchill was far from disposed toward coming to an understanding with him, he considered mounting an attack on the British Isles to secure absolute control over Western Europe before turning to his major objective: the war against Soviet Russia. The battle between the air forces of Germany and Great Britain is one of the most celebrated chapters of World War II. Its significance was summed up in Churchill's ringing statement, "Never in the field of human conflict was so much owed by so many to so few." In September 1940, the Royal Air Force, smaller in size than its German counterpart, forced the enemy to abandon its attack plan, and the Nazis decided to postpone an invasion indefinitely.

In the meanwhile Mussolini, eager to extend his own empire, sent his forces to invade North Africa and advance toward Egypt in August 1940. By the middle of December, however, Sir Archibald Wavell, the commander of the British forces in the Middle East, not only had succeeded in beating the Italians back but also had taken tens of thousands of Italian POWs. Early in February 1941 the British forces reached Bengazi, in Italian-occupied Libya, thus lifting the threat to Egypt and Palestine. In October 1940 Mussolini also tried his strength in the Balkans by sending troops through Albania to attack Greece. But in the following months, he was repulsed there, as well, and the Germans had to come to his aid.

Germany's influence in southeastern Europe, particularly in the Balkans, was enhanced as a result of its victories in the East and the West. In this region, however, the Germans faced a strong and menacing rival: the Soviet Union. The Balkan state that suffered most from the overt and covert struggle going on between these competing powers was Rumania, whose oil resources were coveted by both of them. In effect, the German penetration into Rumania had been in progress ever since Hitler's rise to power and had increased with his military successes. The Germans, who were interested in compensating the Russians for the concessions they had made in the partition of Poland, consented to their demands, and on June 28 Rumania was forced to cede Bessarabia and part of northern Bukovina to the Soviet Union. A few days afterward Rumania joined the Axis powers, and by virtue of an agreement signed in Vienna on August 30, 1940—in the presence of the Italian and German foreign ministers—northern Transylvania was ceded to Hungary and the Dobruja region in the south was given over to Bulgaria. These territorial concessions sparked off such unrest in Rumania that King Carol II was forced to abdicate in favor of his son Michael. The country's real ruler, however, was Ion Antonescu, who proceeded to bring members of the fascist Iron Guard into his government. Whatever remained of the country's democratic constitution was abrogated in September, and in October the German army entered Rumania. The rest of the Balkan states—Bulgaria, Greece, Albania, and Yugoslavia—did not come under direct German influence until the spring of 1941. Hungary held a unique place among this constellation of countries in that it received generous benefits from the Germans, although the German army did not enter the country until March 1944. Above all, the events in Rumania caused a deterioration in the conditions of the country's Jews, who were already suffering from stringent discriminatory laws modeled on those enacted by the Nazis.

As a consequence of all these military and political maneuvers, by the spring of 1941 close to 3 million Jews were under German control: 675,000 in the Reich and the annexed territories and about 2,250,000 in the occupied countries. A strong Nazi influence also threatened the approximately 430,000 Jews in the satellite countries of Slovakia, Rumania, and Italy. And over them all, Himmler cast his net of agencies, thus creating an SS State throughout Europe.

Himmler: Moving from Theory to Practice

Who was Heinrich Himmler—this man whose name is as closely associated with the fate of European Jewry during the Nazi era as that of the führer himself, this man who by his own testimony murdered millions of people in cold blood and was prepared to murder many millions more? Many have wondered but found no explanation for the fact that this man—whose appearance in no way bespoke a demonic character—became the architect and chief prosecutor of genocide. In his book *The Face of the Third Reich,* the biographer Joachim C. Fest describes two faces of Himmler that were revealed in two separate death masks: one portraying grotesque and distorted features, the other showing the simple face of a romantic petit bourgeois.[46] Giving his version of the subhuman, Himmler stated:

A subhuman is a creature of nature that seems biologically equal to all others. He has hands, legs, a brain of sorts, eyes, and a mouth. Nevertheless, he is a totally different, frightful creature. He is merely an attempt at a man; his facial features are similar to those of humans, but from the intellectual and psychological points of view he ranks lower than the beasts. Lurking in his soul is a brute chaos of wild, unbridled lusts, an inchoate desire to destroy, the most primitive craving, shameless vulgarity. For he is a subhuman, nothing more! The bearer of a human face is not equal in every way. Woe to whoever forgets that.[47]

Anyone who knows what Himmler wrought not only to the Jewish people but to humanity as a whole cannot help but think that he unwittingly drew his self-portrait in this statement. According to Fest, Himmler was closer to Hitler than anyone else and on his own initiative carried Hitler's thoughts to their ultimate conclusion. He was also accorded the power to put them into practice, and that is what established his place in the hierarchy of the Third Reich.[48]

Himmler looked upon Hitler as a kind of divine creature whose likes are born only once in a millennium, an incarnation of Jesus Christ or of the Hindu god Krishna. His feelings toward the führer fluctuated between mystical adoration and fear, and this irrational attitude continued to motivate him even after the two men had parted ways toward the end of the war. It was Himmler who translated the führer's ultimate conclusions into action. Fest calls him "Petty Bourgeois and Grand Inquisitor."[49]

The petit bourgeois was born in 1900 to a respected Catholic family in Bavaria. His father, a teacher, raised his sons strictly but also imbued them, or at least Heinrich, with his own love for the history of ancient and medieval Germany. After finishing school, Himmler took up art in the closing stages of World War I and then completed his studies as a certified agronomist. He joined the National Socialist party early enough to participate in Hitler's abortive coup in 1923. Until the end of the 1920s, however, he remained a private citizen, living on his farm and raising an improved stock of chickens. His great moment came when Hitler took notice of him and in 1929 charged him with organizing the SS.

Unlike many of the leaders of the Nazi regime, Himmler fully believed the myth that the German race was destined to rule the world. Since the epitome of the race was its "good blood," it was vital to preserve, improve, and extend it through procreation. To determine the genealogy of the race Himmler founded a special institute within the SS called Heritage of the Forefathers (Ahnenerbe). But its purpose was not just theoretical study, for he also wanted to put principles into practice and encourage as high as possible a birthrate of those with "good blood." Consequently, he issued strict regulations on marriage for the men of SS and established special institutions called Lebensborn (the source of life) for women bearing children out of wedlock when both parents were of pure German stock. Himmler was not content with encouraging the propagation of what he considered the superior race in Germany alone; he also wanted to save the offspring of so-called pure Germans through the world and replant them in their homeland. On September 7, 1940, in a speech to officers of a special SS unit named in honor of Adolf Hitler, he said, "For eleven years now I have been serving as Reichskommissar-SS. As far as I am concerned, there has always been only one immutable, all-inclusive goal: to create an order of good blood capable of serving Germany; [an order] that is unhesitatingly and unsparing devoted. . . . To create an order that will spread a consciousness of Nordic blood until we draw to us all the Nordic blood in the world."[50]

Hitler's Minister of the Treasury, Graf Schwerin von Krosigk, once said of Himmler, "Hitler could not have assigned the task of disposing of his political garbage to a more appropriate character than Himmler. He pedantically created a terror organization and knew neither mercy nor remorse."[51]

Himmler himself remarked of the way he was handling matters in the East that he worked toward achieving his goal with relentless and unflinching determination but was flexible about the means used to achieve it.[52] This dichotomy of the goal remaining immutable but the means of attaining it being varied and adaptable was also characteristic of Hitler's approach—yet another similarity between the two men. It enabled Himmler to combine his mystical and fantasized concepts with an unremitting war of pure might. Without Himmler's clever control of the instruments of power, he would not have been able to establish the SS State that extended to every country in Europe in which the Nazis gained a foothold. It was in occupied Poland that he took the decisive step toward expanding his realm. Here his bureaucracy not only was the power behind the realization of the racial policy but set the objectives and decided on the means of achieving them. The very fact that Himmler and his executors became the central force directing the implacable war against the Jews accorded them, and primarily Himmler as their leader, a crucial position in the hierarchy of Nazi rule wherever it extended. Hitler's hatred of the Jews and the importance he ascribed to solving the Jewish problem according to his concept were among the factors that ensured Himmler's status as the man who carried out the führer's program.

It might have been assumed that in wartime, when stress is necessarily laid on the military struggle, the influence of the SS would have declined, since it no longer held the center stage. If Hitler had lost interest in Himmler's activities, the latter's own political career would have come to an end. He forestalled that danger in two ways: one was by associating the SS with the war effort through the establishment of the armed or Waffen SS while being careful to prevent the army's influence over these corps from overriding his own.[53] The other means of maintaining his focal position was by acting to Germanize the occupied territory in the East and solve the Jewish problem. The more he accomplished in fulfilling these two tasks, the more he could hope to remain in the führer's good graces, thus enhancing his own power, for the authority of the man who realized Hitler's chief ambition would not be open to appeal. In the course of time, Himmler tried to add a third element to these two sources of power by building an SS economic empire, but he had less success in that sphere.

6

The War Against European Jewry: The First Assault (Autumn 1939 to Spring 1941)

The Reich's Jewish Policy in Occupied Poland

The rulers of the Third Reich took the liquidation of Polish Jewry to be a challenge and a test, an inevitable stage in their struggle for sovereignty over all of Eastern Europe. That is why planning the measures against the Jews was comprehensive, far-reaching, and guided by principle. Heydrich issued his orders on this subject to the commanders of the Einsatzgruppen at a meeting held on September 21, 1939, and went on to detail and assign them in an express letter dispatched to the commanders that same day under the heading "The Problem of the Jews in the Occupied Areas." It was one of the prime documents characterizing the process that was to develop into the Final Solution. In his opening remarks, Heydrich stated:

> I refer to the conference held in Berlin today, and again point out that the *planned total measures* (i.e., the final aim [*Endziel*]) are to be kept *strictly secret.*
>
> Distinction must be made between:
>
> 1. the final aim (which will require extended periods of time)
>   and
> 2. the stages leading to the fulfillment of this final aim (which will be carried out in short periods).[1]

Further on the directive stressed that not all the details of its execution should be determined in advance. Thus the instructions that followed were also meant to stimulate further practical thinking on the part of the Einsatzgruppen commanders themselves.

The instructions were divided into six clauses. The first stated that the Jews scattered throughout the country should quickly be concentrated in the large cit-

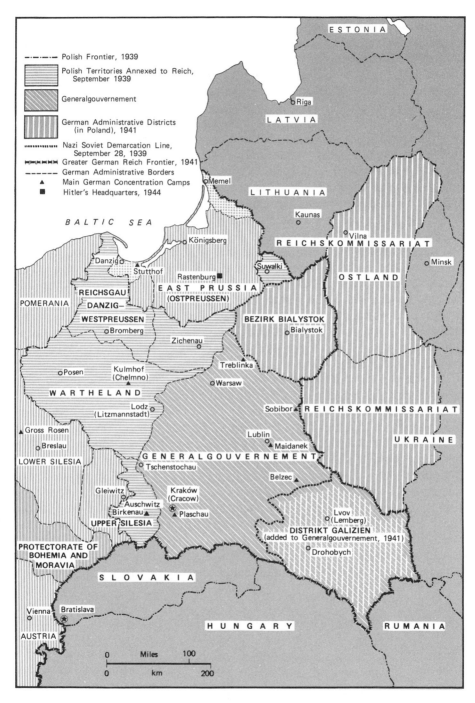

Poland under Nazi occupation. (After Norman Davies, *God's Playground: A History of Poland.* Vol. 2: *1795 to the Present,* Oxford, 1981)

ies, with the districts of Danzig (Gdańsk), West Prussia, Poznań, and Upper Silesia, in particular, being "purged of Jews as quickly as possible." In all the other areas, a few concentration centers were to be established "to facilitate subsequent measures." The cities in question would have to be on or near a railway line. Jewish communities of fewer than five hundred people were to be liquidated and their inhabitants transferred to the nearest concentration point.

The second clause addressed itself to the establishment of the Jewish councils, the Judenräte. Their members were to be rabbis and other people of influence, and each council was to have a maximum of twenty-four members, depending on the size of the community. It would be charged with overall responsibility, in the fullest sense of the word, for the precise and prompt execution of all orders that had been, or would be, issued. The members of the council were to be forewarned that in the event of sabotage in the execution of orders, grave steps would be taken against them. The councils would be obliged to take a census of the Jewish population, classifying it by sex and age, and they were to be responsible for gathering in the Jews of the vicinity. Their concentration in the cities was to be justified by the claim that "[the Jews] have taken a decisive part in sniper attacks and plundering." The councils would bear responsibility for feeding the deportees en route to their points of concentration and for housing them in the cities. Finally, the concentration operation would require the establishment of ghettos; the publication of regulations such as the prohibition against Jews leaving the ghetto or being found in other quarters of the city; the imposition of curfews; and the like.

The third clause discussed the coordination of actions with the other German authorities in the area, namely, the army and the civilian administration.

The fourth clause dealt with the need for the commanders of the Einsatzgruppen to report on the results of their actions, with special emphasis placed on the need to conduct a survey of the Jewish-owned industrial enterprises and workshops that could be put to work for the Four-Year Plan. The prospects of Aryanization were also to be explored, taking the vitality of these enterprises into consideration. The fifth and the sixth clauses dealt with administrative matters.

The directives indicated the means designed to undermine the basis of the Jews' lives. This process was built upon a number of basic measures that, taken together, would drain the Jews of their strength to the point where the Nazis could do with them as they pleased. First came the **eviction of the Jews** from their permanent residences and their deportation to a temporary and as yet undetermined destination. The Jews were to be not only uprooted but deprived of all their household goods, clothing, and other belongings: the baggage they were allowed to take along would not even cover their most immediate needs. Moreover, their apartments and other real estate were to be expropriated. Second was the **concentration and isolation** of the Jews, which would disrupt their lives, overturn social conventions, and lead to insufferable crowding, with all the attendant side effects: dirt, disease, and tension. Third, the burden of the **organization and maintenance** of the deported and concentrated Jews was placed on their communal organizations, the kehillot, which would be administered through the Judenräte. Fourth, the **economic basis** of the Jews' lives would be destroyed by confiscating and exploiting their property to the maximum. Fifth was to **make use of the Jewish labor force.**

As noted at the opening of Heydrich's letter, all these measures were but the initial stages of a program that was to lay the ground for achieving "the final aim," which was still considered secret and not yet articulated in clear-cut terms.

These directives were disseminated throughout occupied Poland even before the fighting came to an end and about a month before Himmler issued his order to initiate the resettlement *(Umsiedlung)* at the end of October. In effect, anti-Jewish actions—including deportations—had begun even before this central order was given. With the Germans' entry into Poland, terror actions were mounted in individual places on the initiative of the commanders and soldiers of the conquering army and the SS men accompanying them. They included physical assaults and beatings, robberies, clipping the sidelocks of elderly people, torture, murder, and so on. Besides observant Jews, women in particular were the target of attack, being forced to strip and clean the streets and all kinds of filth with their underwear. Acts of violence were also directed against Jewish institutions; in many places buildings were taken over and synagogues put to the torch, often with the Jews themselves being forced to set them alight or accused of arson and prevented from extinguishing the flames. The remaining buildings were converted into stables, warehouses, and even houses of prostitution. At the same time, men were abducted for forced labor, such as repairing roads, bridges, and railway tracks; cleaning public and private property; and providing services to the army and its officers. Jews were forced by pay heavy fines for a variety of charges, and hostages were taken with threats being made to kill them if they were not ransomed by a set date. Afterward it was often claimed that the Jews had missed the deadline, so that new punishments and fines were imposed on them—in many places the ransom was demanded in gold.

Deportations soon followed. During this initial period, they were channeled in three main directions: to a nearby place or large area of concentration in the vicinity, such as Łódź; into the Generalgouvernement; or over the border into the Russian zone of occupation.[2] In addition to the deportation of groups of men and women (each sex separately), deportation orders were also issued to individuals who had to leave on very short notice—sometimes as brief as a quarter of an hour. They were left to make their way into the Generalgouvernement or over the Russian border on their own. During this early period, Jews driven out of the western regions of Poland were still allowed to travel on trains, which was later forbidden. To the deportations we must add the exodus of Jews who tried (but did not always succeed) to flee on their own initiative. The overall picture was thus one of total chaos created by the Germans both deliberately and unintentionally.

One of the Jews deported from the town of Koto to Izbica Lubelska related that before being shipped out, the deportees were told by the gendarmes, "You will receive shops and workshops in your new places of settlement and you will be able to start new lives." After the promise came the warning, "Whoever escapes from the march to the railway station or falls out of line will be shot on the spot."[3] The deportees were sent by cattle car on a journey that lasted for days, with no hint of their destination until they finally arrived in Izbica Lubelska. The same deportee reported, "The local Jews did everything they could to make the exile easier on us. We felt that we were among kindhearted Jews. This was not an easy task for them: a few days before we arrived, a transport of 15,000 Jews had come from Łódź, doubling the number of Jews in the town. The overcrowding was unbearable."

During the first four months of the occupation, more than half the Jewish population of 600,000 people disappeared from the annexed Eastern districts. The number of deportees, who came from fifty different locations, is estimated at 330,000,[4] of whom 100,000, at most, were sent to the Generalgouvernement in organized transports; the rest were smuggled out or fled. The number of Jews who fell victim to murder is estimated in the thousands. In the regions of East and West Prussia, hardly any Jewish communities remained. Small communities continued to exist for the most part in the Warthegau and in southern East Prussia and in eastern Silesia as well, with many work camps being set up in all these areas. The largest concentration in the region continued to be in Łódź, where 233,000 Jews had been living before the outbreak of the war. The number of Poles deported during this same period was 325,000.[5]

Developing the Methods of Deportation

The initial period of the deportations served as a preparatory or experimental phase for the mass deportations of Jews from Poland and from all of Europe to the extermination camps. During the deportation to Nisko, on October 6, 1939, Heinrich Müller ordered that the expulsion of seventy thousand to eighty thousand Jews from the vicinity of Katowice be joined by Jews from the area of Ostrava as well as by any Poles living there. (This operation was not carried out.) The reason given was "first and foremost to acquire experience so that on the basis of this experience it will be possible to execute the transport of the masses." According to the protocol of another conversation among Eichmann, his deputy Rolf Günther, and Gauleiter Julius Wagner, which took place in Katowice on October 11, at first four transports (of one thousand persons each) were planned, two each from Katowice and Ostrava. These transports, too, were to be carried out for the sake of experience: "After the completion of all four transports, a report on these experiments should be submitted to the head of the Security Police [Heydrich, who will pass it on] to the RFSS [Himmler]. We can assume that it will also be relayed to the führer. Then one is to await the order for the wholesale deportation of Jews."[6] According to these instructions, the Nisko deportation served as the groundwork for mass deportations.

It is worthwhile trying to sum up the lessons derived by Heydrich's staff from the first resettlement experiment in Poland. Under Eichmann's direction, Heydrich's staff retooled and streamlined the system of the transports during the winter of 1939/1940. The first rule Heydrich had already established in his express letter was to assemble masses of people in places from which it would be relatively easy to move them out by train. One of the early deportation orders explained that trains were to be used, rather than trucks, because it was easier to guard them. It soon became clear that from a technical point of view it was impossible to concentrate all the candidates for deportation in cities, so that transit camps were established in certain areas where Jews and Poles were due to be deported. At this early stage, the German civil administration (meaning the heads of municipalities and local councils) was placed in charge of the local concentrations and had to coordinate between all the executive arms—the security services, the police, the gendarmerie, the *Volksdeutsche* commissars, and the administrative personnel in charge of the population census. They were also responsible for technical matters such as transit camps, food supply, preparation of trains, sanitary conditions, and the like. At the same time, the operation was centralized by the authorities in Berlin, who issued their instructions in November and December in a series of orders detailing the measures to be taken. These implementation orders covered such details as the means of selecting, registering, and searching people for concealed weapons, valuables, and money. They outlined how to deal with the evacuated apartments, how to involve the Judenräte in the evacuation process, and how to register the property of the deportees. They even went into such matters as how to deal with venereal diseases, the recruitment of officials and workers for the Railway Authority, and many other subjects.[7]

What we have before us, then, is one of the hallmarks of the organization of the Final Solution as a whole and the deportations in particular. On the one hand, the onus of organizing and executing these operations fell on the local German authorities, who were also accorded a certain degree of freedom of action. At the same time, however, an attempt was made to direct these operations according to a central plan. As early as November 29, 1939, Heydrich stated, "The factor determining the pace of the evacuation is the Evacuation Plan."[8] Moreover, the operation should not be postponed due to economic or organizational considerations, which were considered to be of secondary importance.

This dictum had to do with one of the prime technical problems determining the pace of the transports and the success of the deportation: the matter of the rolling material *(das rollende Material),* meaning the trains. In fact, the need to obtain and control rolling material was one of the problems that forced Heydrich to establish a central authority to direct the deportations. When it became obvious that a timetable would have to be set up in coordination with the railroad's central authority, this critical task was assigned to Eichmann and remained one of his prime occupations throughout the war. From then on the negotiations regarding the transport of the deportees were handled by Eichmann's office in the RSHA in cooperation with the Ministry of Transport, which issued the orders to the office of the Railway Authority in Cracow and Poznań. Despite this centralized arrangement, many difficulties arose on the local plane. The Railway Authority could not always keep to the schedules owing to such difficulties as "lack of interest on the part of the railway officials," "the refusal to provide services," and even "acts of sabotage."[9] Thanks to his administrative talents, however, Eichmann brought about an improvement in the situation. The Final Travel Plan, as the operation was called, had forty trains setting out from nine places between February 10 and March 3 and included their destinations and times of arrival.[10]

In addition to these improvements on the technical side of the operation, the style of treating the deportees steadily took hold. During the earlier transports to Nisko from Austria, Czechoslovakia, and Upper Silesia, the quota was set at one thousand people per train, and it generally remained frozen until all the deportations had ended. But the treatment of the deportees became increasingly harsh. At first the Germans saw to it that the deportees took food along, but later they actively prevented it. Then the deportees to Nisko were forbidden to drink water, often on the pretext that it was polluted. The passenger cars used for the transports to Nisko were soon replaced by freight cars, and deportees' baggage allotment was set at 44 pounds at most. At first the Jews deported within Poland proper were allowed to take along the sum of 100 zlotys (the equivalent of U.S. $12) in cash; soon thereafter, the sum was reduced to 10 zlotys and all their other valuables were turned over to the German authorities. From the very outset, threats and deception were used to get the deportees onto the trains without resistance or attempts to escape. The inhabitants of Teschen, for example, were told that they were being sent to Cracow and some would be allowed to stay there in the care of the Central Bureau established for that purpose, which would also arrange for their emigration, if possible.[11] Clearly, the whole story was sheer fiction.

Explicit reports on the implementation of the deportations, the discussions of relevant details in the meetings of the main protagonists, and the cooperation with the other pertinent authorities (such as the army and the various Reich ministries) all attested that the deportations were an operation of major proportions and national significance.

Coercion of the Polish Jews

The Regime of Violence in the Generalgouvernement

> While the dictatorship of order that was implemented in Warthegau led to great paralysis, left no room for escape, and no resistance movement worthy of the name was able to develop here, in the Generalgouvernement the oppressive regime that developed was anarchic and, thus, opened the way for arbitrary forces nullifying control.[12]

The anarchy in the Generalgouvernement was heightened by the competition among the various authorities, above all, as mentioned before, between the governor, Hans Frank, and Himmler's representative, HSSPF Friedrich-Wilhelm Krüger. Initially, Frank was at loggerheads with the military authorities in the Generalgouvernement, but after the commanding Marshal von Blaskowitz was replaced—at Frank's insistence—by a man more amenable to National Socialist methods, the army was blocked from interfering with the civil administration and confined itself to matters directly related to its jurisdiction. One sphere in which the army tried to maintain a certain degree of independence was the armament industry. According to Hitler's reasoning, the administration in the Generalgouvernement was to utilize the area's industrial and human potential to the maximum without consideration for the physical, social, or economic state of the inhabitants. Although he, too, subscribed to, and even declaimed, these ideas, Frank nevertheless conceded that unless he took the needs of the Polish population into account, he would not be able to exploit it. This contradiction between the desire to exploit the country's economic potential and the Nazi doctrine propounding the destruction of the population was a salient feature of the German occupation of Poland and also influenced the attitude toward the Jews.

In contrast to these conflicting undercurrents in Frank's regime, the administration of the SS and the police had but a single aim: to achieve complete control over the population without consideration for its needs or economic value. Until the outbreak of the war against Russia, Krüger's objective was essentially to establish and extend his control throughout the Generalgouvernement by virtue of the police forces under his command. Aiding him in this task was the fact that Frank had no armed force at his disposal and was, therefore, wholly dependent on Krüger's police and SS.

The Generalgouvernement was initially divided into four districts: the Cracow District, whose capital was chosen by Frank as the seat of his government; the Radom District; the Warsaw District in the north; and the Lublin District, bordering on the zone of Russian occupation, in the east. All of these areas were heavily populated by Jews. In October 1939 there were about 1.5 million Jews in the Generalgouvernement, representing slightly more than 12 percent of the area's population. The largest number of Jews—some 400,000 people—lived in Warsaw, where they composed one-third of the population. Jews streamed to the Polish capital in the hope of finding safer refuge there than in the outlying cities, although there was also a countermovement of Jews attempting to flee from Warsaw over the Russian border.[13]

The conduct of the German troops—both the army and the SS—was no different in the Generalgouvernement than in the western areas of Poland. Murder, the abduction of Jews for forced labor, deportations, robbery, abuse, the burning of synagogues, the imposition of fines, the arrest and often murder of hostages all created great insecurity among the Jews and undermined the basic conditions of their existence, which had already been severely shaken by the war.

Displacing the Jewish Population

The difference between the policy adopted in the Generalgouvernement and that pursued in the Eastern districts was that in the Generalgouvernement there was no intention of systematically clearing out the Jewish population. It would be wrong to conclude, however, that there was no movement of Jews, some wandering of their own volition but most being forced to do so. The first type of movement was the flight of Jews over the Russian border, primarily from settlements close to the new Russian zone. In the areas that had initially been turned over to the Russians (by virtue of the 1939 Nonaggression Pact) but subsequently reverted to German hands, many young Jews succeeded in joining the withdrawing Soviet forces. For instance, of the seven thousand Jews living in the city of Hrubieszów in the Lublin District prior to the occupation, two thousand accompanied the Red Army; over 75 percent of six thousand Jews managed to flee from Tomaszów Lubelski in this way.[14] There were also many who tried to escape on their own. Considerable movement over the Soviet frontier was effected from the Warsaw District. Flight into the Soviet-occupied zone remained possible, however, only as long as the two armies moved back and forth and the border was not finally drawn.

An eyewitness described the crossings over the Soviet border:

> While a number of refugees managed to escape before the Nazi hordes occupied their towns, most of them were rounded up by the Gestapo and driven to the frontier. There they streamed over the Soviet frontier at three points. . . . During the first weeks of this mass exodus, the Red Army guards permitted everyone to cross the border and frequently showed a sympathetic attitude. About the fifteenth of October, however, the borders were suddenly shut tight.[15]

The witness went on to relate how the civilians were then chased back and forth over the frontier, were shot, or ultimately froze to death in the bitter cold. In the end thousands of people (among them the famed actress Ida Kaminska) remained stuck in no-man's-land, where the Nazis tormented them. An especially gruesome tragedy occurred outside the city of Sokal near the Bug River on the border in the Lublin District. In November 1939 the Germans marched eighteen hundred Jews from the community of Chelm, in the Lublin District, toward the Bug River, presumably to have them cross it and reach Sokal. Many of the Jews were shot in the course of this *"death march,"* one of the first of its kind, and the Soviets prevented the rest from crossing the border.[16] Only four hundred people succeeded in escaping and reaching their destination; all the rest perished. A large proportion of the Jews the Nazis sent to Nisko from Austria and Czechoslovakia were also driven over the Soviet border. The estimated number of more than three hundred thousand Jews who crossed into the Russian zone[17] does not take into account the many who died in the attempt.

Counterweighing this movement of refugees and deportees from the Generalgouvernement into the Russian zone was the influx of Jews deported, in either an organized or improvised manner, from dozens of communities in the western regions of Poland into the Generalgouvernement. They were sent not only to the Lublin area, which was initially earmarked to become a *Jewish reservation,* but also to the three other districts—Radom, Cracow, and Warsaw. Jews were driven back and forth from one place to another inside the Generalgouvernement as well. The following is a brief description of one of the many deportations—this one from Lublin on November 9, 1939, "Panic broke out in the city. It was early morning. Many people were still in bed when they received the order to evacuate their apartments within minutes. . . . About five hundred families were turned out of their homes that day and lost their furniture, linens, towels, and stocks of food."[18]

The Coercive Regime

On the day after the abolition of the military government, when Frank took over the rule of the Generalgouvernement, he issued a series of orders and regulations covering both general and special affairs. In the Generalgouvernement declaration of October 26, 1939, announcing his appointments, he stated, "I have been instructed by the führer, in my capacity as governor general of the occupied Polish territories, to take decisive steps in order to ensure that there will be peace in this country forever, and that the relations of the Poles with the mighty world empire of the German nation shall develop normally."[19] Further on in this statement, he promised the Poles, "Under a just rule everyone will earn his bread by work. On the other hand, there will be no room for political agitators, shady dealers, and Jewish exploiters in a territory that is under German sovereignty." A threat warned anyone against daring to resist the occupying power. Two of the ten orders published that day to settle administrative, security, and financial problems were aimed at the Jewish population. One forbade the practice of ritual slaughtering, under threat of incarceration either in prison or in a concentration camp.[20] The second dealt with conscription for labor. Contrary to the orders imposing the *duty* of labor *(Arbeitslpflicht)* on the Polish population, the order addressing itself to the Jews stated, "Hard labor [*Arbeitszwang*] is being imposed upon the Jews forthwith. For that purpose the Jews are to be concentrated in special battalions. The regulations necessary for carrying out this directive will be discharged by the Higher SS and Police Leader."[21]

This order effectively gave Krüger complete control over all Jewish affairs; this fact was immediately manifest in the first implementation orders he issued on December 13, 1939. These orders determined that beginning on January 1, 1940, Jews would be forbidden to change their places of residence without written permission from the local authorities and that any Jews who "migrate[d] or [were] evacuated into the Generalgouvernement" were obliged to report immediately to the local authority and inform the Judenrat of their arrival. The implication was that the refugees and the deportees were to be incorporated into the conscription pool for forced labor and the Judenrat would be responsible for conducting the registration of these new inhabitants. Finally, the Jews were placed under a curfew from nine o'clock in the evening until five o'clock in the morning; anyone violating these orders risked being sent to prolonged forced hard labor or being punished otherwise.[22]

These implementation orders speak of the Judenrat as an existing fact. The order requiring the establishment of Jewish councils was issued by Frank on November 28, 1939, and went into effect on December 7, that is, only six days prior to Krüger's order. It stated that "representations of the Jews, known as Judenrat" were to be established in communities of up to ten thousand inhabitants and were to include twelve members; in communities of over ten thousand residents, these councils would have twenty-four members. The councils were to be elected by the local Jewish population, but the local authorities in the district or city were authorized to confirm the composition of the council or change it. The order defined the council's role, "It is the duty of the Judenrat through its chairman or his deputy to receive the orders of the German Administration. It is responsible for the conscientious carrying out of orders to their full extent. The directives it issues to carry out these German decrees must be obeyed by all Jews and Jewesses."[23]

Jewish councils had been set up in many places well before the publication of Frank's order. The first Judenrat in the Generalgouvernement came into being on September 4 in Piotrków, in the Radom District, immediately after the German army entered the city. Another was established in Sosnowiec in Eastern Upper Silesia immediately after the German conquest on September 6, 1939. In the latter case, the Germans ordered the leading members of the Jewish community to report to them. After subjecting them to abuse, they asked the members of the community board to identify themselves, but no one dared to do so other than Moshe Merin, who had, in fact, not held any public post. At first Merin was treated to another round of blows, but then the Germans charged him with forming the Judenrat.[24] In the course of time, Merin was to become a prominent figure in the area as a whole (see chap. 7).

The establishment of the Judenrat was accompanied by threats, terror, and arrests in every city and town. Elections were not usually held; in many cases the authorities constructed the Judenrat on previous administrative and self-help organizations, and they often appointed the chairman—sometimes quite arbitrarily.

The establishment of the Judenrat implied an extension of the system developed by the Gestapo in Austria, Czechoslovakia, and Germany in 1938/1939, but under the conditions of occupation in Poland, this system was to become far more harsh. The general atmosphere of terror, which was directed above all against the Jews, made this means of controlling the Jewish public all the more effective. This system of control reached its height with the creation of the ghetto, but even before the Jews were enclosed behind walls, the Germans placed many stringent restrictions on them to manifest the principles set down in Heydrich's order of September 21, 1939: isolation, concentration, and forced labor—now to be joined by the plunder of property. Among the new designs for achieving these goals was marking the Jews with a special symbol. The first step was the order of September 8, 1939, that obligated the Jews to mark their businesses with a Star of David.[25] The decree, stigmatizing them personally, resulted from a combination of improvised actions on the part of local instigators and the will of the regime as expressed in a comprehensive order. The first place in which Jews were made to wear a yellow triangle was the town of Włocławek in Warthegau, following an order issued as early as October 24, 1939, by the commander of the town. During November the same order was issued by the governor of the Łódź District (November 16), the commander of the SS and the police in Cracow (November 18), and the mayor of Sosnowiec in Eastern Upper Silesia (November 25).[26] Eventually, Frank's order that required the wearing of a distinguishing mark throughout the Generalgouvernement was issued on November 23, 1939, and went into effect on December 1. It stated, "All Jews and Jewesses within the Government-General who are over ten years of age are required, beginning December 1, 1939, to wear on the right sleeve of their inner and outer garments a white band at least 4 inches wide, with the Star of David on it."[27]

Spoliation

In occupied Poland the Nazis intensified and accelerated all the steps they had earlier taken against the Jews in the Reich, but here each stage, which had taken years to achieve in Germany and months in Austria and Czechoslovakia, was completed in a matter of weeks. The same was true of the spoliation of property. Robbery and looting by members of all the arms of the regime—the army, the SS, and the civil administration—became everyday occurrences:

> The Germans come to a Jewish family and rob it of virtually all its belongings. They take away pictures, rugs, furniture, shoes, etc. The mother begs them to leave the little bed for her child. The answer is that a Jewish child does not need a bed. German soldiers visit Dr. Brokman's home, and steal. They express their surprise that there are so few shirts. He tells them that he is not a wealthy man. "Yes," confirms the German, "with honesty you cannot get rich," and he steals some more.[28]

These improvised actions were complemented by a legislative campaign composed of four elements: a boycott, the imposition of taxes and fines, the registration of property, and the expropriation of property. We have already referred to the regulation of September 8, 1939, ordering the Jews to mark their businesses with a Star of David. It was reissued in the Generalgouvernement on the same day as the order requiring Jews to wear an arm band (November 23, 1939).[29] Together they were essentially a revival of the boycott system that the Germans had first tested, without much success, on April 1, 1933—except that this time there was virtually no danger that an international outcry would ensue. The imposition of taxes was not restricted to the Jews, however, since the Germans charged the Poles—and thereafter the other occupied peoples—with defraying the costs of maintaining their army. Here they also imposed compensation for damages incurred in the war and a "Defense Tax" for the German war treasury, as "compensation for the German war effort" that had "saved the occupied countries from Russian Bolshevism." Thus Poland paid out RM 1.2 million for its supposed defense against the Soviet Union.[30]

The chief architect of the plunder of Poland was Hermann Göring, who in his capacity as the head of the Four-Year Plan announced, "There must be removed from the territory of the Government General all raw materials, scrap, machines, etc., which are of any use for the German war economy. Enterprises which are not absolutely necessary for the meagre maintenance of the bare existence of the population must be transferred to Germany."[31]

To put this policy into effect, he introduced the trusteeship system, by means of which he had appropriated the property of the Jews in Austria and Czechoslovakia. Göring proceeded to establish the Main Trustee Office East (Haupttreuhandstelle Ost, or HTO). Following Göring's respective orders of November 1, 1939, Frank published a series of directives designed to regulate the handling of foreign currency and the registration, expropriation, and transfer of property to the staff of the regional trustee offices.[32] The large sums confiscated in Poland remained in the country to finance the local German administration. Göring naturally saw to it that a good portion of the plunder from the Polish industrial plants reached the Hermann Göring Works; this included not just simple machinery but furnaces and entire steel plants. The alliance Hitler had concluded with Germany's major industrialists continued to stand them in good stead, for together with the large banks they partook of the spoils.[33]

In their general plunder of the Polish state, private property, and works of art, the Germans focused special attention on the systematic looting of Jewish property. On November 20, 1939, the Foreign Currency Division of the Generalgouvernement published special administrative directives blocking all bank accounts, deposited stocks, and safety deposit boxes held anonymously, under false names, or under Jewish names. In addition, Jews had to transfer all their holdings to the central bank by December 31, 1939. Their right to draw money from these accounts was limited to 250 zlotys (U.S. $30) per month. Similarly, payments to Jews of over 500 zlotys (U.S. $60) per month could be transferred only to the bank or a credit union (loan *kassa*), and any sum over 2,000 zlotys (U.S. $240) in cash had to be deposited in the bank immediately.[34] These details were consonant with the order to block Jewish capital that had been issued by the military government in September 1939.

After depriving the Jews of their liquid assets, on January 24, 1940, Frank issued a general order requiring the registration of all Jewish property. Its clauses were based on the principles that had guided the registration of Jewish property in Germany, and special directives were issued for determining the "Jewish character" of companies with Jewish partners. The order covered both movable property and real estate, and it enumerated all the forms of property, claims, and personal belongings of any value. It also established that the property of anyone who failed to comply with all the orders by March 1, 1940, would be declared ownerless and be confiscated. Heavy punishments were stipulated for anyone attempting to evade the orders.[35] At the close of the summer of 1940, special directives were issued for seizing the capital of "refugees and evacuees," that is, the deportees from the areas annexed to the Reich, and all the tax exemptions of Jewish communities and organizations were revoked.[36] On September 17, 1940, a general order published as a law in the official German newspaper, *Verordnungsblatt,* authorized the expropriation of all Polish property cited in previous edicts,[37] stating that "expropriation will be effected in the case of property belonging to (a) Jews; (b) persons who have fled or are not just temporarily absent." However, the order did not cover real estate that served personal needs or cash and stocks up to the amount of RM 1,000 (2,000 zlotys or U.S. $240). It was signed by Göring, chairman of the Council of Ministers for the Defense of the Reich and commissioner for the Four-Year Plan.[38]

Isaiah Trunk wrote of this measure, "By this single stroke of the pen the Jewish industrialist lost his factory, the Jewish merchant his business, and the Jewish owner his real estate. Thus by February 1941 the *Treuhandstelle* in the Wartheland had taken under its management 216 large industries, approximately 9,000 medium-sized ones, and 76,000 small ones as well as 9,120 large businesses and 112,000 small businesses. Most of these belonged to the Jews."[39]

Seventy-five percent of the Jewish industrial and commercial enterprises in Warsaw had been liquidated by the middle of 1940. The Jews were forbidden to engage in commerce in real estate, precious metals, and jewelry; implementation orders also prevented them from deriving any benefit from their former property. On the German side, however, everyone derived gain from the confiscated property: Himmler, Göring, and their respective organizations and institutions. Confiscated furniture, personal belongings, and clothing were also divided among the *Volksdeutsche* who had been resettled in the annexed areas. Clearly, the property of the evacuees sent to the Generalgouvernement and of the Jews living within its bounds was open to all takers.[40]

As in the Reich, Jewish officials were fired from their jobs in both the public and private sectors; Jewish doctors were forbidden to treat anyone but other Jews; Jewish lawyers were not allowed to practice, their licenses were revoked, and their offices were turned over to trustees; and Jewish schools remained closed even after the Polish schools had reopened.

The official coloration accorded to the economic plunder by orders framed in classically legal language hid the lawlessness and economic chaos that was rife in the occupied territories with no more than a thin veneer. As it was impossible to conduct an orderly and open economy in such circumstances, everyone—the German civil authorities, the SS, the police, the army, the Polish population, and, of course, the Jews—trafficked in the black market to obtain vital necessities. Like the Poles, the Jews suffered heavy damage as a result of the bombings, yet the Poles were allowed to begin to rehabilitate their economy by working for the Germans.[41]

The Method of "Natural Death"

Forced Labor

Kidnapping Jews for the purpose of forced labor was a daily occurrence in occupied Poland. As the occupation went on, two main trends directed the approach to the manpower problem. In one, the Germans tried to exploit the available Poles and Jews for their needs. Their aim was to mobilize about a million Polish laborers for work in Germany, but despite their vigorous propaganda campaign, by March 1940 no more than about eighty thousand workers had been recruited, one-third of them women. Since this number fell far short of their needs, especially in agriculture, and having turned to the method of forced labor, the Germans needed Krüger's police forces; thus the latter were invested with additional powers. Following tried-and-true methods, people were dragged out of their beds at night and hunted down in the streets by day.[42] "Often the workers were ordered to [be ready to] move out in less than an hour. Their baggage was limited to what each could carry easily. . . . Husbands were separated from their wives and children from their parents."[43] In addition to the migration of forced laborers to the Reich, the Germans tried to exploit the labor force within Poland itself.

The second aim that the system of forced labor served primarily affected the Jews. Dozens, if not hundreds, of work camps were set up for Jews in Poland. Admittedly, these camps fulfilled a certain economic role, but they were also an important instrument in the process designed to achieve the "solution to the Jewish problem" by the **method of "natural death."** This trend was closely bound up with the failure of the plan for the Lublin Reservation.

The Lublin Reservation

What motives lay behind the German attempt to concentrate the Jewish population in the so-called Lublin Reservation? The area in question extended southeast of the city of Lublin between the San and Vistula rivers in the west and the Bug River in the east, comprising 300 to 400 square miles.[44] The idea was not entirely new, as it had already been broached at the end of the 1930s. The Germans believed that the focus of the Jews' power and source of their genetic potential lay in Lublin, and during that period a Nazi propagandist, Hermann E. Seifert, published *The Jew on the Eastern Border*. He wrote, "[The Jews of Lublin are] a source of great energy, like a bottomless well from which Jews flow to all corners of the globe, the source of the rebirth of world Jewry. So it is that Lublin has maintained constant contact with world Jewry. So it has been able, again and again, to disseminate its views and decaying force throughout Jewry."[45]

It therefore appeared to the Nazis that by its very nature, the Lublin area would lend itself to the extermination of its Jewish population. For one thing, it was situated far off on the eastern border, and the Germans even believed that it was deserted. In a report on a tour he made in November 1939, Frank's deputy, Artur Seyss-Inquart, quoted the regional governor as having said, "This area, which is noted for its swampy nature, can . . . serve as a reservation for the Jews, and this action may cause a considerable decimation of the Jews."[46]

The area was earmarked for this task not only for the indigenous Jewish population but for *all* the Jews, be they in the annexed territories, the Generalgouvernement, or anywhere else in Europe. On November 25, 1939, Frank informed the leading officials in the Radom District of the proposal to concentrate millions of Jews east of the Vistula River.[47] In 1941 Peter H. Seraphim, one of the "scientific" propagandists of the Third Reich, observed, "It is known that . . . a 'Jewish reservation' of this kind in the eastern part of the present Generalgouvernement, in the Lublin District, has often been considered as a way of absorbing the Jews from the Greater Reich and the rest of the areas of the Generalgouvernement—and perhaps, later on, from all the rest of Europe."[48] Hence, the Germans did not keep the Lublin Reservation Plan secret. It was even reported in the press, and rumors about it spread throughout Poland. Eichmann was the first to try to realize the plan when he effected the deportation to Nisko.[49]

The Nazi leadership believed that the Lublin area had another advantage that made it particularly suitable for the concentration and possibly extermination of European Jewry: the personality of Himmler's representative in the district, Odilo Globocnik. Like many of the Nazi butchers, Globocnik had first proved himself in Austria. In November 1939 he was appointed SSPF in the Lublin District and was immediately placed in charge of "the systematic organization of all matters pertaining to the Jews of the district of Lublin."[50]

The department he established, headed by Dr. Hofbauer, drew up two plans, one dealing with the conscription of Jews for forced labor, the other with the settlement of the Jewish refugees who would be brought into the area. The situation that evolved in the Lublin area was intolerable. Masses of Jewish deportees arrived exhausted and ill from the difficult journey in the bitter cold, lacking sufficient clothing, drugs, or means of support. Thus, they posed a number of very real threats—an outbreak of typhus and typhoid fever being only the most exigent of them. No housing was found for the refugees, to say nothing of sources of livelihood. Even the great effort made by the local Jews was unable to alleviate the situation. These dangers, combined with the fact that news of what was happening in the area had leaked out to the foreign press, were among the factors that prompted Göring to cancel the plan on March 23, 1940, with Himmler's support. In April 1940 Krüger officially informed all the district commanders that the Lublin Reservation Plan had been rescinded.[51] The return of the remaining deportees from Nisko was also part of this turnabout.

The Lublin Reservation Plan was shelved for pragmatic reasons, not out of principle. Not only did the deportations continue—albeit at a slower pace—but the Germans began to seek other ways of neutralizing European Jewry. With the fall of France, this search led to the formulation of yet another outlandish scheme known as the Madagascar Plan (see chap. 10).

Forced Labor Camps

With the abandonment of the Lublin Plan, the Germans were faced with the question of how to continue moving toward a solution of the Jewish problem. Meanwhile, they contended themselves with two other channels of action that had earlier been considered, planned, and to a certain extent instituted: the establishment of forced labor camps and of ghettos.

The forced labor camps steadily developed as a branch of the network of concentration camps. The demand for laborers increased during wartime, and for the most part, camps were established according to the need for working hands. On an administrative level, the labor camps were usually attached to one of the large concentration camps, with dozens of them being so annexed to Buchenwald, Dachau, and Mauthausen, for example. In addition to the network of forced labor camps run by the SS, a second set of camps known as *Einsatzlager* was developed by the German Labor Front (Deutsche Arbeitsfront, or DAF) and Fritz Todt's Building Authority. These were improvised camps whose inmates were transferred from one place to another according to need. As a rule the camps inhabited by Germans and by foreign workers exiled to Germany were kept strictly separate. This huge army of laborers not only built fortifications and roads, cut timber, plowed fields, and brought in the harvest but later on even staffed the various branches of the armament industry. The treatment of the foreign workers was disgraceful, and their living, nutritional, and sanitary conditions fell far below the minimal needs for survival. These conditions continued to deteriorate as the war progressed, with the number of deaths rising concomitantly. From the outset, however, the lowest rank of all in the labor camps was assigned to the Jews, because the explicit Nazi aim was twofold: to exploit the work force and to eliminate the Jews.

From the beginning of the occupation the Germans intended to use the Jews as a work force. Even before Frank's official order was issued at the end of October, the military authorities had set up work centers in Łódź, Warsaw, and Lublin, for example.[52] The German outlook held that it was necessary to teach the Jews "order and work." Krüger sketched a portrait of the Jews in the style of *Der Stürmer* in an article on the actions of the SS and the police—"the bearers of the might of the state"—published in a book of propaganda about the Generalgouvernement. Commenting on one of the tasks of the policing arms, he noted, "By means of police coercion, for the first time many Jews have been induced to engage in fruitful labor in the service of the community." Krüger regarded the Jews as criminals by nature and accused them of dealing on the black market. He described Jews as disgustingly filthy and their wares as defective. Indeed, "it is necessary to maintain constant, meticulous supervision of the dealers' markets, of their apartments, and of the rest of the 'places of trade' not only for the sake of police supervision of the marketplace but also from the standpoint of police supervision of sanitation."[53]

On December 12, 1939, Krüger published the Second Implementation Order of the Forced Labor Decree establishing that, "All the Jewish residents in the territory of the Generalgouvernement from the ages of fourteen to sixty are in principle obliged to engage in forced labor. The term of forced labor is usually two years; it is extended if, during this period, its *educational objective* is not achieved."[54] According to the Nazi Language Regulations, the "educational role" was also one of the purposes of the concentration camps. Thus, the true reason for the camps—to exploit their inmates as slaves until they expired—was camouflaged by a term that suggested a positive social intent.

To set up the Labor Service, it was necessary to prepare an Engagement Card File that would include the names and occupations of all men aged twelve to sixty. The preparation of this file would fall to the Jewish councils, under the aegis of the mayors. The people called up for work would have to bring two blankets and enough food for two days as well as all the tools in their possession. Severe punishments were prescribed for those who tried to sell tools and machinery, those who tried to evade hard labor, or members of the Judenrat who failed to carry out their duties to the fullest.

The order covering these points was issued in Warsaw by the city's mayor on January 20, 1940. The actual registration was described by an eyewitness who left Warsaw at the end of February 1940 and reached Palestine the following month, "The Jews were required to report every day in alphabetical order. Everyone who registered was forced to pay 20 zlotys [U.S. $2.40] for the registration form and had to fill it out precisely, especially with regard to his occupation. . . . After following all these formal instructions, the person being registered had to pay another 20 zlotys for a 'Certificate of Engagement.'"[55] After the completion of this registration procedure, the Warsaw community was obligated to supply 6,000 to 15,000 workers per day.

It would be mistaken to believe, however, that the conscription of men for labor was accomplished in a quiet and orderly fashion. Abductions had been frequent, primarily in the early months of the occupation, and they never stopped completely. A woman resident of Palestine who returned home at the beginning of March 1940 related:

The Jews hunted down for forced labor are tortured in the building of the defunct Sejm [the Polish Parliament]. Not long ago three hundred Jews were taken to the Sejm building and divided into groups of eight, each group placed in a separate room. Their coats were removed, they were made to lie down on tables, and their naked bodies were beaten with iron rods. After the beatings, the Jews were made to stand with their faces to the wall, and the murderous Nazis threatened them by shooting off their guns. After all kinds of brutal torture along these lines, they were sent off to forced labor. The Nazis took the *laissez-passers* from the Jews and ordered them to appear for "work" every day for two weeks. Many of the tortured people fell ill.[56]

During the winter of 1939/1940, the Poles also mounted a number of organized pogroms against the Jews. Emmanuel Ringelblum described the best known of these riots, which took place in February 1940, "Anti-Semitic gangs, composed mostly of young people, were directed by a German who covered them from behind and supervised the '*Aktion.*' Their slogan was 'Jews emigrate!'"[57]

The labor camps were not organized in a comprehensive and systematic fashion until the spring of 1940. The first major *Aktion* in this context was carried out by Globocnik in the Lublin District. It was designed to fill a network of forced labor camps opened near the town of Bełżec, by the Russian border in the southern part of the district, where major fortifications were being built. Jews from Lublin, Warsaw, and Radom were conscripted for this project, and by August 1940 there were 10,000 Jews in these camps. When the fortifications were completed, some of the inmates were transferred to other places, but at the end of October 1940 there were again 12,000 Jews around Bełżec.[58] By the end of the summer of 1940, a system of forced labor had been established throughout the Generalgouvernement, and at the end of October the official Jewish newspaper, *Gazeta Żydowska,* reported the existence of thirty-six camps—a few of them in the Warsaw District but most in the Lublin District—where over 20,000 Jews were working for Todt's enterprises. At the end of 1940 there were over fifty camps in the Generalgouvernement encompassing at least 30,000 Jews.[59] Where no labor camps were established, the Jews were later closed in ghettos and sent out to various work places. Often, however, a ghetto and a labor camp existed side by side, as was the case in Lublin. The Judenrat in the city was usually responsible for the care of the Jews in the adjacent camp.

This same system was also in effect in the territories annexed to the Reich. The systematic *Aktionen* did not begin in these areas until the large-scale deportations had stopped. It was Himmler who ordered the concentration of Jews and unemployed Poles in closed camps and had them put to work in quarries and on road gangs. But the Jews in the annexed areas were also deemed suitable for work in the Reich proper, and in October 1940 the Germans began to transfer hundreds of Jews to Germany. These transports continued through 1942.[60]

In the spring of 1940 a camp was opened in an old Polish barracks in Eastern Upper Silesia. The order to establish it was issued by Himmler himself on March 27, 1940. It was a small camp built close to the town of Oświęcim (Auschwitz, in German), and was meant primarily for Polish political criminals. On May 4, 1940, Rudolf Höss, one of Theodor Eicke's outstanding pupils, was appointed its commander. In the latter half of May, thirty German prisoners convicted on criminal charges were sent there to serve as wardens, and the camp was opened in the middle of June. Although it was then considered a small concentration camp, in the course of 1940 a broad expanse of the surrounding countryside was attached to it—including seven villages that were expropriated and emptied of their inhabitants—thus raising the area of the camp to 15.5 square miles.[61] The purpose of this expansion began to be manifest about a year thereafter.

It was determined in advance that Jews in the Generalgouvernement would not be paid wages for the "educational process." When the work of professionals and skilled laborers was organized by the labor bureaus, the Jews received wages that were 20 percent lower than those of the rest of the workers.[62] Yet even this salary was usually not paid to them, being transferred directly to the authorities, particularly the SS. In December 1940 the Judenräte in a number of cities were instructed to form trade unions for artisans—membership being mandatory, of course.[63] This order was related to a discovery that surprised Frank, namely, that the Jews were good skilled workers. The Germans, moreover, felt constrained to use them and, thus, somehow to protect them. At a meeting of department heads of his ministry, Frank stated, "The Jews in the Generalgouvernement are not always degenerate figures but rather a vital factor in professional work.... We cannot teach the Poles either the energy or the talents [necessary] to replace the Jews."[64]

The Ghetto

As early as October 1938, Göring had raised the possibility of closing the Jews within ghettos along with using them as a work force. As noted before, this measure was also discussed in the meeting held after Kristallnacht (see chap. 4). The wording of Heydrich's express letter makes it clear that he regarded the ghetto not as a permanent institution, but as a temporary concentration until it proved possible to achieve the ultimate solution to the problem by disposing of the Jews. During the first months of the occupation, a few isolated and random attempts were made to establish ghettos and thus segregate the Jewish population from the Poles. The first known instance of the establishment of a ghetto was in December 1939 in Łęczyca, but it was not turned into a closed ghetto until January 1941. The pace of ghettoization in Warthegau began to pick up in February 1940, whereas the rest of the Eastern districts contained a high concentration of Jews in labor camps, so that few ghettos were established in them. A prominent example of the way in which large communities were depopulated was the fate of Kalisz— one of the oldest Jewish communities in Poland with a population of twenty thousand at the outbreak of the war. Both Germans and Poles joined in brutal pogroms against the Jews. Some 20 percent of the Jewish population managed to flee; thousands were deported into the Generalgouvernement, and countless others fled in the wake of the deportations, with some seven thousand reaching Warsaw. The healthy men remaining in Kalisz were sent to work in the camp, whereas the ailing were slaughtered in a nearby forest. By October 1940 only a few hundred Jews were left in the city.[65]

At the beginning of October 1939, the first ghetto in the Generalgouvernement was established in Piotrków, in the Radom District, but it remained open. The first to be established in a systematic fashion was the **Łódź** ghetto. It had been planned since December 10 when the governor of the Kalisz–Łódź District, Friedrich Übelhör, wrote a secret memorandum on "The Establishment of a Ghetto in the City of Łódź." He set out from the premise that it was impossible to evacuate immediately the 320,000 Jews he believed were living there (according to the Jewish estimate, the number was originally around 230,000, but in May 1940 the population of the ghetto numbered only about 160,000).[66] Übelhör proposed that two actions be executed in tandem. The first was to close off most of the Jewish population in the northern part of the city, where the majority of the Jews lived, and to transfer the Jews from other parts of Łódź to this area. The second was to select those fit to labor and concentrate them in another ghetto, actually a labor camp, where they would be organized into labor battalions. To prepare this operation, Übelhör summoned a team made up of representatives of the National Socialist Party, the Łódź municipality, the Order Police and the Security Police, the SS Death Heads (Totenkopf), the Bureau of Industry and Commerce, the Finance Department, and his own office of district governor (Regierungspräsident) with himself as chairman. The first step was to fix the borders of the ghetto and work out the problems of transport through the streets incorporated into the closed section of the city. The place for the resettlement of the Germans and Poles who would have to be evacuated from the area earmarked for the ghetto had to be chosen. Among other factors that required planning were the sealing and guarding of the ghetto and provisions for medical care, sewage, refuse removal, burials, and the fuel necessary for heating.

Once these preparations were completed, the ghetto would be established in one day at a predetermined time, "in a single stroke." A Jewish body for self-administration headed by the Elder of the Jews (Judenälteste) and a large community administration was to be established within the ghetto immediately. The Council of Elders (Ältestenrat) would be responsible for creating individual departments to deal with nutrition, health, finances, security, living quarters, and registration. Foods and other supplies were to be provided only in exchange for merchandise such as textiles and other goods. "In this way we shall succeed in dispossessing the Jews of the valuable assets they have hoarded and hidden." The apartments belonging to Jews who were unfit for labor and who were to be disposed of by sending them to the ghetto would be confiscated and preserved.[67]

Certain changes notwithstanding, the general outline set down here remained characteristic of all the ghettos. In most places, including Łódź, the distinction between Jews who were fit or unfit for labor was not observed. Instead, the overwhelming majority of the Jews were interned in ghettos and the laborers were brought to places of work outside. According to this plan, the ghetto and the labor camps were designed for only a transitional period. Übelhör concluded his remarks, "The establishment of the ghetto is naturally only an interim measure. When and how the ghetto and the city of Łódź will be purged of Jews is something I reserve for my exclusive decision. In any case, however, the final aim will be to burn this fraternity of pestilence to the end."[68]

At first it was planned that the Łódź ghetto would be liquidated by October 1,

1940. Indeed, by then the ghetto had the appearance of "a kind of detention camp or concentration camp" and existed primarily for the purpose of sifting out all the goods and valuables owned by the Jews.[69] The actual preparations for establishing the ghetto in Łódź focused primarily on three spheres: (1) the deportation of as many Jews as possible, with preference given to the wealthy, the educated, and the community leadership, if they had not managed to flee by then; (2) the confiscation of property on as broad a scale as possible; and (3) terrifying the Jews by harassment, depriving the population of food, and abducting people for labor. At the time Übelhör was writing his memorandum, the first deportation train left Łódź carrying most of the members of the first Judenrat, who had been arrested about a month earlier in the most brutal manner and had been kept in a quarantine camp under relentless torture by members of the *Volksdeutsche* Auxiliary Police. One of the community elders was killed on the trumped-up charge of having raised his hand to a policeman. The news of his execution was relayed to the rest of the prisoners in this way, "Contemptible Jews: Take the dirty, lice-ridden clothing of the filthy Jew who dared to raise his hand to a German."[70]

In the middle of January, the German authorities began the large-scale confiscation of property and held a thorough discussion on how to expropriate the real estate of the Jews and whom to appoint as trustees. They were especially interested in seizing the warehouses owned by Jews. A list of the goods they sought included all kinds of textiles, metals, kitchen wares, household goods, electrical appliances, and the like. In addition to expropriating the warehouses, the stock in Jewish stores was confiscated, and the list of items found in them included food, drugs, and cosmetics. Special warehouses were set up for collecting all the goods. The confiscation of the furniture in the evacuated apartments was left to the Łódź municipality, but its efforts to combat the wholesale looting by Germans, *Volksdeutche,* and Poles were futile.[71]

The "single stroke" in the form of the order establishing a ghetto descended on the Jews of Łódź on February 8, 1940. According to the official decree, the transfer to marked sections of streets and buildings was to follow the instructions issued hourly each day; in fact, chaos reigned for weeks as the transfer wore on. As a rule the Jews were given no more than minutes to get a few belongings together, with the rest of their property being abandoned to the looting Germans and Poles.

The Łódź ghetto was closed on April 30, 1940, with the city's mayor issuing the following order to the Elder of the Jews, Mordekhai Chaim Rumkowski (see chap. 7):

> I charge you . . . with the implementation of all the measures that are presently necessary, or will be necessary in the future, to maintain orderly social life in the residential area [*Wohngebiet*] of the Jews. You must particularly ensure an orderly economic life, nutrition, the duty of labor, health, and welfare assistance. Toward that end, you are authorized to determine all the necessary measures and orders and to carry them out with the aid of the Order Service under your control. . . . Negotiations with the German authorities will be conducted by you alone or by your deputy in the administration, whom you must appoint.[72]

Thus Judenälteste Rumkowski was charged with duties such as commercial and economic activities and assuring the supply of food, duties that were usually handled by the municipality or, in a free society, by the citizenry itself. Normally, these spheres, including the labor market, require control or organization in either war or peace; thus they are tended to by the highest ruling authority, usually the government itself. But in this case responsibility for them all—including seeing to housing in the insufferably crowded ghetto and to sanitation in a quarter that lacked sewers—fell upon a single man—one who had little experience in administration, to say nothing of politics; one in whom the public had not expressed its confidence; and one whose authority derived from the edict of a tyrannical regime. Rumkowski served that regime on penalty of death, and to carry out his duties he was equipped with a policing mechanism made up of Jews who were likewise residents of the ghetto: the Jewish police, called the Order Service (Ordnungsdienst).

Without question the Germans knew perfectly well that the task they had placed upon Rumkowski was an impossible one. Indeed, the formula they had devised was meant to ensure the maximum loss of population during the period allotted for the ghetto's existence while facilitating the seizure of the property left behind. To supervise this process the Germans required Rumkowski to be meticulous in his registration of the ghetto's inhabitants and provide them every week with exact lists noting the religion and nationality of all the residents. He was also ordered to draw up lists of all the property in Jewish hands (other than the bare necessities required to meet clothing, nutritional, and housing needs) and to confiscate it, "as all Jewish property was regarded by the laws of the Reich as expropriated." Forced to work without pay, the Jews would presumably self-destruct and disappear on their own by "natural death." The components of the method by which the Germans intended to "do away with the pistules of pestilence" were intolerable living and sanitary conditions, financial ruin, hunger, hard labor, epidemics, terror, and internal social disintegration—all to be achieved by the Judenrat's administration of the ghetto through the instrument of the Jewish police. The ghetto's function was essentially no different from that of the labor camp: both were designed to exploit the Jews and to destroy them "naturally." Josef Goebbels called the ghettos "death caskets," and Alfred Rosenberg decreed that "'living space' for the Jews should be *Lebensraum* in the opposite direction."[73]

Without doubt, considerable importance was ascribed to the systematic starvation of the population trapped in the ghettos. We have evidence that Hitler was aware of the debilitating effect of hunger as far back as the start of his political career. In notes penned in his own hand in the early 1920s, for the purpose of clarifying his outlook and aims for himself, he blamed the Jews for the difficult economic situation then prevailing in Germany and posited the following theses:

> Racial suicide
> Prerequisite for this is
> *mass madness*
> which can be manufactured

through mass misery—*hunger,*

starvation as a weapon
  in all times
starvation in the service of the Jews.

Destroys physical strength and health
and addles the brain

    Systematic starvation of the nation
      by [raising the cost of living].

      Jewish Domination and Starvation of the People

Jews left to themselves are poor.
(Only flourish [in] foreign bodies)

    (Effects like those of creepers)[74]

The implication of these telegraphic notes is clear: the Jews had used starvation to wrest control of the German people. Deprivation of the masses leads to derangement, meaning the suicide of the race (in this case the Aryan race, of course). Thus, care must be taken to remove the Jews from the foreign body (of the nations) and ensure that they remain isolated among themselves, for then they will be destitute and will choke, as though caught in the grip of a creeper. Indeed, the Nazis ascribed to the ghetto the role of the place in which the Jewish race would commit suicide.

Supervision of this process in Łódź was assigned to a special department called the Ghetto Administration headed by Hans Biebow. A loyal Nazi with an academic education, Biebow had been a wholesaler in Bremen and was sent to Łódź specifically for the purpose of running the ghetto on behalf of the municipality. He created a complex bureaucracy to which Rumkowski was responsible—though this apparatus did not prevent the direct intervention of the police and the SS whenever they deemed it necessary or possible. A Special Squad (Sonderkommando) of the Criminal Police (Kriminalpolizei, or Kripo) that viewed its main role as accelerating and supervising the expropriation of property was set up in the ghetto in the second half of May. The reason given for its creation was, "In the final analysis, about 250,000 Jews are living in the ghetto, and most of them are confirmed criminals, to one degree or another." The police confiscated valuables in such quantities that the Ghetto Administration finally protested their activities and succeeded in restraining them, thereby keeping most of the plunder for itself.[75]

The basic lines of the method of "natural death" were followed in all the ghettos established in occupied Poland from 1940 to 1942. Not all of them were hermetically closed like the Łódź ghetto; in some, Jews were permitted to leave and Poles to enter, occasionally during specified hours. Moreover, quite a few ghettos were initially left open and were closed at some point thereafter.

In other places the process of establishing a ghetto was not effected as quickly as in Łódź. For example, in **Warsaw,** one-third of whose residents were Jews, the process took a year. The Gestapo and SS tried to establish a ghetto immediately after the fall of the city, at the beginning of October 1939. As the Generalgouvernement was still governed by the army then, they used the name of the general in command in the order relayed to the Warsaw Judenrat. But the heads of the council made this order known to the military government, and the plan was canceled. In January 1940 the idea was revived. The Jews were to be concentrated in the most heavily populated Jewish area in the north of the city. The main reason given for isolating them was the danger that a typhus epidemic would spread through the city. In March 1940 the Germans declared a quarantine of the Jewish residential area *(Seuchensperrgebiet),* and at the end of the month the Judenrat was ordered to erect a wall around the "infected area."

After long months of discussions, in August 1940 it was decided to shut the Jews of Warsaw in their own sector. On October 2, a year after the first attempt to create a ghetto, the governor of Warsaw, Ludwig Fischer, issued the order to begin transferring the Jews to the area specified for them. Ten days later, on October 12, the Judenrat was informed of the decision, and two days after that it was officially announced to the general public.

In Warsaw, as in Łódź, the governor of the city was in charge of establishing the ghetto. As the argument went, this operation rested on three basic premises: (1) for political and ideological reasons, it was necessary to distinguish between Jews and Poles; (2) the Jews were the main force behind the black market, and the economy could not be rehabilitated without removing them from it; (3) the Jews posed a serious health hazard to the German army and administration because they were infected with communicable diseases. This last reason in particular was widely publicized by a propaganda campaign that stressed the connection between Jews, lice, and typhus. Biology professor Ludwig Hirszfeld, a convert to Christianity, was incarcerated in the ghetto and wrote after the war, "You come up against walls and barbed wire at any turn. This is the way the authorities hoped to isolate the carriers of the deadly germs. People calling themselves doctors supported this theory. [But] science long ago abolished medieval quarantines, not only because they were inhumane but because they were inefficient. Inefficient? Why, their intention is not to wipe out an epidemic but to eradicate the Jews."[76]

As in Łódź, it was necessary to evacuate Poles from the area of the ghetto in order to bring Jews in. October 31 was initially set as the final day of the operation in which 140,000 Poles and over 100,000 Jews were to move, but owing to difficulties in execution it was necessary to extend the deadline to November 15. Actually, the move was not completed by that date either, but the ghetto was closed on November 16 anyway, and the Jews who deliberately kept their businesses and most of their belongings outside it no longer had access to them. The ghetto covered 2.4 percent of the city's area and had 30 percent of the city's population crowded into it. Only seventy-three of the city's eighteen hundred streets were included therein, and some not even along their entire length. The ghetto's border was 11 miles long, and the wall constructed around it was 10 feet high. Estimates as to the number of Jews living behind it on January 1, 1941, range from 300,000 to 400,000. At first there were twenty-two gates and other openings in the wall, but by April 1941 over half of them had been blocked and only thirteen remained, with this number, too, steadily decreasing in time.[77]

The creation of the Warsaw ghetto entailed special problems because of its size and the number of inhabitants it was to contain, the economic power wielded by the Jews of Warsaw, and the economic import ascribed to the Polish capital. The internal struggles among the various authorities of the German administration reached their peak over this issue, because (as in Łódź) the Jewish population was regarded as a source of wealth that would enhance the power of the government agencies controlling it.[78]

Each of the civilian officials and leading members of the SS and the police tried to extend his control over the Jews of Warsaw and do with them as he pleased. As a result conflicting orders were issued, and Adam Czerniakow, the head of the Jewish Council, scurried from office to office and from one man to the next trying to get the German decrees revoked or at least mitigated. Often the Germans resorted to deception, each official or officer claiming that he was not authorized to decide on the matter at hand and sending the Jewish supplicant to another party, only to hear the same disclaimer repeated. Every order was, of course, accompanied by threats of what would befall the leaders of the Judenrat and all the people affected by it if it were not obeyed to the full.

The administrative system of the Warsaw ghetto was copied from the one introduced in Łódź. About a month before its actual establishment, a delegation of fifteen high-level officials led by District Governor Fischer visited Łódź to study how the ghetto there was run. This system was later copied for Warsaw as well as for most of the other ghettos, large and small.[79] Following the system of strict supervision developed by the Ghetto Administration in Łódź, the Warsaw Judenrat was ordered to submit detailed weekly and monthly reports on all aspects of life in the ghetto, including finances, demography, the economy, employment, and health. To produce them the ghetto's Jewish administration not only had to develop an extensive bureaucracy but had to employ professionals such as accountants, statisticians, and economists.[80]

However, in one field—the economy—the administration of the Warsaw ghetto differed in principle from the system followed in Łódź. In the latter all economic activity was concentrated in the hands of Rumkowski and his administration, whereas the economic activities in Warsaw were divided among a variety of private factors. In December 1940 the Transferstelle (Transfer Authority) was established for the purpose of centralizing the supervision of all economic activity within the ghetto. According to the initial conception of this bureau, its role was to bring food and goods into the ghetto; supply Jewish workers with jobs both within and outside the ghetto; serve as an intermediary in all economic transactions between the ghetto and the surrounding world; supervise the Trusteeship Bureau, which handled the Aryanization of property; and oversee the management of warehouses and private businesses. However, this approach did not succeed in Warsaw, and the Economic Department of Frank's administration realized that it was choking the ghetto's economy. Frank's officials wanted to exploit the productive potential of the Jewish population as much as possible while not abandoning the ultimate objective of annihilating the Jews. Therefore, they decided, in a meeting on April 19, 1941, to establish workshops as a means of easing the ghetto's economic isolation so that certain branches of its industry could receive orders directly from Polish clients and German firms. In addition, special Jewish economic institutions were to be established so that the Jews could manage and finance commerce and production by themselves.[81] Max Bischof of the Gestapo was appointed to head the Transferstelle in place of an official from the Łódź Ghetto Administration. There can be no doubt that the liberalization was prompted by the growing need to supply the army in anticipation of the war against Russia. Its significance from a Jewish standpoint will be discussed in chapter 7.

Prominent among the means of control the Germans exercised over the Jews was the tactic of collective responsibility, which proved equally effective in large and small communities, ghettos, and camps. This approach entailed having the entire community, or a certain portion thereof, pay the price for the act of an individual that the Germans deemed a grave infringement of their rule, honor, or interests. Collective punishment was one of the devices whose effect was to stifle resistance—Polish as well as Jewish—to oppression and terror. The Jewish community of Warsaw was introduced to its implications at the very start of the German occupation in Warsaw. On November 13, 1939, two Polish policemen entered a building at 9 Nalewki Street to arrest a man they sought as a criminal. A scuffle broke out in the course of which the suspect shot and killed one of the policemen. In retaliation, the Germans arrested all the men who were in the building at the time—fifty-three in number, including some who happened to be visiting. Czerniakow tried to negotiate their release through the SS and was told to pay 300,000 zlotys (U.S. $36,145) ransom. Naturally he understood that the people would be released in return for the payment. He raised the sum with great difficulty and proceeded to pay it in installments, only to discover after the last payment was made that all fifty-three men had already been executed. The report of this incident in the official German paper *Krakauer Zeitung* had it that the Polish policeman was killed by a "Jewish gang" and that the tenants of the building had interfered with the search, which is why fifty-three of them were killed.[82]

On October 2, 1940, while settling the arrangements for creating a ghetto in Warsaw, Fischer ordered the mayors of cities and towns throughout the Warsaw District to begin establishing ghettos.[83] As usual, not everyone waited for an order, and in some places a ghetto, or "Jewish residential area," was created even earlier. Most of the ghettos that came into being that year were set up between July 1940 and January 1941, though the movement in this direction was still limited and was felt even less in the Radom, Lublin, and Cracow districts.

The Jewish Policy in the Occupied Countries of Northern and Western Europe

With the conquest of northern and western Europe, the Germans encountered Jewish communities that had long enjoyed equal rights and whose members identified with their native lands as full citizens in every respect. In addition to this fully integrated native Jewish population, each of the occupied countries—Norway, Denmark, Luxembourg, Holland, Belgium, and France—also hosted Jews who had arrived between the two wars or in the wake of the Nazi persecution in Germany, Austria, and Czechoslovakia. Before the invasion began on the western front, in February 1940 it was decided that the German occupying forces in Belgium and Holland would have to conduct themselves according to dictates of international law and refrain from any acts of violence or pillage so as to avoid creating the impression that Germany intended to annex these countries. The directives to this effect included the statement, "No initiative should be taken on the racial issue. . . . One must not support special actions against an inhabitant *solely* because he is a Jew."[84] Ultimately, the German approach toward the Jewish population in each of these countries was determined by local conditions. Although these were a composite of many factors, the primary and often decisive one was the form of the German administration. Also of import was the degree of independence that the government of the occupied country was able to assert and the attitude of the local population toward the Jews. As a rule the Nazis tried to replicate the methods they had used within the Reich, but they applied them in the occupied countries at a swifter pace.

In **France** the Jewish problem was treated with greater urgency than in the rest of the occupied countries, both because it was a highly complex matter and because its "solution" held promise of greater spoils than could be expected in the smaller states. The intricacy of the Jewish problem in France stemmed from both the division of the country into two zones—one occupied by German troops, the other ostensibly free under the Vichy regime—and the presence of many foreign Jews within France. It is very difficult to establish the exact number of Jews who were then in France or the breakdown of this population by country of origin. Many of these Jews were in France illegally, and there was a constant fluctuation in the refugee population as its members went on to emigrate overseas or even return to Germany (all in all, 50,000 refugees passed through France in the 1930s). Over 150,000 Jewish refugees had entered France since World War I, 40 percent of them coming from Germany, Austria, and Czechoslovakia and the rest from Eastern Europe or the Balkans. The East Europeans settled mostly in Paris, where they made up about 90,000 of the city's total Jewish population of 150,000. In contrast, the number of German Jews living in Paris at the outbreak of the war was estimated at about 10,000. Hence, native French Jews constituted, at most, only one-third of the capital's Jewish population.[85]

Many of the Jewish refugees who had been living in France for years never acquired French citizenship, so that the Germans had to adapt their attitude toward them as subjects of such friendly states as Slovakia, Hungary, and Rumania, lest they prejudice Germany's relations with those governments. To the native and immigrant Jews who, together with the general population, fled southward to Vichy France we must add Jews who had been expelled from Alsace-Lorraine and the refugees who were pouring in primarily from Belgium, though also from Luxembourg and Holland, in search of refuge from Nazi persecution. The Jews coming from Belgium included a substantial number of refugees who had originated in yet other countries.[86]

Thus, by the summer of 1940 the Jewish problem had become a highly pressing one for the regime in southern France, and the first orders limiting the rights
of the Jews were, in fact, issued by the Vichy French. July 17, 1940, saw the publication of an order prohibiting the employment by public and government institutions of any aliens not born in France—the intent, of course, being Jews—
unless they or their sons had served in the army. About a month later, on August
16, a second order was issued prohibiting aliens to practice as physicians, dentists,
or pharmacists. This order applied to the French colonies as well—its object there
being the Jews in North Africa. These regulations were the first sign of the evolving
policy modeled on the steps taken in Germany from 1933 onward.[87]

The German administration in the occupied zone did not begin to take action
against the Jews until the end of September 1940. The definition of a Jew according to the Nuremberg Laws was published on September 27, after which the
regional and local French authorities were told to take a census of the Jews following these guidelines. Three weeks later, on October 18, the registration of Jewish-owned businesses and factories began in response to the demand to appoint
temporary trustees for them. The military government had decided not to disrupt
the French economy any more than necessary, and on November 1 it issued an
order to have French trustees appointed for Jewish businesses so that the French
population could also benefit from the purge of the Jews from the economy. On
November 12 this trend was consummated by an order to sell Jewish businesses
or expropriate them for Aryanization.[88]

In the meanwhile, far from standing idly by, on October 3, 1940, the Vichy
government published the Jewish Statute *(Statut des Juifs),* which embraced the
definition of a Jew established in the Nuremberg Laws. From then on even French
Jews were forbidden to hold any post in the public or government administration,
the army, the educational system, the judicial system, or the film industry.
Exempted from this rule were people "who have given outstanding service to the
French nation in literature, science, and the arts."[89] The statute applied throughout France, not only in the zone of the Vichy government (though not in Algeria,
the French protectorates, or the colonies), for under the terms of the armistice the
laws of the Vichy government were valid throughout the country. Henri-Philippe
Pétain and his government were also interested in ensuring that France received
its share of the confiscated Jewish property and it was to Germany's advantage to
have the French institute anti-Jewish actions. The day after the *Statut des Juifs*
was published, masses of foreign Jews in the free zone were arrested and incarcerated in camps. By the end of 1940, thirty thousand foreign Jews had been arrested
in Vichy France, compared with twenty thousand in the German-occupied zone.[90]

At the same time, the pace of Aryanization did not meet the Germans' expectations because the French displayed a certain reluctance to take over Jewish businesses. Naturally, the Germans themselves, particularly the owners of the large
industrial concerns, were very interested in the Jewish factories and tried to
acquire them by whatever means possible. Still, the Aryanization process took
years, touched only one-third of the Jewish enterprises, and was completed for
only 21.5 percent of them.[91]

The Germans displayed particular interest in the art treasures owned by Jews in general and by the Rothschild family in particular. They had also pillaged the art treasures in the East, but now Alfred Rosenberg established a Special Action Team for Art (Sonderstab Bildende Kunst) whose work was based on an order personally issued by Hitler on September 17, 1940. Rosenberg's men carried out a methodical search of the castles belonging to the Rothschild family and the homes of other Jewish collectors. Their report summarizing the period from 1940 to 1944 described how, after seizing the art collections on display, they systematically combed storage facilities (mostly of moving companies) and the apartments of Jews who had fled, emigrated, or were deported to the East in search of art that the Jews were trying to conceal—sometimes by using French names. "The unquestionably Jewish origin of the owners was determined in cooperation with the French police and the [German] Security Police, as well as on the basis of the Action Team's political source material, and in each case it was proved on the basis of documents." Rosenberg complained that the French authorities deliberately impeded these investigations, while the French trustees also made things difficult by camouflaging Jewish property. The Germans, he claimed, were merely protecting the art treasures and ensuring that they would not be smuggled out of Europe. As usual, Hitler and the other leaders of the Reich were the beneficiaries of the plunder, with most of the booty being concealed in caches in Germany. Over the years, 29 transports comprising 137 railroad cars carrying 4,174 crates that contained 21,903 items—paintings, furniture, and various kinds of objets d'art of all periods originating from all over the world—were shipped out of France.[92]

Developments in France also influenced the condition of the Jews in the French protectorates in North Africa. The sultan of **Morocco** ostensibly assured his more than 160,000 Jewish subjects equal rights, and to a certain extent the autonomy extended to the Jewish community regarding laws of personal status also protected them. Thus the *Statut des Juifs* was not officially in effect in Morocco. Nevertheless, beginning on October 31, 1940, the French authorities issued one order after the next imposing some of the laws of the Vichy regime on the Jews—and even interpreted them in radical terms. The racial principle was applied throughout the French administration in Morocco, with the result that Jewish officials were summarily dismissed. An atmosphere hostile to the Jews was generated among the public at large, and contact between Jews and the French population in Morocco came to an end. Jews were barred from entering the swimming pool in Casablanca, for example, and Jewish youngsters were drummed out of the scouting movement. Worse yet, Jews were discriminated against in the distribution of food.[93]

The Jewish population of **Tunisia** numbered 90,000 people, most of them merchants and artisans (as was also true in Morocco). During the 1930s hostility toward the Jews intensified, but when riots broke out in one of the cities, the bey used the army to restore order. The Jews enjoyed a recognized independent status that was nullified when the *Statut des Juifs* went into effect on November 30, 1940. First to be affected were the Jews employed in the public services, but soon limitations were placed on the number of pupils and teachers in the schools and there was a decline in the number of people practicing the free professions.

The North African country most closely tied to France was **Algeria,** where French rule had existed for over a century and the Jews were deeply rooted in French society, its language, and culture. In 1940 there were 117,000 Jews in Algeria, most of them employed in the crafts, industry, and commerce. Even so, a large percentage of this population was indigent, with about half of it living in one-room apartments. The Jews in Algeria were protected by the law as full-fledged French citizens. But the Algerian nationalist movement was anti-Semitic, and its attacks on the Jews grew more vigorous. The 1934 anti-Jewish riots that broke out in the city of Constantine had repercussions among the Jewish public in Europe precisely because Algerian Jewry enjoyed equal rights.[94] Pressure on the Jews increased after the outbreak of the war, and the Vichy *Statut des Juifs* was imposed in Algeria as early as October 18, 1940. Even before that, however, on October 7, the Crémieux Statute (of 1865), which assured the Jews French citizenship, was rescinded.[95]

The German regime in **Belgium** was similar to that in northern France; in fact, the orders of the military government were issued by the commander of the occupying army in Belgium and northern France, General Alexander von Falkenhausen. The first order was published on October 28, 1940, and like the Vichy regulations, it, too, followed the German example by prohibiting Jews to work in the public services. Its provisions extended to lawyers; teachers at all levels, including university instructors; newspaper editors; and people working in broadcasting. The date by which Jews had to relinquish these positions was December 31, 1940. A second order defined who was a Jew and required that a census be taken. The Belgian government-in-exile in London responded to these measures on January 10, 1941, in declaring all the orders of the German military authorities null and void. It also promised to see to the return of confiscated property and the punishment of all collaborators. Sharp protests were also voiced in Belgium itself.[96]

In **Holland** the process of discriminating against the Jews began at the end of September 1940, when the ruling Reichskommissar, who had the SS as his instrument of enforcement, demanded that the Dutch public administration officials attest to their Aryan origin. The ruling also stated that "public judicial bodies will not appoint or hire, permanently or temporarily, people who are full or partial Jews; will not take them on by means of a contract; and will not promote them."[97] This order, it was claimed, related only to the hiring of new employees, but as early as November all the Jews and the offspring of Jews were fired from their jobs. On October 22 the Germans demanded the registration of Jewish businesses; in January they ordered a census of the Jews. The Jewish press in Holland had been banned in September 1940. No protest or resistance was expressed by the Dutch public administration, but most of the churches, Protestant and Catholic alike, decried the anti-Jewish measures both in approaches to the German authorities and in public statements. A sharp protest was also expressed by professors and students at the University of Leiden, though none of these denunciations had any practical effect.[98]

The publication of the German orders was accompanied by terror actions, especially against the impoverished population concentrated in the Jewish quarter of Amsterdam, which the Germans declared a "visual ghetto" but did not subject to the same regime they had instituted in the East. Some of the Jews organized for self-defense, and there were instances of clashes between Jews and Dutch Nazis, even German policemen. When a member of the Dutch Storm Troopers was killed and a German guard troop was attacked, the Germans resorted to collective punishment by closing off the Jewish quarter and arresting 430 young people, who were deported to concentration camps in the Reich. Most of them perished within months—about fifty in Buchenwald and the rest in Mauthausen in Austria—with only one man surviving. In response to this action, the Amsterdam dockworkers went out on strike. In essence, this was a Communist-inspired protest action that arose out of the general unrest prompted by the German demand that Dutch workers be sent to Germany. The strike was suppressed and petered out after two days (February 25–26, 1941).[99] But it appears that on the basis of this experience, the Germans concluded they would have to separate Jewish affairs from general politics, see to the complete segregation of the Jewish population, and effect their anti-Jewish measures step by step. Earlier, they had established a Judenrat—the first in Western Europe—and now they used its two chairmen, Professor David Cohen and the diamond merchant Abraham Asscher, to help defuse the resistance movement in the Jewish and general public. Both these men assumed they could protect the Jews by negotiating with the Germans, and the Nazis allowed them to hold to this belief (see chap. 8).[100]

Even though the SS was the ruling force in **Norway,** at first the small Jewish community was not seriously disturbed. But there, too, in the autumn of 1940 a prohibition was issued against employing Jews in the free professions. However, an exceptional situation prevailed in **Denmark,** where the government actually defended the rights of the Jews. An agreement on cooperation between the German occupation force and the Danish government included the tacit condition that the Germans would not assail the Jewish citizens of the country. During the first years of the occupation, the Danish government insisted that this condition be honored, and the Germans appreciated that it was not worth their while to violate it. Hence, the Jews in Denmark continued living their lives much like the rest of the country's citizens and felt no special pressure.

Germany, Austria, and the Protectorate

In **Germany** proper the actions taken against the Jews became steadily harsher. With the outbreak of the war against Poland, the Germans incarcerated Jews of Polish origin still living in Germany in concentration camps, and by the beginning of 1940 their number had reached about 35,000. The supply of food, clothing, and other daily needs to the Jews was reduced. On February 6, 1940, for instance, an order was published allowing the Jews to purchase RM 0.20 (U.S. $0.05) worth of sewing materials only once every three months. The Jews were not issued ration cards for clothing, shoes, and soles. They failed to receive some basic foodstuffs at all and were generally given only half an hour to conduct their purchases. Germans who sold Jews more than the permitted allotment of food or other goods were fined. Yet, at the same time, Jews were drafted by the thousands for hard labor in the cities and on farms, and their remaining property—including public institutions such as hospitals—was confiscated.[101]

For all that, the deportation from western Germany was in a class by itself. After the fall of France, the Germans expelled into the Vichy zone 22,000 French Jews from Alsace-Lorraine, which had been annexed to Germany. Following this action, on October 22 these deportees were joined by 6,504 Jews from the German secondary states of Baden and the Palatinate as well as more than 500 others from the Saar region. With Heydrich's agreement, based on Hitler's orders, the operation was conducted by two Gauleiters, Robert Walter and Josef Bürkel.[102]

As the man responsible for organizing the deportations, Eichmann had to handle the transport. This involved certain difficulties because a ban on Jews moving from one zone to another in France essentially made a deportation of this sort illegal. It was not at all certain that Eichmann would succeed at his task. Indeed, he received a contingency order that if he failed, he was to transfer the Jews to a concentration camp (in the Reich). He described the operation thus, "With this shipment I got as far as Saône sur Chalon, which is the last train station in occupied France. Problems cropped up there. I negotiated with the director of this last station in the occupied area. Finally it was agreed that we would mark this transport as a shipment of the Wehrmacht, which was subject to agreements that would make it possible to transfer shipments of this sort." Further on in this statement, Eichmann related that he personally had made the necessary declaration regarding the army shipments.[103] The Jews were taken to the concentration camps of Gurs, Les Miles, and Rivesaltes. The transport that included mostly ailing and elderly people and children was conducted with extreme cruelty, following the pattern that Eichmann and his men had established in Poland. Many of the deportees died along the way or succumbed to the harsh conditions in the camps. The Germans explained this action to the French by intimating that they intended to deport the Jews to Madagascar at a later date. It appears that in the wake of this operation, they reached the conclusion that the difficulties involved in deportations to the West were excessive; at any rate, they did not repeat the action.

The condition of the Jews who still remained in **Austria** was inordinately grave, and the threat of deportation constantly hovered over them. After the thorough plunder of their property, which had begun in 1938, the Jews of Austria were left with the most meager of resources, and many would not have been able to subsist had it not been for the aid they received from JDC. Eichmann continued to exert relentless pressure on the Jews to spur their emigration from Austria, from Germany, and from the Protectorate of Bohemia-Moravia. Emigration was to serve the dual purpose of ridding the area of Jews while bringing in foreign currency, which would presumably be paid in exchange for their release. That, at least, is how Himmler portrayed the situation to his men.[104] Moreover, the Gestapo continued to cooperate with the people organizing the illegal immigration to Palestine even in the midst of the war.

A systematic operation to confiscate Jewish property was also mounted in the **Protectorate** of Bohemia-Moravia; the orders tailored to facilitate the plunder of this property were published in Prague in January 1940. Once again, the formula followed the lines that had been developed from the spring of 1938 through the publication of Frank's orders in Poland: all property was to be registered; the free sale of businesses and valuables was prohibited; accounts were frozen; and there were explicit orders as to when certain businesses were to be closed. Special emphasis was placed on the fact that jewelry was to be registered but could also be sold under supervision—a provision that practically assured it would go for less than its actual value.[105] A few hundred Polish Jews living in the Protectorate were loaded onto trains and deported to an unknown destination. By the end of the summer of 1939, Eichmann had ordered the concentration of the Jewish communities, first in Prague and then in other cities as well. Of the 120 Jewish communities in the Protectorate, only 18 remained at the beginning of 1940. The Jews were placed under a curfew, and a special hunt was launched to catch anyone who violated this order so that they could be subject to heavy fines. The Nazis had sold all Jewish-owned stocks in February 1940. Since the economic situation was difficult, the Prague community was often short of funds, so much so that it was unable to maintain its soup kitchen.[106] About ninety thousand Jews continued to live in the Protectorate under these conditions.

In the western areas annexed to the Reich, the Germans followed the model established in the Eastern districts to a certain degree. We have already mentioned the deportation of the Jews of Alsace-Lorraine to southern France. A similar strategy was adopted in **Luxembourg,** where close to four thousand Jews had been living prior to the occupation, about one-quarter of them refugees. Luxembourg fell on Sunday, May 10, 1940, and it appears that around one thousand Jews managed to flee during the invasion of France. At the beginning of August the Germans officially announced the annexation of Luxembourg, and a civil administration was established there under Gauleiter Gustav Simon, who governed the area on the left bank of the Rhine between Koblenz and Trier (Treves). By the end of the month, he had already submitted proposals for anti-Jewish measures for Hitler's approval, and his orders were published beginning on September 5. The most important of these edicts proclaimed the confiscation of Jewish property, and within half a year many factories and stores had been transferred to Aryan owners—other than those liquidated on the grounds of a surplus of businesses in specific fields. In addition to land not under cultivation 380 Jewish-owned farms were sold or given over to the management of local farmers. The motivating factor was to step up emigration, and toward that end, on September 12, 1940, Simon announced that unless the community leadership organized the emigration of all the Jews within twenty days, they would be deported on Yom Kippur (the Day of Atonement), which fell on October 12, 1940. However, this order was rescinded. Those who failed to flee or emigrate and were not deported were either concentrated together in Luxembourg or sent to do forced labor in Belgium or France.[107]

Southeastern Europe

A more difficult situation prevailed in the newly independent state of **Slovakia.** According to the 1930 census there were 136,737 Jews living in Slovakia, where

Table 2. Jewish Occupations in Slovakia

Occupation	Jews	General Population
Agriculture and afforestation	7.06%	56.82%
Industry and crafts	20.24	19.07
Commerce and credit businesses	53.04	5.44
Transportation	1.81	4.73
Public services and the free professions	7.34	4.69
Armed forces	0.23	1.62
Other occupations or unskilled	10.28	7.63

Source: Jan Steiner, *Ha-Ḥakikah neged ha-Yehudim ve-Nisholam min ha-Khalkhalah bi-Medinat Slovakia* (Tel Aviv, 1975), p. 8.

they composed 4.11 percent of the population. Table 2 shows the breakdown of the Jewish population by occupation (given in percentages), compared with the population at large.[108]

On November 2, 1938, the First Vienna Award (concluded by Germany and Italy as arbitrators of the territorial dispute between Hungary and Slovakia) established that a sector of southern Slovakia (Felvidék) would be annexed to Hungary. Infuriated, the Slovaks living in the area accused their Jewish neighbors of supporting Hungarian nationalism, attacked them at night, and drove them over the Hungarian border. The Hungarians were not willing to accept them, however, and drove them right back. Hundreds of people of all ages were forced to live for weeks in an open field, and only with great effort was an arrangement found for them.[109]

On March 15, 1939, Hitler took over the Czechoslovak Republic. One day earlier, under the protection of the Nazis, the Slovak leadership had proclaimed an independent state.[110] The new rulers of Slovakia—Monsignor Josef Tiso, head of the clericalist–nationalist Hlinka Party, and his deputy, Professor Vojtech Tuka—copied from their benefactors a number of measures aimed against the Jews. Yet during this early period they still aspired to maintain a certain degree of independence so that they portrayed their anti-Jewish activities as deriving from religious rather than racial principles.

A month after the proclamation of the independent state of Slovakia, on April 18, 1939, the new administration published an order defining the concept of a Jew and imposed restrictions that for the most part affected lawyers. According to the explanation given in the announcement, the concept of a Jew was being defined "out of a desire to rectify the social-welfare, economic, and political conditions within the state of Slovakia." As in Germany in 1933, the government of Slovakia was camouflaging its anti-Jewish measures by trying to make their purpose appear to be the welfare of Slovak society as a whole. Following the Nazi example, the rulers of Slovakia proceeded by means of legislation, propaganda, and terror. The last of these was conducted by the Hlinka Guard (named after its founder, Andreas Hlinka), whose men, like the SA, assaulted Jews and laid synagogues and Jewish cemeteries to waste.

In March 1939 about 90,000 Jews remained in Slovakia. The decline in their number resulted from the reduction in the country's size and the fact that some members of the Jewish community had managed to emigrate overseas or to Palestine. The value of Jewish property, after the deduction of debts, was estimated at 3.2 million Slovakian crowns.[111]

Various orders issued in the course of 1939 proved detrimental to the agricultural economy, Jewish crafts, and innkeepers and wine merchants. At first the government was wary of causing harm to any of the larger Jewish enterprises, which represented an important element of the state's economy, but in the spring of 1940 explicit orders set down restrictions and made it possible to expropriate Jewish concerns. In the meantime, Jews were fired from their jobs in the government and the army, and additional restrictions were imposed on the free professions. The conscription of people for forced labor, especially among the ranks of the unemployed, was also initiated.

After his victory over France, Hitler trained his sights on Slovakia, intent on transforming it into a satellite in the fullest sense of the word. On July 28, 1940, he summoned the Slovak leaders to the so-called Salzburg Meeting and dictated his demands, which included an intensification of anti-Jewish actions.[112] The creation of an oppressive regime over the Jews, following the German example and based on racist anti-Semitism, was envisioned as one way of reducing the influence of the Catholic church and thus advancing German hegemony over Slovakia. The day after this talk with Hitler, Joachim von Ribbentrop ordered the German minister in Slovakia to see to the appointment of German advisers to the Slovak government on matters such as the police, propaganda, the economy, the organization of the Hlinka Guard, and the Jewish problem. At the end of August an "adviser on Jewish affairs," Dieter Wisliceny, was sent to Slovakia; yet he came not on behalf of the Foreign Ministry but from Eichmann's office. Wisliceny worked in cooperation with the official diplomatic representatives of the German Foreign Ministry (the minister then being Manfred von Killinger, who was later transferred to Rumania and was replaced, in turn, by Hans E. Ludin). But most of Wisliceny's work was done in direct contact with the Slovak government, and his aides infiltrated the various ministries that dealt with Jewish affairs.

Slovakia was the first country in which machinery of this sort for handling the Jewish problem was established on the instigation of Himmler and Heydrich. Even though it was not subject to direct Nazi rule, the Slovak satellite joined in striving toward the Nazi aim of ridding Europe of Jews. Until then the SS and the Gestapo had been installed as a guiding or ruling force only in the occupied countries, such as Poland, Holland, and Norway. In France and Belgium, which were ruled by a military government, the program of anti-Jewish measures was not directed by Himmler's emissaries during that period. Thus Slovakia provided Himmler with the opportunity to extend his sphere of direct influence and accelerate the treatment of the Jewish problem according to the Nazi model.

The results were not long in coming. An order issued at the beginning of August, to go into effect on August 30, made the registration of all Jewish property mandatory. But the critical legislative measure was a basic law, Constitutional Law 210, passed by the Slovak Parliament on September 3, 1940, that empowered the government to act in regard to Aryanization. In the following months hundreds of laws and regulations were issued with the aim of undermining the basis of Jewish life in Slovakia by depriving the Jews of their sources of livelihood and all their other rights. The most comprehensive was the Ordinance *Judenkodex* (Jewish Code) of September 9, 1941, comprising 270 articles. Two institutions were created: one a government agency, the other a Jewish one under government supervision. On September 16, 1940, the Central Office for the Economy (Ústredný Hospodársky Úrad, or ÚHÚ) was established to oversee the process of Aryanization.[113] It was subject to the authority of the prime minister, and all the necessary laws and orders were issued on its behalf. The process of expropriation was completed within a year, with the heads of the regime and their close associates benefiting from the plunder. The official who headed the operation, Augustin Morávek, received his training in Germany and applied the theory he had learned with thoroughness and vigor.

Ten days after the establishment of the ÚHÚ (September 26, 1940), the second institution, known as the Center of Jews (Ústredňa Židov, or ÚŽ), was founded and given a mandate to organize Jewish life in Slovakia. In the course of time, it burgeoned into dozens of branches and essentially became a new way of organizing the Jews in a country that was not subject to the direct rule of the Reich. By then there were no longer any nationwide Jewish institutions in any of the occupied countries. The Jewish Council in Holland was not established until half a year later, and even then, like the Judenräte in occupied Poland, it was created primarily for Amsterdam; only later was its jurisdiction extended throughout the country. In fusing the system of the Judenrat developed in Poland with that of a mandatory national organization, like the one that had been operative in Germany since 1939, the apparatus run by Himmler and Heydrich advanced another step toward becoming the prime factor deciding the fate of the Jews in Europe. The ÚŽ was founded as a tool of the government. All the 175 Jewish organizations in Slovakia were disbanded, and their funds, which to a large degree came from JDC, were transferred to the new institution. After these resources ran out, taxes were imposed on the impoverished Jewish population; and as their economic condition deteriorated further, more and more people went on the dole.

Appointed by the government as chairman *(starosta)* of the ten-member council was Heinrich Schwarz, formerly head of the Orthodox kehillot. The ÚŽ's various departments were likewise headed by Jewish officials, many of whom were Zionists. The Center of Jews was a unique institution, and we shall return to discuss its activities.

Of the Balkan states, **Rumania** was perhaps most infamous for its anti-Semitism and the precarious situation of its Jews—along with their struggle, and that of Jewish organizations throughout the world, for their rights. The 1930 census counted 756,930 Jews in Rumania. They were not the only distinct ethnic group in the Rumanian population, for in addition to the Jews, who composed 4.2 percent of the population, there were Hungarians and Germans, Russians and Ukrainians, Bulgarians, Greeks, and Gypsies, together making up 25 percent of the country's population. The government did not take the same approach to all of these minorities; as noted, the Jews were in a particularly bad state. About half the Jewish breadwinners engaged in commerce and banking, many merchants were petty traders, and some 25 percent worked in industry and the crafts. The rest made their living from clerical jobs or the free professions.

Anti-Semitic organizations had long been active in Rumania and were nourished by a widely read anti-Semitic press. During the 1930s these organizations established close ties with the National Socialists in Germany, and the Foreign Policy Department of the Nazi Party, headed by Alfred Rosenberg, stayed in close contact with the anti-Semitic political factions in Rumania. Thus the Rumanian anti-Semitic movement coalesced throughout the decade with German encouragement, including financial support. Among the leading activists were students led by a professor from the University of Jassy (Iași), Alexander K. Cuza. In 1935 this group merged with the National Peasants' Party led by Octavian Goga as the National Christian Party.

The economic depression of the early 1930s had a particularly devastating effect on agriculture, which was the source of livelihood of 78 percent of the Rumanian population. It is, therefore, easy to imagine the farmers' resentment of the Jewish bankers who had extended them credit and of the Jewish merchants who served as middlemen in the distribution of their produce, locally and abroad, when their credit turned into debts they could not cover and markets steadily closed to them. Out of these quarters came the legionnaires of the militant anti-Semitic organization led by Cornelio Z. Codriano, later known as the Iron Guard. From its establishment in 1927, the guard's declared aim had been "to save Rumania from the Jews." It served as a catalyst in the bitter power struggles that raged in Rumania during the 1930s, practicing terror and political assassination. Moreover, in the charged atmosphere of the period, anti-Semitic slogans were common even within the more conservative Rumanian political parties, while the anti-Semitic propaganda disseminated by the press denounced the Jews as parasites, Communists, and enemies of Rumania and the church. Anti-Jewish riots had occurred as far back as the 1920s, but they intensified and spread in the following decade and were joined by statutes and regulations limiting the employment of Jews. The students' demand for a *numerus clausus* became increasingly strident, while doctors, pharmacists, and lawyers found themselves particularly vulnerable to discrimination.

Owing to its electoral success, the Goga–Cuza National Christian Party rose to power at the end of December 1937; although its government lasted only forty days, in that span it managed to enact the most stringent of anti-Jewish laws. It began by ordering a reexamination of Rumanian citizenship, which was directed particularly at the Jews and led to the revocation of the civil rights of one-third of the Jewish population in the autumn of 1939.[114] The influence of the Nuremberg Laws was particularly evident here, and even though King Carol II dismissed this extremist government, many of its laws and regulations remained in force. In essence, the government that followed maintained the same policy, though it conducted itself more cautiously.

After Munich and the dismemberment of Czechoslovakia, Rumania's king was summoned to meet with Hitler on November 24, 1938. At this meeting the führer proposed an expansion of the commercial ties between Rumania and Germany but stressed that he expected rigorous action to be taken against the Jews. Germany's pressure mounted in the spring of 1939 when, in light of the preparations for war, its interest in Rumanian oil increased considerably. It is an intriguing fact that the person who conducted the negotiations on commercial ties between the two countries, Helmut Wohltat, Göring's man, was simultaneously negotiating an agreement with the Western Powers on organizing the emigration of the Jews from Germany. Wohltat saw to it that the commercial pact signed in Bucharest on March 23, 1939, included explicitly anti-Jewish clauses. At the same time, the Rumanian government began to step up its pressure on the Jews to emigrate. With the outbreak of the war, the treatment of the Jews was pursued more aggressively. The covert penetration of German forces into Rumania, primarily by means of the Field Intelligence (Abwehr) headed by Admiral Wilhelm Canaris, began in the autumn of 1939. A year later, at the end of 1940, the German army officially entered the country and quickly established itself on the basis of the footholds it had gained in the course of the year.

Threatened as it was by the USSR on one side and the German Reich on the other, Rumania became so dependent on Germany that in May 1940 it felt constrained to sign an oil agreement it had earlier spurned. Worse yet, it was forced to cede large chunks of territory to its neighbors. The result was considerable ferment in the country that ultimately led to King Carol's abdication. Also characteristic of this period were grave assaults on the Jews in the form of both riots in the summer of 1940 and new laws, the most damaging of which was the Jewish Statute issued on August 8, 1940. These laws banned Jews from serving in government or public positions, limited the number of Jews in all branches of the economy, established a *numerus clausus* in schools and universities, prohibited Jews from working in publishing and the press, extended the examination of the civil rights of Jews, and even prohibited Jews from converting to Christianity. In October of that year, the Rumanianization of Jewish property began, following the model of Aryanization practiced in Germany. Jewish-owned land was expropriated, and the Jews were deprived of the right of ownership in all branches of the economy. As in Germany, these actions were camouflaged by formal statutes. Moreover, following the example of the SA in 1933, the Iron Guard simultaneously mounted terror actions, concentrating most on looting for the benefit of its own members.[115]

While the Jews were expelled from all the trade unions, the legionnaires of the Iron Guard founded cooperatives to replace Jewish trade. Jewish institutions (even schools) were forcibly transferred to the legionnaires. Finally, when the Iron Guard's violent behavior became a threat to the state itself, it was disbanded at the beginning of December 1940. The value of the assets plundered by the legionnaires was estimated at billions of lei.

Hitler was interested in **Hungary** no less than in Rumania, but there the National Socialists did not try to influence the country from within. Instead, they pursued a course of signing agreements and showering Hungary with benefits that would make it amenable to serving German interests. Here, too, Hitler insisted on the encouragement of anti-Semitic tendencies and the limitation of the Jews' rights. At first he rewarded Hungary with a portion of dismembered Czechoslovakia—part of Slovakia and southern Carpathian Ruthenia. Close to 80,000 Jews were living in these two areas, which had been taken from Hungary after World War I by the terms of the Treaty of Trianon of 1920 (which forced Hungary to cede territory to Czechoslovakia, Austria, Italy, Yugoslavia, and Rumania). Hitler took care to continue adjusting these borders, and after the annexation of Bohemia-Moravia, he turned the rest of Carpathian Ruthenia—with more than 70,000 Jewish inhabitants—over to Hungary as well. At the end of August 1940, this trend culminated in the transfer of northern Transylvania from Rumania to Hungary. Thus the number of Jews in Hungary grew from nearly 450,000 in 1930 to 725,000 in January 1941.

It was not by chance that the First Jewish Law, limiting the rights of the Jews, was promulgated in 1938 when Hungary entered the good graces of the Third Reich. This first statute was matched in 1939 by a second one, with the racist principle being established as the basis of them both. Hence, these laws were extended to Jews who had converted to Christianity and their offspring, adding tens of thousands of people to the rolls of the Jews. The ratio of Jews permitted to practice the free professions was reduced to 6 percent and, as in Germany, Jews were fired from the government bureaucracy and the press. At first the proportion of Jews allowed to work in economic enterprises was limited to 20 percent, but in 1939 this was further reduced to 12 percent. Hungarian citizenship was revoked from Jews who had acquired it after 1914, and the Jews were effectively removed from the political system, for they were no longer allowed to vote in either general or municipal elections. The curtailment of civil rights did not preclude the conscription of men aged eighteen to twenty-five for the Labor Service beginning in 1940 (later on older men were drafted). These laws also applied to the annexed areas, but the Hungarians did not content themselves with legal measures alone and went on to stage riots against the Jews, especially in Transylvania. Anyone who could not prove his Hungarian citizenship was expelled into the Rumanian part of Transylvania or to Rumania proper. Nevertheless, most of the Jews were actually pleased about coming under Hungarian rule, because in the first phase of the war it appeared that the Jews of Hungary would be able to hold out even under wartime conditions and that the regent, Miklós Horthy—who was known to be friendly with a number of Jews—would not follow in the wake of the rabid anti-Semites. The Hungarian attitude toward the Jews was also influenced by the latter's role in the economy. Naturally, the aristocracy took advantage of the license issued in 1939 to expropriate Jewish-owned lands, but in the fields of commerce, banking, and industry, Hungarianization did not proceed at the pace desired by the Germans.[116]

With Hitler's conquest of the European continent in the east, north, and west and with the increase of his influence in the south, the war against the Jews entered a new stage. The manner in which the Germans fashioned their repressive regime over the Jews in the occupied countries and their degree of success in doing so were dependent on three factors: the size and character of the local Jewish community, the size and character of the German administration in the country, and the quality of the traditional relations between the general and the Jewish populations. The combination of these factors yielded different results in each of the countries under discussion. The concentrated assault that the Germans mounted on the Jewish community in Poland and the relative tranquility in which the Jews continued to pursue their lives in Denmark represented the two poles between which the gamut of approaches to handling the "Jewish problem" ranged. In each of the Western countries—France, Holland, Belgium, and Norway—the Germans acted primarily on the basis of political and strategic considerations. Usually, they were wary of antagonizing the local population any more than necessary, so that their anti-Jewish measures were effected step by step and with a certain degree of circumspection in countries where Jews were accepted as citizens with full equal rights, or were at least protected by the law. In Holland the SS, which essentially controlled the country and believed it could speed up the process of segregating and dispossessing the Jews, revised its strategy only after realizing that the Dutch population was not indifferent to the fate of the Jewish citizenry. In France the Germans did not work in a consistent manner. Alsace-Lorraine, the area annexed to the Reich, was purged of Jews as much as possible by means of deportations or emigration. (The same was true of Luxembourg.) In France the Germans tried to create the impression that the initiative behind the anti-Jewish measures and their implementation came mainly from the Vichy government, and they were undoubtedly pleased that the French protectorates in North Africa followed the lead of the Vichy regime.

The extent to which anti-Jewish measures were adopted by the satellite countries was an indication of how far these countries had already been taken over by Nazi collaborators. The German pressure exerted on Slovakia, Rumania, and Hungary thus served a double purpose: to further undermine the condition of close to 1.5 million of Europe's Jews while providing a channel of penetration for direct German influence. How strongly the authorities resisted this German pressure depended on the extent of the political independence they had managed to preserve and how much influence was wielded by the anti-Semitic element in the population. The abortive attempts at deporting Jews from the Greater Reich—made in 1939 and 1940 from Vienna, Czechoslovakia, Stettin (Szczecin), and Baden—proved that Hitler was still not capable of cleansing his own house of Jews. He had begun the war against the Jews of Europe, but it was still far from having reached its full dimensions.

7

The Jews' Struggle for Survival
(September 1939 to Spring 1941)

The Jews in Poland Between the Two World Wars

In eastern Europe the Jewish people has come into its own. It does not live like a guest in somebody else's house that must constantly keep in mind the ways and customs of the host. The Jews live their own life without disguise, outside of their homes no less than within them. . . . Eastern European Jewry was a people with a common will and destiny. It was not merely a uniform group, a homogeneous tribe; but a multiform society, uniform in its variety: one language, with many dialects. Social existence was complex, frequently dominated by centrifugal forces, but there was a common center and in most cases also a common periphery. There was even a social dynamic that created groupings in its own fashion.[1]

This Jewish community had been living in Poland for centuries and throughout those years had been an enduring source of the creative energy that animated the Jewish people. The great vitality of East European Jewry found many different, sometimes conflicting, channels. It expressed itself in scholarship, practiced by both the great minds of the age and by simple folk, as well as in a variety of popular religious movements, public and secret alike. It imbued the Jews with the strength to wage a tenacious war for survival, overcoming hardship and violence, deprivation and poverty. It took shape in the organization of the kehillah and national associations, and it found vent in many internal struggles, both social and intellectual. This powerful life force enabled the Jews of Eastern Europe to revitalize their society and culture and to forge new patterns of life for the community and the individual. As their distress mounted, a flow of emigration burst forth that carried the talents and energies of the Jews to new centers overseas, where they made their mark on the Jewish communities in the Americas and laid the foundations on which the State of Israel was established, drawing the new Hebrew culture out of the nation's ancient repositories.

In the opening quotation, Abraham Joshua Heschel noted that a number of sometimes clashing currents existed in Polish-Jewish life. Along with the cultural and political trends that had developed throughout the Western world, especially the Jewish world, the community was strongly influenced by the economic character and political fortunes of Poland, which for centuries had been the victim of the political and territorial designs of its neighbors: czarist Russia, the Austrian Empire, and Germanic Prussia. When Poland achieved independence after World War I, the prime ambition of its rulers was to accord the new state a distinctly Polish national character while consolidating its economic and cultural standing.

Many obstacles threatened to block the achievement of these aims. The makeup of the country's population was two-thirds Poles and one-third ethnic minorities: Ukrainians, Byelorussians, Germans, Lithuanians, and more than three million Jews—about 10 percent of the overall population and, as such, one of the most conspicuous of the minority groups.[2] While the Ukrainians and Byelorussians lived in clearly defined areas, the Jews were scattered among thousands of settlements, large and small, though to a notable degree they were concentrated in a few cities: 466,477 Jews lived in Warsaw and Łódź in 1921, and this number had grown to 555,156 by 1931 and was estimated to have reached 597,000 by 1939. Because of their large numbers, the Jews stood out as concentrated blocks, and in many places they composed 30 percent or more of the population. Moreover, during the interwar period, Poland was basically an agricultural society; 60.06 percent of the population was working in agriculture in 1931, compared with 25.4 percent engaged in commerce and industry. Yet only a negligible minority of Jews was employed in agriculture (6 percent in 1921 declining to 4 percent by 1931), whereas the number employed in the traditional occupation of commerce—especially in retail trade—was salient: Jews accounted for an average of 52.7 percent of all those engaged in commerce, with trade being the source of livelihood of 36.6 percent of the Jewish population. In contrast to the situation in Western Europe, craftsmen and laborers composed 42.2 percent of the Jewish work force in Poland and were concentrated primarily in the lumber, textile, clothing, and food industries. Jews were also employed in middle-sized factories (10 percent) and a small minority (2 percent) in large industrial plants.[3]

The Polish intelligentsia, who assumed the leadership of the independent state, had its roots in the old nobility, whereas the middle class in Poland was weak. Initially, this situation made it possible for Jews not only to flourish in commerce but to penetrate into the free professions, such as medicine and social welfare (21.7 percent), law (33.5 percent), and journalism and publishing (22 percent). Jews accounted for less than 10 percent of the country's schoolteachers—though outside the state school system their proportion rose to 43.3 percent.[4] Still, they were rarely accepted into the state bureaucracy since the authorities were strict about maintaining its Polish national character.

A parliamentary system was adopted in Poland, and in addition to the profusion of Polish nationalist parties represented in the Sejm (the Polish Parliament), the ethnic minorities formed parties of their own and sought to enhance their strength by uniting in a political bloc. On the initiative of President Woodrow Wilson, the Great Powers had introduced a clause into the Treaty of Versailles safeguarding the rights of minorities in the defeated countries and in the newly created states, which Poland was expected to honor. During the 1920s Jews were among the prime movers and leading activists in the struggle to ensure the cultural rights of the minorities, which clashed with the government's ambition of imposing the Polish language and culture on its whole citizenry. Among the members of the Sejm who worked to ensure the cultural rights of minorities was Yitzḥak Grünbaum, one of the leaders of the Zionist Organization.

Poland's backward economy was beset by the dual affliction of inflation and stagnation, which only exacerbated the domestic political unrest. In 1926 Marshal Jósef Piłsudski successfully mounted a coup d'état and set up a dictatorial regime that was supposed to bring quiet and order to the country. During his tenure— and increasingly after his death in 1935—the nationalist forces gained in strength. The world economic depression of the early 1930s hit Poland very hard, further feeding the internal tensions, and the rise of the Nazis in Germany heightened both the country's persistent anxieties about Germany's design on Poland and the nationalistic–fascistic leanings within Polish society.

These developments during the 1920s and 1930s affected the Jews in various ways. From an internal political standpoint, the autonomous life of the Jewish community revolved around three main factors: the Zionist parties; the Jewish socialist party known as the Bund (Yiddisher Arbeter Bund in Lite, Polin un Rusland), which had been growing in size and strength since the emergence of a Jewish proletariat at the end of the nineteenth century; and the traditionalist Orthodox circles organized in Agudat Yisrael. Most of the Jewish working class joined the Marxist Bund in the hope that a change in the social order would eliminate the physical threat to the Jews and enable them to pursue their lives within the autonomous framework they envisioned building upon the foundations of Yiddish culture. The Bundists regarded Zionism as a utopian movement that, while unlikely ever to realize its goals, represented the forces of reaction and impeded the practical solution offered by socialism. By calling for emigration to Palestine, they held, Zionism strengthened the hand of the anti-Semites, who would have liked to oust the Jews from Poland altogether. Similar and even more strident charges were raised against the Zionist movement by Jews in the Communist Party—also equally opposed to the Bund's position on the Jews' right to cultural autonomy.

The Zionist movement embraced a broad spectrum of tendencies from the right-wing, religious-oriented Mizraḥi through the General Zionists in the center to the left-wing Zionist Socialists. Each of these currents was, in turn, divided into smaller factions, so the debate over the course to be pursued by the Zionist movement raged both among and within the three main streams. The Revisionists, under the leadership of Vladimir Ze'ev Jabotinsky, called for the prompt establishment of a Jewish state in Palestine and placed the imperative of emigration there above all others. The friction between the Revisionist Party and the Socialist factions, which accused it of promoting nationalism and of imitating fascistic methods, culminated in 1935 in the Revisionists' secession from the Zionist Organization and the establishment of their own New Zionist Organization. Common to most of the Zionist parties, however, was the desire to base Jewish culture on the Hebrew language. During the 1920s the Zionist youth movements began to come into their own. United in the framework of Heḥalutz, these movements were dedicated to the principle of "personal fulfillment" (meaning emigration to Palestine and settlement on the land), for which they prepared their members in agricultural training groups (Haḥshara).

Operating alongside this varied collection of parties and factions was Agudat Yisrael, a force of major import since broad masses of Jews either belonged to the party or were influenced by it. Agudat Yisrael held the preservation of Jewish tradition as the cardinal principle of its platform, and the influence of ḥasidism was strongly felt within its constituency—to the point where it became the most potent factor of all.

All the elements in this diverse community were deeply rooted in Jewish culture and tradition, but two exceptional groups existed on its periphery: (1) a small but influential class of intellectuals and professionals who chose to live and work mostly within Polish society and (2) members of the Polish Communist Party who had renounced their Jewish identity altogether. This is not to imply that those who cultivated a strong Jewish consciousness did not participate in Polish life or that no lawyers and doctors championed Zionism or were associated with the Bund. The Polish government regarded Agudat Yisrael as its principal source of support in the Jewish public because its members spurned both socialist and Jewish nationalist aspirations. In the latter half of the 1930s, however, the government's anti-Jewish policy worked to the detriment of this constituency as well.

None of the paths taken by the Jewish leadership across this spectrum of sections, none of the doctrines they espoused as the key to improving the Jewish condition led anywhere. The Jews were one of the groups that suffered most from the economic depression that ravaged independent Poland, and during the 1930s their distress was aggravated by the political tension that continued to rise for both economic and political reasons. Moreover, as a result of these pressures, the government took a steadily more stringent attitude toward the minorities in general and the Jews in particular.

Beyond the effects of the economic situation, the Jews of Poland were the object of outright anti-Semitism. It found expression in every social class and wherever social intercourse took place, and it grew especially virulent during the 1930s as a result of domestic developments and the influence of Nazi anti-Semitism from abroad. Nothing was done to halt the anti-Jewish riots or the assaults on Jewish property, synagogues, and persons. By the same token, anti-Semitism found its way into the country's economic, social, and cultural life. In 1921, for example, Jewish students composed 24.6 percent of the student population in Poland; by 1938 only one-third of this number remained. Similarly, it was not by chance that the number of Jews employed in industry was so small. For quite a while before Hitler's rise to power in neighboring Germany, the Polish government had aspired to purge the economy of Jews—beginning in those sectors controlled by the state through a system of economic concentration known as etatism. As a rule, Jewish workers could find jobs only with Jewish employers, and there were few Jewish industrialists. When Poland was hit by massive unemployment, the authorities instituted a system of welfare allowances from which most of the jobless Jews derived no benefit because they belonged to the lowest classification of laborers, who were not compensated for the loss of their livelihood.[5] Thus the economic condition of the Jewish masses steadily declined. The eligibility of Jews to join the free professions was increasingly restricted, and in 1938 the legal profession was closed to them altogether. A quota was placed on the number of Jews permitted to study in Polish secondary schools, while the government ignored the commitment (stipulated by the Versailles treaty) to fund independent Jewish education, so that Jewish schools and other cultural institutions were deprived of any government support.

The upshot of this situation was catastrophic. Various assessments have it that about one-third of Poland's Jews—meaning a million people—were living below the poverty line. As early as 1932 it was said, "Trying to solve the Jewish problem in Poland [is] like trying to collect the water gushing though a sluice in a pot with a soup spoon."[6] And this situation grew steadily worse, so that a large percentage of the Jews found themselves in need of financial assistance. The main source of this social welfare was JDC, in addition to which a number of local Jewish organizations dedicated themselves to improving the condition of the Jewish population. The Organization for Rehabilitation Through Training (ORT)—an association to promote the crafts among the Jews that had come into being after World War I—was active primarily in Eastern Europe (though also in Germany and France). In Poland it sponsored fifty schools serving over two thousand pupils in addition to twelve agricultural farms; its budget in 1931 was $68,000. Two other organizations working on a national scale in Poland were the Society for the Preservation of Health (TOZ) and the National Society for the Care of Orphans (Centrala Opieki nad Sierotami, or CENTOS). Founded after World War I, TOZ's purpose was to combat the Jews' generally poor state of health, especially that of Jewish children. Toward the end it worked in cooperation with Oeuvre Secours aux Enfants (OSE), an international Jewish society established before World War I to aid Jews in the maintenance of their health. In 1924 TOZ had sixty-three branches in Poland employing about one thousand people, and it enjoyed support from JDC. Set up after World War I, CENTOS's mission was to care for the many Jewish children orphaned by that conflict. Its network of committees extended throughout Poland, and although it worked in cooperation with JDC, most of its budget came from its sixty thousand members, who covered about 60 percent of its annual operating costs of 6 million zlotys (U.S. $670,400); an additional 25 percent came from the government and the municipalities and the rest from JDC. Ten thousand orphans were sheltered by CENTOS, about half of them in institutions and the remainder in foster homes. It maintained its own sanitariums, special institutions for retarded children, and the like. These two organizations, TOZ and CENTOS, also worked in cooperation with each other, especially in terms of serving the needs of children.

Following World War I, the JDC largely concentrated its activities in Poland on the younger generation, who suffered not only from malnutrition but from the overcrowding in poverty-stricken neighborhoods. Seventy-three percent of the

Jewish children in Łódź, for example, lived with their families in a single room, and most of these living quarters lacked sanitary facilities. In the years 1931 and 1932, the JDC fed an average of 32,000 children per month.[7] Notwithstanding this assistance, many Jewish children suffered from extremely poor health and others were unable to go to school—and thus benefit from the additional nutrition provided there—for lack of shoes and clothing.

As part of carrying out its centralized economic policy, the government encouraged the establishment of Polish cooperatives, thus further abetting the destruction of Jewish commerce.[8] As in Germany, a boycott movement made itself felt in Poland, especially in the small towns and villages. The government also closed down or took over the management of Jewish factories; either way the Jewish laborers were put out of work. With the aid of JDC, various Jewish organizations provided inexpensive credit and aid to the cooperatives that the government was attempting to destroy. JDC was supported in this venture by the Jewish Colonization Association (ICA), and together in 1924 they established the American Joint Reconstruction Foundation, which took over the financing of the cooperative funds in Eastern Europe. The credit unions established to provide small loans at low interest were organized in a central association (known as the Verband, or Union) backed by both Zionists and Bundists. Those Jews who were able to pay the interest rates—about one-third of the population—availed themselves of these credit unions, while JDC, on the initiative of its European director, Bernard Kahn, established charity funds that offered interest-free loans. By 1930 there were 545 such funds operating in Poland, and they controlled over a million dollars in capital. They fulfilled an important function, especially during the depression years, and by 1939 their number had grown to 841.[9] After visiting Poland that year, the president of the British Board of (Jewish) Deputies, Neville Laski, remarked that he had "never seen such poverty, squalor, and filth. It made one despair of civilization."[10]

During the second half of that year, before the outbreak of the war, a certain improvement could be felt in the relations between the Poles and the Jews. At least for a while, the looming threat from without had the effect of mitigating the tension between them, though there was no change in the government's hostile economic policy.

Characteristic of the Jewish population of Poland was its internal politicization, which clearly differentiated it from the Jewish population of Germany, for example. This factionalization was particularly evident in the sphere of education, where Jewish autonomy found its main expression. The great majority of the Jewish educational institutions operated under the aegis of one political party or another and were shaped by its outlook. Common to all these parties was the problem of financial difficulties, for they had to maintain the educational institutions on their own; the government did not support them and as a rule did not even recognize the diplomas they awarded. Consequently, two-thirds of the Jewish children in Poland studied in public schools.

In these circumstances it is not surprising that the idea of emigration and resettlement in Palestine occupied the attention of the Jewish public. The question of whether the Jews should leave their native land or stand fast and fight for their rights became the subject of ideological debate (just as it had been deliberated in Germany after the Nazis came to power). Even in the face of the disastrous Polish situation, however, many Jewish organizations in Poland and abroad—above all JDC—believed that the Jews should stay and fight for their existence; thus, they mobilized to provide massive economic assistance. At the same time, the organizations not opposed to emigration in principle debated the question of where the Jews leaving Poland should go. Obviously, the Zionists championed emigration to Palestine, whereas the Bund, which was also a strong popular movement outside of Poland (particularly in the United States), was firmly against it. With the exception of the Poalei Agudat Yisrael (Workers of Agudat Yisrael) faction, the members of Agudat Yisrael were opposed to Zionism, and only under the grave pressure of events toward the end of the decade were they prepared to consider Palestine as a possible haven.

Yet the main obstacle to leaving Poland was pragmatic rather than ideological: the number of countries prepared to accept Jewish emigrants steadily diminished. For years the Polish government itself had been seeking a channel of exit not just for the Jews but for the destitute members of the Polish population, especially from the rural areas. It was prepared to consider even so dubious a plan as resettlement on the island of Madagascar, then a French colony. First raised in the 1920s, this idea was discussed with the French but was rejected on the grounds of unfeasibility. It cropped up again in the mid-1930s as a way of disposing of Poland's Jews; and it was looked into yet again in 1937/1938, even receiving a modicum of international attention.[11]

Of the 1,167,568 people who emigrated from Poland in the decade from 1921 to 1931, a total of 292,832 (or 33.5 percent) were Jews. In the 1930s the flow of Jewish emigrants bound for Palestine mounted considerably, and in 1935 alone 24,300 of the 30,703 Jews who entered that country came from Poland.[12] The Poles even tried to persuade the British to change their policy on Palestine. They were supported in this effort by Vladimar Ze'ev Jabotinsky, who put forward a plan for transferring—or, in his term, *evacuating*—the masses of Polish Jewry to Palestine. But nothing came of any of these schemes or thoughts on the matter.

Despite the depressing state of affairs, it must be said that not all the Jews of Poland were destitute. Many businessmen, merchants, professionals, artisans, and workers were still on a firm footing. These well-to-do people believed—each in accordance with his political and cultural outlook—in the ability of the Jews to overcome the hardships and to build a future for themselves in Poland. When the war broke out, Jews volunteered en masse either for the army or for emergency labor and other activities in order to defend the country that, after all, they regarded as their homeland.

The desperate economic situation, the anti-Jewish sentiment so deeply ingrained in broad segments of the Polish population, and the government's anti-Jewish policy, especially during the latter half of the 1930s, all prepared the ground for the Germans' savage treatment of the Jews in occupied Poland. The Nazis merely expanded on and supplemented what had already been done. With great ease they were able to embark on a ready-made program of riots, looting, boycotts, confiscation, exploitation, and discrimination as many quarters in the

Polish population supported, collaborated in, or even instigated these actions. The help proffered to the Jews was negligible, and indifference to their fate prevailed at the hour of crisis for the defeated, oppressed, and smarting Polish people. But the Jews of Poland, schooled as they were in the struggle for their existence, gathered all their strength and prepared for a stubborn fight for life.

"Until the Storm Blows Over": The Jews of Piotrków Trybunalski (Radom District) Under Occupation

Piotrków, like the other Jewish cities in Poland, sank deep into the mire of misery and murder. The term "extermination" had not yet been coined, and the people of Piotrków hoped that even in the shadow of terror, it would be possible to live a relatively ordinary life and maintain their humanity. The effort made by the kehillah's devoted staff was beyond description. . . . Workers and volunteers established clandestine schools, held secret religious services, organized soup kitchens for the masses of the needy, ran private fund-raising campaigns for anonymous donations, set up health and sanitation services, and even managed to tend to the needs of the soul by infusing spirit and providing a measure of culture.[13]

Piotrków was a middle-sized town, one of dozens of similar settlements in Poland in which Jews made up a large proportion of the population. Its Jewish community was one of the thousands of such communities that had once populated the cities, towns, and villages of Poland—and are no more. In turning to discuss their bitter fate, we can portray them only by trying to capture their way of life and by relating the history of a few selected examples. The choice is not an easy one. Each city and area had its own unique character and fortunes. Notwithstanding the fact that the basic problems confronting them stemmed from the policy pursued by the Germans, there were differences in shading and nuance to the situations that emerged in each of these communities owing to both objective circumstances and the behavior of the actors in each individual place: Germans, Jews, and Poles.

The examples given here have been chosen on the basis of various criteria, including the size of the settlement, the composition and character of the Jewish population and its leadership, and the ways in which the people and their leaders reacted to the situation. I wish to show both the characteristic and the range of variety. Thus, rather than discuss the full gamut of problems and manifestations of behavior in each of the selected places, the emphasis has been placed on specific aspects that will cohere into a comprehensive mosaiclike portrait. In the Generalgouvernement I have chosen Piotrków as a medium-sized city. In the Warsaw and Lublin districts I have selected the national and district capitals, respectively, both among Poland's eleven largest cities. In the areas annexed to the Reich, Łódź is the city that stands out; and in Eastern Upper Silesia an entire district, Zagłębie, will be discussed.

The Jewish settlement in Piotrków was a four-hundred-year-old community that in 1931 numbered 11,400 people, or 22.2 percent of the city's population.[14] Though originally located in the Łódź District (close to the border of what became Warthegau), during the occupation Piotrków was incorporated into the Radom

District of the Generalgouvernement. It was a lively city, and among the Jewish organizations there the Bund took pride of place; having won a majority on the kehillah council in 1937, its activists headed the communal leadership. As far back as the 1920s, an alliance between the Bund and the Polish Socialist Party (PPS) gave them—together with the Paolei Zion Party—a preferential position on the City Council, and in 1939 seven members of the Bund and two members of Poalei Zion were, in fact, elected to the council. In addition, thirteen of the forty-five members of the regional council of the General Sick Fund were Jews from Piotrków and the vicinity. Hence, during the period between the wars, the Jews of Piotrków were somewhat better off than their brethren in many other Polish cities and towns. They did not suffer from discrimination either in their work or their political and cultural lives insofar as the situation was under the control of the local authorities and not related to national policy. The community's cultural institutions included a Hebrew high school and an ORT vocational school. The kehillah also maintained its welfare-assistance programs, of which 40 percent of its members were already in need in 1929.[15]

As throughout Poland, however, the situation in Piotrków deteriorated during the 1930s, especially during the latter half of the decade. The Jews and their property came under attack as attempts were made at staging boycotts and even physical assaults were not unknown. However, these displays of enmity were denounced by Polish citizens and the municipal authorities alike.

Piotrków was bombed at the beginning of the war, with low-flying planes pursuing the refugees who fled from the city, so that many were killed by machine-gun fire or in aerial attacks on the nearby towns to which they fled. Included among these victims were thousands of Jewish men, women, and children.[16] The German army entered Piotrków on September 5, and on that very day twenty Jews were shot to death. The following day a section of the Jewish quarter was set afire, and the people fleeing from the blaze were cut down by gun fire. The Jewish New Year fell in the middle of September, and it was especially during the holidays that German soldiers and SS men went on a rampage, with Poles joining in the looting.

On October 8 an official order was issued establishing a ghetto, making Piotrków the first place in Poland in which Heydrich's directive was put into effect. The ghetto was not fenced in or otherwise closed, and on December 20 the six hundred Jews who were still living outside it were ordered to move too within its bounds. All told, the ghetto encompassed 182 buildings, containing 4,178 rooms. After the flight of about two thousand Jews—most of them youngsters, a few others people of means—the indigenous population concentrated in the ghetto numbered close to eighty-five hundred people, who were soon joined by thousands of refugees and deportees. It is estimated that at a later stage, the average density of the population was four people to a room; sometimes this figure reached as high as eight.[17] Within the ghetto, the residents were allowed on the streets only between the hours of 8:00 A.M. and 5:00 P.M., and they were permitted outside the ghetto only between 11:00 A.M. and 1:00 P.M. In December 1939 the hours were reduced to 10:00 A.M. to 1:00 P.M. and 3:00 to 4:00 P.M. within the ghetto. Any Jew who dared to leave the bounds of the ghetto took the side streets and alleyways and avoided the streets on which he was forbidden to step on the sidewalk—a prohibition that pertained to the main streets of the ghetto as well. The punishment for violating the curfew was death.

Naturally, these prohibitions were soon joined by the usual abuses that beset the Jews of Poland as a whole: the marking of their clothing and businesses with a special symbol, forced labor, fines and other forms of payments, the theft of their property, hunger, and physical assaults, beatings, and torture. At the end of October, the army turned the governance of the city over to Hans Frank's civil administration, and a German, Hans Drecksel, was appointed mayor. Two weeks later, in mid-November, Drecksel ordered the establishment of a Jewish Council, or Council of Elders (Ältestenrat), as the Germans referred to it. It was headed by the former deputy chairman of the kehillah, Salman Tannenberg, who chose the rest of the council's members—all well-known, veteran public servants.[18]

The Jewish Council was charged with the same duties that applied almost everywhere: conducting a census, registering the property and goods in Jewish hands, and above all seeing to the payment of "contributions" and the provision of furniture and housewares. Thereafter the Jews of Piotrków were subjected to one fine after the next: 25,000 zlotys, 15,000 zlotys, and then 350,000 zlotys. As noted earlier, it was not a particularly wealthy community, especially as its more affluent members had fled early on. The Jewish Council found it particularly difficult to raise the last sum, which it had been ordered to pay "by 11:00 A.M." on November 29, 1939, lest forceful measures be taken against the leading members of the community, who had already been beaten and tortured, in some cases resulting in death.[19] During the first three months of the occupation, the Germans plundered Jewish-owned warehouses, shops, and apartments. Thereafter the Jews were required to submit whatever merchandise remained, and the Germans, fixing the price, bought it at far below its real value. The authorities also confiscated or "purchased" the raw materials that remained in Jewish hands or that had been reobtained. Yet they turned the clothing, furs, leather, and similar goods over to Jewish craftsmen for processing, so that some tailors, furriers, shoemakers, and the like derived a livelihood from the action.[20] These arrangements resulted from the connections that Tannenberg had succeeded in forming with the German authorities, to no small degree through bribes. Individual Jews and Jewish institutions soon discovered that the Germans were eager to accept such payments, and Tannenberg successfully employed them to get people released from prison. Yet the Germans' avarice also led to acts of cruelty, especially when they learned from informers that a certain individual was concealing property.

In Piotrków, like everywhere else, forced labor in the service of the Germans was one of the sorest problems. At first Jews were snatched off the streets, often just for the fun of torturing them and setting them to senseless hard labor. Yet there was a genuine need for manpower: the trustees who had been placed in charge of expropriated factories wanted to activate them; ruined areas had to be rebuilt; and the Germans planned to pave roads and install drainage systems. The leadership of the Jewish community came to an understanding about the anarchic employment situation and supplied the German-run Labor Exchange with about one thousand people a day. This arrangement did not quite put an end to the abductions because some Germans were unwilling to waive the pleasure; but they did decline in frequency. An order of priority was established to divide the burden more or less equally among the Jews. Here too, however, the well-to-do were able to obtain exemptions from labor duty by paying a ransom, with the council putting this income toward the payment of a minimal wage to the laborers and balancing its budget.

Another area in which the council tried to avoid serious damage by arriving at a reasonable arrangement was the supply of food. First it succeeded in ensuring a certain stock of foodstuffs, which it proceeded to distribute by means of ration cards. Nevertheless, it was soon necessary to set up soup kitchens and provide a hot meal to those unable to purchase food on their own. The most difficult problem confronting the council, however, was the influx of refugees. Thousands of deportees from Łódź and the towns of Warthegau and Eastern Upper Silesia were joined by yet other Jews who were drawn to Piotrków because conditions there were better than in many other places. During the peak period, about twenty thousand extra Jews were living in Piotrków; some estimate as many as thirty thousand.[21] They needed food, clothing, and a roof over their heads, with many also requiring medical attention.

The community overcame these problems in an unusual way: to some extent the refugees were housed in public buildings, but many were taken into private homes. The local residents displayed a great readiness to aid the deportees, sharing their food, clothing, and even their beds with them. Refugees were also absorbed into the labor market, so that a considerable number were able to fend for themselves. Some of the merchants whose wares had been seized turned to opening restaurants—or sweet shops, as they were known—on the same premises, thus providing meals for the refugees and people of greater means.

A good many of the refugees and indigenous inhabitants of Piotrków tried to make their way eastward to Warsaw or "the other side," meaning the territory under Soviet control. This road was difficult and fraught with danger; many were forced to turn back. Groups of youngsters organized in order to steal over the border; at first they seemed to be making headway, ultimately they failed. During a certain period there was a rash of weddings in Piotrków because the parents of young women were loath to have their daughters set out on the perilous journey alone.[22]

Ya'akov Kurz, a Jew from Palestine who was caught in Poland when the war broke out, described the relatively favorable situation in Piotrków, noting that the craftsmen were working in their fields and earning a good living. Many of the city's Jewish merchants also stayed in business by secretly bringing in materials such as iron and fabrics from other cities. On a few occasions these goods were seized by the German or Polish police, but even then they were ransomed with cash and returned to their owners. This clandestine trade went on not only in merchandise but in gold, precious stones, and foreign currency. Certain expressions that were used to camouflage the real goods being exchanged in these deals later became rooted in the Jewish jargon. Thus, gold dollars were referred to as hard ones *(harte)* and paper dollars as soft ones *(weiche)*. These valuables were usually brought in from Warsaw by Christians, and the exchange rate on the black market was transmitted from the capital by phone three times a day in a special code.[23]

As people grew accustomed to the harsh new conditions, they tended to believe that they would be able to hold out "until the storm blows over." Some were even contemplating plans for after the war, and many thought about emigration to Palestine. But the acts of robbery by individual Germans assaulting Jews on the streets never let up. The Germans also plundered the little that the refugees had managed to bring along. An officer who caught a simple soldier in the act of stealing would often push him aside or chastise him and then proceed to complete the robbery himself, with even greater thoroughness. These assaults, which were a daily and nightly occurrence, terrified the community; in a situation of utter lawlessness, the Jews went out of their way to avoid provoking the Germans—to say nothing of the fact that they dared not come to the aid of anyone who was victimized.[24] Here and there a decent or shamefaced German was prepared, at least, to turn a blind eye to outlawed activities; sometimes they even warned the Jews of an approaching action. For the most part, only bribes in the form of cash or merchandise kept Germans at bay.

Owing to the efforts of the Jewish Council, the Jews of Piotrków were at first sent to labor camps in the immediate vicinity or were put to work within the city itself. In July 1940, however, the Germans began sending young people (for the most part) to forced labor camps in the Lublin District. The entire community mobilized to prepare food and suitable clothing for the deportees. Apprised of their destination, many of the youngsters panicked and tried to flee or go into hiding. But once again the Jewish Council managed to calm the public, took charge of dispatching the youngsters' belongings, and tried as much as possible to prevent the arbitrary abduction of Jews to replace those who had fled. All in all, nine hundred people were taken off to the camps in the Lublin District.[25] It soon became clear from letters and the tales borne by people passing through the district that the conditions there were appalling and that, in line with Odilo Globocnik's methods, a previous work force, after completing the fortifications on the Russian border, had been liquidated. As word of all this spread, an uproar broke out in Piotrków. The families of the deportees descended on the council's offices and even made violent threats until the council agreed to co-opt a number of their representatives for consultations. Then, both the council and the families organized to provide assistance to the deportees. Food packages were dispatched to the labor camps—though the council was careful not to send out a large amount at any one time lest the Germans conclude that the Jews of Piotrków were too well-off. When it became obvious that the deportees were meant to be liquidated, their families tried to ransom them. Large sums were raised for this purpose, and when the labor camps were disbanded in the spring of 1941, the Piotrków Jewish Council succeeded in getting 80 percent of its deportees back. The council's efforts on their behalf were genuinely heroic. Many of the ransomed deportees were in such poor condition that they were beyond saving; others survived but never regained their health.

In the winter of 1940/1941, signs of the worsening situation began to proliferate. It was then that the health of the Jewish population was undermined by an epidemic of typhus fever. The Germans had taken over the Jewish hospital at the start of the occupation, but the council established an infirmary and a health service employing twenty doctors, and through their dedicated work the epidemic was finally brought under control.

The Jewish Council divided its work among fifteen departments, including housing, nutrition, labor, finances, and refugees. It also established a special department to organize stores of food and supplies and an information center that tried to gather data on the whereabouts of family members and put them in touch with one another. The council's financial burden by far exceeded its means, but JDC, TOZ, and CENTOS came to its aid, contributing considerable sums and foodstuffs.[26] In the spring of 1940, when the Germans ordered the establishment of a Jewish Order Service—meaning a Jewish police force—the council debated whether or not to comply with this demand. The chairman, Tannenberg, tended toward acquiescence because he hoped that a police force would strengthen the council's standing. Various other members were wary of establishing such an institution, and Rabbi Moshe Haim Lau feared that young people would resort to the use of force without sufficiently considering the moral and social implications of their actions. It was finally decided to establish the unit—essentially because of lack of choice—and a special public committee was formed to review the character and background of the candidates. Initially, the council succeeded in exercising its control over the twenty-four members of the Jewish police, whose main duty was to bring delinquents to their place of work, though it also executed sentences on behalf of the court established by the council and even of the city's rabbinical court. In the course of time, the police expanded its ranks, and a unit of Health Police was formed in the spring of 1941 to combat the typhus epidemic by systematically disinfecting the ghetto's buildings and escorting residents to bathhouses at regular intervals. Later on the police assumed other, more harmful duties.[27]

The Jews of Piotrków were convinced that their tribulations were but a temporary affliction and that if they could hold fast until the storm had spent itself, justice would prevail in the end and all would turn out for the best.[28]

Between the Hammer and the Anvil: The Jewish Council of Lublin

Whereas Piotrków was located close to the western border of the Generalgouvernement, Lublin was a focal point near the eastern border. It was one of the oldest Jewish communities in Poland, and during various periods played an important role in the history of Polish Jewry. It was not by chance that the Germans ascribed it importance as a symbol of the strength and spirit of Jewry. In 1931 there were close to 39,000 Jews in Lublin, composing 34.7 percent of the overall population; by 1939 their number had declined to 37,830, representing 21 percent of the population. Throughout the Lublin district in 1934 there were 80,000 Jews living in forty towns and twenty agricultural settlements.[29] From its inception, Zionism held an important place in the Lublin community and all its factions were represented there. Members of the rest of the movements and organizations, from Agudat Yisrael to the Bund, were also found in the city. Jewish schools of all kinds were operating in the city, and the community conducted a lively cultural life.

Past Experience and Present Reality

Lublin did not fall to the Germans until almost the end of the battle for Poland, on September 18, 1939. As soon as the fighting broke out, however, a stream of refugees descended upon the city, some of them headed for the Soviet-occupied zone. The kehillah's council saw its main task during that period as easing their lot, but as the fighting intensified it also became necessary to provide shelter for the local Jews whose homes had been destroyed in the bombing of the city.

After the German conquest, the structure and composition of the community council remained essentially unchanged at first. A few members of the community council had fled, but others were co-opted in their place and the council continued to operate with twenty-three members. As in other places, however, there was a sharp rise in the number of physical assaults, robberies, and abductions for forced labor, and the Germans immediately imposed heavy payments on the Jews. On October 20 a Department of Forced Labor was organized in an attempt to obviate the abductions.[30]

The members of the kehillah's council assumed that the Germans would essentially conduct themselves on the basis of rational considerations, making it possible to reach an accommodation with them. Indicative of their mood was the oft-repeated comment of one of the council's leaders, the attorney Dr. Mark Alten, "the worst law is preferable to the absence of any law."[31] Like his associates, Alten clung to assumptions and conventions that had evolved and proved themselves in the past but that were inapplicable to the Nazi rulers since the destruction of the rule of law was a sine qua non of their system. In their misapprehension of the situation, the Jews believed that the acts of terror were being perpetrated by the local German authorities alone, that the central regime did not support them, and consequently that the situation would improve once the central government established its control. It took the Jews of Lublin a long time to realize their error. Thus, in 1939/1940 the community's leaders submitted various memoranda informing the authorities of their problems, suggesting ways of overcoming them, and even forcefully demanding their solution. Needless to say, none of these approaches had the least effect. As for bribery, either it did not work in Lublin, as in Piotrków, or the Jews at first did not attempt to use it. Indeed, the community's leaders and the German authorities were acting on the basis of wholly antithetical concepts and a very different perception of the situation in which the Jews found themselves.

This does not mean that the members of the kehillah's council did not do their utmost to help the Jews survive. Their work can be divided into two main categories: actions taken in response to orders from, and in the service of, the Germans; and actions taken on behalf of, and in the service of, the Jews.

With the firm consolidation of the coercive system of rule over the Jews in the

Generalgouvernement, the Lublin community council was turned into a Juden-rat, though a ghetto was not established until the summer of 1941. The list of the twenty-four members of the Judenrat was officially approved on January 25, 1940. Chosen as its chairman was an engineer by the name of Henryk Bekker, who prior to the war had been the chairman of the community council, and Mark Alten was the most prominent of the five deputy chairmen. Alten was then in his late fifties and was highly experienced in the ways of public life, having served in the Austrian government during World War I. Between the wars he had practiced law, been an active and respected public figure, served as chairman of the local Zionist Organization, and for a certain period had also been a member of the Lublin City Council. A quiet, authoritative, and distinguished-looking man, Alten now conducted most of the contacts with the Germans. Some accused him of having ingratiated himself with them, but there is no doubt that he also fought for the interests of the Jews and did not merely do the Germans' bidding. They even arrested him on more than one occasion. Alten was just one of the many Jewish leaders in Poland who erred in their approach because they failed to appreciate the true nature of the outlook guiding the Nazis' behavior. These people, who assumed the tasks of public leadership willingly or otherwise, were genuinely tragic figures whose misreading of the situation ultimately led them to act in ways that ran counter to their conscience and better judgment.[32]

Financial Administration

The Judenrat in Lublin was one of the few such institutions that we are able to study in great detail, as most of the minutes of its meetings have been preserved. From them we are able to see that the community was in a poor financial state even before the occupation began. Its budget for 1939 was 175,155 zlotys, but on September 1 of that year only 64,000 zlotys of that amount was covered, with the deficit running at 200,000 zlotys.[33] A year later, the report submitted to the authorities on its income and expenses between September 1, 1939, and August 31, 1940, showed the Judenrat's income to be 1,617,780.29 zlotys and its expenditures 1,619,438.87 zlotys.[34]

The difference between this accounting and the community's earlier, normal budgets is stark indeed. The sums that the Jews of Lublin paid out to the Judenrat in cash came to a total of 836,973.03 zlotys, or 51.7 percent of the council's total income (see Table 3). The fees collected for the community's standard services amounted to a total of 92,115.74 zlotys, or 5.7 percent of the income. These two sources of funds were joined by payments related to the obligations imposed on the council by the Germans such as ransoming people from labor duty. These payments alone (650,596.77 zlotys) accounted for 40.2 percent of the total income and were expended primarily on wages for the laborers (591,872.73 zlotys). In addition to the kehillah's taxes and fees for standard services (216,636.24 zlotys), 1,401,144 zlotys, or 86.6 percent of the total income, was collected from the public that year. The deficit of the official budget was, thus, relatively small.

The report does not give a detailed breakdown of the expenses, and it was difficult to maintain public control over these outlays. "Contributions," for exam-

Table 3. The Budget of the Lublin Community, September 1, 1939–August 31, 1940

Income (in zlotys)		%	Expenses (in zlotys)		%
Payments			*Independent Activities*		
Taxes	124,520.50		Wages for kehillah workers	143,165.27	
One-time donations A	342,535.40		Administration	21,426.57	
One-time donations B	349,684.59		Preparing new cemetery	10,713.50	
Pledges	20,232.54		Welfare	108,318.26	
	836,973.03	51.7		283,623.60	17.5
Standard Services			*Activities Under German Orders*		
Emigration	1,842.54		Cash payments	260,000.00	
Legal aid	718.60		Supply of goods	47,232.33	
Burial society	75,382.00		Wages to laborers	591,872.73	
Gravestones	3,507.00		Maintaining workshops	343,202.73	
Marriage ceremonies	2,091.50			1,242,307.79	76.7
Birth certificates	3,757.10				
Secretarial work	4,817.00				
	92,115.74	5.7			
Services Caused by the Times			*Miscellaneous*	93,507.48	5.8
Ransom from hard labor				Total 1,619,438.87	100.00
Men	497,276.34				
Women	153,320.43				
Registration department	6,398.20		*Extras Not Included in Budget*		
Mail	23,880.85		Furniture and housewares	200,000.00	
				107,076.00	
	680,875.82	42.1	Miscellaneous	307,076.00	
Miscellaneous	7,815.70	0.5			
	Total 1,617,780.29	100.00		Total 1,926,514.87	

Source: The Polish Report of the Community Council, YVSA, 06/3, vols. 9–11, pp. 6f.

ple—meaning bribes, plunder, expropriations, and the like—were sometimes included under the heading Miscellaneous. As far back as October 14, 1939, a special board of nine council members was set up to deal with such "contributions." The money was collected from hundreds of people by special "fund raisings," and the amounts mentioned in the Judenrat's internal documents are much higher than those cited in the official financial statement.[35]

The administration of the community's funds attests the conflict that the Judenrat faced. Forced to serve as a lodestone for funds that found their way to the Germans, the council was also charged with responsibility for services and other aspects of community life that had formerly been handled by the citizenry or the government. At the same time, the council tried to run its affairs along lines that were appropriate to normal times, maintaining a controlled economy and tending to the needs of the Jewish population. This attempt to live simultaneously in the past and the present inevitably spawned conflicting and destructive forms of behavior: the community tried to rise above the misfortune that had come upon it so suddenly while conducting itself as though nothing at all had happened and that life was going on as usual.

Not only did these two inclinations clash head on but in their desire to serve two masters—the capricious regime and the demands of good order—the members of the Judenrat found themselves at loggerheads. The minutes of the Judenrat's meetings are filled with the details of personal arguments, mutual suspicions, and bitter recriminations. Relations within the community's leadership had been tense even before the occupation, but now they reached their nadir. In contrast to the detailed accounts of these personal spats, including the particulars of salaries and the like,[36] the reports on the matters under discussion at the council meetings are often terse. They state what was on the agenda but do not describe the deliberations or explicitly report what decisions were taken. The reason for this reticence is evidently that these minutes were subject to perusal by the Germans, and often the members of the council did not want the content or conclusions of their debates known to them.

The Council in Action

The official financial report was submitted to the authorities to prove that the Judenrat was incapable of fulfilling the difficult role inflicted upon it. Thus, it goes into great detail about the council's work on behalf of the refugees,[37] for example, showing that it lacked the means to cope with such typical problems as housing, employment, nutrition, supplies and storage, welfare, and health. Once a day a number of soup kitchens supplied these refugees with a hot meal—soup and about half a pound of bread or about a pound of bread to be taken home. But the newcomers were not the only ones to avail themselves of this service; the local poor were also served by the soup kitchens. The need for clothing proved to be an especially difficult problem in which the council depended on three factors: JDC, a one-time shipment of clothing from the United States, and a clothing collection held among the Jews of Lublin. But in the course of the first year of the occupation, most of these sources were blocked, and the council no longer knew how to meet the demand. The funds for running the soup kitchens also ran out, and it must be kept in mind that it was necessary not only to care for the refugees and needy members of the community but to supply food to the entire Jewish population. Ration cards were issued for distributing bread, flour, groats, oil, potatoes, salt, eggs, milk, and soap (the last four items in very small quantities). Beginning in August 1940 the Judenrat also had to care for and support the families of the 3,200 workers sent to labor camps in the vicinity of Bełżec (for a total of 10,200 people). These services were financed by the meager funds and special donations collected each month, while CENTOS and TOZ assisted by providing health services and caring for children.

The conscription of people for forced labor was one of the most unsavory and complex tasks that the council had to fulfill. The minimum payment to ransom a man from labor was 25 zlotys for four workdays per month,[38] and obviously even those unable to ransom themselves tried to evade labor duty. The council found it very difficult to collect these sums—just as it was chronically behind in its collection of taxes—and often its members were forced to appeal to the more affluent members of the community for advances.[39] Forced labor and collection of taxes were the main sources of the conflict and tension between the Judenrat and its constituency. The forced laborers from Lublin were paid between 15 and 50 zlotys per day. Later, the Germans realized that they could not make the Jewish community cover the wages of the skilled workers in their employ, but since the German Labor Bureau fell far behind in the payment of these wages, the Judenrat inevitably had to assume this burden as well.[40]

The Jewish POW Camp

These skilled workers in German employ were engaged in building a camp inside the city named Liprowa—after the street on which it was located—for Jewish POWs from the defeated Polish army.[41] The first men to inhabit the camp, in December 1939, were soldiers who hailed from the territories under Soviet control; they had been assembled under the supervision of the SS ostensibly to be exchanged for German prisoners held by the Russians. Instead, at the end of December, the SS forced the prisoners to make a run for the border and shot most of them to death; only a few survived through the aid of the nearby Jewish community (Parczew). This slaughter was evidently the result of a local initiative because when word of the episode—known at the time as the Death March from Lublin—reached the senior ranks of the German regime, the aftermath was handled by Hitler's head of chancellery, Hans Heinrich Lammers, and by Himmler personally.[42] Beginning in January 1940, thirty-two hundred Jewish POWs hailing from the western areas of Poland were interned in the camp. The treatment they received was appreciably better: some of them were sent back to their homes and others were released in return for a declaration guaranteeing their upkeep. The Judenrat established a special council to deal with the POWs, and it managed to garner two thousand such guarantees from the local population. Later on, almost all the prisoners were released. A Public Council for Prisoners of War was formed to work under the aegis of the Judenrat, and when the released soldiers were required to leave their uniforms in the camp, the two councils held a clothing drive for them. The Judenrat also provided housing and medical care when sponsors could not be found for the men, and it helped the soldiers establish contact with their families. For all that, however, the relationship between the Judenrat and the POWs was not always amicable, if only because the council was eager to free itself of the additional burden.[43]

In the winter of 1940/1941, twenty-five hundred new POWs from the eastern areas came to Lublin and were to remain in the Liprowa camp for about two years. These prisoners were a highly cohesive unit that maintained its military format under the leadership of a few officers and successfully fought for its rights as POWs.[44] As a result of its strong demonstration of unity, the group won the Germans' consent to divide up the work assignments on its own and toward that end was even entrusted with the camp's card file. In addition to successfully resisting the demand to wear a special symbol marking them as Jews, they obtained an increase in their food ration and received permission to conduct cultural activities.

Deportees from Near and Far

At the beginning of 1940, an extraordinary group of refugees was added to the responsibilities of the Lublin Judenrat. These were the deportees from Stettin

(Szczecin) (see chap. 5), and they came at a time when the death rate among the Jews of Lublin was rising markedly. Although 529 Jews had died in the twelve months from September 1938 through August 1939, in the four months between September and December 1939 alone there were 301 deaths, and in the course of 1940 the number of fatalities soared to 1,224. Even though there was a death rate of 2.4 per 1,000 among the local Jews, this bore no comparison to the figure of 18.8 per 1,000 among the deportees from Germany.[45]

The Lublin Judenrat played an ever-broader role with the establishment of labor camps in the vicinity of Bełżec. At the end of May 1940, when it established a special committee of assistance to tend to the workers destined for the camps, the Judenrat had the workers from Lublin in mind.[46] Shortly thereafter, however, the Germans began to send Jews from all over the Generalgouvernement to these camps. The assistance committee sent out food, dispatched two doctors, and tried to help with the organization of the camps around Bełżec, whose number eventually reached fifty. However, aid from Lublin was unable to prevent the tragedies that befell the workers who were building fortifications. The problem of extending aid was greatly complicated by the mixture of people who had been sent to the camps. Jewish councils from cities and towns throughout the Generalgouvernement sent emissaries to Lublin in the hope of influencing the Judenrat to help their deportees, and sharp debates raged within the Lublin Council itself. The main question it had to decide was how much of its budget to allocate for assistance to the workers at Bełżec. To keep up with the demand for aid, the Judenrat attempted to increase its income and cut back on the salaries of its officials. Finally, the council decided to allocate 50 percent of its income to the community and to divide the other 50 percent equally between the committee for Bełżec and the families of the laborers from Lublin.[47]

The Judenrat could not possibly find a reasonable solution to all the problems it faced. Caught between the hammer of the Germans' demands and the anvil of the community's needs, it waged a desperate battle to save lives, keep up health standards, and maintain the usual conventions of public life. Inevitably, perhaps, a climate of tension and suspicion developed between one member and the next, between the Judenrat as a whole and the public it served. In their effort to maintain order, the leaders of the Judenrat sometimes resorted to dubious measures and asked the authorities to assign policemen to guard their offices, help them collect taxes, and track down the people evading labor duty. The men of the Selbstwehr, an auxiliary police force recruited from among the *Volksdeutsche,* participated in these policing duties. Ultimately, the Judenrat decided to establish its own (Jewish) Order Police, and at first the force had only ten men.[48]

Jewish Self-help

Together with the work of the aid organizations (TOZ, OSE, and ORT), JDC played a highly important role throughout occupied Poland. It operated within the framework of the assistance effort mounted by American organizations that made their aid conditional on the Jews being included as its beneficiaries. The reason that the German authorities did not bar JDC from extending assistance to the Jews was apparently twofold. On one level the Nazi leadership, which aspired to take over the whole of Europe, hoped that the United States would remain neutral in the war. They also had a vested interest in the dollars that JDC was pumping into occupied Poland, which were exchanged at the official German rate. This seems to be why the Nazis chose to ignore the blatant contradiction to their policy of oppression toward the Jews. To a certain extent Jews also benefited from the food and clothing that the Americans contributed to the population of occupied Poland.

In the winter of 1939/1940, JDC lent its support to the initiative taken by Jewish intellectuals in founding an independent organization known as Jewish Self-help (ŻSS).[49] The head of the new organization was Michael Weichert, its secretary-general, Emmanuel Ringelblum. Unexpectedly, the ŻSS was officially recognized by the Department of Population and Welfare in the Generalgouvernement's Ministry of the Interior. In March 1940 the department's director, Dr. Fritz Arlt, invited representatives of the Judenrat, JDC, and the ŻSS from Warsaw to a series of meetings in Cracow, the seat of Frank's administration; in May the ŻSS was added to the list of Polish and Ukrainian assistance organizations recognized as part of the umbrella organization known as the Central Council for Social Care, or RGO. The RGO had been established in collaboration with the American aid organizations, and it allocated 17 percent of the aid coming from abroad to the Jews. The governing board of the ŻSS—one of whose seven members was Dr. Alten from Lublin—was officially recognized at the end of the summer of 1940.[50] Meanwhile, on July 23, 1940, Frank issued an order revoking the autonomy of all the independent aid organizations in the Generalgouvernement—Polish, Ukrainian, and Jewish—and expropriating their capital. The TOZ and CENTOS, which fulfilled vital roles in caring for the sick and for children—especially orphans, of whom there was already a substantial number—were able to evade this order by being included under the bureaucratic auspices of the Judenrat or the ŻSS. Thus, the Lublin Judenrat satisfied its desire to bring the assistance organizations under its control. When Alten became a member of the governing board of the ŻSS in the autumn of 1940, representatives of all the aid organizations were co-opted onto the social welfare committees of the Lublin council. But this takeover created friction among the various executives, and the lack of clearly defined spheres of jurisdiction sparked many clashes.

One of the decrees that greatly troubled the Jews of Lublin was the closing of the schools. At the start of the occupation, the educators in the city tried to obtain a license from the local Polish authorities to open schools. A number of courses were renewed in the Hebrew gymnasium and the Tarbut schools, but the SS quickly intervened and closed the schools with the declaration, "From now on we'll deal with the education of Jewish youngsters." Many of the one hundred or so Jewish teachers who remained in Lublin began to run courses in private homes. This was the genesis of the clandestine educational program that, sooner or later, came into being in every one of the communities and ghettos.[51]

The overall picture that emerges from this look into the conduct of the Jewish Council of Lublin is one of contradictions and indecision, internal conflict, suspicion, and fear. Nevertheless, a great effort was made to act in concert for the sake of the common good—of the indigenous community as well as of the new-comers who had fled to Lublin or the vicinity. The leaders of the Jewish community did not have any clear program of action, and it is doubtful whether one could have been composed. Most of the council's members did have a sincere desire to cut a path through the morass that the Germans had created without causing or succumbing to corruption, just by doing their job faithfully. Toward that end, they created supervisory institutions and committees, disciplinary courts, and the like.

Moreover, following the conventions of the prewar period, they served the public on a voluntary basis; their income came from their jobs and other sources. But during the occupation these sources of livelihood were blocked, and ultimately they were forced to admit that they were in need of remuneration for their hard labors at the council, where they often worked day and night. Thus, at a meeting on September 30, 1940, they decided that as of October 1, the members of the Judenrat would be paid a salary. Still, they established an order of priority for expenses: first, the payments demanded by the authorities would have to be covered; second, all the operating expenses of the community's institutions; and only then would the remaining funds be used to cover personal expenses, including salaries for the members of the Judenrat.[52] These men were merely mortals, and like all mortals they were not free of the desire to rule. But it cannot be said that they regarded their roles and the power they wielded during that period as an achievement. On the contrary, they considered them a burden.

Coercive Leadership

Moshe Merin in Zagłębie (Eastern Upper Silesia)

A number of figures stand out among the leaders of the Judenräte for ostensibly being the masters of the fate of the Jews. Certainly, these men were not all cut from the same cloth; indeed, there were major differences between the styles adopted by Moshe Merin in Eastern Upper Silesia and Mordekhai Chaim Rumkowski in Łódź or Adam Czerniakow in Warsaw. The historian Philip Friedman has characterized some of them as "pseudo-saviors" suffering from a messianic complex. Opinion is divided on others of these leaders. But it appears that there is no argument about the character of the man who apparently dreamed of establishing his dominion over all the Jews of Europe in the shadow and under the aegis of the Nazi regime. That man was Moshe Merin, who held sway over the Jewish communities of Eastern Upper Silesia.[53]

This territory, with its seat of government in Katowice, was set apart for a special fate and was annexed directly to the Reich. Its governors were equivalent to the top-ranking members of the administration in the Reich proper—sometimes they were one and the same. Eastern Upper Silesia was among the first areas to be conquered by the German army and the first in which Hitler's legions went on a rampage. The small Jewish communities scattered through the area's villages and towns contained a total of one hundred thousand Jews. They suffered considerably during the early days of the war, with many communities being wiped out altogether. The two larger Jewish settlements in the area, Będzin and nearby Sosnowiec, together had fifty thousand Jews. A large portion of the population in this coal- and iron-rich area lived off mining and related industries; in line with the policy of the Polish government during the 1930s, the part played by the Jews in these fields of the economy was cut back. Nevertheless, they still played a considerable role as both employers and workers, though they were even more active in commerce and the crafts.

In Eastern Upper Silesia the Germans organized the Jewish communities along the lines first established for the Jews of Germany and united them into an umbrella organization patterned on the Reichsvereinigung der Juden in Deutschland. At the end of October 1939, Moshe Merin was appointed as head of this framework, the Union of Jewish Communities of Upper Silesia, and his office was officially known as the Central Committee of Jewish Councils of Elders for Eastern Upper Silesia. Philip Friedman has described this man, who was also known as "Munik" Merin:

> What sort of a man was Moses Merin? Though in his late thirties, he looked no more than twenty-five, because of his slight build; his expression was sharp and energetic, his eyes keen and deep. His family was well known in the town. . . . Before World War II, Merin was a commercial broker. He was separated from his wife, and led a bachelor's life. He spent most of his days and nights in coffeehouses, playing cards and billiards, at which he lost considerable sums of money. Merin's favorite pastime was politics, but his political reputation was not above reproach.[54]

Ringelblum observed that in his desire to become active in politics, Merin flitted from one party to the next. Before the outbreak of the war, he was a member of the board of the Jewish community of Sosnowiec, representing the Revisionist Party. As head of the Central Committee, he extended his sway over all of the thirty-two communities remaining in the area.

Special bylaws were published giving Moshe Merin broad powers. In addition to representing the Jewish councils vis-à-vis the Germans, he was authorized to change their membership—a right he used without reservation to ensure his control over them. Council chairmen or members who did not bow to his will—which was in most cases the will of the Germans—were soon replaced and sometimes disappeared. The Central Committee established departments—at least on paper—to deal with legal questions, welfare assistance, health, nutrition, finances, and of course compulsory labor. In December 1939 they were joined by a special Welfare Association that administered assistance programs on behalf of JDC, which was not permitted to operate in the territories annexed to the Reich. The Central Committee's Financial Department was also authorized to conduct negotiations with other foreign aid organizations such as TOZ and the Red Cross in order to obtain financial support for the Jews of the area. The Forced Labor Department was responsible for organizing the conscription of Jews who would be sent mostly to Germany. All in all, the Central Committee employed about twelve hundred people, with its senior officials—department heads and the chairmen of the large communities—acting as an advisory body to Merin that was called the brain trust.[55]

Merin worked methodically to gain absolute control over all the Jewish councils in his jurisdiction. In Będzin he went through four consecutive chairmen of the Judenrat before finding a man who would carry out his orders without questions; the first three had resigned in protest over his way of doing things. Such changes in personnel were not uncommon among the Judenräte. Usually they were ordered by the Germans, but often they were prompted by the resignation of the council's chairman. Thus in many places veteran local officials were replaced by recent arrivals who were prepared to do as they were told. The exception to this rule was in Eastern Upper Silesia, where Merin ran things himself. His rule reached down even to the small communities, and often his brother Ḥaim served as his envoy to the local councils.

In the sphere of forced labor, the Central Committee's actions were much the same as those of the other Jewish councils, that is, it attempted to fulfill the Germans' demands. In most cases this meant sending men to labor camps either in Germany or in Eastern Upper Silesia itself. At first Merin tried to get young men to volunteer for labor duty, but as soon as they grasped what this duty entailed and got wind of the conditions in the camps, no volunteers could be found. Then he shifted to the system of mandatory conscription, using all means possible to make it work, including threats to the youngsters or their parents.[56] An Order Service, or Jewish police, was formed, and in addition to its various administrative functions it was used to bring the "work dodgers" to the assembly points. Here, too, the system of self-ransom from labor duty was practiced by means of payments. In one instance Merin's extortion reached extraordinary proportions: he demanded the staggering sum of 15,000 zlotys per person. Although the families raised the money—with great difficulty—their loved ones were not released.[57]

As of summer 1940, factories opened under German management began to employ Jews. One of the largest of these enterprises was the plant for sewing uniforms run by a German named Rosner. From a workshop employing a few dozen people, it grew into a factory with three thousand workers whose products were well above the Germans' expectations. All who spoke of Rosner described him as "a rare character not at all like a typical German." He treated his employees with respect, appreciated their work, and fought to protect them; he even warned them when an *Aktion* was about to take place. Rosner kept this position until January 1944 when he was arrested and hanged.[58] A mechanized carpentry shop was established in the area as well as a plant for producing underwear and other enterprises. The workers engaged in these shops (as these industries were called) received a blue card that protected them against being sent to labor camps. Consequently, people did everything possible—including paying out hefty bribes—to secure a place in one of these concerns. They earned a paltry wage, the salary of a skilled worker for two weeks' labor being RM 15, with a third of this sum deducted for the local German Labor Office. Moreover, since no one could subsist on such an income (2.2 pounds of bread, for example, cost RM 24 [almost U.S. $10] on the black market), after using up their savings, the workers were reduced to selling their personal belongings. They did so at no small risk as such trade had been outlawed and anyone caught engaging in it faced the death penalty; there were even instances in which such people were hanged in public.

Together with his efforts to involve the Jews in productive industries, Merin worked to ensure the availability of aid and welfare assistance. He was very proud of his aid projects, and in March 1941 he published a guide to the Central Assistance Department in Eastern Upper Silesia summing up the various welfare programs operating in each of the thirty-or-so places it covered.[59] The longest section discussed food supplements: meals offered in soup kitchens and the distribution of basic foodstuffs. The other sections dealt with the financial support of the local residents and refugees (in thirty communities) and the care of infants, children, and the elderly. These standard activities were joined by special ones such as wintertime assistance through the distribution of coal, potatoes, and clothing; the supply of matzos for Passover; and the like.

Merin's rule also had limitations, the primary one being the German control that was the source of his authority. Yet in terms of the public, the clearest opposition to him came from the youth organizations. The Zionist youth movements in Zagłębie had been well established before the occupation, and after an initial period of disarray they began to reorganize. On the initiative of a number of their members, all these movements united in the Brith Hehalutzim (Alliance of Pioneers) and held their activities clandestinely in private apartments. They were initially aided because in the beginning the restrictions on the movement of Jews were relatively light in this area. No ghettos were established, and there were no limitations on travel from place to place or on the use of transport facilities, though a curfew was in effect during certain hours. In time the youngsters involved in these movements began to act in opposition to the Central Committee, as a matter of principle, and they refused to compromise with Merin. Their vigorous stand forced the "president" to take account of their demands.

After the Germans turned 75 acres of neglected agricultural land around Będzin and Sosnowiec over to the Judenrat, the members of the pioneering youth movements set to cultivating it. This project developed into an agricultural farm on which the youngsters lived and worked. They attracted additional members and held large conclaves at the farm. Even though the land was under the control of the Central Committee, Merin did not really have any influence over what went on at the farm. But he tried to bring this organized force into line at every opportunity, and at one point even tried—and failed—to establish a rival youth movement.[60]

Merin indulged himself with the belief that he had been called upon to fulfill a historic mission for the Jewish people throughout Europe. His readiness to serve the Germans gained him rare advantages: he was allowed to move freely within Poland and the Reich and had access to high-ranking German officials. On various occasions he visited not only Łódź, Warsaw, and other areas in the occupied territories but Berlin and Prague as well. Philip Friedman believes that these visits were related to the Jews who had been deported to Nisko and that their return should be credited to Merin. In Berlin, for example, he met with none other than Eichmann and together with him embarked on planning the mass emigration of Jews from Poland—to the point where he committed himself to obtaining twenty thousand certificates for entry into Palestine. When nothing came of these schemes, Merin shrugged off his failures by blaming them on the other leaders in the East and the West who had failed to cooperate with him or refused to accept his dictates.[61] Here and there his statements suggest that he saw himself as a latter-day Moses chosen to lead the Jewish people out of bondage. He was so blinded by pride that in his mind's eye he saw the way was open before him alone, and he was determined to pursue it—only to find that it was merely a figment of his imagination.

Mordekhai Chaim Rumkowski in Łódź (Warthegau)

Perhaps the most prominent of the Judenräte leaders and the subject of the most heated controversy was Mordekhai Chaim Rumkowski, who served as the Älteste of Łódź. Of all the heads of the ghettos, no one concentrated such absolute power in his hands as Rumkowski. An attractive man of sixty-two when he was appointed head of the Łódź Jewish Council, Rumkowski had been an insurance agent and community activist, primarily in charities, and had once even served as the director of an orphanage. Known as an energetic and domineering man, years earlier he had joined the council of the Łódź kehillah as a member of the Zionist minority (Agudat Yisrael then being the ruling party in Łódź). But when the Zionists left the council in protest to Aguda's policies, he refused to follow suit for fear of losing the public standing he had gained. Friedman contends that he did not take the role of chairman upon himself lightly but willingly accepted it even though he realized that the Jewish community was embarking upon a period fraught with peril. Like Merin, he believed that he was one of a privileged few who had been fated to play a decisive role in those difficult times.[62]

Rumkowski began working immediately after the German conquest. Most of the leaders of the Łódź community—members of the Aguda, the Bund, and Zionist parties—had fled on the outbreak of the war, and when the kehillah reorganized on September 12, 1939, Rumkowski was its deputy chairman. In mid-October the Germans dispersed the community council, appointed Rumkowski as Älteste, and charged him with forming the Ältestenrat (see chap. 6). Most of its members were veteran community officials of high social standing, and we may assume that they balked at the prospect of rendering blind obedience to Rumkowski and expressed opposition to his policy, for on November 11 they were all summoned to come to the Gestapo, never to be seen again.

Trying to put together a new council, Rumkowski encountered great difficulty since prospective candidates were daunted by the fate of the first Judenrat, especially as the appointments were made under the supervision of the Gestapo. When the new twenty-one-member Judenrat was installed on February 5, 1940, most of its participants, who included assimilated Jews and converts, lacked experience in public life, having at best served in junior positions in the Jewish community. Three days after the formation of the new Judenrat, the Germans proclaimed the establishment of the ghetto, which became the "realm" of "King Chaim"—as Rumkowski was known to the local wags.

Rumkowski's general aim was to turn the ghetto into a bastion of independent Jewish life, and he was convinced that he would achieve that goal only if he ruled it with a firm hand. To stress the ghetto's autonomy, German currency was taken out of circulation and was replaced by special bills bearing Jewish symbols, Rumkowski's portrait, and his signature. Some of the public services also became autonomous. When the Łódź Post Office canceled its service to Jews in February 1940, Rumkowski created his own postal service in the ghetto, whose stamps also bore his picture. By the end of its first year, this service employed 139 persons and had handled 10,000 telegrams, over a million letters and postcards, 150,000 packages, and 64,000 checks.[63] Post offices were established in other ghettos as well, but the only other instance of such complete autonomy was in Theresienstadt.

Even as Jewish property was being confiscated for use by the Germans, Rumkowski's broad aim was to transform the ghetto into a center of manufacture. He believed that productive work was the key to survival for the Jews; thus he must impose a regimen of labor and productivity upon the inhabitants of the ghetto for their own good. Two weeks after the ghetto was closed, he gave the Germans a list of close to 15,000 skilled workers and seventy different products that its inhabitants could manufacture. Shortly thereafter he added another few thousand to the list of workers. Isaiah Trunk has observed, "The emergence of an industry in the ghetto was contingent on three main conditions: the self-interest of the authorities, the accessibility of raw materials and equipment, and the availability of skilled labor."[64] Rumkowski succeeded in ensuring all three of these conditions in Łódź. In contrast to the rule in other places—and in Łódź itself prior to the closing of the ghetto—hardly any of its inhabitants were sent out of the ghetto for compulsory labor on a daily basis (as distinguished from deportation to labor camps). The ghetto was hermetically sealed, and that was why a work force was available within it.

At first Rumkowski mostly availed himself of the equipment found in Jewish-owned workshops, and if this machinery was not promptly turned in, he confiscated it. When his improvised industries began operating, the raw materials that fed them were junk and rags because the bona fide materials had been confiscated by the Germans. In the autumn of 1940, however, the Germans realized that the Łódź ghetto would not be just a temporary concentration camp, and they were prepared to take up Rumkowski's proposals to exploit its industrial potential. Workshops of all kinds were added to the existing collection of small-crafts' shops, and the Germans began to open factories that would eventually engage thousands of workers, releasing frozen funds for this purpose. Many white-collar workers also became laborers now, and special occupational retraining courses were given. Once orders began coming in from the Germans, raw materials were supplied as needed.

There were many consequences of the hermetic closing of the ghetto. The Jews of Łódź were unable to obtain food from outside the ghetto, and even within its bounds the exclusive use of ghetto currency impeded smuggling activities. The inhabitants were forced to exchange their money, including foreign currency, for local tender in order to purchase the meager foodstuffs that could be obtained in rationed amounts but that were not always affordable on the piddling wages they received. Hunger was widespread in Łódź, perhaps more than in most places in

Poland. Neither was the city spared the concomitant effects of epidemics and a high mortality rate. The resultant tension found vent in the riots, strikes, and demonstrations that broke out intermittently in the summer of 1940.[65]

Rumkowski's administration tried to cope with the problem of insufficient nutrition by establishing soup kitchens. Between October 1939 and September 1940, the number of portions distributed through these kitchens rose from 500 to 18,060. Food was supplied to an average of 5 percent of the population, but as a rule the recipients preferred money or basic foodstuffs to the poor quality of the soups, and during that year the Department for Social Assistance distributed basic products and cash to 52,058 people. Rumkowski financed some of this aid with money received from abroad, which in the first year reached the sum of RM 1,700,000 (U.S. $390,000). Even so, in September 1940 he was forced to close the department for lack of funds. When, as a result, hunger riots broke out in the ghetto, a new Department of Social Assistance was created to distribute small sums as a monthly allowance. At the close of 1940, this assistance program covered some 100,000 people, some two-thirds of the ghetto's population.[66]

The state of the health services was likewise poor, as most of the doctors had fled the city and those who remained, hampered by a shortage of drugs, were in many cases unable to treat the diseases successfully. Nevertheless, the epidemic of typhus fever that broke out in March 1940 during the establishment of the ghetto and the crowding of masses of people into temporary quarters and hostels was brought under control. In December 1940 a strike of medical workers broke out in the ghetto's only hospital because Rumkowski demanded that the workday be extended beyond eight hours. The strike was abandoned after a number of nurses and some of their relatives had been arrested.[67]

Among the other institutions that Rumkowski created in the ghetto were a network of courts, patterned on the state judicial system, and three prisons. Held in these prisons were both Jews who had violated the strict orders of the German ghetto administration and criminals brought from outside the ghetto. The Gestapo, which supervised the legal system in the ghetto, sent outside prisoners to these jails because they were the worst to be found. Most of the arrests made in the ghetto were for evading labor duty, robbing, failing to pay taxes, or for overt opposition to the Judenrat. When Rumkowski wanted to institute the death sentence, he met with opposition from four of the ghetto's judges and was forced to withdraw his demand. But he took revenge for their insubordination by firing them and seeing to it that they received no other work for a long time, which was tantamount to dooming them to starvation. All these judges were members of the Bund, and the organization supported their families until they were able to get by on their own.[68]

At the end of October 1939 Rumkowski established an Education Department and, with the permission of the German authorities, reopened forty-five Jewish schools. He also integrated welfare activities into this program by opening kitchens in some of the schools, so that almost all the youngsters who were studying could benefit from a nutrition program; in addition they were allocated clothing and provided with medical services. This educational network continued to exist for about two years. Rumkowski devoted special attention to orphans, establishing a compound of orphanages, known as Kolonia, in the Marysiu quarter of the ghetto, which contained agricultural land. These dormitories housed up to fifteen hundred children aged seven to fifteen. They included sickly and invalid children, for whom an infirmary, small hospital, and pharmacy were opened. Kolonia also contained schools, and beginning in the summer of 1940 summer camps were organized for the children in the kindergarten.[69]

At first most of the activities in this area of the ghetto were run by the Zionist youth movements, which had established training farms. At its peak, this enterprise encompassed about one thousand young people working on more than twenty farms. They were joined by a group of youngsters from the Bund, a group of girls from Agudat Yisrael, and twelve groups of young people not affiliated with any political party. This program was administered by the Judenrat's Agricultural Department, with the members of the collective farms working both on the land and in workshops in the city as well as engaging in cultural and social activities. After about a year, however, in the spring of 1941, Rumkowski disbanded all the training farms, concentrating both agricultural work and the youth programs under his direct supervision.

The emphasis in the city's cultural life shifted from the programs sponsored by the Jewish political parties and other organizations to the events held by the Center for Cultural Activities that opened in the winter of 1940/1941. About ten orchestral concerts were given there each month as well as performances by the Zamir Choir, theatrical productions, and children's plays. The theatrical performances included reviews, humorous sketches, and satires on ghetto life—usually a number of performances were staged each week. Art exhibits were held, and the Writers' Union sponsored literary evenings at which members read from their works. The ghetto administration established an archive to collect documentary material on the history of the Jews of Łódź and life in the ghetto. Beginning in January 1941, the archive published a daily chronicle that surveyed life in the ghetto.[70] Many of the ghetto's inhabitants also wrote memoirs and kept diaries; some were saved. A collection of sacred books and works on Jewish subjects has been lost. Another indication of the ghetto's irrepressible cultural life was the lively activity of the private lending libraries serving thousands of people. In spite of the fact that the synagogues had been destroyed, the community's religious activities went on at an intensified level, with worshippers gathering in private homes; during the High Holidays of 1941, public prayer services were held as well. The Judenrat supported the religious functionaries, protected the rabbis, and enabled them to practice under its wing. As in most other communities, it also tried to provide the inhabitants of the ghetto with matzos for Passover, and some of the ultra-Orthodox groups made great efforts to supply kosher food. During the early period of the ghetto's existence, Saturday was the official day of rest, and the observant population tried to give the day both religious and cultural content.

Like most of the other prewar Jewish communities of Poland, especially those in the large cities, Łódź was marked by a lively internal political life. The parties remained intact during the occupation and were joined by workers' committees and trade unions established in the industrial enterprises. To an increasing degree these committees became involved in running mutual-aid activities such as the opening of soup kitchens, the organization of sick funds, and the creation of financial instruments for mutual assistance. As a rule the Socialist parties remained in opposition to the Judenrat and Rumkowski personally, to the point where they organized protests against the council, demonstrations in which the Communist Party, with a large following in Łódź from before the war, was particularly active.

On becoming chairman of the Judenrat, Rumkowski had adopted an apolitical stance. "I have put aside my party card for the duration of the war,"[71] he declared and professed himself to be "both a fascist and a communist," for he understood totalitarianism as the concentration of all power in the hands of an omnipotent ruler who controlled people, their property, and the entire work force. Such absolute rule was bestowed upon him in the Łódź ghetto. According to one premise, he expected that as part of the "New Order of Europe" the Jewish question would be solved by granting the Jews some territory where they would be able to create "a model state."[72] He also believed that through "quiet and labor" he would succeed in protecting the Jews of Łódź.

One of his opponents who survived the Holocaust has pointed out that there was a substantive difference between the two periods of Rumkowski's rule: the earlier phase of the occupation and the later period of the deportations to the death camps. During the first phase, he concedes, Rumkowski displayed great initiative, quickly and skillfully creating a well-organized "realm" that encompassed all spheres of life.[73] He tried to cultivate the image of a caring, paternal ruler, and he took pains to appear in the figure of supreme judge; he was especially fond of having his picture taken at wedding ceremonies. His likeness on the ghetto's stamps portrayed him as a man protecting children and the poor. Friedman relates that hundreds of flattering poems, letters, and solicitations were sent to Rumkowski along with the works of artists and sculptors and that adulation of the chairman became obligatory in the schools.[74] During the first phase of the ghetto's existence, no one could conceive of a program of systematic mass extermination, and Rumkowski undoubtedly believed wholeheartedly that he would save the Jews of Łódź.

The One and the Many: Adam Czerniakow and the Jews of Warsaw

The Man and His Fate

"Adam Czerniakow [was] one of the most tragic of Jewish community leaders during the Holocaust," wrote Josef Kermisz, in the introduction to the published edition of Czerniakow's diary. As chairman of the Judenrat in Warsaw, "he showed the best of his character, his moral strength, and his devotion to his people." Yisrael Gutman remarked, "Czerniakow's diary is an impressive testament to the fairness and courage of the man who was appointed to represent the largest Jewish community in Europe at a time of terror and supreme trial." Yet Gutman asks why, despite all these praiseworthy qualities, a deep breach opened between the Judenrat and the Jewish public in Warsaw.[75]

Among a broad segment of the population, the opposition to Czerniakow grew to the point of outright hatred. According to the definition of the role that the

Germans forced upon him, Czerniakow was above all obliged to fulfill their demands. That was their purpose in creating the Judenrat, and one of their explicit aims was to turn it into an instrument that would lead the Jews to their destruction. According to this thinking, the Jews were supposed to regard the Judenrat as their main and direct enemy so that their hatred for it would further abet their self-destruction. When Czerniakow and the other members of the Judenrat tried simultaneously to comply with the Germans' demands and safeguard the Jewish public, "their efforts were doomed to bitter failure," Gutman wrote.[76] During the early period of the occupation, which is discussed here, neither the leaders of the Judenrat nor the Jewish population grasped the scope and depth of the disaster that would overtake them. When Czerniakow finally did comprehend the full implications of the tragedy, he took the one drastic step left to a man powerless to prevent it.

Adam Czerniakow was Rumkowski's cousin and about three years his junior, but his life prior to the Nazi conquest of Poland was very different from that of the "dictator of Łódź." He came from an assimilated Jewish background and had studied industrial engineering in Warsaw and in Dresden. From his youth onward, beginning in the days before World War I, Czerniakow had taken an active part in Jewish public life. Most of his energies were devoted to the cause of the craftsmen, the largest sector of the Jewish working class, who had great difficulty maintaining their status and livelihoods during the interwar period. Czerniakow became a prominent figure among these artisans, held important posts in their organization, gave speeches and published articles, and fought for their rights against the government's adverse policy. He also worked toward raising the professional level of the workers by establishing vocational schools and taught in the kehillah's vocational schools in Warsaw. At the same time, Czerniakow took an interest in broader Jewish affairs and, as a member of Yitzhak Grünbaum's faction at the end of the 1920s, fought for the national rights of the minorities. He served on the Warsaw City Council from 1927 to 1934 as a representative of the craftsmen and the (Jewish) National Bloc list, and in 1938 he was a member of the Warsaw delegation to the Convention of Polish Jewry for Palestine. When the war broke out, Czerniakow was a member of the Council the Polish authorities had appointed to run the Warsaw kehillah. Again he represented the Union of Craftsmen. He also served as the chairman of the kehillah's Education Department.

Beleaguered and Occupied Warsaw

Adam Czerniakow was, therefore, a well-known figure—at least to part of the Jewish public—and had entrée to the city's ruling circles. At the outbreak of the war, the city fathers tried to prepare Warsaw for the difficult days ahead by founding the Capital Committee for Mutual Social Assistance, in which all the Polish political parties and a number of economic and social welfare experts took part. This committee controlled the stores of food in the city and had a large sum of money at its disposal. At the same time, those leaders of the kehillah who remained in Warsaw tried to form a Civilian Council that would represent the Jewish community in all dealings and cooperative efforts with the Polish authorities (this council began operating on September 12).[77]

There was a great fluctuation in the population of Warsaw—perhaps most of all in its Jewish population—as a result of the mass flight from the city, on the one hand, and the entry of refugees from all over the country, on the other. The diarist Chaim A. Kaplan wrote on September 11, 1939:

> Warsaw is full of refugees from all corners of the country. In the midst of the turmoil an unplanned and undirected flight started, with some fleeing from Warsaw and others fleeing to Warsaw. Among the refugees there is a preponderance of people from the left bank of the Vistula. They were so frightened by the approach of the barbarian enemy that they left a lifetime's labor behind in order to save their skins. Camps, camps of tens of thousands, filled with movable property and children, line all the roads that lead to the capital, when the capital itself is not safe from disaster.[78]

The relentless bombing of Warsaw left many of its inhabitants homeless, and the aid committees had their hands full preparing shelter in public buildings, providing food, tending to the wounded, and burying the dead—all while participating in the defense of the city. Among the countless people who fled Warsaw were many of the leading lights of the Jewish community. On September 23 the mayor of Warsaw, who was also the commander of the civil defense force, appointed Czerniakow chiarman of the Jewish Community Council. "A historic role in a besieged city," Czerniakow wrote in his diary that day. "I will try to live up to it."[79] That was the man's style: terse sentences of sometimes only a few words giving the bare essentials. Here and there he might hint at what he was thinking and feeling, but for the most part his thoughts and sentiments were concealed behind the dry recitation of the facts. It was certainly the recommended style for a diary kept by the chairman of the Judenrat, considering that the Germans could get their hands on it whenever they pleased. Yet evidently it was also the natural manner of a man who was not in the habit of giving his feelings away.

Strikingly different was the style of the Hebrew teacher Chaim A. Kaplan, who regarded the writing of his "Scroll of Agony" as an inescapable duty. Kaplan repeatedly described the sights of the destroyed city. The Jewish neighborhood was worst hit by the German bombs, which had rained down on it—evidently not by chance alone—particularly on the eve of the Jewish New Year (September 13, 1939). Kaplan related that the Jewish quarter was all but wiped off the face of the earth, reduced to mounds of rubble with smoking rods poking out of them.[80] There was talk of thousands of Jews being buried under the wreckage—Czerniakow once wrote that he himself had buried corpses[81]—and hunger and pillage were rife. These were the circumstances in which Adam Czerniakow took up his new role.

Warsaw fell on September 27, 1939, but that was not the end of the agony. On October 4 members of the SS came to the kehillah's offices at a time when Czerniakow was not there. They drove the council's members out of the building, shut the rooms, and left, taking the keys—including the key to the safe—with them. The members of the council met Czerniakow in the street and told him that the Germans had demanded that he report to them. After a brief consultation, it was decided that everyone else would go home and Czerniakow would approach the Germans alone. When he did so, they took him off to the SD headquarters. The incident is indicative of one of Czerniakow's most outstanding personal traits: raw courage. Countless times he stood facing the German authorities alone. They used to summon him at any hour of the day or night, as they pleased, and often he was subjected to threats and blows at these meetings. Still, Czerniakow did not kowtow to the Germans, though he saw no way to avoid complying with their demands. On July 21, 1940, he wrote, "One has to carry the cross but not drag it."[82]

At his first meeting with the SS men, Czerniakow was ordered to establish an Ältestenrat of twenty-four members. One Warsaw Jew accused him of pressing for the position of chairman, but the entries in his diary do not corroborate that,[83] and it was not until three days after the Germans closed down the kehillah that Czerniakow agreed to serve as the chairman of the Judenrat. It was not until October 16 that the keys were returned and the council was able to begin its work.

On October 20 Czerniakow noted in his diary that he believed his main tasks would center on statistical matters, finances, schools, and the work battalion, adding, "I must supply 500 men to the Municipality at seven in the morning."[84] By "statistical matters" he meant the census that the Germans had ordered for October 28. That day dozens of Jewish youngsters went from house to house registering the population, which was shown to be 360,000 people.

Then the blows began to rain down on the Jews one after another: the expropriation of property, the order to wear a special insignia, the marking of businesses, and above all the threat to establish a "pale of settlement"—the ghetto. We now know that Czerniakow managed to have this last decree postponed, but he was less successful in standing up to the Germans' extortion. Their repeated demands for "contributions" from the Jews were enforced by arresting distinguished members of the community and holding them for ransom. Dozens of Jews were killed in these and other exercises in intimidation. In light of all these pressures, on January 26, 1940, Czerniakow approached the SS and asked "to be released from chairmanship since I find it impossible to manage the community under these abnormal conditions. In reply I was told that this would be inadvisable."[85] And so he went on working, remaining at his difficult and perilous post out of a sense of duty toward the people. It was suggested to him that he flee Poland, perhaps even make his way to Palestine—as many other Polish-Jewish leaders had done before him. But as his diary shows, he regarded these people with the contempt reserved for deserters.[86]

Jews Mobilize for Self-help

Czerniakow and the Judenrat were not the only organized Jewish force fighting to keep the Jews of Warsaw alive. The Warsaw council of Jewish Self-help (ŻSS) developed a program of activities so broad that it ultimately surpassed the scope of the Judenrat's assistance work. The ŻSS put together a large and ramified bureaucracy that covered all spheres of life. It was divided into departments for soup kitchens, food stores, housing, clothing, health, finances, and legal affairs as well as a bureau of statistics and special branches for supervision and training, social affairs, theater and the arts, the press, religion, and for youth.[87]

In essence, Jewish society continued to function along the lines that had been established prior to the war. Then, too, jurisdiction over the community and the direction of its activities had been divided among various voluntary organizations working parallel to the kehillah. During the occupation yet another institution came into being in Warsaw: the *house committee.* Having evolved spontaneously on a grass-roots level, these committees proved very successful in their social aid. They were installed in cooperation with the ŻSS.[88] Back when Warsaw had been under siege, the Council of Destroyed Property had made arrangements for seminaries and schools to house people whose homes had been bombed and extended them loans, many of which were returned once they had got back on their feet. On the establishment of the ghetto, a Department of Traffic was created to help people move their belongings to their new apartments. The Jews suffered heavy financial losses in this exchange of apartments. Not only were they forced to turn well-kept, spacious apartments in various parts of the city over to Poles in return for small, run-down ones in the ghetto, they also had to pay the Poles key money for the privilege. The concierges waxed particularly rich during this period, for they had the opportunity to take over for themselves the best of the Jewish apartments, including the furniture, clothing, and other belongings left within. Even at this early date, the Jews were plagued by a severe shortage of money, and the loan funds of the ŻSS did their best to help. The source of their capital at this stage was still the JDC, which was channelling funds into the Generalgouvernement to help all branches of Jewish society maintain their services. In addition, the ŻSS collected monies from wealthy Jews who were still in a position to make donations. But the size of these contributions declined quickly, and the growing impoverishment of the Jewish community was as evident in Warsaw as elsewhere in the areas under Nazi control.[89]

The Ghetto Fighting for Life

At the end of 1940, when the ghetto had been isolated, the Jews lived in a state of chaos and immense anxiety, for suddenly they saw themselves being closed in, as though imprisoned, with their sources of livelihood now beyond reach. Nevertheless, the full gravity of the situation had yet to be grasped. People still had some resources left, it was still possible to obtain stocks of food, and during these early months the mortality rate in the ghetto was not very high. As the winter wore on, the number of people in need of aid increased, but it was not until the following summer that the drop in the funds provided by JDC was sorely felt. In the spring of 1940, soup was distributed by seventy-two kitchens; by September of that year their number had been reduced by half, whereas the number of needy people mounted and hunger increased.[90]

But the vitality and lust for life of Warsaw's Jews soon proved themselves even beyond the framework of the self-help enterprises. We shall try to indicate some of the factors that forged the special character of the Warsaw ghetto and its population. To begin with, the system of total segregation practiced in the Łódź ghetto and the concentration of absolute power in the hands of the Älteste was not followed in the capital. Unlike Rumkowski, Czerniakow had no pretensions to dictatorship. What is more, the regime in the Generalgouvernement was fractionalized and less categorical in its approach than the German administration in the annexed areas, and the real needs of both the Germans and the Poles in Warsaw were greater and more varied. For example, it was imperative to rehabilitate the economy in Warsaw, not worsen its paralysis. Unlike the situation in Łódź and so many other places, the number of Jewish leaders who either remained in or returned to Warsaw was relatively high. But perhaps the most decisive reason for the difference between Łódź and Warsaw was the essential nature of the Warsaw Jewish community.

The range of activities cultivated in the Warsaw ghetto seems almost phenomenal. The Jews displayed incredible initiative and resourcefulness in turning junk and rags into products for which the Poles and Germans alike were prepared to violate all the government's strictures. Most of the movement and contact between the supposedly closed ghetto and the world around took place not through the official Transferstelle but through a variety of alternative, very risky channels that worked beyond all expectations. Had the ghetto been forced to exist solely on the food allocated by the Germans, it would not have survived for long, especially as its population kept rising at a rapid rate. Groups of refugees from other cities and towns continued to stream into Warsaw, and they were joined by Jews from the immediate vicinity who the Germans forced into the ghetto.

As time went on greater amounts of raw materials were brought into the ghetto, and the Jews fashioned them into a wide selection of products. From brushes to electronic instruments, there seemed to be hardly anything that the Jews of Warsaw were not capable of manufacturing. In the spring of 1941, when the Germans realized the potential of this work force and productive capacity and as their own need for various products kept increasing, they effectively gave recognition to the center of commerce and industry that had emerged in the ghetto. The commercial traffic between the two parts of the city was accompanied by the smuggling of food into the ghetto. These operations, on which the lives of the ghetto's inhabitants were dependent, were carried out by individuals and groups alike. Quickness and daring, cunning and unscrupulousness were all required by the successful smuggler (many of whom were children) to get past policemen, guards, and the wall itself (encompassing most of the ghetto), which was about 10 feet high, about 11.25 miles long, and topped with broken glass.[91]

But this vibrant side of Warsaw was only part of the picture. We cannot overlook the thousands who were unable to work and therefore unable to purchase the smuggled goods; the sick and the starving who stand out in the many photographs that have survived from the Warsaw ghetto; the beggars; the shadows of human beings who roamed the streets; and the newspaper-covered corpses left lying where they had dropped. The special life of the Warsaw ghetto created two new, conspicuously diametrical classes. While the number of the weak and dying mounted, the aggressive types—members of the gangs of smugglers and those who traded in smuggled goods—waxed steadily richer. They believed they were living on borrowed time and followed the dictate *"carpe diem."* Not all the Germans' stories of debauchery in the ghetto were fabrications. Although clearly they exploited such phenomena for propaganda purposes, there really were restaurants in the ghetto where it was possible to obtain a selection of choice delicacies.

Unquestionably, Czerniakow knew all this. In December 1941 he even explained the open secret of the smuggling operations to a German official, "We received legally 1,800,000 zlotys' worth of food in the ghetto monthly and illegally 70[000,000] to 80,000,000 zlotys' worth. . . . One might reckon there are 10,000 capitalists, plus or minus 250,000 who earn their living by work, and 150,000 who have to rely on public assistance."[92]

The Jewish Police

Czerniakow's tolerance of the people's behavior and activities was taken in various ways, sometimes as weakness. While opinions are divided on this matter, we find only negative views of his dealings with the Order Service, the Jewish police. Its establishment was ordered by the Germans when the ghetto was closed off in October 1940. Though it was set up by the Judenrat, its members had to be approved by the Germans.[93] The Judenrat employed a long and involved process for choosing among the many candidates who applied for acceptance into the ranks of the Jewish police. They were reviewed by various selection boards that checked into their past, education, health, and so on, but there was a great difference between the conditions for acceptance in theory and in practice.

The commander of the force was Józef Szeryński, formerly a colonel in the Polish police. A man then in his forties, he had served in the Russian army in World War I and was captured by the Germans. After returning from Germany as a POW, he joined the Polish police and at the same time converted from Judaism, changing his name from Sheinkman to Szeryński. Over the years, Szeryński worked his way up the ranks to hold a series of posts in the national headquarters, and when World War II broke out he was the deputy commander of the police in the Lublin District. He came to Warsaw after being released from prison by the Germans, and with the establishment of the ghetto, like many other converts, he was forced to return to the Jewish fold. Szeryński's attitude toward the Jews, and certainly toward Jewish culture and tradition, was at best indifferent, but he was accused of being hostile. When word got out that he was to be appointed commander of the police, there was an outcry from various quarters of the population, especially from the Bund. But despite this opposition, Czerniakow and a number of his associates on the Judenrat decided to confirm the appointment.[94] Their reasons for doing so seem to have been Szeryński's professional experience and his good relations with the Polish police. At a subsequent stage, Szeryński faced opposition from within the Jewish police, as a result of which certain changes were made in its staff. At the end of the recruitment campaign, the force comprised 1,700 policemen, 869 of whom were students or members of the free professions (51.1 percent), with the rest being merchants, technicians, and craftsmen. During the first few months, 184 were replaced and 127 left of their own volition or were dismissed due to absenteeism. Seven hundred of the 1,700 policemen were tried before a disciplinary court at one time or another for violations of discipline or acts of corruption.

From an organizational standpoint, the ghetto was divided into sectors with a police station opened in each. The command hierarchy was similar to that of the Polish police, and the policemen's "uniforms" essentially consisted of a visored cap bearing their symbol of rank and a yellow band with the inscription "Warsaw Judenrat, Order Service" in German and Polish, which was worn on the right sleeve. The policemen were armed with rubber or wooden truncheons. As the Jewish police was subordinate to the three authorities—the Judenrat, the Germans, and the Polish police—the public regarded it as the representative of the tyrannical and arbitrary forces ruling over them.

Initially they were responsible for maintaining order, seeing to the cleanliness of the ghetto, and standing guard on the inner side of the ghetto's gates. Later on they were charged with additional duties that heightened the tension in their relations with the population. When an epidemic of typhus fever broke out, the Jewish police were sent to guard the infected buildings that had been placed under quarantine, and a special unit, the Sanitation Police, was also created for this purpose. Thus, the policemen came into conflict with the house committees, which were interested in preserving their tenants' freedom of movement. In the spring of 1941, when the Germans demanded that Jews be sent to labor camps, it was the Jewish police that rounded up anyone attempting to evade labor duty. In many cases the policemen behaved very harshly in carrying out their duties, and some of them were even punished by being sent to the camps themselves. The population was particularly bitter about the special police tax that the Judenrat instituted to cover the upkeep of the force at a time when the tax burden already weighed heavily on the population.

In two spheres, however, a sense of cooperation did develop between the Jewish police and the ghetto's inhabitants. The first was in the field of smuggling. In many cases it proved impossible to carry on any smuggling operations without the cooperation of the policemen. When that was so, the police tried to exploit the situation to their own benefit, especially since they received a meager wage at best (a fact that had many repercussions). Some policemen even engaged in smuggling themselves. The other sphere of cooperation was with the policemen known as instructors, who played a definite and positive role. Attached to the local police stations in the ghetto, these instructors served as mediators and judges:

> [They] intervened to settle disputes between neighbors and handled problems between people that resulted from life in the ghetto. . . . The kind of work done by the instructors was not bureaucratic in any way and was marked by its large measure of public responsibility. It won the great appreciation of the Jewish population because, among other things, it averted the necessity of handing Jews over to the Polish Police, to which all criminal cases had to be referred.[95]

The paradoxical role played by the Judenrat came out even more sharply in the relations of the Jewish police with its principals, on the one hand, and the population fighting for its life, on the other. The temptation to exploit this situation for personal gain was enormous, and few withstood it. But during the first phase of the ghetto's existence, the Jewish police maintained something of a balance between deeds of corruption and actions carried out for the good of the public.[96]

Hope Against Hope

Naturally the Jews tried to get whatever reliable information they could on the situation at the fronts in the East and in the West, but the ghetto was rife with rumors and fabrications meant to encourage the inhabitants by implying that their misery would soon be coming to an end. One day the word was that Hitler had been murdered, the next that the Russians were at the gates or that victory was imminent for the Allies in the West. Of course, every piece of bad news turned the hopes to despair, so that the mood swung from one extreme to the other. Testimony to this effect can be found in Chaim Kaplan's diary. The entry for January 14, 1940, reads, "It is good that we console ourselves, for even if these are false hopes, they keep us from collapsing under the weight of the persecution." And the following day he wrote, "Between defeat and victory, Polish Jewry is being wiped out. Here the victory is complete. The conqueror regards world Jewry as its enemy, and now it is fighting, so we are kept as prisoners-of-war."[97] Sometimes he criticized those who clung to false hopes, but then again he himself mused, "Which will disappear first, Nazism or Judaism? I pledge! Nazism will go first. We have the remedy that the Prophet Isaiah counselled: 'Come my people . . . and shut your doors behind you; / hide yourselves for a little while / until the wrath is past.' That is what we are doing."[98]

To a certain degree, even Czerniakow was given to mood swings. In contrast to Rumkowski and Merin, most of the Jews fully believed, like Kaplan, that the Nazis would meet their end one day, so they had but one focal aim: to persevere until that day came. Essentially the strategy of the Jewish war for survival was simple: first, it was necessary to see to one's physical existence, which meant obtaining food in any way possible and getting along with the absolute minimum in terms of shelter and clothing; second, it was necessary to work not only to earn the wages that would ensure these minimal conditions but also to earn a place in the Germans' calculations of expediency. The Jews tried to achieve these aims on both the collective and personal planes. But like most of their brethren elsewhere, the Jews of Warsaw knew that man does not live by bread alone, and they tried to tend to their other social and spiritual needs as well. They saw to the education of their children—in defiance of what the Germans had ordained. They practiced their religion, held prayer services, continued the study of the Torah (despite the prohibitions and persecution directed specifically against observant Jews), and accumulated historical evidence of what was taking place. Although the Nazis deprived the Jews not only of a sufficient amount of food but initially of the means to maintain health and medical services, hospitals and pharmacies continued to operate and doctors worked with boundless dedication. When an epidemic broke out, for example, the Germans in Warsaw were forced to organize a special course for the people who worked on the disinfectant squads. The Jews did not capitulate and did not despair. Instead, they mounted their own war: a war for survival.

Schooled in suffering for centuries, the Jews of Poland were well versed in the ways of the difficult and often desperate struggle for survival. Victims there had always been, but one way or another the Jewish people had always overcome their trials. The crowded conditions in which they lived actually gave them a sense of security and enabled them to carry on the active intellectual life for which they were renowned. The impact of this tradition was evident in their behavior during the first phase of the war and the occupation. Deep in their hearts they carried the belief that they would prevail this time as well.

The hardships to which the Nazis subjected the Jews were of various kinds. Much of the Jewish population was uprooted and forced into new and crowded concentrations. This population transfer took place in three stages: (1) the major expulsions from the western territories into the Generalgouvernement, effected through both deportations and conscription for the labor camps, with a thin stream even being siphoned from the annexed areas to the Reich proper; (2) the transfer of population on a local and lesser scale from smaller settlements to larger ones; and (3) the concentration of the inhabitants of cities and towns in a Jewish residential area, namely, a ghetto—though we should note that the ghettoization process was far slower than had been visualized in Heydrich's orders of September 21, 1939. To this forced movement of Jews we must add the movement undertaken on their own initiative. They fled from one place to another—either trying to leave Poland or remaining in the country but streaming toward the urban centers—in the hope of finding conditions more amenable to their struggle for survival. A few statistics will illustrate these facts. The 55,245 refugees and deportees in the Lublin District in the spring of 1941 composed 28.5 percent of the district's Jewish population of close to 194,000 people. The 67,843 refugees and deportees in the Radom District in 1941 accounted for 20.7 percent of that district's Jewish population of 327,583. But the largest concentration of refugees was unquestionably in Warsaw. On December 31, 1940, there were 78,625 refugees from seventy-three cities living in the ghetto, where they composed 20 percent of the population of close to 400,000 people. In the first quarter of 1941, they were joined by another 70,000 Jews from the vicinity, and in the summer of that year the number of refugees reached 150,000, fully one-third of the ghetto's population.[99] The deportations into the Generalgouvernement notwithstanding, there were concentrations of this sort in Warthegau as well.

Among the groups of Jews roaming about within Poland's borders were demobilized soldiers. It is estimated that about 100,000 Jews, or 10 percent of the military, took part in the battle for Poland. The Poles sustained casualties of 60,000 dead and about 133,000 wounded,[100] with Jews again composing about 10 percent of these figures. Some 60,000 Jews were captured by the enemy, but the Germans did not recognize them as POWs, and many suffered a most bitter fate. Estimates run that about one-third were murdered; the rest managed to return to their homes, by one way or another, or they stayed in the settlements where they had been demobilized—most of them only to become victims of later extermination.

Many of the thousands of Jewish soldiers who remained in the Soviet sector were granted Soviet citizenship and drafted into the Red Army. After an agreement was concluded with the Soviet Union in 1941, a Polish army was formed in Russia under the command of General Władyslaw Anders, and it fought alongside the Allies. About 5,000 Jewish soldiers joined this army, some of them even reaching Palestine with its units.[101]

There were also instances of both forced and voluntary movement of the population into the area under Soviet control, and over the years a few hundred people emigrated from Poland, some of them to Palestine. In most cases they had to labor for many weeks, even months, to obtain all the papers necessary in order to leave the occupied country legally. These journeys of escape were handled by international travel agencies. Residents of Palestine who were caught in Poland at the outbreak of the war and the fortunate few who had Palestinian immigration certificates were able to sail from Trieste. The Hebrew Immigrant Aid Society (HIAS) office was the scene of bitter struggles for the right to be included in the lists of immigrants. These people were also the first to bring out word of what was going on in Poland. Naturally, in their desperation to get out of the country, people also took recourse to forged documents acquired for a steep price; on more than one occasion, after the coveted papers finally arrived, they suddenly and mysteriously disappeared, leaving the man who believed he was about to go free again locked in the ghetto.[102] But emigration was brought to a halt by a circular dated November 25, 1940, abolishing the Jews' right to leave Poland. This new prohibition was based on the RSHA order of October 25, which cited two reasons for the new restriction. The first was that Hermann Göring wished to save the option of emigration for the Jews of the Reich and the Protectorate. The second was anchored in the ideological tenet that the source of the Jews' spiritual power was in Eastern Europe. Hence, it was imperative that they be prevented from reaching the United States and contributing to the spiritual renewal and general consolidation of the Jewish community there, which would inevitably intensify the war against Germany.[103]

The policy of expelling the Jews from their places of residence always included plundering their property, exploiting their labor, depriving them of food, and denying them the possibility of conducting a normal social life—all in addition to deliberate acts of humiliation meant to strip them of their humanity. A combination of German self-interest and the initiative and talents of the Jews is what prevented the complete deterioration of the Jewish population. In most places the Jews succeeded in maintaining themselves on a level that enabled them to wage their stubborn struggle for survival. Until the United States entered the war, they also received assistance from abroad, mainly from JDC.

8

Facing a Triumphant Germany

Jewish Communities in Northern and Western Europe

The six countries that came under Hitler's domination at the beginning of the summer of 1940—Norway, Denmark, Holland, Luxembourg, Belgium, and France—had Jewish communities that were distinguished from each other by their size, demographic composition, history, internal organization, and their Jewish and general cultural disposition. These communities also found themselves subject to different patterns of rule by the German occupiers. The three small Jewish communities—Norway (with eighteen hundred Jews), Denmark (with close to eight thousand, including the offspring of mixed marriages), and Luxembourg (with about four thousand)—were subordinate to three different kinds of authority: the first to the SS; the second to the Danish government, by virtue of an understanding between the Danes and the Germans; and the third to the German government, as a consequence of the country's annexation to the Reich.

During the period under review here, the Jews of **Norway** and especially of Denmark suffered no more than the rest of the population in these countries. Immediately after the annexation of **Luxembourg,** the Jews in that country felt the impact of the Reich's racial laws. As stated earlier, about one thousand Jews managed to flee Luxembourg during the first days of the occupation (see chap. 6). For the rest, Rabbi Robert Serebrenik reconstituted the community organization (Consistoire), but essentially no trace of traditional civil liberties remained. On the other hand, close to two thousand Jews managed to leave the country as emigrants through France and Portugal, some in 1940 and most as late as May 1941.[1]

In contrast, and notwithstanding some attacks in the newspapers by a small group of local anti-Semites, the Jews of **Denmark** continued to enjoy the civil rights granted them at the beginning of the nineteenth century. Their property was not expropriated; here and there they were even involved in trade with the Germans. In return, through an understanding with the Danish government, the Jews worked against flight from the country, forbade the members of the community to be associated with any underground, and tried to run their lives in a low-keyed manner, so as not to arouse the attention of the German occupation authorities. Hence, they discontinued the publication of the community newspaper and the activities of its council, which had previously tended to the needs of the Jewish refugees in Denmark under the noncommittal title of the May Fourth Committee. Aid to the refugees was now channeled through the government's Ministry for Social Affairs, which also assumed financial responsibility. The fund-raising drives that had been held for this purpose among the members of the Jewish community were discontinued, but the staff that served the 350 Zionist pioneers undergoing agricultural training in Denmark continued to function. These young pioneers represented a portion of the 1,500 refugees who still remained in the country out of the 4,500 who had found their way into Denmark during the 1930s. A group of Youth Aliyah children and a few dozen Palestinian citizens were allowed to leave Denmark legally for Sweden, and they reached Palestine via the USSR. The Jews of Denmark, regarding themselves as fully equal Danish citizens, placed their faith in their government. They felt obliged to prove their loyalty to Denmark, especially at this hour of trial, by not creating any difficulties. Such conduct, they further assumed, would also ensure their safety.[2]

The three larger Jewish communities—Holland (140,000), Belgium (65,000), and France (300,000)—differed from one another in almost every respect. From an internal viewpoint, the Jews of **Holland** stood apart from their counterparts in the other communities in their outlook and the character of their religious and political leadership. The Ashkenazi community, which was organized in a nationwide union of kehillot, was generally Orthodox in nature, though many of its activists were Liberal Jews. The Ashkenazim were the majority in Holland, with the Portuguese community composing a small minority. Thanks to a long tradition of civil rights, which had been granted at the end of the eighteenth century, the Jews of Holland took their equal status in Dutch society for granted, and many Jews fulfilled leading roles in the country's economic, juridical, and cultural life. As a result of this unqualified identification with the Dutch people and state, Zionism did not take hold among any appreciable portion of the Jewish public in Holland, but several prominent Dutch Jews were associated with the movement, and their influence far exceeded their number. A few of the leading Zionists emigrated to Palestine, where they likewise assumed key positions in the Yishuv.

During the 1930s the Jews of Holland were confronted by the need to care for the tens of thousands of Jewish refugees who had fled to the country. David Cohen, professor of ancient history at the University of Leiden and president of the Ashkenazi Union of Communities, and the diamond merchant Abraham Asscher addressed the needs of these refugees through the Committee for Special Jewish Affairs. The committee was headed by Asscher, while Cohen played a focal role as head of its subcommittee for refugees, which recruited a large staff to care for the refugees' needs.[3]

In the autumn of 1940, the first assaults on their civil status profoundly shocked the Jews of Holland. In the wake of their ouster from the civil service, the attorney Marinus Kan, chairman of the Zionist Organization, deemed it wise to establish a new, comprehensive communal organization that would represent Dutch Jewry vis-à-vis the authorities and otherwise work on behalf of the Jewish community during this trying period. His first step was to expand the Zionist leadership by co-opting representatives from WIZO (Women's International Zionist Organization) and Hanoar Hatzioni on to the board of this communal group. Later on, in December 1940, the Joodse Coördinatie Commissie (Jewish Coordination Committee) was established under the chairmanship of a distinguished figure whose authority was acknowledged by all: Lodewijk Ernst Visser, a judge who had served on the Supreme Court for twenty-five years and became its president in 1939.[4] He was particularly shocked because he saw that his colleagues on the Supreme Court lacked the courage to protest his dismissal by order of the Germans. Since the heads of the Committee for Special Jewish Affairs, Cohen and Asscher, were the most active figures in the community and had a well-trained staff at their disposal, it proved impossible to run the Coordination Committee without them. But almost from the start, these two men found themselves at odds with Visser over matters of principle. Visser believed—and never tired of asserting—that the Jews must not cooperate with the Germans in any way and that there was only one authority to whom the Jews of Holland could address themselves: the Dutch authorities, whose duty it was to protect the rights of the Jews anchored in law. He ignored the fact that the heads of the Dutch administration were now carrying out orders issued by the Germans. The directors-general of the ministries were bureaucrats, not politicians, and they regarded the tribulations of the Jews as a humanitarian problem, not a political one.

While Visser's opposition to cooperation with the Germans bespoke a political orientation, Asscher and especially Cohen invoked the humanitarian principle and believed it was necessary to negotiate with the Germans in order to mitigate the suffering of the Jews through intercession on their behalf. Thus, they essentially held to the approach that had been employed prior to the war to obtain aid for the refugees, except that now they were tending to the Jewish community as a whole.[5]

The organization of Holland's Jewish youth, and particularly of Hanoar Hatzioni in Holland, is a subject in its own right. Until Hitler's rise to power, this youth movement had not made much of an impact in Holland. Yet its structure differed radically from that of the Zionist youth movements in Central and Eastern Europe. Following the philosophy of the Dutch Zionist leaders that their youth should not be split among party-oriented movements, a Federation of Jewish Youth was established as an umbrella organization for all the country's Zionist youth, encompassing about two thousand members.[6] The federation embraced two main youth organizations: Hevrat Ha-olim (The Society of Immigrants [to Palestine]) and Brit Halutzim Dati'im (Alliance of Religious Pioneers), which was essentially an arm of the same movement in Germany. They were joined in the 1930s, especially as of 1938, by members of Hehalutz from Germany—most were members of movements that had established a branch of Hehalutz in Holland in order to provide for agricultural training, either in groups or individually, with local farmers. Some 765 young people were engaged in agriculture under this program.

In the summer of 1940 all the Zionist youth united in an umbrella institution known as the Jewish Center, although the Dutch Hanoar Hatzioni and the members of the German movements did not readily find a common ground: despite their efforts to integrate, they remained two separate entities. Apart from the sense of strangeness that traced to differences of language and cultural background, most of the members of the Dutch Federation of Jewish Youth did not subscribe to the socialist outlook of the German pioneering movements. Toward the end of the 1930s, the Dutch began to take to the kibbutz idea, and immigrants to Palestine found their way to the kibbutz movement there. But most of the Jewish youngsters remained in Holland—and subsequently perished in the Holocaust.

In the late 1930s, as war loomed even closer, the opportunities to enter Palestine legally were sharply restricted, but illegal immigration stepped up considerably. A boat chartered in Scandinavia, the *Dora,* was set to sail from Amsterdam, although the Dutch Hanoar Hatzioni objected on the grounds that "one should not cross borders like thieves in the night"[7]—a legalistic approach that was characteristic of the Jews in Holland. The members of Hehalutz, on the other hand, were grappling with the problem of establishing objective criteria for determining who would be entitled to exploit the opportunity to reach Palestine, and they finally agreed on the principle that only those who had completed at least one year of professional agricultural training would be allowed to emigrate. After repeated postponements of its departure, the *Dora* finally sailed a few weeks before the outbreak of the war. Its passengers were joined by travelers from Antwerp, and it was one of the immigrant boats that succeeded in evading the British blockade and making its way to shore.[8]

During this period the young members of Hehalutz were still assisted by emissaries from Palestine, but in the summer of 1940 these Palestinians were arrested and sent to a civilian detention camp in Germany. At first it was possible to remain in contact with them through letters; among the correspondents from Holland was Yakhin (Joachim) Simon, known as Shushu, who was to become one of the leading figures in the pioneering underground in Holland and in the organization that arose to smuggle people out of the country to safety. In his letters to the emissaries, Shushu described the lives and problems of the aspiring pioneers. On August 16, 1940, he wrote:

> Life has returned to normal. Actually it's amazing to see the peace of mind and the lack of concern of the people here. Everything appears to be as tranquil as it was a year ago. Naturally it takes a great deal of innocence [to believe that this is so], but it is interesting that this atmosphere has affected us all. . . .
>
> We are burying our heads in the sand like the well-known bird [ostrich], you see, but there's no choice; we must devote ourselves to petty concerns and forget the bleak future for a while.

Three months later, however, the danger seemed far more patent because the Germans had begun to take action against the Jews, and within Hehalutz the burning question was whether to allow members to find their own channels of escape and leave (e.g., for the United States) if the opportunity presented itself. Finally, the movement ruled that every member could do as he saw fit, but if he left Heḥalutz, the movement would sever all ties with him. Here is how Shushu put it on November 17, 1940, "We are now grappling with the issue of emigration to America. Proposals have been made to the parents of children [evidently by Youth Aliyah in Holland]. What should we do? Encourage or oppose it, as in the case of an older member? The responsibility is enormous, because the decision is one of life and death."[9]

Hence, these youngsters perceived the full gravity of the situation even then; nevertheless, most of them concluded that they should remain in Holland and face their destiny together.

The situation deteriorated considerably after the clash between Jews and Dutch Nazis and the following deportations to Mauthausen in February 1941 (see chap. 6). The members of Heḥalutz began to approach the institutions in search of aid and advice. Among the plans forwarded at that time was one that called for transferring the entire agricultural training program to neutral Sweden. Nothing came of it, however, and on March 20, 1941, the Gestapo arrived at the Labor Village with seven buses and took off all but a few of the members of the training farm; the remainder were ordered to complete the season's agricultural work. From then the Zionist agricultural training program in Holland entered a new stage.[10]

Similar to Dutch Jewry, the Jews of **Belgium** were not much disturbed by the Germans during the early months of the occupation. As already noted, the composition of the Jewish community in Belgium differed considerably from that of its northern neighbor, for most of it comprised recently arrived immigrants. The Jewish community organization, built along the lines of the French Consistoire, was controlled by the native Belgian Jews, most of whom identified with the Liberal stream of Judaism. The immigrants, on the other hand, represented the full spectrum of views and religious outlooks professed by the Jews of both Eastern and Western Europe, with the Zionist parties being highly active among them. After the return of the Jews who had attempted to flee to France, the economic problem in Belgium became a particularly sore one, and efforts were made to organize self-help. The Consistoire's social welfare arm, *Ezra* (Aid), attempted to centralize control over all the community's welfare activities. It also made a special effort to persuade the American authorities to release the JDC funds—50,000 Belgian francs—that had been frozen in its legation, and indeed the money was turned over to the community. Besides *Ezra,* there were two other, independent assistance organizations in operation: Jewish Mutual Aid, backed by the Leftist Poalei Zion Party, which was established at the end of 1940, and Solidarité Juive, under the influence of the Communists.[11]

The situation in which the Jews of **France** found themselves was considerably more complex. The indigenous French-Jewish community regarded itself as an integral part of the French nation, but the immigrants who had streamed into the country over the years had substantially changed the structure of, and numerical balance within, the community. About half the French-Jewish community was concentrated in Paris, where Jews from Alsace had comprised 90 percent of the community at the end of the nineteenth century but were only 15 percent in 1940. Still, the ruling influence in the Consistoire remained in the hands of the veteran families, led by the Rothschilds; the disparity between these veteran families and the immigrants was conspicuous in all spheres of life, from their occupations to their standards of living and residences in different districts of Paris.[12]

Most of the immigrants (83 percent) were textile workers, but a majority had failed to obtain work permits, so they were not protected by the law and found themselves forced to work under very poor conditions. The French-Jewish community rendered them assistance. Although it regarded such aid as a humanitarian duty, it wanted to avoid having the immigrants become a burden to the state. In addition, schools were opened for the immigrants' children, and the cultural activities provided for the adults were designed to promote their integration. In this way the leaders of the Consistoire hoped to forestall a rise in anti-Semitism while protecting the status of the indigenous Jewish community.

For all that, the tension between the old-timers and the immigrants continued to rise. The latter had organized in small groups based on their places of origin *(Landsmannschaften)* and thus became fractionalized, even though about half of the close to two hundred *Landsmannschaften* united in an umbrella organization, La Fédération des Sociétés Juives de France (The Federation of Jewish Societies of France). The federation conducted a rich cultural program in Yiddish—the language of the leftist circles, such as the Bund and the Communists—and the differences between them and the Zionists—who also encompassed people of various political outlooks—were obvious. At the time, a bitter struggle was going on between the Right and the Left in French society, and the inclination of most of the members of the Consistoire to side with the French Right only aggravated the friction with the many immigrants who championed socialism. In 1937, with the fall of the leftist government of Léon Blum, the crisis within French Jewry reached new heights. The economic condition of the immigrants deteriorated further because the rising xenophobia in France, and the anti-Semitic climate in particular, found expression in the labor market. Despite this precarious situation, groups of French-Jewish youth who were alert to the dangers posed by the radical rightist and anti-Semitic forces rebelled against the leaders of the Consistoire, who were prepared to enter into an alliance with the Right. The more the political situation in Europe became strained, the more the influence of these young people grew along with signs of possible cooperation between the indigenous French Jews and the immigrants.

This entire complex community—old-time Frenchmen and immigrants, leftists and rightists, Zionists and Bundists—was cast into the whirlwind that the war brought upon France. Together with the flood of refugees, all the main Jewish organizations passed into southern France, where they primarily focused their efforts on social welfare needs. The most active Jewish organizations in the Vichy zone were the international ones—JDC, HIAS, OSE, as well as CAR (Comité d'Assistance aux Réfugiés)—whose aid had begun to increase even before the war. Both the Consistoire and the federation concentrated on providing aid to the refugees, deportees, and detainees. Robert de Rothschild, who had been chairman of the Consistoire after the death of his father, Edmund, in 1934, had fled to the

United States. Thus the leadership went to the new chairman of the Consistoire, Jacques Helbronner. The Jewish aid organizations united into a cooperative Jewish council, the Commission Centrale des Organisations Juives d'Assistance (Central Commission of the Jewish Aid Organizations), whose activity branched out further and further as the actions against the Jews became increasingly oppressive.[13]

Jewish Communities in Southern Europe

The Jewish community of **Rumania,** numbering hundreds of thousands of people, was made up of a collection of people distinguished by their history, occupations, and political disposition. After the annexation of the new provinces at the end of World War I, it at first proved impossible to unite the Rumanian Jewish community into a single organization. The Jews living in the original geographical area of Rumania shared a long tradition of struggle for their rights in a prevailing atmosphere of anti-Semitism. Following World War I, in an expanded Rumania, this struggle was conducted in two different ways. One group, under the leadership of Dr. Wilhelm Fildermann, organized into the Union of Rumanian Jews and, being opposed in principle to direct Jewish representation in the parliament, tried to exercise political influence through the country's liberal parties. The other group, led by the Zionists, established a Jewish party and worked to have the rights of the Jews acknowledged and honored along with those of the other minorities in Rumania. After scoring an initial electoral success, the party found that the mounting political and economic pressure in the 1930s reduced the prospects of achieving its goals. Thus, in 1936 the two organizations united in the Central Committee of Jews in Rumania, with Fildermann at its head. Its proclaimed goal was to defend the rights of the Jews against the forces that "propagated to erect a racial regime."[14]

In the 1920s and the 1930s, the struggle for their livelihood led the Jews of Rumania, like those of Poland, to establish cooperative credit institutions. This movement was sustained by the international aid organizations, led by JDC, and quickly spread not only throughout Rumania but to the neighboring countries as well. In 1939 the capital of the Rumanian credit institutions reached 29 million lei (U.S. $213,000).[15]

The Jews of Rumania were sensitive to the dangers posed by Nazi Germany and, as long as it was possible, they denounced and attacked the German regime in the Jewish press. They even organized a boycott of German goods while simultaneously promoting trade with Palestine. But after the installation of the royal dictatorship in the spring of 1938, the political activities of the Jews were forbidden and all Jewish parties in Rumania were abolished except the Federation of Jewish Communities under Fildermann, which remained to conduct general Jewish activities. The government cut back its support of the kehillot and tried to liquidate the cooperative credit unions, so that it was only after a long and stubborn political, diplomatic, and legal struggle that in 1939 these unions were able to continue their activities.[16]

The period of great upheaval began in the summer of 1940, with the general unrest sparked by the transfer of many territories to the neighboring countries. As Jews began fleeing from these ceded territories to the Rumanian heartland, the country experienced a new surge of anti-Semitism. The Federation of Jewish Communities came to the aid of these refugees and was supported in this effort by JDC, which continued to operate in Rumania, albeit on a reduced scale.[17]

On October 6, 1938, **Slovakia** declared its autonomy, though it was then still part of Czechoslovakia, which had become a federative state as a result of the Munich Pact. Throughout the years, the Jews of Slovakia had done their best to aid the refugees who had reached their area, first from Austria, then from Bohemia-Moravia, and in the following year from Poland. The most active and effective clustered around a small group of leaders in the Zionist movement, which had earlier participated in the political life of the republic in the framework of the Jewish Party. Now that they were cut off from the Jewish center in Prague, they decided to establish a central institution to lead the Jewish community in Slovakia. At first they failed to unite all the elements that made up Slovak Jewry, for the Union of Orthodox Communities refused to cooperate with the Zionists. Therefore, they established the Central Jewish Bureau on their own, and it was officially recognized by the new Slovak government. Having won broad support among the Jewish public, the bureau held a national convention to elect its executive, set up its own administrative machinery, and published a bulletin. Among its earliest initiatives was extending assistance to the Jews who were caught in no-man's-land between Slovakia and Hungary (see chap. 6). Representatives of the bureau also conducted talks with the world Jewish organizations, primarily with WIZO and JDC, to obtain their help for the Jews of Slovakia. But these efforts, which were designed to increase the opportunities for emigration, especially to Palestine, yielded meager results and at any rate were nipped in the bud by the outbreak of the war.

After the proclamation of the independent Slovak state in March 1939, and naturally once the war was in progress, the anti-Jewish actions became increasingly ruthless. In light of this situation and under pressure from the Jewish public, the Orthodox leadership finally agreed to a united representation of all the Jews of Slovakia in the summer of 1940. It was made up of delegates from the two community organizations—the Orthodox and the Liberal Neologist—but the Orthodox leadership stopped short of agreeing to have the Zionist Organization represented, as such, on the new body; instead, its members were only allowed to participate as community delegates. Even though the Zionists were essentially the moving force behind this new federation, they agreed to these conditions in order to make its establishment possible. One of the leading figures in the Zionist Organization—the chairman of WIZO and representative of HICEM (a roof organization: Hias–ICA–Emigdirect) in Slovakia—was Gisi Fleischmann. One of the most outstanding Jewish personalities in Slovakia as well as throughout Europe, she was widely known for her devotion, courage, and rectitude. Her husband, a wealthy merchant, died during this period; and having sent her two daughters to Palestine with Youth Aliyah, she was determined to devote herself wholeheartedly to the service of her people.

Shortly after the establishment of their united representation, the Jews of Slovakia were subjected to a series of stinging blows.[18] Even before the founding of the Central Office for the Economy (ÚHÚ) and the Center of Jews (ÚŽ) (see chap. 6), the authorities closed down the Zionist Organization and seized its offices. Even though the police sealed the doors of the Zionist headquarters, nonetheless that same Friday night, the membership files and especially the correspondence with people abroad were spirited out of the building. Thus, the Zionist Organization was able to continue its work underground. When the Center of Jews was established, the Zionists had debated whether to send their representatives to its council, on which the Orthodox faction enjoyed a majority and which was headed by Heinrich Schwarz, the secretary of the Union of Orthodox Communities. After protracted discussions, they again decided to join the council and take part in its general program. As time passed it became increasingly clear that this was a fateful decision that led to one of the more important clandestine endeavors effected by the Jews during the Holocaust period.

So it was that Zionist officials and activists of broad experience and talent were integrated into the framework known as the Center of Jews, which established the same principal departments associated with the Judenrat in most other places. Here, too, the first task of its Statistical Department was to organize a comprehensive card file of the Jews of Slovakia. The Finance Department was ordered to register all Jewish property and collect taxes, and each month it also drew up a budget, which at the start of this period was as high as 30 million Slovak crowns (about U.S. $640,000). Naturally, a heavy burden was placed on the Social Welfare, Housing, and Education departments. The Jewish children and youth had been expelled from the general school system, and as Jews they were forbidden to receive either a high school or a higher education. However, the remaining Jewish elementary schools were in need of buildings, teaching materials, and teachers. During this initial period the Emigration Department continued to function and included the Immigration Bureau of the officially banned Zionist Organization, headed by Gisi Fleischmann. Among the difficult tasks imposed on the ÚŽ was the establishment of labor camps, which the Jews were expected to finance and construct. A special department for occupational retraining was established and served as a cover for the continuing activities of the Zionist youth movements and their agricultural training program. This same department ran a cultural and social program for young people and maintained contact between the various youth groups scattered throughout the country. The Press Department published the center's official newspaper, and a special department was created for converts from Judaism. This wide-ranging bureaucracy had seventy branches scattered throughout the country.

The Jews in Greater Germany

It has already been noted that Hitler and his henchmen failed to purge the German Reich of Jews, as they had done in the annexed territories—although there, too, this mission was not carried out to the full. The attempts to deport the Jews, as from Stettin (Szczecin) in February 1940 and from southwest Germany in October 1940, failed because of opposition from the places in Poland and France that were expected to absorb the deportees, but the Reichsvereinigung der Juden in Deutschland also had a hand in the matter. Moreover, these two deportations were not the only instances of the expulsion of Jews from the Reich, for attempts had been made to deport the Jews from the town of Schneidemühl (Piła), in West Prussia, to Łódź (at approximately the same time as the deportation from Stettin) and from Breisach am Rhein, in western Germany. It appears that the Reichsvereinigung vigorously protested all these cases before the RSHA and further saw to it that the facts were publicized abroad; thus, these deportations were halted in response to domestic and foreign pressure. The Jews of Schneidemühl and Breisach am Rhein were even able to return to their homes, though the leaders of the Reichsvereinigung were unable to bring back the Jews of Stettin.

The Reichsvereinigung's most thoroughgoing action was mounted in response to the deportation of the Jews from Baden. Dr. Otto Hirsch, the council's director, had a talk on this matter with the SD, complaining that these latest and particularly brutal expulsions violated the assurances given after the deportation from Stettin that such actions would not recur. Not content with registering a strong protest, the executive of the Reichsvereinigung saw to it that all the inhabitants of this area who happened to be away at the time were warned against returning to their homes. It also tried to safeguard the deportees' property, although the local authorities moved to confiscate it. To whatever degree possible, the executive also helped to organize the emigration of the deportees from southern France, where they had been deported. A day of fasting was proclaimed in all the Jewish communities in Germany; the activities of the cultural societies were canceled for a week as an expression of mourning and special services were held in synagogues, including sermons that expressed anger over the breach of faith.[19] These actions were undoubtedly designed to catch the attention of the press abroad—as indeed they did.

In return, the Nazis took their wrath out on one of the leaders of the Reichsvereinigung, the lawyer Julius Seligsohn. A proud and particularly astute man, Seligsohn had been one of the moving spirits behind the executive's actions as well as the author of the circular sent to all the communities. He was arrested and sent to the Oranienburg concentration camp; he died a few months later in the Sachsenhausen camp. In November 1938 Seligsohn had been in the United States, where he had sent his family, but he returned to Germany to assume his responsibilities as a member of the community leadership. In this case, the RSHA acted as the German authorities conducted themselves in Poland; punishing the heads of the Judenrat who dared to oppose them. The authorities permitted Seligsohn's burial in the Berlin cemetery, where Rabbi Leo Baeck eulogized him.[20]

This was not the only instance in which the heads of the Reichsvereinigung did their best to resist or mitigate the schemes used against the Jews. They also tried to obtain the release of people being held in prisons and concentration camps. At the same time, despite the increasingly adverse conditions, the Reichsvereinigung kept up its educational activities in the schools and such endeavors as adult education and their cultural societies. Other training centers also contin-

ued to operate. From the beginning of 1939 the communities and the Reichsvereinigung had borne the burden of the assistance effort, whose proportions steadily
grew because of the impoverishment of the Jews and the mounting tide of emigration. The kehillot were forced to sell off their property, usually to the local
authorities, and the return they received for land and buildings was far below their
actual value. The income from taxes was also on the decline because in many
communities the more affluent members had borne the lion's share of the burden,
and it was precisely these people who had succeeded in emigrating in 1939.

Emigration remained the prime issue in 1939 and 1940 and continued to be
a matter of some consequence until the autumn of 1941, when it was prohibited
(see chap. 11). Under relentless pressure from the government, the Jews now
grasped that their lives were in danger in Hitler's Germany. Thus, in 1939 Jewish
emigration surpassed the numbers of 1933—the first year of panic—with at least
68,000 Jews leaving the country. Communities all over Germany, especially small
ones, simply emptied out during that year. The total number of emigrants from
the Greater Reich from 1933 to 1939 is assumed to have been over 400,000.[21]

After the outbreak of the war, potential emigrants came up against new difficulties, and those with visas to countries overseas had only two ways of reaching
their destination: via either Lisbon or Sweden or via the Far East. While the Jews
in the three countries of the Reich—Germany, Austria, and the Protectorate—
enjoyed the support of JDC and HICEM in their efforts to leave, they had yet
another, perhaps even more influential partner in this cause: none other than
Adolf Eichmann. On July 3, 1940, Eichmann called a meeting in Berlin of representatives from Prague, Vienna, and Berlin, and among the subjects on the
agenda was emigration from each of the countries represented by these capitals.[22]
He also took the opportunity to inform them of a comprehensive plan to solve
the problem of European Jewry after the war by resettling the Jews outside the
Continent—the reference being to the so-called Madagascar Plan, which had been
drawn up at about that time. Like Reinhard Heydrich, Eichmann no longer
believed that the Jewish problem would be solved by voluntary emigration on an
individual basis. The practical details related to the matter of emigration were
discussed at the July 3 meeting with one of Eichmann's deputies, Theodor Dannecker, whom we shall meet again during the period of the mass deportations.
Among the subjects raised were so-called special transports to Palestine, meaning
illegal immigration into that country, which Eichmann and his men supported.
One of the Jews particularly active in this means of rescue was Bernhard Storfer
of Vienna, who directed and even financed the better part of it. For example, in
the summer of 1940 he saved a group of emigrants from Prague who had been
stuck in Bratislava (Pressburg) for nine months by helping them reach a Rumanian port, whence they could sail for Palestine.[23] (Afterward these hapless people
were among the Jews whom the British authorities in Palestine deported to the
island of Mauritius in the Indian Ocean.)

The network of the illegal immigration effort extended throughout central and
southern Europe, from Danzig (Gdańsk) to Amsterdam and from Berlin, Vienna,
and Prague to Bratislava and Bucharest. The Palestinians involved in these operations were headquartered in Geneva, where they could weave the strands of the

net while maintaining contact with the free world. Much money was invested in this cause, and the immigrants suffered severe hardship during long waiting periods and on the dangerously overloaded boats that carried them to Palestine. Still, only a few thousand people were saved in his hazardous way.[24]

Conclusion

Nine years had passed since 1932, the "year of decision," when the Weimar Republic had essentially met its doom. Now the Greater German Reich was called on to concentrate all its resources for the great battle that Hitler believed would decide the fate of Europe, a stage in his victorious campaign to take over the world. Adolf Hitler, and the German people together with him, had come a long way since that fateful day, January 30, 1933, when he took power in Germany. Beginning by fashioning his domestic regime, he went on to expand the borders of the new Reich to the west (past the Rhine), south (Austria and Bohemia-Moravia), and north (the Memel [Klaipėda] area) and had now taken the tactics of threat and persuasion to their limit. In the summer of 1939, he had stood poised on the brink of a great offensive, and on September 1 he stepped over the threshold. Eighteen months later, only Great Britain, at one end of Europe, and the Soviet Union, at the other, remained as foci of resistance to his rule. The rest of the Continent had lost its independence to one extent or another, some states being conquered, others being forced into pacts with victorious Germany, and still others being reduced to satellites. Only five countries—Switzerland, Sweden, Turkey, Portugal, and Spain—succeeded in maintaining a neutrality of sorts, and of these, three were able to do so only because it was in Germany's interest.

Millions of Jews had come directly or indirectly under the sway of the Third Reich. The war that Hitler had declared on the Jewish people was a fight to the finish, and he had openly threatened to wage a war of annihilation. Hitler considered racial anti-Semitism as both ideology and praxis, a pillar of his Weltanschauung and a means of achieving concrete political aims. He gave free rein to anti-Jewish sentiments—rousing them, fostering them, according them value and respect—not only wherever his minions trod, not only wherever he sought a foothold and greater influence, but the world over. Germany was not the only place where the Jews rightly felt themselves under siege in the 1930s. The Jewish communities in the democracies that championed human rights (France, England, and the United States, for instance) also felt that their freedom of action had been constrained and that they had to behave with circumspection. Hence, the Nazis' interest in Jewish emigration was twofold: to "cleanse" the territory under their control of Jews and to "inherit" as much of the Jews' property as possible while simultaneously "defiling" the refugees' new host countries with anti-Semitism and Jews—especially destitute Jews. By pursuing this policy, the Nazis believed they would both strengthen Germany and weaken their enemies by corroding them from within. Although politicians in many of the countries of potential refuge shared this evaluation and were consequently reluctant to admit Jewish refugees, hundreds of thousands of Jews, nevertheless, found shelter in the free world. Yet, the Nazis' craving for Jewish wealth hampered mass emigration. During its first years in power, Hitler's regime still allowed Jews to leave Germany with a certain amount of their property, but by 1938/1939 it proposed a foreign currency load to be provided by world Jewry—according to Hjalmar Schacht's scheme—for the same privilege.

Hitler's triumphs on the battlefield effectively turned the Jews into POWs as Chaim A. Kaplan observed in his Warsaw diary.[25] However, they were not protected by an international law or defended by any international organization such as the Red Cross. They had neither standing in the political world nor status in the field of battle. The Jewish people were not recognized as a nation, so its fugitives from tyranny were not acknowledged as political refugees. The rights of Jews as individuals (in the Western democracies) and as an ethnic group (in the Eastern countries) could be annulled with the wave of a hand, thus leaving them subject either to the whip or to the mercies of the peoples among whom they dwelled. The Jews' equal rights were predicated on principles, not power, and when democratic principles were jettisoned or abrogated, the rights of the Jews became as inconsequential as the snows of yesteryear. The creed of humanism still remained of some value in the democracies, but its impact was limited by political considerations, and only when humanism was consonant with political interests did it prompt any action. An instructive example was Britain's willingness to admit Jewish children and adults after Kristallnacht so as not to have to open the gates of Palestine.

Hitler, too, acted on the basis of political interests, which often set limits on the fulfillment of his ideological aims. This dualism of ideology and practical interest coincided, as he saw it, in the general purification policy *(Flurbereinigung)* being carried out in occupied Poland. The establishment of an oppressive regime over the Jews and the adoption of any measures capable of advancing the currently favored "solution" to the Jewish problem fit in with that scheme. In contrast, Hitler did not initially believe that the course of action pursued in Poland would further his political interests in the West. Hence, in Western Europe the anti-Jewish measures were put off at first and then turned out to be different ("Western European") in character. In Denmark, the Nazis actually refrained from taking any action at all.

Nevertheless, difficulties arose in Poland and elsewhere. The expulsion of the Jews from the annexed Eastern districts *(Ostgaue)* was never completed, and the idea of a Lublin Reservation proved unfeasible. Attempts to expel the Jews from the Greater Reich—Germany, Austria, and the Protectorate of Bohemia-Moravia—were similarly unsuccessful, and in the East, the concentration of the Jews in labor camps or ghettos did not proceed at the pace originally envisioned.

The difficulties encountered by the Nazis in implementing their anti-Jewish schemes stemmed, in part, from objective problems of storage, food, transportation, health, and economics that threatened detriment to Germany itself. But, in part, they traced to the Jews' struggle for survival. In this trial Jews organized and created means of livelihood and instruments of mutual aid, on both a local and national scale, with the support of international Jewish organizations—led by the JDC, whose dollars were highly coveted in Germany. On the one hand, the Jews tried to circumvent the onerous prohibitions with which they had been saddled; on the other hand, they sought to institute a dialogue with the Germans to coax them into revoking or mitigating their edicts—first of all by means of bribery. In Amsterdam the Jews initially formed an antiterror organization, but despite the supportive attitude of the Dutch, the results of this effort were counterproductive and ended in deportation and death of hundreds of young Jews. The possibilities of emigration or escape were limited. The mass movements that brought Jews over the Russian border (from Poland) or into southern France (from Belgium and the Nazi-occupied zone of France) succeeded only for limited periods—no border remained unequivocally open—and some refugees had to turn back, just like those who had fled Germany in panic at the start of the period. In both the East and the West, the Jews' behavior was predicated on the faith that Hitler would ultimately be defeated, and until that time the supreme task was to survive, however possible.

The Jews had been engaged in a struggle for existence for countless generations and, conditioned to organizing for this purpose, they found it natural to take recourse to tried-and-true organizational forms by utilizing the frameworks at their disposal. In many places the community was sorely divided, and they labored to overcome the divisions and arrive at a single agency of representation and action. Thus, Germany's Jews began by establishing a nationwide representation (the Reichsvertretung), and their brethren in Slovakia, Rumania, Holland, and France followed suit. The institution known as Jewish Self-help (ŻSS) came into being to sustain the Jewish population in the Generalgouvernement—it reconciled divisions and forged contacts with isolated communities.

The Germans, for their part, realized that the key to seizing control of the Jewish community was to command its organizational talent. Having learned this lesson in the 1930s, they resolved to turn the Jewish institutions into instruments of their own designs, channels through which their plans would be implemented. The tactic was first used in the forced emigration that Eichmann began organizing in Austria. It proved so successful that it was transplanted to Czechoslovakia and Germany itself; in Poland it served as a model for the Judenrat. Of all the measures taken against the Jews at the time, this system was the most successful one, from the Nazis' point of view, precisely because it derived from the traditional *modus operandi* of the autonomous kehillot. The Jews were accustomed to shouldering communal responsibility in this manner, and most communities had already taken the initiative during the early stage of the occupation to establish committees for assisting the victims and refugees of the war. In many places in Poland—some of which have been discussed in these pages—the Germans easily turned these *ad hoc* committees into Nazi-dominated institutions. Though they were not able to form ghettos throughout Poland during the first year of the occupation, they quickly established Jewish councils, under their firm control, almost everywhere. Even in Holland, a Jewish council grew out of the committee that had aided refugees during the 1930s, and as we have seen, the system was employed in satellite Slovakia as well.

These councils were a paradox: the Jews regarded their role as fighting on behalf of the community, whereas the Germans handed them the task of enslaving that selfsame community. The chairman and members of these councils, therefore, faced the impossible mission of reconciling wholly contradictory objectives. They could pretend to maintain normal activity, as in Lublin; maneuver adroitly, as in Piotrków; strive to establish a miniature dictatorship, as Merin and Rumkowski did in Będzin and Łódź, respectively; or behave liberally, as Czerniakow did in Warsaw. But regardless of how these councils conducted themselves, the very ambivalence of their rule doomed their efforts to failure, occasional limited successes notwithstanding.

The Judenrat was caught in the thick netting of cross-purposes and could not extricate itself without self-destructing and imperiling the community. However, the Jewish public sought—and to a certain extent found—its own ways of fighting for its existence, whether in cooperation with, or in opposition to, the council. Life went on despite destruction, persecution, restrictions, and mayhem on all sides. Having subjected the Jews to appalling overcrowding, undernourishment, forced labor, and plunder, the Germans expected them to collapse, lose their humanity, become easy prey, and succumb by the masses to a "natural death." Except for isolated instances, none of these expectations were borne out. On the contrary, the Germans came to realize that the output of skilled Jewish workers was indispensable, and the Jews' resourcefulness and talents in the crafts and industry far surpassed all previous notions.

Since the Jews were fighting for their lives, it should not be surprising that cracks appeared in their solidarity, and there were always people who were ready to spare themselves at others' expense, thus hoping that by serving the new masters they would better their own lot. But these opportunities did not set the standard. Even when starving, Jews did not murder each other. In secret, underground cells, they continued to pray, observe the *mitzvot* (commandments), study, educate their young, and even chronicle their lives and trials.

The relations between the tormentors and their victims developed along somewhat parallel lines, with the Germans taking aim at the "enemy" with the threefold weapon of terror, propaganda, and legislation and the Jews mobilizing to fight their decrees, preserve whatever they could, and save those who could be saved by devoting their economic, organizational, and moral energy to this cause. Objective circumstances, the Nazis' own economic or political exigencies, and even outside factors—Jewish and otherwise—sometimes came to their aid. But just as these factors seemed to cushion the blow, the Nazi assault would rise to yet a new level of pressure and persecution more vicious and aggressive than before. An escalation of this kind occurred in Germany in 1935 and again in the years 1937 to 1939. The drive against Polish Jewry, though harsher than its precursors, still did not yield the desired results, and in the Greater Reich the process was halted altogether. In the summer of 1940, however, the Nazis proposed new plans, some of which were even voiced publicly. Among their salient characteristics were an intensification of the ghettoization process in Poland and the prohibition of Jewish emigration. Nor were these plans arrived at by chance: whenever Hitler devised a new step to enhance the power of his regime, he linked it to an acceleration of his war against the Jews, and the new measure was aimed at rectifying what he considered the failures of the previous phase. Thus, the latest advance toward the "final solution of the Jewish question" was planned alongside the military move to complete the conquest of Europe: the mass annihilation of Jews was viewed as an integral part of Operation Barbarossa.

In contrast to the Nazis, who had built a political system with anti-Semitism at its heart, the Jews neither subscribed to a comprehensive political system nor had any foundation on which to construct one. The Jews living in the democracies usually identified with those forces in the political system that were (or were imagined to be) willing to include them in their endeavors. During the interwar period, the Jews of Czechoslovakia and Rumania conducted themselves as consolidated political minorities, creating their own parties and representations. (For the Baltic countries, see chap. 10.) In Poland, however, these ambitions foundered upon the birth of the nationalist dictatorship. Only on the level of local government did the Jews succeed in securing political representation, and even this faltered under the burden of internal Jewish fragmentation (Bund vs. Zionists, the observant vs. the nonreligious, etc.). Outside of the party framework, the only communitywide operations that the Jews could mount were related to economic and social aid— and these, it should be said, stood the test during the German occupation.

Though aware of performing a broader national mission, the Jewish community in Palestine, still in its infancy and engaged in a fierce existential struggle of its own, concentrated on its political needs. Neither the Palestinian community nor the Zionist movement abroad developed a policy for dealing with the events in Europe. They failed even to address the prospect of a rescue operation until 1939, when it was decided to create a network to handle illegal immigration to Palestine. But by then their response was in a certain sense too late. The emissaries from Slovakia who reached Western capitals during this period were sorely disappointed by the local Jews' meager understanding of the severity of their situation and urgent need for help.

Thus the Jews in occupied Europe fought for their existence with little outside assistance. Against a mighty power that had subdued almost all of Europe, their struggle was tantamount to fighting tanks with sticks. Nothing the Jews in either the East or the West had known, learned, or suspected about the nature of human society had prepared them for the way the Nazis operated. As the nightmare overtook them with stunning speed, they hoped it would pass—if they could only hold out—while the few who foresaw the fate in store for them felt helpless. On February 12, 1940, Chaim Kaplan wrote in his diary, "Distress is growing by the day, even by the hour. This is a period of respite in the war. The sides are gearing up for a terrible battle whose likes the world has yet to witness. A time of momentous events for each side looms steadily closer, yet the war against Polish Jewry does not let up for a single moment."[26] And today we may add: not only did the war against Jewry not let up, but on this front, as well, a "terrible battle whose likes the world has yet to witness" was in the making.

Part III

Holocaust, 1941–1945

And what will ye do on the day of visitation,
and in the desolation which shall come from far?
To whom will ye flee for help?
and where will ye leave your glory?

Isaiah 10:3, King James Bible

9
_____

The Quest for _Lebensraum:_
Germany's Wars (1941–1943)

The Significance of Operation Barbarossa

Emperor Frederick I Hohenstaufen (1152–1190), known as Barbarossa (Red-beard), was a legendary figure in German folklore. He symbolized one of the pinnacles of medieval German history and his mysterious death by drowning during the Third Crusade gave birth to the myth that this great monarch had not died but was waiting in the bowels of the holy great mountain of Kyffhäuser and would emerge some day to lead the German people to victory and to fresh triumphs. The German nationalist movements of the nineteenth century seized on this legend and the myth-enveloped mountain became the focus of national ceremonies and commemorations. At the end of the century, a ceremonial structure was erected there, with a statue of the new ruler, Kaiser Wilhelm I, at its center; a large platform in front of the monument served as a sacred space and thousands assembed there to commune in an act of national identification. The building was funded by the donations of the million members of the Kyffhäuser League.[1] It was no accident that Hitler, in his directive of December 18, 1940, on the preparations for war with Russia, altered the code name of the operation from the nondescript Fritz to Barbarossa. This name not only played on popular associations with a period of national splendor but also implied that the time had come to complete the unfinished task of the medieval monarch and to launch a new "crusade" to overthrow the sworn enemy, Russia, and to erect the worldwide German Empire.

Hitler considered the conquest of the East to be a vital and essential step toward routing Great Britain and winning Germany dominant status in Europe. It was considered a stepping-stone for Germany to become the prime world power. The natural resources in the vast Russian expanses would free Germany from its dependence on imports. Hitler regarded the high population density in

Germany as one of the main threats to the country and dreamed of expanding the Aryan race eastward and settling it in those regions. He perceived the struggle between the National Socialist Reich and the Soviet Union as the mighty battle between two empires with antagonistic Weltanschauung; but only National Socialism offered elevation and salvation to mankind. Hitler's attitude toward the Soviet Union was a blend of two contradictory viewpoints: on the one hand, he never tired of pointing out the great danger to Europe and to all the human race posed by the "Bolshevik–Jewish" state, with its "Asiatic" methods of government and inhuman attitudes. Conversely, he depicted the Russians as inferior beings and their state as a giant body resting on "feet of clay," a body that would collapse as soon as the superior Aryan army invaded it. To one of his generals he remarked, "You have only to kick in the door and the whole rotten structure will come crashing down."[2] This duality of approach underlay his conviction that it was imperative to launch an attack on the mighty Russian state at once and that victory would be almost instantaneous. This, then, was one of the main reasons for Hitler's debacle in Russia.

His erroneous assessment of the internal strength of the Soviet Union probably also stemmed from Hitler's ideological assumption that the Communist state was "ruled by Jews." The Soviet Union, he postulated, was the first place where the Jews had succeeded in their plot to take over the world by undermining the foundations of human society. The Jews' impact, as he saw it, lay in their ability to corrupt and sunder; therefore, communism together with Judaism threatened to proliferate the "germs of division" that would pollute the entire world. The Jews were powerless to resist Hitler's attacks, and this fact ostensibly corroborated his theory that, though dangerous, they could not hold out. But to draw conclusions from the situation of the Jews, bereft of a homeland and lacking independent political and military power, and to relate them to the mighty Soviet state was a patent absurdity.

However, Hitler knew only too well that Stalin's empire could only be subdued through fierce combat. He regarded the Soviet leader as his greatest adversary and, in a certain sense, as an equal, one who must be overcome if the foundations of Germanic rule were to be firmly laid throughout the world. He and his chiefs of staff were preoccupied with preparing the campaign against Russia from July 1940. It seems that no war has ever been so extensively documented as Germany's Russian campaign. The course of strategic events is relatively clear, but the commentaries differ greatly. The present study cannot examine these complex issues in depth, but it is necessary to sketch the general background to the events because they are inextricably linked to the fate of the Jews. Since the entire war was perceived as a confrontation between two conflicting ideologies, with the Jews as the personification of the one that represented *the* divisive force in human society, their annihilation came to be regarded as an integral part of the war effort.

The war was conducted in two main domains: military operations (i.e., the struggle between two mighty armies) and the administration of the areas conquered by the Germans. In the former the German army was entrusted with the task of destroying Russia's military might and, as Hitler phrased it, ensuring that as far as the border of the Urals no Russian troops would remain to constitute a threat to Germany. In the second domain, the army was ordered to implement the task that was the goal of the conquest: to transform the conquered territory into an area entirely under German rule and dedicated to serving the German people's economic needs and enlarged settlement. It was to this end that various functions were allotted to the civilian, police, and military forces operating behind the front line. At a meeting Hitler convened with several of his close associates on July 16, 1941—when he and his generals were convinced that overall victory lay in reach—he defined his objective in a now-famous phrase:[3] "In principle, it is important to divide up this vast cake properly so as to enable us

1. to rule it *(beherrschen)*
2. to administer it *(verwalten)*
3. to loot it *(ausbeuten)*."

From the *Blitzkrieg* to the Defeat at Stalingrad

In his famous directive No. 21 of December 18, 1940, in which he gave the operation its name, Hitler fixed May 15, 1941, as the date of the invasion. It opened with the words, "The German Wehrmacht must be prepared . . . to crush Soviet Russia in a rapid military campaign (Operation Barbarossa)."[4] At that time, a detailed offensive plan had been drawn up by the High Command and practical preparations for mobilization training, evacuation of areas adjacent to the German-Russian border in Poland, and other logistic activities had already commenced. In the winter of 1940/1941 the Soviets expedited the mass expulsion of populations in border regions—people they perceived as dubious and dangerous elements—and they concentrated large numbers of troops in those areas.

Meanwhile, Germany was also focusing its attention on the Mediterranean arena. The Italian debacles in North Africa and Greece forced Hitler to dispatch troops to the Libyan desert and to Greece. He feared both the reinforcement of British forces in the eastern Mediterranean as well as the British air threat to the oil fields in Rumania. The Germans also intensified their pressure on Bulgaria because their plans for the conquest of Greece (Operation Marita) entailed the transportation of troops through the former country.

On March 1, 1941, Bulgaria officially joined the Tripartite Pact (signed on September 27 the previous year by Germany, Italy, and Japan) and on the same day German army units crossed the Bulgarian border. The Axis powers had hoped that Yugoslavia, too, would join the alliance, but two days after the Regent, Prince Paul, signed the agreement (March 25, 1941) with Joachim von Ribbentrop, a coup occurred in Belgrade and the young monarch, Peter II, was placed at the head of the anti-German movement. On April 6 the Germans launched simultaneous offensives against Greece and Yugoslavia, and on that day the Soviet Union and Yugoslavia signed a treaty of friendship. Within three weeks, the Germans had crushed the two Balkan states despite their fierce resistance and the military aid dispatched to Greece by the British. The partisans in the Yugoslav mountains fought on for a lengthy period.

It is generally accepted today that Operation Barbarossa would have been post-poned in any event.[5] Napoleon had launched his campaign against Russia on June 22, 1812, and it is possible that Hitler's choice of June 22 was not fortuitous. The date was also linked to the victory over France since it was the first anniversary of France's official surrender at Compiègne.

As soon as the German offensive in Russia began, Finland, Rumania, and Hungary joined in and their troops took part in the fighting against Russia. Only Bulgaria refused to dispatch troops. On June 26 Hitler declared that the readiness of foreign countries to participate "in this crusade" should be greeted with enthusiasm.[6]

One of the unsolved riddles of this war is why Stalin did not heed the numer-ous warnings that reached him from internal and outside sources, even though these offered him minute details of the German preparations for war. Nonetheless, the Russian army was taken by surprise, and this afforded the Germans their first great advantage. The Northern Army Group made very swift progress. Lithuania, the region closest to the German border, was conquered within three to four days; Latvia, within a week. The occupation of Estonia was completed only after two months. The Central Army Group advanced almost 250 miles in eighteen days and on July 10 attacked Smolensk, which is less than 122 miles from Moscow. In these opening stages of the *Blitzkrieg,* the Germans took 150,000 Russian pris-oners and seized large quantities of tanks and guns. In the south the advance was not initially as rapid as on the other fronts. But by the end of September large Russian forces were compelled to surrender at Kiev and 665,000 Russians were taken prisoner by the Germans. Hitler's main aspiration at that time was to cap-ture Leningrad, but, as we know, he failed. It was not until October 2 that the Germans launched their attack on Moscow. At first they advanced almost to the outskirts of the city and the Soviet government was evacuated to the East. Stalin himself remained in the Kremlin and his appeal to the Russian people to defend themselves and to drive out the invaders has been compared to Churchill's renowned speeches during the Blitz in England. Meanwhile, an unexpectedly early and severe winter paralyzed German troop movements. The renewed onslaught at the beginning of December was checked by a Russian counterattack that inflicted such heavy losses on the Germans that they were no longer capable of conducting an offensive. The German generals advised retreat, but Hitler was ada-mant in his refusal and forced them to hold on. As a result of his intransigence, the Germans retained a large part of their positions, thus staving off defeat. This bolstered Hitler's belief that he alone was capable of conducting this war and that, in any event, persistence would win the day. He dismissed some of his top com-manders and took upon himself, in addition to the supreme command (Oberkom-mando der Wehrmacht; or OKW), command over the general staff (Oberkommando des Heeres, or OKH). As one historian has phrased it, Hitler as supreme commander now issued orders to himself.[7]

By the time they began to plan their summer campaign both sides had suffered heavy losses. Hitler decided to concentrate his main offensive in the south, to con-quer the Crimean Peninsula and cross the Caucasus in order to reach the Caspian

Sea and the Baku oil fields. At the beginning of the summer, it seemed that the German army was succeeding in its mission. The Russians suffered a serious defeat near Kharkov. At the same time, the German generals began to grasp that they had greatly underestimated Soviet military strength. Against their advice, Hitler divided up his forces, dispatching part to the Caucasus and part to the Volga region. This was a momentous, even fatal decision. The Caucasus offensive was eventually checked. At about the same time, German forces penetrated Stalingrad (Volgograd). Here the Russians succeeded in encircling the German Sixth Army commanded by Field Marshal Friedrich Paulus. Bitter fighting raged for some two months. At the end of November, Paulus requested permission from Hitler to retreat; this was denied. Hitler knew that this battle could decide the fate of the entire Russian campaign. On December 12, 1942, at a discussion of the war situation, he declared, "If we abandon [Stalingrad], we are in effect abandoning the whole point of the campaign." Once again he was relying on steadfastness and described the desire to hold on to a position as "a fanatic principle."[8]

The Mediterranean Campaign and the U.S. Entry into the War

Prior to these events, the Axis forces on the North African front had been dealt a decisive blow. In the spring of 1941, the British made an attempt to come to the aid of the Greeks, but at the end of April they were compelled to evacuate the force they had dispatched to Greece only a month previously. In a daring mission the British fleet succeeded in evacuating more than forty thousand troops, but more than ten thousand others were taken prisoner by the Germans, including the Jewish troops from Palestine who had volunteered for service in the British army. One month later the same scenario was repeated when the Germans overran the island of Crete. In the North African desert, General Erwin Rommel threatened the British position in Egypt and, as a consequence, Palestine as well. For some time the armies shuttled to-and-fro and positions changed hands until the campaign reached its height in the late summer of 1942. By the end of October, at the battle of El Alamein, Lieutenant General Bernard Montgomery inflicted a massive blow on the German army. Despite this victory, Montgomery, in pursuing the fleeing Germans, failed to capture Tunis. At the same time, an offensive against the northern coast of Africa from the west was launched by the Americans, who were commanded by a relatively unknown general, Dwight D. Eisenhower. Thus, Italy's flank was exposed to an Allied attack. In reaction to the African events, the German army, on November 11, 1942, entered the so-called free southern region of France, which had been under Vichy rule.

Hitler had meant to prevent the United States from entering the war before he had defeated his enemies in Europe: the Soviet Union and Great Britain. Then came the Japanese attack on Pearl Harbor (December 7, 1941), which was carried out without consulting Germany. It had been Hitler's plan for Japan to launch an offensive on the British positions at Singapore. But the Japanese act brought the United States into the war and compelled Hitler to declare war against the Americans at a time when his Russian advance had been halted and he was far from achieving his objective of defeating Britain.

Administration of the Occupied Territories

At the beginning of 1943, the titanic struggle of World War II had entered a new stage, which was to last for two more years. The Germans had added huge expanses to the territories under their rule. Hitler's proclaimed aim was to exploit these lands for German interests without consideration for the local populations. As in occupied Poland, administration and government in Soviet areas were entrusted to several rival forces. The Ministry for the Eastern Occupied Territories was established, with Alfred Rosenberg as Reich Minister. Its jurisdiction extended over a vast area that encompassed the Baltic states, to which were annexed part of White Russia; the Ukraine (two additional planned areas, Moscow and the Caucasus, were never occupied); the area around Bialystok, which was annexed to East Prussia (i.e., to the Reich itself) like the western regions of Poland; Eastern Galicia—before the war part of independent Poland, which in 1939 came under Soviet rule—now was the fifth district of the Generalgouvernement; the area between Odessa and the Bug River, Transnistria, was handed over to Rumania, although it had never belonged to that country, nor was Ion Antonescu overeager to receive it. Civil administrations (Reichskommissariats) were established in the Baltic states and White Russia, on the one hand, and the Ukraine, on the other. The former, known as Ostland (Eastern country) was administered by Reichskommissar Hinrich Lohse, whereas the Ukraine was placed under the Gauleiter of East Prussia, Erich Koch. Since the Bialystok region was annexed to East Prussia, he administered territory that stretched from the Baltic Sea to the Black Sea. Koch set up his central office in Rovno, the largest city in the Volhynia District (which had also been part of Poland before the war and had come under Soviet rule in 1939). Within Ostland, each of the Baltic states—Lithuania, Latvia, and Estonia—as well as White Russia constituted a Generalkommissariat ruled by a Generalkommissar, with subordinate district commissars (Gebietskommissare).[9] Himmler's forces—dispatched to the region to carry out "special tasks"—operated in parallel to these other bodies. As in Poland, they were made up of police, Gestapo, and SD units. Armed SS units (Waffen SS) also operated in addition to the Higher SS and Police Leaders (Höhere SS- und Polizeiführers, or HSSPF) directly subordinate to Himmler. These police units were augmented by the Einsatzgruppen, who were directly entrusted with the implementation of the "special tasks." Although it had been established in principle that these two branches of government—civil administration and police—would rule over the territories, the army was unable to forgo apparatus of its own since its supply lines cut across these areas, and the supply bases, repair workshops, and other needs of so vast an army, deployed thousands of miles from home, were also located therein. In the battle areas and adjacent territories, military rather than civil administration was established.

Distribution of Functions and Army–SS Cooperation

The apparatus was geared for action in the same spirit formulated by Hitler at the meeting of July 16, 1941, which was reminiscent of the planning session held during the Polish campaign on September 20, 1939 (see chap. 5). This meeting discussed the administrative division of the area, manpower problems, and conflicts among the various authorities. In effect, the network of interrelationships in the newly occupied territories had been prepared long before. The discussion of the line of command begun in March 1941 already emphasized "the special role of the Reichsführer SS," namely, Himmler.[10] The first official formulation appeared in a directive issued on March 13, 1941, by the head of the High Command of the armed forces, Field Marshal Wilhelm Keitel, "In the area of army operations, the Reichsführer SS will be entrusted, on behalf of the Führer, with special tasks for the preparation of the political administrations—tasks entailed by the final struggle that will have to be carried out between two opposing political systems. Within the framework of these tasks, the Reichsführer SS will act independently and on his own responsibility."[11]

In the wake of this directive, negotiations commenced on the same day between Heydrich, as Himmler's representative, and the army quartermaster, General Eduard Wagner; the agreement they signed was ratified on April 28, 1941, by the then chief of the army command Field Marshal Walter von Brauchitsch.[12] The SD was empowered to engage in certain activities in the area of military operations, but its main function was to combat anti-Reich tendencies in the area behind the front line. The Einsatzgruppen were to receive their special "professional" orders from Heydrich as head of the Security Police (Sipo) and the SD. A liaison officer between the army and the police would be appointed in each army group. The Einsatzgruppen were authorized to act toward the civilian population on their own initiative.

This document is of fundamental importance because it attests, for the first time, to official collaboration between the army and Himmler's forces; this had been avoided in Poland. There were two main reasons for this change: first, whereas in Poland administrative arrangements were made after the end of the campaign, in Russia they became operative while the battle still raged. Hence, the army was unwilling to waive its say on administrative arrangements in the areas behind the front line. Second, and perhaps even more significant, this time Hitler ordered the army to collaborate in extermination plans directed against the Russian army as well as against the civilian population. He explained these tasks to his generals at a meeting held on March 30, 1941. What was involved, he declared, was a struggle between two kinds of Weltanschauung, and he exhorted them not to treat the Russian army with the respect due to enemy soldiers. This, he emphasized, was a war of destruction. Only thus was there a chance that the Communist enemy would not raise its head again after thirty years. First and foremost, he demanded the extermination of the "Bolshevik commissars" and the Communist intelligentsia. Since the commissars and the secret police (GPU) were criminals, they should be treated accordingly. This war, he said, in no way resembled the war in the West. In the East, only cruelty could guarantee a tranquil future. It was incumbent on the generals to display self-sacrifice and to overcome their hesitations.[13] The generals—some 200 to 250 in number—heard their führer in complete silence. Some sources claim that a debate broke out among them and that Hitler cut it short by commenting, "I cannot demand that my generals should understand my orders, but I demand that they follow them."[14]

Hitler's directive was issued the following day (March 31, 1941), but the debate on methods of implementation continued throughout April and May until the heinous directive known as the Commissar Order was published on June 6, 1941. It laid down rules for the action to be taken against political commissars attached to Red Army units. In principle it stipulated that they should be executed by arms whenever captured in battle or offering resistance. The explanation was that they fostered the spirit of resistance and could be expected to mete out hostile, cruel, and inhuman treatment to prisoners, for they "had originated barbaric Asiatic methods of warfare." Those political commissars not apprehended while engaging in hostile actions and who were not suspected of such actions should be left alone—for the time being. Commissars captured while engaged in suspicious activity in areas close to the front line should be handed over to the Einsatzgruppen or the SD. The secrecy of the document was emphasized; it was also stressed that the document must not be allowed to fall into the hands of the enemy. At the planning session of July 16, 1941, Hitler also stressed that the true intentions of the Germans toward Russia, its population, and its army must be disguised.[15]

Because of the camouflage efforts, it is difficult to establish to what extent these orders were carried out and how many commissars fell victim to this planned extermination campaign. Military units did not, apparently, act uniformly, and while some strictly adhered to instructions, others were reluctant to do so.[16] This is attested to by a directive, dated August 8, 1941, that states, "Various questions raised by the armed forces make it necessary to emphasize that nothing has changed as regards treatment of these people [the political commissars]."[17] The murders, however, had the opposite effect to that anticipated—they stiffened Russian resistance.[18]

The Fate of Russian POWs

Hitler's theory that the Slavs were an inferior breed found its most blatant expression in the attitude toward Russian POWs. They were captured in the first six months of the war in numbers that stunned the Germans, including Hitler himself. By the end of 1941 their number had exceeded 3.5 million, and the fact that Red Army troops were surrendering in the millions seemed to corroborate the theory that they were lowly beings. The Nazi propaganda machine exploited this fact and the German press published photographs of prisoners, pointing out their "decadent oriental appearance." The word *subhuman* first came into public usage at this time. And SS publications made extensive use of this propaganda. A pamphlet entitled "The Sub-humans" concluded with an appeal, "The sub-humans have arisen in order to conquer the world. . . . Europe, defend yourself!" Another pamphlet produced by the SS Training Authority was entitled "Jewish Sub-human Bolshevism." It depicted the Russian soldier as a machine driven by bestial lusts, "Machines built to attack, to trample, to kill, to destroy blindly ... machines which are incapable of suddenly becoming human again, of intelligence or of feeling pity for the defenceless."[19] The SS instructors were referring not to their own troops, but to the Red Army.

This propaganda accompanied the mass slaughter of prisoners. The German army's preparations to absorb prisoners were provisional and in no way adequate. Nor was the army willing to allocate to its prisoners any of the food that was supplied to its own troops with great difficulty. As a consequence, it was concluded that the POW camps should be "purified."[20] To this end SS units were brought into the camps in the summer of 1941. Heydrich's orders contained the statement that "the task of commando units is political examination of all the inmates of the camp. They must classify the elements and ensure appropriate treatment for: a. those who are intolerable from the political, criminal, or any other aspect; b. those who can be utilized for the rehabilitation of the occupied territories."

This meant that the "intolerable" elements were to be annihilated and only a small number left to be exploited for hard labor. The "intolerable" elements included all Communist activists, all officials and intellectuals, all those defined as agitators or fanatic Communists, and *all Jews.*[21] This directive was issued on July 17, 1941, namely, one day after the fateful meeting of July 16. Here, too, we find a parallel to Heydrich's instructions of September 21, 1939, during the Polish campaign. Masses of prisoners died of hunger; thousands were shot. On December 21, 1941, Heinrich Müller, head of the Gestapo, reported that out of 22,000 prisoners classified, 16,000 had been executed in concentration camps in Germany.[22] However, the cruelest suffering was inflicted on prisoners during the death marches from distant regions westward. Endless processions of defeated, wounded, sick, and starving men were driven by the SS along Russia's poor roads, and those who fell behind or faltered were shot on the spot. The strongest of the prisoners survived these death marches, only to die, for the most part, in the camps in which they were incarcerated.

Why did the Germans choose to exterminate most of the POWs rather than exploit them as a labor force in the occupied territories and in Germany itself? At first the authorities objected to transporting Russians as laborers to Germany, but as time passed they changed their minds and began to select those prisoners who appeared suitable candidates for work in agriculture and other sectors suffering from a lack of manpower. In due course Russian prisoners were also sent as laborers to the occupied countries—their graves may be seen today even in Norway. As the fighting grew fiercer, hundreds of thousands of them were recruited into the German army; during the invasion of Normandy, Russian soldiers were captured by the Allied forces.[23]

The planning of the war and of the civil administration was guided intermittently by ideological and pragmatic considerations. To rule and to exploit were the proclaimed objectives of the military effort. Military victory was intended to impose German rule and the brutal methods of administration were aimed at consolidating this rule and organizing the exploitative activities. But the methods employed by the totalitarian regime actually sabotaged all prospects of maintaining *Lebensraum*. It was impossible to destroy and to exploit at the same time. This inconsistency was one of the characteristic features of the occupation in Eastern Europe. It stemmed from the essence of the National Socialist regime and was compounded by internal strife among the implementing bodies, great and small, each eager to safeguard its own interests and its share of the "vast cake." The German people nicknamed government officials in Eastern Europe golden pheasants because of their overwhelming concern for their own pockets.

In all circumstances Hitler was the supreme arbiter. The inherent conflict of National Socialism echoed his own personal conflict between ideology and realpolitik. He "solved" it by advocating to an ever-increasing degree ideological consistency as the most effective method of guaranteeing success. Hence, his continued pertinacity, even when in the winter of 1941/1942 he apparently began to fear the outcome of the campaign. From the outset, however, he had refused to consider failure as a possibility. According to the German historian Andreas Hillgruber, Hitler now shifted from the virtuoso tactical flexibility he had displayed during the preparations for war with Russia to rigid methods in order to achieve his fixed ideological–racist objectives, namely, "War in the East for the conquest of new *'Lebensraum'* and the 'Final Solution,' meaning extermination, starting with the Jews in the conquered area of the Soviet Union: both [these schemes were] planned simultaneously and commenced on the same day, June 22, 1941."[24]

10

The Final Solution:
The First Stage—Einsatzgruppen

Preliminary Thoughts

We do not know for sure when Hitler finally made up his mind to exterminate the Jews in order to "solve" the Jewish problem. It may be assumed that he considered such a prospect from the beginning of his political career, as suggested by many of his utterances and by his well-known comments in *Mein Kampf* that during World War I thousands of Jews should have been gassed. But at that time, and for many years thereafter, this aspiration was certainly no more than a vision for the distant future. Nor do we know of any statement by Hitler at the time of the conquest of Poland that indicates he perceived the concentration of the Jews in ghettos as a preparatory stage for systematic mass extermination, although he and his henchmen apparently hoped to decimate the Jewish population through poor and hazardous living conditions. However, as the historian Andreas Hillgruber has succinctly stated, Hitler thought it both essential and possible to link up the military campaign against Russia with the liquidation of the Jews. The directives issued to the heads of the army and the SS in March 1941 were probably accompanied by verbal orders to include the Jewish population in the planned extermination operations. It was self-evident that the task would be entrusted to Heinrich Himmler's cohorts.[1] Since the very beginning of the Polish campaign, Himmler had been in charge of implementing the racist plans, and it was he who masterminded the exchanges of populations and the deportations.

The Madagascar Plan

The solution that Himmler envisaged for the Jews in the summer of 1940 was mass migration overseas.[2] This idea, linked to the so-called Madagascar Plan, proposed to banish the Jews of Europe to an island off the east coast of Africa. Cited in anti-Semitic literature since the 1880s, the scheme to settle this island in the Indian Ocean with the surplus East European population had again been aired in the 1920s and 1930s. The possibility was broached in 1937 in the context of the Polish government's desire to reduce the dimensions of its Jewish problem. It was then discussed in international forums and was investigated by a special committee, in which Jews also participated. Eventually, it was concluded that the scheme was impractical. Later, the Nazis displayed interest in the idea, too, and in March 1938 Heydrich instructed Eichmann to examine the matter. After the conquest of France and after the failure of the Lublin Reservation, the idea was raised again; thus, the German Foreign Ministry and the RSHA began to draw up detailed plans. Hitler appeared to favor the scheme and referred to it several times in the summer of 1940.[3]

Eichmann dedicated himself to this new-old scheme with his usual diligence and thoroughness, perceiving it as a desirable solution to the complex Jewish problem. In August 1940 he submitted a comprehensive fourteen-page memorandum, describing the island and proposing that four million Jews from the Reich and the occupied countries be settled there. They would live in a kind of ghetto under the supervision of the Security Police (Sipo). Western Jewry would fund the operation "as reparations for the damage caused to the Third Reich by the Jews in the economic sphere and as a result of the Versailles treaty."[4] Government offices continued to toy with the idea long after Hitler had abandoned it, and it later served as camouflage for the extermination program. Even after it had been officially shelved and while the extermination operations were proceeding apace, Hitler continued to use it as a smokescreen.

Planning and Organization

In May 1940 Himmler was still of the opinion that entire nations should not be exterminated. However, he changed his mind by March 1941 when Hitler propounded his objectives in the planned war against Russia. That same month, at a meeting with several senior SS officers, Himmler explained that the die was cast: they were about to attack Russia. He informed these officers of the "special tasks" that would be entrusted to the SS units, the SD, and the police. "Without remorse, cruel war will develop between nations; in its course, twenty to thirty million Slavs and Jews will perish because of war activities and food shortages."[5] Oral directives were issued by Heydrich to the Einsatzgruppen while they were being trained for their tasks.[6] It is well known that Hitler apparently did not issue written orders on the "Final Solution." Heydrich, however, received an ordinance from Herman Göring on July 31, 1941:

> In completion of the task which was entrusted to you in the Edict dated January 24, 1939, of solving the Jewish question by means of emigration or evacuation in the most convenient way possible, given the present conditions, I herewith charge you with making all necessary preparations with regard to organizational, practical, and financial

aspects for an overall solution [*Gesammtlösung*] of the Jewish question in the German sphere of influence in Europe. Insofar as competencies of other central organizations are affected, these are to be involved. I further charge you with submitting to me promptly an overall plan of the preliminary organizational, practical and financial measures for the execution of the intended final solution [*Endlösung*] of the Jewish question.[7]

According to Eichmann, it was he who drafted the letter that Heydrich then submitted to Göring for his signature.[8] As in numerous other National Socialist procedures, the directive did not launch a completely new initiative but rather bestowed sanction on an operation that was already under way and had to be officially implemented by the various government agencies. The directive refers to an "overall solution" and the final clause even mentions a "final solution." We may, then, assume that by the end of July 1941 a clear-cut decision had been taken to exploit the conquered territories in order to solve the Jewish problem throughout Europe in the spirit proclaimed by Hitler time and again. Hence, it is also reasonable to assume that Heydrich would require the cooperation of other administrative bodies in the operation, for example, the Foreign Ministry or the Ministry of Transport, and to this end required explicit authorization. For the first time, we encounter here, in an official document, the phrase "the final solution of the Jewish question." As we know, this phrase served to disguise the intention to wipe out the Jewish population of Europe and, if possible, throughout the world. Not by chance, the two aspects emphasized in the directive were *totality* and *finality.*

Killing Operations

The millions of Jews with whom the Germans had come into contact in occupied Poland were now augmented by close to four million more in the newly occupied territories. They included more than two million in the Soviet Union,[9] over a quarter of a million in the Baltic states, and a million in the areas that had formerly belonged to Poland. We have seen that in Poland the Germans failed to achieve the comprehensive solutions to which they had aspired. A large proportion of the Jewish community held fast despite persecution, overcrowding in the ghettos, and malnutrition; the process of natural mortality was less rapid than the Germans had hoped. Now they concluded that they could no longer rely on natural factors, and therefore had to do the job themselves, particularly since the plans for reservations in Poland and Madagascar had proved unworkable.

The vast area stretching from the Baltic Sea to the Black Sea was divided into four areas, with one Einsatzgruppe in each. They were known as groups A, B, C, and D, and each was commanded by an officer from the RSHA; each group was composed of several commando units, and most of their commanders were professional SS and Gestapo officers. Each of the Einsatzgruppen was attached to an army corps and, in accordance with prior agreement, acted in collaboration with it. As they advanced almost simultaneously with the fighting force, the speed of the military progress the first few months enabled the Einsatzgruppen to work swiftly.[10] The units moved systematically from place to place, assembling the Jews, conveying them outside towns and villages, and murdering them beside antitank trenches or pits dug especially for this purpose. The victims were ordered to strip and to stand in groups by the pit where they were shot by automatic weapons, the dead and dying falling into the mass graves. Sometimes the victims were even forced to lie down in the pit in neat lines, head to toe alternately, and there they were executed row by row by what the SS called the sardine method. Finally, the pits were covered with earth. Rivers of blood flowed and the earth sometimes heaved and trembled for days afterward.

The Order Police (ORPO) took part in the operations under the command of the Higher SS and Police Leaders (HSSPF) and their local collaborators. But, to the surprise even of the SS, the army cooperated of its own volition, and in certain areas army units played a very active role in mass murder. According to the preliminary planning, the local population was expected to collaborate. At first this method proved successful, but the readiness of the local population did not reach the dimensions the Germans had anticipated. More successful was the activation of local auxiliary police units under German command. The first wave of murders came to an end around the beginning of winter, and it is estimated that by then more than seven hundred thousand Jews had been murdered in these actions: at least four hundred thousand of them in Soviet Russia, close to two hundred thousand in the Baltic states, and the remainder in the areas that had belonged to Poland before the war.[11]

For propaganda purposes the Germans constantly claimed that the Jews were the main organizers of the partisan movement and hence must be exterminated, an argument that was first broached by Hitler at the planning session of July 16, 1941. Stalin had just called for partisan activity behind the enemy lines, and Hitler welcomed this statement as providing him with a pretext for German terror in the occupied areas (see chap. 9). In fact, at this time the partisan movement was tiny and unorganized and did not constitute a real threat to the German army. The claim that it was being run by the Jews was certainly baseless. In many cases the mass murders were described as retaliation for the killing of German soldiers supposedly carried out by Jews, the ratio being 1:100.

The commanding officer of Einsatzgruppe A, Franz W. Stahlecker, sent a detailed report on January 31, 1942, about activities in the Baltic countries and White Russia, covering the period from July 23 to October 15, 1941. According to this report the overall number murdered was 135,567. Among them, the known numbers of Jews killed are 80,311 in Lithuania, 30,025 in Latvia, 474 in Estonia, and 7,620 in White Russia; to this should be added 5,500 Jews killed in pogroms and 5,502 killed in the Tilsit (Sovetsk) sector and near the border with East Prussia. There were undoubtedly also an unknown number of Jews among the 3,387 "communists" and 748 mental patients mentioned in the report.[12]

According to a report submitted by Einsatzgruppe B, 45,467 were killed up to mid-November 1941, within its area of operation, that is, White Russia.[13] Owing to the slower advance of the army in the south, operations began there later. According to a report dated November 3, 1941, there were 80,000 Jews killed in the Ukraine, a large proportion of them (namely 34,000) in Kiev. The Kiev Operation—the Babi Yar slaughter—was one of the bloodiest and most notorious of all. The Einsatzgruppen units reached the city between September 19 and 25, 1941. At this time, Russian sappers set off two explosions, the second one destroying the German headquarters and a large part of the city center; 25,000 people were left homeless. In retaliation, the German authorities demanded resettlement of the Jews and called on them to assemble on September 29 for transfer. The 30,000 Jews who assembled were taken to the forest and slaughtered over the course of two days. According to the German report, "there were no incidents." It also emphasizes that "thanks to the outstandingly efficient organization," the Jews believed up to the last moment that they were being taken to their new homes. The local population—it is further reported—believed the story and were gratified by it. Only *post factum* did the truth emerge. The Germans boasted of having solved the housing problem by evacuating a suitable number of apartments—that is, by exterminating approximately 35,000 Jews.[14] Before the German occupation, 175,000 Jews had lived in the city; thus the victims accounted for only part of the Jewish community, which had comprised both local residents and refugees. A large percentage of these Jews had made their escape before the Germans arrived. Most of the victims were the old, the sick, and women and children who had been left behind.[15]

The Soviet evacuation of the Ukraine was more organized and workers, including Jews, were evacuated with their factories. Thus, for example, a report from Einsatzgruppe D, dated November 19, 1941, states that of the 100,000 Jews in Dnepropetrovsk, 70,000 fled before the Germans arrived; of those remaining, 1,000 were shot on the spot.[16]

Sometimes, economic considerations were brought up, as witness a report sent on December 2, 1941, by the representative of the Industrial Armaments Department of the Supreme Command (OKW) in the Ukraine to General Georg Thomas, who headed the department. The Jewish population of the Ukraine was mainly urban, the report explained, and often constituted more than 50 percent of the population of a town. These Jews "carried out almost all the work in the skilled trades, and even provided part of the labor for small- and medium-sized industries." The murder operations in the Ukraine were vaster in scope than anywhere else in the Soviet Union, but as the report states, "no consideration was given to the interests of the economy."[17]

Marshal Walther von Reichenau, supreme commander of the Sixth Army in the southern army corps, was one of the high-ranking officers who wholeheartedly supported National Socialism and Hitler personally. On October 10, 1941, he issued an order in which he noted that vague concepts were still rife as to how soldiers were to conduct themselves. "The main objective of this campaign against the Jewish-Bolshevik system is to totally destroy the potential for power and to extirpate Asiatic influence on European cultural life." He went on to explain that consequently German soldiers were faced with tasks above and beyond the conventional framework of conduct of warfare, "The soldier must fully understand the need for severe but just atonement of the Jewish subhumans." There follows the customary agrument that all partisan activities behind the front were organized by the Jews, and the soldiers were exhorted to refrain from treating the partisans as "decent soldiers." Only total cruelty could guarantee the safety of the army and ensure victory, "Only thus can we carry out our historic task and once and for all liberate the German people from the Jewish-Asiatic danger."[18]

Hitler was enthusiastic about the marshal's directive and ordered that it be distributed among all the army units; thus it also reached Field Marshal Erich von Manstein, the supreme commander of the Eleventh Army, which was operating in the Crimean Peninsula. At his trial before a British military tribunal in Hamburg, von Manstein claimed that he had known nothing of the extermination of Jews, notwithstanding the fact that he personally signed an order on November 20, 1941, reiterating von Reichenau's statement.[19]

Ghettos and Decrees

Before the occupation, there were some 2.5 million Jews in the Baltic states and those parts of Russia conquered by the Germans. Between 1 million and 1.5 million managed to escape, particularly from the original Russian areas.[20] By the beginning of winter, the Einsatzgruppen had managed to exterminate only about two-thirds of the remaining Jews. This was partly because of economic constraints, that is, the need for skilled laborers, and that the number of people who were engaged in these murderous activities were insufficient to cover the entire area. It also became necessary to deal with the Jewish population by concentrating the Jews in central ghettos and organizing them into forced labor units. The Germans now applied the lessons learned in occupied Poland. In many places, particularly the Baltic states, the Jews were rapidly herded into ghettos, but the intention now was not to keep them there, but to transport them directly to their deaths. Frequently, for example, in Riga, the population was divided in advance into two ghettos; the inmates of one were earmarked for immediate extermination, whereas the others were exploited as a labor force before being sent to their deaths. In Ludmir in the Volhynia District, a two-section ghetto was set up in April 1942. By that time the Jews already knew what awaited them, and they referred to the ghetto where the skilled workers were concentrated as "the ghetto of life" and to the other that housed "nonproductive" elements—women, children, and the old and sick—as "the ghetto of the dead." Some of these ghettos existed for very brief periods: sometimes months, sometimes only a few weeks.[21]

In order to round up the Jews for liquidation purposes, the Germans in addition to employing brute force used various stratagems, explaining that the Jews must enter ghettos for their own safety. In places (e.g., Lithuania and Latvia) where they had succeeded in inciting the local population to conduct pogroms, this argument proved particularly effective.

The Reichskommissar of the Ostland, Hinrich Lohse, soon issued a series of directives that included most of the known prohibitions. First, the Jews were ordered to wear the yellow badge; they were forbidden to use public transport, to enter public places, to study in schools, to own radios, and so on. Their property was confiscated and they were banned from engaging in commerce and exploited as forced laborers. Judenräte were established and ordered to conduct a census.

This procedure was followed, with minor changes, throughout almost all of the occupied areas.[22]

In the Ukraine the army itself dealt with the problem of the ghettos. On August 28, 1941, an ordinance was issued "on the establishment of ghettos."[23] In those places where ghettos had not yet been liquidated, mostly because of the need for manpower, the Einsatzgruppen together with the police searched for Jews who had hidden or fled to the forests. They also apprehended those who were not wearing their yellow badges, a crime usually punished by death. All these activities were accompanied by looting, including millions of rubles (as in Poland) extracted as fines imposed on the Jewish community.

In Poland the Germans had utilized the experience accumulated in anti-Jewish activities conducted over the years in Germany and Austria, carrying it to even greater extremes. Now they utilized their Polish experience in Russia, adding the "final stage" of direct extermination. This time the task was completed within a few weeks. One of the lessons of the Polish experience was that population movement (i.e., deportation) without a clear-cut objective was no solution. Thus, it was decided that the Jewish population should be seized on the spot or else incarcerated in ghettos to prevent their escape—and then liquidated on the spot. Once the Jews were no longer mobile, the Einsatzgruppen moved from place to place engaged in their task of extermination.

The economic and organizational problems were compounded by additional difficulties. Not infrequently witnesses to the murders were shocked at the sights they saw. Moreover, there were indications that the organized slaughter was beginning to affect the SS perpetrators. Himmler himself, when present near Minsk at a mass execution, found it hard to stand this test. In a speech he later delivered to the men who had done the work, he admitted that he was "repelled by this bloody job," but he emphasized that he, too, was merely obeying a supreme law and doing his duty. On the same occasion, Erich von dem Bach-Zelewski, who was in charge of the district, emphasized how shaken the men were. They were "finished," he said, for the rest of their lives and would become either neurotics or savages.[24] These experiences indicated that it was essential to find other ways to carry out the task.

One of the methods chosen to circumvent the need to involve German soldiers in direct acts of killing was the introduction of gas vans (*S-Wagen,* S = *spezial*). A hermetically sealed compartment was mounted on the vehicle and the exhaust gases of the van were pumped in through rubber pipes. Up to sixty people—sometimes more—were jammed into the compartment. The victims were told that they were being transported to some other location for resettlement. The entire operation took fifteen minutes.[25] However, this method did not solve the problem. Numerous hitches occurred and during the rainy season it was impossible to use the vehicles on the muddy roads. Nor was this method any easier from the psychological point of view. The sight of the contorted corpses was so terrible that SS troops usually preferred the previous method of killing. However, despite these reservations, it was apparently decided that the new method had proved itself effective. A report to the officer in charge at the RSHA, dated June 5, 1942, says,

"Since December 1941, for example, 97,000 have been processed [*sic!*] in the three vehicles in operation without any malfunctions in the vehicles."[26]

On the basis of this report, ten additional vehicles were ordered and several technical improvements were introduced in the hope of facilitating the processing of the cargo *(Ladung)*. About thirty gas vans were apparently in use, especially in the southern regions and in Minsk. They represented the transition to killing by gas in the extermination camps.

Annals of the Jews in the Occupied Russian Territories

The Former Polish Areas

In the areas handed over to the Soviet Union in 1939, the Jews welcomed the Russians since they feared the Germans. But they soon realized that their new rulers did not intend to protect them and improve their condition. All Jewish community institutions were shut down and the activities of social, cultural, and political organizations were banned. The private assets of Jews and non-Jews were confiscated, and their businesses and industrial concerns were taken over by the state. Hundreds, thousands, and even tens of thousands of the more than three hundred thousand Jews who had fled Poland during the occupation were now clustered in a number of towns, particularly Bialystok and Lwów. Some of these refugees were evacuated immediately by the Russians to the interior of Russia and to distant regions. The great majority rejected the alternative held out to them, namely, to accept Soviet nationality, which would have obliged the younger men to enlist in the Red Army. They feared being banned in perpetuity from leaving the Soviet Union and returning to their homes in Poland. In the summer of 1940, the Russians launched an additional evacuation scheme that also affected those sections of the indigenous population who, because of their public or economic status, did not appear suitable to the Communist regime.

Lwów

Eastern Galicia was densely settled with Jews, more than a million in number. The district capital, Lwów, had the third largest Jewish community in Poland after Warsaw and Łódź. Before the war, the Jewish population had numbered 110,000, one-third of the total population of the city. Under Russian rule, tens of thousands of Polish and Jewish refugees streamed into the city and its population was doubled. Some of the Jews continued their odyssey or moved to nearby towns. When the Germans occupied the city, 150,000 to 160,000 refugees remained.[27] Just as the Jews had earlier welcomed the entry of the Russians, the nationalist Ukrainians now eagerly awaited the Germans, convinced that together with the eastern Ukraine, they would now be able to establish an independent Ukrainian government. The Germans, however, planned otherwise. The leader of the Ukrainian movement, Stefan Bandera, and several of his associates were arrested, and he was incarcerated in a concentration camp, from which he emerged only after the war. The Germans also separated eastern and western Ukraine administratively by declaring, on August 1, 1941, Eastern Galicia the fifth region under the jurisdiction of the governor of the Generalgouvernement, Hans Frank. Henceforth, the rules and regulations operating in the Generalgouvernement were applicable to the Jews of Eastern Galicia.

In the period between the German occupation of the region and its annexation to the Generalgouvernement, the Jews suffered heavily. Units of Einsatzgruppe C, under the command of Dr. Otto Rasch, encouraged the Ukrainians to give free rein to their disappointment and frustration by conducting pogroms against the Jews. Charges were leveled against the Jews of having committed atrocities against Ukrainians during the Russian occupation.[28] Of those arrested on this charge, some were executed in prisons and in the forests outside Lwów; the remainder were taken to prison cells stained with Jewish blood and were forced to clean the traces of the murders. Then they were executed. The pogroms raged throughout July, claiming thousands of victims. The Ukrainians also rounded up Jews for forced labor—none returned. The killing was accompanied by looting.

One of the Jewish dignitaries, Rabbi Yeheskel Levin, tried to solicit the aid of Catholic Metropolitan Andreas Sheptitsky, who did issue a call to the Ukrainians to refrain from murdering Jews—without noticeable effect. He also invited the rabbi to take refuge in his residence until quiet was restored, but Rabbi Levin refused to abandon his flock. On emerging from the metropolitan's residence, he was seized by rioters and later murdered in prison.[29]

At this time, the Germans tried to set up a Judenrat composed of the leaders of the city's Jewish community, but most of the candidates approached, refused to accept. The Judenrat was eventually appointed on the basis of a list of Jewish intellectuals and public figures. The heads of the Judenrat were replaced in rapid succession, one alone dying a natural death. The slaughter spread throughout Eastern Galicia, and only in the southern area, captured initially by the Hungarians, were mass murders prevented at the outset.[30]

Bialystok

The Germans reached Bialystok on June 26, 1941. Part of the Jewish quarter was burned down immediately; at least one thousand people died when the synagogue in which they had been locked was set afire. The pogroms lasted until mid-July, and another sixty-three hundred people, many of them young men, lost their lives. Here, too, the Germans utilized the methods that had been used at the beginning of the Polish occupation, and hundreds of intellectuals were among the first victims. On August 1,1941, the ghetto was set up and run by the Judenrat, which had been established on the orders of the Germans at the end of July. The Judenrat was composed of people who had been active in community affairs before the war and who had maintained their authority despite the abolition of all Jewish institutions by the Russians. It was headed by Rabbi Gedalia Rosenman, but the dominant figure was Ephraim Barash, an engineer who had served before the war as secretary of the Jewish community.

As noted earlier, Bialystok and the surrounding area were annexed to East Prussia, and the entire district thus came under the rule of Reichskommissar Erich Koch. As a friend of Martin Bormann, who was by then the all-powerful figure in Hitler's staff, Koch managed to gain himself independent standing. Even Alfred

Rosenberg, who, in theory, was his superior, was unable to curb him.[31] Thanks to its annexation to East Prussia, however, a civil administration was set up in Bialystok. The German administration—interested in exploiting Jewish labor as well as Jewish skills in crafts and industry—turned to Łódź in the spring of 1942 to learn from the arrangements made there, just as the Germans in Warsaw had done before them. Because of the special form of its administration and because of the Judenrat activities, in general, and its actual leader Ephraim Barash, in particular, the Bialystok ghetto survived for a relatively long period; its liquidation only began in 1943.

From the outset it was evident that the Judenrat intended to conduct its work systematically. At its first meeting on August 2, 1941, it established thirteen departments, including labor, welfare, health and sanitation, finance and economics, and supplies and housing. At its next meeting, on the following day, the functions in the various departments were divided up among the Judenrat members, and a fourteenth department, industry, was established.[32] A week later, people who engaged in a wide range of trades were asked to register at the Judenrat.[33] Some workshops and factories were in German hands; others were run by the Judenrat or the ownership was private. Most were within the area of the ghetto, but some people also worked outside.

Initially, the Germans tried to divide the ghetto in two, and Barash did not delude himself as to their intention. At a Judenrat meeting on November 8, 1941, he said, "It may be assumed that a program will emerge from this . . . the crux of which is to eliminate all those Bialystok Jews who have no occupations. The danger is great and this is a great catastrophe. We are trying, on the one hand, to win concessions and on the other—to delay." According to his assessment, the number of skilled workers involved was fifteen hundred together with their families, a total of six thousand. At that time, there were fifty thousand people in the ghetto. Barash succeeded in averting the decree.[34]

The situation in the small towns and villages scattered throughout the district was worse than in Bialystok itself, and many people sought shelter in the town. The refugee problem was of great concern to the Judenrat because it was necessary to find housing, to supply food, and to integrate the refugees into the life of the ghetto. In September and October 1941, the Germans demanded the evacuation of the surplus population from Bialystok in order to assemble them in the small town of Pruzany near the border of what was then the eastern Ukraine. From there it was convenient for the Germans to transport them over the border for extermination. The Judenrat, aware of this fact and ordered to prepare lists as a basis for the evacuation, decided not to include in these lists skilled workers of any kind, members of the Judenrat and Judenrat clerks, Jewish police personnel, and firemen. The Judenrat has been charged with "basing the lists on the criterion of rescuing the intelligentsia, the middle class, the privileged and those with influence or money."[35] Most of those evacuated in September/October were from the poorer class or refugees. In the past 4,000 Jews had lived at Pruzany; now the number swelled to 12,000 from thirty towns and villages in the district, apart from Bialystok. They were crammed into a ghetto set up while the deportation was in progress. The Judenrat considered itself responsible for the evacuees and announced that it was necessary to make provisions for the 1,000 families from Bialystok who were in need of heating, food, building materials, beds, and clothing. The outlay was estimated at RM 370,000. Barash summed up the concessions he had won from the Germans: instead of 55 pounds of gold, only 13 pounds had been handed over; instead of 5 million rubles, only 2.5 million had been paid; instead of being located in a poor quarter, the ghetto had been set up in a better area. The demand for 10 million additional rubles had been withdrawn. No more than 4,500 people had been evacuated to Pruzany instead of the 13,000 the Germans had demanded. The order to submit a list of intellectuals had been rescinded.[36] The Judenrat later succeeded in bringing some of the evacuees back to Bialystok.

Barash believed that the key to the survival of the ghetto was stepping up production. On March 1, 1942, he said, "As you know, the focus of our activity, which may be our salvation, is the rapidly developing industry."[37] It was reported at the same meeting that about eighteen hundred workers were employed in ghetto industry. There were saddle-making, tailoring, and glass-polishing workshops as well as shoemakers and the knitwear industry. At the end of March 1942 an exhibition of products was held outside the ghetto and five hundred items were placed on show "which make a stunning impression, like in prewar times." It was described as "a rich and variegated display of human artifacts and military items, displayed and laid out with delicate artistic taste." Responding to the criticism voiced in the ghetto, Barash said, "I would like to declare that we have one sole objective: *to preserve ourselves until the war is over,*" and he cited the methods he was employing to this end:

a. 100 percent compliance with orders;
b. proving useful—this will provide those who champion us [reference is to the Germans] with material that can be used to our advantage;
c. conduct that will satisfy the German authorities *in the manner in which Jews behave in their Diaspora lives.*[38]

On June 29, 1942, at a small-scale celebration held to mark the anniversary of the founding of the Judenrat, Barash said, "There is nobody who could describe what has happened to us, what we survived during these past 365 days—no artist, no writer, no painter. We can scarcely believe it ourselves, and I think nobody will believe it in the future . . . it is lucky that we cannot foresee the future, for if we could, we would not have lived and reached the present stage."

He went on speaking of the achievements and importance of industry and did not forget to mention other spheres of activity: an educational network, vocational schools, social welfare and hospitals "of a scope severalfold that of similar institutions before the war," and concern for improving nutrition by planting vegetable plots. Finally, he defined the situation of the Judenrat:

After all, we are hostages, held responsible for everything that happens in the ghetto. And you have seen what that means in other cities. The devotion, heart and soul, cannot be described in words. If we survive, whole books will have to be written about it. . . .

And he concluded.

> In truth, there is no place for optimism in the ghetto, but when I consider the road
> along which we have come, and our burdens, then I am sure that we will take the
> Bialystok ghetto through to a happy end.[39]

The Bialystok ghetto was not sealed as hermetically as that of Łódź. More
significant, perhaps, is the fact that by the summer of 1941, the dangers facing the
Jews were clearer than they had been in Łódź in 1939. The systematic extermination activities of the Germans in the Soviet regions in 1941/1942 were known
in Bialystok. We have seen that Barash specified three rules for conduct. At the
time he spoke, in late June 1942, he had apparently not yet grasped that the implications of his first rule (i.e., full compliance with German orders) would be so
drastic. The second rule (i.e., the need to remain useful) was based on the belief
that the local German administration would decide the fate of the ghetto Jews and
that they had an interest in Jewish labor; hence, they would "champion" the Jews.
This belief, rather hope, was erroneous. Barash saw no alternative but to live from
one day to the next and to attempt to mitigate the harshness of the decrees.

Volhynia District: The First Stage

The Volhynia District was annexed to the Ukrainian District, and Generalkommissar Erich Koch chose the capital, Rovno, as his headquarters. The greater part
of the town's mixed population were Ukrainians; the remainder were Russians,
Jews, Czechs, and Poles. In 1939 the number of Jews was estimated at 28,000.
The town first tasted war when it was bombed by the Germans on September 14,
1939, but three days later the Red Army entered. The Russians ruled with a heavy
hand, and all those they considered of suspicious appearance or dubious occupation were arrested. These included Jewish activists, particularly Zionists and
Bundists, many of whom were immediately deported to Siberia. Store owners
were deported from Rovno or forced to open their shops, and they hastened to
sell off their stocks without having any opportunity to replenish them or to use
their money. People were mobilized for various forced labor tasks, including
building a new road. The work regime was most arduous and any absenteeism or
tardiness was punished by lengthy imprisonment. Trials were frequently rigged
with the help of false witnesses who accused the defendants of plotting against the
regime. The wages the authorities fixed did not suffice for subsistence.

The Rovno community, like other Jewish communities at the time, came to
the aid of the numerous refugees who flocked to the town, but its efforts were
greatly hampered by the ban on all Jewish institutions. Hebrew schools were
closed down. In their place several schools were opened that conducted studies in
Yiddish, in accordance with the practice of Jewish Communists in the Soviet
Union. The Zionist youth movements, now banned, and the community institutions tried to continue their activities clandestinely. Through joint efforts, they
succeeded in helping the refugees to continue on their way to Vilna (Vilnius) or
to Rumania and Hungary.[40]

When war broke out between Germany and Russia, Rovno was bombed at
once (June 22, 1941); a week later the Germans entered the town. The Russians

had only a few days to organize their retreat, but they succeeded in this short time in mobilizing most of the youth of army age including a large number of Jews—but only a small number of other Jews joined the Russians. The great majority of the Jewish population—families with children, old and sick people—had neither opportunity nor desire to escape.[41] Here, as elsewhere in the Ukraine, the Ukrainians awaited the German army as the liberators who would grant them independence. When they realized that this was not to be, their disillusionment found release in active participation in pogroms and in the plundering of Jews. Some three hundred Jews were murdered when the Germans occupied the town; one thousand more were seized in the streets and shot during July and August.[42] Meanwhile, the town was filling up with refugees from nearby small towns. The widespread slaughter in Rovno was conducted at the beginning of November 1941. It was carried out in the main by the police, not by the Einsatzgruppen.[43] On November 5 the newly established Judenrat, acting on directives from the Germans, announced that all Jews must assemble on the following morning in the central square and bring with them provisions and personal belongings not to exceed 35 pounds. Only skilled workers, who had previously been issued special work cards, were exempted. The Jewish population was gripped with fear, but most accepted the directive as an ineluctable catastrophe and thought that they would be deported—but they did not imagine what awaited them. Only after the mass murders had been perpetrated did the facts come to light from the testimony of the few who succeeded in making their escape. The people were taken to a site in a pine forest where Russian POWs had earlier dug five large pits. Although a severe storm was raging and it was bitter cold, the people were ordered to strip and to jump into the pits. Some of the elderly people and small children froze to death before their turn to be murdered arrived. On November 6 and 7, 1941, at least 17,500 Rovno Jews were executed.[44] The remainder were now concentrated in the ghetto. Some sensed the enormity of the approaching danger and fled the town before the day of judgment. They hid in the neighboring villages, thanks mainly to the assistance of Czechs who took them into their homes and concealed them. But once the *Aktion* was over, they usually had no choice but to return to Rovno and to join the remnants of the Jewish population there. It was not possible to remain in hiding for long, nor could they move onward, since they would then have been rounded up by the Germans or the Ukrainians. Sometimes these survivors returned in order to seek relatives and friends, who, in most cases, had disappeared.

The main problem that now faced these survivors was the need to find work. It was clear that only the redeeming work card could protect them. To the extent that bread rations were given out, they were issued only to workers. Hence, the Jews were ready to do any job in the service of the Germans, who were the main employers. One task was the sorting of the clothes and belongings left by the victims of the slaughter. This tragedy was vividly documented by Emmanuel Ringelblum in his diary:

> This is a tragic complication. The Jews are granted the right to live only when they
> work for the German army; it was thus in Vilna, in Rovno, and in dozens of other

towns where mass exterminations of the Jewish population were perpetrated. There survived only those who worked directly and indirectly for the Germans. . . . There has been no such tragedy in history. A people who hate the Germans with every fiber of their being can redeem themselves from murder only at the price of giving help to the murderer[s] for the sake of a victory, which means the eradication of Jews (of himself) from the face of Europe.[45]

Volhynia District: The Second Stage

In quoting Ringelblum, a remark made in parenthesis was omitted: "In the end, in Rovno, these, too [those who worked for the Germans], were taken to the pits for extermination or deported to an unknown destination."

The final liquidation of the Rovno ghetto was one of the many *Aktionen* that the Germans organized in the summer of 1942 in that region in order to cleanse it of Jews. This was the second phase in the systematic extermination operation which was carried out by the Sipo, largely made up of personnel from the Einsatzgruppen who were no longer mobile. Toward spring the Germans began to plan their next wave of killings by setting up new ghettos divided into the "ghetto of the dead" and the "ghetto of the living," for skilled workers and their families. Toward the end of May the implementation of extermination commenced. The following depicts an example from a small town:

> The Germans reached Koritz on July 2, 1941, and on the following day they issued these directives relating to Jews:
>
> 1. Jews must hand over all weapons in their possession.
> 2. Jews are prohibited from leaving the town without a permit from the authorities.
> 3. Gentiles are forbidden to cross the threshold of a Jewish home.
> 4. All Jews aged twelve and over must wear the yellow badge on the left side of the chest and on the back.
> 5. Jews are permitted to appear on the streets only on their way to and from work.
> 6. Jews are permitted to shop only on Thursdays between 8 to 10 A.M.[46]

There were 5,000 Jews in the town; in August 1941 about 550 men were murdered in two operations.[47] A fine of RM 100,000 was imposed. The Judenrat was ordered to produce this within a few hours, just as it was also ordered daily to supply the Germans and the Ukrainians with whatever produce or goods were demanded—in addition to individual looting.

The large-scale *Aktion* was conducted on the eve of Shavuot, the Jewish Feast of Weeks (May 21, 1942). On that day all the Jews were assembled in the market square, where they were classified; two hundred males who were skilled workers were exempted. The Germans transported about twenty-two hundred people outside the town on that day to a site where pits had been dug in advance. When the *Aktion* was completed, the Gestapo officer told the survivors, "The *Aktion* is over. Tomorrow morning all the remaining Jews must report at their places of work. Jews who were in hiding can return to the ghetto. They are no longer in danger."[48]

Moshe Gildenman (then about forty), chairman of the Artisans Association, was a cultured man active in public life who also wrote. He has depicted the character and appearance of that Gestapo man:

From his quiet voice, with the matter-of-fact intonation of a businessman, one could not discern that he had just taken part in an *Aktion* that had, all at once, robbed fathers of their children, children of their parents, men of their wives. His face showed only satisfaction and slight weariness, as after completion of a difficult but pleasant task. Was this a human being? I asked myself. If so, then I am ashamed of mankind and regret that I was not born some other animal.[49]

Gildenman did not confine himself to rhetorical questions. He succeeded in organizing a group of young people who were ready to follow him to the forest and try to join the partisans. Before he could put this plan into action, however, it became known that the Germans were preparing the liquidation of the ghetto in which fifteen hundred people remained. On the last night he and his group escaped. Gildenman succeeded in establishing a partisan unit and became one of the prominent leaders in the Ukrainian forests, an almost legendary figure. The Germans tried in vain to capture him alive or dead (see chap. 17).

To escape prior to an *Aktion* was a difficult and hazardous undertaking. One of those who succeeded told that his group was sheltered by a Ukrainian villager who had once told him that if he were ever in danger he could take shelter in his home, and he welcomed them most civilly. When the farmer later heard what had occurred in the town, he no longer dared to keep them, but sent them to the nearby forest. His nine-year-old son brought them food, lest the older sons discover the presence of Jews. The refugees later undertook a long odyssey through the forests.[50]

Why did only relatively few Jews attempt to escape? Gildenman describes the apathy—the feeling that nothing mattered any more—that afflicted people as a consequence of the first *Aktion* in Koritz. People found it hard to make decisions, to take initiative, or to launch themselves into the unknown in the forests. Gildenman describes his conversations with various people he urged to join him, but who flatly refused. One of them chose to trust the owner of the printing press where he worked, a person who had told him that only unproductive Jews would be exterminated. "If [Hitler] exterminates us, he will have to replace us by Germans he needs in the front line. And Hitler is not stupid enough to do that." And the man went on to admit that he did not dare go into hiding in the forest since winter was approaching.

Another Jew, when approached, retorted that he had thought Gildenman a cleverer man. After all, the Germans were already standing at the gates of Moscow and would soon be fighting the whole world. The Jews must hold fast until the Germans were weakened and destroyed. The situation in the ghetto had improved slightly and the Jews should hold on. It would take five years. Gildenman adds, "His five years ended about two weeks later."

A third Jew—a refugee from central Poland—whom Gildenman approached, became very agitated and trembled; he shouted, "You will bring down a catastrophe on our heads. When they find that you have gone to the partisans, they might, Heaven forbid, kill all the Jews in the ghetto. Don't dare to do it!"

The fourth Jew was his friend and roommate, the chairman of the Judenrat, Moshe Krasnostovsky, who adamantly refused to flee to the forest. "He argued that after having lost his wife and three children, life had no more value for him and he would live in the ghetto and await the end." All attempts to persuade him were in vain. When Gildenman described to him how the Germans would take pleasure in bringing him to the pit to execute him, he replied that he had nothing to fear; he was preparing petrol and when the time came, he would set himself and his home on fire. This, in fact, was what he did when the Germans launched the last *Aktion;* thus he gave the signal to the entire town.[51]

Amid the dangers and vicissitudes of the forest life, the fugitive Jews found aid and succor in the Polish villages. The farmers did not betray them even under threat from the Germans, despite the fact that they often suffered severely as a consequence. The situation improved somewhat when the Russian partisans became active in the region. The Germans, on their part, balked at nothing in their search for Jews who had gone into hiding. In Koritz there was a shortage of salt, so

> announcements were posted in the streets stating that any person who brought the head of a Jew to the Kommandant would receive 2.2 pounds of salt. The Ukrainian murderers fanned out through the forests to hunt Jews. They murdered them, cut off their heads, and brought them to the Kommandant. It was terrible to see the murderers walking the streets of the town clasping the severed heads of Jews.[52]

Jewish informers also posed a threat. When rumors reached Koritz that there were Russian partisans in the vicinity, the Jews tried to check the facts; two young men, both refugees from central Poland, volunteered to go out of the ghetto and try to establish contact. Because of informers, they were seized by the Ukrainian police and killed while trying to jump into the river and escape.

Although there were Jews who were willing to inform on their brethren, there were also Germans who were willing to help Jews. On the eve of the liquidation of the Koritz ghetto, two Germans came to warn the Judenrat that pits were being dug in the forest. The Judenrat passed on the information but few Jews succeeded in escaping. In these regions there was usually less scope for conducting negotiations with the Germans than in occupied Poland, nor were attempts at bribery as effective. The fact that the Germans now knew that the Jews were earmarked for extermination and that all their assets would then be confiscated, rendered the Nazis impervious to attempts to negotiate with them.

Moreover, under these circumstances many Germans gave free rein to their darkest impulses and displayed almost unimaginably bestial conduct. Many of them acted with particular savagery toward little children. There is eyewitness testimony as to how children were flung alive into the pits, how their heads were dashed against walls as their parents watched helpless, and of children cast alive into the river. In the *Koritz Memorial Book,* Dr. Jakob Wallaḥ tells the following story:

> I would like to bear everlasting witness to a horror that I witnessed in the first days of the occupation of the town by the Nazi beasts; there sat the Kommandant of the town, on the porch of the Oḥmonovitch home, he and his wife and children. At some distance, a Jewish child aged three was wandering about. The Kommandant called one of the murderers, ordered him to seize the child and throw him in the air like a ball. The murderer shot the child as a hunter shoots down a bird. The infant fell to the ground

covered in blood. The Kommandant's family laughed and applauded. The younger daughter clung to him and pleaded, "Daddy, do it again."[53]

And, indeed, the Germans did not refrain from abusing the living and the dead. The following is the story of Yehudit Kirsh on the burial of the victims of the first *Aktion* in Koritz:

> After the completion of the *Aktion* in the Kosak forest, the Germans informed the Judenrat that the Jews had not been buried properly and that workers should be sent to cover the pit with a thicker layer of earth. We all mobilized for this sacred task. What we saw there, so I believe, has no parallel in the annals of the extermination of European Jewry. Three pits were revealed to us: in one men were buried; in the second, women; and in the third, children. They had propped up the old man Leizer Shiher on the mass grave of the men. He sat there upright and the wind moved his white beard to and fro. At first sight he seemed to be alive, praying, lamenting, shrieking, crying out and condemning Heaven for the terrible slaughter. Ironically, it was a clear day. The sun poured light on Reb Leizer's frozen face and white beard. . . . The saintly Reb Leizer swayed to and fro, because underneath him the pit still seethed with life. . . . The pits heaved and sank, heaved and sank, these were the last convulsions of the dying. . . . How can I summon up the strength to describe what I saw and heard. Our cries pierced the heavens, and our eyes wept blood. We buried the sainted Leizer and covered the mass graves with earth, a large amount of earth. The men said the Kaddish prayer for the dead; and as evening fell we returned home.[54]

Thus sadism found expression in acts of brutality against individuals and against the community as a whole. One could cite endless examples of its manifestation from all the occupied areas in all the stages of the war, particularly during the reign of terror of the Einsatzgruppen and their local henchmen. The Germans aimed at systematic and "businesslike" activity, with neither positive nor negative emotional content. In reality, the situation was very different and every kind of savagery of which human beings seem to be capable was practiced.

The Soviet Areas

Our knowledge of events in the occupied areas that were part of the Soviet Union before 1939 is fragmentary and not always verifiable. Here, even more than in other regions, we lack the corroboratory testimony of the victims. But even this partial information gives us some idea of what occurred in White Russia, in the eastern Ukraine, and even in the Crimea and Caucasus. This partial material from Russian sources contains the dates and scope of the *Aktionen* in 173 places, including many important Jewish centers such as Minsk, Zhitomir, and Odess[a]; it is summarized in Table 4. I have used these data to compare the number [of] *Aktionen* conducted by the Germans every month with the number of victim[s].

We see that there was a steep rise in the number of *Aktionen* and the n[umber] of victims between July and September 1941. In September the number [of Akti]onen reached a peak, one-quarter of those carried out between July an[d Octo]ber, claiming close to two hundred thousand victims, almost half the to[tal] of victims during this period. The number of operations and victims [declined gradu]ally until April 1942; from then on, *Aktionen* were infreque[nt]

Table 4. Victims of the Einsatzgruppen *Aktionen* in the USSR

Date	Aktionen Number	%	Victims Number	%	Total Number per Year	Aktionen Overall Annual %	Total Victims Number of Victims Annually	Annual %
1941								
July	13	8.1	6,254	1.4				
August	35	21.7	53,770	12.2				
September	40	24.9	192,663	43.8				
October	32	19.9	74,998	17.1				
November	21	13.0	72,099	16.4				
December	20	12.4	40,042	9.1				
Total	161	100.0	439,826	100.0				
					161	64.7	439,826	71.2
1942								
January	18	25.4	47,057	28.8				
February	12	16.9	27,840	17.0				
March	11	15.5	22,086	13.5				
April	9	12.7	4,480	2.7				
May	7	9.9	12,740	7.8				
June	2	2.8	1,660	1.0				
July	5	7.0	46,021	28.2				
August	3	4.2	1,086	0.7				
September	2	2.8	338	0.2				
October	—	—	—	—				
November	2	2.8	80	0.1				
December	—	—	—	—				
Total	71	100.0	163,388	100.0				
					71	28.5	163,388	26.4
1943					8	3.2	1,815	0.3
Undated					9	3.6	13,060	2.1
Total					249	100.0	618,089	100.0

Source: Based on Wila Orbach, "The Destruction of the Jews in the Nazi-Occupied Territories of the USSR," *Soviet Jewish Affairs,* 6, no. 2 (1976), Table 3. The Russian material was researched by Orbach and is catalogued in a card index in *YVSA* 0-53/29.

the number of victims reached a new height, equal to the figures for January. This brought the entire operation to a conclusion. In 1943 only isolated *Aktionen* were carried out. In the same period, however, there were increased reports that various towns were *judenrein.* These statistics do not cover the complete number of victims, which is estimated to be about one million.

Russia

k, the capital of White Russia, there were 53,686 Jews in 1926, representpercent of the population. Now, as refugees streamed in, the number rose ching 75,000 in 1941. The ghetto was established at the end of July tween 80,000 and 100,000 inmates as the Germans had also round up the Jews of the surrounding areas. This figure remained stable for some time despite the *Aktionen* because the Jews expelled from Germany and Austria were sent to Minsk. The town was an important base behind the German front line, serving as a transportation center and as a central supply base. No doubt, the great demand for labor explains why the ghetto was maintained until October 1943. Here, as in many other places, the intellectuals were the first victims of the *Aktion,* which was carried out in July, immediately after the Germans occupied the town. Three additional *Aktionen* took place in the second half of August, but the number of victims is unknown. A second wave of killings took place in November and the number of victims ranged from 20,000 to 30,000. Even less reliable are the figures for the extermination operations carried out in March and July 1942. It may be assumed, however, that a large number of Jews perished, both local residents and evacuees from the West. In Minsk the Germans utilized the gas vans for killing. What is indisputable is the fact that after four days of killing in July 1942, there were only 9,000 inmates left in the ghetto. At the end of the month, it was announced that Minsk was *judenrein,* although, in fact, the ghetto was only liquidated in October 1943. The total number of Jews exterminated there is estimated at between 90,000 and 100,000, one-third of all inhabitants killed in Minsk. Both Aryan Minsk and the ghetto were very active in establishing underground resistance and making contact with the partisans.[55]

Viteps, celebrated for the paintings of its native son Marc Chagall, was also an important Jewish center. In 1926 there were 37,000 Jews living there, more than 37 percent of the population. It is thought that by the outbreak of war this number had increased to 100,000 as the result of a steady flood of refugees. The great majority of these Jews appear to have succeeded in making their escape, although the German army took the town on July 12, 1941. At that time, 13,000 to 15,000 Jews remained there, the great majority of them women, children, and old people. At the end of July 10,000 to 13,000 Jews were incarcerated in the ghetto. The river that flows through the town played a central part in the German terror. When the ghetto was set up, the Jews were ordered to move from one bank to the other, but they were forbidden to use the bridge. Instead, they were forced to row across or wade across at sites where the water was neck-deep. The Germans shot at the boats, which capsized, and people drowned. At the end of August, an *Aktion* was conducted on the bridge and the corpses were flung into the river. The number of people who perished is not clear; some sources say 200 and others claim 2,000. The reports of the Einsatzgruppen relate that the ghetto was liquidated in the course of two *Aktionen,* one in October and the other in November, claiming together 8,000 victims.[56] Previously, many Jews had perished from hunger and disease as the Germans supplied no food at all. Between August and November, each family received 4.4 pounds of potatoes. These meager rations notwithstanding, the Jews were mobilized for forced labor projects, which often ended in the murder of the workers.

The Eastern Ukraine

We have already mentioned the waves of killings that engulfed the Soviet Ukraine and the mass slaughter of the Jews of Kiev at Babi Yar. Now we turn to Zhitomir, one of the most important centers in the eastern Ukraine. It was first invaded by the Hungarians on July 9, 1941. The 1926 census listed 30,000 Jews in the town, 38 percent of the total population. In 1941 the figure rose to 35,000. Here, as elsewhere, the Hungarians initially prevented the Ukrainians from conducting pogroms against the Jews. On July 15 the command was transferred to the Germans, who immediately launched operations against the Jewish population. In the same month more than 2,500 Jews were murdered, and subsequently several hundred more perished in further operations. These *Aktionen* were marked by cynical brutality and sadism. One of them, apparently in August, was directed at children aged four and five who were found in a children's home. Meanwhile, a Judenälteste had been appointed and the ghetto had been established. Jews were allocated half-rations of food on the pretext that they had been stockpiling provisions. The extermination operations were conducted rapidly: in September 4,000 Jews were shot, in October more than 3,000. These operations were carried out by Einsatzgruppe D.

In October 5,000 Jews remained in the ghetto. As in other places, extermination was justified on the grounds that "they must be considered as bearers of Bolshevik propaganda and sabotage." The Jews were also charged with having fired on the unarmed Ukrainian auxiliary police. In addition to mass slaughter, there were also individual executions, mostly by hanging. Two of the victims were accused of having murdered 1,000 Ukrainians. On November 30, 1941, it was reported that after the *Aktionen* in Kiev and Zhitomir, "137 truckloads of clothing [that had belonged to the victims] have been guaranteed." The total number of people slaughtered at Zhitomir, including POWs, was 43,000. The army, under the command of General Georg-Hans Reinhardt, assisted in the operation, for example, by searching for Jews in hiding and by apprehending those who tried to flee the town.[57]

There is no way of depicting, even in general terms, the scope of the *Aktionen* in the eastern Ukraine and the method of its implementation. Many of the place-names affected by the *Aktionen* are famed in the annals of Judaism and Zionism. One of the towns renowned for its strong and dynamic Zionist movement was Poltava, birthplace of Ber Borochov, one of the founders and philosophers of socialist Zionism, and of Izhak Ben-Zvi, Israel's second president. The historians Benzion Dinur and Eliyahu Cherikover, later professors at the Hebrew University, Jerusalem, were also born there. In 1926 the Jewish population numbered 18,476, some 20 percent of the total. There is scant information, however, on the fate of the town, either before or during the war.

The Crimean Peninsula

The Crimean Peninsula fell into the hands of the Germans in October 1941, excluding Sebastopol, which was captured by von Manstein on July 1, 1942. There were between fifty thousand and sixty thousand Jews in the peninsula at the time, some twenty thousand of them engaged in agriculture. Farming settlements had been established there by Jews in the 1920s with the cooperation of the pioneering Zionist movements, which set up training farms of their own, and with the help of JDC, which planned large-scale Jewish agricultural settlement with the support of the Soviet government.[58] These settlements were gradually transformed into kolhozes, and by 1938 they numbered eighty-six. The urban Jewish population was composed of three separate communities. For centuries the region had been the center of the Karaite community. In addition there were Krimchaks, Jews who spoke the Tartar language. These two communities maintained their distinct identity. The number of Jews increased during the war because the Crimea was one of the regions where refugees from the western areas sought safety in the hope that the Germans would not reach it.

A number of Karaites, former Russian officers who had served in the White Army, had made their way to Germany and were living there when Hitler came to power. When the racial laws were promulgated in Germany, they approached the authorities with the claim that the laws did not apply to them. And, in fact, in October 1938 they were officially informed that the authorities did not consider them to be Jews under the racial laws. Now, when the Einsatzgruppen arrived in the Crimea together with the army, the same claim was put forward again, and the Germans asked for instructions from the central authorities as to how to deal with the Karaites. The previous ruling was reaffirmed. The Germans even consulted Jewish historians such as Zelig Kalmanovitch, who worked for them in the YIVO library in Vilna, and Meir Balaban and Yitzhak Shiffer, both still living in Warsaw at that time. All three confirmed that the Karaites were not Jews by race, apparently in the hope of saving them. The Germans, on the other hand, were unwilling to make an exception with regard to the Krimchaks, who declared themselves to be of Jewish origin and believers in the Mosaic religion according to the rabbinical tradition. The Krimchaks were exterminated together with the other Jews. The Germans were actively assisted in their work by the Tartars who hated the Jews.[59]

There were Jewish concentrations in Kerch, Simferopol, and Sebastopol. The largest town, Simferopol, had 156,000 inhabitants in 1941, of whom 20,000 were Jews. About half succeeded in making their escape, but 11,000 were executed by the SD. It was reported that equipment in good condition that had belonged to Jews had been handed over to the medical units of the army.[60] We learn from the testimony of a Russian eyewitness that the Germans plundered the Jews in very thorough fashion before executing them.

It seems that neither the Jews nor the Russians conceived what fate awaited the Jews. On December 11, 1941, directives were issued ordering Jews and Krimchaks to assemble, each community separately, for transportation to a workplace. They were to take provisions for one week and their apartments were to be confiscated. At the assembly point, the Germans ordered the Jews to hand over all the valuables they had brought, warning that those who failed to do so would be shot. A sheet was spread in the center of the room and the Jews threw in all the valuables they had concealed in their clothing. Then they were transported by trucks to a place of execution.[61]

Most of the Jews who tried to hide in the forests, the quarries, or the villages were caught by German search parties, which were generally actively assisted by the local population. Nonetheless, some Jews succeeded in joining the partisans and fought with them against the Germans. According to Einsatzgruppen reports

17,645 Ashkenazi Jews and 2,504 Krimchaks were killed between November 16 and December 15, 1941. To these the report adds 842 Gypsies and 212 Communists and partisans. It is feasible to assume that there were Jews among the latter as well.[62] On May 22, 1942, it was reported that 6,000 Krimchaks had been executed in all the *Aktionen*. But already in April 1942, the Crimean Peninsula was declared to be *judenrein*. However, one should take into account that at that time Sebastopol had not yet been occupied. The estimates of the total number of Jewish victims in the Crimea range between 85,000 and 90,000.[63]

The Caucasus

The last southern region that fell under Nazi occupation was the Caucasus. A kind of epilogue to the wave of murders in 1941/1942 occurred in Kislovodsk. The town was captured on August 11, 1942. A Judenrat was immediately appointed, fines were imposed, and the Jews were ordered to wear the yellow badge. On September 7, 1942, a delusory directive was issued ordering "the evacuation of the Jews to the Ukraine." They were given precise instructions as to what they were permitted to take with them and what was prohibited: no more than 44 pounds of baggage (valuables, money, clothes, etc.) together with food for two days. Along the route the Germans would provide food for the laborers. Furniture was not to be taken because of transportation difficulties. Each family must lock its apartment and the keys—labeled with the exact address and personal details—were to be handed over to the German authorities at the railway station.

The evacuation order applied to all two thousand Jews, including converts to Christianity. Many of the Jews, however, particularly intellectuals, did not believe the directive and were well aware of what awaited them and hid, but there were also numerous cases of suicide on the night before the evacuation. Yet, next day eighteen hundred Jews assembled at the railway station, from which they were supposedly to be transported to their new homes. Under way, the train came to a halt, and the Jews were forced to leave it and run to the place where the *Aktion* was to be carried out. Those who fled were shot. Only two women survived.[64]

The German *Aktionen* in Soviet Russian areas were among the swiftest and most savage of all. For the Germans, the Soviet Union was a no-man's-land. This approach characterized not only the Einsatzgruppen but also the Wehrmacht, as attested by the collaboration of army units in the murderous tasks on the orders of senior commanders.

The Baltic States

After World War I, the three Baltic states—Lithuania, Latvia, and Estonia—had won independence, and their autonomous national rights had been recognized in the peace treaties and by the League of Nations. The Bialystok area and a large part of White Russia, with Vilna at its center, were part of Lithuania's sphere of political influence. A struggle raged after World War I between Poland and Lithuania over Vilna. Initially, in August 1920, it was declared the capital of independent Lithuania, but by October of the same year it was conquered by the Poles and was ruled by them for the next nineteen years. They tried to make their mark in all spheres of life in the city and to assimilate the non-Polish population—

Lithuanians, White Russians, and Jews—who constituted one-third of the population. Only after the division of spheres of influence between Germany and Russia in 1939 could Lithuania once again annex Vilna and reproclaim it as the country's capital. Now the tables were turned and the Lithuanians made life hard for the Poles.

The Lithuanian Jewish community was the most cohesive of the three groups, and Vilna was renowned as the Jerusalem of Lithuania. In the early years of independence, the Jews enjoyed a considerable degree of autonomy and influence in both the political and the educational sphere. Some 90 percent of Jewish children were educated in independent Jewish schools. In contrast, in Latvia the Jews resided in areas more open to external influences, mostly German and White Russian. The capital, Riga, was marked by social, economic, and cultural division among the Jews. The Estonian Jewish community was much smaller than the other two, and it was particularly influenced by Russia.

After World War I all three Baltic states initially had democratic governments, and they guaranteed the minority rights stipulated in the international treaties that had established their independence. Despite the fact that in the early years of independence the Jews took part in public life, they were not anxious to assimilate but rather endeavored to act as an autonomous national group. However, as was the case in most countries of eastern and southeastern Europe, the democratic regime failed and with it the cultural and political autonomy of minorities. As nationalistic movements gathered force and the governments became dictatorships in each of the countries, anti-Semitic manifestations increased in the political, cultural, and economic spheres. In each of the states, the Jews began to suffer persecution and restrictions, although for the most part they did not suffer from pogroms, as was frequently the case in Poland.

These facts added weight to those movements within the Jewish community that sought an extraneous solution. There were two main movements: the various trends of Zionism and communism, inspired by the Soviet Union. Under the nationalist governments, the Communist Party was banned and operated underground. When the three states were restored to the Russian sphere of influence in July 1940, they were annexed as socialist republics, and the Jewish Communists emerged from the underground to take part in the government.

These developments as well as the prevailing public mood were well known to the Germans, and they assumed that many of the local population would be eager and willing to collaborate with them in implementing the Final Solution. However, the slaughter that the indigenous population conducted against the Jews did not satisfy the Germans, and they soon decided to prefer the planned actions of the Einsatzgruppen, who made use of the local militia organized as auxiliary police.

The escape opportunities of the Jews were largely determined by the pace of the German advance. In Lithuania, which was captured within a few days, few Jews succeeded in fleeing. In Latvia, as noted earlier, Jews were able to join the Soviet evacuation and to cross the border. The small Estonian community had almost two months' respite and most of the Jews left with the Russians; many joined the army and fell in battle. The great majority of the Jews of the Baltic states and tens of thousands of refugees from Poland fell victim to the Einsatzgruppen.

The Einsatzgruppen, the civil administration, and the civilian population competed among themselves in looting in the Baltic states and White Russia. Göring established a special economic headquarters in the East (Wirtschaftsführungsstab Ost)[65] supported by the Wehrmacht Supreme Command, but it did not succeed in organizing systematic confiscation of property as had been done in Poland. The SS Einsatzgruppen ruled the roost, both killing and plundering; whenever they liquidated a Jewish community, they seized its property. In Lithuania, for example, by the second half of September 1941, they had confiscated close to 4 million rubles of Jewish capital. Lohse's protests were to no avail, and he was even criticized by Himmler, who complained to Rosenberg about "the pettiness of Reichskommissar Lohse" and "the ridiculous complaints of Generalkommissar [Wilhelm] Kube" of White Russia about "provision of the required needs of the SS and the police." Nor did Lohse meet with greater success in his efforts to restrain the looting activities of the local population. The civil administration had no other source for profit than the remaining assets of the Jews; consequently, stringent instructions were issued on the procedure for confiscation of the assets of those Jews who had been incarcerated in ghettos.[66]

A similar struggle was conducted around the exploitation of the Jewish labor force. By the autumn of 1941, the civil administrators, particularly Kube, had begun to protest against the indiscriminate killing being carried out by the Einsatzgruppen. The latter made every effort to implement their tasks despite the protests of the local Gebietskommissar, the Generalkommissar, and Lohse himself. The dispute was passed up to the central authorities in Germany, and on December 18, 1941, Rosenberg's office issued its ruling together with general instructions to Lohse not to take economic considerations into account when dealing with the solution of the Jewish question. The evolving problems were to be solved through negotiations on the spot between the administration and Himmler's forces.[67] These bodies had meanwhile arrived at a compromise and, to a large degree under pressure from the army, it was decided to preserve the Jewish labor force. The December 18 directive of Rosenberg's office was not implemented for the time being.

The Jews of Ostland, Bialystok, and Volhynia concluded that they could hope to survive only through labor. The most important document now was the work permit, the *Schein* (paper), which stated that the holder was required by the German authorities. From summer 1942, however, the civil administration succumbed to the demands of the SS and collaborated in efforts to preserve only "the most vital labor force." This second wave of murders was directed primarily against the smaller towns and labor camps, for only a few population centers continued to exist. In the Baltic states the bulk of the remaining Jewish population in the ghettos in Lithuania were in Vilna (Vilnius), 20,000 people; Kovno (Kaunus), 17,000; and Shavli (Šiauliai), 5,000. In White Russia there were 9,000 Jews in Minsk and a similar number were left in Latvia, most of them in the three cities of Riga, Dvinsk (Daugavpils), and Libau (Liepāja).[68]

Vilna

From 1939 to 1941 Jewish Vilna played a special role. At the end of October 1939 when the town was transferred to Lithuania, the frustrated and angry Poles conducted pogroms against the Jews, and the Lithuanian administration did little to prevent this. It was only when the government began to fear that the unrest could also cause harm to the Lithuanian minority in the city that it intervened and restored order. Vilna soon became the center for Jewish organizations whose members had fled Poland. All the youth movements as well as the Heḥalutz pioneering movement set up centers in Vilna and were joined by prominent public figures and by large groups of Orthodox Jews, rabbis, and Yeshiva students. They tried to operate on two levels. On the one hand, they maintained contact with colleagues left behind in occupied Poland, organized their escape when possible, and supplied them with information and assistance; on the other hand, they tried to promote attempts at flight to the free world, in particular to Palestine and the United States. The route to Palestine led through Russia, either directly to the Mediterranean or through Siberia to the Far East. In 1931 there were 54,600 Jews in Vilna. It is estimated that the figure rose by 1939 to approximately 58,000. The added refugees brought the Jewish population of the town close to 70,000, of whom between 4,000 and 6,500 managed to emigrate. At the end of November 1941 the Lithuanians began to evacuate Jews from Vilna to inland Lithuania, and most of those who left were pioneers who set up training farms throughout the country. It is estimated that 60,000 Jews were in the town at the time of the German occupation on June 24, 1941.[69]

A so-called joint Lithuanian-German administration was maintained for a week, in which the Lithuanians were mainly concerned with the Poles rather than the Jews. But at the beginning of July a German military administration was established and operations against the Jews commenced. On July 3, 1941, the military commander issued an ordinance requiring all Jews to wear the identifying badge. The number of stores and markets Jews could enter was restricted, as were the times at which Jews were permitted to purchase food. As in Germany, they were barred from entering public places and all services were reduced. On instructions from Lohse, property was looted and confiscated. Jews were also prohibited from changing their apartments and here, as elsewhere, were seized for forced labor.

Fifty-one leaders from all sections of the community were ordered to convene to set up a Judenrat. They did not delude themselves as to what lay ahead; it was difficult to find ten candidates among them ready to serve on the council, and they were only chosen in the second round of voting. The Judenrat was later expanded to twenty-four members, as specified in Heydrich's notorious letter of the early war days.[70] At first the Jews regarded the members of the Judenrat as their natural representatives and displayed confidence in them; the youth movements and Heḥalutz consulted them on their affairs.

The term of office and life span of the first Judenrat were very limited and, in early September 1941, when the Einsatzgruppen extermination activities began, the Judenrat was liquidated. At the same time the Germans began herding the

Jews into two ghettos. Ghetto No. 1 housed some 30,000 "productive" Jews; the remainder, 11,000, were incarcerated in Ghetto No. 2. These ghettos were set up on September 6, 1941; concomitantly, some 6,000 people were brought to the town prison prior to extermination.

It is estimated that up to the establishment of the ghetto, some 20,000 Jews in all had already been liquidated. The imprisonment was a stage in the extermination process. From the jail they were ostensibly taken out to work, but most were conveyed to the extermination site in the infamous Ponary Forest. At the beginning, the Lithuanian police did the work of seizing the Jews in the streets and carried out the actual killings. In accordance with the almost universal extermination procedures, the first to be rounded up were men, and the police flushed them out of their hiding places, known as *malines*. When the extermination operations entered their second stage, which was carried out by the Einsatzgruppen, the three-stage process continued: kidnapping people, concentrating them in jail, and exterminating them at Ponary. Now, however, whole families were being arrested and women and children were killed en masse. Ghetto No. 2 was liquidated in October. While imprisoned, the Jews were robbed of their money and valuables. The *Aktionen* continued until the end of December 1941; it claimed the lives of more than 20,000 additional Vilna Jews. More than 40,000 in all had been murdered by the end of the year.[71]

After the establishment of the two ghettos, a new Judenrat was set up in each of them. This time the Germans appointed as members people who had been less involved in the Jewish community life of Vilna. One of the first steps taken by the Judenrat in Ghetto No. 1 was the establishment of a Jewish police. It was headed by Jacob Gens. He became the outstanding personality in the ghetto administration and one of the most controversial figures of this period, like Rumkowski in Łódź and Merin in Eastern Upper Silesia. Gens was born in 1903 in a small village near Shavli. At the age of sixteen he joined the Lithuanian army and since he had attended a high school, he was immediately sent to officers school and was rapidly promoted and given the opportunity to complete his schooling. He was an impressive and highly talented man, fluent in several languages. After being discharged from active service, he continued his studies at the University of Kovno and worked as a teacher; later, in the 1930s, he undertook administrative work in the economic sphere. As a Zionist, he belonged to the Revisionists. In the late 1930s he was called back into the army and promoted to the rank of captain, but was dismissed when the Russians took over. He moved to Vilna, where he found work thanks to a Lithuanian officer, an acquaintance from his army days, who headed the city's Sanitation Department. When the Germans occupied Vilna, his friend transferred him to the Jewish hospital as director. On various occasions, several of the leaders of the Jewish community hid from the Germans in the hospital, where they came to know Gens and were impressed with his organizational ability and proud stand against the Germans. Thus, they considered him a suitable candidate to head the Jewish police.[72]

Among the *Aktionen* in late October and early November 1941, the most notorious is known as the yellow *Schein Aktion*. Only people in possession of yellow work permits escaped death. Gens, as police chief, was ordered to conduct the selection. He tried to rescue a few people, mainly children, but by deciding who remained and who had to go he now became involved in the murderous activities of the Germans. His policemen even dragged victims out of their hiding places.[73] At that time, no clear information had reached the ghetto as to what was going on in the Ponary Forest; rumors spread, but they were greeted with disbelief. However, people tried to flee toward White Russia and Bialystok, and many of them were aided by a German sergeant, Anton Schmidt. It was his job to locate German soldiers who had lost contact with their units or had wandered off for other reasons. Hence, he had at his disposal several rooms and trucks, and he used them to hide and transport Jews. Some two weeks after the yellow *Schein Aktion,* a new decree introduced pink work permits. The color was probably altered in order to facilitate supervision of the labor force that the Germans wanted to preserve. The Germans often employed the stratagem of changing the color of work permits; one reason was that the Jews began to forge these lifesaving documents.[74] After the bloody operations, only 13,000 Jews remained in the ghetto at the end of December 1941. In the following months, the number rose again to 20,000 as those who had been in hiding came out into the open.

Eventually, some of the victims transported to Ponary Forest succeeded in making their escape, and with the aid of Polish farmers, they returned to the ghetto to tell their tale. The heads of the Judenrat tried to hide them in the ghetto hospital, banning access to them. Nonetheless, their testimony was recorded. In most cases, it has been lost, but several stories were subsequently written down from memory. This is the report of a teacher who returned to consciousness and found herself in a mass grave:

> Suddenly I heard soft weeping near me in the grave. I listened for a moment and recognized the weeping of a child. I crawled toward the voice and was stunned when, as I crawled, I found the corpse of my husband from whom I had parted only the night before. . . . The child did not cease crying and I summoned up the remnants of my strength and reached it. I discerned a little girl of three, alive and whole, and decided to save myself and the child. As I rested with her, holding her in my arms on the pile of corpses, I knew that if I survived, it would be she who had saved me.[75]

The youth movements were badly hit by these operations and many of their members perished. Several of the Hashomer Hatzair leadership in Vilna succeeded in slipping out of the ghetto and hiding in the convent of the Dominican Sisters near the town. Among them was Abba Kovner, the later well-known Hebrew poet. In those tranquil surroundings, far from the horrors of the ghetto, he tried to gauge the meaning of the events and arrived at dire conclusions.[76] In the last days of 1941 he and his comrades returned to the ghetto, and Kovner shared his thoughts with the fellow members of Hashomer Hatzair:

> We cannot believe that those who have been taken from us are still alive, that they were merely being deported. Everything that has happened to us so far means Ponary—death. And this is not yet the whole truth. Because that truth is infinitely greater and more profound even than this. The destruction of thousands is but the harbinger of the liquidation of millions. . . . Vilna is not Vilna alone. Ponary is no episode. The yellow

Schein is not the invention of the local commander. This is a complete system. We are faced here with a well-calculated method, still concealed from us.[77]

He drew the logical conclusions. On the night of December 31, 1941, members of several youth movements organized by Heḥalutz met together. Abba Kovner read them a manifesto exhorting Jewish youth, "Let us not go as sheep to the slaughter" (see chap. 17).

Kovno

The second largest city in Lithuania, Kovno, served as its capital for most of the period of independence. Before World War II about thirty thousand Jews lived there; when war broke out, they were joined by some five thousand refugees from Poland. Together they constituted some 30 percent of the city's population. This Jewish community was then the focus of Lithuanian-Jewish life, and links with Jewish communities elsewhere in the world were close: many world Jewish leaders visited the country. Although the Jews of Kovno suffered from increasing hostility on the part of the Lithuanians, their economic, cultural, and public achievements were unparalleled among Lithuanian Jewry.

When the German campaign against the Soviet Union commenced, Kovno was among the first cities to suffer. The Russians abandoned the town in great haste on June 23 since the proximity of the German border held out great danger. In fact, on the evening of June 24 the first German army units entered Kovno. Here, as elsewhere, many Jews tried to flee eastward—most failed. Some fell victim to German bombings or were blocked off in their flight by German units. Others were stopped short at the border with Russia, which was closed during those first days of the campaign. Thus, many of the refugees were forced to retrace their steps and return to the city. But, on returning to Kovno, they found a terrible and chaotic situation.

Kovno was the center of Lithuanian nationalist aspirations. Immediately after the Russian withdrawal and before the Germans entered, a Lithuanian National Government was established; simultaneously, Lithuanian partisans came out into the open. Their number throughout Lithuania was estimated at one hundred thousand. These Lithuanian nationalists eagerly awaited the arrival of the Germans and shared their conviction that the Jewish enemy must be eradicated. Rumors were bandied about that the Jews intended to act against the Germans, and the partisans announced that for every German soldier killed, they would execute one hundred Jews in retaliation. As we know, the Germans intended to exploit Lithuanian hatred of the Jews. According to the report of Franz W. Stahlecker, the commanding officer of Einsatzgruppe A, "During the first night of the riots, the night between June 25 and 26, the Lithuanian partisans exterminated fifteen hundred Jews, many synagogues were set alight or destroyed and the Jewish quarter, with some sixty houses, was burned. On the following nights, twenty-three hundred Jews were liquidated in similar fashion."[78]

This slaughter was conducted in Slovodka, a suburb of Kovno, but approximately sixty Jews were also murdered in the heart of Kovno. For more than a week, people were rounded up in the streets, thrown into prison, and then transported to one of the town forts, where the men were separated from the women and children. Czarist Russia had constructed nine forts around the town to defend the border with Germany. During the period of Lithuanian independence these forts had served as prisons, and many inmates met their death there. Now the Germans used them as sites for the extermination of Jews. The first slaughter was carried out by the Lithuanian partisans. Six thousand men had been murdered there by August 8. The surviving women were permitted to return to the city along with thirty men who had previously volunteered for service in the Lithuanian army. These events were accompanied by the usual phenomena: kidnapping of Jews for forced labor, famine, and looting.[79]

At the beginning of July, several community notables were summoned to an officer they thought to be the Gestapo commander but who was actually Karl Jäger, the commander of the Einsatzgruppen and the SD in Lithuania. He announced to the stunned Jews that within one month the entire Jewish population was to be moved into a ghetto to be set up in the suburb of Slovodka. On this occasion, the Jews were also informed officially about the executions in Fort Nine. Their attempts to establish contact with the Lithuanians and to appeal for the aid of the Catholic archbishop were fruitless. On July 11 announcements were posted throughout Kovno in which the mayor informed the Jews of the establishment of the ghetto. They were ordered to liquidate all their property in the city and to exchange apartments with Lithuanians now living within the area of the planned ghetto. The Germans placed responsibility for the move on a Jewish transfer committee made up of the same community leaders to whom they had first conveyed the order. In contrast to the procedure in Vilna, for example, the Jews of Kovno were given one month's notice. During this time the town witnessed horrific scenes similar to those enacted in Warsaw when that ghetto was established. The Jews, though anticipating overcrowding, isolation, and humiliation, hoped that they would be permitted to administer their own lives. One of the urgent functions performed by the transfer committee was the organization of a labor force for the Germans. As was the case elsewhere, they hoped that organization of regular hard labor units would put an end to the random kidnapping of Jews.

Before the ghetto was sealed off, the Germans demanded the establishment of the Council of Elders (Ältestenrat) of the Jewish Ghetto Community in Kovno. The election of the council and its chairman was a highly dramatic act in which thirty community leaders took part. They found it particularly difficult to choose a suitable personality to head the Judenrat. According to Leib Garfunkel, one of those present, "It was not easy to find the suitable candidate for this extraordinary task. . . . The man who headed the ghetto had to have an immaculate public past, to be a good Jew and a good human being, wise and shrewd, courageous, and of strong character so as not to be discouraged and not to bow the knee when he appeared before the Germans as the tragic emissary of the unhappy Jewish public."

The candidate selected after lengthy discussions, with the approbation of all those present, was Dr. Elḥanan Elkes, a physician and a Zionist. He refused, at first, but finally accepted the position that Rabbi Yaakov Mosheh Schmuckler described as an inescapable duty. To encourage him Schmuckler said, "But please understand, dear and beloved Dr. Elkes, that only to the Nazi murderers will you be Head of the Jews. In our eyes you will be the head of our community, elected in our most tragic hour."[80]

Elkes stands out among the Judenrat heads throughout the areas of Nazi occupation as one of those who had no illusions, one who served his community with integrity, courage, and boundless dedication.

Even before the transfer to the ghetto was completed, the Jews suffered a new wave of *Aktionen*. Now the operations were openly directed by the German authorities, but they were still partially implemented by the Lithuanian partisans. Immediately after the sealing off of the ghetto (August 18, 1941), the Germans took special action to liquidate the intelligentsia, who were summoned on the pretext (used elsewhere as well) that they were to engage in special office work, in this case "organizing archives." Five hundred people were summoned but only three hundred arrived, and in order to fill their quota, the Germans rounded up hundreds more in the street and added thirty-four more as "punishment."[81] Only some time later did it become known that all had been murdered. On the following day the Germans launched systematic looting operations to ensure that all Jewish valuables fell into their hands. The searches of Jewish homes did not produce the desired amount of gold and silver, and the Germans then offered the Judenrat the choice between organizing voluntary confiscation or risking the life of any Jew found concealing valuables plus the lives of one hundred of his neighbors. As a result, the Jews hastened to rid themselves of their hidden belongings, even removing them from hiding places. The quantity collected even took the Germans by surprise. The value of the gold alone was estimated at RM 50 million (U.S. $20 million).[82] These two operations were merely overtures to the extermination *Aktionen* that began in mid-September and continued until the end of October. According to the tried-and-tested methods, the Germans used the *Schein* stratagem in order to distinguish between those fit and unfit for work. When Rauke, the officer in charge of Jewish affairs in the Kovno Gestapo, informed the Council of Elders that all ghetto inmates were to assemble on October 29 in Democrat Square in order to classify them into workers and nonworkers, the council fully comprehended what lay ahead. For hours they debated what should be done and finally asked the advice of Chief Rabbi Avraham Dov Shapira as to how to conduct themselves according to Jewish law. After a sleepless night, during which he consulted his books, the rabbi ruled, "If a community of Jews is threatened by persecution, and some may be saved by a specific action, then the leaders of the community have to muster the courage and the responsibility to rescue whosoever may be rescued."[83]

On the following day Rauke decided who would live and who would die. More than nine thousand Jews were transferred that same day to the Little Ghetto and held there until the following day when they were transported group by group to Fort Nine. The Germans then ordered the ghetto Jewish police to round up people who had gone into hiding in the Little Ghetto. The policemen succeeded in saving some of them by giving them police tags as identification.

On completion of the *Aktionen*, Jäger submitted a detailed report on his work throughout Lithuania. It covers the period between July 2 and December 1, 1941.

Table 5. Report on the Extermination of the Jews of Kovno by Einsatzkommando 3, Commanded by SS Standartenführer Karl Jäger

Date	Men	Women	Children	Total	Place	Notes
July 4	416	47		463	Fort 7	Carried out on Jäger's orders by Lithuanian partisans
July 6				2,514		
July 9	21	3		24	Fort 7	Carried out by Ensatzkommando and partisans
July 19	17	2		19		+ 7 Communists
August 2	171	34		205	Fort 4	+4 Communists
August 9	484	50		534	Fort 4	
August 18	698	402				
	771	(intellectuals)		1,811	Fort 4	+ 1 Polish woman
September 26	412	615	581	1,608	Fort 4	
October 4	315	712	818	1,845	Fort 9	Punitive action
October 29	2,007	2,920	4,273	9,200	Fort 9	
Total	7,766	4,785	5,672	18,223		Including 1 male and 1 female U.S. national

Source: Yad Vashem Archives O-18/245

He lists 106 *Aktionen* in fifty-four places; in 38 *Aktionen,* the task was completed on a single occasion; in 14 others, two to four operations were required. He reported that up to 5 *Aktionen* were carried out weekly "through skillful exploitation of time." The bloody reckoning of their work in Kovno can be seen in Table 5, based on Jäger's daily specifications.

In addition to the statistical report, Jäger gives a description of the operation and the methods of organization. He lauds the officer in charge of the commandos, H. Hamann, of whom he says, "He adopted my aims fully," and notes that Hamann succeeded in guaranteeing the collaboration of the Lithuanian partisans and the German civilian administration. Jäger goes on to explain, "The carrying-out of such *Aktionen* is first of all an organizational problem. The decision to clear each subdistrict systematically of Jews called for a thorough preparation for each operation and the study of local conditions. The Jews had to be concentrated in one or more localities and, in accordance with their numbers, a site had to be selected and a pit dug."

Generally speaking, he writes, the pits were located about 3 miles away from the concentration site and the Jews were taken there in groups of five hundred, with a distance of at least 1.25 miles between groups. He emphasizes the hardships of this "nerve-racking" task. But in contrast to the "difficulties" in some places, he notes that in Kovno there were sufficiently trained partisans; hence the work resembled a shooting display *(Parade-Schiessen).*[84]

At the head of the report, Jäger lists the number of Jews who, according to his calculations, remained in Vilna, Kovno, and Shavli, commenting that it was not

possible to liquidate them because of the strong opposition of the civil administration and the army.

Shavli

The Jewish community of Shavli was the third largest in Lithuania and had numbered at least eight thousand before the war. Although not large, this Jewish community excelled in industrial and commercial initiative, conducted a lively community life, and fostered cultural activity. Jewish economic activity was
apparently closely interwoven in the local economy, and one of the community
notables served as deputy mayor of Shavli. Here, too, the Jews encountered fierce
hostility on the part of Lithuanian nationalists and partisans; nonetheless, the
impression is that their close ties with Lithuanians proved to their advantage.
Shavli is one of the Jewish communities that has given us living testimony of the
wartime events. Dr. Eliezer Yerushalmi, a teacher, undertook the task of recording the annals of those years and compiling documentation. He began his records
on his own initiative but later recruited the aid of others; in due course his project
was taken under the auspices of the Judenrat, which he served as secretary. Before
the liquidation of the ghetto in 1944, he buried the material underground in crates
and informed various people of its location, including a Lithuanian Communist.
The latter told the Red Army of its existence when they reached the town. The
Russians then transferred the material to Moscow, where it is stored, inaccessible
to this day. The Soviets did, however, use the manuscript and some of the documents as evidence for the prosecution in the Nuremberg trials. This evidence was
copied and taken to Yad Vashem, which arranged for the records' publication in
1958.[85] Although incomplete, these documents are among the most reliable and
illuminating sources of the period.

The Judenrat was appointed from among Jewish community leaders in the
first few days after the German occupation. The chairman was Mendel Lejbowicz.
From the outset, he and his deputy, Berl Karton, courageously stood up to the
authorities, both Lithuanian and German, and tried hard to save the community.
Although not all the Lithuanians sought to harm the Jews, even the best among
them were usually powerless against the Lithuanian nationalists and the Germans.
Nonetheless, both prominent Lithuanians and simple people did help the Jews
clandestinely, and thanks to their former ties, the Jews managed to trade in goods
and thus obtained food.

First, the Lithuanians started deporting the Jews, who soon discovered that
this meant death. In their struggle against the decrees, the community leaders
found support in the Wehrmacht headquarters, which often prevented the Lithuanian police from torturing Jews. In order to prevent deportation, Lejbowicz and
his colleagues themselves proposed the establishment of a ghetto.[86] During these
tumultuous times, the terrified Jews were arrested indiscriminately, sent to forced
labor, and their property was looted. The "Delegation" (as Yerushalmi called the
Judenrat) after great effort succeeded in saving a group of children who were staying in a holiday camp outside town and had been refused permission to return
home while being kept under terrible conditions.

The ghetto was established in two separate quarters, but could not house all the Jews by August 15 as intended; those who did not succeed in finding places for themselves were sent to the synagogue. From there, they were dispatched to an unknown location. When survivors made their way back, it became known that the deportees had been killed. The Judenrat also failed to save the children from the local Jewish orphanage, even though all arrangements had ostensibly been made to transfer them to the ghetto. At the beginning of September, Gebiets-kommissar Gewecke called for a halt to the killings. In a memorandum dated September 3, 1941, in reaction to Hamann's request (based on an order of Jäger) to exterminate Shavli's Jews, he wrote:

> I unequivocally opposed the extermination and I have pointed out that, on the orders of the Reichskommissar [Hinrich Lohse], additional extermination of Jews should be avoided. At the same time, I have pointed out that the consequence of the extermi-nation of all the Jewish men in Shavli will result in the closing down of all the large enterprises because all the skilled workers are Jews. I have forbidden SS-Obersturm-führer Hamann to carry out the order and asked him to inform the Standartenführer [Jäger] of this.[87]

Gewecke also objected to SS attempts to take over Jewish property. He deemed it necessary to stress his loyalty and to note the "National Socialist sever-ity" with which he had acted against the Jews, while noting that the four thousand Jews who had survived the *Aktionen* were required mainly for the leather industry, which was highly developed in Shavli.[88]

The situation in the two sections of the ghetto was desperate, and the accom-modation shortage was particularly severe. Yerushalmi praises the initiative of the "Delegation," which eased the situation "by constructing new dwelling places in the cellars, the attics, and the animal pens, where nobody would have ever con-templated doing something. To date [November 28, 1941], a sum of 48,690 rubles has been spent on these structures."[89]

Despite the efforts of the Judenrat, the most pressing problem for ghetto inmates was food, and attempts were made to smuggle in provisions. There was considerable opportunity for this since most people worked outside the ghetto and came into contact with Lithuanians. The authorities severely punished smugglers and threatened the ghetto population and the Judenrat with harsh penalties; those apprehended were imprisoned and, in fact, sentenced thereby to death by starva-tion. Despite this, Yerushalmi notes (in March 1942) that "the ghetto is hungry but not dying of starvation." This state of affairs was not to the liking of the authorities and they compelled the Judenrat to issue stringent directives on this matter.

The focus of ghetto life was labor, and the officer in charge of the German Labor Bureau was, in effect, the overseer of the Jews. He sometimes even inter-vened on their behalf when police and SD activities posed a threat to them. Here, as in Kovno, the Jews were put to work building an airstrip; even worse was the condition of the laborers sent in the summer of 1942 to work in the peat fields. In the labor camp, they were held under terrible conditions, starved, and merci-lessly driven. With great effort, the Judenrat finally succeeded in bringing them back to Shavli.

The ghetto population, and even more so its leaders, had no illusions as to the intentions and methods of the Germans. The Shavli records also attest to the fact that the Jews were in possession of extensive and precise information on what was going on elsewhere in Europe. The transports of Jews from the West who passed through the town supplied them with details of what was happening in the Reich itself. They soon learned of the extermination of German mental patients in the Reich itself (see chap. 12). They also learned from the German and Lithuanian press about the decrees against the Jews in southeastern Europe; and in the summer of 1942 they received somewhat truncated news of the extermination of the Jews in Poland and of the conditions in the Warsaw ghetto.

Toward the end of that summer, the situation deteriorated even further, and the directives and restrictions were stepped up. Among other directives was one issued banning births.[90] The food situation worsened and penalties became even more severe. Notwithstanding, the Judenrat heads succeeded in arranging the release of most of the imprisoned Jews on the frequently reiterated pretext: they were needed for work.

Operation Barbarossa launched both the decisive stage of the war and the extermination process aimed at "the final solution of the Jewish question." The *Aktionen* of the Einsatzgruppen were planned and implemented concomitantly with the military operations, both geographically and organizationally. However, both the Wehrmacht and the civilian administration in the occupied areas of Russia soon realized that the indiscriminate mass murder of Jews was a two-edged sword and could constitute a threat not only to production capacity but also to the execution of those services that were vital to the army itself. It was no accident that Gewecke began to protest in Shavli immediately after jurisdiction over Ostland was officially handed over to the civilian administration on September 1, 1941. His objections derived, in part, from the necessity to fulfill the demands of the war effort and the civil administration as well as, in part, from the desire of the administrators—perhaps also of the army—to hold on firmly to the reins of power and, above all, to enjoy its material benefits. The administrators were unwilling to allow the SS State of Himmler and Heydrich to rule unchecked in their area of jurisdiction. The ruling bodies' struggle for power and for the ill-gotten gains created a twilight zone in which the remnants of the Jews could, meanwhile, continue to exist and to maneuver among the various authorities. Their leaders played the hazardous game for the lives of the community and for their own survival. Some of them, such as Barash and Elkes and the Judenrat heads in Shavli, played their mediating role faithfully; others, like Gens, gambled dangerously with lives. All of them trod a tightrope above a yawning chasm.

Barash was right when he said that no artist—and he could have added no historian—could depict accurately what the Jews, both leaders and flock, were suffering. The Jewish community was flung into a maelstrom of planned murder that neither it nor the majority of modern humanity, could have conceived to be possible. The killing was planned and carried out within the framework of military operations as part of the conduct of warfare. The terminology of its implementation was technical and military, and it was accompanied by bureaucratic reports.

When the gas vans were introduced, the work became increasingly technological in nature. The mortal dread of the trapped and screaming victims created a problem that was solved by technical devices.

The Jews had no previous knowledge or experience to guide them at this time. They were acquainted only with the "ordinary" hazards of Diaspora life: expulsions and pogroms. In the Hashomer Hatzair movement in Vilna, young Abba Kovner sensed, with a poet's intuition, what was occurring, and he was able to transform his awareness into a practical driving force. Years later he admitted that he could not say how he would have thought and acted during the war had he then already been a parent. Moreover, Soviet policy during the pact with Germany systematically and deliberately prevented the dissemination of information about the deeds of the Germans in occupied Poland. The stream of refugees and the news they brought with them failed to persuade the Jewish population that they faced a holocaust, nor did they—together with the entire population of the Soviet Union—anticipate the German occupation of Russia. The refugees who remained in the border areas were forcibly deported en masse to the interior and, thus, most of them survived.

Those Jews who survived after the summer of 1942 continued their bitter struggle for life by laboring for the enemy. In the Baltic states, in Bialystok, in White Russia, in Volhynia and the Ukraine Jews worked for the German war effort. At the same time, there was increasing awareness, particularly in the organized youth movements, that another method of struggle must be sought.

11

The Final Solution: The Second Stage

The Jews of the Greater Reich: From Persecution to Deportation

In his programmatic speech before the Reichstag on January 30, 1941, Hitler reiterated the threats that he had been voicing against the Jews ever since his famous Reichstag speech two years earlier. We have seen that shortly afterward, the Germans began to plan the liquidation of the Jews in the Soviet-annexed sector of Poland, and its implementation ran parallel to their military thrust into the Soviet Union proper. The Jewish communities in the rest of Europe were still not being physically molested at this time nor were they covered in the plan linked to Operation Barbarossa. However, we are able to discern a certain change in the conditions to which they were subjected and a stronger sense of design in the measures taken against them. During 1940, while the Germans were preoccupied with their military operations in northern and western Europe, they did not particularly aggravate the persecution of the Jews anywhere on the Continent. To the degree that they devoted their time and attention to any far-reaching plan, it was to the political scheme to deport the Jews en masse to Madagascar. But this overall situation began to change toward the end of 1940, and the Germans stepped up their anti-Jewish measures considerably in 1941. The shift was particularly felt in a number of spheres that, taken together, composed the basic conditions for subsistence: housing, work, and property as well as civil and legal status. In all these areas the erosion of the basic conditions of life was steadily intensified until the way had been paved for the deportation of the outcast and isolated Jews.

Vienna: Concentration Through Eviction from Apartments

A proposal to enclose the Jews in a ghetto within Germany proper was summarily rejected after Kristallnacht. Nonetheless, to a certain degree the Jews began to be assembled in separate neighborhoods or buildings. This relocation operation was possible because as far back as the spring of 1939 the Tenant Protection Law had been partially repealed as it related to Jews.[1] In 1939/1940 no further action was taken in this matter within Germany, but the same cannot be said of Vienna.

The Austrian capital had been suffering from a severe housing shortage for decades. During the tenure of the Social Democrats, the municipal government tried to alleviate the situation by drawing up a comprehensive construction program that was acclaimed throughout Europe. However from 1933 to 1938 Engelbert Dollfus and, after his murder, Kurt von Schuschnigg held power, and consequently the Social Democrats lost control over the city. The new government no longer pursued the same social welfare policy. When the Germans entered Austria, they found that the housing shortage—which was estimated to have reached some 70,000 apartments—was among the most pressing problems they would have to solve. By the end of 1938, the savage descent of the Nazis—both local and from the Reich—upon the Jews and their property had resulted in the evacuation of 35,000 Jewish-occupied apartments. To a certain degree this was the result of emigration, but in all the remaining cases, the Jews had been ousted by force. From then on the eviction of Jews from their apartments became a standard *modus operandi* of the Nazi authorities in Vienna.

In September 1939 there were 10,000 to 12,000 apartments that still remained in Jewish hands; for the most part, the dispossessed Jews had been taken into these premises. Hence, the Jews were inevitably concentrated in neighborhoods that the Nazis called quasi-ghettos, and they proceeded to plan the ejection of the remaining Jews to barracks camps *(Barackenlager)* outside the city.[2]

In August 1940 a new representative of the Reich, Baldur von Schirach, arrived in Vienna and was immediately confronted by the grave housing problem. He saw deportation of Vienna's Jews as part of the answer to this crisis. Thus, when Hans Frank complained—during a dinner conversation at Hitler's residence on October 2—that he was unable to absorb the Jews being deported to the Generalgouvernement, Schirach cut in and protested that he, too, had over fifty thousand Jews in Vienna who should be sent to Poland. Hitler took the opportunity to deliver a lecture on his broader view of things, namely, that overcrowding in Poland should not be a cause for concern because Poland was to serve as a reservoir of cheap unskilled labor for the Reich, nothing more.[3]

Still, the housing problem continued to plague Schirach. In September 1940 he had issued orders to "resume the systematic and total transfer of Jews from their apartments forthwith" and had reported to Berlin on this program. On December 3, 1940, the state secretary of the Reich Chancellery, Hans Lammers, wrote back, "On the basis of your report, the Führer has decided that the sixty thousand Jews still residing in the Vienna district of the Reich should be deported to the Generalgouvernement as soon as possible, that is, while the war is still in progress, [because of] the housing problem in Vienna." The implementation of this decision was put off until "the beginning of next year"; indeed, the transports did begin in mid-February 1941.[4] But the housing problem was not solved by this move. In the autumn of 1941 Schirach urged that building activities be renewed in Vienna, to which the führer's deputy, Martin Bormann, replied on Hitler's behalf on November 2, 1941, that any signs of discontent and unrest must be quashed and the housing problem should be solved by deportations, first of the Jews and then of the "Czechs and other aliens."[5]

Revocation of Social Benefits

One sphere in which far-reaching decisions were taken during this period was labor. It has been noted that starting with the outbreak of the war, the Jews of Germany were increasingly employed as forced laborers. It was in this connection that the question arose whether the Jews were entitled to enjoy the same social benefits and compensations granted to Germans. After the fall of Poland, similar questions were raised about the Poles who were sent to work in the Reich. Proposals to deny the Jews most of the social benefits, bonuses, and other incentives granted to the German laborer had been in existence since 1940, but they had been shuffled between one ministry and the next because Hermann Göring, who was in charge of the Four-Year Plan, apparently was not interested in having the issue decided. On Bormann's insistence, however, the matter was raised for discussion at an interministerial meeting on January 8, 1941. Göring's representative resorted to evasive tactics, and the participants did not reach any clear-cut decision. The debate wore on through October 1941 and was not resolved until November 4 when the labor minister, Franz Seldte, published an order that repealed long-standing terms of employment and promulgated new ones: Jews would no longer be entitled to receive sick pay, accident insurance, paid vacations, or pensions; they could be fired without notice; they could not be employed as apprentices; and work conditions for adults would also apply to youngsters aged fourteen to eighteen. The precise number of Jews employed at the time is not clear. According to Hilberg, thirty thousand Jews were working in the framework of the labor battalions at the beginning of 1941, but many others were employed in factories and, of course, in the institutions run by the Jewish community.[6]

Abrogation of the Civic Status (Implementation Order No. 11)

Among the matters deliberated by the German authorities in 1940/1941 was the civil status of the Jews in the Greater Reich. These discussions evolved into a process that culminated in the revocation of the deportees' status—in effect since the passage of the Nuremberg Laws—as "subjects of the state." This act, then, was a formal manifestation of what was a total abrogation of the Jews' civil rights. Originally, the matter arose not because of any problem entailed in the deportations but because of questions relating to the status of the citizens of occupied Poland. On September 12, 1940, Himmler issued a regulation stipulating four ranks of civil status for those foreign nationals who stood to become German citizens. Everyone else in Poland was classified as a ward *(Schutz-Angehöriger),* one whose civil rights were restricted and whose civic status was revoked. This new arrangement prompted the director-general of the Interior Ministry, Wilhelm Stuckart, to institute deliberations on the addition of a statute to the 1935 Citizenship Law that would redefine the status of the Jews within the Greater Reich. Stuckart proposed that Jews be demoted to the same status of wards applied to those foreign nationals in the occupied areas who were denied the rights of Germans. When his proposal was submitted to the Reich Chancellery, however, it was opposed by the senior official, Wilhelm Kritzinger, for he deemed it singularly inappropriate to define the Jews, of all people, as wards of the German Reich. Moreover, in the opinion that he delivered on this proposal in mid-December 1940, he questioned, "[Is it] at all worthwhile granting them a special legal status, considering the fact that in the not too distant future the Jews will vanish from Germany[?] In any event they are not citizens of the Reich anymore."

Instead, Kritzinger proposed that since Jews who emigrated or were deported would lose their qualification of residence in the Reich, they should then be stripped of their status as German subjects. He raised the question before Hitler, who concurred with his view. The Ministry of Justice and the Treasury took part in the ensuing long and complicated negotiations, trying, together with the Reich Chancellery and the Interior Ministry, to fix the legal status of deportees, including the status of the partners of an intermarriage and their offspring. It was the Council of Ministers for the Defense of the Reich that came up with a formula: the property of Jews who lost their status as German subjects would automatically be consigned to the Reich "if their regular place of residence [was] abroad or if they transfer[red] it abroad."[7] For the purposes of this prescription, the Generalgouvernement fell under the category of "abroad." In the meantime, the RSHA, eager to lay its hands on Jewish assets, began confiscating the property of Jews charged with an offense of any kind,[8] and Himmler wanted to seize the property of the deportees. Göring, as the head of the Four-Year Plan, was no less covetous of these assets and, therefore, tried to postpone the decision on the status of the Jews. It also remained to be decided whether the proposed statute could also be applied to the Jews still residing within the Reich. Eventually, at the meeting held on March 15, 1941, it was decided to raise the matter before the führer; at the beginning of June 1941, Hitler decided that it would be sufficient to revoke the subject status of the Jews residing beyond the borders of the Reich. He considered the other proposals too complicated and, as Lammers wrote to Bormann on June 7, 1941, he believed "that anyway, after the war there will be no Jews left in Germany."[9] We should keep in mind that at the time—the eve of the invasion of Russia—Hitler was confident that within a few months the Barbarossa campaign would culminate in victory, placing him in a position to "solve" the Jewish problem throughout Europe. It was only after the deportations had begun, on October 22, 1941, that Implementation Order No. 11 of the Citizenship Law was circulated among the pertinent ministries for signature. Just over a month later, on November 25, its two principal clauses were published:

> 1. A Jew whose regular place of residence is abroad cannot be a German subject. The criterion "usual place of residence abroad" applies if the Jew is abroad under circumstances recognizable as not being temporary.

2. The property of a Jew who loses his status as a German subject devolves on the Reich upon his so losing it. The property of the Jews who are stateless persons upon the publication of this statute and who were formerly German nationals also devolves on the Reich if their regular place of residence is abroad or they go to live there.[10]

The rider establishing that the Generalgouvernement—where the Jews would presumably "go to live"—came under the category of abroad was not published along with the order; it was unofficially appended a week later (December 3, 1941). Other areas defined as abroad were Ostland, the Ukraine, and "any territory that has been conquered by the German army or is presently or will in future be under German administration."[11]

Hence, it was clear that Implementation Order No. 11 was merely a formality that provided legal approbation to the deportation operation that was then already in progress. Following its provisions, the deportees could now be stripped of their civil and legal rights and divested of their property "legally," as it were.

The Yellow Badge Regulation

The fact that the Jews in occupied Poland had been set off from the rest of the population by a special mark naturally did not remain a secret. From time to time demands were voiced in government, party, and SS circles that the yellow badge should be made mandatory within the borders of the Greater Reich. Yet the proposal was not raised officially until the summer of 1941. This time the prime mover was Goebbels. On August 15, 1941, an urgent meeting was called by the Ministry of Propaganda, with the ministry's director, Leopold Gutterer, in the chair. He argued that the solution of the Jewish problem was urgent because soldiers on leave from the front were incensed that Jews were still strolling freely about the Reich. The matter of the housing shortage was also raised on this occasion, and the suggestion already mooted in Vienna—namely, evicting the Jews from their apartments and sending them to barracks camps—was reiterated here. It was also stated that there were still 70,000 Jews left in Berlin but that only 19,000 of them were working. "All the rest should be checked out to find which of them are capable of working, and the others should be cast out [*abkarren*] into Russia." In addition, a spate of new regulations were proposed, for example, setting aside special cars for Jews on public transport and further restricting their food rations. "The best thing," the minutes read, "would be to kill them altogether." All these ideas would make it necessary for the Jews to be distinguished by some special mark. Not everyone agreed with this radical approach; thus the official representing Albert Speer, the inspector of construction, argued that according to Hitler's decision the Jewish-owned apartments should be held in reserve to compensate for apartments that would be destroyed as a result of hostilities. He added that there was already a shortage of 160,000 apartments in Berlin, and the Jews accounted for only 19,000 of them.[12]

It appears that at the time Hitler was still reluctant to take up Heydrich's suggestion about instituting a partial evacuation of the Jews from Germany while the war was still in progress. However, in a talk with Goebbels a few days after this meeting, the führer promised to provide means of transport for deporting the Jews of Berlin to the East, "where they would be dealt with in a harsher climate." He had also agreed in principle to mark the Jews with a special symbol.[13] On September 1 the regulation was published that obliged the Jews of the Greater Reich to wear the yellow badge.[14]

The Deportations to the East

Hitler's Decision and the Ban on Emigration from the Reich

In the spring of 1941, contradictory orders began to be issued about emigration from the Reich and the annexed areas. Recall that emigration from Poland was prohibited as far back as the autumn of 1940, while the delays that made it so difficult to emigrate overseas from the other spheres of German rule grew steadily worse. In March 1941 Adolf Eichmann issued orders to block the exit of Jewish citizens of the Reich then in Yugoslavia, for there was no longer anything to be gained by allowing them to leave "considering the forthcoming final solution."[15] (At the time this comment was written, the Germans had already begun organizing the Einsatzgruppen.) In May, however, Göring demanded that emigration from the Reich and the Protectorate be accelerated, even though it was simultaneously intimated to Jacob Edelstein that it would be halted altogether.[16] Eichmann spoke in more explicit terms at the end of the summer when the matter at hand was emigrants from Denmark who held entry visas to countries overseas and had requested permission to transit the territory of the Reich en route to ports on the Atlantic. Eichmann's response, dated August 28, 1941, was, "considering the forthcoming final solution of the European Jewish problem, now in the preparatory stage, the emigration of Jews from our areas of occupation should be blocked." His answer seems reasonable considering that Himmler had issued a directive on August 23, 1941, that ordered "the emigration of Jews to be stopped immediately."[17]

Hitler's original plan to solve the Jewish problem after the war had been upset because his assumption that the Russian campaign would end quickly had proved wrong, and by the end of August 1941, it was clear that the fighting would rage on at least until the following summer. Meanwhile, both Goebbels and Alfred Rosenberg were pressing for vigorous action to deport the Jews from the Reich. There is reason to believe that Rosenberg wanted to oust the Jews as retaliation for the Siberian exile of the Germans living along the Volga. At any rate, he was quick to dispatch the deputy director of his ministry's political department, Dr. Otto Bräutigam, to obtain Hitler's approval for the move. To Bräutigam's surprise he received a sympathetic hearing at the führer's main headquarters but was told that the Foreign Office had to be consulted. It appears that some time in the latter half of September Hitler decided to begin deporting Jews from the Greater Reich to the East.[18]

The First Destination: Łódź

In any case, on September 18 Himmler wrote to Artur Greiser in Warthegau, "The Führer is demanding that the original Reich and the Protectorate be cleaned out from west to east and be rid of Jews as quickly as possible. Hence before the year is out, I shall try to transfer the Jews of the Reich and the Protectorate to the areas of the East annexed to the Reich two years ago—as the first stage—so as to move them farther eastward next spring."[19] Himmler also informed Greiser that he intended to dispatch some 60,000 Jews to the Łódź ghetto and have them spend the winter there.

About a month later, on October 14, 1941, the chief of the Orpo, Kurt Daluege, issued the deportation order, and between October 16 and November 4, 1941, there were 19,827 Jews from the Reich sent to Łódź in twenty transports of 1,000 people each, following the model of the deportation to Nisko. Of the almost 20,000 Jews, approximately 5,000 came from Vienna; the same number from Prague; and the rest from Berlin, Cologne, Frankfurt on the Main, Hamburg, and Düsseldorf; in addition there was a transport of about 500 Jews from Luxembourg.[20] And 5,000 Gypsies were deported to Łódź at the same time.

This was not the first deportation in 1941; the deportation of Jews from Vienna to the East had already begun in February of that year. The aim then had been to transfer 10,000 Jews to the Generalgouvernement, but only 5,000 or so were actually deported before the transports came to a halt in mid-March—perhaps owing to the preparations for Operation Barbarossa and the reallocation of all means of transport for that purpose. Moreover, it was probably not advisable to burden the Generalgouvernement with an additional infusion of Jews at just that point in time. This situation would also explain Himmler's decision in the autumn of 1941 to send tens of thousands of Jews from the Reich to Warthegau, that is, far from the front. Friedrich Übelhör, the governor of Łódź, was adamantly opposed to such a large influx of Jews, arguing that he was unable to absorb them in the ghetto; thus the number of 60,000 was reduced to 20,000.[21]

The model followed for organizing the autumn deportation was, once again, the earlier one from Vienna. When rumors spread at the end of 1940 that the deportation of Jews was in the offing, the chairman of the Vienna Jewish community, Josef Löwenherz, approached Eichmann's deputy, Rolf Günther, to ascertain whether there was any truth to them. As was the Nazis' wont, Günther categorically denied any such intent. Still not fully assured, Löwenherz tried to deter the Gestapo by threatening that the JDC would withdraw its support for Jewish emigration from Vienna—meaning the flow of foreign currency to finance their exit—if Jews were deported to the East. But the Nazis were not daunted by such talk; two days after Günther had given his assurances to the contrary, Löwenherz was summoned by the Gestapo and presented with detailed orders to prepare the community for deportation.[22] The Central Bureau for Emigration assumed responsibility for organizing the operation, including the selection of the Jews to be deported, but the community leadership was to be the channel for relaying the necessary instructions to the deportees.

The Jews slated for deportation were assembled at a central point—a building expropriated for this purpose—and were maintained there at the community's expense. Moreover, to prevent anyone from escaping, Jews were forbidden to leave Vienna without express permission. The Germans pledged that the community's own officials would not be placed on the transports, but the intention to liquidate the entire community was obvious from the order to cancel all vocational training and rehabilitation courses that were being run to prepare Jews for emigration. Of all the procedures spelled out in the orders, special importance was ascribed to the orderly transfer of vacated apartments. The Jews were told to turn their keys over to the Gestapo attached to a piece of cardboard bearing the apartment's address, the name of its owner, and his date of birth. With certain variations, this procedure became standard throughout the Reich whenever deportations were carried out.

When it emerged that the plan to "lodge" the Jews from the Reich in Łódź was meeting with difficulties, a decision was taken to send them farther East into Russian territory: the two primary destinations were Riga and Minsk. This decision marked the onset of the systematic annihilation of the Jews of the Reich. It is beyond question that the Germans had any other fate in mind for the deportees or intended to treat them differently from the local Jews, who were falling victim to the Einsatzgruppen—as Himmler himself had witnessed two months earlier in Minsk.[23] On October 24, 1941, Daluege issued another deportation order. It was surely not by chance that on the previous day Himmler had directed the head of the Gestapo, Heinrich Müller, to officially bar all emigration of Jews from the Reich.[24] The new deportation order stated that from November 1 to December 4 the Security Police would deport fifty thousand Jews from the Reich to the vicinity of Riga and Minsk. It mentioned by name sixteen cities from which trains carrying one thousand people each would depart. The necessary arrangements were made for escorts and payments.[25] So it was that the period from October 1941 through January 1942 saw the start of the massive movement in which Jews from all over Europe were borne to their destruction.

German Jewry on the Eve of Deportation

The deportation of Jews from Germany was rumored to be imminent long before it began, and from the spring of 1941 onward the conditions of Jewish existence deteriorated steadily. Probably the most pressing problem in most places was housing because the Jews had been evicted from their apartments. In many places the Jews had been turned out of their homes long before the start of the deportations. For example, in Breslau (Wrocław), the capital of Silesia, the Jews were first evicted from their apartments in the summer of 1941 and at that time sent to remote corners of the Reich,[26] for Hitler had still not agreed to banish them altogether. The Jewish communities tried to handle this problem by doubling up in the remaining apartments as well as by establishing dormitories and old-age homes—though they were often forced to evacuate these "Jewish buildings" without warning.[27] The restrictions placed on obtaining food and clothing also called for resourcefulness, and in 1941 the communities were still managing to provide these essentials—to the point where the deportees who arrived in Łódź attracted attention because they were properly dressed. Yitzhak Schwersentz, who had been active in community work in Germany at that time, described the difficulties involved in this work and the frustrations borne by the communal workers:

> What self-control, what powers of concentration were required by a community worker who found in the morning mail an order to vacate his apartment within twenty-four hours; or received a confiscation notice that a belonging which was vital and dear to him would have to be turned in that very day; or found on returning home from work in the evening a notice that he was being fined RM 500 [U.S. $200] for crossing the street in the wrong direction or for neglecting to append the word *Israel* to his name in signing a request or a receipt.[28]

For all that, even the communities' cultural activities continued apace. However, in the autumn when preparations for the systematic deportations got under way, the situation worsened considerably. First, the Jews were forced to wear the yellow badge and forbidden to emigrate; then, on September 11, 1941, an order was issued abolishing the Cultural Society.[29] The Jews had long been deprived of radio sets and telephones at home; now they were forbidden to use public phones as well.

The most staggering blow was dealt to the young people. Up to this time the youth movements and Hehalutz had continued to maintain their training farms in a number of places in Germany and the Reichsvereinigung continued to offer vocational training in a number of schools, where metalworking and woodworking were taught on a high level. The youngsters were usually glad to work and study in these institutions, not least because the Reichsvereinigung also provided dormitories for the vocational students in the cities. Moreover, Jewish youngsters were brought into these schools from the towns to rescue them from the isolation that the Jews suffered in the smaller communities.[30]

In the summer of 1942 preparations for the mass deportations to the East forced the closure of the training farms. For about a year before that, however, the youngsters had, for the most part, not been able to engage in agricultural or occupational training because the authorities employed them in labor battalions assigned to collect garbage, clean the streets, lay sewer pipes, and the like. Nonetheless, even then, a few hundred members of the youth movements kept up their communal lifestyle and also managed to engage in cultural activities. From February through April 1941 the movements managed to hold a seminar for sixty of their members, for it was still possible to disguise the program as a course for vocational rehabilitation. And an exhibit of the participants' work was held as late as the autumn of 1941.[31]

Especially effective during this period was the Aid Program for Jewish Youth, which assumed responsibility for both the training farms and the Youth Aliyah programs and kept one Youth Aliyah school going in Berlin. The program was then headed by Alfred Selbiger—the director of Hehalutz and a member of the Palestine Office—who left his mark on all the youth activities of the day and united the program's staff solidly behind him.[32] "The office had a special aura about it," one of its staff members wrote. "Anyone who worked in our Youth

Aliyah office can attest to the dedication of the staff of volunteers, for they regarded their jobs not as office work but as a mission."[33] Among these devoted workers were two young women from Palestine who eventually got out of Germany and returned home in 1942. It was they who provided the first reliable information about what was really happening in the Reich.

The curriculum and atmosphere of the Youth Aliyah school were described in a letter written by a number of members of Maccabee Hatzair in May 1941:

> Each group holds a discussion once a week and an outing once a week. The older groups discuss [the philosophy of Aaron Darvid] Gordon . . . the middle-level groups discuss the subject "The Socialism of the People" [and] the youngest group studies the history of Zionism. . . . When we feel the need to give expression to our deepest feelings in our very own way, we hold parties or a roll call. The last one was on the anniversary of [Joseph] Trumpeldor's death and another on Passover. Despite great difficulties, we were able to hold a Passover Seder this year as well . . . on both nights, and it was a stirring experience.[34]

The same letter also mentions a work program, the founding of a first aid service, lessons in Bible and Hebrew, and a variety of other activities.

When the deportations began, these youngsters were confronted by a cruel dilemma: Should they remain together with their peer group or accompany their parents to the East? We should bear in mind that at the time no one so much as imagined that the deportations meant certain death. Everyone believed the deportees would live and work—under admittedly difficult but not necessarily fatal conditions—in the ghettos of Poland. This illusion was fostered because in 1941 it was still possible to correspond with the deportees in Poland and even send them packages containing food, medicine, clothing, and other supplies.[35] Now these youngsters were forced to decide where their duty lay: with parents in order to ease their burden and to stand beside them in the harsh struggle for survival or to remain with their comrades in the movement. They debated the matter with great solemnity and, as in Holland, reached the decision that as members of a youth movement their first obligation was to their comrades. Those who decided to accompany their parents were forced to leave the movement; only in rare cases did a member receive his peers' consent to do so.[36]

The Jews of the Protectorate: Deportation and the Establishment of the Theresienstadt Camp

On September 27, 1941, Heydrich arrived in Prague bearing the title of acting Reich protector.[37] He had come to replace Konstantin von Neurath, whose relatively lenient policy as protector in Bohemia and Moravia was no longer to the liking of his superiors in Berlin. During the summer there had been a dramatic rise in sabotage, interference with the normal work process, and strikes, so that by September it was obvious to the Nazi leaders that the situation called for a man who could rule by the tried-and-proven method of terror. In his maiden speech before the heads of the German administration in the Protectorate, which was not distributed for publication, Heydrich warned that the public unrest simmering beneath the surface demanded a vigorous response before it was too late.[38] He proclaimed the need to change the system of rule, and he proceeded to do just that. From April 28, 1939, the Protectorate had, at least nominally, been under the rule of a quasi-independent Czech government headed by an ex-general, Alois Eliaš. It was this limited independence that Heydrich was determined to abolish because he believed it fostered illusions among the Czech public and hindered the unqualified merger of the Protectorate with the Reich. Indeed, on September 28, 1941, the day after Heydrich's arrival, Eliaš was arrested, and three days later he was tried before a People's Court (Volksgerichtshof) presided over by Judge Otto Georg Thierach, one of the prominent members of the Nazi judicial establishment. Found guilty of espionage, abetting the underground, and aiding the escape of fugitives from the Protectorate, Eliaš was condemned to death, though the sentence was not carried out until after Heydrich's assassination in the summer of 1942. When Eliaš was deposed, a state of civil emergency was declared in most of the country. Thousands of people were arrested, and in the two months from the end of September to the end of November more than four hundred people were shot.[39]

Still, the Germans were divided among themselves on such questions as how the Czech population should be treated and what status the Protectorate should hold within the Greater Reich. The ratio of ethnic Germans to Czechs in the Protectorate was low, which made the Germanization of the country a formidable task. One of the more oppressive means used to accomplish this goal was labor service in Germany, for which young unemployed Czechs were required to "volunteer." This service, usually devoted to hard labor, was considerably expanded by Heydrich, who saw it as a way of achieving the "final solution to the Czech question." He even considered linking this "solution" with the program to dispose of the Jewish question by deporting the "Mongols" to Siberia.[40]

As in the Reich proper, the basic conditions of life steadily deteriorated for the Jews in the summer of 1941—all this on top of the occupational restrictions and the plunder of property that had been in effect since the start of the occupation. An order published on July 5, 1941—and made retroactive to March 16, 1939, the date of the establishment of the Protectorate—extended the Nuremberg Laws to Czech citizens. Restrictions on housing and the eviction of the Jews from their apartments had begun much earlier, while the laws pertaining to the Aryanization of property had become increasingly stringent. In the autumn of 1941 there were still some 88,000 Jews living in Bohemia-Moravia.[41]

The leaders of the Czech-Jewish community had, of course, been sensitive to the decline in the situation since the spring of 1941. The trauma of the deportation to Nisko at the end of 1939 convinced Jacob Edelstein that everything possible should be done to prevent any further deportations to the East. The regulations issued by the Germans had transformed the Prague Jewish community into the focal institution of Czech Jewry, and in the summer of 1941 Edelstein created a special department within the community administration—Department G—to study the possibility of concentrating the Jews in a separate area, essentially meaning a ghetto.[42] Edelstein believed that if he could bring about the self-ghettoization of the Jews and provide the labor force needed by the Germans, he would be able to save his community. He saw cooperation with the Germans as the only way to survive.

In the tense atmosphere that pervaded the country once Heydrich had instituted his reign of terror, the role that the Jews could serve as the victims of the New Order was not lost on the Germans. Although Hitler's aim was to purge the Reich of Jews, in the process they could serve as an example to the Czechs of what awaited those who defied the Germans' bidding. In essence, then, two German aims converged: the broader objective of solving the Jewish problem in the Reich and the specific and local objective of intimidating a population that was chafing under German hegemony.

Heydrich and Eichmann laid down their course of action at a meeting in Berlin on October 4, 1941.[43] The Czech operation was conceived on two planes. First, transports would carry Jews from Czechoslovakia to Łódź within the framework of Himmler's deportation plan—indeed, this aspect of the program began on October 16. At the same time, however, Eichmann ordered the leaders of the Jewish community to draw up a memorandum on concentrating the Jews in a special place within the country. Edelstein submitted the memorandum on October 9. A day later Heydrich convened a meeting in Prague, attended by Eichmann, to discuss preliminary steps for solving the Jewish problem in the Protectorate—and to a certain degree within the original Reich as well.[44] One outcome of this meeting was the policy to be imposed on the press of the Protectorate in the days to come. It was decided, for example, that the press conference scheduled to take place that day would be devoted not only to the Jewish problem but to the matter of the resistance movements within the Protectorate.[45] This is a clear indication that the Germans saw a link between "the solution to the Jewish problem" and the suppression of the Czech insurgents.

Since the plan to deport the Jews from the Protectorate was meeting with resistance from the authorities in Łódź, the minutes of the October 10 meeting spoke of sending the "most troublesome" Jews to Minsk and Riga. Eichmann apprised his colleagues that plans had already been made to transfer the Jews "to camps for Communist prisoners of war in the area of military activity." But his mention of Artur Nebe and Otto Rasch, the commanders of the Einsatzgruppen, leaves no doubt that the intent was to turn the Jews over to these squads.

The main subject discussed at this meeting, however, was "the possibility of [instituting] ghettoization in the Protectorate." Contrary to Edelstein's approach, which accentuated the value of the Jews as a productive element, the Germans characterized the proposed site for the ghetto, "The only [place that can be] considered is an out-of-the-way suburb (never part of the city center, that has not proven itself) or a small village or town with as little industry as possible." As to the productive aspect of the enterprise, it was agreed that the Jews should be employed in cottage industries, "without much machinery" *(ohne maschinellen Aufwand)*. Of the various possible sites mentioned at the meeting, the fortress town of Theresienstadt took pride of place. It was clear that a ghetto of this type would essentially be a way station, for as Eichmann put it, "After the evacuation of this temporary assembly camp and their transfer to the East, it will be possible to turn the whole area into a model German settlement." Another advantage of Theresienstadt was the rich soil suitable for the cultivation of vegetables, and a proposal on this subject had already been submitted to Himmler.

The practical problems of funding and transport were also discussed. Moreover, it was decided that the rooms in Theresienstadt's buildings would be filled with straw ("because beds will take up too much room") and that the better apartments would be assigned to the Council of Elders and the guard units. It was taken for granted that epidemics would break out in the ghetto (Eichmann had remarked that the number of Jews would at any rate be reduced); emphasis was placed on ensuring that they would not spread to the countryside. In summing up the session, it was stressed, yet again, that the führer wanted the Jews to be gone from the German realm by the end of the year; thus it would be necessary to solve all outstanding questions quickly. At this point there was still no mention of using Theresienstadt as an instrument for camouflaging the annihilation campaign.

The first group of Jews—the "construction commando," comprising 342 young people—was sent to Theresienstadt on November 24, 1941, and charged with transforming the fortress town into a camp that would accommodate the Jews of the Protectorate. Since mid-October Edelstein had been trying to persuade the Central Bureau for Emigration to handle the vital needs of housing, sanitary conditions, food, and work for the Jews in order to save them from further deportation to the East. However, his efforts met with only partial success, and he was not allowed to accompany the first group sent to Theresienstadt.[46]

The fortress Theresienstadt had been built by the Austrian Emperor Joseph II and was named in honor of his mother, Empress Maria Theresa. From the end of the eighteenth century onward, it had for the most part served the needs of the army, with its buildings being used as barracks, subterranean stores, and quarters for officers and their families. At a later period a post office, loan fund, and church—and even a hotel—were added. The fortress was built in the form of a twelve-pointed star surrounded by a high wall covered with grass, even with trees. It was into and over this wall that the barracks had been constructed. The town's houses, 219 in number, were old and the worse for wear, as was all the plumbing, the sewage system, and so on. There were swamps in the vicinity of Theresienstadt, which accounted for the area's extreme dampness. This was especially felt in the so-called Little Fortress, which was located a short way from the main town. Having once served as a prison, it was now made into a concentration camp. The Nazi scheme of things was also served by the fact that Theresienstadt lay far from any main road and was not even served by a railway feeder line. Its first commander was Dr. Siegfried Seidel, who had specialized in deportations to the East from occupied Poland (see chap. 6). Undoubtedly, this appointment was not arbitrary, for as we have seen, Eichmann regarded Theresienstadt as essentially a transit camp.

Nevertheless, the development of the camp, which did not officially become a ghetto until the summer of 1942, differed substantially from the lines projected at the October 10 planning meeting. To a large degree this disparity can be credited to Jacob Edelstein, his deputy, Otto Zucker, and their staff, who before and after being sent to the camp worked tirelessly to improve its living conditions. Edelstein reached Theresienstadt on December 4, 1941, and was appointed Elder of the Council by the Germans. With the active support of the youngsters from the pioneering youth movements, who regarded him as their leader, he tried to ensure the survival of the incarcerated Jews by having them work within and outside the town and by making their lives as orderly and cultured as possible. It was largely due to these efforts that the camp was later reclassified as a ghetto, to which, beginning in the summer of 1942, Eichmann began to send elderly and privileged Jews from all over Central and Western Europe. In 1943 he went one step further and decided to use Theresienstadt for propaganda purposes by exhibiting it as a model ghetto.

The Second Destination: Occupied Soviet Territory

For a certain period, at least, the Jews in Theresienstadt fared much better than the deportees sent "farther on eastward" as Himmler had put it. The main destinations of these other deportees from Prague, Vienna, and the cities within the original borders of the Reich were Minsk, Kovno, and most of all Riga and its environs. Under German rule fewer than 10,000 Jews, out of an original population of 95,000, were left in Latvia. (Prior to the German conquest there were 40,000 Jews in Riga, and in the other two large cities of Latvia—Libau and Dvinsk—about 9,000 and slightly more than 13,000, respectively. The rest of the Jews were scattered in towns and here and there in villages [see chap. 10].) Just before the outbreak of war with Germany, 5,000 Jews had been evacuated when the Soviets exiled a total of 30,000 "hostile elements" to the Russian interior. A considerable number of Jews took part with the retreating Soviet army in fighting the Germans, and many fell; the number that made it safely to Russian territory is estimated at 16,000.[47]

The descriptions that have come down to us portray the Latvians as among the more savage collaborators with the Nazis. Their acts of murder, mayhem, and plunder during the first months of the occupation—including the burning of synagogues with Jews trapped inside—were not spontaneous outbursts or even pogroms instigated by the Germans. The Latvians themselves actually planned and organized the massacre of Jews, and the gratified Germans dubbed these brutal rampages self-purging actions *(Selbstreinigungsaktionen)*. In this way most of the Jews of Libau, Dvinsk, and the surrounding towns were wiped out during the summer of 1941.

The Riga Ghetto and the Combined Extermination Action

Consequently, when the ghetto was established in Riga at the end of October, it gave the remaining Jews hope that they would be able to survive within its bounds. The leaders of the ghetto council launched into organizing self-help activities from the very outset. Most of them were associated with circles that had earlier sought means of cooperation with the Latvian nationalists (the Latvian-Jewish Free

Union).[48] When a Jewish police force was established in the ghetto, it was mostly members of the Zionist youth movements who joined it. One account reports that "the best boys volunteered, including the members of the youth movements. Their motive for doing so was conscientiousness and a sense of public spiritedness. They hoped that as part of their role they would be able to help the Jews in their acute distress, and certainly they did help as best they could."[49]

This testimony by one of the survivors of the Riga ghetto was confirmed by others, setting the Riga police apart from the Jewish police forces in many other ghettos. However, this first ghetto in Riga, which was called the Big Ghetto and contained 32,000 people, was short-lived—thirty-seven days. At the end of November some of its inhabitants, particularly those in the labor battalions who left the ghetto daily to work outside, were forced to move to a new area called the Little Ghetto. This was essentially a labor camp, attested by the fact that the women were interned separately. After this shift had taken place, on the night of November 29, 1941, the Germans perpetrated a wholesale massacre among the residents of the Big Ghetto. While some of them were slaughtered within the ghetto proper, the majority, following the method used by the Einsatzgruppen, were first taken to a nearby forest called Rombuli. According to German documents, 10,600 people were killed at that time; Jewish testimonies placed the number at more than 15,000.[50] With the aid of the Jewish police, some people managed to escape to the Little Ghetto. When they told their news, the internees refused to believe that their families were being wiped out. In fact, it was not until the Germans conducted their second *Aktion* on December 8 that they realized the truth. There were 12,000 people killed in this second slaughter, but three women managed to escape to attest to the facts. Altogether 27,000 of Riga's Jews perished during this period,[51] leaving 4,500 men in the Little Ghetto and some 300 women in a separate camp. In all of Latvia only about 9,000 Jews were alive at the close of 1941, a mere 10 percent of the original Jewish population prior to the German invasion.

A short while later transports of Jews from Germany were brought to the deserted Big Ghetto, thus confirming the widely held belief that the purpose of the massacre was to make room for Jews deported from the Reich. A German report dated January 5, 1942, even stated, "Everything has been readied to receive the next transports of Jews, both in Minsk and in Riga."[52]

As the Jews were crowded into the Minsk ghetto, the demeanor of these new arrivals from Germany—the first to come from Hamburg—perturbed the commissar-general, Wilhelm Kube. He found that they were possessed of European culture and ways, and he was particularly troubled that some of them had fought and been decorated in World War I. Kube expressed his doubts to his superiors, but they were not prepared to accept his arguments.[53]

No problems of this sort arose in Riga, but organizational hitches were in evidence. The so-called preparations for receiving the transports had been rather haphazard. When the deportees began to arrive early in December, some of them were sent to a nearby camp improvised from the dilapidated buildings of a deserted farm *(Jungfernhof)*.[54] The transport from Hamburg included the city's chief rabbi, Josef Carlebach, who had joined the deportees of his own volition and until his death in the summer of 1942 provided spiritual succor to the living and the dying.[55] Beginning on December 10 the deportees were taken to the deserted buildings of the Big Ghetto, whose population had gradually risen to 15,000. Then, the Germans began to deplete it again, purportedly transferring people to other places of work while actually leading them to places of slaughter. For all that, however, the deportees housed in the Big Ghetto were slightly better off than the surviving Jews of Riga in the Little Ghetto. For example, they were allowed to conduct their religious life openly, which was forbidden to the local Jews. But most of the transports were now being taken to another camp that was already infamous for its harrowing conditions: Salaspils. Actually, it was a network of camps originally designed for Russian POWs, though civilians had been interned there as well. A group of workers from this camp had prepared the place to receive the deportees. The conditions in Salaspils were inordinately harsh and calculated to kill inmates through hunger, illness, or sheer exhaustion, which is precisely what happened to most of them. In addition, the camp commanders were notorious for their sadistic brutality: inmates were hanged almost daily, for all the others to see.

Some transports from the Reich were sent neither to the ghetto nor to the camp but directly to the killing grounds in the forests of the area.[56] In January transports also began to come in from the Theresienstadt transit camp, and the first two of them, dispatched on January 9 and 15, carried one thousand people each and were sent directly to the forests around Riga. Besides some transports directed to Kovno and Minsk, most of the Jews deported at this time were sent to Riga. It is estimated that from the beginning of December 1941 to the end of January 1942 some twenty thousand of them perished in the city and its surroundings.

The Spoliation of Property

In the bureaucratic division of labor for the task of ridding the Reich of Jews, the RSHA handled the planning and organization of the deportations and Eichmann's department was responsible for their execution. One other branch of the German administration was highly interested in the benefits that could accrue from disposing of the Jews: the Reich Treasury. Through a systematic and sweeping operation, the Reich's financial authorities succeeded in sequestering the property, liquid assets, and real estate of the deported Jews. Once the revocation of the deportees' German citizenship had provided the ostensibly legal grounds for seizing their property, the Nazis barred Jews from sending ("smuggling") capital abroad or from concealing it within the Reich.

On November 4, 1941, the Reich Treasury issued directives on this matter to the heads of the financial authorities in most of the district capitals of Germany. The introductory clauses of this circular stated, "*Jews* not employed in businesses of importance to the people's economy *will be banished* [*werden abgeschoben*] to one of the cities in the territories of the East. The *property* of the Jews who are to be so banished *will be confiscated* on behalf of the German Reich. The Jews will retain RM 100 [U.S. $40] and 50 kilograms [110 pounds] of personal baggage."[57]

Thereafter, extended and detailed instructions listed the cities from which the deportation of Jews had already begun and discussed each stage of the confiscation procedures. Prior to their departure, the Jews were to submit a precise list of their assets, which was to be turned over to the Reich as a "gift" for the Gestapo's organization of the "emigration." The plundered property was divided among various authorities. The handling of apartments was delegated to the municipalities, though the contents of these apartments—furniture, kitchenware, and articles of every other kind—were to become the property of the Reich Treasury. If they were not required for immediate occupancy, they were to be sold, with the proceeds going to the Reich. Works of art were to be turned over to the Reich Office for the Arts. A special point was made about seizing Jewish writings, paintings, sculptures, and folk crafts: as of the spring of 1942, on Hitler's orders, these were "donated" to Alfred Rosenberg's executive staff for the "study of the Jewish problem."[58] In addition to stocks, other securities, bank accounts, and the like, the Jews were to turn in their valuables and stamp collections. The Reich Treasury would handle the management of real estate and the transfer of legal ownership. Finally, the circular requested that the progress of this operation and any difficulties encountered in carrying it out be reported as quickly as possible along with suggestions for streamlining the procedures because "we must assume that the deportation of the Jews will continue."[59]

Considerable attention was paid to the fact that the Jews were liable to conceal their assets and effects. Thus, in October 1941 special orders were issued to forestall the transfer of Jewish property or capital into other hands, that is, to Germans. Even the police received special instructions on this subject. Those issued in Düsseldorf on January 5, 1942, stated, "Generally, one must conclude from a large-scale transfer of capital that the intent was to prevent the state from seizing the assets. It goes without saying that deals that appear to have been [made] due to a forthcoming or anticipated deportation are a priori null and void, so that whatever possessions and rights were transferred revert back to the Jewish seller."[60] Hence they were subject to confiscation as Jewish property whose owners had been banished. The Reich Economic Office sent similar instructions to all banks, loan funds, and other financial institutions that required them to report on any "smuggling of property" *(Vermögensverschiebungen)* that had occurred after October 15, 1941. Similar orders were issued in Austria, but the situation differed in the Protectorate, for the Central Bureau had taken over the Jewish property there and most of the confiscated articles were shipped to Berlin in "sealed and guarded railway cars."[61]

Within Germany proper the RSHA tried to be sure that it would get its share of the spoils; to that end it created its own financial apparatus by opening a special *W* account and officially declaring it a fund to finance the deportations and provide the permissible RM 50 (U.S. $12.50) to those unable to obtain the sum on their own. The fund's capital was raised by requiring wealthy Jews to deposit at least a quarter of their liquid capital into this account (by an order dated December 3, 1941). The sole purpose of this highly complex operation was to channel a portion of the Jewish assets into the coffers of the RSHA.[62]

In addition to these procedures, every deportee was subjected to a thorough search of his clothing and person to prevent the smuggling of cash or valuables, particularly foreign currency. The customs officers were given explicit orders and detailed advice on how to conduct these searches for concealed property. And as we know in retrospect, even if a Jew managed to foil the system and take something along, he was stripped of the little that was left to him—brought out legally or otherwise—on reaching the East to be killed immediately or at some later point.

Implementation Order No. 11 provided the National Socialist regime with the legal formula for deporting the Jews from the Greater Reich while spoliating their property. The long process of drafting the necessary legislation occupied such eminent institutions of the German administration as the Ministry of the Interior, the Reich Treasury, and the Reich Chancellery—in addition, of course, to the RSHA, which was responsible for seeing to the deportations and coordinating the transports to the East with the *Aktionen* of the Einsatzgruppen. Within the Reich proper the national bureaucracy, the bureaucracies of the constituent states, the municipalities, and the banks effected the plunder of Jewish property according to intricate and incredibly detailed instructions. Legions of officials at all levels must have been involved in executing these directives.

Implementation Order No. 11 stripped the deported Jews of their remaining civil and human rights and reduced them to mere numbers, one thousand of whom were loaded onto each transport. At the same time, the stigmatization of the Jews of the Reich by means of a yellow badge consummated the segregation of the entire community after its living conditions had been steadily undermined during 1941 and its own organized activities abolished almost entirely. The orders of deportation to the extermination area were accompanied by a prohibition on emigration. Thus marks the decisive shift in the Nazi policy for ridding the Reich of Jews: from pushing them out to rounding them up and transporting them out of the Reich to be murdered in the East. The process leading to the final stage of the "solution of the Jewish problem" reached its height when extermination camps were built to perpetrate mass murder by the new technique of gassing.

12

The Final Solution: Overall Planning

From Racism to Racial Eugenics

In an article, "The *Völkisch* Idea and the Party," which Hitler wrote in 1922, he attacked the German *völkisch* bloc for its failure to understand that "an idea is valueless as long as its aspirations are not transformed into action but remain forever mere notions."[1] At that time, he already envisaged his main task as accumulating political might so that he could convert theory into practice. It has often been said that Hitler's political strength lay neither in his definition of new objectives, nor in the innovativeness of his political vision, nor in his exploitation of hitherto unused tactics and measures. Rather it stemmed from his ability to concentrate the anti-establishment notions and trends dispersed throughout the German society of his day and activate them. This is true of his military aims, economic methods, and the consolidation of his totalitarian rule in general, and it certainly characterizes the course he steered toward the extermination of the Jews. In the wide and complex range of operations against the Jews—encompassing legislation, terror, spoliation, and finally murder—there were none that had not been proposed—or even practiced before Hitler's day.[2] Anti-Semitic propagandists before him had proposed killing the Jews, and the remote and recent past offered numerous examples of the translation of the proposal into action. Hitler's innovation lay in his desire to solve "the Jewish question" once and for all in a comprehensive fashion. In his efforts to this end, he came to utilize new techniques that transformed his anti-Semitism into the revolutionary scheme of genocide.

The element of racist theory in Hitler's method and in his struggle for power in Germany was gradually implemented within the framework of the struggle of National Socialist Germany for hegemony in Europe. In a speech to the Reichstag on January 30, 1937, Hitler "prophesied" that just as acknowledgment of the existence of the solar system had changed the basic concepts of the world, the National Socialist racial theories would transform historical consciousness of the past and future of mankind.[3] Racism remained the main ideological instrument of the wartime struggle to gain world power. It was the guiding light in three main spheres: the effort to Germanize the areas annexed to the Reich by means of concentrating German ethnic elements from Eastern Europe in these areas; the extermination of both the ruling elite of the Slavic peoples and Russian POWs; and the total extermination of the Jews. Racist theory served both as an ideological basis and as a government instrument. To these three areas should be added a fourth sphere, one in which the Nazis operated from the beginning of their rule: the improvement of the race within the Reich itself. It was no accident that Nazi ideology failed to formulate a precise definition of the Aryan race.[4] After World War I, racial theory as a component of German nationalistic aspirations evolved in two forms: the first was sociopolitical and was adopted by all those organizations, associations, and popular movements that prepared the ground for the National Socialist party. The second based its ideology on the elaboration of a quasi-scientific approach whose aim was the improvement of the biological stock of the German people. The concept of so-called racial eugenics found advocates both among the *völkisch* ideologues and among physicians.

These circles considered an issue that, at the time, was preoccupying many, mainly physicians, in other countries as well: euthanasia, which the Germans called *Sterbehilfe* (aid to the dying). Today physicians and legal experts as well as the public at large wrestle with the question of whether it is permissible to end the suffering of the incurably sick by hastening their death. But the proponents of racism reversed the moral implications, thus distorting its true humanitarian intent. For them, the focus of the dilemma was no longer the desire to alleviate suffering, but an ostensible concern for the health of the nation and the prevention of "squandering" its resources on those who were useless to society and constituted a burden on it. This *Sterbehilfe* became *Vernichtung lebensunwerten Lebens* (the destruction of undeserving life) and the extension of such life was denoted *unsozial* (asocial).[5] According to this approach, which evolved in Germany before World War I, the task of racial eugenics was to develop and improve the human race and, in light of this seemingly noble aim, the individual and his suffering became insignificant. The principle of the absolute value of human life and the ethical demand for its preservation were discarded. The reverse became true, and the individual was now obliged to prove his or her right to life according to the yardstick of the "supreme political morality." The state was now a biological concept, an organism whose health it was incumbent to preserve, just as an individual is concerned for the health of his or her body. People who were no longer useful to the state were perceived as "monsters" in contrast to "true human beings." They were described as *geistig Tote* (dead souls), "an alien growth in human society, and of a lower level than animals."[6] It is only a short step from this concept to the denial of the right to exist of all those regarded as aliens, enemies, or "of a lower level than animals."

Immediately after the installation of the National Socialist regime, this ideological trend moved from a marginal position to center stage. Among the basic laws promulgated on July 14, 1933, was the Law for the Prevention of Progeny of Sufferers from Hereditary Diseases, which established the possibility of sterilizing the sick. The law was gradually extended over the following years, and from 1935 on it was supplemented by a law determining eligibility for marriage.[7] There were two aims of this legislation: "1. To purify the body of the nation and to gradually eradicate hereditary diseases. 2. To guarantee to the state authority and total control over life, marriage and the family." Professor Ernst Bergmann, one of the theorists who provided the ideological sanction for Nazi schemes, said in 1933 that a worldwide campaign should be launched against idiots, the retarded, habitual criminals, and all degenerates. He recommended "quietly throwing away onto the garbage heap a million of the human refuse in the large cities."[8]

The Implementation of "Euthanasia"

The term *ausmerzen* (exterminate) crops up repeatedly not only in the utterances of Hitler and his henchmen but also in the statements and writings of philosophers and scientists who prepared the theoretical framework for the acts of horror.[9] As soon as war broke out, Hitler concluded that the time was ripe to act for the purity of the German race not only through preventive and restrictive laws but also through direct extermination of *Ballastexistenzen* (burdensome life). One of the chief implementers of "euthanasia," Hitler's personal physician, Professor Karl Brandt, claimed at his trial that Hitler had stated as early as 1935 at the party rally in Nuremberg that, in the event of war, he would return to the issue of "euthanasia" and implement it. In fact, in June 1939 at the latest, secret deliberations commenced in his office on the preparation of the project. Among the professors, psychiatrists, and other experts to whom the plan was expounded by Victor Brack, a member of Hitler's private chancellery, only one declared himself unwilling to take part. That was Gottfried Ewald, professor of psychiatry at Göttingen University; later, he was among the physicians who tried to have the plan shelved. The leader of the doctors' organization of the Reich, Leonardo Conti, who also served at the time as secretary of state for health in the Ministry of the Interior (thus, in effect, his own superior), drew up the plan for implementation together with his advisor, Dr. Herbert Linden, who was in charge of all health institutions in the country. Immediately after the victory over Poland, Hitler ordered the head of his private chancellery, Philip Bouhler, to solve the "euthanasia" problem instantly. At the end of October, Dr. Conti sent a circular to all relevant institutions and ordered them to answer questionnaires on the condition of each patient within a month.[10] At the same time, Hitler issued a rare written directive that was predated September 1, 1939—the day on which war broke out. It charged Bouhler to empower physicians to determine personally which incurably sick "may be accorded a mercy death." The operation was strictly confidential and participants took an oath of silence.[11]

The operation was carried out in five stages. First the candidates were selected from among the inmates of the institutions; next they were taken to a transit center from which they were transported to the nearest "euthanasia" installation.

There they underwent a perfunctory medical test and were sent, in batches of twenty to thirty, to a sealed room into which carbon monoxide was piped. Finally, the bodies were removed and burned in an attached crematorium, but not before all gold teeth had been extracted and some of their brains had been excised for purposes of "scientific research." The first experiments were conducted in January 1940; by August of the following year 70,273 people had been exterminated in five installations set up for *Sonderbehandlung* (special treatment). This particular term from the Nazi language of concealment continued to be used when referring to killing by gas, even when it was later conducted in the death camps with no medical connotations. The first killings were carried out by a commissioner in the Criminal Police named Christian Wirth, who was afterward joined by a chemist, Dr. Kallmeyer, who became the professional expert in charge of all killings by gas.[12]

Hitler's assumption that in wartime it would be easier and more simple to implement this scheme was refuted by the great number of people who became aware of what was being perpetrated in these special "curative institutions." Leaders of the Catholic and Protestant churches protested to government ministries and some, including several bishops, even raised their voices in public protest. Dr. Hilfrich, bishop of Limburg an der Lahn near Hadamar, where one of the main installations was located, wrote on August 13, 1941, to the minister of justice with a copy to the minister of the interior and the minister for church affairs. He noted that attempts had been made to silence public outcry by means of threats but that the illegal activities had not been halted. The local children, he wrote, now recognized the buses with blacked-out windows in which the victims were transported and pointed them out, "Look, there's the murder-box coming again" or slandered one another, "You're crazy. They'll take you to the oven at Hadamar."[13]

Such protests and the increasing number of appeals that relatives of the deceased brought to the courts against the physicians, apparently persuaded Hitler that organized action should be discontinued, and on August 24, 1941, he gave the order to halt the "euthanasia" operation.[14] The installations were officially closed down. In practice, however, the operation continued in the form of the so-called wild euthanasia, that is, killing in special, locked-up institutions in which victims were put to death individually by injection, sleeping pills, or starvation. The starvation method was particularly popular in the case of mentally defective and physically disabled children—the number of such victims is estimated at twenty thousand. Persuasion and deception were practiced particularly in the case of child victims: parents were informed that the child had been transferred to a special institution for special treatment. The entire operation was implemented through four organizations acting as fronts. One of these was responsible for deciding which patients were incurable, the second was in charge of financing, the third ran transportation by bus or train, and the fourth served as a registration bureau for the dead.

Initially, the objective of the operation was racial purification for the German people; thus the Jews were not considered worthy of inclusion. But the authorities soon changed their minds and decided to exploit the opportunity to rid themselves of Jewish mental patients as well. The first Jewish transport was apparently dispatched to its fate in June 1940; this was followed by additional groups ostensibly being sent to a fictitious mental institution at "Cholm,"[15] near Lublin. This was apparently a front, for the address was that of a large office building in Berlin (Columbia House), which was the administrative center and registration bureau of the operation. It was there that Jews were ordered to address funds they paid into an account in the Bank of Prussia as "maintenance fees" for patients who were, in fact, no longer alive. The *Reichsvereinigung der Juden in Deutschland* paid RM 350,000 for treatment in the "Cholm State Hospital," and the Hamburg community paid RM 40,000.[16] Then, without warning, standard letters were sent informing relatives of the death of the patients who, in mysterious fashion, had all died on the same day. At the end of August 1940, instructions were issued to concentrate all the Jewish patients in Bavaria in a single institution, Eglfing-Haar, from which not one returned.[17]

From "Euthanasia" to the Gassing of Jews

By summer 1940 the extermination system was extended to the concentration camps as well. This operation, carried out under the auspices of Himmler, had a code name, 14 f 13. Here, too, the candidates for gassing were classified by a committee of doctors that visited the camps. They usually decided the fate of their patients on the basis of reports prepared by the camp commandant and a superficial examination of the selected prisoners. The victims were then transferred in groups to camps in which gas installations had been constructed, such as Mauthausen and Gross-Rosen. Selection of the sick, crippled, those unfit for work, and the Jews was conducted in all the large camps in Germany such as Buchenwald, Sachsenhausen, Neuengamme, Ravensbrück, and others. One of these physicians, Dr. Friedrich Mennecke, wrote letters to his wife during the selections at Buchenwald that are extant. On November 28, 1941, he started his morning letter with a well-known German phrase, "Hurray! We are going out on the merry hunt."[18]

The operation continued until 1944, and its victims included forced laborers, Russian POWs, and children of mixed marriages. The number of German victims is estimated at about 120,000; the total number is much higher. It is also known that mental patients in Poland were killed as early as 1939; in East Prussia a similar operation, launched in the autumn of 1940, encompassed Poles as well.[19]

It has already been noted that the Einsatzgruppen used gas cells installed on trucks (see chap. 10). Meanwhile, the civilian administration in the Baltic states and in Alfred Rosenberg's office were debating the question of how to exploit this system in order to expedite the Final Solution. It is not clear who was the initiator. However, in the autumn of 1941 with the launching of deportations from the Reich eastward, there was an exchange of letters on this matter between Hinrich Lohse, Reichskommissar of Ostland, and Rosenberg's office. From this we learn that a meeting took place between Rosenberg's expert, Judge Alfred Wetzel, Victor Brack of Hitler's chancellery, and Adolf Eichmann. With Eichmann concurring, Brack expressed his agreement to help in the preparation of gas installations by utilizing equipment and experts who had managed the "euthanasia" scheme to solve the problem of the Jews deported to the East. He proposed that Dr. Kallmeyer be dispatched to Riga because he was now unoccupied due to the official disbanding of gas installations for "euthanasia." The general conclusion drawn from the meeting was that "in light of the given state of affairs, there should be no hesitation about using Brack's methods to eliminate those Jews who are unfit for work."[20]

In the end the death camps were established in occupied Poland—not in the Russian areas—most of them in the Generalgouvernement, where their construction commenced in early 1942 on the initiative and under the supervision of Odilo Globocnik. In doing this job, he utilized the services of most of the personnel who had taken part in the "euthanasia" operation in Germany headed by Christian Wirth. With time, the number of experts rose to ninety-two.[21]

While these preparations were under way, the use of gas trucks began in early December 1941 in the Chełmno extermination camp about 40 miles northwest of Łódź. In the spring the same method was then developed at Bełżec, Sobibor, and Treblinka in the Generalgouvernement; here, too, diesel engines were used, but in contrast to Chełmno fixed installations were constructed. The same was true of Auschwitz in Eastern Upper Silesia; however, there, as later in Majdanek near Lublin, hydrocyanide (prussic acid) was used for the killing. This chemical, marketed as a disinfectant, went by the trade name of Zyklon-B. According to the testimony of the commandant of Auschwitz, Rudolf Höss, Himmler ordered him in the summer of 1941 to prepare a large-scale extermination camp at Auschwitz, stating explicitly that the extermination of the Jews was being carried out by order of the führer. The first experiments with Zyklon-B were conducted in September 1941 in the bunker at Auschwitz on Russian POWs; systematic operations, though not yet on a full scale, commenced in early January 1942.[22]

The idea of employing gas to eliminate the sick, women, children, Jews, and others seems to have been popular in various circles of the National Socialist regime. This fact made it easy for the leadership to use this method to achieve the central racial objective: liquidation of the Jewish people. For example, in the summer of 1941, Himmler consulted the chief physician of the SS, Dr. Ernst Grawitz, as to the most effective method of carrying out mass killing. The latter advised him to use gas chambers.[23] The gas truck method was developed that same summer by the Technical Department of the RSHA.

Thus, the Nazi regime was contemplating the introduction of these measures at the time it dispatched the Einsatzgruppen to execute Jews by shooting.[24] We may conclude that the various methods were developed concomitantly. This fact serves as additional proof that the Nazi leadership was already devising the extermination of Jews on a European scale when Göring signed the directive to Heydrich on July 31, 1941, charging him with implementation of the "intended final solution of the Jewish question." Hence, the deportations from the Reich, which commenced in the autumn of 1941, may be perceived as the first stage in the execution of the overall plan. Since comprehensive and systematic mass extermination by technological means had never before been carried out, the Nazis experimented with various methods in order to achieve their goal; thus they developed a number of techniques that were tested and used at the same time.

The Wannsee Conference

We have frequently noted that the Nazis often began to act, but it was only later that they summed up their actions systematically and accorded them official sanction. This important gathering convened on January 20, 1942, in the Berlin suburb of Wannsee. Chaired by Heydrich, it is a striking example of these tactics. It is often assumed that the decision to launch the Final Solution was taken on this occasion, but this is not so. It was only after varied experiences had been accumulated, after the practical measures were already in full swing, and after certain difficulties had emerged that seemed liable to impede implementation in all the countries of Europe that the planners of the vast operation felt the need to give it the official stamp of approval and to harness all the relevant authorities of the Third Reich to ensure coordination among them.

Heydrich sent out invitations on November 29, 1941, calling the meeting for December 9. This was after Implementation Order No. 11 had been published and rendered deportation the proclaimed policy of the government (see chap. 11). At the time, Eichmann, too, summoned his representatives from all over Europe to a meeting at which his men reported on the situation regarding *Aktionen* and described the technical problems of assembling the victims and planning railway transportation. This meeting was undoubtedly convened in preparation for the Wannsee Conference and Rudolf Höss, as commandant of Auschwitz, was one of the participants.

The official nature of the Wannsee meeting is evident from the phrasing of personal letters of invitation in which Heydrich cited Göring's official directive of July 31, 1941. He emphasized that the task entrusted to him required "the participation of all the other central agencies." He dwelt on the need for an overall solution to the Jewish problem in Europe and went on to explain that he proposed to hold joint discussions of "all the relevant central agencies on the other activities involved in this final solution." He stressed, in particular, the importance of arriving at a consensus because the transporting of Jews from the Reich and the Protectorate to the East had begun on October 15. Nor did he forget to note in detail other agencies that had been invited to the conference,[26] which, however, did not take place on the original date but was postponed the day after the Japanese attack on Pearl Harbor on December 7 and the subsequent U.S. declaration of war on Japan. The postponement was brief, and the meeting convened on January 20.

One of those invited was the director of Abteilung Deutschland (Deutschland Department) of the Foreign Ministry, Martin Luther, who was the RSHA liaison on Jewish affairs and acted as the counterpart and loyal supporter of Eichmann's department in the RSHA. Luther handed down the invitation to his deputy, Franz Rademacher, with instructions to prepare a memorandum detailing the department's thoughts and wishes on the Jewish question. In eight points, Rademacher proposed the evacuation of all Jews from the Greater Reich, including Croatian, Slovak, and Rumanian Jewish citizens residing within the Reich's borders, it being taken for granted that their governments would agree to the deportation of these nationals. The memorandum also proposed deporting those former German Jews in the occupied countries who had been declared stateless and the Hungarian Jews employed in labor camps. The German authorities, Rademacher continued, should also proclaim their readiness to evacuate the Jews of Rumania, Slovakia, Croatia, Bulgaria, and Hungary. Bulgaria and Hungary should be persuaded to promulgate anti-Jewish legislation and pressure should be brought to bear on all other European governments to pass similar laws. These steps, Luther's deputy stated, should be implemented in close collaboration between Abteilung Deutschland and the RSHA as in the past.[27]

Almost all of those invited were in attendance when the meeting finally convened on January 20, 1942: those present were a representative of Rosenberg's Ministry for the Eastern Occupied Territories; Hans Frank's delegate from the Generalgouvernement; an agent of Göring's Four-Year Plan; the director-generals of the Interior and Justice ministries; Martin Luther representing the Foreign Ministry; Martin Bormann's delegate from the chancellery of the Nazi party; Wilhelm Krizinger from the chancellery of the Reich; numerous representatives of the various branches of the RSHA, including the commanders of Sipo in the Generalgouvernement and in Ostland; and, of course, the head of the Gestapo, Heinrich Müller, and Eichmann.[28]

Thus Heydrich, in charge of implementing the Final Solution, harnessed both the civilian and economic administrations of the occupied territories in which he was about to carry out his mission and the Reich agencies responsible for their citizens from the administrative and legal points of view as well as the Foreign Office, the agency in charge of relations with the satellite governments. All these bodies were expected to approve the uniform methods of action propounded to them and to cooperate with the implementing agency, the RSHA. In this fashion, the Final Solution enabled Himmler and Heydrich to guarantee and extend their influence and authority over the official apparatus. It was by deliberate intent that Heydrich in his keynote opening address emphasized that responsibility for dealing with the final solution of the Jewish question rested with the "Reichsführer-SS and the Head of the German police [namely, Himmler] *irrespective of geographical boundaries*" (emphasis added). Thus, he included the geographical dimension to the demand for ruling authority as reflected in the composition and scope of the list of invitees. There can be no doubt whatsoever as to the ideological motives guiding Himmler, who perceived the liquidation of the Jews as the *conditio sine qua non* for realization of the dream of global supremacy for the Aryan master race.[29] But Heydrich also exploited the Jewish problem as an effective instrument for imposing his authority on Reich apparatus throughout Europe. This interpretation is substantiated by Eichmann's statements at his trial. In answer to the query of his counsel, Robert Servatius, he said that Heydrich's over-ruling consideration in summoning the meeting had been "beyond any doubt, the expansion of his authority and domination." He went on to explain that, previously, the operation had been impeded by bureaucratic red tape "and we never succeeded in achieving a clear-cut solution in one fell swoop." Heydrich achieved his aim and an "atmosphere of general agreement" prevailed.[30]

Heydrich described the evolution of the Jewish problem since the Nazi rise to power and noted the "achievement" of the organized emigration of the Jews from the original German Reich, from the Ostmark (Austria), and from the Protectorate. The number of emigrants had been 537,000, he said, and the Jews had paid a total of U.S. $9.5 million for this emigration. But emigration had since been banned "on account of the dangers of emigration in wartime and the possibilities in the East." Hence, with the führer's approval, there had been a change of policy to "evacuation to the East." And he hinted at the possibilities inherent in this evacuation, "We are already concentrating the practical experiments [the gassings], which are of vital importance in light of the future final solution of the Jewish problem."

He then cited dubious data on the number of Jews living in Europe, arriving at a total of eleven million, including all the neutral countries such as Sweden, Switzerland, Turkey, and Spain. He did not, of course, explain that the number of Jews, particularly in Eastern Europe, had already shrunk considerably. After mentioning "certain difficulties" in countries such as Hungary and Rumania, he announced that the Jews were being evacuated to the East in order to work in labor units that were building roads; "thereby a large proportion will undoubtedly disappear through natural reduction." Those who survived the process of "natural selection" would be dealt with "appropriately" because of the danger that they might constitute the nucleus for Jewish renewal.

In order to complete the mission, "Europe must be combed from west to east"; the Jews of the Reich and the Protectorate were to be dealt with first because of the housing problem and other social needs. In discussing deportation, Heydrich excluded Jews over sixty-five who were to be assigned to a "ghetto for the aged" in Theresienstadt. This ghetto was to serve as a kind of shopwindow. Eichmann even went to the trouble to visit it a day before the conference convened,[31] apparently in order to ensure that it was suited to its allotted function. The Nazis intended to use this camp to silence criticism voiced in Germany itself against the treatment of the old.

Heydrich went on to survey the various countries in which action was to be taken and detailed those in which Foreign Ministry cooperation would be required. In the discussion that followed, Luther claimed that he foresaw no particular difficulties in the countries of western and southeastern Europe but proposed temporary postponement of "more thorough handling" in the northern countries since problems could be anticipated there. This should not be regarded as a significant concession, he said, since only a small number of Jews were involved.[32]

The second half of the conference was devoted to the complex problem of the progeny of mixed marriages, the regime having wrestled with it for many years in order to determine criteria for its resolution, but without success.

At the conclusion of the meeting, Frank's representative, Dr. Josef Bühler, suggested that it was desirable to expedite the implementation of the Final Solution in the Generalgouvernement. Special transportation problems were not to be anticipated there and, in any event, it was advisable to eliminate the Jews as rapidly as possible since they constituted both health and economic hazards. The great majority were, in any case, unfit for work.

From Eichmann's testimony at his trial, we learn that the participants at the Wannsee Conference openly discussed the various methods of killing Jews and did not mince words, referring explicitly to extermination and liquidation.[33] Eichmann claimed that he fulfilled only three functions at the conference: preparing material for Heydrich's speech, sending out the invitations, and writing the minutes.[34] But there can be no doubt that he was a central figure in the implementation of the Final Solution. Although he was subordinate to Müller, he was allotted special powers, and in several instances received his orders directly from Heydrich and even from Himmler himself. We have seen that in the spring of 1941, he began to issue explicit directives on the banning of emigration, citing the preparations for the Final Solution of the Jewish problem. In the context of the official sanctioning of the Final Solution, he was also promoted on November 9, 1941, to the rank of *Obersturmbannführer* (colonel).

One of Eichmann's close associates, Dieter Wisliceny—who played a decisive role in the fate of the Jews of Slovakia, Greece, and Hungary—stated in his postwar testimony, "Eichmann had special powers on behalf of the Head of the Division, Müller, and the Head of the Security Police [i.e., Heydrich]. He was responsible for what was called the solution of the Jewish problem in Germany and all the territories conquered by the Reich."[35]

Wisliceny also claimed that in the summer of 1942 Eichmann had shown him a directive signed by Himmler that ordered the implementation of the Final Solution and that this directive had been composed in April 1942 and had also been dispatched to the controller of concentration camps, Richard Glücks. According to Wisliceny, Eichmann boasted that he was personally responsible for carrying out the order and was well aware that it involved the killing of millions of human beings. Eichmann denied this at his trial and argued that Wisliceny and others had made him their scapegoat.

No such official directive from Himmler was ever found—if it ever existed, it may be assumed that it was destroyed together with other RSHA documents before the collapse of the Third Reich. It seems feasible to assume that in the spring of 1942, when the Final Solution had become, as it were, official policy, Himmler felt the need to make an explicit statement of intent. A few days after the Wannsee Conference, on January 25, 1942, he ordered Glücks to prepare the concentration camps for the absorption of one hundred thousand men and up to fifty thousand women, Jews "who would be evacuated from the Reich" *(die aus Deutschland ausgesiedelt werden)*.[36] They were to be transported to camps as laborers "since we can no longer expect Russian prisoners." He goes on to emphasize that important economic tasks are shortly to be imposed on the concentration camps. It appears that Himmler at that time was endeavoring to extend his powers in the economic sphere, and the concentration camps were to serve this end.[37] The man who was in charge of organizing the camps, Oswald Pohl (Glücks's superior), was also reorganizing his administration at the time. Since 1940 he had wielded control over all the SS concerns in the concentration camps and the labor camps. He was also in charge of the Main Office for Administration and the Economy (Hauptamt Verwaltung und Wirtschaft). On February 1, 1942, he combined all his agencies under the Economic and Administrative Main Office (Wirtschafts-Verwaltungschauptamt, or WVHA).[38]

Thus, Himmler had at his disposal the Waffen SS; the Sipo; the SD; the Gestapo under Heydrich, head of the RSHA; and the economic–administrative sector under Pohl. The destruction of the Jews was an integral and central part of this administrative system, and in the wake of the Wannsee Conference, the central agencies of the civilian administration were now harnessed to the task.

Hitler's Harangues

This was a time of problems, tensions, and even apprehension for the Nazi regime. The campaign against Russia had been stalled before Moscow and Leningrad and the rigors of the Russian winter had inflicted a heavy blow on the unprepared German army. Not only were the troops inadequately clothed but the equipment was unsuited to the harsh climatic conditions; supplies were often cut off because of the collapse of the railway network. The Japanese attack on Pearl Harbor had changed the war situation. After the U.S. declaration of war on Japan, Hitler had no alternative but to declare war on the United States, though he could have been in no doubt as to the dangers that now faced him.[39] On December 11 he convened the Reichstag, as was his wont at fateful moments, particularly in the international arena, and delivered a speech in which he tried to answer various urgent questions while declaring war on the United States.[40]

Analysis of this speech suggests that Hitler felt a strong urge to explain and justify his actions and to bolster the confidence of his followers. As always, he claimed that his only desire was peace and that his enemies had forced war on him. At the same time he proclaimed that "a historical correction of unique proportions has been imposed on us by the Creator,"[41] meaning the salvation of Europe. He described the triumphs of the German army in all the war arenas, but felt the need to cite climatic conditions as the reason for his postponement of the attack on Russia from May to June 1941. He had launched the war, he said, because otherwise the Russians would have attacked first and conquered all of Europe.

Hitler's main verbal onslaught, however, was directed against Roosevelt, whom he described as a slave to the Jewish warmongers, eager to enter the war because of his economic debacles in the United States. He accused the U.S. president of violating international law and of having, in contravention of all concepts of justice and law, restricted the freedom of movement of German nationals living in the United States. In fact, he accused Roosevelt of all those acts of deception and aggression of which he himself was guilty. Thus he spoke of "the deliberate incitement by this man who plays the peace lover and all the time is inciting to war." Roosevelt, Hitler claimed, together with Great Britain, was aiming at "untrammelled dictatorial rule over the world," and to achieve this aim would stop at no crime. The force behind him was the "eternal Jew."[42] According to Hitler's political calculations, the confrontation with the United States was essential, but he certainly had had no intention of launching this battle before he had triumphed over Russia. Now he knew only too well that the Russian *Blitzkrieg* had failed and that for the first time he had not been the initiator of an additional move but had been forced to adopt it as a result of the initiative of others.

Hitler's speech on the anniversary of his rise to power, January 30, 1942, can be seen as the continuation of his diatribe against his adversaries. This time he was not addressing the Reichstag, as was the tradition, but a popular meeting in the largest auditorium in the Berlin Sports Palace. He felt the need to appeal to the people directly in order to instill new spirit in them and strengthen their faith in him and in the future of the Reich. Again, he spoke of "international Jewry" that backed the misdeeds of all his enemies, but the main brunt of his attack this time was leveled at Great Britain. Then he reiterated his well-known interpretation of the history of Germany after World War I, whose collapse was brought about by the "eternal Jew." The greatest catastrophe at the time was class war, which the Jews had encouraged since they "had interests in both camps. On the one hand, they directed capital and, on the other hand, they controlled the anticapitalists. Sometimes, in one family there were two brothers, one in each camp."[43]

His main theme was the war, which had been brought about, so he asserted, by the hatred of others, mainly the British and the Americans. In contrast to the creative projects he had initiated, the leaders of those countries—"the chatterer and drunk, Churchill, and the madman, Roosevelt"—were not capable of creating anything, only of destroying. And since they hated the Germans, the Germans were obliged to hate them in return; and he went straight on to identify this hatred with the hatred of the Jews, "It is evident to us that this war can end only in the elimination of the Aryan peoples or the disappearance of Jewry from Europe." He then repeated his "prophesy" of January 30, 1939:

> This war will not end as the Jews imagine, namely, in the liquidation of all the European and Aryan peoples; the outcome of this war will be the extermination of Jewry. For the first time it will not be other nations who will bleed to death. For the first time we will practice the ancient Jewish law: an eye for an eye, a tooth for a tooth!

The wider the struggle, he said, the more anti-Semitism would speread!

> It will find fertile soil in every prison camp, in every family to whom we explain why, in the end, they must make sacrifices. And this world enemy, the wickedest of all times, will play his role no longer, at least for one thousand years.[44]

Hitler went on to rant and boast, but again felt the need to justify the fact that the attack on Russia had been checked not, he claimed, by the Russians, but by the winter cold. At the end of the speech, he promised that the coming year would again be one of great victories, although he did not promise that it would bring the end of the war.

Hitler delivered this address ten days after the Wannsee Conference. Just as his speech of January 30, 1939, had provided the official sanction for the appointment of Heydrich to run the Emigration Center, he now endorsed the Final Solution as an integral part of his war policies and even set it up as the yardstick for success. Now that new difficulties faced him and new dangers threatened, Hitler attributed great significance to the plan for the extermination of the Jews, as if their destruction would confound his enemies and their death would symbolize his triumph.

Preparation for Full-Scale Extermination

The Wannsee Conference marked the beginning of the full-scale, comprehensive extermination operation and laid the foundations for its organization, which started immediately after the conference ended. According to the plans, the Jews of the Reich were to be deported first, and as noted before, Himmler intended the operation to encompass 150,000 victims. Eichmann immediately set to work. On January 31, 1942, he sent an express letter *(Schnellbrief)* marked "secret" to all the state police stations *(Stapoleitstellen)* in the Greater Reich that opened, "The evacuation of the Jews to the East, recently carried out in several areas, is the beginning of the final solution of the Jewish problem in the original Reich, in Ostmark, and in the Protectorate of Bohemia and Moravia."[45]

He went on to explain that the operation had initially encompassed only isolated places and that only partial operations had been carried out, but now a full-scale operation was in preparation. He, therefore, requested precise data on the location of Jews in the Reich and gave instructions for compiling the data. He also specified which categories were to be excluded from the deportations—Jews who were partners in mixed marriages, foreign nationals, Jews employed in industry working for the war effort, and those over fifty-five who were "*particularly* weak and, hence, cannot be transferred." Also to be excluded were those over sixty-five. The number of people in the various categories, including, of course, those who were to be deported, should be determined. He ordered this information to be submitted within ten days. Next, Eichmann's office sent out "directives for the technical implementation of the evacuation of Jews to the Generalgouvernement."[46] These directives listed the categories already noted in the express letter; in addition, they provided detailed instructions for the organization of the transports that were more or less identical with those familiar to us from the wave of deportations organized in the autumn of 1941. They stressed the need to include all tools and equipment of any kind in the possession of the evacuees.

The instructions were conveyed not only in writing. On March 4, 1942, Eichmann convened all his representatives from the territories outside the Reich in his office to discuss the organizational problems of the deportations.[47] The participants were by now all well versed in the resolutions of the Wannsee Conference. Moreover, at the beginning of January instructions had already been sent in Himmler's name to stop further emigration of former German Jews from the occupied territories. At an additional meeting on March 6, the representatives were shown the plan for the evacuation of 55,000 Jews from the Greater Reich, among them 20,000 from Prague and 18,000 from Vienna. It was again emphasized that aged Jews should not be included in the transports since they were earmarked for dispatch to Theresienstadt. The remaining instructions were identical with those given in the "directives," but special stress was placed on the confiscation of property. The Jews were to be encouraged to make large "contributions" to Account W.[48]

We also learn from the report of this meeting about transportation techniques. It was explained that since the operation was to utilize the trains bringing Russian laborers from the occupied territories to Germany, it was not possible to draw up exact schedules ahead of time. Dates would be reported by telephone to the local police headquarters six days prior to the planned departure, using codes to ensure secrecy. The trains could hold only 700 persons, but since it was necessary to convey 1,000 Jews at a time, freight wagons for the load of luggage and passenger carriages for the escorts should be provided.

These details indicate the scope and systematic nature of the technical planning once the Final Solution entered the decisive stage, which had been developed over an entire year—ever since Eichmann had been appointed director of the department now designated 1V B 4 *(Judenangelegenheiten, Räumungsangelegenheiten)* on March 1, 1941.[49] We have now seen how in the summer of 1941—concomitantly with the killings by the Einsatzgruppen—preparations for the mass murder of the Jews commenced. Toward the end of the summer, the situation of the Jews in the Reich deteriorated greatly and steps were taken to isolate them and to deprive them of their remaining rights. The practical and legal framework for the confiscation of their assets was also formulated. Once the organized "euthanasia" project was shelved, the opportunity arose to use the method and the experience of the trained team for the preparation of gassings in the special extermination camps in occupied Poland. Now, in the spring of 1942, all the instruments were ready and there had been established a general consensus among all government agencies on the implementation of the Final Solution. This wide-scale murderous operation was accorded vital importance, despite the fact that the German army and industry were expected and required to invest tremendous effort to overcome the debacles of the winter and to create new impetus so as to achieve the longed-for victory.

Poland's Jews: From Subjugation to Extermination (1941–1942)

Chełmno: The First Extermination Camp in Operation

The organized and systematic extermination operations in occupied Poland actually commenced before the Wannsee Conference was convened. In July 1941, when the murderous work of the Einsatzgruppen in the newly occupied territories was in full swing, the commanders of the SS in the Poznań district were pondering the question of how to implement the Final Solution and find the most effective method of ridding themselves of the approximately 250,000 Jews left in the districts incorporated in the Reich, 150,000 of them in Łódź. Erich Höppner, after recommending the concentration of all the Jews of the Wartheland in a giant concentration camp, suggested, "Would it not be the most humane solution [!] to liquidate the Jews through some means that operates swiftly, to the extent that it is not possible to allocate them for labor?"[1] It may have been as a result of this proposal, addressed to "dear colleague Eichmann," that the first extermination camp, Chełmno, was established in the Wartheland. It was at about the same time that Rudolf Höss was summoned to Himmler and given the task of preparing a large extermination camp at Auschwitz.

The extermination activities at Chełmno started on December 8, 1941, that is to say, one day before the Wannsee Conference was originally scheduled to begin. Chełmno was a small village about nine miles from the district town of Kolo, to which it was linked by a railway branch line, while a main line and a good road connected Kolo with Łódź. In addition to the advantage of good communications, there was an unoccupied castle on the site and the camp was set up around it and walled in by a high wooden fence. The Jews were transported from the nearby railway station in trucks closed in by canvas. After they were unloaded in the castle courtyard, they were addressed by H. Lange, the commander of the Sonderkommando unit, who explained to them that they were to be sent to work in Germany, but that first they would shower and change their clothes. They were herded into a large hall in the castle, ordered to strip, and even received towels and soap. The Germans then hustled them along a corridor in the cellar where signs pointed the way to the "washroom." At the end of the corridor the people were rammed into a van awaiting them, ninety at a time. The doors were slammed shut, a pipe attached to the exhaust was linked up to an aperture under a wooden grating in the floor of the "washroom," and the engines were started. For several minutes screams, weeping, and supplications were heard—when silence reigned again, the van was driven to the "forest camp," two and a half miles away. After all the gold teeth had been extracted from the corpses by Ukrainians, who also searched for hidden valuables, the Jews were buried in a large pit in a forest clearing. The unloading of the corpses and their burial were done by a Sonderkommando unit of Jews. The operation was repeated some twelve to thirteen times a day. In other words, about one thousand people were murdered daily. During the summer the stench increased and spread to the neighborhood; as a result ovens were brought in, the graves were opened, and the corpses were incinerated. The bones that remained after incineration were ground in a special mill, and the ashes were scattered in the nearby river. If it transpired, when the truck doors were opened, that there were unconscious survivors, the SS men shot them in the nape of the neck. The Jewish Sonderkommando was used for the sorting of garments, for burial, and for cleansing tasks, particularly in the vans before they were sent back to the castle for reloading; between operations these workers were incarcerated in a cellar not far from the place where the Jews were loaded into the vans. After escape attempts were made—several of them successfully—these workers were chained by their legs. One of those who succeeded in making his escape was Michael Bodhalevnik of Kolo.[2]

One day, while laboring in the forest, he found among the dead the corpses of his wife and two children, aged five and seven, "I lay down by the corpse of my wife and pleaded with them to shoot me. One of the SS men came over to me and said, 'This fellow can still work well' [those whose strength failed them were shot]. [He] gave me three blows with his stick and forced me to go on working."[3]

That evening he tried to commit suicide, but his comrades prevented him. It was apparently then that he made the decision, born out of despair, to escape. Bodhalevnik was the central witness at the postwar Chełmno trial.

Kolo was one of the first towns affected by the "cleansing" operation in the Wartheland. Between December 7 and 11, 1941, all the Jews were rounded up and rapidly transported by truck to the extermination camp. They were told that they were being taken to western Poland for agricultural labor and the laying of railway tracks.[4] The Germans operated systematically and emptied the subdistrict within a month. Of the remnants of the Jews in the small towns and villages, all died at Chełmno. The grim reaper did his work in the neighboring Kutno subdistrict as well. In the town of Kutno itself there had been close to 7,000 Jews before the war, of whom there remained in April 1941 only 5,239 local Jews together with 1,365 refugees. By mid-July this number was reduced by close to 600. This mortality rate was also raised by the famine rife in the ghetto. The conditions

within the ghetto were intolerable and there was bitter conflict between the Judenrat and the masses of the poor. As resentment grew, demonstrations took place
and the Judenrat treasurer was attacked. The trucks in which the Jews were to be
transported to Chełmno arrived in March 1942; the Jews refused to board them
at first, but eventually they submitted.[5] Here, too, the operation emcompassed the
entire district.

Łódź

In the same period, the Germans began to weed out the inmates of the Łódź
ghetto. After the Chełmno camp became operative, the Germans demanded, in
December 1941, that Rumkowski select twenty thousand people to be deported
from the ghetto (it was thus that the German authorities responded to the evacuation of twenty thousand Jews from the Reich to Łódź; see chap. 11).
Rumkowski was unaware of the objective of the deportation but tried his best to
avert the decree; he succeeded in reducing the number of deportees to ten thousand, who were deported from the Łódź ghetto between January 16 and 29, 1942.
A committee was set up and charged with the task of choosing the victims. They
selected those designated *unsocial* (asocial)—namely, people who had been tried
for various offenses—together with their families. In addition, the committee
chose those who were supported by welfare agencies. It exempted the gravely sick,
whose fate was decided by a committee of physicians. Also exempted from the
deportation were sick children, residents of old-age homes, community workers,
and rabbis. The assembly point was the ghetto prison. Those who did not report
as ordered were brought in by the Jewish police.[6]

It will be recalled that among those deported from the Reich in October 1941
were 5,000 Gypsies. They were housed in the ghetto in a separate area surrounded
by a barbed wire fence. There they succumbed in the thousands to starvation and
disease. Those who survived were among the first to be sent, in January 1942, to
the death camp.

The liquidation of all the deportees from the Reich was completed only in May
1942 when close to 11,000 of them were transferred to Chełmno. Those who
remained behind in the ghetto were people with regular employment or, as in the
case of the previous deportation, those who were severely ill or inmates of old-age
homes. Also exempt from deportation were interpreters fluent in several languages
and people who had been decorated by the Germans.

On May 1, Artur Greiser, the district commandant, wrote to Himmler, to
inform him that "in the coming two to three months the operation of the special
treatment [*Sonderbehandlung*] of some one hundred thousand Jews, as approved
by you and the Head of the Main Office for Security of the Reich, SS Obergrup-
penfuhrer Heydrich, will be completed in my district."[7]

The main subject of this letter was not the Jews, but the proposal that sufferers
from active tuberculosis, whose number was increasing among the Poles, receive
"special treatment" similar to that accorded the Jews.

In areas in which extermination operations took place in the first few months of 1942, they were accompanied by extensive terror activities. These activities were launched prior to the opening of the extermination installation of Chełmno. In October 1941, some three thousand Jews who had been hiding in the forests in the Kolo subdistrict were murdered. Antismuggling measures were tightened and those caught red-handed were sentenced to death and executed. The same fate also awaited many of the community leaders. The executions were frequently carried out in public. Occasionally, some people succeeded in making their escape. Rumors were rife about the gassings at Chełmno.

On the same day, May 1, 1942, on which Greiser informed Himmler of the prospect that the Wartheland would be "cleansed of Jews," he reissued an ordinance directing that the Łódź Ghetto Administration (Ghettoverwaltung) inherit all property left in the destroyed communities. A contract signed on April 20 had established that all machinery, foreign currency, gold, silver, and valuables were to be handed over to the Ghetto Administration, while buildings, furniture, and food were to be sold on the spot and the money, after deduction of costs, was also to be paid to it.[8] In mid-May, the transports were halted for about one month. In this interval the Gestapo in Łódź prepared a summary report.

In the period from January 16 to June 1942, according to this report, some 55,145 Jews had been transported to Chełmno from Łódź and 15,200 from Łódź district. Together with the victims from the three subdistricts of Koło, Kutno, and Lanica, the number of Jews murdered totaled about 100,000. Thus, within seven months, Greiser had filled the specified quota. By the end of the year the number of victims at Chełmno had reached 145,000.[9] Their clothes, including many furs, filled 370 railroad wagons. The Gestapo went on to explain, "It is necessary to evacuate all the Jews who are incapable of working and to assemble those fit for work from throughout the district in the Litzmannstadt ghetto [Łódź]. . . . During the preparation of the district ghetto, it transpired that there was a need to vacate space [in the ghetto] for those Jews who are to be brought in."[10]

The Extermination Process: Opening Stages in the Eastern Generalgouvernement

Concomitantly with the launching of the implementation of the Final Solution in the Warthegau, extermination operations began at the other end of occupied Poland, in the areas near the eastern border that, before Operation Barbarossa, had separated German from Russian territory.

Lwów

Since eastern Galicia was incorporated in Hans Frank's area of jurisdiction in the Generalgouvernement, the activities of the Einsatzgruppen did not proceed here as in other parts of the Ukraine, though the Jews of Lwów and other towns were, nevertheless, exposed to Ukrainian attacks and German persecution. Whereas during the first days of the occupation, in June and July, heavy fines had been extracted from the Jews, they were now ordered to supply the Germans with goods and equipment on a wide scale. To this end a special *Supply Office* was established, whose employees went from house to house and confiscated the items ordered by the Germans. These items included jewelry and silver, household utensils, expensive furniture, carpets, and so on. This organized robbery was accompanied by individual looting carried out in particular by SS and Gestapo personnel. When they encountered a refusal, they usually did not hesitate to remove the items by force and even to kill.[11]

As elsewhere in the Generalgouvernement, an autonomous Jewish Self-help unit (ŻSS) functioned in Lwów. It established an apparatus that worked parallel to the Social Department of the Judenrat, and tension was generated between the two rival institutions. The need for aid was very great since the living conditions of most of the population were appalling. The allocated food rations were small and of poor quality. Once every two months less than a pound of dark flour, which the Germans called Jewish flour, were doled out. The only salt available was animal salt. Wood and charcoal were sold only in the stores of the Judenrat. Vegetables were not rationed, but the Jews were permitted to visit the market only for two hours in the afternoon when most of the supply had run out. Black market dealings were dangerous and frequently people caught red-handed disappeared without trace. As time passed, the Jews not only spent all their money but bartered clothing as well. Under these circumstances, the face of Jewish society was transformed, as had occurred all over occupied Poland. A privileged class emerged— composed of Judenrat officials, policemen, and community workers—to whom the Germans allocated better rations and housing, thereby fostering their illusion that they enjoyed immunity. In November/December 1941, as was now routine practice, a Jewish "residential area" was established in one of the poorer quarters. The ghetto was not yet sealed, but the Jews now suffered from drastic deterioration in their living conditions.[12]

However, the heaviest blow inflicted on the community was forced labor. The Germans recruited Jews for labor by means of their labor office and, in parallel, the labor registry of the Judenrat allocated Jewish labor *(jüdischer Arbeitseinsatz)*. This registry was adjunct to the municipal labor office.[13] Most of the labor was carried out in the numerous camps set up by the Germans, in which the overseers were mostly Ukrainian auxiliary police. The Jews labored at road building in swamp areas; in winter, in particular, the mortality rate was very high as a result of the arduous twelve-hour working day, disease, starvation, and the blows inflicted by the Ukrainian guards. The first head of the Judenrat, Dr. Parnas, was murdered by the Germans when he refused to provide workers for labor camps. The Jewish police carried out the order in his stead in contravention of his explicit instructions.[14] The commander of the Sipo and the SS in eastern Galicia, Fritz Katzmann, boasted in a report he wrote in the summer of 1943 that he had begun setting up labor camps on the road and that "despite the many obstacles, we set up seven new camps and were able to report the existence of fifteen such camps, in which some twenty thousand Jews labored."[15]

Janowski Camp

The main camp set up for the Jews of Lwów, however, was one of the most noto-rious concentration camps. The Janowski Camp was located in Janowska Street, one of the main thoroughfares leading out of the city. A textile factory under Jew-ish ownership had once stood there and had been confiscated by the Russians; now the SS turned it into a concentration camp.[16] The commandant was Fritz Gebauer. Conditions in the camp were appalling, with inmates jammed into huts with four levels of bunks. The sanitary conditions were also appalling, and the filth bred disease. Food was of very poor quality and people suffered constant hun-ger, but the community's attempts to supply supplementary food were not very successful. To some extent a black market evolved, assisted by Polish and Ukrai-nian prisoners who enjoyed greater freedom of movement than the Jews, who left the camp only en route to death.

The commandants conducted special operations to discover the inmates who were still fit for work and could endure the almost superhuman effort required. The men were forced, after an exhausting day's work, to run through the camp, or else they were left for three days in confinement without food. Those who failed the test were immediately taken outside the camp and shot. The same fate awaited the sick who were unable to hide their condition. The killing was done at the sandy area called the Valley of Death or the Sands, some distance away from the camp, by the method of the Einsatzgruppen. The prisoners were forced to dig their own graves and to lie down in them; then they were shot. At first small groups were brought there, but as time passed it became the site of mass killing, and it is estimated that some two hundred thousand human beings were murdered in the Sands.

In due course workshops were established in the camp and the SS set up one of the German Equipment Plants (Deutsche Ausrüstungswerke, or DAW) that operated in concentration camps; these usually manufactured uniforms. In the Janowski Camp they utilized machinery already in place, left over from the for-mer textile factory. Some Jews, including women, worked in the kitchens or at cleaning, packing, tailoring, and other tasks.

The camp fulfilled an additional function. A separate area served as a concen-tration area for the transports earmarked for extermination at Bełżec. The inmates of the transit camp *(Durchgangslager* or *Du-lag)* were eventually herded into wag-ons that conveyed them to the death camp. An SS officer, Gustav Willhaus, was appointed commandant of this transit camp. He took up the duties at the begin-ning of March 1942 when operations commenced in the extermination camp. He and his deputy, Richard Rokita, an older man, were notorious for their cruelty, as was Gebauer. Rokita had been a violinist, but this did not prevent him from displaying inhuman conduct. The relations between the two senior commandants were very strained and the tension between them usually found outlet in the per-secution of Jewish prisoners. In this camp killing was engaged in for sport and recreation, sometimes carried out by strangling or sometimes by shooting—Jews serving as targets for marksmanship contests. Here, as in many other places, the Jews were forced to play musical accompaniments to the acts of savagery and murder. When a prisoner escaped, ten were executed in retaliation, and any of the escapee's relatives still living in the Lwów ghetto were hanged.[17]

In light of these facts, the situation in the original area of the Generalgouvernement appeared better and, whereas the direction of flight at the beginning of the war had been eastward, there was now a general movement from eastern Galicia westward. It consisted mainly of refugees trying to return to their homes, but they were often accompanied by Lwów Jews.[18]

The Jews of Lwów Face Deportation to Bełżec

Spring 1942 marked the beginning of the execution of Frank's plan that the Jews of the Generalgouvernement would be the first victims of the Final Solution. The deportations to Bełżec commenced in the areas close to the former Russian border. The large-scale deportation from Lublin began on March 17, 1942, but Lwów's turn came a week prior to that, on March 10. By April 1, 1942, the first night of Passover, the *Aktion* had ended, with more than 15,000 Lwów Jews transported to the extermination camp. The Germans ordered the Judenrat to organize the transport, claiming that the deportees were being transferred to new homes in order to alleviate the crowded living conditions in the Jewish quarter.[19] They explained that they intended to evacuate both the asocial elements in the community and the recipients of social welfare. The deportees were given explicit instructions as to what belongings, money, clothing, blankets, and so on could be taken, 110 pounds in all. At the fixed assembly points, a committee composed of representatives of the authorities and of the Judenrat would decide who was to be evacuated and who would be left behind.

The Jewish community leaders were divided on the question of whether to cooperate with the Germans. The head of the Judenrat, Dr. Henryk Landesberg, the third successive holder of the post, apparently thought that by cooperating, the Judenrat could protect part of the population. On German orders, small Jewish units were to round up from their homes those listed for deportation. These units brought in so few prospective deportees that after three days the Germans revoked the order and rounded up the victims themselves. The Judenrat members were widely cautioned by fellow Jews not to collaborate. A deputation of rabbis approached Landesberg and urged him to take no part in the evacuation. In reply, he explained that the Judenrat members were not free to act as they chose and were utterly dependent on the German authorities.[20] The fact that the deportees were dispatched to an extermination camp became known only months later.

However, once this blow had fallen, the Jews deemed that there was some prospect of improvement. After the *Aktion* ended, the Germans distributed to working Jews new identity cards that were intended to protect them against kidnapping. The workers were also given identifying armbands and their families were allocated special cards. This Labor Office protection was extended to 50,000 men and 25,000 women. New industrial undertakings were established, "municipal workshops" set up on the joint initiative of a Jew from Cracow and a German national *(Volksdentscher)*. These workshops, which operated with the approval of the municipality, were also subsidized by the ŻSS. They manufactured haberdashery, luxury items, baskets, brooms, lingerie, hats, paper items, and so on; very soon they employed more than 3,000 Jews. The workers brought with them sewing machines and other equipment. The economic competition between the civil administration, patron of the venture, and the SS eventually caused its ruin. This, however, was not the sole initiative. As in Warsaw, Bialystok, and elsewhere, private German firms became interested in exploiting the cheap available labor. One of these engaged in mending and refashioning articles of clothing supplied by the SS. These were, in fact, the clothes of the Jews murdered by the Einsatzgruppen. After mending, the clothes were sent to charitable institutions in Germany, particularly to the Winter Aid. Some 3,000 Jews were employed by this firm. People usually paid for the privilege of working there.[21]

On March 23, 1942, the chronicler Chaim Kaplan wrote in his diary that the explusions in Lwów were being conducted slowly but steadily. There was no ghetto "because they did not deem it feasible to create one for just a short period."[22] Kaplan was aware of the difference between the situation of the population of the institutionalized Warsaw ghetto, which was battling for survival, and the rapid destructive actions of the Germans in the eastern regions. Moreover, word had arrived of the extermination of the Jews in the Russian areas.

Most of the ghettos in eastern Galicia were set up only in the summer or autumn of 1942, after the Germans had already liquidated part of the Jewish population by employing the Einsatzgruppen methods or in the Bełżec extermination camp.

Lublin and the District

In Eichmann's instructions to the Gestapo on organizing the deportation of Jews, he mentioned locations in the Lublin district as the destination. The gas chambers at Bełżec and apparently also at Sobibor were in preparation by the beginning of 1942. There is no way of knowing why the Germans again chose this area that had once before been selected to absorb deported Jews, but this time it was transformed from a "Reservation" into a liquidation center. In the spring of 1942, the Germans began transporting to it not only Jews from the Reich but also the first transports from other countries—among them Slovakia. Perhaps an even more significant factor than Frank's desire to expedite the Final Solution in the Generalgouvernement was the need to find temporary accommodation for these deportees, and for this reason the Germans began emptying the region itself of Jews. On March 3, 1942, Frank's deputy, Josef Bühler, informed the district governor of Lublin, "Within the framework of the overall solution of the Jewish problem in the European arena, we require the establishment of a transit camp in Lublin for Jews to be evacuated from certain parts of the Reich."[23]

From March 17, 1942, additional directives deal with the way in which these Jewish deportees were to be treated.[24] First, it was deemed necessary to distinguish between those capable of working and those who could not be used for work; the latter were to be sent to Bełżec. Meanwhile, the number of Jews deported from the Reich had increased greatly, and it was asked where sixty thousand Jews could be "unloaded" along the Dęblin–Trawniki railway line. It was added that four to five transports of one thousand Jews each could be accepted daily for the final destination of Bełżec, "These Jews will be transported across the border and will never return to the Generalgouvernement."[25] Special attention was directed to the need to consider "the allocation of labor Jews" *(Einsatz der Arbeitsjuden)* who were not to be evacuated.

A memorandum dated March 20, 1942, reports on "the state of the *Aktion* for resettlement of the Jews" *(Stand der Juden-Umsiedlungsaktion)* carried out so far. For example, "Pjaski: 3,400 Jews out; 2,000 Reich Jews in; 1,000 Reich Jews expected."[26]

The minutes of the Judenrat meeting of March 14, 1942, contain as yet no reference to imminent deportation. The sole indication of what lay ahead was the comment, "With reference to the urgent proposals, Judenrat member Levi asked whether community aid was being extended to refugees now arriving from Czechoslovakia." The reply was that food provisions had been prepared for them. At the next meeting, on March 17, however, it was reported that on that same morning an ordinance on evacuation had been read out to the presidium of the Judenrat, "Only those Jews whose labor cards have been stamped by the Security Police will remain in Lublin with their wives and children. These Jews should be instructed to carry out their tasks conscientiously."

These people were then ordered to move to Ghetto B, the Small Ghetto set up near Lublin. There, additional stringent restrictions were imposed on them. Anyone leaving the ghetto for purposes of smuggling or dissemination of information would be shot. The deportees would be allowed to take one parcel weighing 15 pounds as well as money and valuables. The number of deportees was fixed at fourteen hundred daily. All members of the Judenrat were also ordered on that same day to move to Ghetto B. The memorandum ends with the words, "The Judenrat takes note of the implementation of the above order."[27]

The Judenrat continued to issue announcements in accordance with the German directives. On March 21 it called on all those selected for deportation to report to the assembly point "for their own good." On March 23 it issued an additional directive ordering the Jews now concentrated in Ghetto B to search the cellars, attics, and hiding places to find any Jews in hiding there without Security Police endorsement. Reports on the presence of such Jews were to be submitted to the Judenrat. This order was accompanied by the threat that if any fugitives were found in hiding, all the ghetto population would be deported.[28]

The financial straits of the Judenrat are indicated by the decision to cease payment of salaries to Judenrat members and staff from April 1, 1942. The Judenrat apparently tried to bring about the halting of the deportations by paying bribes to the Gestapo, but three members who handed over the money and valuables that had been collected never returned.[29]

The Judenrat session of March 31, 1942, was attended by SS officers who appointed a new Judenrat only partly composed of members of the previous council. The minutes stated, "The members of the previous Judenrat who have not been included in the Judenrat appointed today will be evacuated with their families and will leave Lublin today with the first transport."[30] There is no way of knowing why this punishment was meted out. Possibly they had not displayed the necessary submissiveness. At the same meeting, the SS commanders announced that the labor card would be replaced by a new document bearing the letter *J*, and that this document alone would guarantee exemption from evacuation. (The tactic of replacing documents has already been noted.) The *Aktion* apparently ended on April 24, 1942. Some four thousand Jews remained in the new ghetto, while more than thirty thousand had been sent to Bełżec.

On April 25, 1942, this information was conveyed by the head of the Judenrat, Dr. Mark Alter, to the presidium of the Social Self-help organization in Cracow. About two weeks later, on May 9, he sent them a letter in which he asked for help in locating the deportees, for whom 10,000 zlotys had been collected. And he adds, "I must admit that I do not understand why the presidium cannot obtain an answer to this question."[31] It is obvious that he never considered the possibility that these people were no longer alive. The presidium does not appear to have answered the question.

On April 17, 1942, Kaplan wrote in his diary, "We trembled when we heard of the Lublin events. Some refugees, risking their lives, fled the town of death and came to the Warsaw ghetto. Their tales freeze the blood in your veins. . . . Jewish Lublin, a city of sages and writers, a place of learning and piousness, is totally and utterly destroyed."

After describing the horrors of the deportations, he adds, "When the hunt began, hordes, hordes, thousands of Jews assembled like silent lambs being conveyed to slaughter. Conveyed—where? No living soul knows the answer."[32]

The Jews of the Generalgouvernement—Caught Between the Extermination Centers to the East and the West

Most of the Generalgouvernement territory lay between the two extermination centers that began to operate in the winter of 1941 and the spring of 1942. Here, too, the situation deteriorated in that period. New ghettos were established, and those that had been open were now sealed. Jews were evacuated from the smaller towns, mostly to the Warsaw ghetto. The Germans imposed stricter control on smuggling and harsher punishments were meted out. At the same time, they now had greater need of laborers since the Generalgouvernement was the hinterland of the conquering army, and a labor force was required for production and for repairs to support the armed forces. Thus, we observe paradoxical manifestations: on the one hand, increasingly stringent restrictions directed against the Jews, who sensed the growing danger, and on the other hand, the development of labor opportunities in factories and workshops.

The Piotrków Trybunalski Illusion

Our discussion of the early years of occupation in Poland depicted the efforts of the Judenrat at Piotrków Trybunalski to preserve Jewish life and to care for the

numerous refugees who reached the town. The Judenrat, headed by Salman Tannenberg, succeeded initially in protecting the community. When the German-
Russian war broke out, the local people were witnesses to the preparations for war
because the trains carrying equipment and troops to the East passed through the
town. Distressing news soon arrived from the East about mass murders of Jews in
the newly occupied areas, and Germans, too, reported that a similar fate awaited
the Jews of the Generalgouvernement. They reiterated the Nazi assertion that the
Jews were to blame for the war, hastening to add, however, that the local Jews
were innocent and "decent Jews." The refugees followed in the wake of the
rumors. They related what they had seen in strict confidence, for fear of the
Gestapo, but they also made it clear that the operations had been carried out by
"experts" and according to a system.[33]

In that same period, the local Jewish community suffered a severe blow. By
chance, during a search conducted on a train, the Germans discovered Bundist
underground newspapers destined for distribution in several towns. The courier
was a Polish woman who also kept a list of addresses, including some in Piotrków.
Thus the Gestapo found out that a Jewish underground movement was operating
in the town and that the heads of the Judenrat were connected with it. The ties
that the Jews had fostered with Germans proved to no avail. On July 5, 1941, the
German police arrested the Judenrat chairman, Tannenberg, and then almost all
of the community leaders. Among those arrested were some people who had never
been members of the Bund. All were cruelly tortured and on September 11 the
prisoners were sent to Auschwitz.

In the spring of 1942, an ordinance was issued closing the ghetto, in which
Poles had also lived till then. The latter were ordered to leave by March 31, 1942,
and on the following day the ghetto was sealed off. At that time, disturbing news
reached Piotrków from both east and west. Two young men from a group that
had succeeded in escaping from Chełmno arrived in Piotrków during Passover;
they revealed the terrible truth that Jews in the thousands were being gassed there.
Most people refused to believe their ears.[34]

Similarly horrifying information also arrived from the Lublin District and
from eastern Galicia, and the Piotrków community sent an emissary there to find
out what had occurred, all too soon learning that the Jews of Lublin had been
"transported" to an unknown destination. Dread gripped the Jews. At an official
discussion of community leaders, attended by the Piotrków rabbi, the gravity of
the situation was exposed. The participants, desperately seeking reassurance,
argued that Lublin was different from Piotrków, and they attributed the catastrophe to Odilo Globocnik, thus trying to comfort themselves with the thought that
nothing like it could happen in the Radom District.[35]

Warsaw

In early spring 1941, several new appointments were made among the personnel
responsible for the Warsaw ghetto. Commissar Waldemar Schön was replaced by
Heinz Auerswald, a lawyer by profession. His assumption of his post in mid-May
was preceded in April by a meeting attended by Frank. The participants empha-

sized, among other things, the need to augment the work force in the ghetto for the benefit of the German authorities. In the same period, the official in charge of the Transfer Authority (Transferstelle) was also replaced by Max Bischof, an economist who had formerly worked in banking in the Generalgouvernement. Bischof acted with great liberality. He wanted to promote and develop industry in the ghetto and did not impede German and Polish firms from conducting business directly with factories and workshops in the ghetto; neither did he institute strict supervision. His policy was anathema to Auerswald, and Adam Czerniakow was also dissatisfied with the fact that economic activity was being conducted outside the aegis of the Judenrat. He maintained close contact with Auerswald, and his diary reveals that he met with him almost daily.[36]

It was apparently the war against Russia that created improved economic opportunities for the Jews. Their work in production and repairs was vital to the army. This situation enabled Ephraim Barash of Bialystok to develop local industry; it also operated to the advantage of the Jews of Warsaw. The total sum of wages paid to the Jews rose between June 1941 and May 1942 from 332,836 to 6,340,000 zlotys. No figures are available on production in the ghetto from 1941 onward, but between January and July 1942 it rose from 3,700,000 to 15,058,558 zlotys.[37] In the course of this year, before the large-scale deportation, the economic situation in the ghetto improved considerably. The rise in production, however, benefited only part of the population and concomitantly this year witnessed a steep decrease in the standard of living of the general population from both economic and health aspects. Auerswald increased the ghetto's isolation from the surrounding world. It is difficult to establish whether this was his own initiative—as the ghetto inmates believed—or whether he was implementing the general policy laid down by Frank. Be that as it may, Auerswald separated from the ghetto area those buildings that bordered on the Aryan side and that had served as transit points for the smuggling of food. The food ration for the nonworking population was reduced. On October 15, 1941, Frank issued an ordinance stating that the death penalty would be imposed on any Jew caught outside the ghetto without permission. This threat was carried out, and a number of Jews, including women, were shot by the Polish police as the Jewish police refused to carry out the sentences of the German court. On that same day, October 15, a meeting was held in Frank's office, at which the problems of the Warsaw ghetto were discussed and one of the participants stated that the ghetto "will constitute a provisional concentration camp until the right time, when it will be possible to remove and rid ourselves of the Jews." Frank rejected a proposal to increase the rations for the Jews.[38] There is no question but that the heads of the Generalgouvernement were fully cognizant of the progress of the Final Solution and awaited further operations.

Throughout the period of the extermination activities, there are two conflicting trends: on the one hand, the administration, particularly the military, was anxious to exploit the Jewish work force. On the other hand, there were those, particularly Himmler's staff, who urged the liquidation of the Jews irrespective of the benefit they might bring to the war effort. These two trends operated simultaneously throughout that year in Warsaw. The ghetto suffered from increasing poverty and a spiraling death rate because of famine and disease, and, at the same time, it enjoyed a kind of economic boom. This contradiction also heightened the social contrast within the population. The streets of the ghetto were filled with peddlars, beggars, and even abandoned corpses covered with newspapers. On the other hand, there were numerous well-stocked cafés and restaurants in which licentious parties were held.[39]

The disease that claimed the largest number of victims was typhus. In 1941 there were 14,661 cases officially registered, but it is estimated that this registration encompassed only 25 to 30 percent of the sick; some sources cite an even larger number of cases. The war against disease was extremely difficult not only because people had been debilitated by hunger and hard labor but also because of the severe lack of drugs. Despite this lack of preventive and curative medicines, the epidemic was checked toward the summer of 1942.[40]

In addition to disease and hunger, the ghetto inmates suffered from the cold. Fuel was available only in very limited quantities and in the winter of 1941/1942 a new decree was inflicted on the Jews of the occupied areas: they were ordered to hand over all their furs. It is well known that when the German army launched its war on Russia it was woefully unequipped for the Russian winter. Hence, the urgent demand for furs, one of the main sources of which was the Jewish population. On December 24, 1941, an edict was issued in the Generalgouvernement that ordered the collection of all furs in the possession of men and women in the ghettos within four days. In Warsaw, Czerniakow was made personally responsible for carrying out this task.[41]

The Jewish Public: The Struggle for Survival Versus Extermination Operations

The year 1941 was indeed a transition time. The Nazi administration developed its Final Solution scheme in this year and prepared the "legal" and organizational foundations for its implementation as well as providing the necessary ideological and political rationale. But the methods of implementation adopted in various regions of occupied Poland and the newly occupied areas were not uniform and were still at the experimental and preparatory stage. The first form of implementation of the overall plan was through the activity of the Einsatzgruppen. After the tremendous impetus of the first wave of extermination, the Jews were herded into provisional ghettos for the preparation of the second wave. It soon became evident that this was not the effective means of total liquidation of the millions of Jews in the East, particularly since it was planned to add to them the Jewish communities of the other countries under German rule or influence. In order to carry out the comprehensive objective, therefore, it was decided to prepare an effective and rapid means of extermination that was not dependent on direct operation by German personnel. The solution was found in poisonous gas fumes. The experience that had been accumulated through the "euthanasia" project was now exploited for the preparation of the extermination sites. Chełmno represents the transition stage from the use of van engines to fixed installations. In the first extermination camps set up and operated in the East—Bełżec, Sobibor, and Treblinka—the vans were completely eliminated, although the diesel engine was again used. At Treblinka, tank engines were also used (see chap. 15).

According to the Germans' psychological planning, the Jews were not to know what awaited them. In addition to the delusive tactics they employed, they also endeavored to isolate the Jews and to disrupt all contacts among Jewish communities. Those ghettos in the Generalgouvernement that were still open were sealed, and the Germans made every effort to liquidate the Jewish communities still scattered in towns and villages. This activity was not carried out to the same extent and with the same degree of thoroughness in all towns and districts. One of the reasons was apparently the need for manpower and, in particular, the army's interest in Jewish labor. The lack of system undoubtedly also stemmed from the conflicting interests and objectives of the various German agencies. The concentration of the Jews may be perceived as a preliminary step toward the transports to the death camps. Sometimes it appeared more convenient not to transport the Jews twice, first to the central ghetto and then to a camp; quite often the Germans preferred to carry out the *Aktionen* on the spot rather than taking the trouble to transport the victims to a death camp. This tendency was particularly evident in eastern Galicia. In many of its towns and villages, slaughter was conducted *in situ* in addition to the transports to Bełżec. At the same time, Judenräte were appointed and the Jews were incarcerated in ghettos. However, these ghettos more closely resembled those in the areas captured from the Russians than the institutionalized ghettos of the Generalgouvernement.

Consequently, the situation of the Jews differed from region to region, and this is true even of various locations within the same region. While whole communities were being liquidated in the Warthegau, Łódź too suffered, but industrial activity there was not disrupted; in fact, it flourished. In Warsaw, into which one hundred thousand Jews from the surrounding area were crammed, industry expanded and permission was even granted for the reopening of schools. Vilna held its own, after a horrific bloodbath, as did Bialystok and Kovno. The situation in Volhynia and eastern Galicia was worse. These discrepancies were not predetermined, but were the outcome of various developments and conflicting aspirations. In retrospect, however, they helped the Germans to foster illusions among the Jews and to prevent the Jews from realizing that their fate was sealed according to a comprehensive scheme. In each ghetto the local Jewish Council fought for the survival of the community, each in its own way, determined by the quality of the leadership and the local conditions.

This was a struggle for life, a struggle to hold fast in the hope that eventually Hitler would be defeated and at least part of the Jewish population would survive until after the war. The Judenräte gradually came to realize that this was not a struggle for survival, but for respite before death. This realization was the inherent tragedy of the Jewish councils.

Most of the Jews of the Warthegau, apart from Łódź, were not allowed respite to grasp what lay in wait for them and what was the end aim of the "resettlement." This was not the case in the areas conquered by the Germans in 1941. There the Jews knew from the outset that the Germans intended to liquidate them. Notwithstanding, Judenräte were established here and ghettos were set up. The process was swifter and crueler than in the Generalgouvernement after 1939, but the predicament of the Jewish councils was essentially the same.

In most towns, the Judenräte were initially composed of members of the intellectual leadership of the community. Sometimes the nucleus was established through Jewish initiative and sometimes by order of the Germans. Some of the traditional leaders refused to undertake this burden, but often they succumbed under pressure, usually from the community. In some places the leadership was composed of people who had not previously been prominent in community life. The approach and activities of the council members, particularly the chairmen, were based on conceptions shaped in the course of previous public experience. They undoubtedly comprehended, on the basis of what they saw around them, how grave the situation really was, but most of them believed it possible to mediate between the conquerers, who wielded authority over Jewish life, and the Jews who had to continue their lives under these conditions. They strove to maintain a kind of compromise between the need to conciliate the authorities and the desire to preserve the community. They had not foreseen that it was impossible to combine the two functions and to act as go-betweens for those who aimed at death and those who strove for life. There were some who reached the breaking point more rapidly than others who were able to trod the tightrope longer. But sooner or later all, in one way or another, faced the moment of truth. In most places, the Judenrat heads and often the members as well were constantly replaced—either because they resigned or because they were removed by the Germans for refusing to obey orders or because they themselves chose death. As time passed the Germans became more skilled at selecting council heads to their taste, those who would carry out the will of their masters in the vain hope that thereby they would save themselves and their families. A striking example is in the town of Stanislawów in the southern part of eastern Galicia, where three Judenrat heads in succession were executed because of their refusal to hand over Jews. The Germans then found a candidate who was willing to carry out their orders.[42] Everywhere bitter debates raged—within the councils, between the council members and the community, and within the community—on whether or not to hand over those earmarked for evacuation.

The basic problems were always the same, but they encountered a variety of responses depending on the local conditions and the character of those involved. Many were convinced that property should be handed over to the Germans in order to satiate their greed and that they should be supplied with the laborers they demanded in order to demonstrate how useful the Jews could be to them. They believed that by meeting these two demands they could save lives but when the Germans demanded lives they should meet with refusal. In Bursztyn, in the Rohatyn district of eastern Galicia, the Judenrat members first consulted with the councils of nearby towns with regard to "contributions"—the fines the Germans imposed on Jewish communities. Later, the second chairman of the Judenrat, Mine Tobias, convened the community in the synagogue and said, "Up till now I was ready to take your assets but, now that they are demanding Jewish lives, I no longer wish to live. I am going to hand myself over to the Germans and let them kill me. I thought that in return for assets I could redeem your lives."[43]

Others decided that they had reached the borderline when they were ordered to provide forced laborers. In many places, particularly in the smaller communities, the heads of the Jewish councils succeeded in preserving the confidence of the public, but the inner logic of the impossible mediating role frequently led the person who bore responsibility to the community to decide on the need to use coercion in order to force the recalcitrant to hand over their property or to report for labor. In some places, however, the crisis point had not yet been reached because the Final Solution had not yet been put into operation.

14

European Jewry Prior to Deportation to the East (1941 to Summer 1942)

The Foreign Ministry Enters the Picture

Once the Wannsee Conference had laid the foundations for the wholesale transportation of the Jews of Europe to the extermination sites that were under construction in occupied Poland, preparations commenced for the implementation of this project. It was a complex operation. In addition to the technical problems entailed in the organized transfer of myriad human beings, it was necessary to take into account local conditions, the nature of the indigenous population, the form of government, and the degree of authority or influence wielded by the Reich representatives. There were fundamental differences between satellite countries and occupied areas. The RSHA—or to be more precise, the staff of Adolph Eichmann's section, IV B 4—could not operate freely, but required the assent and sometimes the cooperation of other agencies such as the army or the Foreign Ministry. The agreements concluded in the spring of 1941 between Reinhard Heydrich and the army command were not applicable to the Western countries such as Holland, Belgium, France, or Norway, and certainly had no validity in the Balkan states, in Finland, or Italy. In each, it was necessary to develop specific instruments that would enable activities to proceed. The prerequisite for these preparations was the support and collaboration of all the agencies operating in those countries on behalf of the Reich, including the Foreign Ministry.

It was not easy for Foreign Minister Joachim von Ribbentrop to hold his own within the Third Reich leadership. Göring, Goebbels, and Himmler were avid to expand their sphere of influence to encompass the occupied and satellite countries. Despite the keen competition, the foreign minister succeeded in introducing his representatives into all the countries, with the exception of the eastern territories, which came under the jurisdiction of Rosenberg's office. Foreign Ministry diplomats were present in all the satellite states with autonomous governments as well as in the occupied countries such as Holland, Belgium, France, Denmark, and even Tunsia.[1] Some of these diplomatic representatives were part of the ministry's traditional cadre from the pre-Nazi period, while most were SA or SS men. The ministry was headed by State Secretary Ernst von Weizsäcker, and within the framework of the wide-spread network of departments, it also dealt with the affairs of the neutral states and even those of enemy countries.

Supervision of matters pertaining to the Jews was one of the central functions of the special German Department, which safeguarded the political interests of the Foreign Ministry, headed at that time by Martin Luther, one of the minister's henchmen. Franz Rademacher was the official in charge of Jewish affairs.[2]

Holland

As noted earlier, a Jewish Council was set up in Holland in early 1941, and the process of isolating the Jews from the general population was intensified (see chap. 6). Additional restrictions were soon introduced: the Jews were ordered to hand over radio sets, and most of those in the liberal professions were prohibited from providing services to non-Jewish clients.[3]

Himmler's representatives in Holland were Hanns A. Rauter, the commissar for Internal Security, and Dr. Wilhelm Harster, the commander of the Sipo. They operated largely independently of Reichskommissar Artur Seyss-Inquart. At the end of August 1941 a special department, Sonderreferat J, was established under Harster's direct command. It was entrusted with the mission of combating Judaism as a whole, with the aim of achieving the final solution of the Jewish question through "the evacuation of all Jews abroad" *(Aussiedlung)*. This department was also empowered to deal with all matters pertaining to Jews including "emigration," property questions, the Jewish Council, and so on. The Central Bureau for Jewish Emigration, as it was officially denoted, was ordered, according to the plan, to prepare the Jews for future evacuation abroad.

The concentration of Jewish property commenced at the same time in accordance with the plan drawn up on May 19, 1941, at a meeting of all the heads of the German administration in Holland and the Sipo personnel. At this gathering "Seyss-Inquart declared that he agreed in principle to the concentration of Jewish capital to be placed at the disposal of the financing of the final solution." The detailed planning of the operation was carried out by Dr. Hans Fischböck, the expert who had already organized the looting of Jewish property in Austria and recommended to Göring adoption of these methods at the meeting after Kristallnacht (see chap. 4). This suggests that in May 1941 it was already evident to all those involved that the Jews of Holland must vanish from the country. Their destination was not yet stated.[4]

Implementation commenced on September 15, 1941, when a decree was issued instructing Jews to transfer all sums of 1,000 gulden or more in cash to the Lippmann-Rosenthal Bank, which had formerly been under Jewish ownership and was now under German control.[5] Bonds were to be deposited separately; a second directive expropriated all Jewish real estate. Jews were also banned from appearing in public places, including shops and places of entertainment. They were allowed to change domicile only by special permit. Internal directives, regulating the relations among the various German agencies, stated explicitly that the Jewish Council was the agency for transmitting the orders of the relevant German authorities.

Immediately after the Wannsee Conference, Harster promoted his department to the supreme authority dealing with Jewish affairs and changed its name to IV B 4. He defined its task as preparing for the Final Solution; channeling people *(Durchschleusung)* through the Central Bureau for Jewish Emigration; taking action for resettlement *(Umsiedlungsaktionen);* managing the Westerbork transit camp; and preparing for evacuation abroad.[6]

Already in January 1941, a special expert in population statistics had been charged with the precise registration of the Jews of Holland. The data showed that in Holland there were 140,000 "full Jews," 14,500 "half-Jews," and almost 6,000 "quarter-Jews."[7] At the beginning of the winter, the heads of the Jewish Council carried out German instructions by recruiting dozens of typists to copy the files of Jews collected in the Central Bureau of Statistics in The Hague. Thus, an accurate and detailed index file of all the Jews of Holland was compiled.[8]

In January 1942 the concentration of the Jews in camps commenced. This was done under the guise of mobilizing Jews for labor camps, thus paralleling the recruitment of Dutch unemployed.[9] Some half a dozen such camps were established in various parts of the country. In March the Nuremberg Laws were promulgated, and marriages between Jews and non-Jews were prohibited—probably because they were increasing; however, the trend continued despite the ban.

Meanwhile, Eichmann's office had begun the overall planning of the deportation of the Jews from Holland, Belgium, and France. At the end of April and the beginning of May 1942, the Jews of these countries were ordered to wear the yellow badge. In Holland Harster personally issued the order to the heads of the Judenrat, Abraham Asscher and David Cohen. In his report he noted that the two men were stunned and struck dumb, "for apparently they had not taken such a step into account." They tried vainly to protest against the directive, but the yellow badges were eventually distributed by the Jewish Council.[10]

The year 1941 had been devoted to the systematic undermining of the situation of the Jews. Activities were patterned on the system primarily devised in Germany and then applied intensively and swiftly in Austria and the Protectorate. The differences between these measures and the process adopted in Holland, however, lay not solely in the streamlining of techniques and the rapidity of implementation—there was a fundamental difference: in Holland the final objective was evident from the outset and this time there were no provisional experiments such as improvised deportations or impractical schemes such as the trial to establish the Lublin Reserve or the Madagascar Plan. While the German authorities in Holland were impoverishing the Jews, undermining their civil status, and isolating them, tens of thousands of Jews were being murdered in the occupied areas in the East by the Einsatzgruppen, while in Poland the death camps—where the Polish Jews and those of the rest of Europe were to be exterminated—were already under construction. It is unlikely that the new rulers of Holland, all SS officers, were unaware of the end aim of the preparatory measures they were implementing.

France

Initially, Eichmann's representatives in France were not granted as free a hand as in Holland, since supreme authority was vested in the military commander, General Otto von Stülpenagel. The German ambassador, Otto Abetz, also wielded considerable authority, Hitler granted the latter wide-ranging powers in the sphere of political relations, and he was allotted the task of coordinating German policy with Henri-Philippe Pétain's Vichy government, which remained the source of constitutional authority for all of France. The Germans' aspiration to work with the Vichy government and to exert influence indirectly obliged them to carry out anti-Jewish measures through Vichy or with its concurrence. In accordance with this political setup, the Pétain government promulgated dozens of laws and regulations relating to the Jews, whereas the military authorities issued only a few. Therefore, Eichmann's henchmen—the head of the Sipo in France and Belgium, Helmut Knochen, and the RSHA official in charge of Jewish affairs, Theodor Dannecker—did not succeed in establishing in France a Central Bureau for Jewish Emigration along the lines of the institutions in the Reich and in Holland. They were obliged to operate through a French institution that was expected to do the work for them.[11]

It was against this background that the General Commissariat for Jewish Affairs (Commissariat Général aux Questions Juives) was set up on March 29, 1941. Its establishment was preceded by protracted discussions between the German agencies and the Vichy government. The Pétain government was willing to organize a central body to deal with Jewish problems according to the wishes of the German military authorities because it feared that Aryanization activities by the Germans in the north would prevent it from seizing confiscated Jewish property. In disregard of various German suggestions, Xavier Vallat was appointed commissar on April 3, 1941. He had won a reputation as a French nationalist and anti-Semitic propagandist but, at the same time, he was not an anti-Semite of the Nazi ilk and did not advocate a final solution. His views were in line with those of the conservative Vichy rulers, who wanted to discriminate against the Jews and to dispossess them, but not kill them. Vallat was aiming first against the "foreign" Jews, the tens of thousands of Jewish refugees who had found refuge in France.

The establishment of the commissariat was made possible by the changes in the Vichy government, namely, the appointment of Admiral François Darlan as deputy president and premier. In discussions between Darlan and Ambassador Abetz on March 5, 1941, they agreed on the setting up of the new body. Darlan stressed the reservations of Pétain, who insisted that French Jews, particularly those who had served in World War I, should not be harmed. Abetz, on the other hand, perceived the establishment of the commissariat as an opportunity "to wield German influence in such fashion that the unoccupied area will be forced to join in the measures being employed."[12]

Of the three German agencies that dealt with Jewish affairs—the military administration, the ambassador, and the RSHA personnel—Eichmann's representative, Dannecker, was the most active. He focused his efforts on four targets, with the aim of preparing the ground for the Final Solution. On his own evidence, he acted *auf kaltem Wege* (in a cold way), in other words, without using violence or terror.[13]

The first objective was to conduct a census of the Jews. In the occupied zone, the initial directive ordering a census was issued on September 27, 1940, and was implemented, in the main, by the Paris police. As a first step toward depriving the Jews of their civil rights, their French identity cards were confiscated. On June 2, 1941, Vichy adopted the same measure and a census was conducted in the south of France as well.

The second objective was the undermining of the economic standing of the Jewish community by cutting off all sources of livelihood and ejecting Jews from all state institutions. On July 22, 1941, Vichy promulgated a law that directed the registration of Jewish businesses and appointed "provisional directors" in both zones. The Jewish situation was further worsened by various professional restrictions.[14]

The third objective was the concentration of the Jews. As it was not possible to close them up in ghettos as in Eastern Europe, decrees were issued, reminiscent of ghetto ordinances, that ordered nighttime curfews for Jews and that prohibited a change of domicile (February 2, 1941).

From the outset Dannecker aimed at solving the problem of the segmentation of the Jewish population by amalgamating their organizations. This, according to his conception, would facilitate achievement of the fourth objective—the establishment of a Judenrat. The heads of the Consistoire, however, refused to accede to his demands, citing French law in their support. Only in January 1941 did he succeed in inaugurating the Coordinating Committee for Jewish Charities in Paris, which amalgamated several French Jewish charitable organizations.[15] After setting up the commissariat and the enactment of Vichy's stringent laws, the Germans submitted to Vallat in August 1941 the demand for the establishment of a central Jewish institution with jurisdiction in both zones. The Vichy government was wary of this new demand, but finally acquiesced when Stülpenagel threatened at the end of September 1941 that the military administration would issue the directive itself if Vichy did not do so within one month. Concomitantly with the protracted negotiations between the Pétain government and the German authorities, conducted through Vallat, the commissar began to negotiate with the Jews to guarantee their cooperation in the scheme.[16]

Most of the Jewish organizations in the south were amalgamated within the framework of the Central Commission of the Jewish Aid Organizations, but almost all of them were relatively autonomous. The Central Consistoire had not joined this commission. Between October and December 1941, these organizations repeatedly debated the demand of the French authorities that they collaborate in the creation of a central Jewish organization. Despite the negative resolutions, several of the organization heads began to respond to Vallat's exhortations and to negotiate with him.[17]

Finally, all of them faced the choice between accepting the mandate and undertaking responsibility for the Jewish community vis-à-vis the authorities or of being subordinated to an institution whose leaders would be appointed by the authorities. In light of this dilemma, most decided to acquiesce but several refused, including Marc Yarblum, the leader of the Poalei Zion party in France and head of the Federation of the Jewish Societies of France. The Consistoire, led by Jacques Helbronner—a distinguished lawyer who before the war had been honorary president of the Conseil d'État (the corresponding position to that of Lodwijk Visser in Holland)—succeeded in maintaining the independence of its institutions and activities. On November 29, 1941, a law was enacted setting up the Union Générale des Israélites en France (UGIF).

This organization operated from two separate centers, one in the occupied zone in Paris, the other in the unoccupied zone. The nine-member board was officially set up only on January 8, 1942, since the negotiations on its form and composition lasted throughout December, accompanied by the repeated protests and reservations of the Jews. The first president in the south was Albert Levi, and the chief director was Dr. Raymond-Raoul Lambert, who had conducted most of the negotiations.[18] The head of the organization in the north, with the title of deputy president, was André Baur, and the director was Marcel Stora. In the north, an individual was coopted to the board who aroused considerable apprehension. Dannecker had brought two Jews from Vienna and appointed them advisers to the Coordinating Committee. One of them, Israelowicz, was now attached to the UGIF in the occupied zone and served there as liaison officer to the German authorities.

Simultaneously with the establishment of the UGIF, the authorities proclaimed the abolition of all the Jewish organizations that had been active until then in France. These organizations, however, were not disbanded; they were, instead, incorporated as departments within the new umbrella organization and, thus, they continued to function, each in its own sphere. Many were able to operate clandestinely and evade official supervision. This method was particularly successful in the south and, with time, especially during the period of deportations, it developed into effective underground operations. On the other hand, the UGIF, notably in the north, was forced to accept the dictates of the authorities and to undertake tasks that were part of the deportation and extermination scheme. The organization chiefly concerned itself with the welfare of the detainees in concentration camps.

The situation had deteriorated in the summer of 1941 when the Germans ceased employing what Dannecker had called "cold" methods. In May the first roundup of foreign Jews took place. Thousands of Polish Jews were summoned on administrative pretexts to the French police, and the 3,710 who responded to the summons were arrested. They were detained in two camps, Pithiviers and Bon-la-Rolande, but hundreds succeeded in making their escape. This first *Aktion* roused ferment, and thousands of the wives of the detainees assembled at the offices of the Coordinating Committee to demand the return of their husbands. The demonstration was eventually dispersed by the police. On August 20, 1941, an additional 3,477 foreign Jews were arrested on trumped-up political charges.

They were taken to the Drancy camp, which then became the main transit camp for the deportation of Jews from France to Auschwitz.[19]

In December 1941, some two weeks after the UGIF was set up, the military commander, Otto von Stülpenagel, exploited the attempted assassination of a German officer in Paris to step up anti-Jewish measures. He requested permission to shoot some 100 hostages, to impose a fine of Fr 1 billion on the Jews and to deport 1,000 Jews to the East. Permission for these actions was granted by Hitler,[20] and on December 12, 1941, 743 Jews were arrested in Paris and incarcerated in Compiègne. On December 15, 95 hostages—"Jews, Communists, and anarchists," including 53 Jews—were executed at the Mont Valérien prison (despite the protests of the Vichy government).[21] The UGIF was ordered to collect the fine.

The deportation did not take place at once because there were severe transportation difficulties. But at the meeting Eichmann convened with his representatives on March 4, 1942, to plan the implementation of the Wannsee Conference resolutions (see chap. 12), Dannecker raised the demand that 5,000 Jews be deported from France immediately. This was the first time that an organized deportation of Jews from the Western countries to Auschwitz was planned. Eichmann approached the matter with caution. On March 9, 1942, he informed his colleague, Rademacher at the Foreign Ministry, of the intention to deport 1,000 Jews from France to the detention camp at Auschwitz on March 23, 1942, and asked to be informed if the ministry had any reservations on this action. A correspondence ensued; eventually, Eichmann raised the quota by another 5,000 Jews. The Paris Embassy's reply that there were "no reservations" was conveyed by Rademacher to Eichmann on March 20.[22] The first train left on March 27, with 1,012 Jews aboard, half from Compiègne and half from Drancy. The 5,000 additional Jews earmarked for deportation were sent in five batches: one at the end of April, four during June.[23]

This initial success encouraged the heads of the RSHA and they began to prepare for mass deportations from the West. The supreme commander of the SS and the police in northern France and Belgium, Karl A. Oberg, regarded Xavier Vallat as an impediment.[24] Hence, Vallat was dismissed at the end of April and was replaced by Louis Darquiers de Pellepoix, a racist anti-Semite, one of the German administration's original candidates for the position.[25] On May 5, 1942, Heydrich visited Paris and agreed with the head of the French police on the deportation of stateless Jews, those detained in Drancy to be dispatched first. As an essential measure preceding the deportations, a decree issued on May 29, 1942, ordered the Jews to wear the yellow badge, stipulating that it was to be worn by the Jews of the Reich and by French, Polish, Dutch, Belgian, Croatian, Slovakian, and Rumanian Jews.[26] This list encompassed nationals of those countries that did not oppose the deportation of their nationals from France to Auschwitz (seen in this chapter). The measure encountered opposition on the part of Jews and non-Jews, and the German authorities began to arrest and punish Frenchmen who displayed various badges or distinguishing marks, sometimes deliberately ridiculous, in order to protest against anti-Jewish discrimination.[27] After all these preparations, it remained only to arrest the Jews in their thousands and to organize railway transportation.

At the first press conference that Vallat convened on April 6, 1941, he asserted that, in his opinion, there was no special Jewish problem in North Africa.[28] Notwithstanding, the restrictions against Jews in Algeria were tightened in the summer of 1941. Children, in particular, were affected, since they were almost totally excluded from elementary and secondary schools. On July 1 an order was promulgated rescinding the law that had previously banned racist propaganda; this was followed by a second directive ordering a census of the Jews. On August 14 yet another ordinance established a General Association of the Jews of Algeria, patterned on the UGIF in France. This organization never became operative because of the opposition of the Jews, many of whom were very active in the underground movement and became especially effective during the occupation of Algeria by the Allies in November 1942.

Belgium

Preparatory operations were also conducted in 1941 in Belgium. The first statutes regulating the Aryanization of Jewish businesses were issued in March 1941. The economic scope involved was much smaller than in Holland and France. The total number of businesses owned or controlled by Jews was 7,729, of which 6,388 were liquidated, and only 600 were Aryanized. Together with the securities and bank accounts that were expropriated, the Germans seized capital worth BΓ 600 million.[29] They displayed particular interest in diamonds; thus in early 1942 they liquidated all diamond concerns owned by Jews. The Germans complained that the Belgian authorities were carrying out anti-Jewish measures reluctantly and in slipshod fashion. According to the official census, 43,000 Jews were registered, only 4,000 of them Belgian nationals. It is not clear how many Jews succeeded in evading the census.[30]

On November 25, 1941, while the UGIF was being established in France, the establishment of an Association of the Jews in Belgium (AJB) was also proclaimed. In the first clause, the directive defined who would be considered a Jew,[31] and special bans were placed on mixed marriages. Supervision of the association was assigned to the Belgian Ministry of the Interior and Health, but all regulations passed by the latter required the endorsement of the military administration. The association was empowered to collect taxes and was also accorded legal status, whereas financial responsibility was assigned to the Belgian state. In contrast to France, the various Jewish organizations in Belgium were not disbanded, but were granted permission to join the association.

In Belgium, the German authorities encountered problems when, on May 27, 1942—simultaneously with France—they issued the decree ordering the yellow badge to be worn by all the Jews. The distribution of the badges was to be carried out by AJB and the local authorities. But, with the exception of the municipality of Antwerp, all refused to carry out the job. The chairman of the Council of Mayors of Greater Brussels informed the military administration by letter on June 5, 1942, that they were unable to be partners in any act that so greatly injured the self-respect of human beings.[32] The Germans had no choice but to deal with the matter themselves. These circumstances undoubtedly helped a large number of Jews to go into hiding and remain inaccessible to the Germans.

Rumania

The story of Rumania during the German-Russian war is a unique chapter in the annals of the war in general and in the history of the Jews of the region. The Rumanian army took an active part in the German offensive against the southern areas of Russia. The German advance was rapid, and Northern Bucovina and Bessarabia were captured first. From there the armies continued their advance into Transnistria, waging fierce battles along the way. They crossed the Bug and continued on to the Dnieper. Odessa fell later, on October 10, 1941. In all the areas conquered by the German and Rumanian armies, massacres of Jews were conducted by the German and Rumanian troops and by the Einsatzgruppen from Unit D, commanded by Otto Ohlendorf.

The number of Jews in Transnistria was then estimated at 300,000, with the largest concentration in Odessa, where the 180,000 Jews constituted close to 30 percent of the town's population. The siege of Odessa was lengthy, and in its course some 80,000 to 90,000 Jews succeeded in making their escape by sea. Those who remained suffered a grim fate. Several days after the occupation, an explosion rocked the Rumanian army headquarters in the town (it will be recalled that a similar event had occurred in Kiev), and in retaliation, the ruler of Rumania, Ion Antonescu, ordered the execution of 200 "Communists" for every Rumanian officer killed, and 100 for each soldier. Most of the victims were Jews, 35,000 of whom were executed by cruel and barbarous methods. An additional 5,000 Jews were arrested and deported to concentration and death camps in Southern Transnistria, in which 70,000 other Jews, formerly residents of the area, had been detained. Almost all of them were killed in the winter of 1941 by the Germans, the Rumanians, and the Ukrainian auxiliary police. The SS units, recruited from the German residents of the region, also took an active part in the slaughter. The deportations continued throughout the winter, and on February 23, 1942, Odessa was proclaimed "cleansed of Jews."[33]

The situation in the traditional Rumanian territories (the Regat) had long-since deteriorated.[34] Already in the spring of 1941, as the German army began to move through the Balkan states, persecution of Rumanian Jews was rife. In January 1941 Antonescu had suppressed the uprising of the Iron Guard with the aid of the army, and from then on the Germans, who had supported his struggle, wielded greater influence in Rumania. There were scattered pogroms against the Jews, but most of the activity was conducted through legislation. They were deprived of voting rights and most other laws and decrees were aimed at confiscating their property and restricting their occupational activity. A special law enabled the seizing of Jewish homes and, as time passed, 40,758 homes worth a total of L 60 billion were expropriated.[35] A directive was issued establishing ghettos in Bucharest and several provincial towns, but it was never promulgated thanks to the activity of the Jewish leadership. In April clerical workers and wage earners were banned from entering into mixed marriages, and in May obligatory forced labor for all Jews between the ages of sixteen and sixty was instituted. After the outbreak of the war between Germany and Russia, pogroms by Rumanians and Germans became frequent occurrences. One of the gravest cases occurred at the end of June in Iași (Jassy). The Jews were charged with signaling to Russian aircraft and thereby abetting the bombing of the city. This was one of the anti-Semitic myths that were prevalent at the time in Rumania (and elsewhere as well). It was a deliberate attempt to cast responsibility on the Jews for the heavy destruction that the war had inflicted in the provincial towns. Jews were arrested in their thousands. Some were shot on the spot and others were dispatched by the so-called death train. En route both Rumanians and Jews were forbidden to supply the passengers with food and water. Of the close to twenty-five hundred who were loaded onto this train, more than fourteen hundred died en route—and fewer than one thousand returned to Iași.[36]

The Rumanians soon began evacuating Jews, and German influence was clearly evident in their operations. Immediately after the outbreak of war, a directive was issued ordering the concentration of all Jewish males from Moldavia and Bucovina aged sixteen to sixty in the Târgu-Jiu concentration camp; women, children, and the elderly were transferred to district capitals. The evacuation operations spread westward and even reached southern Transylvania. A total of 50,000 Jews were deported. Constance, on the shores of the Black Sea, and Ploiești, in the oil field region, were emptied of Jews. Night curfews were introduced, and community leaders were seized as hostages.

On August 30, 1941, an agreement on the administration of the territory between the Dniester and the Bug rivers was signed between the Germans and the Rumanians at Tighina (Bendery, USSR) in Bessarabia. In accordance with Hitler's own decision, however, it was agreed in early September that the northern region, Moghilev district, would be attached to Rumania as compensation for previous territorial losses. In September most of the Jews of Bessarabia, Bucovina, and even the Dorohoi district were evacuated to Transnistria and in the course of two months close to 120,000 Jews were deported. The victims were transported in cattle trucks to a site close to the Dniester and from there were force-marched in convoys to the other side of the river. Many perished en route—sometimes mothers carried the corpses of their children for days until they reached a Jewish cemetery and agreed to their burial.[37]

The association of Jewish communities, headed by Dr. Wilhelm Fildermann, made every effort to bring a halt to the deportations. But despite Antonescu's apparent willingness to discontinue them, they lasted until November. When they ended, there were some three hundred thousand Jews in Transnistria. They were detained in various camps—forced-labor camps, punitive camps, and detention camps for political prisoners. The Jews were also dispersed in dozens of towns and villages where they lived in ghettos of a kind. They suffered severely from hunger, disease, forced labor, and the brutality of the Rumanians and the Germans. Occasionally, individual officers or units displayed a humane attitude and even proffered assistance, but it was mainly Rumanian Jews who came to the aid of their brethren. At the beginning of the winter of 1941, they were permitted to organize aid for the deportees, and sent them clothing, drugs, and money. The funding was raised among prosperous Jews in Rumania and, in the main, from JDC.

The Tighina Treaty stipulated that the Jews in Transnistria should not be deported to the Ukrainian territories beyond the Bug and Dnieper rivers. Notwithstanding, the Rumanians tried to drive the Jews across the Bug into the area of operations of the Einsatzgruppen. This activity was not to the liking of the German authorities and, in a sharply worded letter, Eichmann demanded that the Rumanian government be prevailed on at once to cease the "illegal" dispatch of Jews. He expected the Rumanian government to accede to the demand "unconditionally," but in order to ensure this, he threatened that otherwise measures would be taken by the Sipo.[35]

Here, we discern the limits of the influence of the German advisors, felt in Rumania from the spring of 1941. The two main advisors were the German minister, Manfred von Killinger, and his specialist on Jewish affairs (Eichmann's representative), Gustav Richter. It was under their influence that a regulation was issued on September 3, 1941, ordering Jews to wear the yellow badge. However, the efforts of Dr. Fildermann and Chief Rabbi Dr. Alexander Shafran bore fruit, and Antonescu withdrew the order on September 8, just as he had previously suspended the construction of ghettos. In several areas where the Germans were particularly influential, Jews were forced to wear the yellow badge. In November the Rumanians appointed their own official in charge of Jewish affairs, Radu Lecca. Together with Richter, he drafted anti-Jewish legislation in line with Nazi policy that ordered a census of the Jews and abolished the federation of Jewish communities. The authorities accepted these proposals, and in January 1942 they replaced the federation by the Center for Rumanian Jews, to be supervised by Lecca on behalf of the Rumanian government.

The members of the center, who were appointed by the government, were not deemed trustworthy by the Jewish public. The main task of the center was to extract funds from the Jews, monies which Lecca transferred to the Rumanians and the Germans. The community leaders continued to operate illegally at the same time maintaining contact with Antonescu and other members of the government with whom they had old, established ties. Eventually, several of the heads of the former federation as well as several Zionists were added to the center. There was a constant hidden conflict between Lecca's henchmen and the unofficial Jewish leadership. Community representatives infiltrated the center in the capacity of clerical workers and tried to foil the schemes of the authorities from within. For example, when a census of the Jews was proclaimed in January 1942, they ensured that it was never completed; again, in contravention of regulations, they prevented the distribution of special ration cards to Jews, thus making it possible for Jews to obtain normal supplies of food.

Community mutual-aid activities continued. They were particularly effective in the provincial capitals where organized efforts were directed at helping Jews who had been expelled from villages and provincial towns. The center did not intervene in these operations: the reverse was true; it endorsed community autonomy. The main efforts were conducted by the Aid Committee, headed by Dr. Fildermann. Helping evacuees was only part of his activity. In his desperate attempts to prevent the deportations, he sought all possible spheres of influence and he and his colleagues gained access to the queen mother and the leaders of the church. Prominent Rumanians, including the queen, approached the Germans on behalf of the Jews, but their intercession was haughtily rejected. Nor were diplomats from neutral countries more successful when they tried to persuade their governments to act and to sway the U.S. ambassador to bring influence to bear on his government. The ambassador sent detailed reports to Washington about the Jews' situation, but his forecast was gloomy, "The program of systematic extermination is continuing nonetheless [in spite of Rumanian denials] and I see little hope for the Rumanian Jews as long as the present German-controlled regime continues in power."[39]

It is not easy to understand the situation in Rumania, and even more difficult to assess it accurately because it was marked by ambiguity: the Rumanians, known for their anti-Semitism, had been persecuting the Jews since they arrived in large numbers from Russia in the nineteenth century; they treated their Jewish inhabitants brutally, killing, looting, humiliating, and expelling them. At the same time, the leaders of the Jewish community succeeded in maintaining relations with the heads of state and though they could not prevent drastic measures, they did succeed in limiting and mitigating them. On the one hand, every last ley was squeezed out of the Jews; on the other hand, astute Jewish officials succeeded in impeding the census of the Jews and in guaranteeing food supplies for the Jewish population (it is interesting to note that here, in contrast to German methods, it was considered a privilege *not* to receive a ration card). Antonescu openly took part in anti-Semitic incitement and accused the Jews both of hostile acts toward the retreating Rumanian army after the Russians captured Bucovina and Bessarabia and of inciting the Soviet army to acts of terror against Rumanians. He was thereby ostensibly providing justification for Rumanian revenge on the Jews. Conversely, the very same Antonescu promised to halt the deportations, cancel the yellow badge regulation, and, as a result of the intercession of his personal physician, even rescinded several deportation orders. These were unique occurrences, unparalleled in either occupied or satellite countries.

The impression is gained that in Rumania—more than in other spheres of German influence—the traditional form of anti-Semitism reigned; and although unbridled persecution was the norm, it was not characterized by the systematic purposefulness that the Germans succeeded in introducing in those countries that they controlled totally. The traditional Jewish means of self-protection such as bribery, intercession, evasion, and mutual aid proved relatively effective, particularly since the Jews had been accustomed to this form of struggle for decades. The Germans apparently failed to comprehend the underlying factors of Rumanian conduct. They interpreted the reactions of the Rumanians according to their own preconceptions and were not attuned to the ambiguities involved. The Rumanians, for their part, were undoubtedly resentful of Killinger's discourteous response to the queen mother when she tried to intercede on behalf of the Jews.

It should be recalled that the Rumanians had suffered a bitter blow before the war when the Germans forced them to cede territories to their neighbors. They were now seeking any available opportunity to demonstrate independence of action. The Jews served this end: sometimes they deported them against the wishes of the Germans; sometimes they failed to carry out anti-Jewish instructions handed down by the Germans. Richter, Eichmann's representative, claimed in April 1942 in a Bucharest daily that no European country could now refrain from the solution of the Jewish problem because "this problem has ceased to be an internal problem of the various countries." The Rumanians, for their part, chose to regard it as their own particular problem and to take their own decisions—for better or worse. Just as the Germans exploited the Jews to bolster their rule in other countries, so the Rumanians employed the Jews to demonstrate their own independence.

Hungary

Although Hungary retained a greater degree of independence than most of the Balkan states, tension increased there as the war progressed. In the year of German victories in Western Europe, at the beginning of the summer of 1940, the Hungarians prepared to go to battle in order to recapture northern Transylvania, which they had been forced to hand over to Rumania after World War I. At the end of May 1940, mobilization was proclaimed; at that time, Jews were still being recruited into the army, but according to a 1939 law, all those who were unfit or ineligible for military service were obliged to serve in labor units. This category included not only Jews but also those considered enemy nationals: Serbs, Slovaks, Ruthenians, and even Gypsies. The Hungarians had previously introduced draconian anti-Jewish legislation and now, in 1941, they mobilized into the labor units not only Jews aged twenty-five to forty-eight—as in the case of other minorities—but all Jews up to the age of sixty, ostensibly in order to prevent subversive activity on the home front. Thus, 260 labor units were set up in which 52,000 Jews served. Living and labor conditions were appalling, although the regime was still relatively liberal.[40]

The Hungarian army first saw action in Hitler's Balkan campaign in the spring of 1941. During the occupation of Novi Sad in Yugoslavia, the Hungarians murdered thirty-three hundred citizens, including one thousand Jews (see chap. 18). When Hungary joined the German offensive against Russia on June 27, 1941, the labor units were attached to the armed forces as auxiliaries. The conduct of the Hungarian troops was marked by certain contradictions. As noted earlier, the Hungarians acted decently toward the Jews in several occupied towns in eastern Galicia, and even protected them (see chap. 10). In contrast, in that very same period the Hungarian authorities deported some twenty thousand Jews without Hungarian nationality. They had reached Hungary as refugees or lived there for lengthy periods. On the pretext that they had originally come from Galicia, these Jews were deported to eastern Galicia, which was officially claimed to be controlled by the Hungarian army; in actual fact, however, they were handed over to the Einsatzgruppen, who murdered most of them at Kamenets-Podolsk shortly afterward. Both Ukrainians and Hungarian troops took part in the slaughter.[41]

In the same period the new Hungarian government, headed by László Bárdossy, enacted the Third Jewish Law. This law redefined the term *Jew* in line with racial criteria and prohibited mixed marriages. Despite the protests of the Hungarian church, all those with two Jewish grandparents were defined as Jews. Accordingly, the number of Jews in Hungary at the time was estimated at 825,000 to 850,000.[42] In 1941, under the rule of the Hungarian Life Party, pressure on the Jews increased but their situation was still essentially tolerable. There was even a change for the better in the spring of 1942 when Miklós Kállay came to power. He wanted to liberate Hungary from the strong German influence exerted on his predecessor and displayed a more moderate and decent attitude toward the Jews. On the other hand, in this same period the Jewish auxiliary units were dispatched to the front line in the Ukraine, where they suffered very heavy losses. Kállay enacted laws aimed at restricting Jewish economic activity even further; conversely, he also found ways of exempting young Jews from labor duties.

Yugoslavia

After the German occupation of Yugoslavia in April 1941, the country was divided up into several regions. Only one area, Serbia and Banat, with a population of German origin, was under direct German military administration. It included the capital, Belgrade, where most of the Jews of the region lived, some eighty-five hundred in number. In Yugoslavia proper there were some eighty thousand Jews, organized in a national federation. They were distinguished by internal cohesion and by social and cultural activity. Hungary reannexed the territories it had lost after World War I (notably Bačka), where close to thirty thousand Jews lived. Macedonia was attached to Bulgaria. Italy took over the western coastal area, Dalmatia and Montenegro, and even part of Croatia. The greater part of Slovenia in the north was attached to the German Reich, and the rest of this territory came under Italian rule.

Most of the country became an independent Croatian state, where Ante Pavelić, leader of the Croatian nationalist movement, Ustaše, came to power. This movement, founded in 1929, represented the national aspirations of the Croats, who were eager to break free of Serbian rule. Before the German occupation, Pavelić had been in exile in Italy together with a large number of members of the movement, and from there he made contact with the Nazi regime in Germany. The national differences between the Croats and the Serbs were exacerbated by religious conflicts, which were complex in themselves: the Croats were Roman Catholics, whereas the Serbs were Orthodox. There was also a Greek Orthodox community and several hundred thousand Moslems. When the Ustaše seized power, the Croats launched savage persecution of the Serbs, killing them by the thousands or forcing them to convert. In these attacks the Ustaše supporters were abetted by the Moslems. It is estimated that at the end of the summer of 1941, the number of Orthodox Serbs slaughtered or deported to Serbia totaled hundreds of thousands. It was only then that the Croatian Catholic church condemned the use of violence and forced conversions.[43] In the Free Croation State some three hundred Greek Orthodox churches were destroyed and tens of thousands of priests were killed in addition to hundreds of thousands of men, women, and children.[44]

The fate of the Jews was no kinder, particularly as the Germans directly or obliquely influenced their "removal." Before the war some forty thousand Jews had lived in Croatia. Immediately after the occupation, the Germans acted in conjunction with the Croats, attacking Jews and looting their property wherever possible. On April 30, 1941, the new state proclaimed Croatian nationality, and went on to promulgate racial laws, based on the Nuremberg Laws. The Jews were placed outside the law; an additional statute of May 22, 1941, obliged them to wear the yellow badge.

Bosnia and Herzegovina were annexed to newly independent Croatia. Sarajevo, the ancient Sephardic Jewish center, was captured by the Germans on April 17, 1941, and the Croats and the Germans immediately burned down the ancient and renowned synagogue. The Moslems collaborated in this (one of their units later joined the German forces fighting in Russia). The first concentration camp was already established in May 1941.

Alexander Arnon, then secretary of the Jewish community in Zagreb, capital of the Ustaše state, gave evidence at the Eichmann trial.[45] Zagreb was the largest community, with a Jewish population of 12,000. Arnon was also a representative of JDC in Yugoslavia before the war. He was ordered by the Gestapo to prepare 10,000 yellow badges. After the indiscriminate arrests of the first few weeks, all members of the B'nai B'rith lodge were arrested on May 16, 1941. After the outbreak of the war with Russia, they were dispatched to a camp in Lithuania. This was apparently the first deportation of Jews to the East from one of the satellite states. In that period the Jews were usually killed or incarcerated in camps inside the country; the number of detainees was estimated at 25,000. The Judenrat, however, was allowed to assist the detained Jews by sending food, drugs, and clothing. The Jews lacked the required funds to supply all needs. Arnon testified that he approached the authorities and was granted permission to travel to Budapest, in order to telephone the European director of the JDC, Joseph Schwartz, who was then in Portugal, and ask for his help. The means of preparing supplies for the camps were, in fact, placed at the disposal of the Jews. A large part of these supplies, however, was stolen by the Croats who were in charge of the camps, and the Jews never received them.

The Jews met with less success in their efforts to save children. They requested exit permits for fifty children they hoped to send to Palestine. The request was granted on condition that they supply the exact addresses of the children, most of whom had been left solitary after the arrest of their parents. The Judenrat supplied only one address—its own—but the Germans insisted that their condition be met. Thus, only eleven children were able to leave for Palestine—the remainder were killed. This is only one example of the activity of the Gestapo in the "independent" Croatian state. Overall responsibility for Yugoslavia was lodged with the German military administration, which controlled the entire area, including Croatia. Hence it also bore responsibility for implementing the Final Solution in all the former Yugoslavian territories.[46]

In a conversation with the Croatian minister of war, Marshal Sladko Kvater-nik, on July 21, 1941, Hitler gave his blessing to the policy of slaughter that the Croatian government was employing against the Serbs, stating openly that "par-asites" and "scoundrels" had to be exterminated, or—when they did not consti-tute a danger to society—should be imprisoned in concentration camps "from where they should never be released." Nor did he miss the opportunity to reiterate his convictions and plans regarding the Jews, "If there were no Jews left in Europe, the unity of the European states would be disturbed no longer. It does not matter to where the Jews are deported."[47]

In the summer of 1941, the Jews were ousted from most professions, heavy fines were imposed on them, and their valuables were seized. In accordance with a tried and tested method, the Croats arrested prosperous Jews and held them as hostages until they were redeemed for gold or the equivalent in cash. They expro-priated cultural institutions and all other community assets. About half a dozen concentration camps were established; most became death camps. Both Jews and non-Jews were incarcerated in the Jasnow camp, where the inmates were mur-dered in the thousands; twenty thousand Jews perished. In many camps there was strict separation between the men and the women and children. Some few Jews succeeded in fleeing Croatia to the Italian zone (see chap. 16).

In the Serbian region the Germans employed such familiar methods as terror and looting. They proclaimed a census, a special police force was established to supervise the Jewish population, the Jews were forced to wear yellow badges, and they were mobilized for forced labor. The Judenrat was ordered to collect and hand over "contributions." A cross between a ghetto and a concentration camp was established in Belgrade itself, and the Jews of Banat, some twenty-five hun-dred in number, were also crammed into it.

In the fall of 1941, an affair occurred in Belgrade in which all the German agencies—the military administration, the Foreign Ministry, and Eichmann's office—were involved. A Serbian partisan movement began to operate in the region, greatly harassing the Germans. Jews also took part in it, and the Germans exploited this pretext to retaliate mainly against the Jewish community. The rep-resentative of the Foreign Ministry, Felix Benzler, wrote on September 12, 1941, to the Foreign Ministry claiming that it was now impossible to concentrate the Jews in labor camps because security there could not be guaranteed due to parti-san activities. First, Jewish men must be removed in order to restore order. He, therefore, reiterated his request to evacuate these Jews. He proposed that they be sent at once to the Generalgouvernement or to Russia, implying, of course, that they should be liquidated there. Eichmann refused to accede to this request; when urged,[45] he shouted into the telephone that responsibility rested with the military administration and added, "Shoot them!"[49]

The problem was apparently too complicated to be solved by telephone; after protracted correspondence, consultations were held in Belgrade in the second half of October 1941. It then emerged that not eight thousand Jews were involved, as had previously been specified, but four thousand to five thousand, since two thou-sand had already been killed in retaliation for partisan attacks on German soldiers: for every German soldier killed, one hundred Serbs were executed, but most of them were Jews. Rademacher, who took part in the discussions, explained in his report why it was impossible to deport the Jews to Rumania or to the Generalgouvernement or to the eastern territories. Where Rumania was concerned, the reasons were political, while deportations to the East were out of the question for technical reasons. Hence, the men would be shot "within a few days." And he added, "The remainder, about twenty thousand Jews (women, children, and old people) as well as fifteen hundred Gypsies, whose men will also be shot, will be concentrated in the so-called 'Gypsy quarter' in Belgrade. Food for the winter will be supplied sparsely."[50] They fell victim to the gas vans.[51]

Slovakia

The first country outside the borders of the Greater Reich from which large-scale and systematic deportations to the East were organized was the satellite state of Slovakia. At the beginning of the war, Dieter Wisliceny had been appointed adviser on Jewish affairs on behalf of the RSHA; this opened up the opportunity for Eichmann to try out methods of dispatching Jews to the East (on previous activities in Slovakia, see chap. 6). It was actually the Slovakian government itself that provided the occasion for deporting the Jews. In May 1941 the official in charge of Jewish problems on behalf of the Slovakian government, Augustín Morávek, proposed transferring Jews to the Generalgouvernement or putting them to work in Germany itself. It is unlikely that at that time he knew of the fate awaiting deportees in Eastern Europe; he was trying to free the Slovaks of the obligation to supply the Germans with laborers. It was only in the autumn of 1941, while the Slovakian leaders Josef Tiso and Voitech Tuka were visiting Hitler's headquarters, that they learned that a plan existed to "cleanse" Europe of Jews and to concentrate them in the eastern territories. When deportations commenced from the Reich (at the beginning of the winter of 1941), an attempt was made to include nationals of several satellite countries among them and also to examine to what extent these states would be willing to join in the scheme. As Luther wrote—in a comprehensive report in August 1942—it seemed immediately feasible to include the Jewish subjects in the Reich from those countries that had taken steps against the Jews *(Judenmassnahmen)*. He went on to relate that "for reasons of courtesy," the German diplomatic representatives in Slovakia, Croatia, and Rumania had approached the governments and offered them the choice between including those Jews in the deportations to the ghettos in the East or returning them to their countries. All three governments chose the former path. The Rumanians stressed that they were not interested in having the Jews back; the Croats expressed gratitude to the German government for its initiative; and the Slovakian government expressed its consent on principle, but emphasized that "the justified Slovakian claims to the property of those Jews should not be placed at risk."[52] This was the background to Luther's statement at the Wannsee Conference that no difficulties were to be anticipated on the part of the governments of Rumania, Croatia, and Slovakia. Indeed, in the framework of implementation of the Wannsee resolutions, Luther cabled the German Embassy at Pressburg (Bratislava) on February 16, 1942:

> In the course of the activity for the final solution of the problem of the Jews of Europe, the German Reich is ready to accept at once twenty thousand young, strong Slovakian Jews and to transfer them to the East, where there is a demand for manpower. Please inform the government there. As soon as the Slovakian government approves this on principle, the details will be clarified orally by the advisor on the Jewish question.[53]

This message reveals several of the characteristic features of the organization of evacuation from countries outside Greater Germany:

1. The organizers were confident a priori of the consent of the Slovakian government.
2. They still adhered to the pretext that they were mobilizing Jews for labor.
3. The etiquette of normal diplomatic relations between the Reich government and the satellite government was maintained, since the message was conveyed by the Foreign Ministry.
4. The implementation was entrusted to Eichmann's office, whose representative was on the spot.

Wisliceny immediately set to work, and once the Slovakian government had accepted the offer with great eagerness, practical preparations commenced. The Germans, however, did not intend to do this favor without reward; they demanded of the Slovaks RM 500 in payment for each deported Jew, arguing that "accommodation, food, clothing, and training of the Jews in new occupations, plus families, entail expenses, that at present cannot be covered by the labor of the Jews themselves."[54] The Slovakian government debated the various aspects of the operation and even prepared a special law to serve as the legal basis for the illegal act.

At the beginning of March, the Slovaks launched practical preparations, which included the adaptation of special railway carriages for the task, taking care of all details such as provision of containers for drinking water, locks, and other devices. Later, when they saw the first carriages that had returned from the trip, they decided to install a lavatory in each carriage.[55] On March 12, 1942, the Slovaks submitted a precise plan for the transportation of twenty loads scheduled to start at the end of the month. A special meeting to draw up the final transportation schedule was convened in the third week of March in Passau, Germany. In attendance was a representative of the Slovakian Ministry for Public Works and Transportation. The transports that left after April 4, 1942, were to contain the laborers and their families.[56]

In actual fact, the Slovaks arrested Jews indiscriminately and sometimes even deliberately selected those unfit for work. There is extant evidence by Alfred Wetzler (who was later to win renown as one of the two men who succeeded in the spring of 1944 in escaping from Auschwitz and bringing out the first authentic testimony). He describes the first deportation from his hometown of Tarnów:

> When the members of the guard came to take my parents, I asked them to leave them behind and I would go in their stead. . . . In the carriage I was in, there were forty-three

people, and it was locked and sealed. During the journey we had no possibility even of relieving ourselves since the necessary installations were lacking. . . . The people in the carriage were mainly old people from our street, mostly cantors and rabbinical assistants, and most were fifty to sixty years old.[57]

The formal negotiations between the Germans and the Slovakian government were concluded on May 1, 1942, in an oral proclamation *(Verbalnote)* by the German Legation stating that "the German Reich government in principle will not bring back to Slovakia those Jews who have been deported and will be deported in the future to Reich territory." The legation went on to promise that the Reich government would raise no demands about the property of the evacuated Jews and pointed to the arrangement "proposed" by the Germans concerning the payment of RM 500 "for each Jew that the Reich receives into its care."[58] The Slovakian government stripped the deported Jews of their Slovak nationality in accordance with the German practice.

The mass deportation of the Jews from Slovakia served as a trial run for the planned deportation method, and its organizational and political success was so important to Eichmann that he personally visited Slovakia several times and made contact with Slovak leaders. Among other matters, he assured the Slovaks that the Jews being deported to Poland were being treated there in humane fashion. On June 4, 1942, he received word while in Bratislava of the death of Heydrich in Prague.[59]

At the time of Heydrich's death (the assassination was organized with British support), the foundations had been laid and the instruments prepared for the comprehensive extermination operation. In the European countries outside the occupied territories in the East, the preparations proceeded in accordance with a master plan, adapted in each case to local conditions.

The two countries in which the operation was most meticulously planned— with the exception of the Reich itself—were Holland and Slovakia. In Holland this was made possible by the unbridled rule of the RSHA and the almost unquestioning submission of the senior bureaucracy in the country, which had been left without political leadership. In Slovakia, on the other hand, the political leaders collaborated with the Germans; the sole condition they stipulated was that the Jews should not be returned to Slovakia. This ensured that the Slovaks would be able to enjoy their ill-gotten gains of looting without any impediment.

The situation was different in France and Belgium. In the former, Eichmann's henchmen could not operate as smoothly as in Holland because of the complex structure of the German administration, on the one hand, and French interests, on the other. In the southern zone, in particular, these circumstances enabled the Jews in the first years to preserve a certain independence of action. In Belgium, the Germans did not benefit from collaboration and submission on the part of the local authorities and population, as was the case in Holland. Because the Jewish population consisted largely of immigrants and refugees, many were able and willing to go into hiding because they enjoyed the support of the Belgian underground movement.

We have seen that in southern and southeastern Europe, the situation was by no means uniform. There is a wide gap between Slovakia, which collaborated enthusiastically, and Italy, which gave shelter to Jews persecuted by the Croats and the Germans in Yugoslavia (see chap. 16). Anti-Semitic Rumania, whose intentions were in harmony with German policy, did not conform as Slovakia did, because of its own aspirations and because of the intense efforts of the Jews. Notwithstanding, in this transition period, 1941 to the spring of 1942, the Jews were persecuted in Rumania more than in any other country in Europe outside the East, and their fate resembled that of the Jews of Poland, Soviet Russia, and the Baltic states.

15

The Death Factories
in Action (1942)

The tide of death that swamped the Jews throughout Europe continued to mount in the summer of 1942 and would, in fact, not abate until the conclusion of the war. The initiation of the extermination program in Chełmno and Bełżec and the first deportations from Slovakia epitomized the system by which the envisioned mass extermination was organized. It was during this summer that the main death camps on the eastern border of the Generalgouvernement—Bełżec, Sobibor, Treblinka, and Majdanek—were placed in operation. Other than Majdanek, these camps came under the jurisdiction and direction of the police and were directed by Odilo Globocnik. Majdanek, outside Lublin, was in his sphere of influence, though in the course of time it came directly under the control of Richard Glücks, the RSHA man responsible for the entire network of concentration camps. Glück's authority also extended to the largest of the camps (from the standpoint both of its size and the number of victims it claimed): Auschwitz in Upper Silesia.

Bełżec had started out as a labor camp (see chap. 6) but was then used exclusively for annihilating Jews, whereas Sobibor and Treblinka were established explicitly for that purpose. Majdanek and Auschwitz served as both extermination and concentration camps in which the prisoners were exploited as a labor force. This dual role was also characteristic of a number of veteran concentration camps established within the bounds of the Reich, such as Dachau, Buchenwald, Sachsenhausen, and Mauthausen.

The Bełżec Camp and Kurt Gerstein, the Supplier of Gas

We have already noted that the Jews from eastern Galicia, the Lublin District, and Slovakia were sent to Bełżec, where they were joined by others from Germany

356

and Hungary. The gassing facilities operated there from the beginning of March 1942 until the end of the year, and it is estimated that from its inception in 1940 until its dismantlement in the spring of 1943, some six hundred thousand Jews perished in Bełżec.[1]

Regarding those gassing facilities, we have the testimony of Kurt Gerstein, a member of the SS and one of the strangest and most obscure figures of the period. Gerstein did not lack expressions of human ambivalence, and his personality, paradoxical behavior, and unexplained death in a French prison after the war have been the subject of many inquiries, though none has fathomed these enigmas.[2] Gerstein was born into a typical Prussian family; all his brothers were dedicated National Socialists, whereas he turned to the church while still in high school and became an active member of the Protestant youth movement. There is no doubt that he was a true believer. In May 1933 he joined the National Socialist Party as a twenty-eight-year-old mining engineer. Shortly thereafter he came into conflict with the regime, for his involvement in the Protestant youth movement had left him closely attached to the Confessing Church (Bekennende Kirche), led by Pastor Martin Niemöller, who tried to remain independent of National Socialism. Gerstein provoked the ire of Baldur von Schirach, the leader of the Hitlerjugend, and consequently, he spent various periods in prison and even concentration camps during the latter half of the 1930s. Thereafter Gerstein remained unemployed, but meanwhile he had acquired something of a medical education. It was thanks to this combination of skills that he was accepted into the Waffen SS, where he took on the task of setting up the apparatus for disinfectants meant to be used for medical and sanitary purposes. Gerstein's work was considered so important that he was allowed to pursue it even though the party's legal authorities continued to persecute him. As a result, he became privy to information about the "euthanasia" program, to which one of his relatives fell victim.

In January 1942 Gerstein was appointed chief disinfection officer in the Office of the Hygienic Chief of the Waffen SS and the police. In this capacity—so he later testified—he was charged by Adolf Eichmann's deputy, Rolf Günther, with transporting hydrogen cyanide (prussic acid) to "a secret place." That is how he came to Bełżec, where he witnessed the extermination operation in the gas chambers run by the architect of the killing centers, Dr. Christian Wirth. As had happened on so many other occasions, something broke down during Gerstein's visit, and for a long time the diesel engine remained inoperable. For two hours and forty-nine minutes (Gerstein used a stop watch), seven hundred to eight hundred people were kept standing naked in four chambers measuring 5 square yards each. When the motor was finally activated, it took thirty-two minutes to kill all the victims. Their corpses were removed by the Sonderkommando and taken to large pits, where they were buried in layers.[3]

Gerstein claimed that the gas he had brought along to Bełżec was no longer ready for use, so he buried it in the ground. But that was not the end of the matter. Although Wirth insisted that the diesel engine continue to be used, despite frequent breakdowns, Rudolf Höss chose to employ hydrogen cyanide in Auschwitz, and Gerstein had to supply it from the company known as Degesch (Deutsche Gesellschaft für Schädlingsbekämpfung, or German Vermin-Combating Corpo-

The main camps in the Third Reich and the Nazi-occupied territories. (*The Nazi Co*
tration Camps. Proceedings of the Fourth Yad Vashem International Conference, J
lem, 1984)

FINLAND

Leningrad

Stockholm

Klooga Vaivara

ESTONIA

Kaiserwald

Riga LATVIA

tic Sea

LITHUANIA

Pravieniskis

Kovno Vilna

Stutthof

USSR

Treblinka Bialystok

elmno

Warsaw POLAND

Trawniki ☼

odz

Poniatowa ☼ Sobibor

Lublin-Majdanek

Plaszow Belzec

Janowski

Cracow

hwitz–Birkenau Lwow

☼
Novaky

☼ Vyhne

TRANSNISTRIA

Peciora

Bogdanovka

Acmececta

Mostovoi

Berezowka

Budapest

NGARY

RUMANIA

Djakova

miste

ac Belgrad

Bucharest

GOSLAVIA

Nis

BULGARIA

Sofia

ALBANIA

Salonika

Istanbul

Black Sea

GREECE TURKEY

Legend

International boundaries, 1933	—·—·—
City	○
Death Camp	
Concentration Camp	
Murder Camp	
Ghetto–Camp	⬦
Transit and Assembly Camp	▢
Labor Camp	☼

ration), which produced the gas in large quantities during the war for the army.[4] Gerstein conducted all the negotiations with the company and claimed that he tried to sabotage the use of gas for killing human beings. He also explained that he did not try to get out of doing this job because he felt obligated to serve as a witness to the Nazis' crimes. To his credit, it must be said that the regime did not readily part with the kind of people upon whom it had imposed tasks of this sort. After the war (and Gerstein's death), a German court charged that he had collaborated with the government in the perpetration of crimes, though it also took note of his good intentions. Clearly the man led a double life, and the great tension between the two manifestations of his split personality repeatedly drove him to the brink of suicide, so that it is reasonable to believe that he ultimately did take his life in prison.

Gerstein's story is the tragedy of a man who resolved to do lone battle with a totalitarian regime, became hopelessly ensnared in the net of its machinations, and not only failed in his mission but precipitated his own downfall. The root of this tragedy lies in the fact that one cannot fathom the ways of a dictatorial regime until one penetrates the regime itself, but whoever gives himself over to a totalitarian authority—even with the intention of thwarting its schemes—inevitably becomes its slave and is doomed to serve it, willingly or unwillingly. The designs and methods of a tyrannical government cannot be undone by collaboration with it, and certainly this is beyond the power of a lone individual.

Sobibor

The second extermination camp to begin operating in eastern Poland was Sobibor, which had been built specially for this purpose. It functioned from May 1942 to October 1943, claiming the lives of some 250,000 Jews from eastern Poland, the occupied parts of the Soviet Union, and from those European countries in which deportations were then being organized.[5] Sobibor was divided into three areas (known as *Lager,* or "camps") in addition to an ante-camp inhabited by the SS men and their Ukrainian aides. Area A included the barracks housing the Jews working in the camp as well as the sanitary facilities and a number of workshops. Railroad tracks brought the trains directly into the camp, and the "selection"— the choice between the candidates for destruction and those chosen for labor— was carried out on the ramp. The former were directed to large halls in Area B, where they were ordered to undress and turn in their valuables and where they had their hair shorn (the Germans having come up with various uses for this hair). From there, they were sent to what was supposedly the showers in Area C—actually they were five gas chambers in which it was possible to kill up to four hundred people within twenty to thirty minutes. At first, pits were used for burial here, too, but later the Germans began to burn the corpses. After the selection, the people chosen for labor (a total of about one thousand prisoners worked in the camp) were told that the members of their families would emerge on the other side of the camp and be taken to additional places of work in the East. Of course, the bitter truth soon became known (see chap. 17 on the uprising in Sobibor).

Treblinka

For three months the commander of the Sobibor camp was Franz Stangl, an Austrian police officer chosen for this position after he had served in the "euthanasia" program. Stangl was one of the people who had been specially assigned to Globocnik, and he arrived at the camp while it was still being built and first put in operation—a period during which about one hundred thousand were gassed or shot to death.[6]

Then Stangl was transferred to Treblinka—the main camp in the area—and commanded it until its dismantlement. He was tried by a German court after the war. Initially, he had managed to flee Germany—first to Syria and then to Brazil—but was caught and extradited in 1967, dying in prison in Düsseldorf in 1971.[7] Globocnik—according to Stangl—had sent him to Treblinka because he held that the Jews' valuables were not reaching him and that order had to be established in the camp, which was still in the process of getting organized.[8] Like Sobibor, Treblinka was officially called a transit camp (Du-lag). It began operating in July 1942, with its first victims being more than three hundred thousand Jews of Warsaw; it was gradually closed down following the revolt that broke out on August 2, 1943. In the intervening months, according to the estimate of a Polish government commission, over seven hundred thousand people—some claim as high as one million people—were put to death in the camp's gas chambers.[9] Most of these victims were brought to Treblinka in seventy-eight hundred railroad cars from central Poland, Bialystok and its surrounding area, Germany, Austria, Czechoslovakia, and Greece.

In his interrogation by the Israeli police prior to his trial, Adolf Eichmann told of his visits to Treblinka at the bidding of his superior, Heinrich Müller, in order to draw up a report. He described the bogus railway station that looked "exactly like a railway station somewhere in Germany."[10] Like Gerstein, he also saw naked Jews being chased through the passage between barbed wire fences to the partially concealed gas chambers. The Germans called this walkway the hose *(Schlauch)* or the Way to Heaven *(Himmelstrasse),* the same term was used in Sobibor.

One of the survivors of the camp who testified at the Eichmann trial described this passage to the gas chambers:

> The people came through the infamous *Himmelstrasse,* which led from Camp 1 to Camp 2. Standing in the Himmelstrasse were SS men with dogs, whips, and clubs. The people walked quietly; that was at the beginning, in the summer of 1942. They didn't know where they were headed for. When they entered the gas chambers, two Ukrainians were standing by the door. . . . They provided the gas. . . . The last people to enter the gas chambers were pricked with bayonets, since they could see what was going on inside and didn't want to enter. Four hundred people were placed in the small gas chamber . . . so that they barely managed to close the chamber's outer door. When they did close it, we were on the other side. Then we heard only the shouts: "Hear O Israel!" "Papa!" "Mama!" Within thirty-five minutes they were dead. Two Germans stood listening to what was happening inside. Finally, they said, "They're all asleep." They told [us] to open the door. We opened the door and removed the corpses.[11]

The Sonderkommando assigned to the gas chambers had about two hundred men. Moreover, as in all the other extermination camps, the gold teeth were extracted from corpses in Treblinka, with most of the gold being sent to Globocnik—though the SS men also helped themselves to it. (In Sobibor, Stangl had kept a young jeweler whose job was to fashion the gold into jewelry, decorative pieces, and the like.[12]) Other than the Jews who worked as jewelers, tailors, shoemakers, carpenters, and in other crafts in Treblinka, Stangl picked out a group of intellectuals, usually older people from Warsaw and Czechoslovakia, to improve the level of work and organization in the camp. They were treated to special privileges and did not suffer from hunger because the Jews coming into the camp—especially those coming from the West—usually brought along food and the intellectual groups managed to get their hands on it, so that they did not have to eat the camp's revolting fare.[13]

Death was manifest in Treblinka not only as a consequence of the gas chambers, for corpses lay scattered all along the railroad track in and around the camp. It is assumed that many people died in the trains and others were shot on arrival.[14] The stench is said to have been unbearable, and since the camp's security fence was bordered by fields in which Polish farmers worked every day, no one in the vicinity was unaware of what was going on in the camp.

Treblinka's existence can be divided into four distinct periods.[15] The first was prior to Stangl's arrival at the end of August or beginning of September 1942 when caprice and confusion were the order of the day and everyone tried to snatch whatever he could. The second period was during the first stage of Stangl's command, when the SS men still did whatever they pleased, allowing one Jew to remain alive, for example, and sending another to the gas chamber at will. This period continued as long as the transports arrived with great frequency. The third phase began at the start of 1943 when fewer transports came in and the SS became more interested in proving their efficiency and running the camp in an orderly fashion. At this time, they also began to appreciate the value of good workers who could aid them in this task, so that a more stable situation evolved. It was during this third phase that Himmler visited Treblinka and ordered the obliteration of all traces of mass murder, meaning that the corpses were to be burned and even the buried ones were to be disinterred so that mass graves would not remain as evidence (see chap. 16). The fourth and final period of Treblinka's existence was during the months preceding the August 1943 uprising, when tension in the camp was steadily on the rise (see chap. 17).

Majdanek

The fourth camp in the Generalgouvernement, Majdanek, was situated 1.25 miles from the city of Lublin. It was built in the winter of 1940/1941 by Jewish POWs who had earlier been held in a camp in Lublin (see chap. 7); Russian POWs were first brought to the camp on July 21, 1941.[16]

Majdanek was built after the model of Dachau but had been planned as a larger camp and was subsequently expanded even further, its 144 barracks housing up to 45,000 prisoners. The camp was divided into five parts, the fifth eventually being called the death camp. During its first years, Majdanek served as a labor camp for Jews and Polish political prisoners in addition to the POWs. Most of the 5,000 Russian prisoners died of starvation, torture, or the cold. In 1942 the first Jews arrived from Slovakia and the Protectorate. They were followed by Dutch, Belgian, French, and Greek Jews and then again by Polish Jews—for a total of 130,000 people during 1942–1943. A Soviet commission of inquiry found passports and other identifying documents belonging to people from all over Europe. The camp's food, sanitation, and living conditions in general were vile, and many of the inmates died of dysentery.[17]

The gas chambers operated according to the same system employed in Auschwitz, though the Germans also used death vans and executed many people with weapons. The SS men in Majdanek were particularly sadistic and tortured people for their pleasure; they were especially fond of slaughtering infants and children before their mothers' eyes. At roll calls, which were held every morning and evening—as in all the camps—inmates were harassed with particular zeal, for example, by being ordered to put on and take off their caps in rhythm. At times, one of the prisoners was ordered to step forward and was informed that he had been condemned to death, the sentence being quickly carried out by hanging.[18] The transports of Jews from outside Poland were brought straight to the gas chambers, in line with the system followed in all the extermination camps. Eichmann visited Majdanek at the end of 1942; before his arrival, the inmates were made to stand in parade formation for an entire day. When he finally arrived, according to the testimony of a witness at the Eichmann trial,"he gave a cursory glance, one could say, [and] because I was standing at the edge in a low spot, I heard him say, 'Get rid of the whole pile [meaning pile of garbage].'"[19]

The worst massacre occurred in the third camp on November 3, 1943, when 17,000 Jews were mowed down by machine-gun fire in a single day. The few hundred remaining in Majdanek were put to work covering up the evidence of this mass murder. According to the official Polish estimate, 200,000 people were killed in the camp, of whom 125,000 were Jews. Most of them were from Poland and came either from the immediate vicinity—that is, Bialystok—or from Warsaw after the uprising. In the summer of 1943, 10,000 Jews who were "fit for labor" were transferred out of Majdanek, some to Auschwitz and some elsewhere. Among them was Israel Gutman, today an authority in the field of Holocaust history.

Auschwitz

The Development of the Camp's System

As we have already noted (see chap. 6), Auschwitz started out as a camp for political prisoners—mostly Poles (together with a few Jews) who had been sent there for their resistance to the German authorities. From the outset the prisoners had been given numbers and were known to the camp's administration solely by this means of identification. On March 1, 1941, two prisoners were issued the numbers

10901 and 10902, respectively. This does not mean that there were close to 11,000 prisoners in the camp at the time, for many of the inmates had already died by then, either of "natural causes" or by execution in the "bunker" in Block 11— the punishment block—or at the "Wall of Death" where they were shot in the back of the neck.

On that same March 1, Himmler paid a visit to Auschwitz, and his entourage included, in addition to a number of SS officers, the inspector of the concentration camps, Richard Glücks, and the chief directors of the large concern of I. G. Farben,[20] the latter being an innovation on such visits. After reviewing the camp and its surroundings, Himmler issued orders to extend the camp at Auschwitz so that it would be capable of holding thirty thousand prisoners; to establish a camp on the site of one of the villages in the vicinity of Birkenau (the name derived from a nearby grove of birch trees) that would be able to absorb one hundred thousand POWs; and to build a factory in another place in the vicinity, Dwory, for I. G. Farben and to put ten thousand prisoners at the company's disposal.

Work on these projects began immediately. In swift and brutal actions, the towns of the area were emptied of their inhabitants, among them the Jews living in the town of Auschwitz (Oświęcim). As stated earlier, in the summer of 1941, Himmler extended the role Auschwitz was to fulfill by transforming it into the main camp for the extermination of European Jewry. In the wake of his order to do so, Eichmann visited Auschwitz and discussed the technical side of the extermination program with Rudolf Höss. He even showed Höss the deportation plan—to the degree that it had been developed by then.[21]

Why did Himmler choose Auschwitz as the place to establish a "death factory"? The population in this sector of Upper Silesia—annexed to the Reich with Eastern Upper Silesia—was purely Polish. From the standpoint of transport connections, the area could be reached from all parts of Europe without any special difficulty. The area itself was also known for its unfavorable topographical and climatic conditions. Owing to its many swamps, it suffered from chronic dampness that was aggravated in the winter by the brutal cold. In short, there was every reason to believe that nature would contribute to the aim of destroying human beings. Upper Silesia was also relatively far from the eastern front, so that the Bunawerke (Buna Works) for the manufacture of artificial rubber, which I. G. Farben was to establish there, could be expected to function without disturbance from enemy planes from the East or the West. Moreover, the massive concentration of prisoners and POWs ensured the factories the necessary manpower, and it was no problem to replace anyone who perished.

The opening of the factories also provided the SS with a substantial income. After seven months of labor by male prisoners and nine months of labor by female prisoners, RM 12,753,526 were paid to the Auschwitz camp. Subsidiary camps rose up one after the next around the original camp to accommodate additional factories and supply the manpower they required. These camps were geared not solely to industry, for Himmler took an interest in agriculture and saw to the construction of experimental fish ponds and even an experimental farm for gardening.[22]

The original camp at Auschwitz was known as Auschwitz I. Auschwitz II was the camp at Birkenau, whose capacity was originally planned as one hundred thousand prisoners but, following Himmler's orders, was soon expanded to accommodate two hundred thousand. Moreover, Birkenau continued to expand and it had essentially become a constellation of camps—known as BI, BII, and BIII—that were further divided into subcamps. Auschwitz III was the industrial center in Monowitz. Auschwitz II-Birkenau became the extermination camp.[23] Primarily during Eichmann's visit a secluded structure was chosen as the site for the gassing, and the first trial was conducted on September 3, 1941, with nine hundred Russian POWs being killed. This structure, originally chosen because of its isolation—being hidden behind a grove of birch trees—was later abandoned because it took too long to ventilate.[24] (Care was taken to conceal the gas chambers behind trees and bushes in Treblinka and Sobibor as well.) Later, additional gas chambers were built in Birkenau under the crematoria—the corpses were sent up by elevator). The construction work continued from the winter of 1941 throughout 1942 and essentially up to the summer of 1944. The deportees on the first transports were not killed immediately. They were put to death in very sadistic ways but were not sent to the gas chambers because the latter still were not operating at full capacity. Initially, the corpses were buried in pits and only later were they burned, first out in the open and subsequently in the crematoria.

The Extermination Process

The first Jews sent to Auschwitz came from the immediate vicinity, primarily from Eastern Upper Silesia. They were soon followed by transports from Slovakia—the first, containing women, arriving on March 26, 1942—and then from France. Each train was dispatched by order of the RSHA and was accompanied by a directive to the camp headquarters that was worded according to a standard formula, "This transport conforms to the standing orders and should be included in the special operation [*Sonderaktion*]."[25] These transports were also known as Eichmann shipments.

Himmler's original order was to do away with all the Jews, but as early as the summer of 1942, it became clear that the Reich was suffering from a shortage of working hands. Therefore, in July an order was issued to conduct a selection, that is, to single out the strong and healthy among the masses of deported Jews and put them to work. This task was assigned to the SS doctors in Auschwitz. Thus, the notorious drama began to be played out: after the deportees had been removed from the sealed railway cars, to the accompaniment of shouts and blows, they had to pass in front of the SS doctors, who directed them with a wave of the hand to the right or to the left—to death or hard labor inside or outside the camp. Especially infamous was Dr. Josef Mengele, who became the omnipotent arbiter of life and death. For the most part, the deportees did not grasp the significance of this division, although many had a sense of impending disaster. Families were overcome by emotion on being separated, with mothers and young children going to one side and older boys and girls fit for labor going to the other, sometimes with their fathers and sometimes alone. Both categories of people were told to leave all their belongings behind, with the promise that they would be returned to them later on. Those sentenced to death were led to the anterooms of the gas chambers, where they were ordered to undress, purportedly in order to shower. They were told to tie their shoes together and remember the number of the hook on which they had hung their clothing so that they would be able to find their belongings on emerging from the shower. To complete the deception, each person was given a piece of soap, and the gas chambers were equipped with shower heads. Höss took great pride in these arrangements, claiming that they ensured a calm atmosphere by avoiding the wave of terror that gripped the victims in the other camps when they were sent running to their deaths.[26]

The pellets of hydrogen cynanide, Zyklon-B, were supplied in metal canisters that were carried to the crematoria in a Red Cross ambulance. These pellets were poured into the gas chambers in the basement through the looped course of hollow metal shafts and were thrown out through evenly spaced openings. As soon as Zyklon-B came into contact with the air in the chamber it became gas. It worked in an upward direction, so that the first to die were the children and the last were the young and the strong who struggled to climb upward on the piles of corpses. The Germans turned off the electricity when the gas chambers were in operation, and they did not turn it on again until all was quiet. After checking the situation through the peephole in the steel door, they activated the ventilators set in the chambers' walls. Only then did they open the door and wash down the interior of the chamber with jets of water, after which the members of the Kommando removed the corpses and transferred them to an elevator that carried them to the cremation room. Both the SS men responsible for releasing the pellets and the prisoners removing the corpses were protected by wearing masks. No one made mention of any odor being perceptible inside or outside.[27]

Those who remained alive were transferred to one of the camp's blocks. The women were in a special camp in Birkenau. All personal effects were concentrated in central warehouses, and special units of Jews were employed to sort them for shipment to Germany. This warehouse was known in the camp as "Canada," some say because the first units of workers were told that working there would earn them the privilege of emigrating to Canada, others because these workers lived in affluence, "as though they were in Canada." One way or another, the name stuck, and this was only one of the bitter jokes that spread through the camp.

The Plunder

One of the main objectives of the extermination campaign was the plunder of the victims' property. Not only were their clothing and personal belongings systematically collected, classified, and passed on, but special emphasis was placed on salvaging money and valuables, and gold teeth were extracted from the corpses before their cremation. The valuables were passed on to the Deutsche Reichsbank (Reich Central Bank). Even though carloads of personal belongings of all kinds were sent to Germany, the Germans failed to exploit all this plunder. In January 1945, when the camps were about to be evacuated, the Germans tried to burn the "Canada" warehouses, but six of them remained intact and were found to contain 349,820 men's suits, 836,255 women's outfits, 38,000 pairs of men's shoes, 5,525 pairs of women's shoes, close to 14,000 rugs, and an unstated number of false teeth, eyeglasses, toiletry items, and the like. As in Treblinka, food from "Canada" reached the inmates in Auschwitz, especially in the camp of Polish prisoners, and a black market developed in it. Some of the items of food found their way into the general kitchen and led to an improvement in nutrition. "The camp soup became thicker," one survivor related, "but it was necessary to be on the lookout, because sometimes an old razor blade or button or five-dollar gold piece turned up in the bowl." Private pillage and a black market thrived despite the obligatory oath taken by SS men dealing with "the evacuation of Jews." Among the punishments meted out for violating this oath was the death sentence for anyone caught stealing Jewish property.[28]

As indicated earlier, Globocnik made a great effort to collect the belongings of the Jews murdered in Treblinka, and the same held true for the other camps under his supervision. This enormous enterprise was one aspect of the extermination operation dubbed *Aktion Reinhard* (Operation Reinhard) after Heydrich's assassination, indicating that he had orchestrated the "Final Solution" and the massive plunder.[29]

Valuables were accorded special attention, so that it was necessary to count, register, and weigh all the gems, gold, other precious metals, watches, and so forth. The centralized apparatus did not always function properly, however, and many items found their way into the pockets of the SS men and supervisors in the camps or were turned directly over to certain quarters in the hierarchy. Still, the lion's share of the booty was channeled according to the orders passed down from Oswald Pohl's Economic and Administrative Main Office (WVHA). He referred to the plundered property as "goods that derived from theft, the receipt of stolen goods, and concealed goods," thus implying that it had all been taken from the Jews by right, since they had acquired it by underhanded or illegal means. This formula was repeated in WVHA's various statements about what was to be done with the goods. Watches and fountain pens, for example, were handed out by the thousands to the SS and elite army units or were given to wounded soldiers as Christmas presents. Clothing was turned over to the state's Winter Aid Project. Sometimes unfortunate oversights occurred: blood stains were left on articles of clothing or the yellow patches were not removed. According to Globocnik's final report to Himmler, he passed on valuables worth RM 100 million and goods that filled 825 railway cars, for which Himmler thanked him, writing, "I wish to express my gratitude and appreciation for the great and singular right you have won for yourself by carrying out *Aktion Reinhard* for the sake of the entire German nation."[30]

On the basis of a special agreement, money and valuables were turned over to the Deutsche Reichsbank, whose president, Economic Minister Walter Funk, entered into this accord with Himmler in the summer of 1942. The details were worked out by Pohl and the directors of the bank at a luncheon held in the Reichs-bank. The transfer of the property was handled by one of the senior officials in Pohl's office, and according to his testimony the bank received seventy-six or sev-enty-seven truckloads of valuables. After being sorted in the bank's storehouses, the haul was divided up: coins were turned over to the Precious Metals Depart-ment; stocks and checkbooks were sent to the Securities Department; and the gold from teeth was transferred to the Prussian coinery to be melted down. In 1943, however, a workshop for melting down this gold was opened in Crematorium 3 at Auschwitz, with dental technicians chosen from the prisoners employed at this task. The completed gold bars were taken to the camp's collection point by ambu-lance. The amount of gold converted into bars sometimes reached as much as 11 to 22 pounds per day.[31] Jewelry was sent to the Berlin Pawn Bureau, where it was sold under supervision. The money derived from the sale of the stocks and pre-cious metals was passed on to the State Treasury and credited to a special account under the name of Max Heiliger. The Germans did not always succeed in pro-cessing and exploiting the booty as planned; specifically, they could not always keep pace with the inundation of transports. Thus on conquering Germany, the Americans discovered 2,007 containers filled with gold, foreign currency, and other valuables hidden in a salt cave. Still, the SS was allowed to benefit from this huge stash in another way: the Reichsbank and the Gold Discount Bank were obliged to establish a special reserve, known as the Reinhard Fund, from which the SS borrowed substantial capital for its operations. This enabled the SS to pay debts of millions of marks—to the German Red Cross, among other creditors—and to develop industrial enterprises.[32]

Medicine in the Service of Murder

Doomed to die in the gas chambers were not only the elderly, the children, and the weak—essentially the great majority of the deportees—but also all those Jews whose strength had been drained by hard labor in the camp, who had fallen ill, or who had been caught in the act of some grave transgression by camp standards. Gassing was not the only means of murder, however. A special expedient that had been developed as far back as 1941 (before masses of Jews were brought to Ausch-witz) and that was employed against Jews and non-Jews alike was death by injec-tion. At first, various poisons were used, but later the Germans restricted them-selves to the use of phenol injected directly into the heart. The disease most prevalent in Auschwitz was typhus, with the epidemic reaching its height in the summer of 1942. Terrified that the lice carrying the typhus germ would infect them, the SS men began killing masses of the sick either by injections or by gas, even though by that point they had begun to be concerned about maintaining a certain level of manpower. In contrast, the camp hospital was staffed by a team of doctors and aides who worked with great dedication to save human lives.

The SS doctors, however, were engaged at the time in an additional kind of "medical" operation, conducting experiments on prisoners. Himmler looked on Auschwitz as a place to exterminate the inferior and hated race of the Jews, but he also intended to use it, along with other camps, to advance the recognition of racial theory as well as other issues related to man's physical nature. This ostensibly scientific research, carried out on human beings, was yet another aspect of how the Nazis turned society's conventional value system on its head, placing humans on the same level as the animals on which the medical and biological sciences conducted their experiments.

In Auschwitz the aim of the experiments was primarily to find the most expeditious way of sterilizing human beings. The results of the "research" were to be used both to advance the war against the Jews—especially the offspring of mixed marriages—and to enhance the Aryan race. One of the SS physicians working on the sterilization research, Dr. Horst Schumann—who had been transferred to Auschwitz directly from one of the "euthanasia" institutions—conducted his experiments in the women's camp in Birkenau, sterilizing his subjects by means of X-rays. Men and women in their twenties and thirties were chosen for his work from among the deportees and shortly thereafter usually died in great agony as a result. Other trials were conducted in isolated Block 10 of the men's camp in Auschwitz I. Supervised by the chief SS physician, Dr. Eduard Wirths, working in collaboration with a number of aides—the most prominent of whom was Dr. Carl Clauberg—these experiments were carried out by chemical means. Sylvia Friedman, a prisoner from Slovakia, who worked as an assistant in the program and survived the war, subsequently gave testimony about the sterilization experiments conducted in Block 10 on 350 young Jewish women from Holland and Greece. The experiments were repeated at regular intervals, using various preparations, and this is how she described the results:

> After each injection the women ran a high fever, suffering from an infection of the ovary, resulting in sharp pains and contractions that often ended with them fainting. Each woman had one or both ovaries removed, and they were sent to Berlin.... Various parts of the women's sex organs were removed, photographed on the spot, and likewise sent on to Berlin.... The prisoners smuggled all the preparations out of the camp [through underground connections with a Belgian doctor by the name of Frank].[33]

The Nazis regarded the sterilization experiments as so important that Dr. Clauberg actually paid the camp administration for the women on whom they were performed. Clauberg took on the task on direct orders from Himmler after the two had consulted on June 7, 1942. Himmler also sent Clauberg to conduct a sterilization program at the women's camp at Ravensbrück, as a result of which, a year later, Clauberg reported to Himmler that an experienced doctor could sterilize hundreds, perhaps even thousands, of people a day.[34]

The most notorious of the SS physicians in Auschwitz was Dr. Josef Mengele, who conducted "scientific experiments" in addition to presiding over the selection, especially during the systematic destruction of Hungarian Jewry in 1944. Mengele was particularly interested in the subject of twins and made a point of picking them out during the selection. In Block 10 they were subjected to tests to ascertain their response in varying situations and judge whether or not these reactions were identical. To assure the validity of the results, the twins often were treated to a more nourishing diet, as a consequence of which a certain number of them survived. After the war Mengele managed to flee to South America and was in hiding there for decades.[35]

The Camp Way of Life and Death

When Auschwitz was still in the process of being set up, Höss brought with him thirty inmates from Sachsenhausen who had been imprisoned on criminal charges and turned them into Kapos, or supervisors over the prisoners. (The Italian word *capo,* meaning "head," was first used by the Italian laborers who worked on building roads in southern Germany. From there, it entered the jargon in Dachau and then spread to all the concentration camps established in Germany and beyond.) This system of supervisor-prisoners was headed by two inmates, one responsible for the work program, the other for the blocks in which the prisoners were housed. Kapos also presided over the labor details. In each block of living quarters, a prisoner was responsible for order, discipline, and the distribution of rations. The Kapos wore yellow armbands and the block supervisors red ones. Added to these two instruments of supervision were various other figures of authority—such as the people responsible for the kitchens, workshops, building sites, and the like—who wielded great power—sometimes exceeding that of the Kapos and block supervisors. These erstwhile criminal prisoners controlled the routine administration of the camp by means of a ruthless regime. They were present twenty-four hours a day and unabashedly exploited the authority placed in their hands.[36] Of course, there were also exceptions to such conduct, but in general they behaved according to the rules and ethos of the underworld society, and they enjoyed the full backing of the SS because they were a convenient tool. In the course of time, the number of these petty despots grew in all the camps, reaching into the thousands—including also Jews.

One of the characteristic traits of all the concentration camps was the division of the prisoners into categories and the creation of a hierarchy that determined the precise nature, rank, and value of the inmates. These categories were noted by the colored triangles sewn on the prison cloth to distinguish among political prisoners, asocial prisoners, common criminals, homosexuals, and even Jehovah's Witnesses. The Jews were marked with the same symbols except the standard triangle had a second, yellow triangle superimposed on it, thus creating the effect of a Star of David. Special marks were appended for prisoners sentenced to the punishment block or suspected of attempting to escape. The number tattooed on the arms of the women was joined by a small triangle, probably to distinguish them from men; since all the inmates had their hair shorn, were emaciated, and wore the same clothing and rags, it was apparently difficult to differentiate between the sexes on sight.

The daily schedule in Auschwitz was similar to that in all the camps. After being awakened at dawn, the prisoners reported for the morning roll call and were then taken out to their places of work. A systematic search was carried out for anyone attempting to evade work by hiding; those caught were sent directly to the gas chamber. On their way to work outside the camp, prisoners were obliged to sing as they marched to the music of the camp band. The SS men were posted at the camp gate to count the marchers filing in rows of five, while other SS guards, aided by specially trained dogs, accompanied the prisoners to their places of work, where their labor was supervised by Kapos. "The relish with which these supervisor-prisoners persecuted, harassed, and tormented their comrades was incredible. . . . Only those who won over their supervisors with a bribe enjoyed any relief."[37] When the prisoners returned to the camp, another roll call was held. Only then were they released to their barracks, where they received a watered-down soup that had come from the kitchen at lunchtime and was, of course, cold by then.

The portions of food would not have sufficed for an average person under normal conditions and certainly did not satisfy those engaged in hard labor. Yet even these inadequate rations did not reach the prisoners intact: much of the bread and other items of food had been seized by the SS men and rerouted to their own kitchen. The same fate befell the packages occasionally sent to Jewish prisoners from the neutral countries. Often they were confiscated and turned over to the Kapos and block supervisors as a prize of sorts, even though their food was, at any rate, superior to that of the Jewish prisoners.

A Polish physician who survived Auschwitz and became a professor after the war described the symptoms of starvation in Auschwitz and reported his conclusions. He distinguished between two phases in the development of the condition. During the first stage the sufferers grow steadily thinner, their muscles become weak, their movements become slower. The transition to the second phase may be sudden or gradual. In the second stage the victims' expression changes and they become apathetic, dull, and sad; their skin grows dry, its color becoming ashen, and it begins to peel; their eyes sink in their sockets, their cheekbones become prominent, their heads become elongated, and their hair grows wild. Edema and swelling begin to appear in various parts of the body, and the victims are afflicted by severe diarrhea.[38] In this condition the prisoners were forced to go out to work as long as their legs would carry them. The sanitary conditions in the camp further reduced their ability to persevere. During the first phase, the prisoners tended to be irritable and arguments often broke out, usually over food. During the second stage, the prisoners continued to be affected by emotional disturbances, and there was an increasing loss of self-control.

When a group of these emaciated figures, crushed to the ground, was viewed from a distance, they resembled Muslims at prayer—which is probably the source of the term *Muselmann* that was given to the starving prisoners. They were completely apathetic to their surroundings and were no longer able to function—not even able to commit suicide. When the number of such prisoners soared in the winter of 1941/1942 (i.e., before the period of mass extermination), the Germans found a way to speed up the process of their demise: they gathered them in the courtyard of Block 11 and kept them there for days, pouring cold water on them from time to time.

"It is not likely that a decent prisoner will live for more than three months" went the SS estimate of a prisoner's life span in the camp. "If he does, he's a thief." Willpower and above all a strong will to live were necessary for a man to hold on any longer. It is interesting to note that it was not necessarily the hearty types who were able to adapt themselves to the trying conditions and keep body and soul together.

The most onerous problem of all, perhaps, was that of water. There was no drinking water in Birkenau, and from lack of choice both the sick and the healthy drank the polluted water that was channeled into the camp from the swamps of the area. The poor nutrition, unpotable water, and hard labor all led to a high incidence of disease and endangered the lives of every one of the prisoners. Neither were they given any opportunity to rest: on official holidays and rest days, the SS men amused themselves by "drilling exercises" and "sports activities" for the prisoners or put them to work at pointless tasks, for example, carrying rocks from one place to another. These activities were usually accompanied by murderous beatings. To the many who died from these beatings or from illness and physical exhaustion must be added the desperate people who committed suicide by hurling themselves against the electrified fence or who deliberately provoked the guards. And one who withstood all the torture and deprivation could look forward to a wooden slab as his place of rest and refuge. These bunks were three-tiered arrangements, with each prisoner allotted less than one square yard (31 square inches)—occasionally, there was merely an empty sack on the floor. Forbidden to go out at night, the four to five hundred people living in a block were provided with two barrels for the purpose of relieving themselves. Eight thousand prisoners had a single faucet for washing. The black market price of a bottle of water was equal to that of half a loaf of bread. Only during the last phase of the camp's existence were showers installed; even then the prisoners hardly used them because of the great difficulty in obtaining soap or a towel. To add insult to injury the signs hanging in the blocks read: "One louse—your death!" "Work makes you free!" "The block is your home!" "Maintain cleanliness!"

In light of these conditions, it is not surprising that the mortality and disease reached mass proportions. In contrast to the tolerable conditions in the hospital in Auschwitz I—making it possible for the Polish underground to use it as a headquarters—the situation in Block 7, the hospital in Birkenau, was so insufferable that whoever fell ill did everything possible to stay out of the *Revier* (as the hospitals in all the camps were called). The premises were crawling with lice, and the sick lay side by side with the dead without being administered drugs or any other kind of therapy to ease their suffering. "On some days as many as 225 prisoners died out of a total of 860." It is estimated that between May 1941 and August 1943, 70,000 people died in Block 7 or were sent to the gas chambers.[39] For the most part, the SS doctors never even examined the sick or helped in any other way. Jewish orderlies who tried to save these patients were highly limited in their ability to do so. From time to time a German doctor would help in these efforts, of course, but he, too, barely had the means to do much good.

Punishments

In addition to the usual hardships of daily life in the contrasociety of slavery and death that the Nazis created in the concentration camps in general and at Auschwitz in particular, they instituted the special regimen of punishment. The inmates of Auschwitz were severely chastised for every transgression, large or small, with the punishments being varied and graduated on a scale of brutality. Regulations in this regard had been laid down in 1933 by the commander of Dachau, Theodor Eicke, and were passed on to all the concentration camps.[40] Occasionally, they were appended by order of a camp commander to make them harsher. Observing these regulations supplied the SS men and their aides with countless opportunities to give their sadistic impulses free rein.

Political prisoners received relatively light punishment: their special rights were revoked or their mail was withheld from time to time. Among the more popular punishments imposed on all the other prisoners were "drilling exercises," usually accompanied by special torture, and work during free time. These were the punishments stipulated for anyone caught smoking or sleeping on the job or for anyone who lost a cap or other article of clothing. In such cases the transgressor's Sunday rest was canceled for ten weeks. A harsher punishment was the denial of food: usually a prisoner was not permitted to eat the meager lunch doled out at his place of work; as a result he often deteriorated into a Muselmann and died. Death by starvation was most likely if a prisoner was also denied the evening meal, which usually had a higher nutritional content.

Beating was a very common form of punishment in Auschwitz. According to standing written orders, a doctor had to confirm that the prisoner was capable of surviving a flogging, but this precaution was never observed. The prisoner had to lie over a simple wooden horse with his feet secured in a crate and his arms stretched forward so that his body was taut. He would then receive twenty-five lashes on the buttocks; often the blows were also applied to the kidney area. In line with Himmler's special orders, from April 1942 onward the blows were delivered to the naked body.[41] The prisoner was responsible for counting the strokes, and if he erred—this happened particularly to people who did not speak German—he had to go back and count from the beginning. When the flogging was over, the prisoner had to get up, stand at attention, and declare that he had received his punishment. In many cases he was immediately placed in the bunker without receiving medical attention and generally without any food or water. The results were usually fatal. These beatings were carried out in front of all the prisoners or in the courtyard of Block 11. Even those fortunate enough not to be placed in the bunker afterward were denied medical attention and suffered from grim aftereffects unless hospital workers managed to hide them, operate on them, and nurse them in secret. Countless people simply died as a result of such punishment.

Flogging was not the worst punishment dispensed in the camp. Even more savage was the practice of suspending a prisoner by his hands, which were crossed behind him and tied with a rope that was attached to a beam. Höss took credit for having originated this punishment as an alternative to incarceration; his intention was to avoid the prisoner's extended absence from work.[42] But there were other highly cruel forms of imprisonment, for example, the standing cells. These compartments, four in number and about 1 square yard each, were situated in the basement of Block 11. Entering through a small aperture, four people were crammed into each cell and were only able to stand, having no way of resting their legs, to say nothing of lying down. Air entered the cell through a 2-inch opening, so that the prisoners were doomed to suffocate. Höss claimed that this punishment never extended beyond three nights; in fact, it was usually imposed for a period of ten days. One prisoner was punished in this way for asking for two portions of soup; another was placed in the standing cell for six weeks because he accidentally broke a cement pipe. Women were also subjected to this form of punishment for picking apples, for example. The basement of Block 11 also contained regular-sized cells where prisoners were incarcerated for long periods. They were always in danger of falling victim to one of the "cleansing operations" *(Säuberungsaktion)*: to make room for new prisoners the purged ones were shot at the Wall of Death in the block's courtyard.

The conditions of imprisonment ranged from confinement without food to being jammed into an unlit cell, from which only a few emerged alive. Collective punishment was applied in the form of making the prisoners stand perfectly still for hours, sometimes whole nights, in the freezing cold, with murderous blows being administered for the least movement.

Even the death sentence took different forms. Many prisoners were shot to death on different occasions and for different pretexts, but this penalty was used especially for those suspected of, or caught engaging in, underground activity. Prisoners apprehended while trying to escape were hanged, usually in public during a roll call and in the presence of the camp command. In cases where the fugitives succeeded in getting away, other prisoners from the same block were closed up in a dark cell and left to die of starvation. These examples reflect merely a selection of punishments used in the system; the range of tortures by which the prisoners were harassed, humiliated, and killed was far more extensive.

On July 17, 1942, Himmler visited Auschwitz for the second time, spending two days in the camp. On the first day, he toured the camp from end to end, reviewing many of the agricultural and construction projects in which the prisoners were employed and visiting the Bunawerke for the manufacture of artificial rubber. "After touring Birkenau he viewed the entire process of exterminating a transport of Jews. Thus he was witness to the unloading of the transport, the *selection* of those fit for labor, the gassing in Bunker 2, and the emptying of the gas chamber. The corpses were still being buried in pits at that time."[43] In the evening he took part in a number of social events and, as Höss reported, "[he] was in the best of spirits . . . I had never known him like that before!" The next day Himmler visited Auschwitz I and viewed all the facilities there, including the "Canada" storehouses. At his request, the punishment by flogging was demonstrated for him in the women's camp so that he could "observe the effects." He was not interested in hearing about the problems and difficulties raised during his tour and at one point even castigated Höss, "There are no difficulties for an SS officer; his job is always to overcome every possible difficulty by his own devices!" During their final talk, Himmler gave orders to expand the armament works, enlarge Birkenau, and eliminate all the Jews and Gypsies unfit for labor. Finally, as a sign of appreciation he promoted Höss.[44] Some time after this visit, Höss was also given orders to burn the corpses. The first cremation took place on September 20, 1942, and marked the initiation of the effort to cover all traces of the crime (see chap. 16).[45]

The Bureaucracy of Murder: A Source of Information

For our knowledge of what went on in this hell on earth, we can essentially credit two sources: (1) the recollections—and occasionally the memoirs written during or after the experience—of those who managed to flee or miraculously survived the camp; and (2) the bureaucratic precision of the Germans themselves. The administrative offices in Auschwitz maintained fastidious records of the prisoners kept alive for the purpose of labor. These offices were staffed by prisoners who knew every detail of what was happening in the camp and did their best to memorize the information and even pass it on to the outside world. Two German-Jewish women worked in the Registration Department and another two in the Population Registry, both branches of the Auschwitz Secretariat known as the Political Division.[46] The first dealt with the day-to-day affairs of the prisoners, whereas the latter was in charge of recording births, marriages, and deaths—the major work was, of course, registering the deaths. Specific details on all prisoners were kept by the Registration Department on a special form that recorded, among other things, the date of their arrest. In addition, all prisoners were photographed. When prisoners died, their files were turned over to the Population Registry, where the cause of death was duly noted. As the recording of this data was done for the purpose of camouflage, the cause of death was invariably given as an illness of one sort or another, chosen at random. Never was it recorded that a prisoner had been executed or maltreated in any way. The cause of death of those who had been gassed was given as SB, the initials of the expression for special treatment *(Sonderbehandlung)*. Every month these fabricated reports were sent to Berlin, while the "Books of the Dead" were kept in the camps' secretariats. The trouble that the Germans went to in covering up their acts of murder by this elaborate clerical fraud, conducted as meticulously as all their government operations, seems rather odd. At the same time, they failed to keep any record of the Jews sent directly from the trains to the gas chambers, making it very difficult to determine their number.

Separate records were kept in Block 11, the punishment block, where all the events and details were recorded there in the bunker log. The prisoner who kept this record was associated with the underground and accepted the difficult and perilous task of keeping a record parallel to the official SS log. In the course of time, it turned out that the SS needed the precise details that the prisoner had managed to record, so that the parallel record became a semiofficial one. At the beginning of 1944, the members of the underground decided that the log should be smuggled out of Auschwitz. It was copied by two prisoners—both former Polish army officers—and spirited out of the camp. An analysis of this record provides a clear picture of the special regime of terror that existed in Auschwitz—above and beyond the mass extermination of the Jews.[47]

The Transport System

For quite a while, Hans Frank, the head of the Generalgouvernement, had aspired to clear all the Jews out of his sphere of rule, despite the fact that he recognized their value as laborers. On December 16, 1941, in a meeting with a number of senior local officials and SS leaders, he hinted at the preparations being made to exterminate the Jews and even intimated that this was the reason why they were being sent to the East. He also called upon his men, "Gentlemen, I must ask you to steel yourselves against all considerations of compassion. We must destroy the Jews wherever we find them and wherever it is possible, in order to maintain the whole structure of the Reich."[48] No one asked why it was necessary to transfer masses of Jews from the Reich and the countries of the West into the General-gouvernement. It appears that all the officials and SS men present understood that masses of human beings could not be murdered within the Reich proper—or any-where else in Western Europe—and that the only place where it was possible to do so was in the occupied countries of the East. In most of the countries of the East, the Germans would not have to mount the major camouflage operation they deemed necessary in Germany in regard to a cover-up from their own people. In fact, this was among the reasons for the creation of the immense mass transpor-tation apparatus, the scheme developed by Adolf Eichmann and his subordinates as early as the winter of 1939/1940, beginning with Operation Nisko. In contrast, the actual extermination program was the task of the SS units stationed in the camps.

Conducted as it was in the midst of a global war that drew upon all the mate-rial and human resources available to the Reich, the massive extermination oper-ation was and remains one of the least comprehensible of the Nazis' actions and represented the acme of their digression from the moral maxims and rational premises of human society. To effect this program, an entire apparatus had to be built and put into operation, including the construction of technical facilities, pro-curement of chemical materials, and the mounting of complex organizational devices such as the assembling of people for deportation and the seizure of their property. It was necessary to work out a train schedule for directing the transports to their various destinations so that the program could proceed with ease and effi-ciency, free of the disruptions caused by either a dearth or glut of victims. This planning was accomplished through coordination and cooperation among various places, hierarchies, and administrations scattered across Europe. The regulation of this traffic was the key to ensuring that the gassing facilities in Sobibor and Treblinka, Majdanek and Auschwitz would be able to work at full capacity.

Obviously, neither Eichmann nor Franz Novak, the man in his department responsible for transportation, carried this operation off singlehandedly. In addi-tion to the members of the police and the administrative officials who participated in each of the originating cities and ghettos were the railroad officials and their staffs. We know of practically no case in which the men working on the technical level balked at carrying out their orders. In one instance, however, the commander of a transport to Riga complained about a stationmaster in Germany who did not respond to his requests in a very polite manner. He believed it advisable to bring this behavior to the attention of his superiors so that they could inform the stationmaster that "he must treat the members of the German police differently from the Jews. I had the impression that before [me] was one of our people who was still speaking of the 'poor Jews' and to whom the concept of 'Jew' is entirely alien."[49]

Even though it was accorded a priority second only to the transport needs of the army, the transport of Jews to the East was not free of hitches.[50] As a rule, breakdowns in the operation were due not to a lack of zeal on the part of the staffs in question, but to technical problems that could not be solved with satisfactory speed or thoroughness. From time to time, the exigencies of the war were responsible for an interruption in the supply of trains for deportations. The surprising thing is not that these disruptions occurred, but that they were usually overcome so quickly.

In 1942 we twice hear about the halt of deportations owing to the intervention of the army, which demanded that the trains be placed exclusively at its disposal. The first time—in the summer of 1942, when the Germans mounted their attack on Kharkov—the commander of the SS in the Generalgouvernement, Friedrich W. Krüger, feared that it would be impossible to continue evacuating the ghettos until August, although he managed to persuade the head of the railways in the East "to make a number of trains available for Jews here and there."[51] Since the transports from Warsaw to Treblinka were then at their height, Himmler intervened this time by having the head of his bureau, Karl Wolff, appeal directly to the state secretary of the Transport Ministry, Theodor Ganzenmüller. The exchange of letters between the two is well known because in it Ganzenmüller informed Wolff (on July 28, 1942) of the deportation of the Jews from Warsaw to Treblinka since July 22. Wolff replied to this news on August 13, 1943, "heartily" thanking the state secretary on Himmler's behalf as well as his own, "It was with special satisfaction that I received your report that for two weeks now a train with five thousand members of the Chosen People has been traveling to Treblinka daily, and hence in this fashion we were able to effect the movement of this population at an accelerated rate."[52]

The second time an extended halt occurred was in the winter of 1942 when the train service to the Ukraine broke down. On that occasion Krüger informed Himmler that because of a "transport stoppage," the trains would be suspended for a month as of December 15, 1942. This time Himmler intervened personally, writing to Ganzenmüller (in the midst of the debacle at Stalingrad [Volgograd], January 20, 1943) that since the Jews were responsible for the breakdown because of acts of sabotage against the trains, the management of the railroad should be interested in abetting their elimination as a way of putting an end to further partisan activity.[53] However, it appears that his argument failed to win over the relevant parties, who knew that the main reason for the disruptions were the weather and the shortage of trains. Thus, the transports to the death camps came to a halt at the start of the winter, but they were renewed at full pace on January 20, 1943. For all that, Raul Hilberg observes that from a quantitative standpoint, the impact of the deportations on the railway system was negligible: the total number of German trains traveling throughout Europe was twenty thousand per day, so that there was no significance whatever to the "one or one hundred" trains that carried Jews.[54]

Himmler's Order to Liquidate the Ghettos

Following his visit to Auschwitz in the middle of July 1942, Himmler conducted a visit to Lublin, and on July 19 he ordered Krüger to see to it that the Jewish population in the ghettos was liquidated by the end of the year and that any remaining Jews—meaning those employed in projects vital to the war effort—were assembled in concentration camps near the large cities (Warsaw, Cracow, Częstochowa, Radom, and Lublin were mentioned by name). Three days later, the transport of Warsaw's Jews to Treblinka began under the command of the SS officer Hermann Höfle, whose company had been sent to Warsaw expressly for that purpose. According to an estimate, by that point 250,000 of the 1.6 million Jews living in the Generalgouvernement had already been put to death.[55]

The Jews of Warsaw Are Sent to Their Deaths

The destruction of Warsaw's Jews in the period between July 22 and September 12, 1942, was one of the tragedies unparalleled among the atrocities perpetrated by the Nazis. By that point this major Jewish community—numbering at least 350,000 people at the start of the deportation[56]—was well versed in the struggle against persecution and hardship; in containing the spread of disease amid terrible crowding and inhuman sanitary conditions; and in fighting off starvation. In the face of these daunting circumstances, the Jews of Warsaw had managed to establish productive enterprises virtually out of nothing, to educate their children in secret, to feed and shelter a flood of refugees, to organize cultural activities, to publish a varied underground press, and to maintain the historical archive "Oneg Shabbat" in order to document the events of their plight[57]—all despite the Germans' endless machinations; the need to relinquish the best Jewish property to them; the forced hard labor service; and the reign of terror the Nazis conducted in the ghetto. In spite of the many setbacks, oppression, and the countless dead from starvation and disease—to say nothing of German bullets—the population of the Warsaw ghetto persevered. But when it came to the ultimate trial, Jewish Warsaw was defenseless. It had failed to break through the barrier that surrounded it, and its people—famished and in despair—were even prepared to report to the assembly point, the *Umschlagplatz* (the place for transmission of merchandise), in return for a promise of three loaves of bread and portions of jam. The suicide of Adam Czerniakow, who refused to acquiesce in the murder of his fellow Jews and felt helpless to prevent the tragedy, was somehow symbolic of what happened to the Jews of Warsaw that summer. Only after the terrible slaughter were the remaining Jews in the ghetto able to take the desperate and difficult step of shifting from a struggle for life, which had led them into the abyss, to a struggle for honor and vengeance as they faced certain death (see chap. 17).

Although the Germans had operated according to their tried-and-true system of first summoning the weak—the elderly, children, and others unfit for labor—most of the Jews in the beginning evidently did not realize that rather than bringing them to labor camps in the East, this "resettlement" *(Umsiedlung)* meant their deportation to the Treblinka extermination camp. When the destination of the transports became unavoidably clear, many tried to find a place of work in the ghetto or otherwise equip themselves with documents that would presumably exempt them from deportation.[58] Even after the Germans changed their method and began to systematically empty out whole streets, it still appeared to many that work documents would gain them an exemption. On the eve of their *Aktion,* the Nazis replaced the German policemen guarding the walls and gates of the ghetto—most of them aging soldiers—with Lithuanians, Latvians, and Ukrainians serving in the auxiliary police. Within the ghetto, however, they placed the task of rounding up the Jews and leading them to the *Umschlagplatz* on the Jewish police, against the promise that these policemen and their families would remain safe. Some of the Jewish policemen were involved in the underground or otherwise avoided carrying out the task—sometimes at the cost of their lives. But the great majority of them did not stand up to this difficult test. Yet their obedience to the Germans did them little good, for here, as everywhere else, the Nazis eventually killed those who served them. On the Day of Atonement (September 21, 1942), the Jewish policemen and the members of their families were loaded onto transports; only 380 of them remained behind.

As long as the Jewish police engaged in their deplorable labors, it was sometimes possible to evade deportation by resorting to bribery. But this chance at salvation was ruled out almost completely once the work of tracking down the Jews was turned over to the SS, Lithuanians, Latvians, and Ukrainians. The latter did not always bother to bring the Jews—especially those who resisted or otherwise tried to slip out of their grip—to the hospital that was then being used as a concentration point. Instead, they killed them on the spot. The number of people so murdered in the ghetto was close to 7,000, to which we must add an appreciable number of suicides and deaths from so-called natural causes—thus the total is over 10,000 dead. By the end of July 1942—that is, in little over a week after the start of the *Aktion*—close to 65,000 people had been "evacuated" by train, with more than 7,000 human beings crammed into each transport. At the end of August, the operation was halted for a brief spell during which the Germans emptied out the ghettos and towns in the vicinity. By early September a large portion of Warsaw's Jewish population had been liquidated, with only about one-third of the ghetto's inhabitants remaining. Among the deportees were the children of the orphanage run by the venerated educator Janusz Korczak, who chose to go to his death at the head of the line of children, even though he had an opportunity to save himself. He led his wards to the train dressed in their Sunday best, as if they were going off on an outing or celebration.

The final phase of the operation was carried out with dizzying speed. Penetrating the ghetto in a pincer movement, the Germans collected the remaining third of the inhabitants and sent more than half of them out to Treblinka. Among this last group were many people who had been employed in workshops and industry, and it was with great difficulty that the German factory owners managed to keep a certain percentage of their workers. When the *Aktion* was over, the Warsaw ghetto had been reduced to a number of mutually isolated sectors containing 65,000 Jews, 35,000 of them equipped with papers and the rest wildcats who were in hiding. About 8,000 people managed to steal over to the Aryan side of Warsaw and go into hiding there.[59]

The Warsaw Ghetto on the Eve of Its Liquidation

What had life been like in the Warsaw ghetto on the eve of the mass deportation? As the spring of 1942 approached, the situation in the ghetto seemed to ease somewhat, although there was a spate of signs that new perils lay ahead for the Jews in the Generalgouvernement. I have already noted that word of the slaughter of Jews in the eastern and western territories had reached the Jewish underground in Warsaw through emissaries who had returned from these areas with precise and reliable information. Particularly successful at this work were a number of young women whose Aryan appearance enabled them to move freely through the length and breadth of occupied Poland with the aid of forged papers.[60] Indeed, we can see from Emmanuel Ringelblum's notes that his clandestine archive, Oneg Shabbat, had received exact detailed information on what was going on in Jewish communities throughout Poland.

In May 1942 Ringelblum reported on the murders that had claimed the lives of about fifty people in each of a number of ghettos.[61] They are mentioned in connection with a similar event that had occurred in the Warsaw ghetto on the night of April 17, 1942, when the Germans, working from prepared lists, had murdered about fifty people, including a number of members of the underground. The victims had been dragged out of their homes and summarily shot in the street. This calculated and cold-blooded massacre shocked the ghetto's inhabitants and for a while left them terrified at the prospect of deportation, which, rumor had it, could be expected at any moment. Even the name "penal camp of Treblinka" had been explicitly mentioned by Ringelblum on April 23; he had learned that 164 young Jews originally from Germany—most of them members of pioneering youth movements—had been sent there. Moreover, on the day after the shooting of the fifty people in the ghetto, Czerniakow had reported in his diary that Heinz Auerswald, the German commissar of the ghetto, had given him "a list containing seventy-eight names from the last transport [from Germany]; these people are to be sent to Treblinka." At that same time, Czerniakow had also been given two letters that deportees had been forced to write before being murdered: he notes, "One [of the deportees] is asking for phonograph records, the other for tools."[62]

Before the April 17 massacre, there was a certain degree of optimism in the ghetto, as the Jews tried to convince themselves that Hitler's fall was near. Any scrap of news about German losses at the front was seized on and quickly spread; reports of this kind were even fabricated. Ringelblum observed as early as January 1942, for example, that people were buying up books at bargain rates in order to resell them after the war. But in the weeks after the April 17 murders, the residents of the ghetto vacillated between optimism and fear. On May 8, for instance, Ringelblum reported that the people had calmed down somewhat and had gone back to believing that the war would soon be over.[63]

The April 17 massacre naturally had a profound effect on the activities of the Jewish underground. Before these killings the underground had operated in a quasi-open fashion that Ringelblum dubbed a legal conspiracy. Its outlawed newspapers were not only distributed openly but even competed in the frequency of their publication. But all this changed after that night of terror; now the conspiracy was genuinely clandestine.[64] Still, one event planted hope in even Ringelblum's breast: with the aid of the Polish underground, Oneg Shabbat managed to send the information it had gathered to England, where a representative of the Bund, Shmuel A. Zygelboym, was at work collecting and passing on news of the state of the Jews in Poland. When the BBC began to report this information in June 1942, Ringelblum characterized Friday, June 26, as the greatest day for Oneg Shabbat. "This morning the English radio broadcast about the fate of Polish Jewry. They told about everything we know so well." He described how angry he and his comrades had been with the world for not responding to the destruction of Polish Jewry, but now it seemed that finally their efforts were bearing fruit. "The OS group has fulfilled a great historical mission. It alarmed the world to our fate." As it turned out, Ringelblum was tragically mistaken on this point; for although the Oneg Shabbat had fulfilled a historical mission, the hundreds of thousands of Jews still alive in Poland would not be saved as he had hoped. Indeed, within a few days Ringelblum had returned to his dire predictions, having come to the conclusion, "whether we live or die depends on how much time they [the Nazis] have. If they have enough time, we are lost."[65]

In the meantime the ghetto continued in its ways. Shortly before Ringelblum penned this comment, the Germans had permitted the schools to reopen, and the children were able to come out of the hiding places in which they had been studying with great zeal. Now it was even possible to hold a celebration out in the open. Indeed, "a large children's program was presented in the big Femina Theater hall, with children from all the schools performing and being rewarded with sweets. Procession after procession of schoolchildren marched through the streets toward the Femina."[66] That was at the end of May. Less than two months later, the children again marched through the streets of the ghetto—to the *Umschlagplatz.*

In his diary entry for July 11, Czerniakow remarked on an improvement in the economic situation. Whereas in January 1942 the German Labor Bureau had provided work to 1,268 men and 165 women, by June these figures had risen to 9,250 men and 1,802 women; the overall number of Jewish workers handled by the bureau was 24,357 men and 5,739 women. The total of 79,000 people who had been working in their respective fields in April had grown to 95,000 by June. And export from the ghetto, which had been 2 million zlotys in December 1941, had risen to 12 million zlotys in June 1942.[67]

Nevertheless, rumors of an impending deportation abounded. On July 17 Czerniakow recorded that the commissar's secretary had phoned him "saying that today we must empty the synagogue of the refugees. The building is to be placed at the disposal of the SS. . . . The day has started badly."[68] As a wave of anxiety spread through the ghetto, Czerniakow on July 20 went from one man to the next among his German contacts trying to ascertain whether there was any truth to the rumors. One said that he knew nothing about a deportation; another claimed that the matter was not related to his department and sent Czerniakow to a third person, who likewise claimed ignorance and insisted that if the rumors were true, he would know about it. The fourth contact expressed surprise at the idea, and the fifth person dismissed it as utter nonsense. Yet others pretended to be appalled at the very thought and promised to check the matter out. But Czerniakow was not reassured. The next morning, July 21, a detail from the German police appeared in his office and ordered him to call in all the members of the Judenrat who were on the premises. The remaining members were summoned according to a list; with the sole exception of Czerniakow, all of them were arrested. Later, Czerniakow's wife was likewise taken into custody. The day after that Höfle, the commander of the *Aktion,* turned up in Czerniakow's office and informed him of the impending deportation. Czerniakow wrote, "We were told that all the Jews irrespective of sex and age, with certain exceptions, will be deported to the East. By 4:00 A.M. today a contingent of six thousand people must be provided. And this (at the minimum) will be the daily quota."[69] When he learned that he had to hand over the children, Czerniakow decided to take his life. In a note he left, he said, "I am powerless, my heart trembles in sorrow and compassion. I can no longer bear all this. My act will show everyone the right thing to do."[70]

The Ghettos Throughout Poland Are Razed

Ringelblum was right to draw an analogy between the massacre on the night of April 17 in Warsaw and similar murders in other cities in the Generalgouvernement. They truly were an omen of things to come. In all the other places he mentioned in this context, *Aktionen* were, indeed, carried out sometime after the killings, with the Jews being sent to Treblinka. Transports containing a few thousand Jews had been directed to Auschwitz from **Sosnowiec** and **Będzin,** the twin cities in Eastern Upper Silesia, as far back as May and June 1942, but the main deportation operation began in August when a total of close to twenty thousand Jews were dispatched from these two communities.[71]

During the three successive selections conducted in **Cracow** in June 1942, hundreds of people were being killed in the ghetto itself and five thousand were sent to Bełżec. The next *Aktion* there did not take place until the end of October, when six thousand people were again sent to Bełżec; patients in the hospitals, residents of the old-age home, and children in the city's orphanages were murdered on the spot.

The ghettos in the **Radom District** were emptied out in August 1942, their tens of thousands of Jews being deported to Treblinka.[72]

Częstochowa was one of the relatively strong and better organized Jewish communities in Poland. Prior to the war it had numbered 28,500 people, and even though the Germans had embarked on a series of pogroms immediately after capturing the city on September 3, 1939, in the subsequent months many refugees came to Częstochowa. A ghetto was not established there until April 9, 1941—

during the round of creating ghettos that preceded the attack on the Soviet Union—and it was closed on August 23, 1941. As in other communities in the district, 1,000 young people had been sent to labor camps in the Lublin District in August 1940, with almost all of them perishing there. And from September 21, which was Yom Kippur (the Day of Atonement), to October 5, 1942, there were 39,000 people sent to Treblinka, 2,000 others having been killed in the *Aktion* itself.[73]

Like Warsaw, Częstochowa experienced a certain degree of economic development in the period just prior to the liquidation. With the aid of ŻSS, a mechanized metal workshop was created along with other new shops for carpentry, tailoring, and the manufacture of brushes. At the same time, the Germans concentrated a number of industrial plants in the area, primarily for the production of arms—the most important one being Hugo Schneider's Hasag. The hundreds of Jews employed in this factory and four others had good reason to believe that their situation was more or less secure, for they were supplying a product vital to the German army.

At the same time, there was certainly cause for concern in Częstochowa. Individual acts of terror increased, and the Judenrat was given just two days to vacate the building it had inhabited throughout the ghetto period, rousing fears that the entire street was about to be evacuated. At the end of August, rumors circulated that a Kommando was being dispatched to Częstochowa for the purpose of annihilating the Jews, and many people began to prepare hiding places in cellars and attics. Then, without warning or explanation, the Judenrat was ordered to pay a fine of 550,000 zlotys. As the council had nowhere near that sum in its coffers, it appealed to people of means (who could still be found in Częstochowa) for a loan, promising to pay it back as soon as the money could be collected from the community. Considering the threat hanging over the ghetto if the sum was not paid, the prospective donors were accommodating, and a committee formed to determine the quota each one donor would pay. Most of these people fulfilled their obligations, but those who tried to evade making the payment were forced to do so by the police.[74]

After this incident, apprehension increased from day to day in Częstochowa, especially as reports filtered in about the boasts of a group of Ukrainians that for two months they had been engaged in liquidating the Warsaw ghetto and that it was for this same task that they had now been sent to Częstochowa. Here, as in Warsaw, the members of the Judenrat began to ask the Germans what the spurt of police activity near the ghetto was about; and, as in Warsaw, they received soothing replies—and believed them. To enhance that reassuring impression the Germans submitted new orders to the shops, until the Day of Atonement arrived. The *Aktion* began in the wee hours of the morning, with the local commander of the police, Degenhardt, standing in the market and passing judgment on who would live and who would die, "With a baton in hand, like a conductor, he reviewed the groups passing before him and whenever he spied some strong man or attractive young woman, he waved that baton as a sign that the person should be removed from the line. They were taken out and placed on the side, meaning that they would stay behind."[75] The Jewish doctors and their families together with the Jewish policemen were spared during this round, and some of the bachelor doctors managed to couple up with young women, thereby saving them as well. Before being placed on the trains, the Jews were ordered to remove their shoes, so that "mountains of shoes immediately gathered and shot up, each pair being tied together by the laces." Those who remained behind in Częstochowa were concentrated in the Little Ghetto. Extending over the three worst streets, it now contained some sixty-five hundred people, including about one thousand illegals.

The fifth and last *Aktion* of this period was conducted on October 4, 1942. As it was drawing to a conclusion, Degenhardt entered the Jewish hospital, called all the doctors and nurses together, and ordered them to kill all the patients by injection. At first the doctors argued that they lacked the necessary drugs, but "the commander retorted that if the task was not completed within two hours, he would order all the doctors and nurses shot to death along with all the patients." After a consultation, the doctors decided to carry out the order. "As all [the patients] lay dying, all the doctors and nurses stood at their bedsides weeping over their deaths and their own deeds." The remaining Jews of Częstochowa no longer harbored any illusions, "A few days after we were transferred to the Little Ghetto, some people who had fled from the extermination camp at Treblinka reached us and revealed that the Jews taken to the camp had been exterminated in gas chambers."[76]

On March 20, 1943, the Germans mounted a special operation to wipe out the intelligentsia remaining in the ghetto. It took place on Saturday, the eve of the holiday of Purim, with Degenhardt portraying it as a "trip to Palestine." All the doctors, members of the Judenrat, and others regarded as belonging to the intelligentsia, together with their families—for a total of 127 people, including 10 small children—were taken to the cemetery and shot. One of those children, a kindergarten tot named Lilka, was immortalized in the following description, "One day the kindergarten children—defying fate—put together a play on the subject of brotherhood among the nations. The day of the presentation was also Lilka's birthday. Dressed in her blue velvet frock, she sang, danced, laughed, and was happy. That same afternoon she was taken with her family to the assembly point and from there to the cemetery." The story has it that she begged the Gestapo man, "Let me live."[77]

The Częstochowa ghetto was completely liquidated in the summer of 1943.

Himmler's order to do away with all the Jews in the Generalgouvernement by the end of 1942 was not carried out in full, though the overwhelming majority of these Jews had been exterminated by then. According to the summary report drawn up by Richard Korherr, Himmler's statistical expert, the result of the Nazis' persecution and extermination campaign against Europe's Jews through the end of 1942 was a total of 1,419,467 Jews "filtered through" *(wurden durchgeschleust)*—meaning exterminated—in the camps in the East, 1,274,467 in the Generalgouvernement, and 145,301 in Warthegau. These figures included the Jews who had previously been deported to camps and ghettos from the Greater Reich and the rest of Europe as well as those who had been sent directly to the extermination camps. Hence, it is difficult to determine precisely how many Polish Jews had been murdered in the extermination camps by that date, especially since the number who had perished in the ghettos and labor camps was very high. According to the German account, on December 31, 1942, a total of 385,094 Jews remained in Łódź and the five districts of the Generalgouvernement (87,180 in the former; 297,914 in the latter). This number represents only those Jews who had been counted in a census and is unquestionably too low, as the following statistics indicate. At the outbreak of the war, 2,350,000 Jews had been living in the Generalgouvernement and the areas annexed to the Reich. To this number we must add the 1,150,000 Jews then living in the area of Russian occupation—500,000 of them in eastern Galicia (the Lwów area)—bringing the total number of Jews under German domination in the East to 3,500,000 people, of whom no more than about 300,000 succeeded in fleeing to the Soviet Union and other countries and who were not subsequently captured.[78]

The Internal German Struggle over Jewish Labor

Himmler's directive of July 19, 1942, that called for all the Jews remaining after the *Aktionen* to be concentrated in "collection camps" was only partially fulfilled. Among these camps were some of the more notorious of their kind, such as Majdanek near Lublin; Poniatowa and Trawniki in the same area, which received many Jews from Warsaw; and Płaszow near Cracow, whose construction was begun in June 1942. The number of Jews employed in Płaszow in the production of glass, metal, clothing, and brushes reached a high of twenty thousand people, including six thousand sent there from Cracow in April 1943. Skarżysko-Kamienna, a large "Jewish camp" (or *Julag,* short for *Judenlager*), was established in the Radom District to exploit the labor of the Jews from that area, including Częstochowa.[79]

The summer of 1942 was marked by a struggle raging within the Generalgouvernement over the issue of Jewish labor, especially as it proved to be a significant factor in the munitions industry. By that point the shortage of manpower had begun to be felt quite keenly in the Third Reich. Thus Fritz Sauckel, whom Hitler had appointed on March 21, 1942, to mobilize manpower for agriculture and industry in the Reich, was demanding the release of workers from Poland to be transferred to the Reich proper.[80] At that time, the systematic extermination of the Jews had begun, though even Hans Frank was forced to admit the value of the Jewish work force. On December 9, 1942, a year after his fiery speech calling for the elimination of the Jews as quickly as possible, Frank told his subordinates, "Clearly the labor situation is aggravated when, at the height of the war effort, an order is given to prepare Jews for annihilation."[81]

The solution to this paradox was sought in an attempt to achieve both objectives—eliminating the Jews and exploiting them as a work force—by adopting the official doctrine of "extermination through labor" *(Vernichtung durch Arbeit).* Ever since their occupation of Poland, the Germans had, in fact, been practicing this doctrine by forcing the Jews to do hard labor—whether in a random or organized manner—as a consequence of which thousands of them died in the camps and the ghettos. At the Wannsee Conference, Heydrich unequivocally commended this system and its aims. On September 18, 1942, it received an official stamp of approval in the form of an agreement between Himmler and the new minister of justice, Dr. Otto Thierack, by which asocial elements would be turned over to the SS and the police without a trial. The determination of these asocial elements had earlier been established by Goebbels in a meeting with Thierack, "Dr. Goebbels's view is that Jews and Gypsies should be eliminated altogether, as should Poles sentenced to three or four years of harsh imprisonment, Czechs, and Germans sentenced to death, life imprisonment, or security detention. Extermination through labor would be the best idea."[82]

An RSHA memorandum of November 5, 1942, informed all the departments of the SD and the police that "the agreement has been confirmed by the Führer" (meaning that it was legally binding). These people were not to be tried according to criminal law, which took an offender's motives into account. Instead, "what counts is that the act [committed by the asocial] imperils the order of the German nation."[83] Turning people over to the SD and the police meant that they would be incarcerated in concentration camps, joining the host of workers doing hard labor. Hence, there were now two kinds of camps: extermination camps per se and the work camps in which the doctrine of extermination through labor was put into practice.

Throughout the summer of 1942, internal discussions were held on the exploitation of the Jewish labor force, which seemed to be vital but ran counter to the urgency with which the extermination program was being conducted. Thus Alfred Rosenberg's office, which was responsible for the occupied territories in the countries of the East *(Ostland),* warned of the danger that "precisely because of the economy, in many cases the Jews will be declared indispensable manpower." Rosenberg further contended that no effort had been made to find an alternative work force "and this will ruin the plan of total deportation of the Jews from the territories we occupy."[84]

As the army was then the principal employer of Jews in the Generalgouvernement, on July 17, 1942, Krüger tried to reach an agreement with General Schindler, who was in charge of the armament industry in the Generalgouvernement, on replacing the industry's Jewish workers. The compromise reached in these negotiations had the army promising to "discharge" all the barracks camps housing the Jewish workers, whom it agreed to forgo, in return for which the SS relented on its demand for the "total deportation" of the Jewish armament workers. Krüger promised to set up and manage Jewish labor camps in accordance with the demands of the Armament Inspectorate (Rüstungsinspektion) and likewise to conduct the liquidation of the ghettos in coordination with its needs.[85] It may be assumed that Himmler's order that explicitly stressed the imperative of emptying all the ghettos—issued as it was two days after this compromise was reached—was designed to foil the agreement and remind Krüger that he was supposed to be liquidating the ghettos and dispatching the Jews to extermination camps; thus, he was not to yield too readily to the army's demands.

Within two months this conflict of interests between Himmler and the army had reached the point of an open clash. On September 5, Field Marshal Wilhelm

Keitel yielded to the demands of the SS by issuing an order to replace the Jewish workers with Poles. General Curt L. Freiherr von Gienanth, commander of the military authorities in the Generalgouvernement, responded to the order in a report to the OKW, dated September 18, stating that up to that point the Polish and Ukrainian laborers transferred to the Reich had been replaced by Jewish workers, who were concentrated in special plants. But now that the SS had removed these Jews from many of the plants without prior notice, it was proving impossible to find substitutes for them. He also noted that three hundred thousand of the one million industrial workers were Jews; that one hundred thousand of these Jews were skilled workers; and that in some branches of the economy the Jews composed the key production personnel. The number of private firms working for the army, particularly in the textile and leather industries, was also considerable. Hence, Gienanth concluded, "The immediate removal of the Jews would cause a considerable reduction in Germany's war potential." To avert this problem, he recommended that the Jews not be released until replacements could be trained—this in his estimation would take anywhere from a few months to over a year. He, therefore, requested that the removal of the Jews from the industrial enterprises be postponed until the needs for the winter had been ensured.[86]

The background to this struggle over the Jewish work force and other sources of labor in the Generalgouvernement was the Reich's overall war effort. By the beginning of 1942, it was already plain to see that Göring's Four-Year Plan had not met its schedule; the armament industry had fallen severely behind and would not reach the specifications set for it. In place of Dr. Fritz Todt, who had died in a plane crash on February 8, the führer appointed Albert Speer as minister for armament and ammunition. The enhancement of Germany's war potential required one decisive factor: a larger work force. Thus Speer wanted to create a central authority for recruiting this work force, and Hitler accepted his thinking, assigning the job to one of his Old Warriors, the ruthless Gauleiter Fritz Sauckel. Within a few months Hitler had invested Sauckel with broad powers to mobilize manpower in all the countries under German control.[87]

Himmler wished to exploit this restructuring of the war economy to expand his own economic domain, and in February 1942 he established the WVHA under Pohl, who likewise believed it necessary to revamp the organization of the concentration camps to conform with their new economic role. Himmler intended to build some of the new factories in the camps and set the prisoners to work under SS supervision. But Speer and the army had no intention of allowing him to gain control over the manufacture of arms and ammunition. Moreover, they won Hitler over to their view, and it was decided that while the concentration camps would make prisoners available to the armament industry, these worker-prisoners would constitute only a limited portion of the personnel in any workplace at any one time. Although Himmler was promised 3 to 5 percent of the production, Speer and the army managed to foil that plan as well.[88]

Following the Wannsee Conference, at which the Final Solution became official state policy, the question arose: What should be done with the Jews, who constituted a substantial portion of the skilled work force of the armament industry in both the Generalgouvernement and the Reich proper? This question was discussed, among other issues, by Speer and Sauckel at meetings with Hitler on September 20 to 22, 1942. According to the minutes of these talks, Hitler's decision on the matter was, "The Führer accepts Sauckel's suggestion that for the present the skilled Jewish workers should remain in the Generalgouvernement, but he stresses the importance of removing the Jews from the armament industry in the Reich."[89] Thus in the conflict between the principle of extermination and the need to exploit the work force, Hitler decided to continue using Jewish labor in the Generalgouvernement for the time being but to step up the deportation of the Jewish workers from Greater Germany. The second part of this decision was carried out in the spring of 1943 (see chap. 16).

A few days before these decisions were taken, Gienanth had sent off his memorandum underscoring the importance of the Jewish skilled workers for the armament industry in the Generalgouvernement. Thus Himmler sustained a triple blow: he was prevented from establishing armament plants within his own domain; the commander of the army was protesting the extermination of the Jews engaged in the plants working for the military; and Hitler, together with Sauckel and Speer, had blocked him from concluding the job he had projected in the Generalgouvernement. His reaction was vehement. On September 30, 1942, General Gienanth was dismissed, and at the beginning of October Himmler issued an order spelling out his counterinstructions, "I have given orders that all so-called armament workers who are actually employed solely in tailoring, furrier, and shoemaking workshops be collected in concentration camps on the spot, i.e., in Warsaw and Lublin."[90] Thus the army would have to submit its orders for goods to the SS Economic Office headed by Pohl. Himmler railed against all those who opposed the evacuation of the Jewish workers in the "alleged interest of armament needs" and demanded that they be treated "ruthlessly." He further proposed that the Jews who were genuinely needed in the armament plants be concentrated in large special camps, preferably in the eastern part of the Generalgouvernement. But there, too, the day would come when the Jews would be eliminated "in accordance with the Führer's wishes."

We have seen that despite Himmler's orders, not all the ghettos had been liquidated by the end of 1942, and as matters turned out neither were all the Jews concentrated in a limited number of camps. To the 300,000 Jews remaining in the ghettos of the Generalgouvernement (by Korherr's count) we must add those imprisoned in the labor camps. In the autumn of 1942, Krüger also confirmed the existence of fifty-five "residential areas in Galicia" (out of one thousand that had existed there beforehand!), and it is estimated that there were still 600,000 to 700,000 Jews in the Generalgouvernement at the end of 1942.[91]

When Himmler arrived in Warsaw at the beginning of January 1943 to take stock of the situation there, he complained that the ghetto still had not been eradicated and that "the order issued directly by the Führer" had not been obeyed.[92] Finding that 35,000 to 40,000 Jews were living openly in the ghetto—32,000 of whom were working "in so-called armament plants"—Himmler set February 15, 1943, as the new deadline for the fulfillment of his demands. The private enterprises in the ghetto, especially those of W. C. Többens (whom he accused, not without reason, of making millions in profits), were to be liquidated. Többens was to be sent to the front, and the 16,000 Jews working in his textile plants were to be sent to a concentration camp, "preferably to Lublin." Himmler also insisted that 8,000 Jews be eliminated in the coming days. This was the background to the *Aktion* conducted in the ghetto on January 18 when the Germans met with armed resistance for the first time and were prevented from discharging their task to the full (see chap. 17).

Himmler wanted to concentrate the Jewish workers in as few camps as possible under SS supervision; in addition, he tried to get his hands on the machinery and other equipment left idle in the workshops and factories whose workers were being deported to extermination camps. His objective was twofold: to broaden the economic base of his dominion while disposing of the Jews. Toward that end, in March 1943, he founded a company named OSTI (Ostindustrie), designed to become his economic mainstay, and he placed Pohl at the head of this new enterprise. During the summer of 1943, OSTI established five plants, two of them in Lublin (under Globocnik's aegis) employing 14,300 workers. They augmented the existing labor camps, such as Janowska in Lwów and Płaszow in Cracow, which were likewise under the supervision of Pohl's office. Nevertheless, OSTI failed to establish itself as a going concern because it lacked two elements essential for the consolidation of an industry—capital and manpower—and it was disbanded a year later, in April 1944. On the other hand, Jews continued to work in the army's enterprises.[93]

The Deportations from the West

Just as the extermination program in Poland was reaching massive proportions, the planned and systematic transport of West European Jewry to the death camps in Poland began. In accordance with the conclusions of the Wannsee Conference, the Germans now embarked upon the extermination of all the Jews living in countries under German domination or in the Reich's sphere of influence. On June 11, 1942, Eichmann summoned his agents in Holland, Belgium, and France to a meeting in his office in Berlin, where he laid down the general lines for initiating this phase of the extermination program.[94] Auschwitz was chosen as the main site for the extermination of the Jews of Western European countries, though some of the transports from the West were directed to the eastern border of the Generalgouvernement, primarily to Sobibor.

France

The quota for France was set as the deportation of 100,000 Jews by the end of 1942. On June 23, 1942, Eichmann informed Franz Rademacher, his contact in the Foreign Ministry, that from mid-July onward trains would be leaving the Western countries daily carrying 40,000 French Jews, the same number of Dutch Jews, and 10,000 Belgian Jews to the East.[95] Indeed, Eichmann's office saw to it that a transport left France or Holland each and every day. The operation began in France—or, to be more exact, it continued at an accelerated pace, for these were not the first deportations from France (see chap. 14). Even so, the operation did not work out exactly as planned. A card file and lists of the Jews had long been ready, but political and organizational problems impeded the implementation of the plans. As there were not enough German policemen in France to handle a major operation of this sort, it was necessary to obtain the cooperation of the French police, who had to obey the orders of the Vichy government. Toward that end, HSSPF Karl Albrecht Oberg, who had recently been assigned to France, conducted negotiations with Pierre Laval, adding threats to his false assurances that the Jews would be allowed to establish a state of their own in the East. Invoking the distinction that the French made between native and immigrant Jews, Laval consented to the deportation of the "foreigners" from both zones of France, including children from the free zone.[96] This qualification forced the Germans to reduce the previously set quotas. In Bordeaux, for example, they failed to fill the train with one thousand Jews as planned because only 150 "foreign" Jews could be found. Consequently, they had to cancel the transport, which infuriated Eichmann, who was not one to take the abortion of his plans lightly.[97]

The main operation was, of course, conducted in Paris, where, according to the police card file, 28,000 immigrants—both veterans and recent arrivals—were still to be found.[98] The Germans laid the groundwork for the *Aktion* by mounting a broad propaganda campaign and preparing an organizational master plan. For weeks they showed a film called *The Jewish Peril,* which described the lives of the Jews in the most backward areas of Eastern Europe and the ghettos of Poland.[99] At the same time, official German posters warned that the death sentence awaited not only anyone who demonstrated resistance to the German occupation but also the members of his family.

Once the secretary-general of the French National Police in the Vichy government, René Bousquet, agreed to cooperate, thousands of policemen were assembled in Paris, divided into 888 squads of three to four men apiece, and given the names and addresses of the people to be arrested. As usual in German-run operations, all the squads were to go into action simultaneously. The policemen were given explicit instructions not to accept any argument or defer to any situation that might be grounds for postponing the arrest—such as illness—and to bring in all the people and their children. No child was to be left behind in an apartment or with a neighbor, whereas a family's dog or cat was to be left with the concierge.[100]

The operation was scheduled to begin at 4:00 A.M. on July 16, 1942, and to end the following day. Rumors of its approach had begun to circulate, and despite the heavy cloak of secrecy, Frenchmen were warning their friends and acquaintances that something was afoot. All told, not 22,000 (as planned) but 12,884 Jews were captured, including 4,051 children. Most of the 3,000 men were sent directly to the transit camp at Drancy, while close to 7,000 other family members were taken to a Parisian stadium known as the Vélodrome d'Hiver. There, in the bird cage—as it was called by the commander of the operation, Heinz Röthke, who was soon to replace Theodor Dannecker—the families remained for days on end without food, water, or sanitary facilities until the situation began to resemble the condition in the concentration points in Eastern Europe. At one point André

Baur, the chairman of UGIF in the occupied zone, managed to bring Röthke to the stadium, and as a result a number of pregnant women and war invalids were released. Thirty people died in the stadium, and there were instances of others going insane. Eventually, the more than 4,000 children were wrested from their parents and held in a separate camp, from which they were later deported to the East in groups. Eichmann phoned specially from Berlin to assure the Gestapo men—who were engaged in a dispute with the French over the fate of the children—that trains would, indeed, be made available to carry these Jews to the Generalgouvernement. Finally, the transports began departing at regular intervals; between July 19 and August 31, twenty-two such trains left France, each carrying 1,000 people. All told, some 25,000 Jews were sent to the East during this period, most of them stateless persons or "foreigners."[101]

As Drancy was the largest camp in France, the majority of the trains left from there. It was run by a French police officer—under the supervision of the German commandant—assisted by a number of inspectors responsible for the civil status of the prisoners and by French policemen to guard the camp. The internal administration of the camp was given over to the Jews themselves, who dealt with such matters as housing, sanitation, welfare assistance, and the care of children. The camp's economic management and medical service were run by professionals in the employ of the French police.[102]

While this operation was in progress, Dannecker tried to sort out the situation in southern France and speed up the deportation to Auschwitz from there as well. He visited various camps in the south but did not find many Jews in them. Finally, after various postponements and delays, at the beginning of September the Vichy government turned 7,100 Jews over to the SS, and they were added to the transports. Naturally, the pressure on the southern zone increased once the Germans conquered it in the wake of the Allied invasion of North Africa in November 1942. According to Korherr's figures, 41,911 Jews had been deported from France to the East by the end of 1942—certainly not 100,000 (50,000 from each zone) as had originally been planned.[103]

Holland

The deportation action in Holland began at the same time as the operation in France, with the first trains leaving for Auschwitz on July 15. It has already been noted that on July 18, 1942, Himmler was present at a selection of Dutch Jews when this first train reached its destination.[104] By September 24, 1942, Hanns A. Rauter was able to inform Himmler, "To date we have shipped a total of 20,000 Jews off to Auschwitz—including those who were sent to Mauthausen as punishment." He then explained the stratagem by which he intended to catch another 30,000 Jews "in one lightning blow" on October 1. He was referring to the 7,000 Jews who had already been drafted and were in labor camps, to which he hoped to add another 1,000 together with all their relatives, whom he estimated at 22,000 people. "I want to try to obtain three trains a week, instead of two," he wrote, adding his hope that "by Christmas we shall also be rid of these 30,000 Jews, so that by then 50,000 Jews, or half of Dutch Jewry, will have been eliminated."[105]

Notices to report for labor duty were sent out by the Central Bureau for Jewish Emigration in Amsterdam. Unlike earlier summonses, which demanded that the recipient report for work in Holland, this time notices spoke of "service to increase employment in Germany under the supervision of the police."[106] After being interned in the camps, the Jews were given preworded forms that read:

> I have been in a labor camp since September 3. I am fine. We receive sufficient and very tasty food and drink. For the present we are forbidden to receive mail. We have been told that our stay here will be short, so that it is not necessary to send me anything. The camp provides us with underwear. As you can see, you needn't worry about me. In closing, I wish you well. Hearty regards.[107]

All the prisoner had to do was fill in the date and name and address of the addressee and append his signature.

The Dutch underground published a statement giving a precise description of the organization, course, and objective of the deportation and warning the Jews not to respond to the notices. It also reported on the murder of the Jews in Poland, basing the story on official Polish communiqués from London. The Dutch public was asked to send unsigned letters of protest to the German military command in Holland.[108] The local Catholic church officially protested the deportation of Catholics of Jewish origin, in response to which the Germans organized a special manhunt for such Jews (one of whom was the philosopher Edith Stein) and sent them to Auschwitz. Among the means used to get the Jews to report for deportation was the threat that anyone who failed to come to the assembly point would be tracked down and sent to Mauthausen. The Jews already knew that deportation to Mauthausen meant all but certain death, whereas they still did not know, or refused to believe, that deportation to Auschwitz meant exactly the same.

The campaign to deport the Jews from Holland had been well prepared by the German authorities. After the regulation to wear a yellow badge was put into effect at the end of April, the Jews' right to a legal defense was officially revoked in May, and the police were granted broad powers of arrest and the drafting of indictments. Moreover, the Jews were forbidden to move their belongings from one place to another without a special license in order to prevent the concealment of property. On June 30, 1942—that is, two weeks before the start of the deportations—severe limitations were placed on the Jews' freedom of movement, with a curfew being declared from 8:00 P.M. to 6:00 A.M. and shopping hours being restricted. These limitations were joined by prohibitions against working in any economic field and any branch of medicine or related professions. All these provisions were designed to force the jobless Jews, who were also denied freedom of movement, to report for "labor service" or even directly for deportation to the East.[109]

In the cited report to Himmler, Rauter praised the conduct of the Dutch police—who were working in cooperation with the German police and the Dutch National Socialist squads—in writing, "The new squads of the Dutch police are outstanding in their handling of the Jewish question and are arresting the Jews by the hundreds, day and night." The concentration point from which the Jews were sent to Auschwitz was the Westerbork Camp, which had formerly been a refugee camp. Initially, the camp's day-to-day affairs were run by the remaining 1,000 refugees from Germany, but in 1944 they, too, were placed on transports and sent to the East. It must be said, however, that despite all the careful preparations and the systematic and sophisticated management of the operation, Rauter failed to fill the quota he had set for himself. According to Korherr's figures, by the end of 1942, when the army halted the train traffic to Auschwitz, 38,571 Jews had been dispatched from Holland.[110]

Belgium

The difficulties that arose in Belgium when the Germans instituted their actions against the Jews have already been noted. For various reasons the SS did not obtain complete control over the Belgian civil service or the public at large, as they did, for example, in Holland. On July 22, 1942, the first *Aktion* was carried out, and the candidates for deportation were taken to the transfer camp at Malines (Mechlen). Reports and rumors of the plan to deport the Jews to work in Germany—or so it was assumed—had been rife even earlier because 2,250 Jews had been sent out of Belgium to work for the Todt organization in factories in northern France (we shall return to them further on).[111] As early as July 9, Werner von Bargen, the representative of the German Foreign Ministry in Belgium, had reported difficulties in organizing the deportation to the East because the Belgians failed to display "sufficient understanding" of the Germans' objectives. When Jews were rounded up for the transport—the majority of them immigrants and refugees—voices of protest were raised in the Belgian public. Through the mediation of various people connected to the Belgian court, leaders of the AJB requested an audience with Queen Mother Elizabeth, and two days later, on August 1, 1942, three distinguished members of the community met with her. They described the harrowing deportation to Germany of infants, children, and old people without consideration for familial ties.[112] Promising to intercede, the queen mother appealed to Hitler through the military governor, General Alexander von Falkenhausen, while the head of the military administration in Belgium, Eggert von Reeder, left for Berlin to clarify the matter with Himmler. As a result, the RSHA agreed not to deport Jews who were Belgian citizens or break up families. An agreement was also reached with the Gestapo whereby no men over the age of sixty-five or women over the age of sixty would be liable to deportation. How could such people—the Belgians argued—be "recruited for work" (which was ostensibly the reason for the deportations)? Afterward, the queen mother again intervened whenever it was brought to her attention that the agreement was not being honored.

On August 1, however, Eichmann's office cabled an order to Hermann Ehlers, the commander of Sipo and the SS in Brussels, to deport the stateless Jews. The first transport apparently left on the following day, August 2, and reached Auschwitz on August 5. As usual, it included about 1,000 people (998 to be precise), of whom 744 (426 men and 318 women) were deemed fit for hard labor and were transferred to the camp; the remaining 25 percent, sent directly to the gas chambers, undoubtedly included the 80 children on the transport. This ratio changed for the worse as time went on, so that in the transport that reached Auschwitz on

October 12, only 28 men and 88 women were sent to the camp and about 88 percent of the deportees were killed.[113] Notwithstanding the delays that followed the queen mother's intercession, by September 15, in accordance with the predetermined quota, 10,000 Jews had been deported in ten transports. In contrast to the developments in Holland and France, even though more and more Jews were going underground in Belgium, Eichmann's people managed to exceed this quota, so that by the end of October seventeen transports had been sent to Auschwitz with a total of 16,622 people: 6,894 men, 6,386 women, and 3,342 children under the age of sixteen.[114]

Belgian Jewish Communists tried to sabotage the deportation operation by destroying the card file in the offices of AJB. Then Robert Holzinger, a Jew from Austria who had been appointed to head the machinery for the "recruitment for labor" *(Arbeitseinsatz),* was shot down. In response to the threats of Sipo and to a manhunt conducted by the Germans after these incidents, Chief Rabbi Salomon Ullman resigned as head of the AJB; shortly thereafter, he was arrested together with five of the leading Jewish officials in Brussels. The five Belgian citizens were sent to the concentration camp in the Breedonk Fortress; the sixth detainee, of Hungarian origin, was placed on a transport to Auschwitz. The other five were released two weeks later following the intervention of high-level Belgian figures, including Cardinal Roey and Queen Mother Elizabeth. Even the military government, which was the highest authority in Belgium, did not agree with the way Eichmann's people were operating, but essentially the latter achieved their objective, and the new leaders of the AJB were more submissive than their predecessors. The Jewish population, however, increasingly dissociated itself from them.[115]

Norway

From the outset of the German occupation of Norway, the administration of the country was placed in the hands of Reichskommissar Josef Terboven (see chap. 5) without giving Vidkun Quisling a chance to rule the country. In fact, it was not until February 1942 that the Germans were prepared to install Quisling in power—so to speak—and allow him to run his own government. During the summer of 1942 he made various efforts to free himself of German tutelage, in one case proposing to Hitler that Germany enter into a peace treaty with Norway, for Quisling hoped that such an arrangement would enable him to conduct an independent policy. But his efforts met with opposition from all concerned: Hitler, the Germans stationed in Norway, and the Norwegian people, who refused to lend a hand to any political body under Quisling's leadership. In the course of September 1942, it became increasingly clear that Quisling had no hope of realizing his ambitions. The struggle going on in Norway was marked by considerable unrest and insurgent counteractions, particularly from within the labor unions and clerical circles. Under these circumstances, it appears that Quisling decided to seize upon action against the Jews as a life buoy, for he believed that an initiative of this kind would enhance his status in German eyes. The action against the Jews was duly discharged, but Quisling did not improve his lot. On the contrary, from then on he was little better than a lackey to his German masters.[116]

During the first months after his return to "power," in the spring of 1942, the Jews' identity cards were stamped with the letter *J.* On November 17 a law was passed requiring Jews to register with the police for the purpose of conducting a new census, which was structured according to the principles of the Nuremberg Laws. Even before then, Jews had been arrested from time to time, and there had been isolated cases of executions, primarily in the northern city of Trondheim. But these incidents were not distinguished in any way from similar measures taken against the Norwegian population at large. For example, all the Norwegians (with the exception of members of the Norwegian Nazi Party) were forbidden to keep radio sets—though this restriction was initially applied to the Jews alone. Widespread arrests increased during August and September, with the chief rabbi, Julius Samuel, being among those detained. He was taken into custody on September 2 along with a number of other Jews who had all been called in by the Gestapo a number of times before but who were now held in Norway's main detention camp, Grini.[117] The main thrust in the roundup of Jewish men came on the night of October 25; the following day the Quisling government issued a law expropriating all Jewish property. Close to a month later, on November 20, eighteen Jews, including Rabbi Samuel, were deported from the country by boat, first to Germany and then on to Auschwitz, where they perished.

The main deportation, however, was executed on November 26. Women and children were arrested on the previous night in yet another lightning operation; then, together with all the remaining men, they were placed aboard the *Donau,* which was waiting to sail. It is not clear who decided on this action and what role Quisling played in it—beyond the fact that the Norwegian police, under Quisling's command, participated in making the arrests alongside German policemen. It appears that the head of the Sipo and the SD in Oslo, Hermann Y. H. Reinhard, organized this deportation on his own initiative. (We should recall that Eichmann had no agent of his own in Norway—as he did in Holland, for instance—and that in light of Martin Luther's remarks at the Wannsee Conference, no operation of this kind was planned for the Scandinavian countries.) Essentially, Reinhard presented Eichmann's office with a *fait accompli,* leaving Eichmann's deputy, Rolf Günther, with no choice but to take the steps necessary for receiving the deportees in the Baltic port of Stettin (Szczecin) and transferring them to Auschwitz. The 532 men, women, and children arrived at Auschwitz on December 1, and 186 of the men were kept in the camp—all the others were sent to their deaths.[118]

Forewarned of this action by members of the police, the Norwegian underground made great efforts to place the Jews in hiding until they could be smuggled over the long, mountainous border with Sweden. Over 800 Jews, including Rabbi Samuel's wife, Henrietta, and three children, were saved in this way.[119] But a number of others who had been sent to Oslo from the northern areas and arrived after the *Donau* had sailed, together with dozens of Jews whom the Germans had meanwhile arrested with the aid of Norwegian Nazi policemen, were deported by boat at the end of February 1943. Docking at Stettin, they were sent on to Berlin, on Eichmann's orders, and then attached to one of the transports to Auschwitz. Of the more than 760 deportees, only 24 returned to Norway after the war. At least 20 other Jews died in Norway itself. On the other hand, about 900 of the approximately 1,700 Jews who had been living in Norway in the spring of 1940 reached safety in Sweden—most of them with the aid of the underground. Thus about 750 Jews perished.[120]

Other than the activists in the Norwegian underground, church people also came to the defense of the Jews. Many members of the Lutheran Church of Norway, the official state religion, as well as of other Protestant sects, had long resisted Quisling's government, and for months an appreciable number of clergy had been refusing to accept their salaries from the government as an expression of their opposition to the regime.[121] On November 11 the Lutheran bishops in cooperation with clergy from several other Protestant sects sent a letter of protest to Quisling; in December it was twice read from the pulpit and was published as the New Year's message for 1943. After noting the arrest of all the Jewish males over the age of fifteen and the order confiscating Jewish property, the protest stated:

> For 91 years Jews have had a legal right to reside and to earn a livelihood in our country. Now they are being deprived of their property without warning. . . . Jews have not been charged with transgression of the country's laws, much less convicted of such transgressions by judicial procedure. Nevertheless, they are being punished as severely as the worst criminals are punished. They are being punished because of their racial background, wholly and solely because they are Jews. . . . Thus, according to God's Word, all people have, in the first instance, the same human worth and thereby the same human rights. Our state authorities are by law obliged to respect this basic view. . . . To remain silent about this legalized injustice against the Jews, would render ourselves co-guilty in this injustice.[122]

This proclamation not only was circulated in Norway and Sweden but was read over the Norwegian-language and other broadcasts of the BBC.

Greater Germany: The Deportations to Theresienstadt and the East

During the summer of 1942, alongside the preparations for the mass deportations to extermination camps in the East, the Germans were planning the transports to Theresienstadt. These were to come primarily from Bohemia-Moravia—the Protectorate—but to some degree from Germany and Austria. Accordingly, the Gestapo sent explicit orders to the officers responsible for arranging "Jewish emigration" from the Reich, detailing which Jews were to be exempted from the transports to the East. They explained, however, that "at the appropriate time, all those who are not to be sent to the East, for the aforementioned reasons, [should be] sent to the Old People's Ghetto Theresienstadt."[123]

Transports left Germany and Austria for Theresienstadt beginning early in June 1942, and a steady stream of Jews flowed there from the Protectorate throughout the year. By the end of December, seventy-three transports had delivered 61,490 Jews from the Protectorate, including 30,837 people sent in thirty-four large transports from Prague. But the standard formula of 1,000 people per transport was not always observed; occasionally individuals or a few dozen people came in from one place or another. One hundred and fifty-five transports dispatched to Theresienstadt from Germany brought in 33,554 Jews.[124]

The largest deportation to Theresienstadt from any one place was from Berlin: about 10,000 people arriving in small groups of 50 or 100 people, with only a few transports numbering as high as 1,000 people. Eighty-two such contingents were transported to Theresienstadt in standard railway passenger cars from July 2 to December 17, 1942, while from March 28 to December 14, 1942, the same number of people were sent from Berlin to the East, for a total of close to 21,000 people deported from the capital that year.[125] The destination of the transports to the East had to some degree changed from the last quarter of 1941 and January 1942. Then, as will be recalled, the deportees were sent to Łódź and the Baltic countries (see chap. 11), but in accordance with the orders issued after the Wannsee Conference, the destination of the trains was officially changed to Trawniki, near Lublin—that is, not a ghetto way station, but the labor and extermination camps in the eastern Generalgouvernement. Transports were also dispatched to Riga, but we do not know in every case where they actually ended up. Toward the end of 1942 the trains were usually directed to Auschwitz, which remained the destination of the transports from Berlin throughout 1943.

The rest of the 73 (out of a total of 155) transports that were sent to Theresienstadt from the Old Reich in 1942 came from all over Germany—including the annexed Sudetenland—and from Danzig (Gdańsk). To a certain extent these transports were small, like those from Berlin, but for the most part the deportees were collected from a number of locations to make up the quota of 1,000 people in a single special train. The data in our hands do not enable us to establish with any certainty how many Jews from the Reich (excluding Berlin) were sent directly to the East during that period—compared with the transports to Theresienstadt—though it does appear to be less than the number of Jews deported from Berlin. People were likewise collected from various places for these transports to Poland, with individual cars being joined into a single long train that carried the Jews to the death camps. Their destination was not always in the Lublin area; a few groups of Jews from Greater Germany were directed to Auschwitz as early as the summer of 1942; on March 1 of that year 800 Jews from Hanover had been deported to Warsaw.[126]

It was probably no coincidence that the number of Jews sent to the East was parallel to the number dispatched to Theresienstadt, for this ratio was similar in both Austria and Berlin. The deportations from Austria were well organized, with the Jews from Vienna and the rest of the *Ostmark* being assembled, according to the standardized formula, in groups of 1,000 people. Between June and October 1942, about 14,000 such Jews reached Theresienstadt in thirteen transports, whereas between April 9 and October 5, 1942, some 15,500 Jews were deported to the East in sixteen transports, 9,500 of them to Minsk and 6,000 to Izbica in the Lublin District—most, if not all, of them perished.[127]

All in all, by the end of 1942 about 109,000 Jews had been sent to Theresienstadt and close to 50,000 of them were still there. Some 16,000 of the others had died in the camp and 40,000 had been sent on to the East between March and October 1942. Here again, the destination of the transports was initially the Lublin area and from the summer onward Minsk and its environs; only the last of the transports dispatched that year, at the end of October, was sent to Auschwitz.[128]

The East Transports *(Ostentransporte),* as they were officially called in the camp jargon in Theresienstadt, were organized in an official manner according to standard administrative procedures. The candidates for the transport that left on September 8, 1942, for example, had been summoned four days earlier by the Jewish Council of Elders, which took its orders from the camp command. In this particular case, Jews from Prague who had recently arrived in Theresienstadt were attached to the transport; they were allowed to appeal this decision until seven o'clock the following morning. After that hour they had to gather in the building known as *Die Schleuse* (The Dam), for just as water is collected and passes through a dam, so human beings were assembled and passed through this building. Special orders were issued regarding the baggage they were permitted to take along; other inmates were allowed to report for the transport of their own volition—this often happened in order to keep families together when one or more members were summoned for deportation. A thousand people traveled on the September 8 transport for four days until they reached the vicinity of Minsk. There the train first stopped by an open field, 44 people were picked out, and they were sent to the Trostinez labor camp. All the others were murdered in gas vans. The breakdown of the victims by age was: 111 up to the age of fourteen (11.1 percent); 513 in the fifteen to forty-five bracket (51.3 percent); 303 in the forty-six to sixty bracket (30.3 percent); and 73 above the age of sixty-one (7.3 percent).[129]

The high percentage of people under the age of sixty can be explained by the fact that they were mostly Jews from the Protectorate. The majority of the people included in the transports from Germany and Austria were elderly, that is, over the age of sixty; in the first transports in June, the average was even over seventy. They had remained behind after younger people had either emigrated from the country or been deported to the East with their families—a fact that also explains the high mortality rate in Theresienstadt in August to December 1942 when 14,000 people died.

Theresienstadt was called the "privileged camp" in all official orders and RSHA documents. As a ghetto it was designed to fulfill a number of conflicting functions. It should be recalled that the initiative in establishing Theresienstadt came from both the Jewish leadership in Prague and the RSHA. But whereas Jacob Edelstein believed that a ghetto within the Protectorate would obviate the deportation of the Jews to the East, the Gestapo planners regarded it as a way station for deportations. This paradox accorded the camp a special character, from the outset, and for quite a while the Jews believed that even if they were building an artificially forced society, they were at least able to save lives and preserve their humanity.

At that time the RSHA had evidently realized that the prosecution of the Final Solution entailed certain problems and difficulties that were not readily solved by the deportation program as it had been planned. For example, there were people, particularly within the Reich, who enjoyed special privileges or had influential German friends intent on saving them or, at least, making things easier for them. It was also difficult to claim that elderly men and women were being sent out of the Reich to be "recruited for work." But a "privileged camp" could absorb both the elderly and the well connected. The notion of "prerogative" also came into play within Theresienstadt, and two kinds of privileged people—whose number reached into the hundreds—were set off from the rest. The first were so designated by the SS; the second were people of high standing in the Jewish community—professors, physicians, political figures, and the like—who had this distinction conferred on them by the Council of Elders. Both groups enjoyed special rights regarding housing, nutrition, and exemptions from work. They were even allowed to engage in scientific research, and above all they were protected against deportation.[130]

In order for the transfer of these privileged people to Theresienstadt to achieve the effect envisioned for it by Eichmann's office, it had to be conducted in a civilized manner and with apparent regard for the special needs of the people involved. A number of practices served this aim: the deportees were sent in passenger cars, sometimes attached to a regular train and sometimes joined onto a special one. Moreover, suitable arrangements were made for the sick and the infirm. The Jews were permitted to take along two kinds of baggage: hand luggage and suitcases; the latter were shipped separately in the baggage car. Naturally, no one imagined that they would never again see the belongings that were presumably to serve them in their new home. The deportation was referred to as a "change of residence" *(Wohnsitzverlegung),* and the word *evacuation* was scrupulously avoided. The fact that these people underwent a meticulous search of their person and belongings prior to boarding the train might have aroused suspicions, for many personal items were already being taken from them at this stage, even when they were devoid of all value. Another curious detail that might have provoked misgivings was the appearance of the court clerk who, invoking Implementation Order No. 11, stripped them of their German citizenship and served them with an order announcing the confiscation of their property.[131]

But to ensure that all would go smoothly, the Germans employed a special rule whose purpose was to make the deportees feel secure while divesting them of their capital in favor of the RSHA. Many of the people sent to Theresienstadt at this time had been living in homes for the elderly or had intended to move into such a facility in the near future. It was customary for a person to purchase the entitlement to enter such an institution—often through the auspices of the Social Welfare Department of the kehillah. Hence, neither the candidates for such a transaction nor the kehillah suspected anything when the Germans offered them the opportunity to sign similar contracts purchasing the right to be accepted in a "home for the elderly in the Protectorate." In fact, the campaign to acquire these rights was organized by the Reichsvereinigung, whose circular on this subject was signed by no less than its chairman, Paul Epstein, and one of its leading officials, Johanna Kaminski, who was also director of the Social Welfare Department. Neither were the terms of purchase particularly demanding. In order to be accepted into the program, it was necessary to pay out the sum of at least RM 1,000 in cash or securities, and it was also possible to receive a loan against the collateral of one's life insurance. Yet while supposedly being paid to the Reichsvereinigung, this sum was, in fact, deposited in a special account that effectively belonged to the RSHA. In recommending this option and explaining its terms, the Reichsvereinigung circular stated, "In these contracts the Reichsvereinigung der Juden in Deutschland commits itself to supply living quarters and nutrition in the institution for the rest of [the signees'] lives."[132]

People turned over all the money they had left—often considerable sums—under the illusion that they were ensuring themselves the necessary minimum for the rest of their lives. It is not difficult to imagine how they felt on reaching Theresienstadt and beholding the living conditions in the ghetto, to say nothing of the deportations to the East. It was certainly not by chance that among the personal effects confiscated from the deportees were the postcards they had brought along to keep in touch with friends and family back in Germany. No communications were allowed to or from Theresienstadt until the deportations came to a stop in the autumn of 1942; then, an arrangement was arrived at, but it was subject to strict conditions and limitations.[133]

The transports from Theresienstadt to Auschwitz were resumed in January 1943, with the overwhelming majority of the 7,000 deportees being "specially accommodated" *(gesondert untergebracht)*, in the words of a report sent to Pohl.[134] As a result of these deportations, Theresienstadt began to suffer from a shortage of working hands, and in February the head of the RSHA, Ernst Kaltenbrunner, personally appealed to Himmler on this point. According to the survey he had taken, 46,735 Jews remained in the ghetto. Over half of them were under the age of sixty, but between a quarter and a half of this group was unfit for labor; the proportion of Jews sixty and older found capable of labor was 13.1 percent.[135] Kaltenbrunner also gave a breakdown of the work in which the prisoners were engaged: 6,000 in various construction jobs, manufacture, crafts, and the like; 15,000 in work related to the maintenance of the camp, for example, agriculture and provisioning, sanitation and medical care, organization and administration, cleaning, and the like. The care of the elderly and the sick, including the 406 people suffering from typhus, placed a heavy burden on the camp administration, prompting Kaltenbrunner again to propose "removing from Theresienstadt, for the meanwhile, 5,000 Jews over the age of sixty and sending them to Auschwitz or to the Generalgouvernement." He promised not to include people with special connections or those who had been decorated in the war in these proposed transports; nonetheless, on February 16 he received a negative reply, on Himmler's behalf, explaining that "otherwise the purpose of allowing Jews to live and die peacefully in the old people's ghetto of Theresienstadt will be disturbed."[136] As a result of this decision, all deportations from Theresienstadt were suspended until September 1943.

The Jews of Slovakia: The Struggle Against Deportation

It has already been noted that Slovakia was both the first German satellite to realize the Nazi anti-Semitic program in full and the first to organize deportations to the East on a large scale. These transports were halted primarily at the end of July 1942 after Heydrich's death and the initiation of the mass transportation of Jews to the death camps from Western Europe and Poland proper. The onset of these deportations may have been the reason for stopping those from Slovakia, though it is somewhat difficult to accept that the halt was due to transportation difficulties, as the Slovaks claimed, since the deportations from other countries were in no way affected by such difficulties. Fifty-four thousand people had been deported from Slovakia in fifty-four transports between the end of March and July 1942, most of them destined for the Lublin area and some for Auschwitz. The census taken in August showed that 25,000 Jews were still living openly in Slovakia, and for the time being the Germans intended to allow 20,000 to remain. Some of these Jews were skilled workers who were needed for various kinds of labor; others were the "privileged people"—many of them converts or bona fide Jews passing themselves off as converts. They were concentrated for the most part in the Sered, Vyhne, and Nováky labor camps, though some were still to be found in Bratislava and a few of the provincial cities. It should be noted that Slovakia resembled the Western countries in that no ghettos had been established in the cities. To further reduce the number of Jews, in September and October, the Germans sent three additional transports directly to Auschwitz, bringing the number of deportees close to 58,000; they also sent about another 700 people to the Lublin area and its extermination camps in the following winter of 1942. Then, however, the mass deportations were halted until the autumn of 1944.[137]

This pause was related to important changes in the internal organization of the Jewish community that influenced the conduct of the Germans and the Slovaks alike. Beginning in April 1942, people who had succeeded in escaping from the camps in Poland began to turn up in Slovakia bringing detailed information about what was taking place in Poland. Thus, it became clear beyond a doubt that deportation meant extermination, even though some of the deportees were still being held in labor camps in the Lublin area. In light of these eyewitness reports, a group of activists began to organize within the framework of the Jewish Council. Essentially, they had been the active nucleus of all the assistance and rescue operations in Slovakia even earlier. Known simply as the Working Group, these activists formed a shadow cabinet unbeknownst to the Germans, the Slovak authorities, or even the chairman of the Jewish Council, the *starosta,* who was an obeisant servant of the regime. Among the prominent figures in the Working Group were Gisi Fleischmann and Rabbi Michael Ber Weismandel, who was an extraordinary figure in many ways. Oskar Neumann, one of the leading Zionists in Slovakia, wrote of him, "Whoever met this man for the first time—a man whose unattractive face was fringed by a wild black beard and long sidelocks and whose rather neglected appearance hardly made an appealing impression—could not imagine the personality hidden behind this exterior."[138] Yet in those days Weismandel not only dared to walk openly through the streets of Bratislava looking this way, but also initiated contact with Jews and non-Jews alike, even with people who were far removed from his spiritual world and way of life. Weismandel came from the district capital of Nitra, one of the centers of Orthodox Jewry in Slovakia. The city's yeshiva was headed by his father-in-law, Rabbi Shmuel David Ungar, whose authority was recognized and honored far beyond the borders of Slovakia. The large and famous center of learning (facetiously called the Vatican) now became a focus of spiritual resistance and efforts to rescue Jews by smuggling them over the nearby border into Hungary. Combining the virtues of a warm-hearted Jew with a strong impulse to act, Weismandel soon became a leading figure in the Working Group's far-reaching plans and desperate actions to save Jews. As Oskar Neumann observed, these operations defied all the rules of logic. But he asked, "Could this work have been done at all by the rules of logic? Did it not require the likes of the *Partisanenrebbe*'s creative imagination, courage, and wonderful lack of a realistic outlook on practical issues?"[139]

Weismandel came to realize that the Jews had only one way of influencing their oppressors, namely, the time-honored method of saving Jews: interceding on their behalf with the aid of money, or, in blunt terms, bribery. He happened to hear of a Jew who got himself released from deportation by bribing Dieter Wisliceny and drew the obvious conclusion, "I thought to myself: if he takes a bribe for *one* person, why shouldn't he take it for *many?*"[140] Weismandel immediately raised this notion with a number of officials in the Bratislava kehillah and recommended involving a man who had played a rather dubious role in the fate of Slovakian Jewry, the engineer Karl Hochberg. This ambitious and probably emotionally disturbed young man had succeeded in getting a seat on the Jewish Council and had established a special relationship with Wisliceny. Through skillful jockeying, Hochberg had obtained a focal position on the council and began to make his views felt in all its affairs. But the equally shrewd Weismandel maneuvered Hochberg into working for the rescue effort by persuading him that through such work he would earn himself a reputation as the savior of the remaining Jews of Slovakia, winning the support and appreciation of even the members of the council who had opposed him.[141] But the figure with whom Weismandel worked most closely, however, was Gisi Fleischmann, and through her he obtained the trust of the other members of the Working Group. His plan was to bribe Wisliceny in the hope of bringing the deportations to a halt. Accordingly, Hochberg was sent to see Wisliceny, and although the latter was amenable to the arrangement, he demanded the exorbitant sum of U.S. $40,000 (U.S. $50,000 by Weismandel's account) to be paid within ten days. The main problem was to obtain the money, which was to come from JDC, within so short a time. As noted earlier, the mass deportations were, indeed, halted until the autumn of 1944, but it is not certain that the bribe was the decisive reason for their cessation.[142]

In the course of these activities and efforts, the Working Group consolidated to the point where, in Neumann's words, it became "one heart, one pulse, one mind. . . . It became the factor . . . that created all the necessary political ties, broadened and enhanced the connection with countries abroad, and slowly won the faith of the Jews through the country as a result of its achievements, which became increasingly noteworthy."[143] Among its activities was aiding the flight of

Jews from Poland to Slovakia and from Slovakia to Hungary; within the country it pursued the same course that the Jews had adopted almost everywhere: proving to the Germans the concrete benefit to be derived from productive Jewish labor.

Under the direction of the Working Group, factories and workshops were opened in the three camps containing some three thousand people; twelve hundred in Sered, sixteen hundred in Nováky, and five hundred in Vyhne (formerly a vacation resort in the mountains that was now inhabited mainly by Jews who had succeeded in fleeing to Slovakia from Sosnowiec in Eastern Upper Silesia at the start of the war). In 1943 the three camps together had 130 workshops producing a turnover of 40 million Slovakian crowns. They manufactured carpentry products, mainly furniture (the factory in Sered becoming one of the largest in the country whose products were in great demand by Slovaks and Germans alike), toys, clothing, chemicals, leather and silver products, pipes, and bricks. There were also workshops for car repairs, light mechanics, and graphics. Run by professionals, they enabled many people to retrain in new occupations. Moreover, the workshops had their own salesmen who established the contacts to supply their products to public authorities and private businesses throughout the country. All of this, including the necessary machinery, was created from scratch—like the factories in the ghettos of Poland without start-up capital and in contravention of the official anti-Jewish laws. The internal management of the camps was handled by the local Jewish Council; Slovak forces did guard duty. As a rule life in these camps went on in an orderly fashion, the health and sanitary facilities were well kept, and welfare and educational institutions were established to care for the children. Overcrowding was severe here, too, but for the most part, activities were conducted freely. These camps were supplemented by work centers, which were essentially labor battalions working on drainage, road building, and similar projects and whose turnover in 1943 reached some 6 million Slovakian crowns.[144]

16

Erntefest (The Harvest Festival): The Destruction of the Jews (1943)

Hitler Proclaims the Annihilation of European Jewry

On December 17, 1942, the House of Commons rose to its feet in tribute to the memory of the Jews who had been murdered by the Nazis. Only then were the Allies willing to admit and to acknowledge officially and publicly that the Nazis were conducting a slaughter of the Jews of the occupied countries—particularly in the vast killing ground in Poland and Russia. How did it come to pass that even official recognition and proclamation did not generate rescue action and lead to the cessation of the killings? Why were the Nazis able to continue the implementation of the final solution of the problem of European Jewry until the end of the war almost without impediment? This is one of the most perplexing and troubling questions in our discussion of this period of horrors, and it will continue to haunt us as we describe the course of events in the final years of the war.

The debacle at El Alamein and the great defeat at Stalingrad must have aroused doubts in the minds of all reasonable persons as to Germany's prospects for winning the war. Hitler was certainly aware of this. Under these circumstances he felt the need to pay a personal visit to the southern front commanded by Marshal Erich von Manstein so as to influence strategic plans and to raise the spirits of the weary and demoralized troops. On February 17, 1943, he flew to Zaporozhye for consultations, at the very time when the Russian onslaught was reaching its height. Two days later he issued a proclamation to the troops telling them that the outcome of the battle would determine the fate of the world and that the present and future destiny of Germany lay in their hands. The army was fighting a defensive battle, he admitted, but they could turn it into a victory. Surprisingly enough, von Manstein succeeded within a short time not only in checking the Russian advance but also in compelling the Russians to abandon Kharkov again.

Once more it seemed that Hitler had prevailed by sheer conviction and determination.[1]

On February 24, when the Nazi party members were celebrating the anniversary of the party's establishment, Hitler sent them a message describing the situation:

> The German army, which has again fought in outstanding fashion this winter, is conducting a bitter struggle against the global threat that was devised by the banks of New York and London in conjunction with the Bolshevik Jews in Moscow. . . . Think what fate would have awaited our people, and Europe as a whole, had we not proclaimed the slogans of the National Socialist revolution that restored the soul of the German people and developed within it the strength that now enables it not only to check the world Jewish danger but also, at long last, to destroy it.

Now—he emphasized—the mission was to foil the satanic schemes of the Jewish world criminals. And he went on to declare that the party's road to success had not been easy and secure, that problems had always arisen and failures had occurred, but just as the movement had overcome all failures and all crises and emerged stronger than before, so the struggle must now continue without surrender. "Accept my assurance that I myself am guided today by that same fanaticism as then, and it will never leave me as long as I live . . . the schemes of our foes and their so-called successes will only reinforce my determination not to shift one step from my path."

In response to the proclamations of the Allies, Hitler said that the Jews in London, New York, and Moscow had spelled out clearly what fate they planned for the German people. His conclusion:

> Truly, this struggle will not end, as they intend, in the destruction of Aryan humanity but in the liquidation [*Ausrottung*] of Jewry in Europe. Then our movement's conceptions will become the shared asset of all nations. State by state, even as they fight us, they will be compelled to use the National Socialist slogans in order to conduct the war they initiated. And, hence, awareness of the criminal and accursed activity of Jewry will be spread by this very war throughout the nations. . . . This war will prove beyond any doubt that plutocracy and Bolshevism are the same and that the eternal objective of all Jews is to plunder all nations and to subjugate them as the slaves of their international guild of criminals.[2]

It was on the basis of this knowledge—he went on to explain—that the German people had fought successfully against the internal Jewish enemy (i.e., the Jews of Germany) and were even about to destroy them totally. The same (he believed) would be done by other nations as the war continued.

As on previous occasions (see chap. 12), Hitler referred explicitly to his desire to destroy the Jewish people, but this time he added that the implementation was now in full swing and that in Germany it was about to be concluded. He was no longer "prophesying," but speaking of hard facts. And he again clearly spelled out his conviction that there was an essential link between the war and the destruction of the Jews and that furthermore the war itself would lead other nations, even those now fighting Germany, to arrive at the same conclusion and adopt the same measures. Employing the reverse logic so characteristic of his thinking, he transformed the Allied threat to punish the war criminals into a threat against the Jews; and he leveled at them all the charges of plunder and subjugation that had been directed by Nazi Germany. It is certainly no accident that at this precise hour, when it appeared that all his efforts and gains and all the sacrifices of the German people had been invested in vain that Hitler reverted to the lifeline of hatred of the Jews.[3] In so doing, he provided the slogan and set the target for Himmler and his henchmen, and it was in this spirit that they now approached the extermination operation with the intention of completing it rapidly and in full.

Judenrein Germany

It has been noted here that in 1942 Himmler endeavored to reserve manpower for industry in the labor camps and the concentration camps. But, in essence, two conflicting trends were at work among those charged with the solution of the Jewish question. According to the one—whose advocates were the heads of the RSHA, led by Dr. Ernst Kaltenbrunner, with Adolf Eichmann and his staff as implementers—the process of extermination was to be expedited and the concentrations of Jews in the Reich itself and the occupied countries were to be liquidated as soon as possible.[4] These intentions were hampered to some extent by objective circumstances such as the war situation, the shortage of trains, and the capacity of the death camps. For all these reasons, the transports did not always reach their destination or were shuttled from camp to camp, so that the extermination process did not end at the scheduled time. The main sufferers from these mishaps were, of course, the victims, who were often shut for days in boxcars without food or water or lavatories and in inhumanly overcrowded conditions. The second trend was to create an independent economic system for the SS State and to this end to exploit the labor of the concentration camp inmates. The commandant of Auschwitz, Rudolf Höss, once said that no office was more interested in increasing the number of dead Jews than the RSHA Jewish Department, but that, at the same time, the WVHA was instructed by Himmler to recruit as many prisoners as possible for the armaments project. "The RSHA and the WVHA, therefore, had diametrically opposed aims," but both agencies cited Himmler in their support.[5] Himmler did not succeed in reconciling these conflicting demands, and thousands of prisoners who were fit for work were exterminated. This conflict was among the reasons that prevented the SS from creating its own economic empire based on the concentration camps and OSTI.

The conflict also left its mark in the Reich, from which the Jews were scheduled to disappear within a brief period. According to Richard Korherr's report, at the beginning of 1943, no fewer than 185,776 Jews were still employed in the "work project" *(Arbeitseinsatz)* within the area of the Greater Reich. 40,000 of them were in the original Reich, including Austria: 15,100 were in Berlin; 18,531 in Königsberg (Kaliningrad, USSR) in eastern Prussia (of whom 18,435 were denoted as Soviet Jews); and the remainder—close to 6,500—were dispersed among fourteen towns in the Reich. Some 53,021 Jews, most of them apparently from Eastern Upper Silesia, were working in the Breslau (Wrocław) region.[6]

According to Albert Speer, it was he who prevented the deportation of the skilled Jewish armaments workers, mainly from Berlin, in the period from the beginning of 1942 to the beginning of 1943. But then, as a result of the activities of Fritz Sauckel, an increasing number of Poles were dispatched as forced laborers to Germany, and pressure increased from Himmler and Goebbels to fulfil the führer's demand and cleanse Berlin of Jews.[7]

Eichmann was ready well in advance. In November 1942 he summoned one of his most experienced henchmen, Alois Brunner, to Berlin in order to prepare the operation. From January 12 onward, consecutive trainloads of Jews set out for the East, and this traffic continued throughout February and March. Simultaneously with the deportations to Auschwitz, the transports of the sick, the old, and the priviledged personages to Theresienstadt were renewed and among the deportees were two of the leaders of the Jewish community: Rabbi Leo Baeck, chairman of the National Association of Jews in Germany, and Dr. Paul Epstein, one of the leading figures on the board of the Berlin community. On June 16, 1943, the last of the Jewish employees of the National Association and of the Berlin community were dispatched to Theresienstadt, and the capital was then declared *judenrein*.[8]

The sending to Auschwitz of those employees, who had until then been exempt from deportation, was organized as a characteristic lightning stroke. In January and February 1943 rumors were rife in Berlin that negotiations were being conducted between the Gestapo and the Wehrmacht on the exemption of these staff members. Employees of the community and the National Association were given yellow documents (known as *Scheins* in Eastern Europe), certifying that the bearer was a clerk in the community and listing the members of his family. They were ordered to display the documents in a prominent place in their homes; some kept them in their pockets—a move that proved effective when the Germans began rounding up Jews in the streets. In order to carry out the organized deportations, Brunner brought with him from Vienna collaborators from the ranks of the Jewish police. Their conduct toward the Jews was so cruel that when they, too, were eventually dispatched to Theresienstadt, the Jewish inmates did not fail to take their revenge. Even the SS did not succeed in protecting their lives.

When the blow fell, on February 27, reality proved even worse than anticipated: the SS men burst into factories and seized all the men and women workers, loaded them onto trucks, and conveyed them to four concentration spots in the city. The Berlin community, then numbering some 27,000, was gripped with panic. Between January 12 and March 12, more than 13,000 of them were sent to Auschwitz and some 2,000 to Theresienstadt.[9] The community employees tried to arrange for supplies as well as to bring the deportees some of their own belongings; they even made every effort to locate children so as to reunite them with their parents.

This, more than any other evidence, attests to the fact that both parents and community staff were unaware what fate awaited the deportees. Nobody apparently considered the possibility of concealing, and thereby saving, at least some of those children—as was being done at that time in Holland, Belgium, and France. At the end of March, 18,500 Jews remained in Berlin, half of them with non-Jewish spouses or exempt for some other reason from wearing the yellow badge.[10]

An extraordinary event occurred in the course of the deportations. Among those rounded up on February 27 and 28 were many Jews married to non-Jewish German women. They were assembled at a special concentration spot. It was apparently still unclear what their fate was to be:

> Then the wives took action. During the morning they already discovered where their husbands were being held. As if by prearranged signal they appeared at the place en masse. The police guards tried in vain to disperse the demonstrating women, some 6,000 in number. They assembled again and again, crowding forward, calling out to their husbands—who, despite the strict ban, showed themselves at the windows—and demanded their release.[11]

Indeed, the Gestapo was forced to concede, and the husbands were released. Goebbels complained in his diary that there had been manifestations of protest and sympathy on the part of the German public.[12]

Berlin, and Germany as a whole, were almost completely emptied of Jews. At the end of 1942, the number of Jews in the capital had been estimated at some 33,000, including those married to non-Jews. At the end of June 1943, there were fewer than 7,000. On May 16, 1933, the Berlin community had numbered 160,564 men, women, and children, of whom, at the end of 1943, there were 238 "full" Jews out of a total of 6,681 registered by the Gestapo. For obvious reasons, we do not know how many succeeded in going into hiding in Berlin. Their number is estimated at between 2,000 and 4,000. At the end of 1942, the number of Jews in the whole of Germany was given as 51,327. At the end of March 1943, the number had dropped to 32,000, and by September 1, 1943, there were only 14,574 left. Only 1.6 percent of the Jews of the Reich were then "full" Jews.[13]

The Destruction of the Salonika Jewish Community

Occupied Greece and Its Jews

By 1943 the extermination operations in the East and the West were almost over. The concluding operation in Poland, conducted in the camps in the Lublin region toward the end of the summer of that year, was known as the *Erntefest* (harvest festival). The deportations from the West continued throughout that period, but in three countries in southern Europe—Bulgaria, Greece, and Italy—extermination activities only began in that year. In Slovakia the suspension of transports, agreed on in 1942, continued; in Hungary operations had not yet been launched. In Greece and Italy the situation was somewhat unusual, at least from the German viewpoint.

After the conquest of Greece in the spring of 1941, the country was divided into several zones: Italy annexed part of the western coastal area and the Greek islands; western Thrace, eastern Macedonia, and part of the Aegean Islands were handed over to Bulgaria; and a small part of the Greek mainland was declared "independent" territory. But the bulk of the country became the Greek State headed by a quisling of sorts. The country's center, including its capital, Athens, and the Peloponnesus were handed over to the Italian occupying forces; the northern regions, including Salonika, were attached to the German Eastern Aegean Military Administration Division, which entrusted the administration of the civilian population to Kriegsverwaltungsrat Dr. Max Merten, Sipo, and the SD, the last two represented by W. Paschleben. Formally speaking, Greece was considered an independent state; hence the German Foreign Ministry was represented in Salonika by a consul-general, Schönberg, and in Athens by a diplomatic legation.

Whereas most of the territory and population of Greece were not under direct German rule, the great majority of the Jews resided in the German-occupied areas. The total number of Jews was estimated in 1940 as some 77,000 (within a population of 8 million), and they were organized in twenty-four communities. In the largest of these, Salonika, there were about 56,000 Jews—several hundred more were in the surrounding towns; another 6,000 lived in areas attached to Bulgaria; and at least 13,000 lived in that part of Greece the Italians ruled.[14]

Jews had lived in Greece and its islands in ancient times and in the Middle Ages. Then, and later, they experienced intermittent prosperity and persecution— and even suffered banishment. Refugees reached Greece from other countries, including Hungary, but the most influential factor shaping the character of the Greek community was the Sephardic and Portuguese Jews who settled in the Turkish Empire after the exile from Spain in the fifteenth century. It was in this era that the Salonika community flourished, and in due course its destiny was linked up with the Sabbatean movement. Salonika's rabbis and its seminaries, libraries, and printing presses were renowned. The situation of the Jews worsened in the nineteenth century in the wake of the Greek war of independence from Turkey. The Jews were believed to be the allies of the Ottoman Empire and suffered greatly at the hands of the Greeks both on the mainland and in the islands. Their number increased again as Greece expanded on the eve of World War I when it took over areas to its north.

After the war the Jews were detrimentally affected by the exchange of populations between the Turks and the Greeks, carried out from 1923 onward. In the north the economic standing of the 90,000 Jews was still firm and they were also active in trade and industry. They generally enjoyed equal rights but their autonomous cultural activity was curtailed. Emigration to Western Europe and to Palestine commenced. In 1940/1941 during the Greek war against Italy and the brief campaign against the Germans, close to 13,000 Jews served in the Greek army; 613 of them fell in battle and 3,750 were wounded.[15]

The Tranquil Period

In the early days of the German occupation, anti-Jewish activities were relatively restricted, and the conquerors did not treat the Jews markedly different from the general population. The press was closed down, and Jewish papers also ceased publication. There were, however, a very large number of Jewish-owned apartments among those expropriated by the Germans. Anti-Semitic propaganda was also intensified; on April 15, 1941, all the members of the Community Council were arrested—and subsequently released. Also significant was the confiscation of all Jewish libraries in Salonika, with their collections of ancient books and renowned manuscripts. On May 5, 1941, a special—ostensibly scientific—unit representing Alfred Rosenberg's bureau arrived in Salonika in order to ensure that this valuable material would be transferred to the "Institute for the Study of Judaism," which had been established in Frankfurt on the Main.[16] Meanwhile, the chief rabbi, Dr. Zvi Koretz, was arrested on May 17 and sent to Vienna. There he was imprisoned for eight months on the charge of having conducted anti-German propaganda.[17]

After the events of the first few weeks, a lull set in. The Greek population as a whole suffered considerably during the occupation, particularly during the severe winter of 1941/1942 when food and fuel were in short supply and all, including the Jews, suffered from hunger and cold. The International Red Cross made great efforts at the time to supply the Greeks with their vital needs, and its representatives included the Jews among the recipients of aid. The number of needy Jews increased and was swelled by refugees who had reached Greece from Central Europe. The Jewish community was also forced to cover the cost of maintaining the Gestapo offices. The mortality rate among the Jews rose from 15 per week before the war to 80 per day.[18] The community began to organize self-help activities. A joint committee of all the Jewish aid organizations began to supply meals to thousands of needy people. Particular efforts were invested in improving the nutrition of the children. Some 25,000 sick people received aid in the community hospitals and clinics.[19]

The Black Sabbath

For the time being the military administration and the Gestapo maintained an almost decent attitude toward the Jewish community, and the Jews were lulled into illusions hoping that it would be possible to hold fast until the war ended.[20] However, these hopes were shattered in July 1942 when the Germans decided to mobilize the Jews for forced labor. On July 7, 1942, an ordinance was issued requiring all Jewish men aged eighteen to forty-five to assemble on Saturday, July 11, at 8:00 A.M. in Liberation Square—the central square in Salonika. The ordinance stated that "a Jew is any person who belongs to the Jewish nationality, irrespective of the Jew's religion. . . . Failure to report will be punished by a fine and imprisonment in a concentration camp." Only those with Italian and Spanish nationality were exempted (see later discussion).[21]

The German attitude toward the Jews changed abruptly and drastically. Conducting a census that lasted several days, the soldiers and Sipo now adopted all the familiar methods of persecution: they forced the Jews to perform various "physical exercises" and to dance, beat them, set dogs on them, and humiliated and mocked them—before the eyes of German spectators, particularly women, who were entertained by the spectacle.[22]

Shortly afterward the first two thousand of nine thousand registered Jews were ordered to report. They were sent to various distant labor projects in quarries, at airfields, on roads, and so forth. Their accommodations, food, and working conditions were appalling, and they lacked the necessary tools and implements. The community tried to extend aid to those interned in the labor camps and entered into negotiations with the authorities to improve their conditions and to obtain the release of the increasing number of ailing workers by paying ransoms. More than one thousand were released. With the concurrence of the authorities, a committee of three members of the Community Council undertook responsibility for dealing with all problems related to forced labor, including releases; but its decisions required endorsement by the German headquarters. Soon another three thousand forced laborers were mobilized. All members of the Jewish community were required to pay a redemption tax and aid was organized for the laborers and their families. The situation, however, did not improve.

Meanwhile, winter was approaching, and people lacked warm clothing and shoes. Now it was the German contractors who recommended that the Jews be obliged to pay ransoms and that the money be used to hire local laborers able to withstand the harsh conditions. The Germans demanded a sum of Dr 3,500 million, which was reduced, after negotiations, to Dr 2,500 million. The German representative, Dr. Merten, threatened to desecrate and destroy the ancient community cemetery if the sum was not paid. A contract was subsequently signed, according to which the Jews would pay part of the sum by December 15, 1942. They eventually succeeded in mobilizing close to Dr 2,000 million, but the cemetery was destroyed notwithstanding. There were numerous incidents of confiscation of Jewish property and businesses, plundering, and looting.[23]

Facing Deportation

The practical preparations for the deportation of Greek Jewry—first and foremost the Jews of Salonika—were only made in January 1943. The operation was prepared and implemented in close conjunction between Eichmann's bureau and Martin Luther's department in the Foreign Ministry, which employed its diplomatic channels to transfer the relevant instructions. On January 22, Eichmann's deputy, Rolf Günther, flew to Salonika to discuss the organization of the operation.[24] On January 20, 1943—two days before Günther's arrival in Salonika—Dieter Wisliceny was summoned to Eichmann in Berlin and told that he was to move to Salonika. Arriving at the beginning of February, he was unpleasantly surprised when Brunner, who had been working in Vienna up till then, was sent to join him.[25]

Until then no special steps had been taken to organize the Jewish community, except for one significant change: on December 11, 1942, the chief rabbi, Dr. Zvi Koretz, was appointed chairman of the Community Council. After the war debates ensued as to the advisability of the rabbi's consent to accept the dual functions of chief rabbi and Community Council head as well as on his activities during the subsequent deportation period. There were those who accused Koretz of collaborating and of displaying domineering tendencies; another theory holds that he undertook the position with great hesitation and only on condition that a council of community notables be established. In any event, the Germans apparently wanted to guarantee that, throughout the deportations, the community would be headed by a man of authority and influence.[26]

On February 6, 1943, Merten sent the first directive that launched the deportations. It was addressed to the Jewish community and ordered that (1) all the Jews of Salonika, their businesses, and homes be clearly tagged; (2) the Jews be concentrated in special quarters of the town, a ghetto. The cost was to be borne by the Jews themselves, and implementation was entrused to the local SD. On February 12, Wisliceny issued the first implementation orders that specified the form of the yellow badge and where it was to be worn by every Jew from the age of five upward. To the badge was added a numbered identity card; the same number was stamped on the badge. At this time a numerical list of all the Jews was prepared. The directive also contained a shortened version of the Nuremberg Laws' definition of Jews, with the added comment that if a Jew had left the community, it would not exempt him from the marking. No requests for exemption would be accepted. An additional directive prohibited the Jews from leaving their places of residence and using public transportation; a nighttime curfew was imposed on them.

By February 25 all the Jews had been concentrated in two ghettos. On that day Merten issued another ordinance annulling all financial or organizational claims by Jews and canceling their membership in public legal bodies, organizations, and associations. Most of the Jews were concentrated in the Baron Hirsch quarter of the town near the railway station, which later served as a transit camp for deportations. On March 13 a new directive was issued that was aimed at guaranteeing the confiscation of Jewish capital and valuables.

Wisliceny's orders for the implementation of the deportations were published on March 15 and 17, 1943. The first trainload of Jews left Salonika on March 15 for Auschwitz, with 2,800 men, women and children aboard. It arrived at its destination five days later, on March 20. At the selection, 2,191 victims were sent to the gas chambers; 417 men and 192 women were sent to the labor camp.[27]

Dr. Zvi Koretz conveyed the orders to the community and mobilized a staff that diligently implemented them. The Germans themselves were amazed at the rapidity with which the orders were carried out. In his efforts to placate the Germans, the rabbi earned the hatred of the Jews at the time and, particularly in retrospect, most of them condemned his conduct. Before the deportations commenced, the Germans demanded that hostages be handed over to them to guarantee the submissive conduct of the Jews. The Community Council submitted a list of 102 notables. Koretz explained to them that he had succeeded in averting their arrest but had given his pledge that they would report to the SD when called. "Any disobedience on the part of any of us—and you will pay with your lives," he told them. He also promised the ghetto inmates that their lives and livelihoods would not be affected; but on the following day, March 6, the Germans banned any departures from the ghetto and the Jews were no longer able to reach their shops and businesses scattered throughout Salonika.[28]

While the SD personnel were preparing the deportations, Fritz Todt's organization (the Building Authority) approached headquarters and requested that manpower be placed at its disposal. Merten proposed that laborers be recruited from the Jewish population. Eichmann agreed to release 3,000 Jews from the deportation for this purpose. When Koretz heard this news, he appealed to Wisliceny to increase the number of laborers to 15,000 in the hope that in this way he would succeed in halting the deportation; Eichmann, however, refused. Koretz made an additional attempt to prevent the deportation, proposing to the Germans a ransom equal to half the property of the Jewish community in Salonika. To this end, he called a meeting of community officials and prominent personalities and asked them to sign individual obligations to hand over half of their property. This proposal, too, was transmitted to Berlin and was rejected—so Merten told Koretz—because of the protests of the Greek population.[29]

The deportations continued. At the end of March or beginning of April, the Greek prime minister, Rhallis, visited Salonika. Through the mediation of the metropolitan of the Greek Orthodox church, Genadios, Koretz met with the premier and pleaded with him to intercede with the German authorities and persuade them to halt the deportations. Rhallis informed his German masters of Koretz's request; in response, they arrested Koretz and his family and interned them in the transit camp. They were held there for a lengthy period against the wishes of Brunner, who wanted to dispatch them straight to Auschwitz.

It is hard to gauge Koretz's motives. He may have believed that it was incumbent on him to act so as to achieve two ends simultaneously: to conciliate the Germans and thereby win their trust and to try at least to mitigate the decree. He apparently failed to grasp that such a double game was impossible. Nor can one guess to what extent he himself believed the deceptive tactics that the Germans employed in order to allay the fears of the Jewish population. Koretz disseminated the German version that the Jews were being sent to Cracow, where they would be resettled. They were even permitted to change a certain sum of money into zlotys, as testimony to the sincerity of the German intentions; people were even given promissory notes for plots of land around Cracow.

At the end of March, Wisliceny ordered the reorganization of the community. The reorganization plan sketches along general lines the network of functions that characterized ghetto organizations, but everything was directed to one main end: deportation. The directive itself served as a smokescreen by suggesting that the Jews were being permitted to reestablish a stable and autonomous organization, whereas it actually served the Germans' true intention: deportation.

Here, as elsewhere, the looting of Jewish property both before and after the deportation was one of the most important German aims. Cash, jewelry, silver, and carpets were heaped up in quantity, and the Germans did not hesitate to invest effort in feathering their own nests. Most of the plunder was sent to Germany: to the consignments were also added works of art, which had previously been confiscated by the committee representing Rosenberg's office. Jewish apartments and businesses were seized after their owners had been arrested and deported. As usual, the businesses were handed over to new managers, or "trustees."

The pace of the deportations indicates to what extent the Germans had streamlined their techniques. The trains were placed at their disposal by the military command and left at intervals of a few days. Between mid-March and mid-May, at least seventeen trains left Salonika for Auschwitz; the smallest load was 1,000, the largest 4,500.[30] There are no figures on the number of Salonika Jews who lost their lives at Treblinka.[31] One of the last transports departed on June 1, 1943, with 880 passengers—collaborators, officials, intellectuals—"the cream of the Jewish community." They reached Auschwitz—not Theresienstadt as they had been promised—on June 8 and 512 of them were sent straight to the gas chambers.[32] The last transport from Salonika to Auschwitz arrived on August 18, 1943, and consisted of the 1,800 laborers who had been assigned to the Todt organization. Altogether, the records show that nineteen trains left Salonika conveying 48,533 Jews. Of these, 6,713 men and 4,234 women were sent to the camp; 37,386, constituting 77 percent of all those deported from Salonika, were exterminated on arrival. To these were added Jews from small towns in eastern Thrace and central-eastern Macedonia.

An Avenue to Rescue: Foreign Nationality

There were several hundred Jews with foreign nationality in Salonika at that time, most of them Italian and Spanish nationals. All official proclamations and decrees issued by Merten and the SD emphasized that these nationals were excluded. The attitude of the Italians and Spaniards to the Jews differed from that of the Germans. As long as the Italians ruled part of Greece, this area served as a refuge for those who succeeded in fleeing or in reaching there by legal means, particularly holders of Italian passports.

The problem of foreign nationals was not exclusive to Greece. Nationals of neutral countries, satellite states, and countries that were fighting Nazi Germany resided in all the countries the Germans had reached as conquerers or allies. The systematic plan for the extermination of Jews throughout Europe placed this problem on the agenda, and it became the subject of protracted and complex debates between Eichmann's department in the RSHA and Luther's department in the Foreign Ministry. Germany's foreign ties obliged the Foreign Ministry—and hence Luther—to take note of the complaints and protests of other countries with regard to the treatment of their nationals. The discussions continued for years; at the beginning of 1943, various criteria and principles were formulated to which Eichmann's office was forced to acquiesce. In January 1943 Eichmann drew up draft directives to be distributed to his representatives throughout Europe: but it was only two months later, on March 5, 1943, that Kaltenbrunner, the head of RSHA, signed them and dispatched them to the commanders of the SD who were engaged in deporting Jews. These directives listed fifteen countries whose nationals were to be included in the extermination operations: "former Poland, former Luxembourg, Slovakia, Croatia, Serbia, Rumania, Bulgaria, Greece, Holland, Belgium, France, former Estonia, former Latvia, former Lithuania, Norway." Directives sent to the East included a sixteenth country—the Soviet Union. To these were added all stateless Jews. However, the directive then stated, "[Deportation] activities are not yet to be extended to Jews from other countries, whether enemy, neutral or friendly, whether conducting hostilities or not. All Jews who can claim

British or American nationality, together with some other nationality—even if they were only born in those countries—should be excluded from the general activities against Jews and interned in camps."[33]

Repatriation

What fate, then, was planned for those Jews with foreign nationality who were excluded from the deportations and who—for some reason—included British and American nationals, that is, citizens of countries that were at war with Germany? It transpires that in the agreement arrived at between the Foreign Ministry and RSHA two possible solutions were contemplated: the first was to enable the respective countries to take back those of their Jewish subjects who were living under German rule; the second was to exchange Jews with foreign nationality (or Jews whose case had aroused interest abroad) for Germans detained in those countries. In both cases the Foreign Ministry was acting counter to the intentions of RSHA. The latter was not anxious for Jews to leave the country and relate what they had seen and heard in the Nazi state; RSHA also held that the release of Jews from its control would obstruct objectives of the Final Solution. Nonetheless, the RSHA was forced to succumb to pressure exerted by the Foreign Ministry, which had become the target of queries, complaints, and protests from both neutral and friendly countries aiming at rescuing Jews. It was no accident that the problem was regarded as particularly pressing after December 1942 when the Allies publicly announced that the Nazis were exterminating Jews.

The fate of foreign nationals was decided at the highest echelons. On January 13, 1943, Joachim von Ribbentrop ordered the German embassy in Rome to inform the Italian Foreign Minister, Count Galeazzo Ciano, that Jews with Italian nationality would be permitted to remain in areas under German rule until March 31 of that year. After this date—"for weighty military and political reasons"—the government would no longer be able to make exceptions. In other words the Italian government was urged to carry out the repatriation of several hundred of its nationals by the specified date. A similar announcement was conveyed to the Swiss government at the end of December 1942.[34] Operation Homecoming *(Heimschaffungsaktion),* as the arrangement was called, encompassed—in addition to the two countries noted—Spain, Portugal, Denmark, Sweden, Finland, Hungary, Rumania, and Turkey (ten countries in all). The final date for the repatriation was postponed several times, since the transfer could not be completed within so brief a period. Finally, the patience of the RSHA ran out, and on July 5, 1943, the Foreign Ministry was notified of the "final" date—July 31, 1943. Several days later, the Foreign Ministry responded, "The fixing of final date, after which Jewish foreign nationals will, on principle, be denied exit permits from the areas under German rule, and will be treated like German Jews . . . is of such far-reaching significance for foreign policy that it is vital that all the relevant agencies in the Foreign Ministry examine it carefully."[35]

Hence, the statement continued, haste was not recommended, and the countries should be allowed a last respite of at least four weeks to settle matters. As a consequence, the matter dragged on until September 23, 1943, when Heinrich

Müller of the RSHA sent an additional directive, stating that from October 10, 1943, the nationals of the ten listed countries were to be included in activities aimed at implementing the Final Solution.[36]

The problem was particularly pressing in Greece, as noted earlier, since several hundred Jewish foreign nationals were living there, most of them Italians and Spaniards.[37] For the Germans, the Italian problem was particularly complicated. Not only did the Italian consul in Salonika protect Italian nationals and ensure that they were able to move to Italian-ruled areas of Greece, but he also agreed to bestow Italian nationality on additional applicants. The SD and Sipo tried to mobilize the Foreign Ministry against the consul with the aim

> of persuading the Italian government—by pointing out the case of Salonika—to cancel the granting of Italian nationality to Jews who [were] not residing in areas under Italian rule, retroactively from the date of Italy's entry into the war. In any event, to instruct [Italian] diplomatic legations to refrain in future from granting nationality.[38]

At first the Italians gave evasive replies, but some time later the Italian government announced its decision:

> Jews with Italian nationality [in the occupied area] are to be treated in the same fashion as [Jews] in Italy. Dangerous elements are interned in camps or transferred to Italy. This has already been done in many cases. Jews with Greek nationality are interned in a camp in the Greek islands or in Italy.[39]

Unsurprisingly, this answer did not satisfy the implementers of the Final Solution. The matter was brought to Ribbentrop's attention in a memorandum that emphasized that the RSHA insisted that anti-Jewish activities in the area of Greece under Italian rule correspond to those being conducted in the German zone.

The Germans had good reason to be concerned, since at the time when they launched the deportations, an escape movement was under way from Salonika to the Italian area. Among those who made their escape was the legal adviser of the community, Yom-Tov Yakuel, and several senior Jewish policemen. The escapees found guides who took them over to the Italian area in return for high payment in foreign currency or in gold. As always, there were informers and swindlers and several Jews were caught and publicly executed in the Baron Hirsch Camp.[40]

The curfew hours for Jews were extended from 4:00 P.M. to 10:00 A.M. Notwithstanding these restrictions, some Jews succeeded in fleeing. The Italian consul sent some 750 Jews to the Italian zone, including about 300 Greek Jews. Some 2,000 other Jews reached the Italian area by their own efforts.

The Exchange Scheme

In his directives of March 5, 1943, related to repatriation, Kaltenbrunner demanded the exclusion from the deportation of those Jews who were candidates for exchange with citizens of the Reich held in enemy countries. This directive was also the outcome of negotiations with the Foreign Ministry. Ribbentrop's initiative was preceded by an exchange of German nationals for Jews from Palestine carried out in the fall of 1942. On the basis of this experience, the head of the Legal Department, Dr. Emil Albrecht, proposed on February 4, 1943, that Jews with foreign nationality be exploited for purposes of exchange. In this fashion, he argued, Jews with British or American nationality could "be used advantageously." Ribbentrop approved of the idea, and a missive was sent to the RSHA on February 8, 1943, in his name, requesting that thirty thousand Jews with British, American, Dutch, Belgian, French, Norwegian, and Russian nationality be reserved for use in exchanges. "If negotiations for exchange do not produce results, it will always be possible to deport these Jews." It was recommended to concentrate initially on Dutch, Belgian, and Norwegian Jews to be selected on the basis of their familial, friendly, political, or commercial ties with people of influence in enemy countries.[41] Approximately in mid-April, Himmler apparently decided to accede to the Foreign Ministry request, but he reduced the number of candidates for exchange to ten thousand.[42] A special camp was allotted for these candidates that was relatively close to the western border of the Reich—the now-notorious Bergen-Belsen. At first, it was regarded as a "civilian detention camp," but its name was soon changed to "sojourn camp" *(Aufenthaltslager).* This change (it was stated) was required since, according to the Geneva Convention, any civilian detention camp must be open to visits by international commissions. Administratively speaking, the camp was attached to the concentration camp administration headed by the WVHA; in actual fact, it was under the jurisdiction of the RSHA. This nebulous administrative arrangement encouraged anarchy to reign in the camp.[43]

In mid-July 1943 the first candidates for exchange were dispatched from Poland to Bergen-Belsen. The members of the second group to reach there were apparently Jews from Salonika, most of them Spanish nationals.

Jews with Spanish Nationality

Negotiations were conducted between the German and Spanish governments on the fate of Jews with Spanish nationality who were residing in many countries under German rule, in both East and West. The discussions commenced with France, where three thousand Jews claimed Spanish nationality. Madrid's stand was not as unequivocal as that of the Italian government. The Spaniards introduced stringent tests to determine the right to Spanish nationality. This was of particular significance in Salonika because of a 1924 decision of the Spanish government (under Miguel Primo de Rivera) to enable Spanish Jews in Salonika to purchase Spanish nationality. An anomalous situation ensued whereby the German Foreign Ministry was almost more eager to return Spanish nationals to Spain than were the Spaniards to receive them. The Germans in this case displayed patience and did not rush to exploit the hesitation of the Spanish government. When the Spanish finally agreed to take back their nationals, they stipulated as a condition that these "homecomers" would stay in Spain only in transit and only after other refugees, who had reached Spain by other means, had moved on and vacated space in the transit camps. This emigration was guaranteed by a promise of JDC to the Spanish Foreign Ministry. Consequently, the Spanish authorities informed the Germans that they were ready to accept the Jews; however, only part of the Salonika Jews benefited from the arrangement.[44]

The Spanish government was torn between its desire to respond to humanitarian and political demands, specifically to rescue Jews it considered citizens of Spain, and the problems stemming from the absorption of large numbers of refugees. Its readiness to take into account humanitarian considerations was undoubtedly affected by political calculations. As the Allies gained power in the global struggle, Spain displayed increasing willingness to serve as a haven—or at least as a transit station—for refugees and survivors. But, as noted, it did not adopt an unequivocal stand and altered its policy two or three times in the course of 1943. The Spanish reservations and the administrative obstacles it placed in the path of rescue activities enabled Eichmann and his henchmen to exploit the situation and treat Spanish nationals as they chose, or at least to attempt to act thus. Their efforts, however, were obstructed by Sebastian Romero Radigales, who was appointed Spanish consul in Athens in April 1943. He resolved to save the Spanish Jews in Salonika and to this end acted in conjunction with the Spanish vice-consul there, Solomon Azrati. This was no easy task. His reports and missives were transmitted by means of the German ambassador in Athens, Günther Altenburg, through the Foreign Ministry in Berlin. Thus, it frequently happened that his messages did not reach his government—nor did he receive responses when the issues involved were uncongenial to the Germans.[45]

While Madrid was making up its mind, the SD in Salonika managed to deport 38 Jews of Spanish nationality or their Jewish spouses, all of whom vanished without trace at Auschwitz. When the Spanish government finally approved a list of names of 510 Spanish nationals resident in Salonika who it was willing to take in, a new problem arose: no way was found, either by sea or land, to transport these people to their destination. As a provisional solution, von Thadden suggested to Eichmann that they be sent to a detention camp and held there for three months. He insisted that the internees be treated in such fashion that no complaints could be lodged "in the event that later all or some of them are granted exit permits."[46]

Meanwhile, Radigales and Azrati were not idle, nor were they swayed by the conduct of the Spaniards. They arrived at an agreement with the Italians for the transfer of Spanish nationals to Athens and succeeded in smuggling 150 people onto a train that was taking Italian troops home on furlough. On July 29 Wisliceny summoned all the male heads of households to a meeting in the Salonika synagogue: 117 out of 184 came. The place was surrounded by the German police, and all the men were taken to the Baron Hirsch Camp. Their relatives had no choice but to join them; thus 367 Spanish Jews were interned. Radigales tried in vain to prevent their deportation; he succeeded in meeting with Solomon Azrati, who was among the detainees, and the latter handed over to him part of the funds confiscated from the deportees. On August 2, 1943, these Jews were sent together with a group of 74 of the community dignitaries—including Rabbi Koretz and his family—to the sojourn camp, Bergen-Belsen. They reached the camp on August 13. In accordance with the Foreign Ministry demand, they were transported in railway passenger carriages, and the Spaniards were detained under tolerable conditions in a special section of the camp. Once again, protracted negotiations were conducted between the German and Spanish governments. Finally, at the beginning of February 1944, they reached their haven.[47]

Greek Jewry: The End

The Jews in the Italian zone felt relatively secure under the protection of the Italian army, even though the Germans were present in Athens and the SD and Gestapo representatives there tried to harass them and utilized their staff in Salonika to this end. Initially, the Italians had no desire to become deeply involved in Jewish affairs, but when they became aware of the German intentions, they became more alert. For example, when the Germans ordered Rabbi Eliahu Barzilai to serve as chairman of the Jewish community, the Italians appointed him under their auspices without mentioning the German appointment. The Germans, for their part, supported a group of anti-Semitic students and assisted them when they attacked the community offices. The Greek underground movement retaliated later by destroying the offices of the student group. Jewish refugees from Salonika set up a committee in Athens and during the deportations made desperate but vain attempts to help their brethren.

A new and dangerous situation evolved after Italy's capitulation on September 8, 1943, when the Germans took over the Italian-occupied areas. On September 20 Wisliceny appeared in Athens together with SS General Jürgen Stroop, destroyer of the Warsaw ghetto. On the day after his arrival, Wisliceny summoned Rabbi Barzilai and demanded that he carry out a series of steps aimed at organizing the Jews of Athens for swift and efficient deportation. He demanded that the Jews prepare four different lists: (1) all the Jews of Athens, with addresses and occupations; (2) all the Greek Jews who had fled from Salonika to Athens between the beginning of 1940 and September 1943; (3) all the Italian Jews from Salonika; and (4) all the people who had been active in transferring Jewish refugees from Central Europe to Palestine.

In addition, he demanded the establishment of a Jewish council. The rabbi was expected to implement all these orders within twenty-four hours. Barzilai called a meeting of all the Jews of Athens, at which a committee was elected that was given the task of appealing to Metropolitan S. B. Damaskinos to intervene on behalf of the Jews. He told the delegation that they had no alternative but to go into hiding and agreed at once to offer the Jews refuge in churches. A similar appeal to premier Rhallis, the collaborator, did not, of course, produce results. On the following day, Rabbi Barzilai told Wisliceny that he had not succeeded in carrying out all the instructions, that he did not have community records in his possession, and that there were no people available to prepare such records. Wisliceny allotted him another forty-eight hours to complete the task, but on the same day took over the community offices and turned them into Gestapo headquarters. He found no records there; most of the people who had been candidates for membership in the council fled and went into hiding. The leaders of the Jewish community consulted with the Greek underground and decided that the rabbi must disappear from Athens. His escape was organized on September 25, and he hid with his family in mountain villages until the war ended.

When Wisliceny realized that the Jews were not cooperating, he persuaded Stroop to issue a directive obliging the Jews to register and prohibiting them from leaving their places of residence; those residing in Athens were ordered to report to the community offices for registration. Certain restrictions were imposed on them—for example, a curfew from 5:00 P.M. to 7:00 A.M.—and special statutes were introduced for Jews outside Athens and those with foreign nationality.

In Athens the registration proceeded slowly at first. In the first two weeks, 200 Jews were registered, and the Germans decided to postpone the deportation until the spring of 1944.[48] They adopted tactics aimed at reassuring the Jews that they would merely be expected to report every two weeks at the synagogue on Saturday. The number of registrants gradually rose, and within two months had reached 2,000. Many tried meanwhile to ensure their safety by undergoing baptism or acquiring forged papers. Not all those who fled or went into hiding were able to hold out, either because they lacked means or because those who had given them shelter could not continue to do so. Particularly hazardous was the escape route chosen by those who tried to make their way to the Turkish coast in small boats. Among these were Jews with Spanish nationality who had no faith in the Germans. There was no shortage of informers and traitors, who exploited the predicament of the Jews, took money from them, and later abandoned them or handed them over to the Germans. Thus, more and more Jews were apprehended. Finally, Wisliceny adopted the same tactic that had helped him to trap the Spanish Jews in Salonika. At the end of March 1944, when the Jews reported as usual at the synagogue, the doors were locked: 350 men were trapped and their families were forced to join them. All were transported to the Haidar concentration camp. Here the Germans also interned Jews caught while trying to escape as well as those hunted down in the Greek towns and villages. In only a few of the ten provincial towns did several hundred Jews succeed in escaping or go into hiding. At the beginning of April, 5,200 Jews were dispatched in eighty railway trucks to Auschwitz; among them were 155 Spanish Jews who had previously fled Salonika, and 19 Portuguese Jews. The latter were taken to Bergen-Belsen.[49]

After the deportations of 1943 and the spring of 1944, Jews only continued to live on the islands, particularly Corfu and Rhodes. There were about 2,000 Jews in Corfu, and the Germans arrested them in June 1944. Some 200 succeeded in fleeing to the mountains. Most of the community were sent to Auschwitz on June 20, 1944.

At the beginning of this century, Rhodes still had a large Jewish community of 10,000 souls, but the number dwindled gradually owing to migration overseas. As long as the island was under Italian rule, the situation of the Jews resembled that of their brethren in Italy. As the Italian attitude toward the Jews changed for the worse, from 1938 on, emigration increased. At the time of the German occupation, there were some 2,000 Jews on the island. The Germans arrested them on July 24, 1944, and transported them by boat to the Greek mainland and then to

Auschwitz. Only 275 Jews who lived on the island of Zante (Záteinthos) were saved thanks to the help of the local population, the Greek authorities, and even the commander of the German garrison (who was of Austrian origin). They suffered hunger, penury, forced labor, and appalling living conditions in remote places—but survived them all.

The Jews of Corfu and Rhodes, on arrival at Auschwitz, were usually in better health than those dispatched from Salonika. At the end of July, the Germans decided that 435 young men from this group would be attached to the Sonderkommando that worked at the gas chambers and the crematoria. These Jews refused to take part in burning corpses and were themselves immediately sent to the gas chambers. Their conduct left a strong impression on the camp inmates.

As with most other countries, there can be no certainty as to the number of victims in Greece. Among other reasons, not all the transports ended up at Auschwitz; apparently several arrived—in entirety or in part—at other camps. Be that as it may, the figure of 54,533 deported to Auschwitz appears too low, and the actual figure ranges between 60,000 and 68,000. After the war, slightly more than 10,000 Jews were counted in Greece.[50]

There can be no doubt that the percentage of victims among Greek Jewry was one of the highest (about 80 percent). The question is how it came about that the Germans succeeded in operating so successfully here, even though the persecution commenced relatively late and the conditions were seemingly conducive to escape. The country is mountainous; the population in remote regions was usually willing to take in refugees; in the area under their control, the Italians protected Jewish inhabitants, and they even extended their activities to areas under direct German rule; the commander of the Greek police in Athens was ready to issue forged documents; the church also helped Jews—though in many cases by easing the procedure for baptism; and, last but not least, the underground proffered assistance and was ready to absorb Jews. Why, nonetheless, were more Jews not saved? This question is, as yet, unanswered.

Italian Jewry: The Vicissitudes of Fate

The deportation of Italian Jews from Greece was planned at the very time when Stalingrad was about to fall. This may help to explain why the Germans attributed such urgency to the liquidation of the Salonika community; they attempted to complete the operation within six to eight weeks and recruited such experts as Wisliceny and Brunner to expedite the task. Moreover, General Erwin Rommel's defeat in North Africa and the Allied landing there in November 1942 undoubtedly heightened German awareness that Italy was under threat, and hence the Balkans as well. The threat to Italy materialized when the Allies landed in Sicily on July 10, 1943, and Mussolini's regime collapsed. Thus, a new situation was created on the southern front for the Italians, the Germans, and the Jews. New and hazardous conditions were created for Italian Jews on September 8 when an armistice was proclaimed between Italy and the Allies, and the Germans took over central and northern Italy. On the night of September 9/10, the Germans entered Rome, and it was only on June 5, 1944, that the city was conquered by the Allied forces.

The Jews in Fascist Italy

We have observed the conduct of the Italians in Greece and shall return later to their activities in other occupied areas—Yugoslavia and France. There is a seeming contradiction between the readiness of the Italians to protect the Jews in those occupied territories and their attitude—as it evolved under Mussolini's Fascist rule—toward the Jews in Italy itself. For various reasons the Italians objected to handing over Jews to the Germans, but their own conduct toward the Jews was colored by other considerations. In the early twenties Italian fascism developed a racist anti-Semitic ideology that found expression in literature and the press and was given voice by Mussolini himself.[51] But from Mussolini's rise to power (in 1922) until 1938, the Fascist rulers did not apply this ideology in practical policies. There were various reasons for this, among them the disinclination of the Italian population for engaging in active anti-Semitism and such practical considerations as the desire to mobilize Jewish support for the Fascist regime. Although it was opposed on principle to Zionism, the Fascist movement apparently regarded the Jewish community in Palestine as a possible factor in weakening British influence in the Mediterranean. In 1930 a law was enacted that defined and consolidated the status of the Jewish communities. A number of Jews held important positions in the state administration, although the number of Jewish party members was not great.

This situation began to change in 1936 in the wake of the Spanish civil war (many Italian Jews supported the Republicans) and after Mussolini launched his Ethiopian campaign. Not only did the tension between Britain and Italy increase, but Italy now adopted a pro-Arab policy. These two combined trends naturally fostered an anti-Zionist attitude—and, consequently, an anti-Jewish attitude as well—on the part of the Italian government. There had always been a marginal anti-Semitic group in Italy, and its impact now increased and was reflected in literature and the press. These manifestations increased in 1937. Catholic anti-Semitism blended with racism. In July 1938 the "Manifesto of the Italian Race" was published; it claimed Aryan origin for the "Italian race" and called for the removal of the Jewish population from its midst. At the beginning of September 1938, the first anti-Jewish laws were enacted. These events were, of course, closely linked to Italy's rapprochement with Nazi Germany and the latter's burgeoning power in Europe. The first to be affected were the Jewish refugees who had recently reached Italy, but in addition to them, all those Jews who had received Italian nationality after January 1, 1919, were ordered to leave the country within six months. A series of restrictions and bans were imposed on Italian Jews who had enjoyed full civil rights for many years. The new laws included a definition of who was to be considered a Jew. They also banned mixed marriages; excluded Jews from military service, public office, and economic posts; restricted their rights to own land; banished them from elementary and higher education; and, finally, barred them from the liberal professions. Only some 3,000 exceptions to the rule were eventually specified. The Jewish community, numbering 46,850 in 1938, was stunned; some 10 percent of the Jews converted to Christianity and more than 5,000 emigrated.[52]

However, like the Jews of Germany in the 1930s, the majority tried to reorganize their lives. The Union of Jewish Communities established Jewish elementary and secondary schools and erected public aid institutions for those ejected from the Italian economy. From November 1939 the union was headed by Dr. Dante Almansi, who had been dismissed in 1938 from his post in the civil service, in which he had served from 1900 in various prominent positions.[53] Considerable attention was devoted to the problem of the refugees residing in Italy, and in 1940 a special joint Jewish–gentile organization was established, known by its initials as Delasem (Delegazione assistenza emigranti ebrei). It supported refugees in Italy and helped them and Italian Jews to leave, mostly to Switzerland.

It should be emphasized that throughout this period the Italian population at large did not take part in anti-Jewish activities, and there were only isolated incidents of violent attacks on Jews and their institutions. After Italy entered the war, forty-three detention camps were set up in which foreign nationals were interned—particularly nationals of the Allied powers—including several thousand foreign Jews who until then had succeeded in remaining in Italy despite the expulsion orders. These camps did not enforce as stringent a regime as the German concentration camps. From May 1942 Jewish men aged eighteen to fifty-five were ordered to report for so-called obligatory labor; in actual fact not more than two thousand or so were recruited.[54]

A unique situation existed in Libya. Here, the Italians began to harass the Jews in 1936; they even marked their passports with a distinguishing stamp. The Italian anti-Jewish legislation of 1938 was strictly implemented in Libya. The Italians in Libya gave priority to Arab interests and adapted their conduct toward the Jews to that of the Arab community. They undermined the civil status of the Jews, hampered their economic interests, and restricted their professional, cultural, and educational activities. During the 1941/1942 fighting, the region changed hands several times. The Jews, in particular, suffered from Italian acts of vengeance; among them foreign nationals were expelled or transported to Italy or even handed over to the Germans. Some Jews were interned in labor camps and many died there; a large part of Jewish property in Tripoli and Benghazi was expropriated. All this occurred despite the fact that the local Arab population did not take part in the acts of persecution. The status quo ante was restored only after the decisive victory of the British at the battle of El Alamein.

Under German Rule: The Deportation of the Jews of Rome

Both before and during the war, the Italians on various occasions displayed interest in German racial research, legislation, and even in the organization of the concentration camps. Nonetheless, they did not emulate German actions; even when they arrested Jews, they did not erect concentration camps along the German model.

All this changed at one fell swoop with the overthrow of the Fascist government in Italy. Those Jews who had been interned in camps in the south were released by the Allied forces; however, the great majority of the Jews of Italy were living in Rome and the north where the Germans now ruled. During the brief rule of the government of Marshal Pietro Badoglio (July 25 to September 9, 1943), Mussolini was rescued from imprisonment in a daring operation and taken to Germany, Hitler now returned him to quasi power, and in mid-November the Italian Socialist Republic was established under his leadership. On November 14, 1943, the Fascist Party conference formulated the principles of the new regime. One of the eighteen clauses of the Verona platform stipulated, "Members of the Jewish race are aliens. During this war they are to be considered as members of an enemy nation."[55] As a consequence, on November 30 the minister of the interior issued instructions to arrest all Jews without exception, to incarcerate them in concentration camps, and to confiscate their property. This ushered in the second stage in the persecution of the Jews of Italy.

The first stage had commenced immediately after the German occupation. In the first few weeks, chaos reigned in the German-occupied areas; thus there was a proliferation of spontaneous, unplanned acts by German forces aided by the Fascist militia. However, the SS soon started planned actions whose success was based on the surprise element. The cooperation among the German army, the SS, and Fascist organizations served as the background for all the anti-Jewish activities in that period. The Germans had long been trying to reinforce SS influence, and as early as 1939 an SD representative, Herbert Kappler, had been sent as police attaché to the German embassy in Rome. In August 1943—that is, in the most critical period from the point of view of German influence in Italy—Himmler sent one of his closest associates to Rome, SS General Karl Wolff. When the Germans took over, he became the head of the military administration in northern Italy. He was joined by two men with greater experience in deportation: Dr. Wilhelm Harster (previously head of the SD in Holland, where he was in charge of organizing transports) was appointed Gestapo commandant; and Theodor Dannecker (who had demonstrated his abilities mainly in France and with less success in Bulgaria [see chap. 20]) was put in charge of the deportation operation.

The explicit order to arrest and deport the Jews of Rome apparently arrived on September 25, and Kappler immediately set to work. The number of Jews, including those in the surrounding area and refugees, was estimated at more than ten thousand.[56] On September 26 he summoned the president of the Rome community, Ugo Foa, and the president of the Union of Italian Jewish Communities, Dante Almansi, and demanded that the Jews hand over 110 pounds of gold within thirty-six hours—or else, two hundred Jews would be deported. Foa called the community leaders for consultations. A debate ensued in which doubts were expressed as to whether the Germans would keep their promise not to deport Jews if they received the gold; grave doubts were also voiced as to the ability of the relatively poor community to raise so great a sum within such a brief period. It was finally resolved to try to fulfill the German demand. Feverish activity commenced, and from all corners of the ghetto Jews brought their jewelry and gold. It still seemed that the required amount would not be collected. Then the idea was broached of appealing to the Vatican for a loan to make up the difference, guaranteeing to repay the loan when possible. Various people apparently made contact with the Vatican and the pope agreed to place the required gold at the disposal of the Jews; but after the deadline had been extended by several hours, it transpired that there was no need for this loan, and the gold was handed over to the Gestapo. At first they tried to claim that the amount of gold was insufficient but finally it was proved that 50.3 kilograms of gold packed in crates had been brought. The Jews hoped that they had thereby redeemed themselves.

It has been claimed that Kappler and several officers of the German high command tried to avoid carrying out the deportation order and—with the support of the army commander, Marshal Albert Kesselring—proposed exploiting the Jews for work on building fortifications. This proposal was modeled on the arrangement introduced previously by the Germans in Tunis, where Eitel Friedrich Mölhausen had served as consul during the German occupation. On October 6, 1943, he sent Ribbentrop an urgent cable in this spirit; yet the reply he received three days later was emphatic: the deportation of the Jews of Rome was being carried out on Hitler's instructions and he was to avoid interfering in the action of the SS.[57] On October 16, in the intermediate days of *Succot* (the Feast of Tabernacles), the German police surrounded the quarters in which Jews lived and began arresting them on the basis of prepared lists. Many of the Jews had previously abandoned their homes and gone into hiding in the homes of Italian friends outside the city or in Catholic institutions; others now fled under cover of darkness through the lanes of Rome. The Germans seized a total of 1,259 Jews in this operation, but they released the children of mixed marriages. On October 18, they dispatched 1,007 Jews directly to Auschwitz—where they arrived on October 23, one day after the feast of *Simhat Torah* (the Rejoicing of the Law).[58]

The People and Their Leaders in the Hour of Crisis

The fact that the Germans succeeded in apprehending only part of the Jews of Rome indicates that the Jews were capable of swift reaction and obtained the necessary help from the population in hiding from the Germans. In this, Rome and in due course all of Italy differed from many other countries. The situation was unique in that, according to personal testimony, the Jewish population as a whole did not suspect that the Germans would deport them to Poland. Nor did the community leaders imagine when the persecution commenced that the community was in mortal danger. Immediately after the affair of the gold, the Germans conducted a search in the office of the community president, Ugo Foa, and in the adjacent central synagogue. They displayed particular interest in the community's ancient libraries and gave their promise not to touch holy vessels and silver and gold utensils in the possession of the synagogue. The two community leaders—Foa and Almansi—were highly apprehensive as to the intentions of the Germans, but they continued to operate within the frame of reference of their relations with the Italian authorities. They wrote letters to the Library Department of the Ministry of Education, the General Administration of Religious Rituals, the General Administration of Public Security, and the Civil Administration in the Ministry of the Interior. In these letters they related what had taken place that same morning and protested against the intention to confiscate and remove the libraries. The Minister of the Interior, who was responsible for security, was a Fascist, and later designated a war criminal. It is not surprising, therefore, that the appeal did not produce results: but the fact that it was submitted indicates the lack of awareness on the part of the Jews of what was happening in Rome. In a report written after the war, Foa noted that he suffered at the time from a "vain illusion."[59] On October 13, between the Day of Atonement and the Feast of Tabernacles, the Germans appeared at the community offices in order to pack the books and load them on trucks, which awaited outside; implementation was delayed until the following day. This postponement enabled Foa and his staff to find hiding places for the synagogue treasures, thus preventing the Germans from seizing them as well. It was decided to utilize the *mikveh* (ritual bath) for this purpose. It was emptied of water, and while the Germans were occupied with the books, all the silver and gold artifacts were concealed in this hiding place. Other objects were divided among private homes and buried in gardens. Full crates, entrusted to banks for safekeeping, were later transferred to a clandestine storeroom. The Germans never discovered these caches.[60] It may be assumed that these operations could not have succeeded without the aid of non-Jews. Some must have known the secret, yet the Germans never came to know of it.

Even after these happenings, the community leaders continued to reassure the Jewish population, claiming that one could not deduce from crimes against books that crimes would be committed against human beings as well. Foa refused for some time to leave his apartment and go into hiding. Although some of his staff fled, he tried to continue running the community office. Almansi acted otherwise. He wanted to preserve his office from the experience of the Community Council, where Foa was forced to open the safe, which the Germans then emptied. Almansi and his staff gradually removed the entire archives and all the funds. Stocks and bonds were handed over to the bank in which they had been invested and which secured them and all interest accruing to them until after the war. Almansi himself went into hiding, as did the active members of the Delasem—Renzo Levi and Settimio Sorani. Before the German occupation of Rome, the latter removed all material that was liable to serve the Germans as a source of information, particularly on the 650 refugees then residing in Rome. Sorani knew what had befallen the Jews of Europe, including the gassings, and he urged the Jews of Rome to make their escape. He organized the underground existence of 400 of the refugees remaining in the city.[61]

One of the strangest (even dubious) figures of the period was the chief rabbi of Rome, Rabbi Israel Zolli. He and his family left their apartment as soon as the Germans entered Rome because he was convinced that they would immediately arrest and execute him. Zolli was not Italian-born; he came from Brody, but had studied in Italy. He later claimed that he had tried to persuade Foa to organize a clandestine exodus of the Jews from Rome and to go into hiding wherever possible.[62] But as his opinion was dismissed, he did not take part in the discussions or the activities of the community leaders. Hence, they accused him of dereliction of his duties in those troubled times. Zolli was among the survivors, and after the war he returned to Rome and to his post as chief rabbi. However, he encountered adamant resistance on the part of the community. Having apparently nursed a predilection for Christianity for some time, he then openly converted, changing his name to Euginio Maria. This act shocked not only the survivors of the Rome Jewish community but also Jews the world over.

One cannot attribute the survival of part of Rome's Jews to the actions of their official leadership. A contributing factor was the character of the city, with its hidden lanes, as was the fact that the Jews still had telephones, so that relatives and friends could warn them. But the overriding factor operating to the benefit of the Jews was the spirit that prevailed among the Italian people. It found expression in the response of the underground whose organ published a strong protest, "All night and throughout the day the Germans moved through Rome, seizing Italians for their furnaces in the north. The Germans would like us to believe that these people are alien to us, that they belong to a different race; but we feel that they are flesh of our flesh and blood of our blood. They have always lived, fought and suffered with us."

The article went on to describe how old people, children, and women had been rounded up and taken away in trucks.[63]

Statistics show that for every Jew caught, nine made their escape.[64]

Concentration Camps and Deportation

On October 17 Kappler sent a report on the deportation operation. He described the difficulties in capturing the Jews, who were scattered in twenty-six quarters of the city. The Germans had not succeeded in sealing all of them off, and the Italian police had not been brought in "because of our lack of confidence in them." At first he claimed that the Italian population "displayed passive resistance, which only in a few cases found expression also in active aid"; but several lines later he wrote, "the great majority of the inhabitants tried to smuggle Jews away from the police." On the same day von Thadden and Heinrich Müller discussed the problem of the deportation of the Jews of Italy. Müller commented that the SS lacked sufficient forces to carry out simultaneously a rapid and decisive operation throughout Italy. The Foreign Ministry, on the other hand, feared the reaction of the pope. German fears of church intervention proved unfounded, since the pope—as is well known—did not intervene in his official capacity. It was the head of the German Catholic church in Rome, Episcopus Hudal, who wrote on the day of the operation to the German city commandant asking for an immediate halt to the arrest of the Jews.[65]

The Rome operation was not, in fact, the first. It was preceded by an operation conducted on October 9 in Trieste, to which another expert on liquidation of Jews had been dispatched—namely, Odilo Globocnik. The sole concentration camp in Italy, which was also a death camp with a crematorium, was set up at San Saba near Trieste. Two thousand Jews and political prisoners in the camp were exterminated.[66]

Most of the camps set up in this period were transit camps. Some existed for only a few weeks until the people who were rounded up in the vicinity had been transferred to one of the central camps and from there sent eastward. In most of the large towns and many small places, about one-half the Jews were taken systematically and deported from Italy, usually to Auschwitz. The Germans were generally equipped with lists of names and addresses, which they had received from the Italian authorities. The mass arrests ended in the second half of November 1943 before the promulgation of the November 30 law mentioned earlier. As was frequently the case with the Nazis, this law also served to sanction an existing situation. Then, a new stage commenced in which the Germans hunted down Jews who were trying to make their escape or were in hiding. In this operation they succeeded in rounding up the same number of Jews as in the first deportation activities. All in all, 8,360 Jews were deported out of the 35,000 members of the Italian-Jewish community at the time of the German conquest. Some 250 were killed in Italy itself; 2,000 to 3,000 joined the resistance movement. Of the Jews who fell fighting for the underground 7 were posthumously awarded the highest Italian decoration.[67] The operations were accompanied everywhere by the looting and robbery of the Germans. Apart from private property, they destroyed many of the cultural treasures of the ancient communities held in synagogues and public and private libraries. In all the camps, the supreme command was in German hands, but there were Fascist militiamen among the guards and gendarmes. These were, then, concentration camps in every sense of the term, but they differed from the camps in Germany in several details of administration and regime.

A considerable number of Italian Jews succeeded in escaping to Switzerland, mostly with the help of the Delasem. A group of students who had previously made their way to Lausanne set up a committee known as "The Committee for Aid to Italians Persecuted for Political or Racial Reasons." The committee tried to assist refugees and to collect and disseminate information on what was occurring in Italy; it assembled eyewitness testimonies describing the situation in the concentration camps. In a prison in Milan (we learn), the Jews were allowed freedom of movement and the possibility of supplying their own vital needs. There were old and sick people and children in the camps—all were candidates for deportation. It is noted, however, that "there were no grave acts of violence." Generally, the Jews conducted themselves with courage and tranquillity despite severe difficulties. There were numerous manifestations of fraternity, sympathy, and mutual aid, particularly when the candidates for deportation were being taken away.

Some twenty-five hundred Jews passed through a large camp at Fossoli. The internal arrangements permitted families to live together, and special efforts were made to care for children. The internees were not forced to wear prisoners' garb. They received food parcels and were allowed to receive and to write letters. They were greatly helped by a priest, Father Francesco Venturelli. Those who did not receive aid suffered severely from hunger. The Germans, for their part, conducted searches and used torture and interrogation to force the inmates to reveal where their relatives and friends were hiding.[68]

The Massacre of Croatian Jewry

The Italians protected the Jews in their area of occupation in Yugoslavia and helped them to escape both the Germans and the Croatians. As in Greece, the situation lasted until Italy capitulated to the Allies and Germany took over the formerly Italian-occupied areas. The tension between the Ustasha and the Italians was of a general political origin: the Germans did not allow the Croat leader, Ante Pavelić, to annex those areas that the Italians claimed for themselves. When the so-called independent Croatian state was set up in April 1941, the head of the German Foreign Ministry, Baron Ernst von Weizsäcker, told the future German minister, Siegfried Kasche, "As long as the war goes on, we must handle Italian sensitivities with care."[69] And he added that in the event of conflicts between the Italians and the Croats, he should always support the Italians. The Croats were particularly enraged by the fact that the Italians maintained an occupying force in the area formally belonging to Croatia and that they defended the Serbs and the Jews.

At the end of July 1942, the legation in Zagreb informed Luther that in the first half of August, the deportation of Jews would commence in northern Croatia; unfortunately, in the south, namely, the area under Italian military rule, problems were to be anticipated. By the end of 1942, more than five thousand Jews had been deported to the East. On October 14 Kasche announced that the Croatian government was ready to pay RM 30 for every Jew deported from the country.[70]

All this time, the debate continued between the Ustasha and the Italians while the Germans were trying to exert pressure on Mussolini and proffering advice to Pavelić. The Italians adopted the tactic of seemingly agreeing to the demand while, in fact, sabotaging implementation by delay. Mussolini himself often succumbed to the heavy German pressure and promised to hand over the Jews in the Italian area to the Croats. But subsequently he took note of the arguments of his Foreign Ministry officials and generals and authorized them to use delaying tactics to prevent the handing over of the Jews. Thus, for example, the Italians transferred the Jews to islands under their rule, the largest concentration being on the island of Rab. Even Jews who had already been rounded up by the Croats were saved in this way. In the course of these spurious negotiations, the Croatian government announced that it was willing to leave the Jews to the Italians and that they would be transferred to Italy on condition "that the Croat state will inherit their property, and that the Jews will forfeit Croatian nationality."[71] The Italians did not accept this offer, but some of the Jews were, in fact, transferred to Italy.

The tension in the region was heightened in this period because of the striking successes of the partisans. In response the Germans reintervened in the military command, which had previously been assigned to the Croatian forces. Since the latter had not demonstrated military skill, command of numerous areas was transferred to the German units in January 1943. In March 1943 Himmler, too, attempted to bolster his influence in Croatia by augmenting the German police forces under command of his men. In addition to Kasche, Jewish affairs were being dealt with by the police attaché, Hans Helm, an SS officer representing Eich-

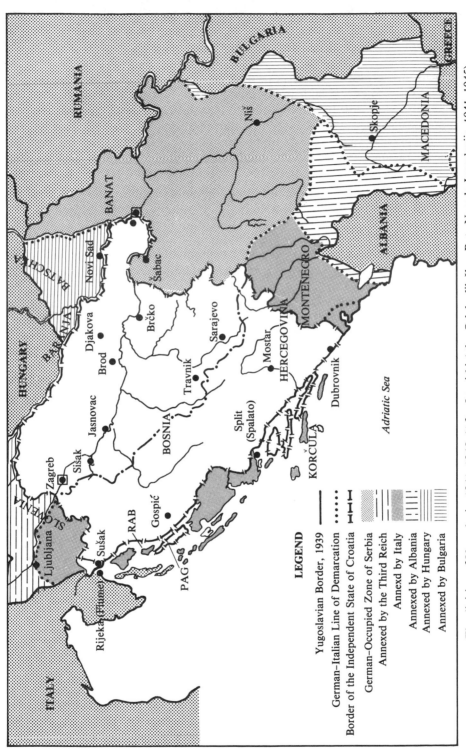

The division of Yugoslavia, 1941–1945. (After Istoriski Atlas Oslobodilačkog Rata Naroda Jugoslavije, 1941–1945)

LEGEND

——	Yugoslavian Border, 1939
•••••	German–Italian Line of Demarcation
I—I—I	Border of the Independent State of Croatia
	German-Occupied Zone of Serbia
	Annexed by the Third Reich
	Annexed by Italy
	Annexed by Albania
	Annexed by Hungary
	Annexed by Bulgaria

mann's bureau. No wonder, then, that there was now, once again, pressure to "cleanse Croatia of Jews."[72]

On March 4, 1943, Kasche and Helm sent a joint cable reporting a new *Aktion* against the Jews. It would begin in the middle of the month and small groups of 20 to 150 would be deported in special railroad cars to be attached to regular trains. They requested that the necessary technical arrangements be made for the deportation of some 2,000 people. The implementation was postponed. Thus on April 10 Horst Wagner of the Foreign Ministry inquired when the 2,000 Jews would finally be sent. Eventually, the deportation took place in May 1943. The Croats were hesitant, but it was apparently Himmler himself—on a visit to Zagreb on May 5—who settled the matter. Some 1,400 Jews were then deported. On July 15, however, Horst Wagner again urged that the deportation of "800 Jews, mostly women and children" be expedited, since he had learned from a highly confidential report that they were still in concentration camps in Croatia. It seems that they were never dispatched, but were killed in gas vans, which were widely used in Croatia. According to estimates, 6,000 to 7,000 Jews from Croatia reached Auschwitz, of whom 24 were found in the camp when it was liberated.[73]

Croatian acts of cruelty were among the most barbaric committed in this era of horrors. The literature is filled with descriptions of mass murders by the most savage means, mutilation of corpses, murder of women and children. The island of Pag was handed over in April 1941 by the Italians to the Ustasha; at the end of August it reverted to the Italians who had maintained a small garrison there all the time. It was through this force that word first reached the Italian headquarters of the Croatian atrocities against Serbs and Jews (according to one source, they numbered 4,500 and 2,400, respectively). All of them were interned in two concentration camps and almost all were brutally murdered there. People were executed daily by axe. The Italians found on the island corpses of men, women, and children in their hundreds in mass graves. A report, accompanied by photographs, written by military physicians, "had a profound impact on the Italian stand with regard to the Jewish refugees and their decision to help them."[74]

Children—both Serbs and Jews—were concentrated in Croatia in special camps where they were murdered in gas vans. In 1942 there were 24,000 children in the infamous Jasenovač Camp. Half of them were murdered; the remainder were released owing to Red Cross pressure. Many, however, later died of the aftereffects of their imprisonment. Particularly notorious for his savagery in that camp was a Franciscan brother known as Fra Sotona (Brother Satan). For four months—from the fall of 1942—he ruled the camp, and in this period 40,000 inmates lost their lives. It is estimated that the number of victims in the camp approached 200,000.[75]

The End of the Harvest Festival in Western Europe

France

The most serious obstruction to the work of Eichmann's staff occurred in France. According to his plan, the operation there was to be completed by mid-1943. At a meeting held in his office on August 28, 1942, Eichmann announced that all stateless Jews were to be deported by the end of the year and all foreign Jews by the end of June 1943. But, in a report dated March 29, 1943, the head of Sipo, Helmut Knochen, stated that in the near future there would be no need to organize trains from France. He listed two main impediments to future action: (1) the attitude of Pétain, who was refusing to deport Jews with French nationality; (2) the conduct of the Italians, who had declared that they would not treat the Jews as the Germans did but would oppose continued activity against them; this stance, he claimed, was providing the French with a pretext. He expressed the hope that the French would pass a law annulling the naturalization of Jews who had arrived in France after 1932. Thus, when they lacked nationality, it would be possible to transfer 100,000 Jews to the East.[76] Two days previously it had been determined that the number of Jews dispatched by that date was 49,902; and the author of the memorandum (apparently Heinz Röthke) wrote that these constituted only one-seventh or one-eighth of the 350,000 Jews in France. Of these, 13,000 had been deported from the southern region, 4,000 since the occupation of the south by the Germans in November 1942. Most of them were probably attached to the transports that left Drancy in the first half of February 1943 for Auschwitz. The writer considered it essential to concentrate the Jews in Drancy and Beaune la Rolande in northern France as soon as possible in order to avoid a recurrence in southern France of what had happened during the Allied occupation of North Africa. This is an oblique reference to the fact that the Jewish underground resistance movement played an important part in Algeria. So, Jews should be arrested irrespective of nationality; the French government should be urged to transfer all Jews from the southern zone to the north; and it was to be anticipated that the führer himself and the Foreign Ministry would shortly bring about a change in the conduct of the Italians.[77]

Prior to this, on January 13, 1943, Knochen had complained in a letter to Heinrich Müller that the Italian government had conveyed a message to Pierre Laval that it did not object to operations in the Italian-occupied French zone directed against French nationals, but that it "is opposed to any measure against Jews with foreign nationality; that is to say, they are protecting not only the Italian Jews but at the same time all other foreign Jews."[78] He requested that Himmler be invoked to persuade the Italians. On the same day, Ribbentrop wrote to his ambassador in Rome and devoted most of his letter to the fact that the Italian government was defending Italian Jews abroad. It was clear to the Germans that no activity could be conducted against the Jews in the southern zone of France as long as the Italians refused to cooperate. In response to complaints about the attitude of the Italian forces in France to the Jewish question, Rome asserted that this was an important political question that should be regulated at the government level and not between military commanders.[79] Ribbentrop now decided that the matter must be discussed with Mussolini, and he acted accordingly during his visit to Rome on February 25, 1943. He brought along a memorandum—composed for this purpose by the RSHA—informing him of the current state of affairs and listing the SS demands. The main one was that the Italians put a halt to their sabotage of anti-Jewish operations in France and Greece. The SS also cast the blame on the Italian government for the difficulties it was encountering at the time in Bulgaria, Rumania, and Slovakia, but it placed particular emphasis on Italian influence on the French government. Ribbentrop broached the Jewish problem to *Il Duce*, explaining that the war had illuminated the Jewish problem with great clarity and consequently Germany had dispatched all the Jews from its own country and from the occupied territories to reservations in the East. There were, of course, those who considered these actions cruel, but they were essential to the proper conduct of the war. In light of the tremendous importance of the problem, the steps adopted seemed relatively moderate. He was well aware that in Italian military circles—as sometimes within the Germany army—the Jewish problem was not treated with the required understanding; only thus could one explain actions seemingly ordered by the Italian high command being canceled in the Italian-occupied area of France.[80]

Mussolini refuted this charge and seemed to be concurring with the views of his visitor. To the Germans' disappointment, however, there was no discernible change in the stance of the Italians, and they continued to prevent the arrest and deportation of Jews.[81] The German ambassador in Rome, Eberhard von Mackensen, reverted to the subject in a talk with Mussolini on March 17, 1943. *Il Duce* again responded politely and appeared to agree, but he defended his generals, claiming that they did not grasp the far-reaching importance of the anti-Jewish measures. Three days later, the Germans discovered that Mussolini had again changed his mind and decided to entrust all dealings with the Jewish problem to the Italian police. To this end he dispatched to the French zone a distinguished police chief named Lospinoso as commissar for Jewish affairs; thus he removed the matter from the hands of the military. When this too failed to produce the desired results, Heinrich Müller flew to Rome on April 2 to attempt to change the outlook of the police chief, his "colleague." The latter continued, however, to employ delaying tactics and to cite the pretexts that the Italians had been exploiting all along. Particularly active in the rescue of Jews was Angelo Donati—an Italian businessman with good contacts in the army—who was Lospinoso's chief assistant.[82]

Fifty thousand Jews, six thousand of them French nationals, had been deported from France by June 23, 1943.[83] Since this slow pace was not to the liking of the Germans, they changed the procedures in Drancy. The expert on swift deportations, Alois Brunner, appeared, and on July 2, 1943, he took over the administration of the camp. It was now run by the SS, but subordinate to it was a Jewish "order service," whose task was to supervise the prisoners. Several of its members helped the inmates and fostered clandestine links between the camp and the outside world. With the aim of arresting as many more Jews as possible, Brunner tried to exploit inmates whose families were with them in the camp by sending them to bring in other Jews whose addresses were known. This method did not prove effective and was abandoned after one month.

Brunner divided the inmates into six categories:

1. Aryans, partners in mixed marriages, or half-Jews.
2. The unclassified.

3. Camp laborers employed in cleaning, hygiene, clerical work, and so on.
4. People of protected nationality.
5. Wives of POWs.
6. People awaiting the arrival of their relatives still at large.

Categories (1) and (3) were the privileged ones. Those in category (2) were in the worst situation. They constituted the majority of the inmates and were candidates for deportation. Most of those in category (1) were sent to the coastal area near Cherbourg. Some were sent to the island of Aurigny (Alderney) where their living conditions were harsh and they were employed as forced laborers. Those who fell seriously ill were returned to Drancy and attached to category (2) for deportation. Other groups of category (1) were deported to other camps in the Paris area in order to work in furniture repositories in which the Germans packed and stored the contents of the households of arrested Jews.[84]

From September 1943 onward—after the fall of Italy—German interest waned concerning Jews who had survived or were in hiding in the northern zone. Brunner spent September and October in Nice, organizing the rounding up and deportation of some fifty thousand Jews who had been trapped there after the Italian retreat. Many of them succeeded, nonetheless, in hiding and going underground or in fleeing to Switzerland or Spain, although quite a few were caught in flight. Here again, Brunner did not succeed in capturing as many victims as intended because the Vichy government was no longer interested in abetting him. To the surprise of the Germans Laval informed them that he would not agree to annul the French nationality of émigrés, and he even rescinded his previous signature on this matter. He asserted that he had not realized at the time that the intention was to arrest masses of French Jews.[85] The French were undoubtedly influenced by the changes that had occurred on all fronts and perhaps also by the proclamations of the Allies and the news of the extermination activities in Poland, which could no longer be ignored.

The last period of deportations extended from the beginning of July to mid-August 1944. In the course of 1943, twenty-one transports had been sent: eighteen to Auschwitz and three from the eastern border areas of France apparently to Sobibor; all in all, they included 20,000 people. From the spring of 1944, the Germans invested special efforts in capturing Jews, including those categories previously regarded as exempt. However, the war conditions, particularly after the Allied landing in Normandy on June 6, 1944, did not enable them to carry out their schemes in full. Notwithstanding, in April they deported 41 children from an orphanage near Lyons. One of the last actions of the Germans was the deportation of 300 children from UGIF orphanages in the vicinity of Paris. They emptied these institutions within two days in July, but the last deportation, planned for July 13, 1944, could not be carried out. In 1944 the number of victims transported from Drancy to Auschwitz was 15,316, and some 250 wives of POWs were sent to Bergen-Belsen. Together with another 4,000 persons deported from other places in France, the Germans succeeded in dispatching to Auschwitz another 20,000 victims in the last months of that year. In all, 84,000 Jews were sent from France to death camps, to which should be added those executed in France.

Before making their escape from Drancy on August 17, 1944, the Germans burned the camp archive, unaware that a copy had been smuggled out in good time. On the following day, the Red Cross entered the camp and found the last 500 survivors.[86]

More than two-thirds of the estimated 350,000 Jews who were living in France in 1940 were saved.

Belgium

Among the Jews deported from Drancy were some 5,000 from Belgium.[87] They probably included Jews who had fled to the south of France at the beginning of the war and been arrested by the Germans as foreign Jews. It has been noted that by the end of October 1942 close to 17,000 Jews, most of them foreigners, had been deported from Belgium in seventeen transports. As in other Western countries, the deportations from Belgium were temporarily suspended in the winter of 1942 until the beginning of 1943. This does not mean that alert officials in Germany were slacking. At the beginning of December, complaints were sent from Martin Luther's office to Werner von Bargen, Foreign Ministry representative in Brussels, pointing out that Belgian Jews were not being deported nor were deportations being planned.[88] However, in January 1943, the activities were renewed on a relatively limited scale. By July 1943 four trains had been sent to Auschwitz, carrying some 4,570 victims.

The transport prepared at the beginning of September was unusual and aroused considerable reaction. The operations against the Jews were planned to parallel those in Brussels and Antwerp for Friday night, September 3/4, 1943. All the technical details were prepared: units of military police accompanied by the Gestapo were to arrest the Jews and bring them to the assembly point from which they would be transferred the following day to the Malines camp. A unit of the *Kommando Devisenschutz* (Currency Preservation) was attached to these forces. Its task was to break into the apartments while the Jews were preparing to leave and to seize valuables, money, and documents.[89] Particularly brutal was the operation conducted in Antwerp: the people were shut into a hermetically sealed, metal boxcar for transporting furniture. The journey to Malines was to have taken half an hour but was deliberately extended to three hours. When the doors were opened, a horrific sight was revealed. Nine people had been asphyxiated and hundreds were taken to a hospital in serious condition. During September two transports left for Auschwitz and on September 20 eight hundred Belgian-born Jews were included for the first time.[90]

It was, however, the transport that left Malines on April 19, 1943, that became famous. Through collaboration between the Jewish and general underground movements, it was planned to free the people and enable them to make their escape. Still, this unique initiative was only partially successful.[91] By coincidence on the same day two additional significant events occurred: the outbreak of the Warsaw ghetto revolt and the opening of the abortive Bermuda Conference at which the American and British delegates were supposed to prepare a refuge for the persecuted.

This was not the sole escape operation carried out in the course of the deportations from Belgium. At one time, the Germans sent some 2,200 laborers to Todt labor camps in northern France; most of them, some 1,700, were later returned to Belgium and from there were deported to Auschwitz. Close to 200 fled the camps in France and another 150 escaped the transports from Belgium. Another example: the Jews succeeded in smuggling files aboard the train that departed from Malines on January 15, 1943. These were used to break open the doors and 30 to 40 Jews escaped.[92] In 1943 a total of six trains were dispatched to the East with 6,000 Jews aboard. In 1944 another six trains were also sent to Auschwitz, delivering 2,701 Jews. Smaller numbers were sent to camps in Germany— Buchenwald and Ravensbrück; candidates for exchange or privileged categories were sent to Bergen-Belsen as well as Vittel in France, for a total of 200 persons. The overall number deported from Belgium was 25,437.[93]

The fact that the deportations from Belgium were relatively restricted can be attributed both to the fact that Jews tried to escape and hide and to the conduct of the Belgian people and their leaders. Had it not been for the readiness of the population to assist those Jews who went into hiding, the frequent intervention of the leaders of the church and the activities of its institutions, and the responsiveness of Queen Mother Elizabeth, it is unlikely that Jews would have succeeded in evading the SS and the Gestapo. A special role was played by the Belgian underground. It constantly warned the Jews and appealed to the population to aid them, and, moreover, it collaborated with the Jewish underground in all its activities: preparing forged documents, obtaining ration cards, hiding individuals, and, in particular, concealing four thousand children.

Holland

Among the occupied countries of Western Europe, the Dutch-Jewish community was the most severely affected. By the liberation, in the fall of 1944, some 107,000 of the 140,000 Jews who had been living in the Netherlands had been deported. Less than 5 percent of them (5,200 in number) survived the war. By the end of 1942, some 38,600 had been deported and an additional 14,000 were deported by April 1, 1943, for a total of 52,600—most perished at Auschwitz. From March onward most of the transports were directed to Sobibor. Some 90,889 Jews were dispatched from Holland to those two death camps; another 2,000 or so Dutch Jews were loaded on trains that departed for the East from France and Belgium. Table 6 summarizes these deportations by destination.[94]

Thus, 105,000 Jews were deported from Holland: half of them by April 1943 plus another 52,400 from then up to the fall of 1944. In France the number of deportees in April 1943 was about 50,000 and to that number another 34,000 deportees were added by August 1944. The number of Jews in France was more than double that in Holland—and the Germans also occupied the south of France from the end of 1942. Notwithstanding, the percentage of Jews deported from France did not exceed 24 percent, in contrast to Holland, whence 76 percent were deported. These controversial figures call for explanation.

Table 6. Deportations According to Destination

Buchenwald and Mauthausen	(1941–1942)	1,750
Auschwitz	(1942–1943)	56,576
Sobibor	(1943)	34,313
Theresienstadt	(1943–1944)	4,894
Bergen-Belsen	(1943–1944)	3,751
Other camps in Germany and Upper Silesia		3,800
From France and Belgium (apparently to Auschwitz)		2,000
Total		107,084

The deportation operation in Holland was relaunched in January 1943 in accordance with the plan devised by Wilhelm Zöpf, who was in charge of Eichmann's office in Holland. It called for the initial deportation of some 8,000 sick people along with their medical attendants and their relatives. The Auschwitz timetable notes that on January 24 a transport arrived from an institution for the insane in Holland that consisted of 921 Jews and included, in addition to the patients, children from an adjacent institution for retarded children as well as a medical staff. Of these, 16 men and 36 women were transferred to the camp—the remainder, 869 in all, were exterminated. According to eyewitness testimony, they were thrown into pits where wood was thrown on top of them, saturated with gasoline, and then set alight—and they were burned alive.[95] The Germans went on to empty old-age homes and hospitals one by one.

From April to June 1943, tension in Holland was heightened. In February Himmler had given Hanns Rauter orders that reflected a drastic worsening of German policy. He even proposed to Hitler the detention in Holland of 300,000 people as POWs who were to be sent to Germany and put to work.[96] Hitler approved the scheme and in April the Germans tried to implement it. In reaction the Dutch government-in-exile ordered the proclamation of a general strike. About a million people ceased work, but the strike soon collapsed and some 100 strikers were shot by the Germans. In February orders were also issued to continue the deportation of the Jews at full steam. According to Harster, Himmler demanded "dispatch this year whatever possible in the way of human resources"[97] and this, in fact, was done. The main *Aktionen* took place in Amsterdam, after the Jewish communities in the provincial towns had already been liquidated either by deportation to the camps or by means of a directive ordering them to move to Amsterdam. In May Community Council employees—who had thought themselves exempt from deportation—were demanded by the Germans for the first time. Under pressure of threats, the Jewish community leaders decided to comply with these demands and to select candidates for deportation from among their officials. The people themselves, however, did not carry out the orders; of the 7,000 called to report for transportation to Westerbork, only 500 appeared. The Germans then conducted the *Aktion* through Sipo and Orpo as well as a unit of the Jewish Order Service that was brought in from Westerbork.[98] A larger *Aktion* was conducted on June 20 when 5,550 Jews were rounded up in the southern part of Amsterdam. On

June 25, Otto Bene, the Foreign Ministry representative, reported proudly that the 100,000th Jew had been removed from the midst of Dutch society.[99]

In addition to the looting of valuables that were confiscated at the Westerbork Camp by the German clerks of the expropriated Jewish bank, Lipman Rosenthal Ltd., the Germans competed successfully against Dutchmen who were also eager to lay their hands on Jewish possessions abandoned in deserted Jewish apartments. On September 9, 1943, Artur Seyss-Inquart responded to Göring's demand that the contents of the confiscated apartments be sent to the Reich. He concluded his long letter, "Between March 1942 and August 1943 we emptied 25,000 Jewish apartments and transferred them in 666 barges, with a capacity of 267,682 tons, and in more than 100 boxcars. We placed them at the disposal of the various areas of the Reich damaged by bombing."[100]

The assembly place of the Jews in Amsterdam was the Dutch Theater, at that time called the Jewish Theater. Within the building and in the back courtyard, several hundred Jews at a time were assembled, and from there were taken to the railway station en route to the transit camp at Westerbork. Despite the strict supervision of the SS and the officials of the Central Office for Jewish Emigration, several Jews managed to slip away. Some wore armbands of the Jewish Order Service (operating under the auspices of the Judenrat), which had been printed in the underground. Detainees were mostly smuggled out through the stage entrance of the theater, which was used by the Jewish Council itself. Without the knowledge of the heads of the Jewish Council, Abraham Asscher and David Cohen, this activity was organized by Walter Süsskind, a German-Jewish refugee who worked on the card index. He managed to conceal his clandestine activities and his work was considered so essential that he was returned from Westerbork to Amsterdam on German orders on October 22, 1943. He was even permitted to travel by streetcar and to be out of doors until 11:00 P.M.; his permit was extended seven times up to September 30, 1944. He was eventually deported to Theresienstadt and from there, with his entire family, to Auschwitz. Among those who helped him was SS Corporal Alfons Zündler. The latter was caught and sent, as punishment, to the eastern front. These two men rescued adults as well as children of all ages. Among those who helped them was one of Professor Cohen's daughters.[101]

In the summer of 1943, the Germans estimated that 20,000 Jews were in hiding in Holland. They were also aware that many Jews had entrusted their children to Dutch families, and they tried to prevent this by ordinances promulgating rewards for betrayal and by threats.[102]

There was, in fact, an official, legal way to avoid deportation. In Holland various categories of Jews had been established, and these people enjoyed privileges and were supposedly exempt from deportation. First and foremost among the privileged were the council staff and their families. In the peak period, their number reached 17,500. In addition, there were fifteen lists of such exempt Jews[103] that included, for example, "armaments Jews," who worked in that industry; "diamond Jews," who were employed as polishers; and Jews with foreign nationality, who were candidates for exchange—the last group included a large number of Jews with immigration certificates to Palestine. Special place was assigned to Jews with non-Jewish spouses and their offspring, Protestant Jews, and those who had declared themselves to be of Portuguese origin—the last, by some quirk of the racial theories, were considered Aryans. These lists, which sometimes encompassed thousands of people, "exploded" (as the phrase went) sooner or later, and those whose names appeared on them were deported. Rules were also established for partners in mixed marriages and several other privileged categories—these people were later deported to Theresienstadt. Of the Portuguese Jews, who initially numbered 4,000, only 362 were recognized as Aryans; the remainder were deported.

Decisions as to the racial affiliation of Jews were handed down by Hans G. Calmeyer—a German who, for unknown reasons, was entrusted with the fate of thousands of Jews. De Jong writes that he carried out his tasks with heavy feelings of guilt, "He knew that he, as a senior official, was taking part in a criminal system. He knew that once the decision on the final solution had been taken, his were life-and-death decisions. He knew that he could save one life only by abandoning another. His shame at the latter was greater than his satisfaction at the former."[104] Calmeyer appears to have maneuvered between his desire to help and the need to examine and verify the facts brought before him—and the pressure brought to bear on him by the SS.

After the war Calmeyer wrote to Jacob Presser, author of *The Destruction of the Dutch Jews,* "To despair and to remain in despair—this is the sole honorable attitude and valuable response possible to us when we try to confront what happened."[105]

Just before the Jewish New Year, September 28, 1943, the last great *Aktion* was conducted in Amsterdam. Among the 2,000 Jews taken from the Jewish Theater to Westerbork were the heads of the Judenrat.[106]

The last of the privileged Jews—foreign nationals, holders of certificates, wives of POWs, partners in mixed marriages, and the Jewish Council heads—were transferred from Westerbork to Bergen-Belsen or Theresienstadt. The last of the council officials were deported in the summer of 1944. In March 1944 most of the diamond workers were deported, apart from a small group who were taken to Bergen-Belsen in order to practice their craft.

Particularly problematic for the Germans was the question of mixed marriages. These proliferated during the occupation, and their number was estimated at 12,000. It was proposed to the couples that they provide proof that they were unable to produce children—either because the wife had passed the childbearing age or because they had "volunteered" to undergo sterilization operations. In fact, they were faced with a choice: deportation or sterilization. Such operations were performed on hundreds of people, but close to 6,000 did not respond to the directives. Some 9,500 Jewish men or women were partners in privileged mixed marriages because they had children. They survived and were even exempted from certain restrictions, but they were forced to join the labor service.[107]

As for those who went into hiding, the following calculations have been made: 107,000 Dutch Jews were sent to camps. About 2,700 fled Holland illegally and another 1,000 left legally. Thus, 110,700 Jews left Holland and 900 were eventually released from Westerbork. The total, therefore, is 111,500. This means that of 140,000 Jews living in Holland during the occupation, 28,400 were still there after the war, 10,000 of whom had been allowed to continue living there openly. Accordingly, it can be calculated that 18,000 Jews, including 4,500 children, survived by hiding until the war was over. It is, of course, difficult to estimate how many Jews tried to go into hiding and were apprehended, but their number is assessed at 25,000. If we add to these figures those who left the country legally and illegally (about 4,000), we see that some 30,000 Jews tried to evade the Germans in Holland. The historian Louis de Jong writes, "These figures seem to refute the claim that the Jewish community in Holland in general succumbed without resistance to deportation."[108]

Yet our question still remains unanswered: How did it happen that the Jews of Holland fell victim in such great numbers? Several factors were apparently at work here. The first—and possibly decisive one—was German domination of the local administration that accepted the situation unresistingly. It should be stressed that Eichmann's emissaries in the local office of IV B 4 were under the command of Sipo officers Rauter and Harster. They ruled the local population with an iron hand and regarded the "cleansing of Holland of Jews" as their prime, even sacred, task. On March 22, 1943, Rauter addressed his team and said that almost all the Jews of Holland were candidates for deportation to the East. He added:

> I intend to remove the Jews as rapidly as possible. This is not a pleasant task. It is dirty work. But it is a step of great historical importance. We cannot even guess what it means to cast out from the body of a nation 120,000 Jews, who within a century might have reached 1 million. What we are doing for the benefit of the body of the people must be done without mercy, and there is no room for softness and weakness. . . . We only want to recover from this distress, and the Jewish problem must be clarified finally and conclusively.

There had apparently been protests and indications of compunction on the part of the policemen engaged in this task, hence he added:

> I do not understand why these people [the policemen] do not cast the responsibility on us, since they say that they cannot bear it before God. I will willingly expiate in Heaven with my soul for my sins against the Jews.[109]

It should be noted, in contrast to the conduct of the Belgian government, for example, that the Dutch government-in-exile did not give the Dutch general secretaries, who operated under orders of the German commissars, clear instructions with regard to the Jews. No special agent was ever dispatched with the task of establishing contact with the Jews or producing intelligence reports. The Dutch broadcasting station in London did not display alertness and solidarity; it never admitted that the Jews were singled out within the Dutch population for a special fate. The result was (de Jong concludes) that the Jews were abandoned. Speaking on the Dutch radio in London on October 21, 1943, the Dutch prime minister of the government-in-exile delivered a kind of eulogy, "In the Netherlands the curtain is beginning to descend on the Jewish drama. In the last nights of September, the last five thousand Jews from Amsterdam joined their brethren in slavery under the domination of their persecutors."[110]

It is strikingly evident that in Holland, the Germans operated in a highly sophisticated fashion, adapting themselves to the mood of the population and of the Jews. The large number of lists of privileged persons fostered an illusion of false security among many Jews. Nor did the Dutch, and certainly not the Jews, imagine that all these official stamps would prove useless once it was decided to cancel the lists. To the same extent they did not suspect the veracity of the letters they received from Birkenau informing them how well the Jews were being treated there.

The living conditions in the Westerbork Camp were different and in many ways better than those prevailing in concentration camps and labor camps. People were allowed to maintain limited contact with the outside world and to receive mail, parcels, and foodstuffs. They enjoyed freedom of movement within the camp. The camp hospital provided proper, skilled, and dedicated care. People married in the camp and were then allocated married quarters for a time (this was later abolished). Children attended school, and a bar mitzvah ceremony was once held. Cultural activities took place, and the reading of newspapers was permitted.[111] In the course of time, 210 people succeeded in escaping from Westerbork; however, the camp commandant, Albert K. Gemmeker, retaliated by deporting 10 inmates out of each hut from which an escape had been made.[112] The camp is described as dirty, with intolerable overcrowding, and there were frequent grave incidents and acts of humiliation committed by the Germans and even by Jews. The hour of trial came every Tuesday—the day on which the deportation train departed; in the peak period, 2,000 to 3,000 deportees were crammed aboard such trains.

The surviving Dutch Jews took a very critical view of the activities of the Jewish Council—mainly of the two chairmen, Cohen and Asscher. This was already evident in Westerbork. Suddenly, the chairmen were reduced to the same level as the other prisoners and were obliged to take orders from the Order Service.[113] People generally considered them as tools of the Germans.

On the orders of the German authorities, the Dutch administration sent 100,000 Dutchmen to Germany as laborers—most returned alive. But most of the Jews did not return. De Jong, pointing to the differences between these two types of deportation and their outcome, notes that if the leaders of the Jewish organization had refused to carry out orders, they would have thereby placed their lives at risk, whereas "this danger did not usually face non-Jews." He believes that, despite the difference between the dependence of the civil administration on the Germans and the forced organization of the Jewish Council, the methods of collaboration were not unique to Jewish institutions, but constituted *"a special form of the general collaboration in the Netherlands."*[114]

Most Jews were undoubtedly unaware that the trains they boarded were conveying them to their deaths. They believed that they were being sent to Germany as laborers. On the other hand, there was growing apprehension that they faced eventual annihilation; therefore, Jews went into hiding or tried to escape (on the flight of Jews from Holland, see chaps. 17 and 20).

Liquidation in Eastern Europe

Bialystok

Far away from Holland, in the district and town of Bialystok, the Germans were preparing in the winter of 1942/1943 to conclude their work of extermination. The situations in the East and the West differed, and events unfolded quite disparately. Although the Germans introduced Jewish councils in both Bialystok and Holland, they differed in character. The Bialystok Council and its leader, the engineer Chaim Barash, were well aware that they were fighting for the life of the community and for their own survival—they nursed no illusions as to the aim of the deportation. They knew only too well what had been happening since the summer of 1941 to Jewish communities throughout Russia, the Balkans, and Poland. As in Łódź and Warsaw, extensive Jewish economic activity evolved, which supplied various vital needs of the German war effort. Barash's great hope was that the economic value of the ghetto would preserve it and enable it to hold fast until the Allies vanquished the Nazi empire.[115] The eyes of the Jews in this Eastern region were fixed on the Russian army, whose triumphs in the winter of 1942/ 1943 aroused great hopes. At the same time, the Jews were attuned to the dangers, which were exacerbated by the threat of defeat hanging over the German army. The message Hitler sent on February 24, 1943, to the party convention in Munich was known in Bialystok, and its significance was clearly grasped.[116]

Most of the Jews in the towns and villages of the Bialystok district had been deported in November 1942—some to Treblinka and Majdanek, some to Auschwitz. The Germans managed to carry out this operation before transportation was halted by order of the military. In order to implement the deportation scheme, the civil administration of the area was transferred to the Gestapo, and deportations from Bialystok itself were also planned. At this time, the ghetto population was on the increase because refugees were arriving who had escaped from deportation in the district's towns. Concomitantly, the Jewish Council was forced to reduce the area of the Bialystok ghetto. The Jews regarded this as the lesser evil. "It is better to lose streets than people," Barash said at the council meeting of November 8, 1942, when there were 45,000 inmates in the ghetto.[117]

At this time, one of the outstanding personalities in the pioneering Jewish youth movements, Mordeḥai Tennenbojm-Tamaroff—a leader of Dror—came to the ghetto. He had gained considerable experience in the struggle waged by the youth movements. Born in Warsaw, during the war he went to Vilna and was active there in the pioneering underground movement, first under Russian, then under German occupation. Later, he returned to Warsaw and was one of those who brought the Jewish underground there the bitter message of the German slaughter of Jews in 1941. In Bialystok he soon became the central figure in the Zionist underground and later in the planning of the uprising.

Before the young people could organize an armed uprising planned to take place during the liquidation of the ghetto, the Germans inflicted the first blow. In the last few days of January 1943, they informed Barash that they intended to transfer 17,600 Jews from Bialystok to the Lublin District. Barash tried to barter with them, citing the economic argument and pointing out the value of the ghetto industry, but the Germans claimed that the decision stemmed from Berlin. Tennenbojm ordered that leaflets be prepared for distribution in the ghetto. Originally in Yiddish, they read:

The evacuation of Jews from the town—means death.

Do not go to your death of your own free will.

Defend your children. Avenge the death of your mother.

Destroy the factories.

On leaving your home, burn it and its contents.

Do not go to Treblinka.

Jewish policemen—do not aid the hangmen.

On the eve of the *Aktion,* February 4, 1943, a meeting was held at which Barash reported on the situation. He did not reveal the truth, did not say that the *Aktion* would commence that same night, and only admitted this to Tennenbojm in a private conversation. On the basis of this information, Tennenbojm said at the meeting that in light of the situation at the frontline and the assumption that every day could bring a change, a small number of victims was to be preferred to the destruction of the ghetto.[118]

The Jews of Bialystok grasped the significance of the call to go into hiding and prepared caches en masse. After the *Aktion,* which lasted for a week (from February 5 to 12), Tennenbojm summed up: 700 people were killed for displaying resistance; dozens committed suicide; but "18,000 people are 'under the ground,' the whole of Bialystok ghetto is a great hiding place. They know that there is nothing to lose." He also attests that the Jewish police responded to his appeal and did not collaborate. "Often—at risk of life—the policemen saved dozens and hundreds of Jews in hiding places." But he goes on to query, "What will happen during the next *Aktion?*"[119] And, in fact, during the next and final *Aktion,* which started on August 16, 1943, the community conducted itself differently. Despite the passive resistance of the Jews in hiding, the Germans in February 1943 ferociously deported 9,000 people to Treblinka, Majdanek, and Auschwitz.[120]

The situation in the ghetto immediately after the *Aktion* was very difficult. On February 13, Tennenbojm described it with great emotion in Yiddish (he usually wrote in Hebrew):

Only now is the extent of the horror revealed. Dozens of people who have lost their minds are running through the city calling for their relatives. They run and stumble, run and stumble. Smothered babies are taken out of the hiding places—they started crying during the searches and were smothered. Everyone is carrying bundles. People are weeping everywhere. Policemen move through the cellars, attics, and all nooks and crannies collecting the dead. The apartments of the deportees are sealed. In the cemeteries great piles of corpses. They are buried in mass graves. Weeping and wailing.

In contrast, Mordeḥai Tennenbojm was amazed when he visited the dining hall of the Dror kibbutz of Tel Ḥai on the following day, "As if nothing had occurred. Heat. Light. Laughter. A sense of confidence and satisfaction." His conscience troubled him, "The responsibility for failure to react rests with us; those who follow will judge us and exonerate us or declare us culpable."[121]

Not all those who hid in bunkers were saved. This was due to informers who bought their release from deportation in this way—but they did not escape popular vengeance. Haike Grossman, a leading member of the underground (today a member of the Knesset), wrote,

> In the Bialystok ghetto at that time there was an eruption of mass rage against the informers. Nobody knew how the groups of avengers were organized, but they operated with precision on the basis of accurate information, and no innocent person was ever punished. . . . The informer would make his way confidently down the street, certain that his crime was unknown in the ghetto . . . but suddenly, as if from the bowels of the earth, Jews would appear at his side armed with sticks and axes, and begin to beat him about the head and face, and the passersby would help them.[122]

One day a man arrived who had succeeded in escaping from Treblinka and reported in detail on what was happening in the extermination camp. His testimony was recorded in writing and distributed widely.[123] The ghetto continued to exist, and hope burgeoned that it might hold fast. But just then, when least expected, the liquidation operation began early in the morning of August 16, 1943. The Germans, who had learned the lesson of the Warsaw ghetto uprising, sent one of their archbutchers, Odilo Globocnik, to Bialystok to prepare the surprise operation, which was carried out on the explicit orders of Himmler.[124] The underground, which had been preparing for this moment for many months, was taken by surprise. It made desperate attempts at defense and tried to rouse the masses to self-defense and flight—but in vain. Barash headed the procession of deportees. "Barash marched in the front row, his wife at his side. His grey head gleamed from afar. He was followed by other members of the Judenrat, and behind them hundreds of Jews—the dignitaries."[125]

Bialystok was cleansed of Jews.

Himmler's Plan

The liquidation of the Bialystok ghetto was part of an overall plan on which Himmler had resolved in May 1943. The German security forces in Warsaw were still occupied with stamping out the last sparks of the ghetto uprising when Himmler ordered the liquidation of the remaining ghettos as soon as possible. In light of the situation at the front and the strengthening of the partisan movement, completion of the liquidation scheme became an urgent priority. These trends merged with Himmler's desire to promote the industrial enterprises of OSTI, his pet scheme since March 1943. As in the second half of 1942, he now wanted to combine the exploitation of the Jewish labor force with its liquidation. On May 25, 1943, he gave the order to evacuate the remaining Jews, and to dispatch to the East "whatever possible in the way of human resources."[126] It was certainly no accident that he employed the same phrase that Harster had used (quoting Himmler) in Holland on May 5, 1943 (see p. 437). Himmler's demand was raised at a heavily attended meeting that Hans Frank convened in Cracow on May 31, 1943, in the presence of representatives from the Reich—among them Dr. Ernst Kaltenbrunner, on behalf of the RSHA; a representative of Hans Lammers, the head of Hitler's chancellery; several generals; and Friedrich Wilhelm Krüger. It was noted that the Jews had already been concentrated in camps, and that some had been sent as laborers to the munitions industry. Now, Himmler was demanding that this employment, too, be halted. After a detailed discussion with the head of the munitions industry, General Schindler, it became obvious that "this request of the Reichsführer-SS [could not], in the final analysis, be fulfilled" because there was no substitute for the skilled Jewish workers. Those Jews—called Maccabeans—remaining in industry were in better physical condition and "worked excellently."[127]

It appears that, in light of the opposition to his schemes voiced in military circles, Himmler felt the need to ensure the führer's backing. On June 19, 1943, he expounded his views to Hitler at his residence in the Bavarian Alps, and he later noted, "After my lecture on the Jewish question, the Führer expressed the view that the evacuation of the Jews should be carried out in radical fashion in the coming three to four months. Despite the unrest stemming from this, it must be insisted on."

Two days later, on June 21, 1943, Himmler gave the decisive order to liquidate all the ghettos in Ostland, and to concentrate the remaining Jews in camps. He also prohibited the removal of Jews from the camps for labor purposes and ordered that a concentration camp be set up near Riga, to which the workshops manufacturing clothing and equipment for the army would be transferred. Private firms should no longer be used. The "unneeded" relatives of the workers should be "evacuated to the East," that is, exterminated. August 1, 1943, was fixed as the date for the implementation of the reorganization. In fact, no new camp was set up; the existing Kaiserwald Camp near Riga was extended and several subcamps were attached to it.

The hour of liquidation of the ghettos had arrived: Bialystok—in August; Vilna and Minsk—in September; Riga—in November.[128] For unknown reasons, the Lithuanian ghettos—Kovno and Shavli—survived for the time being.

Vilna

In Vilna, as in Bialystok, production was stepped up in 1943. In April more than 10,000 Jewish laborers were counted; by the end of June their number had risen to 14,000. Most worked in factories outside the ghetto, some of them in the heavy timber and metal industries. Within the ghetto only 3,000 were employed in light industry and workshops for tailoring, shoemaking, and so on. Jacob Gens, the head of the Vilna Judenrat, was another who believed that it was possible to save the Jews through the essential work they were doing. He recommended this to the public in lectures and speeches he delivered; he even reduced the labor age to thirteen and requested that children be taught trades.[129]

In the spring of 1943, the Germans began to empty the smaller ghettos and the labor camps around Vilna. They employed subterfuge and tricks, claiming that the people would be sent to work in Kovno. In truth, they were transported by train to Ponary and murdered there. When the Jews learned what awaited them, many tried to escape or to defend themselves, mostly without success. Several dozen, however, did succeed in stealing back into the Vilna ghetto. This time the Germans did not hide their actions from Jewish eyes, and the Jewish police of Vilna, who were forced to bury the dead at Ponary, were permitted to return to the ghetto.[130]

These *Aktionen* continued throughout the summer of 1943. Finally—on Himmler's orders—the Germans began the task of liquidating the ghetto. From August 1943 there were eighty-five to ninety-five hundred laborers taken by transports, which left one after another, for the labor camps in Estonia where there was a shortage of workers. The women and children were murdered, with the exception of some seventeen hundred young women who were taken to the Kaiserwald Camp near Riga. Close to five thousand were sent to extermination camps in Poland. Officially, twenty-two hundred Jews were left in the Vilna labor camps. The ghetto was totally liquidated on September 23/24. About two thousand Jews succeeded in hiding in *malines,* but many of them were later caught. Others succeeded in joining groups who had previously made their way to the forests and the partisans. Since they had no further use for Gens, the Germans executed him on September 14, 1943.[131]

The Remnants of the Warsaw Ghetto

The annals of the Warsaw ghetto from the end of the great *Aktion* in September 1942 to the uprising in April 1943 epitomize Jewish armed resistance and will be rendered in this context (see chap. 17). The Jewish survivors the Germans dragged out of the bunkers were taken to labor and extermination camps in the Lublin region, such as Travniki, Poniatowa, and, above all, Majdanek. Himmler ordered the ghetto area razed to the ground.[132]

However, in 1942 and the beginning of 1943 and even while the uprising was in progress, thousands of Jews succeeded in escaping the ghetto to the Aryan side of the city and joining the 8,000 Jews living there at that time. Among them were Emmanuel Ringelblum (who had been liberated in a daring operation from Travniki) and his wife and son. There he wrote his book on the relations between Poles and Jews during World War II. In his conclusion he estimated that 15,000 Jews were hiding in the Polish capital.[133]

How did these Jews survive? Almost all lived clandestinely. All required places of residence and were dependent on Polish families who agreed to provide them with shelter. Ringelblum calculated that the number of such families was at least equal to the number of Jews in hiding. But these Jews also needed to support themselves, to purchase clothing, and so on, but almost all were penniless. They were assisted by the Council for Aid to Jews,[134] established at the time of the *Aktion* in the ghetto. Most of its members were Poles affiliated with various parties: lawyers, politicians, intellectuals. The activity was organized by Dr. Adolf A. Berman, a member of Poalei Zion, together with Yitzḥak Zuckerman (Antek). Both men represented the Jewish National Committee and the Jewish Combat Organization of the ghetto on the Polish side of Warsaw. Berman was the secretary of the Council for Aid to Jews, and its deputy chairman was a Bund representative, the lawyer Leon Feiner. The committee made contact with the Warsaw representatives of the Polish government-in-exile. The committee's funds came mainly from Jewish organizations abroad. Among the most difficult tasks the committee faced was the need to solve the accommodation problem. A wide network of agents sought out the suitable locations and directed Jews there. As in all the general and Jewish underground movements, a "factory" was set up for the forging of documents. It followed the instructions of a special department, the Legalization Office. This "factory" produced thousands of birth, baptism, and marriage certificates; prewar identity cards; German identity papers from the occupation authorities; residence papers; labor cards; and so on. It sometimes even forged documents purportedly issued by SS and Gestapo offices. The man who headed this project, the former governor of a Polish town, finally fell into the hands of the Gestapo and was shot. Only those Jews able to pass as Aryans could work and were obliged to do so. They guaranteed their livelihood thereby, but they were also exposed to extra risks. A special department was set up to care for the hundreds of children who had been orphaned or whose parents wanted to find them a safe refuge. Catholic monasteries assisted in this.

The numerous blackmailers constituted a grave problem. They were ready not only to extract large sums of money but even to hand Jews over to the Germans. Their activities intensified after the liquidation of the ghetto. "The war against this plague became one of the central tasks of the Council for Aid to Jews and the Jewish underground organizations," and death sentences were passed against blackmailers and informers both in Warsaw and Cracow.[135] The Jewish underground operated in so systematic and organized a fashion that it even submitted financial reports on the sums of money received from abroad. In the period between June 1943 and October 31, it received U.S. $40,000 and 10,000 pounds sterling, equivalent in value to 3 million zlotys. Between November 1, 1943, and May 20, 1944, the underground received U.S. $126,000. Of this sum, about 15 percent was expended on support for parties, organizations, writers, and artists; 10 percent for the Jewish Combat Organization; and the remainder, 75 percent, was spent on "general aid activities for the Jews of Warsaw, for internees in camps, and for provincial towns."[136]

Lwów

The liquidation of the remaining ghettos in the Generalgouvernement—in the wake of Himmler's instructions— commenced in eastern Galicia in the second half of June 1943, after the first *Aktionen* in the region in 1941/1942, mainly in Lwów, and the establishment of the concentration and Janowski labor camps. More than 40,000 Jews were exterminated, some at Bełżec, some at other camps.[137] Then the ghetto was set up in Lwów on November 10, 1942, and surrounded by a high barbed wire fence. At that time, "254,989 Jews [from eastern Galicia] had already been evacuated or transferred elsewhere."[138] The remainder were declared "working prisoners" and concentrated in factories and camps. The ghetto was proclaimed a Jewish camp *(Julag)* and placed directly under SS command. Fugitive Jews or escapees who were apprehended were given "immediate special treatment," in other words, shot on the spot. Fritz Katzmann, the commandant of the SS and the police in eastern Galicia, boasted, "By June 27, 1943, a total of 434,329 were evacuated." Another 21,156 Jewish laborers remained in twenty-one camps. It emerges, therefore, that from November 1942 to June 1943 another 180,000 Jews were murdered in eastern Galicia.[139] From among the half million Jews who had been living in the region, 24,000 survived because they were working in munitions factories or other vital industries. Katzmann had to admit that "almost 90 percent of the trades in Galicia were in the hands of the Jewish labor force. We could solve the problem only step by step because immediate removal was not in line with the interests of the war economy."[140]

In 1943 Katzmann was plagued by the partisan movement, which was on the increase in the forests of Galicia. Jews were active in the movement, and they also tried to defend themselves during the *Aktionen* in the ghetto of Lwów. The Germans encountered determined resistance; eight of their men were killed and twelve injured. In order to smash the resistance, they used similar measures to those that had been employed in Warsaw: blowing up or burning down buildings. To their surprise they found 8,000 Jews in hiding in the ghetto in addition to the 12,000 Jews of whose presence they were aware. Many Jews were executed in the notorious place near the Janowski Camp (see chap. 13). And 3,000 murder victims were reported to have committed suicide; 7,000 Jews were sent to the labor camp, and several thousand succeeded in hiding—mostly in the town of Lwów.[141]

Erntefest

In July 1943 a census was conducted in the Generalgouvernement according to which there were 14.8 million inhabitants in the region, of whom 306,000 were Germans—including local Germans—and 60,000 were military and police personnel. According to the census the number of Jews was 203,000. Two weeks later, Frank boasted, "If someone should ask what will happen to the National Socialist Party, we can answer: be assured that the National Socialist Party will live longer than the Jews. We started here with 3.5 million Jews, of whom only a few labor battalions are left. All the rest, let us say, have emigrated."[142]

In fact, 21,643 Jews were employed at the time in the munitions industry; moreover, their number was to increase. On January 27, 1944, General Schindler reported that of the 140,000 workers employed in industry, 26,000 were Jews. He anticipated (correctly) that their number would increase.[143]

The situation with respect to OSTI was different. After the failure of the enterprise, most of the Jews employed there were liquidated in the early winter of 1943. The executors called this operation *Erntefest.* By the end of the summer, Himmler had succeeded in annihilating a large proportion of the Jewish concentrations remaining in the western areas of Poland, those which had been annexed to the Reich. In August 1943 the ghettos of Sosnowitz and Bendin in Eastern Upper Silesia were liquidated. The Warthegau had been almost totally emptied of Jews in 1942. On the orders of the RSHA, 20,000 "nonproductive" Jews were dispatched from Łódź to reopened Chełmno in 1944. After this bloodletting, 87,000

Jews remained in Łódź, and the ghetto was turned into a labor camp. As such, it held as the very last of its kind until August 1944.

In Łódź, as a labor camp, it was no longer possible to keep up the illusion of self-rule—fostered by Rumkowski. The administrative apparatus of the Judenrat was greatly reduced, and Rumkowski's powers were curtailed. The ghetto inmates realized that their survival depended on labor, and production was developed to such a degree that the commandant, Artur Greiser, was able to boast that he had at his disposal "one of the greatest industrial networks in the Reich."[144]

The Warsaw activists maintained contact with all the other ghettos and labor camps. On November 15, 1943, they informed Dr. Isaak Schwarzbart—the Jewish representative on the Polish Council in London—of the liquidation of the camps in the Lublin region where (so they calculated) 40,000 Jews had been incarcerated. Operation *Erntefest* commenced on November 3, 1943, and was carried out by the SS in person without the participation of the Ukrainian guards. The Germans feared—and not without cause—that the Jews might attempt an uprising or defensive action. Consequently, they brought in a large number of troops—thousands, according to the report. The greatest slaughter was conducted at Majdanek, where at least 17,000 prisoners were killed on November 5.

In October 1943 the number of Jews surviving in the Generalgouvernement had been estimated in Warsaw as 250,000 to 300,000. Six months later in a report written on May 24, 1944, the number of Jews present "legally" (quotation marks in original) was assessed at 160,000. To this was added some 40,000 Jews in hiding. "We are a handful of community leaders who have survived," the report declared, "and we have undertaken—despite the dangers and constantly increasing difficulties—the task of proffering social assistance to the remnants of our tortured populace."[145]

Covering the Traces

Among the numerous and often weird contradictions in Himmler's actions and aspirations, one of the most striking is his desire to cover up the traces of mass murder. It may be assumed that he was motivated, in part, by the fact that word of the extermination was spreading in the Reich and outside it as well as by the fear that the Germans would not be able to hold on to all the conquered territories. His attempt at concealing was first revealed in the summer of 1942 when, after his visit to Auschwitz in June of that year, he ordered the burning of all the corpses. According to the testimony of Höss, the order was conveyed by "Standartenführer Blobel from Eichmann's bureau." Paul Blobel was an Einsatzgruppen commander, who took part in the murder of the Jews of Kiev. Now he was selected as commander of Kommando 1005, known as the Enterdungs Kommando (commando for removal from the ground).[146]

In the summer of 1942 Blobel conducted experiments at Chełmno to determine the best method of digging up corpses from mass graves, incinerating them, and obliterating traces. These methods were later employed at all the extermination sites where such graves existed (ranging from southern Russia to the Baltic states) and in the extermination camps, where there were mass graves from the period preceding the introduction of outdoor incineration or cremation.[147] The units were trained by commanders who had passed a course in the school for special SS units at the Janowski Camp. The process was described at the Nuremberg trials by the Russian prosecutor, "The chief of Sonderkommando Number 1005, Scherlok, taught the commandants on the spot how to organize the exhumation of the corpses from the graves, how to pile them on stacks, burn them, how to scatter the ashes, how to crush the bones, how to fill up the ditches, and how to plant trees and brushwood on the graves as camouflage."[148] In some places tens of thousands of corpses were not removed from their graves; gasoline was poured into the pit and ignited. Sometimes these pits burned for days.

Jews were employed in all these tasks. Their legs were chained; on completion of their task, they were shot. The 1005 units of the SS usually served as guards. If members of the local auxiliary police units were present, they, too, were shot after the work was over.[149] Nonetheless, a few Jewish prisoners did succeed in slipping off their chains and escaping. In one case, twenty-four out of thirty escaped under cover of thick mist.

The main operation was carried out in 1943 and lasted into 1944. As the Red Army advanced, the cover-up work became more urgent; but it was precisely for that reason that Blobel did not succeed in achieving his aim in full.[150] Even when the graves were obliterated, traces of the action remained in most places: heaps of soil, bones, belongings, and so on. Nor were the facts unknown to the local population. They knew about the covering up of the traces, just as they had known previously of the Einsatzgruppen murders.

On October 4, 1943, when Himmler delivered his famous speech to SS commanders at Poznań, he tried to justify the killing by assuring his audience that the weighty task they had carried out to implement the Final Solution and their responsibility for it would be kept secret and would never become known.[151] On the other hand, the leaders of Hitler's Third Reich publicly boasted of having "cleansed" Europe of Jews. This contradiction reveals not only illogical reasoning but also lack of self-confidence. They apparently needed the figleaf of secrecy in order to conceal their naked lust for murder.

Nazi attempts to hide their horrendous deeds from the eyes of the world did not begin in 1942. The concentration camp specter haunted National Socialist rule from its beginnings in 1933. Although the authorities endeavored through threats and terror to prevent the dissemination of information on happenings within the camps, word was spread both inside Germany and abroad by escapees and by released inmates. Hence, the Germans were anxious to deny the "atrocity propaganda" and to improve their image by bringing visitors to the camps and presenting them as orderly places where inmates could survive despite the harsh conditions. In the 1930s German and foreign deputations visited camps, initially Dachau, later Buchenwald. Among the visitors were German army officers, journalists, and Red Cross representatives—they were even escorted by Himmler, Heydrich, Julius Streicher, and others.[152] In anticipation of the visits, special measures were taken and arrangements were made in order to create a good impression. Any elements liable to disrupt this illusion—the sick, the injured, and the starving—were kept out of sight.[153]

In the summer of 1942, Eichmann broached the idea of exploiting the "site of Jewish settlement" *(Jüdisches Siedlungsgebiet),* Theresienstadt, for propaganda purposes. In the summer of 1943, he permitted the German Red Cross to visit the ghetto. But at that time, the appearance of the camp had not yet been improved and the impression gained by the delegation was not sufficiently positive. The overcrowding had a particularly negative impact.[154] Therefore, when visits by foreigners were scheduled for 1944, it was decided to alleviate the problem by deporting thousands of inmates to Auschwitz between September and December 1943 and in May 1944. This deportation was planned in such a fashion as to serve propaganda purposes as well: a special camp, the "family camp," was set up for these deportees at Birkenau, where they were permitted to continue their lives together, to enjoy a certain degree of self-rule, to organize the education of their children, and to receive food and medicines from the Red Cross. If Eichmann ever intended to display this special camp to the outside world, he changed his mind because he did not bring many foreign visitors to visit. Only once, at the end of February 1944, did he come to the camp with a delegation that included the head of the German Red Cross—subsequently, extermination of the inmates started.[155]

In the same period, Eichmann was concentrating on preparing Theresienstadt for visits. The Danes were demanding the right to visit their deportees and had been doing so since immediately after the deportation of close to five hundred Danish Jews to the ghetto in October 1943. The special attitude the Germans displayed toward the Danes also found expression in the fact that Eichmann was forced to agree to unprecedented concessions. But this time he decided to do a perfect job, and for months he prepared the ghetto for the special show that was put on for the deputation of Danish and International Red Cross representatives who visited the camp in June 1944. Although this act of deception proved highly successful, the Germans never repeated the experience.[156]

Interim Summary

The years 1942–1943 marked the height of the struggle between the armies of the Reich and the Allies. These years saw the tide of battle turn and the first signs of the coming defeat of the Nazi tyrant together with the destruction of the vast empire he had established from the Atlantic Ocean to the Caucasus and from the Arctic Circle to the North African desert. But even though these years marked the turning point in the war, the struggle still continued until the beginning of May 1945. Moreover, 1942–1943 were the years in which the major share of the "final solution of the Jewish problem" was carried out. As the operations of the Einsatzgruppen drew to an end, the summer of 1942 saw the inauguration of the master plan that projected the annihilation of most of the Jews in the occupied countries—beginning with the millions living in occupied Poland and the territories formerly under Soviet control. What the Nazis did not accomplish in 1942, they tried to complete in the following "harvest" year. The special death camps were used mainly for annihilating the Jews of Poland, who were transported to them in well-planned, thoroughly coordinated, smooth-running operations, notwithstanding occasional snags. The task of transporting the Jews of Western Europe to the East was similarly characterized by its systematic and sophisticated nature, although it should be noted that in quantitative terms, the task was far less formidable than the mammoth transport operation being run within the bounds of occupied Poland. The number of Jews transported to the East from Holland, France, Belgium, Norway, Germany, Slovakia, and Croatia in 1942 was about half the number of Jews carried from Warsaw to Treblinka during that summer alone. The suffering and tragedies of individuals and families were much the same everywhere, but from the viewpoint of the fate and the figuration of the Jewish people, the millions murdered in the East during these years were the focus of the Holocaust. The number of Jews who perished is of both qualitative and substantive significance. A few countries, principally Greece and Italy, were not drawn into the circle of destruction until 1943.

At the same time, particularly in 1943, it was possible to discern the effects of the military turnabout on the extermination operation—and this fact was equally evident among the Germans, the peoples of the occupied territories, and the Jews. Especially blatant was the contradiction between the desire to "purge" Europe of the Jews and, at the same time, to exploit Jewish manpower, which the war effort required with an urgency that mounted in direct proportion to the increasing difficulties in production and supply. This contradiction was manifest in the confrontation between the extermination apparatus, headed by Himmler, and the army and armament industry, headed by Speer, but it also obtained with the SS state itself between the extermination machine, on the one hand, and Himmler's production enterprises, on the other. Himmler failed in his bid to build an independent economic base for the SS partly because he was in the throes of this contradiction. But the impulse to destroy—which he shared with Hitler—won out in him. Following the rule that "might makes right," Himmler gained the upper hand in his contest with the army in the Generalgouvernement and with Speer in the Reich proper. Yet he failed to reach the goal of the extermination program, and tens of thousands of Jews remained an integral part of the production process. He also failed to cover up the traces of the slaughter, despite his pledge that the truth would never come out.

Other problems interfered, as it were, with the extermination process. One was the issue of the progeny of mixed marriages—the RSHA wanted to include them among the candidates for extermination. Despite the many attempts to settle this question by establishing different categories of "crossbreeds" and through a sterilization program, no solution was found. Another difficulty was created by the presence throughout Europe of thousands of foreign Jewish subjects whose governments—neutral, friend to, or at war with Germany—began to take a growing interest in their welfare. Many of these Jews were crushed between the opposing forces of the Germans that were bent on their destruction and the governments that wanted or hesitated to save. The problem was particularly irksome to the Germans in those instances in which their allies refused to cooperate—as was the case with the Italians in their areas of occupation, the Rumanians in the center of their country, and to some extent the Vichy government with regard to French Jews. Unique in this context was the development that occurred in Slovakia, where the deportations were brought to a halt in the autumn of 1942. The efforts of the Working Group to delay the deportations by bribing Wisliceny stand out prominently in this context, though it appears that the deportations were halted for a variety of reasons that can be traced to both the German administration and the Slovaks. Certain qualms had evidently overtaken the Slovak government.

The acceleration of the extermination process and the changing strategic and political situation engendered far-reaching changes among the Jews as well. The annihilation operation brought the tension in relations between the Germans—implementing the extermination—and the Jews—struggling for survival—to a climax. This crisis demanded a fateful decision from the Judenrat, on the one hand, and the Jewish underground, on the other—with the masses influenced by them both and often unable to decide for themselves which path was the right one.

The structure of the Judenrat did not leave its members and chairman much room to maneuver when confronted with the fact that the *Aktion* to liquidate the ghetto was already in progress. By the time the members of the Judenrat realized what was happening, they did not have much choice about how to respond. Adam Czerniakow committed suicide; both Jacob Gens and Moshe Merin tried to traffic in human lives in the vain hope of saving some; Chaim Barash headed the line of the last people led off to death. In each case the start of the liquidation process was the terrible moment of truth; the struggle for the life of the ghetto had come to an end. The struggle had mainly been waged by the councils in three ways: (1) by organizing the ghetto's population in an attempt to preserve order, maintain health, and serve individual needs to the greatest degree possible; (2) by maintaining a channel of mediation with the German authorities; and (3) by creating and developing possibilities for production.

As to the first task, the Judenrat and the Jewish self-help organizations alongside it could rely on their long experience in the spheres of social welfare, education, and cultural life. The mediation with the Germans, however, now took the place of the political struggles by which the Jewish communities in Poland, the Baltic states, Rumania, and Czechoslovakia had attempted to establish and secure their status among the host peoples. Interceding with the authorities had been a common practice prior to the modern period and, in fact, had opened up before the Jews the political arena in which they proceeded after the French Revolution to struggle for civil rights. Previously interceding had been based on the economic benefits—in trade, finance, and production—that the Jews could offer the sovereign. As long as these advantages were assured, the lives of the Jews were secure; if their economic value declined, however, the Jews faced the prospect of expulsion or even slaughter. In effect, the heads of the Jewish councils in Eastern Europe tried to revive this system. It was commended to them by none other than the Germans, who robbed the Jews of their capital and property and exploited them as laborers while ostensibly granting them the right to govern their own affairs. The councils could claim certain successes to their credit as long as they were able to convince the local German authority of the benefits to be derived from the Jews—both on a personal level through bribery and on a general scale by skilled labor and production. Barash and Merin even tried to extend the scope of this "lobby" beyond the local authorities to the central ones. We can assume that they were aware of the internal struggle over manpower going on within the German administration and hoped that the workers would carry the day on the basis of rational consideration and by dint of sheer necessity.

It was a vain hope, however. Admittedly, for a time these leaders managed to exploit the cracks in the German polyarchy created by conflicts of interest and the competition among the heads of the different branches of the administration. Ultimately, however, two things defied their understanding and their powers. First, they failed to appreciate the potency of the Nazi ideology, which linked the destruction of Jewry with the very purpose of the war and the probability of achieving its aims, therefore making the annihilation of the Jews a sine qua non. Second, in their darkest dreams they never imagined that human beings were capable of creating "death factories" instead of production plants—or that the two could exist side by side as they did in Auschwitz—to say nothing of transporting millions of people from all over Europe to these camps at the height of the war effort. Few, very few, were the people within or beyond the bounds of the German occupation who were capable of contemplating such an apocalyptic vision. The administrative transformation and moral deterioration that took place in many councils on the Germans' initiative; the decline in the powers of resistance of the Jewish public afflicted by overcrowded conditions, hunger, illness, and epidemics; the terror of new ordeals and outbursts of violence at any moment; the awful isolation from the immediate (even if generally hostile) surroundings; and the silence of the world outside all added up to the condition intended by the Germans for executing their final blow.

The Nazis were well aware that their "final solution of the Jewish question" was beyond the comprehension of the Jews—or anyone else in the world, for that matter—and that they were operating according to a conception that departed radically from the one common to mankind. Society at large was based on life and strived toward life, and it was incapable of imagining the existence of a countersociety based on, and striving for, death. Moreover, the Germans cynically exploited this anomaly to deceive people by luring them with the trappings of life during the *Aktionen*. For example, they got people to report for deportations by threatening—and manifesting the threat—to shoot anyone who resisted or tried to hide. It was only during the actual final stages of the extermination operation that the Germans permitted Jewish policemen to return from Ponary to Vilna— that is, once they no longer saw the need for ruses. A similar phenomenon was reported from Auschwitz: In contrast to the deliberate deception of the victims outside the gas chamber—including a soothing speech by one of the SS men, Obersturmführer Hössler, whose sobriquet among the men of the Special Unit was Moishe the Liar—immediately prior to the gassing the Germans spoke and behaved with unabashed brutality if they thought the Jews knew what awaited them.[157]

What is surprising is not that people were taken in—as the arrogant wisdom of those acquainted only with the society of life and untried by the ordeals of the kingdom of death would have it. The wonder is that despite everything the Jews summoned up the strength to mount resistance and that they found ways to escape and the means of staying alive (we shall discuss these phenomena in later chapters).

The Nazis instituted the system of the Judenrat almost everywhere they or their satellites ruled, and its basic purpose was universally identical: to serve as an instrument for effecting their anti-Jewish policy, whether it was conducted by the Germans themselves or by the local authorities of the country in question working under the guidance of German agents. Jewish councils were not established in any form in the Scandinavian countries (Denmark, Norway, and Finland) or in the satellite lands of southeastern Europe (Italy, Greece, and Bulgaria). Neither were ghettos established in these countries or in Central and Western Europe. Yet in some of these places the Germans took pains to concentrate the Jews, usually in camps, or to transfer them to a central city, such as Amsterdam. In Eastern Europe a council was appointed either prior to the establishment of a ghetto or at some time during its existence. This was so even in Russia, where the Jews were, for the most part, not incarcerated prior to their execution by the Einsatzgruppen. In a number of areas—for example, Eastern Upper Silesia, Łódź, Warthegau, and the vicinity of Radom in the Generalgouvernement, as well as in Vilna—a number of ghettos were merged into a local administration headed by a central council. In this way some chairmen, such as Merin and Gens, were made responsible for additional ghettos in outlying cities, which heightened their delusion of enjoying a preferential status.

The system of having a central Judenrat for an entire country was first developed in Germany itself in the Reichsvereinigung der Juden in Deutschland, officially established in the summer of 1939. It was subsequently applied first in Slovakia and then in Western Europe in Holland, Belgium, and France (where, owing to the last-named country's special political status, there were essentially two parallel bodies). The Council of the Jews in Salonika was also a regional body, whereas in Vienna and Theresienstadt there were local councils. The situation was particularly complex in Rumania and (ultimately) in Hungary, where influential semiofficial Jewish bodies operated alongside the councils.

Although the structure of the Judenrat was, as has been noted, essentially identical everywhere, the councils in the West differed from their counterparts in the East in a number of ways. The Jew in the Western democracies not only identified fully with the nation and state within which he lived, but trusted his fate to the national government, the administration that represented it, and the parliamentary institutions that endorsed its authority. Once this rule was arrogated by the German conquerors, the Jews found themselves in a vacuum politically speaking. They could not fall back on any tradition or a political collective, and they barely had any experience in waging an independent and organized political struggle. The leaders of the Jewish Council in Holland deferred to the new rulers precisely as the Dutch administration had. The French Consistoire also tried to take recourse to its ostensibly sovereign government, and even though the Vichy regime collaborated with the Germans, the French Jews appealed to it again and again in the hope that it would protect them—and to some degree it ultimately did. The sizable body of refugees and immigrants, who were forsaken by the Vichy government, tried to organize for mutual aid and self-help activities. A relatively large number of French Jews joined the underground as individuals, each according to his own political conviction. The situation was different in Belgium, for the government-in-exile and the Belgian administration identified with the Jews. Even if they were not always in a position to save Jews, the Belgians for the most part did not collaborate with the Germans in persecuting them. Both for that reason and because of the composition of the Jewish population—it was made up mostly of refugees and immigrants—the Jewish Council, composed of Belgian Jews, was ostracized and isolated. Moreover, its work was disrupted by the Jewish underground, which received aid and support from the general underground in Belgium.

In addition, from the standpoint of both their social and professional makeup, the Jews of the West were less equipped to fight for their lives. But besides the disparities in the character of Jewish society in the East and the West, another differentiating circumstance existed. From the earliest days of the occupation, the Jews in the East witnessed atrocities, pogroms, and ruthless persecution day in and day out. There were gradations of savagery in these deeds, too, so that the awareness that a holocaust was in progress was stronger in the expanses of Russia, where the Jews had immediately been subject to extermination by the Einsatzgruppen and their accomplices, than was the case among the Jews sealed up in the ghettos of Poland. Still, both these groups knew they were engaged in a life-and-death struggle, whereas the Jews of the West did not even know that they were marked for destruction. Neither did the Jews of Slovakia, Salonika, Italy, Germany, Vienna, and Theresienstadt. They were less capable of conceiving of death camps, gas chambers, and crematoria than were the Jews of the East. Dutch Jewry knew that most of the deportees to Mauthausen perished there; consequently, the German threat to deport people to Mauthausen succeeded in convincing people to report for "labor service" in the camps within Holland—from which they never returned.

Fear is a function of the survival instinct. It grows to the degree that life-securing necessities—food, shelter, health, a livelihood, and a family and social framework—are denied or destroyed. This can and often does happen as a result of natural disasters or war. But for the Jews these necessities were deliberately and systematically destroyed by the Germans, who added torture, humiliation, and the isolation of people to the list of ordeals, until inevitably they began to prey on the Jews. How can we account for the fact that fighters rose up and resistance forces emerged under these conditions? Chapter 17 will deal with this subject.

17

The Armed Struggle of the Jews in Nazi-Occupied Countries

Background

The armed struggle of the Jews in the Nazi-occupied countries was part and parcel of the overall struggle of all nations persecuted and oppressed by the Nazis during World War II. But the situation of the Jews, condemned to isolation, starvation, and total extermination, differed drastically from that of other subjugated peoples. Hence, the motives for Jewish resistance differed, as did the conditions under which Jews were able to organize armed resistance.

Generally speaking, one can point to three main motives for anti-Nazi organization and armed resistance within the conquered peoples.

1. National and political motives and the desire to demonstrate that the people had neither relinquished their liberty nor accepted their fate and were seeking, through continuing their struggle underground, to guarantee their future political status. The commander of the underground Polish Army defined the objectives of the Armia Krajowa (AK) as follows: "In the underground army, people of varied political opinions were united in a common aim: the expulsion of the Germans from Poland and the recovery of independence."[1]
2. Active resistance for ideological, religious, and moral reasons. The leftist and Communist sectors waged an ideological–political struggle after the German invasion of the Soviet Union.
3. Resistance to the occupation. The mass murders, execution of hostages, mass evacuations, incarcerations in concentration camps, dispatch of slave

This chapter was written by Israel Gutman.

laborers to Germany, and so on, drove part of the population to take up arms.

The Nazi racist theories and the Final Solution policy did not, as we know, distinguish between Orthodox Jewry, Jews who identified with Jewish national aspirations, assimilated Jews, and first- or second-generation converts to Christianity. But in examining the motivation of Jews who chose the path of armed resistance and in attempting to ascertain the singular traits of Jewish combat, it is necessary to take note of the differences among the approaches of the various Jewish groups.

In Western Europe in the main, but frequently in Eastern Europe as well, some Jews joined the general resistance movements and took part in their activities not as Jews but as citizens of the countries in which they lived or as supporters of certain political frameworks.

In Eastern Europe and in several of the countries of the West, there were Jewish resistance movements with two distinguishing characteristics: (1) affiliation with a Jewish framework; or (2) the nature of the combat was determined by the treatment meted out to the Jews. These separate Jewish organizations were usually found in the mass Jewish concentrations in Eastern Europe. A group composed of Jews but operating within the framework of the Communist underground movement was the Baum Group in Berlin, headed by Herbert Baum.[2] However, in the Soviet partisan movement, the Slovakian uprising in August 1944, and the Polish revolt in Warsaw in 1944, we find Jewish units marked by strong Jewish self-awareness.

There were three types of specific Jewish organization for resistance:

1. The resistance and uprising in the ghettos.
2. Revolts in the death camps.
3. Jewish participation in the partisan movement.

In Nazi policy toward the Jews in the Third Reich and in the occupied and satellite countries, we can observe an ever-worsening trend proceeding stage by stage.[3] In the first period—that of the gradual and indirect extermination, which lasted until 1941—the Jewish effort was focused on attempts to foil Nazi decrees and to guarantee the physical survival of the Jewish masses. The individual Jews and the community frameworks, whether so-called legal or underground, directed all their physical and spiritual endeavors to achieving that same aim. At this time, the underground did not confine itself to efforts to ensure physical survival, although it, too, saw it as a central task, but also initiated widespread activity on other spheres, for example, publishing underground newspapers, fostering illegal educational frameworks, dispatching couriers to establish liaison with isolated Jewish centers, and striving to continue their activities in the political, social, and cultural fields. Particularly active were the Jewish youth movements of all trends, first and foremost among them being the Heḥalutz movements. The traditional political parties forfeited much of their influence as numerous political leaders and public personalities joined the exodus from such countries as Poland and Lithuania. Under wartime conditions, the remnants of the political parties concentrated mainly on mutual aid and welfare in their own circles and on cultural projects. It was mainly the youth movements, whose leaders remained with them, that distinguished themselves through intensive work and bold initiative in the underground. The young—not burdened with responsibility for the well-being and support of families—were more suited to hazardous underground activity, since it is in the nature of the young to plunge themselves into struggles that entail risk and challenge and offer little reward. Moreover, the public potential inherent in the young generation, which had previously been involved in the pioneering effort of *Hahshara* (agricultural training on farms) and *Aliyah* (immigration), was now diverted to underground tasks and to the armed struggle.[4]

During the period of the struggle for survival, the general and pioneering underground movements did not propose an alternative to the path of the existing leadership (the Judenräte and the mutual-aid associations). Still, in addition to their efforts to keep themselves alive, the youth movements wanted to preserve the spiritual image of the Jew and foster ideological and political awareness. And certain religious circles sought not only to preserve life but also to observe the religious injunctions, despite the prohibitions, and to cling to the tenets of morality and charity rooted in Jewish traditions.

Attempts to Organize Armed Resistance

The first reliable information on the mass murders in the areas of the Soviet Union that had recently been occupied by the Germans reached Warsaw in the fall of 1941 in secret messages and through Jews who had escaped from Vilna (Vilnius) and Bialystok. The community leaders and the underground circles, to whom the detailed information was secretly conveyed, were confronted with a dilemma. What was the meaning of this murderous onslaught? Did it have threatening implications for Jews outside the affected area? It was, of course, impossible to receive any official information that would bear out or refute the various conjectures. It was also impossible to conduct an open and public discussion. Although the underground press published eyewitness descriptions of the slaughter, it did not initially make clear reference to the consequences and to the threat to the Jewish population as a whole.[5] Many experienced public figures argued that mass murders in the occupied areas of the Soviet Union could not be considered indicative of the general situation of Jews in the occupied countries. The slaughter, they claimed, represented the unrestrained outburst of brute force in an area under military occupation. The Jews had been particularly affected because they were the object of racial hatred and were considered to be loyal to the Communist regime that had granted them privileged status. Thus it was for these reasons that the Nazis and sections of the local Lithuanian and Ukrainian populations had taken revenge on them. They sought substantiation for this theory in the fact that the pogroms and murders were followed by a kind of stabilization: ghettos were established in the large towns. Jews were taken as forced laborers, and it appeared that in the occupied areas in the East a situation was evolving similar to that prevailing for close to two years in central and western occupied Poland. The Jews, particularly prominent figures in Warsaw, continued to assert that the Nazis would never dare to conduct mass murders openly in their city, the former Polish capital, to which the eyes of the world were still turned; the slaughter in the East had been conducted only in remote areas while fighting was still raging.

The leaders of the young generation took a different view of the situation. The members of the pioneering youth movements in Vilna were particularly cognizant of the true implications. On January 1, 1942, a pamphlet was read out at one of their meetings, declaring among other matters that

> Jewish youth, do not be led astray. Of the eighty thousand Jews in the "Jerusalem of Lithuania," only twenty thousand have remained. Before our eyes they tore from us our parents, our brothers and sisters. . . . Ponar is not a camp—all are shot there! Hitler aims to destroy all the Jews of Europe. The Jews of Lithuania are fated to be the first in line. *Let us not go as sheep to slaughter!* It is true that we are weak and defenseless, but resistance is the only reply to the enemy! Brothers! It is better to fall as free fighters than to live by the grace of the murderers. Resist! To the last breath![6]

The authors had no official information in their possession, but they based their conviction that "Hitler aims to destroy all the Jews of Europe" on sharp intuition and a sense of danger. This was typical of youth movement members, who were educated in a radical anti-Fascist spirit and who were convinced that the Nazi regime was capable of anything. Only against such a background could this daring and perceptive assertion have been made, namely, that the slaughter was no mere local outbreak but the first stage in the scheme to annihilate the Jewish people. At the end of January, the United Partisans' Organization (Fareinikte Partizaner Organizatzia, or FPO) was established. This was an armed organization that set itself the tasks of preparing to resist whenever an attempt was made to liquidate the ghetto, committing deliberate acts of sabotage against the Nazi forces, and joining up with the organized partisan units in the forests. The Communists, Hashomer Hatzair, Beitar, the Zionist Youth, and the Bund all joined the FPO.

In the second half of January 1942, escapees from the first extermination camp, Chełmno, reached Warsaw and brought eyewitness testimony of the horrors being committed there. Their stories constituted irrefutable proof that the mass murders were not restricted to the occupied areas of the Soviet Union and that there was apparently a much more comprehensive plan for the extermination of the Jews by mass killing.

The underground political parties and youth movements in Warsaw now resolved to go over to defensive action and to prepare an armed force. Consultations were held in March 1942 with the participation of most of the political bodies active in the underground, but the Bund representatives refused to join the proposed body at this stage. They claimed that they were unwilling to act in conjunction with Zionist–bourgeois elements and, above all, that there was no place for the creation of a separate Jewish framework for combat. They also announced their intention to operate in liaison with the Polish underground. The secession of the Bund precluded the establishment of a wide organization, since the other groups had hoped to establish contact with the Polish armed resistance forces through the Bund and to obtain, thereby, guidance, arms, and other vital assistance.

This did not spell the end of attempts to establish an armed force in the Warsaw ghetto. In March/April 1942, an anti-Fascist bloc, set up on Communist initiative, undertook political and military tasks. Political bodies and youth movements of labor and leftist orientation joined the new bloc. The Soviet Union was then the object of great esteem because of its unremitting struggle against Nazi Germany, and the Jewish bodies assumed that links with the Communists opened up prospects of receiving arms and aid. It was only natural to assume that the Communist underground was backed by the might of the Soviet Union. It soon transpired, however, that this belief was erroneous. The Communists in Poland did not maintain direct and continuous contact with the Soviet Union. They were also isolated from the Polish public and their resources were meager. The "arms" that the ghetto received from this source consisted of a single revolver. The Jewish force began to plan how to join the partisan forces, but this activity brought no real results. The bloc was disbanded after several of the Communist leaders were denounced to the authorities and arrested, including bloc member Andrzej Schmidt (whose real name was Pinkus Kartin), who had been in charge of the armed brigade. Despite this failure, the bloc had provided the initial impetus for amalgamation of the various political organizations in Warsaw in a first attempt to set up an armed force, and it blazed the trail for the fighting Jewish organizations set up at a later stage in Warsaw and other large towns.

The question is why so long a period lapsed between the realization by the underground movement in the large ghettos that the Nazis had resolved to annihilate all Jews and the initiation of extensive resistance activity. There was a gradual process of changeover from the concept of an underground organization dealing with political and educational activity to an armed fighting corps. Each armed cell and local nucleus experienced growing pains and organizational problems shaped by this particular milieu, their wider surroundings, and their chances for conducting significant activity in that particular ghetto. But above and beyond the local, specific problems and obstacles, one can point to basic causes that were valid everywhere and that checked and limited action until the appropriate time.

Internal Cohesion

It took some time for the political bodies to overcome past conflicts as well as ideological differences and rivalries. Each had evolved its own singular method of organization and fostered separate social links. In Warsaw the debate continued to rage in the underground press during the occupation and was a very real obstacle to unity. A similar phenomenon may be observed elsewhere. It is evident that the establishment of a united armed organization required the breaking down of barriers and the reinforcement of awareness that all former differences were meaningless in the face of the vast mission confronting the Jews and the common fate awaiting them at the hands of the Nazis. Most of the organizations eventually arrived at this conclusion, thus enabling the establishment of wider associations. At the same time, one cannot deny that the underground and the armed organizations were marked by division and dissent to the end.

Divisions and Responsibilities

The ever-increasing scope of the deportations and the testimony brought back from the death camps might have been expected to convince even the most skeptical. But the mechanism of denial was highly complex. It was not simply the psychological and intellectual constraints of those educated in the spirit of European culture that made it difficult to digest the truth. The confusion and uncertainty stemmed, to a large extent, from the Nazis' calculated methods of deception. They generally claimed that the evacuees from the ghettos were being transferred to distant places of work; on the other hand, they claimed that they did not intend to deport all the Jews but only those who were not employed and constituted a burden on a ghetto. Ghetto inmates received letters—or reports of letters—from deportees, telling those they left behind that they had been brought to labor camps and were interned with other acquaintances. Each *Aktion* was accompanied by promises that this was the last of its kind and that consent to deportation would guarantee survival for the remaining ghetto inmates. In other words, each *Aktion* held out the lure that the many might be saved at the expense of the few if they accepted the deportations and even collaborated in them. Community leaders, who were innocent of any selfish urge to save their own skins at the expense of others, also found themselves trapped in a tragic dilemma because of their public responsibility. Thus many Jews, for example, including the well-known historian and distinguished public figure Yitzhak Schipper, claimed that the younger underground militants might be right in believing that the Germans were aiming single-mindedly at total annihilation of the Jews. However, it was also possible that there was partial truth in the repeated German assertions that they intended to employ the Jews as slave laborers and let them live.[7] The process of killing and destruction not only was unprecedented but also was at odds with the interests of the murderers themselves because the Jews were working for the war effort. This was not the first time in history that the Jewish people had been forced to pay a bloody price to an oppressor, but this price had assured that the core had always remained alive, thus ensuring continuity. Did not the Jews of the occupied countries now face that same tragic choice? And was not it permissible under these circumstances to offer a categorical unequivocal response that precluded the prospect of survival?[8]

When the underground nuclei overcame all doubts and hesitations and decided to disregard caution and organize for action, the road was not yet open to them. They were obliged to take into account a cruel and powerful weapon wielded by the Nazis, namely, collective responsibility. Those who resolved to resist were endangering not only themselves. It was clear that the acts of an individual or a group could bring down German retribution greatly outweighing the impact of the act itself. In the first few days of the deportations from the Warsaw ghetto in the summer of 1942, stone splinters hit a car carrying SS men from the unit conducting the operation. It was not even clear whether a brick had fallen from the roof of a house or whether the stone had been thrown deliberately. All the inhabitants of the building adjacent to the site of the incident were seized indiscriminately and sent with the next transport to a death camp. This was no isolated incident but one of many. Hence, it could be assumed with certainty that a large-uprising in the ghetto would be regarded as the pretext for general retaliation and would bring down destruction on the entire ghetto.

Yet, it was not the threat of collective responsibility alone that deterred the masses of Jews in the ghetto. A more decisive factor was the objective the fighters had set themselves. The struggle was a hopeless one as it could neither bring rescue nor offer a way out. Most did not fight to save themselves or the community. Their aim was to take revenge on the murderers, insofar as possible, and to offer personal testimony that the Jews had fought as part of the wider human struggle for freedom. The common people, harassed and weary by their concern for themselves and their families and having undergone bitter and humiliating experiences in order to survive—detached and abandoned by the world—could not identify with the call of the fighters. The latter's ideas attracted only a handful of people with firm ideological motivation. These succeeded under the ghetto conditions in preserving a freedom of spirit that bolstered their resolve and allowed them to sense that they were linked to their fellow Jews in the free world. This situation was later depicted by Abba Kovner, the commander of an armed fighting organization, "We alone saw our Vilna, saw the thousands who chose to be dispatched to detention camps and passed by our barricades, casting pitying glances at us."[9]

At a certain stage, tension was generated and there was an explicit confrontation between the underground movements that had adopted the path of armed resistance and the Judenräte. The latter generally favored the notion that Jewish labor and productivity would serve as a protective barrier and would save the lives of at least some of the Jews. The Judenrat leaders perceived Jewish resistance as a threat to the existence of the ghetto or as a personal threat. Hence, the conflict and the struggle that raged in several ghettos such as Vilna and Warsaw.[10]

Liaison, Weapons, and Contacts with the Non-Jewish Underground

In addition to their sufferings at the hands of the Germans, the Jews in most countries, particularly in Eastern Europe, faced the hostility of the local population. The Ukrainians, the Lithuanians, and the Latvians collaborated in the task of annihilating the Jews. They were also marked by their cruel conduct and appetite for Jewish property and assets. The White Russians were more restrained, whereas among the Poles who did not play an active part in the killings, there were still many who handed over fugitive Jews—though others helped those in hiding. Thus, the Jews in addition to their relentless Nazi enemy faced the anti-Semitism and hooliganism of the subjugated peoples. In Western Europe the popular anti-Jewish movement was of little weight and in certain countries the population displayed sympathy toward the Jews. In Denmark, a daring and decisive operation was launched to rescue the Jews. In France, Belgium, Holland, and Norway, local police forces took part in the search for Jews and in their arrest.

These conditions made the task of the resistance organizations even harder. The underground movements in various countries and the military units operating against the Nazis enjoyed the support of governments-in-exile and received arms and guidance from Allied military forces. It is estimated that some seven thousand emissaries reached the occupied countries from the free world to train underground forces and help in the armed struggle. Underground movements in Poland and Yugoslavia, France and Denmark maintained constant courier traffic and received parachuted equipment, and considerable amounts of weapons and funds were dispatched to reinforce the focal points of armed resistance.[11] The partisan territories under Russian control were known in an advanced state of the campaign as the "little land," that is, the small liberated area linked to the "great land," which was fighting Russia. A stable contact with the "little land" was established from 1943 onward, and men and supplies were parachuted in.

The Jewish resistance movement in the occupied countries was totally cut off most of the time from the free world and largely from the Jewish world as well. In periods when exchange of letters was possible, information was passed by hints and the full picture was never conveyed. The rare and sporadic couriers from Jewish communities abroad who reached the occupied countries arrived very late (in 1944); for example, in Poland and Lithuania the few Jews who survived were in detention camps, in hiding, and in a small number of ghettos. The couriers played a certain role in extending material aid to the Hungarian and Rumanian underground, but they could not be treated with absolute confidence in the sphere of underground activity and even more so where armed action was concerned. Throughout the war not a single Jewish underground emissary ever reached central Poland with the aim of learning the situation of the Jews firsthand, of building up a system of aid and liaison, or of instructing, assisting, or equipping the armed resistance units. The few attempts to establish contact with Jews deported to Poland were carried out with the aid of Slovakian non-Jews (see chap. 20).

Since no such aid arrived from abroad, the Jews were dependent on the existing underground movements around them. There were no weapons in the ghettos, and few of the young resistance fighters had ever received training in the use of arms or studied methods of combat. Most of them were beneath the age of military service and had never held a gun. Arms could only be obtained through non-Jewish elements. As for intelligence, contact with the free world, and military training, the ghetto was utterly dependent on the goodwill of the local bodies—Polish, Soviet, and others.

The Jews of Poland usually maintained only tenuous ties with their Polish surroundings, particularly the stratum that made up the leadership of the Polish underground. Of the few Jews who had formerly been active in political life and had established political links, most left Poland at the beginning of the war. The sole party that continued its links with Polish socialist circles was the Bund, which did, in fact, for a time exploit these links for political ends in the underground. The Communists maintained similar ties, but they constituted a weak and isolated factor in Polish life, and they were more anxious to exploit the Jews to further their own political and military consolidation than to help them. A number of Jews left the ghetto and joined the Communist organizational network on the

Polish side; they were numbered among the first members of the Communist partisan units. However, most of the Jews who escaped from the ghettos under Communist guidance fell into German hands because the promised contacts never arrived, they did not receive arms, and no force was ready to absorb them. The pioneering youth movements had friends among the Polish Catholic scouts, who stood by them during the war, carried out political missions, and supplied their emissaries with the addresses of Polish underground contacts. The Beitar movement, particularly members who had been officers in the Polish army, were in contact with those Polish military men who were active in various branches of the wide-ranging Polish underground. Beitar succeeded thereby in obtaining quantities of arms, which equipped Żydowski Związek Wojskowy, or ŻZW (Jewish Military Union) in the Warsaw ghetto. Jews from Vilna, Kovno (Kaunas), and Bialystok—particularly Communists—also made contact with cells of members and supporters outside the ghetto, thanks to which they made their escape to the forests.

These contacts, however, were of local and marginal character and did not open up access to the centers of general underground activity or to the abundant resources at their disposal. The extensive Polish underground, with its strong military arm, was well organized and equipped; it was, however, subordinate to the Polish government-in-exile in London and its representation in the occupied area, which displayed little interest in the Jews and certainly took no action to defend them. The many reports it transmitted from Poland to London contain a great deal of information on happenings in the Jewish sector, but they are written in a vague and complacent fashion. The Jews were treated as a foreign element whose fate did not concern the Polish underground. The underground's military arm, the AK, was led by prewar professional officers and was imbued with anti-Semitism. When details of the Nazi extermination methods were revealed, the AK issued a directive in reaction to the events. It contains no hint of the need to protect the Jews or to aid either those who wished to defend themselves or who succeeded in escaping death. It relates the assumption that the Germans might adopt similar methods toward the Poles and what to do in this eventuality.[12] Out of political and religious motives, certain circles in Polish society revealed sensitivity to the Jewish tragedy and demanded that aid be extended to the Jews. However, when members of the Jewish fighting organizations sought contact, they encountered a blank wall of evasions and refusals to meet their representatives. After they succeeded in meeting with those in charge and obtaining aid from them, General Stefan Rowecki, supreme commander of the underground armed forces in Poland, sent the following message to London on January 4, 1943, "Jews from a variety of groups, among them Communists, have appealed to us at a late date, asking for arms, as if our own arsenals were full. As a trial, I offered them a few pistols. I have no confidence that they will make use of any of these arms at all. I will give no additional arms because, as you know, we ourselves do not have any."[13] However, the Polish government in London was obliged to make some gesture toward the Jews, and after it was demonstrated that the Jews were, in fact, intending to defend themselves, the Jewish fighting organization was given aid on an infinitesimal scale. This happened only in Warsaw, not in the provincial towns, where the appeals of the Jews were totally ignored. Moreover, the AK even condemned those Jews who escaped from the death trains and reached the forests as well as the groups of Jewish partisans in the forests. Many individual Jews and whole groups were liquidated in these forests by the right-wing and extremist sections of the Polish underground.[14]

The Jews were forced to obtain arms by stealing weapons and weapons' parts from German arsenals and smuggling them into the ghetto. In Warsaw, where it was impossible to obtain arms in this fashion, weapons, particularly revolvers, were obtained from the Polish underground, but they were mostly bought for high prices and the quantities were sparse and the quality poor.

These were the weak spots to be taken into consideration in arriving at the decision to fight and in preparing for the struggle in the ghettos. These difficulties were enervating and time-consuming; thus when the hour of decision came, the organizations were insufficiently prepared.

As noted earlier, in Poland and Lithuania the Jewish armed struggle took place in the ghettos, in partisan units in the forests, and in the form of uprisings in the death camps. Each form was based on its own ideological approach and set itself distinct objectives. There were gains in each, although these were meager when weighed against the energies invested in the preparations and the iron resolve displayed by the fighters.

The Ghetto War

The fighting in the ghettos was the consistent and the clear expression of resistance based on Jewish nationalist and public motives. This is reflected in the leaflets and appeals of the organizations and in the reminiscences of fighters who took an active part in the uprisings. From the operative military point of view, the ghetto was the most problematic arena. The stage of preparations in a closed populated area under stringent supervision by the enemy was precarious and hazardous. The restriction of combat to built-up areas in the midst of a densely populated urban area limited mobility, precluded flexible maneuvering, and barred paths of retreat. Not only was the surrounding population incapable of proffering aid, the very presence of civilians, including old people and children, cast heavy obligations on the fighters. Thus, it is clear that the ghetto was an unfavorable arena from the viewpoint of tactical considerations and from the prospect of developing long-term action and remaining alive after battle. The resistance deliberately undertook to fight under these circumstances since it was their motivation to react and revenge that determined the location of the battle.

An additional and important problem was timing. The ghetto rebellion could only be launched in response to the final evacuation, so that the Germans controlled the timing—and it was they who delivered the sudden blow. At times of *Aktionen,* the German assembled force was alert to signs of resistance. On the other hand, the ghetto fighters were forced to forgo minor raids and attacks on individual Germans in the periods preceding, or between, German operations. Such small-scale attacks would have exposed that there were arms and armed people in the ghetto and would have invited relentless acts of retaliation by the Germans. In most cases the fighters did not take up arms during the first *Aktion.* Thus, for example, Mordeḥai Tennenbojm-Tamaroff, commander of the Bialystok ghetto revolt, was convinced in February 1943 that it was necessary to accept the Germans' demand that part of the ghetto Jews be handed over to them. In his diary for February 4, 1943, he wrote, "We are sacrificing 6,300 Jews in order to save the remaining 35,000."[15] In Bialystok, as in Warsaw, the fighters refrained from activity during the *Aktionen* in order to gain time and to reserve their strength for an additional *Aktion.*

The almost certain outcome of an uprising in the ghetto would be that the fighters would die in battle. But in ghettos that were close to areas where partisan activity was beginning to burgeon, such as Vilna and Bialystok, integrated schemes were broached: after carrying out their mission, the rebels would leave the ghetto and assemble in the forests. In Warsaw, which was not close to a forest area and where the few attempts to smuggle people out to partisan units ended in abysmal failure, the Jewish fighting organization had no plan for a line of retreat.[16]

The Uprisings in the Large Ghettos

Vilna

In Vilna the Jewish fighting force began to operate at a relatively late stage; in the final analysis, its main impact and achievements were reflected in partisan combat not in the ghetto.

The FPO was a wide-ranging organization that encompassed members from Beitar on one end of the spectrum to the Communists on the other end. The Dror movement refrained at first from joining, and it established a separate group with associates. Only in the final stage of the ghetto did this group join the FPO.

The first commander of the FPO was Yitzḥak (Itzik) Witenberg, the Communist representative. The first task confronting the FPO was to obtain weapons that had to be taken from German arsenals; their introduction into the ghetto entailed great risk. After pistols had been smuggled in, the organization began to bring in rifle parts and to assemble them in the ghetto. An attempt was also made to make contact with the AK in order to obtain weapons and support for the armed struggle. But the AK replied, "By orders received from the Polish government in London, we are forbidden to give arms to Jews in border regions adjacent to the Soviet Union."[17] The danger existed (so they claimed) that the Jews would some day use these arms against the Poles when the latter fought the Soviets. The FPO also organized a fund-raising campaign for the purpose of buying weapons from the local farmers who had hidden arms that had reached them during the war. Although considerable quantities of weapons were bought, there was not a sufficient number to equip the hundreds of fighters with personal weapons. However, such arms as were obtained instilled confidence in the members of the organization, helped them to train fighters, and enabled them to equip groups of men with revolvers, guns, and hand grenades.

Those members of the underground who worked in German factories engaged in sabotage activities there, and in June 1942 the FPO derailed a German freight train en route to the front line. This was one of the first partisan operations in the region and had considerable impact, though few knew that it had been carried out by Jews.

In the last few months of 1942, Soviet paratroopers reached the area, having been sent to set up a partisan movement. In their search for potential supporters, they encountered the FPO and were impressed with the force concentrated in the ghetto. They discouraged the idea of fighting within the ghetto and proposed transferring the fighters to the forests. As a result of these contacts, the FPO assisted in consolidating, under Soviet auspices, the general underground and the partisan movement. Pamphlets were prepared in various languages, including German, directed at the Wehrmacht troops, and the FPO conducted intelligence activities for the partisans. Only 18,000 to 20,000 Jews were then left in the Vilna ghetto and it was impossible to hide the existence of the underground force. The head of the Judenrat, Jacob Gens, and the police chief, Salek Desler, were aware of its existence. After the Germans succeeded in tracking down the Communist organization in Vilna, they then learned from the non-Jewish captives of the presence of Witenberg in the ghetto and demanded that he be handed over. Thus, Witenberg's name was revealed not in his capacity as chief of staff of the Jewish organization, but as a Communist militant. The Germans threatened the entire ghetto if their demand was not met. The Jewish police succeeded in diverting the anger of the ghetto population against the fighters who were claimed to be placing the entire ghetto at risk after relative quiet had prevailed for some time. Owing to this massive pressure and to the demand of his comrades, Witenberg gave himself up to the Germans and was never seen again. After his death, Abba Kovner of Hashomer Hatzair became commander of the FPO. The Witenberg affair served as proof in support of those in the FPO who argued that the fighters should make their way to the forests. It was also deemed necessary to remove well-known people from the ghetto lest they suffer a fate similar to that of Witenberg. Shortly after his surrender to the Germans on July 16, 1943, a group of more than twenty armed FPO fighters escaped into the Naroch forests, some 125 miles from Vilna. En route a clash occurred, and some of them were killed, but most reached their destination. The group was headed by Yosef Glazman, Beitar representative at FPO headquarters. This group then established a base in the forests. At the time, smooth contact was initiated between the ghetto and this base. In the ghetto itself a defensive plan was drawn up, built on the principle of defending the ghetto when the *Aktion* was launched. The aim was to breach the wall and enable the greatest number of inmates as possible to escape to the forest. On September 1, 1943, the Germans demanded 5,000 Jews; they claimed that they were to be sent to camps in Estonia. The organization regarded this step as the onset of the *Aktion* and interpreted the Nazi claim as the well-known tactic of luring Jews out of the ghetto in order to transport them to their deaths. It published a leaflet calling on the population to defend themselves and proclaimed a state of alert among its members. However, implementation of the plan was disrupted by the rapid and sudden deployment of the German forces before the fighters had taken up their positions. The Jewish police, who wanted to prevent an armed confrontation, persuaded the Germans to leave the ghetto and assured the Jews that the Germans were planning deportations for labor purposes and that, if the ghetto obeyed, an *Aktion* could be prevented.

Meanwhile, the FPO and its associated groups had begun erecting barricades in the streets and assembled all the arms in their possession. As the Germans approached the barricades, the signal was given to open fire on them. In the German counterfire, the commander of the Jewish fighters, Yehiel Sheinbojm, was killed. The fighters expected the combat to be renewed on the following day, but the Germans did not appear; on September 4 the state of emergency in the ghetto was canceled.

Young people from the ghetto began to slip away to the Rudniki forests. The FPO decided that there was now no hope of a popular uprising followed by directing many of the ghetto inmates to the forests. Consequently, the FPO forces were removed from the ghetto to the forest. Between September 8 and 13 five groups, consisting of 150 people, left by clandestine means for the forest, where the FPO launched a new era of partisan combat.[18]

Kovno

In the first few months after the outbreak of war, members of the Zionist youth movements and the Communists established underground groups in the Kovno ghetto. The period of mass liquidation and pogroms after the commencement of German-Soviet hostilities was followed in 1942 by a period of relative calm. In March 1943 a Public Committee for Rescue and Self-Defense was set up; it encompassed representatives of the various sectors in the underground. The committee set itself the task of rescuing children and those adults for whom a hiding place could be found as well as planning escape routes to the forests. Affiliated with this committee was the Military-Technical Committee, which began to organize a combat force. A plan of action was devised according to which the ghetto wall was to be breached and an escape route opened up for as many ghetto inmates as possible.

In Kovno ghetto there was cooperation between the Judenrat, headed by Dr. Elḥanan Elkes, and the police, whose commander, Moshe Levin, a Beitarite, was active in the underground. The central figure in the underground movement was Chaim Yelin, a Communist activist. He succeeded in establishing effective contact both with the Communist underground outside the ghetto and with the commanders of the local partisan movement, which was under Soviet guidance. A certain amount of arms were concentrated in the ghetto and training commenced. As ties with the Communists outside grew stronger, the Jewish underground composed of various political sections, mostly Zionist youth, resolved to dispatch forces to the forests. The first groups that left the ghetto never reached their destination: they lost their way, and nobody was waiting for them in the forests. They encountered patrols and were handed over to the Germans by Lithuanians. Most of them fell into the hands of the Gestapo. Some fifteen were separated from the rest and transferred to the Ninth Fort—the site of mass murders—where they were forced to engage in burning the corpses of other victims. A joint escape was organized by the Jewish resistance fighters from Kovno and the Soviet POWs. Eleven members of the group returned to the ghetto and after some time set out again. The remaining twenty-one were imprisoned and the Nazis tortured them in order to extract information on underground activities in Kovno, without success. They were eventually executed. In the ghetto, activities were resumed and the breakout was now planned both from within and from without. The destination of the escapees was a base that had been prepared for them in the Rudniki forest, some fifty-six miles from Kovno. In all, two hundred to three hundred fighters left the ghetto at fixed intervals in groups of twenty to thirty. Chaim Yelin, who had organized their departure and safe journey, was himself apprehended by the Germans in one of the operations outside the ghetto and never seen again.

There was no uprising in Kovno nor did fighting take place within the ghetto. However, the constant contact between the ghetto and the forest, the aid proffered by the ghetto inmates to the fighters in the forest, and the effort invested by the latter in ensuring continued exodus from the ghetto transformed the ghetto into an active partner in the partisan effort.[19]

Bialystok

The Bialystok ghetto was a kind of crossroads for emissaries from Vilna and Warsaw. In many spheres the fighting force here adopted the middle road between the methods employed in Vilna and those used in Warsaw. There were two main underground forces preparing for the armed struggle in Bialystok. The main core of one of them consisted of Communists and members of Hashomer Hatzair; the second group was based on a pioneer-training group of the Dror organization that was concentrated in Bialystok. In the summer of 1942, the latter was reinforced when Mordeḥai Tennenbojm-Tamaroff arrived from Warsaw and took over its leadership. All the organizations were preoccupied with the question of which strategic plan to prefer—ghetto fighting or forest combat. Even the Communists, who were usually known for their monolithic stand, were divided on this issue. The majority favored parallel action on both fronts. The Communists refused to establish a joint front with Dror and the efforts to overcome this division squandered precious time. It was only close to the date of the last *Aktion* that a united organization was established with Tennenbojm at its head.

Arms were supplied by Jewish workers in German industrial plants, but in the course of 1942 only isolated items were smuggled in. The partial *Aktion* in January 1943 spurred the fighting organization to redouble its efforts to obtain arms. Revolvers and rifles as well as their parts—in one case even an automatic rifle— were smuggled into the ghetto. Twice during 1943 organization members conducted raids on German arsenals, and in these two operations seized more than seventy rifles and their parts. Workshops were set up in the ghetto for assembling weapons' parts, repairing faulty items, and producing homemade hand grenades.

Attempts were made to contact the AK for help. Tennenbojm appealed by letter to the leader of the district Polish underground asking for arms and even proposing "immediate transfer of our fighters to the general campaign [that is, to the partisans]."[20] No reply was ever received.

During the January *Aktion,* the underground did not operate at full capacity, but there were isolated acts of resistance. The best known is that of Yitzhak Melamed, who flung sulfuric acid into the face of an SS soldier. The injured SS man began to shoot indiscriminately and killed one of his comrades. Melamed fled and in retaliation 120 Jews were rounded up and executed. But the Germans did not content themselves with this act. They threatened that if Melamed were not handed over to them, they would destroy the entire ghetto. Melamed surrendered, as Witenberg had done in Vilna, and was hanged by the Germans.[21]

Between February and August, a Jewish unit crystallized in the forests around Bialystok. There was no general partisan force there as yet, so that the Jews from Bialystok were the trailblazers of the partisan movement in this area. The first to move into the forests were Jews from the surrounding small towns who had reached Bialystok as refugees. People were also sent from the underground in Bialystok and the new unit was in contact with the ghetto by means of a group of girls who operated under Aryan guise in the Polish sector of Bialystok.

The ghetto uprising began on August 15, 1943, when the Germans attempted to evacuate the population of the ghetto, then numbering some 45,000. The plan was for groups of fighters to barricade themselves in the largest and strongest buildings in the ghetto. Experience from the time of the first *Aktion* had taught them that most of the Jews would not submit to the Germans and would go into hiding, refusing to respond to calls and threats. Hence, the fighters believed that it would be possible to rally them to the uprising. This time, however, many of the ghetto inmates flocked to the place of assembly, abandoning the houses that had been chosen as the centers of combat. Thus the fighters were forced to change their tactics. They decided to go out at the head of the convoy, to attack the Germans face to face, and to break open an escape route in the wall through which the deportees could flee in the wake of the fighters. According to Haika Grossman, a member of the command of the fighting organization:

> This was the last possible strategic plan. . . . We knew that we would be the first to fall. We knew that those who broke through would be shot and that few would come unscathed through the volley of fire. But the masses were behind us. If the barrier was opened, thousands would flee. There were apparently more than 20,000 Jews at the place of assembly. If dozens fell—hundreds would go forward—if hundreds fell— thousands would come. And we? We would be the bridge. Our bodies, our sacrifice would be the living bridge, the bridge of life for these masses.

As to the arms and the number of fighters:

> One hundred units of long weapons [rifles] were distributed, apart from revolvers and hand grenades, and there were numerous fighters; more than 200 remained unarmed or armed only with short weapons [revolvers] for self-defense.[22]

A pile of hay was ignited, giving the signal to the fighters that the operation was to commence. Groups of fighters, mainly girls, engaged in sabotage in factories in the ghetto, setting alight the finished products and the stocks of raw materials. This part of the mission succeeded. The fighters fired their weapons and advanced toward the fence that closed off the ghetto. The Nazis had learned the lesson of the Warsaw ghetto uprising and assumed that the Jews might decide to defend themselves. The German troops concealed by the fence opened fire, igniting the wooden houses in whose shelter the fighters were advancing. The Jewish resistance forces found themselves exposed. A battle was waged in which the Nazis used heavy weapons. At the height of the combat, two SS units appeared and fired continuously from automatic weapons, thus isolating the fighters from the crowd and surrounding them. Most of the fighters perished, among them their commander, Mordeḥai Tennenbojm. Those apprehended by the Germans were placed against a wall—the "wall of the seventy-one"—and shot. This battle was the culmination of the Bialystok ghetto rebellion. For several days and nights clashes continued in the ghetto, and the survivors of the Jewish fighters and the ghetto inmates in hiding tried to make their way to the forest where their comrades in arms awaited them.

Będzin–Sosnowiec

The situation of the Jews of the towns of Będzin–Sosnowiec and the surroundings in the Zaglembie region, which had been annexed to the Reich, was somewhat better than that in most other places throughout most of the occupied areas—and immeasurably better than that of the Jews of the Generalgouvernement. This enabled the Judenrat, particularly its head, Moshe Merin, to argue that the Jewish communities there did not face the threat of evacuation. The Jews seized eagerly on this hope and tried to avoid giving the Nazis pretexts for worse treatment. This made the underground movement's task more difficult. Merin attempted to harness the political organizations and youth movements to his schemes, but when he discovered that the underground in the ghetto was making preparations for armed resistance and that control was slipping out of his hands, he did not hesitate to hand over underground militants to the Gestapo.[23]

The idea of armed resistance was broached by emissaries from Warsaw, including Mordekḥai Anielewicz, who helped crystallize a core of resistance in the youth movements. There was no possibility under the prevailing conditions of obtaining arms in this area; thus weapons were smuggled in from Warsaw by hazardous tactics. On one of the missions, Edzia Pesaḥzon of Hashomer Hatzair fell into the hands of the Germans. The weapons were discovered and she was tortured in an attempt to extract information, but she said nothing. It was rumored that the Germans executed her by hanging, believing her to be a Polish-woman.

At the beginning of June 1943, Mark Polman, who was active in Dror and had been a partisan in a Communist unit for some time, visited Będzin. Thanks to his contacts, an attempt was made to link up with a nearby partisan unit. His Polish guide, a supposedly reliable person Polman had known in Warsaw, was revealed to be a Gestapo agent; he succeeded in deceiving two armed groups from the ghetto and betrayed them to the Gestapo.

Letters were sent from Zaglembie to Germany that told the truth about the fate of the Jews, and the Germans were exhorted to resist the Nazi regime. The letters were sent from post office boxes in the towns to chosen addresses. Leaflets were also printed and directed to Jews, thus revealing the true significance of the deportations and calling for both passive and armed resistance. Acts of sabotage, usually initiated by the underground, were carried out in factories. It was sometimes possible to slip across the border from the Zaglembie towns to Slovakia and thence to Hungary. Border-crossing schemes were devised in Warsaw and continued even after most of the Zaglembie towns had been emptied of Jews. Not many could take advantage of this escape route, and there were numerous setbacks, but a handful of people succeeded in crossing the border, and a few of them managed to reach Palestine during the war.[24]

In the last stage of the existence of the ghetto here, the underground movement took up arms. The various groups, organized by movement affiliation, barricaded themselves with their arms in underground bunkers. On August 1, 1943, when the Nazis launched the total liquidation of the region's ghettos, the bunkers could not withstand the Germans for long. All of them were discovered and their occupants captured. Only a few Jews remained in the Aryan sector or in the labor camps, and they continued rescue efforts, including crossings into Slovakia.

Cracow

Most of the activities of the Cracow underground were outside the ghetto, which had been established in March 1941 and, at its peak, housed 17,000 Jews. In Cracow there were two underground Jewish combat organizations. The first was focused around members of the Akiba Orthodox youth movement and of Dror;[25] the second consisted of members of Hashomer Hatzair and the Communists. At a certain stage, in October 1942, the two groups amalgamated. As was the case elsewhere, emissaries from the Warsaw fighting organization were sent to Cracow as well.

An attempt was made to break through to the partisans, but, as in other parts of western Poland, the operation ended in failure. Those who left the ghetto encountered a German patrol and most of them were murdered.

The Cracow Jewish underground conducted most of its operations while bearing false identity as Poles or Germans. All operations in this city—the capital of the Generalgouvernement, which was filled with SS and police forces—entailed great risk, and thus the fighters took great care not to bring down German wrath on the ghetto as a whole through their actions. They succeeded in acquiring a small amount of arms, in establishing contact with groups of the Polish leftist underground, and in carrying out propaganda activity and acts of sabotage.

The most important operation that was carried out in Cracow was a concerted attack on German cafés and clubs on December 22, 1942. It was executed in retaliation for the deportations from the ghetto. The fighters were successful in their raid on the SS officers club, Cyganeria. They threw hand grenades and fired shots from revolvers. According to German sources, a large number of Germans were killed and wounded. This wave of actions led to the uncovering of the organization and the arrest of most of its members. A group of young women from this organization later became the moving spirit behind the revolt of women prisoners in the Cracow jail.[26]

The Uprisings in Small Communities

In 1942 an armed struggle took place in a number of small towns in eastern Poland, in the area that since the beginning of the war had been in Soviet hands and had come under German control when the German-Soviet hostilities began. The aim of the militants was to prepare the population for the anticipated deportations. The Jews were exhorted to resist deportation, to destroy and set alight the ghettos, and to escape en masse to the forests. Examination of these uprisings shows that those who urged resistance did not plan to conduct a battle within the ghetto but rather to remove as many Jews as possible to the forest areas surrounding the towns and villages in the East.

Information on the uprisings in the smaller ghettos and communities is fragmented. It is by no means certain that we know of all of them because there were undoubtedly communities where nobody survived to tell the tale.

The revolts in the small communities occurred earlier than in the larger ghettos—they were spontaneous in nature, without prior complex and protracted organization efforts, hesitations as to which arena to choose, efforts to establish contact with the Polish underground, and so on. The outburst in these smaller places was usually the outcome of the joint decisions of individuals from various circles or sometimes the implementation of a resolution taken by a representative public body, including the Judenrat and the local rabbi.

Table 7. Manifestations of Resistance by Small Jewish Communities in Poland During Their Liquidation by the Nazis (in chronological order)

Name of Community (ghetto)	Number of Residents*	Date of Liquidation	Storing arms	Igniting of houses	Hand-to-hand combat	Flight	Suicide	Community Leaders	Underground Group
				Form of Resistance				**Initiators of the Resistance**	
Markuszów	1,600	5.9.42				+		+	
Szarkowszczyzna	1,500	7.18.42		+		+		+	+
Nieśwież [Nesvizh]	5,000	7.22.42	+	+	+	+			+
Pilica	2,700	8.5.42	+			+		+	

Why do we find less dissension and debate in the smaller ghettos than in the larger ones? Why did mass spontaneous outbreaks occur in small towns, but hopes of attracting the masses were dashed in the larger ghettos? There are no unequivocal answers to these questions. In many small towns, there were close and intimate ties between the Jewish inhabitants and the community at large. In addition, the leaders of the community council were on familiar terms or even related to many members of the community, so that there was greater confidence in the institutions and a greater readiness to act together. It is possible that the German techniques of deception and smokescreening were not applied so systematically in smaller towns so as to arouse confusion and uncertainty. Moreover, the forest areas, being closer to the smaller ghettos, seemed to hold out the prospect of rescue if a spontaneous outbreak took place. One may also assume that in small towns the Jews were readier to believe the worst than in cities. Small-town Jews had none of the restraints and illusions fostered by a wider European education nor did they believe in the power of public opinion in the free, enlightened world; they were hardened and better acquainted with the brutal exposed face of Jew-hate.

The following are two examples of mass escapes to the forests (see Table 7).

Biographical Details of Community Leaders (heads of the Judenräte)			
Locally Born	Fate	Estimated Number of Escapees (during the liquidation)**	Comments
		Several hundred	Just prior to the liquidation, the Judenrat, headed by Shlomo Goldwasser, unofficially declared that every Jew who could should save himself.
+	Killed during liquidation	900	As a result of the warning by the chairman, Hirsch Barken, a watch was posted and at the last moment the signal given to flee and set fire to the ghetto.
	Killed during liquidation	25	The chairman, Megaliff, who opposed the activities of the underground, refused to fulfill the demands of the Germans on the day of the liquidation.
		Several hundred	Prior to the liquidation, the chairman, Fogel, encouraged many Jews to flee and afterward he went out to the forest and supplied arms to the fugitives.

Table 7 *(continued)*

Name of Community (ghetto)	Number of Residents*	Date of Liquidation	Form of Resistance						Initiators of the Resistance	
			Storing arms	Igniting of houses	Hand-to-hand combat	Flight	Suicide		Community Leaders	Underground Group
Zdzięciol	3,000	8.6.42	+			+			+	+
Lakḥwa	2,300	9.2.42	+	+	+	+	+		+	+
Serniki	1,000	9.9.42				+				
Tuczyn	4,000	9.23.42	+	+	+	+	+		+	+
Korzec	5,000	9.24.42		+		+	+		+	
Marcinkańce	370	11.11.42	+		+	+			+	+
Rohatyń	2,000	6.6.43	+						+	+

*The figure has been derived by averaging a number of estimates, but there is no doubt that on the day of the liquidation the figure was much smaller (as in the case of Nieśwież).

**This figure, too, is an average of a number of estimates, the number of those who actually survived being much smaller.

Source: Dov Levin, "The Fighting Leadership of the Judenräte in the Small Communities in Poland," *Patterns of Jewish Leadership in Nazi Europe, 1933–1945* (Jerusalem, 1979), pp. 148–149.

Biographical Details of Community Leaders (heads of the Judenräte)			

Locally Born	Fate	Estimated Number of Escapees (during the liquidation)**	Comments
+	Killed fighting in the ranks of the partisans	800	After Dvoretski, a member of the Judenrat, initiated and organized the underground in the ghetto, which included ten policemen. Even after his flight to the forests, he tried to encourage others to escape and some, in fact, did.
+	Killed fighting in the ranks of the partisans	600	The chairman, Berl Lopatin, cooperated with the local underground on the day of the liquidation, and he himself was the first to set fire to the ghetto and to attack the Germans: 120 succeeded in reaching the forest with arms and other booty.
+	Killed during liquidation	270	Before escaping, the fugitives gathered in the home of the chairman, Shlomo Turkenitz. His deputy joined the fighters and was killed while with the partisans. In total, some 150 were saved.
+	Killed during liquidation	2,000	The chairman, Getzl Schwartzman, and his deputy, Himmelfarb, incited the Jews to revolt and were the first to set fire to the ghetto. The Judenrat prepared kerosene and assisted in the acquisition of arms. In total, some 15 Jews were saved.
+	Committed suicide during liquidation	Several dozen	Judenrat member Moshe Gildenman failed to convince Judenrat chairman Moshe Krasnostavski to support their flight to the forests. Yet, on the day of the liquidation, the chairman and his colleagues set fire to the ghetto.
+	Killed while defending himself	200	The chairman, Aaron Kovrovski, gave prior warning and gave the signal to set the ghetto ablaze.
		Isolated few	Groups of Jews were smuggled out of the ghetto with arms, with the assistance of the Judenrat and the Jewish police. The police later paid for this with their lives.

Lakḥwa

The town of Lakḥwa is located in the swampy area of Polesie, east of Pinsk, and had a population of 2,300 Jews, people on whom the youth movements—the Zionist Youth, Beitar, and Hashomer Hatzair—had considerable impact. When the ghetto was established in April 1942, the youth movement members held meetings and hoarded cold weapons: axes, hammers, pitchforks, and so on. On the night of September 3, 1942, the ghetto was surrounded. The Judenrat gave the order to burn the ghetto, and were among the first to set their houses alight. A young man, Yitzḥak Rokḥczin, attacked a German, smashed in his head with an axe, and was shot while trying to escape by swimming away. Another German was attacked with an axe by Asher Ḥefetz. The German managed to open fire and killed Asher. The brother of the murdered man, Chaim Ḥefetz, snatched a rifle from another German and attacked the gate of the ghetto; at that point a crowd stormed the exit. The Germans and their henchmen opened heavy fire. Some 600 Jews made their escape, but this act was only the beginning. Local farmers took part in the hunt for the fugitives. Some 120 of the Jews managed to reach the forests. Only part of them were accepted into the partisan units—most were obliged to wander the forests. The great majority were murdered before they had had a chance to fight. Only a handful of the partisans survived.[27]

Tuczyn

In this small town (in the Volhynia area) in which 4,000 Jews were living, several workshops were set up that filled German orders. As a result, Tuczyn was preserved longer than other communities in the vicinity, but the Jews did not delude themselves. At the end of the summer of 1942, the ghetto was set up; when it became known at the end of September that pits were being dug near the town, the Jews grasped the meaning of this news. When an SS unit reached the town, a member of the Judenrat addressed the community assembled in the synagogue and proposed "that every Jew prepare incendiary material in his home, and those who have none, should come to me to receive a bottle of petrol [gasoline]. When the right time comes, each will set his home alight."

When the Germans and the Ukrainian auxiliary police arrived, the Jews launched their operation. Each burned down his home and the few who had weapons of any kind tried to defend themselves. The Germans opened fire and the crowd, including women and children, fled in the direction of the forests. At least 1,000 were killed and those who reached the forests—men, women, children, and old people—wandered without food or shelter. About 300, mainly old people and children, returned to the ghetto after the Germans promised them immunity. They were concentrated in the few remaining buildings and several days later, all of them were murdered. Only a few of the Tuczyn Jews succeeded in gaining entry to partisan units; for a long time families and orphaned children wandered the forests trying to preserve themselves against beasts and men. Several groups set up eight bunkers, but they, too, were discovered and murdered. Of the 4,000 Tuczyn Jews who rebelled and fled to the forests, about 15 survived the war.[28]

The Warsaw Ghetto Revolt

The Warsaw ghetto revolt was the most extensive and important Jewish military endeavor in the occupied countries of Europe. The combat in the Warsaw ghetto was the fruit of lengthy planning. Organized and armed fighting units as well as numerous ghetto inmates took part, forcing the Germans to deploy a large force and to engage in protracted combat in the center of a large European city.

In Warsaw, as elsewhere, perhaps even to a larger extent, the Jews did not believe the news of mass murders and did not grasp the significance of the Final Solution. The underground movement, particularly that section focused around the youth movement, began to organize on a wider scale as an armed organization, but these efforts were not notably successful.

On July 22, 1942, when the great evacuation of Warsaw began, there were no weapons in the ghetto. As soon as the deportations commenced, attempts to consolidate a united front of the political underground and to devise a line of resistance were made but failed. As a consequence a meeting was held on July 28 among representatives of three movements—Hashomer Hatzair, Dror-Heḥalutz, and Akiba—at which a Jewish fighting organization, Żydowska Organizacja Bojowa, or ŻOB, was set up in the Warsaw ghetto. A command was established and emissaries were sent to the Aryan side of Warsaw with the task of establishing contact with the Polish underground and obtaining weapons by all possible means.

The deportations from the ghetto continued until mid-September. During the *Aktion,* which was conducted savagely and at a breathtaking pace, there were isolated incidents of resistance. The ŻOB obtained a small amount of arms from the Communists—a few revolvers and hand grenades—but as they were being transferred from place to place, these weapons fell into the hands of the Germans. Two members of the command, Yosef Kaplan and Shmuel Braslaw, were murdered. Attempts were also made to smuggle groups of fighters out to the forest, but some were caught en route and others reached their destination but were unable to join up with the partisans. The Jewish police took part in the *Aktion* and the ŻOB passed a death sentence against their commander, the apostate Jozef Szeryński. The execution of the sentence was attempted during the deportation by a member of Akiba Yisrael Kanal, and had wide repercussions, even though Szeryński was only wounded in the face and took up his post again after some time.

Despite failures and setbacks, the organization succeeded in protecting a considerable proportion of its members. Thus, on completion of the *Aktion,* on September 12, 1942, it had at its disposal a considerable cadre of highly motivated fighters.

At the height of the *Aktion,* the ghetto inmates were engaged in feverish attempts to survive and save their families. When the operation ended and the survivors began to suffer feelings of remorse and bereavement, the hour of reckoning arrived. Emmanuel Ringelblum wrote:

> Husbands tore out their hair because they had let the Germans, unharmed, take away those dearest to them, their wives and children; children loudly reproached themselves

for allowing their parents to be taken away. Oaths were sworn aloud: Never shall the Germans move us from here with impunity; we will die, but the cruel invaders will pay with their blood for ours.[29]

This mood of grief and the desire for revenge provided the impetus for the expansion and consolidation of the ŻOB. In October/November 1942, the fighting organization was set up, encompassing all the political and public trends in the ghetto underground, apart from the Revisionists and Agudat Yisrael. Its command was made up of representatives of the main bodies and was headed by Mordekḥai Anielewicz[30] of Hashomer Hatzair.

A national committee was set up as the political umbrella organization assisting ŻOB. The Bund representatives established a coordination committee, a federative body that operated in conjunction with the national committee, which represented the organization both in the ghetto and outside it. This committee helped raise funds for the purchase of arms and other equipment. Externally—to be more precise, in relations with the Poles—it was significant that this body was authorized to represent the entire Jewish public. Initially, Aryeh Vilner of Hashomer Hatzair represented the organization on the Polish side. He was arrested shortly before the revolt and was replaced by Antek (Yitzḥak Zuckerman), of Dror. Vilner had already succeeded after persistent efforts in establishing contact with the evasive Polish underground and after the establishment of the national committee, its emissary was given accreditation and results were finally achieved. Aid was given, infinitesimal but, nonetheless, significant in light of the conditions in the ghetto. The Polish attitude changed after the armed uprising in the ghetto in January 1943. Henceforth, the AK could no longer claim that the Jews would never fight. They now supplied slightly more weapons and military instruction as well. However, they also tried to curb Jewish militancy, and they were ready to guarantee the exit of the fighters from the ghetto and to provide assistance on the other side on condition that the organization abandoned the idea of an uprising.[31] They feared that the revolt in the ghetto might break out at an inconvenient time for them. They preferred to conserve strength until the hour was ripe and it would be possible to direct the Polish force simultaneously against the Germans and the Russians. They apparently worried that the ghetto uprising was liable to disrupt this plan and stir up the Poles to emulate it.

The events that began on January 18, 1943, constituted a decisive turning point that, more than any other occurrence, shaped the scope and character of the great uprising of April. This renewal of deportations did not come as a surprise, although the timing was not anticipated. The dimensions of the first deportation indicated that the second deportation would be the final one. This was how the situation appeared to the Jews, and only a small part of the ghetto inhabitants responded now to the German summons to report for deportation; the great majority sought shelter in provisional hiding places. The ŻOB did not have time to coordinate action between the groups and to proclaim general mobilization, and thus each group took defensive action in its own fashion. A group, commanded by Mordekḥai Anielewicz and armed with revolvers, left its assembly point in Mila Street, and deliberately joined a large convoy of Jews being taken to the central square for deportation. Close to the site, on a given signal, they broke out of line and commenced hand-to-hand combat with the Germans escorting the convoy. Most of them fell fighting: Mordekhai Anielewicz survived miraculously. On the German side, the first troops fell in battle with Jews. Simultaneously, other groups, led by Yitzhak Zuckerman, engaged in armed combat in a building. This form of combat proved more suitable to urban conditions and clashes between such uneven forces; it was adopted as the basic tactical method of the ŻOB.

Not all of the ŻOB's force was deployed in January as the groups that had not yet been mobilized did not have time to prepare for action. But the use of firearms by Jews and the losses inflicted on the Germans came as a stunning shock to the conquerors. Deportation of Jews was considered an easy task that did not involve risk. From that day on, the Germans took precautions in breaking into apartments and buildings, and they preferred not to search cellars and attics.

The January deportation ended after four days. Some five thousand Jews were deported from the ghetto, most of them having been apprehended on the first day of the *Aktion*. It is now known that the Germans had planned only a partial operation, and this is why it was halted. The people in the ghetto and also the Polish underground press interpreted the "little" *Aktion* (in comparison with the summer 1942 deportation) as a German debacle and as an indication of fear of confrontation with an armed force. Thus, the January clash instilled in the ghetto population a sense of confidence, which in retrospect appears naïve. It appeared to confirm that the Nazis understood only force and that the force employed by the Jews could serve to protect the ghetto effectively for a certain period. This optimism was bolstered by the encouraging news from the front after the decisive Soviet victory near Stalingrad and the developments in the North African campaign. Many hoped that the war would end within a few months and believed that the goal was to hold fast until then. An alliance was forged between the fighters and the Jews remaining in the ghetto, according to which the ŻOB conducted the armed struggle while the masses barricaded themselves in their hiding places and adopted a policy of passive resistance. The ŻOB, however, did not share the prevalent optimism and took a totally different view of the combat and the outcome of the approaching battle.

Operating in parallel to the ŻOB was the Jewish Military Union (ŻZW) representing Beitar, which was also joined by individuals outside the Revisionist camp. These two frameworks, which operated separately from one another, eventually conducted negotiations on the allocation of arms and the distribution of military command positions, extraction of payments, and so on. At this stage, the fighters became the true rulers of the ghetto, and the head of the Judenrat, who was approached by the Nazis to restrain illegal activities, replied that he was no longer master of the ghetto and that control had passed into the hands of others.[32]

A considerable number of weapons reached the ghetto, mainly revolvers (it transpired during the revolt that these were not very effective in battle) as well as a small number of rifles, several submachine guns, one machine gun, and a relatively large number of hand grenades and homemade bombs. The period up to

April 1943 was used for combat training. The fighters were concentrated near fixed positions at central spots, with constant lookouts observing the gates of the ghetto, and the force was made ready for battle. The two organizations, some seven hundred to eight hundred men and women in all, were joined by a number of unorganized volunteers. The bunkers, or hiding places, were prepared over much time and considerable thought and expense were invested in them in order to ensure that they could withstand attack for lengthy periods. The entries and exits were well camouflaged and many bunkers were connected to the electricity network and sewage pipes. Food and medicine were also stockpiled there. Thousands of people worked at night excavating the hiding places and carrying out skilled tasks. People paid for places in the bunkers, just as they had once paid to work in supposedly safe industries.

On April 19 the uprising broke out. The Germans had been prepared for the eventuality of resistance and assembled troops and large quantities of arms for the final *Aktion*. More than two thousand SS soldiers and police units, under tank cover, took part in the operation. On the first day of the *Aktion,* which was the first day of Passover, the German units entered the ghetto in military formation and found no Jews above ground. The ghetto inmates were hidden in their bunkers while the fighters had taken up their positions in the attics. Upon entry, the Germans were attacked at two crossroads and suffered losses. The German tanks were forced to retreat from the ghetto after one of them was hit. At this stage, the commander of the police and SS in Warsaw district, who was commanding the operation, was dismissed and replaced by SS General Jürgen Stroop. He wrote a detailed report on the course of the uprising and daily descriptions of the battles. In summary, he said, "After a few days it was already clear that the Jews would under no circumstances consider voluntary resettlement but were determined to fight back by every means and with the weapons in their possession."[33]

For several days battles raged, as the mighty, well-armed German forces faced a handful of fighters who would open fire suddenly, flee, and reappear at a new location. The Germans did not succeed in discovering how the Jews were moving from place to place. In a letter to Yitzhak Zuckerman (then ŻOB representative on the Aryan side of Warsaw), Mordekḥai Anielewicz reported on April 23, the sixth day of the revolt, "One thing is clear; what happened exceeded our boldest dreams. The Germans ran twice from the ghetto. One of our companies held out for forty minutes, and another, for more than six hours. The mine set in the 'brushmakers' area' exploded. Our losses in manpower are minimal."[34]

After the first days the Germans adopted a new tactic. They began to burn down the stone buildings in the ghetto from which shots had been fired. This destroyed the positions on the roofs and blocked the secret passages leading through the attics. They then systematically ignited blocks of buildings throughout the ghetto. The fires did not defeat the fighters nor did they flush out the many Jews in hiding under the buildings. The Nazis then used listening devices in order to discover where people were hiding, blew up those buildings where they discerned signs of life, and used forced informers to whom they promised survival as the reward for revealing the location of bunkers. This stage, accompanied by armed clashes, lasted weeks. On May 15 Stroop blew up the central synagogue in

Warsaw and was able to declare, "There is no longer a Jewish residential quarter in Warsaw!"[35]

Tens of thousands of the inhabitants of the ghetto took part in the revolt and identified with it. They transformed the ghetto into an indomitable fortress from which they had to be extracted one by one, requiring thousands of German troops—who suffered losses. The struggle went on for weeks, and this uprising of the last Jews in Warsaw became the first mass revolt in Nazi-occupied Europe. Its message extended far beyond the walls of the ruined ghetto.

The Revolts in the Death Camps

The revolts in the death camps were isolated outbreaks that were aimed at opening up escape opportunities. They did not resemble the escapes of individuals or organized groups from concentration camps or labor camps, and there was no corresponding phenomenon in concentration camps where people of various nationalities were imprisoned.

Revolts occurred in three death camps—Sobibor, Treblinka, and Auschwitz. There is a difference between the first two and the last. In Sobibor and Treblinka a certain number of prisoners were singled out and taken from the transports, while most of the people were conveyed to their deaths. They were employed as service personnel (e.g., there were eight hundred of them at Treblinka) and they were the sole Jews who survived in the death camps for longer periods, were allowed human contact, and were well acquainted with the camp's conditions. In both Treblinka and Sobibor, the rebels, who organized mass escapes, came from these ranks.

In the factory of death at Auschwitz–Birkenau, as well, special units of prisoners, the Sonderkommando, were employed at the crematoria. In the later stage of the camp's existence, most of these forced workers were Jews. They were replaced from time to time, and the Jews who were forced to engage in this terrible task in all three camps were well aware that, as eyewitnesses, they were seen by the murderers as a threat.

The Jews who rebelled in these camps knew, of course, that successful escape did not guarantee survival. It was obvious to them that the Nazis would invest great effort in pursuing fugitives and that even if they managed to evade pursuit, they faced the arduous task of surviving in a country where no Jews were left, where the regime had condemned all Jews to death, and where they could not expect much help from the local population.

Treblinka

The first rebellion in a death camp was the Treblinka uprising, which broke out on August 2, 1943. The underground was organized by a fifty-year-old doctor from Warsaw, Dr. Ilya Horonzitzki, who assembled around him a small group, including Zelio (Zelomir Bloch), a Jew who had been an officer in the Czech army. The team of forced laborers at the camp included a small group of Jews from

Czechoslovakia who were linked by ties of mutual friendship and trust. Several of them had received military training and were ready for an uprising. The facts that these Jews could move more or less freely through the camp, were acquainted with every inch of it, and knew people from the surroundings facilitated the planning of the operation.[36] The group sought ways of acquiring arms or seizing weapons within the camp, although these were well guarded and inaccessible to them. An attempt was made to purchase weapons from Ukrainians. The Jewish serving personnel were forbidden to take money or jewelry from the murder victims, but these Jews succeeded, notwithstanding, in hoarding money and valuables. After several small-scale attempts, a sum of money was discovered in the possession of Dr. Horonzitzki. The SS man who found it was attacked by the doctor. They struggled, but the Nazi overcame the older man, who managed to swallow poison and thus to escape torture and interrogation. The Germans tried to investigate his contacts but discovered nothing. The underground did not cease to exist after the death of its initiator. The new leader was an engineer, Galewski, who had been in charge of the Jewish workers in the camp for some time. One day the Germans brought the door of the armory for repair, and the Jewish artisans succeeded in making a wax impression of the lock so as to duplicate a suitable key. A plan was devised, with the participation of about sixty conspirators from among the then twelve hundred Jewish inmates of the camp, which involved seizing arms, killing as many guards and SS men as possible, and engineering a mass escape toward the nearby forest. The date was fixed several times, but for various reasons the prisoners were forced to postpone it. On August 2, 1943, a shot was fired from a pistol, giving the signal for the start of the operation.

One of the survivors of the revolt, Stanislaw Kon, describes the revolt as follows:

> Exactly at four in the afternoon, emissaries are sent to the groups with the order to come immediately to the garage to receive weapons. Rodak from Płock is in charge of distributing them. Everyone who comes to receive a weapon is obliged to state the password: "Death!" To which comes the answer: "Life!" "Death–life," "death–life"—the ardent messages are repeated in quick succession and hands are stretched out to grasp the longed-for rifles, pistols, and hand grenades. At the same time, the chief murderers in the camp are being attacked. Telephone contact is immediately cut off. The guard towers are set alight with petrol. Captain Zelomir attacks two SS guards with an axe and breaks through to us. He takes over command. By the garage stands a German armored car whose engine Rodak has immobilized in good time. Now the car serves him as shelter, from which he fires at the Germans. His shots fell Sturmführer Kurt Meidlar and several of Hitler's hounds. The armory is captured by force by Sodovitz's group. The weapons are divided up among the comrades. We have two hundred armed men. The remainder attack the Germans with axes, spades, and pickaxes. The crematoria are set alight. The false railway station with its signs "Bialystok-Volkowisk," "Ticket Office," "Cashier," "Waiting Room," etc., burns. The Max Bull barracks also burn. The flames and the echoes of the shots summon Germans from all around. SS men and gendarmes from Kosov [USSR], soldiers from the nearby airfield, and even a special SS unit from Warsaw arrive. The order is given to destroy and to breach the siege to the nearest forest. Most of our warriors fall, but Germans fall as well. Few of us are left.[37]

The gas chambers remained operational after the uprising and for two weeks a limited number of deportation trains continued to arrive at Treblinka, among others one from Bialystok. The demolition of the camp took about two more months.[38]

Sobibor

Sobibor camp lay close to a forest and was sealed with three layers of barbed wire fence, a minefield, and a deep surrounding trench. There were several dozen SS men in the camp and several hundred armed Ukrainian guards. Some five hundred Jews were employed in sorting the clothes of the victims and other skilled tasks. A separate group of Jews worked in Camp 3 near the gas chambers.

On October 14, 1943, a prisoners' revolt broke out in Sobibor; in its wake, the camp ceased to function and was liquidated. In Sobibor, as in Treblinka, escape attempts were made and isolated prisoners managed to flee from both. In the summer of 1943, the organization launched the general uprising and mass escape. The operation was planned by a group of prisoners led by Alexander (Sasha) Pechorsky, a Jewish Soviet officer, who was a POW. The tactic was based on groups of prisoners, mainly skilled artisans, who were to liquidate the SS men in the camp. Each group was to undertake the killing of one SS man. A large group was to seize the armory and to arm the prisoners. Other prisoners would break open the gate and designated spots along the barbed wire fence, which were thought to be clear of mines. The operation was only partially successful. The prisoners managed to murder the SS men who were summoned on various pretexts to the workshops and were attacked there with implements prepared in advance. The group that was to have taken the armory failed in its mission because it came under heavy fire from the guard towers. Only part of the prisoners knew of the conspiracy, and those who learned of it at the last moment were gripped with panic and stampeded—many of them were killed in the minefields. One group made for the gate, overcame the guards, and broke out. Others found openings in the barbed wire without encountering mines. All the Jews in the camp took part in the breakout and escape. Many were killed by bullets and mines, but a considerable number reached the forest, which was only some 22 yards from the camp. Of the escapees, some groups succeeded in reaching partisan units, but most were apprehended or murdered by the local farmers and the right-wing sectors of the Polish partisan movement. Several dozens of the Sobibor rebels survived, including Alexander Pechorsky, who wrote his memoirs of his imprisonment in the camp, of the preparations for the revolt, and of the uprising itself.[39]

Auschwitz–Birkenau

The prisoners' revolt at Birkenau broke out on October 6, 1944. The mass extermination of the Jews of Hungary was coming to an end, and the Sonderkommando, most of them Jews, knew that their days were numbered. They had established contacts with the international underground movement in Auschwitz, and urged it to launch the overall revolt that had been in preparation for some time.

But the general underground, headed by political prisoners of various nationalities, was motivated by considerations of its own and did not respond to the urgent appeals of the Sonderkommando.

The Sonderkommando succeeded in acquiring only one type of ammunition, explosives, from the German Union ammunition factory inside Auschwitz where hundreds of prisoners worked day and night. A group of Jewish girls from Birkenau worked in the room where the explosives were handled. The international underground approached one of the women prisoners from Birkenau, Rosa Robota, a young Jewish woman from Ciechanow, who was active in the underground in the camp. She was asked to try to obtain explosives for the underground through the Union workers. The girls agreed to smuggle out small quantities of explosives and these reached both the general underground in the central camp at Auschwitz and the Sonderkommando at Birkenau. One of the Sonderkommando workers, a munitions expert, succeeded in preparing an active mine from the explosives.

The forced laborers in the Sonderkommando—tragic figures from different countries (e.g., Poland, Greece, Hungary) and different social backgrounds—were a closely knit group and constituted the core of the conspirators who prepared the uprising. Details of events during the days preceding the uprising can be learned from the diaries kept by Sonderkommando workers, which were hidden in the ground near the crematoria and found after the war.[40]

The Sonderkommando demanded that a general uprising be launched immediately in the camp; when this proposal was rejected, they decided to disobey the orders of the general underground to await instructions, and they went ahead with their plan. On October 6 they blew up Crematorium 3, destroyed the installations, and killed the Kapo and the SS men on the spot. Alone in their struggle and in their escape efforts, they broke through the fence and dispersed over the terrain in an attempt to slip through the net of guards around the camp and to move as far away from it as possible. As soon as the uprising began, hundreds of SS men in the camp were mobilized and a relentless pursuit began. As far as we know, all the escapees were rounded up and executed.

This, however, was not the end of the affair. The Nazis brought in special investigators to study the uprising. It was soon discovered that the explosives used to blow up the crematorium had been stolen from the Union factory. A few of the girls who had worked there were arrested and one of them disclosed the name of Rosa Robota. The latter was severely tortured in the Political Department at Auschwitz, which specialized in breaking experienced underground militants. But her lips remained sealed. She was executed by hanging on the camp parade ground together with three of the girls who had worked at the factory.[41]

The Partisan Struggle in the Forests

The partisan movement in World War II consisted of mobile forces that operated behind enemy lines in suitable terrain, attacking the enemy at its weak spots through sabotage, sudden sorties, or sporadic battles. Relatively small partisan units immobilized large enemy concentrations, disrupted transportation lines, and hampered free enemy action over widespread areas. In 1944 large areas in the occupied Soviet Union and Yugoslavia became partisan areas.

The forests in eastern Poland and the Soviet Union as well as the Alps and the Carpathian Mountains were considered suitable territory for partisan operation. The first partisans in the occupied areas of the Soviet Union were assembled from among Soviet POWs who had escaped from camps as well as people who had sought political refuge in the forests. It was only at the end of 1942 and the beginning of 1943 that Soviet commanders were parachuted into the forests. Discipline and political orientation were then instilled in the scattered and semiwild units, and the partisan movement under Soviet command took on the character of an organization with a political–military center. This had important consequences for the Jews. The Soviet partisan movement was a significant force, but only one of many on the partisan map, which also included Poles, Ukrainians, and others. In a number of countries—particularly Yugoslavia, Greece, and later Italy, France, Slovakia, and Bulgaria—there were national partisan movements, as well as various sectors, that were often at loggerheads with one another.

Thus, partisan combat was not unique to Jewish units, but the situation of the Jews who sought to join partisan units was different from that of other nationalities. This difference was particularly striking when organized Jewish groups reached the forests and tried to establish separate units. Moreover, in addition to the young people who reached the forests in order to fight as part of the partisan units, special frameworks were established that were unique to the Jews, namely, so-called *family camps* for the women, children, and old people who sought shelter in the forest (see later discussion).

To escape to the forests and join the partisan units was a difficult decision for young Jews to make for several reasons:

1. Jews were town dwellers and the outdoor life in the thick of the forest was alien to their traditional way of life.
2. One of the preconditions for life in the forest was the backing of the rural civilian population, which supplied food and vital information to the partisans. The Jews had no allies among the local population and parts of the national groups—especially Ukrainians—were markedly hostile toward them.
3. In order to find shelter in the forest, the young Jews were obliged to leave their families behind in the ghetto, thereby abandoning them to their fate.
4. The Jews did not have the option of retreating from the forest or leaving it temporarily. In Poland, as in other areas in the East, there were units (most subordinate to the AK) whose members conducted normal lives during the day and operated in partisan units by night. Some farmers were called to action only for large-scale operations. The Jews could not live normal civilian lives while taking part in guerrilla action.

But the overriding factor was time. In 1942 when the implementation of the Final Solution was in full swing, there were only a few irregular cells of local partisans in the forest, including criminal elements. This situation was not to the advantage of those Jews who wanted to establish strongholds in the forest, and many of those who found their way there were robbed and murdered by the Germans as well as by the roaming bands and the villagers. In this period a relatively large number of Jews sought shelter in the forests. There are no reliable figures on the number who tried to reach the forests, fled the ghettos and transports, and were murdered or rejected by the partisans. The partial data available suggest that the figures ran into the tens of thousands. In the Lublin, Kielce, and Radom districts, hundreds of Jews reached the forests in 1942, whereas in the spring of 1943 only a few isolated groups remained.[42] From mid-1943 through 1944 the partisan movement grew considerably but by then only remnants of the Jewish community survived in isolated ghettos, labor camps, and hiding places. But even at the peak of the growth of the partisan movement, those Jews hiding in the forests could not feel secure as quite a number of partisan leaders were infected with Jew-hatred. Despite the claims of discipline and strict supervision, the lower-rank partisan leaders were given considerable leeway and could act arbitrarily. The Jews were very frequently told to bring personal weapons, as the precondition for being accepted into organized partisan units, whereas this condition did not apply to non-Jews. However, even a Jew who succeeded in acquiring a firearm could not be confident that he would be accepted. Sometimes the weapon was confiscated and the Jewish applicant was sent to a service unit or even abandoned in the forest without protection. The extremist right-wing sector of the Ukrainians and some armed Polish underground (Narodowe Siły Zbrojne, or NSZ, which never fully accepted the authority of the AK) often engaged in pursuit of isolated Jews and small units, murdering those it captured. It should be noted that among the leaders of the partisan brigades, Russian and Polish, there were some who accepted Jews into the ranks and protected them against other partisans. There were even some Jews among the Russian commanders who were parachuted in to help build up the units. Their Jewish origins were usually kept secret and they were not always ready to help fellow Jews, but several of them endeavored to save those survivors they encountered. There were numerous Jewish senior officers among the commanders of units founded by the Gwardia Ludowa (People's Army) under the auspices of the Polish Communists. Several of them tried to protect the isolated Jewish units in the forests.

As noted earlier, a large proportion of the Jews in the forests were unfit for combat and were merely in search of shelter. The inhabitants of the family camps maintained by partisan units or larger camps tried to make themselves useful. They helped as handymen, grew vegetables, tended the wounded, and so on. But objectively speaking, this noncombatant population constituted a burden and during German raids or searches they were a dangerous focal point. They also helped to fan hatred of Jews because a large concentration of people increased the food quotas that the partisans had to requisition from local farmers. This aroused hostility toward the partisans and even more so toward the Jews in hiding. The adoption of the family camps by partisan brigades greatly curtailed the mobility of the forces owing to the presence of children and old people. Large-scale movement was liable to draw German attention and was particularly threatening when the Germans were closing in to search the forest for partisans. Mobility was the foremost strategy of guerrilla warfare and the family camps were apt to hinder quick movement.[43]

For Jews, the chance of reaching shelter in the forests was also conditional on the topography of the terrain and dependent on the military and political forces ruling the area. In the East, areas formerly under Soviet rule contained wide expanses of dense forest where Soviet forces enjoyed hegemony. We find relatively large numbers of Jewish partisans in mixed units, Jewish units, and family camps. In central Poland the forests were sparser, the partisan movement was not homogeneous, and because of the rivalry among the various sectors there were generally fewer Jews. In the West there were few forest areas and the main partisan force was affiliated with the right wing; thus very few Jews participated in partisan activity.

Partisan fighting offered the Jews several alternatives to revolt in the ghetto as regards both the nature of the combat and the prospect of surviving it. The Jews here felt like true fighters, taking revenge without forgoing the prospect of survival. In several ghettos, such as Vilna and Bialystok, a debate raged as to whether it was preferable to fight in the ghetto or to transfer most of the young people to the forests.[44]

The separate Jewish units could stay together in the forest only if they found a partisan group willing to grant them protection. In the main, the Polish Aruna Ludowa and the Soviet partisan movement were more ready than others to accept Jews. But the latter objected to separate Jewish units and forced the Jewish fighters to disband and operate within mixed units.[45]

Despite the obstacles that faced the Jews who fled to the forests and sought entry into partisan units and despite the fact that most of them never achieved their aim, there were, nonetheless, thousands of Jewish partisans in the Soviet Union and Poland—some sources believe as many as twenty thousand. Many of these Jews reached positions of command and carved niches for themselves as guerrilla fighters, wreaking revenge on the Nazi perpetrators.[46]

The Soviet Area

In areas formerly under Soviet rule, the Jews found it relatively easy to gain entry into partisan units. Those who came from small towns or Jewish villages encircled by forests were more adaptable to living conditions there. In addition, their escape from the ghetto and entry into the forests were less hazardous than for those who resided in central or western Poland. Moreover, the constitution of the partisan force in these places—particularly in the later stages after the partisan organizational pattern was consolidated—was conducive to a more tolerant attitude and readiness to absorb Jews who wished to fight.

A large concentration of Jewish partisans was based in the Rudniki forests near Vilna. In September 1943 FPO members reached there and established a Jewish brigade composed of four battalions. Abba Kovner was one of the commanders. When the fighters led by Yosef Glazman from Vilna reached the Naroch forests, they joined up with a Jewish group that was already operating there; together they founded the *Nekamah* (Vengeance) unit. Some two hundred to three hundred Jews from the Kovno ghetto also found their way to the Rudniki forest and established a large and cohesive Jewish group in the Lithuanian Brigade. Around the town of Slonim there were several Jewish groups and family camps in the forests. The best known of these was the unit headed by Dr. Yehezkel Atlas, who became a legend among the partisans. In Central White Russia (Byelorussia) in the Naliboki forests, there was a large camp of more than one thousand Jews, some active as partisans and the rest living in family camps. This group was led by the Belski brothers and was composed mainly of Jews from the surrounding small towns. This camp later split into the Ordjonikidze combat battalion and the Kalinin family camp.

In Minsk, the prewar capital of Soviet White Russia, the ghetto was the prime mover behind the wide-ranging local partisan organization; this force was largely composed of Jews from the ghetto. Thousands of Jews from Minsk joined various partisan units and family camps and were among the founders of partisan units, although most of them were concentrated in two specifically Jewish frameworks— Prahomenko's unit and the Zorin family camp. The former consisted of 130 fighters, some 85 of them Jews, many of whom played leading command and combat roles. This unit wandered some distance from its place of origin and settled in the Ivanitz area. The Zorin camp was strongly influenced by the character of its commander. A simple Jew from Minsk, Zorin became very friendly with Soviet officers who had escaped from captivity and commanded the active partisan forces in the area. He organized a unit, composed mainly of people who had not been accepted into the regular fighting force, and "gathered in any Jew, any woman or child, who had been treated cruelly by the forest." With the small amount of arms in his possession and a retinue that hampered mobility, his unit traveled more than 65 miles and established its base in the expanses of the Naliwoki forests. He gathered together a fighting force 80-strong, but he perceived his main task as rescuing surviving Jews from the surrounding towns as well as individuals who were wandering through the forests. His camp eventually encompassed approximately 700 Jews, from Russia and Poland.[47]

In the Kazian forests, even before the partisan units arrived, there was a Jewish family camp composed of fugitives from the towns in the vicinity as well as Jewish forest workers. When the forest became an active partisan arena in 1942, a large Jewish bloc joined the Spartac unit, and there were subsequently some 150 Jewish fighters in the partisan units in these forests.[48]

The swamps and forest expanses of Polesye (Pripet Marshes) were suited to partisan action. This vast area between White Russia in the north and the Ukraine in the south was split by rivers and their tributaries that emptied into a swamp. Amidst this area of treacherous boggy soil and forests there were a few small islands of firm cultivable soil with sparsely populated villages. A high proportion of Jews lived in these villages, deeply rooted in the region and familiar with its geographical conditions. General partisan units were established at a relatively early stage, and the Jews of the villages—who decided to abandon their homes when danger threatened—sought refuge in the forests. A free partisan area was created in Polesye—German rule was tenuous or restricted to the daylight hours, but the partisans were the true masters. Partisan units moved to Polesye from other regions, and Sidor A. Kovpak's renowned partisan camp was located there for some time. Many Jews from the towns and villages in northern, central, and southern Polesye penetrated the forest areas, coming from near and far. They organized separate Jewish units that underwent various metamorphoses and finally became affiliated with mixed units under Soviet command. There were also numerous family camps here. Jews interned in labor camps who were released or escaped also reached Polesye and joined these camps, which numbered between five hundred to one thousand members each.[49]

In the Ukraine the partisan movement under Soviet auspices was very weak. In 1943 as the situation began to change on the southern Soviet front, the Soviet partisan movement began to make progress in the Ukraine. Those Jews who had survived or were living in small groups in the forests joined the units then being consolidated. There were Jewish units here, one of them a battalion commanded by the engineer Moshe Gildenman, from the Koretz ghetto (see chap. 10). He gathered around him individual Jews or groups and set up a combat unit that won renown in the forests and that eventually took in non-Jewish fighters, too.

There is no way of estimating the number of Jewish partisans in the overall guerrilla movement in Lithuania, White Russia, and the Ukraine. Those Jews who were fortunate enough to be granted the opportunity of fighting proved their mettle in countless actions. The guerrilla movement, which was mainly activated by the Soviets, demonstrated that it was capable of constituting a viable factor even under the conditions of modern warfare. The partisans transformed areas that were sensitive and vital to the Nazi war effort into focal points of constant danger and instability. They learned to evade pursuit, to move rapidly from place to place, and to exploit the surprise factor in essential combat. Their losses were very heavy; only a proportion of the initial force survived the years of struggle and the vicissitudes of fugitive life in the forests. The Nazis, of course, regarded the partisans as robbers and executed them without hesitation. Thousands of Jews took part in combat in these areas. Many of them received high decorations, and proportionally many were paratroopers dropped into areas in order to found partisan units in places where guerrilla action at the time had not been strongly felt.

The Generalgouvernement

The Generalgouvernement area was a more difficult objective for partisan action because it was very densely populated and forest cover was sparse. The attitude of the inhabitants, which was influenced by the stance of the Polish underground, did not help promote the spread of the partisan movement and placed obstacles in the path of the Jews. In the first years of the war, AK did not favor partisan methods of resistance. The nuclei of partisan units founded by the AK began to emerge only at the end of 1942 and the beginning of 1943.

The AK sometimes charged that the groups of Jews who had fled to the forests were gangs of robbers who were acquiring provisions by violent measures and harassing the rural population. This interpretation implied that the Jews could be attacked with impunity. At the same time, there were AK units under Socialist and liberal auspices; thus an AK commander would occasionally take a humanitarian and sympathetic stand. Such units accepted Jewish groups and some others accepted individual Jews or those who concealed their identity. As noted earlier, the extreme right wing of the NSZ refused, in part, to accept AK authority and engaged systematically in hunting down and murdering Jews in the forests.

The Communist underground, both out of a desire to increase its force and as a matter of principle, adopted Jewish groups and accepted Jews into its ranks. Several of the founders of the partisan movement affiliated with the Communist underground and some of its senior commanders were Jews. The attitude toward Jews was usually quite correct, although anti-Semitism reared its head at times. When Communist strength increased in the summer of 1942, there were few Jews left in the towns and only remnants in the forests.

Thousands of Jews escaped to the forests around Lublin from the surrounding towns and villages. For a period part of the rural population maintained contact with the Jews in the forests and Jewish artisans worked to order for the peasants. With time, however, the relations worsened and the groups in the forest were faced with survival problems. Most of the Jews who reached the forests—a spontaneous flood of escapees from deportation—died at the hands of both foreign and local enemies, others died of starvation. Only those who survived the winter of 1942/1943 came into contact with Gwardia Ludowa (later Armia Ludowa, or AL) forces.

In addition to these Jews, the forests around Lublin were peopled with groups of escaped POWs who had been interned in the camp for Jewish prisoners in Lipowa Street in Lublin (see chap. 7). These groups, who had combat experience, helped shape the Jewish fighting units in the forests. In 1944 most of the Jewish partisans in the Lublin area were assembled in the Parczew forests. A series of Jewish partisan units operated in the district. One was composed of the survivors of the ŻOB who had escaped from the Warsaw ghetto through the sewers. They reached the Wishkov area and founded the Mordekḥai Anielewicz partisan battalion. This force suffered harassment by the AK, which ruled the region, and most of the battalion perished at AK hands. Isolated groups, like that in the Częstochowa area, wanted to launch partisan action, but the prevailing conditions and the attitude of the population largely frustrated their plans. The commanders of the ŻOB and the National Committee, who were operating clandestinely in the Aryan sector of Warsaw, maintained contact with other units such as those in the Wishkow forests or the Częstochowa area.

There were considerable numbers of Jews in the ranks of the AL partisan movement. Among others, Colonel Robert Satanowski and Major Alexander Skotnicki commanded partisan battalions. Four of the twelve AL units that established bases in the forests during the summer and fall of 1944 were commanded by Jews. Hanka Shafran-Savicka was the leading figure in the young Communist fighters' organization.

In Warsaw Jews took part in the Polish uprising that began in August 1944. Jews who hid in the city, prisoners in the Ganshowka Camp, and the Jews who were employed in removing the debris from the destroyed Warsaw ghetto joined the ranks of the AK and the AL. Also participating in the struggle was a platoon—commanded by Yitzḥak Zuckerman—composed of the survivors of the ŻOB in Warsaw.

In all, the number of Jews who joined the partisan units at various stages and belonged to the guerrilla movement in the Generalgouvernement was some fifteen hundred.[50]

Slovakia

The Slovakian national revolt erupted in August 1944. This reflected the changing mood in Slovakia as a result of the anticipation of a German debacle and in response to the call to arms issued by Czech leaders in exile. The participants were officers and soldiers of regular Slovakian army units, partisan units, and groups of escaped prisoners of various nationalities. The uprising was based on a wide-ranging political front, including the Communists.

The remaining Jews in Slovakia left Bratislava (Pressburg) and the western areas for the rebel capital, Banská Bystrica, in central Slovakia and for the liberated areas. Here, there also assembled young people who had been interned since 1942 in Jewish labor camps, Novaki and Sered. The organized groups in these camps, members of the pioneering Zionist youth movement and Communists, had been preparing for the struggle for some time. They acquired arms, joined partisan units, and fought in Jewish units. Several Jews played central roles in the leadership of the rebellion and as unit commanders.

At the height of the uprising, four paratroopers from the Yishuv reached Slovakia. Two of them tried to make their way to Hungary while Haviva Reik and Zvi Ben-Yaakov remained in Slovakia. The Germans rallied large forces to suppress the revolt. At the end of October 1944, the last rebel strongholds fell. The partisans who refused to surrender and fall into German hands headed for the Tatra Mountains to make a stand there and to continue the armed fight. The Nazis pursued the units as they made their way into the mountains and bitter battles were waged. The two paratroopers leading a camp of 250 Jews also headed for the mountains. En route they were apprehended by the Germans and the two Palestinian Jews were shot in November 1944.

It is estimated that among the 12,000 to 15,000 fugitives who hid deep in the mountains in partisan units were some 1,500 to 2,000 Jews.[51]

Yugoslavia

In Yugoslavia, particularly in Serbia, the immediate response to the German invasion was partisan organization. Hence, the Nazis had difficulty in gaining total control of Yugoslavia. The consolidation of the guerrilla movement was a clearly defined and consecutive process that took on the dimensions of a mass wide-ranging movement.

It is estimated that some two thousand Jews fought in the ranks of Tito's movement and in various partisan frameworks. This cannot be checked because the Jews were not registered as such and did not set up separate units, apart from the Rab battalion, which played a unique role in the struggle of Yugoslavia's Jews.

When the Italians conquered the island of Rab, they turned part of it into a detention camp where Jews were held together with other nationalities. A clandestine
organization operated there, one in which Jews were active. When Italy surrendered in September 1943, the young Jewish prisoners, men and women, organized
an independent Jewish battalion that joined the Banjeska division, the Seventh
Division of the Yugoslavian Army of Liberation. Later, however, the battalion
was dispersed among various units. Most of its members fell in battle. Of the Jews
among the leaders of the guerrilla movement, the best-known was Moshe Piada,
a personal friend of Tito and one of the outstanding personalities in the leadership.

In an article in the (Yugoslav) *Jewish Almanac* in 1954, A. Moreno, a former
member of the Hashomer Hatzair in Belgrade, describes the experience he and his
comrades had undergone at the time:

> In 1941, a week after the occupation of Belgrade, the Jews were already ordered, under
> threat of death, to report to the German headquarters. In this situation the Communist
> party organized groups of Jewish youth commanded by party members. The groups
> met in secret, read and disseminated illegal leaflets, collected medical supplies for the
> partisans and saboteurs, took courses in first aid, collected "red aid" (clothes and
> money for the partisans), learned driving, burned enemy publications, took part in
> sabotage, and so on. All this was done by young Jews who remained behind the front
> line until the mass deportations began. According to plan they were to have gradually
> joined the partisan ranks, but the roundups and sudden raids surprised many of them
> and dozens were executed. In August 1942 a first group of young Jews responded to
> the party appeal and went to join the partisans. Most, almost all, fell in battle all over
> the country. No members of their families survived. Many remain nameless heroes.[52]

Jews from many strata—particularly young people and intellectuals—who
survived the great roundups joined the ranks of the popular liberation movement.

France

The Jews encountered no discrimination in the underground movement or in the
armed organizations in France. There is no way of establishing with certainty the
number of Jews in the underground and the fighting organizations because most
of them fought as Frenchmen. At the same time, it is estimated that the Jews of
France—who accounted for approximately 1 percent of the general population—
constituted 12 or even 15 percent of the resistance. According to Léon Poliakov,
they made up to 15 to 20 percent of the underground.[53] Among the six founding
members of the liberation movement, Liberatio, three were Jews, including Daniel Mayer. There were Jews among the founders and leaders of the Combat (Fight)
associations and the Franks Tireurs Partisans, or FTP. Jean Bingen was one of
the Jews who joined the Free French forces in exile and distinguished himself in
the ranks of the army. In 1943 he was sent back to France and appointed the head
of the general delegation of Free France in the northern zone. Like most of the
Jewish militants, he paid with his life for his activity, and his name was commem-
orated on a French postage stamp. One of the central activists of the underground
in the southeast was the distinguished historian Marc Bloch. He, too, was arrested

and executed. In the National Committee of the Resistance, which had sixteen members at the time of the liberation, there were three Jews, representing the central bodies in the underground.

There were two sectors among the Jewish groups. One consisted of religious or Zionist youth, mostly French, who were committed to the aiding of Jews in distress and to the armed struggle. The second sector was composed of Eastern European Jews with Communist leanings, some of them veterans of the Spanish civil war. They founded separate groups because of comradely ties, different language and customs, and so on. The outstanding circle among the separate Jewish groups was made up of members of the Jewish scout movement of religious orientation, Éclaireurs Israélites de France, or EIF. These young people, who before the war had not been distinct from other French scouts, changed their image during the war. The wartime events fundamentally altered their outlook and many adopted Zionist views. They carried out rescue operations, particularly of children; ran orphanages; and organized studies, vocational training, and social activities among groups of orphans and foreign Jews in France. But in 1942 when conditions changed and the foreign Jews were exposed to the danger of arrest and deportation, the scouts (particularly the Sixth Unit) shifted the focus of their activities to obtaining forged documents, seeking hiding places and shelter, and transferring Jews in danger from place to place and district to district within France. The organization members who operated in Toulouse managed to arrange a route for smuggling Jews to Spain. Thus, during the war, the Toulouse underground smuggled some five hundred young Jews to Spain—most of whom made their way to Palestine—as well as one hundred children to that country and two thousand more through the OSE to Switzerland. A daring group of Jewish pioneers of German origin came from Holland and wanted to reach the free world and Palestine through France and Spain. The outstanding figures in the organization of the operation in Holland were Joachim Simon, called Shushu, and the Dutch gentile Joop Westerweel. Both were caught by the Germans and perished. This group played an active part in the smuggling operation. Its central figure, Kurt Reilinger, was also caught and executed by the Nazis.[54] Young members of the Zionist youth movements were also active in transporting people in danger of deportation and in forging documents. There was also a widespread underground press.

At a later stage, the groups moved on to active resistance and became part of the armed underground movement. The initiator of the establishment of a fighting unit among the scouts was Robert Gamzon, who emigrated to Israel after the war. The Jewish Maquis, founded by the scouts, distinguished itself in the battle of Castres. A Zionist group was active as a combat unit in the vicinity of Toulouse. The various Jewish groups, members of the scout movement and the Zionist associations, together founded the Armée Juive (Jewish Army), which later became the Organisation Juive de Combat (Jewish Fighting Organization). It had branches in various towns and a particularly strong cell in Paris. They took part in numerous acts of sabotage against the railroads, against factories working for the Germans, against electricity pylons, and against bridges, and they fought in operations against the conqueror. Hundreds of these Jewish fighters fell.[55]

Eastern European Jews constituted another sector of the Jewish underground that was organized on a language basis. Jews also played an important part in the ranks of the Communist underground and in the fighting force under Communist control. Groups of immigrants were associated with the Communist party, although they adopted an oppositional stand as long as the Ribbentrop–Molotov agreement was in force. They saw action for the first time in Paris in 1942 when a German battalion on the march was attacked by Communist forces. The operation was led by the nineteen-year-old Jewish fighter Marcel Raymon, who displayed heroism in later actions as well and who was eventually caught by the Germans and executed in 1944. There were numerous Jews in the command of the Communist military forces. The supreme commander in the Paris area was Colonel Jules, the underground name of the Warsaw-born Jewish engineer Yosef Epstein. The leader of the Toulouse organization was Capitaine Philippe, the code name of Zeev Gottesman. In the summer of 1944 Ernst Lambert, who was in charge of the Jewish underground at Lyon, was caught by the Gestapo and executed.

The Jews of Algiers played an important role in the Allied landing in November 1942. In the cadre of four hundred fighters who collaborated with the Allies from within, more than half were Jews. The members of this underground, who trained at length for the task, immobilized the Vichy forces by breaking into key positions and seizing senior Vichy officers, including Admiral François Darlan.[56]

Jews played a decisive part in running the daring spy network known as the Red Orchestra. This was headed by Polish-born Leib Tropper, who had spent some time as a pioneer in Palestine, moved to France, and during the war became a master spy whose network reached out into Belgium, Germany, and the Soviet Union.

Belgium

In Belgium many Jews took part in the underground and in Le Front de l'Independance. By means of the Communists, a group of Jews established contact with the Front and established the Comité de Defense des Juifs (Committee for Jewish Defense). This committee initiated rescue activities and hid Jews. The Jewish underground hampered the work of Jewish institutions and prevented them from handing over to the Germans the card index of Jewish names—most of those on the list were not Belgian citizens. The rescue activities in Belgium were of considerable dimensions: among others, some 4,000 Jewish children were hidden. This activity was coordinated between Jews and various non-Jewish circles. The aid provided by members of the Catholic church was of special impact. The committee had a team that planned resistance operations. The most important operation that the committee undertook with the aid of the Belgian resistance was the attack on a trainload of deportees—the twenty-second transport that set out from the Maline Camp on April 19, 1943, headed for Poland. In coordination with a group at Maline that had been prepared, the attackers succeeded in releasing 150 Jews. In the confusion the Germans fired wildly, killing 220 and wounding others of the deportees; but the 150 who escaped were assisted and hidden by the committee.

This was the sole operation throughout Europe in which a train taking Jews to a death camp was attacked.[57]

Acts of resistance, flight, and rescue in Holland have been described several times elsewhere (see chaps. 6, 8, 16, and 20 as well as earlier data in this chapter).

The Jews of Italy, Greece, and Bulgaria took an active part in the partisan movement in their countries, and they left their mark on the struggle and the achievements of these movements.

Several Jewish authors who have written about the Holocaust, particularly certain Jewish scholars in the United States, have attempted to depict the lack of resistance (as it were) of the Jews in the face of the Nazi murder machine as a characteristic phenomenon stemming from an outlook anchored in the tradition, lifestyle, and conduct of the Diaspora Jew. In the opinion of these writers, it was the dominant traditional approach of the Jewish masses in Eastern Europe that paralyzed the will to resist among the Jews and rendered them meek victims, bowing their heads before the slaughterer.

This theory cannot be considered totally groundless. Philip Friedman, historian of Eastern European Jewry and chronicler of the Holocaust, does not ignore the fact that within the extremely Orthodox Jewish community, there was considerable weight to the attitude that

> can be epitomized by the saying: "not by force but by strength of the spirit," an attitude maintained during many centuries of religious persecutions, and reinforced by various philosophical and mystical movements (the Kabbalah, messianism, hasidism, and so on). The guiding principle is that the evil of the world should not be fought; that the struggle between good and evil will be decided elsewhere, by Divine Providence. In accordance with this view, the true weapons of resistance are conscience, prayer, religious meditation, and devotion—not military arms. Orthodox Jews did not believe that it was possible or even desirable to resist the Nazis in any other way.[58]

In fact, although this tradition of reckoning with the evildoer and the persecutor on the theological–transcendental plane may have had a certain meaning, we should not exaggerate its importance. Toward the end of the nineteenth century and during the present century, Eastern European Jewry underwent a process of dynamic change. The Jewish communities experienced demographic, social, and economic changes; modern secular trends emerged; and the Orthodox community itself was no longer a uniform monolithic bloc impermeable to the winds of change. Thus, for example, on the night when the Warsaw ghetto revolt commenced, several of the fighters visited the apartment of Rabbi Maisel in the ghetto. He blessed them and wished them success, saying: "I am old and grey, but you who are young in years, do not be afraid, fight and prevail, and may God be with you."[59]

It is not only this anachronistic view of the Jewish community that cannot stand up to scrutiny. Also lacking in basis is the view that passivity is a specifically Jewish way of behavior, unknown among other nations. It has been proven that people who are cruelly oppressed and cut off from the free world are not marked by organizational ability and the power of resistance. The ostensibly logical assumption that a man who faces danger and the prospect of death will risk everything and fight without considering the consequences does not stand the test of reality, particularly in totalitarian regimes. Those sectors of the general population in the Nazi-occupied countries that suffered and were persecuted more than others—and paid the heaviest price—did not rebel or fight. We know of almost no cases of uprisings in the concentration camps, although the proportion of non-Jews and the mortality rates were high there. It is interesting to note that of some 5.7 million Soviet POWs, the Nazis liquidated between 65 and 70 percent. Nobody would cast aspersions on the courage of Soviet soldiers who fell into enemy hands; yet we know of no revolts of Soviet POWs, with the exception of isolated escapes. Furthermore, this phenomenon of acquiescence—acceptance of one's fate on the threshold of death—can be found in Soviet detention camps as well. And those personalities who had led the Soviet Communist movement and in the course of Stalin's rule were stamped as traitors and enemy agents also went unresisting to their certain death.

Examination of these phenomena belongs largely to the sphere of psychological and sociological research, and findings are still awaited. It transpires that for individuals to rebel, to choose the path of resistance, requires an expanse of inner freedom, contact with the world, and faith in some ideological outlook. Without these basic conditions they usually lack the will and the spirit to fight even if their condition is hopeless; they certainly cannot organize, plan, and rebel. Very few choose the path of "May my soul perish with the Philistines!"

It is in this light that one should examine the conduct of the Jews and assess the facts presented herein. Facts that reveal Jewish resistance did, in fact, exist—and on a not inconsiderable scale.

18

The Last Phase of the Final Solution (1944–1945)

Let us now take a look at the strategic and the consequent political situation that had evolved in Europe during 1943 and 1944 as prelude to the collapse of the Third Reich in the winter of 1944/1945. After the debacle at Stalingrad in January 1943, the Allies launched their assault on Hitler's Fortress Europe on all fronts. Extending about 9,500 miles in circumference, Hitler's bastion was attacked first on the eastern and southern fronts. The Germans were keenly aware that they stood in danger of having the signal victory they had scored during the first years of the war reversed into defeat. It was not merely fortuitous that in a speech delivered on February 18, 1943, Josef Goebbels called for "total war" and that in closed discussions the heads of the Nazi regime confessed their apprehension to one another. On March 2, 1943, for example, Goebbels recorded in his diary, "Göring knows perfectly well what awaits us all if we run out of our strength in this war. We have no illusions about it. Especially when it comes to the Jewish question, we are so deeply mired in it that we no longer have any way out. And it's just as well, for experience shows that a movement and a people who have burned their bridges behind them are more likely to fight without reservation than those who have options of retreat."[1] This statement reflects the identity of Goebbels's perception of the war and the extermination campaign against the Jews. For just as they were "so deeply mired in it" that they could no longer disengage from their campaign to annihilate Jewry, so had they passed the point of no return in their conduct of the war: all their bridges had been burned, leaving no avenue of retreat. This was the rationale behind the total war for which Albert Speer would have to increase the industrial and armament effort, Fritz Sauckel would be accorded the power to bring millions of workers in from the occupied countries, and Goebbels would amplify his propaganda program while continuing to stress the anti-Semitic motif—on Hitler's personal recommendation. The führer also tried to encourage the German people, particularly the party leadership, imbuing them with faith in ultimate victory. In his speech before the Gauleiter and Reichsleiter on May 8, 1943, he reconfirmed "his undiminished certitude that the Reich will rule over all of Europe," adding that the Germans would have to fight yet many more wars, but they would be crowned with brilliant victories, "And then, essentially, the road to world dominion will be paved. Whoever owns Europe will dominate the world. Questions of justice or injustice naturally do not come into this discussion." And Hitler reiterated his dauntless, unshakable resolve not to abandon the struggle.[2]

As the führer was sounding these words, the Allies were about to complete the conquest of North Africa. Two months later, in July 1943, they landed in Sicily under Dwight D. Eisenhower's command; in another two months, on September 9, 1943, Italy had surrendered—though the advance of the Allied forces northward through the Italian boot was subsequently halted in bitter fighting with German troops at Monte Cassino. Thus Rome was not taken until early June 1944.

By the summer of 1944, the Russian advance was in full swing, threatening the Balkans in the south and liberating the Baltic states in the north, although in the central sector of its thrust, the Red Army had halted at the gates of Warsaw in July. The tragedy of the Polish underground in Warsaw is one of the more intriguing and disputed episodes of the war. Expecting the Red Army to capture the city in August 1944, the AK mounted an uprising to ensure Polish rule over the capital before the Russians entered it. To this day historians are divided over the question of why the Russians allowed the Germans to quash this rebellion so brutally. In any event, the Russians did not take Warsaw until January 1945. They then continued their advance toward the Reich, reaching Łódź on January 19 and liberating the 830 people left in its ghetto.

The already tense relations between the Soviets and the Poles had deteriorated to the point of a complete break in April 1943 after the Germans uncovered a mass grave of Polish officers in the Katyn Forest near Smolensk. Goebbels exploited this gruesome discovery in strident propaganda that denounced the Russians' barbarity. As far as he was concerned, the incident had come at just the right moment, giving even greater force to his call for a total war. He was also hoping to counterbalance the Allies' publication of information about the extermination of the Jews by exposing the Allies' own savagery and thus to skirt the Jewish issue entirely. This strategy had been decided on in mid-December 1942; from then on Goebbels targeted his propaganda most of all against the British by focusing on their conduct in India, Iran, and the rest of the Middle East. He even availed himself of the mufti of Jerusalem for that purpose. A report on closed meetings with his staff noted, "The minister believes this to be the best opportunity to rouse a general outcry against the atrocities [committed by others] in order to get away from the irksome matter of the Jews."[3]

In the summer of 1944, the Allies in the West were preoccupied with overcoming the stiff German resistance to their June 6 landing in Normandy. But by the time Paris was liberated on August 25, the strategic and political situation in southeastern Europe had begun to shift as well. From the end of 1942 onward, especially after the German defeat at Stalingrad, the satellite states in the Balkans—Bulgaria, Rumania, and Hungary—were prompted to take stock of their political position. Not only had the Rumanians incurred heavy losses in fighting on the Russian front, but Hitler also blamed them, along with the Hungarians, for the debacle at Stalingrad.[4] This provoked a quarrel between the führer and Prime Minister Ion Antonescu when they met in April 1943. By that point the Rumanians had already begun to put out feelers to the West, primarily through American ministers in neutral countries, and they continued to maintain contact with the Italian government after it had gone over to the Allies. The Russian assault on Rumania began in mid-May 1943. On August 23 King Michael declared a truce; on August 25—the day of the liberation of Paris—he joined in the war against Germany. The Red Army entered Bucharest on August 31, 1944, and had completed the conquest of Rumania by the end of September.

Germany and Hungary

The Kállay Government

The last German attempt to save the crumbing front in southeastern Europe was made in Hungary. The debacle of the Hungarian troops in the war against the Soviets had been, if anything, even more disastrous than that of the Rumanians. The Hungarian army collapsed completely and its regiments were routed from their positions on the Don.[5] In April 1943 Miklós Horthy was invited for a talk with Hitler and was confronted with two main complaints: first, that in 1942 Prime Minister Miklós Kállay had attempted to establish contact with the Americans in Turkey; second, that the Hungarian government was not fulfilling Germany's demands on the Jewish question. Ascribing Germany's problems to the bombing of its major cities, Hitler boasted that despite supply difficulties, no black market had developed in Germany. To which Horthy replied that Hungary was also beset by these problems but that he had not yet succeeded in wiping out the black market. Hitler saw this as his opportunity to move on to his second complaint and argued that the Jews alone were responsible for the black market because wherever they lived, they were busy cheating and hoarding. Horthy had brought along a draft of the arguments he would put forth in just such a contingency. He conceded that the Jewish problem was a Pan-European one; he objected to the introduction of the yellow badge in Hungary; and he absolutely ruled out the deportation of the Jews on the grounds that "the state lacks the legal and technical means" to effect such a venture.[6] According to the German report on the meeting, Horthy's reply to Hitler's comment on the matter was, "What, then, should he do with the Jews after they had essentially been denied almost every opportunity to earn a living. Why, he couldn't kill them." In response, Hitler and Joachim von Ribbentrop decided to teach Horthy a lesson in how to deal with the Jews. Hitler described the Jews' condition in Poland: "In places where Jews were left to themselves, as for instance in Poland, cruel misery and decay prevailed. Jews were mere parasites, he said. In Poland they [the Germans] put an end to this state of affairs. Jews who would not work there would be shot, and those who could not work should go to the dogs. They were to be treated like T.B. bacilli, which were dangerous for a healthy organism."[7]

Hitler also took this opportunity to demand that Horthy dismiss Prime Minister Miklós Kállay, whom the Germans regarded—not without reason—as the dominant factor behind Hungary's diffident attitude toward German interests, including the Jewish question. It was under the influence of Kállay and the Hungarian defense minister, Vilmos Nagy, that the Hungarians had refused to deport the Jews, knowing that their refusal to yield to German demands would serve them in their contacts with the Allies and enable them to be trusted. Nevertheless, they did not stand up to German pressure for long or, indeed, to the pressure from the radical right within Hungary itself. In June 1943 Nagy was forced to resign for refusing to accommodate Speer's demand to send ten thousand Hungarian Jews to the copper mines in Bor, Yugoslavia, which supplied some 50 percent of the needs of the German armament industry. Following his resignation, on July 2, 1943, the Hungarians signed an agreement committing them to send three thousand Jewish laborers to Bor. In fact, they doubled this quota, dispatching Jewish labor battalions numbering some six thousand men; in return, the German Ministry of the Economy supplied Hungary with 100 tons of unrefined copper a month.

Although the living and working conditions of these labor battalions were appalling, with the German labor bosses and some of the Hungarian guards subjecting the workers to physical abuse, most of the men withstood these trials. The fact is that few died before the German retreat in the autumn of 1944 when about thirty-six hundred of these laborers were transferred to concentration camps in Germany and some twenty-five hundred were sent back to Hungary on a death march in which most of them were shot by the Germans along the way.[8] The worst massacre of all, in the style of the Einsatzgruppen, took place at Cservenka. We have testimony about it from one of the few survivors, Zalman Teichmann, whose recovery after being badly injured is regarded as a medical miracle. Teichmann and others who fled the scene were aided by Serbian partisans.[9]

The labor battalions that had earlier been sent to the eastern front fared little better: of the approximately 50,000 people dispatched to the front, only 6,000 to 7,000 returned. Those not killed in the fighting itself—felled by German or Hungarian bullets—or not overwhelmed by exhaustion on their way back were taken captive by the Russians and suffered terribly at their hands, too. Most of the losses were incurred by the labor battalions in 1943 when the number of Jewish victims is quoted as being 23,308.[10]

The Délvidék Trial: Background and Implications

Toward the end of 1941 there was a rise in partisan activity by the Serbs in the Banat region of northern Yugoslavia, which was under German control. These guerrilla actions began to provoke the Hungarian regime as well. When it became obvious that the Hungarian gendarmerie was helpless to quell the riots that had erupted in this district, the Hungarian Council of Ministers decided (with

Horthy's consent) to send the army into action. The campaign was headed by Ferenc Feketehalmi-Czeydner, the commander of Hungary's Fifth Army Corps (in Szeged), who was a supporter of the Germans and a Jew-hater.[11] By the time his troops reached the troubled area, the situation had essentially settled down. But by filing false reports, Feketehalmi-Czeydner created the impression that rioting and heavy fighting persisted, in response to which he had decided to take "punitive measures." Thousands of local inhabitants, including women and children, were killed in these actions for allegedly "supporting the partisans." Feketehalmi-Czeydner justified the murder of the children by asserting that "when they grow up they will want to take revenge" (the same argument, incidentally, that Heinrich Himmler used in addressing the commanders of the SS in Posen [Poznań] in October 1943 to justify the murder of Jews). Among the murdered were also hundreds of Jews.

The main massacre, however, took placed in the Délvidék region's largest city, Novi Sad (Újvidék). It was mounted in contravention of express orders from the government, which had by now received reliable information on the state of affairs in the area and regarded the army's actions as atrocities. The Novi Sad massacre was organized by the local army commander. First the city was placed under curfew and completely isolated by cutting the phone and telegraph lines. Then masses of hostages were taken, especially from among the Jewish population, which was believed to be the wealthier class. Thousands of people were arrested on false charges of "collaboration with the partisans," and their "interrogation" usually ended in death. To justify the operation the army staged partisan attacks on the local gendarmerie, after which the purportedly wounded gendarmes wore bandages on their heads and hands as ostensible proof of the violence. The troops' appetite for mayhem was stoked by a stiff drink of rum. The massacre was conducted systematically, street by street. In actions reminiscent of the atrocities committed by the Ustasha movement in neighboring "independent" Croatia, some of the victims were chased or brought by truck to the banks of the Danube, where they were herded into the swimming club two by two, forced to undress in temperatures reaching − 20 degrees Fahrenheit, and were shot, with their bodies being cast into the river (after a hole had been made in the ice by cannon fire). Others were thrown alive into the freezing water. It was not until four days later that the city's governor, Leó Deák, managed to get through to his superior and that same evening the army's actions in Novi Sad were halted—although the massacre continued in the surrounding area. The toll of deaths in Novi Sad and its environs was 4,116 people: 2,842 Serbs, 1,250 Jews, 11 Hungarians, and 13 Russians.[12]

When word of the massacre got out in Hungary, it sparked off a great outcry, especially in liberal circles, and questions were raised in both houses of Parliament. The prime minister, László Bárdossy, a pro-German right-winger, duly sent a commission of inquiry to the area, but its report essentially gave the army's version of the affair, making it easy to cover up the matter. A new investigation was held after Bárdossy's government was replaced on March 9, 1942, by the Kállay regime. Yet it was not until December 1943—in the wake of the Hungarian army's defeat on the eastern front and the Allies' announcement of November 1, 1943, of their intention to prosecute war criminals—that fifteen army officers responsible for the massacre were brought to trial. Four death sentences were passed together with long prison terms, but four of the men found guilty—including Feketehalmi-Czeydner—managed to escape to Germany.[13] The Germans delved into the affair quite thoroughly, and Ribbentrop even briefed Hitler on it in a series of memoranda to elicit his decision on how to deal with the case. The führer reasoned that it should not be assumed that the Hungarian army had slaughtered women and children, but reports to that effect should be taken as typical Jewish propaganda. His decision was, "Anyone in Europe who has been persecuted for his war against the Jews will be accepted in Germany as a political refugee and be treated as such."[14] This statement not only underscores the perception of the Jewish question as a political problem but lends the impression that Hitler was trying to offset the Allied declaration regarding the punishment of war criminals.

The German Occupation

The Délvidék affair may have had an effect, however, on the discussions in progress within the senior ranks of the German government to decide whether to forestall Hungary's break with the Axis in order to join the war on the side of the Allies. On March 7, 1944, when the Red Army was about 100 miles from the Hungarian border, the Germans decided to launch Operation Margarete. Hitler's secret order of March 12 that explained the need to invade Hungary contended that Kállay's negotiations with the Allies had been induced by the Jews and the Hungarian aristocracy "married to the Jews,"[15] although it also portrayed the Hungarians as being influenced by the "betrayal of the Italians" and similar instances of "treachery." On March 15, after consultations with Himmler and Ribbentrop, Hitler decided to invite Horthy for a talk that was held three days later in Schloss Klessheim, outside Salzburg. Apparently the exchange between them was a heated one, but ultimately Horthy capitulated, agreeing to dismiss the Kállay government and replace it with a new Council of Ministers that would do the Germans' bidding. By the time Horthy had returned to Hungary on March 19, the German army had already entered the country without firing a shot. An extra car was secretly attached to the special train carrying the regent back to Budapest, and in it the new German minister plenipotentiary of the Reich, Edmund Veesenmayer, traveled together with a staff of German officials and envoys sent to brief the yet-to-be formed government. The new prime minister, Döme Sztójay (formerly the Hungarian minister in Berlin), took office on March 22, 1944.

The German representation in Hungary included a large special team dispatched by the RSHA and headed by HSSPF Otto Winkelmann. Also attached to it was Himmler's special representative, Kurt A. Becher. The Special Operational Commando Hungary, which had earlier been constituted by Eichmann in the Mauthausen camp, came to Budapest on the very day of the occupation for the purpose of organizing the deportation of the country's almost eight hundred thousand Jews. Counted among the team of sixteen men were some of Eichmann's most experienced office and field aides, including Dr. Siegfried Seidel, the first commandant of Theresienstadt; Theodor Dannecker, who had organized the deportations from France, Bulgaria, and Italy; and Dieter Wisliceny, who had functioned in Slovakia and Greece. Among the men from Eichmann's office now posted to Budapest were the transport expert Franz Novak and two of his senior aides, Hermann A. Krumey and Otto Hunsche.

In both their takeover of Hungary and the deportation of its Jews, the Germans demonstrated the degree to which they had perfected their efficiency in implementing their plans and their proficiency at adapting to local conditions. In no time at all they had eradicated the last traces of the democratic system in Hungary. Parties were disbanded and ministers and senior officials throughout the country were replaced by people acceptable to the Germans; however, members of the radical right and the terror group Arrow Cross were not invited to join the new government. Nevertheless, two men from the Hungarian radical right, László Endré and László Baky—both unabashed anti-Semites—were installed in the Interior Ministry by Ernst Kaltenbrunner, the head of the RSHA, as chief aides to the minister, Andor Jaross, in all matters related to the Jews.[16] Appointed to command the Hungarian army were generals known for their pro-German and anti-Semitic posture, and in the economic field the Germans took over factories that were of value to their war effort.[17]

The Destruction of Jewry

Eichmann and the Hungarian Government

The RHSA's strategy toward the Jews of Hungary differed from the one that had generally been followed in the occupied countries. Apparently it was copied from the Slovakian model, improved and adapted to the specific circumstances of time and place. As Eichmann himself testified, in this case the Germans preferred to have the Hungarians carry out the operation themselves. He explained this decision by recalling the failure the Germans had suffered in Denmark in October 1943 and observed, "Over the years, I have learned from experience which hooks I have to use to catch which fish."[18] He claimed that as a German he could not force the Hungarians to hand over the Jews. The fact that he personally had come to Hungary (on March 21) to head such a large staff of aides belied this claim. Nevertheless, this time the Germans tried to orchestrate the operation from behind a screen of Hungarian decrees and actions while reserving direct influence over the Jewish public for themselves. This tactic worked as long as the *Gleichschaltung* of the Hungarian state was in effect and its leaders were fully prepared to act against the Jews according to the "advice" of Eichmann and his men.[19]

Back on March 25 Veesenmayer had already received confirmation that the Hungarian government would deal with the Jewish problem; on March 31 the order was published requiring every Jew to wear a yellow badge as of April 5—an obligation that extended to Christians of Jewish origin. In response to the protests of Jusztinian Cardinal Serédi, the head of the Roman Catholic church in Hungary, priests of Jewish origin, the families of demobilized soldiers, Jews who had intermarried, and foreign Jews were exempted from this order. Other decrees that followed within days of this first measure to isolate the Jews included travel restrictions, the expropriation of bicycles and cars, a night curfew in most cities, and the confiscation of all telephones. Moreover, the Jews were denied any opportunity to make a living: they were fired from their jobs, their businesses were confiscated, and they were to be conscripted for labor service. Jewish notables and other men of stature were arrested throughout Hungry, and some of them were later among the first to be deported.[20]

On April 7 at a secret meeting held in the Ministry of Interior, the decision was taken to initiate preparations for deporting the Jews. Secret orders signed by Baky that were sent to all provincial governors, mayors, the gendarmerie, and the police explained, "The Hungarian Royal Government will soon have the country purged of Jews. I order the purge to be carried out by regions. As a result of the purge, the Jewry—irrespective of sex or age—is to be transported to assigned concentration camps. In towns or large villages a part of the Jews are later to be accommodated in Jewish buildings or ghettos." The arrests, the order continued, were to be effected by the gendarmerie and the police in close cooperation with the German Sipo, which acted as "an advisory body." Special committees were to be appointed to deal with the Jews' apartments and businesses and see to it that valuables, money, securities, and the like were safely delivered to the local authorities, who would be required to turn them over to a branch of the national bank.[21]

Hungarian Jewry in Crisis

According to the state census taken in 1940/1941, there were 725,007 Jews living in Hungary. To this figure we must add the 100,000 or so people who had converted to Christianity at one time or another but were defined as Jews by the racial laws, bringing the total number of "racial" Jews in Hungary in 1941 to 825,000. After subtracting the estimated 63,000 who died throughout Greater Hungary up to the time of the German occupation—half of them in the territories that had been retransferred in 1938 to 1941—we arrive at a figure of 762,000 as the number of Jews (including apostates) living in Hungary in 1944.[22]

In 1941 the close to 185,000 Jews living in Budapest represented about 25 percent of the country's Jewish population.[23] The other 75 percent—about 544,000 people—were the object of the first and fateful stages of the deportation to Auschwitz.

The many changes in the composition of the Jewish population of Hungary led to the splintering of the community, a process that had already been set off by waves of immigration from neighboring countries. Clearly manifest in Hungary were a variety of distinct social classes and religious groupings that had each created its own communal organization. One group, which hailed mainly from Moravia and identified primarily with Magyar culture, had made a considerable impact on the Hungarian economy. Many of its members were also highly successful in the free professions and took an active part in the country's political life through the Liberal and Social Democratic parties. To the degree that they still maintained ties with organized Jewry, they belonged to the reform wing of the

Hungarian community: the Neologists. Almost totally set apart from them was the class of shopkeepers and petty merchants mostly from Germany, Austria, and Poland who made up the Orthodox sector of the community. A third, much smaller group was referred to as the status quo and rejected the positions of the two major groups. Each of these groups maintained its own communal body (kehillah), so that there was no unified, centralized Jewish leadership in Hungary; only a few social-assistance and cultural organizations existed on a nationwide scale.[24]

Neither was there any Jewish political body in Hungary dedicated to pursuing a distinctively Jewish policy that was comparable to the Jewish parties in Rumania and Czechoslovakia. Like their counterparts in Germany, France, and Holland, the Jews of Hungary were not recognized as a national minority, and thus they strove to solve the problems they confronted as Jews—including anti-Semitism, which had steadily intensified between the two world wars—in the broader framework of Hungarian national policy. The Jews of Hungary had been deeply scarred by the anti-Jewish White Terror that had swept through the country upon the fall of the short-lived Communist regime of Béla Kun and with which many members of the radical Jewish intelligentsia had identified. Hundreds of Jews were murdered in this outburst of violence as pogroms ravaged a number of communities. Under the leadership of a few prominent economic figures, the Jews tried to defend themselves, especially by means of apologetic protestations of loyalty to the Magyar regime.

The historian Béla Vago has characterized the unique situation in Hungary:

> This was one of the paradoxical phenomena of the Hungarian regime, which contained a mixture of vestiges of feudalism with democratic-parliamentary elements; the authoritarianism of a quasi-fascistic regime with tolerance toward the democratic opposition; an official anti-Semitic policy with tolerance toward Jews in the fields of journalism, the arts, and other areas of culture. The Jews could be active as members of Parliament until the German occupation in 1944.[25]

Until the outbreak of the war, Zionism had not been a very influential factor in Hungary. The conventional Jewish leadership functioned within the framework of the kehillot, and the government was particularly attuned to those notables belonging to the capitalist bourgeoisie who had excellent connections with the leading Magyar business circles. One of the outstanding figures among these Jews was the chairman of the Pest Neologist kehillah, Samu (Samuel) Stern.

By the time of the German occupation, Stern was a septuagenarian with a rich and active life behind him. For years he had presided over the export of most of the country's agricultural products, to the point where the anti-Semites referred to him as the King of Milk and Eggs. He was also on close terms with members of Horthy's regime—even with the regent himself—and hoped that Horthy and Kállay would keep Hungary free of direct German rule.

Together with the great majority of the country's population, ruling circles, and the government opposition, the Jews of Hungary had not anticipated the German occupation. Samuel Stern survived the Holocaust and, in memoirs written after the war, tried to clarify and justify his actions and those of his colleagues during the tragedy that befell Hungarian Jewry. In this self-defense, dismissing the many grave accusations raised against him during and after the persecutions, he wrote, "It looks to me like accusing a man awaiting execution of collaboration with the hangman." Stern also insisted that he had accepted the chairmanship of the Jewish Council despite the fact that he knew "what the Germans had done throughout the occupied Europe."[26]

The Jewish Council was formed as soon as the Germans arrived, and all other Jewish organizations were promptly outlawed. On March 19, the first day of the occupation, Wisliceny and Krumey appeared in the offices of the kehillah in Pest and issued an order to have the notables assembled the following morning. The frightened Jews knew only one mode of action: to seek the aid of the Hungarian authorities. They appealed for help to the Ministry of Education, which was responsible for the kehillot—of course, to no avail. Finally, they were referred to the police, where they were told that they would have to obey all of the Germans' commands. The next day, the appearance of Eichmann's men in the kehillah's office, accompanied by soldiers armed with submachine guns, made the nature of this order obvious. Wisliceny then informed the assembled notables that they must constitute the Jewish Council, that all matters related to the Jews would be handled by the Germans, and that the Jews were to have no contact with the Hungarian authorities except through the auspices of the Germans. Yet, at the same time, Eichmann's experienced operatives proceeded according to the well-known stratagem: reassuring the Jews and promising them a certain measure of independence and, above all, safety if they did as they were told. These assurances were, of course, juxtaposed with the threat that whoever defied or tried to deceive the Germans would be put to death. They explicitly promised that there would be no deportations. Wisliceny even remarked that the suitcases they had brought along in the expectation of being arrested were superfluous. Despite the prohibition on contacts with the Hungarians, Stern tried to get through to Sztójay's government and to erstwhile friends, but his efforts proved fruitless. Yet he still hoped to exploit his connection with Horthy, not knowing that the regent had completely dissociated himself from the Jewish problem and made it clear that he had no intention of intervening in the matter.[27]

Again and again, Stern reiterated in his own defense that he had accepted the heavy responsibility because he believed that not only his connections but also the long experience of his life would stand him in good stead in serving Hungary's Jews and saving them from destruction.[28] The essence of the tragedy lies in the fact that it was this lauded experience that failed Stern and his comrades. Wittingly or otherwise, even though the circumstances had been revolutionized, the Jews continued to conduct themselves as though they were still confronted by the ambivalent Hungarian attitude to which they had grown accustomed over the decades. Somehow they did not grasp that with a wave of the hand the Germans had swept away all the old conventions and together with their Hungarian collaborators were now operating on completely different assumptions. Moreover, hatred had become lucrative through the benefit to be derived from the plunder of Jewish property; the Jews had never even suspected the magnitude of the Hungarians' rapacity. It was the Germans who told Stern how surprised they were by the number of tips they had received from Hungarian informers: no fewer than 35,000 had come into their offices during the very first days of the occupation.[29]

Stern claimed in his account that the Jewish Council "regulated" the wild arrests of wealthy people and community notables by giving people a day's notice before they were to report for detention. That way they could either prepare themselves for arrest or flee—though in no way was it ever intimated to these people that they should try to escape and go into hiding. Quite the opposite was true: in every official summons as well as in personal talks, the members of the council stressed that their instructions, issued according to the Germans' orders, were to be strictly obeyed.

The first announcement of the new format was issued on March 23, 1944, in the *Journal of Hungarian Jews,* the only organ with official sanction, in a "Call to Hungarian Jewry":

> On the basis of the position taken by the competent authorities, we may point out that Jewish religious, cultural, and social life will continue. This should have a reassuring effect on all.
>
> Jewry has been requested to establish a Central Council, which will, as the need arises, establish its own internal committees. The Central Council is the only authorized and responsible organ of all of Jewry, and is the competent organ to maintain contact with German authorities.[30]

Thereafter the announcement cited various limitations on the Jews' freedom of action and demanded their "strict and conscientious adherence to all these regulations." On April 6, 1944, a corollary announcement spelled out the relationship between the council and the Hungarian authorities: "The Hungarian authorities deal exclusively with the Central Council, and it is to this body that they send all instructions relating to the Jews throughout the country." Hence, by this point, official responsibility for dealing with the Jews had already been given over to the Hungarians. On April 27 the *Journal of the Jews in Hungary* (the change of name being, as usual, at the demand of the Germans) published an order of the Hungarian Royal Government in which the new organization headed by the Jewish Council was called the Association of the Jews of Hungary, and its jurisdiction was extended "to all the Jews compelled to wear the Yellow Star."[31] Clearly the leaders of the council still believed in the assurances they had received about the safety of the Jews.

Less than a month later, on May 19, 1944, the Jewish leadership felt it necessary to urge the Jewish masses to have faith in them. With the initiation of the ghettoization process and the deportations, doubt and criticism were being aired on all sides, and the council responded by charging that the complaints leveled against it were based on "vague rumors spread by dubious sources." Its members repeatedly stressed the weight of the responsibility they bore and chided their constituents, "We must not expect explanations. They cannot be given in any case. We must trust and have faith!"[32]

Ghettoization and Deportation

The process of ghettoization began in the middle of April; in preparation for it the first two areas to be closed—Sub-Carpathian Ruthenia and Transylvania—were declared areas of military operations. Seventeen temporary ghettos were established in the main cities of Ruthenia, and 144,000 Jews were concentrated in them. In Transylvania the Jews were gathered into seven ghettos containing a total of 97,000 people. All in all, as the action proceeded in the five main sectors of Hungary, forty ghettos and three concentration camps were established in order to intern 427,400 Jews.[33] The larger concentrations were situated at some distance from the cities, occasionally in an open field. Many Jews, especially from the less populous communities, were also incarcerated in small, temporary concentration facilities, with synagogues, factories, schools, or even private homes being used for this purpose.

The deportations to Auschwitz began on May 15, and by May 24 between 12,000 and 14,000 Jews were being sent out of one or two areas every day, for a total of 116,000 people in a ten-day period. All the squads working in the gas chambers, crematoria, and the "Canada" warehouses in Auschwitz were reinforced, and the crematoria were kept working twenty-four hours a day. Many of the Jews chosen as workers in the selections were sent on to one of 386 other camps, but most of them were kept for work in Auschwitz or one of the other main concentration camps—Mauthausen, Dachau, Buchenwald, or Ravensbrück.

After emptying Sub-Carpathian Ruthenia and Transylvania of their Jews, in

Table 8. Data Relating to the Ghettoization and Deportation in the Five Areas*

Name of Area	Concentration in Ghettos		Deportations		Difference
	Number of Ghettos	Number of Jews	Dates	Number of Jews	
Sub-Carpathian Ruthenia	17	144,000	5/15–6/7	289,357	+48,357
Transylvania	7	97,000	5/15–6/7		
Northern Hungary	5	69,000	6/11–6/30	50,805	−18,195
Southern Hungary east of the Danube (Tisza River basin)	4	73,000	6/25–6/30	41,499	−31,501
Transdanubia, suburbs of Budapest	7	36,400	6/29–7/9	55,741	+19,341
Total	40	419,400	5/15–7/9	437,402	+18,002
Concentration Camps	3	8,000		8,000	
Grand Total	43	427,400		445,402	

Source: Randolph L. Braham, *Eichmann and the Destruction of Hungarian Jewry* (New York, 1961), pp. 20, 23; Jenö Lévai, ed., *Eichmann in Hungary: Documents* (Budapest, 1961), pp. 108–10.

*For a slightly different table, see Randolph L. Braham, *The Politics of Genocide: The Holocaust in Hungary* (New York, 1981), vol. 2, p. 607.

June the Germans turned their attention to the three other sectors of Hungary: the northern district stretching between Budapest and the German border; the southern sector east of the Danube (the Tisza River basin); and the fifth area, west of the Danube. At first, they did not touch Budapest, but finally the Jews living in its suburbs were added to the transports. Also included in these transports were apparently some of the people who had earlier been held in concentration camps. Altogether, in the course of less than two months, 445,000 people were sent to Auschwitz.[34]

Table 8 indicates that in no place was the number of Jews incarcerated in ghettos identical to the number deported from the area. More Jews were deported from Sub-Carpathian Ruthenia, Transylvania, and the Transdanubia than had been closed in ghettos, but in the other two areas the number of deportees was lower than the number of detainees. All told, 18,000 more people were deported than had been enclosed in the ghettos. These discrepancies can be explained in a variety of ways, and the addition of people to the transports is not surprising. More difficult to explain are the instances in which fewer people were deported than the number living in the ghettos. In one of his reports, Veesenmayer complained that it was impossible to achieve the maximum number of deportees because the Hungarians were conscripting people for their labor battalions. In another report he bemoaned the flight of Jews to Rumania, where they were accorded political asylum; the number of such fugitives was estimated at 5,000 to 7,500.[35] It was also possible that on occasion Jews from one area were included on trains from another.

On another level, Eichmann and his transportation officer, Franz Novak, had difficulty obtaining the necessary number of railway cars. The shortage of trains was sorely felt by the Reich at that time because of the pressing needs of the retreating German army. Eichmann appealed to Himmler on this issue—in a number of similar instances in the past, the Reichsführer-SS had successfully interceded on his behalf—and the matter was again referred to Karl Wolff (see chap. 16). Wolff, in turn, invoked Hitler's order giving the military's transport needs first priority only when the army was on the offensive. Thus, since the Wehrmacht was now mainly in retreat, it could be argued that Eichmann's demand for rolling stock took precedence. In any case, Eichmann was forced to make do with four trains a day, instead of the six he had requested through the offices of the Hungarian government—but he crammed eighty to one hundred people into each car with a normal capacity of forty. The trains traveled via Ruthenia and Galicia. As far as the border station of Kassa (Košice), the Hungarians were responsible for the transports; at Kassa they were turned over to the SS, who opened the sealed doors primarily to remove the bodies of those who had died along the way. Keeping to strict formality, Eichmann did not initiate the deportations until he had received Hungary's "demand" that the ghettos be liquidated, supposedly because of the intolerable conditions in them.[36]

Among the countless lies that were being circulated by the Germans, this was actually the truth. From all over Hungary the Jewish Council received reports of the harassment of men and women, children, and old people as well as of the torture inflicted to make them reveal "where they had concealed their valuables."

In many cases their hastily abandoned apartments were not sealed (as the official order demanded) and became an easy mark for plunder. There seemed to be no limit to the lies, deception, and the false propaganda that were being disseminated by the Nazis. Eichmann and his men often traveled to the sectors placed under their control, and upon returning they reported to all who would lend them an ear on how perfectly everything had been arranged. Eichmann told Horthy, "The provincial ghettos are like sanitariums. Finally the Jews have started living in the fresh air and have exchanged their old way of life for a healthier one."[37] The Hungarian officials followed his lead. Here, for example, is what Endré wrote on May 15 in the Arrow Cross journal, "We have carried out measures which have always taken place with humanitarian methods and with due regard to moral factors. In fact, [the Jews] suffer no injury. They may live among themselves, after their own racial and popular laws. . . . I have given instructions that their personal safety should be carefully guarded."[38]

The Jews were told that rather than be taken to Germany, the deportees were being held in a special labor camp in Hungary. To reinforce that impression, deportees from the first transports were forced to write postcards reporting that they were in a pleasant place—the Waldsee Labor Camp—where they had been housed in comfortable quarters and put to work. This supposedly "pleasant place" was, in fact, Auschwitz, but many Jews were tempted to believe the false claims and reports.[39]

And so, in a swiftness without precedent, Eichmann emptied all the districts of Hungary of their Jews. Despite heavy pressure from the Hungarians, for the present he still would not touch Budapest out of fear that the presence of foreign diplomats would make it impossible to keep word of the destruction of Hungarian Jewry from quickly getting out to the neutral countries and Western Allies. He even provided for the possibility that Jews from the provinces would attempt to flee to Budapest and go into hiding there.

Even so, the Jews in the capital were not left unmolested, and preparations were being made to deport them as well. These began on May 3 with an order to conduct a census; and on June 15 the Hungarian Ministry of Interior issued a decree requiring the Jews to leave their apartments and move to alternative quarters that would be marked with the yellow star. The tenants of these Jewish houses were to be allowed out for only a few hours each day. Needless to say, this operation met with enormous difficulties: instead of 28,000 only 2,500 apartments were turned over to new owners in the course of a week. One member of the committee responsible for this transfer, a representative of the Budapest municipality, tendered aid to the Jews.[40]

Labor Versus Deportation

As in all the occupied countries, a confrontation developed in Hungary between the forces intent on destroying as many Jews as possible and those hoping to use the Jews as vital manpower. It appears that in his talk with Hitler on March 19, Horthy had agreed to make one hundred thousand Jews available to the Germans for work in subterranean aircraft factories supervised by Speer's ministry. Eichmann was the one placed in charge of implementing this manpower transfer; on the other hand, the RSHA wanted to dispatch Hungary's Jews earmarked for destruction to Auschwitz and then filter them through the labor and concentration camps under its control. Both the Hungarians and Eichmann's people also demanded that the workers be joined by their families in order to "heighten their desire to work." But then something paradoxical occurred: the Hungarian Labor Ministry, the instrument through which the Jewish labor battalions of the army had earlier been sent to the eastern front, now became a factor in saving Jews. As the need for manpower was also strongly felt in Hungary proper, additional labor battalions of Jews were established to work within the country. The historian Randolph L. Braham writes, "It is one of the ironies of history that the Ministry of Defense, which had been viewed as one of the chief causes of suffering among Jews during the previous four to five years, suddenly emerged as the major governmental institution actively involved in the saving of Jewish lives."[41]

Thus, something of a struggle developed between the SS men who came to take the Jews off for deportation and the commanders of the Hungarian army who wished to use them in labor battalions. The Hungarian plan was to increase the number of these battalions from 210 to 575, and, indeed, a mobilization order was issued to every Jewish male aged eighteen to forty-eight.[42] The lot of the men conscripted for these battalions was not an enviable one, but thousands of Jews, nevertheless, were saved in this way because their working and living conditions were comparatively good—especially as they were regarded as something akin to POWs. In contrast, most of the people employed in the German subterranean factories perished.

The Turnabout Ends in Failure

When the persecution of Hungarian Jewry first began, the members of the Jewish Council had failed to activate their connections with the members of the Hungarian regime, and above all with Horthy. But on June 23, 1944, through the good offices of his son, the council did succeed in getting a petition through to Horthy that described the tragedy of Hungarian Jewry in great detail. As the council had garnered precise information on the ghettoization and the deportations, the petition cited exact figures as well as the places where Jews were still being detained. It also described the torture, humiliation, and torment to which the Jews were being subjected. The principal intent of the petition was to save the Jews of Budapest, "Being in full knowledge of the above-mentioned facts, we are filled with the deepest anxiety at hearing the rumours according to which in the near future the deportation of the Jewish population of the capital is also to be started to the end that all the Jews should be driven out from Hungary."[43]

In the meantime reports on these developments in Hungary were being published in the press throughout the free world, leaving the Sztójay government embarrassed. The prime minister sent a memorandum to all Hungary's diplomatic representations abroad; he argued that the government had merely yielded to the German demand for manpower, but lies of this sort no longer impressed anyone. On June 27 Sztójay proposed to the Germans that they accept the offers of the countries prepared to take in Jews, but the Germans were unwilling to accept this suggestion.[44] However, for the first time in the history of the Holocaust, an international effort was made to halt the extermination operation. President Roosevelt, Pope Pius XII, King Gustav of Sweden, and the president of the Red Cross all appealed to Horthy to stop the deportations and to save, at least, the Jews of Budapest, whose number was then estimated at a quarter of a million (more on this in chap. 21).

At that point Horthy came to the realization that he could no longer ignore or exempt himself from what was going on. His change of heart was prompted not only by the pressure coming from abroad but also by developments on the battle-field. Units of the Red Army were approaching the Carpathian Mountains, and there was no longer any question that it was only a matter of time before the Wehrmacht collapsed. Moreover, a large contingent of the Hungarian gendar-merie had been deployed around the capital for the purpose of deporting the Jews of Budapest, but fears were growing that this concentration of forces had been engineered as a prelude to a putsch—by Horthy's rivals on the radical right—to bring the regent's rule to an end. Thus, as in so many previous cases, the action against the Jews was to serve as a vehicle for the political ambitions of Germans and Hungarians alike. Alerted to this situation, Horthy summoned a few regi-ments of the army to Budapest and ordered the gendarmerie dispersed. Seizing the opportunity, he ordered the deportations of the Jews to be halted on July 7.[45]

This refusal to allow the deportations to continue together with the cancella-tion of the major action planned for Budapest caught Eichmann by surprise. "In all my long experience, such a thing has never happened to me before," he fumed, " . . . that won't do . . . this is contrary to our agreement. . . . It cannot be toler-ated!" And as if such defiance were not enough, Eichmann's two chief aides in the Hungarian Ministry of Interior, Endré and Baky, were barred from all involve-ment with the operation. When he saw that the Hungarians would absolutely not acquiesce in the deportation of ten thousand Jews from Budapest, Eichmann decided to go into action on his own, with the aid of 150 SS men who were answerable to him. On July 14 he was about to deport half of the two thousand Jews who had been crowded into the Kistarcsa concentration camp when word of his plan became known to the Jewish Council, and its leaders immediately appealed to Horthy as well as to the diplomatic envoys of the neutral countries. Summoning the minister of interior, Horthy ordered him to halt the deporta-tion—by force if necessary. The transport, which had already left the camp, was stopped en route and the deportees returned to Kistarcsa. Eichmann did not yield, however: five days later, on July 19, he made a second attempt to deport the same Jews. But this time he invited the Jewish Council to his office "for consultations," and he kept the members there from early morning until his men managed to deport a total of twenty-seven hundred Jews from Kistarcsa and a second camp. By the time the council members grasped what was happening, the transport had already crossed the Hungarian border.[46] The news was immediately transmitted abroad.

At the time, Hitler's regime was rocked by the attempt on the führer's life on July 20, 1944; for the rest of that summer, the Germans were careful to treat

Horthy's regime with a measure of deference.[47] Nevertheless, on August 25 Eichmann attempted to renew the deportations—but the action was again annulled by Horthy's command. That same day Himmler likewise ordered the deportations from Hungary to Auschwitz suspended until further notice. Eichmann was forced to leave Budapest, but his special commando was not disbanded until the end of September.[48]

By then certain changes had been effected in the Hungarian regime. During July and August Horthy had tried to revise its format, and on August 24, 1944, he appointed a new government headed by General Géza Lakatos. It can be assumed that Horthy was decisively influenced by the Rumanian surrender to the Allies on August 23. He aimed at restoring Hungary's home rule and independence even though German troops were still stationed on Hungarian soil. He also wanted to lay the groundwork for Hungary's departure from the war and put an end to the persecution of the Jews, which had elicited such a strongly negative reaction in the West, but which the Germans and the Hungarian radical right were consistently trying to renew. He tried his hand at a double game: negotiating with the Germans, on the one hand, and attempting to reach agreement on a truce with the Allies, on the other. The general condition of the Jews improved during this period, although conscription to the labor battalions continued. At 3:00 P.M. on October 15, 1944, a truce was announced over the Hungarian radio, but it soon became clear that the wave of exultation that spread through the country and the sense of salvation that settled over the Jews were premature. Aided by the Germans, Hungary's radical right-wing opposition staged a coup to wrest control of the government. Left isolated, Horthy was forced to resign on the night of October 15/16. Ferenc Szálasi, the leader of the Arrow Cross, became prime minister, and his regime lasted until the Red Army completed the conquest of Hungary in the winter of 1945.[49]

Jewish Organization Outside the Council

The Jewish Council under Stern's leadership was not the only organ operating among the Jewish public or maintaining contact with the authorities throughout this fateful period. Neither did the council retain the composition that had been established at the beginning of the occupation because many of its members were replaced just before the deportations began. As we have seen, the council was not a very influential force. Notwithstanding the German order determining that the Jewish Council represented all the Jews of Hungary, other groups formed to deal with the needs of the Jewish community and effectively maintained even closer contact with the Germans. Orthodox Jewry, for example, was represented by Rabbi Philip von Freudiger, and the most effective of these *ad hoc* groups functioned under the leadership of the Zionists.

Prior to the war the Zionist movement had not been a factor of major consequence, though it gained in importance after the annexation of the new areas, particularly Transylvania, where the Zionists had considerable influence. They were also experienced in the political activity at which the Jews of Rumania were particularly successful. The Jews living in Transylvania (a province of pre-World

War I Hungary that had been ceded to Rumania by the Treaty of Trianon) had long tried to preserve a measure of independence from the indigenous Rumanian-Jewish community, and this disposition contributed to the extensive politicization as well as to the Zionist orientation of its community. After northern Transylvania was annexed to Hungary in 1940, some of the local Zionist leaders moved to Budapest and reinforced the Zionist nucleus there. Yet they were not the only Zionists to reach Hungary and influence the Jewish public; the Jews of southern Slovakia, which had likewise been annexed to Hungary, played a similar role. The flow of Jewish fugitives into Hungary had been steadily mounting since the onset of the persecutions in Slovakia. These Slovak Jews were joined by refugees from Poland, some of whom came directly through the Carpathian Mountains but most of whom made their way via Slovakia. For the most part, they were members of the Zionist youth movements and became an invigorating force within the Hungarian-Jewish community, despite—or perhaps because of—the difficulties they faced in Hungary.[50]

This miscellany of Zionist groups coalesced into a new, quasi-legal public body that called itself the Relief and Rescue Committee (Vaadat Ezra ve'Hatzala). Its first attempts to rally forces outside the country to the aid of Hungarian Jewry proved fruitless, but in the autumn of 1942 the committee established contact with the rescue delegation of the Yishuv (Jewish commonwealth in Palestine) in Istanbul, which relayed funds to Budapest. At the beginning of January 1943, the Relief and Rescue Committee began to function in a systematic fashion, launching an operation in which representatives of most of the Zionist parties took part. The chairman of the committee was the engineer Otto Komoly, who maintained contact with the Hungarian authorities; his deputy and the secretary of the committee's executive was Dr. Rezsö Kasztner; relations with parties abroad were handled by Samuel Springmann in cooperation with Moshe Krausz, the director of the Palestine Office of the Zionist Organization dealing with *aliyah;* and the smuggling of people out of the country—referred to as the *tiyul* (excursion)—was directed by Joel Brand. These were supplemented by representatives of the Polish and Slovak refugees as well as local members of Heḥalutz. At first the committee's work focused on smuggling people out of the country and caring for the refugees within Hungary, whose number was estimated at the end of November 1943 (in a report sent to Istanbul and to the Jewish bodies represented in Switzerland) at 15,000.[51]

Working alongside the organizations formed by the refugees themselves, the committee tried to help the newcomers overcome the many practical and legal difficulties they encountered in Hungary and to protect them from arrest and deportation. They resorted to various stratagems to circumvent the strict Hungarian laws and to some extent were also able to avail themselves of aid from the Red Cross and Christian Poles living as refugees in Hungary, openly and officially, under the protection of the representatives of the Polish government-in-exile. Of course, it was necessary to feed, clothe, and house these people and, as far as possible, provide them with work. Despite these combined efforts, however, many of the refugees were arrested by the Hungarian Alien Police and interned in its prisons and concentration camps.

The committee's contacts with factors abroad were effected through a varied collection of emissaries, ranging from the official envoys of neutral countries to Hungarian and even German intelligence people and to outright adventurers. Consequently, these ties were always vulnerable to severance, exposure, or exploitation by the emissaries for blackmail and service to German or other intelligence. The main unofficial channel to the Germans was via the Wehrmacht's counterespionage division, the Abwehr. A few days before the German army entered Hungary, the members of the committee had learned of Hitler's plans from this source, but they lacked sufficient time to make the necessary arrangements or take preemptory action. Once the occupation was a *fait accompli,* the contacts that the committee had cultivated with Hungarian groups opposed to the regime—for example, the Social Democrats or circles seeking contact with the Allies—were no longer of much practical value. On the other hand, there had always been a certain degree of cooperation between the committee and both the Orthodox group led by Freudiger and the leaders of the Neologist community who headed the Jewish Council.

As matters turned out, the Orthodox community and representatives of the Relief and Rescue Committee each tried to establish contact with Eichmann's Jewish commandos. In both cases negotiations with Wisliceny were initiated through the mediation of the Working Group of Slovakia, which had considerable experience in dealing with him, particularly by means of bribery. Freudiger and Kasztner leaned toward adopting the same strategy. Although they succeeded in making inroads among the SS men and notwithstanding the large sums invested in this effort, they failed to forestall the deportations.[52]

The Consequences of the Fascist Coup

At the time of the coup on October 15, 1944, there were still some two hundred thousand Jews living in Budapest, many of them crowded into the two thousand buildings marked with a yellow star. Two days afterward, on October 17, Eichmann returned to the Hungarian capital and gleefully informed the Jewish leaders, "You see, I'm back"—assuring them of his intention to deport the Jews of Budapest.[53] This marked the end of the three-month period during which the Jews of Budapest were able to breathe somewhat more freely.

Eichmann knew that the time he had to manifest his designs in Hungary was limited and that he would have to work quickly if he hoped to complete the deportation of the country's remaining Jews. On November 2 the Russian troops began to approach the capital; three days later the Hungarians permitted Eichmann to begin deporting the Jews. As it was impossible to transport the deportees on trains and the operation in Auschwitz was being phased out at the time, Eichmann chose to send the Jews to the Austrian border. He did so by the same method that had been employed wherever the Germans had tried to "save" the Jews from the approaching Russian divisions: by marching them over hundreds or thousands of miles on foot. These death marches were the last performance of the Final Solution, and they were conducted with the same brutality practiced in the extermination camps. Such were the marches that Eichmann organized for the Jews of

Budapest in November/December 1944, sending tens of thousands of them trudging toward the Hegyeshalom border station.[54] The first group of 25,000 Jews—of
every age and regardless of their state of health—set out on November 8 and
walked more than 125 miles in seven to eight days. Whoever was unable to continue was left to his own devices or shot. The marchers were not given sufficient
food, and at night they had to rest in whatever shelter they could find in the fields.
By the time they reached the border, the survivors were barefoot, half naked, and
exhausted from the rigors of the journey and the blows they had received from
the Hungarian escort. Even Raoul Wallenberg (see chap. 21), who raced after the
column in a car, supplying bread and clothing, was unable to help them all. In
reporting on this march, the head of the Swiss legation in Budapest, Charles Lutz,
wrote, "Their conditions may not be compared to persons afflicted by any other
spiritual distress or physical suffering. . . . Poverty and want will still leave a man
his dignity if there remains security based on law. But human dignity vanishes in
the event of a total deprivation of rights and total defenselessness." Even SS officers who encountered these columns en route expressed misgivings about what
they saw. Eichmann ordered Wisliceny, who met and assumed responsibility for
the survivors at the Austrian border, to assign them to places of work without
regard for their physical condition. Since it was by then impossible to exterminate
masses of people in Auschwitz, he reverted to the method of extermination
through labor.[55]

These latest anti-Jewish measures were based on an agreement with the new
Hungarian minister of interior, Gábor Vajna, which Eichmann concluded on
October 18, the day after his return to Budapest. In addition to the deportation of
50,000 people to Germany, the agreement envisioned the concentration of the
able-bodied in four camps near Budapest and the internment of the remaining
Jews in a ghetto. Thus the government announced the conscription of Jews for
"national defense service," mandatory for men aged sixteen to sixty and women
aged sixteen to forty (later on women up to age fifty were conscripted for "sewing
work"). On October 20 policemen and members of the Arrow Cross bands forced
the Jews out of their homes, assembled them at two points, and, organizing work
squads, sent them to the fortifications being built to defend the capital against the
forthcoming Russian attack. From there, however, most of these people were
snatched by Eichmann's men and sent on the death marches to the Austrian border, thus adding about 25,000 deportees to the previously dispatched 50,000.[56]

Particularly bitter was the fate of the Jews who were turned over to the Germans to build fortifications. They were assigned to hard labor while having to
endure appalling conditions in terms of food and living quarters as well as the
abuse of their guards, and in the end they were slaughtered by the thousands.
Some were cast into the icy waters of the Danube; others were buried in mass
graves. At least 9,000 of them were killed in Budapest itself by the men of the
Arrow Cross, who began ranging freely through the city on October 15. The suffering of the people in the labor battalions did not end with the Russians' conquest
of Pest on January 17/18, 1945; the battle for the capital was not decided until
February 13, 1945. Hungary was not completely conquered until the beginning
of April. On March 22/23, during the evacuation of the city of Kőszeg (where the

Hungarian government had taken up temporary quarters), ninety-five sick and exhausted members of a labor battalion were locked in their barracks and killed with gas by three German special units. They were buried together with 2,500 others who had perished in the same area.[57]

We noted already that 825,000 Jews—or rather people regarded as Jews—were living in Hungary in 1941 and that 762,000 of them were still alive on March 19, 1944. Of this number, 618,000 were deported or killed and 5,000 succeeded in escaping, so that when Hungary was liberated early in April 1945, there were only 139,000 Jews who remained—20,000 of them outside of Budapest. An estimated 116,500 others returned from their places of deportation and from the labor service that year, bringing the number of survivors up to 255,500 at the end of December 1945. Some 65,500 of them had returned to the territories that had been annexed to Hungary from 1938 onward and that were given back mostly to Rumania at the end of the war. Thus, there were some 190,000 Jews in the reduced state of Hungary: 144,000 in Budapest and 46,000 in the provinces.[58]

Spoliation of Jewish Property

The theft of Jewish property by the Hungarians and, as we shall presently see, by Himmler himself is a subject in its own right. The Jews played a focal role in the Hungarian economy, for much of the wholesale trade within the country as well as the import and export trade and a healthy portion of the country's industry were in Jewish hands. Jews were also a prominent force in banking. "It can be stated," observed a concluding assessment of the subject, "that the Jews were the moving force behind the industrialization of the country, the development of its commercial life, and the use of modern and scientific methods in agriculture."[59] Consequently, the Hungarians found it difficult to eliminate the Jews' economic base completely, especially since the most important factories in the armament industry were owned by Jewish families and, thus, even the Germans could not avoid dealing with them. Nevertheless, in the course of 1943–1944, the Hungarians brought the activity of many Jewish commercial enterprises, especially wholesale businesses, to a halt, and they also expropriated about half of the agricultural land in Jewish hands.[60] The upshot of these measures was that many of the Jews were left unemployed—a fact that made it even easier for the authorities to conscript them for the forced-labor battalions.

The Hungarian authorities carried these measures to their completion after the German occupation. In addition to the spate of regulations issued in March and April 1944 that ousted officials and members of the free professions from their positions, orders were published in March that closed 40,000 of the 110,000 Jewish businesses throughout Hungary. Of 30,000 Jewish businesses, 18,000 were closed in Budapest alone—a few of them subsequently reopened under Hungarian "trusteeship." At the end of April, the Jews' bank accounts were seized, and in May the remainder of the Jewish agricultural property was expropriated.[61]

At about the time that his attempt to build an economic empire through OSTI was judged a failure, Himmler hoped to exploit the German takeover there to realize his ambition in another way. His representative in Hungary, Kurt Becher, was charged with this task. One of the most prominent enterprises in the Hungarian armament industry was the Weiss-Manfred plant, owned by the Weiss and Chorin families. Fearing, perhaps, a repeat of what had happened in the Protectorate when Hermann Göring appropriated the greater part of the Jewish industries to his private industrial empire, Himmler moved very quickly. As the negotiations between the SS and the factory owners were conducted in complete secrecy, word of them did not reach the rest of the interested German parties— and through them the Hungarian government—until after an agreement had been signed and the owning families had been taken out of Hungary through Vienna. According to this agreement, the management of the enterprise was turned over to Himmler for a twenty-five-year trusteeship. In return, the SS promised to transfer close to fifty members of the two families, most of them Jews, to a neutral country and to pay them the equivalent of RM 3 million in foreign currency as partial compensation for the "losses they incurred." The Sztójay government tried to prove that the deal was illegal and prevent it from being carried out. Even the German Foreign Ministry made an effort to block Himmler, but the members of the families, nevertheless, reached Lisbon on a special Lufthansa flight. For all that, the changes that had begun to affect Hungary in July together with the swift advance of the Soviet armies during the autumn and winter months prevented Himmler from reaping the fruits of the holdings he had acquired in Hungary in the hope of strengthening the SS empire.[62]

The Final Liquidation of the Ghettos in Eastern Europe

Other than Auschwitz and the labor and concentration camps, three ghettos remained in the area under German rule in the East: Shavli and Kovno in Lithuania and Łódź in Warthegau. All three were liquidated in the summer of 1944.

Shavli

The first sign of the impending liquidation in Shavli came on Friday, November 5, 1943, when the Germans conducted a special *Aktion* to isolate and deport the children, the old, and the sick from the ghetto. First they allowed the Jewish laborers to leave the ghetto for their places of work; then they brought in the SS and a team of Ukrainians to conduct a hunt for children. These Ukrainians, who were particularly sadistic in their treatment of the children, also used this opportunity to loot and destroy Jewish property. "The Ukrainians broke down walls, attics, and pillars and tore up the floors of the buildings in their search for booty and an opportunity to do ill." In the course of committing such havoc, they conducted a thorough search for all the hiding places where people had tried to conceal their children, emitting whoops of victory each time they found one. In this context, the diarist in the Shavli ghetto, Eliezer Yerushalmi, found cause to speak of the Jewish police in a positive light, "Forced to take part in this terrible work, [the Jewish police] did its best to save children or, at least, prevent their being beaten. Many policemen were themselves beaten but, nevertheless, continued to place themselves in jeopardy in order to help."[63] The Germans similarly prevented the chairman of the Jewish Council, Mendel Leibowitz, and his colleagues from rescuing children when they attempted to intervene. This *Atkion* in Shavli continued from 7:30 A.M. to 4:00 P.M., with the distraught parents standing helplessly behind a fence in the nearby factory compound watching the harrowing spectacle. That day's transport, which also included the sick and the elderly, was joined by two members of the Jewish Council. The Germans suggested that their presence would ensure the proper treatment of the children—who, they contended, were merely being transferred to alternative accommodations. In actuality, the two council members and the rest of the adults were removed from the train at a point along the way and summarily shot; the children were taken not to the town designated as the transport's destination but to Auschwitz, where they were sent directly to the gas chambers.

By coincidence, a description of the processing of this transport was found among the notes kept by members of the Sonderkommando who worked at the gas chambers; the notes were found near the crematoria after the war. The anonymous author relates:

> The head of the Kommando sent them [the children] to the disrobing hall to undress the little ones. There stood a little five-year-old girl undressing her year-old baby brother. When one of the members of the Kommando walked over to her to undress him, the girl cried out, "Get away from here, Jewish murderer! Don't touch my beautiful brother with your hand stained with Jewish blood. I am now his good mother, and he will die in my arms, together with me."
>
> A seven- or eight-year-old boy standing beside her asked the member of the Kommando if it was really worth his while to lead lovely children to their death by gas just to save his own life.[64]

In his diary, Yerushalmi described the uniqueness of the ghetto's children:

> No Jewish community has ever had such a large proportion of talented and cute children as the proportion of these children in the ghetto. The bitter life has brought out all their latent powers of spirit. Early on the children displayed talents in all fields of life and study. The toddlers ran to school as if it were a place of entertainment. They prepared their homework thoroughly, meticulously, and at the same time kept house, cooked, did the shopping, and watched over their little brothers and sisters. And yet they were always cheerful. The streets of the ghetto rang with the sound of their lively play and laughter.

The Shavli *Aktion* claimed the lives of 506 children up to the age of ten and 68 between the ages of ten and thirteen. Together with the adults on the transport, the total number of victims was close to 800. As similar *Aktionen* were conducted in the immediate vicinity, the inhabitants of the ghetto were gripped by despair. On November 11 Yerushalmi wrote in his diary:

> It is as if we are living in a nightmare and are unable to exercise our reason. We are acting on impulse and live by our instincts, but it is doubtful whether we are functioning properly.[65]

The liquidation of the Shavli ghetto, with its remaining 2,000 people, took place in the summer of 1944 as the Red Army was marching on the Baltic states.

The concentration of the inhabitants—as the prelude to the evacuation—began on July 8, but the transport from Shavli and subsequent trains carrying the remaining Jews of the vicinity did not leave until the following week. The last inhabitants were removed from the ghetto—on foot—on July 22 and were sent to the Stutthof and Dachau concentration camps. Leibowitz was killed in the bombing of the ghetto toward the end, but Yerushalmi escaped in the confusion.[66]

Kovno

The fate of the Kovno ghetto during the final months of its existence resembled that of Shavli, except that the liquidation was effected somewhat differently because of the circumstances prevailing there. Kovno, it will be recalled, was one of the foci of active Jewish resistance. Contrary to the situation in so many other places, the Jewish police in Kovno actually collaborated with the underground, as did the Judenrat itself (see chap. 17). The Germans were surely aware of these ties when on March 27 they ordered 140 members of the police to report for duty and led them directly to the infamous Ninth Fort, where most of the Jews of Kovno and many of the Jews deported from the West European countries had been murdered by the Einsatzgruppen (see chap. 10). After the execution of the policemen and the departure of the adults to their places of work, an *Aktion* began against the children, the sick, and the elderly—the operation conducted modeled on in Shavli.

The *Aktion* continued for two days, during which the Germans had difficulty finding the children because of the many hiding places that had been prepared in the ghetto. To uncover them they used a number of Jewish policemen who had been held in detention in the fortress and, succumbing to threats, agreed to accompany the Ukrainians on their search. Most of the policemen bore up under the brutal interrogations and threats and did not reveal any information about the underground, but 40 of them, including the top-ranking members of the police, immediately paid for this with their lives. The rest were returned to the ghetto; in place of the Jewish police, the Germans now established an Orpo of their own. Among those arrested during the *Atkion* and taken to the Ninth Fort were Dr. Elḥanan Elkes, Leib Garfunkel, and Jacob Goldberg, all members of the Ältesten-rat. Dr. Elkes was soon returned to the ghetto, and thanks to his efforts, his two associates were also sent back—though Garfunkel was released only after a prolonged interrogation in which he was tortured to make him disclose information about the underground. The Kovno ghetto was liquidated in the middle of July, and its inhabitants—4,000 to 5,000 in number—were transferred to the same camps in Germany as the remaining inhabitants of Shavli. Dr. Elkes died in Dachau on July 25, 1944.[67]

Łódź

In the autumn of 1942, when the mass deportation of the inhabitants of the Łódź ghetto to Chełmno drew to an end, Mordekhai Rumkowski's independent institutions were disbanded one after another, until hardly a trace remained of the "autonomy" in which he had taken such pride. Still, the ghetto continued to exist until August 1944; despite prohibitions, Rumkowski did keep up a few of the assistance programs for the children, the youth, and the ailing. The ghetto had remained fairly stable, at least through the end of 1943, with the exception of a few deportations to other labor camps—the largest of these, in February/March 1944, of 1,700 men. Thereafter, the condition of the remaining inhabitants improved somewhat, in terms of both housing and nutrition, and the ghetto was apparently maintained at this level because of its importance as a center of the textile industry.

On June 15, 1944, there were still 76,000 Jews living in Łódź, but then the Germans began to empty the ghetto out gradually, and about 7,000 people were sent to other labor camps. On August 1 the remaining inhabitants put up a show of passive resistance by refusing to report for work as ordered in the "rosters" (workplaces). Beginning in the second week of August, however, the ghetto's inhabitants were rounded up, by force when necessary, and sent to Auschwitz. The last of the transports departed from Łódź on August 29, leaving some 600 Jews in two collection camps within the ghetto and a scattered number of people who had managed to hide. Rumkowski and his family were among those sent to Auschwitz. After the Red Army liberated the city on January 19, 1945, the Red Cross found 900 Jews in Łódź—all that remained of what had been the second largest ghetto in Poland.[68]

The Last Jews of Slovakia

Among the last victims of the extermination operations at Auschwitz in the autumn of 1944 were the remaining Jews of Slovakia. The uprising that had broken out in Slovakia at that time and in which Jews took part served as a convenient pretext to resume the deportations that had been halted at the end of 1942 (see chap. 17). On September 5, 1944, a new government was formed in Slovakia under the leadership of Stefan Tiso (a relative of President Josef Tiso). The uprising left the Slovak leaders in a ticklish position, and they were only too happy to place the blame on foreign subjects and forces, be they Russians, Czechs, or Jews. Hence, the new Slovak government was prompted to declare that "the Jewish problem in Slovakia demands a thorough solution," and the Germans were prepared to take responsibility for providing it. It was they who conducted the manhunt for the Jews and organized the transports through the Slovak railways.[69] These deportations were going on as the victorious Russian columns neared the borders of Slovakia; unfortunately for the Jews, they did not cross the frontier until the spring of 1945.

In preparation for the deportation campaign, Eichmann sent one of his most trusted and experienced men, Alois Brunner, to Bratislava (Pressburg). Brunner arrived before the Slovaks had officially agreed to the resumption of the deportations, though Jews were already being rounded up throughout the country and sent to Sered, which had been declared a concentration camp and was controlled by especially ruthless SS who maltreated the inmates with particular cruelty. A delegation from the Jewish Council that visited the camp to ascertain whether it would be possible to convert it back into a labor camp found the Jews there covered with bruises and lacerations from beatings. The first victims had been shot for failing to bear up during the "games" organized by the guards.[70] On September 28 Brunner conducted a manhunt for Jews in Bratislava and arrested the heads of the Jewish Council. The next day eighteen hundred people were sent to Sered, where they witnessed the first transport being dispatched to Auschwitz. Peering through a bathroom window to see what was happening outside, the chairman of the council, Oscar Neumann (pseudonym Dr. Alt) spotted his elderly mother among the people moving out.[71]

Initially, the trains were dispatched at a rather brisk pace, but when the revolt of the Sonderkommando broke out in Auschwitz on October 7, operations there became less regular and slowly came to a halt. It has been assumed that Himmler gave the order to stop the killing by gas at the end of October or the beginning of November. From that time onward, there no longer were reports of mass murder being practiced in Auschwitz. The gas chambers continued to operate on a limited scale until the end of the month, but then Himmler ordered the destruction of the crematoria, and their systematic demolition began on November 25.[72] The deportation of the camp's prisoners westward to labor and concentration camps in the Reich steadily picked up pace; the Jews from Slovakia were also sent there. Gisi Fleischmann was placed on one of the last transports from Slovakia to Auschwitz with a "special order" that she be sent to the gas chamber promptly upon arrival.

In the meanwhile, Oscar Neumann and his colleagues succeeded in having labor resumed in Sered, primarily in the workshops of the textile industry. Evidently Brunner realized that there was benefit to be derived from allowing the Jews to work, and they were allowed to use the facilities and materials to equip the deportees—at least to some extent—with clothing and other needs. As in the past, an ambitious aid program was conducted under the cover of the camp's official activities. The courage of the communal leaders and the enormous experience they had gained over years of clandestine activity now stood them in good stead. They were helped by the funds they had managed to smuggle into the camp, the ties they had had the foresight to establish with the outside world, and the intelligence network that had organized within Sered itself. They were even able to dispose of traitors and informers.[73]

Toward the end of the year, women and children began to be transferred from Sered to Theresienstadt; at the end of March 1945, all the camp's remaining inmates and equipment were sent there too. As they were leaving Sered, these last deportees could already hear the cannons of the approaching Russian forces. Altogether, 13,500 people were deported between the end of September 1944 and the end of March 1945, 1,477 (or 10.7 percent) of them to Theresienstadt. Of the 90,000 Jews who had been living in "independent" Slovakia, close to 70,000 were lost and 4,000 to 5,000 went into hiding within the country. If we add to these figures the Slovak Jews deported from the territory that had been annexed by Hungary, the total number of victims comes to 110,000 out of the Jewish population of 136,737 that had been living within the bounds of the Czechoslovak Republic in 1930.[74]

The Last Days of Theresienstadt

On arriving in Theresienstadt at the beginning of April 1945, Oscar Neumann found the camp in a state of disintegration. We have seen that the ghetto was marked by a certain degree of stability from January through the autumn of 1943. The first transport bound for Auschwitz left on September 6, and by the end of that year 10,000 people had been deported in two large transports.[75] The deportees on these transports did not undergo a selection in Auschwitz but instead were placed in the family camp. (This was part of the preparations made in anticipation of the visit of the Danish delegation and the International Red Cross that was scheduled for the spring of 1944; see chap. 16.) In connection with the beautifying restoration of the "model ghetto," it was deemed necessary to thin out its population—then living in highly crowded conditions—so that the deportations were resumed in May 1944. This new group of deportees was also housed in the family camp, which had in the meantime been emptied of its initial inhabitants.[76] However, most of the deportees were transferred from Theresienstadt to Auschwitz for gassing in the autumn of 1944, just before the crematoria were put out of action.

In the course of 1944 and early 1945, another 14,147 people were added to the population in Theresienstadt. They included Jews from Holland, Germany, the Protectorate, Austria, and Slovakia, which brought the total number of deportees to Theresienstadt from 1942 to 1945 to almost 139,000.[77]

From November 1942 to April 1945, close to 87,000 people were deported from Theresienstadt to Auschwitz: 3,000 survived and 33,419 others died in Theresienstadt itself, bringing the total number of victims to over 117,000. When the camp was liberated in May, there were 17,320 people found in Theresienstadt; 1,200 inmates had been sent to Switzerland in a special convoy in February 1945 and 425 Jews from Denmark were returned to Scandinavia in April 1945 (see chap. 21). Thus, of the 139,000 people deported to the "model ghetto," some 22,000 survived—slightly less than 16 percent.[78]

On resumption of the deportations at the end of 1943, certain changes were effected in the camp's format. It was then that Jacob Edelstein was dismissed from the camp leadership. It may be assumed that his forceful personality, great influence on the young people in the camp, and courageous stand in dealing with the Germans seemed dangerous to them. Edelstein was arrested on November 10 on charges of "assisting escape," and in December he was placed on a transport to Auschwitz. His wife, young son, and mother-in-law were deported with him; all three were placed in the family camp in Birkenau, whereas Edelstein was held under arrest in the bunker of the political prisoners in Block 11. On June 20, 1944, SS men informed him that a death sentence had been passed and that he was to accompany them since it would be carried out forthwith. He and the other members of his family were taken to the execution site by car and shot there—first the family, then Edelstein.

Ten months before Edelstein's arrest, in January 1943, Paul Epstein—a leader of the Reichsvereinigung der Juden in Deutschland who had been one of that union's chief liaisons with Eichmann since the late 1930s—had been sent to Theresienstadt on a transport from Germany. On arrival, Epstein was appointed Älteste, Edelstein was demoted to the position of his deputy, and Dr. Benjamin Murmelstein, a rabbi from Vienna, was appointed Epstein's second deputy. Long accustomed to dealing with the Nazis, Epstein tried to create a workable relationship with them; in Theresienstadt he was accused of being rather too solicitous in his dealings with them. On December 13, 1944, he was arrested; rather than being sent to Auschwitz, he was held in the Little Fortress—the concentration camp attached to the ghetto—from which he never returned. Murmclstcin was appointed Älteste and continued to hold this position until the camp's liberation. The inmates of Theresienstadt were generally appreciative, even admiring, of Edelstein; they tended to be critical of Epstein and treated Murmelstein with suspicion. Even Oscar Neumann's impression of Murmelstein, immediately on arrival in Theresienstadt, was negative.[79]

Added to the internal disintegration of the ghetto was the terrifying shock its inhabitants experienced when 15,000 to 20,000 people were brought to Theresienstadt on death marches. Standing by the barbed wire fence, the inmates saw the head of the column approaching them. Here are some of the impressions that Oscar Neumann describes:

> And then suddenly the creeping terror, that awful, mute column, the ghosts of living skeletons, came closer. They are dragging their feet after having marched hundreds of kilometers without food and water . . . tired to death, stumbling, holding one another up as they walked and suddenly collapsing silently—they are no longer human. . . .
>
> Fear settles over the entire ghetto, for in their animal wildness, mad with starvation, they are dangerous. It is impossible to mete food out to them in the usual way; they immediately attack each other, choking and beating one another for every scrap.

Many of the marchers were beyond the point where they could digest food, and they died while eating. Even though they were locked away at night so that they would not come into contact with the inhabitants of the ghetto, a typhus epidemic then broke out. Despite everything, many of the people who had been marched to Theresienstadt began to recover within a short time.[80]

Theresienstadt was liberated by Soviet troops on May 7, 1945, and was turned over to the care and supervision of the Red Cross.

The Death Marches and Evacuation of the Camps Inside the Reich

The death marches were a corollary of the German retreat in both the West and the East, though primarily in the latter. The swift advance of the Allied armies forced the Germans to move the industries they had founded in the occupied countries into the Reich and to dismantle the labor camps that had supplied a large proportion of the workers. This evacuation had begun in the summer of 1944. As Auschwitz was the largest center of all, starting in July 1944 men and women prisoners, in large and small groups, were transferred out of it to camps in the Reich. At first these were mainly the Polish inmates—by moving them out the Germans hoped to avert the possibility of a revolt in the camp—but this same process also resulted in the dispersion of those Hungarian Jews who had been assigned to labor camps rather than to gas chambers. Often these laborers were moved from one camp to the next according to the various stages of the German retreat, so that groups of Hungarian Jews reached camps in the Baltic countries first and then were sent westward from there.

The year 1944 was marked by a rising demand for labor in the Reich. In a meeting with Hitler on January 4, 1944, at which Sauckel, Speer, Himmler, and Field Marshal Wilhelm Keitel were present, a quota was set that required the Germans to mobilize 4,050,000 laborers for the war effort. However, Sauckel conscripted only 1,024,000 foreign civilian laborers, all told, to which number he added 186,000 POWs, for a total of 1,210,000 new workers. According to the assessment of Speer's ministry, at the end of 1944 there were over 8 million foreign civilian laborers and POWs in Germany, making every fifth worker a foreigner. It is estimated that over the entire period of the war, no fewer than 12 million foreign workers were employed within the Reich. While the POWs and civilian workers from the occupied countries and satellite states were employed in both agriculture and industry, the Jews and other inmates of concentration camps were apparently used in industry alone, with hundreds of satellite camps being built and attached to the jurisdiction of the main concentration camps for that purpose.

In light of the severe shortage of manpower, it is difficult to understand the rationale behind the acceleration of the extermination process in the summer and autumn of 1944. This clash of interests between the two dominant trends within the Nazi leadership reached the height of absurdity at that point, and as the historian Edward L. Homze noted, the history of the foreign labor program exemplified the weakness of the Nazi brand of totalitarianism.[81] It was especially during the disintegration of the Third Reich that the disarray within the polyhierarchy was most pronounced and essentially culminated in anarchy on a mass scale. Cast into this chaos and maelstrom were the columns of the surviving Jews being marched by the SS from the areas about to fall to the Russians to areas that would fall in a matter of weeks, sometimes days, to the American and British forces.

The Evacuation of Auschwitz

The cluster of camps known as Auschwitz underwent a number of changes in structure and management from 1942 to 1944. In the autumn of 1943, the central headquarters was divided into three distinct divisions—Auschwitz I, II, and III—and Auschwitz I, which now included Birkenau, was declared a concentration camp. In November 1943 Rudolf Höss was promoted to supervisor of the network of concentration camps and was replaced in Auschwitz by Arthur Liebehenschel. However, Höss was brought back to Auschwitz in May 1944 when the Germans were preparing to exterminate Hungarian Jewry. He set the pace of the extermination process at an unprecedented level, using all five crematoria—including No. 1, which had been in use before the four main crematoria, equipped with gas chambers, had been built in the first half of 1943. The capacity of each of the gas chambers in the cellars of Crematoria No. 2 and No. 3 was 3,000 people per day, but the cremation ovens were unable to process more than 1,400 corpses, which explains why it was necessary to burn corpses in outside pits as well. The furnaces of Crematoria No. 4 and No. 5 were capable of handling only 770 corpses per day (the capacity of the attached gas chambers is unknown). Altogether there was a total of forty-six cremation ovens. The maximum number of people who could be gassed in a twenty-four-hour period is estimated differently in sources, but it was apparently at least 8,000.[82]

The Sonderkommando working in these crematoria initially numbered four hundred men, but this number was augmented during the Hungarian period to about one thousand. Crematorium 4 was destroyed in the revolt of the Sonder-kommando on October 7, 1944 (see chap. 17). Crematoria 2 and 3, also damaged in the rebellion, were subsequently dismantled on orders from Himmler. They were not finally demolished until January 20, 1945, whereas Crematorium 5 was blown up on January 26—the day before the Russians reached the camp. The number of people gassed to death in Auschwitz could not be documented until now: estimates range from two million to almost twice that figure.[83]

As far back as July 1944, secret orders had been issued to begin liquidating the prisons in the Generalgouvernement. The directive to evacuate the concentration and extermination camps came at a later date, and Himmler did not, in fact, issue a general liquidation order until January 1945.[84] The man who was to see to the liquidation of Auschwitz was the HSSPF in Silesia, Ernst H. Schmauser, whose mandate included all the fields of action that had been organized in Auschwitz. He tried, for example, to save the huge amount of booty that had been collected and stored in the "Canada" warehouses. Despite the transport difficulties, hundreds of thousands of articles of men's, women's, and children's clothing were, indeed, transferred to the Reich in December 1944 and early January 1945. Even so, the Germans failed to empty out all the storehouses. To prevent them from falling into the hands of the Russians intact, Schmauser had them put to the torch, but he only managed to burn twenty-nine of the thirty-five structures. Hundreds of thousands of articles were found in the six remaining buildings and the six full railroad cars that the Germans had not had time to dispatch.

No less urgent for the SS was the destruction of the documents attesting to the tasks that Auschwitz had fulfilled and the actions that had been performed there. They tried to burn them. Actually, they had started burning these papers as far back as July 1944 after the liberation of Majdanek, where many such documents fell into Russian hands. Now, with the end approaching, the SS were possessed by panic. During its final days, Auschwitz looked like one huge bonfire; throughout the camp's passages between the huts files and documents were set ablaze, and the wind spread the crackling and smoldering debris around the camp. Consigned to the flames were all the files in the infirmary and the secretariat as well as the card file of Soviet POWs. Still, in the general confusion caused by the frantic haste, with the burning being interrupted from time to time by air raids, members of the camp underground managed to salvage important documents and conceal them in various caches. The burning of documents did not stop until the night before January 18 as the Russians neared the camp.[85]

As they began demolishing the crematoria, the Germans made a point of transferring some of their equipment to the Gross-Rosen concentration camp in Lower Silesia. Their plan was to make Gross-Rosen the first stop for the prisoners evacuated from Auschwitz; only if they could not be absorbed there would it be necessary to send them on to the Reich. Gas chambers had earlier been set up in Gross-Rosen, so that the camp was apparently considered a suitable place to dispose of at least some of the prisoners who had yet to be exterminated. During the summer and autumn of 1944, the Germans had operated on two planes in Auschwitz: gassing the prisoners or evacuating them westward. Extermination was prescribed first and foremost for those who could bear witnesses to the Nazis' crimes. Other than the members of the Sonderkommando, in addition to the Russian POWs, these were primarily the clerks among the inmates who kept the records. During the final months, however, the stress was placed on the evacuation effort, which began on August 11 and continued until December 25. After that date it was no longer possible to use the railway because all available trains were transporting the retreating army. Thus, the Germans began to march the prisoners on foot, except on the occasions when they did manage to commandeer trains found parked in one station or another. Since the main arteries in the area were similarly jammed with army units and their vehicles, the columns of prisoners had to be directed over side roads. More than once the officers in charge lost their way and had no idea where to lead their charges.

In the midst of all this turmoil, it proved impossible to report on the progress of the evacuation program, so that Oswald Pohl—who was responsible for the overall network of concentration camps—sent Höss to check on the situation in Auschwitz. By that point, however, Höss was no longer able to reach the camp. He met with the marching columns on the way:

> On all the roads and tracks in Upper Silesia, west of the Oder, I now found columns of prisoners struggling through the deep snow. They had no food. Most of the non-commissioned officers in charge of these columns of corpses had no idea where they were supposed to be going. They only knew that their final destination was Gross-Rosen. But how to get there was a mystery. On their own authority, they requisitioned food from the villages through which they passed, rested a few hours, and then trudged on again. There was no question of spending the night in barns or schools, since these were all crammed with refugees. The route taken by these miserable columns was easy to follow since every few hundred yards lay the bodies of prisoners who had collapsed or been shot.[86]

According to the statement of the underground in Auschwitz, on August 21, 1944, there had been a total of 105,168 people in all the sectors of the camp. By the middle of October, there were still close to 95,000 inmates, but in the interim over 10,000 additional prisoners had been brought in, most of them after the Polish uprising in Warsaw. During this period transports of 2,000 to 3,000 prisoners each were dispatched to the Buchenwald, Sachsenhausen, and Flossenbürg camps in Germany. At the final prisoner count, on January 17, 1945, 66,020 inmates were accounted for in Auschwitz, so that since mid-October their number had decreased by close to 28,000 people. The remaining prisoners were evacuated with incredible speed on the day and night of January 18, but 7,600 people too sick and weak and thus incapable of embarking upon a journey by foot remained in the central concentration camp. A representative of the Polish Red Cross who reached Auschwitz on February 6, 1945, reported finding 3,800 civilians from twenty-two countries in the sick bay; 95 percent of them were Jews.[87]

Mauthausen

The Mauthausen concentration and extermination camp (near the Austrian city of Linz) is known to have been one of the more brutal of the camps that existed within the Reich proper. Its commandant, Franz Ziereis, had served in the army until 1936 and then as a training officer in the Waffen SS. Unlike many other commanders of concentration camps who were transferred from one camp to another, Ziereis remained in Mauthausen from the autumn of 1939 until the camp's liberation in May 1945. Referred to by the inmates as Babyface, he instituted and conducted a regime of terror and torture of the most harrowing kind. Mauthausen was established in the autumn of 1938 by special order of Himmler, who wanted to exploit the local granite quarry for Hitler's construction enterprises. Over the years, forty-nine satellite camps opened in *Ostmark* (Austria) and were attached to the administration of Mauthausen, the two largest and most notorious being Gusen and Ebensee.[88]

Few Jews were to be found in Mauthausen prior to 1941; then hundreds of Dutch Jews were sent there (see chap. 14). The methods of murder practiced in this camp varied from starvation, beatings, and exposure to the cold to sheer hard labor in the quarry, especially when it took the form of pushing a cart of stones from the quarry up the mountainside to the camp—if a prisoner lost his footing, he was often crushed by the sliding wagon. The Dutch prisoners, moreover, were forced to carry stones weighing 110 pounds or more up the 168 steps leading from the quarry to the camp. Over and above these punishing labors, prisoners were sent to their deaths by being forced to run into the camp's electrified fence or were chased outside the camp perimeter so that it could be noted in the ledger that they had been "shot while trying to escape." Jews were even cast hurtling down the mountain cliff into the quarry—this particularly gruesome form of murder was stopped because it disrupted the work. Sometimes prisoners were subjected to a "bath" or a "shower," meaning that they were sprayed with a strong jet of cold water until they expired. Shootings (in the back of the neck) and hangings were quite common forms of execution, as were injections directly into the heart. Gas was first used in 1941, initially in gas vans. Later on scores of prisoners were sent to the nearby Schloss Hartheim, which had earlier been a sanitarium for invalids and the chronically ill. But when "euthanasia" was practiced, it had been turned into an institution for extermination by gassing and was also used for this purpose once gassing was extended to the concentration camps in 1941. At first the Germans put out the story that the prisoners taken to Schloss Hartheim had been transferred to Dachau and that the sick had been sent to a "recuperation camp." However, in 1942 a gas chamber was installed in Mauthausen proper. According to testimonies, it was operated three times a week, and sometimes an entire transport was put to death immediately on arrival. From May 1940 onward all the corpses were burned in the crematorium.[89]

At the beginning of February 1941, as preparations were being made to launch Operation Barbarossa, Himmler established a scale of stringency for the concentration camps based on the categorization of prisoners. Mauthausen, together with its satellite camps, was classified as No. 3, the most severe, and most people sent there were essentially doomed to extermination.[90] The prisoners came from all over Europe and included refugees from republican Spain who had been deported from southern France by the Vichy government—most of whom perished in the camp; Italians; members of all the Balkan peoples, the last of these being tens of thousands of Hungarian Jews; Czechs, including (before the establishment of Theresienstadt) many Jews; Poles, naturally including Jews; thousands of Russian POWs; soldiers and citizens of all the other countries embroiled in the war; citizens of the neutral states—even some from overseas; and a considerable population of German political prisoners and common criminals. The number of deaths that occurred in Mauthausen in 1941 is assessed at 8,114, with the Gusen camp reporting 5,782 of them; some 1,600 of these victims were Jews. From the beginning of 1940 to the end of 1943, there were 2,760 Jews registered in the camp, including close to 900 from Holland, all of whom were quickly eliminated.[91]

At the beginning of October 1942, Himmler issued an order that all the Jews imprisoned in concentration camps within Germany be sent to Auschwitz. At that time 33 people were transferred out of Mauthausen, and in August 1943 they were joined by another 5. A year later, in August 1944, when the Germans had already begun sending Jews from Auschwitz to work in Germany—including Mauthausen—two transports were dispatched from Mauthausen to Auschwitz with more than 850 Jews, including children and teenagers. Half these prisoners died along the way, and only 93 of the survivors were assigned to work in the camp.[92] There were 65,545 prisoners registered in Mauthausen in 1944, of which 13,826 were Jews; of the 14,766 people who died in the camp that year, 3,437, or 23.3 percent, were Jews.[93]

During the summer and autumn of 1944, a tent camp was put up as an extension of Mauthausen, and in December it was filled mainly with Hungarian Jews.[94] They belonged to the group that had been deported from Budapest to the Austrian border in November, including people who had been sent to work in Austria back during the summer and even a company from a labor battalion that had been working in Russia. All of these people had been brought to Mauthausen either by train or on foot and were in grave physical condition; in fact, only a few of those who came on foot made it to Mauthausen. The men, women, and children living in the tent camp were subjected to the harshest conditions, particularly extreme malnutrition. Those who survived were later sent to a satellite camp called Gunskirchen for extermination. The flow of Jewish prisoners from Hungary mounted substantially in March/April 1945 at the height of the evacuation effort. At that same time, the main camp and its satellites were filling up with masses of evacuees coming from all corners of the Nazi empire in the same state of prostration. The number of people found dead when the trains arrived reached into the hundreds.

Ziereis tried to send the new arrivals on to one of the other camps or, alternatively, to gas them. Mauthausen was already in such a state of chaos that few of the new arrivals—the prisoners sent on or the dead—were being recorded, making it virtually impossible to estimate their number with any degree of accuracy. Unquestionably, the number of Hungarian Jews reached into the thousands, but only some of them were registered. On March 21, 1945, there were over 85,000 registered prisoners in the complex of camps known as Mauthausen, but it must be assumed that the number who reached the main camp and were sent onward, those who died on arrival at or within the camp, or those who died en route from the main camp to one of the satellites was higher.[95] The crematoria in Mauthausen worked day and night up to almost the last. The extermination facilities in Schloss Hartheim, however, were dismantled in the latter half of December 1944, and in January the castle reverted to its original appearance.[96]

According to the latest calculations, close to 200,000 people passed through the Mauthausen complex and about 120,000 of them met their death there—the highest percentage of victims among all the concentration camps in the Reich. Nearly one-third of these victims—over 38,000 people—were Jews.[97] During the camp's last days, a representative of the Red Cross appeared in Mauthausen and managed to free a few dozen prisoners. Reaching the camp on May 5, the American forces found masses of sick and dying people lying helpless alongside the dead. Ziereis remained in the camp almost until the end. Only at the last moment did he try to flee and hide but was found a few days later. He was wounded while trying to escape and subsequently died in the hospital, but his captors still managed to take testimony from him.[98]

Stutthof

Far from Mauthausen near the northern port of Danzig (Gdańsk) was the Stutthof concentration camp—another objective for the prisoners evacuated from Auschwitz as well as for many of the Jewish prisoners the Germans had sent marching westward out of the Baltic countries. Established on September 2, 1939, Stutthof had been inhabited mainly by non-Jewish prisoners from Poland and the immediately surrounding area until a few hundred Jews from Bialystok and Warsaw were sent there—particularly in the autumn of 1943 after the liquidation of the Bialystok ghetto and the uprising there. At the beginning of 1944, those Jews who were still alive were transferred to Auschwitz. At that time the camp was enlarged and seventy-four satellite camps were attached to it. From then on Stutthof also served as an extermination camp with its own crematoria; as in Mauthausen Jews were killed by injection or by being shot in the back of the neck. From the autumn of 1942 until the liquidation of the camp in January 1945 its commandant was Paul W. Hoppe, one of the Dachau trainees.

In December 1941 Josef Katz, a fifteen-year-old German Jew from the city of Lübeck, was deported with his mother to Riga and then transferred on to Salaspils, the labor camp outside the city that was one of the worst of its kind. Katz acquired skills in a number of fields and as a skilled laborer was sent from place to place until finally reaching Kaiserwald. He was evidently a resourceful young man and made friends everywhere; although they helped one another, most of his comrades simply did not share his luck, which held out until the last days of German rule in Riga.

Katz's next stop after the evacuation of Kaiserwald was Danzig, which the prisoners reached after a three-day journey in the hold of a ship on a stormy sea. They received food only once—a mere 10 ounces of bread per person—and when they were brought water, the SS man amused himself by throwing it in the faces of the prisoners who climbed up to the hatch to take it. Once, the hatch opened and above on the deck a Jew was standing wrapped in a prayer shawl reciting the prayer for Rosh Hashanah (the Jewish New Year). Everyone rose, all repeating after him in a chorus, and the familiar melodies filled the air, "Suddenly we were all one big family. It is a miracle how a destiny and common faith can forge human beings into one unit. 'To a Happy New Year. . . . This will be the year of our liberation.' These words are heard everywhere. A festive mood has taken hold."

From Danzig the prisoners were transferred to Stutthof on open cargo barges used for hauling sand and stones on the Vistula River—500 men, women, and children were crammed onto these barges and could only rest by lying one on top of another. The distance between Danzig and Stutthof is 14 miles, but it took three days and three nights of traveling this way in the freezing cold, over the sea, the river, and the canals to reach their destination. "Each one of us was longing for the dubious paradise of Stutthof. Even a concentration camp seemed like a haven after a trip like that."[99] They soon learned what "paradise" really held in store.

Stutthof then contained prisoners from almost all the countries of occupied Europe, including Norwegians and Danes, most of them Communists who had been joined by 200 Norwegian policemen who had refused to collaborate with the Nazis. Regarded as Aryans, the Scandinavians were kept separately in the German camp *(Germanenlager)*. At the end of the summer of 1944, however, it was mostly Jews who flowed into the camp, the majority of them Hungarian women who had been brought from Auschwitz. Up to the onset of its liquidation, from January 25 to 27, 1945, there were 110,000 prisoners registered in Stutthof—70 percent of them Jews, about 20 percent Russians, and the remaining 10 percent divided among all the other people of Europe, including Germans and Gypsies. The prisoners worked in the satellite camps and in the vicinity of Stutthof. Many of these inmates, and above all thousands of Jewish women, were killed in Stutthof; starvation and disease also had a part in the reduction of the camp's population.

In January 1945 as the Red Army was drawing near, the Germans decided to evacuate 33,000 women and 18,000 men of the camp's remaining population; 30,000 of the women were Jewish, but this was true of only 3,000 of the men. On January 25 the death march began in the midst of a snowstorm and bitter cold.[100] Most of the prisoners were sent trudging westward escorted by SS men with dogs. Some of the SS men on motorcycles shot the stragglers while driving along; many of the marchers simply froze to death. Especially cruel was the fate of those who had been sent marching eastward in the direction of Königsberg (Kaliningrad, USSR), for at night the Nazis pushed them into a hole made in the ice covering a small inlet of the Baltic Sea. Even though the Nazis shot anyone who tried to climb back on dry land or simply threw them back into the icy water, a few of these prisoners managed to escape. There are no figures on the number of killed or of survivors.

After the conquest of Danzig, the Germans continued to hold out in an enclave on the Hel Peninsula at the northwestern tip of the Gulf of Danzig. Still open, the Stutthof camp contained—in addition to the ailing women, who were unable to set out on the march in January—Norwegians, members of Jehovah's Witnesses, and a smattering of other prisoners. In fact, the camp continued to exist until the latter half of April. Then the remaining inmates were evacuated westward by sea just as it was about to be conquered by the Russians. Those considered healthy were placed on two double-decker barges, each tied to a lead boat; the sick, accompanied by the doctors and nurses, were placed on a third barge that served as a quarantine ship. When this convoy reached Lübeck Bay, it was awaited—along with prisoners brought from the Neuengamme camp outside of Hamburg—by a unique fate of doom and rescue. Of the ten thousand assembled prisoners the Germans intended to kill, either on land or in the sea, some seven thousand perished during the last days of April 1945 and over three thousand were saved, including seven hundred inmates from Stutthof. Much of the credit for the rescue of the Stutthof prisoners goes to their Norwegian fellow prisoners.[101]

Buchenwald

In the very heart of Germany, alongside Goethe's city of Weimar, Buchenwald, one of the main and most brutal of the concentration camps in the Reich, was established in the summer of 1937.[102] Initially, it was not a very large camp, and it housed mainly political prisoners. But in 1938 it prepared to take in a massive number of Jews, the first of them German Jews sent as early as June of that year in the operation against the so-called asocial characters who were subsequently joined by 2,400 Austrian Jews (see chap. 4). Additional barracks built that summer were filled after Kristallnacht by over 10,000 Jews. By August 1939 there were 5,382 prisoners still being held in the camp; after the outbreak of the war 2,000 to 2,500 Polish and Austrian Jews were brought to Buchenwald and placed in a separate tent camp enclosed by barbed wire that was referred to as the little camp. Held under conditions of severe overcrowding and poor sanitation, these prison-

Table 9. The Condition of the Jews in Buchenwald, 1941–1942

Prisoners	In Camp		Died		Percentage	
	1941	1942	1941	1942	1941	1942
German	4,704	5,681	167	283	3.6	5.0
Polish	2,368	2,417	372	386	15.7	16.0
Jewish	2,158	1,575	542	609	21.5	38.7
Total	9,230	9,673	1,081	1,278	11.7	13.2

Source: Falk Pingel, *Häftlinge unter SS-Herrschaft: Widerstand, Selbstbehauptung und Vernichtung im Konzentrationslager* (Hamburg, 1978), pp. 99–100.

ers died by the masses. In addition to 941 Jews in the little camp, 1,257 of the 12,000 or so inmates held in the general camp in October 1939 were Jews.[103] In 1942 a few hundred Jews and Gypsies were transferred from Buchenwald to Auschwitz on Himmler's orders, whereas other Jews were sent to Dachau and Mauthausen.

The movement of prisoners into and out of the camp picked up considerably in 1943; at the same time, the death rate decreased among all the categories of prisoners. In October 1944 more than 800 Hungarian Jews were sent to Auschwitz to be gassed. All told, from the beginning of 1937 to March 31, 1945, there were 238,989 people who entered Buchenwald, including prisoners subsequently assigned to satellite camps.[104] Buchenwald was one of the main centers where the concentration camp prisoners were exploited for the benefit of German industry—a trend that, as we have seen, greatly intensified in 1943 and 1944. Many of the deportees who came to Buchenwald remained in the camp for only a few days before being sent on to satellite camps scattered throughout Germany, which at their height were 134 in number. Most of the prisoners were employed in Speer's armament industry. The administration of Buchenwald also organized prisoners from other camps to be sent to new places of work without passing through Buchenwald proper. This hiring out of hundreds of thousands of workers brought Buchenwald a profit of millions of Reichsmarks.[105]

In the camps known as Dora and the S III (also in central Germany, in the hilly sectors of the Thüringen region), subterranean factories were built for the manufacture of the secret V-1 and V-2 missiles (the letter *V* standing for the word *Vergeltung,* meaning "reprisal action"). These factories were established in caverns far below ground, and the laborers worked and slept in them. They were devoid of even the most elementary sanitary facilities such as water for washing and often the prisoners could not even change their underwear for months at a time. Hangings were held almost daily for imaginary acts of sabotage or attempted escapes, and the SS men working in these plants were extraordinarily sadistic and bloodthirsty even by concentration camp standards. The planning and general direction of the work were handled by scientists, headed by the renowned physicist Wernher von Braun, who wore an SS uniform in those days. This is what one of the former prisoners stated in his testimony about him, "Every day countless [corpses of] prisoners who had been tortured to death lay beside the infirmary barracks. . . . From a distance these human remains looked like one big pile, and he, Professor von Braun, passed so close by that he almost touched the corpses. Didn't that sight make any impression on him? Even the prisoners who happened upon this corner were seized by horror."[106]

The evacuation of the camps in the East brought a massive infusion of prisoners into Buchenwald from Auschwitz, the industrial center alongside Częstochowa, Gross-Rosen, and Stutthof. Altogether some 24,500 people, at least half of them Jews, came from these areas between the end of December 1944 and March 1945. On April 6 there were still 47,000 prisoners in Buchenwald, but by April 11 over 28,000 of them had been evacuated to camps in southern Germany, with thousands dying on the way. Buchenwald was liberated on that day, and the prisoners' clandestine organization, coming up from underground, seized control of the camp. On April 13, however, an American officer assumed command of Buchenwald.

Buchenwald's first commandant, Karl Koch, later became infamous as the commander of Majdanek. He was succeeded by Hermann Pister, who remained in command of the camp until the end. As in so many other camps, dogs specially trained to attack people in the striped uniforms of the prisoners were used in Buchenwald, particularly against Gypsies who refused to submit to sterilization. These people were shut up in their barracks with hands tied; the dogs were unleashed and literally tore them to pieces. The uproar lasted for hours and the blood-chilling shrieks could be heard throughout the night until the dogs tired of mangling their prey. It is not known how many of the Gypsies met their death.[107] In Buchenwald people were not killed in gassing installations, but they were sent, fully clothed, into gas-filled chambers—supposedly for disinfectant purposes— and were left there for hours, most of them dying in the aftermath. In addition, as in most of the camps in Germany, medical experiments were conducted in the camp.[108]

It is difficult to estimate the death toll to be ascribed to Buchenwald because its inmates were transferred to other camps to be exterminated, some of them dying along the way. One group was sent to Bergen-Belsen but had to turn back to Buchenwald en route owing to the advance of the British army. Close to 10,000 people came to Buchenwald during the camp's final days and were apparently sent on, though the close to 3,000 prisoners incapable of walking any further were killed either in the camp or along the way after being sent out again.[109] We should, therefore, treat the total number of victims with a measure of reservation and assume that the figures were actually far higher than those eventually recorded.

1937–1945

Died in Buchenwald or the satellite camps (except for women)	33,462
Executed: Russian POWs hanged	8,483
Others	1,100
Evacuees in April 1945 who collapsed and were shot (estimate)	13,500
Total	56,545

To these figures we must add the prisoners who were transferred from Buchen-wald to other camps, primarily for extermination.

1941	To "euthanasia" camps	472
1942	Jews to Dachau, Mauthausen (Dutch), and Auschwitz (with Gypsies), and Jews who died in Dora (1943–1944)	4,055
1943	Adults and children to Auschwitz	1,380
1944	Jews to Auschwitz, adults and children to Bergen-Belsen	7,110
Total		13,017

Thus the verifiable number of victims comes to close to 70,000—about 30 percent of those who were imprisoned in or passed through Buchenwald.[110]

Dachau

At 4:00 P.M. on April 29, 1945, in his final demonstrative act, Hitler signed his last will and testament, reiterating his faith in the racial laws and his abysmal hatred of Jewry.[111] At that very same hour, units of the American army were liberating the 32,335 prisoners left in Dachau, the Nazis' first concentration camp and the model for the rest of the Kingdom of Death.[112] Sometimes seemingly random coincidences suggest some deeper significance. Here, at the very moment when Hitler was attempting to immortalize his "merciless fight" against Jewry, this paradigm of the Nazi hell was being shattered.

The Dachau concentration camp existed for twelve consecutive years (except for a short interval in the winter of 1939/1940 when it was used for training SS men and its 5,000 prisoners were temporarily divided among Buchenwald, Mauthausen, and Flossenbürg, later to be returned to Dachau). Altogether, over 200,000 people passed through the camp, 80 percent of them between 1940 and 1945.[113]

From May 1940 through the end of April 1945, some 67,000 Dachau prisoners were sent to other camps in Germany and to Auschwitz. Registered among the prisoners in April 1945 were thirty-seven groups of foreign citizens—including Turks, Spaniards, Arabs, Armenians, and even a Chinese prisoner—as well as a group of stateless persons. Estimates have it that 32,000 people died in Dachau, but it is assumed that this figure is too low, especially as it does not take into account the executions. About 50 percent of the camp's victims died in 1945. An epidemic of typhus spread through the camp in the winter of 1944/1945, but this was not the first of its kind; typhoid and typhus had broken out in Dachau back in 1942. At that time, the severely ill were disposed of by sending them to the gas chambers in Schloss Hartheim; thirty-two such transports were dispatched that year.[114]

It is generally posited that the gas chambers found alongside the crematoria in Dachau were never used, and certainly systematic mass extermination was not practiced there as in the euthanasia facilities or the main camps in Poland. But it is possible that the use of gas was practiced by Dr. Sigmund Rascher, who directed the infamous experiments on human beings in Dachau.[115] The use of gas was, therefore, standard in a number of camps within the Reich proper, as we have seen in Gross-Rosen and Mauthausen. Another camp in which gas was used in connection with experiments on human beings was Natzweiler-Struthof in Alsace. Its commandant, Josef Kramer, was another graduate of training in Dachau who later became the commandant of Auschwitz–Birkenau and ultimately commanded Bergen-Belsen. Following the instructions of August Hirt, a professor of anatomy at the German University of Strassburg (Strasbourg), Kramer gassed to death eighty prisoners sent to Natzweiler-Struthof from Auschwitz specifically for that purpose, through Eichmann's intervention. The professor proposed to Himmler that the war in the East be exploited to ensure a steady supply of "the skulls of Jewish-Bolshevik commissars for scientific research." The gas chamber was built for such experiments. In answer to a question posed to him at the Nuremberg trials, Kramer stated, "I did these things without any feeling because, as I told you, I had received an order to kill these eighty prisoners in this manner. That, by the way, is how I was educated."[116] The "research" was carried out under the aegis of The Ancestral Heritage *(Ahnenerbe),* one of the SS institutions in which Himmler was particularly interested because its main purpose was the study of the Nordic race. Hirt also conducted other experiments in those gas chambers.[117]

In Dachau the experiments were conducted primarily under the supervision of Dr. Rascher, an odd and rather dubious character who was eventually executed by the Nazis. The best known of his experiments began in February 1942 at the request of the German air force, which was interested in clarifying three issues: the body's response under conditions of low air pressure; preserving body temperature in an environment lower than normal body levels; and the possibility of desalinating seawater. Through this research they hoped to find a means of saving pilots who were forced to bail out, especially over the sea.[118]

The first time Himmler witnessed an experiment being performed on human beings at Dachau, he evidently felt the need for backing from Hitler and raised this matter before the führer. As might have been expected, Hitler decided, "In principle, experiments on humans should be allowed when the matter at hand is the good of the state. . . . It is unreasonable that anyone in a concentration camp or prison should not be harmed at all by the war."[119]

These experiments were performed not only on POWs, a variety of non-Aryans, and, of course, Jews and Gypsies, but also on asocial Germans. There does not seem to be any precise information on the number of people involved, but we do know that the guinea pigs who survived these ordeals (whose number is likewise not known) usually remained invalids of some kind.

The fact is that most of the problems that the Germans addressed in their experiments occupy the attention of medicine and technology to this day. This is also true, for example, of guided missiles, which the Germans were the first to develop and use. But the Nazis' attitude toward these problems and their means of solving them was determined by an ideology that recognized the value of a human being and his right to life only in terms of the service he provided to the regime of the master race.

In Dachau, as in other concentration camps, Russian POWs were executed. The directive for their execution, issued in July 1941 by the head of the Gestapo, Heinrich Müller, was based on the "Commissar Order" that read, "The executions are not in public, they have to be carried out in the nearest concentration camp without arousing attention." It is estimated that the number of Russians killed in Dachau was approximately eight hundred. They were dispatched by the same tested method used by the Einsatzgruppen against the Jews: shooting the victims in the back of the neck before open pits, where these Russian officers had to kneel down after removing their clothes.[120] Many executions were effected by hanging. In addition to the men and women from the satellite camps transferred to Dachau to be executed, the Gestapo sent people from the Munich area who had been sentenced to death. The number of people so executed in Dachau is not known. Among those shot to death was an Italian-born Jew from the Yishuv in Palestine, Enzo Sireni, a pioneer who had promoted illegal immigration and was caught parachuting into Italy on behalf of British intelligence with the aim of contacting Jews in occupied Europe.[121]

Apparently out of some sense of superstition, all the last-minute evacuees were directed to Dachau, so that tens of thousands of people were crammed into the camp after having roamed by train or foot for days, sometimes weeks. Just as the Germans had begun to evacuate Buchenwald merely days before the arrival of the American army, so they waited until the last minute before dispatching the prisoners from Dachau. Death marches of close to 20,000 people left the Dachau complex between April 24 and 27 (some 15,000 people from Dachau itself). These prisoners wandered around in circles in Bavaria, at the foot of the Alps, until the Americans liberated them, group by group. Many, of course, were not fortunate enough to make it to that moment. Prisoners who had been left in Dachau organized an international committee that took over the administration of the camp after its liberation.[122]

Rescue from a Death March: A Personal Testimony

During these last months of Nazi rule, when tens of thousands of people were sent plodding over trackless wastes in the cold and rain for seemingly endless distances, only a small percentage of the marchers survived. Most of these prisoners had already passed through a succession of camps, suffering untold torment in each of them, and now, perhaps more than ever before, their survival depended on a combination of luck, resourcefulness, and a spirit of comradeship.

In their testimonies the survivors of the death marches often portray their salvation as a miracle. One of them was a middle-aged woman from the city of Ungvár in Carpathian Ruthenia (which prior to 1938 had been part of Czechoslovakia under the name of Užhgorod). Reska Weiss related her story in *Journey Through Hell*.[123] It began with the well-known process of ghettoization, in this case on the Passover holiday (April 21–24), followed by deportation to Auschwitz in May. During the five days of traveling to the unknown, the deportees suffered not only from a lack of food and water and from terrible overcrowding but also at various stations along the way the SS fired into the cars, killing and wounding people. After passing the selection, where she was, of course, separated from her husband, Reska Weiss apparently managed to adapt to camp life relatively quickly; in a second selection she was assigned to a transport to Riga. After passing through a series of camps in Latvia, she reached Stutthof.

In one of those Latvian camps, near Dvinsk (Daugavpils), in June 1944, she had been attached to a battalion ordered to cover over a pit—temporarily hidden by branches—with lime and squares of turf. When the job was completed, all the members of the battalion were shot by the SS, group by group, at the lip of a new pit. That night Reska and another woman, who were not only alive but had not been wounded, climbed out of the corpse-filled, branch-covered pit, and the next day they surreptitiously joined the new battalion that had come to cover this pit, eventually returning to the camp with these laborers. That same evening all the women prisoners were transferred to another camp.

Despite bouts of hunger, wounds, dysentery, and pneumonia, Reska Weiss managed to survive. At one point she was treated by a Jewish doctor, who, before discharging her from the infirmary, prevailed upon her to overcome her present apathy and fight for her life. She had kept the photographs of her two sons—last known to be in Budapest. Seeing them, the doctor said, "Don't you want to return to them? If you have the will to survive you'll go back to your home. We Jews have only one duty and that's to keep alive." From then on she fought tenaciously to survive. She, too, understood that there were only two possibilities: to capitulate, lose all sense of self-respect, sink into apathy, and lose all will to live or to overcome the initial shock, despair, and stupefaction and accept the situation for what it was and fight with an animal passion for daily needs, for a better place to lie down, for a crust of bread. Still, she wrote, "To this day I cannot understand how we bore it. But it seems there is no limit to human suffering or, perhaps, those who did survive were the eternal affirmation of a miracle. . . . A fierce strength possessed me, a desire to live and an inexplicable conviction that I was entitled to life."

Most of the time she was together with one of her sisters and a few other women relatives from her large family. Finally, all the women still capable of walking were evacuated by a death march not toward Germany (which evidently could no longer be reached) but back to an area in Poland still controlled by the Germans. The march lasted twelve days, during which time the women trudged through deep snow in temperatures of -20 degrees Fahrenheit in worn clothes and almost without food. The SS would shoot not only those who dropped from exhaustion but also anyone who fell to the back of the column as well as people resting during the breaks or in the temporary quarters where they spent the night. Reska Weiss continues:

> Had weeks or months elapsed since we started on this death march? Neither; just a few days. But we could measure time only by the number of our dead. The living were constantly dwindling, and the racing row, running at whatever speed it could summon up, had already become pathetically short. . . . We were really no longer human beings in the accepted sense. Not even animals, but putrefying corpses moving on two legs. . . . But the dead were no concern of ours. We still wanted to survive.

One night she and a number of friends managed to hide in a haystack. Then began a period of wandering on their own through the area, which was still controlled by the Germans. Here and there they found people who were willing to help by giving them work or food and shelter. During this period, she relates in an amusing vignette, she once claimed to know how to milk a cow—though she had never done so in her life—and figured out this complex task on her own. She even tried her hand as a fortune-teller—and the Germans believed she was just that. Finally, the coveted day arrived when she and her friends were liberated by the Russians. Together with her sister, she walked as far as Cracow and was helped there by the JDC, which had set up an aid station and soup kitchen for aiding refugees trying to return to their homes. When she finally made it back to her native city of Ungvár and was reunited with some of her relatives, she learned that her husband had been shot in Dachau on the day before the camp was liberated.

It was then that she fell into despair, to the point where she was contemplating suicide. But then another miracle occurred: suddenly her two sons reappeared. They had returned from the place to which they had been deported in Austria, albeit sick and weak but alive. Once they recovered, mother and sons moved first to Paris, then to South Africa.

This is but one story of many, the tale of a single year embracing a world of torment and atrocities, only some of which have been cited here; the narrator herself confesses to omitting some incidents "even more abysmally evil." But it is also a story full of luck and miracles that few were privileged to enjoy.[124]

There is no way of estimating how many people were lost on the battered roads of the Third Reich during those last months, especially during those last mad days of Nazi rule:[125] they traveled by train while the railway cars and tracks were being bombed incessantly by the Allies; they were left locked in railway cars in out-of-the-way places when their guards fled; they dragged themselves down bombed-out roads crowded with refugees. Whole days passed without an opportunity for them to eat or drink. They slept outdoors in the frost and rain or they didn't sleep at all. And all the time, around them and behind them, their guards were just waiting for the moment when they would fall behind the column, try to rest, or simply collapse; terror and menace closed in on them from all sides.

The Nazis, who had pretensions of being the master race and imagined that they would rule the world, who thought they could turn the social order on its head and dictate new laws nullifying the ethics that had preserved humanity over the ages were now shattered and scattered in all directions. But up to the last they could not believe that fate would overtake them; right to the last they continued hatching their plans in the belief that they could go on executing them as before and dominate their victims even as dominion was being wrested from their hands. Incapable of letting their victims go, they wreaked their vengeance on their prisoners precisely because the prisoners were even more defenseless than they themselves had become. But in the end nothing remained and they were reduced to scampering frantically about searching for refuge like rats in a burning barn.

Hitler and Goebbels, the latter with his family, committed suicide in the bunker in Berlin, but most of their entourage tried to flee. A few of them succeeded in getting away; the fate of others is unknown to this day. Some of the captains of the Third Reich who were captured and placed on trial in Nuremberg, the city where Hitler proclaimed the racial laws, drew the same conclusion as Hitler and, sooner or later, committed suicide. Himmler tried to escape disguised as a wounded soldier. He was caught while attempting to reach a Scandinavian country, but he managed to evade trial and justice by killing himself. (At the Sachsenhausen trial, one of the accused testified that toward the end of the war, one of the prisoners was forced to bite down on a cyanide pellet to determine how quickly the heads of the regime could kill themselves.)[126] In memoirs penned in prison, Rudolf Höss described his last meeting with Himmler:

> I shall never forget the last time I reported to the Reichsführer-SS and bade him farewell. He was beaming and in high spirits, even though an entire world—*our* world—

was in decline. If he had said: Well, gentlemen, this is the end, you know what to do—
I could have understood that. It was congruent with what he had preached to the SS
over the years: self-effacement for the sake of the ideal. Instead, the last command he
gave us was: Hide yourselves within the army![127]

And that is precisely what Höss did, but he was eventually caught.

Oblivious to what awaited them, these diehard Nazis never grasped that in
addition to bringing destruction upon millions of human beings, they had failed
themselves. Instead, they clung to the belief that their deeds were laudable. Thus,
even as late as January 1945, SS Gruppenführer Richard Glücks was decorated
for his role in the arming of the Reich, for he had managed fifteen large concentration camps and their five hundred satellite camps, in which no fewer than
40,000 SS men had kept guard over 750,000 prisoners.[128]

19

Rescue from the Abyss

Rescue: The Specific Problems

The process of liquidating the camps affected all their inhabitants, Jews and non-Jews, with all being subjected to the same ordeals. The SS annihilated masses of prisoners inside and outside the camp without discerning between Jews and other people. Nevertheless, we would not be wrong in estimating the number of Jewish victims alone in the tens of thousands. At the end of the war, in addition to the multitude of POWs, there remained in Germany eight million civilians who had been brought there from all the nations of Europe to do forced labor. Among them were about forty thousand Jews who had been liberated either in camps or in the course of death marches. Most of them had originated in the occupied countries—Poland, the Baltic states, Hungary, Slovakia, and Italy—but Jews from Western Europe or Germany proper were relatively few.

Why were so few of the millions of Jews who had been living in Europe prior to the Holocaust saved? The debate surrounding this question has gone on for over a generation. Bitter accusations have been leveled at all the parties involved, the Nazis first of all but also the bystanders: the peoples of the world; the great bodies such as the Christian churches and the Red Cross, which were charged with a special moral obligation; and even the Jews themselves, who, according to some arguments, failed to exploit rescue opportunities and surrendered without resistance to the Holocaust that descended on them.

In the following chapters we shall attempt to examine the conditions, prospects, and deeds that prompted or prevented rescue during these fateful years. As it is clearly impossible to exhaust this subject in the framework of this book, we shall limit ourselves to a number of aspects and illustrate them, as far as possible, with appropriate examples.

Three Basic Factors

In approaching the subject of rescue, one must address three factors: Nazi Germany, the Jews both in the sphere of Nazi influence and in the free world, and all the other nations of the world, meaning the governments, populations, and organizations operating within them. We have seen that the twelve years of Hitler's rule were not uniform in character in terms of either the Nazis' conduct, the attitude of other nations toward the Third Reich, or the fate of the Jews, whether under the Reich's direct or indirect rule or in the free world. I have attempted to describe the changes that characterized the various stages of the period, but it remains to delve into the specific issue of rescue, whose components formed something of a triangle. One side was the **information** known to all the parties concerned regarding the Germans' intentions and the facts they had already established. The second was the degree of **acknowledgement** evoked by this information. And the third was the **action** prompted by this acknowledgement. Each one of these factors was activated and functioned according to certain patterns.

Information was wholly dependent on the ability to obtain authoritative reports and was not in equal supply during each stage of the period, as will be seen later. For the most part, **acknowledgement** was not necessarily a corollary of the receipt of information, unless such information came from firsthand experience or from an authoritative source for which there was corroborating evidence. The factors that influenced acknowledgement were complex. The fundamental political, social, and moral tenets of the nations, including the Jews, differed from those of the Nazis, as the latter had broken all the rules by which twentieth-century man was accustomed to judge and act. Hence, the world did not properly assess the Nazis' intentions, even when they were declared quite openly. No one imagined that the Germans would actually translate the declarations being made by their leaders into action. Moreover, it appears to be an empirical fact of human nature that it is difficult for people to adapt their way of thinking to new circumstances—a point that helped Hitler make unimaginable strides forward, particularly at the beginning of his career. And at a later stage, this made it possible for the Nazis to carry out the extermination campaigns in broad daylight without the recipients of information throughout the world to acknowledge it actively and to draw the conclusions it demanded.

Yet there was another obstacle to a full and proper acknowledgement of the facts: interests, both personal and political, in the broadest sense of the word. The disparity between recognizing the situation for what it was and the tendency to ignore it is manifest in all sectors of the conflict during this period and was true of all the parties in times of crisis. In discussing the events of 1932, it was emphasized how recognition and delusion existed side by side among the Jews of Germany—and not only among them (see chap. 1). One factor that is common to the reactions of all the parties involved—Jews, members of other peoples, and even Germans—is the propensity to disregard the true, radical implications of the situation in which they found themselves as a result either of their own doing or of sheer bad luck. Thus Neville Chamberlain chose to believe that at Munich he had safeguarded the peace; Stalin believed that Hitler would not attack Russia; the majority of the American people deluded itself that the United States would avoid being dragged into the war; the Allies failed to draw the proper conclusions from the fate being suffered by the Jews under Hitler's rule even when they had ample and accurate information about what had befallen them; and the Jews did not believe it possible to plan and execute the annihilation of millions of people even after they had witnessed countless acts of murder.

The rescue of Jews and others depended first of all on acknowledgement, for without a full appreciation of what was happening, one could not expect a suitable response in the form of **action.** The process was cogently described by a founder of the ecumenical movement and secretary of the World Council of Churches, the Dutch theologian W. A. Visser't Hooft, who spent the war years in Geneva, where information flowed in from all parts of Europe. The International Red Cross, international Jewish organizations, the consuls of the neutral countries in Europe and beyond, and church figures all maintained official and unofficial ties with the occupied and satellite countries as well as with the many Germans who came to Switzerland. Swiss citizens served as agents for various welfare institutions in remote regions; on their return to Switzerland, they brought evidence of what they had seen with their own eyes. In this way information and messages were passed from one person and one organization to the next, which is how Visser't Hooft heard about the massacre of Jews in Poland. The witness, a Swiss citizen, described an *Aktion* at which he had been present. Rumors and other information to this effect had reached Visser't Hooft earlier, but he confessed:

> From that moment onward I had no longer any excuse for shutting my mind to information which could find no place in my view of the world and humanity. And this meant that I had to do something about it.
>
> Hitler's strength was that he did the unimaginable. . . . A considerable number of people in Germany, in occupied countries, in the allied and neutral countries heard stories about mass killings. But the information was ineffective because it seemed too improbable. Everyone who heard it for the first time asked whether this was not a typical piece of wildly exaggerated war-time propaganda.

He did not believe that anti-Semitism was the reason for suppressing this information but rather that

> people could find no place in their consciousness for such an unimaginable horror and that they did not have the imagination, together with the courage, to face it. It is possible to live in a twilight between knowing and not knowing. It is possible to refuse full realization of facts because one feels unable to face the implications of these facts.[1]

Thus, we have before us a highly complex situation, for even the availability of information and the acknowledgement thereof did not ensure that action would be taken in the direction of rescue. Every rescue attempt—and all we can speak of are attempts—required a *decision* about what conclusion was to be drawn from the acknowledgement of information. It might be a decision to take or avoid to take action; to mount a rescue attempt or to resign oneself to the situation and abandon the victims to their fate. A decision of this sort was demanded as much of the persecuted Jews as of the party capable of assuming the task of rescue—be it within Europe or beyond—and it was affected by the conditions prevailing at any one time in any one place. Thus, it is necessary to examine when and by whom it was decided to rescue Jews and when and by whom it was decided to abandon them as well as when and how Jews attempted to save themselves and when and why they surrendered to the inevitable.

Entirely separate is the matter of the actual odds of saving people and the objective and subjective factors necessary for rescue to succeed. In terms of the subjective factors, what has come under scrutiny particularly in recent years is the character and behavior of the survivor. As a rule, however, the studies of this facet of the rescue issue have focused on the extreme situations that characterized the concentration and extermination camps. Far less attention has been paid to the many other situations—in the ghettos and the labor camps, in the forests and hiding places—in which people were forced to make decisions. The objective factors were essentially the local conditions and circumstances that affected the prospects of rescue and chances of success in any one place.

The Jewish Condition as a Reflection of the Developments of the Period

Phase One: 1933–1937/38

The years from 1933 to 1937/38 established a number of facts that were among the hallmarks of the Holocaust, although they were expressed in different ways according to the changing circumstances:

1. The behavior displayed toward the persecuted Jews was determined by both the global political situation and the prevailing circumstances in each country. It was likewise influenced by domestic economic and social problems, the nature of the regime and its attitude toward the Third Reich, and the relations that traditionally obtained between the Jews and the peoples among whom they lived. The degree and character of anti-Semitism exhibited by the population and government were, of course, of special moment.[2]

2. The Jews did not enjoy a recognized, institutionalized political status, so that their activities qua Jews could only be conducted on the periphery of the general political arena. The means of leverage available to them were national or international intervention, propaganda, and public protest, but their collective effect was highly limited and was usually relative to the standing of the Jewish community in each country.

3. The Jewish community was plagued by division and bewilderment, and its established frameworks—of Zionists and Liberals, Orthodox and Reform Jews— had lost much of their significance and decisions were no longer being made along these lines. One of the basic points of controversy was whether or not to negotiate with the Germans to improve the condition of the Jews or to facilitate their emigration. Clearly it was necessary to offer the Nazis some kind of advantage to obtain concessions from them, as was done in the case of the *Haavara* (Transfer Agreement). Yet as soon as the Germans felt there was no longer much signifi-

cance to its economic benefits, Hitler concluded that its political drawbacks out-weighed them, and the *Haavara* was curtailed and eventually rescinded altogether (see chap. 4).

For the Jews there were two issues at stake: first, whether it was proper, from a political and moral standpoint, to conduct negotiations with the Germans; and second, whether such negotiations, or even an agreement, would yield the desired results in terms of saving Jews. The example of the *Haavara* was not chosen at random, for there was usually only one advantage that the Jews had to offer the Third Reich—an economic one—and during the 1930s it was still open to nego-tiation. The Nazis believed that the Jews wielded enormous political influence in the world; in the pre-Hitlerite period some of the Jewish leaders in Germany had tried to play this card. But even then, and certainly later on, their influence did not extend beyond lobbying and its erratic results.

Thus, whether and how to pursue negotiations with the Germans was one of the focal issues of the Jews' struggle for survival and rescue. The problem first became manifest at the end of March 1933 when Göring summoned a number of the community's leaders and ordered them to go abroad and deny the atrocity propaganda about Nazi acts of terror against the Jews. He also told them to deter these Jews from conducting propaganda against the New Germany—lest their efforts backfire and cause harm to the very people they were trying to save. This particular circle closed twelve years later, in April 1945, when Himmler invited a representative of the WJC, Norbert Masur, to come from Sweden to Germany and negotiate the release of Jews from concentration camps (see chap. 21). Throughout the period, a debate went on between the supporters and opponents of negotiation, each declaring that its sole aim was to save Jews.

4. But the decisive factor was the gulf between the captains of the Nazi regime—and none more than Hitler himself—and the Western democracies because the basic assessments and approaches of each side were predicated on fundamentally opposing doctrines. The Nazi ideology provided the Germans with a doctrine that negated all the concepts and values that motivated their opponents. Not only did the ends justify the means in this system but as the Nazis saw it there was essentially no need to justify them: Germany had an absolute right to fight for world domination. And that determined their theory and practice of what was permissible, what was not, and how to exploit the existing situation. Freed of the constraints of moral judgment and the norms of human society, their behavior was directed by practical and rational considerations in implementing their doc-trine. Thus, although their basic approach was informed by irrational drives, their actions were governed by practical logic. They forged their irrationality into an ideology that drove the immense bureaucratic machine of the Third Reich. This was the source of the unique combination of fervor and cold calculation, of Hitler's blend of firm purpose and impromptu strategy.

In contrast to the dynamism of the Nazi regime, whose aim was to change the world order, the democracies aspired to preserve the status quo. Indeed, their efforts were directed toward compromise, and during his first years in power, Hit-ler exploited this policy for all it was worth. The Western world based its actions mainly on rational thinking. Its great mistake was in assuming that Hitler did so too, that his frenzied ideology was merely a frill, as it were. In effect, each side was operating on a completely different plane, but whereas the Western powers failed to appreciate the essence of the Nazi regime, Hitler fully understood the nature of the democracies and was sensitive to their weaknesses. And the Jews, who likewise had an interest in maintaining the status quo, were an integral part of the democratic world and partners in its rationalizing conduct.

Anti-Semitism held a focal position in the Nazi Weltanschauung. The Jew was the antitype, the epitome and incarnation of evil (see chap. 2). In a paradoxical way, hatred of the Jews became a way of rationalizing irrational drives. The elimination of the Jews was meant to vindicate the Nazi cause and to guarantee its success besides serving as an instrument of strategy and propaganda. Yet the crucial role assigned to the Jewish problem was appreciated by neither the Jews nor the other nations. They were accustomed to seeing anti-Semitism used as a political tool or emerge as a spinoff of radical political aims, especially of the Right. But they never imagined it being cast as the foundation of an entire ideological system: the fuel, so to speak, that feeds the motor. As the nations of the world did not recognize the political motive behind the persecution of the Jews, they refused to accord the Jewish refugee the right of political asylum. This basic misapprehension of the essential nature of the National Socialist regime and the role played by anti-Semitism for it was one of the cardinal errors of the time, and millions of Jews paid for it with their lives. Indeed, it was perhaps the main factor blocking the rescue of the Jews. In 1939 these same nations learned for themselves that rather than ensure peace, compromise had been its downfall. Thus, it was not until very late that they drew the conclusions that ultimately led them to go to war. Their outlook on the persecution of the Jews, however, remained static *in that they persisted in viewing it not as a political but as a humanitarian problem.*

The condition of the Jews differed from that of all the other peoples of the world owing to their geographical dispersion and lack of official political status, on the one hand, and to the negative image of the subhuman antitype ascribed to them, on the other hand. Yet they, too, failed to perceive the enormity of the peril looming ahead. A long history of bitter experience had taught Jews the taste of rape and pillage, slavery and massacre; but never had they known persecution that stemmed from a denial of their very essence as human beings. The gap between the Nazis' approach and the Jews' grasp of it had yet to become apparent.

Phase Two: 1938–1941

As already noted, the strategy the Nazis adopted toward the Jews changed in accordance with the political and economic developments preceding the outbreak of the war. The new style first became evident in Austria. In Germany the leaders of the national representation of the Jews, the Reichsvertretung, had been accustomed to negotiating with the authorities. But in Austria Eichmann introduced the principle of controlling the Jewish leadership, thus setting the precedent for the institution of the Judenrat. On one decisive point, however, the Jews realized that they were working toward the same goal as their persecutors: to promote the exodus of Jews from Austria. That is precisely what the SS had in mind from 1936 onward in recommending that emigration be stepped up by destroying the Jews' economic base and using terror against them. This spur to leave *Ostmark* gave rise to another form of exit: illegal immigration to Palestine.

Once the war had broken out, the problem assumed major proportions. The Germans' grandiose deportation plans, designed to rid the areas of Poland annexed to the Reich of Poles and Jews alike, prompted the movement of hundreds of thousands of people in a mixture of deportation and flight (see chap. 5). From then on, any attempt at escaping the bounds of Nazi rule was made to avoid deportation, and even where the Germans permitted emigration to continue, it assumed the character of flight and was tantamount to expulsion.

In imposing their rule on the millions of Jews in Poland who for the time being stayed in place, the Germans employed the tactics they had earlier tested on a smaller scale in Germany—and particularly in Austria—perfecting and adjusting them to the new dimensions. Like its Polish counterpart, the Jewish population of Poland was initially stunned by the Wehrmacht's *Blitzkrieg* and was quite unprepared to cope with the Germans' calculated methods of repression and terror. As a result the Jewish communal leadership underwent some far-reaching changes. In some communities the prewar kehillah took new responsibility upon itself; in others the chairman and often many members of the newly formed Jewish councils were people who lacked experience in Jewish public life or had at best held marginal positions in the community and were now forced into the role of liaisons between the Nazi regime and the Jewish population. Under the circumstances it was impossible to organize a mass exodus, nor were the Germans interested in one; in fact, they prohibited emigration from Poland as early as the autumn of 1940 (see chap. 6). Hence, the main problem facing the Jews was how to preserve Jewish life and endure in the hope that sooner or later Hitler would be defeated.

One reason for changes in the Jewish public leadership was that many of the communal, organizational, and party leaders fled as the German troops advanced into Poland.[3] This was also a reason for the difficulties involved in rescue. There is no doubt that most of these people saved themselves; several went on to hold important public positions, particularly in Palestine. To a certain degree they also brought out information about what was happening in the areas under German rule. But a major ethical question comes into play: in fleeing Poland they left the Jewish public bereft of its veteran leadership. Many of those who remained in Poland even though they had had an opportunity to escape—for example, Adam Czerniakow—denounced the leaders who fled for saving themselves while abandoning the community. In the beginning the heads of the Zionist youth movements joined in the flight, but many of them later returned to occupied Poland and worked in their movements toward the establishment of the underground. Most of these youngsters perished in this struggle, just like the older leaders and council chairmen, veterans and new ones, who tried to stand in the breach.[4]

Flight from the occupied countries was equally problematic on the personal level. Once the border between the German-occupied area and the Russian-controlled part of Poland was closed, flight eastward became a perilous and arduous affair that only people of daring, usually youngsters, were likely to essay. Even those who succeeded in stealing across the border so closely guarded on both sides did not always manage to keep going once on the Russian side, and they were forced to make their equally hazardous way back. Yet even people with the stamina and resourcefulness to stage a successful escape confronted a fateful dilemma. While fleeing toward an obscure future, invariably these young or more established people left behind wives or girlfriends as well as parents and siblings who were ill equipped to pit themselves against the dangers entailed in flight. At first it was thought that the Germans would not harm women, children, or the elderly, but it soon became clear that such assumptions were wishful thinking and that any Jew, qua Jew, was a potential victim. Here the issue is not the responsibility of a leader who had abandoned his community but of matters that touch on the heart and soul of every individual. Had anybody the right to save himself by abandoning those who would need him most in the struggle for survival? Many answered "No" and refused to leave for this very reason; others even returned to their homes after luck had shined on them and they had successfully escaped.

Thus, it was both on the public plane and on the personal level that a moral decision had to be taken—a decision for which there were no norms, conventions, or even precedents. Some decided to go, others to stay, still others even to return based on the information at their disposal and their assessment of its implications. Which of these decisions was the right one is a matter of debate to this day. Again and again, throughout the Holocaust period people faced dilemmas of this kind—decisions that actually meant choosing between life and death for themselves and for others.

As a rule the Jews in Poland soon came into possession of highly accurate information about what the Germans were doing. The question is whether they were also suitably aware of what the Nazis intended to do and how far this awareness influenced their own actions. Within a short time of their swift defeat of Poland, the occupiers revealed how they were going to deal with the population; what people did not see for themselves they learned from the droves of refugees streaming into the large population centers from every corner of the country. The only practical course, it seemed, was to adapt to the new situation as quickly as possible and try to survive. The essential task was to preserve one's basic way of life or even create a new one to replace the foundations destroyed by the war itself as well as by institutionalized theft, private plunder, forced labor and harassment, disease, starvation, deportation to labor camps, and ghettoization. Communities and individuals throughout Poland organized for this purpose, some more successfully, others less so (see chap. 7). Hence, at that time rescue meant simply continuing to endure.

The struggle to survive was conducted simultaneously on three planes. The first was the level on which life was directed by each Jewish Council under the supervision of the German authorities. This effort entailed conscripting people for forced labor—as demanded by the Germans—and dealing with such needs as housing, nutrition, health, and sanitation. The second level straddled the border between overt and clandestine activity: it included the creation of new sources of livelihood in industry and trade, welfare and self-help activities, and the internal organization of the population—sometimes with the support or even direction of the council, sometimes contrary to it. The third level was the clandestine activity that quickly evolved and branched out to embrace the provision of food supplements; education for children; cultural activities; the keeping of a chronicle of events; the maintaining of ties with other communities in the immediate vicinity as well as in more distant places and with parties abroad; the dissemination of information by word of mouth and through the underground press; and, finally, the continuation of political activity.[5] The dividing line between each of these levels was not always clear and definite, so that sometimes they overlapped, depending on local conditions and the character and approach of the people working on each plane. In this way the Jews in occupied Poland were able to keep going, despite the grave state of affairs and the high toll it took in lives—all in the hope that one day soon suffering would come to an end and those who had managed to bear up would be saved.

In Germany, Austria, and the Protectorate, the approach to perseverance changed as the German attempts to deport Jews made their victims more sensitive to the danger they faced. Jacob Edelstein learned of the Germans' true intentions in Poland from what he saw during the Jews' deportation to Nisko. He hoped to save Czech Jewry from a similar fate if only he could ensure its survival within the bounds of the Protectorate, but the Germans turned his attempt at rescue into a death trap.

From the outbreak of the war onward, it became increasingly evident that within the sphere of German rule the choice was not between good and evil—that is, a secure life and a precarious one—but only between the greater and the lesser evil—that is, an inexorable threat to life or some chance of survival. It was for this chance that Jews struggled wherever they were to be found.

Phase Three: 1941 Onward

It was no coincidence that the decision to put up armed resistance did not crystallize until 1942. In the discussion of the circumstances surrounding such resistance, its development, and results, it has been shown that it was the Jews of the small communities in the Russian zone who were the first to try their hand at organized opposition and flight in large numbers. Most of the leaders of the kehillah, the organized youth, and the public at large joined in this endeavor (see chap. 17). The communities previously controlled by the Russians had been savaged by the first wave of slaughter conducted by the Einsatzgruppen beginning in the summer of 1941. Considering this experience, they no longer had any doubt what the Germans had in mind for them. Nevertheless, when the second stage of the liquidation campaign began in the summer of 1942, indecision reigned in most places. A combination of delusion, fear, and despair served to deter many people from joining the ranks of those prepared to take their fate in their hands. The tragedy that had already afflicted almost every family was so overwhelming, so unexpected and unfathomable that, feeling stunned and helpless, many walked quietly toward the inevitable. Their only defense was to retain their dignity in the face of those who had lost all trace of humanity (see chap. 10).

The chances of surviving and escaping to safety were very slim. In those places where individuals or whole sectors of the community risked flight into the forests, only a meager few came through the war alive. We know of attempts at flight and resistance in forty-five small and medium-sized communities in addition to the more renowned uprisings (see chap. 17), but we must assume that we shall never know the full scope of these acts of heroism because eventually no witnesses survived to tell of them.[6] Jews perished in the course of the *Aktionen* or in attempted flight and in hiding, their lives were constantly threatened by man and by nature, especially in the forests—only by dint of iron will were they able to endure these trials. Yet in addition to an indomitable spirit, a measure of sheer luck was necessary for survival.

The incidents of mass murder did not come to an end after the second phase of the Einsatzgruppen campaign in occupied Soviet territory in the summer of 1942. Tens of thousands of Jews were shot to death in 1943 as well. The Germans referred to these massacres—conducted by SS units throughout Eastern Europe— as *Sonderbehandlung* (special treatment) or as *Umsiedlung* (resettlement), that is, deportation to forced labor and extermination camps. This differentiation was evidently of import, for in 1942 the Jews in the East were still easily deceived, believing that the purpose of the deportations was indeed "resettlement," and when the truth came out they were astounded. But once they came to appreciate the real significance of these terms, they had four options of active response: self-defense, flight to the forest, refuge in a nearby place, or an attempt to secure survival by being of benefit to the Germans through productive labor.

In grasping onto the last of these options, "rescue through labor," the Jews essentially resorted to the same tactic they had been using to conduct their struggle for existence throughout the occupation. It was employed not only by the chairmen of the Judenräte but by many of those who remained in the ghettos after the liquidation operations in 1942. Seeing that until then productive work had protected them, and often their families, these laborers presumed that it was the only effective means of influencing the Germans' actions. As for all the other options, the risk seemed greater than the odds of succeeding. We know that the assumption that Jewish labor was of value to the Germans was not an unfounded one because both a trenchant debate and vigorous struggle were being waged within the regime over this very issue, reaching as high as Hitler (see chap. 15). Indeed, among those who survived the war were thousands of people who held out because of their work.

Self-defense was the least promising of the options, and in places where the underground was resolved to mount armed resistance, the organizers were aware of the poor odds. Only in the event that it was possible to combine an uprising with flight—as was attempted even in the death camps—was there reason to hope that at least some of the insurgents would be lucky enough to escape. But even those who fled a ghetto before or during its liquidation were assured neither survival nor even an opportunity to join the partisans. Today it is assumed that tens of thousands of people took this course but only a few thousand lived to tell the tale. The dangers were especially great when not only young and strong people fled a ghetto but whole families, for whom special camps were established (see chap. 17).

Those who chose to go into hiding tried either to prepare a place of concealment within the ghetto or to get out of it, obtain Aryan papers, and find a place
to hide among the local inhabitants. This option was a viable one particularly in
the large cities, where thousands did, indeed, hide on the Aryan side. Still, only a
portion of these people were saved.

There was no sure path to salvation, and a constellation of factors had to exist
in order for a Jew to be saved. Objective circumstances such as the natural conditions in the vicinity, the climate, the military situation, an effective Jewish
underground organization, and a sympathetic non-Jewish population were decisive. Also of great importance were the subjective prerequisites of age, health, the
habit of getting by on little, and the ability to endure harsh conditions; a good
sense of local orientation; and the strong resolve of a fearless, iron will. Added to
all of these was that measure of luck without which—or so it seems in all the
testimonies and recollections—no one could get away. Under these circumstances, it was fortune that reigned.

Forced to go over to the defensive while withdrawing from eastern and southeastern Europe, the Germans were well aware of the change that had befallen
them, and it heightened their fury. Early on they had pretended that the Jews were
partisans and had, therefore, to be destroyed—thus prompting the exodus to the
forests. Now, they actually were being harassed by the partisan movement, which
was directed by Moscow and which Jews tried to join—not always with success.
The Germans also learned a lesson from the uprising in the Warsaw ghetto; thereafter, whenever they came to liquidate a ghetto—such as Bialystok, for instance—
they planned the operation carefully so as to foil the plans of the Jewish underground. Although the Germans faced growing difficulties and occasionally paid a
price for pursuing the Final Solution, Jewish lives remained as vulnerable as
before. For even though the Jews had become increasingly aware of what lay in
store for them, each German reversal on the battlefield tempted them to believe
that the war would be over in a matter of months and all those who endured till
then would be saved. Such hopes, like others before them, proved to be vain, and
the masses of Jews who were unwilling or unable to embark on one of the risky
courses turned into easy prey, like those before them. Whoever offered resistance,
fled to the forest, or went into hiding knew that his life hung by a thread but at
the same time he had recovered an important human quality: he had cast off the
yoke and regained his freedom of decision and action. He remained subject to the
Kingdom of Death that was closing in on all the Jews, but it no longer dominated
his spirit. He faced the enemy standing upright; rather than yield by his death, he
was defeated by it. Indeed, if ordained by fate to survive, he emerged the victor.

Rescue and Faith

The problem of rescue and the preservation of their own distinct ethos was particularly vexing for the Orthodox and traditionalist Jews. For these people were
distinguished by a way of life shaped by the injunctions and proscriptions of Jewish law, whereas the injunctions and proscriptions of the Nazis and the subhuman

conditions to which they subjected the Jews deprived them of the ability to observe this law. A believing Christian, even if forced to go underground or interned in a concentration camp, was not beset by the torment that a practicing Jew suffered when the Nazis denied him not only liberty, livelihood, property, and food but the possibility of observing God's commandments.

The Orthodox Jew and the Struggle for Survival

It is estimated that at least half of the Jews in Eastern Europe (not including the Soviet Union) were faithful to traditional Jewish ways,[7] and a substantial proportion of these people belonged to distinct groups for which religion was the very essence of life. The traditionalists came from all walks of life, ranging from rabbis and their disciples, teachers, public servants, merchants, industrialists, artisans, and laborers to members of the poorest classes, right down to street beggars. How did these Jews construe the afflictions of the era? How did they respond? What effect did their conduct have on the life of the community as a whole?

The Nazis had a special interest in assailing the Jewish religion and its institutions, customs, and adherents. Their wave of terror in November 1938 began with the burning of synagogues; dozens of years earlier the hatred of the anti-Semites had already found expression in the desecration of Jewish cemeteries. On entering Poland, not only did the Germans set to destroying Torah scrolls and holy objects and burning synagogues and Batei Midrash (houses of learning, seminaries)—often with Jews locked inside them—they deliberately abused Orthodox Jews even more conspicuously than the rest. It was not difficult to recognize these people as most of them were set apart by their style of dress, sidelocks, and long beards—in addition to which they gathered together three times a day for prayer. The sadistic Nazis took special satisfaction in tormenting these Jews by forcing them to perform humiliating acts and special exercises and ordering them to remove their long outer garments. Elderly Jews were especially popular targets of abuse. One of them, Rabbi Shimon Huberband, who kept a chronicle of events for Emmanuel Ringelblum's Oneg Shabbat archive, penned a description of these brutal assaults:

> Any Jew with a beard and moustache was first of all soundly beaten and then had his beard plucked out by hand. Those with short beards had them cut down to the flesh with bayonets. Many were wounded. . . . Any time was appropriate for an assault on a beard: upon meeting a bearded Jew in the street; while abducting him off the street or out of his home for work; . . . while assailing him with the aim of robbing him; on a streetcar, on a train . . . wherever [he was] in reach.[8]

Rabbi Huberband also related that sometimes the Nazis held a collective shearing of all the bearded men in a public square—or bearded Jews were penalized with a stiff fine. Cutting off rabbis' beards was a favorite pastime for the Germans, and one rabbi actually agreed to submit to a hundred strokes rather than forfeit his beard. Sometimes Jews were taken to barbers to have their beards shaved and had to pay for the privilege; sometimes well-dressed young women were stopped in the streets and forced to cut off a Jew's beard. As the final humiliation, "Jews were often made to swallow the hairs of their shorn beards."

The Jewish holidays were a particularly desirable time for the Nazis to carry out their actions. There was a pragmatic reason for this: Jews are concentrated together at such times. Often the Germans announced in advance that the Day of Atonement, for example, would be the date of a deportation if the Jews did not fulfill one demand or another by then.

The way in which the Nazis attacked the Jewish tradition attests to the same double message that has already been noted in the discussion of the Nuremberg Laws (see chap. 4). On the one hand, they proclaimed that a Jew was defined on the basis of racial origin, not religion. Ostensibly, one's faith did not come into play at all, and the fact is that even apostates continued to be regarded as Jews. But in practice the Germans made a point of choking every expression of the Jewish religion because they regarded it as the source of strength and key to the longevity of the Jewish people. In the beginning they often turned to rabbis with the demand that they form the Judenrat on the spot.

The rabbis' response to the unfolding events varied, as did that of the Jewish population at large. A good many leaders of the Orthodox community fled Poland at the outbreak of the war and even managed to reach safety in the United States or Palestine. In contrast, there were rabbis who regarded their personal fate as inexorably linked to that of their congregation, and some went so far as to shave off their beards and change their style of dress as a safety measure. Here are a few examples of such fidelity from among hundreds. Rabbi Neḥemiah Alter of Łódź refused to flee to Warsaw with the members of his family, declaring, "Since the good times of my life all had to do with the Łódź community, I shall remain here in times of tribulation as well."[9] Rabbi Joshua Heschel Halevi of Alkosh, the Admor of Tanczyn—and at age ninety the dean of these heads of ḥassidic "courts"—refused to shave his beard, as his disciples had implored him, when the Germans began sending the Jews of Alkosh to their deaths. Like Rabbi Alter, he was shot by a German soldier or SS man as he boarded a transport and died on the spot. Rabbi Israel Shapira, who had been the Admor of Grodzisk for close to fifty years, declined to make use of the immigration papers his disciples in the United States had obtained for him. Instead, he was sent to Treblinka with the rest of the community "and preached to them at the entrance to the gas chambers, singing *Ani Ma'amin* ('I Believe') with them."[10]

All over occupied Europe there were rabbis who accepted the difficult role of chairing their local Judenrat or at least serving as a member of the council. And there were also rabbis who refused to do so. Either way, the Jewish layman regarded his rabbi as the authority who was entitled, indeed obliged, to interpret the Torah and determine what was permissible and what was not in those fearful circumstances. For daily, almost hourly, questions arose that an observant Jew had to have answered: What should a Jew do when ritual slaughter was prohibited (this was usually one of the first of the regulations that the Germans published)? Under what, if any, circumstances was it permissible to eat nonkosher meat? When public communal prayer was prohibited, should Jews take the risk of defying the ban or should they pray individually? Or together but clandestinely? When the teaching of the Torah and all other forms of Jewish education were prohibited, should the yeshiva students continue to study? And what of the children? How could the adults observe the commandment of studying a page of Talmud each day when they were forced to work ten to twelve hours at hard labor? How could they keep up the Torah schools and save the ritual objects and the holy books when the man keeping them might have to pay for it with his life? What should a Jew do on the Sabbath and holidays when the Germans demand that he work? What should a pregnant woman do when it was forbidden to bring a Jewish child into the world?

These are but a few of the questions with which a religious Jew was forced to grapple every day of the year. Because most of these Jews did not know what the Oral Law required in these exceptional cases, they turned to rabbis for rulings. Questions were posed and answered both orally and in writing, and just as some of these rulings have been passed down in writing or by word of mouth, others have been lost. From the ones that have reached us, however, we can appreciate the quandary of the people who were trying to preserve the glowing embers of traditional Jewish life while enabling the Jews themselves to survive. They turned to the traditional sources—the ancient sages, the commentators, such figures of authority as Rabbi Akiva, Sa'adiah Gaon, the Rambam, and Rashi—and found that all these difficult questions had already been raised at one time or another in the long history of Jewish adversity, but for most there were no consistent or definitive answers. One sage permitted what another would not; one stipulated a certain condition and another a different one. In most cases no halakhic ruling had been passed, and each authority invoked the interpretation he deemed most appropriate. And that is precisely what happened again, in the period of modern persecution: the decisions of the rabbinical authorities varied.[11]

In no few cases the Jews did not ask for rulings but did as they thought best. Many made a supreme effort to keep kosher, hold communal prayers, observe the Sabbath and holidays, conceal Torah scrolls and other holy books, study, and even teach under the most trying conditions, thus placing their lives in constant danger. To a certain degree Jews were able to display their faithfulness to the Torah and Jewish tradition even in the camps. It was not unknown for a man to forfeit his tiny ration of bread, a sine qua non of survival, in order to buy a prayer book, prayer shawl, or phylacteries that a Jew or a *Kapo* had smuggled into the camp.[12]

As his life could only be lived within the framework of Jewish law, the Orthodox Jew was willing to risk it in order to observe that law in the hope that the day of salvation would soon arrive. Rabbi Ephraim Oshry of Kovno (Kaunas), who was fortunate enough to have survived and subsequently collected his memories in a book of responses, relates that at the beginning of the occupation he continued to give lessons on the Talmud and tried to encourage the young people so that they would understand that just as they bless the Lord for all the good in life, they must also bless Him for the bad. According to the Talmud, he argued, the Jewish people were to wait passively for God's aid and salvation.[13] Worth mentioning is the Admor of Piaseczno, Rabbi Kalonymus Kalish, who preached in Warsaw on the Sabbath and holidays from 1940 to 1942, trying to encourage his listeners through allusions to the affairs of the day. He wrote down and collected these sermons, and they were found and published after the war in *The Book of Holy Fire*.[14]

The halakhic authorities were confronted with a fateful and highly vexing question when the Germans began to demand that the Jewish councils decide who would live and who would die. As soon as the council members, or occasionally only the chairman, realized that the Germans intended to transform them into a tool for implementing their murderous designs, they had to make a fatal decision—and no matter what they decided, it would not conform to society's principles of justice and certainly not to the canon of Jewish ethics. In these circumstances the leaders of the community often asked a rabbi or rabbis for a ruling based on the *Halakhah*. The fact of the matter is that Jewish tradition addresses itself to the problem of extradition, but the Jews had never had to face it on such a massive scale. The best-known halakhic precept quoted in the postwar discussion of this subject was Maimonides' ruling, invoking the Talmud, "... If heathens said to Israelites, 'surrender one of your number to us, that we may put him to death, otherwise we will put all of you to death,' they should all suffer death rather than surrender a single Israelite to them. But if they specified an individual ... they may give him up, provided that he was guilty of a capital crime."[15]

However, there is no consensus on this difficult question in Jewish tradition, neither was there a common opinion among the rabbis who were asked to rule on it during the Holocaust. The two most outstanding examples are the rulings of Rabbi Avraham Dov Shapiro in Kovno and the rabbis in Vilna. On hearing the terrible news of the impending *Aktion* from the members of the Jewish Council, the elderly Rabbi Shapiro fainted. After being revived he spent the entire night going through books and finally ruled that the Gestapo's order to classify the Jews into workers and nonworkers should be obeyed in the hope of saving part of the community (see chap. 10 for an expanded discussion). In Vilna some twenty of the rabbis had perished in the first *Aktionen* in 1941; the remaining rabbis established a Religious Council as part of the Judenrat's Cultural Department. Convening after the Yellow Certificates *Aktion*—in which Jacob Gens, then commander of the Vilna Jewish police, executed a German order to allow all those bearing yellow work certificates to remain alive and turn everyone unable to work over to be killed (see chap. 10)—the Religious Council sent a delegation of rabbis and teachers to Gens to cite Maimonides' ruling and reproach him for what he had done. Gens, in turn, justified his action by arguing that by turning a portion of the community over to the Nazis, he had saved the rest from death.

The Sanctification of the Holy Name or the Sanctification of Life

This was not the first time in Jewish history that whole communities found themselves having to choose between life and death. In earlier periods, especially during the Middle Ages, Jews had been killed for refusing to renounce their faith, and their self-sacrifice came to be known as the Sanctification of the Holy Name *(Kiddush Ha-Shem)*. Ever since the time of Rabbi Akiva, in the days of the Roman Empire, Jews had been going to their deaths, as individuals and communities, to prove their faith and sanctify God's holiness. Following Maimonides, Rabbi Huberband wrote:

> The Sanctification of the Holy Name is accomplished in three ways:
>
> 1. a Jew surrenders his soul when he is about to be converted;
> 2. a Jew imperils himself in order to save another Jew or many Jews;
> 3. a Jew falls in battle defending other Jews.

One tradition has it that Maimonides ruled that if a Jew is killed, even if it is not because of an attempt to convert him, but simply because he is a Jew, he is considered to have been martyred.[16]

During the Holocaust the first way did not apply: no Jew sacrificed himself because an effort was made to convert him. But the other two ways applied in abundance, especially that Jews were massacred simply for being Jews. Therefore, it was usual during the Holocaust, as it is in our own day, to refer to all the victims as holy martyrs. At the same time, it was felt that the persecution of the Jews by Nazi Germany was markedly different from the murder of Jews during the Crusades or the Black Death or even during the Chmielnicki pogroms of 1648/1649. One expression of this feeling is ascribed to Rabbi Yitzḥak Nissenbaum of Warsaw, "In these times, the Sanctification of the Name is practiced by sanctifying life. In the past, when our enemies demanded the soul, the Jew sacrificed his body for the Sanctification of the Name in order to save his soul. Now, when the enemy wants to take the body's life, we must not give him what he wants; rather we must defend the body, preserve life."[17]

These words express not only an awareness of the difference between the situations in the past and the present but also the Jews' instinctive response, namely, to fight for life. This struggle—conducted with great tenacity and by every means possible, conventional and otherwise—like every desperate struggle, also had its negative and destructive sides. The overwhelming majority of the Jewish population behaved as Ephraim Barash of Bialystok observed, "they lived from one day to the next and each day tried to secure their existence for the morrow day" (see chap. 10). This struggle was a stubborn one. As Ringelblum put it, "The Jews demonstrated resistance and strong and beneficial perseverance from a physical and psychological standpoint. No people in the world would have held on so tenaciously for so long. The proof is the small number of suicides among the Jews of Warsaw. The Germans had complaints against the Jews of Poland for this."[18]

The innovation in Rabbi Nissenbaum's conception is **the Sanctification of Life:** In the ghetto and the camps man's rebellion against the conditions forced upon him came out not in a willingness to die but in a struggle to live. This struggle was a demonstration of heroism, because to stand up against the Kingdom of Death meant placing oneself in mortal danger every hour of every day. Evidence to this effect are the many people who testified that it was easier to surrender and to die at the hands of the tyrants than to struggle in order to outlast the Nazis—who were destined, Jews everywhere firmly believed, to be swallowed up in the abyss of their own creation.

Yet the meaning and form of resistance changed as soon as all possibility of striving for life was foreclosed. Facing the gas chambers or a firing squad at the edge of a pit, there was only one way of remaining a "free man": by retaining one's dignity, through silence. Resistance of this kind is exemplified by the story of the Jew who resolved not to cry out when the Nazis beat him. An officer demanded, "Jew, shout!" ("Jude, schrei!"), but he stood his ground even when beaten harder, until the Nazis gave up.[19]

As long as the Jews could exercise self-control they did not shout or plead in most cases. Often they went to their deaths reciting the Shema Yisrael or other confessional prayers said before dying. Despite these declarations and reiterations of their creed, the ghettos, the camps, and most of all the extermination camps set before religious Jews—Liberals as well as Orthodox—the difficult test of reiterating their faith. How was it possible to believe in the God of Israel, who had created man in his image, in a place like Auschwitz? The question disturbs philosophers and Christian and Jewish theologians to this day.

One way of preserving one's faith was to deny or shut out reality—the course taken primarily by a number of groups of Ḥassidim. General Jürgen Stroop's famous photo collection, assembled during the fighting in, and destruction of, the Warsaw ghetto, contains a snapshot—captioned "Jewish rabbis"—that shows a group of religious Jews who had retained all the outward signs of their piety: beard, sidelocks, style of dress.[20] This was one of several groups of Gur Ḥassidim who had gone underground and lived in bunkers and other hiding places while they continued their studies and traditional way of life by completely isolating themselves even from the ghetto. The people in this picture were discovered when the Germans began destroying all the bunkers. Underground groups of this kind, composed primarily of young people, existed in a number of other places in Poland, including Cracow and Łódź. They were well organized and even maintained contact with one another.

At the opposite pole of Jewish response in the ghettos were those who sacrificed themselves in an armed uprising. This act was likewise perceived as the Sanctification of the Name; they, too, cut themselves off from reality by refusing to capitulate to it. On April 23, 1943, the fifth day of the revolt in the Warsaw ghetto, the commander of the Jewish Fighting Organization, Mordekhai Anielewicz, wrote to Yitzḥak Zuckerman, its envoy on the Aryan side of Warsaw, "Farewell, my friend. Perhaps we shall meet again. The most important thing is that my life's dream has come true. I have lived to see Jewish resistance in the ghetto in all its greatness and glory."[21] Thus these Jews divorced themselves from the *dictates* of reality but not from reality itself; instead, they fought against it.

The Struggle for Survival in the Labor and Extermination Camps

Limited though the prospects of rescue may have been in the ghettos and forests, they still left some room for struggle for anyone determined to fight for his life. Could the same be said of those interned in camps? And what were the chances of surviving in a concentration camp, labor camp, or transit camp—to say nothing of an extermination camp? Much has been written about the condition of the prisoners in the camps as a whole and the death camps in particular, especially those that also served as labor camps, such as Auschwitz. Survivors have told their stories in thousands of testimonies (some subsequently published, others collected in archives), and among them were people capable of analyzing their experiences. The subject of rescue cannot be discussed without delving into the traits of the camp survivor as well as the factors and circumstances that saved him from death. In the framework of the present work, however, it is possible to point to only a few salient issues and phenomena without claiming to exhaust the subject.

The varying patterns of concentration camp life were influenced at different stages by the general situation and the Germans' strategies in a variety of spheres that affected the condition of the prisoners as a whole and the special condition of the Jewish prisoners in particular. Throughout the period the Jew was treated as unworthy of being included in human society—not even in a society of criminals. The only other prisoners in the camps who received similar treatment, from 1941 onward, were Gypsies and Russian POWs.

The Initial Shock

Eugen Kogon notes in his book that only a few of the prisoners held in protective custody during the early years of the Nazi regime knew what awaited them in a concentration camp before arriving there. Usually, they were in a state of stupefying fear. Those who had heard about atrocities or had already undergone interrogation by the Gestapo expected the worst, "But such concepts were always obscure; reality was far more appalling."[22] Indeed, it appears that hardly anyone failed to be stricken by shock when cast into the reality of the camps. Viktor E. Frankl—a psychiatrist and philosopher and himself a survivor who did extensive research on man's suffering in the camps and his struggle for life—has written, "If one wanted to classify the entrance-shock phase psychiatrically, one would have to enter it among the abnormal affective reactions. Yet one must not forget that in a situation which is itself abnormal to the degree represented by a concentration camp, an 'abnormal' reaction of this sort is something very normal."[23]

Far from being fortuitous, this "entrance-shock" was a deliberately engineered effect, one means of "education" by which the organizers of the concentration camp intended not just to break their opponents' will but to shatter their psyche so thoroughly that even after being released they would be incapable of acting against the regime.[24] Whether or not he was released, an Aryan German prisoner remained part of his nation's broader society. The same could not be said of the Jew, however. His "education" in a concentration camp was designed to excise him from German society: during the first and second stages (until 1941) by means of his emigration (provided he survived) and during the third stage by eliminating him—in other words, exterminating him.

During the first stage (until 1938), the political and racial aspects of the camp system were mixed together, and most of the Jews were arrested on an individual basis for their political, public, legal, or economic activity. The majority were sent to Dachau. There they were tortured with special savagery and held under the most stringent conditions in the punishment unit *(Strafkommando)*. Yet, even though they underwent a tough and parlous process of acquaintance with abnormal reality, they still did not sever their ties with their former, normal condition. The homes and families of these prisoners remained intact, and they were permitted to maintain a limited and controlled correspondence with them. Through this channel to the outside world, it was possible to make arrangements to emigrate, which held out the most promising chances of securing one's release. One's past reality was not completely destroyed, and the future offered some hope.

These two facts were highly important, perhaps decisive, in helping Jewish prisoners to adjust to, understand, and resolve to endure the aberrant situation in the camp. Certainly, not all of them succeeded, either because their mental or physical powers did not sustain them or because the destructive drives of the SS ruined any chance of leaving the camp alive. It was difficult for a Jew to withstand the combination of poor housing conditions, insufficient food, hard and often humiliating labor—assigned to the Jews in particular—along with beatings, individual and collective punishments, torture and mortal blows, all accompanied by obscenities, deliberate humiliation, and demonstrations of contempt. Facing all of this day in and day out, it was hard to retain one's sense of self-worth, to say nothing of the convictions and values that once upon a time had informed one's life in the outside world in the past—and that might now be to one's detriment.[25]

Was Survival Possible?

It is not easy to establish the characteristics that enabled a man to hold out in a concentration camp for a long period of time. The discussions and analyses of this subject since the end of the war rely primarily on material from Auschwitz, where the situation was most extreme.[26] Of course, it is possible to conclude that the basic conditions there held for other kinds of camps as well, including concentration camps during the initial period. But even if we manage to isolate the traits and behavior that might have helped the inmate or POW persevere, one unquantifiable but decisive factor must always be taken into consideration: happenstance. Without a certain degree of luck, it was evidently impossible for even the resourceful and strong-willed to find a way to save themselves. One instance will serve to exemplify this. After the war one of the survivors of Auschwitz, the Italian writer Primo Levi, wrote a highly candid and insightful book about life in that camp. A chemist by profession, Levi came to Auschwitz in 1944 and, thus, was imprisoned there for only a year or so. Fate had it, moreover, that a Special Chemistry Team was created for one of the industrial plants at about that time. This factory was bombed before it was ready to go into production, but three chemists were, nevertheless, sent to work in its laboratory in the winter of 1944/1945, and Levi was one of them. Here is his assessment of his own prospects of surviving:

> So it would seem that fate, by a new unsuspected path, has arranged that we three, the object of envy of all the ten thousand condemned, suffer neither hunger nor cold this winter. This means a strong probability of not falling seriously ill, of not being frozen, of overcoming the selections. In these conditions, those less expert than us about things

in the Lager might even be tempted by the hope of survival and by the thought of liberty. But we are not, we know how these matters go; all this is the gift of fortune, to be enjoyed as intensely as possible at once; for there is no certainty about tomorrow. At the first glass I break, the first error in measurement, the first time my attention is distracted, I will go back to waste away in the snow and the winds until I am ready for the Chimney.[27]

After analyzing the condition of the prisoner and his chances of survival, the sociologist Anna Pawelczyńska, who had been a Polish inmate of Auschwitz, concluded, "The increase or decrease of a prisoner's chances for survival, whether he survived or perished was purely a matter of luck."[28] Moreover, the odds of a Jew surviving were far poorer than those of a non-Jew, and to the Jews themselves the odds seemed infinitesimal.

Two prime characteristics appear to have disposed a prisoner toward behavior that increased his chances of survival. On the one hand, prior to coming to the camp these potential survivors either had dedicated their lives to some public cause (political or social) and had lived according to a defined ideological outlook or they had been noted for their lively intellectual life or profound religious faith. Providing that they had also a bit of luck, they were able to nurture a sense of self-sufficiency that enabled them, by adjusting to the camp conditions, to maintain a certain distance from or indifference to the torment and misery. They were also able to find loopholes in the system by which they could improve or at least mitigate their situation.[29] Moreover, the prisoners who adhered to a clear political philosophy, such as the Communists and Social Democrats, were in most places involved in clandestine organizational work that greatly increased the level of mutual aid and solidarity. For the most part, these were the people who managed in one way or another to make contact with the world outside the camp and knew how to use bribery effectively.

The other prominent characteristic of the survivor was a lust for life, the burning desire to remain alive that moved him to act decisively in his own best interests without consideration for others. He was able to exploit opportunities that seemed likely to be to his benefit; he mastered the art of bribery; and he was prepared to help anyone who might, in turn, act in his behalf. A KZler (inmate of a *Konzentrationslager*) of this sort was always in control of himself, was marked by his ability to concentrate, and acted out of an understanding of the situation and a determination to survive. Dr. Elie A. Cohen, another inmate of Auschwitz, quoted one such survivor, "We camp prisoners had only one yardstick: whatever helped our survival was good, whatever threatened our survival was bad and to be avoided."[30]

Naturally, in the course of the years there were many variations in the behavior and responses of the various types of survivors. During the first phase, a relatively high number of the incarcerated Jews came from a background of political activism. Some of the intellectuals, physicians, and lawyers likewise demonstrated the above-mentioned traits and tried, successfully or otherwise, to cope with the inherent risks. Although there were instances of special cruelty and atrocities in Dachau from 1933 to 1937, the total number of victims, including Jews, was still relatively low.[31]

However, this situation changed radically during the second stage—the period of the mass arrests in Germany. With the deportation to Dachau of thousands of prisoners from Vienna and the entry of the asocials to Buchenwald and Sachsenhausen, the SS men changed their tactics. In addition to lowering the housing and nutritional conditions considerably, they instituted large-scale torture in the form of collective punishments, mass beatings, and the like. This mass assault reached its peak during the influx of tens of thousands of people following Kristallnacht, as a result of which the entry-shock was considerably exacerbated and the incidence of collapse soared. Yet these prisoners had a better chance of being rescued than the Jews who had been arrested individually under the protective custody provision. The intent of the mass arrests was to force people to investigate avenues of emigration, which was an essential condition of their release. Thus, though hundreds perished, most of these prisoners succeeded in leaving the camps within a matter of months.[32] A considerable number of Jews were detained in the wave of arrests that followed the outbreak of the war. Yet even in 1940 it was still possible to obtain release from the concentration camps if emigration was a viable option.

In the Forced Labor Camps

The system of the forced labor camp, which was primarily a by-product of the concentration camp, developed steadily during the war years.[33] As noted earlier (see chap. 6), it was initially employed mainly in occupied Poland. For the most part, the regime of forced labor was applied to the Jews, but Poles found themselves subjected to it as well: The number of permanent labor camps within the Generalgouvernement multiplied from the spring of 1940 onward. At first these camps were built mostly in the vicinity of the settlements from which Jews were being conscripted, whether by the arbitrary method of snatching them off the streets or in a systematic manner with the aid of a Jewish Council. In many places these councils were also charged with caring for the needs of the conscripted laborers. Thus, their upkeep constituted an important item on the agenda of the Jewish Council in Lublin, for example (see chap. 7). But the Germans did not content themselves with employing Jewish labor close to home; they began to send the laborers, who were mostly young people, to distant labor camps. We know of the efforts made by the Jewish councils in Warsaw and Piotrków, for example, not only to keep in contact with the deportees to the Bełżec camps but also to ease their lot as much as possible by sending parcels of food and drugs.

The Sending of Parcels

Throughout the entire period of Nazi persecution, sending parcels was one of the ways in which the Jews, as individuals and organizations, tried to provide support for those who had been trapped by the Nazis in the camps and ghettos. The scope of this endeavor and its degree of effectiveness have yet to be investigated, but there is no doubt that it was a venture of major proportions and significance. The Germans alternately permitted and prohibited the receipt of these parcels. Many of the packages were sent from one place to another within Germany or Poland and many dispatched from foreign countries into Poland never reached their destination, having been pilfered by the Germans or the Poles. But the ones that did arrive contributed not only to the nutrition of the inmates of the ghettos and camps but also to their morale by proving that the Jews had not been forsaken, that someone still cared about them.

Hugo Burkhard, a prisoner of Buchenwald, related that during the first months of 1933, packages reached his camp by the carloads (naturally, they were not for the Jewish prisoners alone) and included basic foodstuffs, warm underwear, and the like. In 1940 small parcels were sent from Sosnowiec to the deportees in the labor camps; when the dispatch of such packages was forbidden, someone traveled daily to "those towns in the vicinity where the prohibition still had not been put into effect and sent [the parcels] from there. Even if these small packages, which did not always reach their destination, could not do very much to help maintain the body, they certainly went a long way toward keeping up spirits." The Danish prisoners in Theresienstadt testified that the parcels they received from their homeland from 1943 onward were a factor in enabling them to prevail both physically and psychologically. These parcels, if not filched by the SS, supplied important goods for the black market on which prisoners could purchase vital items such as bread or soup. The contents of these parcels were the equivalent of legal tender in the camps, and their value varied according to the supply and demand for the particular items being traded. After the liberation of Bergen-Belsen, the British forces found warehouses full of parcels sent from Sweden by the WJC that the SS had declined to distribute while prisoners were starving to death by the thousands.[34] It must be said, however, that while these packages carried an expression of support for the prisoners, they did not represent a means of rescue.

Efforts to Get People Released

In many places attempts were made to save people from being transferred to distant camps or ghettos. Thus, we know of a case in Sosnowiec, for example, in which the Jews being sent to labor camps in Silesia, within the Reich proper, were first detained in a transit camp, and at the demand of the camp's commander, Lagerführer Novak, the Sosnowiec community sent nurses to care for the deportees. One of these women told of the attempts to get people released. There was not very much to be done in terms of practicing medicine. Instead,

> the work was . . . to bribe Novak, to buy him with money and expensive gifts, or to drink with him until he was "loaded" and would comply with a request to release "a relative." Sitting with Novak for hours, drinking and joking with him, was not the most pleasant task. Other means were used as well. We knew that an injection of milk causes a high fever and dizziness, so we administered such shots, and the "sick" man was sent home. Old x-rays and plaster casts were also part of our equipment, to prove that someone had a broken hand or foot and was unable to work so that he could return home. Consider how much sangfroid was required to engage in such manipulations, how much tension and danger they entailed.[35]

The underground of pioneers also attempted to get people back from the labor camps, especially those youngsters who, responding to Moshe Merin's initiative, had volunteered to go to the camps, which had been described to them as a kind of *Haḥsharah* (training farm). A major campaign to get people released from Bełżec was mounted by the Jewish Council of Piotrków, and through vigorous action a woman emissary succeeded in getting some 80 percent of the deportees back (see chap. 7). In 1942 the underground newspaper of Hashomer Hatzair in Warsaw emphatically instructed its members not to go to labor camps, characterizing their refusal as "passive but adamant resistance." Once there, however, it was a cardinal rule in these camps to conserve one's strength, not to work quickly or at full capacity. Whoever invested all his energy in his work—to obtain an extra portion of soup, for example—was regarded by the rest of the prisoners with the contempt reserved for the strikebreaker in normal society.[36]

The Hazards of Escape

Escape attempts were mounted in almost every camp, and the successful escapees were the ones who brought the information on the harsh conditions prevailing in the camps to the ghettos. The SS intended the labor camps to serve two purposes: as a supply of cheap labor and for the extermination of the Jews by "natural death" as a result of hunger, hard labor, poor housing and nutritional conditions, epidemics, and torture. The chances of getting away safely were not very good, and anyone who was caught was, of course, promptly executed. But there were also two other daunting problems: if the escape attempt succeeded, the remaining laborers were subjected to severe punishment in retaliation. Consequently, the Jews themselves often objected to the idea of trying to escape. There were also prisoners who doubted whether the effort was worthwhile, particularly during the later days of the Holocaust. After the ghettos had been liquidated, many believed they would be safer in a labor camp where they could be of benefit to the Germans. The two sides of this question were explored in a description of the labor camp in Korowitz near Lwów (established after the German occupation of the area in 1941):

> From the very beginning escape was our greatest desire. Some fled the camp during the first days; others tried their luck during their second month there. Occasionally people fled on the very day they arrived in the camp, unaware that the commanders would respond to their escape by killing some of us—the sick, sometimes the healthy too— so that this threat did not deter them. We were constantly debating the basic expedience of escape. Some of us felt we should flee; others argued that the camp was the safest place of all, because the ghetto was going to be liquidated anyway and only "people who were of no benefit," as the Germans put it, were concentrated there, whereas we were people they needed.[37]

Rescue from the camps was an increasingly difficult feat. From the outset the German system had determined a limited period in which the prisoners—particularly Jewish prisoners—were to be exploited for their labor. This system was not adjusted even in light of the severe labor shortage during the latter half of the war. On the contrary, the system of extermination through labor received official, thus essentially legal, sanction by being approved by Hitler (see chap. 15). The projected life span of a working prisoner in Auschwitz was a maximum of three months. Even if a prisoner knew that he was doomed to die in the camp, flight was usually beyond his strength or capability. In addition to the deterrent effect of the many guards and the threat of death under torture, the system of collective punishment also affected the prisoner's decision. When the camp command discovered someone missing, the entire camp was usually kept closed in its quarters until the Germans found out what had become of the absent prisoner; in the event that he had escaped, the confinement often continued until he was caught. Moreover, since escape was usually impossible without the aid and support of other inmates, these accomplices were in danger of being exposed and executed. Finally, in the first years of the occupation, a Jew escaping within the Generalgouvernement could try to return to, and hide in, a ghetto. But as the war progressed, the liquidation of the ghettos precluded this possibility.

Hence, anyone who succeeded in stealing out of a camp had only two options: either to join the partisans or to get beyond the sphere of direct German rule, usually by crossing the border into Slovakia. Both were conditional on geographical conditions and either the proximity of partisans willing to accept Jews in their ranks or the willingness of people to supply the fugitives with food, clothing, or even a night's shelter along the way. Much also depended on the season in which the escape took place. It was more difficult to negotiate the unpaved roads in the rain and snow, and, of course, the colder seasons were more inclement toward those who had to sleep outside. To all these hazards and hardships we must add the element of treachery by those who pretended to be benefactors. The difficulties of escaping are known to us from the few people who were saved, and there is no way of estimating the number of those who failed at the attempt.[38] The problem was particularly complicated for Jews, but it must be said that all the other prisoners faced similar perils, especially when they were not inhabitants of the country in which they were interned, did not speak the language, and were unfamiliar with the territory.

Most difficult of all was escape from an extermination camp. The number of such attempts appears to have risen during the later years of the war, and statistics are available for a number of camps. In Mauthausen, for instance, escapes ranged between 4 and 11 attempts per year from 1939 to 1942; but in 1943 there were 44 people who attempted to escape; and in 1944 this figure rose to a total of 226 people, including a group of Russian officers who for the most part failed to get away. The rise in the incidence of escape during the later years was related to the division of prisoners among a large number of satellite camps where the security arrangements were less effective than in the main camps. As a rule one-third to one-half of the escapees were caught. The Jews had less of a chance of effecting a successful escape because they were held under more stringent conditions and were usually suffering from malnutrition; only those who maintained a fair degree of physical fitness could withstand the rigors of an escape attempt. Between October 1944 and March 1945, 93 prisoners escaped from Dachau, including 9 Jews; 8 of them were among the 44 escapees who were caught.[39]

It was the escapees who brought word of what was happening in the extermination camps, first to the ghettos and later on to the outside world.[40] Five Jews who fled from Auschwitz—Hungarians, Czechs, and a Pole—all made it to Slovakia. Some of them had served as clerks in the camps; thus they were in a position to know what was going on and their strength had not been drained by hard physical labor. One way of improving the odds of a successful getaway was to hide for a few days in a bunker in or near the camp until the search for the fugitives was over. Preparing such a bunker inside the camp was an understandably hazardous venture and could not be done without help from other prisoners. In one case in particular, it was even done with the knowledge of the Jewish *Kapo,* but people who hid in that particular bunker almost smothered to death because the ventilation arrangements were faulty.[41] It is, therefore, all the more surprising that they, nevertheless, managed to escape and cross the Slovakian border. In 1940 to 1944 at least 647 people attempted to flee from Auschwitz, and 270 of them were caught; 16 percent of these escapees were Jews.[42] The motive for such flight was unquestionably a desire to save one's life; however, many of the Jewish escapees in particular were also hoping to get word of the mass extermination out to the world at large in the belief that if the Allies knew what was really going on in Auschwitz, steps would be taken to halt the extermination. That this belief was never justified is a matter we shall go into later.

Facing Death

One might imagine that an extermination camp was the place where all illusions were finally put to rest, where knowledge and acknowledgment became one and the same. This was not so. There are testimonies that people living in the family camp of Czech Jews, for instance, deluded themselves that they would be saved even though they were living alongside the crematoria and saw fire and smoke rising out of them day and night.[43] Still, the psychological processes undergone by the prisoner in the extermination camp differed radically from the reactions in society outside and even from those of the inmates in labor camps. Just as the society in an extermination camp was based on principles diametrically opposed to those of a normal society, so the behavior of the incarcerated human being differed from what his norms had been before.

In a unique way the extermination camp prisoner found himself in a state of stress between hope and despair. He had been deprived of all the elements on which his life and identity had always been based—his name, family, social life, profession, clothing, and the minimal physical conditions necessary to sustain life. Moreover, he lived in complete ignorance of what would happen the next day or even the next hour; nor had he any possibility of conceiving of a future. Under these circumstances, he was all but totally incapable of making his own decisions or planning his actions. In this sense the Jews were far worse off than the other prisoners, for in addition to being at the bottom of the camp hierarchy, with the threat of death looming far closer to them than to the other prisoners (with the exception of the Gypsies and Russian POWs), they were entirely cut off from their families and either did not know what had befallen them or were sure that they had already perished. Mourning is a critical experience for everyone, even under normal circumstances; here this crucible had to be faced in the "society of death" of the extermination camp. Despair may overwhelm any man upon sight of a dead loved one, but here such despair threatened to destroy once and for all his power of resistance. Elie Cohen holds that it took months for a man to get over the entry-shock and mourning period.[44] As a result of this emotional stress and the hardships of camp life, many reached a state that Frankl calls emotional death, a condition of indifference or apathy that worked as a defense mechanism but that also harbored the threat of psychological and physical deterioration, "for he who loses all often easily loses himself."[45] As a consequence, the prisoners shunned all independent decision making. Frankl describes the phenomenon: "The camp inmate was frightened of making decisions and of taking any sort of initiative whatsoever. This was the result of a strong feeling that fate was one's master, and that one must not try to influence it in any way, but instead let it take its own course."

On the other hand, Frankl and others make a point of stressing that decisions—often fateful ones—were demanded of the prisoners. As an example he tells of his own irresolution about whether to exploit an opportunity to escape that presented itself during the final days of Auschwitz or to remain with the sick people who were in his care. In the end he decided to stay. "I did not know what the following days would bring, but I had gained an inward peace that I had never experienced before."[46] This is a well-known emotional response known to affect people who have made a clear-cut moral decision in a trying situation. Indeed, Frankl and others emphasize that the possibility of making such a decision was open even to a prisoner in a death camp and was an expression of the inner freedom that a man retains even under such conditions.

Frankl also stresses the importance of the tie with a loved one that a prisoner hopes to see again, for this, he believes, is one of the effective motives helping him persevere. It nurtures his hope for a future, even when he suspects that such hope might be senseless. Sometimes hope was fed by a desire to return to one's profession. Thus Frankl relates that at a time when he was close to collapse, he overcame his own despair by imagining the day when he would stand in a university lecture hall and hold forth on a certain psychological problem on which he had gained insight in Theresienstadt. He told of this daydream as it was coming true.[47]

Anna Pawelczyńska concludes, "He who under conditions of terror and coercion achieved inner freedom, at least to some extent, carried off the only form of victory possible within the existing situation." She also notes that such inner freedom, which is the supreme expression of resistance, could be achieved only through mutual support among the prisoners. It was provided in simple, everyday matters and required the prisoners to treat one another with tolerance.[48] Still, certain traits were necessary to elicit such expressions of solidarity: affability and an impulse to aid and protect the weak; patience, self-discipline, and daring; quick-wittedness and a sense of humor.[49] One of the many paradoxes inherent in camp life was this: each of the prisoners was more lonely and fortified than he had ever been before, yet the individual prisoner who withdrew from the community could not survive. Sometimes solidarity derived from personal friendship, occasionally from actual kinship. Groups formed on the basis of political or ideological affinities, national or local origins; and occasionally help of this kind was offered by the laborers with whom the prisoners came into contact outside the camp.

Primo Levi told of one such laborer, an Italian named Lorenzo who brought him leftover food or used clothing, wrote home for him, and served as the address for the replies. Levi believed that it was because of this laborer that he survived, ". . . And not so much for his material aid, as for his having constantly reminded me by his presence, by his natural and plain manner of being good, that there still existed a just world outside our own, something and someone still pure and whole, not corrupt, not savage, extraneous to hatred and terror; something difficult to define, a remote possibility of good, but for which it was worth surviving."[50]

Everyday life went on, however, in the world of deprivation ruled by the SS, the *Kapos,* and other men of "stature"—and all who tried to imitate them. A running debate in the Holocaust literature revolves around the question of whether it was inevitable that the prisoner should be drawn to emulate those who enslaved him. Without question this phenomenon existed, but it was undoubtedly less prevalent and unavoidable than some have assumed.[51] Evidence can be found of two contrary responses by prisoners who were unable to adapt to the camp norm. One type was represented by those who identified psychologically with the SS and their helpers and tried to emulate their aggressiveness. This was the behavior of most of the "criminals," for example, but it appears that relatively few Jews were willing or able to resort to the raw aggression characteristic of most of the *Kapos,* including those few Jews who attained that status. We should note, however, that there were also exceptions among the *Kapos,* Jews and non-Jews, who used their positions to help others, lent a hand in escape attempts, and participated in organizing revolts. The other type identified not with the demeanor of the SS men but with their intentions. These were the people who surrendered inwardly—the figure of the Muselmann being their most radical incarnation. Frankl relates that when anyone was seen to be smoking a precious cigarette rather than trading it for a portion of soup, you knew that he had succumbed to despair and abandoned the struggle for existence. Those who were beyond exercising self-discipline, who neglected themselves and failed to maintain personal hygiene and order (to the degree that it was possible in the camp) were also generally understood to be in a state of decline.[52] Even a frail physical type who was blessed with strong willpower, concentration, and a rich inner strength was often better equipped to survive than a man of physical prowess who lacked such motivation. But these qualities were at best factors fortifying the prisoner against the winds of blind, cruel fate that buffeted him—whether to his benefit or detriment being a matter of pure chance.

If there is anything certain in a man's life, it is the knowledge that one day he must die. And if there is anything uncertain in a man's life, it is when that day will come. But in a normal life, a man does not stand before the gates of death every day, indeed every hour, and its terror only descends on him in special circumstances. The Jew in an extermination camp was in mortal danger every hour of every day. He was doomed, though not for anything of his own doing, and he had no means of defending himself. If in normal life a man is in danger of dying because of a disease or an accident, doctors, medical institutions, family, and friends can come to his aid. But in the concentration camps, the Nazi doctors regarded the death of the Jewish prisoner as the "solution." From the outset, the weak, the children, and the old all were doomed. Death was a daily occurrence, and people turned into corpses before one's eyes—hanged or shot to death or killed en masse in gas chambers. How did the prisoners generally and Jewish prisoners in particular react to this? All have testified that they ceased to react: they got used to it. Within minutes they pounced upon the dead and relieved them of whatever could be put to use: clothing, shoes, and any other paraphernalia.

Frankl relates that as his gaze settled on the corpse of a man with whom he had spoken just two hours earlier, he continued eating his soup. "If my lack of emotion had not surprised me from the standpoint of professional interest, I would not remember this incident now, because there was so little feeling involved in it." Habit became a protective wall.

The prisoners grew accustomed not only to seeing others die but to living forever in the "realm of death." They lost their fear of dying and even of the gas chamber.[53] Why did so many people who knew what awaited them go to their deaths so quietly? Cohen's answer is that "the adaptation to concentration-camp life and living in the 'realm of death' caused death to lose its terror, for it had become normal" and "people will not as a rule resist the normal." Even the political prisoners did not rebel when they were led to their deaths. But in certain circumstances the defense mechanism of delusion was at work. Thus we hear of sick people who believed they were being taken to another hospital or a sanitarium when they were, in fact, being taken to the gas chambers.[54] This happened in Auschwitz, but the same was essentially true in Mauthausen.

For the prisoners who maintained their inner freedom, the desire to live grew as the fear of death subsided. One witness quoted by Cohen stated, "Life belongs truly, completely, and without restriction to anyone who has ceased to fear death." This evidently explains what appear to be the surprisingly few incidents of suicide in the extermination camps, for as Cohen puts it, "In the realm of life one can escape from life by committing suicide; in the 'realm of death' one can escape from death by living."[55]

No study has yet been done on the incidence of suicide and the circumstances or character of the victims, and it is a difficult problem to attack for a number of reasons, especially in the concentration camp setting. Often the SS listed a prisoner who was killed as having committed suicide. People were coaxed into killing themselves and sometimes told forthrightly to do so. But since suicide is a common response to persecution, it is necessary to submit the phenomenon and its significance to closer scrutiny in terms of the circumstances of each period. Here I shall restrict myself to sketching a few aspects of the issue, which is a highly complex one.

It is usually argued that suicide was more common among Western than Eastern European Jews owing to the influence of German culture, in which death is a prevalent motif; to a false sense of security; and to the abandonment of Judaism and its values following the Emancipation. All of these elements undoubtedly played some role, but it seems to be that they were not the decisive factor. For, as we have seen, it was precisely the spiritual values of Western culture that might have enabled the prisoner to build the inner defense he needed to survive the camps. Let us, therefore, look into the question of when people committed suicide in great numbers.

The first wave of suicides occurred not in Germany but in Austria during the months immediately following the *Anschluss*.[56] People who had lived more or less normally until then were suddenly assailed by a wave of unbridled terror, mass arrests, economic ruin, unprecedented harassment, and humiliation. While the framework of their lives had been destroyed in a single stroke, they remained bound by the concept of a society striving toward equality and the rule of law and were themselves still in a physically and psychologically normal state. They were not given time to adjust to the situation and ascertain how to behave in it. Whoever could flee over the border did so, but many could not escape—or at least so they believed. A relatively high number of those who committed suicide in those first months after the *Anschluss* were intellectuals and members of the free professions who had held respected positions in society and were gripped by the feeling that their world had fallen apart. Shock and despair combined with the verve they still retained seemed to drive them to flee from life, which had lost its meaning and prospects for them. Still, these people accounted for just hundreds among the almost two hundred thousand Jewish residents of Vienna; the majority tried to flee the country or withstand the assault at home.

The incidence of suicide rose again when the deportations began in 1941, and each new wave of expulsions in the years to come was attended by dozens of cases. By then people had somehow managed to adjust to the situation and bear up despite poverty, overcrowding, hunger, and hard labor; but the prospect of deportation seemed to snuff out all hope. Even some of the people who had succeeded in going into hiding (popularly referred to as U-boats) drew radical conclusions when their hiding places were destroyed by the bombings in 1943 and abandoned both hope and life.[57] Yet this phenomenon was not unique to the Jews of the West. As Yisrael Gutman observes:

> There was another, no less tragic, option open to the Jews of the ghetto. Many diarists had commented that the Jews of Poland differed from their German and Austrian counterparts in that they did not break down and take their own lives but kept up a long, stubborn struggle to survive despite everything. This was indeed true from the beginning of the occupation until July 1942. But during the period of the mass deportation, many people surrendered and, as Levin put it, there were "scores of suicides."[58]

He goes on to cite some of the sources, including Ringelblum, who "put the number of suicides at hundreds, particularly among the intelligentsia." I, too, believe that it is an exaggeration to speak of a multitude of suicides solely in the West, especially from 1933 to 1941. Suicide is sometimes characterized as passive death, and the expression is used to denote the diametrical opposite of an activist response, meaning armed resistance. But suicide is a conscious act stemming from an animating desire and is, therefore, an active form of death: a man takes steps to put an end to his life, whereas in a passive death he no longer exercises his will. I believe it is no coincidence that the rate of suicide rose at the last stop of life before deportation, that thin dividing line between the realm of life that existed before the onset of the persecutions or in the shadow of their menace, and the realm of death, in which the pursuit of the "Final Solution" reached its apogee. As Cohen quotes one of the survivors, "The only thing one had to do was to give up the grim struggle for life, i.e., the struggle to do everything possible to obtain food and keep up one's spirits. When one did give this up, then death came by itself."[59] Perhaps we can say that this was the most common form of passive death in the camps.

20

Attempts at Rescue

Possibilities of Liberation from Fortress Europe

In approaching the problem of rescue, my purpose is not to sit in historical judgment but rather to raise a number of salient issues and outline the tendencies that forged the historical constellation of the time. The following are what seem to be the crucial questions that have direct bearing on the subject:

1. Which factors *led to the rescue of Jews?* In which countries?
2. Which factors *prevented the rescue of Jews?* In which countries?
3. Which countries served as a *haven for Jews?* When? Under what circumstances?
4. How did the *course of the war* affect the prospects of rescuing Jews?
5. Did the *Christian world* take action to rescue Jews? If so, how?
6. What did the *underground and resistance movements* of the other oppressed peoples do to help rescue Jews?
7. Did *the Jewish people* stand up to the test of rescue?

In turning to discuss these matters, it must again be noted that the concept of rescue, like that of genocide, did not fully come into its own—nor was it grasped by the world at large—until after the war. Despite the murderous zeal displayed by Hitler and his henchmen, the rescue of Jews was not of paramount concern to the world he threatened, and then only infrequently—and briefly—was it a prime aim or focal event.

Denmark

One such hour of grace came at the beginning of October 1943 when the Danish people, in a signal effort, rescued the great majority of the Jews in their country from the grip of the Nazis by ferrying them to safety in Sweden. The success of this operation and the drama of a concerted action accorded this rescue mission a unique character. It became a legend that quickly spread, including as it did the courageous and popular figure of the aged Danish king, Christian X. People grasped at this tale of collective rescue as proof of man's basic moral good, which had been placed in severe doubt by the atrocities of the Holocaust. Just as a spot of light can drive out much darkness—as the ancient Jewish sages taught—the humane character of this small Scandinavian nation, many of whose citizens took their lives into their own hands to save Jews, shone over the inhumanity of mass extermination and became a subject of glorification.

I certainly do not mean to deny the value or special significance of this great deed. Whoever surveys the history of this era and is familiar not only with its terrors but also with the bootless displays of heroism, the efforts that came to naught, and the circumstances and coincidences of the times cannot but praise the rescue of almost 8,000 people.[1] Yet one must also ask: Doesn't the rescue of 18,000 Jews in Holland, out of the 25,000 who tried to evade arrest and lived in hiding not for a few days but sometimes for years in a country that was essentially abandoned to its helpless indigenous administration and was among the most subjugated from the standpoint of SS domination—doesn't their salvation attest to the bravery of people who were willing to imperil themselves to save others? And what was the difference between these two instances? The 7,220 Jews and several non-Jewish relatives who were smuggled into Sweden and another 425 who, thanks to the efforts of the Danes, remained alive in Theresienstadt and were brought back before the end of the war represented almost 100 percent of the Jews who had been living in Denmark during the occupation, whereas in Holland 75 percent of the Jews (some 105,000 out of a total of 140,000) perished and 35,000 (or 25 percent of the original Jewish community) were saved.[2]

The rescue in Denmark resulted from a constellation of three factors: available opportunities, topical circumstances, and human actions—on the part of Danes as well as Germans. It should be noted that as part of the agreement concluded between the occupying Germans and the submitting Danes, the status of the country's Jews was not prejudiced during the early years of the occupation. Thus, in essence, their condition had not been undermined, and the Danish government, which continued to function, protected them. Although German troops were stationed in the country, the Danish army had not been disbanded, and the relations between Denmark and Germany were conducted through standard diplomatic channels. This compromise was equivocal, however, as the authorities in Germany interpreted it differently from the German representatives in the field, who had been influenced to one degree or another by Denmark's democratic way of life. These same representatives helped to suppress attempts to introduce the Nazi brand of anti-Semitism, which sparked the indignation of the Danish elite.

This first occurred—and not by chance—in the winter of 1942 when the Germans tried to extend their influence and tighten their hold over Denmark. In light of the uncompromising resistance, however, the participants at the Wannsee Conference concluded that the implementation of the Final Solution should be postponed in the Scandinavian countries, the number of Jews there at any rate being relatively small. The more the situation at the front bode ill for Germany, the more the strains in the relations between the Germans and the Danes became manifest, and by 1943 the Danish underground had gone into action. Germany's chief representative in Denmark, Dr. Werner Best—who had been one of Reinhard Heydrich's chief aides before he was ousted from his high post in the Nazi hierarchy—tried to paper over the conflict, but his rival for power, Hermann von Hanneken, the commander of the German troops in Denmark, forced matters to a head. At the end of August, a state of emergency was declared, the king's activities were halted, the army was confined, and the government was forced to resign; only the civil service remained intact under the direction of the state secretaries. Best then began playing a double game, initiating the deportation of the Jews to shore up his position as a loyal servant of the regime in Berlin and to obtain additional police units under his command while concomitantly trying to undo the deportation plan. His tactics came to naught, however, owing to Hitler's explicit order to carry out the action.[3] Still, he left the Danes the option of foiling the implementation of the deportation and rescuing the Jewish inhabitants of their country.

In this case, the triangle of *information, acknowledgement,* and a *decision in favor of action* (see chap. 19) was at work in the rescue. The reliable *information* was given to the Danish political leadership by the Germans themselves, the key figure in this instance being the maritime attaché in the German legation, Georg F. Duckwitz. Best apprised him of the deportation plan—presumably so that he would pass it on to the country's leading Social Democrats, with whom he maintained contacts—and the Danes never doubted the reliability of the information. Since the crisis that had erupted between the occupying authorities and the Kingdom of Denmark a month before, the Danish populace and leadership had feared a serious assault on their national freedom and the democratic character of their society. Now they took the threat to the Jews to be just the tip of the iceberg, and this *acknowledgement* led to the spontaneous identification with the Jews—after which the *decision to act* in order to save them was a natural conclusion. By this action the Danes expressed both resistance to the Nazi occupier and loyalty to their government and way of life. They warned the Jews, hid them, and, once it became clear that Sweden was prepared to take the fugitives in, organized the operation to smuggle them out at a number of different points.

The guiding hand of the Danish underground could soon be felt, moreover; during that period it boosted its influence among the Danish public and established an all but regular means of transport over the strait to Sweden. Most of all, however, it was the widespread participation in this practically overt operation that accorded its participants a large degree of security, for the Germans had neither the will nor the way to conduct mass arrests. The Danish underground was not the only force to strengthen its ties with Sweden in the autumn of 1943, however. Denmark's politicians were conducting negotiations to reach an agreement on political goals common to the two countries once the war drew to an end, and rescue of the Jews was but one element in the fabric of the political underground being woven against the background of a turnabout in the war.[4] The Danish civil service, headed by the state secretaries of the ministries, did not take part in the rescue operation, but it did fight for the lives of almost five hundred Jews the Germans had arrested during the manhunt and had sent to Theresienstadt.

One of the paradoxes of this period was the relationship between the passivity of the Jewish leadership and public and the proportion of Jews who were saved through the actions of their countrymen. Protected by the authorities for three and one-half years, the Jews of Denmark scrupulously avoided any activity that might have embarrassed their government or in any way prejudiced its relations with the Germans. This fact came out most clearly when a number of Zionist pioneers undergoing agricultural training in Denmark sought ways of escaping to Sweden or to the southern part of the Continent. In the spring of 1943, a group of these pioneers working as fishermen succeeded in fleeing to Sweden. But the attempt to reach the southern shores of Europe failed, and at the behest of the Danish authorities, the leaders of the Jewish community did everything in their power to prevent such actions from recurring.[5] When the crisis erupted about half a year later, the mood of rebelliousness among the Danish public was what above all saved the Jews. Thus, the situation in Denmark, which was exceptional from almost every point of view, shows how risky it is to draw generalizations about the direct connection between independent Jewish endeavor and the likelihood of being rescued.

Finland

Even more exceptional than the rescue from Denmark was the fate of the Jews in Finland.[6] The Jewish community there was a small one, numbering close to two thousand people during the war, including about three hundred refugees who had escaped from Germany and Austria and a few who had evidently come from Denmark and Norway after those countries fell to the Germans. Jewish life had not developed in Finland until the nineteenth century when the country was under Russian domination; the largest of the Jewish communities was in its capital, Helsinki. At the time, these communities were oppressed by a series of severe restrictions and heavy taxes, but matters improved appreciably when Finland was liberated from Russian rule and became a democratic state in 1917. The country's new constitution accorded the Jews full equality, and the small Jewish community developed its own lively cultural life. The Zionist movement became increasingly influential, and the Helsinki community even had a Jewish secondary school whose matriculation examinations were recognized by the state. In 1932 the chief rabbi, Simon Federbusch, united the country's kehillot into the Center of Jewish Communities in Finland, which safeguarded the rights of the Jews and, with the aid of leading Finnish political figures, succeeded in defeating a 1934 attempt to pass legislation outlawing the practice of ritual slaughter.

As noted earlier, Jewish refugees from the West (some of them actually apostates) began to reach Finland in 1933 and were aided by the Jewish communities (primarily in Helsinki) acting together with Finnish groups. Some of these refugees managed to emigrate overseas via Sweden, which had granted them transit visas. Although there were groups of anti-Semitic nationalists in Finland, their influence was marginal, and the Finnish political system was composed primarily of Conservatives, Liberals, and Social Democrats. It cannot be said that anti-Semitism was a prominent force in the army either, although close ties did exist between Finnish and German officers, especially as most of the Finns had received their military training in Germany.

The outbreak of the war did not affect this situation at all. In the Winter War against the Soviet Union, which had tried to exploit the hostilities in Europe to reassert its hegemony over its weaker neighbor, Jews served in the Finnish army alongside the country's other citizens. Contrary to what had happened in much of the rest of Europe, the Jews retained their equal status even after Finland had joined Germany in its campaign against Russia in 1941, for the Finns regarded the fighting against Russia as an extension of their struggle against Soviet aggression, not as an expression of support for Germany's ideology or political system. They did not indulge in anti-Semitism, to say nothing of deportations and extermination, and their posture on this issue was expressed quite clearly in the state's free press. What is more, since Jews served in the Finnish army in this war, as well, the Germans found themselves in a situation in which Jewish officers and enlisted men were fighting as their comrades-in-arms.

It should not be surprising that the leaders of the German regime, including Hitler, found this situation strange, so that as of the summer of 1942 attempts were made to lure Finland into the embrace of the New Order that was being established throughout Europe—and hence into the operations of the Final Solution. Visiting Finland, Himmler tried to promote the extermination plan among the Finns. He was accompanied on this trip by his personal physician, masseur, and therapist, Felix Kersten, a Finnish citizen who exercised a certain degree of influence over Himmler by virtue of his special art of massage, which relieved the Reichsführer of the severe pains he suffered from intestinal spasms. Kersten's role is a matter of dispute, but there is no doubt that on various occasions he saved people by using his sway over Himmler to thwart or mitigate Nazi plans for plunder or extermination. He claimed that Finland also exploited this relationship and that in collaboration with the Finns he tried to dissuade Himmler from his plans.[7] In any case Himmler was told in no uncertain terms that there was no Jewish problem in Finland.

The attitude of the Finnish authorities differed, however, when it came to the refugees who had entered Finland in the 1930s. At the beginning of the war, the Finns had assembled these refugees in labor camps in the northern part of the country, which was under the control of the German army, but in response to their requests subsequently transferred them to Finnish labor camps on the island of Suursaari (Hogland) in the Gulf of Finland. The head of the Finnish police, Arno Anthony, developed contacts with both the SS men assigned to Finland and with the Gestapo in Berlin, and reached an agreement to turn over to them for "repatriation" foreign citizens together with other aliens (primarily Russians) suspected of espionage. Among the "undesirable aliens" Anthony included a number of Jewish refugees against whom complaints of administrative and other minor infractions had been filed with the police. In accordance with an agreement contracted between Anthony and the head of the Gestapo in Estonia, refugees were deported by boat to that country in October 1943. Meanwhile, sixteen Jews were transferred from Suursaari to Helsinki with the intention of including them in the deportation. However, they succeeded in getting word of this action to one of the heads of the Jewish community, Abraham Stiller. He enlisted the aid of influential Finnish political figures, including the Social Democratic minister K. A. Fagerholm, who threatened to resign if the deportation was not canceled. Yet despite the debate within the government and the sharp response of the press, seven Jews were ultimately deported—one of them accompanied by his wife and nine-year-old son. Only one of these deportees survived the war. After lengthy negotiations most of the refugees were transferred to Sweden in the spring of 1944.

On September 19, 1944, an armistice agreement was signed between Finland and the Soviet Union. Two months later the Central Committee of Jewish Communities in Finland published a memorandum stressing the full equality that the Jewish citizens of Finland had enjoyed during the war, both in the army, in which some 20 percent of the Jewish community had served, and in civilian life. The Helsinki community had also been permitted to extend aid and certain services to the Jews among the Russian POWs. On December 6, 1944, Finnish Independence Day, Marshal Carl Gustaf von Mannerheim, who had been the country's leading military personality during the war and was now Finland's president, came to the synagogue in Helsinki to attend a memorial service for the thirty-six Jewish soldiers who had fallen in battle.

Bulgaria

The third country in which concerted activity to rescue Jews proved successful was Bulgaria, but developments there were very different from the two cases cited above. Close to fifty thousand Jews composed 0.8 percent of the population of Bulgaria, with about half of them living in the capital, Sofia, and the majority being middle-class merchants and artisans. Their kehillot were recognized as a national minority and enjoyed autonomy in their organization and management, which was conducted by a community council, the Consistoire. The state did not interfere in their affairs, but neither did it accord the kehillot financial support. Similarly, there were no laws discriminating against the Jews, but neither did they wield economic or political influence in Bulgaria. During the 1930s there was a certain rise in anti-Semitism as Nazism gained in influence. Yet one could not speak of a decline in the condition of the Jews until 1940, at which time Bulgaria began to lean toward Germany (as a result of which it was awarded part of the Dobruja area of southern Rumania, on which the government had long had designs). The definitive step was taken in March 1941 when Bulgaria joined the Axis powers and the German army, entering the country, proceeded to invade Greece and Yugoslavia at the beginning of April. The new Bulgarian government constituted at the time was headed by Bogdan Filov, a supporter of Germany.

After the conquest of Yugoslavia and Greece, Bulgaria fulfilled another territorial aspiration: it received control of part of southern and eastern Macedonia as well as Greek Thrace, thus giving it access to the Mediterranean. Before long, the Bulgarians were resorting to harshly repressive measures to exert their control over the economy, culture, and religious life of these "new territories." On May 14,

1941, they officially annexed Thrace, but the Germans insisted that the final borders of Macedonia not be determined until after the war, for they themselves were interested in the area for military and economic reasons. Meanwhile, the Bulgarians exploited an uprising in Thrace in order to pare down the Greek population: thousands of people were murdered, others fled or were deported, and Bulgarian citizens were settled in their place.[8]

Bulgaria did not play a significant role in the military operations in the Balkans. Of even greater import was the fact that it not only refrained from declaring war on the Soviet Union but continued to maintain diplomatic relations with Moscow. To the Germans' great irritation, a Soviet legation continued to function in Sofia throughout the war, and the Bulgarian Communists even set up a radio station in Moscow to broadcast to their homeland![9] It was not until after Pearl Harbor that Bulgaria joined in Germany's declaration of war on the United States and the other Allied powers, though the government did not really intend to become involved in the war.

It is against this general background that we can understand Bulgaria's behavior on the Jewish question, although the domestic situation in Bulgaria also played a considerable role. Throughout the period Bulgaria formally maintained the parliamentary format of its regime, and even though the opposition parties may not have had any real influence on the dictatorial rule of Czar Boris III and his government, they were, nevertheless, allowed to air their views and enjoyed public support—a factor that the government had to take into account. To this we must add the sway of the Communist underground, whose arm in the Soviet Union constantly warned against persecuting the Jews—likewise out of a desire to stoke opposition to the Bulgarian regime. Toward the end of the summer of 1940, when the government decided to pass anti-Jewish legislation—entitled the Law for the Defense of the Nation—a debate broke out in the parliament as well as among the public at large, so that alongside the enthusiastic proponents of the law were broad sectors that publicly protested the passage of discriminatory legislation against the Jews. The debate continued for months, during which the Holy Synod of the Bulgarian church sent a letter of protest to the prime minister, with a copy to the chairman of the parliament, proposing that rather than devote itself to passing special laws against the Jews, the government should be taking meaningful steps to counter the real danger facing the Bulgarian people.[10] Thus, it was not until the second half of January 1941 that the government managed to get the law passed, and Boris signed it on February 15. The bill was modeled after the Nuremberg Laws, though a number of clauses exempted certain types of Jews from its provisions. The protesting Jews were told that the intent of the law was "to pave the way for rapprochement with Germany and firmly to establish Bulgaria's position within the Axis."[11] Indeed, it was less than two weeks after the law was signed that Bulgaria officially joined the Axis.

In the course of time, the Bulgarians added new laws and regulations that generally restricted the Jews' economic activities, while a good part of their property was plundered through special taxes, confiscation, expropriation actions, and various prohibitions. The situation deteriorated further in the summer of 1942 when the government passed a special law authorizing it to take whatever measures were deemed necessary against the Jews. This bill was likewise passed despite vocal opposition, and at the end of August the Commissariat for the Jewish Problem was established under Alexander Belev, a well-known anti-Semite. Its mandate was twofold: to preside over the confiscation of Jewish property and to lay the groundwork for deporting the Jews to the East by passing laws and regulations modeled on the German precedents. Back in the winter of 1941, Belev had been sent to Germany for a few months to study this very matter.[12] Yet in Bulgaria there was a difference between passing laws and enforcing them, which was particularly obvious in the case of the regulation requiring the Jews to wear a yellow badge. The government agreed to supply the badge, but by October 1942 it had provided only 20 percent of the required number, claiming that it was technically impossible to distribute any more.[13] On another plane, a few of the cooperative banks under Jewish control succeeded in merging with similar institutions run by the Social Democrats, thus saving at least a portion of the Jewish capital.[14]

In the autumn of 1942, the German pressure on the Bulgarians to join in the execution of the Final Solution began to mount; in November the German minister, Adolf H. Beckerle, announced that after a long debate, the Bulgarian government had decided to comply with the German demands. Once again the Bulgarians claimed they faced great difficulties in honoring their commitment because they needed the Jewish work force.[15] Indeed, over the previous years Jews, especially young Jews, had been conscripted for hard labor in building roads.

This was the period in which the Germans began to implement the Final Solution in Greece, and just as Dieter Wisliceny had been sent there to organize the operation, so Theodor Dannecker (who had earlier been stationed in France) was now transferred to Bulgaria for the same purpose. He arrived in January 1943 and at the beginning of February reached an oral agreement with Belev that the Jews in the new territories would be deported first. The number agreed on was 20,000, although it was known that the Jewish population of eastern Macedonia and Thrace did not exceed 12,000, so that from the outset the plan was to fill the quota by using 6,000 Jews from Bulgaria proper. Once again the consent of the Bulgarian government was obtained, though not without a debate. The Dannecker–Belev agreement, including all the technical and organizational details (e.g., that twenty trains were to be sent out of six collection centers in Macedonia, Serbia, and southwest Bulgaria) was committed to paper and signed on February 22. The government officially approved it on March 2, 1943, evidently being cognizant that full-fledged Bulgarian citizens would be deported, too.[16]

In the new territories Jews were not allowed to acquire Bulgarian citizenship as other people could. In the community of Skopje, Macedonia, the Jews tried to protest against this discrimination, which was legally turning them into aliens, by arguing that they and their ancestors had been living in Macedonia for centuries.[17]

Immediately after the establishment of the Commissariat, Belev appointed representatives to various areas and charged them with carrying out the preparatory actions: expropriating Jewish property, prohibiting economic activities, limiting freedom of movement, and enforcing the requirement to wear the yellow badge (under pressure from the Germans, the required number of these patches had finally been supplied). Beginning in February 1943, secret preparations were made to round up the Jews and concentrate them in camps by lining up the necessary trains and escorts. The system that Dannecker was later to use on a larger scale in Hungary was inaugurated here. The country was divided into five regions: Thrace, Macedonia, Pirot (in Serbia), Sofia, and the rest of Bulgaria. The first in line to be deported were the 4,273 Jews in Thrace—farthest from their destination in Poland. The *Aktion* began on March 4.[18]

Then came the turn of the 7,381 Jews of Macedonia. Following what had become the standard system, this operation was carried out at a single stroke with great cruelty. On March 11, just after midnight, the Bulgarian troops in Macedonia surrounded the three cities containing large Jewish communities, and at three o'clock they began transferring the Jews to a central camp in Skopje. Two days earlier, two members of the Skopje Community Council had been warned of the impending operation by a city official who was a personal friend; both fled to Albania. About two hundred other Jews followed in their wake, though not all of the people who got wind of the plot tried to escape, either because they refused to leave their families in a time of trouble or because they failed to appreciate what actually lay ahead for them. The policemen who carried out the arrests were told to persuade the Jews that they were being taken to other areas of Bulgaria for a time. They also counseled the Jews to take their money and jewelry along, "just in case they needed it."[19]

In the collection camps, the Jews suffered from all the well-known hardships, their remaining property was plundered, and they became the targets of humiliation. Yet during the two weeks or so that the Jews of Macedonia spent in the camp, it appears that only 4 of the 7,314 prisoners perished; 165 others were released, including doctors and pharmacists (and their families)—whose services were needed by the state—as well as the Turkish, Italian, and Spanish citizens whose governments had protested their arrest.

In Thrace the action had been handled in a similar fashion, and a few days after their arrest, Jews were transferred to concentration areas within Bulgaria. From there, 4,058 together with 161 Jews from Pirot were sent in open cargo cars through a succession of stations (where they had to change trains) until they reached Lom, a port on the Danube at the country's northern border. This journey took two weeks, and the deportees arrived at their destination in very poor condition. Children were born and people died during this train journey, which the Bulgarians conducted in a way that resembled the Nazi deportations in its barbarity. A non-Jewish nurse who came upon one of these trains in Lom did all she could to help the deportees by courageously and tenaciously surmounting the obstacles of apathy, bureaucracy, and sheer malice. She later related the story of this struggle, in which local Jews and children of Gypsies helped her distribute food and water.[20] The fate of these people remains obscure. In Lom they were placed on four boats and some barges to take them to Vienna, the stop on the way to Poland. But only three boats were reported to have arrived in Vienna. There is reason to believe that at least some of the deportees, mostly men, were drowned in the Danube, but the fate of the others is equally unclear, for none of them returned after the war. Of the Jews of Macedonia, 7,144 were sent by train to Treblinka, where 7,132 of them were murdered.[21] By the end of March, 11,363 of the Jews who had been living in the new territories, mainly Thrace and Macedonia, had been deported from Bulgaria.[22]

Dozens of isolated Macedonian Jews were interned in concentration camps in Yugoslavia and within the bounds of the Reich. Of the 196 who returned at the end of the war, 65 had been in concentration camps, 116 had been in Albania, and 15 had been taken prisoner in the fighting in 1941 and spent the war in POW camps in Germany. The total number of survivors (those who were liberated and returned) was 604, representing 5.1 percent of the Jews who had been living in the Macedonia new territories in 1943.[23]

How can we explain the fact that in contrast to the vigorous and brutal action taken to deport the Jews from the new territories, the Jews of Bulgaria did not suffer similar treatment? That Bulgaria was, in fact, counted among the few countries whose Jewish population was for the most part saved? And how are we to explain the flagrant contrast between the ruthlessness shown toward the Jews of Macedonia and Thrace and the halt of the extermination campaign called by the same government acting under the dictatorial rule of the czar?

Preparations for a campaign to deport the Jews of Bulgaria were made together with those for the action in the new territories—and with quite the same thoroughness. As early as February 22, for example, the agents of the Commissariat throughout the country were given twenty-four hours to prepare lists of Jews characterized as "rich, prominent, and well known to the public," influential people who were strengthening the "spirit of Judaism," and opponents of the regime, real and imagined. The lists were also to include the most minute details about these figures and their families. As a result of this groundwork, the Commissariat drew up a comprehensive list of 9,000 candidates from Bulgaria proper; 8,400 of them were marked for deportation together with the Jews from Thrace and Macedonia; 2,600 from Sofia; and the rest from provincial cities, mostly in the west and southwest, that were close to the departure points. These Bulgarian Jews were meant to fill out the deportation quota of 20,000 people. The *Aktion* was to be effected beginning on March 8, and in Sofia it was set for March 10 and 11.[24] Everything was ready, including the trains to carry the victims to their initial concentration points in the cities of Dubnitsa and Radomir. And then, at the very last moment, something happened and the plan was not carried out.

During the night of March 9/10, which was set as the date for inaugurating the *Aktion* in Bulgaria's cities, the minister of the interior, P. Gabrovski, ordered Belev to call off the deportation operation because the government had decided to postpone it. This order was relayed by phone to the directors of the operation throughout the country. In some of the provincial cities, where Jews had already been arrested a day or two earlier, they were released and sent to their homes (which in the meantime had been looted by the police and local residents). What brought about the sudden, last-minute change, this eleventh-hour rescue—in the literal as well as the metaphorical sense of the term?

Rumors and even definitive information about the deportation plan had begun to reach Jews in the last days of February. One of the sources of this information was, surprisingly enough, Belev's own secretary, Liliana Fanitsa, who simultaneously relayed his orders to the Commissariat's agents throughout the country and warned her acquaintances among the leaders of Sofia's Jewish community.[25] In a chance meeting in Sofia—and in exchange for a fee—a relative of the minister of the interior revealed a "great secret" to Chaim Raḥamim Bakhar, a resident of the provincial city of Kiustendil who happened to be in the capital that day. Bakhar passed the information on to the leaders of the Jewish community and to well-connected Bulgarian acquaintances, but the Bulgarians denied it. On the other hand, after Bakhar returned to Kiustendil, the frightening news was confirmed by the local Bulgarian area commander, who took the initiative and warned Bakhar of the impending action—though not without demanding an exorbitant payment in return.[26] In the meantime the preparations being made to establish collection camps in various locations alarmed Jews and non-Jews alike. On orders from the Commissariat, equipment such as beds, barrels for water, and various other paraphernalia were collected and stored mostly in empty tobacco warehouses. Ordered to supply these things, the Jews were gripped by anxiety, while the Bulgarians were exhibiting contradictory tendencies: some protested, resisted, and came to the aid of the Jews, including influential figures who decided to go to Sofia and intercede with members of the regime; others—incited by Belev's men—tried to prevent such attempts at intercession, and they ridiculed and assailed the Jews.

The city of Kiustendil became the center of the struggle over the fate of Bulgarian Jewry, and it mirrored both the forces and the doubts that were at work throughout the country.[27] One resident of the city during that period was Shimon Barukh, the brother of Ya'akov Barukh, the Jewish Agency's representative in Bulgaria and one of the members of the underground-operating Zionist Executive. Shimon succeeded in getting information about the planned action from Kiustendil to Ya'akov, who had also received word of it from other sources. Together with other leading figures, Jewish and non-Jewish alike, Ya'akov Barukh tried to approach various officials and members of the government. Their efforts were fruitless, however, as the latter either held that it was impossible to act contrary to a German order or argued that the government decision should not be revoked. Finally, on March 8, Ya'akov Barukh appealed to an old school friend, Dimiter Peshev, the delegate from Kiustendil and deputy speaker of the parliament, who had not as yet heard of the deportation plan but now received confirmation of it from the commander of the Kiustendil area and the chief of police. The next day a number of Jews and other Bulgarians met for consultation in Peshev's office and decided to try to rouse opposition in parliament, which was convening that evening. Citing the demur exempting Bulgarian Jews from deportation in the wording of the government's decision, they managed to obtain an unlimited postponement of the operation. It is not absolutely clear whether Prime Minister Filov acted on his own initiative or on the czar's orders in this matter, but considering the nature of Bulgaria's dictatorial regime, it is difficult to imagine that Filov would have decided on such a measure by himself.[28]

Not content with a postponement alone, Peshev got forty-two parliamentary delegates—many of them leading personalities and some even supporters of Germany—to sign a petition protesting the intention to deport the Jews of Bulgaria and submitted it to Filov on March 19. The wording of this public protest was a work of art: couched in terms of an expression of confidence, loyalty, and concern for the government's honor, it essentially accused the government of plotting the deportation and warned it against damaging Bulgaria's interests or reputation or violating the law by deporting the Jews, which was tantamount to committing mass murder.[29]

This was not the only protest addressed to the government or parliament. Among the opponents of the move were individual church leaders as well as the Holy Synod, which likewise submitted a petition to the prime minister on April 2. It demanded that "Christians of Jewish origin and *Jews in general* should not be denied their elementary rights as human beings and citizens or their right to live in the country and work for a decent human existence" (emphasis added). Adopting a line of argument similar to the one voiced by the Protestant clergy in Denmark, these protesters invoked the right to defy the authorities and denounced the "principle of racism, by virtue of which hatred can be spread and acts of oppression and cruelty committed."[30] Other circles, including the Bulgarian Writers' Association, joined in this expression of civil disobedience.

However, there were also forces that supported the action—out of either fear of the Germans or a mixture of political conviction and anti-Semitism—and with their aid Filov succeeded in mounting a retaliatory move against Peshev in parliament: on March 24 a large majority voted in favor of full support for the government's actions, including the measures to be taken against the Jews, and repealed the Peshev petition. Two days later, in the midst of an uproar and calls of protest from the floor, a motion was passed ousting Peshev from his position as deputy speaker of the parliament.[31]

In Berlin it was understood that the original plan, which was regarded as the first step toward the Final Solution in Bulgaria, had been carried out only in Macedonia and Thrace. The results satisfied neither Eichmann in the RSHA nor Ribbentrop in the Foreign Ministry, and their disappointment found expression when Czar Boris arrived in Germany for a meeting with Hitler. The czar's visit extended from March 31 to April 3, 1943, and his talk with Hitler revolved around the position Turkey would be likely to take in light of the situation on the fronts after Stalingrad and the Allied conquest of North Africa. It was in a talk with Ribbentrop that the deportation of Bulgaria's Jews came up, and Boris clearly stated that he had consented to a deportation to the East, but only of the Jews of Macedonia and Thrace. As for the Jews of Bulgaria proper, he again took shelter behind Bulgaria's need for labor to build roads, but he did promise to deport "a small number of Bolshevik Communist elements" and to close the rest of the Jews in provincial cities and camps within Bulgaria.[32]

By the second half of March, the Bulgarian government had queried its envoys in Rumania and Italy about how these countries were relating to the Jewish problem and the German demand regarding deportations to the East. In both cases the answers were that the authorities were opposed to deportation and not being responsive to the German entreaties. The reply of the Bulgarian minister in

Bucharest was unequivocal, "The Rumanian plan to deport the Jews of Rumania has been shelved."[33]

But the struggle in Bulgaria continued. At first Belev resigned in response to the cancellation of the operation. However, following the parliamentary motion, and at the urging of Interior Minister Gabrovski, who evidently promised him that the action would be resumed, he withdrew his resignation. Then broader events in Bulgaria came to his aid. During these early months of 1943, there was a rise in the incidence of political murder against members of the radical Right. The perpetrators were not caught, and various assumptions and rumors circulated about their identity, but the government naturally found it very convenient to accuse the Communists and Jews.[34] It was against this background that Belev embarked upon a new plan in mid-April: to establish the exact number and location of the Jews, he published an order (on April 14) stating that "every man of Jewish origin has to submit a 'family card' . . . that will include precise details on all the members of his family." This operation was to be completed by May 16; Belev planned to execute the deportation on May 30.

Before being placed before the czar for his approval, the plan was discussed with Dannecker and Gabrovski and the decision was made to propose two alternatives: (1) Belev's plan, which included the deportation to Poland and (2) deportation only to provincial cities and camps within Bulgaria. On May 20 the minister of interior submitted both plans to the czar, who decided on the second one, which was also in agreement with what he had told Ribbentrop. And once again the information was leaked to the Jews by Belev's secretary.

Since the middle of March a movement had been afoot to mobilize public opinion against the deportation of the Jews.[35] Among the quarters that came to the aid of the Jewish community were the two parties representing the socialist movement—both operating underground—whose war against anti-Semitism was part and parcel of their struggle against the regime. In contrast, the bourgeois democratic circles had a direct influence on members of the regime, and although their parties were likewise suppressed, "almost all [their] leaders extended a hand to help the Jews in these fateful days." Finally, the Holy Synod, under the leadership of the Metropolitan Stefan, raised its voice in support of the Jews. When it became known that a deportation from Sofia was in the offing, the coalition leading this struggle tried to galvanize all these forces and turned to the papal nuncio and the ministers of Spain and Italy, as well. To counter all this activity, Gabrovski tried to sway public opinion by publishing communiqués that blamed the Jews for the political murders.[36]

On May 21 the government began distributing the deportation order forms among the Jews. May 24 was a national religious holiday on which it was customary to hold processions, but when agitated Jews who had gathered near one of the synagogues tried to hold a demonstration with the intention of marching to the czar's palace, even the leaders of the community tried to stop them, for fear of the consequences. Indeed, the police were sent to stop the march, scattering the demonstrators by force and arresting over 400 people, for the most part youngsters. They were later sent to the Samovit camp on the shore of the Danube, which had been operating as a concentration camp for a year. That same night, after arresting the Jews, the police broke into their apartments and looted them. All attempts at intercession proved futile, and between May 26 and June 7, a total of 19,153 Jews from Sofia were transferred to twenty provincial cities, where they were crowded into temporary quarters and the apartments of local Jews (their own apartments in Sofia had been sealed, following the procedure adopted in Macedonia and Thrace). These Jews were soon joined by deportees from three other cities.[37] But this was essentially the end of the anti-Jewish actions in Bulgaria. In response to pressure from Eichmann and from Horst Wagner of the Foreign Ministry, on August 18 and 19 Beckerle explained that pressuring the Bulgarian government on the matter of the Jews was "pointless."[38]

On August 14, 1943, the czar had made a one-day visit to Hitler's headquarters, and shortly after his return in the führer's private plane, he fell ill and died a few days later. Ever since then, there has been a nagging suspicion that Boris was poisoned on that flight. But even if that were so, the murder did Germany no good, for from then on the successive governments in Bulgaria increasingly dissociated themselves from the Germans, and on September 8, 1944—the day on which the Russians crossed the Bulgarian border—the government declared war on the Reich. The next day a coup took place, and the Communists emerged as the dominant political force among the group that came to power. During that last year, from the autumn of 1943 to the autumn of 1944, the Jews found their situation gradually easing until all the anti-Jewish laws were officially revoked on September 7, 1944.[39]

In 1943 the Jewish population of Greater Bulgaria numbered 63,403 people;[40] 18 percent of this population, or 11,363 Jews, were deported. One of the Bulgarian government's primary objectives in passing the anti-Jewish legislation was to get hold of Jewish property, even though this was not particularly extensive. The value of this property in Bulgaria proper was over Lv 6 billion (U.S. $75 million or, according to another estimate, Lv 7.5 billion, which was equivalent to U.S. $91 million). Almost all of it was confiscated: 25 percent taken in the form of taxes and Lv 4.5 million (U.S. $74.7 million) expropriated outright. In the new territories, the Jews' property was assessed at Lv 1.5 billion (U.S. $18.2 million), but here the Bulgarians succeeded in collecting only a small proportion of it— Lv 356 million (U.S. $4.3 million), of which Lv 21.3 million (about U.S. $257,000), or 6 percent, were discounted as the cost of the deportation.[41] Some of this property was returned to the Jews of Bulgaria, and the law provided for partial payment for whatever was not restored. What happened, in effect, was that the Jews were pauperized—but they survived.

In their treatment of the inhabitants of the new territories—especially the Jews of Thrace at the time of the deportation—and the Jews of Sofia during the deportation from there, the Bulgarian authorities displayed a savageness comparable to that of other peoples in similar circumstances. And the rapaciousness of the regime and the individuals whose aid and support had to be bought was extraordinary. Yet, there were also people like Dimiter Peshev and Liliana Fanitsa who put themselves in jeopardy without asking for reward. The contradictory trends were characteristic of the country's situation between the fronts, its dualistic behavior in foreign affairs, and the way in which it swayed between dictatorship and a parliamentary regime. They also shaped the dichotomy in Bulgaria's attitude toward the Jews.

Still, Bulgaria was not the only country that abandoned "foreigners." The same can be said of Vichy France, and even in Finland the chief of police would have surrendered Jewish refugees to the Germans had it not been for the pressure of public opinion on the government. In each case the critical factors were the broader political situation and the odds that one side or the other stood to win the war. In the Balkans the mutual influence of the countries in the area also played a role; perhaps of decisive importance was the fear of an Allied invasion via the Mediterranean or the Soviet Union.

There is no cause to doubt the motives of those who came to the aid of the Jews in an hour of crisis. However, it was the political and strategic circumstances of the day that reinforced their arguments and served as the background to the rescue activities. Sweden's readiness to establish clandestine ties with Denmark and take in the Danish Jews was to a large extent in response to the turn in the tide of war in 1943. The same can be said of the Bulgarian czar's refusal to abandon his citizens to the Germans. However, two phenomena are common to all three of the countries in which the rescue of the Jews was largely successful. The first is that authoritative information on the planned deportation came from the side of the perpetrators: in Denmark, from the Germans stationed there; in Bulgaria, from the Commissariat and its representatives; and in Finland, from the police. The second was that in all three cases, the deportation was foiled at the very last moment—in response to an attempt to effect it in a surprise, lightning move. The authoritative source of the information left no question about acknowledgement, which, in turn, facilitated a quick response that averted tragedy.

The Probability of Rescue from Areas Under German Rule

It still has not been explained why, in these particular circumstances, a decision was made to save people—and was successfully executed—or why these cases are exceptions to the rule. Hence, I now shall attempt to sketch the development of events and analyze the reasons for the magnitude of the loss and the exigency of the rescue effort. It must be stressed, however, that this is merely an attempt to diagnose and indicate a direction and as such is far from an exhaustive presentation. A fuller investigation of this subject would require a research effort in its own right.[42]

Within the sphere of German influence and the bounds of the actual German occupation, it is possible to discern four main factors that, in various combinations, had a decisive impact on the treatment of the Jews and their fate:

1. the degree of subjugation to, or dependence on, the National Socialist regime;
2. the political tradition of the country in question and the way it was implemented by an independent administration;

3. the degree of anti-Semitism found among the people and the independent regime;
4. the organized public forces—overt or clandestine—that were opposed to Nazi Germany.

The complex circumstances in which these factors operated and their mutual influence were not identical in every place. In examining the historical situation it becomes clear that their evolution in one country bears no resemblance to that in another. To elucidate this point, the problem of rescue must be examined in two types of regimes: the occupied countries and the satellite states.

Nazi-Occupied Countries

Though there is a striking resemblance between the circumstances that emerged in the areas captured from the Soviet Union in 1941 in which the Einsatzgruppen systematically perpetrated their mass murder operation, nonetheless, differences existed. In the Baltic states the SS made extensive and calculated use of the violent anti-Semitism found among broad sectors of the population. The rule of these countries was concentrated exclusively in German hands, and no organized forces of resistance remained (as much as possible they had joined the retreating Russian troops); actions to aid the Jews were carried out solely on an individual and incidental basis.[43] A similar situation prevailed in the other areas captured from the Soviet Union, especially those that had belonged to Poland prior to the war. The factors of time and timing were of critical importance everywhere, regardless of the specific conditions that prevailed in any one place. Thus, the Jews of Estonia had greater opportunities to flee because it took the Germans a month to reach the country. And in the southeastern Ukraine, not only was the Russian administration a stabilizing factor, there was also time to organize a retreat—with Jews joining it, in many areas, as Soviet citizens. It is estimated that as a result of this move, at least a million Jews were saved from slaughter by the Einsatzgruppen.[44]

German rule was absolute in Poland, as well, but the treatment of the Jews there progressed through a number of stages. On the one hand, the escalation of the war was attended by a step-up in the slaughter of Jews; yet the turn in the tide in 1943 did nothing to change that. The Poles, for their part, had an underground resistance organization and a government-in-exile, but their support for the Jews can only be characterized as too little, too late. And, as we noted, the nationalist partisans who fought the Germans became their allies when it came to killing the Jews who had succeeded in escaping to the forests. At the same time, however, thousands of individual Poles displayed support for the Jews despite the risks entailed.[45]

In the occupied countries in the West, the most stringent situation existed in Holland and Norway.[46] Both of these countries were ruled by a Reichskommissar—an SS man appointed by Hitler and supported by the machinery of the SS and the German police. Both countries had governments-in-exile resident in England together with their royal families, which had also fled. A large German contingent of troops was stationed in both, and the local administrations were subordinated to the SS apparatus. In Norway the support for Vidkun Quisling was marginal, so that the Germans did not take him very seriously. The Norwegian police took their orders directly from the occupiers—willingly or under duress—with rebellious elements within the force being deported to concentration camps in Germany. The Jews' turn to be deported came when the war was at its height, in 1942, but more than half of the small Jewish community was smuggled out to Sweden.

There was no equivalent of a Quisling in Holland, but the senior ranks of the local civil service lacked both independence and initiative. The fact of the matter is that even the Dutch government-in-exile did not issue orders to display resistance to the Nazis until practically the end of the war, and no such orders were ever given in regard to the Jews. As far back as the 1930s, the Dutch government had tried with increasing urgency to dam the flow of Jewish refugees. During the occupation the Dutch underground and churches in Holland met with an emphatic response from the Nazis and ever-greater difficulties when they attempted to protest the persecution of the Jews. The Dutch population at large, on the one hand, displayed a mixture of a leaning toward self-preservation and even service to the Germans—often for financial reward—and, on the other hand, resistance to them combined with solidarity with the Jews and sincere efforts to rescue them. Amid the general confusion, which often deteriorated into apathy, multitudes of Jews were deported to their deaths.[47]

The German occupying regime in Denmark was the least rigorous in all of Europe. Until the crisis that erupted in August 1943, the German military presence was hardly felt there, and no SS machinery had been established in the country. An important factor in Denmark was that until the crisis, the country's political echelon operated openly, and afterward it cooperated with the underground, which had replaced it as the country's most influential political force. It should be stressed, however, that the heads of the Danish civil service, who took the administration of the country upon themselves after the government's resignation, showed no more political acumen when the deportation crisis broke out than had their Dutch counterparts.

Other countries that were subject to an occupying regime but were able to protect a substantial proportion of their Jewish population were Belgium, France, and Italy. In Belgium and the northern sector of France, the German occupational regime was in the form of a military government, but the Himmler–Eichmann apparatus, nevertheless, enjoyed a rather free hand. The governments of these countries were able to preserve a certain degree of political independence, and although the conduct of King Leopold III of Belgium is a subject of controversy, the fact remains that his presence—and particularly that of Queen Mother Elizabeth—was felt during the occupation and a sense of independent authority was maintained in domestic affairs. (The influence of the royal house was felt even more strongly in Denmark.) But contrary to the Dutch example, the Belgian government-in-exile remained alert and involved at all times and tried, by means of its communiqués and directives, to set down a political line in the spirit of a legally constituted democratic regime. Moreover, the well-organized and highly active Belgian underground cooperated with the Jews. It is true that these combined forces, which enjoyed some public support, failed to prevent the deportation of more than 25,000 Jews; but at least it can be said that about the same number were saved.

The intricate situation in France left potent aspects of rule in the hands of the Vichy government.[48] What is more, the French government remained in power and Henri-Philippe Pétain retained his position as president even after the German army entered the southern zone in November 1942. The Vichy government's attitude toward the Jews vacillated between xenophobic anti-Semitism and a democratic tradition that stood for offering refuge to the persecuted; a sense of loyalty to French citizens, but also greed for Jewish property; the fact of capitulation to the Germans—out of both desire and necessity—and finally a desire to maintain some measure of independence. The fluctuation between these poles led to the abandonment of the Jews, on the one hand, and the provision of opportunities for them to escape, and for various forces active within the French populace to aid them, on the other. These forces were to be found in the state administration (especially in the south), the resistance movement, and to a certain degree in the church. Thus, over two-thirds of the Jewish population of France could be saved.

As long as Mussolini remained in power in Italy, the attitude toward the Jews oscillated between the dictates of a liberal tradition and a humane approach and latent or overt anti-Semitism that was affected by both a desire to conform to the strong ally, Germany, and a will to remain independent. Mussolini was motivated above all by tactical considerations, whereas the humanistic approach was the more evident trend in the Foreign Ministry and the army. Consequently, as we have seen, the Italians—in contrast to the Bulgarians, for example—took the Jews in the territories occupied by them in Yugoslavia, Greece, and France under their protection, to the obvious dissatisfaction of the Germans (see chap. 16). This situation changed, however, after Mussolini's fall and the armistice with the Allies, when the Germans occupied central and northern Italy and also wrested control over the Italian-occupied areas. Then, even Italian anti-Semitic elements raised their heads, but the majority of the Italian people did not let the Jews down, and thousands of them found refuge among the population and in church institutions.

Satellite Countries

The four traits that characterized the occupied countries in their treatment of the Jews also applied to the satellite states.[49] Worst of all was the situation in the countries that had been granted their independence by Germany, such as Slovakia and Croatia, because they were most willing to comply with the Germans' demands, especially after aides and advisers had been sent in to implement the Final Solution. In Serbia, on the other hand, the Germans exercised direct rule and the situation more closely resembled that in the countries of Eastern Europe, except that here the partisans were both a political factor and extremely active, thus providing the Germans with a convenient pretext for annihilating the Jews.

In Rumania, indigenous anti-Semitism stood out prominently, and the violent anti-Semitic outburst in the summer of 1941 dealt the Jews of north Transylvania, northern Bukovina, and Bessarabia a stunning blow in the form of murder, harassment, and deportation to Transnistria. By the turn of the year, however, there were growing signs that when it came to the Jews of the country's heartland (the Regat), the leaders of the Rumanian regime had no intention of allowing the Germans to do as they pleased. The following summer the government reached the decision not to surrender the Jews living within the state's traditional borders. What stands out most strikingly here is the extent to which the changing attitude toward the Jews was a function of the Rumanian authorities' complicated relationship with Germany.[50]

Just as France was both an occupied and a satellite country, and just as Yugoslavia was divided between satellite Croatia, occupied Serbia, and the area under Italian influence (until it, too, became an occupied area), so Greece was not all of a piece in terms of its status. In the occupied area in the north, the Germans treated the Jews of Salonika with a high hand, but it was not until the fall of Italy that they gained control of the south. And in contrast to the situation in Salonika, where the local population exhibited no support whatever for the Jews, in the south the Greek underground helped them to the degree that it was able.

An exceptionally negative case, from the standpoint of timing and the way in which the Final Solution was carried out, is the harrowing fate of the Jews of Hungary. It was about a year before the conclusion of the war—at a time when the ruling powers and grass-roots elements everywhere else had begun to dissociate themselves from the Germans and when the Allies as well as the neutral and subjugated countries were all anticipating Hitler's inevitable defeat. Then it was that Hungary was not only conquered but that its government, and the surrounding world, permitted the Germans to execute the most concentrated, rapid, and extensive *Aktion* in which Jews had ever been deported to their destruction from a country with a self-dependent regime.

Help and Jewish Self-help

In no place were the Jews in a position to work toward their rescue, to say nothing of actually being saved, without the aid of confederates and supporters. Such allies ran the risk of losing their own and their families' freedom, property, or lives. The story is told of a Dutch farmer's family who found hiding places for hundreds of Jews in addition to the scores concealed on their farm—and three of its members paid for it with their lives.[51] This is but one example of the many that can be cited in every country. The individuals who took their lives in their hands for the sake of this cause have come to be known as "Righteous Among the Nations," and their number among every nation, including the German people, reaches into the thousands. Not all of them are known to us, especially as many perished along with the Jews they were trying to protect. Their deeds are a living testimony that there is still hope for man's future.

At the same time, not all those who helped the Jews acted out of moral, political, or ideological conviction. In many cases aid was obtained in exchange for payment, which was usually exorbitant. All of Europe's professional smugglers took in a tidy sum during those years. Even Danish fishermen usually demanded a hefty fee for each person they ferried to safety, and it was only due to the intervention of the underground that their prices were reduced. On the Swiss border, in the Pyrenees on the route to Spain, and in the passes between Poland and Slovakia, Slovakia and Hungary, and Hungary and Rumania the trade in human lives flourished.

In other cases political considerations entered into the decision to help Jews. When aid was particularly well organized, it was usually a sign that it was being extended on political or ideological grounds. The larger the organizations behind these efforts and the more of the population they encompassed, the better the chances of success and the less the risk to the individual. Denmark serves as a good example of this rule, as well.

Both a supply of money or valuables and connections with the immediate vicinity—and sometimes distant areas—were vital to planning any means of escape. We have seen that Jews everywhere tried to hold onto their money—preferably in foreign currency, with a premium on dollars—and to hide valuables in their clothing or on their person, and their captors worked with the same consistency and diligence to uncover these hidden treasures. Nevertheless, there were Jews who managed to keep a hold on their cash, and thus purchase or otherwise "organize" the funds they needed. Much of this money was lost, either because it was given as a down payment on the purchase of arms to a dealer who promptly absconded with it or because it was paid in advance to a smuggler who abandoned his charges in the middle of a forest or allowed them to be caught by the border police and returned to their country of origin—thus their money was spent for naught and more had to be found to make a fresh attempt. In addition, the role paid by bribes, large and small, has to be mentioned.

Even if money were no object, if a Jew could not make contact with the outside world—with people who enjoyed freedom or influence—there was no way he could realistically attempt to save himself. For this reason there was great importance to the Jewish bodies that initiated rescue attempts by mobilizing funds and exercising their connections. These organs worked in various ways during different periods and according to changing conditions. When the Germans believed that a Jewish initiative of this sort served their own interests, they collaborated with its organizers and in due course even accorded them official recognition. This was particularly so both at the beginning of the era when they entered into the *Haavara* agreement with the Zionist institutions and from the end of the 1930s into the early years of the war when they collaborated with the organizers of illegal immigration to Palestine from Germany and Austria. Within the Generalgouvernement, not only did the Germans refrain from interfering with ŻSS, which developed independently of the Judenräte, but they cooperated with the organization and in the summer of 1940 even granted it an official status. The ŻSS represented a combination of the Jewish mutual-aid organizations that had been active during the 1920s and 1930s and the new forces that had emerged during the days of crisis, such as Emanuel Ringelblum and his comrades and the organizers of the building councils in Warsaw—these became an important element within ŻSS.

In western and northern Europe, where the Jews had enjoyed equal rights and full citizenship for generations, they never doubted that the law of the land would protect them or that the authorities were responsible for their safety. The state determined the organizational form of the kehillot, but it left them free to act as they deemed best to fulfill their special needs. Hence, it was only natural that when Jewish refugees began to stream out of Germany, *ad hoc* committees of Jews as well as mixed groups of Jews and non-Jews formed in all of these countries to come to their aid.

Independent Jewish Organs in the Satellite Countries

In three satellite countries, the Jews built clandestine organs on the foundations of their prewar communal bodies. Organizations of this sort operated in France, Slovakia, and Rumania. The machinery of the UGIF in France and the ÚŽ in Slovakia served as a cover for secret rescue operations. An alternative leadership of this sort had to take responsibility not only for mobilizing funds but also for maintaining a network of communications throughout the respective country and beyond. These connections were used to collect and relay information and funds and to pass on operational orders.[52] In the case of each of these activities, the Jews required the services of intermediaries and other helping hands. In France, especially in the southern zone, the Jews benefited from the fact that various prewar institutions—relief, refugee, and youth organizations—remained generally intact, and some of them were integrated into the activities of UGIF after having operated overtly for a year and a half.[53]

Rumania represented a special case in terms of independent Jewish activity on behalf of rescue. If the Jews obtained the repeal of already activated or planned measures or were permitted to extend aid to their brethren (e.g., the deportees sent to Transnistria), it was as a result of the labors of all the veteran Jewish organizations in Rumania.[54] The underground Jewish Council continued operating in the winter of 1941/1942; in essence its activities were quasi legal because its members had worked hard to maintain their connections with the heads of the regime, church circles, and representatives of foreign countries, including the papal nuncio. Contrary to the desires of the Germans assigned to Rumania and Eichmann in Berlin, the Palestine Office continued to operate openly, directing emigration to Palestine until the spring of 1942, at which time it was forced underground. The Zionist youth movements, which had been strictly forbidden because of their leftist outlook, also continued to exist underground.

The most ambitious and important mission undertaken by the Jews of Rumania was their endeavor on behalf of the deportees to Transnistria. This was a two-pronged effort that consisted of providing relief and conducting a struggle to bring the surviving deportees back. Most of the Rumanian Jews were living in ghettos scattered throughout the country, yet their organizational abilities and cooperative spirit stood them in good stead on this front. Autonomous committees were formed, and their chairmen—newcomers to Jewish public life alongside veteran personalities—tried to solve the pressing problems facing their communities: finding work and a livelihood for members of the community, extending support and mutual aid, caring for the many orphans, educating the children, tending to the sick, fighting against disease, and establishing contact between the deportees in various places and the outside world. Here I should note the fundamental difference between this independent organizational effort, which traced solely to Jewish initiative, and the Jewish councils created by the Germans in Poland specifically to serve as their tool. As one of the Rumanian activists testified, "I resorted to every means imaginable to prevent the civilian and military [Rumanian and German] authorities from interfering with the management of the ghetto. We established a kind of state-within-a-state." Indeed, the Jewish organizational effort "had to its credit achievements on a nationwide scale that surprised the persecutors and changed their way of thinking, to the point where even German soldiers and officers recognized the authority of the heads of the ghetto." This was not Poland, of course, but the phenomenon, nevertheless, indicates what Jewish self-help was capable of accomplishing—provided it enjoyed a certain freedom of maneuver.[55]

Naturally there is great importance in the fact that this independent effort had the support of Rumania's Jews and that their leaders obtained permission to have funds, food, clothing, shoes, drugs, equipment (including surgical instruments), coal, heaters, building materials, and raw materials for manufacture sent to the deportees. Not that there weren't difficulties in getting these shipments safely through; some arrived after a great delay, and not all of them reached their destination intact because of confiscations and thefts.[56] Nevertheless, at the end of December 1942, a delegation representing the Autonomous Committee of Assistance was allowed to go to Transnistria to check on whether the shipments had reached their destination and to examine conditions in the ghettos firsthand. The delegation spent about two weeks in the area, meeting with the heads of the ghettos, and the report written on its return to Bucharest was even distributed abroad. During that period—meaning the time of the Russian victory at Stalingrad—Dr. Wilhelm Filderman and his colleagues were negotiating the return of the deportees, and ultimately Ion Antonescu agreed to allow certain types of deportees back. But it was not until the end of 1943 that the government permitted the return of a substantial portion of the deportees and that the first of them began to arrive. The Committee of Assistance devoted a major effort to organizing the operation, and once again a group of activists left for Transnistria, where they joined a delegation of representatives of the International and Rumanian Red Cross. The operation met with many difficulties—political and technical—and it was only under the pressure of the advancing Russian forces, who had crossed the Bug River on March 14, 1944, that on that same date the government announced its agreement "to repatriate all the deportees." Not all of them made it back to Rumania. Some were killed by the Germans at the last minute; others failed to get out before the conquering Russians closed the border and were forced to wait another year—during which many of the men were conscripted into the Red Army. Of the close to 150,000 Jews who were deported to Transnistria in 1941–1942, fewer than 60,000 survived and returned to Rumania—88,000 perished.[57]

Europe's Neutral States as Islands of Refuge

The neutral countries in Europe were like islands in the stormy sea of war. Although life went on in regular order in these states, their governments were forced to grapple with issues created by the times, among them the problem of refugees. The countries in question are Switzerland, Spain, Portugal, Sweden, and Turkey. Each was affected differently by the events of the period, but in one way or another their conduct proceeded along parallel lines. Their declared and focal aim was to preserve their neutrality and, thus, their independence, and their policies underwent reversals and revisions according to developments on the battlefield. Thus, from 1940 to 1943, Sweden permitted German forces to cross its territory on their way to Norway, and throughout the war it sold Germany iron ore and industrial products that were of great importance to the German war economy.[58] Spain, which Hitler was particularly interested in drawing into his camp, managed to avoid that level of commitment but did feel constrained to send a company to the Russian front that was not relieved until 1943.

As far back as 1938 there was a tendency in most countries to limit the entry of Jewish refugees as much as possible (see chap. 4). Among the states that had stiffened their laws and regulations limiting the entry of Jews were Sweden and Switzerland. During the war these countries naturally became centers of espionage for all the belligerent states—a fact that left them highly suspicious of all foreigners. Added to this was the matter of economic difficulties, for the war limited opportunities for manufacture, import, and export; for the most part the neutral states (with the exception of Sweden) were unable to profit from the war. In Spain, for instance, the economic situation grew so desperate that many people were suffering from hunger. Hence, accepting refugees from the warring countries, including soldiers of the Allied armies (in 1940), was bound to create serious difficulties for these countries. As for the Jews, each of these states feared that it would be "inundated" by Jewish refugees, which would have kindled the wrath of Nazi Germany and exacerbated the anti-Semitism in their own societies and make them vulnerable to the influence of Nazism. On the other hand, there were liberal circles in those free countries that hoped to preserve their humanist tradition by granting fugitives the right to asylum.

International law established rules regarding certain types of refugees. For example, soldiers of belligerent states who reached neutral countries were to be denied access to places from which they could reach the front. Switzerland was meticulous in observing this rule, but Spain permitted fugitive soldiers from the defeated Dutch, French, British, Polish, and Czech armies to leave its borders and treated the Jews among them as all the rest. The situation differed for the Jewish civilian, who was not recognized as a political refugee and was, thus, in danger of being sent back over the border. But the Jews also enjoyed certain advantages in the neutral countries because the worldwide Jewish organizations were permitted to operate freely there. For that same reason free-world Jewish organizations established footholds and centers first in Switzerland and Turkey and toward the end of the war in Sweden. Representatives of the Jewish Agency for Palestine, the

JDC, HICEM, the WJC, and the Orthodox Rabbinical Council opened lines of communication from these centers to all the occupied and satellite countries.

The problems arising in all the neutral countries were of a similar nature, for their governments were unanimous in a desire to ensure that refugees did not remain within their borders for very long. Thus, even when a refugee had a valid passport and a visa to another country, he was allowed only a limited stay and was sometimes granted only a laissez-passer valid for a short time. When a government was forced to consent to a refugee's extended stay, he was usually not granted a work permit or, alternatively, was put to work at one of the specially instituted jobs of the Labor Service. In most instances only a few people were permitted to reside in the country freely, whereas most of the refugees were concentrated in camps or were assigned to obligatory housing arrangements. Most difficult of all was the state of those who had slipped over the border, especially as they usually lacked valid papers and belonged to the persecuted category of stateless people. This situation obliged the local and world Jewish organizations to make special efforts and exercise their influence on the authorities, particularly the police, to soften their attitude. In addition, the Jewish organizations operating in most of these countries were obliged to bear most of the expense of maintaining the refugees.

Switzerland

Although Switzerland took pride of place among the neutral countries, situated as it was at the very heart of Europe, the crises of war seemed to threaten it from all sides. The Swiss government was keenly aware that neither the country's mountains nor its well-trained but tiny popular army would succeed as a protective buffer if its powerful neighbor was intent on involving it in the war. Hence, its main task was to make sure that Germany never had any excuse to do so. Not only did the persecuted of Europe—first in Germany and Austria, then in France, and finally Italy—look to their country's border with Switzerland as an avenue to safety and freedom, but they were soon joined by soldiers from the defeated armies and POWs who had managed to flee from their captors. Like France and Holland, Switzerland had a tradition of offering refuge to fugitives from tyranny, and its regime was predicated on the principles of humanism and democratic freedoms. Yet, the government took the position that the right of asylum is the sole prerogative of the state—not that of the refugee. Thus the state can exercise this right as it sees fit, and this was the basis for establishing the arrangements, restrictions, and obligations of all the fugitives. From the earliest days of the Nazi regime until the last stages of the war, when Switzerland ceased to fear a German invasion, both the Swiss authorities and the general public incessantly debated the question of how to keep the country safe and still fulfill its moral duty.

After the war the conduct of the Swiss government was attacked both at home and abroad. Dr. Carl Ludwig was commissioned by the government to investigate, and his report then served as the basis of the discussion in parliament.[59] Most of the criticism was directed against the chief of police, Dr. Heinrich Rothmund, who was responsible for many of the initiatives and activities that effectively spelled the doom of countless Jews. Rothmund's first initiative, which in 1938 led to having the passports of Jews stamped with the letter *J,* proved to be disastrous for all the Jews of Germany, not only those heading for Switzerland (see chap. 4). This designation served all the parties who were intent on preventing the entry of Jews into any country. This included the Swedish government, which had contracted a similar agreement with Germany so as not to interfere with the free entry of Aryan Germans, who did not require visas, and to limit as much as possible the entry of Jews, who did. Clearly, however, Dr. Rothmund would not have acted as he did without the backing of the Swiss government (Bundesrat), which set down the rules and regulations in the matter of refugee affairs. These rules became increasingly stringent each time the vicissitudes of war prompted a rise in the flow of refugees trying to enter Switzerland legally or otherwise. For all that, Switzerland did host a total of close to 300,000 foreigners for shorter or longer periods; this number does not include those who crossed the border by black entry without their presence becoming known to the police—a number that is believed to be far from small. About one-third of all those who entered Switzerland were soldiers of various nations. Three categories of civilian refugees were recognized: emigrants, who were permitted to stay in the country for a limited period while being apprised of their obligation to find some way of continuing their journey; refugees, who were obligated to move on as quickly as possible and were placed under special scrutiny; and political refugees, who were mostly granted asylum. Over the entire period, these three categories of registered refugees were divided as follows:[60]

Emigrants	9,909	Includes	6,654 Jews or 67.2%
Refugees	55,018	Includes	21,858 Jews or 39.7%
Political refugees	251		
Total	65,178	Includes	28,512 Jews or 43.7%

A special operation was mounted from 1940 to 1942 to send close to 60,000 children from France and Belgium to enjoy a period of rest and recuperation in Switzerland. In December 1943 the government agreed to take in 1,000 to 1,500 children of Jewish refugees from France, evidently meaning orphans. These activities were conducted under the aegis of the Red Cross.[61]

On the outbreak of the war, the restrictions posed by the Swiss government became stricter, and in 1940 the police were ordered to deport any refugee who violated any of its directives (one of which was the establishment of a labor camp for aliens). From 1940 to 1942 orders were repeatedly issued to turn back anyone attempting to cross the border illegally, with the exception of unaccompanied children, parents with children up to the age of six, elderly people, and pregnant women. Notwithstanding its qualifications, this directive blocked the route of escape for the thousands of Jews trying to flee from southern France after the Germans took over the Free Zone in November 1942. But thousands of others fleeing from Holland, Belgium, and France, including Jews, did enter Switzerland during those years.[62] By the end of December 1942, the number of refugees and emigrants had reached 16,200, including 8,467 illegals who were allowed to stay.[63] This situation changed radically in the autumn of 1943, following developments in Italy, when some 74,000 foreigners—about half of them military personnel—

entered Switzerland legally. Included among these tens of thousands of Italians were 10,000 partisans and a few thousand Jews.[64]

In July 1944 the directives of 1942 were abolished and replaced by one that read: "Foreigners in mortal danger for political or other [sic!] reasons are allowed to enter if they have no other chance of surviving but by fleeing to Switzerland." On December 1, 1944, the total number of refugees of all types present in Switzerland was 103,162.[65] The 1,685 Jews who had been sent in the "Rescue Train" from Hungary to Bergen-Belsen (see chap. 21) arrived from there in two transfers in August and December 1944.[66] In February 1945 another transport brought 1,200 Jews who had been released from Theresienstadt.[67] Before the armistice there were 115,000 refugees in Switzerland, of whom fewer than 50,000 were military men.[68]

Over the years, the number of people who were turned back at the border and presumably caught by the Germans came to no fewer than 10,000. Close to 30,000 Jewish refugees spent time in, or passed through, Switzerland legally during the war (including those categorized as emigrants), representing a total of 10 percent of all the foreigners who found asylum there. It appears impossible to establish the exact number of Jews who passed through the country, not only because the number of those who entered illegally and were not caught is unknown but because from 1933 until the outbreak of the war there were fluctuations in the flow of Jewish refugees into Switzerland, with their number rising sharply after the *Anschluss* and Kristallnacht to close to 10,000 at the end of 1938.[69]

During the early years of the Nazi era, many of these Jewish refugees still had means at their disposal and did not require support during their stay in Switzerland or to continue on their journey. But this situation changed drastically as of early 1938. Then, as Rothmund himself observed, the absorption of Jewish refugees was made possible by the action and support of the Jewish organizations and institutions.[70] This burden was shouldered mainly by the Union of Swiss Communities, on the one hand, and the JDC and HICEM, on the other. The Swiss-Jewish institutions offered counseling, placed the refugees, supported them in Switzerland, and organized their emigration. The umbrella organization known as the Swiss-Jewish Union for Aiding Refugees (Verband Schweizerischer Jüdischer Flüchtlingshilfen) had been established in 1936, with its main office in Zurich and nineteen branches operating throughout the country. There were 18,000 Jews living in Switzerland (out of a population of slightly more than 4 million people), and the funds necessary for these activities from 1933 to 1937 did not exceed SFr 150,000; but over SFr 1.5 million were already being expended in 1938; by 1943 this sum had doubled. The state participated only in the expenditures that were related to the continuation of emigration. Fund-raising drives were held among Swiss Jewry as well as the population at large, and a government decision taken in March 1941 required the wealthier emigrants to pay a special mutual-aid tax. The funds were apportioned among the various organizations that aided refugees according to a special scale. In the decade 1933 to 1943 the following sums were donated for the work in support of Jewish refugees:

Swiss Jewry	SFr 7,039,536	
JDC and HICEM	SFr 6,332,330	
Mutual-aid payments	SFr 1,289,314	
		Total: SFr 14,651,180
General Swiss fund drives	SFr 1,255,215	
State and canton allocations for emigration	SFr 428,072	
		Total: SFr 1,682,287

Sum Total: SFr 16,333,467

Thus, the Jews of Switzerland and the United States accounted for 90 percent of the funds collected for supporting the refugees.[71] I must also add the contribution of the Swiss families who took mothers with infants and children into their homes without charge—and there were numerous such families.

The Swiss-Jewish Union for Aiding Refugees handled 34,328 cases throughout the period, the peak years being 1938 (8,980 cases) and 1943 (16,000 cases). The minority of the refugees approached it mostly for advice, and in the early years the problems were relatively simple. At the end of 1937, for example, only 103 out of the 841 cases it had received were still in its care. More difficult were the problems related to emigration. Throughout the above-mentioned years, some 4,500 people emigrated via Switzerland with the aid of the union, about 1,500 of them to other European countries that subsequently came under German influence or domination and over 2,400 to twenty-nine countries overseas, including 505 to Palestine and 840 to the United States. A few hundred reached Britain, and a few dozen went to Spain and Portugal.[72] Also sent to Spain and Portugal, with the aid of the JDC and the state, were trainloads of Jews—traveling on collective papers—that traversed French territory on the basis of an agreement with the Vichy regime. Other than providing aid for the upkeep of refugees in the cities— with families, in special housing, and in work camps, whose number reached into the dozens—the union established laundries and workshops for tailors and shoe-makers, promoted vocational retraining, and worked to obtain apprenticeships with Swiss artisans and professionals.

Many testimonies describe the tragedies that occurred on the Swiss border, particularly that with France. The official report on the refugee problem likewise noted, "Often people committed suicide right in front of the Swiss soldiers rather than fall into the hands of the Germans."[73] It is impossible to estimate the number of people who were lost as a result of being refused entry into Switzerland or who never even attempted to cross the border because they knew what awaited them, but it must have totaled many thousands. We have seen that toward the end of the war the country's borders were opened to multitudes of people and that in the winter of 1944 even Rothmund reported, "We are taking [the effort] to save the remaining Jews very seriously." But in 1942 when the first reports of the slaughter in Poland reached Switzerland and were featured prominently in the press, he repeatedly explained why the state had to beware of being flooded by "the alien Jewish element."[74] Unquestionably, similar sentiments were voiced by the Swiss populace, for since the 1930s Nazi anti-Semitic propaganda had been increasingly prevalent in Switzerland and the supporters of the Nazis had carried on a strident debate with those who championed the cause of asylum for the refugees. Another part of the populace was simply averse to sharing the reduced wartime supply of goods with the refugees.[75]

Proof that the borders were, nevertheless, porous can be seen in the ties that the Jewish underground in France succeeded in maintaining with the Jewish organizations in Switzerland throughout the period. Most of the underground's support from the JDC came to France through these contacts, and the connection was reinforced and extended after Marc Jarblum's flight from France to Switzerland in March 1943.[76]

Spain

The pressure that Spain experienced from both Germany and the Allies was heavier than the parallel demands made on Switzerland. At the beginning of the war, Francisco Franco declared Spain a nonbelligerent, and it was not until the war's latter half that he was able to change Spain's status to neutrality. However, the Iberian Peninsula remained one of Europe's main avenues to the free world and was, thus, the objective of refugees who hoped either to find asylum there or to move on to safety abroad.

From 1933 to 1939 it was Jews, for the most part, who tried to sail overseas from Lisbon and the ports of Spain. By 1936 an estimated six thousand Jews had reached Spain, but not all of them managed to move on before the outbreak of the civil war, which naturally ruled out the use of Spain as an intermediate country for flight from the Nazis.[77]

When a heavy flow of refugees again turned toward Spain with the fall of France in 1940, the Spanish consul in Marseilles was at first given a free hand to grant visas, especially to people whose citizenship gave them a good chance of being accepted by one country or another in the free world. After a short while, however, the Spanish authorities began to place obstacles in the path of the candidates for visas by demanding that they present valid travel documents and by causing delays—not the least of which was created by the erratic opening and closing of Spain's border. Also revised was the attitude toward refugees who had entered Spain illegally, either in the vicinity of the official crossing points or by embarking on a difficult and dangerous trek over the Pyrenees. Despite all these difficulties, tens of thousands of Jews reached Spain in the great flood of 1940/1941, most of them traversing the country and, with the aid of the Jewish organizations, continuing overseas. The number of Jews who sailed from Spain and Portugal by the end of the summer of 1942 is estimated at thirty thousand.[78] Within Spain itself, however, the situation was far more complex: (1) the government did all it could to prevent the refugees from remaining within the country; those who, nevertheless, did so were interned in camps (the main one being Miranda de Ebro); (2) the representatives of the relief organizations were not per-

mitted to open offices in the country. Even the Red Cross had difficulty functioning in Spain, and the situation was all the worse for the Jewish organizations such
as JDC and HICEM, whose agents lived in constant fear that their activities would
be halted and were, thus, highly circumspect in their handling of illegals. It is estimated that during this period, no more than five hundred Jews were detained in
Spain.

The situation did not begin to change until the latter half of 1942. At first,
during that summer, the Spanish raised difficulties toward refugees trying to enter
the country, but after the German army took over southern France in November
1942, they were forced by pressure of the Vichy regime and the British to open
the borders to their citizens, most of them military people. Some 10 to 12 percent
of the tens of thousands of refugees who reached Spain in this wave were Jews,
and those with a military background even became active in organizing the flight.
They also succeeded in getting out of the country with the general stream of refugees, part of which was channeled to North Africa. At the end of the winter,
however, the Spanish authorities not only closed the border again but even sent
some of the people who had already crossed it back into France, interning others
in a camp. Although the Germans maintained patrols and a heavy guard on the
French side of the frontier, refugees—some of them Jews and all of them regarded
as illegals—nevertheless managed to filter through. At the beginning of the summer of 1943, the number of Jews in Spain was estimated at more than two thousand, most of them stateless persons. The overall number of Jews who passed
through or spent time in Spain from the summer of 1942 through the end of 1943
is estimated at fifty-three hundred.[79] In 1943 the turn in the tide of battle took the
chill out of the atmosphere in Spain, so that many of the refugees were allowed to
live in the country's cities and towns.

At the end of March 1943, Wilfrid Israel, an emissary of the Jewish Agency,
reached the Iberian Peninsula. The scion of a distinguished German-Jewish family
that was among the founders of the large department stores in Germany, Israel
had been active in relief and rescue work in Germany since 1933, and he continued working in this field after moving to England in 1939. His mission was to find
ways of reaching Palestine from Portugal and Spain, and in the two months he
worked in these countries, he laid the foundation for an emigration program. On
returning to Britain on June 1, 1943, he was lost when his plane was shot down
by the Luftwaffe. (There has been speculation about the reasons behind this
action, but the enigma has never been solved.)[80] His work was completed a few
months later, however, by Fritz Lichtenstein (Peretz Leshem), a kibbutznik from
Palestine, and in January 1944 a boat left Lisbon for Haifa. In October 1944 a
second boat set sail for the same destination, followed in April and in the summer
of 1945 by another three ships that also picked up passengers in Morocco and
Italy. Altogether about two thousand people—many of them pioneering youth
and children—immigrated to Palestine in these operations.[81]

The children and young people had entered the Iberian Peninsula—under the
direction of the Jewish youth organizations of Holland and France—mostly from
the summer of 1943 onward, when the illegal movement of Jews across the Spanish border increased again. In addition to the hardships of the journey, the need

to resort to professional smugglers, and the difficulties mounted by the Germans on the French side of the frontier, this traffic was burdened by the fact that the refugees had no source of support on the other side. The few representatives of Jewish organizations—such as JDC—who were active in Spain treated them with a measure of suspicion, and those who actually succeeded in traversing the border could expect to be arrested on the other side. This daunting situation remained in force until 1944.[82]

It is estimated that between the summer of 1942 and the autumn of 1944 a total of some seventy-five hundred Jews entered Spain from France, about six thousand of them together with the general flow of refugees. According to these estimates, the number of Jews who were saved by escaping via Spain from 1940 to 1945 was at least forty thousand, most of them having entered the country with the flood of military and civilian refugees.[83] Some of these fugitives were pioneering youth who had escaped from Holland and in a daring action made their way through Belgium and France, where a number of them were captured; but eighty young people managed to get across the Pyrenees; from Spain most of them made it to Palestine.[84]

Sweden

Like Switzerland, Sweden maintained its neutrality throughout World War II, just as it had in World War I. This time, however, the occupation of Denmark and Norway brought the war right up to its border. The shifting events in Finland were also significant for Sweden, and part of its population tended toward Nazi Germany, but this definitely changed when the war was drawing to an end.

The Jewish community in Sweden numbered slightly fewer than seven thousand people at the beginning of the 1930s, most of whom were concentrated in Stockholm in addition to smaller communities such as Malmö and Göteborg. As the decade progressed, the persecution of the Jews in Germany confronted the Swedes with the question of whether, and to what degree, they would be willing to take such fugitives from oppression. By 1937 the Swedish authorities deemed it necessary to issue regulations on the entry of refugees: after an extended discussion, they legislated a new law defining the conditions under which foreigners would be permitted into the country. As in other countries, the emphasis was placed on the definition and rights of political refugees, and a complex legal apparatus was created under the jurisdiction of the Welfare, Justice, and Foreign ministries.[85] The Swedes chose to regard the refugee issue as essentially a political problem that had bearing on the country's domestic and foreign policy, which is why the decision on the reception of refugees was delegated to the ministries. The law came into force on January 1, 1938, but shortly thereafter the general problem was severely exacerbated by the *Anschluss,* and the Swedes, like the Swiss, responded by requiring everyone entering their country to have a visa (the custom had been to allow all visitors free entry and a three-month stay, at the end of which they were required to apply for a residence visa and work permit). Even though such visas were now granted primarily to transmigrants, the fact that the United

States had limited entry so stringently and the growing difficulties faced by those wishing to immigrate to Palestine gave the Swedish authorities reason to fear that even these transmigrants might ultimately be stranded in their country, especially at a time when various labor unions were vigorously protesting the entry of aliens as potential competitors. Those able to claim a familial connection with Jewish citizens of Sweden were treated with greater magnanimity, but the government's apprehensions rose again after the failure of the Evian Conference, in which Sweden had been an active participant. A secret government circular conveyed a new order to the border police requiring bearers of German passports stamped with the letter *J* to produce a visa or border recommendation granted them by a Swedish consulate.[86]

These arrangements had just gone into effect at the end of October 1938 when the turmoil of Kristallnacht placed the Swedes under renewed pressure from a fresh wave of refugees. Whereas about 30 to 60 people a day had applied to the Swedish consulate in Vienna in April 1938, the number of people now requesting visas had soared from 200 to 300 a day. At the beginning of November 1938, there were at most 2,300 Jewish refugees in Sweden; between November 10, 1938, and January 10, 1939, a total of 196 visas were granted, 104 of them to Aryan political refugees and 92 to non-Aryans. Of the Aryans, 98 were granted residence rights in Sweden and 6 emigrated elsewhere; of the Jews, 29 remained and 63 continued on to other countries.[87] As an extraordinary gesture, the Swedes approved a special quota for 500 children, most of whom were brought from Germany, Austria, and later from Czechoslovakia by the local Jewish Relief Council in collaboration with a Swedish women's organization. At the outbreak of the war, there were a total of 24,000 foreign citizens in Sweden, that is, less than 0.4 percent of the overall population. They included about 3,000 Jewish refugees with residence permits and at least 1,000 transmigrants, a few hundred of whom were members of pioneering youth movements and had been accepted for agricultural training in Sweden.[88]

During the war Swedish representatives in both the Greater Reich and in occupied and satellite countries relayed precise reports on the persecution of the Jews. In 1939, for instance, they had information about the deportation of the Jews of Vienna and the Protectorate to Nisko, and in 1941 they knew the exact number of Jews who remained in Berlin and of those who had been deported to Łódź. Moreover, while traveling on a train in Poland one night, the supplier of gas to the death camps, Kurt Gerstein, spoke about his work with the Swedish diplomat Baron von Otter and told of what was going on in the extermination camps, but the Swedish government did nothing with this information.[89] The number of Jews who made it to Sweden from the various areas of the Reich in the course of the war was very small. The last of them arrived between September and December 1941, and with the prohibition of emigration from Germany, even this trickle came to a total halt.

Quite different was the attitude toward refugees from other Scandinavian countries—a typical expression of the solidarity among these countries. In March 1943 a member of the Swedish Foreign Ministry supplied Shalom Adler-Rudel (who had come to Sweden on a mission for the Jewish Agency for Palestine) with the following figures: there were 140,000 refugees in the country at the time: 25,000 Norwegians, 30,000 Swedes from the Baltic countries, 75,000 Finns (including 45,000 children), 5,000 POWs who had escaped from camps in Norway, and 5,000 Germans.[90] The first to arrive were the Norwegians, whose number reached about 50,000 over the years. As the development of Swedish industry accelerated during the war, workers were in great demand, with the Norwegians— and later Danish Jews and non-Jews—answering this need, especially from 1942 to 1944.[91] In the autumn of 1943, moreover, about 8,000 people arrived in the flight of the Jews from Denmark, and some 9,000 other Danes followed in their wake. By the spring of 1944, the number of Jewish refugees in Sweden, including children and pioneering youth on training farms, was estimated to be 12,000, at most.[92] However, the attitude toward the victims of the Nazi regime began to change significantly that year (see chap. 21).

These events confronted the Jews of Sweden with a new and difficult challenge. Until the Nazi era they had barely been active in general Jewish affairs. Few of them were Zionists—one being Chief Rabbi Marcus Ehrenpreis (a Hebrew author who also wrote extensively about Jewish subjects in Swedish and also translated Hebrew literature into Swedish)—but now they felt called on to act on behalf of the Jews being persecuted by the Nazi regime. Thirteen relief committees came into being, some of them encompassing Jews and non-Jews alike. The non-Jewish activists were all opponents of the government's restrictive policy, but their attempts to influence the authorities to act more leniently and admit the Jews who applied were all but futile. Thousands of such applications reached the Stockholm community, but it felt constrained to turn most of them down—a few after the government had rejected them but most without even submitting them to the authorities. Swedish Jewry extended aid to the Jewish refugees who reached their shores while also working to establish contact with the Jewish communities in the occupied and satellite countries. Thus, for example, Swedish Jewry sent parcels and funds to the Łódź ghetto and maintained ties with France, Rumania, and other countries. Most of these activities were paid for directly by the community or through fund drives; JDC and HICEM were also active factors, primarily on behalf of the transmigrants.[93] Moreover, a number of Swedish Jews played special roles in the system of illegal traffic organized by the Danish underground after the Jews of Denmark had been smuggled out, and it was a Jew of Hungarian origin who proposed the idea that ultimately led to Raoul Wallenberg's mission in Budapest.[94] As a rule the German Jews and others who had settled in Sweden prior to Hitler's rise to power were most prominent among the proponents and organizers of rescue activities. During the war a number of Jews also came in from the Baltic countries. One of them, Hillel Storch, became chairman of the Swedish branch of the WJC and worked energetically to rescue Jews. Initially, the Jews were involved mostly in providing relief for the ghettos and camps, primarily by sending parcels. This effort did not take on major proportions until after the International Red Cross agreed to take part in 1943, and it was not until the summer of 1944 that the operation truly developed momentum.[95]

The Allies' War Against Hitler Versus Hitler's War
Against the Jews

One blatant paradox that obtained throughout this period was the Allies' perception of the war's objectives in contrast to the Holocaust that had descended upon the Jewish people. The Allies' prime concern was to defeat their enemies; but rather than view the war as a struggle for world domination, they saw it as a fight to preserve their freedom as nations and individuals. The misfortune of the Jews was looked on as a regrettable, even tragic, by-product of this clash of Titans but not as having any bearing on the fate of the world as a whole. The fact that the Jews lacked an independent political status and were regarded as nationals of one country or another obviated the need to recognize the shared fate of the Jews as a people. This approach was clearly evident in a statement by A. Walker of the Refugees' Department of the British Foreign Office:

> So long as the Jews are the nationals of various States they must speak as nationals in those States so far as official action is concerned. They can hardly ask to be in a privileged position which would enable them to be, e.g., Poles, Roumainians, British, etc., etc., and at the same time to be represented by a supernational body of Jewish spokesmen.

Moreover, in Walker's reading of the situation, the Jews and their tribulations were receiving more than enough consideration despite the fact that they lacked political leverage.[96]

This catch, as it were, was exacerbated by a second paradox, namely, that although the Allies did not take the Germans' preoccupation with the "Jewish problem" very seriously, they categorically rejected the Nazi racial principle. Indeed, it was their rejection of this principle that justified their refusal to recognize the Jews qua Jews as either political refugees or any other category of fugitives—that is, military personnel, POWs, or even partisans—to whom international convention required them to grant asylum.

As far as the free nations were concerned, politically the Jewish problem was regarded as of negative import. Conscious of the impact of anti-Semitism as a tool of National Socialist propaganda and influence, they were interested in quashing any expression of it—on either the tangible or propaganda plane—in their own societies. In these countries the propaganda of anti-Semitic groups was closely associated with the subversive activities of a fifth column, and the combination of collaboration with the Germans and the persecution of the Jews in the satellite countries confirmed the potency of anti-Semitism as a political force. Hence, the Allied powers deemed it imperative to prevent their fight against the Nazis from being branded a Jewish war. Similar calculations were at work in the neutral states. It is often difficult to determine the degree to which a country's attitude toward the Jewish problem was shaped by political and economic factors and the degree to which its population and government were themselves tainted by anti-Semitic leanings. Documents published since the war show, for instance, that anti-

Semitism was at work to a noticeable—sometimes frightful—extent among officials of the United States and Great Britain.

One of the more complex and perhaps most tragic facets of the war was the
relations between the British government and the Zionist movement. Despite
Churchill's support for Zionism, which was manifest at least until the end of 1944,
throughout the war the British authorities held tenaciously to the policy set down
in the white paper of 1939. As a result, the gates of Palestine were not thrown
open to refugees, and it served as a haven for only the very few who, one way or
another, were able to reach it by their own devices.

As the war intensified, the contrast between the declared humanitarian aims
of the Allies and the paucity of aid extended to the victims of the war—especially
the Jews—became increasingly stark. Other than the refusal to admit the existence
of a special Jewish problem, the gap between the basic common ethos of the Western countries and the ideologies behind the acts of the National Socialist regime
was also a factor here. The Western world, which set out to defend its society and
culture in the belief that they were of value for all mankind, refused to credit that
human beings were needlessly committing mass murder, contrary to even their
own interest, and were intentionally denying the value of human life. Even as late
as December 1944, only 4 percent of the American population believed that over
5 million Jews had been exterminated, whereas 27 percent acknowledged the murders but thought that the number of victims was one hundred thousand.[97] The
Soviets, for their part, deliberately suppressed the information for both pragmatic
and ideological reasons.

The International Jewish Assistance Organizations: Actions and Obstacles

The Jewish people found itself in something of a political vacuum, as though
trapped in a kind of no-man's-land between the fronts and borders of Europe. The
Jewish communities and organizations in the free world were able to act solely
within the limits set by the various national governments, which were inevitably
determined by what these governments deemed to be the national interest. Thus,
it was mainly the international Jewish organizations—including the JDC, the
umbrella organization of HICEM (which devoted its efforts primarily to the problems of maritime transport), the WJC, and the Jewish Agency for Palestine—that
came to the aid of the Jewish communities in Europe.

The World Jewish Congress (WJC)

Officially established in 1936, the WJC's goal is "to assure the survival and to
foster the unity of the Jewish people."[98] From an organizational standpoint, the
WJC embraced representatives of the main Jewish communities and leading orga-
nizations in most of the world. Since its establishment, it had been headed by
Rabbi Stephen Wise, the president of the AJC, who was assisted by Dr. Naḥum
Goldmann—both of them Zionists. During the war the WJC made great efforts

to maintain contact with its agents wherever they were able to function. As with other Jewish organizations, Switzerland served as its center of operations and the collection of intelligence. So it fell to Gerhard Riegner, the WJC's representative in Geneva, to play a role in one of the most fateful episodes of the period.

Riegner was on close terms with many members of the international community based in Switzerland, and at the beginning of August 1942 he received a visit from the German industrialist Eduard Schulte, who had access to Hitler's headquarters and reported that the führer had decided systematically to destroy all the Jews of Europe, using poison gas for this purpose.[99] With some misgivings, Riegner passed this information on to Stephen Wise in the United States by means of the American consulate, relaying a copy of the cable to Benjamin Sagalowitz, the WJC's representative in London, through British channels (the use of diplomatic channels was necessary for security and for maintaining secrecy). When the cable reached the U.S. State Department, Undersecretary of State Sumner Welles stopped it from being passed on to Wise. When Wise, nevertheless, received the information on August 28 via London, Welles prevailed on him not to make it public. The suppression of this report was communicated to the American minister in Switzerland, Leland Harrison, and justified on the grounds of "the apparently unsubstantiated nature of the information."[100]

This is perhaps the most extreme case of the yawning gap between the Western and National Socialist outlook on the situation. Riegner's message was actually not the first reliable report on the systematic annihilation of the Jews to reach the West. In May 1942 the Jewish underground in Warsaw sent an account to the Polish government-in-exile in London, and the BBC broadcast its information on June 2, 1942, noting that the number of Jewish victims in Poland had reached seven hundred thousand—less than the actual number of people who had been murdered by that time. On June 10 the Bund's representative in London, Shmuel Zygelboym, and the Zionist representative Ignacy Schwarzbart, both members of the Polish National Council in London, brought the underground's report before that body, which officially relayed it to the legislatures of all the Allied countries. On June 26 the item was again broadcast over the radio, and the Polish government-in-exile raised the matter before the British government. Yet it was not until July 9, a month after the information was first made public, that the British minister of information deigned to hold a press conference, together with the Poles and the Jews, at which the contents of the report were made public—even then, only one British paper published the news, burying it on an inside page. The same was true of the great majority of the American papers. The information was forthcoming, but acknowledgement was not. Ultimately, word of the slaughter reached the Jews in the free world through the reports of the Jewish Telegraphic Agency, which were given prominence in the Jewish press. The response was a series of protest rallies and days of mourning, fasting, and prayer, but even this public acknowledgement of the tragedy did not lead to far-reaching decisions. On the contrary, it in no way changed either the situation or the Allies' attitude toward it.[101]

Since the war, attempts have been made to explain this failure to act by noting that the information was regarded as atrocity propaganda; that people were paralyzed by a sense of helplessness; that, conscious of the mood in Washington and of manifestations of anti-Semitism on the popular level, the Jews of America were fearful of provoking the powers that be; and, over and over again, that it was inconceivable that human beings—even Nazi Germans—would sin so unconscionably against all that was sacred to mankind. Nevertheless, toward the end of 1942, it was no longer possible to deny the facts, and the Allies' declaration of December 17 was the first public acknowledgement of the mass murder of the Jews. They took this step at a time when there was growing evidence that the war had reached a turning point, but they were still far from adopting any significant measures to save the Jews.

On the other hand, since it was becoming clear that the war would leave in its wake the painful problem of millions of displaced persons seeking refuge, and in response to the mounting public pressure, in April 1943 the British and American governments convened their representatives on the island of Bermuda to draw up new guidelines for dealing with the refugee problem. The Jewish organizations were not allowed to participate in these sessions—not even as observers—and the participants continued to deny the existence of a special Jewish problem. Unfortunately, the outcome of this conference was no more constructive than the meeting at Evian had been five years earlier.[102]

The irony of it is that the Bermuda Conference opened on April 19, 1943, the very day on which the residents of the Warsaw ghetto rose in revolt against the Germans—knowing that they had no chance of prevailing—and the very day that a joint underground group of Belgians and Jews attempted to halt a deportation train. There is no way of bridging the moral abyss between those few, weak fighters struggling against the multitude of the strong and the failure of the Allied powers to come to the aid of the persecuted Jews.

In November 1943 Britain, the United States, and the Soviet Union published a declaration in Moscow putting the Axis powers on notice that anyone guilty of having committed atrocities would be brought to justice at the war's end. This declaration enumerated all of the nations that had suffered from persecution at the hands of the Germans and even cited specific ethnic groups, but the Jewish people was not mentioned among them.[103] As far as these three Allied powers were concerned, it simply did not exist.

The Establishment of the War Refugee Board (WRB)

In the spring of 1943, working through Leland Harrison, Riegner asked the U.S. State Department to permit the transfer of funds for the purpose of saving Jews in two places: southern France and Rumania. In southern France he was referring mainly to the efforts to smuggle children into Spain, and in Rumania there were talks under way regarding the return of the deportees from Transnistria. Ever since America's entry into the war, the relief organizations had experienced great difficulties in getting funds transferred for the rescue of Jews in enemy countries, including the satellite states, but one of the few positive results of the Bermuda Conference was the order making it possible to transfer monies to the neutral countries for the purpose of saving refugees. Riegner's request for $25,000 was, in fact, approved by the Treasury Department within a day, but officials in the State Department held it up for eight months. This long delay was brought to the attention of Treasury Secretary Henry Morgenthau, Jr., by some of his aides who had investigated the reasons for it and found that the action had been deliberately sabotaged. Basing himself on the memorandum drawn up by these officials, "Report to the Secretary on the Acquiescence of This Government in the Murder of the Jews," Morgenthau wrote a "Personal Report to the President" describing the delaying tactics in great detail and took it along when he went to see Roosevelt on January 16, 1944, accompanied by two of the investigators, John W. Pehle and Randolph Paul. His report also contained a subtle warning that the matter might leak out and create a public scandal.

Roosevelt was highly sensitive about the specter of a scandal, especially as criticism about the lack of action in regard to rescue had recently been voiced in both Congress and the public, and various quarters had called for the appointment of a special committee to deal with the matter. At the same time, groups of both Jews and non-Jews had begun to search out ways of organizing rescue activities. Among them were four hundred Orthodox rabbis who held a march in Washington on October 6, 1943, and submitted a petition to the Congress and the president. Especially active in this sphere was a group known as the Bergsonites—after the alias adopted by its leader, Hillel Cook (Peter H. Bergson)—which had split off from the Irgun Zvai Leumi, the Revisionists' armed underground in Palestine. However, the Jewish establishment dissociated itself from their activities.[104]

It was against this background that Morgenthau presented the president with a plan for creating the WRB. Within six days, on January 22, 1944, it had been established by executive order, with Pehle as its director. The order charged the board with carrying out "the policy of this Government [which is] to take all measures within its power to rescue the victims of enemy oppression who are in imminent danger of death and otherwise to afford such victims all possible relief and assistance consistent with the successful prosecution of the war."[105] Pehle was a man in his thirties who brought extraordinary dynamism to the position and built a small but energetic and dedicated staff around him. The WRB opened offices in three neutral countries. Ira Hirschmann was assigned to Turkey. A businessman who had dedicated himself to the problems of refugees ever since attending the Evian Conference in 1938, he was appalled by its failure. After Evian, Hirschmann traveled to Vienna, where he helped hundreds of people obtain highly coveted American visas. His work for the WRB helped to promote rescue actions via Turkey. In Switzerland the WRB's representative was a Quaker named Roswell D. McClelland; in Stockholm the board was represented by Yver C. Olsen, a financial attaché at the American legation. These men were involved in two major efforts to save Jews: one took place in Hungary and the other was the transfer of concentration camp prisoners to Sweden (see chap. 21). In Spain the American minister refused to accept the representative of the WRB, and although an office was opened in Portugal, its activities were very limited due to the stalemate in Spain.

Through his agents in the neutral countries, Pehle warned the Axis powers and the satellite states that they stood to face severe punishment after the war for their actions against the Jews. At the same time, Leland Harrison was told to deliver a similar warning to Rumania, Bulgaria, and Hungary on behalf of the new undersecretary of state, Edward R. Stetinius, Jr.[106] These admonitions had an especially potent effect on Rumania and Bulgaria, where government and other official circles were already reconsidering each country's position in light of the turnabout in the war. Hirschmann's contacts with envoys from the Rumanian government in Ankara also contributed to the decision on returning the surviving Jews from Transnistria. In Rumania the threat attending the advance of the Russian army, the government's desire to rid itself of Germany's yoke, the rise of American influence through the work of the WRB, the self-help actions of the local Jewish leadership, and the ransom paid to the Rumanian authorities for liberating the Jews all worked together to save at least part of the Jewish population. It appears that only a combination of factors such as these was capable of generating decisive action in the case of rescue.

Hirschmann's meetings with the Rumanian and Bulgarian envoys took place at the home of the International Red Cross representative in Ankara, and this was not by chance. For Pehle had begun pressuring the International Board of the Red Cross in Geneva to drop the argument that it was barred from intervening in the actions of the German government and to extend its protection and relief work to the inmates of concentration camps, which had been denied until then on the pretense of not being allowed to interfere with a country's handling of its citizens.[107] One result of his efforts was the active role played by the Rumanian Red Cross in effecting the return of the deportees from Transnistria.

It goes without saying that the activities of the WRB also made it possible for the WJC to expand its work. The congress was headquartered in the United States, and among its leading activists were Naḥum Goldmann, Aryeh Kubovy (Leon Kubovitzki), Arieh Tartakover, and his chief aide, Kurt R. Grossman. In February 1942 it established a Committee for European Affairs, "whose object will be the establishment of a united front of European Jewry in regard to its war, peace and postwar problems."[108] The leaders of the WJC, unaware that the general apparatus for exterminating the Jews of Europe had been forged a few days earlier at the Wannsee Conference, of course had no idea what fate awaited these Jews. What stands out so sharply here is the contrast between the reality the Nazis had created in Europe and the perception of it held by the Jews in the United States. When the facts came out in 1942, the WJC established a Rescue Department, headed by Kubovy, and a Department for Relief and Rehabilitation, headed by Tartakover. That same year negotiations were instituted with the International Red Cross to have it extend its efforts to camp inmates and the residents of ghettos, especially through the sending of parcels. In cooperation with the WRB, the WJC redoubled its efforts in 1944 in light of the disaster overtaking Hungarian Jewry. During the final months of the war, after word arrived of Hitler's order to kill off the concentration camp inmates as the Allied forces closed in on the camps, the WJC concentrated on the effort to save the lives of these remaining Jews (see chap. 21).

The American Jewish Joint Distribution Committee (JDC)

It has already been noted that alongside the WJC, the Jewish Agency and the JDC were also operating out of Switzerland—the latter being represented by Saly Mayer, formerly the head of the Swiss Union of Jewish Communities. Like the other organizations, the JDC encountered difficulties in having money transferred from the United States to Europe, but it, too, was ultimately allowed to send funds to the neutral countries, whence arrangements were made to smuggle them into occupied areas—France, for example. Supplementing these funds was a unique system of credit, developed by the JDC, whereby banks and individuals on the spot lent it large sums of money that it undertook to pay back after the war (at the black market rate). Providing funds to the beleaguered communities was, of course, an important part of JDC's activities throughout the era—especially from 1942 onward—but only one part. Here, it is possible to give only an idea of the efforts undertaken by American Jewry to save Jews in Europe through the auspices of the JDC.[109]

Oscar Handlin, a sociologist and student of American society, observed that "the American Jews bore almost the whole burden. . . . The central responsibility [for relief and rescue] . . . rested in the United States, and that meant in the JDC."[110] The men responsible for the organization's activities in the war years were its executive vice-chairman, Joseph C. Hyman, and its secretary, Moses A. Leavitt; in Europe the work was directed first by Morris C. Tropper and from 1942 onward by Dr. Joseph Schwartz, who was headquartered in Lisbon and was a focal figure in the rescue operations. While scrupulously observing the legality of its operations, in conformity with American law, the JDC tried to lend support to every kind of rescue action—official, secret, and even some that were illegal according to the laws and ordinances of one country or another.

The nature of the JDC's activities underwent certain changes, however, during the various periods of rescue outlined earlier. During the first phase, from 1933 to 1937, the organization continued its support to the countries with needy Jewish populations (e.g., Poland and Rumania) along existing lines. However, a sharp change took place in regard to Germany—whose Jews had not required support until then—as well as in regard to a number of the countries that sheltered fugitive and emigrant Jews. During the second phase, beginning in 1938, the entire picture was altered radically. In 1938 and 1939 alone, the JDC's expenditures came to over $12 million, compared with a total of less than $8 million from 1933 to 1937. It is clear that in 1938 the JDC was not prepared for the tragedy that descended upon the Jews of Austria and Germany. The condition of Polish Jewry also deteriorated at a drastic rate, to the point where it became necessary to spend 85 percent of the overall budget on these three countries and on the maintenance of refugees. As a result, in 1939 the JDC's expenditures in Europe were $3,106,500 and its overall budget grew by 123 percent—the increase in donations being proof of a certain awakening of the Jewish public in the United States.[111]

The JDC, and to a certain degree HICEM as well, were the barometers most sensitive to the changes taking place in the Jewish communities of Europe as a result of the war and the intensification of persecution. Their representatives maintained close ties with the leadership and the public in each country and reported on what was going on, so that the JDC's headquarters received a more or less accurate picture of the pauperization and the series of calamities that hit the Jewish communities. Therefore, adapting its efforts to the rising needs, the JDC developed new methods for increasing the extent of its aid. By the end of 1941, the organization had supplied food to 260,000 people in the Generalgouvernement, including 42,000 children. It supported the Jewish ŻSS institutions, official and clandestine, and contributed to the activities of the building councils in Warsaw.[112]

As noted, the JDC and WJC were wholly dependent for their funds on the donations of American Jewry, which increased but never sufficed. The latter organized protest rallies to urge the American government to take steps in order to save the Jews in Europe, but during the critical years the Jews of America essentially did not have a consistent policy or independent position on the Holocaust. Instead, they subscribed to the government's claim that only an Allied victory would save the Jews and resigned themselves to the lack of action on the part of their government. Consequently, the escape of the Jews from Europe appeared to depend upon *themselves alone,* and help could be tendered only after they had succeeded in extricating themselves.[113]

The people of the JDC, however, regarded themselves as active partners in the rescue endeavor and were prepared to participate in any effort made by Europe's Jews that supported overt and clandestine actions, emigration wherever it was possible, and escape wherever it was attempted. They even lent support to the preparations for the uprisings in the Warsaw and Bialystok ghettos. Beyond that, their hands were tied by limited resources and the law in the United States.[114]

The Struggle for Rescue in Slovakia

As the Final Solution entered its third and final stage, the JDC was compelled to go well beyond the legalistic approach it had followed at the beginning of the persecution campaign in the 1930s. A prominent example of this change in approach was its involvement in bribing the Germans to halt the deportations from Slovakia in the summer of 1942. Here, too, the JDC employed the credit system, both by depositing the borrowed money in a bank in Switzerland and by promising to return it after the war. At first the members of the Working Group mobilized the necessary funds in Slovakian crowns from Jews and Slovak merchants who had clients abroad, especially in Switzerland. They also used these people, in addition to various diplomats, as messengers for their correspondence with the Jewish organizations in Geneva and Istanbul. (This service was, of course, not provided free, and it cost a considerable sum to maintain these postal ties.) The problem did not end there, however, nor after further bribes were made to the Slovakian authorities to halt the deportations and thus forgo the profit they would have derived from them. The Working Group also developed a ramified network of contacts with various arms of the regime, including the police, for the purpose of obtaining information and mounting rescue actions, but its main task was to put a stop to the deportations. Both the Germans and the Slovaks insisted on receiving their payments in foreign currency as ostensible proof that it had come from the Jews in the United States. Rabbi Michael Ber Weismandel took this as a sign that the Germans were mainly interested in having a channel to American Jewry—meaning broader political considerations. This seemed especially meaningful since all signs pointed to the fact that Himmler knew about the deal made in Slovakia and had approved it. Therefore, the Jews, for their part, did everything they could to create the impression that they were backed by people of great influence abroad. Yet today it is also assumed that the Germans halted the deportations from Slovakia for reasons of their own (see chap. 15).[115]

As already noted, the activities of the Working Group were not limited to efforts to rescue Jews within Slovakia proper. In addition to the aid it extended to the flight from Poland to Hungary, which passed through Slovakia, it also sent emissaries into Poland to report on what had befallen the people deported there, and the deportees who could be located in camps in the Lublin area were sent parcels in the summer of 1942 (likewise funded by the JDC). Yet it was not long before these envoys to the East, who were Germans—including one Gestapo man—brought word of the systematic extermination being perpetrated in Poland, and Weismandel decided that there was no longer any point in sending parcels. Letters from Poland that were attached to his report about the extermination campaign explicitly mentioned the name of Treblinka.[116]

In light of these "maddening" reports of mass extermination, as Gisi Fleischmann had characterized them in August 1942, the members of the Working Group became acutely impatient. They not only were encountering delays in the transfer of funds but also sensed a lack of trust and understanding on the part of the officials headquartered in Switzerland. The latter were unable to appreciate the aberrant and revolutionary situation the Jews were subject to in the countries under Nazi rule. In this sense there was essentially no difference between the JDC and Hehalutz, for example, to which Gisi Fleischmann sent her letters. On one occasion she was told to submit a "budget proposal," even though such standard bureaucratic procedure, which is appropriate to the dispensing of public funds in normal times, was absurd during those days of calamity. She was forced to explain that all the Working Group's decisions regarding the use of the money had to be made on the spot. "We regret that we will not be able to consult in advance and, most of all, unfortunately, we will not be able to wait. Please show some trust," she wrote.[117]

These exchanges of letters never fully bridged the gap between the reality of life in Switzerland and life in Slovakia and could not change habits of thinking and working overnight. Besides the fact of lacking the necessary funds, Geneva failed to understand the urgency of the requests, while Bratislava complained that the money needed to save what remained of the Jewish community of Slovakia was not dispatched immediately.

The Europa Plan

Yet the most serious clash between the Working Group and the JDC—as well as the other relief organizations that represented the Jews of the free world—emerged in the context of the Slovaks' plan to rescue the remaining Jews of Europe. Known as the Europa Plan, it was the culmination of their thinking on the subject of rescue; the moving force behind it was again Rabbi Weismandel. When it appeared that the Working Group had succeeded in bribing Wisliceny in 1942 and thus saved the thirty thousand Jews remaining in Slovakia after the deportations, Weismandel suggested it would be possible to rescue all of Europe's remaining Jews in the same way and expected that "for the *Europaplan,* for the sake of two or three million Jews, [the officials of the relief organizations] would overcome every obstacle and delay and rise above all their fears and hairsplitting—and not only they, but the ministers of the Allied countries would agree to it as well."[118]

At the end of 1942 the Working Group embarked upon a two-pronged effort to lobby both Wisliceny (and through him Eichmann and Himmler) and the Jews of the West (and through them the governments of the free world) to free the remaining Jews of Europe from the Nazi grip. Gisi Fleischmann and Rabbi Weismandel began sending letters to Saly Mayer in Switzerland, Nathan Schwalb, the Heḥalutz representative in Geneva, and various rabbis. The result was that all the Jewish organizations effectively became involved in the negotiations, which continued until Himmler ordered them to be broken off in August 1943. Eichmann was not enthused by the idea (which is hardly surprising) but, nonetheless, relayed it to Himmler, who approved the conduct of negotiations. Considering what we know of his extermination orders during 1942/1943, it is hard to believe that Himmler seriously intended to suspend the Final Solution at that time—or even ease the conditions for the Jews in the camps. However, it is reasonable to assume that he wished to ascertain how much Jews of the world were prepared to pay for their brethren in Europe and whether they wielded enough influence with the Allied governments to get their approval for such a deal. Other than that, the Germans may well have regarded the negotiations as a convenient means of camouflage and deception, as attested by Wisliceny's behavior on his occasional visits to Slovakia. At the beginning of March 1943, when he presented the terms by which Germans would ostensibly agree to the proposed arrangement and received an additional payment of $20,000, he assured the members of the Working Group that the Jews of Greece would not be deported—even though he personally had directed the preparations for their deportation from Salonika, which began on March 15, 1943 (see chap. 16). Thus, in reality there were no grounds for these negotiations, and the odds of achieving an agreement and actually rescuing the Jews were nil—quite apart from the qualms and limitations of the Jews in the West, who had not the slightest chance of getting the Allied powers to agree to such a deal, as was clearly illustrated in April 1943 when the abortive Bermuda Conference drew to a close. Still, the Working Group was bitterly disappointed that its proposal had not elicited a positive response.[119]

Escape Routes to the Far East

The review of the efforts to rescue Jews—particularly on the part of the JDC—would not be complete without mentioning one of the more complex, curious, and remarkable rescue operations of all: the creation of a center in Shanghai where 17,000 refugees found a haven during the war. For a time this free port and cosmopolitan city, in which Chinese, Europeans, Americans, and Japanese rubbed shoulders and competed with each other, was the only place in the world that could be entered without a visa.

As a result of the competition of the Western powers in the Far East, Shanghai had had a stormy history but, nevertheless, developed into an international center of trade in which the European powers ran their own colonies, in separate sectors of the city, independently of the Chinese regime. Native Chinese also streamed to this free and open city, giving rise to a relatively small class of inordinately wealthy people alongside masses of Chinese living in egregious poverty and filth. The Japanese had long had designs on Shanghai and finally conquered it during the Sino-Japanese War (which was an extension of their campaign against Manchuria). Despite being an open city, Shanghai was bombed and heavily damaged in August 1937 with great suffering to its population of between three and four million people. A unit of the Japanese fleet established itself in the destroyed area of Hongkew, not far from the "international settlement" of the "White" powers, which also maintained defense garrisons there. After conquering Chinese Shanghai, however, the Japanese became the dominant influence in the city.[120]

Two separate Jewish communities existed in Shanghai: the Sephardim, who had arrived in the nineteenth century from Baghdad, numbered 700 people, and boasted wealth and influence; and the Ashkenazim, who had come from Russia, numbered 4,000 people, and were not wealthy. In 1939 these communities were confronted by a virtual flood of refugees, the likes of which had never been known in Shanghai. Whereas in December 1938 there were 1,500 refugees from Germany and Austria in the city, by the end of May 1939 the number had soared to 14,000.[121] Many of these refugees were penniless, and even their passage—usually on ships that sailed from Italy—had been covered by the Jewish relief organizations. The accommodations found for them in Shanghai were primitive, causing no little suffering. Some were assigned to large halls in improvised shelters—dormitorylike setups that were referred to as "homes"; others were placed in the bombed-out Hongkew quarter, which was being temporarily and minimally renovated for this purpose. Later on, the inhabitants themselves completed the renovations, opening shops, restaurants, and cafés in the area, which came to be called Little Vienna. People tried to eke out a living any way they could, as the welfare they received—through assistance committees funded mostly by the Sephardic community—was hardly sufficient to make ends meet.

At first the Japanese did not interfere with the entry of the refugees, but neither did they offer any aid. It was the local Jews, fearing an "excess of refugees," who turned to the JDC for help, but their appeal was rejected. Then something of a strange "international conspiracy" evolved to prevent refugees from sailing for Shanghai. The partners to this "conspiracy" were the JDC, HICEM, the Committee for German Jews in London, the B'nai B'rith, and even the governments of the United States, Britain, and France (which were evidently opposed out of concern for their colonies, then being threatened by the Japanese). In addition to the directives along these lines issued to the Ezra Society *(Hilfsverein)* in Germany, which organized the emigration of Jews overseas, approaches were even made to the Germans to prevent people from leaving for Shanghai and to the Italians to block them from booking passage to the Far East. In February 1939 none other than U.S. Secretary of State Cordell Hull and Undersecretary Sumner Welles issued orders in this spirit to their legations in London and Berlin.[122]

For the most part, these measures seem not to have conveyed their message to the Japanese authorities, although they also received complaints about the matter from the municipality and foreign representations in Shanghai. At the end of May 1939, the leaders of the Sephardi community advocated the introduction of entry restrictions on the grounds that they were consonant with the wishes of the Jewish organizations in the United States and Britain; in the middle of August the Japanese military authorities, indeed, published new regulations restricting the terms of entry for refugees. In order to step ashore, a refugee was required to show that he had a sum of $400 or to prove either that a job was awaiting him or that he was married to a resident of the city. The required sum was usually provided by relatives in the United States or by HICEM, in the latter case with the attached condition that $300 be returned in order to be recirculated. As a consequence of these restrictions, only a few hundred refugees managed to reach Shanghai from the summer of 1939 onward. With Italy's entry into the war in June 1940, passage to the Far East via the Suez Canal was blocked altogether.[123]

At the same time, however, a surprising new route was opened from beleaguered Europe to the Far East: the railroad leading from Vilna—via Kovno, Moscow, and Siberia—to Vladivostok, where the passengers boarded a ship to Japan and completed their journey by train to the port city of Kōbe. An alternative route passed through Manchuria and likewise led to Kōbe. Over forty-six hundred people fled the Germans through these channels, and they included about two thousand Jews.[124]

By 1939 there were already eight Jewish communities, numbering thirty thousand people, living under Japanese rule either in Japan proper or in Manchuria and occupied northern China (where the majority were found).[125] The Japanese attitude toward them derived from a mixture of diverse and often conflicting influences: anti-Semitic sentiments that had been absorbed first from the White Russians and later from the Nazis, the huge loan that had been floated for Japan during the Russo-Japanese War by the great American-Jewish financier Jacob Schiff, and Japan's introduction to the Zionist enterprise in Palestine. All these elements helped to create the belief that it was possible to exploit "the power of the Jews" to promote Japan's economic and political objectives. However, in 1938, after a Jewish intermediary sent to enlist the cooperation of the American-Jewish community was rebuffed by Stephen Wise—whom the Japanese believed had considerable influence with President Roosevelt—the attitude toward the Jews began to change, and it suffered a major setback after the outbreak of the war in the Pacific. Beyond their political maneuvers, however, Japan's officials and people in general were moved to aid the persecuted Jews by humanitarian impulse and "our declared policy of racial equality."[126]

Many Japanese tendered aid to the refugees in one way or another,[127] but a few figures stand out for taking the particularly courageous action without which even the two thousand Jewish refugees who reached Japan would not have been saved. One was the diplomat Sempo Sugihara, who had been assigned as Japan's consul in Kovno, the capital of independent Lithuania, in the autumn of 1939. Sugihara's main task was to observe and report on the movements of the German and Russian armies on the eastern front to ascertain whether Germany really intended—ultimately—to attack its Soviet ally, as had been promised to the mistrustful Japanese. We do not know how well he handled this mission, but we do know of another task he assumed on his own initiative: providing Jewish refugees, who were streaming into Kovno via Vilna, with Japanese transit visas. Sugihara issued these documents ostensibly on the basis of assurances that no visa was required to enter Curaçao in the West Indies, which was under Dutch control. In something of a conspiracy of rescue, this point had been confirmed, through resort to a linguistic ruse, by the Dutch chargé d'affaires in Riga, L.P.N. Dekker. Both Sugihara and Dekker acted solely on their own, the former even contrary to instructions from the Foreign Ministry in Tokyo. From August 10 to September 1, 1940, when he left Kovno—on orders from his principals—Sugihara signed thousands of transit visas. It was on the basis of these documents that the Russians permitted their bearers to pass through the Soviet Union if they could pay the fare, in dollars, for the train trip across Siberia.[128]

Sugihara's visas were valid only for a sojourn of less than two weeks on Japanese soil, though clearly it was impossible for the refugees to arrange the continuation of their journey in so short a time. About half of the two thousand refugees who arrived in Japan through this arrangement had entry visas for Palestine, the United States, or Canada; the rest had no visas whatever. When the Japanese authorities adamantly refused to extend the transit visas beyond their two-week limit, the leaders of the small Jewish community of Kōbe appealed to an extraordinary personage in Japanese society, Professor Setzuso Kotsuji, an expert in the Bible and in Semitic languages. He had served as a senior official in Manchuria and had helped the Jews there—astounding them with his knowledge of Hebrew. It was likewise in Manchuria that Professor Kotsuji had come to know the man who was now Japan's foreign minister, Yōsuke Matsuoka. Following some subtly tendered advice from the minister, Kotsuji began to entertain—and thereby cultivate the friendship and support of—the ranking members of the police in Kōbe. And they extended the Jews' right of sojourn repeatedly until the last of these refugees were able to leave the city in the summer of 1941. The one thousand or so refugees who lacked entry visas to any other country were transferred to Shanghai.[129]

All the Jewish organizations were enlisted on behalf of this rescue action, with special emphasis on the JDC and the Rescue Committee of the Rabbinical Council of America, headed by Rabbi Abraham Kalmanowitz. Jewish relatives in the United States were also solicited for the money to purchase train tickets. Particularly active in Lithuania was the JDC's agent there, Moses W. Beckelman.[130] In 1941 the organization finally sent a representative to Shanghai, Laura Margolis, whose imaginative approach and irrepressible activity did much to improve the condition of the refugees. Together with her colleagues in Shanghai and abroad, she worked tirelessly to obtain the funds necessary for the upkeep of the refugees, even after the American government had forbidden the JDC to transfer funds to Japan as an enemy country. In 1942, however, as American citizens, the workers from the JDC were forced to leave Shanghai, which had been completely taken over by the Japanese after the attack on Pearl Harbor. Thereafter, the state of the Jewish refugees steadily declined and, under the growing influence of the Nazis, anti-Semitism also began to flourish. In February 1943 all the refugees were forced to move to the Hongkew section, which effectively became a ghetto. To leave the area for their places of work, for example, the inhabitants were required to show a pass, which was always issued for only a limited period. Soon the residents of Hongkew began to suffer from shortages and, particularly, from the tyranny of the Japanese controlling them. At the end of 1943, however, the JDC renewed contact with the community and was able to transfer it funds via Switzerland. About 15,000 Jews were liberated at the beginning of September 1945 when the Japanese retreated and the Americans entered Shanghai.[131]

Entry Visas to Latin America: Rescue and Deceit

The road to Japan was not the only means of escape overseas sought by the Jews. Just as the Japanese consul in Kovno had opened that route, there were Latin American consuls were who prepared—usually for a high fee—to provide Jews with genuine or forged passports that were used in a bid to escape the Nazi grip. The saving power of these passports first became evident in Warsaw during the days of the mass deportation to Treblinka. On July 20, 1942, two days before the *Aktion* began, the bearers of U.S., British, and Latin American passports were summoned to the ghetto prison, purportedly to register again. Surprisingly, the Germans respected the validity of these passports; even though their bearers usually did not even speak the language of the country in question, they and their families were usually exempted from deportation. Instead, they were interned in the prison for weeks, sometimes months, during which they were able to follow the events taking place in the ghetto and even witnessed the executions performed in the prison courtyard. One of the first documents on the fate of the Warsaw ghetto published in the West was the diary of Mary Berg, a young woman who was saved together with her family because her mother was an American citizen. About a month after the July *Aktion* was completed, the men of the families protected by these passports were sent to transit camps in Germany and France opened specifically for this purpose. The women and children left to join them on January 17, 1943, a day before the second *Aktion* in Warsaw. This was how Mary Berg and her family reached the Vittel camp near Nancy.[132]

Naturally, when word reached the West that foreign passports might save Jewish lives, a major effort was mounted to obtain such documents. Requests were submitted to the Latin American consuls in Switzerland and other neutral countries, sometimes through the mediation of Latin American diplomats in New York.[133] According to a report dated February 1944, four thousand such passports were issued in Switzerland alone. Their total number is not known, but estimates range between five thousand and ten thousand.[134] The price of the passports was

$200 to $300 in New York and about SFr 700 in Switzerland; only one consul provided them for free. Some of the redeeming documents, known as "promises," consisted merely of a letter confirming that its bearer was entitled to receive a passport. By the time these protective documents reached Warsaw, many of the people for whom they were intended were no longer alive, and the Germans began to traffic in these passports and "promises," using Jewish intermediaries to convey them to new candidates able to pay the price. For the most part, these dealings developed after the uprising in the ghetto and were exploited by survivors who had escaped to the Aryan side of the city. Designated as candidates to be exchanged for German citizens, they were held in two hotels in Warsaw until they were sent mostly to the Vittel and Bergen-Belsen camps beginning in May 1943.[135]

The first exchange of German citizens for Jews from Palestine took place in the autumn of 1942 when Jewish residents of Palestine were traded for Germans who had been kept in detention there or in Iran (see pp. 414ff.) As a result, 180 people, mostly women and children, reached Palestine in November 1942; only 69 were bona fide residents of Palestine, the rest were British nationals. Most of the Jews had come out of Poland, and they supplied the first authoritative information on the mass murder taking place there.[136] Based on this precedent, the rescue organs in Geneva and Istanbul hoped that the Germans would honor the Latin American documents.

When the supply of these protective papers began to make the Swiss authorities uneasy, however, they queried the Latin American governments as to whether, indeed, they recognized the documents being issued on their behalf. Not only were the replies to this question negative, some of the consuls who had issued the documents were recalled. Consequently, there was reason to fear that the Germans would renege on the exchange operation and that the remaining candidates for exchange would be returned to Poland and sent to extermination camps—an option that the Germans had considered from the beginning.

Leland Harrison, the American minister in Berne, had alerted the State Department to this danger back in August 1943, and he reiterated the warning in December of that year; but it was not until the establishment of the WRB in January 1944 that a way was found to involve Secretary of State Hull in the matter. At the end of March, the State Department ordered its envoys in the Latin American and neutral countries to urge these governments to acknowledge the forged passports, confirm their validity to the Germans, and thus make it possible for the bearers of these documents to remain in transit camps where they were apparently safer and conditions were to some degree more bearable. The Americans assured the countries in question that cooperating in this way would not oblige them to open their borders to the refugees during or after the war, and they promised to find other places of refuge for these Jews. Later on, the United States made it known to the German government that it was expected to honor these protective documents and to draw up proposals for exchanges immediately so that the people holding them would be released.[137]

The effort to obtain the documents was carried on by individuals working in collaboration with Jewish public bodies. Among the first organizations to become involved in this field was Agudat Yisrael, but the focal figure in the operation was

Dr. Abraham Silberschein, a Polish-born activist in the WJC who was staying in Geneva. He established a special organ (the Relief Committee for the War Stricken Jewish Population, or RELICO) whose offices sent thousands of rescue documents not only to Poland but also to Holland, for example. The funds needed to obtain the papers were solicited either from relatives of the people involved or from the relevant Jewish organizations; sometimes they were even supplied by Jews in Poland. When the possibility of acquiring such documents became known, a special public committee was formed in the Warsaw ghetto to draw up a list of distinguished personalities who were to be equipped with them. Similar papers, usually "promises," also reached other places in Poland and were even instrumental in getting prisoners released from Poniatowa and Trawniki, to which many of the survivors of the Warsaw ghetto had been sent after the uprising.[138]

Beginning in the summer of 1943, the bearers of these documents were sent to a new camp that had been opened for them in Bergen-Belsen, with the first twenty-three to twenty-five hundred arriving in July. Of course, the Germans knew these documents were forgeries, but during that period they were still interested in assembling a large number of Jews who could be exchanged for German citizens. Eichmann, on the other hand, wished to keep the number of candidates for exchange as low as possible and had only agreed to the program for lack of choice. Indeed, in August 1943 the Germans embarked upon a rigorous check of the "good will passports" *(Gefälligkeitspässe)* to uncover any "fake" ones *(Schwindelpässe).*[139] These examinations quickly revealed the full scope of the forgeries. The documents had been issued on behalf of entire families, but only rarely had a family survived intact. Thus, new families—as large as possible—were constituted at the departure points by joining together the surviving members of destroyed ones.[140] The Germans were quick to sense this, despite the forged Polish papers confirming the composition of each of these fabricated families, and as early as October 1943, eighteen hundred people were returned to Poland from Bergen-Belsen and sent directly to Auschwitz. These people were, of course, told that they were being transferred to another exchange camp.

Beginning in mid-September 1943, Jews marked for exchange arrived in Bergen-Belsen from the Westerbork camp in Holland. However, not all the documents earmarked for Jews in Holland reached their destination. On explicit orders from Eichmann, the German censor held up five hundred of the registered letters containing the passports and claimed they had been lost due to "belligerent actions." Over the course of a year, almost thirty-five hundred people came to Bergen-Belsen from Holland, among the most famous of them being Anne Frank and her sister, Margot. Four hundred of these people had either a certificate for Palestine or written confirmation that they were entitled to one.[141]

In most cases the American action came too late because the Latin American countries did not begin to acknowledge the passports until the beginning of May 1944. However, back in the middle of March—half a year after the passports had first been disqualified in Bergen-Belsen—the Germans initiated an *Aktion* in Vittel, confiscating the Latin American passports from most of the Jews in the camp and sending close to three hundred of them to Auschwitz via Drancy. One of these deportees was the famous poet Yitzhak Katzenelson, who was accompanied by his eldest son. Later the Germans again accepted the validity of these Latin American documents. Before the deportation from Vittel, the bearers of American passports, including Mary Berg's family, were sent to the United States via Spain; the fifteen people with Latin American passports who remained in Vittel were likewise saved.[142]

Bergen-Belsen in Action

Bergen-Belsen, which had originally been opened as a transit camp, soon underwent a transformation.[143] At first mostly Jews with foreign passports were sent there and were held in relatively satisfactory conditions: they did not have to wear a yellow patch and were not forced to work. The camp was divided into sectors that were set off by barbed wire fences. The largest of these sections was dubbed the Star Camp *(Sternlager)* because the Jews detained there were required to wear a yellow badge. First to be interned in this sector were Jews from Salonika, later to be joined by Jews from Holland and North Africa carrying British passports (caught by the Germans in northern Italy), and finally, in the summer of 1944, by a few hundred women from France and Jews from Croatia. By then the camp contained a total of four thousand inhabitants. But there was a large turnover in Bergen-Belsen: some of its inmates were transferred to Theresienstadt, others were sent to an unknown destination, yet others were released in the exchange operation, by virtue of which they reached Palestine. Men and women were housed in separate camps but were allowed to meet during the day and families were allowed to eat together. However, the inmates were required to engage in hard labor, and their living, sanitary, and nutritional conditions were poor. Citizens of the neutral countries were held in a separate part of the camp, to which Sephardi Jews from Greece and Turkish Jews (mostly from France) were assigned. Polish Jews with immigration certificates for Palestine or entry visas to the United States or Latin America were held in another part of the camp and were not allowed to come into contact with the rest of the inmates—probably because they had knowledge of the extermination camps in Poland. Their isolation was not absolute, however, and the news spread to the other prisoners. Also held separately were the Jews who had come from Hungary on the famous "Rescue Train." Non-Jews who were not considered to belong to the "privileged people" were held in concentration camp conditions and employed primarily in construction work.

The internal management of Bergen-Belsen's various sections was similar to the system employed in Theresienstadt. Of course, the camp was commanded by the SS, but Ältestenräte were established in each sector under the chairmanship of an Älteste who was responsible for maintaining order and for the appointment and supervision of people in various positions. The Star Camp was run by people from Salonika, who were the first to be interned there. Its Älteste was Jaques Albala, who had held a similar position by German appointment, in Salonika and on the way to Bergen-Belsen. When the Jews from Holland arrived in the camp, outnumbering the Greek contingent, their representatives were co-opted onto the council, with Joseph Weiss serving as deputy chairman. In contrast to Albala, who became a hated figure and was accused of treachery, Weiss acquired the reputation for treating the camp inmates well. As in many other camps, tension developed between the prisoners from different countries.[144]

Although all these Jews had been brought to Bergen-Belsen with the aim or under the pretext of being exchanged for German citizens held in enemy countries, the Germans also turned Bergen-Belsen into a unique kind of extermination camp. Officially it was called a recuperation camp *(Erholungslager).*[145] But from the summer of 1944 onward, it essentially took in Jews from other camps who were no longer able to work because of illness or exhaustion. A large proportion of them came from the notorious Dora camp, but they were also sent in from Auschwitz, Theresienstadt, Neuengamme, and other camps. This section of Bergen-Belsen was a concentration camp in the fullest sense. When the extermination operation was halted in Auschwitz in November 1944, the commandant, Josef Kramer, was appointed as the new commander of Bergen-Belsen.[146] Toward the end of the war, during the period of the death marches, an incessant flow of half-dead people reached the camp, where they were further ravaged by an epidemic of typhus. We lack statistics on the huge turnover of prisoners who were brought to, sent from, or died in Bergen-Belsen. But we do know that while in March 1945 there were over 40,000 people in the camp, on April 15, the day of its liberation, Bergen-Belsen contained 60,000 people—in addition to the mounds of corpses. Most of these prisoners were sick and starving, to the point where 14,000 died after the liberation. Estimates have it that in the course of its existence, close to 40,000 people perished in Bergen-Belsen—and this number does not take into account the prisoners who were dispatched from the camp, only a few of whom reached freedom outside Germany or survived within the country.[147] Bergen-Belsen was liberated by the British Army on the basis of a special local armistice concluded with its German counterpart. The photographs taken there by the appalled British soldiers brought the free world the first concrete proof of the mass murder that had been perpetrated by the Nazis.

Rescue Operations of the Yishuv

Legal Immigration

The Jews exchanged for German citizens were not the only ones to reach Palestine legally during the war. In September 1939 there were still close to three thousand families in Europe that had immigration certificates for Palestine; naturally, they made very effort to reach their destination. But they encountered a series of major obstacles. First, regardless of the route they chose, they were required to obtain transit visas, and some of the countries along the way were already parties to the war. The situation was further complicated by the British government's refusal to recognize the certificates held by residents of enemy countries. After months of negotiations, the Jewish Agency for Palestine finally reached an agreement with the British government whereby the candidates for immigration would undergo a joint security check by British and Jewish factors so that no enemy agents would slip into Palestine.[148] All these difficulties were further aggravated by the highly pragmatic problem of transport.

In addition to the route to Japan, a means of escape to Palestine via the Soviet Union opened through the Black Sea port of Odessa and was successfully exploited mainly by some three thousand immigrants from the Baltic countries. According to one version of events, the Odessa route came into being owing to the efforts of the chief rabbi of Palestine, Isaac Herzog, who interceded with the Soviet ambassador in London, Ivan Maisky. Initially, four hundred yeshiva students who had fled from Poland to Lithuania were granted permission to use it, and others followed in their wake.[149] Another escape route crossed through Holland and France to Marseilles, but it was blocked when these countries fell to the Germans beginning in May 1940. What is more, after Italy entered into the war, it was no longer possible to sail from Trieste, whence close to six thousand people had reached Palestine.

The Jewish Agency tried to ensure that immigration certificates were granted to as many Jews as possible. The focal points of this activity were the two centers from which contact was maintained with the Jews of occupied Europe: Istanbul and Geneva. The Turkish authorities—anxious to guard their neutrality—at first refused to grant transit visas to people on their way to Palestine, but they relented after negotiations that went on from October 1940 until February 1941. The terms of transit were spelled out in a special law published in the Turkish press on February 12: other than an entry visa to the "country of destination," the Jews were required to have transit visas for all the countries en route and tickets for some means of transport out of Turkey, their stay in the country being limited to two weeks.[150]

As noted before, the first candidates for exchange were residents of Palestine who had been stranded in Europe at the outbreak of the war and wished to return home—altogether fewer than 3,000 people. Negotiations on this issue with both the Germans and the British, which had started in 1939, were long and complex. Only two additional groups reached Palestine via Turkey, one at the beginning of 1943 (283 people), the other in August 1944 via Spain (200 people, including 61 who had been held in the Vittel camp).[151] But efforts to develop this avenue of rescue met with objections from the Germans and British alike.[152] Other than the resistance of certain quarters (primarily in the SS) to releasing Jews in large numbers, it was impossible to find many Germans who were willing to return to the Reich. There were German citizens in South Africa and Australia, for example, who refused to be repatriated, as did the German women living in Palestine.

In order for a Jew from occupied Europe to immigrate to Palestine legally, he had to have an immigration certificate from the Jewish Agency that had been ratified by the British Mandatory government, receive permission to leave one of the occupied countries or satellite states, be able to pass through the intervening countries, have some means of transport to Palestine available to him on land and over sea, and obtain the money to cover his travel and living expenses during the journey, which often lasted for weeks. As we have seen, all these problems were equally true of emigration to any country overseas. But Palestine was unique on grounds of principle, for the Jews' right to immigrate there had been officially recognized by the British government and was one of the underpinnings of Britain's mandate, which had been granted by international consensus and was subject to review by the League of Nations. Under pressure from the Arabs, however, the British government limited this right—with the publication of the white paper in May 1939—in terms of the extent of Jewish immigration and the amount of time allotted for it to continue. There was nothing new in the Mandatory government setting a quota on immigration certificates; the change introduced by the white paper was the restriction of future Jewish immigration to 75,000 people over a period of five years, after which no Jews would be allowed to settle in the country.

The Jewish Agency's demand to open the country's gates to fugitives from persecution was rejected by the British with a number of arguments. One was on grounds of security; indeed, the fear that enemy agents would enter the country disguised as Jewish refugees was a valid one in wartime. Yet in this case, it was also a convenient excuse for denying Jewish refugees access to Palestine. Another reason given was economic, namely that the shortage of basic goods and logistic difficulties of supply created by the war precluded any growth in the country's population.[153] Efforts to circumvent the white paper's restrictions by bringing immigrants into the country illegally resulted in a reduction of the immigration certificates approved for the Jewish Agency because the authorities made it a practice to deduct the illegal immigrants who were caught and allowed to remain in the country from the annual quota. Thus, in the winter of 1939/1940, for example, no certificates were approved at all; the same applied between October 1940 and June 1941. Nevertheless, close to 17,000 legal and illegal immigrants reached Palestine between the outbreak of the war and the end of 1940.[154]

As the war spread to the Mediterranean in 1941/1942—with Rommel's Afrika Korps thrice approaching the Egyptian border, Greece falling to the Germans, and the Wehrmacht's thrust into southern Russia threatening the northern flank of the Middle East—the possibilities of immigration to Palestine, legal or illegal, declined. During these two years, in fact, fewer than 10,000 immigrants reached the country, and it was not until after the tide had turned on the battlefield that avenues reopened, with 23,000 people arriving in 1943/1944.[155]

In apportioning immigration certificates, preference was given to people who were specially recommended by the Zionist organizations and institutions in their native countries. The lists of names were relayed by clandestine channels or Red Cross mail, and after the applicants were approved by the Jewish Agency in Palestine, the certificates were issued by its office in Istanbul or Geneva.[156] In essence, the applicants were equipped with three different documents at each of the three stages of the operation: the first form confirmed that the candidate had requested an immigration certificate and that the office had recommended swift approval; the second informed him of the receipt of a cable confirming that he had been placed on the list of recipients of immigration certificates as part of the exchange program; the third was an announcement that the immigration certificate had been approved and the applicant assigned a number on the list. In many cases, especially in Poland, they arrived too late—just as the Latin American passports had. If the recipients of immigration certificates were still alive when they arrived and were not murdered afterward, they stood a chance of being transferred to one of the holding camps in the West. But even then, most of them were not freed—the exception being the contingent of sixty-one people from the Vittel camp who were included in the group exchanged in 1944.

All in all, seventeen lists of candidates for immigration were approved, for a total of scores of thousands of names. Ten thousand names were relayed via Geneva alone, yet only 800 to 840 people immigrated to Palestine in the exchange operation—fewer than even the 900 agreed to by the British in January 1943. To these 800 to 840 people one must add an unknown number of others who were saved by their ability to produce such documents. According to Chaim Barlas, then head of the Jewish Agency's Aliyah (Immigration) Department, during the war some 40,000 people passed through Istanbul on their way to Palestine, legally or otherwise.[157]

Throughout the period a special effort was made to rescue children and teenagers from Europe. The negotiations with the Mandatory authorities in Palestine and the government in London on this matter were more productive, and on a number of occasions they complied with the Jewish Agency's requests to allocate immigration certificates. The bid to save young people was aimed mainly at the Balkan countries—Rumania, Bulgaria, and Hungary. At first it was hoped that twenty thousand children could be brought out of Rumania—most of them orphans from Transnistria—and by the end of 1942 there was even talk of releasing seventy thousand people from Transnistria in exchange for a payment of 200,000 ley (about $50) per person. Although this plan never came to fruition, there did seem to be a chance of getting five thousand children out of the country. The Turks agreed to have them cross their territory, and the British approved their entry into Palestine, but in the end the operation was sabotaged by the Germans. In fact, the first one thousand children and their escorts were already on their way out of Rumania in mid-March 1943 when the Germans intervened with the Bulgarian government to have them turned back at the border, and the organizers in Rumania were told to abort the operation. Eichmann had been vehemently opposed to the plan, insisting that "the emigration of the children of Jews should be denied as a matter of principle." He was prepared to allow five thousand children to leave the bounds of the occupation if, in return, twenty thousand Germans living abroad were returned to the Reich. "However," he qualified, "it must be emphasized that we are talking not of twenty thousand old people but of Germans under the age of forty who are capable of producing offspring." At the same time he stressed that any negotiations on this proposal would have to be consummated quickly, otherwise "it will no longer be technically possible to organize the departure of five thousand Jewish children owing to the mounting of our actions against the Jews."[158]

Attempts were then made to transfer the children not overland via Bulgaria, but by sea. The main problem here was obtaining ships. Two large Rumanian boats were anchored off Istanbul. Because the authorities feared that they would fall into German hands, they agreed to have them used for transferring children from Rumania and Bulgaria to Palestine. But it was for precisely this same reason that the Germans opposed the idea and even ordered their submarines on patrol in the Mediterranean to act accordingly. The Turkish government did not release the ships, and transport by sea was effected on a more limited scale by the Mossad for Illegal Immigration.

Attempts to organize the departure and legal immigration of Jews from the Balkan countries were resumed with greater impetus at the beginning of 1944 after the establishment of the WRB and Ira Hirschmann's arrival in Istanbul. This time an effort was made to obtain Bulgarian ships; it, too, encountered difficulties, for even as late as 1944 the Germans were still able to delay their departure.[159]

Illegal Immigration

The endeavor into which the Jewish community of Palestine poured its major effort to save Jews from Europe is known as illegal immigration or *Aliyah Bet.* (*Bet,* the second letter of the Hebrew alphabet, stands for "second.") As has already been noted, it began in the 1930s and mounted considerably from 1938 until the outbreak of the war. During those years forty-five immigrant ships sailed to Palestine: sixteen of them organized by the Labor movement through the Mossad for Illegal Immigration and twenty-nine organized by the Revisionist movement and private factors.[160] Altogether these ships brought close to 20,000 illegals to the country, accounting for 50 percent of all the Jewish immigrants during that period. From September 1939 through the end of 1941, only fifteen boats sailed for Palestine with over 12,000 refugees, ten having been organized by private individuals, two by the Mossad, and three by the Revisionists. Most of these ships set sail from the Balkan countries. This movement essentially came to an end in February 1942 with the sinking of the *Struma* just off Istanbul in the Black Sea. The boats that managed to sail from Rumania in 1942 were few, small, and chartered privately. The organized transfer of refugees did not resume until 1944 when the Mossad brought a total of 4,650 people over from Rumania in ten ships, though one of them, the *Mafkura,* sank with some 400 people aboard.

Although there were differences in approach and practice between the organizations and circles that dealt with illegal immigration, all of them were forced to grapple with a number of basic problems. One was the difficulty in obtaining boats. Prior to the war there were still shipping companies and ship owners who were willing to engage in a bit of adventure—providing the price was right. But once the war began, their number declined sharply, leaving the various organizers of illegal immigration to compete for the same few ships. Readying them to sail, outfitting them with the equipment necessary to accommodate the people, and provisioning them with food and water were other major problems that entailed considerable expense. Not only did the cost of the ships themselves rise appreciably, whether for charter or for sale, but further outlays were required—for insurance, materials, and the like—and all of these costs had to be paid in foreign currency.

One of the greatest obstacles, however, was raised by the British government, whose consistent opposition to the mass entry of Jews into Palestine prompted it to resort to every political, legal, and military means of fighting illegal immigration. The British Foreign Office, usually in coordination with the Colonial Office and the High Commissioner in Palestine, did all it could to have the countries of transit and embarkation detain the fleeing Jews and block them from sailing out of their ports. The British even asked such neutral countries as Spain and the Latin American countries not to allow immigrant ships to fly their flags. They explored every legal course of action and used every means of force to deter ship owners and potential immigrants from attempting to defy their naval blockade of Palestine. Above all, the British were convinced that Germany was exploiting the flow of immigrants to plant agents in the Middle East and to provoke the Arabs by citing it as evidence that London was not adhering to the 1939 white paper. They accused the Jewish Agency, and particularly the Revisionists, of political rather than purely humanitarian motives in pursuing this venture—namely, to force the repeal of the 1939 white paper—and the charge was not entirely unfounded.[161]

Pitted against all these obstacles was but a single force: the irrepressible drive of the Jews who were desperate to flee the Reich and its satellites. None of the dangers lurking along the way—on their journey to the coast, on the high seas, and even upon reaching the Palestinian shore—could match the fear of the Nazi demon. This was emigration for the sake of rescue, and the young and the workers were no longer given priority. Young and old, the Jews fled on foot, by train, and by boat down the Danube; sometimes they were forced to wait months for transport, and often they boarded ships whose ability to withstand the rigors of the open sea and reach their destination was dubious. But the people jammed onto these ships nonetheless, filling them well beyond capacity and willingly suffering hunger, thirst, and disease—all for the chance to reach safety. Only a few of these travelers actually did make it safely ashore, then mixing with, and vanishing into, Palestine's Jewish population. Most of them were caught by the British, often on the high seas, and were interned in the Athlit detention camp until the authorities saw fit to release them in return for deducting their number from the immigration quota.

Seeing that its policy failed to stem the tide of illegal immigration, the British government decided upon another approach to deter the Jews, namely, to send the illegal immigrants into exile far from the Middle East. In October 1940, when they learned of the departure of three ships from Rumania bearing thousands of people, the Mandatory authorities resolved to catch these undesirable immigrants and ship them off to the British island colony of Mauritius in the Indian Ocean. This was the background to the disaster of the *Patria* on November 25, 1940.

After being held in Haifa harbor for a number of weeks on two of the seized boats, the *Milos* and the *Pacific,* the immigrants were transferred to the *Patria,* which was to carry them to Mauritius. Meanwhile, a decision had been reached in the Haganah, the mainstream Jewish underground in Palestine, to sabotage the ship so that the deportation could not be carried out. But the action went awry, and the boat sank, claiming a toll of 267 lives. The survivors of the *Patria* were sent to Athlit and were later permitted to stay in the country by a special decision of Churchill's cabinet. But the passengers on the third ship, the *Atlantic*—spared from the tragedy—were, indeed, exiled to Mauritius.[162] The *Patria* affair symbolized the dilemma of the Jewish leadership and population of Palestine in its resolve to cooperate with Britain in the war against the Nazis while actively fighting it over its white paper policy.

It was only natural that all those who came into direct contact with European Jewry and were subject to the enormous pressure of the Jews fighting for their lives tended to support any means of getting them to Palestine. This sense of urgency came on top of the pragmatic problems of arranging emigration in places where the Palestinian operatives had to make decisions under circumstances that did not always allow them to consult with their headquarters. Thus inevitably, perhaps, the agents in the field found themselves in conflict with the establishment in the rear, which directed operations according to considerations and priorities of its own. This phenomenon was common to both the Jewish Agency and the Revisionist movement, and the frustrating difficulties of execution only exacerbated the friction.[163]

Most of the funding for illegal immigration came from the JDC. Under the direction of its European director, Dr. Joseph Schwartz, the organization even found ways to circumvent the American directives that prohibited the transfer of funds to areas under the control of the Germans or their allies. The Jewish Agency also allocated funds for this purpose, as did the Histadrut, the national labor federation of the Jews in Palestine. And, of course, one should not ignore the efforts made to raise funds from the Jews at the points of departure.

In March 1941 the Germans stopped collaborating in the organization of illegal immigration, and it appears that this reversal was not merely fortuitous. If the assumption is correct that during this period the Final Solution was decided on in principle, there was no longer any point in arranging the departure of the Jews through illegal channels. Thus, the organized flight to Palestine essentially subsided as of the summer of 1941, but the movement reached a nadir and a turning point in February 1942 with the sinking of the *Struma*.

The *Struma* was an old vessel of Greek registry that had served as a cargo boat on the Danube.[164] After a number of attempts had been made to refurbish it, a private agent began selling tickets for passage on the *Struma* at exorbitant rates, assuring potential passengers of its excellent condition. On boarding it in the Rumanian port of Constanţa, however, its 769 passengers discovered that the shipping agent had perpetrated a monstrous fraud. Not only was the ship not technically fit for service, so that its motor soon broke down, but it also lacked the most elementary facilities for passengers and did not even have a kitchen. Neither did the crew meet even the minimal professional standard. Nevertheless, as they could not return to Rumania, the passengers had no choice but to remain on board, and the *Struma* sailed on December 12, 1941, reaching Turkish waters three days later, despite a series of breakdowns. Among all the other lies, the passengers had been told that immigration certificates were awaiting them in Istanbul and would enable them to continue on to Palestine legally. They were to discover that this, too, was a hoax.

Facing Istanbul, the *Struma* remained docked in an isolated part of the harbor for ten weeks. The Turkish authorities supplied a small amount of food but they adamantly refused to allow the passengers off the boat—even to be held in a camp for which the JDC was prepared to assume full responsibility. Stricken by hunger and disease, the people were ravaged above all by rising tension. The Turks' obduracy in this matter traced to the implacable stance of the British. At the time, Lord Moyne was the colonial secretary, and his stand on the subject of Jewish immigration to Palestine had always been as intransigent as that of the high commissioner, Sir Harold MacMichael: under no circumstances were illegal immigrants to be allowed into the country. Consequently, even though the British were then prepared to allow the immigration of children from Rumania, they refused to include the children on the *Struma* in that project. MacMichael's arguments were the usual claims of "information" that there were German agents aboard the ship and that the tight supply situation in Palestine precluded the entry of any more people.

The Turks demanded that the British solve the problem of the *Struma,* while the latter either evaded the issue or openly refused to become involved. Finally, on the night of February 23, 1942, the Turks towed the *Struma* to a point outside their territorial waters and, despite the passengers' appeals for help and even attempts at resistance, cut the ship loose and sent it floating without food, water, or fuel. A few hours later an explosion occurred and the *Struma* sank. Turkish rescue boats were not dispatched until the next day, and they returned with a single survivor. To this day it cannot be satisfactorily clarified who was responsible for the disaster. One theory has it that an explosion occurred while the crew was working on the engine, but there have also been reports that the ship was sunk by a torpedo—German or Russian.[165]

The tragedy of the *Struma* precipitated a crisis for all involved in the illegal immigration drama: the Jews who were trying to flee from Nazi-dominated Europe; the Zionist movements in Europe and the Mossad for Illegal Immigration in Palestine; the Turkish government; the British government and the British High Commissioner in Palestine, as the executor of the government's policy; and finally the Jewish Agency, which did not have much control over the ships leaving the Balkan countries by private initiatives but was the only body authorized to conduct negotiations with the British both in London and Jerusalem. Still, in the case of the *Struma* it turned out that its influence on the decisions of the Mandatory government was virtually nil.

Thus, the disaster of the *Struma* forced all of these parties to reconsider their policies in this matter. Despite the grim news, Jews in the Balkan countries pursued their efforts to flee by this same perilous route, if to a somewhat lesser degree. The Mossad doubted its ability to resume organized immigration from Europe to Palestine, not least because of the inflexibility of the Turks. On the other hand, by establishing a center in Teheran it tried to create a land bridge to the Jews who had fled to the Soviet Union and been sent to its Asian hinterland. Its agents did not actually penetrate into Soviet territory, but they did make contact with pioneering young people who had reached the Iranian shore of the Caspian Sea by their own devices. Another channel for bringing refugees to Palestine opened as a result of the agreement between Stalin and General Wladyslaw Sikorski, the head of the Polish government-in-exile, to allow Polish civilians in the Soviet Union to leave for the Mediterranean. Of the 10,000 Poles, 7,000 were Jews. Among the thousands of Polish children who had been living in the Soviet Union with their families or had been cared for in orphanages were hundreds of Jewish youngsters, many of whom had been camouflaged as Christians so that they would be accepted into these institutions. Agents from the Jewish Agency and the Mossad succeeded in collecting them in a separate Jewish camp—despite efforts by the Poles to keep them out of Jewish hands by sending them to India and South Africa—and the British consented to grant them immigration certificates. These 1,400 youngsters, who reached Palestine in February 1943, came to be known as the "Teheran children."[166] Many were orphans or had left their parents behind somewhere in Russia and had no idea what had become of them, so that older children took care of their younger siblings. Having suffered hunger and disease, they treated every slice of bread as a precious possession that was best hidden from coveting eyes. Immigration certificates were also obtained for 325 Jews who had reached Teheran via Bukhara.[167] With the aid of the JDC, another large center was established in Teheran for sending parcels to Jews in the Soviet Union, most of whom were suffering from hunger.

The prominence given to the tragedy of the *Struma* in the British press, and the strong editorials that accompanied the news, elicited a sharp public response. On the initiative of the new colonial secretary, Lord Cranborne, and his successor, Oliver Stanley, the government deliberated the issue and displayed a tendency toward mitigating its immigration policy. Although in principle the British adhered to the white paper and the prohibition against permitting illegal immigrants to enter Palestine, in practice they decided to allow those refugees who had reached the country to remain there. In 1943 this change was supplemented by an order to grant an immigration visa to any Jewish refugee who had made it to Istanbul. But it must be said that the concrete results of this order were meager. In part, this was due to the conduct of the Turkish government, which continued to place obstacles in the path of Jewish refugees, notwithstanding its February 1941 decision to allow them to pass through the country. Thus, it appears that the British order did not really begin to have an effect until much later.[168]

21

Rescue on the Brink

Attempts in Hungary

By 1944 Jews and other people of all nations and denominations the world over could have been well aware of the slaughter the Nazis were perpetrating against the Jews of Europe. Considering this knowledge, was it really impossible to prevent the tragedy that could be foreseen once the Germans conquered Hungary on March 19, 1944?

From both a general European and a specifically Jewish standpoint, the developments in Hungary reflected the complexity of the situation that evolved toward the close of the war and the continued helplessness of the Jewish people. It can fairly be said that all the actors in the European conflict and their clashing aspirations were involved in this drama. Above all there was the German regime, whose various arms were working against one another, each trying to save itself from the debacle looming ahead for Germany; and facing it was the Allied camp, equally beset by rising internal frictions as victory came into view. Vacillating between these two poles were the satellite states, which were out to save their own skins, as it were, by distancing themselves from the soon-to-be vanquished Germans and hoping to gain whatever benefits could be had from the presumptive victors—and Hungary aspired to these ends no less than Rumania and Bulgaria. The neutral countries also read the handwriting on the wall and expressed this cognition in their growing dissociation from Germany and their heightened readiness to extend aid to the Jews. The pope was caught in the pincer of conflicting interests in his relations with Germany and the Allies, which were then engaged in pitched battles up the length of the Italian boot. The Red Cross broadened its activities and set aside a number of restrictions that had previously blocked aid to the Jews. And given these circumstances, the international Jewish organizations—

above all the WJC and the JDC—likewise stepped up their activities while the Jewish public throughout the free world, but primarily in North America, displayed an ever greater willingness to donate to the cause of rescue.[1] The relations between Great Britain and the Jewish community in Palestine improved: the British were seriously considering the Jewish Agency's proposal to send Jewish parachutists into occupied southern Europe; the odds of forming a Palestinian brigade within the British army rose appreciably; and even the restrictions on immigration were eased. Why, then, was it not possible to save the Jews of Hungary? And to what degree did their salvation depend on these Jews themselves? In other words, was it really within the power of the Aid and Rescue Committee to become the driving force aiming at the rescue of Hungary's Jews?

Joel Brand's Mission

Many writers and scholars have explored the abortive mission of Joel Brand, who brought Eichmann's offer of "blood for goods" to the West. The historian Béla Vago has observed of the treatment of this affair:

> The Brand mission . . . has been examined in sharply contradictory contexts. Its failure has been interpreted along a broad spectrum on which there is room for saints and sinners, heroes and traitors, selfless martyrs and paid agents. On the one hand, there are those who present it as having been doomed to failure from the very beginning; on the other hand, many view it as a missed opportunity, a glaring blunder on the part of the Allies, and even of the Jewish Agency. In the estimation of some, the whole mission was fictitious, designed only to camouflage other goals unrelated to the fate of European Jewry, while for others it constituted a feasible means of saving hundreds of thousands of Jewish lives.[2]

It is impossible to delve into all the aspects and renditions of the Brand mission in the confines of the present work. I shall, however, briefly review the facts of the matter. On May 17, 1944, Joel Brand left Budapest for Istanbul carrying a proposal that had been drawn up by Eichmann. It offered to release a million Jews in return for ten thousand trucks (to be used solely on the eastern front), 800 tons of coffee, 200 tons of cocoa, 200 tons of sugar, 200 tons of tea, and 2 million pieces of soap.[3] The deportations from Hungary to Auschwitz had begun three days earlier, but Eichmann promised to suspend them until the Allies had given an answer expressing their readiness to enter into a deal. Brand did not leave Budapest alone; he was accompanied by a man who went under the name of Bandi Grosz, a multiple agent who, in a colorful career, had served the Germans, the Hungarians, the Allies, and the Jewish Agency.[4] In Hungary it was assumed that his ramified connections would suffice to obtain entry visas to Turkey on arrival there; although both men managed to get past the passport control in the airport, neither received a visa.

On Brand's arrival in Istanbul, his message was immediately conveyed to all the parties concerned and was relayed to London, Washington, and Jerusalem. Vanya Pomerantz (Hadari), one of the members of the Yishuv's rescue delegation in Istanbul, conveyed it to the Jewish Agency in Jerusalem in person; in the wake of his report, with David Ben-Gurion's support, Moshe Shertok (Sharett) applied for a visa to travel to Turkey to meet with Brand. He even had the backing of the British high commissioner in Palestine, Sir Harold MacMichael. But the Turks were hostile to the mission from Hungary and went so far as to threaten to deport the emissaries back to their homeland. This would have meant turning them over to the Germans, who in that case—the consensus had it—would surely murder them. Brand himself was undecided about how to proceed, especially as he had left his wife and children in Budapest at the mercy of the Gestapo. The Jewish Agency wanted him to go to Palestine, where he would have direct access to Jewish and British authorities, but the Turks were not prepared to allow him to continue his journey, and it took the intervention of the American minister, Laurence A. Steinhardt, to make them relent.

On June 5, therefore—one day before the Allied landing in Normandy—Brand left for Palestine accompanied by a member of the delegation in Istanbul, Ehud Avriel. On reaching Syria, however, he was promptly arrested and interrogated by British agents. It was four days before Moshe Shertok, who was waiting for him in Aleppo, was allowed to meet with Brand. Then the British spirited him off to Cairo, where they continued to interrogate him under the direction of Lord Moyne. Ira Hirschmann, representing the U.S. War Refugee Board (WRB), also came to Cairo and debriefed Brand. Finally, at the beginning of October, Brand was released from custody and allowed to go to Palestine. The offer he had brought out of Hungary was deliberated in London and Washington, and an exchange of views initially indicated a willingness to enter into negotiations so as to gain time. The idea was to hold these negotiations through the aegis of the Swiss, who represented the Allies in Berlin. But the United States and Britain believed it necessary to involve the Russians in the discussions (a point on which Chaim Weizmann was in full agreement),[5] for the Western Allies were anxious to avoid creating the impression that they were negotiating separately with the Germans. The Russian response was an unequivocal *nyet*. Moreover, Churchill, too, expressed his adamant opposition to any negotiations with the Germans on the subject. Thus, at its meeting on July 13, 1944, the British government's Committee for Refugee Affairs decided against the proposal to negotiate.[6]

As matters turned out, Eichmann did not honor his promise to suspend the deportations until receiving a reply to his offer, and their cessation at the beginning of July 1944 was in no way connected with the Brand mission (see chap. 18). Judging by their systematic arrangements and precise implementation, there is no reason to assume that Eichmann ever intended to halt the deportation of Jews to Auschwitz, even briefly. The discord among the competing arms of the German administration in Hungary and the odd match of Joel Brand with the agent Bandi Grosz suggest that varying—perhaps even conflicting—interests were at work here. According to Grosz's version of the affair, his task and the prime objective of the mission was to feel out the representatives of the Allies and try to open the way for negotiations with Himmler. The British, and even more so the Russians, viewed Eichmann's proposal as a bald-faced attempt to divide the Allies and enter into negotiations with the Western countries alone. On the other hand, it was impossible to ignore the outcry being voiced by the public and legislatures in both

Britain and the United States in light of the word then spreading about the Holocaust. Thus, almost two months passed between Joel Brand's arrival in Istanbul and the final negative decision.[7]

Negotiations with Himmler

Brand's mission, like the Europa Plan before it, was an incontestable failure, but it did highlight the benefit that could be derived from negotiating with the Germans. The maneuver had made it possible to gain time and postpone for as long as possible the extermination actions threatening the surviving Jews of Europe as a whole and of Hungary in particular. During this time, efforts were directed at saving the hundreds of thousands of Jews still alive in the Nazis' labor and concentration camps, in hiding, and in the forests. Moreover, it was not only the Jewish Agency and the international Jewish organizations that came to this conclusion about the potential inherent in negotiations as a delaying tactic; the Americans and the British showed an interest in them as well.

Thus, a paradoxical situation arose: on the one hand, the Western leaders were determined not to negotiate with the Germans because they were striving for their unconditional surrender; on the other, negotiations were clearly a prerequisite for saving Jews. Himmler and those of his associates who were interested in negotiations of this sort sought them for political reasons of their own—both as a way of obtaining the materials of which Germany was running short and as a way of building an image of themselves as "the saviors of the Jews" in the hope that that would shield them after the defeat of the Third Reich. Yet it appears that in addition to these factors, Nazi superstition about the boundless power of world Jewry was at work here—to the point that they believed it would turn the sentiments of the Western leaders in their favor. It must be said, however, that figures such as Kaltenbrunner and Eichmann were firmly opposed to this approach and even tried, often successfully, to counter it.

In the face of this welter of conflicting aspirations and doubts, the Jews tried to exploit the atmosphere created by Joel Brand's mission. The chief figure in Hungary who continued to hold talks with the Germans was Dr. Rezsö Kasztner, working with a few members of the Aid and Rescue Committee. During these summer months, two unusual events occurred. The first was the transfer of at least 18,000 Jews from Hungary to Austria, where some of them were set to work and their families were allowed to remain with them. They lived under relatively tolerable conditions until the last months of the war. In fact, this transfer was the result of an order Eichmann had received to send workers to Vienna, but he portrayed it as a gesture of good will on his part—to keep the Jews there "on ice," as he told Kasztner—and demanded in return the payment of SFr 5 million in advance. After negotiations, the sum demanded of U.S. $100 per Jew was agreed to, with the funds to be raised by the committee. But when Eichmann demanded that the committee also supply the staff to run the office in Vienna under the supervision of one of his own men, Hermann A. Krumey, its members balked, and an administrative staff was later chosen from among the people sent to the Strasshof camp outside Vienna.[8]

The choice of who would be saved and who left to his fate was a difficult one that ultimately billowed into a controversy. In speaking of this problem, Kasztner stated, "Once again we faced the harsh dilemma that featured in all our work: Would we leave the choice to blind chance or try to direct it?" The decision they arrived at was to try to choose candidates according to some sort of guideline: to save people of stature and importance in one way or another; to tend to people who had already been interned in work camps; to promote the reunification of families; and to favor orphans who had no one left to care for them. Often these good intentions were thwarted; some of those chosen to leave Hungary were frightened and hesitated to join the transports or changed their minds at the last moment—and were replaced by others. Kasztner told of one instance in which only thirty people from provincial cities reached Vienna instead of the eighty chosen, but none of these had been included on the original list. Some of the deportees worked in industry; others in agriculture. They received a minimal wage that was deposited in a special account of the Vienna Jewish community, after the deduction of expenses for their upkeep and that of their families. They were housed in apartments but were forbidden to leave them except to go to work. Anyone caught on the streets of Vienna was punished, usually by being sent to Auschwitz. Medical care was available in the labor camp outside the city. As a result of these relatively comfortable conditions, about 15,000 people were still alive in 1945, but many of them were to perish in the death marches to Mauthausen or in the camp.[9]

The transfer to Vienna removed the largest number of people, relatively speaking, from threat of direct deportation to their deaths. Efforts were also made to save smaller groups, one being a number of Orthodox Jews under the direction of Philip von Freudiger, who succeeded in bribing Dieter Wisliceny to transfer to Budapest about eighty Jews living in ghettos in the provincial cities. Most of these people, including Freudiger, managed to flee to Rumania in August. Similarly, the Rescue Committee had "privileged people" brought from outlying cities to the capital where they were held in a special camp.[10]

The second instance in which a group of Jews was set apart for an unusual fate—from the German viewpoint—in the summer of 1944 was the famous "Kasztner Train," or "Rescue Train." It carried 1,684 Jews who were supposed to reach Lisbon via Spain; they were first taken to Bergen-Belsen but were then sent to Switzerland before the end of the year (see chap. 20). The choice of candidates for this rescue train led to grave charges that Kasztner had given preference to his own family and friends. The affair culminated in a tragic epilogue when, years after the fact, it became the subject of a trial in an Israeli court that held up some of the aspersions cast on Kasztner's reputation. After the trial he paid for the controversy over his accomplishments and failures with his life: he was assassinated on a Tel Aviv street. Israel's Supreme Court posthumously cleared him of all charges.[11]

In the detailed report he composed after the war on the Rescue Committee's activities, Kasztner devoted considerable space to the history of the "Rescue Train." The negotiations over it were conducted in June when the systematic deportations to Auschwitz were still in progress. They were initiated because there seemed to open the possibility of getting Jews to Palestine via Rumania and Istanbul. Eichmann turned down the idea on the grounds that Germany's relations with the Arabs, particularly his personal relationship with the mufti of Jerusalem, Haj Amin el-Husseini, precluded a transfer of this sort. The impression of a deportation had to be preserved so that it would be necessary to send the Jews first into the bounds of the Reich proper and from there to Palestine via neutral countries. A heavy payment was demanded for their release this time as well; after lengthy negotiations, Eichmann and the Rescue Committee "compromised" on a sum of U.S. $1,000 per person. Initially, the number under consideration was six hundred to seven hundred Jews, but gradually this number doubled, and on June 30, the day on which the rescue train actually left, the official quota was thirteen hundred. As noted earlier, the number of people on board was, in fact, even higher. According to Kasztner's report, its passengers included Orthodox Jews who had been chosen by Freudiger; refugees from Poland, Slovakia, and Yugoslavia who had been selected by their own representatives; Liberal Jews who had been selected by Samuel Stern, the head of the Jewish Council; Zionists and holders of immigration certificates who had been chosen on the recommendation of the Palestine Office; pioneering youth from Hungary and other countries (chosen from the refugee population); Revisionists; the people who had paid the ransom out of their own resources and, thus, funded the entire transport; survivors from the ghettos in outlying cities; intellectuals, writers, scientists, doctors, and artists chosen by a committee chaired by Ottó Komoly (many of whom refused to exploit the opportunity to escape); and finally a group of children from the Budapest orphanage. After a series of delays, the train finally reached Vienna, where the passengers were sent to a disinfecting station. When they were sent to the showers, many of the Jews were overcome by panic, but it turned out that the showers were precisely what they purported to be. On July 8—the day on which the transports from Hungary were halted—the rescue train reached Bergen-Belsen, whereupon a new episode of exhausting negotiations began over the release of the passengers to a neutral country.[12]

Both these rescue actions were the outcome of extraordinary negotiations conducted with the Germans by the Jews themselves. Yet a seemingly insoluble complication arose; the Jews were negotiating with the Germans in order to save people under the Germans' control, and they did score some successes. But in the case of the Brand mission, they also discovered that even if an understanding was reached with the Nazis, there was no guarantee that the Allies would accept and honor it. Thus, their only option was to conduct their negotiations as though the Western Allies were prepared to compromise with the Germans—even though the British media clearly publicized the government's adamant refusal to negotiate "blood for goods." Rabbi Weismandel, for one, tried to explain away this contradiction by telling Wisliceny that these public statements were "a cover" and actually proved Britain's willingness to make a deal. One wonders if he himself believed this sophistry, but the Germans seemed to buy his explanation.[13]

In the course of these pseudonegotiations, however, when the Germans demanded proof of their enemies' willingness to comply with their demands for money and particularly for goods, the problem was that it proved impossible to supply such proof without some degree of cooperation from the uncompromising Allies. On the other hand, the Jews demanded of the Germans tangible proof of their willingness to release people, implying that there was a genuine prospect of rescue.[14] This complex and delicate task of mediation was assumed by a number of Jews operating out of Switzerland alongside Kasztner in Hungary.

All the rescue efforts made first in Slovakia and then Hungary were dependent on making large sums of money available to the Germans. For the most part, the Nazis calculated the figure in dollars according to the number of Jews they were prepared to release. The only organization capable of supplying such large sums was the JDC, but its hands were tied by U.S. government regulations prohibiting the transfer of money into enemy hands or to areas under enemy control. The European director of the JDC, Dr. Joseph J. Schwartz, was forbidden even to negotiate with the Germans. Hence, this task was assigned to the JDC representative in Switzerland, Saly Mayer, who was told to conduct the talks on behalf of the Swiss Funds for Aid to Refugees, not as a representative of JDC—although it would, of course, be JDC's money that actually changed hands. As in the case of Brand's mission, the course of these negotiations was subsequently described differently by various people. It is clear, however, that Saly Mayer was fully conscious of his ticklish position when he assumed the impossible task of saving Jews by conducting long and involved negotiations with the Germans over the terms of an agreement that he was essentially unauthorized to conclude. His partner in this endeavor was Kasztner, working with Himmler's representative in Hungary, Kurt A. Becher.[15]

In conducting these negotiations, it was necessary to outmaneuver the German, Swiss, and U.S. authorities alike. The Germans had to be convinced that their demands would be met—on condition that they, too, kept their word and released Jews. The Swiss authorities, above all Chief of Police Heinrich Rothmund, were asked to allow negotiations to take place on the Swiss border and thereafter within Switzerland proper in addition to taking in the Jews released from the German camps. U.S. Secretary of State Cordell Hull and his deputy, Edward Stetinius, Jr., were asked to approve the deposit in Switzerland of SFr 20 million (U.S. $4.65 million), ultimately to be turned over to the Germans for the purchase of goods. These negotiations wore on from the latter half of August 1944 until the beginning of 1945. They resulted in the passengers on the "Kasztner Train" being transferred from Bergen-Belsen to Switzerland. Following the putsch in Hungary, a new crisis erupted in mid-October, and the situation deteriorated in November as a result of the death marches being run by Eichmann from Hungary to Austria. At the same time, Himmler ordered the gassing in Auschwitz to be stopped.

In the meanwhile, the talks had branched out and been joined by other actors and bodies. Especially active were the Sternbuch brothers, particularly Isaac Sternbuch (who represented the Rescue Committee of the Union of Orthodox Rabbis) working out of Switzerland. Dealing on his own, Isaac Sternbuch promised the Germans tractors, despite the definitive American prohibition on supplying them with machinery of this sort. In the end he was forced to turn to Saly Mayer for financial help, and the latter complied, acting expressly contrary to the American orders in this matter.[16]

Isaac Sternbuch also tried to enlist a former president of Switzerland, Jean-Marie Musy, to act as an intermediary with the Germans. Known as a right-wing supporter of the Nazis, by 1944 Musy evidently felt it necessary to spruce up his image by involving himself in an effort to save Jews; thanks to his connections with the Third Reich, he was able to contact Himmler, with whom he concluded an agreement to free the remaining Jews for a ransom of millions of dollars. The first quota of 1,210 Jews was brought to Switzerland from Theresienstadt on January 7, 1945. The effort backfired when Musy—at Himmler's request—had their release publicized in the Swiss and American press, for it consequently became known to Hitler, who reacted vehemently and forbade Himmler to release any more Jews.[17]

No Bombing of Auschwitz–Birkenau

Alongside the attempts to negotiate with the Germans came an effort to pursue another tack, namely, to halt the deportations to Auschwitz and the operation of the gas chambers by bombing the camp and the rail routes leading to it. By the spring of 1944, everyone of consequence knew about the extermination campaign, although precise information on its scope and the means used to pursue it were still lacking. But this too changed after Jewish prisoners mounted two successful escapes from Auschwitz. The most informative of the escapees were two Slovakian Jews, Alfred Wetzler and Rudolf Vrba (Rosenberg), who had hidden in a bunker on April 4, 1944, and three days later managed to get away and reach Slovakia. The other two fugitives, the Slovak Ernst Rosin and the Pole Czeslaw Mordowicz, fled on May 27 and also made it to Slovakia. The testimony provided on April 25 by Wetzler and Vrba contained extensive information, describing not only the Auschwitz and Birkenau camps down to the last detail, including sketches, but citing the number of victims and reporting on the extermination process by gassing. Rosin and Mordowicz, for their part, brought out information about the fate of the first Hungarian Jews sent to Auschwitz.[18] The Slovaks who wrote down the reports naturally wanted to pass them on to the free world in the hope that on the basis of the detailed and reliable information an effort would be made to halt the deportations and gassings. However, owing to various delays and hitches, the information did not reach the West until the summer. The same was true of the cables and letters related to the testimonies sent by Rabbi Weismandel, who suggested bombing the gassing installations at Auschwitz and the railway tracks leading to the camp.[19]

On the initiative of the Geneva-based Zionist representative Richard Lichtheim, the British minister in Bern, John Clifford Norton, cabled the information and proposals for action to London, where his wire was received on June 27. Among the suggestions for actions recommended by Lichtheim were the "bombing of the government ministries in Budapest." Indeed, British and American bombers carried out an especially heavy air raid on the city on July 2 in which five hundred people were killed, including many Jews. It is noteworthy that Lichtheim's cable was intercepted by German Intelligence, and once the code was deciphered, on July 5, the Foreign Ministry relayed it to Kaltenbrunner, who transferred it to Budapest.[20] Two days later Miklós Horthy ordered the deportations from Hungary brought to a halt.

Meanwhile, the Jewish Agency in Jerusalem had also begun to contemplate the use of violent means to halt the slaughter. As early as June 2, in a cable to the United States, Yitzhak Grünbaum proposed the bombing of the railway tracks, and from then until October these suggestions and similar attempts to prod the Allies into bombing the extermination installations and the routes leading to them continued relentlessly.[21]

As is well known, however, no such bombing ever came to pass. Equally known is the fact that the I.G. Farben plant and the Buna Works for the production of synthetic oil and rubber in Monovitz, just outside Auschwitz, were bombed by the Allies and that British planes bombed Warsaw in support of the Polish uprising there. The natural question is, then, Why didn't they bomb the gassing facilities at Auschwitz?

Research has shown that the refusal of the American and British air forces to bomb these installations stemmed from their disinclination to be involved with rescue actions per se. As early as February 1944, the U.S. War Department determined:

> It is not contemplated that units of the armed forces will be employed for the purpose of rescuing victims of enemy oppression unless such rescues are the direct result of military operations conducted with the objective of defeating the armed forces of the enemy.[22]

Throughout the summer of 1944, the Americans invoked this decision in response to every appeal. In Britain Moshe Shertok and Chaim Weizmann found that their importunate suggestions consistently met with indifference or a pronounced lack of desire on the part of the Foreign Office to prompt any action, despite the fact that upon being apprised of the information sent by Norton, Churchill himself wrote on July 7 to Foreign Secretary Eden, "Get anything out of the Air Force you can and invoke me if necessary."[23] "To the American military," wrote David S. Wyman, "Europe's Jews represented an extraneous problem and an unwanted burden."[24] The same could be said for the British Foreign Office, which was the Jewish Agency's only channel to the air force.

The Horthy Offer

These rescue efforts were not the only moves on behalf of Hungarian Jewry to be thwarted by delays and by the refusal of almost all the relevant parties to take decisive action. During the summer of 1944, opportunities arose for thousands of Jews to emigrate from Hungary—and were blocked.

Horthy's decision to halt the deportations came after deliberations in the Council of Ministers and the Crown Council in which the regent had taken part. In essence, these internal discussions traced back to the time when the deportations began; but the first penetrating debate of the matter was held only on June 21 when the U.S. Senate Foreign Relations Committee and the U.S. House Foreign Affairs Committee publicly warned the Hungarian government against allowing the deportations to continue. The Hungarian Foreign Ministry also received various protests from abroad as well as reports on the reaction to the information provided by the escapees from Auschwitz that was being published throughout the free world. Their report had earlier been relayed to Hungary's ruling circles through Horthy's son, with whom a member of the Jewish Council was in close contact.[25]

The intervention of Pope Pius XII, President Roosevelt, and Sweden's King Gustav also demonstrated to the Hungarians how well aware the free world was of what was happening in their country. The pope's appeal reached Horthy on June 25, 1944, in a direct cable from Pius XII—the first of its kind during the Holocaust period. On June 26 Roosevelt communicated an explicit warning, demanding the cessation of the deportations (as noted earlier, the heavy bombing of Budapest took place on July 2). Sweden's king had received various appeals for intervention, mostly from Jews. The first, from the Jewish Council in Hungary, had been relayed to the Swedish Foreign Ministry on June 20, 1944, by the Swedish minister in Budapest, Ivar Danielson. Four days later the minister sent a report giving details of the deportations, citing the number of people murdered in Auschwitz according to the Wetzler–Vrba report and noting the intention to deport all the country's Jews by July 15. The chief rabbi of Zurich, Zvi Taubes, sent Sweden's chief rabbi, Marcus Ehrenpreis, a cable urging him to appeal to the king. Ehrenpreis received the same request from Yitzḥak Grünbaum of the Zionist Executive in Jerusalem, who likewise mentioned the plan to deport all of Hungary's Jews by July 15. On June 30 the king sent his telegram to Horthy.[26]

Prime Minister Sztójay summed up the reasons behind the halt to the deportations:

1. an improved attitude toward the Jews had begun to mark the policies of neighboring Slovakia and Rumania, and this fact placed the Hungarians in an embarrassing position;
2. mounting pressure against the deportations at home and from abroad; and
3. the revelations about what befell the Jews deported to Auschwitz.[27]

Also discussed in the course of the Hungarian internal deliberations were proposals to enable Jews to emigrate from Hungary. The candidates for emigration were 400 Jews holding Swedish passports and 1,457 families (for a total of over 7,000 people) with immigration certificates for Palestine. The processing of these potential emigrants was to be handled by the Swiss legation, which represented Britain's interests in Hungary. The plan called for seven families to be sent each week to Constanţa, Rumania, whence they could sail for Palestine. Also proposed was the departure of 10,000 children under the age of ten who were to be accompanied by 100 adults. The funding and other arrangements for their departure were guaranteed by the American WRB through the aegis of the Red Cross.

Veesenmayer relayed this proposal to Germany on June 29, and on July 6 it was raised before Ribbentrop with emphasis placed on the Hungarian argument commending the proposal in light of the Hungarian citizens and capital being held in the United States.[28] Apparently the WRB suggested canceling the debt owed by Hungary to the United States in return for accepting this suggestion. These considerations together with Horthy's new policy seem to have impressed Hitler, for in a cable dated July 10 Ribbentrop announced, "The führer has decided, at my suggestion, to accommodate the Hungarian government on the matter of the foreign proposals on sending Jews abroad. Thus the proposals of the Swedish, Swiss, and American governments may be complied with."[29] Ribbentrop's cable also spoke of the assumption that these Jewish emigrants would be settled in Sweden, Switzerland, and the United States, and he cautioned, "The transfer of Jews to Palestine is to be avoided as much as possible, in consideration of our policy vis-à-vis the Arabs." But Hitler also made the program contingent on Horthy's willingness "to allow the speedy resumption of the deportation" from Budapest.[30]

The details of this emigration scheme, known as the "Horthy Offer," reached Britain on July 18, whereupon the British and American governments consulted on how to respond to it. The Americans were in favor of the idea, whereas the Jewish Agency, which had received an erroneous report that it pertained to seven thousand families (or some forty thousand people), began to pressure the Mandatory authorities in Palestine. But the British government, of course, had misgivings about the arrival of such a large contingent of Jewish immigrants in Palestine and thus suggested that the entire matter be referred to the Intergovernmental Committee on Refugees—a move the Americans regarded, not without reason, as a delaying tactic. When the problem was discussed by the British government's Committee for Refugee Affairs on August 3, its members found themselves facing a dilemma: if they declined the offer, the government would be open to pressure from public opinion; if they accepted it, they could expect difficulties in Palestine. Yet other reasons for rejecting the proposal were the difficulties of transporting and settling such a large number of Jewish emigrants in the Mediterranean area. One of the many suggestions raised during the board's discussions was, "we should accept the 'Horthy Offer' as a gesture, informing the Americans at the same time that they must not face us with the impossible in the question of providing for accommodations."[31] And it was in this spirit that the government decided to act on behalf of the potential migrants once they reached neutral territory or an area under the control of the United Nations. At that point the British would be prepared to seek temporary places of refuge (!) for them. The Americans, for their part, bowed to the British reservations, and the said decision was published in the name of both governments on August 17, 1944. No commitment was made to allow Jews into the United States or Palestine. Evidently the assumption was that after the war these refugees would return to Hungary. Meanwhile, the two allies suggested, the Jews should be allowed into neutral countries.[32]

Hence, Eichmann had found an ally in his resolve to block the departure of the Jews. He had been far from pleased about Hitler's consent to have Jews leave Hungary, and although it was unthinkable to oppose the führer's decision openly, he could at least try to reverse it. At that time, moreover, he was planning to resume the deportations. On July 24 Eichmann asked the RSHA for a decision from Himmler on whether the Jews should be allowed to leave for Palestine via

Rumania. Out of consideration for the mufti of Jerusalem, he proposed that their exodus be solely westward (the same condition he had set at the time of Joel Brand's mission), and this suggestion was ultimately accepted.[33]

Thus, the outcome of the offer was the creation of a deadlock or vicious cycle fed by the political interests, real and imagined, of the Allies and the German desire to prevent the emigration of Jews. The upshot of this essential convergence of views was that countless Jews—whole families or children on their own—who had been chosen as candidates for emigration in July remained imprisoned in Budapest until Ferenc Szálasi's rise to power put an end to all the emigration plans and ushered in the period of the death marches to the Austrian border.

Protected-Citizens' Passports for Budapest's Jews

Just as the failure of Brand's mission prompted further negotiations with Himmler's men, so the abortive "Horthy Offer" led to Hungary's recognition of preferred status for Jews holding passports from the neutral countries. Veesenmayer reported this at the end of September, "The Hungarians no longer intend [to allow] the emigration [of people with such passports] but are merely according these Jews the status of foreign subjects, which assures them special, better treatment when [the Hungarians] engage in internal actions against the Jews."[34]

The first to grant the Jews these coveted passports were the Swedes, who recognized the right to Swedish citizenship of people with family or commercial ties with Sweden. In this case the people in question were four hundred Jews who had been candidates for emigration under the terms of the "Horthy Offer." The *volte-face* in the attitude of the neutral representatives in Budapest came during the suspension of the deportations. Considering the marked effect that the intervention of various governments and international factors had had upon the Hungarian government, some of these diplomatic legations began to extend their protection to the Jews. When other missions followed the Swedish example and the Hungarian authorities honored the documents they issued, the Germans were likewise forced to recognize the various types of protective passports (or *Schutzpässe*). The number of these documents issued by the end of the interim period of the summer of 1944 is:[35]

Switzerland	7,800
Sweden	4,500
Vatican	2,500
Portugal	698
Spain	100
San Salvador	1,600
Total	17,198

The most prominent representatives of the neutral countries, in terms of their work on behalf of rescue, were Charles Lutz of Switzerland and Raoul Wallenberg of Sweden. Wallenberg is the better known of the two because of the tragic conclusion of his mission, but Lutz was no less actively involved in the rescue operation. Both men were citizens of countries that had preserved their neutrality in the two world wars and took pride in their democratic and humanitarian traditions. As it turned out, both had studied in the United States for a number of years. Lutz, a man in his early forties, was a professional diplomat; Wallenberg, ten years his junior, was an architect by profession, but he had been recently engaged in commerce and banking. He was the son of a distinguished family and was related to the banker Jakob Wallenberg, who had handled the commercial negotiations between Sweden and Germany during the war. Born after his father's death, Wallenberg grew up in the home of his stepfather, Frederik von Dardell, and was strongly influenced by his grandfather, Gustav Wallenberg, a professional diplomat. He was well traveled, spoke a number of languages, and both he and Lutz had spent some time in Palestine.[36] Together they saved the lives of tens of thousands of Jews.

Since the German conquest of Hungary, the Swiss legation had been representing, in addition to Great Britain and the United States, fourteen other countries associated with the Allies. Lutz, who headed the department handling the interests of these foreign states, was assigned to deal with matters of *aliyah* and other emigration from Hungary, and in this capacity he maintained close contact with the head of the Palestine Office, Moshe Krausz, and with the pioneering Zionist movements.[37]

Rescue by the Zionist Pioneering Underground

The operations of the Zionist youth movements were originally directed by the need to serve and protect their members who had fled to Hungary from Slovakia long before the German conquest. Hence, they had already adopted clandestine practices and after the German occupation of Hungary had only to adapt the form of their underground activity to the new situation. In the beginning, at least, the youth movements found themselves at loggerheads with Moshe Krausz as well as with Kasztner.[38] Whereas the latter was trying to save Jews through negotiations with the occupier, the youngsters were convinced that the Germans could not be trusted, that their sole intention was to destroy Jews, and thus that Jews should have nothing to do with them. Only when Kasztner succeeded in sending the "Rescue Train" out of Hungary did the youth movements relent and add their own candidates to the list of emigrants, and a few hundred youngsters not included on the official list boarded the train just before departure. Eventually, a kind of division of labor evolved whereby Kasztner dealt with *haut politique*—the Rescue Committee's efforts to achieve the best possible solution through negotiations with the Germans—while the members of Heḥalutz engaged in the day-to-day clandestine activities for rescue.[39]

From the very start of the occupation, the mood and outlook of these youngsters was far more realistic than that of the Jewish population at large. Quickly grasping the real purpose of the deportation that the Germans were about to effect, the members of Heḥalutz sent emissaries to provincial cities throughout Hungary to warn the Jews and persuade them to go into hiding—or at least not to board the trains. Yet few were the Jews who heeded this advice. Instead, they continued to cling to the illusion that nothing like that could possibly take place in Hungary.

Occasionally, the absurd happened as a result. For example, the members of Heḥalutz offered a newly married young man interned in a work camp an Aryan identity document for his wife and an address in Budapest where she could hide, but he refused their help—two days later she had to board the train to Auschwitz. In another instance one of the emissaries happened upon a closed railway car filled with Jews standing unguarded in a field. He opened the doors and exhorted the Jews to get out and flee—but they refused to act.[40]

Even before the occupation, one of the main activities of the youth movements had been to supply documents, genuine or forged, that would accord their bearers a legal status. This operation was stepped up to an impressive degree during the occupation by the establishment of a workshop that turned out no fewer than eighty-five varieties of documents with the aid of 150 different stamps. Some were produced singly or by the dozens, others by the hundreds, and certain types by the thousands. The youngsters managed to keep the location of this workshop from the Hungarian police and the Germans for quite a while, and each time it was in danger of being uncovered—particularly after a comrade involved in the operation had been caught—the facility had to be moved. Thus, it was relocated sixteen times in the course of 1944 before finally being destroyed by members of the Arrow Cross on December 21, just prior to the Russian assault on Budapest. Naturally, the people caught in the workshop were arrested, but thanks to their resourcefulness and that of their comrades, most of them were saved at the last minute. In addition to the movement members themselves, tens of thousands of other Jews and even members of the Hungarian underground used and were saved by these documents.[41] Moreover, throughout the period the youth movement underground mounted daring operations to free its members from Hungarian and German prisons and camps.

Another equally perilous form of rescue was known as the *Tiyul,* or "outing," meaning escape over the border. Before the German occupation, this flight was directed mainly to the Rumanian border, but beginning in March 1944 the youth movements began organizing what they called the *Recontra-Tiyul* to Slovakia, where the situation appeared to be safer and there was at least a possibility of joining the partisans. Most of the youngsters who were accepted by the partisans subsequently fought and died in the Slovakian uprising in the autumn of 1944. An unsuccessful attempt was also made to cross into Yugoslavia. Having learned the bunker system from the Jewish refugees who had come in from Poland, the youth movements made a number of attempts to build such bunkers in the provincial cities of Carpathia, for the most part, as well as in Budapest and its environs, but with only partial success.[42]

The Protected Houses

To arrange for the emigration of Jews from Hungary at the time when the "Horthy Offer" appeared to be a viable option, it was necessary to establish a central office to process the formalities for thousands of people. Such a center was created in a building known in Budapest as the Glass House, which had been placed at the disposal of the Swiss legation for this purpose by a wealthy Jewish merchant, the largest glass wholesaler in Hungary, Arthúr Weisz. The result was the creation of an extraterritorial area that was off bounds to both the Hungarian and the German police. During the negotiations over the "Horthy Offer," thousands of Jews streamed to the Glass House in the hope of obtaining the redeeming document.[43] Within its premises, the project was essentially controlled by Weisz and Moshe Krausz, but the Glass House also served as a headquarters from which the youngsters of the pioneering youth movements could direct their own activities.

Following the Arrow Cross rampage through the streets of Budapest and the homes of Jews in the wake of the October 15 putsch, many Jews fled to the Glass House seeking shelter and soon filled the building to capacity (it ultimately held 2,000 people). It goes without saying that severe problems of accommodations, sanitation, and food supply resulted, but here, too, the members of Heḥalutz displayed extraordinary resourcefulness and organizational talents that helped to ease the situation.[44] In the meantime, Lutz had managed to multiply the number of official safe-conduct passes to 7,800; the youth movement workshop turned out no fewer than 120,000 additional copies. The documents did not always protect their bearers, as Eichmann and the Arrow Cross frequently ignored them. Thus, 17,000 bearers of safe-conduct passes were arrested and earmarked to be sent to Austria, though many were ultimately freed by the members of Heḥalutz and representatives of the neutral states, above all Wallenberg and Lutz.[45]

In view of the chaotic situation, the neutral representatives involved in the effort to protect Jews decided to embark upon a joint venture. On November 17 the papal nuncio and the Swedish minister in Budapest sent the Szálasi government a communication, on behalf of all the neutral diplomatic missions, protesting the deportations and violation of the government's commitment to honor the safe-conduct passes. They also demanded that the government ensure satisfactory conditions for the Jews conscripted for labor camps. Szálasi responded the next day by setting down guidelines for his policy toward the Jews that attempted to comply with the demands of both the Germans and the neutral states. Ostensibly in response to these demands, his government announced the establishment of two ghettos: the Big Ghetto, which was envisioned as a closed one, and the International or Little Ghetto, to be run by the neutral representations.[46] To create them it required the removal of Hungarian Christians living in 133 buildings side by side with Jews. Other locations had been allocated for Jews alone and marked with the yellow Star of David as far back as the summer, but the homes of Christians were interspersed among them. Now all these Christians—about 12,000 in number—were obliged to leave the area allocated for the ghetto, and 86,000 Jews were crammed into the same apartments, for an average of 14 people per room. On November 29, when the population switch had been completed, the Hungarian government proclaimed the establishment of the ghetto, and Christians were forbidden to enter it. Two weeks later, on December 10, it was closed.[47]

The buildings controlled by the neutral legations were far from sufficient to house the thousands of people who sought shelter under their aegis. At the end of December, they contained 33,000 people; as the overcrowding increased, it was compounded by supply difficulties, so that despite the enormous effort—especially on Wallenberg's part—to find food and heating materials, it proved necessary to transfer some of these people to the Big Ghetto. On January 17, 1945, when the Russians broke into Pest, where both ghettos were located, they contained a total of 94,000 Jews—about 25,000 in the International Ghetto and 70,000 in the Big Ghetto. In addition to the people liberated from the ghettos, another 25,000 Jews came up from underground, so that a total of 119,000 people were saved in Budapest. Fifteen thousand had been killed in the city prior to the German occupation and another 105,000 from March 19, 1944, onward—98,000 of them between October 15, 1944, and January 18, 1945.[48]

These tens of thousands of people were saved thanks to the combined efforts of the foreign diplomats and of the Jews themselves. Among the survivors were 6,000 children. Initially the International Red Cross had housed them together in thirty-five buildings, but on orders from the authorities was subsequently forced to transfer them to the Big Ghetto. The task of assembling the children was proposed and directed by the engineer Ottó Komoly, with the International Red Cross creating a special department for the project in collaboration with the Jewish Council. The members of Hehalutz also played an active part in the operation, thereby acquiring the protection of the Red Cross. Komoly, a figure of distinction in the Jewish community, did not live to witness the liberation. Like Weisz, he was murdered during the Russian siege by the Arrow Cross. Many children also fell victim to the vengeful Arrow Cross, but 4,000 were saved.[49]

All the major Hungarian Jewish figures and organizations involved in the rescue effort were in contact with parallel institutions and bodies in Geneva and Istanbul. The Rescue Committee in Palestine contributed significantly to funding the operation, while money from the JDC usually came through Geneva. Vicarious contact with Palestine was created for a fleeting movement through the parachutists who tried to enter Hungary in the summer of 1944 via Yugoslavia. Of the three volunteers for this mission—Yoel Palgi, Peretz Goldstein, and Hannah Szenes—only the first managed to escape the enemy. Despite the failure of the mission and the cost in lives, Rafi Benshalom wrote of the parachutists' effort, "During those tragic times, when we stood abandoned and isolated, [their mission], nevertheless, had great symbolic import that will not be overlooked in the history of Jewish defense and rescue."[50]

Raoul Wallenberg and the Swedish Passports

It has already been noted that as of early 1943, the Germans began to attend to the matter of repatriating foreign citizens caught within the bounds of the occupation. It was in the context of this policy that the Swedes first addressed the problem of saving Jews on the Continent. The prime mover behind this effort was the Stockholm Jewish community, led by Chief Rabbi Marcus Ehrenpreis, but the Swedish authorities were also approached by individual Jews whose relatives were trapped in one of the occupied countries. The matter was assigned to the Swedish minister in Berlin, Alvin Richert, to whom all requests regarding candidates for repatriation from Belgium, France (particularly the Vichy zone), Holland, and Germany were to be addressed. Later on, these requests were joined by appeals to bring Jews out of the Baltic states, the Generalgouvernement, and Italy. The Swedish government was then strict in granting passports, especially visas, only to blood relations of Swedish citizens. They received the same temporary passports designed for people who had lost their Swedish citizenship for one reason or another, for example, as a result of having been naturalized by another country. These efforts to save Jews on the Continent were not very successful, however. Sometimes the requests came too late, for their objects had already been deported to extermination camps; in other cases, the Germans refused to recognize the citizenship that had been granted or restored to a Jew. Very few people got out of the occupied countries as a result of this system, and the Swedes contended that it was necessary to pay considerable sums for them.[51] These cases were still being dealt with in the spring of 1944 when the problem of the Hungarian Jews arose.

The former trial and error in saving Jews[52] had come to a climax by the time the Hungarian problem evolved. Both the Swedish representatives in Budapest and various people in Stockholm were aware of the matter.[53] At first, the Swedish government displayed reluctance, dismissing the idea of its own initiative and stipulating that any dealings about a rescue action must be conditional upon an agreement with the Hungarian authorities. At the beginning of May, however, Dr. Karl Lauer, a Jew of Hungarian origin who was a director of a company that maintained ties with Hungary, asked Gösta Engzell, the head of the Foreign Minstry's legal department, to intercede on behalf of his in-laws. Since Lauer was not a Swedish citizen at the time, he could not request that they be awarded a Swedish passport and entry visa (and when he became a citizen on July 14, his wife's parents were no longer in Hungary, so that he asked for intervention on behalf of his sister alone). This was not the whole of the matter, however. Through the mediation of members of the WJC in Stockholm and the representative of the American WRB—the financial attaché in the American legation, Yver C. Olsen—the suggestion was raised that the Swedish Foreign Ministry send a special representative to Hungary to handle the issuance of the passports. A similar suggestion also came from Ivar Danielson in Budapest. The sponsors of the idea in Stockholm, apparently at the instigation of Dr. Lauer, proposed one of Lauer's fellow directors, Raoul Wallenberg, for the position of special attaché in the Budapest legation, and the suggestion was accepted.

Wallenberg reached Budapest after Horthy had suspended the deportations to Auschwitz on July 7, and on the day after his arrival Ribbentrop announced Hitler's agreement to the "Horthy Offer." Thus, he found himself bound to fulfill a double role: to equip as many people as possible with passports and to ensure that they left Hungary headed for Sweden. His office—known as Department C of the Swedish legation—issued three kinds of passports:

1. a full-fledged Swedish passport, whose covers were black and therefore referred to as a black passport;
2. a temporary passport, which was granted to people with family or occasionally commercial ties with Sweden, was printed on blue-and-gray paper;
3. a safe-conduct pass, which was ultimately distributed to thousands of peo-

ple and was printed on yellow-and-blue paper—the colors of the Swedish flag. By the second half of July 1944, there were 650 to 700 of these safe conduct passes already in circulation.[54]

As the number of candidates for emigration increased, the Swedes also began to assemble them in special buildings. An operation of this size required substantial funding, and the necessary sums were obtained from the United States—meaning the JDC—through Olsen. To transfer them to Hungary a special account was opened in Wallenberg's name in the Schweizer Bankverein in Zurich.

Most of the Swedish buildings were not opened until after the putsch. They were located in the International Ghetto; by the beginning of December, 15,000 people had been crowded into thirty-one such hostels under Swedish control. To manage them the Swedes put together a bureaucratic framework replete with departments and bureaus for handling housing, food, social affairs, health (including two hospitals), and contacts with the authorities that employed hundreds of people, most of them Jews.[55] As mentioned earlier, Wallenberg was subsequently forced to transfer some of the residents of these buildings to the Big Ghetto. Once the ghettos were officially established, he moved his office to Pest, while the Swedish legation remained in Buda on the opposite bank of the Danube. Attempts by the Arrow Cross to assassinate him forced Wallenberg to go underground but did not stop him from continuing his work.

On December 24 the Russians reached the outskirts of Budapest, and roads out of the city were gradually blocked until Budapest was totally surrounded on December 27. The last reports from the Swedish legation reached Stockholm on December 23; thereafter the fate of the staff was not known until its members reached Bucharest during the latter half of March. Stockholm was not briefed on the full story until April, when the entire staff returned home via Moscow—everyone, that is, but Wallenberg.

During the Russian siege of Budapest, Wallenberg established what was effectively a branch of the Swedish legation in Pest, and on January 13 his driver took him to the Russian headquarters, evidently to request recognition for his office and to place it under Soviet protection. Accompanied (or guarded) by a military escort, he returned to Pest on January 17, the day on which the ghetto was liberated. He gathered a few belongings, issued instructions, and left money for the staff, intimating that he was not sure whether the Russians regarded him as a guest or a prisoner. He was never seen again.[56]

Eleventh-Hour Rescue

By the summer of 1944, it was impossible to keep the truth about the extermination camp at Auschwitz hidden any longer. Together with the German reversals on the frontlines, this fact finally forced Himmler to put a stop to the gassing in November and enter into negotiations on the fate of the surviving Jews. The harrowing death marches and the attempts to liquidate the camps before the Allied armies reached them from Italy and the East have already been discussed (see chap. 18). The Jews of the free world were seized by the fear that the Germans would liquidate the remaining camps together with their inmates while they, like the advancing armies, would be helpless to avert this disaster. The Jewish organizations then made a last desparate effort to save the surviving remnant of Jews in Europe.

The Jews, however, were not the only party concerned about the surviving prisoners in the German camps. Intimations of impending danger also reached Scandinavia, and in October 1944 warnings were also relayed to the Scandinavian countries by the WJC.[57] Sweden and Denmark had long been involved in providing relief for their citizens held in camps within Germany, and particularly active in this sphere were the Norwegians, above all N. C. Ditleff, who had been Norway's minister in Warsaw prior to the war and fled the city after the outbreak of hostilities. Escaping to Stockholm, Ditleff had initially attempted to better the condition of the prisoners by sending them parcels. The Germans were prepared to make relatively generous concessions when it came to Norwegians, so that their condition improved compared with that of other prisoners. This project was made possible by the existence of an information exchange that had been founded by a number of Norwegians who had been expelled and forced to live in Germany. It was headed by the rector of the University of Oslo, D. A. Seip, who, together with his aides, compiled an accurate card file of Norwegian prisoners and where each one was interned, so that it was possible to fulfill the Germans' demand to send the prisoners personally addressed packages.

Obviously, the Jews lacked the advantage of such precise information. What is more, the attempts by the WJC to get parcels through to the imprisoned Jews were wholly dependent on the good will of the International Red Cross and the intercession of the WRB, and it was not until the spring of 1943 that the Red Cross was disposed to comply with its requests. Among the first to benefit from the collective shipment of food were the inmates of Theresienstadt, who received parcels from the Portuguese Red Cross in 1944.[58] But the operation did not reach major proportions until the autumn of that year. Through the collaboration of the WRB and the International Red Cross, the parcels were delivered to the Swedish port of Göteborg, where the representative of the WJC in Sweden, Hillel Storch, managed to ship large quantities out by boat and train mostly to Ravensbrück, Sachsenhausen, and Bergen-Belsen. Another center of activity was Switzerland, where parcels were sent by truck not only to camps further south, such as Mauthausen, but to northern Germany as well—until the fighting made transport impossible.[59] Not everywhere were the Jews able to benefit from the food; in some places it was filched by the Germans, and in others it was simply not distributed to the people for whom it was meant.

Other efforts were invested in trying to persuade the Allies to make their voices heard on behalf of the camp inmates. The Norwegians were particularly active in this cause as well—through the auspices of their government-in-exile in London—while the WJC tried to get the WRB to act. Its aim was to have the supreme Allied commander, General Eisenhower, issue a statement admonishing the Germans not to harm the prisoners in the labor and concentration camps. After a round of negotiations, in which the British were included, a statement of this sort was, indeed, published on November 7, 1944, and was circulated by dropping leaflets by the thousands over German territory. Eisenhower called upon the Germans not to obey orders to harm the prisoners "regardless of their religion or nationality." The original draft of the statement made explicit reference to the Jews, but Eisenhower changed the wording, evidently still sensitive about placing too strong a stress on the fate suffered by the Jews during the war.[60]

Anticipating the Allied victory, from early 1944 Ditleff and his people had been making a supreme effort to get the Norwegian prisoners freed before Germany's total collapse because they justly feared what might befall the prisoners in the midst of the foreseeable chaos. At first they clashed on this point with the Allies, who wanted the inmates of the camps to stay where they were and await the arrival of workers from the United Nations Relief and Rehabilitation Authority (UNRRA), which had been established expressly to deal with the millions of displaced persons within Germany. But Ditleff persuaded his government, along with the Swedes, to take the initiative in getting their citizens out. Following talks that went on from the summer of 1944 to January 1945, the Swedish Red Cross committed itself to conduct the transfer of the Scandinavian prisoners to Denmark and Sweden. The job was assigned to the organization's vice president, Count Folke Bernadotte, who negotiated the matter with Himmler and got him to agree to the transfer. Initially, it was understood that the prisoners would be assembled in the Neuengamme camp outside Hamburg, but as the front drew closer in April, they were transferred to Denmark and Sweden, with the full cooperation of the Danes in both the planning and execution of the operation. Hundreds of white buses marked with red crosses carried the prisoners from the various camps to the assembly point and from there to freedom.

Among the last to be saved from the German camps were the Danish Jews interned in Theresienstadt. At literally the last minute, before passage between the two fronts converging from the East and the West was blocked, the buses reached Theresienstadt and within hours had carried the astonished and shaken Jews through the conflagration that was Germany to their homeland. At the same time, the president of the International Red Cross, Karl J. Burkhardt (who prior to the war had been the representative of the League of Nations in the free city of Danzig), tried to persuade Himmler to let him provide relief for the prisoners in the camps.[61] The WJC had long been urging the Red Cross to take the "protected prisoners" under its own aegis, discussing the matter with Burkhardt several times prior to the latter's departure from Switzerland for a meeting with the SS. Now, however, for the first time, Aryeh Kubovitzki (Kubovy) found that Burkhardt was lending the notion a sympathetic ear. Between March 12 and 14, Burkhardt met with Kaltenbrunner, representing Himmler, and with officials from the German Foreign Ministry. Their talks ended with the Germans consenting to have food sent to the prisoners on the death marches and allowing the Red Cross to supervise the distribution of the parcels within the camps. But the concrete results of this agreement were meager. It was not until the final days of the war, for example, that a Red Cross representative managed to get into Mauthausen. And when asked actually to release the prisoners from the camps, the Germans responded with evasions.

Behind the scenes yet another intermediary was at work: Himmler's personal physician, Felix Kersten. Kersten was living in Stockholm at the time, and the Swedish government had no qualms about exploiting his good offices. Of even greater significance, however, were the contacts between Kersten and the agents of the WJC in Sweden; as liaison between Himmler and this international Jewish body, he conveyed Himmler's readiness to meet with Hillel Storch and discuss the possibility of saving the remaining Jews in the camps. Just as Himmler had negotiated with Bernadotte in the hope of opening an avenue to talks with the Western Allies and of concluding a separate peace, he now apparently believed that the Jews could help him in this cause. Therefore, Himmler was prepared to opt for another departure from policy, following the precedent of the earlier negotiations in Hungary and with the JDC in Switzerland. Talks had been going on through Kersten's mediation for a few weeks when suddenly, on April 19, 1945, word arrived that Himmler was prepared to meet with Storch. At the last minute, however, Storch refused to go and was replaced by another of the organization's officials, Norbert Masur. Accompanied by Kersten, Masur was flown to Berlin in a German plane and, under the relentless bombing, continued on to Kersten's estate outside the city. Himmler did not join them until the following night, and it was in the wee hours of the morning that the bizarre two-and-a-half-hour talk took place between the archbutcher of the Jews and the Jewish envoy suing for their release. Most of the exchange was essentially a monologue by Himmler in his own defense, giving a highly distorted account of the extermination campaign he had conducted against the Jews. The only concrete result of the talk was his agreement to release 1,000 Jewish women from Ravensbrück in addition to the French women imprisoned there.[62] The next morning Himmler again met with Bernadotte and confirmed the previous night's agreement and even broadened it. In the end 14,000 women of all nationalities were released from Ravensbrück and transferred, either by ship or by train, first to Denmark and then on to Sweden.[63]

The northern sector along the Baltic coast was the scene of both tragedy and eleventh-hour rescue in a way that was characteristic and perhaps even symbolic of the last days of the Third Reich. Countless Jews and other prisoners succumbed during the death marches. The troops of the victorious armies stood aghast at the mounds of corpses littering the camps and were appalled by the sight of the human skeletons who still found the strength to greet them with cheers. Here and there Jews in hiding emerged out of the ruins and rubble of the bombed cities, and throughout Europe others began wandering toward their homes in the hope of finding surviving family and friends. Millions of people of all nationalities who had been enslaved in subterranean factories, quarries, and camps set off on the roads of Germany, hungry for any crust of bread. Many Germans were also left homeless, and together with defeated troops and deserters, they roamed the countryside seeking shelter. German refugees who had fled before the advancing Russian forces continued to push westward, hoping to cross the border to Denmark to safety. Among them was the man who had planned to build an Aryan empire in greater Germany and make himself lord over life and death: Reichsführer of the SS Heinrich Himmler. However, when caught by the British army, he eluded his captors by committing suicide. So did Hitler in the depths of his bunker in the Reich Chancellery as the Red Army fought its way across Berlin. Helpless to control Germany's fate, he played out his final performance. Bereft not only of the power of rule but of his own physical powers, sick and palsied, Hitler was still possessed by searing hatred and wanted to drag the German nation into the grave with him because it was "undeserving." The same Germany he had intended to lead to the summit of world rule he now wished to render "scorched earth." Neither had he abandoned the vision of the hell into which he had intended to cast the Jewish people—"those who bear the real guilt for this murderous struggle"—and to the last he exhorted his people "to observe the racial laws most carefully, to fight mercilessly against the poisoners of all the peoples of the world, international Jewry."[64]

So ended "The Final Solution of the Jewish Question."

Epilogue

In the grotesque, apocalyptic drama of his final hours, Hitler, having appointed an imaginary government, urged it to honor and consummate the principle on which he had based his regime: the racial doctrine whose actual meaning was the destruction of Jewry. There is no better testimony to the centrality of racial anti-Semitism in Hitler's life and in the National Socialist revolution he wrought than this behest. From his own standpoint, this design had been only partially realized because important sections of "international Jewry," as was his wont to call it, were still alive.

Hitler and those implementing his design regarded the Jewish question as a **political problem** and its so-called solution as a political necessity, a sine qua non, that had to be addressed in the framework of Germany's foreign and domestic policy. Hence during the 1930s, when the Nazis still attempted to bring about the segregation and emigration of the Jews, they used legislation, propaganda, and limited terror to achieve their aims, though taking Germany's economic needs into consideration. Even during the prewar period, but especially after the war broke out, the Jewish problem became an integral part of the Nazis' struggle for predominance; hence the means of dealing with it were determined according to what the Nazis regarded as political and military exigencies. Gradually mass terror and a regime of oppression, total isolation and concentration, plunder and destruction of the economic infrastructure, forced labor and starvation, forced emigration and deportation were introduced and perfected in occupied Poland alongside the political purge *(politische Flurbereinigung)* aimed against the Polish population. Eventually, in preparing their attack on the Soviet Union, the Germans' operational plan included the "special tasks" to be handled by the Einsatzgruppen, the SS immediately training these units to operate against "the Communist commissars" and to murder the Jews en masse. This was the start of the overall operation of the Final Solution planned for the millions of Jews in occupied Europe, which was deemed inevitable for attaining the objectives of the war.

Based as it was upon the antithesis of the basic values upon which human society is grounded the world over, National Socialism necessarily led to the perversion of public and private morality and to the deviation of law and justice, to say nothing of crime. Speaking of the Nazis' crimes at the Nuremberg trials, the American judge, Robert H. Jackson, observed:

> These crimes are unprecedented ones because of the shocking numbers of victims. They are even more shocking and unprecedented because of the large number of persons who united to perpetrate them. All scruple or conscience of a very large segment of the German people was committed to Nazi keeping, and its devotees felt no personal sense of guilt as they went from one extreme measure to the other. On the other hand they developed a contest in cruelty and a competition in crime.[1]

Such basic principles as the value of human life and equality before the law were not just violated, they were renounced by the Nazis. Their racial ideology predicated the existence of three categories of beings: the superior man, or Aryan; the subhuman, a concept applied mainly to the Slavic peoples; and the lowest rank, the nonhuman, which was reserved for the Jews alone. Thus a Nazi judge ruled, "The National Socialist has recognized: The Jew is not a human being. He is a manifestation of putrescence"[2]—and so the Nazis concluded that the noxious element "that is poisoning humanity" must be destroyed. In the "counter-society" they created in the concentration camps, and above all in the extermination camps, "Thou shalt not kill," which society holds to be one of its axioms, was converted into "Thou shalt kill." And it was no coincidence that this injunction was applied first and foremost against the Jewish people, for the Nazis regarded it as the author of the social rules they negated and rejected. Yet Hitler left a legacy behind him, namely, the belief, common to totalitarian governments and movements that aspire to overthrow incumbent regimes, that it is permissible, even desirable, to perpetrate murder for the sake of ideological goals or political interests of whatever kind. Not that this is a new phenomenon; similar doctrines had been advanced prior to the modern era. Since World War II, however, this scourge has spread the world over.

More and more, scholarship has traced the foundations and sources of Nazism to the recent and distant past and has found that there was hardly a concept or method associated with the Nazis that had not been known before but that they amalgamated these elements into a revolutionary doctrine and then put their theory into practice. One element, however, was wholly a Nazi innovation: the use of technology not to develop weapons, as was conventional, but for the projected murder of masses of defenseless people. Moreover, the fact that the murder was not perpetrated for the sake of any benefit and that the detriment in destroying a great human potential available as a work force was deliberately ignored attest to new norms that were uncommon in contemporary society. This approach was so inconceivable to the peoples of the free world, including the Jews, that they had great difficulty in acknowledging the Nazis' murderous intentions. Hannah Arendt noted this during an early phase of her research into totalitarianism, "The extraordinary difficulty which we have in attempting to understand the institution of the concentration camp and to fit it into the record of human history is precisely the absence of such utilitarian criteria, an absence which is more than anything else responsible for the curious air of unreality that surrounds this institution and everything connected with it."[3]

But the Nazis knew how to exploit their adversaries' misapprehension of their methods and deeds to their own advantage. It was also difficult to understand ambivalence in Nazism that allowed for the coexistence of myth and pragmatism, dogmatism and improvisation, the denial and astute exploitation of reality, the rejection of rational norms and pragmatic organization. Very early on, in an attempt at characterizing Hitler, Theodor Heuss stated, "Rational considerations of power and rampant emotion exist side by side with no relation between them."[4]

From Hitler's point of view, these two factors—the pragmatic power struggle and ideological fanaticism—did not contradict one another; together they served the struggle for existence that he saw as life's chief aim and meaning. Thus, politics not only constituted life's essence but became its driving force and source of inspiration. According to Uriel Tal's definition, Nazism was based on the fusion of faith and politics, "The very idea of 'political' became absolutized; hence politics served as both ideal and reality, sacred and profane, divine and terrestrial."[5]

As a consequence of this concept, the humanitarian approach became devoid of meaning. Indeed, the Nazis despised "humanitarian silliness" (*Humanitäts-duselei*, a coinage they likewise inherited from the nineteenth century)[6]—yet the humanitarian approach, more than anything else, was the touchstone of the age.

In contrast to the Nazi outlook, the humanitarian approach basic to Western culture, as shaped by the Jewish as well as the Christian religion, is predicated on the recognition that mortal men are all fundamentally equal and are, therefore, bound to fulfill the commandment "Thou shalt love thy neighbor as thyself" and display solidarity with other human beings, especially when they are facing calamity. Human solidarity was put to a severe test during the Holocaust, and clearly it was demonstrated only under special circumstances. What were those circumstances?

When an individual Jew was lucky enough to experience solidarity, it was usually displayed on the grounds of kinship or the personal loyalty of friends or colleagues, sometimes even under the harsh conditions prevailing in the camps. However, it also occurred that perfect strangers demonstrated solidarity with a persecuted Jew—at a danger not only to their own security but often to that of their family—by acting out of religious or moral conviction, often without being associated with any underground organization.

When did organized groups and public bodies (by which I mean sovereign governments in the Allied, satellite, and neutral countries, governments-in-exile, parliaments, armies, churches, national and international relief organizations, resistance movements, and underground organizations of different kinds) come forth to assist Jews? Our research has shown that such public organizations and forces were ready to help Jews and acted upon a humanitarian-moral impulse mainly under the impact of international and domestic political circumstances. In this respect, decisions depended on the economic situation, the Germans' display of power, the form of occupation or association with the Reich, and last but not least the situation on the battlefield that suggested the outcome of the war. Reaction to the plight of the Jews was also influenced by certain sociopsychological factors, that is, political opinions and interests, acknowledgment of the aims of the Nazi policy toward Jews, rapacity, the desire to be the beneficiaries of the Jews' property, and, of course, the sway of anti-Semitism versus democratic principles.

Thus the public's moral commitment was effective if the humane motive was sustained by political interests, or at least was not adverse to them. Only when the humane impulse dominated public opinion—as in 1938 after the Kristallnacht pogrom—did it become a political factor that governments had to take into account. The outstanding examples were the need, perceived by Roosevelt in 1938, to call the Evian Conference and the British government's consent at the end of 1938 to open the country's gates to thousands of children and adults fleeing from Germany—albeit thus keeping this wave of refugees from entering Palestine. Similar were the motives for convening the abortive Bermuda Conference in the spring of 1943 in response to the public outcry when the mass murder was first officially acknowledged. The failure of both these international conferences to find a way of rescuing Jews was clearly due to the predominance of adverse political interests and the pragmatic calculations of the respective governments.

Right from the start of the Hitler period, the conflict between the humanitarian and political approaches was striking when it came to the problem of Jewish refugees. In most cases the political factor was the decisive one, as demonstrated by the fact that Jews were disqualified from enjoying the rights accorded to political refugees. Throughout the Holocaust period the Jews' fateful condition was marked by the crucial fact that they were not defended by a national representation of their own acting under internationally recognized public law. Thus their fate was decided—for better and, mostly, for worse—by the politics of the world's nations. Not without reason, Hitler ridiculed the Western governments that took him to task for his behavior toward the Jews but did not open their own gates to Jewish refugees, thus, like himself, giving political considerations preference over humanitarian impulses. The same notion of the "exigencies of war," in which the Nazis included the annihilation of the Jews, served the Allies as an argument or excuse for shunning activities to rescue Jews that were deemed to be unusual or dangerous. This was especially obvious during the last year of the war, despite a greater willingness in the Western Hemisphere to come to the aid of Jews in mortal danger.

Every country, occupied or satellite, in which a genuine political authority exercised power or influence had some ability to affect the attitude toward the Jews living within it. During the early stages of the persecution, before the systematic application of the Final Solution, many countries exploited the situation and atmosphere created by Germany to act against the Jewish communities in their midst. This was true of Poland before the outbreak of the war and particularly prominent in the satellite states of southeastern Europe: Rumania, Hungary, and Slovakia. In Bulgaria the government encountered resistance from the population, the parliament, and the church, so that even in 1942 it did not strictly enforce its own anti-Jewish laws and regulations. The Vichy government in France exploited the opportunity not only to isolate "Jewish aliens," meaning refugees, but to push French Jews out of the public arena and effect the plunder of their property by means of Aryanization.

In contrast to the Belgian government-in-exile, which openly condemned persecution and spoliation, its Dutch and Norwegian counterparts did not exercise any influence on behalf of the Jews. And in both these countries the civil service, which was under the command of the SS, capitulated to the Germans' demands. In Norway it was Quisling who participated in the anti-Jewish action, especially prior to the deportation in 1942. The case of Denmark is exceptional, as the government, with the support of the public and its organizations, successfully protected the Jews until the crisis of August 1943 forced it to resign.

At the critical moment, when the Germans demanded that the Jews be turned over to them for deportation to Poland, the governing echelon had to decide between two choices: to relinquish the Jews or to protect some or all of them. In most of the satellite states, the attitude of the governments was ambivalent and changed over time in accordance with developments in the broader political and military situation. The most independent in their attitude toward the Jews during the period of the deportations were Germany's allies: Italy (before being conquered), Finland, and distant Japan. Most active in defense of the Jews was Italy; the Finnish government was for the most part careful to safeguard the Jews' rights as citizens. In Denmark and to a certain degree in France and Belgium, consensus emerged between the general population and the underground, leading to cooperation in saving Jews—and the results speak for themselves.

In almost every case in which official public or underground forces acted to save Jews, they were roused and spurred on by individual personalities whose names are known to us and who acted out of moral or political motives, many times a combination of the two. These instigators galvanized others into mounting rescue operations, often at the very last moment. Their initiatives may not always have been successful and sometimes failed outright, but without them even fewer Jews would have been saved. We may, therefore, conclude that at a time of great moral crisis arising from political turmoil, the initiative of individuals who dare to follow the dictates of their conscience is of great significance. According to Jewish tradition, personalities as such are considered "the Righteous Among the Nations."

Most of the people and deeds known to us from the Holocaust period come from outside the sphere of Soviet rule. The fact that the largest number of Jews was saved within that sphere was not the result of any special rescue effort on behalf of the Jews—to which the Russians were opposed—or to the existence of a humane approach; it was a function of political and military decisions that sometimes worked in the Jews' favor and sometimes to their detriment.

The Holocaust placed the Jewish people at the crossroads between life and death. Jewish life had essentially always been conducted between these two poles,[7] and each time in their long history that the Jews found themselves in situations that forced them to choose between life and death, there were always some—occasionally many—who preferred to sacrifice their lives rather than abandon their faith. Yet the Jews never deprecated the value of life, and the ancient sages spoke of a single human soul being an entire world.[8] Throughout the vicissitudes of the ages, the Jews also proved adept at protecting their lives and evading calamity. By their wandering and integration into the lives of other nations, they developed patterns of survival, traditions of relations with the peoples among whom they lived—gladly or for lack of choice—and ways of preserving their distinctiveness while adapting to the way of life around them. Still, no definitive solution was ever found to the challenge of being both unique and secure, and in the modern era, when religion no longer played a decisive role in the lives of individuals or societies, the Jews found they had to contend with a hostile pan-European movement that spread to other parts of the world as well: anti-Semitism.

For almost two centuries the Jews sought solutions to the problems of their existence in modern Europe in the emancipation, as individuals, and as communities; in the political systems of various countries; in social revolution; in their own religion and tradition; and in the establishment of an independent state in Palestine. This searching went on despite pogroms, economic distress, a massive emigration movement, and growing integration into Europe's economic and cultural life through a display of extraordinary resourcefulness and creativity—all while wars and revolutions were rocking Europe and much of the rest of the world, causing profound and far-reaching changes in all walks of life. When the National Socialist revolution erupted, the Jews viewed it as an alarming phenomenon fraught with great, perhaps even new, forms of peril but not essentially different from the dangers they faced in any case. Thus, they continued the struggle for their existence, way of life, and future, never imagining and certainly not cognizant that a life-and-death struggle lay in store for them. At first they did not even have at their disposal concepts and means different from those that had served them in conducting their lives in the past.

It was the Jews of Germany who quickly sought means of ensuring their existence under the new circumstances by uniting in a national representation, intensifying mutual self-help, seeking ways to strengthen their internal economy and culture, grasping at the Palestinian initiative and setting up the *Haavara,* and increasingly working on behalf of emigration. Step-by-step the Nazis undermined their status until they had destroyed it completely throughout the Third Reich. This process repeated itself with certain variations, at a fixed pace and under increasingly adverse circumstances, wherever the conquering Nazis set foot or exercised influence. Everywhere the Jews were captive to circumstances that were not of their own making, circumstances that had grown out of international situations and in which they had only the narrowest room for maneuver in waging their struggle for survival. Above all, however, this struggle was affected by two factors: (1) the Jews' way of life and integration into the host country prior to the Holocaust and (2) the quality of Jewish leadership during the Holocaust.

In many Jewish communities there was little change in the national or local leadership at the outset of the period of persecution.[9] New people did rise to positions of public leadership, however, especially in places where the existing leaders had been quick to flee (as happened, for example, in Łódź and Warsaw). In the occupied countries, though also in some satellite states, it happened that additional Jewish bodies were operating—openly or clandestinely or simultaneously on both levels.

In the underground it was the young people who made the strongest mark, above all, the members of the youth movements. Their prominence grew as the situation deteriorated and the Jewish councils found it increasingly difficult to influence affairs or extricate themselves from the position of intermediaries between the oppressive regime and the Jewish public fighting for its life. At the crucial moment when they were ordered the turn the Jews over for slaughter, they had reached a dead end. The illusion that intercession with the Germans could save the surviving remnant was shattered, and the council members were doomed together with the Jewish masses.[10]

The tragedy of the Judenrat epitomizes the helplessness of the Jewish people and the political disaster it suffered during the Holocaust period. This is undoubtedly the reason why the internal Jewish debate on the Holocaust period has focused so sharply on this subject. One of the Germans' intentions in creating the institution of the Judenrat was to shift the rage and despair of the trapped Jews onto it, for ostensibly the Judenrat had the authority to make the most critical of decisions. The Nazis were interested in sowing dissension and strife among the Jews as another way of exacerbating their condition; indeed, in many cases the Jews blamed the Judenrat for the tragedies that afflicted them. Such charges, justified or otherwise, also fueled the bitter postwar debate, so that the Nazis' ambition of setting the Jews against each other succeeded even after their defeat.

If the Judenräte erred in their assessment of the situation, so did most of the rest of the world in failing to arrive in time at a proper understanding of the Nazis' essential character, intentions, and means of operating. The difference was that the Jews of Europe, and the Jewish councils at their head, paid the full price for the world's mistake. In fact, the world, including its Jews, grasped the enormity of its error only in hindsight. The tragedy of the Judenrat was both national and personal, as can be seen in the role and fate of Warsaw's Adam Czerniakow. In his book on the Jews of Warsaw, Yisrael Gutman concludes, "It is clear in retrospect that even if the Judenrat had been faultless, the efforts of its members were doomed to bitter failure. As in a classical tragedy, the Judenrat's fate was sealed from the outset, and its members were like fish caught in a net."[11] Yet it was in this same Warsaw that an uprising broke out. Many perceived the defenselessness of millions of murdered people not as a tragedy but a shameful failing, and the blame for it was placed not only on the Nazis, the peoples of the world, and the Jews living in freedom, but even on the victims themselves. However, the uprisings in the ghettos and the war waged by the partisans in the forests are universally regarded not only as displays of courage but as a moral victory. The ghetto fighters sacrificed themselves as a matter of conscious decision and free choice. They chose to fight in the realization that there was no avoiding death; they gave their lives as an act of preserving their freedom and self-respect, which they saw as sureties of a future for the Jewish people. By their free choice they accorded their deaths moral and national significance, voiding the negative import of the Nazis' countersociety. They were no longer motivated by a struggle for life because they had lost all hope of winning it; instead, they wished to sanctify their lives through an armed struggle that stood no chance of being victorious. As partisans, Jews could nurture some hope of surviving. Unfortunately, only a small contingent could make it; the multitude was not able to manifest the opportunity because of the adverse powers of men and nature.

The masses of Jews in the ghettos—women, children, and the elderly, many of them ill and all of them hungry—did not have much of a choice in their response, for even hiding or fleeing, individually or in groups, was rarely successful. As they stood facing death, the many knew but one way of maintaining their dignity: silence. Yet the Jew whose life had been destroyed, who remained alone in the Valley of Death, pinned his hopes on the Jewish people and believed in its future. And for the sake of that future, he saw to it that descriptions—pictorial or in writing—were left behind as a living testimony from the inferno.

When the liberation came, the joy of the survivors was mixed with unbearable sadness and dismay. The Italian Jew Primo Levi, who was liberated from Auschwitz, gave expression to these feelings in portraying the meeting with the first Russian troops to reach the camp:

> They did not greet us, nor did they smile; they seemed oppressed not only by compassion but by a confused restraint. . . . It was that shame we knew so well, the shame that drowned us after the selections, and every time we had to watch, or to submit to, some outrage: the shame the Germans did not know, that the just man experiences at another man's crime; the feeling of guilt that such a crime should exist, that it should have been introduced irrevocably into the world of things that exist.[12]

At the end of the war, a new chapter opened in the history of the Jewish people, with the establishment of the State of Israel taking prominence. This chapter goes beyond the scope of this discussion, but when they were liberated many of the surviving Jews of Europe were aware of history's order of the day. Alongside their longing for kin, their search for family and friends, and the strong desire to reconstruct their lives, they lifted their sights to the nation emerging in Palestine. And at the first conference of the survivors in Germany in July 1945, the people who had just been released from the concentration camps declared:

> We the remnant of the masses of European Jewry, who have been murdered as a people, whose sons and daughters have fought the hateful [enemy] in the forests of Europe, in the bunkers of the ghettos, in underground movements, in the ranks of the Allied armies, in the Jewish Brigade, and in the units of the Palestinian services, raise our voices as a people and demand: the immediate establishment of a Jewish state in Palestine, the recognition of the Jewish people as an equal with all the Allied nations, and its inclusion in the peace conference.[13]

Appendix:
Wartime Currencies

Exchange Rates in Relation to U.S. $

Country	Year	Annual Average Official Exchange Rate	Other Rates	Currency
Austria	1938 until March 17	4.18	5.35	Schilling
	until 12/13/1945	no rates		
Belgium	1940	29.63	—	Franc
	until 9/5/1944	no rates		
Bulgaria	no changes	81.75	—	Lev
Czechoslovakia	1939	28.474	29.232	Crown
	Oct. 1941–May 1945	25	25	
Denmark	1939	4.92	—	Krone
	1940–1941	5.18		
	1942–1945	4.8		
Finland	1939–1943	49.35	—	Markka
France	1939	37.85	35.9	Franc
	1940–1943	43.8	42.3	
	1944	44.45	42.3	
Germany	1933	3.4	4.198	Reichsmark
	1934–1945	2.5	2.479	
Greece	1939	125.01	—	Drachma
	1940	151.34	—	
	1941–1943	—	—	
	Nov. 1944	151		
Hungary	1939	3.46	—	Pengö
	Aug. 1941–1945	no rates	—	
Italy	1939–1941	19.23	19	Lire
	1942–1944	no rates	—	
Netherlands	1939	1.876	—	Guilder
	1942–1944	no rates	—	

Exchange Rates in Relation to U.S. $ (*continued*)

Country	Year	Annual Average Official Exchange Rate	Other Rates	Currency
Norway	1939	4.316	—	Krone
	1940–1945	4.4	—	
Poland	until 9/5/1939	5.306	—	Zloty
	1940–1945	no rates	—	
Rumania	1939	98.74	—	Lei
	1940	98.74	204.39 from March 11	
	1941–1945	98.74	187.6	
Spain	1939	9.359	—	Peseta
	1941–1945	10.95	—	
Sweden	1939	4.169	—	Krona
	1940–1945	4.2	—	
Switzerland	1939	4.438	4.37282	Franc
	1940–1945	4.3 (minor changes)	4.37282	
Tunisia	1939	37.85	43.8	Franc
	1940–1943	43.8	43.8	
	from Nov. 1944	49.62	49.62	
USSR	1939–1945	5.3	—	Ruble
Yugoslavia	1939	44.189	—	Dinar
	1941–1944	no rates	—	

Source: Adapted from information provided by the *American International Investment Corporation,* San Francisco, 1977.

Notes

Introduction

1. See Saul Friedländer, "From Anti-Semitism to Extermination: A Historiographical Study of Nazi Policies Toward the Jews and an Essay in Interpretation," *YVS Studies*, 16 (1984), pp. 1—50.

2. See *"Historiker Streit": Die Dokumentation der Kontroverse um die Einzigartigkeit der nationalsozialistischen Judenvernichtung*, Piper Verlag ed. (Munich and Zurich, 1987).

3. Quoted in Shmuel A. Horodetzki, *Zikhronot* (Tel Aviv, 1957), p. 143.

4. George N. Kren and Leon Rappaport, "Dimensions of the Historical Crisis," in *The Holocaust and the Crisis of Human Behavior* (New York, 1980), pp. 1–15.

5. Emil L. Fackenheim, "The Holocaust and the State of Israel: Their Relation," in *EJ Yearbook* (Jerusalem, 1974), pp. 154f. Reprinted in *The Jewish Return into History: Reflections in the Age of Auschwitz and a New Jerusalem* (New York, 1978), pp. 173–386.

6. Other Israeli memorial and research institutions include: Ghetto Fighters' House, in Kibbutz Lohamei ha-Gettaot, named after Yitzhak Katzenelson (1950); Moreshet, at Givat Havivah (1963); and Masua, at Kibbuz Tel Yitzhak.

7. Avraham Shapira, ed., *The Seventh Day: Soldiers Talk About the Six-Day War* (New York, 1970), p. 181.

8. Alfred Gottschalk, "United States of America, Perspections," in *The Yom-Kippur War: Israel and the Jewish People*, ed. Moshe Davis (New York, 1974), p. 39.

9. See Jacob L. Talmon, *The Age of Violence* (Tel Aviv, 1975) (Hebrew).

10. Horodetzki, *Zikhronot*, p. 143.

11. Yitzhak Katzenelson, *Dos Lid fun Oysgehargetn Yidishn Folk* (Song of the Murdered Jewish People) (New York, 1963).

12. Philip Friedman, *Roads to Extinction: Essays on the Holocaust*, ed. Ada J. Friedman (New York and Philadelphia, 1980).

13. Raul Hilberg, *The Destruction of the European Jews* (Chicago, 1961), new rev. ed. 3 vols. (New York, 1985). The 1985 edition was published after my Hebrew edition. How-

ever, for practical reasons, my numerous references to this work are to the 1961 edition. Gerald Reitlinger, *The Final Solution: The Attempt to Exterminate the Jews of Europe, 1939–1945*, 2d rev. ed. (London, 1968).

Chapter 1

1. The quotation is from a meeting in Berlin in *CV Ztg*, January 22, 1932, p. 30. On the CV and its newspaper (*CV Ztg.*), see Jehuda Reinharz, *Fatherland or Promised Land, The Dilemma of the German Jew, 1893–1914* (Ann Arbor, Mich., 1975); and Ismar Schorsch, *Jewish Reactions to German Anti-Semitism, 1870–1914* (New York, 1972).

2. Isa. 29:6.

3. Esra Bennathan, "Die demographische und wirtschaftliche Struktur der Juden," in *Entscheidungsjahr 1932: Zur Judenfrage in der Endphase der Weimarer Republik*, ed. Werner E. Mosse (Tübingen, 1965), pp. 87–131, esp. pp. 124f.

4. Erich Eyck, *A History of the Weimar Republic* (New York, 1970), vol. 2, pp. 253–57.

5. See Oscar I. Janowsky, *Nationalities and National Minorities* (New York, 1945).

6. See Michael N. Dobkowski and Isidor Wallimann, eds., *Towards the Holocaust: The Social and Economic Collapse of the Weimar Republic* (Westport, Conn., 1983).

7. Heinrich A. Winkler, "Die deutsche Gesellschaft der Weimarer Republik und Antisemitismus," in *Die Juden als Minderheit in der Geschichte*, ed. Bernd Martin and Ernst Schulin. (Munich, 1981), pp. 271–84.

8. *The Path to Dictatorship, 1918–1933: Ten Essays by German Scholars* (New York, 1967), p. 117; Eyck, *A History of the Weimar Republic*, vol. 2, pp. 25f.

9. *Path to Dictatorship*, p. 208.

10. On Papen's coup, see Eyck, *A History of the Weimar Republic*, vol. 2, pp. 410–25.

11. Josef Goebbels, *Vom Kaiserhof zur Reichskanzlei: Eine historische Darstellung in Tagebuchblättern (vom 1. Januar 1932 bis zum 1. Mai 1933)* (Munich, 1943), July 21, 1932, p. 133.

12. William L. Shirer, *The Rise and Fall of the Third Reich: A History of Nazi Germany* (New York, 1960), pp. 179–83.

13. Eyck, *A History of the Weimar Republic*, vol. 2, p. 476.

14. Martin Mendelsohn, "Die Pflicht der Selbstverteidigung," in *Jahresbericht des Vorsitzenden in der ersten ordentlichen Generalversammlung des, C.V.* (Berlin, 1894).

15. See Jehuda Reinharz and Walter Schatzberg, eds., *The Jewish Response to German Culture: From the Enlightment to the Second World War* (Hanover, NH, 1985).

16. H. I. Bach, *The German Jew: A Synthesis of Judaism and Western Civilization, 1730–1930* (New York, 1984), pp. 107f., 137ff.

17. Shulamit Volkov, "The Dynamics of Dissimilation: Ostjuden and German Jews," in Reinharz and Schatzberg, *The Jewish Response to German Culture*, pp. 195–211.

18. *CV Manuscript, 1929*, p. 3; quoted in Reinharz, *Fatherland or Promised Land*, p. 48.

19. Leni Yahil, "Jewish Assimilation Vis-à-vis German Nationalism in the Weimar Republic," in *Jewish Assimilation in Modern Times*, ed. Béla Vago (Boulder, Colo., 1981), pp. 41–55.

20. Max Kollenscher, *Zionismus und Staatsbürgertum* (Berlin, 1929), p. 6.

21. Jacob Lestchinsky, *Gorala ha-kalkali shel Yahadut Germania* (The Economic Fate of German Jewry) (Hakibbutz Hameuḥad, Merḥavia, 1963), p. 162; E. Kahn ("Die Zukunft

der deutschen Juden," *JR*, May 8, 1934) has 510,000; WJC (*Der wirtschaftliche Vernichtungskampf gegen die Juden im Dritten Reich* [1937], p. 13) has 515,000. Also see Abraham Margaliot, "The Political Reaction of the Jewish Institutions and Organizations in Germany to the Anti-Jewish Policy of the National Socialists in the Years 1932–1935 (Ph.D. diss., The Hebrew University, Jerusalem, 1971), vol. 1 p. 14 (Hebrew, with English abstract); Helmut Genschel, *Die Verdrängung der Juden aus der Wirtschaft im Dritten Reich* (Göttinyen, 1966), p. 274; *CV Ztg.*, March 3, 1935, Supplement 2.

22. Zentralwohlfahrtsstelle der deutschen Juden, *Führer durch die jüdische Gemeindeverwaltung und Wohlfahrtspflege in 1932–1933* (Berlin, 1933), pp. 70ff.

23. Bennathan, "Die demographische . . . Struktur der Juden," p. 91.

24. Ibid., pp. 106f.

25. Donald L. Niewyk, "The Economic and Cultural Role of the Jews in the Weimar Republic," *YLB*, 16 (1971), p. 163; also see Wilhelm Treue, "Zur Frage der wirtschaftlichen Motive im deutschen Antisemitismus," in *Deutsches Judentum in Krieg und Revolution, 1916–1923*, ed. Werner E. Mosse (Tübingen, 1971), pp. 387–408.

26. Treue, "Zur Frage der wirtschaftlichen Motive," p. 392.

27. Fritz Theilhaber, *Der Untergang der deutschen Juden* (Munich, 1911), passim; Uziel O. Schmelz, *Jewish Demography and Statistics: Bibliography for 1920–1960* (Jerusalem, 1961).

28. See Volkov, "The Dynamics of Dissimilation"; Steven E. Aschheim, *Brothers and Strangers: The East European Jew in German and German Jewish Consciousness, 1800–1923* (Madison, Wis., 1982), passim; Jack L. Wertheimer, *Unwelcome Strangers: East European Jews in Imperial Germany* (New York, 1987).

29. Schalom Adler-Rudel, *Ostjuden in Deutschland, 1880–1940* (Tübingen, 1959), passim; Volkov, "The Dynamics of Dissimilation"; Aschheim, *Brothers and Strangers*.

30. Robert Weltsch, "Germany," *EJ*, vol. 7, col. 485. The estimate of the number of locations is based on Zentralwohlfahrstelle, *Führer durch die jüdische Gemeindeverwaltung*, passim.

31. Ismar Freund Archive in the Central Archives for the History of the Jewish People, Jerusalem, P2/T1, 4; see also Max P. Birnbaum, *Staat und Synagoge 1918–1938* (Tübingen, 1981).

32. Giora Lotan [Georg Lubinski], "Zentralwohlfahrtsstelle," *YLB*, 4 (1959), pp. 185–207.

33. Joseph Walk, *The Education of the Jewish Child in Nazi Germany: The Law and Its Execution* (Jerusalem, 1975), pp. 19–21 (Hebrew, with English synopsis).

34. See Reinhard Bendix, *From Berlin to Berkeley: German-Jewish Identities* (New Brunswick, N.J., 1986).

35. Ismar Freund's lecture at the central meeting of the CV, 1931, Ismar Freund Archive, P2/Or, 24.

36. Jehuda Reinharz, "The Zionist Response to Antisemitism in Germany," *YLB*, 30 (1985), pp. 105–40.

37. Alfred Wiener, "Die deutsche Adelsgenossenschaft und Wir," *CV Ztg.* January 22, 1932, p. 33.

38. Ernst Simon, *Aufbau im Untergand: Jüdische Erwachsenenbildung im nationalsozialistischen Deutschland als geistiger Widerstand* (Tübingen, 1959), pp. 22f. Simon claims that the Jewish middle class in Germany lived in a fool's paradise. He excludes the Zionists, but this positive evaluation is, in our opinion, mistaken (discussed later).

39. See *CV Ztg.*, 1932. Quotations from Nazi propaganda and information on assaults can be found in almost every issue.

40. Werner Jochmann, "Die Ausbreitung des Antisemitismus," in Mosse, *Deutsches Judentum in Krieg*, pp. 497–500.

41. Arnold Paucker, "Der jüdische Abwehrkampf," in Mosse, *Entscheidungsjahr 1932*, pp. 405–99.

42. Reinharz, "The Zionist Response," pp. 131f.; Yahil, "Jewish Assimilation," p. 46.

43. The white paper was entitled *Die Stellung der Nationalsozialistischen Deutschen Arbeiterpartei (NSDAP) zur Judenfrage* (Berlin, 1932). See Shaul Esh, *Studies in the Holocaust and Contemporary Jewry*, ed. Joseph Walk (Jerusalem, 1973), p. 112 n. 139 (Hebrew); Arnold Paucker, *Der jüdische Abwehrkampf* (Hamburg, 1969), pp. 137–39; idem, "Abwehrkampf," in Mosse, *Entscheidungsjahr 1932*, p. 499; see *CV Ztg.*, February 12 and August 19, 1932, front pages.

44. Paucker, *Abwehrkampf*, pp. 74–84; *CV Ztg.*, December 30, 1932, p. 535.

45. Eva Reichmann-Jungmann, "Wider die Nörgler und Kleinmütigen," *CV Ztg.*, July 7, 1932, p. 178.

46. Yahil, "Jewish Assimilation," p. 44.

47. Paucker, *Abwehrkampf*, pp. 126f.

48. Ibid., passim.

49. "Jüdische Kinder in der Schule," *CV Ztg.*, January 15, 1932, p. 19.

50. Eva G. Reichmann, "Diskussionen über die Judenfrage, 1930–1932," in Mosse, *Entscheidungsjahr 1932*, pp. 503–35.

51. Reinharz, "The Zionist Response," pp. 132f., 139 n. 162.

52. Paucker, *Abwehrkampf* pp. 110–28.

53. Ibid., p. 111; Reinharz, "The Zionist Response" pp. 121–24.

54. *CV Ztg.*, July 7, 1932, passim.

55. Ibid.

56. *Stellung der NSDAP.*

57. Utterances of Bauer, member of the Prussian Parliament (Landtag), June 20, 1932, and Martin Mutschmann, member of the *Reichstag*, June 30, 1931, *Stellung der NSDAP.*

58. Utterances of an SA leader in Rhine region, quoted in a Nazi paper, July 13, 1932, *Stellung der NSDAP.*

59. *Stellung der NSDAP.*

60. *CV Ztg.*, August 5, 1932, Börger, a member of the Reichstag, in a meeting in Cologne, January 31, 1932, said, "When we are in power and a Frenchman crosses the border, the next day all the Jews in Germany will die," *Stellung der NSDAP*, appendix; quotations from newspapers.

61. Ludwig Holländer, "Deutsche Juden in der Krise," *CV Ztg.*, June 7, 1932, pp. 246f.

62. Kurt Blumenfeld, "Die Zionistische Aufgabe im heutigen Deutschland," *JR*, September 16, 1932, pp. 353f.; Jehuda Reinharz, ed., *Dokumente zur Geschichte des deutschen Zionismus* (Tübingen, 1981), pp. 530–42; Reinharz, "The Zionist Response," passim.

63. Kurt Blumenfeld, *Erlebte Judenfrage: Ein Vierteljahrhundert Deutscher Zionismus* (Stuttgart, 1962), p. 196.

64. Blumenfeld, "Die Zionistische Aufgabe" pp. 353f.

65. Eva Reichmann-Jungmann, "Die Judenfrage neu gestellt?" *CV Ztg.*, September 23, 1932, pp. 1f.

66. Selma Schiratzki, "The Rykestrasse School," *YLB*, 5 (1960), p. 300.

67. Kurt J. Ball-Kaduri, *Das Leben der Juden in Deutschland im Jahre 1933: Ein Zeitbericht* (Frankfurt on the Main, 1963), pp. 33f.

68. Recha Freier, *Let the Children Come: The Early History of Youth Aliya* (London, 1961), p. 20.

Chapter 2

1. Jacob Wassermann, *My Life as German and Jew* (New York, 1933), p. 226.

2. Harry Zohn, "Fin-de-siècle Vienna: The Jewish Contribution," in Jehuda Reinharz and Walter Schatzberg, eds., *The Jewish Response to German Culture: From the Enlightenment to the Second World War* (Hanover, NH, 1985), pp. 137–49.

3. Erich R. Jaensch, *Der Gegentypus* (Leipzig, 1938), p. XXVI; also see Uriel Tal, "The Intellectuals and the Third Reich," *Yalkut Moreshet*, 19 (1975), 175–84 (Hebrew).

4. Uriel Tal, *Christians and Jews in Germany: Religion, Politics and Ideology in the Second Reich, 1870–1914* (Ithaca, N.Y., 1975), p. 276.

5. Joseph Arthur, Comte de Gobineau, *Essai sur l'inégalité des races humaines* (Paris, 1853–1855).

6. Shmuel Almog, "The Racial Motif in Ernest Renan's Attitude to Jews and Judaism," *Zion*, 32, nos. 3–4, (1967), 175, 200 (Hebrew). Almog emphasizes the internal contradictions in Renan's theory.

7. Quoted in French in Houston S. Chamberlain, *The Foundations of the Nineteenth Century* (London, 1914), vol. 1, p. 331. Geoffrey G. Field, *Evangelist of Race: The Germanic Vision of Houston Stewart Chamberlain* (New York, 1981).

8. Alex Bein, "The Jewish Parasite: Notes on the Semantics of the Jewish Problem, with Special Reference to Germany," *YLB*, 9 (1964), pp. 3–40.

9. Steven E. Aschheim, " 'The Jewish Within,' the Myth of 'Judaization' in Germany," in Reinharz and Schatzberg, *Jewish Response*, pp. 212–41.

10. Wilhelm Marr, *Der Sieg der Judenthums über das Germanenthum* (Bern, 1879). This pamphlet ran into twelve editions in 1879 alone. On Marr and his activities as a propagandist of anti-Semitism, see Moshe Zimmermann, *Wilhelm Marr: The Patriarch of Anti-Semitism* (New York, 1986).

11. See *Man, Race, and Darwin: Papers Read at a Joint Conference of the Royal Anthropological Institute of Great Britain and Ireland and the Institute of Race Relations* (London, 1960); Jacques Barzun, *Darwin, Marx, Wagner: Critique of a Heritage* (Garden City, N.Y., 1958); Jacob Katz, *The Darker Side of Genius: Richard Wagner's Anti-Semitism* (Hanover, NH, 1986).

12. Hermann Rauschning, *Hitler Speaks* (London, 1939), p. 229. The statements ascribed to Hitler by Rauschning were the target of criticism that cast doubts on their authenticity. The most comprehensive summary of evaluation and research on the subject is in Theodor Schieder, *Hermann Rauschnings "Gespräche mit Hitler" als Geschichtsquelle* (Opladen, W. Ger., 1972). In spite of some reservations, Schieder concludes, "[The conversations] are a document of incontestable value as a source, inasmuch as they include explanations based on direct insight" (p. 62). It is in this spirit that I have used the quotes.

13. Rauschning, *Hitler Speaks*, p. 230. On the theological–metaphysical aspect of the Holocaust, see George Steiner, "The Long Life of Metaphor: An Approach to 'the Shoah,'" *Encounter*, 68, no. 2 (1987) 55–61.

14. Jaensch, *Der Gegentypus*, p. 57.

15. Norman H. Baynes, ed., *The Speeches of Adolf Hitler, April 1922–August 1939* (London, 1942), vol. 1, p. 741; quoted in *DOH*, p. 135.

16. Quoted in Lüdeger Graf von Westphalen, *Geschichte des Antisemitismus im 19. und 20. Jahrhundert* (Stuttgart, 1964), pp. 45f.

17. For the most comprehensive description, see Norman Cohn, *Warrant for Genocide: The Myth of the Jewish World Conspiracy and the "Protocols of the Elders of Zion"* (London, 1967).

18. For comprehensive research on the issue, see Jacob Katz, *Jews and Freemasons in Europe, 1723–1939* (Cambridge, Mass., 1970).

19. Michael Müller-Claudius, *Der Antisemitismus und das deutsche Verhängnis* (Frankfurt on the Main, 1948), p. 49.

20. Cohn, *Warrant for Genocide*, p. 147: Reinhard Rürup, *Emanzipation und Antisemitismus: Studien zur "Judenfrage" des Antisemitismus* (Göttingen, 1975), p. 95.

21. Houston S. Chamberlain, *Deutschlands Kampfziel: Hammer oder Ambos* (Munich, 1916), pp. 55, 61. For a more exhaustive analysis of Chamberlain's views, see Tal, *Christians and Jews in Germany*, pp. 280–89; and Uriel Tal, "Political Faith of Nazism Prior to the Holocaust," annual lecture of the Jacob M. and Shoshana Schreiber Chair of Contemporary Jewish History (Tel Aviv, 1978); Field, *Evangelist of Race.*

22. Houston S. Chamberlain, *Rasse und Nation* (Munich, 1918), pp. 5f.

23. Robert Cecil, *The Myth of the Master Race: Alfred Rosenberg and Nazi Theology* (New York, 1972), pp. 17f.

24. Benzion Dinur, *Biimei Milḥamah u-Mahapeḥa: Zikhronot u-Reshumot mi-derekh Ḥayim, 1914–1921* (In War and Revolution: Memoirs and Records from a Lifetime) (Jerusalem, 1960), pp. 19–21.

25. Cecil, *Myth of the Master Race*, p. 24.

26. Alfred Rosenberg, *Das Parteiprogramm* (Munich, 1922); *DOH*, pp. 15–18.

27. Hugo Valentin, *Antisemitismus* (Stockholm, 1962), p. 57.

28. Ibid., p. 79.

29. Rauschning, *Hitler Speaks*, p. 234.

30. Joachim C. Fest, *Hitler* (London, 1974), p. 211.

31. Werner Maser, ed., *Hitler's Letters and Notes*, comp., with commentary, by Werner Maser (New York, 1976), pp. 209–12; quotation, pp. 210f, Bantam Books.

32. Rauschning, *Hitler Speaks*, p. 238; Robert A. Pois, "Jewish Treason Against the Laws of Life: Nazi Religiosity and Bourgeois Fantasy," in *Towards the Holocaust: The Social and Economic Collapse of the Weimar Republic*, ed. Michael N. Dobkowski and Isidor Wallimann (Westport, Conn., 1983), pp. 364f.

33. Henry Picker, *Hitlers Tischgespräche im Führerhauptquartier, 1941–1942* (Bonn, 1951), p. 321.

34. The literature on Hitler is vast. I consulted a number of biographies, but for general information I relied on Allan Bullock, *Hitler: A Study in Tyranny*, completely rev. ed. (New York, 1964).

35. Hugh R. Trevor-Roper, "The Mind of Adolf Hitler," in *Hitler's Table Talk, 1941–1944* (London, 1973), p. xxv.

36. Bullock, *Hitler*, pp. 31–36, 46f.

37. The papers Hitler sought were preserved by a jurist who published them after the war; Frank Jetzinger, *Hitlers Jugend, Phantasien, Lügen—unddie Wahrheit* (Munich, 1956), pp. 247–72.

38. Fest, *Hitler*, p. 382.

39. Adolf Hitler, *Mein Kampf* (New York, 1939), pp. 45–50.

40. See Rudolph Binion, *Hitler Among the Germans: Psychohistory* (New York, 1976).

41. Hitler, *Mein Kampf*, p. 158.

42. Ibid., p. 54.

43. See Binion, *Hitler Among the Germans*, passim.

44. Rosenberg, *Das Parteiprogramm*; *DOH*, pp. 15–18.

45. Bullock, *Hitler*, p. 66.

46. Hitler, *Mein Kampf*, pp. 455–62.

47. Quoted in Fest, *Hitler*, p. 325.

48. Ibid., p. 324.

49. Houston S. Chamberlain, *Demokratie und Freiheit* (Munich, 1917), pp. 78–82. Chamberlain's intention was to denounce the parliamentary system; his arguments were used by Hitler in *Mein Kampf.* On Chamberlain and Hitler's mutual admiration, see Field, *Evangelist of Race*, pp. 434–42.

50. Hitler, *Mein Kampf*, pp. 448f.

51. Ibid., p. 219f.

52. Ibid, p. 984.

Chapter 3

1. Eliot B. Wheaton, *The Nazi Revolution, 1933–1935: Prelude to Calamity* (New York, 1969), p. 227.

2. Martin Broszat, *The Hitler State* (London, 1981), p. 61. On the whole process, also see idem, *Hitler and the Collapse of Weimar Germany* (Hamburg, 1987).

3. Wheaton, *The Nazi Revolution*, p. 232.

4. See Fritz Tobias, *Der Reichstagsbrand: Legende und Wirklichkeit* (Rastatt, W. Ger., 1962); Hans Mommsen, "Der Reichstagsbrand und seine politischen Folgen," *VJHZ*, 12, no. 4 (1964), pp. 351–415; Wheaton, *The Nazi Revolution*, pp. 251–64; Edouard Calic, *Unmasked: Two Confidential Interviews with Hitler in 1931* (London, 1971), p. 56.

5. "The apparent opportunism upon which Hitler based his daily actions did not therefore change the fact that his ends were preconceived" (C. Robert Cole, "Critics of the Taylor View of History," in *The Origins of the Second World War: Historical Interpretations*, ed. Esmonde M. Robertson [London, 1971], p. 144).

6. Eberhard Aleff, ed., *Das Dritte Reich* (Hannover, W. Ger., 1970), p. 21.

7. Ibid., p. 27; Wheaton, *The Nazi Revolution*, p. 242.

8. Aleff, *Das Dritte Reich*, p. 21.

9. Ibid., pp. 19f.

10. Wheaton, *The Nazi Revolution*, p. 431.

11. Cornelia Berning, *Vom Abstammungsnachweis zum Zuchtwart* (Berlin, 1964), p. 82. See B. Zeller, ed., *Klassiker in finsteren Zeiten, 1933–1934*, "Morbacher Kataloge" 38, no. 1, (1983), p. 99, quoted by Herbert Freeden, "Bleiben oder Gehen, " *BL*, 70 (1985), p. 50 n. 7.

12. Broszat, *The Hitler State*, pp. 16f.; Helmut Krausnick, "Stages of Coordination," in *The Path to Dictatorship, 1918–1933: Ten Essays by German Scholars* (New York, 1967), pp. 133–52.

13. Aleff, *Das Dritte Reich*, p. 33.

14. Karl D. Bracher et al., *Die Nationalsozialistische Machtergreifung: Studien zur Errichtung des totalitären Herrschaftssystems* in Deutschland 1933/34 (Frankfurt on the Main, 1960), pp. 205f; idem, *The German Dictatorship: The Origin, Structure, and Effects of National Socialism* (New York, 1970).

15. Broszat, *The Hitler State*, pp. 80–84; Karl D. Bracher, "The Technique of the National Socialist Seizure of Power," in *The Path to Dictatorship*, pp. 113–32.

16. Wheaton, *The Nazi Revolution*, pp. 283–86.

17. Ibid., pp. 329–32.

18. Ibid., pp. 352, 365f.; Broszat, *The Hitler State*, pp. 86–91.

19. Josef Goebbels, *Vom Kaiserhof zur Reichskanzlei: Eine historische Darstellung in Tagebuchblättern (vom. 1. Januar 1932 bis zum 1. Mai 1933)* (Munich, 1943), April 22, 1933, p. 302.

20. Helmut Genschel, *Die Verdrängung der Juden aus der Wirtschaft im Dritten Reich* (Göttingen, 1966), p. 65.

21. See Bracher et al., *Machtergreifung*; also Karl Dietrich Bracher, *The German Dictatorship*; Broszat, *The Hitler State*; Martin Broszat, *German National Socialism, 1919–1945* (Santa Barbara, Calif., 1966); Peter Diehl-Thiele, *Partei und Staat im Dritten Reich: Untersuchungen zum Verhältnis von NSDAP und allgemeiner innerer Staatsverwaltung* (Munich, 1969).

22. Diehl-Thiele, *Partei und Staat*, p. 10.

23. The order is reproduced in *DOH*, pp. 32–35.

24. Ibid.

25. For details of attempts to control the terror campaign, particularly by Reich Minister of Interior Wilhelm Frick and even Hitler, see Genschel, *Die Verdrängung der Juden*, pp. 45f. and notes.

26. Ibid., p. 44 n. 4. Genschel states that during April and May, more than a hundred protests were lodged by foreign governments in the wake of conspiracies against, and imprisonment of, their nationals.

27. Abraham Margaliot, "The Political Reaction of the Jewish Institutions and Organizations in Germany to the Anti-Jewish Policy of the National Socialists in the Years 1932–1935" (Ph.D. diss., The Hebrew University, Jerusalem, 1971), vol. 1, p. 46 (Hebrew with English abstract).

28. *VB*, April 3, 1933, p.00; Josef Goebbels, diary entry of April 1, 1933, *Vom Kaiserhof zur Reichskanzlei*, pp. 291–93; *DOH*, pp. 35f.

29. Broszat, *The Hitler State*, p. 140.

30. Wheaton, *The Nazi Revolution*, p. 311.

31. Goebbels, *Vom Kaiserhof zur Reichskanzlei*, pp. 288–91.

32. Uwe D. Adam, *Judenpolitik im Dritten Reich* (Düsseldorf, 1972), pp. 50ff.

33. Ibid., p. 65.

34. *DOH*, pp. 39–41.

35. Wheaton, *The Nazi Revolution*, p. 315.

36. *RGBL* (1933), pp. 175–77. See Karl A. Schleunes, *The Twisted Road to Auschwitz: Nazi Policy Towards German Jews, 1933–1939* (Chicago and London, 1970), pp. 92–132.

37. *Das Schwarzbuch: Tatsachen und Dokumente* ed. Comité des délégations juives (Paris, 1934), pp. 201–3.

38. *RGBL* (1933), p. 222.

39. *Das Schwarzbuch*, p. 204.

40. Bracher et al., *Machtergreifung*, p. 323.

41. *RGBL* (1933), p. 225; also see Ulrich Walberer, ed., *10. Mai 1933, Bücherverbrennung in Deutschland und die Folgen* (Frankfurt on the Main, 1983), passim.

42. *RGBL* (1933), p. 212.

43. Ibid., p. 195; *DOH*, p. 41f.

44. Walter Hubatsch, *Hindenburg und der Staat* (Göttingen, 1966): correspondence between Hindenburg and Hitler, April 4–5, 1933, pp. 375–78; *DOH*, pp. 37–39.

45. Adam, *Judenpolitik*, p. 80f.

46. *RGBL* (1933), pp. 479f.

47. Adam, *Judenpolitik*, p. 87.

48. *CV Ztg.*, March 14, 1935, Supplement 2.

49. *RGBL* (1933), p. 699.

50. *Das Schwarzbuch*, pp. 122–25.

51. *RGBL* (1933), p. 531.

52. Wheaton, *The Nazi Revolution*, p. 335.

53. *RGBL* (1933), pp. 661, 713.

54. Genschel, *Die Verdrängung der Juden*, p. 106.

55. *CV Ztg.*, June 29, 1933, front page; and *JR*, July 4, 1933, p. 302.

56. See the protest in *JR*, May 4, 1934, front page; the confiscation order (May 18, 1934) actually came too late as the issue had already been bought up by the public. See *Pinkas Hakehillot, Encyclopaedia of Jewish Communities: Germany–Bavaria*, ed. Dr. Baruch Zvi Ophir et al. (Yad Vashem, Jerusalem, 1973), p. 30.

57. *CV Ztg.*, February 28, 1935, front page.

58. Ibid. Lippert was editor-in-chief of Goebbels's newspaper, *Der Angriff*, from 1927 to 1933. Adam, *Judenpolitik*, p. 33 n. 61.

59. *CV Ztg.*, June 6, 1935, front page.

60. Adam, *Judenpolitik*, pp. 123f.; Genschel, *Die Verdrängung der Juden*, pp. 110–13. The conflict is detailed in *DOH*, pp. 73–75. Also see Abraham Barkai, "Der wirtschaftliche Existenzkampf der Juden im Dritten Reich 1933–1938," in *The Jews in Nazi Germany, 1933–1943*, ed. Arnold Paucker et al. (Tübingen, 1986), pp. 153–66.

61. *RGBL* (1935), pp. 472, 609, 769.

62. Norman H. Baynes, ed., *The Speeches of Adolf Hitler, April 1922–August 1939* (London, 1942), vol. 1, pp. 731f.; quoted in *DOH*, p. 81.

63. Genschel, *Die Verdrängung der Juden*, p. 114.

64. Paragraphs 4–6 of the party manifesto as published by Alfred Rosenberg, Munich, 1930; *DOH*, p. 15.

65. For details, see Adam, *Judenpolitik*, pp. 28–33.

66. Bernard Lösener, "Das Reichsministerium des Innern und die Judengesetzgebung," *VJHZ*, 9, no. 3 (1961), pp. 262–313.

67. *CV Ztg.*, February 20, 1934, front page.

68. *RGBL* (1935), pp. 1146f.; *DOH*, pp. 76–79.

69. Quoted in Hans Lamm, "Über die innere und äussere Entwicklung des deutschen Judentums im Dritten Reich" (Ph.D. diss., University of Erlangen, W. Ger., 1951), p. 50. See Kurt Pätzold, ed., *Verfolgung, Vertreibung, Vernichtung: Dokumente des faschistischen Antisemitismus 1933 bis 1942* (Leipzig, 1973), p. 115.

70. The German Information Agency (Deutsches Nachrichtenbüro, or DNB), published in *JR*, September 17, 1935, front page. Also see *DOH*, pp. 82f.

71. *RGBL* (1935) p. 1333; *DOH*, p. 80.

72. *CV Ztg.*, March 30, 1933, pp. 106–07; April 6, 1933, front page.

73. *JR*, April 4, 1933 front page; quoted in *DOH*, pp. 44–47.

74. According to a public opinion poll by *Israelitisches Familienblatt* published in *CV Ztg.*, June 1, 1933, pp. 203f. On Kareski, see Francis R. Nicosia, "Revisionist Zionism in Germany (II): Georg Kareski and the Staatszionistische Organisation, 1933–1938," *YLB*, 32 (1987), pp. 231–67.

75. *JR*, April 28, 1933, p. 167.

76. Margaliot, "Political Reaction," vol. 1, pp. 186f.; *CV Ztg.* March 14, 1935, Supplement 3; for the proclamation, see *DOH*, pp. 47–50.

77. Abraham Margaliot, "The Struggle for Survival of the Jewish Community in Germany in the Face of Oppression," in *Jewish Resistance During the Holocaust. Proceedings of the Conference on Manifestations of Jewish Resistance, April 7–11, 1968* (Yad Vashem, Jerusalem, 1971), pp. 100–111. On labor controls, see *JR*, August 10, 1934, p. 7.

78. Margaliot, "Political Reaction," vol. 1, p. 200.

79. Decree of August 5, 1935, in the Central Archives of the History of the Jewish People, Jerusalem. See also *DOH*, pp. 67f.

80. Werner Levie, "Der Kulturbund als soziale Institution," *JR*, September 15, 1933,

p. 532; Lamm, "Über die innere und äussere Entwicklung"; Margaliot, "Political Reaction," vol. 1, pp. 71, 141.

81. See Ernst Simon, *Aufbau im Untergang: Jüdische Erwachsenenbildung im natio- nalsozialistischen Deutschland als geistiger Widerstand* (Tübingen, 1959), passim; also *DOH*, pp. 51–53.

82. Margaret T. Edelheim-Muehsam, "The Jewish Press in Germany," *YLB*, 1 (1956), pp. 172–88. For details, see p. 174.

83. Lamm, "Über die innere und ässere Entwicklung," pp. 198f.

84. Max Gruenewald, "The Beginning of the Reichsvertretung," *YLB*, 1 (1956), pp. 57–62. Abraham Margaliot, "The Dispute over the Leadership of German Jewry (1933– 1938), " *YVS Studies*, 10 (1974), pp. 129–48; for additional bibliography, see Shaul Esh, *Studies in the Holocaust and Contemporary Jewry*, ed. Joseph Walk (Jerusalem, 1973), p. 276, no. 3.

85. *JR*, September 29, 1933, p. 589, quoted in *DOH*, pp. 57–59. See also Friedrich S. Brodnitz, "Memories of the Reichsvertretung: A Personal Report," *YLB*, 31 (1986), pp. 267–77; Paul Sauer, "Otto Hirsch (1885–1941): Director of the Reichsvertretung," *YLB*, 32 (1987), pp. 341–68.

86. *DOH*, pp. 57–59.

87. "Authentische Äusserungen zu den Nürnberger Gestzen," *CV Ztg.*, December 5, 1935, Supplement 2.

88. *CV Ztg.*, September 26, 1935, front page; *JR*, September 24, 1935, front page f., quoted in *DOH*, p. 84.

89. *DOH*, pp. 84–86.

90. See Naumann's speech quoted in *CV Ztg.*, September 7, 1933, Supplement 2.

91. Margaliot, "Political Reaction," vol. 1, p. 90. Also see, idem, "The Dispute over the Leadership of German Jewry." Hans J. Schoeps, "Der Jude im neuen Deutschland," (October 1933), reprinted in Schoeps, *Bereit für Deutschland! Der Patriotismus deutscher Juden und der Nationalsozialismus* (Berlin, 1970), p. 112. See Carl J. Rheiss, "Deutscher Vortrupp, Gefolgschaft deutscher Juden," *YLB*, 26 (1981), pp. 207–29.

92. Reinhard Heydrich, "Wandlungen unseres Kampfes," *Das Schwarze Korps*, 1, no. 11 (May 15, 1935), p. 9.

93. On October 21, 1935, the council of the CV decided to change its name from Central Verein deutscher Staatsbürger jüdischen Glaubens to Jüdischer Central Verein. The name of the newspaper was changed to *Allgemeine Zeitung des Judentums*.

94. On Max Warburg and his stance, see Genschel, *Die Verdrängung der Juden*, passim.

95. Margaliot, "Political Reaction" vol. 1, pp. 94–96.

96. See the call by the Reichsvertretung and large Jewish organizations to donate funds to support Jews in need (seventy thousand in Berlin alone). *CV Ztg.*, October 17, 1935, front page; October 31, 1935, Supplement 1.

97. See Otto D. Kulka and Aron Rodrigue, "The German Population and the Jews in the Third Reich," *YVS Studies*, 16 (1984), pp. 421–35. Also Otto D. Kulka, "Major Trends and Tendencies in German Historiography on National Socialism and the Jewish Question (1924–1984)," *YLB*, 30 (1985), pp. 235–38. See also the publications of Jan Kershaw quoted in these two articles.

98. Gestapo report for February 1935. Otto D. Kulka, " 'The Jewish Problem' in the Third Reich" (Ph.D. diss. The Hebrew Univeristy, Jerusalem, 1975), vol. 2, p. vii (Hebrew).

99. Kommission zur Erforschung der Geschichte der Frankfurter Juden, eds., *Dokumente zur Geschichte der Frankfurter Juden, 1933–1945* (Frankfurt on the Main, 1963), p. 339.

100. *DOH*, pp. 71f.

101. Joseph Walk, *The Education of the Jewish Child in Nazi Germany: The Law and Its Execution* (Jerusalem, 1975), pp. 66, 100f, (Hebrew with English synopsis).

102. Ibid., p. 73; table no. 1, p. 284.

103. Solomon Colodner, *Jewish Education in Germany Under the Nazis* (New York, 1964), pp. 43ff.

104. Hans Gaertner, "Problems of Jewish Schools in Germany During the Hitler Regime," *YLB*, 1 (1956), pp. 123–41.

105. Colodner, *Jewish Education in Germany*, pp. 43f.

106. H. Meier-Cronemeyer, "Jüdische Jugendbewegung," *Germania Judaica*, 8, 1/2 (1969), 20, 42; Chaim Shatzker, "The Jewish Youth Movement During the Holocaust," in *Studies in the History of Jewish Society During the Middle Ages and in the Modern Times: Presented to Professor Jakob Katz on His Seventy-fifth Birthday*, ed. E. Etke and Y. Salmon (Jerusalem, 1980), pp. 446–49 (Hebrew).

107. Quoted in Meier-Cronemeyer; "Jüdische Jugendbewegung," *Germania Judaico*, 8 no. 3/4, 101. On Ludwig Tietz, see Gustav Horn ed., *Jüdische Jugend im Übergang, Ludwig Tietz 1897–1933. Sein Leben und seine Zeit* (Council of Jews from Germany, 1980), (Hebrew introduction.)

Chapter 4

1. Eberhard Aleff, ed., *Das Dritte Reich* (Hannover, W. Ger., 1970), p. 129.

2. Andreas Hillgruber, "Kontinuität and Diskontinuität in der deutschen Aussenpolitik von Bismarck bis Hitler," in *Grossmachtpolitik und Militarismus im 20. Jahrhundert* (Düsseldorf, 1974), p. 16.

3. Ibid., p. 27.

4. Allan Bullock, *Hitler: A Study in Tyranny*, completely rev. ed. (New York, 1964), p. 365.

5. Speech on November 2, 1933, in *Hitler, Reden und Proklamationen 1932–1945*, ed. Max Domarus (Neustadt an der Aisch, W. Ger., 1962), vol. 1, p. 325.

6. Address to the Reichstag, January 30, 1934, in *The Speeches of Adolf Hitler, April 1922–August 1939* ed. Norman H. Baynes (London, 1942), vol. 2, p. 1,162; Martin Broszat, *Nationalsozialistische Polenpolitik 1939–1945* (Stuttgart, 1965), pp. 12ff., argues that at the time this was Hitler's opinion.

7. Hermann Rauschning, *Hitler Speaks* (London, 1939), p. 116.

8. Avraham Barkai, "Schicksalsjahr 1938. Kontinuität und Verschärfung der wirtschaftlichen Ausplünderung der deutschen Juden," in *Das Unrechtsregime: Verfolgung, Exil, Belasteter Neubeginn*, ed. Ursula Büttner et al. (Hamburg, 1986), vol. 2, pp. 45–68; *DOH*, pp. 72–75.

9. Theodor Vogelsang, "Neue Dokumente zur Geschichte der Reichswehr, 1930–1933," *VJHZ*, 2, no. 4 (1954), p. 435.

10. Wilhelm Treue, "Hitler's Denkschrift zum Vierjahresplan 1936," *VJHZ*, 3, no. 2 (1955), p. 204; *Hitler's Secret Book* (New York, 1961), pp. 44f., 140–45; *DOH*, pp. 88f.

11. Treue, "Hitlers Denkschrift," para. 6, p. 206; pp. 208f. On Hitler's foreign policy, see Éberhard Jäckel, *Hitlers Weltanschauung: Entwurf einer Herrschaft, erweiterte und überarbeitete Neuausgabe* (Stuttgart, 1986), pp. 29–54.

12. Treue, "Hitler's Denkschrift," p. 210.

13. The number of emigrants is based on the report of the Security Police of May–June 1934, which includes the estimate of the Committee for Matters Concerning Refugees

from Germany Under the League of Nations, cited in Otto D. Kulka, *Tendencies Regarding "The Solution of the Jewish Problem" in the Third Reich* (Akadmon, Jerusalem, 1968), p. 52 (Hebrew). See Herbert A. Strauss, "Jewish Emigration from Germany: Nazi Policies and Jewish Responses," *YLB*, 25 (1980), pp. 313–61; 26 (1981), pp. 343–409; Michael R. Marrus, *The Unwanted: European Refugees in the Twentieth Century* (New York, 1985), p. 135.

14. According to *JR*, June 8, 1934, p. 2, eight thousand Jews returned to Poland during the first year of the Nazi rule. By 1936 the number of returnees to East European countries had risen to eighteen thousand. Also see Hans Lamm, "Über die innere und äussere Entwicklung des Deutschen Judentums im Dritten Reich" (Ph.D. diss., University of Erlangen, W. Ger., 1951), p. 212. See Schalom Adler-Rudel, *Jüdische Selbsthilfe unter dem Naziregime, 1933–1939* (Tübingen, 1974), pp. 94–97.

15. See our later discussion of such countries of refuge as Holland, Switzerland, and Sweden in chap. 20 "Attempts at Rescue."

16. *JR*, April 28, 1933, p. 167; *DOH*, pp. 49f.

17. The Gestapo published their instructions on May 17, 1935; quoted in Abraham Margaliot, "The Political Reaction of the Jewish Institutions and Organizations in Germany to the Anti-Jewish Policy of the National Socialists in the Years 1932–1935 (Ph.D. diss., The Hebrew University, Jerusalem, 1971), vol. 1, p. 292 (Hebrew with English abstract). On the practice and organization of emigration and its pitfalls, see Arthur Prinz, "The Role of the Gestapo in Obstructing and Promoting Emigration," *YVS Studies*, 2 (1958), pp. 205–18; Jacob Touri, "From Forced Emigration to Expulsion: The Jewish Exodus over Non-Slavic Borders of the Reich as a Prelude to the 'Final Solution,' " *YVS Studies*, 17 (1986), pp. 51–91.

18. Protocol of the meeting of the Committee for Occupational Retraining, which was part of the Central Committee of German Jews for Relief and Reconstruction, April 25, 1934, CZA, S25/9703; Adler-Rudel, *Jüdische Selbsthilfe*, pp. 54–71; Lamm, "Über die innere und äussere Entwicklung," p. 188.

19. The Hilfsverein had eighteen branches throughout Germany. See *DOH*, pp. 69–71; Prinz, "Role of the Gestapo."

20. Max J. Kohler, a specialist in immigration and naturalization law, represented B'nei Brith and the American Jewish Committee, when he gave evidence before the Immigration Committee of the U.S. Congress; quoted by David Brody in "American Jewry, the Refugees and Immigration Restriction," *Publications of the American Jewish Historical Society*, 45 (June, 1956), 221f.

21. David B. Wyman, *Paper Walls: America and the Refugee Crisis, 1938–1941* (Amherst, Mass., 1968), pp. 94ff., 210; Arthur D. Morse, *While Six Million Died* (London, 1968), p. 261.

22. The numbers according to Dan Michman, "The Jewish Refugees from Germany in the Netherlands, 1933–1940" (Ph.D. diss., The Hebrew University, Jerusalem, 1978), vol. 2, app. A, p. 367 (Hebrew).

23. See Sir John Hope Simpson, *The Refugee Problem* (London, 1939); Norman Bentwich, *The Refugees from Germany: April 1933 to December 1935* (London, 1939); Arieh Tartakover and Kurt R. Grossman, *The Jewish Refugee* (New York, 1944), contains the most comprehensive bibliography on the whole problem; Yehuda Bauer, *My Brother's Keeper: A History of the American Joint Distribution Committee, 1929–1939* (Philadelphia, 1974), pp. 141–53.

24. Eliahu Ben-Elissar, *La Diplomatie du IIIᵉ Reich et les Juifs, 1933–1939* (Geneva, 1969), pp. 102–10; James G. McDonald, letter of resignation in Bentwich, Refugees from Germany, app.; Marrus, *The Unwanted*, pp. 160–65.

25. Hans Habe described the situation in his novel, *The Mission* (New York, 1966).

26. *Proceedings of the Intergovernmental Committee, Evian, July 6–15, 1938, . . . Resolutions and Reports* (London, 1938); quoted in *DOH*, pp. 95–98.

27. Henry L. Feingold, *The Politics of Rescue: The Roosevelt Administration and the Holocaust, 1938–1945* (New Brunswick, NJ, 1970), passim; Saul S. Friedman, *No Haven for the Oppressed* (Detroit, Mich., 1973), passim.

28. Wyman, *Paper Walls*, p. 44.

29. Ben-Elissar, *La Diplomatie*, p. 27.

30. Memorandum on the Jewish situation in Germany, American Jewish Committee, May 1, 1933, CZA, S25/9703.

31. Shaul Esh, "The Reactions of World Jewry During the First Stage of the Nazi Regime," in *Studies in the Holocaust and Contemporary Jewry*, ed. Joseph Walk (Jerusalem, 1973), pp. 51–57, (Hebrew); Joseph Tenenbaum, "The Anti-Nazi Boycott Movement in the United States," *YVS Studies*, 3 (1959), pp. 141–59.

32. Report of Leo Motzkin, July 27, 1933, CZA, S25/9705. Confidential memorandum of the American Jewish Congress about the situation of the Jews in Germany, July 1, 1933, CZA, S25/9705; Nathan Feinberg, *Ha-Ma'arakhah ha-Yehudit neged Hitler al Bimat Ḥever ha-Leumim* (Jerusalem, 1957), chap. 3.

33. Hjalmar Schacht, *My First Seventy-Six Years* (London, 1955), pp. 284f.

34. Stephen S. Wise, Address at the Peace and Democracy Rally at Madison Square Garden, March 15, 1937, in *Joint Boycott Council of the American Jewish Congress and Jewish Labor Committee* (New York, 1937), pp. 16–22.

35. On the Bernheim Petition, see Nathan Feinberg, "Jewish Political Activities Against the Nazi Regime in the Years 1933–1939," in *Jewish Resistance During the Holocaust: Proceedings of the Conference on Manifestations of Jewish Resistance* (Yad Vashem, Jerusalem, 1971), pp. 76–83; Marrus, *The Unwanted*, p. 160.

36. CZA, S25/18, p. 20. Ben-Gurion emphasized the time factor more than once during the talks; he had already stated, "Tens of generations have been looking forward to this historic moment. It is in our generation that this historical hope must find its fulfilment." CZA, S25/18, p. 3.

37. See Yisrael Gutman and Shmuel Krakowski, *Unequal Victims: Poles and Jews During World War II* (New York, 1986), pp. 1–26.

38. Yoav Gelber, "The Reaction of the Zionist Movement and the Yishuv to the Nazis' Rise to Power," *YVS Studies*, 18 (1987), pp. 41–69. Interview with Chaim Arlosoroff, *JR*, May 23, 1933, pp. 214f.

39. Margaliot, "Political Reaction," vol. 1, pp. 238f.

40. See Weizmann's evidence before the Peel Commission, November 11, 1936, Great Britain, Colonial Office, Palestine Royal Commission Report, 1937.

41. Address at the Zionist Convention in England, October 7, 1934, Weizmann Archives.

42. Gelber, "Reaction of the Zionist Movement," pp. 83–99.

43. *VB (Süddeutsche Ausgabe)*, August 23, 24, 28, 29, 30, 1933, supplement nos. 235, 236, 240, 241, and 242, respectively.

44. Margaliot, "Political Reaction," vol. 1, pp. 69, 275–78, 286; letter from Martin Rosenblüth in London to Weizmann (then in Palestine) of December 23, 1935, CZA, S25/9703. On Kareski, see Francis R. Nicosia, Revisionist Zionism in Germany (II): Georg Kareski and the Staatszionistische Organisation, 1933–1938, *YLB*, 32 (1987), pp. 231–67.

45. For the different categories of privileged immigrants to Palestine, see Werner Feilchenfeld et al., *Haavara-Transfer nach Palästina und Einwanderung deutscher Juden 1933–1939* (Tübingen, 1972), p. 28.

46. Ibid., pp. 20f. The emigration tax was a regulation from the time of the foreign

currency crisis in Germany in 1931. About the raise of the cost in Reichsmarks, see ibid, pp. 68f.

47. See Gelber, "Reaction of the Zionist Movement," pp. 70–83; Yoav Gelber "The Zionist Policy and the Transfer Agreement," 1933–1935 *Yalkut Moreshet*, (a) 17 (1974), 97–152; (b) 18 (1974), 23–100 (Hebrew).

48. Esh, "The Reactions of World Jewry," passim; David Yisraeli, "The Third Reich and the Transfer Agreement," *Journal of Contemporary History* (London), 6, no. 2 (1971), 129–48; Moshe Gottlieb, "The Anti-Nazi Boycott Movement in the American Jewish Community 1933–1941" (Ph.D. diss., Brandeis University, 1967); and Edwin Black, *The Transfer Agreement: The Untold Story of the Secret Pact Between the Third Reich and Jewish Palestine* (New York, 1984). Black's book is about an agreement that was not "secret," but that has been extensively examined. The work is an emotionally laden, pseudohistorical product, one among many journalistic and sensational publications through which authors with unclear motives try to falsify the history of the Holocaust and discredit Zionism. For an excellent review of the book, see Richard S. Levy, "Dealing with the Devil," *Commentary*, 78, no. 3 (1984), 68–71.

49. Yisraeli, "Third Reich," p. 131.

50. Gelber, "Transfer Agreement," *Yalkut Moreshet*, 18 (November, 1974), pp. 41f.

51. Feilchenfeld, *Haavara-Transfer*, pp. 29f.; Ernst Marcus, "The German Foreign Office and the Palestine Question in the Period 1933–1939," *YVS*, 2 (1958), pp. 179–204.

52. See letter written in Göring's name, September 20, 1937, in Rolf Vogel, *Ein Stempel hat gefehlt: Dokumente zur Emigration deutscher Juden* (Munich, 1977), pp. 312f.

53. Yisraeli, "Third Reich," p. 136. Consul Heinrich Wolff had a Jewish wife and was, therefore, forced to resign.

54. Ibid.; *DGFP*, ser. D, 5, nos. 566–69, 572, 574, 576–78, 581–92; and see Vogel, *Ein Stempel*, pp. 107–53.

55. *DGFP*, ser. D, 5, no. 569 (earlier version, no 561). See Francis R. Nicosia, *The Third Reich and the Palestine Question* (London, 1985), pp. 134–44.

56. Yisraeli, "Third Reich," pp. 135f. About the internal German discussion, especially from the economic point of view, see Nicosia, *Palestine Question*.

57. Feilchenfeld, *Haavara-Transfer*, p. 32; Marcus, "German Foreign Office," pp. 190–93.

58. *Eichmann Trial*, text of recorded interrogations by the Israeli police Headquarters Bureau, Dept., 06, vol. 1, cols. 45f., 63ff. Excerpts of the interrogations were published: Jochen von Long, ed. *Das Eichmaum Protocoll: Tonbandaufzeichnungen der israelitischen Verhöre* (Frankfurt on the Main and Berlin, 1984).

59. Shlomo Aronson, *Reinhard Heydrich und die Frühgeschichte von Gestapo und SD* (Stuttgart, 1971), p. 201.

60. Central report by the head of the Intelligence Department of the SD (II, 112), Hagen, April 1, 1937, Bundesarchiv Koblenz, reproduced in Otto D. Kulka, " 'The Jewish Problem' in the Third Reich" (Ph.D. diss. The Hebrew University, Jerusalem, 1975), vol. 2, p. 287 (Hebrew).

61. *Eichmann Trial*, T/124; Eichmann's own story, police interrogations, Dept. 06, vol. 1, cols. 87–94; Heinz Höhne, *The Order of the Death's Head: The Story of Hitler's SS* (London, 1969), pp. 336f.

62. "Sicherheitsdienst des RFSS, SD-Hauptamt. Zusammenfassende Berichte der Abtg. II 112," *Zum Judenproblem Januar 1937*. For the best description of the whole process, see Karl A. Schleunes, *The Twisted Road to Auschwitz: Nazi Policy Towards German*

Jews, 1933–1939 (Chicago and London, 1970), pp. 178–213. Kulka, " 'The Jewish Problem'," vol. 1, pp. 185–203.

63. "SD-Hauptamt," Lageberichte der Zentralabteilung (II, 1, January 1 to January 31, 1938), Bundesarchiv Koblenz, reproduced in Kulka, " 'The Jewish Problem'," vol. 1, pp. 304, 306f.

64. Leni Yahil, "Jews in the Concentration Camps in Germany Prior to World War II," in *The Nazi Concentration Camps: Structure and Aims, the Image of the Prisoner, the Jews in the Camps.* Proceedings of the Fourth Yad Vashem International Historical Conference, ed. Yisrael Gutman and Avital Saf (Jerusalem, 1984), pp. 69–100.

65. *Eichmann Trial*, police interrogations, Dept. 06, vol. 1, cols. 109f.; Schleunes, *The Twisted Road*, pp. 230f., 235; Leni Yahil, " 'Memoirs' of Adolf Eichmann," *YVS Studies*, 18 (1987), pp. 143f.

66. Herbert Rosenkranz, "The Anschluss and the Tragedy of Austrian Jewry, 1933–1945," in *The Jews of Asutria: Essays on Their Life, History, and Destruction*, ed. Josef Fraenkel (London, 1967), pp. 486f.

67. Generally, it is assumed that the director of the Jewish community of Vienna, Josef Löwenherz, suggested the formation of a central office in order to facilitate the process of emigration; see Rosenkranz, "Anschluss," p. 491. It seems to me, however, that the system subsequently implemented was the logical consequence of the deliberations that had been held by the SD for years.

68. Testimony of Dr. Franz Meyer, former chairman of the ZVfD, at the Eichmann Trial, Proceedings, Session, 17, p. 56.

69. See Uwe D. Adam, *Judenpolitik im Dritten Reich* (Düsseldorf, 1972), pp. 166–72.

70. *RGBL* (1938), p. 338; published *DOH*, p. 91; the Ismar Freund Archive in The Central Archives for the History of the Jewish People, Jerusalem, P2/N9a; Adam, *Judenpolitik*, p. 199.

71. *DOH*, p. 98.

72. Helmut Genschel, *Die Verdrängung der Juden aus der Wirtschaft im Dritten Reich* (Göttingen, 1966), pp. 136, 205. Also see Barkai, "Schicksalsjahr 1938."

73. *RGBL* (1938), p. 627; also see Schleunes, *The Twisted Road*, pp. 159–66.

74. Genschel, ibid., p. 150.

75. *RGBL* (1938), pp. 404, 414f.

76. Genschel, *Die Verdrängung der Juden*, p. 153.

77. Ibid., pp. 157f. Nevertheless, the official institutions sought to prevent excessive exploitation of Aryanization; on more than one occasion they turned down proposals for the process that were not in keeping with the established rules.

78. Ibid., p. 161, n. 100; p. 207.

79. Ibid., pp. 165f.

80. Schleunes, *The Twisted Road*, p. 225.

81. Genschel, *Die Verdrängung der Juden*, p. 172.

82. The so-called Hossbach Protocol of the meeting of November 5, 1937 (named after the officer who drew it up), *DGFP*, ser. D, 1, pp. 29–39. See William L. Shirer, *The Rise and Fall of the Third Reich: A History of Nazi Germany* (New York, 1960), pp. 303, 308.

83. Yahil, "Jews in the Concentration Camps," passim.

84. Carl Ludwig, *Die Flüchtlingspolitik der Schweiz in den Jahren 1933–1955* (Bern, 1957), p. 56. Joseph Tenenbaum, "The Crucial Year,1938," *YVS Studies*, 2 (1958), p. 52; also see chap. 20 "Attempts at Rescue."

85. Tenenbaum, "The Crucial Year, 1938," p. 55.

86. According to Genschel, *Die Verdrängung der Juden*, there were 169,000 Jews who

emigrated from Germany between 1933 and 1938, see p. 291; Bauer, *My Brother's Keeper*, reports 164, 369, see tables 7, 19; and Herbert Rosenkranz, *Verfolgung und Selbstbehauptung: Die Juden in Österreich, 1938–1945* (Vienna, 1978), reports 57,226 emigrants between March and October 1938, see p. 284.

87. Sybil Milton, "The Expulsion of Polish Jews from Germany: October 1938 to July 1939—Documentation," *YLB*, 29 (1984), pp. 169f.; Bauer, *My Brother's Keeper*, p. 262.

88. Schleunes, *The Twisted Road*, pp. 227f.

89. Quoted by Touri, "From Forced Emigration to Expulsion," p. 58; idem, "Ein Auftakt zur Endlösung: Judenaustreibungen über nichtslawische Grenzen, 1933–1939," in Büttner, et al., *Das Unrechtsregime*, pp. 164–96.

90. Milton, "The Expulsion of Polish Jews," specifies the local division of the refugees, p. 171; also see summary, p. 174.

91. Helmut Heiber, "Der Fall Grynspan," *VJHZ*, 5, no. 1 (1957), pp. 154–72; and see n. 94 below.

92. Hermann Graml, "Der 9, November 1938: 'Reichskristallnacht'," *Beilage zur Wochenzeitschrift "Das Parlament,"* no, 45 (November 11, 1953), passim; John Mendelsohn, *The Holocaust: The Crystal Night Pogrom*, vol. 3 (New York, 1982), passim; Lionel Kochan, *Pogrom: 10. November 1938* (London, 1957).

93. Heydrich's directive, *IMT*, 31, PS-3051, pp. 515–19; *DOH*, pp. 102–4. Also see *IMT*, 20, p. 146. Graml, "Der 9. November 1938," p. 10.

94. Kurt Ball-Kaduri, "Die Vorplanung der Kristallnacht," *Zeitschrift für die Geschichte der Juden* (Tel Aviv), no. 4, (1966): 211–18. Yahil, "Jews in the Concentration Camps," p. 89. As in the case of the Reichstag fire, fears and suspicions were expressed immediately—mainly abroad, but even from Ernst vom Rath, the dead third secretary's father—that the act may have been a provocation organized by the Nazis in order to launch a pogrom against the Jews. See account in PRO, FO 371/25053, January 14, 1939.

95. Shaul Esh, "Between Discrimination and Extermination (The Fateful Year, 1938)," *YVS Studies*, 2 (1958), pp. 91f.

96. For details about actions and destruction see n. 92; Board of Deputies, *The Jews in Europe: Their Martyrdom and Their Future* (London, 1945) reports five hundred destroyed synagogues, p. 16; Heydrich's report, *IMT*, 32, PS-3058, pp. 1f.

97. *IMT*, 28, PS-1816, pp. 499ff.; Helmut Krausnick in *Anatomy of the SS State* (London, 1970), p. 58.

98. Yahil, "Jews in the Concentration Camps," pp. 88f.

99. Kurt J. Ball-Kaduri, "The Central Jewish Organizations in Berlin During the Pogrom of November 1938," *YVS Studies*, 3 (1959), pp. 261–81.

100. Herbert Rosenkranz, *"Reichskristallnacht": 9. November 1938 in Österreich* (Vienna, 1968), p. 49.

101. Idem, *"Reichskristallnacht,"* pp. 38, 45, 49, 56; quotation, pp. 40f.

102. Ibid., SD report quoted, p. 57; also see summary report of the SD in Tuvia Friedmann ed., *Die Kristallnacht: Dokumentarische Sammlung*, no. 33 (Haifa, 1972).

103. Hildegard von Kotze et al., eds., *"Es spricht der Führer"* (Gütersloh, W. Ger., 1966), pp. 268–86; quotations pp. 279, 281f, respectively. Wilhelm Treue, "Rede Hitlers vor der deutschen Presse (November 10, 1938)," *VJHZ*, 6, no. 1 (1958), pp. 182f. For the same interpretation of Hitler's speech see Hermann Graml, *Reichskristallnacht: Antisemitismus und Judenverfolgung im Dritten Reich* (Munich, 1988), p. 176.

104. *IMT*, 28, PS-1816, pp. 499ff.; quotation p. 501. See also *DOH*, pp. 108–15.

105. On November 12, 1938, four orders were published: Order of the Restoration of the Look of the Street at Jewish Enterprises; Order of the Mulct [Penalty] Imposed on Jews of German citizenship; Order to Oust the Jews from the German Economy; *RGBL* (1938),

pp. 1,579, 1,580; and that of Goebbels, acting as president of the Chamber of Culture, the Order Forbidding Jews to Take Part in Public Events. Also see *DOH*, pp. 115–17.

106. Joseph Walk, *Das Sonderrecht für die Juden im NS-Staat: Eine Sammlung der gesetzlichen Massnahmen und Richtlinien, Inhalt, und Bedeutung* (Heidelberg, 1981), pp. 254–76.

107. Herbert Freeden, "Eine gespenstige Theater-Aufführung," *BL*, no. 1 (1957), pp. 19–23.

108. Norman H. Baynes ed., *The Speeches of Adolf Hitler*, pp. 738–41; see also *DOH*, pp. 132–35.

109. Adam, *Judenpolitik*, pp. 217, 219; for the regulations, orders, and counterorders, see pp. 216–26.

110. Ibid., p. 220.

111. *IMT*, 26, PS-710, pp. 266f.; *DOH*, pp. 125f. Administratively the Reich Center was affiliated with the Ministry of Interior.

112. Shaul Esh, "The Establishment of the 'Reichsvereinigung der Juden in Deutschland' and Its Main Activities," *YVS Studies,* 7 (1968), pp. 19–38.

113. *RGBL* (1939), pp. 1097–99; *DOH*, pp. 139–43. Otto D. Kulka, "The Reichsvereinigung' of the Jews in Germany," in *Patterns of Jewish Leadership in Nazi Europe 1933–1945. Proceedings of the Third Yad Vashem International Historical Conference*, ed. Yisrael Gutman and Cynthia J. Haft (Jerusalem, 1979), pp. 45–58; Esriel Hildesheimer, "The Central Organization of the German Jews in the Years 1933–1943: Its Legal and Political Status and Its Position in the Jewish Community," (Ph.D. diss. The Hebrew University, Jerusalem, 1982) (in Hebrew with English summary).

114. Ruth Bondy, *Edelstein Neged ha-Zman* (Tel Aviv, 1981), pp. 177–96. Livia Rothkirchen, "The Jews of Bohemia and Moravia, 1938–1945," in *The Jews of Czechoslovakia*, ed. Avigdor Dagan et al. (Philadelphia, 1984), vol. 3, pp. 3–28.

115. B. Amann, *Das Weltbild des Judentums, 1939* p. 351, quoted in Artur Eisenbach, "Nazi Foreign Policy on the Eve of World War II and the Jewish Question," *Acta Poloniae Historica*, 5 (1962), 62.

116. In the spring of 1938 Jewish property and assets had been valued as RM 8 billion (U.S. $3.2 billion); this was already reduced by RM 2 billion (U.S. $800 million) because of Aryanization and further by the fine imposed after the pogrom. Genschel, *Die Verdrängung der Juden*, p. 205.

117. The best description is in Eisenbach, "Nazi Foreign Policy," pp. 113–31. For the deliberations of the British government, see PRO, Cabinet Conclusions, November 30, 1938 and December 21, 1938, Cab. 23/96; see also A. J. Sherman, *Island Refuge: Britain and Refugees from the Third Reich, 1933–1939* (London, 1973), pp. 195–203; for the inter-Jewish discussion and additional details, see Bauer, *My Brother's Keeper*, pp. 272–85; on resettlement, see Henry L. Feingold, "Roosevelt and the Resettlement Question," in *Rescue Attempts During the Holocaust. Proceedings of the Second Yad Vashem Historical Conference*, ed. Yisrael Gutman and Efraim Zuroff (Jerusalem, 1977), pp. 123–81.

118. *DGFP*, ser. D, 5, p. 927; Raul Hilberg, *The Destruction of European Jews* (Chicago, 1961), p. 97.

119. Mark Wischnitzer, *To Dwell in Safety* (Philadelphia, 1948), p. 199.

120. PRO, Cabinet Conclusions, December 14, 1938, p. 391; for estimate of the number of refugees accepted by Great Britain, see Sherman, *Island Refuge*, p. 270.

121. PRO, Premier, 1/326, pp. 73–82.

122. Wischnitzer, *To Dwell in Safety*, pp. 197f.; Gordon Thomas and Max M. Morganwitts, *The Voyage of the Damned* (London, 1974); Bauer, *My Brother's Keeper*, pp. 278ff.

123. Bernard Wasserstein, *Britain and the Jews of Europe, 1939–1945* (London, 1979),

passim; Leni Yahil, "Select British Documents on the Illegal Immigration to Palestine (1939–1940)," *YVS Studies*, 10 (1974), pp. 241–76.

124. *DGFP*, ser. D, 5, no. 664, pp. 780–85.

125. James G. McDonald, *My Mission in Israel, 1948–1951* (New York, 1953), p. 251.

126. Genschel, *Die Verdrängung der Juden*, p. 291; Bauer, *My Brother's Keeper*, has 54,451 emigrants from Austria, see table 19.

127. David H. Popper, "International Aid to German Refugees," *Foreign Policy Reports*, 14, no. 16, (1938), 189, 196.

Chapter 5

1. Quoted in Eberhard Aleff, ed., *Das Dritte Reich* (Hannover, W. Ger., 1970), p. 173. For a detailed description, see William L. Shirer, *The Rise and Fall of the Third Reich: A History of Nazi Germany* (New York, 1960), chap. 15.

2. Albert Speer, *Inside the Third Reich: Memoirs* (London, 1970), pp. 161f.

3. Carl J. Burckhardt, *Meine Danziger Mission 1937–1939: Gesammelte Werke* (Bern, 1960), vol. 3, p. 272.

4. See *Hitler's Secret Book* (New York, 1961), p. 104; Andreas Hillgruber, "Die Endlösung und das deutsche Ostimperium: Als Kernstück des rassenbiologischen Programms des Nationalsozialismus," *VJHZ*, 20 no. 2 (1972), 136.

5. Alfred Rosenberg, *Das politische Tagebuch 1934/5, 1939/40,* ed. H. G. Seraphim, (Göttingen, 1964), p. 104; Eduard Calic, *Unmasked: Two Confidential Interviews with Hitler in 1931* (London, 1971); p. 73.

6. Calic, *Unmasked,* p. 72; Hillgruber, "Die Endlösung," pp. 137f.

7. Calic, *Unmasked,* p. 42.

8. Martin Broszat, *Nationalsozialistiche Polenpolitik, 1939–1945* (Stuttgart, 1965), p. 20; Anklageschrift gegen Karl Wolff, Landgericht München, 19.4.1963, *YVSA,* TR-10/475, pp. 87–89.

9. *TWC,* 2, pp. 447ff.

10. See Helmut Krausnick, "Denkschrift Himmlers über die Behandlung der Fremdvölkischen im Osten (Mai 1940)," *VJHZ,* 5, no. 2 (1957), 194–98.

11. *IMT,* 26, PS-864, pp. 377–82.

12. Broszat, *Polenpolitik,* pp. 25f.

13. See Martin Broszat, *The Hitler State* (London, 1981), pp. 307f.

14. Diary of Adjutant Gerhard Engel, cited in Broszat, *Polenpolitik,* p. 45. See Gerald Reitlinger, *The Final Solution: The Attempt to Exterminate the Jews of Europe, 1939–1945,* 2d rev. ed. (London, 1968), pp. 35ff, 47.

15. Broszat, *Polenpolitik,* pp. 48–51.

16. Urteil gegen Karl Wolff, 30.9.1964, *YVSA,* TR-10/639, pp. 68f.

17. Hans Buchheim, "The SS—Instrument of Domination," in Helmut Krausnick et al., *Anatomy of the SS State* (London, 1968), pp. 127–291.

18. Raul Hilberg, *The Destruction of the European Jews* (Chicago, 1961), pp. 182–86.

19. Buchheim, "The SS," p. 177.

20. Martin Broszat, "The Concentration Camps, 1933–1945," in Krausnick et al., *Anatomy,* pp. 426–428; Buchheim, "The SS," pp. 153–55; Heinz Höhne, *The Order of the Death's Head: The Story of Hitler's SS* (London, 1969), passim.

21. Broszat, "Concentration Camps," pp. 438f.

22. For comprenhensive research on the concentration camps, see Falk Pingel, *Häftlinge*

unter SS-Herrschaft: Widerstand, Selbstbehauptung, und Vernichtung im Konzentrationslager (Hamburg, 1978).

23. Broszat, "Concentration Camps," pp. 458, 476. On the situation of the Jews in the camps during the years 1933–1941, see Leni Yahil, "Jews in Concentration Camps in Germany Prior to World War II," in *The Nazi Concentration Camps: Structure and Aims, the Image of the Prisoner, the Jews in the Camps. Proceedings of the Fourth Yad Vashem International Historical Conference, January 1980,* ed. Yisrael Gutman and Avital Saf (Jerusalem, 1984), pp. 69–100.

24. Yisrael Gutman, "Social Stratification in the Concentration Camps," in Gutman and Saf, *Nazi Concentration Camps,* pp. 143–76.

25. Eugen Kogon, *Der SS-Staat: Das System der deutschen Konzentrationslager* (Frankfurt on the Main, 1946); Rudolf Höss, *Kommandant in Auschwitz: Autoibiograpische Aufzeichnungen,* ed. Martin Broszat (Munich, 1963), pp. 55–58, 67.

26. Broszat, *Polenpolitik,* p. 67.

27. Ibid., p. 79.

28. Ibid., quoted on p. 135.

29. The agreement to transfer these Germans from the Soviet Union in the testimony of Dr. Ehlich, head of the Department of National Quality and Racial Health in the RSHA (Dept. III Ba of Sec. III), NO-5179. In fact, separate agreements on mass transfers of people were signed with each of the various countries involved between September 1939 and January 1940; *TWC,* 4, pp. 829–42.

30. *Biuletyn Głównej Komisji Badania Zbrodni Hitlerowskich w Polsce,* 12 (1960), doc. 2, 9f. The execution of the directive was planned at a meeting with Hans Frank in Cracow on November 9, 1939. Ibid., doc. 3, 11Γ–14Γ.

31. Czeslaw Madajczyk, *Polityka III Rzeszy w Okupowanej Polsce* (Warsaw, 1970), vol. 1, p. 72.

32. *Biuletyn Głównej,* doc. 3, 15F–17F; ibid., Heydrich's order, doc. 9, 32F.

33. Ibid., doc. 3, 26F.

34. *Eichmann Trial,* T/179; for role distribution in the RSHA, February 1, 1940, see T/647.

35. Broszat, *Polenpolitik,* pp. 89ff.; *Biuletyn Główej,* doc. 12, 37F; doc. 17, 50F. Also see Kurt Pätzold, ed., *Verfolgung, Vertreibung, Vernichtung: Dokumente des faschistischen Antisemitismus* (Leipzig, 1973), pp. 256f.

36. *Biuletyn Głównej,* doc. 12, 37F; doc. 17, 50F.

37. Ibid., doc. 18, 61F.

38. Broszat, *Polenpolitik,* pp. 92–97; Hilberg, *Destruction of the European Jews, (1961),* pp. 138ff.

39. *Biuletyn Głównej,* doc. 22, 65F–75F. The deportation from Stettin was perhaps linked to the establishment there of a central office for the resettlement of the *Volksdeutsche* in the Warthegau (testimony of Ehlich, NO-5179); the office apparently needed apartments. . . . On other occasions, too, Jews who owned large apartments were particularly singled out for deportation.

40. The Nisko Operation featured prominently in the Eichmann trial, T/148, T/795, T/797, T/798, T/801. The Attorney-General v. Adolf Eichmann, *Testimonies* (Jerusalem, 1963), vol. 1, pp. 113, 120, 125–33, 134–43 (Hebrew). See Seev Goshen, "Eichmann und die Nisko-Aktion im Oktober 1939: Eine Fallstudie zur NS-Judenpolitik in der letzten Etappe vor der 'Endlösung'," *VJHZ,* 29, no. 1 (1981), 74–96; Jonny Moser, "Nisko: The First Experiment in Deportation," *Simon Wiesenthal Annual* (1985), vol. 2, pp. 1–30.

41. Report by Chaim Barlas to Dov Joseph, February 20, 1940, CZA, S25/9703.

42. Quoted in Louis L. Snyder, *The War: A Concise History 1939–1945* (New York, 1961), p. 109.

43. Michael R. Marrus and Robert O. Paxton, *Vichy France and the Jews* (New York, 1981), p. 36.

44. Dan Michman, "The Jewish Refugees from Germany in Holland, 1933–1940," 2 vols. (Ph.D. diss., The Hebrew University, Jerusalem, 1978). (Hebrew).

45. Maxime Steinberg, *L'Étoile et le fusil,* vol. 1, *La Question juive, 1940–1942* (Brussels, 1983), pp. 83–85; vol. 2, Les cent jours de la déportation des juifs de Belgique (Brussels, 1984), pp. 24f. The often-quoted number of ninety thousand Jews was based on inflated figures disseminated by the Germans; see, for example, Hilberg, *Destruction of the European Jews (1961),* pp. 383f. In the beginning the German authorities, for their part, tried to dispose of thousands more of these people by expelling them to France. Later, however, they actually encouraged the refugees to return (particularly skilled Jewish workers).

46. Joachim C. Fest, *The Face of the Third Reich* (New York, 1970), p. 111.

47. Josef Wulf, *Heinrich Himmler: Eine biographische Studie* (Berlin, 1960), p. 23.

48. Joachim C. Fest, in *Himmler: Geheimreden 1933 bis 1945 und andere Ansprachen,* ed. Bradley F. Smith and Agnes F. Petersen (Frankfurt on the Main, 1974), pp. 14f.

49. Fest, *Face of the Third Reich,* p. 111.

50. Quoted in Josef Ackermann, *Heinrich Himmler als Ideologe* (Göttingen, 1970), p. 101.

51. Wulf, *Heinrich Himmler,* p. 12.

52. The German version: "Stur, unbeugsam stur im Ziel, sehr anpassungsfähig in der Art wie es durchgeführt wird," *Himmler: Geheimreden,* p. 128.

53. For example, two letters: a threatening one from Himmler to Friedrich Wilhelm Krüger (December 29, 1939), accusing him of concentrating more on consolidating his regime than on supplying the SS with arms, including machine guns, as Himmler had instructed him; the second, dated March 5, 1942, to SS general Hans Jüttner, in which the conflict is clearly revealed. Helmut Heiber, ed., *Reichführer! Briefe an und von Himmler* (Stuttgart, 1968), pp. 70f., 107f.

Chapter 6

1. *TWC,* case 9, 4, PS-3363, doc. EC 307–1, pp. 119–23; case 11, 13, pp. 133–37. *DOH,* pp. 173–78.

2. For instance, on the deportation from Katowice see the testimony of Moshe Zeiger to the Historical Commission that operated in the displaced person (DP) camps in Germany, *YVSA,* M1/E968. Zieger and others managed to escape to Lwów. (The testimony is in Yiddish.)

3. P. Rauf, "In Izbica Lubelska," in *Sefer Kolo,* ed. Mordekhai Halter (Tel Aviv, 1958), pp. 313f. (Yiddish).

4. P. Friedman, "Zagłada Żydów polskich w latach 1939–1945," *Biuletyn Głównej Komisji Badania Zbrodni Niemieckich w Polsce,* 1 (1946), p. 168.

5. Martin Broszat, *Nationalsozialistische Polenpolitik, 1939–1945* (Stuttgart, 1965), p. 97. Also see chap. 5, "Toward the Struggle for World Domination."

6. *Nazi Dokumente Sprechen,* Rat der jüdischen Gemeinden in den Böhmischen Ländern, ed., (Prague, n.d.), entries October 8–11, 1939.

7. *Biuletyn Głównej* doc. 12, p. 2–6, 38–39F.

8. Ibid.; quote from doc. 8, 22–31F; doc. 4, 16F.

9. Ibid., doc. 17, 58–59F.

10. Ibid., doc. 18, 16F.

11. Report by Chaim Barlas to Dov Joseph, February 20, 1940, CZA, S25/9703.

12. Broszat, *Polenpolitik,* p. 158.

13. The population of the Generalgouvernement totaled 11,836,510, including 1,457,376 Jews, that is, 12.3 percent, see Yisrael Gutman, *The Jews of Warsaw 1939–1943: Ghetto, Underground, Revolt* (Bloomington, Ind., 1982), pp. 13, 34.

14. *EJ,* vol. 8, col. 1054; vol. 15, col. 1214.

15. David Grodner, "In Soviet Poland and Lithuania," *Contemporary Jewish Record,* 4 (1941), pp. 137f.

16. *EJ,* vol. 15, col. 83.

17. Gutman, *The Jews of Warsaw,* p. 17.

18. "Memoirs of Ida Glickstein" in *Faschismus—Ghetto—Massenmord,* ed. Jüdisches historisches Institut Warschau (Berlin, 1961), p. 167.

19. *GG* (Cracow, 1941), A110, p. 1; English trans. in Raphael Lemkin, *Axis Rule in Occupied Europe* (New York, 1973), p. 524.

20. *GG,* A480.

21. Ibid., A425.

22. Ibid., A426, pp. 1f, *DOH,* pp. 179f. Two days later, on December 13, 1939, a parallel directive aimed at Poles and Jews alike was issued in Warthegau.

23. *GG,* A910; *DOH,* pp. 191f.

24. The story appears in Aharon Weiss, "The Jewish Police in the Generalgouvernement and East Upper Silesia" (Ph.D. diss., The Hebrew University, Jerusalem, 1973), p. 152 (Hebrew).

25. "Auftrag des Chefs der Zivilverwaltung Krakau, 8, September 1939," in *Eksterminacja Żydow na Ziemach Polskich w Okresie Okupacji Hitlerowskiej, Zbior Dokumentow,* ed. Arthur Eisenbach et al. (Warsaw, 1957), p. 69.

26. Edward Kossoy,"Judenkennzeichen," in *Handuch zum Entschädigungverfahren* ed. Edward Kossoy (Munich, 1947), pp. 120–131, has a complete list of the issue of the yellow sign all over Europe, indicating place (in alphabetical order), date, authority, form, incidence, and source of the information.

27. *GG,* A405; *DOH,* pp. 178f.

28. Ludwig Hirszfeld quoted in Philip Friedman, ed., *Martyrs and Fighters* (New York, 1954), p. 23. Leni Yahil, "Readings on the History of the Holocaust" (Jerusalem, 1970, Mimeographed), pp. 55f. For translation of the quote from the original Polish, see Gutman, *The Jews of Warsaw,* p. 37.

29. See n. 27. *Verordnungsblatt des Generalgouvernement,* November 23, 1939.

30. Joseph Tenenbaum, *Race and Reich: The Story of an Epoch* (New York, 1956), p. 148.

31. Ibid., p. 127. Letter from Göring to the Reich ministers and plenipotentiaries of the Four-Year Plan, October 19, 1939.

32. *GG,* E860.

33. Tenenbaum, *Race and Reich,* pp. 138–40.

34. *GG,* E336, no. 4; *Verordnungsblatt,* November 20. 1939. Also see Isaiah Trunk, *Judenrat: The Jewish Councils in Eastern Europe Under Nazi Occupation* (New York, 1972), p. 62. On loan *kassas,* see Yehuda Bauer, *My Brother's Keeper: A History of the American Jewish Joint Distribution Committee, 1929–1939* (Philadelphia, 1974), p. 36. Also see chap. 7, "The Jews' Struggle for Survival."

35. *GG,* A435.

36. Ibid., A450, E342V. See Lemkin, *Axis Rule,* pp. 511–16.

37. *Verordnungsblatt,* September 17, 1940, determined, "The property of citizens of

the former Polish state in the sphere of the Greater German Reich, including the annexed Eastern Districts, is liable to expropriation, trusteeship and confiscation."

38. *RGBL,* 1940, vol. 1, p. 1270.

39. Trunk, *Judenrat,* p. 64.

40. Ibid., see pp. 64–67 on the implementation of the law.

41. Broszat, *Polenpolitik,* p. 103; Gutman, *The Jews of Warsaw,* pp. 19f.

42. Broszat, *Polenpolitik,* pp. 79–102.

43. Malcolm J. Proudfoot, *European Refugees: A Study of Forced Population Movement* (London, 1957), p. 81.

44. Benjamin Mintz and Yisrael Klausner, eds., *Sefer ha-Zvaot* (Jerusalem, 1945), p. 20.

45. Hermann E. Seifert, *Der Jude an der Ostgrenze* (Berlin, 1940), pp. 11f.

46. Nachman Blumenthal, ed., *Documents from the Lublin Ghetto: Judenrat without Direction* (Yad Vashem, Jerusalem, 1967), p. 24 (Polish with Hebrew translation). Our translation is according to the German text in the footnote on p. 24.

47. Eisenbach et al., *Eksterminacja,* p. 123.

48. Professor Peter H. Seraphim's lecture to mark the opening of the Institute of Jewish Research in Frankfurt on the Main, March 26, 1941. His subject, "Bevölkerung und wirtschaftspolitische Probleme einer europäischen Gesamtlösung der Judenfrage," *Weltkampf: Die Judenfrage in Geschichte und Gegenwart,* 1 (1941), p. 50.

49. For a comprehensive description of the Lublin Reservation episode and its end, see Hans G. Adler, *Der verwaltete Mensch: Studien zur Deportation der Juden aus Deutschland* (Tübingen, 1974), pp. 126–40.

50. Philip Friedman, "The Lublin Reservation and the Madagascar Plan: Two Aspects of Nazi Jewish Policy During the Second World War," in *Roads to Extinction: Essays on the Holocaust,* ed. Ada J. Friedman (New York and Philadelphia, 1980), pp. 35–37 also see Christopher R. Browning, *The Final Solution and the German Foreign Office: A Study of Referat D III of Abteilung Deutschland 1940–1943* (New York, 1978), pp. 7f.

51. P. Friedman, pp. 39–41. Contrary to Friedman, I think that the publications abroad also influenced the decision to shelve the Lublin Reservation Plan. See chap. 8, "Facing a Triumphant Germany."

52. Trunk, *Judenrat,* p. 48.

53. Max du Prel, "Krüger, Träger der Staatsgewalt," in *Das Generalgouvernement* (Würzburg, 1942), pp. 65f.

54. *GG,* A427, emphasis added; see also n. 22 above.

55. Mintz and Klausner, *Sefer ha-Zvaot,* p. 31.

56. Ibid., p. 41.

57. Emmanuel Ringelblum, *Polish-Jewish Relations During the Second World War,* ed. Joseph Kermish and Shmuel Krakowski (Jerusalem, 1974), p. 51.

58. Raul Hilberg, *The Destruction of the European Jews* (Chicago, 1961), p. 166; Mintz and Klausner, *Sefer ha-Zvaot,* pp. 170, 175.

59. *Gazeta Żydowska,* August–October 1940, quoted in Mintz and Klausner, *Sefer ha-Zvaot,* pp. 170–75.

60. Correspondence between HSSPF of Silesia, Erich von dem Bach-Zelewski, and the head of Himmler's office, Karl Wolff: *Anklageschrift gegen Karl Wolff, YVSA,* TR-10/475, p. 114; *Jüdische Fürsorge in Ost-Oberschlesien, YVSA,* 06/16; Tenenbaum, *Race and Reich,* p. 202. Hilberg, *Destruction of the European Jews (1961),* p. 228.

61. Rudolf Höss, *Kommandant in Auschwitz: Autobiographische Aufzeichnungen,* ed. Martin Broszat (Stuttgart, 1958), pp. 88 n.1; 92 n.4.

62. Tenenbaum, *Race and Reich,* p. 202.

63. Trunk, *Judenrat*, pp. 345–47.

64. The Diary of Hans Frank, September 12, 1940; *IMT*, 29, PS-233, p. 380.

65. *EJ*, vol. 16, col. 1348; also see Trunk, *Judenrat*, p. 130.

66. Pinkas Hakehillot: Encyclopaedia of Jewish Communities, Poland, vol. 1, The communities of Lodz and Its Region, ed. Danuta Dombrowska and Abraham Wein, eds., (Yad Vashem, Jerusalem, 1976), p. 24. (English trans. of Hebrew preface and introduction.)

67. *Dokumenty Materialy*, (Warsaw, 1946), vol. 3, pp. 36–31.

68. Ibid., p. 31.

69. Letter from Dr. Marder, the German deputy mayor, to Governor Friedrich Übelhör, July 4, 1941, *Dokumenty*, pp. 77f. Mintz and Klausner, *Sefer ha-Zvaot*, pp. 66f.

70. Mintz and Klausner, *Sefer ha-Zvaot*, pp. 66f.

71. Memoranda and directives of mid-January, *Dokumenty*, pp. 52–68.

72. Ibid., pp. 74f.

73. Quoted in Philip Friedman, "The Jewish Ghetto in the Nazi Era," in A. J. Friedman, ed., *Roads to Extinction*, pp. 62, 69.

74. Werner Maser, ed., *Hitler's Letter and Notes*, comp., with commentary, by Werner Maser (New York, 1976), pp. 234, 236, Bantam Books. The text was translated from Hitler's original notes, a photocopy of which appears in the book; the original format has also been preserved.

75. Trunk, *Judenrat*, pp. 281–84; *Dokumenty*, pp. 93–101.

76. Quoted in Gutman, *The Jews of Warsaw*, p. 55.

77. Ibid., passim.

78. Trunk, *Judenrat*, p. 273.

79. Ibid., p. 285.

80. For special reports, see "The Reports of a Jewish Informer in the Warsaw Ghetto: Selected Documents," introduction by Christopher R.Browning and Israel Gutman, *YVS*, 17 (1986), pp. 247–93; for reports from the "Early Days," see ed. Joseph Kermish, *To Live with Honor and Die with Honor: Selected Documents from the Warsaw Ghetto Underground Archives "O.S." (Oneg Shabbath)* (Yad Vashem, Jerusalem, 1986), pp. 131–48.

81. *Okupacja i Ruch Oporu w dzienniku Hansa Franka 1939–1945* (Warsaw, 1979), vol. pp. 334–39.

82. Quoted in Gutman, *The Jews of Warsaw*, p. 32.

83. Report by Waldemar Schön, who planned the ghetto's construction, in Eisenbach et al., *Eksterminacja*, pp. 99–104.

84. Sonderbestimmungen für die Verwaltung und Befriedung der besetzten Gebiete Holland und Belgien, February 22, 1940, NOKW, 1515.

85. David H. Weinberg, *A Community on Trial: The Jews of Paris in the 1930s* (Chicago, 1977), pp. 3–6, 8 n. 12.

86. Richard I. Cohen, *The Burden of Conscience: French Jewish Leadership During the Holocaust* (Bloomington, Ind., 1987), pp. 16–19.

87. Hilberg, *Destruction of the European Jews (1961)*, p. 394. The statutes of the Vichy government were published in *Contemporary Jewish Record*, 4, 1941, pp. 673–75. Michael R. Marrus and Robert O. Paxton, *Vichy France and the Jews* (New York, 1981), pp. 65–71.

88. Hilberg, *Destruction of the European Jews (1961)*, p. 394.

89. *Contemporary Jewish Record*, 4 (1941), p. 675, sec. 8.

90. Gerald Reitlinger, *The Final Solution: The Attempt to Exterminate the Jews of Europe, 1939–1945,* 2 rev. ed. (London, 1968), p. 77; Marrus and Paxton, *Vichy France,* pp. 65–71.

91. Hilberg, *Destruction of the European Jews (1961)*, pp. 395f. In 1943, different and

even higher numbers were given, see Robert P. Paxton, *Vichy France, Old Guard and New Order: 1940–1944* (New York, 1972), p. 176.

92. *IMT,* 26, PS-1015(b), pp. 524ff.; Hilberg, *Destruction of the European Jews (1961),* pp. 419f.

93. *EJ.,* vol. 12, col. 342; H. Z. Hirschberg, *Toldot ha-Yehudim be-Afrika ha-tzfonit* (Jerusalem, 1963), vol. 2, pp. 319–23.

94. Joseph Ariel, "An Unknown Document About the Pogroms in Constantine," *Yalkut Moreshet,* 3 (1965), 139–51 (Hebrew).

95. On Algeria and Tunisia, see Hirschberg, *Toldot ha-Yehudim,* pp. 92f., 167f; for both countries under Italian rule, see Daniel Carpi, "The Italian Government and the Jews of Tunisia in the Second World War (June 1940–May 1943)," *Zion,* 52, no. 1 (1987), 57–106 (Hebrew, English summary).

96. Betty Garfinkels, *Les Belges facent à la persécution raciale, 1940–1944* (Brussels, 1965), pp. 15–36; Maxime Steinberg, *L'Étoile et le fusil,* vol. 2, Les cent jours de la déportation des juifs de Belgique (Brussels, 1984), p. 47 n. 43, denounces this source as one-sided and apologetic. His own description of the Jewish question and the fate of Belgium's Jews, based on minute research, reveals a multitude of unknown facts but lacks coherence.

97. H. Wielek, *De Oorlog die Hitler won* (Amsterdam, 1947), p. 14.

98. Ibid., pp. 18–21; Jacob Presser, *The Destruction of the Dutch Jews* (New York, 1969), passim; Leni Yahil, "Methods of Persecution: A Comparison of the 'Final Solution' in Holland and Denmark," *Scripta Hierosolymitana* (Jerusalem) 23 (1972), 288–90.

99. Yahil, "Methods of Persecution," 285–90.

100. Joseph Michman, "The Controversial Stand of the *Joodse Raad in the Netherlands: Lodewijk E. Visser's Struggle,"* YVS Studies, 10 (1974), pp. 9–68.

101. *Contemporary Jewish Record,* 3 (1940), pp. 175f.

102. Jacob Touri, "The Anarcho-Totalitarian Chain of Command: Or Who Was Responsible for the Deportation to Camp de Gurs (October 22/23, 1940)?" *Yalkut Moreshet,* 40 (1985), 41–66 (English summary).

103. *Eichmann Trial,* T/673, T/674; Proceedings, Session 77, pp. 26–30. See Reitlinger, *Final Solution,* pp. 77–79.

104. Bradley F. Smith and Agnes F. Petersen, eds., *Himmler: Geheimreden 1933 bis 1945 und andere Ansprachen* (Berlin, 1974), pp. 138ff.

105. *Contemporary Jewish Record,* 3, (1940), pp. 320–25.

106. Ibid., pp. 173ff. On the population concentration of the Jews, see Otto D, Kulka, "A Clarification of the SD's Jewish Policy in the First Nazi-Occupied Countries," *Yalkut Moreshet,* 18 (1974), 382 (Hebrew).

107. Declaration by Rabbi Dr. Robert Serebrenik, *Eichmann Trial,* T/648; Hilberg, *Destruction of the European Jews (1961),* p. 382. See also Ruth Zariz, "The Jews of Luxemburg During the Second World War," *Dapim, Studies on the Holocaust Period,* 6 (1988), pp. 151–68 (Hebrew).

108. Jan Steiner, *Ha-Ḥakikah neged ha-Yehudim ve-Nisholam min ha-Kalkala bi-Medinat Slovakia* (Tel Aviv, 1975), pp. 8f; also see Martin Broszat, "Das deutsch-slowakische Verhältnis und seine Rückwirkungen auf die slowakische Judenpolitik" in *Gutachten des Instituts für Zeitgeschichte* (Munich, 1958), vol. 1, pp. 221–31.

109. See Randolph L. Braham, *The Politics of Genocide: The Holocaust in Hungary* (New York, 1981), vol. 1, p. 130. On the basis of documents of the JDC, Yehuda Bauer estimates that the number of those deported to Czechoslovakia or trapped there during that period totaled several thousand, see *My Brother's Keeper,* pp. 260ff.

110. Yeshayahu Yelinek, *The Parish Republic: Hlinka's Soviet People's Party 1939–1945* (New York, 1976), passim.

111. Livia Rothkirchen, *The Destruction of Slovak Jewry: A Documentary History*, (Jerusalem, 1961) pp. xiiif. (Hebrew with English introduction).

112. *DGFP*, ser. D, 10, p. 376.

113. Steiner, *Ha-Ḥakikah neged ha-Yehudim*, passim. For the German compilation of the orders and laws, see Dr. Ludwig A. Dostal, *Der slowakische Judenkodex* (Pressburg, 1941). Dostal's introduction states, "Der Kodex fusst völlig auf rassischer Grundlage, führt den Begriff Mischling ein und sein Judenbegriff unterscheidet sich von den Nürenberger Gesetzen überhaupt nicht." For quotations of the laws, see L. Lipscher "The Jews of Slovakia: 1939–1945," in *The Jews of Czechoslovakia*, vol. 3, ed. A. Dagan et al. (Philadelphia, 1984), pp. 165–261.

114. The description is based on the introduction to *Pinkas Hakehillot: Encyclopaedia of Jewish Communities, Rumania*, vol. 1, ed. Dr. Theodor Lavi et al. (Yad Vashem, Jerusalem, 1970) (Hebrew); also see Béla Vago, "The Jewish Policy of the Royal Dictatorship of Romania (1938–1940)," *Zion*, 19 no. 1, (1964), 133–51 (Hebrew).

115. *Pinkas Hakehillot: . . . Rumania*, vol. 1.

116. Braham, *Politics of Genocide*, vol. 1, passim.

Chapter 7

1. Abraham J. Heschel, "The Eastern European Era in Jewish History," *Yivo Annual of Jewish Social Science*, 1 (1946), pp. 88, 91.

2. The official number according to the census of 1931 (the last before the war) was 3,113,993 (9.8 percent). Ezra Mendelsohn, *The Jews of East Central Europe Between the World Wars* (Bloomington, Ind., 1983), p. 23.

3. The numbers are based on Raphael Mahler, *Yehudei Polin bein shtei Milḥamot ha-Olam* (Tel Aviv, 1968), pp. 37f., 68, 79, 102f. Mendelsohn, *Jews of East Central Europe*, passim, relies on the same source. See also Celia S. Heller, *On the Edge of Destruction: Jews of Poland Between the Two World Wars* (New York, 1977).

4. Mahler, *Yehudei Polin*, p. 159.

5. This refers to workers employed in plants with less than five employees; 80 percent of Jewish workers fell into this category. Georges Castellan, "Remarks on the Social Structure of the Jewish Community in Poland Between the Two World Wars," in *Jews and Non-Jews in Eastern Europe, 1918–1945*, ed. Bela Vago and George L. Mosse (New York, 1974), p. 198.

6. Quoted from JDC files in Yehuda Bauer, *My Brother's Keeper: A History of the American Jewish Joint Distribution Committee, 1929–1939* (Philadelphia, 1974), p. 52. I shall rely extensively on this book hereafter.

7. Ibid., p. 49.

8. Ibid., p. 189; an estimated thirty thousand Jewish shops were closed between 1933 and 1938; approximately the same number of Polish shops were opened. Mendelsohn, *Jews of East Central Europe*, pp. 73–75.

9. Bauer, *My Brother's Keeper*, pp. 37, 199.

10. Ibid., quoted pp. 188f.

11. Leni Yahil, "Madagascar: Phantom of a Solution for the Jewish Question," in Vago and Mosse, *Jews and Non-Jews in Eastern Europe*, pp. 315–34.

12. Based on Szyja Bronsztejn, *Ludnosi żydowska w Polsce w okresie miedzywojennym* (Warsaw, 1963), p. 97; Bauer, *My Brother's Keeper*, pp. 191–94.

13. Jacob Maletz and Naphtali Lau, eds., *Piotrków-Trybunalski ve-ha-Svivah, Sefer Zikaron* (Tel Aviv, 1965), p. 22.

14. Reuben Maletz, "Toldot Yehudei Piotrków ve-ha-Svivah, Hemshekh u-Miluim," in *Piotrków-Trybunalski,* ed. Maletz and Lau, cols. 156, 190.

15. Ibid., col. 157.

16. Jacob Kurz, *Sefer Edut* (Tel Aviv, 1944), p. 19. This is the story of a Jew from Palestine who was staying in Poland at the outbreak of war and had first-hand experience of events there until, in the autumn of 1943, he was among the few to be saved in an exchange deal.

17. Joseph Kermish, "Der Ḥurbn," in *Piotrków-Trybunalski,* cols. 707f., 728; Kurz, *Sefer Edut,* pp. 55f. Isaiah Trunk, *Judenrat: The Jewish Councils in Eastern Europe Under Nazi Occupation* (New York, 1972), p.129, states that in July 1940, there were 3,762 refugees, who constituted 45.6 percent of the population, which thus totaled only 8,250 persons. But it is probable that the number had decreased by several hundred after September 1939. Lucy C. Dawidowicz, *The War Against the Jews, 1933–1945* (New York, 1975), p. 159, apparently also relies on a similar calculation.

18. Kermish, "Der Ḥurbn," cols. 715f. According to another version, a twelve-member council was set up on October 14 and later enlarged to twenty-four. See Naphtali Lau (Lavi), "Shivat Medurei Gehinnom," in *Piotrków-Trybunalski,* col. 784.

19. Kermish, "Der Ḥurbn," col. 718. The amount of the sums of money changes in various sources, see col. 738 n. 34.

20. Kurz, *Sefer Edut,* pp. 65, 88.

21. Kermish, "Der Ḥurbn," col. 739 n. 60.

22. Kurz, *Sefer Edut,* pp. 71–73.

23. Ibid., pp. 139, 144.

24. Ibid., pp. 81–82.

25. Kermish, "Der Ḥurbn," col. 739 n. 50.

26. Trunk, *Judenrat,* pp. 255f.

27. Aharon Weiss, "The Jewish Police in the Generalgouvernement and East Upper Silesia" (Ph.D. diss., The Hebrew University, Jerusalem, 1973), pp. 219f. (Hebrew), also see Lau, "Shivat Medurei Gehinnom, col. 789.

28. Kurz, *Sefer Edut,* p. 69.

29. For sources for the numbers, see Mahler, *Yehudei Polin,* p. 35; M. Lerman and M. Litvin, eds., *Dos Bukh fun Lublin* (Paris, 1943), p. 534, states that there were 43,000 Jews in Lublin. A German census of October 24, 1939, gives a total of 37,034 Jews—a low figure, presumably because a large percentage of the refugees who had arrived in the meantime were not included.

30. Trunk, *Judenrat,* p. 48.

31. Nachman Blumenthal, ed., *Documents from Lublin Ghetto: Judenrat Without Direction* (Yad Vashem, Jerusalem, 1967), p. 40 (Polish with Hebrew translation).

32. Ibid., pp. 35f.

33. Ibid., p. 44.

34. Judenrat report, *YVSA,* 06/3, 9–11, pp. 6f. (Polish).

35. Blumenthal, *Lublin Ghetto,* p. 107 n. 5; see also protocol 15, para. 5.

36. Ibid., for example, see protocols 18, 20, 42–49.

37. Judenrat report, *YVSA,* 06/3, 9–11, p. 7f.

38. Blumenthal, *Lublin Ghetto,* protocol 15, March 16, 1940, details forced labor regulations.

39. Ibid., protocols 38, 55, 59, 60.

40. Ibid., protocol 48.

41. For a comprehensive description of the camp's history and the fate of its inmates,

see Shmuel Krakowski, *The War of the Doomed: Jewish Armed Resistance in Poland, 1942–1944* (New York, 1984), pp. 260–64; Trunk, *Judenrat,* pp. 132f.

42. Blumenthal, *Lublin Ghetto,* p. 83.

43. Ibid., pp. 76f.

44. Testimony quoted in Krakowski, *War of the Doomed,* p. 262.

45. Trunk, *Judenrat,* pp. 145, 159.

46. Blumenthal, *Lublin Ghetto,* protocol 27.

47. Ibid., protocols 33, 36, 38–40, 42–47, 48. Altogether, the council allocated 150,000 zlotys to the workers at Bełżec.

48. Trunk, *Judenrat,* 539. On occasion, the organization was also called Selbstschutz. See Blumenthal, *Lublin Ghetto,* p. 129, protocols 48, 51; Weiss in "The Jewish Police," p. 226, assumes that the police force was established in the wake of a German directive, but there is no proof of this.

49. Yisrael Gutman, *The Jews of Warsaw 1939–1943: Ghetto, Underground, Revolt* (Bloomington, Ind., 1982), pp. 40–45. On the activities of the JDC in occupied Poland, see Yehuda Bauer, *American Jewry and the Holocaust: The American Jewish Joint Distribution Committee, 1939–1945* (Detroit, 1981), chap. 3.

50. Gutman, *The Jews of Warsaw,* pp. 40–45; Trunk, *Judenrat,* pp. 299f., 340–42.

51. Nachman Korn, "Educational Problems and the Sufferings of Children in the Ghetto," in *Encyclopedia shel Galuyot: Lublin* (Jerusalem, 1957), cols. 725f.

52. Blumenthal, *Lublin Ghetto,* pp. 190f.

53. Philip Friedman, "The Messianic Complex of a Nazi Collaborator in a Ghetto: Moses Merin of Sosnowiec," in *Roads to Extinction: Essays on the Holocaust,* ed. Ada J. Friedman (New York and Philadelphia, 1980), pp. 353–64.

54. Ibid., p. 354.

55. Ibid., p. 355.

56. Ibid., pp. 355f.

57. Trunk, *Judenrat,* p. 243.

58. *Pinkas Bendin: A Memorial to the Jewish Community of Bendin (Poland),* ed. Avraham Stein (Tel Aviv, 1959), p. 187. (Yiddish and Hebrew).

59. *Führer der Zentralen Fürsorgeabteilung in Ost-Oberschlesien,* YVSA, 06/16.

60. This account is based on Aryeh Lior, "Which Shall Not Be Forgotten, " in *Pinkas Bendin,* pp. 347–56; David Lior, "The Underground in Bendin and its Environs," pp. 356–60. P. Friedman, "Messianic Complex," pp. 360f.

61. Friedman, "Messianic Complex," pp. 356f.

62. Philip Friedman, "Pseudo-Saviours in the Polish Ghettos: Mordekhai Chaim Rumkowski of Lodz," in *Roads to Extinction,* ed. A. Friedman, pp. 335f.; Leonard Tushnet, *The Pavement of Hell* (New York, 1972), pp. 3–70. Opinions about Rumkowski are controversial to this day; see Yisrael Gutman, "The Uniqueness of Ghetto Lodz," in *The Chronicle of the Lodz Ghetto,* vol. 1 *January 1941–May 1942* (Yad Vashem, Jerusalem, 1986), pp. 58f. (Hebrew).

63. Trunk, *Judenrat,* p. 178; P. Friedman, "Pseudo-Saviours," pp. 338f.

64. Trunk, *Judenrat,* p. 78.

65. P. Friedman, "Pseudo-Saviours," pp. 343–45.

66. Trunk, *Judenrat,* p. 123. P. Friedman, "Pseudo-Saviours," According to another source, eighty thousand people were already receiving aid in April 1940: *Pinkas Hakehillot: Encyclopaedia of Jewish Communities, Poland,* vol. 1, The Communities of Lodz and Its Region, eds. Danuta Dombrowska and Abraham Wein (Yad Vashem, Jerusalem, 1976), p. 26 (English trans. of Hebrew preface and introduction).

67. Trunk, *Judenrat*, p. 359.

68. Ibid., pp. 184f., 365, 540–43.

69. The facts on the youth movement and cultural activities are derived from Dombrowska and Wein, *Pinkas Hakehillot: . . . Lodz and Its Region,* vol. 1, introduction, passim.

70. See n. 62.

71. P. Friedman, "Pseudo-Saviours," p. 335.

72. Ibid., pp. 341f.

73. Fivel Pudah, "Thoughts on the Jewish Underground in Lodz Ghetto," *Yalkut Moreshet,* 11 (1970), 66 (Hebrew).

74. P. Friedman, "Pseudo-Saviours," p. 610.

75. *The Warsaw Diary of Adam Czerniakow: Prelude to Doom,* ed. Raul Hilberg, Stanislaw Sharon, and Josef Kermisz (New York, 1979), pp. 1f.; Gutman, *The Jews of Warsaw,* p. 38; Yisrael Gutman, "Adam Czerniakow: The Man and His Diary," in *The Catastrophe of European Jewry: Antecedents, History, Reflections, Selected Papers,* ed. Yisrael Gutman and Livia Rothkirchen (Yad Vashem, Jerusalem, 1976), pp. 451–89.

76. Gutman, *The Jews of Warsaw,* p. 38.

77. *Czerniakow Diary,* September 12, 1939, p. 74.

78. *The Warsaw Diary of Chaim A. Kaplan,* ed. Abraham I. Katsh (New York, 1965), September 11, 1939, p. 29.

79. *Czerniakow Diary,* September 23, 1939, p. 76.

80. *Kaplan Diary,* September 14, 1939, p. 30. The English translation is very much shortened and does not contain some of my quotations.

81. *Czerniakow Diary,* September 29, 1939, p. 77.

82. Ibid., July 21, 1940, p. 176: "Man darf [must] das Kreuz tragen, aber nicht schleppen."

83. For details, see Gutman, *The Jews of Warsaw,* p. 37.

84. *Czerniakow Diary,* October 20, 1939, p. 84.

85. Ibid., January 26, 1940, p. 111.

86. Ibid., December 18, 1939, p. 100.

87. Jonás Turkow, *Hayoh Haytah Varshah Yehudit* (Tel Aviv, 1969). pp. 202.

88. On ŻSS and the house committees (here called building councils), see Gutman, *The Jews of Warsaw,* pp. 45f.; *Kaplan Diary,* November 29, 1940, pp. 27–29.

89. Turkow, *Hayoh Haytah,* p. 39.

90. Gutman, *The Jews of Warsaw,* pp. 103f.

91. Ibid., pp. 66–72.

92. *Czerniakow Diary,* December 6, 1941, p. 305.

93. In describing the Jewish police in Warsaw, I shall rely principally on Weiss, "The Jewish Police," which deals with the subject in depth on pp. 44–145.

94. The decision of Szeryński's appointment was taken on October 9, 1940, that is, before the ghetto's closure had been officially announced. Weiss, "The Jewish Police," p. 48; and see pp. 57f., 61. Of special interest are the memoirs of police officer Stanislaw Adler: *In the Warsaw Ghetto, 1940–1943: An Account of a Witness* (Yad Vashem, Jerusalem, 1982), "Part II: The Jewish Order Service."

95. Weiss, "The Jewish Police," p. 53.

96. On the role of the police, also see Gutman, *The Jews of Warsaw,* pp. 86–90.

97. The quotations are from Chaim A. Kaplan's *Scroll of Agony: Hebrew Diary of Ch. A. Kaplan, September 1, 1939–August 4, 1942* (Tel Aviv, 1966), January 14 and 15, 1940, pp. 141f. It would be worthwhile to issue a new and complete translation of this important document.

98. Ibid., August 15, 1940, p. 301. The quotation is from Isaiah, 26:20.

99. T. Berenstein and A. Rutkowski, "Liczba Ludności żydowskiej i obszar przez nia zamieszkiwany w Warszawie w latach okupacji hiterlowskiej," *BZIH,* 26 (1958), pp. 73–114.

100. T. Rawski, Z. Stapor, and J. Zamojski, *Wojna Wyzwoleńcza Narodu Polskiego w latach, 1939–1945: Wezlowe Problemy* (Warsaw, 1963), vol. 1, p. 130.

101. Shimon Redlich, "Jews in Anders' Army in the Soviet Union, 1941–1942," *Yalkut Moreshet,* 14 (1972), 143–54 (Hebrew); Yisrael Gutman, "Jews in General Anders' Army in the Soviet Union," *YVS Studies,* 12 (1970, pp. 231–96; Shmuel Krakowski, "The Fate of Jewish Prisoners of War in the September 1939 Campaign," *YVS Studies,* 12 (1970), pp. 297–353.

102. For a description of the conditions for emigration to Palestine during that period, see Kurz, *Sefer Edut,* pp. 68, 81f., 96, 98.

103. "Regulations for the Ban on Jewish Emigration from the Government-General, November 1940," *DOH,* pp. 219f.

Chapter 8

1. For details of the efforts to arrange emigration from Luxembourg through Lisbon with the help of the JDC, see Yehuda Bauer, *American Jewry and the Holocaust: The American Jewish Joint Distribution Committee, 1939–1945* (Detroit, 1981), pp. 53f. Also see Ruth Zariz, "The Jews of Luxemburg During the Second World War," *Dapim, Studies on the Holocaust Period,* 6, (1988), pp. 151–68 (Hebrew).

2. Leni Yahil, *The Rescue of Danish Jewry: Test of a Democracy* (Philadelphia, 1969; ppbk. ed. 1983), passim. On the *halutzim* and the Youth Aliyah in Denmark, see Jörgen Haestrup, *Passage to Palestine: Young Jews in Denmark, 1932–1945* (Odense, 1983).

3. Joseph Michman, "The Controversial Stand of the *Joodse Raad* in the Netherlands: Lodewijk E. Visser's Struggle," *YVS Studies,* 10 (1974), pp. 9–68. Most of the description herein is based on this article.

4. Ibid., p. 13.

5. See Leni Yahil, "Methods of Persecution: A Comparison of the 'Final Solution' in Holland and Denmark," *Scripta Hierosolymtana* (Jerusalem) 23 (1972), 279–300.

6. Adina Kokhava and Rina Klinov, *Ha-Mahteret ha-halutzit be-Holand ha-kvushah* (Hakibbutz Hamenhad, 1969), p. 29.

7. Ibid., p. 39.

8. On the illegal immigration in the years 1938–1939, see Dalia Ofer, *Derekh ha-Yam: Illegal Immigration During the Holocaust* (Jerusalem, 1988), pp. 26–30, 73.

9. Quoted in Yakhin Simon, *Mihtavim miimei ha-Shoah ve-ha-Mahteret* (Tel Aviv, 1963), pp. 31f.

10. Kokhava and Klinov, *Ha-Mahteret ha-halutzit,* passim.

11. Lucien Steinberg, *Le Comité de défense des Juifs en Belgique, 1942–1944* (Brussels, 1973), pp. 18f. On the more problematic side of the period, see Maxime Steinberg, *L'Étoile et le fusil,* vol. 1, *La Question juive 1940–1942* (Brussels, 1983), passim.

12. Most of the data on the French-Jewish community is derived from David H. Weinberg, *A Community on Trial: The Jews of Paris in the 1930s* (Chicago, 1977), passim.

13. See Richard I. Cohen, *The Burden of Conscience: French Jewish Leadership During the Holocaust* (Bloomington, Ind., 1987), pp. 24–26, 40–47.

14. *Pinkas Hakehillot: Encyclopaedia of Jewish Communities, Rumania,* vol. 1, ed. Theodor Lavi et al., (Yad Vashem, Jerusalem, 1970), p. 149 (Hebrew).

15. Moshe Ussoskin, *Struggle for Survival: A History of Jewish Credit Cooperatives* (Jerusalem, 1975), chap. 5, fig. p. 151.

16. Ibid., pp. 253–59.

17. Yehuda Bauer, *My Brother's Keeper: A History of the American Jewish Joint Distribution Committee, 1939–1945* (Philadelphia, 1947), p. 218.

18. The description of the events in Slovakia is based on Oskar J. Neumann, *Im Schatten des Todes* (Tel Aviv, 1956), passim; and Livia Rothkirchen's English introduction to *The Destruction of Slovak Jewry: A Documentary History* (Jerusalem, 1961), pp. vii–xviii (Hebrew).

19. Otto D. Kulka, " 'The Jewish Question' in the Third Reich as a Factor in National Socialist Ideology and Policy and the Determination of the Status and Activities of Jews" (Ph.D. diss., The Hebrew University, Jerusalem, 1975), vol. 1, pp. 239f.; vol. 2: notes, p. 229 n. 96.

20. Leo Baeck, "In Memory of Two of Our Dead," *YLB,* 1 (1956), pp. 55f.

21. Schalom Adler-Rudel, *Jüdische Selbsthilfe unter dem Naziregime, 1933–1939* (Tübingen, 1974), p. 216; Also see Bauer, *American Jewry and the Holocaust,* table 1, p. 26. On the other hand, 78,000 is the number given by Helmut Genschel, *Die Verdrängung der Juden aus der Wirtschaft im Dritten Reich* (Göttingen, 1966), p. 241.

22. *Eichmann Trial,* T/802.

23. The story is related in Aaron Zwergbaum, "From Internment in Bratislava and Detention in Mauritius to Freedom," in *The Jews of Czechoslovakia,* vol. 2 (Philadelphia, 1971), pp. 599–658.

24. Ofer, *Derekh ba-Yam,* passim.

25. Chaim A. Kaplan's *Scroll of Agony: Hebrew Diary of Ch. A. Kaplan, September 1, 1939–August 4, 1942* (Tel Aviv, 1966), February 13, 1940, p. 173. (The English translation does not have this passage.)

26. Ibid., February 12, 1940, p. 170.

Chapter 9

1. George L. Mosse, *The Nationalization of the Masses: Political Symbolism and Mass Movements in Germany from the Napoleonic War Through the Third Reich* (New York, 1975), see index.

2. Alan Clark, *Barbarossa: The Russian-German Conflict* (New York, 1965), p. 38.

3. *IMT,* 38, No-221-L, pp. 86–94; present at the meeting were Alfred Rosenberg, Hans Lammers, Field Marshal Wilhelm Keitel, and Göring.

4. Hans A. Jacobsen and Arthur L. Smith, *World War II: Policy and Strategy, Selected Documents with Commentary* (Santa Barbara, Calif., 1979), p. 105.

5. Albert Seaton, *The Russo-German War, 1941–1945* (London, 1971), p. 41 n. 31.

6. Walter Warlimont, *Im Hauptquartier der deutschen Wehrmacht, 1939–1945* (Frankfurt on the Main, 1962), p. 166 n. 34.

7. Seaton, *The Russo-German War,* p. 31.

8. Hans A. Jacobsen, *Der Zweite Weltkrieg in Chronik und Dokumenten* (Darmstadt, 1961), p. 364.

9. Raul Hilberg, *The Destruction of the European Jews* (Chicago, 1961), pp. 227–30.

10. Franz Halder, Chief of the High Command of the Army, on March 5, 1941, in his war diary: Franz Halder, *Kriegstagebuch,* ed. Hans A. Jacobsen (Stuttgart, 1963), vol. 2, p. 303.

11. Hans A. Jacobsen, "Kommissarbefehl und Massenexekutionen sowjetischer Kriegs-

gefangener," in Helmut Krausnick et al., *Anatomie des SS Staates* (Olten, Switz., 1965), vol. 2, pp. 198–201. See also *DOH*, p. 375.

12. Jacobsen, "Kommissarbefehl," pp. 202f. Directive of Field Marshal Walter von Brauchitsch (April 28, 1941), pp. 204f.

13. For the main points of the speech, see Halder, *Kriegstagebuch*, pp. 336f. See Andreas Hillgruber, "War in the East and the Extermination of the Jews," *YVS Studies*, 18 (1987), pp. 113f.

14. Alexander Dallin, *German Rule in Russia, 1941–1945: A Study of Occupation Policies* (London, 1981), p. 30 n. 2.

15. Jacobsen, "Kommissarbefehl," p. 225f., partly published in *DOH*, p. 376.

16. Warlimont, *Im Hauptquartier*, p. 182.

17. Jacobsen, "Kommissarbefehl," pp. 233f.

18. See Gerald Reitlinger, *The House Built on Sand: The Conflicts of German Policy in Russia, 1939–1945* (London, 1960), pp. 94ff.

19. Dallin, *German Rule*, p. 69.

20. *IMT*, 38, No-221-L, pp. 86–94.

21. Jacobsen, "Kommissarbefehl," pp. 244ff.

22. Hilberg, *The Destruction of the European Jews (1961)*, p. 224. Hans-Heinrich Wilhelm, "Die Einsatzgruppe A der Sicherheitspolizei und des SD 1941/42: Eine exemplarische Studie," in Helmut Krausnick and Hans-Heinrich Wilhelm, *Die Truppe des Weltanschauungskrieges: Die Einsatzgruppen der Sicherheitspolizei und des SD/1938–1942* (Stuttgart, 1981), p. 402.

23. See Reitlinger, *The House Built on Sand*, chap. 3; Alfred Streim, *Die Behandlung sowjetischer Kriegsgefangener im "Fall Barbarossa,"* (Heidelberg, 1981), passim; Christian Streit, *Keine Kamaraden, Die Wehrmacht und die sowjetischen Kriegsgefangenen 1941– 1945,"* (Stuttgart, 1978), passim.

24. Andreas Hillgruber, "Die Endlösung und das deutsche Ostimperium als Kernstück des rassenideologischen Programms des Nationalsozialismus," *VJHZ*, 20, no. 2 (1972), p. 138.

Chapter 10

1. See chap. 9, also see Helmut Krausnick, *Hitlers Einsatzgruppen:Die Truppen des Weltanschauungskrieges, 1938–1942* (Frankfurt on the Main, 1985), chap. 3.

2. Helmut Krausnick, "Denkschrift Himmlers über die Behandlung der Fremdvölkischen im Osten," *VJHZ*, 5, no. 1 (1957), p. 197.

3. See Leni Yahil, "Madagascar: Phantom of a Solution for the Jewish Question," in *Jews and Non-Jews in Eastern Europe, 1918–1945*, ed. Bela Vago and George L. Mosse (New York, 1974), pp. 315–34 ; Christopher R. Browning, *The Final Solution and the German Foreign Office: A Study of Referat D III of Abteilung Deutschland 1940–43* (New York, 1978), pp. 35–43.

4. *Eichmann Trial*, T/174.

5. *Anklageschrift gegen Karl Wolff*, *YVSA*, TR-10/475, pp. 98–100.

6. Alfred Streim, "Zum Beispiel: Die Verbrechen der Einsatzgruppen in der Sowjet Union," in *NS-Prozesse*, ed. Adalbert Rückerl (Karlsruhe, 1971), p. 70. Krausnick, Hitler's Einsatzgruppen, chap. 3.

7. *IMT*, 26, PS-710, pp. 266f; *DOH*, p. 233.

8. Leni Yahil, "'Memoirs' of Adolf Eichmann," in *YVS Studies*, 18 (1987), pp. 133– 62.

9. Wila Orbach, "The Destruction of the Jews in the Nazi-Occupied Territories of the USSR," *Soviet Jewish Affairs*, 6, no. 2 (1976), pp. 14–51. The number of Jews killed in the Ukraine, 1,533,000; Byelorussia, 375,000; Crimea, 50,000; other areas, 200,000—the total, 2,158,000.

10. See Raul Hilberg, *The Destruction of the European Jews* (Chicago, 1961), pp. 188f. On cooperation between the Einsatzgruppen and the army, see Krausnick, *Hitlers Einsatzgruppen*, passim.

11. It is difficult to arrive at an exact overall reckoning of the number of these victims.

12. *TWC*, 4, L-180, pp. 154–70; *DOH*, pp. 389–93. For a detailed description see Hans-Henrich Wilhelm, "Die Einsatzgruppe A der Sicherheitspolizei und des SD 1941/42: Eine exemplarische Studie," in Helmut Krausnick and Hans-Heinrich Wilhelm, *Die Truppe des Weltanschauungskrieges: Die Einsatzgruppen der Sicherheitspolizei und des SD 1938–1942* (Stuttgart, 1981). For Krausnick's part see n. 1 above.

13. Einsatzgruppen-Report USSR, no. 133, November 14, 1941: *TWC*, 4, NO-2825, pp. 170–74.

14. Einsatzgruppen-Report no. 106: NO-3140 and report no. 128: *TWC*, 4, NO-3157, pp. 146–54.

15. Orbach, "Destruction of the Jews," p. 16.

16. Einsatzgruppen-Report no. 135: *TWC*, 4, NO-2832, p. 181.

17. *NCA*, 5, PS-3257, pp. 994–97. Also see part of this report in *DOH*, pp. 417–19.

18. *IMT*, 35, pp. 84–86. On this order and that of Manstein (see pp. 475, 504ff.), see Yehuda L. Wallach, "Feldmarschall Erich von Manstein und die deutsche Judenausrottung in Russland," in *Jahrbuch des Instituts für deutsche Geschichte* (Tel Aviv, 1975), vol. 4, pp. 457–72.

19. Wallach, "Feldmarschall Erich von Manstein . . ."; Gerald Reitlinger, *The Final Solution: The Attempt to Exterminate the Jews of Europe, 1939–1945*, 2d rev. ed. (London, 1968), pp. 210–12.

20. Dov Levin, "The Attitude of the Soviet Union to the Rescue of Jews," in *Rescue Attempts During the Holocaust: Proceedings of the Second Yad Vashem International Historical Conference*, ed. Yisrael Gutman and Efraim Zuroff (Jerusalem, 1977), pp. 225–36; see especially pp. 234f.

21. Einsatzgruppen-Report no. 133: *TWC*, 4, NO-2825, pp. 170–74; Orbach, Table 2 summarizes data on forty-two ghettos, giving dates of their establishment and liquidation as well as the number of inhabitants.

22. *IMT*, 27, PS-1138, pp. 18–25; *DOH*, pp. 378–83.

23. NOKW-1586.

24. Quotation from *Aufbau*, August 23, 1946, in Hilberg, *Destruction of the European Jews (1961)*, p. 219.

25. See details on the gas vans in Ino Arndt and Wolfgang Scheffler, "Organisierter Massenmord an Juden in nationalsozialistischen Vernichtungslagern," *VJHZ*, 24, no. 2 (1976), pp. 105–35. See *DOH*, pp. 419f.

26. Streim, "Zum Beispiel," pp. 75–77. Also see Christopher R. Browning, "The Final Solution in Serbia: The Semlin Judenlager—A Case Study," *YVS Studies*, 15 (1983), pp. 55–90, which deals with the use of gas wagons.

27. Philip Friedman, "The Destruction of the Jews of Lwów, 1941–1944," in *Roads to Extinction: Essays on the Holocaust*, ed. Ada J. Friedman (Philadelphia, 1980), p. 245. According to a report by the JDC, there were three hundred thousand refugees in Lwów in 1939 in *Jewish Daily Forward*, November 23, 1940.

28. Testimony of Erwin Schulz, *TWC*, 4, NO-3644, pp. 135–38; quoted in P. Friedman, "Jews of Lwów, p. 246.

29. See P. Friedman, *Jews of Lwów*, pp. 247f.

30. Ibid., pp. 251f.; see *EJ*, 10, col. 1171; *Pinkas Hakehillot: Encyclopaedia of Jewish Communities, Poland, vol 2: Eastern Galicia*, ed. Danuta Dombrowska, Abraham Wein, and Aharon Weiss (Yad Vashem, Jerusalem, 1980), p. 484.

31. Otto Bräutigam, *Überblick über die besetzten Ostgebiete während des 2. Weltkrieges* (Tübingen, 1954), p. 13.

32. Fifty-two protocols of the activities of the Judenrat and hundreds of its announcements to the public are at our disposal in Nachman Blumenthal, *Conduct and Actions of a Judenrat: Documents from the Bialystok Ghetto* (Jerusalem, 1962) (Hebrew and Yiddish. English introduction, pp. vii–L); protocols nos. 1 and 2, pp. 2–8.

33. Ibid., announcement no. 44, p. 302.

34. Ibid., pp. 70, 76.

35. Ibid., pp. 34, 36, 64.

36. Ibid., p. 66.

37. Ibid., pp. 138f.

38. Ibid., p. 148 and n. 9, (emphasis added).

39. *DOH*, pp. 265f.

40. See Shmuel Spector, *The Holocaust of Volhynian Jews, 1941–1944* (Jerusalem, 1986), pp. 28–41, 50. The book deals with the district in general (Hebrew, English translation in preparation).

41. Ibid., pp. 45–50.

42. *Sefer Rovno*, ed. Arieh Avtihai (Tel Aviv, 1957), p. 522.

43. Einsatzgruppen-Report no. 143 of Commando 5 of Einsatzgruppe C, December 8, 1941; *TWC*, 4, NO-2827, pp. 183–85.

44. Spector, *Holocaust of Volhynian Jews*, pp. 97–99, gives the figure of 18,000 to 21,000 killed in that *Aktion*.

45. Quoted, without mentioning the source, in *Sefer Rovno*, p. 513.

46. *Sefer Koritz*, ed. Eliesar Launo (Tel Aviv, 1959), p. 369.

47. Ibid., p. 372; Spector, *Holocaust of Volhynian Jews*, Table 8 p. 67.

48. Spector, *Holocaust of Volhynian Jews*, p. 146; *Sefer Koritz*, pp. 388f.

49. *Sefer Koritz*, p. 390.

50. Ibid., pp. 345f.

51. Ibid., pp. 401–3, (translation from Yiddish).

52. Ibid., p. 365, reported by the physician Dr. Jakob Wallaḥ.

53. Ibid., p. 362.

54. Ibid., pp. 351f.

55. Orbach's "Destruction of the Jews," passim, serves as the main source for details. On Byelorussia, see Shalom Cholawski, *Al Naharot ha-Neiman, ha-Neiman ve-ha-Dneipr: Yahadut Bierlorussia, ha-Ma'arakhot be-Milḥemet ha-Olam ha-Shniyah* (Jerusalem, 1982); idem, *In the Eye of the Hurricane: The Jews in Eastern Belorussia During World War II*, (Tel Aviv, 1988).

56. Einsatzgruppen-Report no. 124, October 25, 1941, NO-3160; Henri Monneray, *La Persécution des juifs dans les pays de l'Est* (Paris, 1949), pp. 299–301.

57. Streim, *Zum Beispiel*, pp. 73f.; YVSA, card index, O-53/29,3, no. 127, 797–802, 804a; Hilberg, *Destruction of the European Jews (1961)*, pp. 197, 199, 238 n. 61; *Quotes in DOH*, p. 416 (also see pp. 430–32) and card index 53/3, no. 800.

58. On the activities of the Agro-Joint, see Yehuda Bauer, *My Brother's Keeper: History of the American Jewish Joint Distribution Committee, 1929–1930* (Philadelphia, 1974), pp. 57–104.

59. On the history of the Karaites and their fate, see W. P. Green, "The Nazi Racial

Policy Towards the Karaites" (M.A. thesis, University of Wisconsin); Philip Friedman, "The Karaites Under Nazi Rule," in A.J. Friedman, *Roads to Extinction,* pp. 153–70.

60. For reports on Kerch and Simferopol, see YVSA, card index, 0-53/F24, 202–3, 605–9; see also Hilberg, *Destruction of the European Jews (1961),* p. 199.

61. Binyamin West, *Be-Ḥevlei Kliyah: Yehudei Russia ha-Sovietit be-Shoah ha-Natzit* (Tel Aviv, 1963), p. 139.

62. Einsatzgruppen-Report no. 150, January 2, 1942: *TWC,* 4, NO-2834, pp. 185f.

63. Einsatzgruppen-Report of February 1–April 15, 1942, NOKW-628. On January 31, 1942, it was stated that a total of some 85,201 Crimean citizens had been murdered by the Einsatzgruppen, see NOKW-3401. Otto Ohlendorf, in his testimony at Nuremberg, gave an estimate of 90,000. *TWC,* 4, pp. 414–16.

64. Testimony of seven survivors of Vislovodsk recorded by the Soviets on June 5, 1943. Published in West, *Be-Ḥevlei Kliyah,* pp. 270–72; *DOH,* pp. 428f.

65. See diagram in Hilberg, *Destruction of the European Jews (1961),* p. 235.

66. Ibid., pp. 239f.

67. *IMT,* 32, PS-3666, p. 437; *NCA,* 6, p. 402; also see the correspondence in *DOH,* pp. 394f. On the course of events see Yitzhak Arad, "The 'Final Solution' in Lithuania in the Light of German Documentation," *YVS Studies,* 11 (1976), pp. 234–72.

68. Arad "Final Solution in Lithuania," p. 190.

69. Yitzhak Arad, *Ghetto in Flames: The Struggle and Destruction of the Jews in Vilna in the Holocaust* (Jerusalem, 1980), pp. 31f.

70. Ibid., pp. 58–64.

71. Ibid., pp. 115f. Philip Friedman, "Jacob Gens, 'Commandant' of the Vilna Ghetto," in A.J. Friedman *Roads to Extinction,* pp. 365–80. His figures are 21,000 killed in September 1941 and 27,000 more up to December 21, see p. 365.

72. The principal details are from Leonard Tushnet, *The Pavement of Hell* (New York, 1972), pp. 150–55.

73. P. Friedman, "Jacob Gens," pp. 366f.

74. Arad, *Ghetto in Flames,* pp. 161–63.

75. Rosa Korczak, *Lehavot be-Efer* (Tel Aviv, 1961), p. 59. Reizl Korchak (Ruz'ka), *Flames in Ash,* 3d augmented ed. (Merḥavia, 1988), p. 57 (Hebrew).

76. The Mother Superior was Anna Borkorska. The young Jews whom she sheltered called her "Mother." In Warsaw in 1984, she was awarded the title of Righteous Gentile by Abba Kovner, on behalf of Yad Vashem. See Abba Kovner's speach at the occasion addressing her with the Hebrew "Ima"- also see "Arieh Vilner's letter to the Mother Superior of the Dominican Convent," *Yalkut Moreshet,* 38 (1985), 7–12 (Hebrew translations from Polish).

77. Korczak, *Lehavot be-Efer,* pp. 51f; new ed. p. 49.

78. Quoted in Zvie A. Brown and Dov Levin, *The Story of an Underground: The Resistance of the Jews of Kovno (Lithuania) in the Second World War* (Jerusalem, 1962), pp. 25–29 (Hebrew; English introduction); quote from *IMT,* 37, L-180, p. 682.

79. Leib Garfunkel, *Kovno ha-Yehudit be-Ḥurbana* (Jerusalem, 1959), pp. 33f.

80. Ibid, pp. 47f; for quote see *DOH,* pp. 384–386.

81. Garfunkel, *Kovno ha-Yehudit,* pp. 56f, states that only the two hundred "missing" Jews were rounded up, and 534 altogether. According to a German report, 1,811 men and women were murdered that day August 18, 1941; see Table 5 on p. 283.

82. Ibid., p. 62.

83. Ibid., p. 72. Lucy S. Dawidowicz, *The War Against the Jews, 1933–1945* (New York, 1975), pp. 282–85; and chap. 19, "Rescue from the Abyss."

84. *YVSA,* 0-18/245; *DOH,* pp. 319–21; see especially material on Vilna in excerpt from Jäger's report pp. 398–400.

85. Eliezer Yerushalmi, *Pinkas Shavli: A Diary from a Lithuanian Ghetto (1941–1944)* (Jerusalem, 1958) (Hebrew).

86. Ibid., p. 33.

87. Ibid., app. 5 (1), p. 407.

88. Ibid., Gewecke's letter of September 10, app. 5 (4), pp. 410f.

89. Ibid., p. 47.

90. *DOH,* pp. 450f.

Chapter 11

1. Gerhard Botz in *Wohnungspolitik und Judendeportation* (Salzburn, 1975), p. 62, erroneously dates the law to 1938. It was published in *RGBL* (1939), p. 864. See also Raul Hilberg, *The Destruction of the European Jews* (Chicago, 1961), p. 116.

2. Botz, *Wohnungspolitik,* pp. 17, 55, and passim.

3. *IMT,* 39, 172-USSR, pp. 425–29.

4. Ibid., 29, PS-1950, pp. 175–77; Botz *Wohnungspolitik,* pp. 108f.

5. Botz, *Wohnungspolitik,* pp. 112, 199f.

6. Uwe D. Adam, *Judenpolitik im Dritten Reich* (Düsseldorf, 1972), pp. 285–91; Hilberg, *Destruction of the European Jews (1961),* pp. 98–100.

7. Hans Mommsen, "Aufgabenkreis und Verantwortlichkeit des Staatsekretärs der Reichskanzlei Dr. W. Kritzinger," in *Gutachten des Instituts für Zeitgeschichte* (Stuttgart, 1966), vol. 2, pp. 369–98; Adam, *Judenpolitik.,* pp. 294–296.

8. Adam, *Judenpolitik,* p. 296. In the ordinance of March 26, 1941, Himmler relied on the law of July 14, 1933 *(RGBL* [1933], pp. 479f.), which provided for "the confiscation of the property of the enemies of the people and the state" (see chap. 3).

9. Adam, *Judenpolitik,* pp. 299f.

10. *RGBL* (1941), p. 722; Wolgang Scheffler, *Judenverfolgung im Dritten Reich 1933 bis 1945* (Frankfurt on the Main, 1964), p. 60.

11. Adam, *Judenpolitik,* p. 301; Mommsen, "Aufgabenkreis und Verantwortlichkeit," pp. 387f.

12. Bernard Lösener, "Als Rassereferent im Reichsministerium des Innern," *VJHZ,* 9, no. 3 (1961), pp. 302f.

13. Hans G. Adler in *Der verwaltete Mensch: Studien zur Deportation der Juden aus Deutschland* (Tübingen, 1974), pp. 152f., indicates that another meeting took place on March 20, 1941. According to Adler the same problems were dealt with there. He quotes minutes that are partly identical with those of the meeting in August. The important talks between Goebbels and Hitler are discussed by many researchers. The unpublished fragments of Goebbel's diaries, vol. 1, August 1941, pp. 225f., 237f., 240, provide the basis for data on the talks and are quoted by Jochen Thiess, *Architekt der Weltherrschaft: die "Endziele" Hitlers* (Düsseldorf, 1976), p. 172 nn. 45–48; Gerald Reitlinger, *The Final Solution: The Attempt to Exterminate the Jews of Europe, 1939–1945,* 2nd rev. ed. (London, 1968), pp. 86f.; Adam, *Judenpolitik,* pp. 308, 335; Martin Broszat, "Hitler und die Genesis der Endlösung: Aus Anlass der Thesen von David Irving," *VJHZ,* 25, no. (1977), p. 755 (English translation in *YVS Studies,* 13 (1979), pp. 88f.). Also see Kurt Pätzold, ed. *Verfolgang, Vertreibung, Vernichtung: Dokumente des faschistischen Antisemitismus 1933–1945* (Frankfurt on the Main, 1984), pp. 278, 288f., passim. Also see Eberhard Jäckel,

Hitlers Herrschaft: Vollzug einer Weltanschauung (Stuttgart, 1986), pp. 114f. (This is an augmented version of the author's *Hitler in History* (Hanover, N.H., and London, 1984.)

14. *RHBL* (1941), p. 547.

15. *Eichmann Trial*, T/679; quoted in B. A. Sijes, *Studies over Jodenvervolging* (Assen, Neth., 1974), p. 59.

16. Adam, *Judenpolitik,* p. 306; Helmut Krausnick, "Judenverfolgung," in *Anatomie des SS-Staats,* ed. Hans Buchheim et al. (Olten, Switz., 1965), vol. 2, p. 371. For the text of the RSHA directive of May 20, 1941, see Plätzold, *Verfolgung,Vertreibung, Vernichtung,* pp. 288f.

17. *Eichmann Trial,* T/683; Leni Yahil, *The Rescue of Danish Jewry: Test of a Democracy* (Philadelphia, 1983), p. 199; Pätzold, *Verfolgung, Vertreibung, Vernichtung,* p. 306; Jäckel, *Hitlers Herrschaft,* p. 115.

18. Adler in *Verwaltete Mensch,* pp. 176f., dates the decision between September 15 and 18, whereas Jäckel in *Hitlers Herrschaft,* pp. 176f., concludes that the decision was taken between September 22 and 24. I tend to accept Adler's version in view of Himmler's letter to Artur Greiser of September 18 (see n. 21 below). The meetings to which Jäckel refers may already have dealt with the implentation of the decision. It is also noteworthy that Himmler's directive of August 23 came after he had witnessed an *Aktion* by the Einsatzgruppen in Minsk on August 15, see Jäckel, *Hitlers Herrschaft,* pp. 107, 113. For a comprehensive analysis of the whole process, see Christopher R. Browning, *Fateful Months: Essays on the Emergence of the Final Solution, 1941–1942* (New York, 1985), chap. 1.

19. Adler, *Verwaltete Mensch,* p. 173; Adam, *Judenpolitik,* p. 309.

20. Report of the commander of the German police in Łódź, November 13, 1941, in *Faschismus—Ghetto—Massenmord,* ed. das Jüdische historisches Institut Warschau (Berlin, 1961), pp. 253ff.

21. A sharp exchange of letters dealing with the issue developed between Artur Greiser and Friedrich Übelhör, on the one hand, and Himmler and Heydrich on the other. See Adler, *Verwaltete Mensch,* p. 174.

22. Ibid., pp. 148f.; *Eichmann Trial,* T/810.

23. See n. 18.

24. For the order banning emigration, see *Eichmann Trial,* T/394, published in *DOH,* pp. 153f.

25. *Eichmann Trial,* T/720; this deportation order was discussed in Session 43, May 17, 1961. Though Kurt Daluege's order was published on October 24, 1941, Himmler's command fixing the date of the deportations was issued on October 31; the difference is due to the fact that the schedule had to be worked out with the railway administration. Eichmann explained the way Himmler's commands were communicated, "Major commands of Himmler were transferred by circular letter to the attached stations . . . on that ground the commanders of State police stations could delegate additional authorization for their execution," Session 78, June 23, 1961. On Daluege, see Adler, *Verwaltete Mensch,* pp. xxix, 451.

26. This process is described in the diary of Dr. Willy Cohn, *Als Jude in Breslau 1941,* ed. Joseph Walk (Ramat Gan, 1975), passim.

27. Rahel Behrend, *Verfemt und Verfolgt: Erlebnisse einer Jüdin in Nazi-Deutschland, 1933–1944* (Zurich, 1945), p. 117; also see *DOH,* pp. 150–53.

28. Yitzhak Shwersentz, *Mahteret Halutzim be-Germania ha-Natzit* (Tel Aviv, 1969), p. 36.

29. Ibid., pp. 37, 204 n. 50.

30. Ibid., p. 41; also see Chaim Schatzker, "The Jewish Youth Movement in Germany

in the Holocaust Period (I): Youth in Confrontation with a New Reality," *YLB,* 32 (1987), pp. 157–81.

31. Anneliese-Ora Borinski, *Erinnerungen* (Kvutzat Maayan-Zwi, 1970), pp. 17–21.

32. On Selbiger and his murder by the Gestapo, see Borinski, *Erinnerungen,* pp. 7–13.

33. Schwersentz, *Mahteret Halutzim,* p. 68.

34. Ibid, p. 89.

35. Behrend, *Verfemt und Verfolgt,* pp. 101–12.

36. Borinski, *Erinnerungen,* pp. 23f.

37. On Heydrich's appointment by Hitler, see Jäckel, *Hitlers Herrschaft,* p. 116.

38. Detlef Brandes, *Die Tschechen unter deutschem Protektorat* (Munich 1969), vol. 1, p. 208.

39. Ibid., pp. 41, 212.

40. Gerhard Jacoby, *Racial State: The German Nationalities Policy in the Protectorate of Bohemia-Moravia* (New York, 1944), pp. 226–32; Brandes, *Die Tschechen,* pp. 238f., and see the German discussion, pp. 124–37.

41. Jacoby, *Racial State,* pp. 86–88, 119f., 140f., 228, 236.

42. Hans G. Adler, *Theresienstadt, 1941–1945: Das Antlitz einer Zwangsgemeinschaft* (Tübingen, 1966), p. 21.

43. Philip Friedman, "Communal Crisis in Germany, Austria, Czechoslovakia," in *Roads to Extinction: Essays on the Holocaust,* ed. Ada J. Friedman (Philadelphia, 1980), p. 111.

44. The minutes of the meeting are found in *Eichmann Trial,* T/299. The quotations related to this issue are from this source.

45. The press conference was held as planned. See Livia Rothkirchen, "The Zionist Character of the 'Selfgovernment' of Terezin (Theresienstadt): A Study in Historiography," *YVS Studies,* 11, 1976, p. 57; for a general survey, see idem, "The Jews of Bohemia and Moravia:1938–1945," in *The Jews of Czechoslovakia,* ed. Avigdor Dagan et al. (Philadelphia, 1984), vol. 2, pp. 3–74.

46. On the development of the Theresienstadt ghetto and the role of Jacob Edelstein, see Ruth Bondy, *Elder of the Jews: Jacob Edelstein of Theresienstadt* (New York, 1989).

47. See Dov Levin, "The Jews of Latvia Wavering Between Reservations and Accomodations to the Soviet Rule," in *Behinot Studies: Jews in the USSR and Eastern Europe,* 5 (1974), 70–96.

48. Max Kaufmann, *Churbn Lettland: Die Vernichtung der Juden Lettlands* (Munich, 1947), pp. 67–71.

49. Avraham Itai and Mordekhai Neustadt, *The History of a Movement: NEZAH in Lettland* (Tel Aviv, 1972), p. 192 (Hebrew; NEZAH stands for *N*oar *Z*iyoni *H*alutzi).

50. Hilberg, *Destruction of the European Jews (1961),* p. 193; Kaufmann, *Churbn Lettland,* p. 102.

51. Kaufmann, *Churbn Lettland,* pp. 111–16, 122f.

52. Quoted in Adler, *Verwaltete Mensch,* p. 184.

53. Kube's story is well known, see Hilberg, *Destruction of the European Jews (1961),* pp. 232f.; Wilhelm Kube to Hinrich Lohse *DOH,* pp. 408f. (See chap. 10.)

54. Kaufmann, *Churbn Lettland,* pp. 231f.

55. Josef Katz *One Who Came Back: The Diary of a Jewish Survivor* (New York, 1973), pp. 17–29; he describes the transport from Hamburg.

56. From the early days of the occupation, two places were notorious for the atrocities perpetrated: the forests of Bikerni and Jugla, both situated near the White Lake. See Kaufmann, *Churbn Lettland,* pp. 221f. Adler, *Verwaltete Mensch,* p. 185.

57. *TWC,* 13, NG-4905, pp. 181–84; quoted in Adler, *Verwaltete Mensch,* p. 506.
58. NG-5789; quoted in Adler, *Verwaltete Mensch,* p. 532.
59. Quoted in Adler, *Verwaltete Mensch,* p. 509.
60. Quoted ibid, pp. 529f.
61. Quoted ibid., p. 536.
62. Ibid., p. 567; during his trial, Eichmann explained that this was a "trick"; see Session 79, June 26, 1961.

Chapter 12

1. "Der völkische Gedanke und die Partei, Denkschrift Hitlers," in *Ausgewählte Dokumente zur Geschichte des Nationalsozialismus 1933–1935,* ed Hans A. Jacobsen and Werner Jochmann (Bielefeld, W. Ger., 1966), vol. 1, doc. 1922.
2. For a summary and analysis of these anti-Semitic theories, see Uriel Tal, *Religious and Anti-religious Roots of Modern Anti-Semitism,* Leo Baeck Memorial Lecture, 14, New York, 1971.
3. R. Deisz, *Das Recht der Rasse: Kommentar zur Rassengesetzgebung* (Munich, 1938), p. 13.
4. Zvi Bachrach, *Racism: The Tools of Politics: From Marxism Towards Nazism* (Jerusalem, 1985), pp. 61ff. (Hebrew).
5. See Klaus Dörner, "Nationalsozialsmus und Lebensvernichtung," *VJHZ,* 15, no. 2 (1967), pp. 121–152. Also se Leni Yahil, "Euthanasia contra Racial Extermination: The Moral Aspect," *Remembering for the Future: The Impact of the Holocoust and Genocide on Jews and Christians* (Oxford, 1989), vol. 3, pp. 495–504.
6. Karl Binding and Alfred E. Hoche, *Die Freigabe der Vernichtung lebensunwerten Lebens: Ihr Mass und ihre Form* (Leipzig, 1922), pp. 28f; Dr. Hoche's definitions are on pp. 49–54.
7. Deisz, *Das Recht der Rasse,* passim. The book contains laws, executive legislation, explanations, and specimen questionnaires and permits.
8. Quoted in Dörner, "Nationalsozialismus," pp. 130f.
9. For example, Dr. Fritz Reuter, *Aufartung durch Ausmerzung: Sterilisation und Kastration im Kampf gegen Erbkrankheiten* (Berlin, 1936).
10. Alexander Mitscherlich and Fred Mielke, *Medizin ohne Menschlichkeit: Dokumente des Nürnberger Ärzteprozesses* (Frankfurt on the Main, 1960), pp. 184, 189, 204, 286 n. 4; idem, *Doctors of Infamy: The Story of the Nazi Medical Crimes* (New York, 1969) passim.
11. The name, Adolph Hitler, formed the only letterhead—this was a private order. *IMT,* 26, PS-630, p. 169. Since Hitler's chancellery was housed in the former home of the painter Max Liebermann in one of Berlin's prestigious streets (no. 4 Tiergartenstrasse) the operation was codenamed T-4.
12. From the literature on "euthanasia," Ernst Klee, *"Euthanasie" im NS-Staat: Die "Vernichtung lebensunwerten Lebens"* (Frankfurt on the Main, 1983); idem, *Documente zur "Euthanasie"* (Frankfurt on the Main, 1985); Willy Dressen, "Euthanasie," in *Nationalsozialistische Massentötung durch Giftgas,* ed. Eugen Kogon et al. (Frankfurt on the Main, 1983); Robert Jay Lifton, *The Nazi Doctors: Medical Killing and the Psychology of Genocide* (New York, 1986), pt. 1. Robert N. Proctor, *Racial Hygiene: Medicine Under the Nazis* (Cambridge, Mass., 1988).
13. Mitscherlich and Mielke, *Medizin ohne Menschlichkeit,* pp. 199f.
14. Hans G. Adler, *Der verwaltete Mensch: Studien zur Deportation der Juden aus Deutschland* (Tübingen, 1974), p. 239; also see Eberhard Jäckel, *Hitlers Herrschaft: Voll-*

zug einer Weltanschauung (Stuttgart, 1986), p. 115. Thus the order was given close to the decision to start exterminating the Reich's Jews in the East (see chap. 11).

15. Adler, ibid., pp. 240–45 (should read Cholm).

16. Report by Dr. M. Plaut, head of the Jewish community in Hamburg, 1939–1941. *Eichmann Trial,* T/655, Session 93, July 12, 1961; T/447, T/476, T/1420–1422. "Cholm" (Chelm) was a central railway station in the Lublin district. Eichmann, at his trial, revealed that in 1942–1943 transports earmarked for Sobibor and Majdanek were sent to this station.

17. On the fate of the patients and unanswered queries concerning their welfare, see NO-1141–1143; NO-1310.

18. Adler, *Verwaltete Mensch,* p. 247.

19. Benno Müller-Hill, *Tödliche Wissenschaft: Die Aussonderung von Juden, Zigeunern und Geisteskranken, 1933–1945* (Reinbek bei Hamburg, 1984), pp. 67ff; English edition: *Murderous Science: Elimination by Scientific Selection of Jews, Gypsies, and Others, Germany 1933–1945* (Oxford, 1988). For bigger numbers of the victims, see Fredric Wertham "The Geranium in the Window: The 'Euthanasia' Murders"in *Death, Dying, and Euthanasia,* ed. Dennis J. Horan and David Mall (Washington, D.C. 1980), p. 607.

20. *TWC,* NO-365, vol. 1 pp 870f.; NO-996.

21. Shmuel Spektor, "Tötungen in Gaswagen hinter der Front," in Kogon, *Nationalsozialistische Massentötungen,* pp. 81–109.

22. Various dates have been given for the first experiment using gas at Auschwitz, but there is no doubt that it took place in September 1941. See Rudolf Höss, *Kommandant in Auschwitz: Autobiographische Aufzeichmungen,* ed. Martin Broszat (Stuttgart, 1958), pp. 122f., 155ff. For Himmler's order to Höss, also see Rudolf Höss, *Commandant of Auschwitz: The Autobiography of Rudolf Höss* (London, 1961), pp. 206–08; quoted in *DOH,* pp. 350–53.

23. Raul Hilberg, *The Destruction of the European Jews* (Chicago, 1961), p. 562.

24. Höss expressed himself unequivocally on this matter: "Zugleich und neben diesen beweglichen Tötungskommandos [Einsatzgruppen] wurde die Judenvernichtung in festen Lagern betrieben," *IMT,* 11, p. 440.

25. Höss, *Kommandant in Auschwitz,* p. 154.

26. *TWC,* 13, PS-709, pp. 192f. Also see Robert M. W. Kempner, *Eichmann und Komplizen* (Zurich, 1961), pp. 126–32.

27. *TWC,* 13, NG F (6)-2586, pp. 198f. Christopher R. Browning, *The Final Solution and the German Foreign Office: A Study of Referat DIII of Abteilung Deutschland* (New York, 1978), p. 77.

28. NG-2586 (G). The minutes of the meeting have been reproduced in many publications. *DOH,* pp. 249–61; Kempner, *Eichmann und Komplizen,* pp. 133–47.

29. See Josef Ackermann, *Heinrich Himmler als Ideologe* (Göttingen, 1970), passim.

30. Quoted in Hilberg, ed., *Documents of Destruction: Germany and Jewry, 1933–1945* (Chicago, 1971), pp. 99–106.

31. Theresienstadt, order of the day, January 19, 1942, signed in the name of the Ältestenrat: *Eichmann Trial,* T/846.

32. Leni Yahil, *The Rescue of Danish Jewry: Test of a Democracy* (Philadelphia, ppbk. ed., 1983), pp. 54–58.

33. Hilberg, *Documents of Destruction,* pp. 102f.

34. Ibid.

35. *IMT,* 4, pp. 356–60. On the presentation of Wisliceny's testimony to Eichmann and the latter's reaction, see *Eichmann Trial, Police Interrogations,* Dept. 06, vol. 1, col. 465–521.

36. *Eichmann Trial,* T/1461; quote from defendant Robert Servatius, Session 78; *TWC,* 5 NO-500, p. 365.

37. For Himmler's economic aspirations and the use of Jewish labor see chap. 15, 16.

38. See Hilberg, *Destruction of the European Jews* (1961), pp. 556–60.

39. Eberhard Jäckel, *Hitler in History* (Hanover, N.H., and London, 1984), pp. 81–87.

40. Speech to the Reichstag, December 11, 1941, special ed.; also see Max Domarus, *Hitler: Reden und Proklamationen 1932–1945* (Neustadt, W.Ger., 1963), vol. 2, pp. 1794–1811.

41. Domarus, *Hitler,* pp. 1,794f.

42. Ibid., p. 1,805.

43. Adolf Hitler, *Rede zum 9. Jahrestag der Machtübernahme, 30.1.1942* (Berlin, 1942).

44. Ibid., pp. 33f. On other occasions, Hitler claimed that he had made his "first prophecy" speech (of January 30, 1939) on September 1, 1939. This was not an error: his intention was to link the extermination of the Jews directly to the war.

45. *Eichmann Trial,* T/730, undated; T/1102.

46. These directives were sent to numerous locations and gave the exact destination of the transport, for example, Pawniki bei Lublin; Izbice bei Lublin; T/644, T/713, T/717, T/737.

47. Report by Theodor Dannecker in France on the proposed deportation of five thousand Jews. *IMT,* 38, AF-1216, pp. 745f.; also see Kempner, *Eichmann und Komplizen,* pp. 182f.

48. Report of the meeting written by a policeman from Düsseldorf by the name of Sticker, May 9, 1945. *Eichmann Trial,* T/734. On account *W,* see chap. 11 and n. 62 there.

49. *Trial,* T/99; *IMT,* 37, L-185, pp. 1–24: "Verteilung der Ämter des Reichssicherheitshauptamtes vom 1. März 1941—Amt IV—Gegner-Erforschung und Bekämpfung. Amtschef SS-Brigadeführer, General-Major der Polizei Müller."

Chapter 13

1. Erich Höppner, stationed at Poznań District Headquarters, to Eichmann, July 16, 1941; quoted in Hans G. Adler, *Der verwaltete Mensch: Studien zur Deportation der Juden aus Deutschland* (Tübingen, 1974), pp. 119f.

2. From a description by Michael Bodhalevnik in *Sefer Kolo,* ed. Mordekhai Halter (Tel Aviv, 1958), pp. 284–88 (Jiddish). Bodhalevnik also testified at the trial of one of the van drivers (Laabs), that took place in Bonn, West Germany, in 1962–1963 *Anklageschrift und Urteil: Chelmno,* YVSA, Tr-10/174 (henceforth; *Chelmno Trial).*

3. Halter, *Sefer Kolo,* p. 287; *Eichmann Trial, Testimonies* (Jerusalem, 1963), vol. 2, p. 1068 (Hebrew).

4. *Pinkas Hakehillot: Encyclopaedia of Jewish Communities, Poland,* vol. 1, The Communities of Lodz and Its Regions, ed. Danuta Dombrowska and Abraham Wein (Yad Vashem, Jerusalem, 1976), entry on Kolo; p. 232. (Hebrew preface and introduction translated into English.)

5. Ibid., entry on Kutno, p. 229.

6. Ibid., p. 37.

7. Léon Poliakov and Josef Wulf, *Das Dritte Reich und die Juden: Dokumente und Aufsätze* (Berlin, 1955), p. 197; NO-246.

8. Isaiah Trunk, *Judenrat: The Jewish Councils in Easter Europe Under Nazi Occupation* (New York, 1972), pp. 107, 315.

9. The numbers cited are from *Chelmno Trial,* pp. 113, 117f.

10. Ibid., p. 99; when asked at the trial about his reactions, Laabs said, "One gets used to it after a while. It's like crushing a beetle." Later on, however, he observed: "If people had only known then what would happen now [meaning the trial]." Ibid., pp. 129, 131.

11. Philip Friedman, "The Destruction of the Jews of Lwów 1941–1944," in: *Roads to Extinction: Essays on the Holocaust,* ed. Ada J. Friedman (Philadelphia, 1980), pp. 249f.; *Pinkas Hakehillot: Encyclopaedia of Jewish Communities, Poland,* vol. 2, *Eastern Galicia,* ed. Danuta Dombrowska, Abraham Wein, and Aharon Weiss (Yad Vashem, Jerusalem, 1980), entry on Lvov.

12. P. Friedman, "Destruction of the Jews of Lwów,"

13. Stefan Szende, *Der letzte Jude aus Polen* (Zurich, 1945), p. 186.

14. Aharon Weiss, "The Jewish Police in the Generalgouvernement and East Upper Silesia During the Holocaust" (Ph.D. diss., The Hebrew University, Jerusalem, 1973), p. 242 (Hebrew).

15. Report by Fritz Katzmann to the HPSSF Friedrich-Wilhelm Krüger, June 13, 1943; *IMT,* 37, L-18, pp. 391–431. In the report Katzmann also boasted that as a result of the well-known "Fur Campaign" he had dispatched thirty five railway cars filled with furs; *DOH,* pp. 336f.

16. On the establishment of the Janowska camp, conditions there, and its functions, see P. Friedman, "Destruction of the Jews of Lwów," pp. 301–03.

17. All the details are taken from *Eichmann Trial, Testimonies,* vol. 1, pp. 199–201 (Hebrew).

18. On the ideas formed by the Jews in Eastern Galicia on the situation in the Generalgouvernement ghettos, see Zvi Radlitzki, "Notes from the Period of the German Occupation of Lvov," *Yalkut Moreshet,* 21 (1976), 8 (Hebrew).

19. P. Friedman, "Destruction of the Jews of Lwów," pp. 268–70.

20. Ibid., p. 269

21. Ibid., pp. 270–73.

22. Chaim A. Kaplan, *The Warsaw Diary,* ed. Abraham I. Katsh (New York, 1973), p. 306.

23. *Documents from the Lublin Ghetto: Judenrat Without Direction,* Nachman Blumenthal ed. (Yad Vashem, Jerusalem, 1967), app. 5 (Polish with Hebrew translation).

24. Ibid., discussions at "The Internal Administration Department for Local Affairs and Welfare, Lublin," March 17–24, 1942, app. 6–9.

25. Ibid., document signed by the deputy director of the department, Türk.

26. Ibid., app. 10, which also mentions that 18,000 Jews were "evacuated" from Lublin.

27. Ibid., pp. 308–12.

28. Ibid., p. 313 n. 14.

29. Ibid., pp. 310f., 315 n. 1.

30. Ibid., p. 317.

31. Ibid., p. 67.

32. Chaim A. Kaplan, "Pages from the Diary," *Yalkut Moreshet,* 3 (1964), 19–21 (no English translation).

33. Jacob Kurz, *Sefer Edut* (Tel Aviv, 1944), pp. 171f.

34. Ibid., p. 217.

35. Ibid., p. 232.

36. Yisrael Gutman, *The Jews of Warsaw, 1939–1943: Ghetto, Underground, Revolt,* (Bloomington, Ind., 1982), pp. 97, 101.

37. Trunk, *Judenrat,* p. 82.

38. Quoted in Gutman, *The Jews of Warsaw,* on the basis of a Polish source, pp. 98–100; *The Warsaw Diary of Adam Czerniakow,* ed. Raul Hilberg, Stanislaw Sharon, and

Josef Kermisz (New York, 1979), November 14, 1941, p. 299 (henceforth, *Czerniakow Diary*); Hilberg, *Destruction of the European Jews* (Chicago, 1961), p. 169.

39. Gutman, *The Jews of Warsaw*, pp. 107f.; Mary Berg, *Warsaw Ghetto: A Diary* (New York, 1945), May 20, 1941, and passim.

40. Gutman, *The Jews of Warsaw*, pp. 100f.

41. *Czerniakow Diary*, December 24, 1941, p. 309.

42. Aharon Weiss, "The Course of the Judenräte in South-East Poland," *Yalkut Moreshet*, 15 (1972), 111f. (Hebrew); *Pinkas Hakehillot: . . . Poland*, vol. 2, p. 375.

43. Weiss, "Judenräte in South-East Poland," pp. 69, 83; *Pinkas Hakehillot: . . . Poland*, vol. 2, p. 102.

Chapter 14

1. On the structure of the German Foreign Office, see Raul Hilberg, *The Destruction of the European Jews* (Chicago, 1961), pp. 349–55.

2. Ibid., p. 350 n. 12; on the problems of the German Foreign Office Under Ribbentrop's directorship, see pp. 245–80. Also see Christopher R. Browning, "Unterstaatssekretär Martin Luther and the Ribbentrop Foreign Office," *Journal of Contemporary History* (London), 22 (1977), 313–44; idem, *The Final Solution and the German Foreign Office: A Study of Referat DIII of Abteilung Deutschland* (New York, 1978); Leni Yahil, *The Rescue of Danish Jewry: Test of A Democracy* (Philadelphia, pbck. ed., 1983), pp. 399–406.

3. H. Wielek, *De Oorlog die Hitler won* (Amsterdam, 1947), p. 27.

4. Louis de Jong, *Het Koningkrijk der Nederlanden in de Tweede Wereldoorlog,* (The Hague, 1974), vol. 5, p. 590. Joseph Michman "Planning for the Final Solution Against the Background of Developments in Holland in 1941," *YVS Studies*, 17 (1986), pp. 145–80. This detailed study contains many new facts and aspects that cannot be discussed here. According to Michman, the prospect of emigration of Jews from Europe was held open together with the implementation of mass murder in the East—a concept that may be disputed. More convincing is the argument of Hitler's direct involvement even in specific decisions concerning the implementation of the final solution, which is shown by the fact that already on August 20, 1941, it was known that he had decided on deportation *(Aussiedlung)* in preference to concentrating Jews in camps in Holland, pp. 172f. On Hitler's decision see chap. 11 "The Final Solution: The Second Stage,"

5. At first, the order to transfer only applied to those Jews who possessed at least 10,000 gulden; in March 1942, however, it became applicable to all Jews. See de Jong, *Het Koningkrijk* vol. 5, pp. 609f.

6. Quoted in Leni Yahil, "Methods of Persecution: A Comparison of the 'Final Solution' in Holland and Denmark," *Scripta Hierosolomytana*, (Jerusalem) 23 (1972), 293 n. 41.

7. De Jong, *Het Koningkrijk*, vol. 5, pp. 464, 530–33.

8. Ibid., pp. 1,046f.

9. *Documenten van de Joden vervolging in Nederland, 1940–1945Joods Historisch Museum* (Amsterdam, 1965), no. 447, p. 69.

10. Yahil, "Methods of Persecution," p. 294 n. 48; Wielek, *De Oorlog die Hitler won,* pp. 82, 124, 126.

11. See report on a meeting of the military administration on February 3, 1941, with RSHA representatives, Kurt Lischka and Theodor Dannecker, in *Die Endlösung der Juden-*

frage in Frankreich: Deutsche Dokumente 1941–1944, ed. Serge Klarsfeld (Paris, 1977), pp. 14f.

12. Joseph Billig, *Le Commissariat général aux questions juives* (Paris, 1955), vol. 1, p. 54. Leni Yahil, "The Jewish Leadership in France," in *Patterns of Jewish Leadership in Nazi Europe 1933–1945: Proceedings of the Third Yad Vashem International Historical Conference,* ed. Yisrael Gutman and Cynthia J. Haft (Jerusalem, 1979), pp. 321f. See Michael R. Marrus and Robert O. Paxton, *Vichy France and the Jews* (New York, 1981), passim.

13. Henri Monneray, *La Persécution des Juifs en France* et dans les pays de l'ouest (Paris, 1949), pp 84–116. This report was completed by a supplementary report (February 22, 1942), ibid., pp. 117–21.

14. Robert O. Paxton, *Vichy France, Old Guard and New Order: 1940–1944* (New York, 1972), pp. 176–80. Marrus and Paxton, *Vichy France and the Jews,* pp. 98–105.

15. See Richard I. Cohen, *The Burden of Conscience: French Jewish Leadership During the Holocaust* (Bloomington, Ind., 1987), pp. 24–40; Marrus and Paxton, *Vichy France and the Jews,* pp. 108f.

16. Billig, *Le Commissariat,* p. 52; Yahil, "Jewish Leadership," pp. 322ff.

17. The whole process is described in detail in Cohen, *The Burden of Conscience,* chap. 3.

18. See Raymond-Raoul Lambert, *Carnet d'un Témoin, 1940–1943,* ed. Richard R. Cohen (Paris, 1985), passim.

19. Georges Wellers, *L'Étoile jaune à l'heure de Vichy: De Drancy à Auschwitz* (Paris, 1973), pp. 78f. According to Hilberg, *Destruction of the European Jews (1961),* p. 403, the total number of persons arrested in the two *Aktionen* was 7,443, including 1,602 French citizens.

20. *IMT,* NG-3571.

21. Wellers, *L'Étoile jaune,* p. 85.

22. The correspondence between Eichmann and Radernacher is quoted in Robert M. W. Kempner, *Eichmann und Komplizen* (Zürich, 1961), pp. 182–92.

23. Wellers, *L'Étoile jaune,* p. 131.

24. Billig, *Le Commissariat,* p. 222.

25. Marrus and Paxton, *Vichy France and the Jews,* p. 44.

26. Hilberg, *The Destruction of the European Jews (1961),* p. 405.

27. Reports on the subject in Leon Poliakov and Josef Wulf, *Das Dritte Reich und die Juden: Dokumente und Aufsätze* (Berlin, 1955), p. 192.

28. Hilberg, *Destruction of the European Jews (1961),* pp. 400f.

29. Ibid., pp. 389f.; I. Schirman, *La Politique allemande à l'égard des juifs en Belgique, 1940–1941* (Brussels, 1970–1971, Mimeographed), passim.

30. Betty Garfinkels, *Les Belges facent à la persécution raciale, 1940–1944* (Brussels, 1965), pp. 27f. The author claims that 25,000 Jews evaded registration. This seems to be exaggerated (see chap. 6 n. 96). According to the German source, the estimate is that 50,000 to 60,000 Jews lived in Belgium at the time. "Sonderbericht, Das Judentum in Belgien," in *Die Endlösung der Judenfrage in Belgien: Dokumente,* ed. Serge Klarsfeld and Maxime Steinberg. (New York, n.d.), p. 10.

31. Garfinkels, *Les Belges,* pp. 39–41.

32. Ibid., pp. 43f.

33. *Pinkas Hakehillot: Encyclopaedia of Jewish Communities, Rumania,* vol. 7, ed., Theodor Lavi et al. (Yad Vashem, Jerusalem, 1969), entry on Odessa, pp. 390ff. (Hebrew).

34. Ibid. for sources for the history of Rumanian Jewry during the period in question;

also see *Pinkas Hakehillot: . . . Rumania,* vol. 2, ed. Jean Ancel and Theodor Lavi (Yad Vashem, Jerusalem, 1980), introduction (Hebrew); Jean Ancel, ed., *Documents Concerning the Fate of Romanian Jewry During the Holocaust* (The Beate Klarsfeld Foundation, (Jerusalem, 1986), vols. 1–12.

35. *Pinkas Hakehillot: . . . Rumania,* vol. 1 p. 155 (the U.S. dollar was worth 187.60 lei).

36. Ibid., pp. 169f.

37. Manfred Reifer, *Masa ha-Mavet: Perakim mi-Shoat Yisrael be-Romania u-ve-Polin* (Tel Aviv, 1946), pp 223f.

38. *IMT,* NG-4817.

39. Bela Vago, "The Ambiguity of Collaborationism: The Center of the Jews in Rumania (1942–1944)," in *Patterns of Jewish Leadership in Nazi Europe,1933-1945* pp. 287–309; *Pinkas Hakehillot . . . Rumania,* vol. 1, pp. 165ff; Report of the U.S. minister to Rumania, Franklin M. Gunther, November 4, 1941, in *Foreign Relations of the United States, Diplomatic Papers, 1941,* (Washington, D.C., 1959), vol. 2, pp. 871–74; quotation p. 874.

40. Nathaniel Katzburg, "Hungarian Jewry in Modern Times," in *Hungarian Jewish Studies,* ed. Randolph L. Braham (New York, 1966), vol. 1, pp. 160–62; Randolph L. Braham, *The Hungarian Labor Service System 1939–1945* (New York, 1977), pp. 19–31.

41. Randolph L. Braham, "The Kamenets Podolsk and Délvidék Massacres: Prelude to the Holocaust in Hungary," *YVS Studies,* 9 (1973), pp. 133–56.

42. Ernö Lasló, "Hungary's Jews: A Demographic Overview, 1918–1945," in Braham, *Hungarian Jewish Studies,* (1969), vol. 2, pp. 163–67.

43. Carlo Falconi, *The Silence of Pius XII* (London, 1970), pp. 288, 293. Menahem Shelah, "The Murder of Croatian Jewry by the Germans and Collaborators During WWII, (Ph.D. diss., The Hebrew University, Jerusalem, 1980), pp. 68f. (Hebrew).

44. Ladislaus Hory and Martin Broszat, *Der Kroatische Ustascha-Staat, 1941–1945* (Stuttgart, 1964), pp. 91f.

45. *Eichmann Trial,* Session 46, May 19, 1961.

46. Christopher R. Browning, "The Final Solution in Serbia: The Semlin Judenlager— A Case Study," *YVS Studies,* 15, (1983), pp. 73–85.

47. Andreas Hillgruber, ed., *Staatsmänner und Diplomaten bei Hitler,Vertrauliche Aufzeichnungen 1939–1941* (Munich, 1969), pp. 307, 310.

48. *Eichmann Trial,* T/874; Kempner, *Eichmann und Komplizen,* pp. 289–93; Hilberg, *Destruction of the European Jews (1961),* pp. 436f.

49. Details of the above document and Rademacher's commentary, NG-3354: *Eichmann Trial,* T/875. Eichmann was correct, the military administration was responsible. See Christopher R. Browning, "Wehrmacht Reprisal Policy and the Murder of the Male Jews," in his *Fateful Months: Essays on the Emergence of the Final Solution, 1941–1942* (New York, 1985), pp. 39–56; idem, "The Final Solution in Serbia," pp. 55–73.

50. Report by Rademacher on his journey to Belgrade, October 25, 1941, *Eichman Trial,* T/883. Browning, "Wehrmacht Reprisal," passim.

51. Browning, "The Final Solution in Serbia," pp. 73–85 ; On gassing, see chap. 12.

52. *Eichmann Trial,* T/196; Kempner, *Eichmann und Komplizen,* pp. 179–87, 228f.; *IMT,* NG-2586 (J).

53. Quoted by Livia Rothkirchen, *The Destruction of Slovak Jewry: A Documentary History* (Jerusalem, 1961), p. 140 (Hebrew with English introduction); *Eichmann Trial,* T/ 1084. The Archive of Auswärtiges Amt (AA), Inland II, Pressburg 312/5, K-403503.

54. Draft of the German ambassador's letter to the Slovakian Foreign Office, April, 29,

1942, AA, Inland II, Pressburg, 312/5, K-403547; Rothkirchen, *Destruction of Slovak Jewry*, p. 141.

55. YVSA, M-5/18 (1); 5/18a (22).

56. Contrary to Eichmann's intention, the Slovaks wanted to deport the families that would constitute an economic burden, YVSA, M-5/12 (2); 5/18a (10); *Eichmann Trial*, T/1080.

57. Testimony before the National Tribunal of Bratislava, 1946, YVSA, M-5/31 (3); Rothkirchen, *Destruction of Slovak Jewry*, p. 158.

58. *Eichmann Trial*, T/1084, 1086.

59. Wisliceny's testimony at his trial in Bratislava on June 5, 1946, *Eichmann Trial*, T/1074, Session 49, May 23, 1961.

Chapter 15

1. According to *EJ*, The Polish authorities' official number of victims of the gas chambers is 250,000, but according to other sources, the number was much higher. See Adalbert Rückerl, *NS-Vernichtungslager im Spiegel deutscher Strafprozesse* (London, 1977), p. 136.

2. The most comprehensive treatment of the subject is in Shaul Friedländer, *Counterfeit Nazi: The Ambiguity of Good* (London, 1969).

3. Kurt Gerstein compiled a number of reports; see Friedländer, "Introduction," *Counterfeit Nazi*, pp. xiif. His report has been widely reprinted; *DOH*, pp. 347–50. On Gerstein's attempts to bring the matter to the attention of the free world, see chap. 20, "Attempts of Rescue."

4. On Degesch, see Raul Hilberg, *The Destruction of the European Jews* (Chicago, 1961), index; Friedländer, *Counterfeit Nazi*, pp. 188–200. Two additional companies supplied the gas: Tesch and Stabenow. Also see Gerald Reitlinger, *The Final Solution: The Attempt to Exterminate the Jews of Europe, 1939–1945*, rev. ed. (London, 1968), p. 156. On the bills for gas sent by Degesch to Gerstein, see *IMT*, 27, PS-1553, pp. 340–42.

5. Rückerl, in *NS-Vernichtungslager*, pp. 145–97, gives a minimum estimate of 151,000 victims. Also see Miriam Novitch, *Sobibor: Martyrdom and Revolt* (New York, 1980).

6. According to Novitch, *Sobibor*, p. 25, Franz Stangl arrived in Sobibor on April 28, 1942. Rückerl in *NS-Vernichtungslager*, pp. 155–57, states that at least 32,000 persons arrived by the end of May; by August, the number had risen to 61,300. However, he notes that a large number of people were shot or died on the way. See Alexander Donat ed., *The Death Camp Treblinka: A Documentary* (New York, 1979); Yitzhak Arad, *Belzec, Sobibor, Treblinka: The Operation Reinhard Death Camps* (Indianapolis, Ind., 1987), passim.

7. Simon Wiesenthal, *The Murderers Among Us* (London, 1967). For Franz Stangl—the man, his actions, and even his sentiments as a prisoner in jail—see Gitta Sereny, *Into That Darkness: From Mercy Killing to Mass Murder* (London, 1974).

8. Sereny, *Into That Darkness*, p. 133.

9. Rückerl, *NS-Vernichtungslager*, pp. 197–200, and n. 74, states that there were 900,000 victims; Arad in *Belzec, Sobibor, Treblinka* has the figure 874,000.

10. *Eichmann Trial*, police interrogations, vol. 1 col. 229. See the testimony of Jacob Wiernik in *DOH*, pp. 353–55.

11. Testimony of Eliahu Rosenberg, a *Sonderkommando* worker in Treblinka, *Eichmann Trial, Testimonies* (Jerusalem, 1963), vol. 2 pp. 1,103f. (Hebrew).

12. Sereny, *Into That Darkness*, pp. 120f.

13. Ibid., pp. 181, 191.

14. Reitlinger, *The Final Solution*, pp. 149f.

15. According to the testimony of a Czech, Richard Glazar, see Sereny, *Into That Darkness*, p. 179.

16. A detailed description of Majdanek was given by one of the Jewish prisoners, Joseph Reznik, at the Eichmann trial. He was also one of the witnesses who testified in 1944 before a Polish–Soviet commission of inquiry investigating the "crimes of the Germans in the extermination camp Majdanek in the city of Lublin." *Eichmann Trial, Testimonies*, vol. 2, pp. 1,012–18. The results were published in London on September 19, 1944, in the *Soviet War News* [London]. At the same time, a journalist, Konstantin Simonow, published a report in a number of languages, including Yiddish: *The Lublin Extermination Camp* (Moscow, 1944).

17. *Soviet War News* (London), p. 3.

18. Testimony of Yaakov Friedman, *Eichmann Trial, Testimonies*, vol. 2, pp. 1,019–26.

19. Ibid., pp. 1,022f.

20. Danuta Czech, "Kalendarium der Ereignisse im Konzentrationslager Auschwitz-Birkenau," *Hefte von Auschwitz*, 2 (1959), 100. (Hereafter "Calendar of Events.")

21. Rudolf Hoess, *Commandant of Auschwitz: The Autobiography of Rudolf Hoess* (London, 1959), pp. 183–85; also see chap. 12. "The Final Solution: Overall Planning."

22. Józef Garlinski, *Fighting Auschwitz* (London, 1975), pp. 83f.

23. Ota Kraus and Erich Kulka, eds., *The Death Factory: Documents on Auschwitz* (Oxford, 1959), pp. 8–17.

24. Hoess, *Commandant of Auschwitz*, p. 146. Birkenau's total area was never utilized to its fullest extent. The greatest number of prisoners there was one hundred thousand, see Helmut Krausnick et al., eds., *Anatomy of the SS-State*, (London, 1968), p. 475.

25. The first transport, which was sent straight from the train to the gas chamber, came from Sosnowiec (May 12, 1942); the second gas chamber began operating on June 30, 1942, see Garlinski, *Fighting Auschwitz*, pp. 85f. In January 1942 Jews from Eastern Upper Silesia were still killed in the original installation. "Calendar of events," *Hefte von Auschwitz*, 2 (1959), 49.

26. Hoess, *Commandant of Auschwitz*, pp. 148f.

27. Filip Müller, *Auschwitz Inferno: The Testimony of a Sonderkommando* (London, 1979), pp. 60, 81, 117f., 122; the details are based on Filip Müller's experiences as a member of the Sonderkommando.

28. Garlinski, *Fighting Auschwitz*, p. 88 fn., p. 92; the details are in "Calendar of Events," *Hefte von Auschwitz*, 6 (1962), 9.

29. Operation Reinhard comprised four operations—murder, which was at integral part, was not mentioned expressively: 1. *Aussiedlung*, 2. *Verwendung der Arbeitskraft*, 3. *Sachverwaltung*, and 4. *Einbringung verborgener Werte und Immobilien*. See *IMT*, 34, PS-4024, pp. 58–92; Hilberg, *Destruction of the European Jews, (1961)* pp. 609–18; Léon Poliakov and Josef Wulf, eds., *Das Dritte Reich und die Juden: Dokumente und Aufsätze* (Berlin, 1955), pp. 43–62. The description of systematic plunder is based on these sources, which often hold that plunder was the sole meaning of *Aktion* Reinhard.

30. Poliakov and Wulf, *Das Dritte Reich*, p. 45.

31. F. Müller, *Auschwitz Inferno*, p. 68.

32. On the use made of plundered gold in Switzerland, see Werner Rings, *Raubgold aus Deutschland, die "Golddrehscheibe,": Schweiz im zweiten Weltkrieg* (Zurich, 1985).

33. The translation is according to the Hebrew edition of Ota Kraus and Erich Kulka,

Bet Ḥaroshet le-Mavet (Jerusalem, 1961), pp. 93f.; the text in the English edition, *The Death Factory*, pp. 99f. (see n. 23), is somewhat different.

34. Kraus and Kulka, *Bet Ḥaroshet le-Mavet*, pp. 98f. On Drs. Horst Schumann and Carl Clauberg, see Robert Jay Lifton, *The Nazi Doctors: Medical Killings and the Psychology of Genocide* (New York, 1986), pp. 270–84.

35. Lifton, *Nazi Doctors*, chap. 17; Benno Müler-Hill in *Tödliche Wissenschaft: Die Aussonderung von Juden, Zigeunern und Geisteskranken, 1933–1945* (Reinbek bei Hamburg, 1984), passim, describes Mengele as a student and associate of Professor Othmar, Freiherr von Verschuer. (English ed.: *Murderous Science: Elimination by Scientific Selection of Jews, Gypsies and Others, Germany 1933–1945* [Oxford, 1988].)

36. Garlinski, *Fighting Auschwitz*, pp. 26–28. Concerning the internal struggle between the different categories of prisoners and their privileges, Garlinski states, "It was not an easy struggle, for it was fought for the right to live, and was carried on in conditions beyond the wildest imaginations, and there was no room for fair play."

37. Translation from: Kraus and Kulka, *Bet Ḥaroshet le-Mavet*, p. 45.

38. Professor Dr. Wladislaw Fejkiel, "Der Hunger in Auschwitz," *Hefte von Auschwitz*, 8 (1964), 3–14.

39. Kraus and Kulka, *The Death Factory*, p. 70.

40. The description is based largely on Henryk Kuszaj, "Strafen, die von der SS an Häftlingen des Konzentrationslager Auschwitz vollzogen," *Hefte von Auschwitz*, 3 (1960), 3–32. For the code of punishments in Dachau, see ibid., 35–37.

41. "Calendar of Events," *Hefte von Auschwitz*, 3 (1960), April 4, 1942, 55.

42. As claimed by Höss at his trial, quoted in *Hefte von Auschwitz*, 3 (1960), 18, fn., 42.

43. "Calendar of Events," (*Hefte von Auschwitz*, 3 (1960), 71. On July 17, 1942, two transports, comprising 2,000 Jews, arrived from Holland. Of these, 449 were gassed, whereas the majority—1,251 men and 300 women—were sent to the labor camp.

44. On Himmler's visit to Auschwitz, see Hoess, *Commandant of Auschwitz*, pp. 205–12.

45. "Calendar of events," *Hefte von Auschwitz*, 3 (1960), 91.

46. See testimony of Raiyah Kagan, *Eichmann Trial, Testimonies*, vol. 2, pp. 1,183–1,202 (Hebrew).

47. For the story of the Block 11 record and a description of it, see Franciszek Brol, Gerard Wloch, and Jan Pilecki, "Das Bunkerbuch," *Hefte von Auschwitz*, I (1959), 7–44.

48. Summary of the December 16, 1941, meeting, PS-2233; Hilberg, *Destruction of the European Jews*, (1961) p. 308, In this instance, Hans Frank greatly exaggerated the number of Jews in the Generalgouvernement; DOH pp. 247–49; the quote is on p. 248.

49. The transport that left Düsseldorf on December 11, 1941, reached Riga two days later. Hauptmann der Schutzpolizei Salitter was in charge of the escort. The report is quoted in Hans G. Adler, *Der verwaltete Mensch: Studien zur Deportation der Juden aus Deutschland* (Tübingen, 1974), pp. 463–65. The problems regarding railroad transportation are described comprehensively in Raul Hilberg, "German Railroads, Jewish Souls," *Society, A Review of Social History* (November/December 1976), 60–74.

50. Testimony of Wisliceny, Bratislava, November 18, 1946, quoted in Léon Poliakov, *The Harvest of Hate* (Paris, 1954), p. 144.

51. Reitlinger, *The Final Solution*, p. 74; Hilberg, "German Railroads," p. 69.

52. Adler, *Verwaltete Mensch*, p. 439. According to Hilberg in *Destruction of the European Jews* (1961), pp. 313f., and in his "German Railroads," the breakdown was technical, caused by a fault on the Sobibor line, thus the transports from Warsaw were diverted to Treblinka. Probably both explanations are correct. During that time, a second train carrying five thousand Jews ran twice a week from Przemyśl to Bełżec.

53. Krausnick et al., *Anatomy of the SS-State,* pp. 104, 114.

54. Hilberg, "German Railroads," p. 67.

55. Poliakov, *Harvest of Hate,* p. 141; Reitlinger, *The Final Solution,* pp. 272f.; *TWC,* 8, NO-5574.

56. The figures are based on Yisrael Gutman, *The Jews of Warsaw, 1939–1943: Ghetto, Underground, Revolt* (Bloomington, Ind., 1982), pp. 207–11, 270.

57. Extensive material is now available on the Warsaw Ghetto: Joseph Kermish, ed., *To Live with Honor and Die with Honor: Selected Documents from the Warsaw Ghetto Underground Archives "O.S." ("Oneg Shabbath")* (Jerusalem, 1986), passim.

58. Ibid., p. 38.

59. Ibid., pp. 691–716; Gutman, *The Jews of Warsaw,* pp. 207–11, 270.

60. Emmanuel Ringelblum, *Notes from the Warsaw Ghetto* (New York, 1974), p. 273.

61. Ibid., p. 262.

62. Ibid., p. 257; *The Warsaw Diary of Adam Czerniakow: Prelude to Doom,* ed. Raul Hilberg, Stanislaw Staron and Josef Kermisz (New York, 1979), April 18, 1942, p. 344.

63. Ringelblum, *Notes from the Warsaw Ghetto,* pp. 255, 260, 274.

64. Ibid., pp. 269, 275. See Leni Yahil, "The Warsaw Underground Press: A Case Study in the Reaction to Anti-Semitism," in *Living with Antisemitism: Modern Jewish Responses,* ed. Yehuda Reinharz (Hanover, N.H., 1987), pp. 413–42.

65. Ringelblum, *Notes from the Warsaw Ghetto,* pp. 295, 298.

66. Ibid., p. 287.

67. *Czerniakow Diary,* July 11, 1942, p. 378.

68. Ibid., July 17, 1942, p. 381.

69. Ibid., July 22, 1942, p. 384.

70. Ibid., quoted in Foreword, p. 23.

71. *Pinkas Bendin: A Memorial to the Jewish Community of Bendin (Poland),* ed. Avraham Stein (Tel Aviv, 1959), pp. 353–57; on resistance, see chap. 17, "The Armed Struggle of Jews in Nazi-Occupied Countries."

72. *EJ,* vol. 5, cols. 1,038f.; vol. 13, cols. 1,501f.

73. *EJ,* vol. 5, col. 1,212; Nathan Eck, *The Holocaust of the Jewish People in Europe* (Yad Vashem, Hakibbutz Hameuḥad, Merḥavia, 1975), p. 177 (Hebrew).

74. *Sefer Czestochov (Encyclopedia shel Galuyot,* ed. M. Schutzman [Jerusalem, 1968] vol. 1, cols. 101–9 (Hebrew).

75. Ibid., col. 112.

76. Ibid., cols. 117, 119, 125, 197. On the history of the underground in Czestochowa, see Shmuel Krakowski, *The War of the Doomed: Jewish Armed Resistance in Poland, 1942–1944* (New York, 1984), passim.

77. *Sefer Czestochov,* col. 139f.

78. The full report by Richard Korherr, NO-5194 (Der Inspekteur für Statistik beim Reichsführer-SS) is in YVSA, DN/31, DN/33. A shortened version (6½ pages) was given to Himmler in mid April 1943 "to be submitted to the Führer." Quoted in Poliakov and Wulf, *Das Dritte Reich,* pp. 239–48; partially in *DOH,* pp. 332–34. Korherr's figures are lower. See also the numbers in chap. 5, "Toward the Struggle for World Domination (1939–1941)."

79. Hilberg, *Destruction of the European Jews* (1961), pp. 341f.

80. Ibid., p. 333; *IMT,* 5, p. 498.

81. Hans Frank added, "Not unimportant labor reserves have been taken from us when we lost our old trustworthy Jews *(unsere altbewährten Judenschaften),*" Hilberg, *Destruction of the European Jews* (1961), p. 336.

82. *NCA,* 3, PS-682, p. 496.

83. *IMT,* 26, PS-654, pp. 200–203; 38, L-316, pp. 98–100.

84. *Trial of Karl Wolff, Verdict,* YVSA, TR 10/639, pp. 252–54. *TWC,* 1, NO-205, pp. 721f. On June 23, 1942, a day after the Germans began to deport Warsaw's Jews to Treblinka, Victor Brack from Hitler's personal chancellery, the chief designer of the "euthanasia" program, wrote Himmler a letter suggesting rather than destroy the Jews that he sterilize them to maintain the labor force, *DOH,* pp. 272f.

85. *Trial of Karl Wolff, Verdict,* p. 255; Hilberg, *Destruction of the European Jews* (1961), p. 334.

86. Krausnick et al., *Anatomy of the SS-State,* pp. 107–10; *DOH,* pp. 287–89.

87. Albert Speer, *Erinnerungen* (Frankfurt on the Main, 1969), pp. 207–10, 232f. According to Speer's estimate, a million workers were lacking. *IMT,* 3, pp. 427f.

88. *IMT,* 3, pp. 515f.

89. *IMT,* R-124; *YVSA,* JM/2139. The date of the issue of the protocol is given as September 29, 1942.

90. Krausnick et al., *Anatomy of the SS-State,* pp. 110f. The quotation is taken from *DOH,* p. 290. According to the *Trial of Karl Wolff, Verdict,* p. 262, Himmler's order was sent on October 2, 1942; officially the order was given on October 9.

91. Krausnick et al., *Anatomy of the SS-State,* p. 113; Hilberg, *Destruction of the European Jews* (1961), p. 337; Korherr's report (see n. 78).

92. Krausnick et al., *Anatomy of the SS-State,* pp. 114f. Full documentation, *Trial of Karl Wolff, Verdict,* pp. 267–71. See also Reitlinger, *The Final Solution,* p. 291.

93. Hilberg, *Destruction of the European Jews* (1961), pp. 337–44; Reitlinger, *The Final Solution,* index. On OSTI, see *TWC 5,* NO-1271, pp. 513ff., NO-1611, pp. 616ff; NO-4651; NO-4652 (the last two are unpublished).

94. Hilberg, *Destruction of the European Jews* (1961), p. 406.

95. Reitlinger, *The Final Solution,* p. 337.

96. Michael R. Marrus and Robert O. Paxton, *Vichy France and the Jews* (New York, 1981), pp. 224–49.

97. Hilberg, *Destruction of the European Jews* (1961), pp. 407f.; Reitlinger, *The Final Solution,* p. 342.

98. Reitlinger, *The Final Solution,* p. 339; Marrus and Paxton, *Vichy France and the Jews,* pp. 250–52.

99. Claude Lévy and Paul Tillard, *Betrayal at the Val d'Hiver* (New York, 1967), p. 7.

100. Ibid., pp. 9f.

101. Reitlinger, *The Final Solution,* pp. 340–42.

102. Georges Wellers, *L'Étoile jaune a l'heure de Vichy: De Drancy à Auschwitz* (Paris, 1973), pp. 147f.

103. Marrus and Paxton, *Vichy France,* pp. 255–61. They give the number of deportees as 42,500.

104. See n. 43.

105. Hilberg, *Destruction of the European Jews* (1961), p. 376; *TWC,* case 11, NG-183; quote from *Documenten van de Joden vervolging in Nederland, 1940–1945,* Joods Historisch Museum (Amsterdam, 1965), pp. 90–92.

106. *Documenten van de Joden,* p. 85.

107. H. Wielek, *De Oorlog die Hitler won* (Amsterdam, 1947), p. 88.

108. *Documenten van de Joden,* pp. 156f.

109. Wielek, *De Oorlog die Hitler won,* pp. 68, 80, 88, 101, 133.

110. According to Reitlinger, *The Final Solution,* p. 359, the number was 38,606. See Korherr, n. 78 above.

111. According to *Liste des Israélites domiciles en Belgique en mai 1940: Déportés, évadés, libérés et décédés* (Brussels, 1977), Belgian government publication.

112. Betty Garfinkels, *Les Belges facent à la persécution raciale, 1940–1944* (Brussels, 1965), pp. 47ff.

113. *Eichmann Trial,* T/513; "Calendar of Events," *Hefte von Auschwitz,* 2 (1960), 78, 95.

114. According to the Belgian government list, see n. 111. Korherr states that 16,886 were sent. Also see Serge Klarsfeld and Maxime Steinberg, eds., *Die Endlösung der Juden-frage in Belgien: Dokumente* (New York, n.d.).

115. Maxime Steinberg, "The Trap of Legality: The Association of the Jews of Belgium," in *Patterns of Jewish Leadership in Nazi Europe 1933–1945. Proceedings of the Third Yad Vashem International Historical Conference,* Yisrael Gutman and Cynthia J. Haft, eds. (Jerusalem, 1979), pp. 366–76; idem, *L'Étoile et le fusil,* vol. 2, *Les Cent jours de la déportation des juifs de Belgique* (Brussels, 1986), passim.

116. Paul M. Hayes, *The Career and Political Ideas of Vidkun Quisling, 1887–1945* (Newton Abbot, Eng., 1971), passim. For a minute description of the events in Norway, see Oskar Mendelsohn, *Joedernes Historie i Norge,* vol. 2, *1940–1986,* (Universitetsforlaget, Nor., 1988).

117. On Julius Samuel and the events in Norway, see the rabbi's widow, Henrietta Samuel, in *Eichmann Trial, Testimonies* (Jerusalem, 1963), vol. 1, pp. 475–80.

118. On the deportation and the arrangements for its implementation see Tuvia Friedmann, ed., *Dokumenten-Sammlung über die Deportierung der Juden aus Norwegen nach Auschwitz* (Ramat Gan, Israel, 1963).

119. See testimony of Mrs. (Henrietta) Samuel, see n. 117; Myrtle Wright, *Norwegian Diary* (London, 1974), pp. 110–18.

120. There are varying estimates concerning the number of victims of Nazi persecution in Norway as well as the number who returned from Auschwitz: Marcus Levin, *The Norwegian Jews During the Occupation,* YVSA, 0/48–28/5, 1946; *EJ,* vol. 12, col. 1,224; Ragnar Ulstein, *Svensketrafikken: Flyktinger till Sverge, 1940–1943* (Oslo, 1974), p. 190; *News of Norway,* September 11, 1952 and April 27, 1961.

121. Bjarne Joeye and Trygre M. Ager, *The Fight of the Norwegian Church Against Nazism* (New York, 1943), pp. 144ff.

122. Johan M. Snoek, *The Grey Book* (London, 1979), pp. 117ff.

123. Heinrich Müller's directive of May 21, 1942, *Eichmann Trial,* T/742.

124. These numbers are according to tables in Zdenek's Lederer, *Ghetto Theresienstadt* (London, 1953), pp. 247–62, that are very detailed; slightly different figures in Hans G. Adler, *Theresienstadt, 1941–1945: Das Antlitz einer Zwangsgemeinschaft* (Tübingen, 1960), pp. 40–43.

125. Three sources mention the transports from Berlin: (1) Lederer, *Ghetto Theresienstadt;* (2) Robert M. W. Kempner, "Der Mord an 35,000 Berliner Juden: Der Judenprocess in Berlin schreibt Geschichte" in *Gegenwart im Rückblick,* ed. Herbert A. Strauss and Kurt R. Grossmann (Heidelberg, 1970); and (3) H. G. Sellenthin, *Geschichte der Juden in Berlin* (Berlin, 1959).

126. *Leben und Schicksal, zur Einweihung der Synagoge in Hannover* (Hanover, W. Ger., 1963), p. 35.

127. Jonny Moser, *Die Judenverfolgung in Österreich 1938–1945* (Vienna, 1966), pp. 34–46.

128. Lederer in *Ghetto Theresienstadt,* p. 250, states that the exact number was 40,071. Probably Korherr's estimate that 87,000 Jews were sent to Theresienstadt is too low; also see Adler, *Theresienstadt, 1941–1945,* p. 59. The peak months for deportations to Theresienstadt were June to September (66,400), whereas September to October (22,870) were

the peak months for deportations from the camp, see Lederer, *Ghetto Theresienstadt, p. 247.*

129. Hans G. Adler, *Die Verheimlichte Wahrheit: Theresienstädter Dokumente* (Tübingen, 1958). pp. 98f.

130. Adler, *Theresienstadt, 1941–1945,* pp. 310f.

131. Ibid., p. 110; Adler, *Verheimlichte Wahrheit,* pp. 16–20.

132. Adler, *Verheimlichte Wahrheit,* pp. 48–54.

133. Ibid., pp. 68f., 229f.; Adler, *Theresienstadt, 1941–1945,* pp. 108f.

134. Adler, *Theresienstadt 1941–1945,* pp. 59f.; "Calendar of Events," *Hefte von Auschwitz,* 4 (1961), 67–71.

135. At the end of 1942 there were, according to the figures we have cited, 49,397 Jews in Theresienstadt: 7,001 Jews were deported; 2,473 died in January 1943; and 4,803 Jews arrived. There could not, therefore, have been more than some 45,000 inmates at that time. Lederer, *Ghetto Theresienstadt,* p. 247.

136. Adler, *Verheimlichte Wahrheit,* pp. 296–99.

137. According to records of the Slovakian railroad company, 57,752 Jews were deported; according to figures given at the trial of war criminals in Slovakia, there were 57,837, including 7,063 children under the age of ten. Livia Rothkirchen, *The Destruction of Slovak Jewry: A Documentary History* (Jerusalem, 1961), doc. 37, p. 104 (Hebrew with English introduction).

138. Yeshayah Oskar Neumann, *Im Schatten des Todes* (Tel Aviv, 1956), p. 111.

139. Ibid., pp. 174f.; the nickname *Partisanenrebbe* occurs on p. 155.

140. Michael Ber Weismandel, *Min ha-Metzar* (New York, 1960), p. 45.

141. Hochberg's activities were suspect in the eyes of the Slovakian authorities as well. He was arrested in the winter of 1943 and the members of the Working Group feared greatly that his large stock of information would be divulged. In the fall of 1944, he was captured by the partisans, tried, and sentenced to death for collaboration, see Neumann, *Im Schatten des Todes,* pp. 149–51. On his participation in the bribing of Wisliceny, see ibid., pp. 136–41; Weismandel, *Min ha-Metzar,* pp. 47–54.

142. According to Weismandel, the money was paid in two installments: the first was handed over in July, resulting in a seven-week halt in the deportations; the deportations were partially resumed, however, as the second payment was not made. The accuracy of Weismandel's dates cannot be accepted unequivocally, see *Min ha-Metzar,* pp. 60f. Wisliceny claimed that he received the money in September. On his testimony, see Rothkirchen, *The Destruction of Slovak Jewry,* pp. 243f. On the complicated issue of aid from the JDC and relations with Wisliceny, see chap. 20, "Attemps at Rescue."

143. Neumann, *Im Schatten des Todes,* p. 116.

144. Ibid., pp. 121–31; Rothkirchen, *The Destruction of Slovak Jewry,* p. 34.

Chapter 16

1. For a description of the strategic position and discussions, see Alan Clark, *Barbarossa: The Russian-German Conflict* (New York, 1965), pp. 300–306. On Hitler's proclamation to the troops see Max Domarus, ed., *Hitler: Reden und Proklamationen, 1932–1945* (Munich, 1963), vol. 2, pp. 1,988f.

2. Domarus, *Hitler,* vol. 2, pp. 1990–93.

3. Goebbels reviled the Allied proclamation of solidarity with the Jews, observing in his diary: "The [English] parliament is a 'Jewish stock exchange' and the English are 'the

Jews among the Aryans.'": Josef Goebbels, *Tagebücher aus den Jahren 1942–1943,* ed. Louis P. Lochner (Zurich, 1948), December 19, 1942, p. 232. Notwithstanding the arrogant tenor of his remarks, some of Goebbel's subsequent comments reveal his growing qualms regarding not only the general situation but also the negative reactions to the extermination of the Jews.

4. See the report of a meeting chaired by Eichmann on August 28, 1942, NG-1965 in Robert M. W. Kempner, *Eichmann und Komplizen* (Zurich, 1961), pp. 200–223.

5. Rudolf Höss, *Kommandant in Auschwitz: Autobiographische Aufzeichnungen,* ed. Martin Broszat (Stuttgart, 1958), p. 134.

6. See report by the statistician Richard Korherr, NO-5194, p. 13.

7. On the activities of Fritz Sauckel's department, see *IMT,* 16, pp. 519, 568f.; *NCA,* 7, L-156, p. 905; Goebbels, *Tagebücher,* March 9, 1943, pp. 262f.

8. Hildegard Henschel, "Gemeindearbeit und Evakuierung von Berlin (Oktober 16, 1941–June 16, 1943), *Zeitschrift für die Geschichte der Juden* (Tel Aviv), 9, nos. 1/2 (1972), 33–52.

9. H. G. Sellenthin, *Geschichte der Juden in Berlin* (Berlin, 1959), p. 85.

10. Henschel, "Gemeindearbeit und Evakuierung," p. 48. Surprisingly enough, even after the war, when the report was compiled, Henschel viewed the reunion of families as an achievement.

11. K. J. Ball-Kaduri, "Berlin Is 'Purged' of Its Jews: The Jews in Berlin in the Year 1943," *YVS Studies,* 5 (1963), pp. 277–80.

12. Goebbels, *Tagebücher,* pp. 261f., 294.

13. Ball-Kaduri, "Berlin Is 'Purged,'" pp. 310–16.

14. As with the rest of Europe, it is difficult to estimate the number of Jews here with complete certainty. I have based my figures on Miriam Novitch, *Le Passage des barbares* (Nice, 1973), pp. 11f. In Raul Hilberg, *The Destruction of the European Jews* (Chicago, 1961), p. 442, the numbers are lower. The figure of 56,000 Jews in Salonika also appears in a report by the German consul dated February 26, 1942, *Eichmann Trial,* T/970.

15. According to the Hebrew manuscript in my possession written by Shimon Marcus for the entry on Greece in the *EJ.*

16. Michael Molho and Joseph Nehama, *The Destruction of Greek Jewry, 1941–1944* (Jerusalem, 1965), pp. 40–42 (Hebrew).

17. Joseph Ben, "The Destruction of Greek Jewry (1941–1944)" (MA thesis, Tel Aviv University, 1977), pp. 35f. (Hebrew).

18. Novitch, *Passage,* p. 28.

19. Molho and Nehama, *Destruction of Greek Jewry,* p. 45; Novitch, *Passage,* pp. 20, 28.

20. Molho and Nehama, *Destruction of Greek Jewry,* p. 46.

21. *Eichmann Trial,* T/956, T/974.

22. Novitch, *Passage,* passim; Ben, "The Destruction of Greek Jewry," pp. 17f.

23. Molho and Nehama, *Destruction of Greek Jewry,* pp. 48–53.

24. The consul-general in Salonika was notified of the operation so that he would support Rolf Günther's activities and enlist the aid of the military authorities. Martin Luther's telegrams of January 22/23, 1943, *Eichmann Trial,* T/951, T/958. Seemingly, the statement, reiterated by a number of historians, that Eichmann himself was then visiting Salonika is founded on error.

25. Günther's letter of January 25, 1943, to the Foreign Ministry, *Eichmann Trial,* T/959. According to Günther, the deportation plans were discussed in Athens at the beginning of January with the Foreign Ministry representative in Greece and the commander of the

Salonika-Aegean corps. Also see, *Eichmann Trial,* Dieter Wisliceny's statement at his trial in Bratislava (Pressburg) on June 27, 1947, T/992; on February 5 Franz Rademacher of Luther's department informed the German legation in Pressburg of Wisliceny's transfer. *Eichmann Trial,* 06-1001 (the document was not submitted at the trial).

26. Molho and Nehama, *Destruction of Greek Jewry,* p. 58; *Yad Vashem News,* 34 (1965), pp. 5–11 (Hebrew).

27. On all these orders and directives see Molho and Nehama, *Destruction of Greek Jewry,* pp. 61f; report of the German consul, *Eichmann Trial,* T/970, T/971. The total number of transports given is an approximate estimate. See Danuta Czech, "Deportation und Vernichtung der griechischen Juden," in *Hefte von Auschwitz,* 11 (1970), 5–37; idem, "Kalendarium der Ereignisse im Konzentrationslager Auschwitz-Birkenau," (Calendar of Events) *Hefte von Auschwitz,* 4 (1961), 85.

28. For Koretz's announcements, see Molho and Nehama, *Destruction of Greek Jewry,* pp. 65, 74.

29. A description of the episode is in Dieter Wisliceny's testimony (see n. 25), pp. 3f. He discourses at length in order to demonstrate that he tried to prevent deportations and save Jews. Wisliceny's telegram to Eichmann is not extant. Molho and Nehama, *Destruction of Greek Jewry,* pp. 77–88: The Germans carried out raids to conscript the laborers, whose numbers totaled less than two thousand. There were no volunteers.

30. See table in Czech, "Deportation und Vernichtung," p. 191. It is quite likely that there were additional transports of which we have no knowledge as the Germans did not carry out a selection and all the deportees without exception were sent straight to the gas chambers.

31. Among the papers found in the Treblinka railway station was a document concerning a train with forty-six carriages that brought "resettled" people from Salonika.

32. According to the table in Czech, "Deportation und Vernichtung"; Molho and Nehama, *Destruction of Greek Jewry,* pp. 90f, give the figure as 820, which has been repeated by others, and they state that all the deportees were immediately killed in the gas chambers. According to one opinion, they were sent to Treblinka.

33. NG-2652; *Eichmann Trial,* T/271, T/340, T/761.

34. Eberhard Kolb, *Bergen-Belsen* (Hannover, W. Ger., 1962), pp. 123f; see Ribbentrop's directive in NG-4961.

35. *Eichmann Trial,* T/779, T/781; NG-2652.

36. For the internal discussions in the Foreign Ministry, see *Eichmann Trial,* T/782; Heinrich Müller's letter of September 23, 1943, Kolb, *Bergen-Belsen,* p. 26.

37. According to a letter dated February 26, 1943, from the German consul in Salonika (*Eichmann Trial,* T/971), there were 281 Italian nationals; 311 Spaniards; 39 Turks; a few Portuguese, Swiss, Egyptians, Hungarians, and Bulgarians; 3 Americans; 3 English nationals; and 2 Persians.

38. *Eichmann Trial,* T/989, NG-1965. On the episode as a whole, see Daniel Carpi, "Notes on the History of the Jews in Greece During the Holocaust Period: The Attitude of the Italians (1941–1943)," in *Festschrift in Honor of Dr. George S. Wise* (Tel Aviv, 1981), pp. 39–41 and passim.

39. *Eichmann Trial,* 06-1002; T/990, T/991; Carpi, "The Jews in Greece," contains additional clarification and details.

40. Molho and Nehama, *Destruction of Greek Jewry,* pp. 85f.

41. Quoted by Kolb, *Bergen-Belsen,* pp. 27f.; draft and letter to the RSHA of March 2, 1943, *Eichman Trial,* T/769. Ribbentrop apparently was unaware that the Norwegian Jews were no longer in the Germans' hands as they had already been exterminated in Auschwitz or had escaped to Sweden.

42. Kolb, *Bergen-Belsen,* p. 35. Ruth Zariz, "Officially Approved Emigration from Germany After 1941: A Case Study," *YVS Studies,* 18 (1987), pp. 282–87.

43. Oswald Pohl and his subordinates who controlled the concentration camp network neglected this camp because it did not correspond to the general principle that had evolved at that time whereby the concentration camps served clear-cut economic interests. On the other hand, the RSHA, which controlled the camp on the political level, did not regard itself as responsible for administrative concerns. Kolb, *Bergen-Belsen,* pp. 38–41.

44. Chaim Avni, *Spain, the Jews, and Franco* (Philadelphia, 1982), pp. 66f. and chap. 3; idem, "Spanish Nationals and Their Fate During the Holocaust," *YVS Studies,* vol. 8 (1970), pp. 31–68.

45. Avni, *Spain, the Jews, and Franco,* pp. 98, 171, 175.

46. Ibid., pp. 98, 254 n. 32, 33: the total number of Spanish-Jewish nationals in Greece was at least 640. See *Eichmann Trial,* T/988; NG-5050.

47. *Eichmann Trial,* T/993, T/994. Also see Molho and Nehama, *Destruction of Greek Jewry,* pp. 92f.

48. *Eichmann Trial,* T/996. This section is largely based on Molho and Nehama, *Destruction of Greek Jewry,* pp. 119–71. Joseph Nehama escaped from Salonika and was an active member of the Jewish underground in Athens.

49. *Eichmann Trial,* T/621, T/997; Molho and Nehama, *Destruction of Greek Jewry,* pp. 153f.; table on p. 191.

50. Czech, "Deportation und Vernichtung," table on page 191; Molho and Nehama, *Destruction of Greek Jewry,* pp. 222–24.

51. For a concise description, see Daniel Carpi, "The Origins and Development of Fascist Anti-Semitism in Italy (1922–1945)," in *The Catastrophe of European Jewry: Antecedents, History, Reflections, Selected Papers,* ed. Yisrael Gutman and Livia Rothkirchen (Yad Vashem, Jerusalem, 1976), pp. 283–98. Also see, Meir Michaelis, "On the Jewish Question in Fascist Italy: The Attitude of the Fascist Regime to the Jews in Italy," *YVS Studies,* 4 (1960), pp. 7–41; idem, "The 'Duce' and the Jews. An Assessment of the Literature on Italian Jewry Under Fascism 1922–1945," *YVS Studies,* 11 (1976), pp. 7–32; idem, *Mussolini and the Jews: German-Italian Relations and the Jewish Question in Italy* (Oxford, 1978), passim.

52. Jacob Robinson, *And the Crooked Shall Be Made Straight: The Eichmann Trial, the Jewish Catastrophe, and Hannah Arendt's Narrative* (New York, 1965), pp. 247, 288–90; Carpi, "Fascist Anti-Semitism," p. 290.

53. According to the defense sheet drawn up at the recommendation of YIVO, by his son, Dr. Renato J. Almansi, *Dante Almansi, President of the Union of Italian Jewish Communities 1939 to Oct. 1944* (New York, 1971, Typewritten).

54. Carpi, "Fascist Anti-Semitism," p. 292; idem, "Prisons and Concentration Camps in Italy During the Holocaust Period," in *Dapim le-Heker ha-Shoah ve-ha-Mered,* 2d ed., vol. 1, p. 183; Michaelis, *Mussolini and the Jews,* p. 293.

55. Carpi, "Prisons and Concentraton Camps," p. 178.

56. *EJ,* 14, col. 252. The number of Jews in Rome itself was estimated at eight thousand.

57. The events in Rome at the end of September and in October 1943 have been described dramatically on the basis of reliable—but somewhat biased—historical and private sources, by Robert Katz, *Black Sabbath: A Journey Through a Crime Against Humanity* (London, 1969), Katz claims that a larger number were deported. On problems surrounding the operation and its background, see Michaelis, *Mussolini and the Jews,* pp. 348–69. For Friedrich Mölhausen's telegram and the reply, see the documentary collection,

Judenverfolgung in Italien, den italienischen besetzten Gebieten und Nordafrika (URO, 1962), pp. 193f.

58. Carpi, "Fascist Anti-Semitism," pp. 294ff.

59. Katz, *Black Sabbath,* pp. 124, 189.

60. Ibid., pp. 148f.

61. Ibid., pp. 31–34, 146f.

62. Euginio M. Zolli, *Before the Dawn* (New York, 1954), pp. 140–55.

63. Katz, *Black Sabbath,* pp. 221f.

64. Michaelis, *Mussolini and the Jews,* p. 368 n. 1.

65. Carpi, "Fascist Anti-Semitism," pp. 294f.; URO documents (see n. 57), pp. 195, 197.

66. Carpi, "Fascist Anti-Semitism,", p. 218.

67. Ibid., for the number of victims. For the number of underground fighters, see Michaelis, *Mussolini and the Jews,* p. 388.

68. Carpi, "Fascist Anti-Semitism," pp. 180, 186, 196f.

69. Ladislaus Hory and Martin Broszat, *Der Kroatische Ustascha-Staat, 1941–1945* (Stuttgart, 1964), pp. 61, 133. On the events of 1941, see chap. 14 "European Jewry Prior to Deportation to the East (1941 to Summer 1942)"; on Sigfried Kasche see Menaḥem Shelaḥ, "The Murder of the Jews of Croatia by the Germans and Their Henchmen During World War II" (Ph.D. diss., The Hebrew University, Jerusalem, 1980), p. 139 (Hebrew).

70. URO documents, pp. 48, 50, 96; Hory and Broszat, *Kroatische Ustascha-Staat,* p. 131; Shelaḥ, "Murder of the Jews of Croatia," pp. 146–51; Ribbentrop to Luther, September 24, 1942, URO documents, p. 85; *IMT,* 13, NG-1517, pp. 255f.; Richard Korherr, NG-2367 in Arad ct al., cds., DOH, p. 333.

71. Léon Poliakov and Jacques Sabile, "Attitude of the Italians to the Persecuted Jews in Croatia," in *Jews Under the Italian Occupation,* ed. Poliakov and Sabile, (Paris, 1955), pp. 131–50. Michaelis, *Mussolini and the Jews,* pp. 304f., 330f. Daniel Carpi, "The Rescue of Jews in the Italian Zone of Occupied Croatia," in *Rescue Attempts During the Holocaust. Proceedings of the Second Yad Vashem International Historical Conference* ed. Yisrael Gutman and Efraim Zuroff (Jerusalem, 1977), pp. 465–525. URO documents, pp. 111, 117f., 120, 125.

72. Hory and Broszat, *Kroatische Ustascha-Staat,* pp. 140f., 148f.

73. Shelaḥ, "Murder of the Jews of Croatia," pp. 158–60; URO documents, NG-2348, p. 157; NG-234, p. 170; NG-2413, p. 186. Also see Gerald Reitlinger, *The Final Solution: The Attempt to Exterminate the Jews of Europe, 1939–1945,* 2d rev. ed. (London, 1968), p. 397.

74. Menaḥem Shelaḥ, *Blood Account: The Rescue of Croatian Jewry by the Italians, 1941–1943* (Tel Aviv, 1986), pp. 34–38, 185f. (Hebrew, English summary); Edmond Paris, *Genocide in Satellite Croatia, 1941–1945: A Record of Racial and Religious Persecutions and Massacres* (Chicago, 1959), p. 129.

75. Paris, *Genocide,* pp. 4, 9, 133, 136f.; Carlo Falconi, *The Silence of Pius XII* (London, 1970), p. 298. The bloodbath of Croatia is estimated to have claimed 700,000 to 750,000 Serbs; 60,000 Jews; 20,000 Gypsies; all told, approximately 800,000.

76. *Eichmann Trial,* T/451; 06–704; this is the reply to Eichmann's telegram of March 18, 1943, in which he asked when to send trains for transporting deportees; N 44 (N standing for defense documents). Various dates are mentioned in connection with the annulment of citizenship: 1927, 1932, and 1933.

77. *Eichmann Trial,* T/477; according to Georges Wellers, *L'Étoile jaune à l'heure de Vichy: De Drancy à Auschwitz* (Paris, 1973), p. 247: on February 9, 11, and 13, 1943, three

trainloads of prisoners were dispatched from among the four thousand then incarcerated in Drancy.

78. URO documents, p. 128.
79. Ibid., pp. 126f., 133, 143.
80. *Eichmann Trial,* T/610, T/611; NG-4956.
81. URO documents, pp. 155f.; *NCA,* 7 D-734, pp. 188–90; Hilberg, *Destruction of the European Jews* (1961), p. 415.
82. URO documents, pp. 163, 164, 167, 168, 180. *Eichmann Trial,* 06-717, N 43; Hilberg, *Destruction of the European Jews* (1961), pp. 416f.; Reitlinger, *The Final Solution,* pp. 343–48.
83. Wellers, *L'Étoile jaune,* p. 75. "Calendar of Events," *Hefte von Auschwitz,* 4 (1961), 1943, pp. 109f. See also Leon Poliakov and Josef Wulf, eds., *Das Dritte Reich und die Juden: Dokumente und Aufsätze* (Berlin, 1955), p. 247.
84. Wellers, *LÉtoile jaune,* pp. 191–97; table of deportations, p. 256. Wellers was married to a non-Jewish woman and was sent from Drancy to one of these storehouses at the end of October 1943. In the summer of 1944, he was brought back to the camp and then deported to Auschwitz at the end of June.
85. Hilberg, *Destruction of the European Jews* (1961), p. 417; Michael R. Marrus and Robert O. Paxton, *Vichy and the Jews* (New York, 1981), pp. 321–29.
86. Wellers, L'Étoile jaune, pp. 197, 218f.; table, p. 256.
87. According to *Liste des Israélites domiciles en Belgique en mai 1940 . . . déportés, évadés, libérés, et décédés* (Brussels, 1977), Belgian government publication, concluding statistical data. The exact number was 5,105, most of whom were among the victims in France.
88. NG-5219.
89. Serge Klarsfeld and Maxime Steinberg, eds., *Die Endlösung der Judenfrage in Belgien: Dokumente* (New York, 1980), pp. 77–83. The plan is dated September 1, 1943, Betty Garfinkels, *Les Belges facent à la persécution raciale, 1940–1944* (Brussels, 1965), p. 54. *Eichmann Trial,* T/519. Maxime Steinberg, *L'Étoile et le fusil,* vol. 2, *Les Cent jours de la déportation des juifs de Belgique* (Brussels, 1986), passim.
90. According to a German document (November 15, 1943) quoted by Garfinkels, *Les Belges facent à la persécution raciale,* p. 62.
91. Lucien Steinberg, *Le Comité de défense des Juifs en Belgique, 1942–1944* (Brussels, 1973), pp. 130–38. See also chap. 17, "The Armed Struggle of Jews in Nazi-Occupied Countries."
92. See n. 87 above; Reitlinger, *The Final Solution,* p. 369.
93. See n. 87 above; *Eichmann Trial,* T/520; Henri Monneray, *La Persécution des Juifs en France et dans les autres pays de l'Ouest* (Paris, 1947), pp. 202–28.
94. Louis de Jong, *Het Koningkrijk der Nederlanden in de Tweede Wereldoorlog* (The Hague, 1978), vol. 8, p. 708, Table ix.
95. "Calendar of Events," *Hefte von Auschwitz,* 4 (1961), 68; de Jong, *Het Koningkrijk,* p. 324; Jacob Presser, *The Destruction of the Dutch Jews* (New York, 1969), pp. 178–84. The institution was next to the town of Apeldoorn–Het Apeldoornse Bos, Neth.
96. *De SS en Nederland: Documenten uit SS-Achieven, 1935–1945,* In't Veld, N.C.K.A., ed. (The Hague, 1976), vol.2, no. 334, p. 969; no. 387, p. 1031. This was actually aimed at all members of the Dutch armed forces who had previously been released. Konrad Kwiet, *Reichskommissariat Niederlande: Versuch und Scheitern nationalsoziolistischer Neuordnung* (Stuttgart, 1968), pp. 150f.
97. De Jong, *Het Koningkrijk,* vol. 8, p. 307.
98. Ibid., vol. 7, pp. 296–302.

99. See Leni Yahil, "Methods of Persecution; A Comparison of the 'Final Solution' in Holland and Denmark," *Scripta Hierosolomytana* (Jerusalem), 23 (1972), 297ff.

100. *De SS en Nederland,* no. 462, p. 1203.

101. H. Wielek, *De Oorlog die Hitler won* (Amsterdam, 1947), pp. 263f.; Presser, *Destruction of the Dutch Jews,* pp. 281f.; de Jong, *Het Koningkrijk,* vol. 8, p. 258.

102. Wielek, *De Oorlog die Hitler won,* pp. 182, 192; de Jong, *Het Koningkrijk,* vol. 8, pp. 358, 360–68.

103. *Documents of the Persecution of Dutch Jewry, 1940–1945,* ed. Joodse Historisch Museum (Amsterdam, 1969), pp. 124–30.

104. De Jong, *Het Koningkrijk,* vol 8., pp. 304, 307–09; Philip Mechanicus, *Waiting for Death: A Diary* (London, 1968), p. 21. The diary was written in Westerbork between March 28, 1943, and February 21, 1944. See reproduction of Wilhelm Harster's orders (May 5, 1943) in de Jong, *Het Koningkrijk,* between pp. 366, 367.

105. De Jong, *Het Koningkrijk,* vol 8, p. 311, Calmeyer's letter is on p. 315.

106. *Het Koningkrijk,* vol 8., pp. 318, 416f.

107. Ibid., vol. 6, p. 292; vol. 7, p. 296. In Holland, as in Germany, a distinction was made between the two categories of mixed marriages: couples with children were privileged, whereas Jewish partners in childless marriages were liable for deportation. Hanns Rauter even requested that a non-Jewish wife be deported, "otherwise we shall always have problems with these cases."

108. Ibid., vol. 6, pp. 356–59.

109. Ibid., vol. 7, pp. 331f.

110. Ibid., vol. 7, p. 312f., p. 374f.

111. Mechanicus, *Waiting for Death,* passim.

112. De Jong, *Het Koningkrijk,* vol 8., pp. 738f.

113. Mechanicus, *Waiting for Death,* pp. 167–69.

114. According to de Jong, *Het Koningkrijk,* vol. 8, p. 708.

115. The appendix to Nachman Blumenthal's *Conduct and Actions of a Judenrat: Documents from the Bialystok Ghetto* (Jerusalem, 1962), pp. 551–53 (Hebrew and Yiddish, with English introduction), gives seventy-five places of employment, factories, and workshops: forty-five within the ghetto area, twenty outside of it, and ten outside the city. Those in the last two locations were under Polish or German proprietorship (private or state).

116. Nina Tennenbojm-Becker, *Ha-Adam ha-Lohem* (Jerusalem, 1974), p. 183.

117. On the deportation in November from the Bialystok district, see "Calendar of Events," *Hefte von Auschwitz,* 3 (1960), 1942, 100–104; Blumenthal, *Bialystok Ghetto,* pp. xliv–xlvii, 266, 270.

118. Diary entry of January 31, 1943, in Mordekhai Tennenbojm-Tamaroff, *Dapim Min ha-Dleka: Pirkei Yoman, Mikhtavim u-Reshimot* (Hakibbutz Hameuhad, 1948), pp. 57f., 67f. On Chaim Barash and his relations with Tennenbojm see Yisrael Gutman, "Problems of Jewish Labor for the Germans in Eastern Europe During the Second World War," *Zion,* (Jerusalem) 43, nos. 1–2 (1968), 136–38 (Hebrew).

119. Tennenbojm-Tamaroff, *Dapim Min ha-Dleka,* pp. 94f.; on February 9 he wrote that twenty thousand were in hiding—"it is impossible to find them" (p. 76).

120. "Calendar of Events," *Hefte von Auschwitz,* 4 (1961), 72; Tennenbojm-Becker, *Ha-Adam ha-Lohem,* p. 175, and fn.

121. Tennenbojm-Tamaroff, *Dapim Min Ha-Dleka,* pp. 79–81.

122. Ḥaika Grossman, *Anshei Maḥteret,* ed. Mordekhai Amitai (Tel Aviv, 1965), p. 234.

123. Tennenbojm-Tamaroff, *Dapim Min Ha-Dleka,* pp. 192f.

124. Report on the operation by the Königsberg department of the Ministry of Propa-

ganda to Goebbels, September 24, 1943. Grossman, *Anshei Maḥteret,* facing p. 402; Tennenbojm-Tamaroff, *Dapim Min Ha-Dleka,* facing p. 224.

125. Grossman, *Anshei Maḥteret,* pp. 312f.; see chap. 17, "The Armed Struggle of Jews in Nazi-Occupied Countries."

126. *Anatomy of the SS-State,* ed. Helmut Krausnick et al. (London, 1968), pp. 119 f.; NO-5179.

127. *Das Diensttagebuch des deutschen Generalgouverneurs in Polen, 1939–1945,* ed. Werner Präg and Wolfgang Jacobmeyer, (Stuttgart, 1974), pp. 678ff. 682, 950.

128. *TWC,* 5, NO-2403, p. 626; *DOH,* pp. 456f.; *Anatomy of the SS-State,* pp. 120–23.

129. Yitzḥad Arad, *Ghetto in Flames: The Struggle and Destruction of the Jews in Vilna in the Holocause* (New York, 1982), pp. 333–38. On the controversial aspects of Gens's actions, see *DOH,* pp. 438–46.

130. Arad, *Ghetto in Flames,* pp. 355–64.

131. Ibid., chap. 23, pp. 425ff.

132. Himmler's directive of June 11, 1943, NO-2496, *TWC,* 5, pp. 623f.

133. Emmanuel Ringelblum, *Polish-Jewish Relations During the Second World War,* ed. Joseph Kermish and Shumuel Krakowski (Jerusalem, 1974), p. 274. Ringlelblum and his wife and son were captured in their hiding place in Warsaw on March 7, 1944, and murdered.

134. Aldolf Berman, *Mi-Mei ha-Maḥteret* (Tel Aviv, 1971), pp. 92f.

135. Ibid., pp. 94, 133f., 136f.

136. The document is quoted in Meilekh Neustadt, ed., *Destruction and Rising: The Epic of the Jews in Warsaw* (Tel Aviv, 1947), pp. 128f. (Hebrew).

137. Reitlinger, *The Final Solution,* p. 282; Phillip Friedman, "The Destruction of the Jews of Lwów," in *Roads to Extinction: Essays on the Holocaust,* ed. Ada J. Friedman (Philadelphia, 1980), pp. 276–78.

138. According to a report of June 30, 1943, by SS and police commander Fritz Katzmann, *IMT,* 37, L-18, pp. 394–432. Published in *DOH,* pp. 335–41.

139. P. Friedman, "Jews of Luów," passim, Table p. 288.

140. See Katzmann's report, n. 138 above.

141. Reitlinger, *The Final Solution,* p. 302; Friedman, "Jews of Luów," pp. 295–303. Regarding new slogans coined at the time, it is interesting that just as the Jews in Holland said of lists of privileged people that they "exploded" if they were declared invalid and the people were deported, so the Jews in Poland said of apartments that they "exploded" when hiding places were discovered by the Germans.

142. *Das Diensttagebuch,* p. 700. The numbers of Poles and Ukrainians are given as approximately 10.2 million and 3.9 million respectively.

143. Ibid., p. 715, August 2, 1943, and p. 776. n. 70. In May 1944 the number was 27,439—almost a hundred less than noted in April. On the Red Army's advance during the summer, many Jews were "evacuated" to Auschwitz; Hilberg, *Destruction of the European Jews* (1961), pp. 341f.

144. Quoted from Artur Greiser's trial in Poland after the war; Isaiah Trunk, *Judenrat: The Jewish Councils in Eastern Europe Under Nazi Occupation* (New York, 1972), p. 89.

145. M. Neustadt, *Destruction and Rising,* pp. 119–21, 126, 137.

146. NO-4498 B; *TWC,* 4, NO-3240, pp. 146–50.

147. Ino Arndt and Wolfgang Scheffler, "Organisierter Massenmord an Juden in nationalsozialistischen Vernichtungslagern," *VJHZ,* 24 (1976) no. 2, pp. 126f.; Adalbert Rückerl, *NS-Vernichtungslager im Spiegel deutscher Strafprozesse* (London, 1977), pp. 205f., 273f. Paul Blobel was condemned to death at the Einsatzgruppen trial in Nuremberg and executed in 1951.

148. *IMT*, 7, pp. 592f.

149. Declaration in Paul Blobel's sworn testimony, June 18, 1947, NO-3947.

150. *IMT*, 7, p. 653; *IMT*, 36, pp. 94–97; NO-3947.

151. Among many other sources, see Reitlinger, *The Final Solution*, pp. 317f.

152. Paul Bergen, *Dachau, the Official History, 1933–1945* (London, 1975), pp. 80f.; Hugo Burkhard, *Tanz mal Jude: Von Dachau bis Shanghai* (Nürnberg, 1965), pp. 83f. Testimony of A. Platz, *YVSA*, 02/236, p. 10; Falk Pingel, *Häftlinge unter SS-Herrschaft: Widerstand, Selbstbehauptung und Vernichtung im Konzentrationslager* (Hamburg, 1978), p. 246 n. 90. Also see Leni Yahil, "Jews in Concentration Camps in Germany Prior to World War II," in *The Nazi Concentration Camps: Structure and Aims, the Image of the Prisoner, the Jews in the Camps. Proceedings of the Fourth Yad Vashem International Historical Conference,* ed. Yisrael Gutman and Avital Saf (Jerusalem, 1984), pp. 69–100.

153. Eugen Kogon, *Der SS-Staat: Das System der deutschen Konzentrationslager* (Frankfurt on the Main, 1965), p. 134; *Buchenwald: Mahnung und Verpflichtung: Dokumente und Berichte,* 4th rev. ed. (Berlin, 1983), pp. 127f.; Burckhard, *Tanz mal Jude,* pp. 127–29.

154. Report brought to Geneva by a member of the International Red Cross, see Hans G. Adler, *Die Verheimlichte Wahrheit: Theresienstädter Dokumente* (Tübingen, 1958), pp. 304–06.

155. Erich Kulka, "Five Escapes from Auschwitz and their Repercussions," *Yalkut Moreshet,* 3 (1965), 23–26 (Hebrew); Ota Kraus and Erich Kulka, *The Death Factory: Documents on Auschwitz* (Oxford, 1959), pp. 167–81.

156. Leni Yahil, *The Rescue of Danish Jewry: Test of a Democracy* (Philadelphia, ppbk. ed, 1983), pp. 302–13.

157. Filip Müller, *Auschwitz Inferno: The Testimony of a Sonderkommando* (London, 1979), pp. 69f., 77–86. Also see chap. 15.

Chapter 17

1. Tadeusz Bor-Komorowski, *The Secret Army* (New York, 1951), p. 42.

2. Ber Mark, "Herbert Baum's Group: The Jewish Resistance Group, 1937–1942," *Bleter far Geshichte,* 14 (1961); Helmut Eschwege, "Resistance of German Jews Against the Nazi Regime," *YLB,* 15 (1970), pp. 168–80.

3. This is discussed at length in chap. 10–15.

4. See Yisrael Gutman in *The Jews of Warsaw 1939–1943: Ghetto, Underground, Revolt* (Bloomington, Ind., 1982), pp. 132–44; Leni Yahil, "The Warsaw Underground Press: A Case Study in the Reaction to Anti-Semitism," in *Living with Antisemitism: Modern Jewish Responses,* ed. Yehuda Reinharz (Hanover, N.H., 1987). pp. 413, 442.

5. See Yahil, "Warsaw Underground Press," pp. 437f.

6. Ruźka Korczak, *Flames in Ash* (Tel-Aviv, 1961), p. 54 (Hebrew); *DOH* 1981, p. 433.

7. See report of Yitzhak Zuckerman (or Cuckierman) of May 24, 1944, *DOH,* pp. 277f.

8. Ibid.

9. From a speech by Abba Kovner, December 1945, "Ha-Nes be-Hidalon": Dvarim be-Kinus be-Modiin," *Sefer Hashomer Hatzair* (Merhavia, Isr., 1956), vol. 1, pp. 643–54.

10. Isaiah Trunk, "The Attitude of the Judenrats to the Problem of Armed Resistance Against the Nazis," in *Jewish Resistance During the Holocaust: Proceedings of the Conference on Manifestations of Jewish Resistance* (Yad Vashem, Jerusalem, 1971), pp. 202–27.

11. For more details about the European resistance movement, see Henri Michel, *The Shadow War: Resistance in Europe, 1939–1945* (London, 1970).

12. J. Caban, Z. Mankowski, "Zwiazek Walki, Zbrojnei Armia Krajowa w Okregu Lubelskim, 1939–1944," in *Dokumenty* (Warsaw, 1971), vol. 2, p. 60.

13. Quoted from Yisrael Gutmam and Shmuel Krakowski, *Unequal Victims: Poles and Jews During World War II* (New York, 1986), p. 159; *DOH*, pp. 304f. Also see Yisrael Gutman, "Jews and Poles in World War II," in Reinharz, *Living with Antisemitism,* pp. 443–72.

14. Gutman and Krakowski, *Unequal Victims,* pp. 120–33.

15. Mordekhai Tennenbojm-Tamaroff, *Dapim Min ha-Dleka: Pirkei Yoman, Mikhtavim u-Reshimot* (Hakibbutz Hameuhad, 1948), pp. 67, 79, 235–39.

16. According to the minutes of a meeting between Yitzhak Zuckerman and Moreshet in Tel Aviv on February 2, 1973.

17. *Sefer ha-Partizanim ha-Yehudim* (Merhavia, Isr., 1959), vol. 1, p. 26.

18. On the resistance movement in Vilna, see Yitzhak Arad, *Ghetto in Flames: The Struggle and Destruction fo the Jews in Vilna in the Holocaust* (New York, 1982); Meir Dworzecki, *Yerushalayim de-Lita be-Meri u-ve-Shoah* (Tel Aviv, 1958); Korchak, *Flames in Ash,* pp. 275–79.

19. On the underground organization of the Jews of Kovno and the revolt movement there, see Leib Garfunkel, *Kovno ha-Yehudit be-Hurbanah* (Jerusalem, 1959); Dov Levin, *Fighting Back: Lithuanian Jewry's Armed Resistance to the Nazis, 1941–1944* (New York, 1985); Zvie A. Brown and Dov Levin, *The Story of an Underground: The Resistance of the Jews of Kovno (Lithuania) in the Second World War* (Jerusalem, 1962) (Hebrew).

20. Tennenbojm-Tamaroff, *Dapim Min ha-Dleka,* p. 111.

21. *Eichmann Trial, Testimonies* (Jerusalem, 1963), vol. 1, p. 355 (Hebrew).

22. Haika Grossman, *Anshei Mahteret,* ed. Mordekhai Amitai (Tel Aviv, 1965), pp. 281–85.

23. Hannah Wiernik-Schlesinger, "One Testimony," *Yalkut Moreshet,* 1 (1964), 73–78 (Hebrew).

24. For details of the operation's organization, see "Internal Correspondence," in *Dapim le-Heker ha-Shoah ve-ha-Mered,* ed. Nachman Blumenthal (Hakibbutz Hameuhad, 1951), vol. 1, pp. 153ff.; see also David Lior, *Ir ha-Metim* (Tel Aviv, 1946); Shmuel Ron, "Fragments of Memoirs," *Yalkut Moreshet,* 14 (1973), 43–74.

25. Gusta Davidson, *Yomana shel Justina* (Tel Aviv, 1953).

26. Hava Perlman, "The Attack on the Cyganeria Café," in *Sefer Milhamot ha-Getaot,* ed. Yitzhak Zuckerman and Moshe Bassok (Hakibbutz Hameuhad, 1956), pp. 319–22 (Hebrew); Arieh L. Bauminger, *The Fighters of the Cracow Ghetto* (Jerusalem, 1986).

27. Arnon Schworin et al., "Revolt in Lachwa," in *They Fought Back: The Story of the Jewish Resistance in Nazi Europe,* ed. Yuri Suhl (New York, 1967), pp. 165–67.

28. Shalom Cholawski, "The Story of Tuczin," *Yalkut Moreshet* 2 (1964), 81–95 (Hebrew).

29. Emmanuel Ringelblum, *Polish-Jewish Relations During the Second World War,* ed. Joseph Kermish and Shmuel Krakowski (Jerusalem, 1974), p. 165.

30. Idem, "Comrade Mordechai," in Suhl, *They Fought Back,* pp. 85–91.

31. Yitzhak Zuckerman in the conversation with Moreshet. (see n. 16).

32. Yitzhak Zuckerman, "Mered ha-Yehudim," in *Mibifnim,* 12 (1947), 426 (Hebrew). Also see Gutman and Krakowski, *Unequal Victims,* pp. 143–71; Gutman, *The Jews of Warsaw,* passim.

33. Quoted in *DOH,* p. 311.

34. Ibid., p. 315.

35. Ibid., p. 310.

36. Gitta Sereny, *Into That Darkness: From Mercy Killing to Mass Murder* (London, 1974); Yankiel Wiernik, *A Year in Treblinka* (New York, 1944); Shmuel Krakowski, *The War of the Doomed: Jewish Armed Resistance in Poland, 1942–1944* (New York, 1984), chap. 12.

37. Stanislaw Kon in *Sefer Milhamot ha-Getaot*, p. 538.

38. Yitzhak Arad, *Belzec, Sobibor, Treblinka: The Operation Reinhard Death Camps* (Indianapolis, Ind., 1987).

39. See Alexander Pechersky's memoirs, "Revolt in Sobibor," in Suhl, *They Fought Back*, pp. 7–50; idem, "The Revolt in Sobibor," *Yalkut Moreshet*, 10 (1969), 7–33 (Hebrew); Miriam Novitch, *Sobibor: Martyrdom and Revolt* (New York, 1980).

40. See fragments of diaries by Levental and Gradowski in Ber Mark, *The Scroll of Auschwitz* (Tel Aviv, 1977), pp. 286–384, 377–435 (Yiddish); Filip Müller, *Auschwitz Inferno: The Testimony of a Sonderkommando* (London, 1979).

41. Details of the Rosa Robota episode can be found in Yisrael Gutman, *Anashim ve-Efer: Sefer Auschwitz-Birkenau* (Merhavia, Isr., 1957), pp. 151–57; Yuri Suhl, "Rosa Robota: Heroine of the Auschwitz Underground," in Suhl, *They Fought Back*, pp. 219–25.

42. Gutman and Krakowski, *Unequal Victims*, pp. 102ff.

43. Yitzhak Arad, "Jewish Family Camps in the Forest: An Original Means of Rescue," in *Rescur Attempts During the Holocaust. Proceedings of the Second Yad Vashem international Historical Conference*, ed. Yisrael Gutman and Efraim Zuroff (Jerusalem, 1977), pp. 333–53.

44. Tennenbojm-Tamaroff, *Dapim Min ha-Dleka*, pp. 100ff.

45. Korczak, *Flames in Ash*, pp. 275–79.

46. On Jews in the partisan movement, see *Sefer ha-Partizanim ha-Yehudim*, 2 vols.; Moshe Kahanowicz, *Milhemet ha-Partizanim ha-Yehudim be-Mizrah Europa* (Tel Aviv, 1954); Reuben Ainsztein, *Jewish Resistance in Nazi-Occupied Europe* (London, 1974), pp. 393–96.

47. See the chapter "One Fate" in *Sefer ha-Partizanim ha-Yehudim*, vol. 1, p. 529; Shmuel Cholawski, "Minsk: Its Struggle and Destruction," *Yalkut Moreshet*, 18 (1975), 101–12 (Hebrew); Ainsztein, *Jewish Resistance*, pp. 463–85.

48. *Sefer ha-Partizanim ha-Yehudim*, vol. 1, pp. 172–188.

49. See Ainsztein, *Jewish Resistance*, pp. 379ff.

50. See Krakowski, *The War of the Doomed*, pp. 417–25; passim.

51. Emil F. Knieza, "The Resistance of the Slovak Jews," in Suhl, *They Fought Back*, pp. 176–81.

52. On Jewish membership of the resistance movement against fascism and the struggle to liberate Yugoslavia, see Emma Chasser, *Lohamim Yehudim be-Milhama neged ha-Nazim*, ed. Marion Mushkat (Tel Aviv, 1971), p. 192 (Hebrew).

53. Léon Poliakov, "Jewish Resistance in France," *YIVO Bleter*, 37 (1953), 185–97 (Yiddish); idem, "Les Différentes Formes de la résistance juive en France," in *Jewish Resistance During the Holocaust* (see n. 10), pp. 524–32.

54. Chaim Avni, "The Zionist Underground in Holland and France and the Escape to Spain," in Gutman and Zuroff, *Rescue Attempts During the Holocaust*, pp. 555–90.

55. Lucien Steinberg, *Jews Against Hitler* (London and New York, 1978), pp. 81–118; see also Renée Poznanski, "A Methodical Approach to the Study of Jewish Resistance in France," *Yad Vashem Studies*, 18 (1987), pp. 1–39; Shmuel R. Kapel, *Le combat juif en France occupée dans les camps d'internement et dans slen de l'organisation de combat, 1940–1944* (Jerusalem, 1981) (Hebrew); Annie Latour, *The Jewish Resistance in France* (New York, 1981).

56. L. Steinberg, *Jews Against Hitler*, pp. 119–27.

57. Lucien Steinberg, *Le comité de défense des Juifs en Belgique, 1942–1944* (Brussels, 1973).

58. Philip Friedman, "Jewish Resistance to Nazism," in *Roads to Extinction; Essays on the Holocause*, ed. Ada J. Friedman (Philadelphia, 1980), p. 393.

59. Tuvia Bozikowski, *Bein Kirot Noflim* (Tel Aviv, 1964), p. 38.

Chapter 18

1. Josef Goebbels Tagebücher aus den Jahren 1942–1943, ed. Louis P. Lochner (Zurich, 1948), p. 242.

2. Hans A. Jacobsen, "Deutsche Kriegsführung, 1939–1945: Ein Überblick" in *Schriftenreihe der Niedersächsichen Landeszentrale für politische Bildung Zeitgeschichte*, 12 (Hanover, W. Ger., 1961), p. 61.

3. Willi A. Boelke, ed., *Wollt Ihr den totalen Krieg? Die geheimen Goebbels Konferenzen, 1939–1941* (Stuttgart, 1967), pp. 312f.; *The Secret Conferences of Dr. Goebbels, October 1939–March 1943* (London, n.d.), pp. 308f. The Russians denied that the Katyn Forest massacre had taken place, whereas the Germans attempted to have it confirmed by an International Medical Commission of Inquiry working in conjunction with the Red Cross. In retaliation for Polish protests, Stalin broke off relations with the Polish government-in-exile.

4. *Pinkas Hakehillot: Encyclopaedia of Jewish Communities, Rumania*, ed. Theodor Lavi et al. (Yad Vashem, Jerusalem, 1969), vol. 1, pp. 179, 189 (Hebrew).

5. See Mario D. Fenyö, *Hitler, Horthy and Hungary: German-Hungarian Relations, 1941–1944* (New Haven, Conn., 1972), p. 105.

6. Béla Vago, "Germany and the Jewish Policy of the Kállay Government," in *Hungarian Jewish Studies*, ed. Randolph L. Braham (New York, 1969), vol. 2, pp. 196f., 204–6.

7. Randolph L. Braham, *The Destruction of Hungarian Jewry: A Documentary Account* (New York, 1963), vol. 1, doc. 103; English translation in Jenö Lévai, ed., *Eichmann in Hungary: Documents* (Budapest, 1961), p. 54.

8. Braham, *Destruction of Hungarian Jewry*, doc. 103, pp. 100, 102, 104–12; idem, *The Hungarian Labor Service System, 1939–1945* (New York, 1977), pp. 50–58.

9. Nathan Eck, "The March of Death from Serbia to Hungary and the Slaughter of Cservenka," *YVS Studies*, vol. 2 (1958), pp. 255–94.

10. Braham, *Hungarian labor Service System*, p. 37; on the losses sustained by the Hungarian army see also Fenyó, *Hitler, Horthy and Hungary*, p. 108.

11. See Randolph L. Braham, "The Kamenets Podolsk and Délvidék Massacres: Prelude to the Holocaust in Hungary," *YVS Studies*, 9 (1973), pp. 119–30. The description that follows is derived from this article. Also see idem, *The Politics of Genocide: The Holocaust in Hungary* (New York, 1981), vol. 1, pp. 207ff. Szeged was a district town near the Baska border. See idem, "The Holocaust in Hungary: An Historical Interpretation of the Role of the Hungarian Radical Right," *Societas: A Review of Social History*, 2, no. 3 (1972), 196.

12. Braham, "The Kamenets Podolsk and Délvidék Massacres," pp. 123f.; Andras Deak, *Razzia in Novisad und andere Geschehnisse während des zweiten Weltkrieges in Ungarn und Yugoslavien* (Zurich, 1967), pp. 7–25.

13. "Declaration of German Atrocities," *TWC*, 6, p. x.; Braham, "The Kamenets Podolsk and Délvidék," pp. 127f.

14. Braham, *The Destruction of Hungarian Jewry,* doc. 63–65, pp. 114–24; ibid., Hitler's directive of January 19, 1944, pp. 117f.

15. Fenyö, *Hitler, Horthy and Hungary,* p. 160.

16. Braham, *The Destruction of Hungarian Jewry,* p. 215.

17. For a list of Eichmann's staff, see Randolph L. Braham, *Eichmann and the Destruction of Hungarian Jewry* (New York, 1961), p. 15. A more complete list in Raul Hilberg, *The Destruction of the European Jews* (Chicago, 1961), p. 528, Fenyö, *Hitler, Horthy and Hungary,* pp. 179–81.

18. "Eichmann's Story," *Life,* January 9, 1961, p. 17.

19. Braham, *Destruction of Hungarian Jewry,* doc. 48, pp. 89f.

20. Hilberg, *Destruction of the European Jews* (1961), pp. 534f.; by the end of April 8,225 people had been arrested; NO-5597; the Kistarcsa concentration camp near Budapest was reopened; Rafi Benshalom, *We Struggled for Life* (Tel Aviv, 1978), p. 40 (Hebrew).

21. Quote is according to Lévai, *Eichmann in Hungary,* pp. 72f. A slightly different, shorter version is in Fenyö, *Hitler, Horthy and Hungary,* p. 103.

22. Ernö Laszló, "Hungary's Jewry: A Demographic Overview, 1918–1945," in Braham, *Hungarian Jewish Studies,* vol. 2, passim. Laszló gives the official number of apostates, 58,320, on p. 154; another source has 61,548. It is generally agreed, however, that these figures are too low. Ze'ev Rotitz, "Statistical Data on Apostacy Among Hungarian Jews During the Years 1900–1941," *Dapim, Studies on the Holocaust Period* (1979), vol. 1, p. 222.

23. Laszló, "Hungary's Jewry," p. 158.

24. For background data see Ernö Marton, "The Family Tree of Hungarian Jewry," in Braham, *Hungarian Jewish Studies,* (1966), vol. 1, pp. 54f. In 1930, there were 292,159 Jews who belonged to the neologist community; 134, 972 to the Orthodox, and 17,440 to the status quo. Braham, *Politics of Genocide,* vol. 1, pp. 85–90. Laszló, "Hungary's Jewry," pp. 150–53.

25. Béla Vago, "Changes in the Leadership of Hungarian Jewry During World War II," in *Hanhagat Yehudei Hungaria be-Mivḥan ha-Shoah,* ed. Yisrael Gutman, Béla Vago, and Livia Rothkirchen (Jerusalem, 1976), p. 62; Nathaniel Katzburg, *Hungary and the Jews: Policy and Legislation, 1920–1943* (Ramat Gan, Israel, 1981), 212–35.

26. "Stern, Memoirs," *Yalkut Moreshet,* 16 (1973), 157–78; 17 (1974), pp. 153–80; Nathaniel Katzburg, "Memoirs of Samu Stern, President of the Pest Community, 1938–1939," in *Pedut, Rescue in the Holocaust: Texts and Studies,* ed. Nathaniel Katzburg (Ramat Gan, Isr, 1984), pp. 203–33 (Hebrew, English summary); and see Samu (Samuel) Stern, "A Race with Time," in Braham, *Hungarian Jewish Studies* (1973), vol.3, pp. 1–47; the quote is from "Stern, Memoirs," pp. 160–62.

27. Braham, *Politics of Genocide,* vol. 1, pp. 418–34; idem, "The Role of the Jewish Council in Hungary: A Tentative Assessment," *YVS Studies,* 10 (1975), pp. 69–109.

28. "Stern, Memoirs," *Yalkut Moreshet,* 16 (1973), p. 163.

29. Ibid., p. 166.

30. Braham, *Politics of Genocide,* vol. 1, pp. 431f.

31. Ibid., pp. 446–49.

32. Ibid., pp. 165f.

33. *Journal of the Hungarian Jews,* May 19, 1944, p. 1; Braham, p. 462; Jenö Lévai, *Black Book on the Martyrdom of Hungarian Jewry* (Zurich, 1948), pp. 192f.

34. Braham, *Eichmann and the Destruction of Hungarian Jewry,* pp. 25f.

35. On the flight from Hungary to Rumania, see Braham, *Politics of Genocide,* pp. 905ff.; Asher Cohen, ,The Ḥalutz Resistance in Hungary, 1942–1944 (Hakibbutz Hemeu-

ḥad, 1984), pp. 124–31; an estimate of the number of fugitives who reached Rumania is on pp. 130, 341 (Hebrew, English summary); NG-5617.

36. Lévai, *Eichmann in Hungary,* pp. 101–3, 105.

37. Braham, *Eichmann and the Destruction of Hungarian Jewry,* pp. 21. On Hungarian-German cooperation, see Braham, *Politics of Genocide,* pp. 596–604.

38. Lévai, *Eichmann in Hungary,* p. 107.

39. *IMT,* 31, PS-2604, p. 6; Moshe Sandberg, *My Longest Year: In the Hungarian Labour Service and in Nazi Camps* (Jerusalem, 1968), p. 18.

40. Lévai, *Eichmann in Hungary,* pp. 108, 112; "Stern, Memoirs," *Yalkut Moreshet,* 16 (1973), pp. 154f.

41. Braham, *Hungarian Labor Service System,* pp. 60–62; the motives of the ministry are unclear. Braham surmises that humanitarian sentiments on the part of the battalion commanders coupled with the pressing need for manpower were behind the change.

42. Telegram from minister Edmund Veesenmayer dated May 8, 1944, in Braham, *Destruction of Hungarian Jewry,* doc. 158, p. 372; NG-2059. Sandberg: *My Longest Year,* pp. 23f.

43. For the entire text of the petition see Lévai, *Eichmann in Hungary,* pp. 112–17 the quote is on p. 16.

44. Ibid., pp. 118–20.

45. Fenyö, *Hitler, Horthy and Hungary,* pp. 202f. The Crown Council had already made the decision to stop deportations on Jun 26, but Eichmann, nevertheless, planned for the deportations to begin on July 6.

46. Lévai, *Eichmann in Hungary,* pp. 126–29.

47. Fenyö, *Hitler, Horthy and Hungary,* pp. 210f.

48. Ibid., p. 215; Braham, *Destruction of Hungarian Jewry,* doc. 214, p. 481; doc. 220, p. 492.

49. Fenyö, *Hitler, Horthy and Hungary,* pp. 228–39. The events of those momentous days are somewhat confused and have engendered controversy among historians.

50. For a description of the fugitives' position see Benshalom, *We Struggled for Life,* pp. 15–25; A. Cohen, *The Ḥalutz Resistance,* passim.

51. Ernest Landau, ed., *Der Kastner-Bericht über Eichmanns Menschenhandel in Ungarn,* (Munich, 1961), pp. 42–45; Braham, *Politics of Genocide,* pp. 103–10.

52. Braham, *Politics of Genocide,* pp. 934–40.

53. Lévai, *Eichmann in Hungary,* pp. 146

54. *EJ,* 8, col. 1,104, gives the number 76,000; Braham, in *Politics of Genocide,* pp. 838–43, refrains from quoting a specific figure.

55. The quotation is in Lévai, *Eichmann in Hungary,* pp. 164; see Braham, *Hungarian Labor Service System,* pp. 70–73.

56. Braham, *Politics of Genocide,* pp. 834–38.

57. Braham, *Hungarian Labor Service System,* p. 74.

58. Braham, *Politics of Genocide,* pp. 1,143–45. Among those who returned to the formerly annexed territories were 56,500 deportees and 9,000 former labor service men.

59. Ivástázi Veghazi, "The Role of Jewry in the Economic Life of Hungary," in Braham, *Hungarian Jewish Studies,* vol. 2, p. 82.

60. Hilberg, *The Destruction of the European Jews* (1961), pp. 511, 516f.

61. Ibid., pp. 521f.

62. Braham, *Destruction of Hungarian Jewry,* docs. 409, 410, 415, 420, 421, 425, 426, 431, 434, 437; Hilberg *The Destruction of European Jews* (1961), pp. 532f.

63. Eliezer Yerushalmi, *Pinkas Shavli: A Diary from a Lithuanian Ghetto (1941–1944)* (Jerusalem, 1958), pp. 304f. (Hebrew).

64. "Inmitten des grauenvollen Verbrechens: Handschriften von Mitgleidern des Sonderkommandos," in *Hefte von Auschwitz*, Sonderhelt (Special issue) 1, (1972), 125.

65. Yerushalmi, *Pinkas Shavli*, pp. 306, 309–15.

66. Ibid., pp. 381–93.

67. Leib Garfunkel, *Kovno ha-Yehudit be-Ḥurbanah* (Jerusalem, 1959), pp. 176–99.

68. *Pinkas Hakehillot: Encyclopaedia of Jewish Communities, Poland,* vol. 1, *The Communities of Lodz and its Regions,* ed. Danuta Dombrowska and Abraham Wein (Yad Vashem, Jerusalem, 1976), pp. 35–37 (Hebrew).

69. Livia Rothkirchen, *The Destruction of Slovak Jewry: A Documentary History* (Jerusalem, 1961), docs. 78, 79, 81, pp. 206–8, 210 (Hebrew with English introduction).

70. Jirmiahu O. Neumann, *Im Schatten des Todes* (Tel Aviv, 1956), pp. 224–29.

71. Ibid., p. 237. The author used the pseudonym in Dr. Alt to describe his own experiences. His Hebrew name Yiruiahu was not in daily use.

72. *IMT,* 33, PS-3762, pp. 68–70. Ino Arndt, and Wolfgang Scheffler, "Organisierter Massenmord an Juden in nationalsoziolistischen Vernichtungslagern," *VJHZ,* 24 no. 2 (1976), p. 134 n. 62; H. G. Adler, *Theresienstadt, 1941–1945: Das Antlitz einer Zwangsgemeinschaft* (Tübingen, 1960), p. 186. "Calendar of Events, 1944," *Hefte von Auschwitz,* 8 (1964), states that the last large-scale gassing of a transport from Sered took place on November 3, 1944; thereafter only small numbers are mentioned in a few specific cases.

73. Neumann, *Im Schatten des Todes,* pp. 249–53.

74. Rothkirchen, *Destruction of Slovak Jewry,* p. 43. It should be noted that there is no record of the number of Jews living in Slovakia in 1938 and that the figure cited was probably slightly lower. On the deportees to Theresienstadt see Zdenek Lederer, *Ghetto Theresienstadt* (London, 1953), p. 249.

75. All the numerical data on Theresienstadt are taken from the tables in Lederer, *Ghetto Theresienstadt,* pp. 247–51.

76. Adler, *Theresienstadt, 1941–1945,* pp. 58f.

77. Lederer, *Ghetto Theresienstadt,* pp. 247–51.

78. Ibid., most of the numbers are from thie source. The number of Jews from Denmark is according to Leni Yahil, *The Rescue of Danish Jewry: Test of a Democracy* (Philadelphia, pbbk. ed. 1983), p. 318.

79. Neumann, *Im Schatten des Todes,* pp. 287.

80. Ibid., pp. 291–93; a similar description is found in Adler, *Theresienstadt, 1941–1945,* pp. 208–11. Adler sharply criticizes the camp inmates for their attitude toward this last group of new arrivals. He also includes the latter in the total number of camp inmates, which he estimates at 155,000 (p. 215).

81. Edward L. Homze, *Foreign Labor in Nazi Germany, 1939–1952* (Princeton, N.J., 1967), pp. 147–53, 311; Malcolm J. Proudfoot, *European Refugees: A Study in Forced Population Movement* (London, 1957), p. 80.

82. Arndt and Scheffler, "Organisierter Massenmord," pp. 131, 133–35; Ota Kraus and Erich Kulka, *The Death Factory: Documents on Auschwitz* (Oxford, 1959), pp. 127–30 (Crematoria Nos. 2 through 5 are counted as Crematoria Nos. 1 through 4 in this source).

83. Eugen Kogen, *Der SS-Staat: Das System der deutschen Konzentrationslager* (Frankfurt on the Main, 1965), p. 157. Kogon estimates that 3.5 to 4.5 million people were murdered. Arndt and Scheffler, "Organisierter Massenmord," report "over a million."

84. Halina Wrobel, "Die Liquidation der Konzentrationslagers Auschwitz-Birkenau," *Hefte von Auschwitz,* 6 (1962), 6f.; Rudolf Höss, *Kommandant in Auschwitz: Autogiobraphische Aufreighnungen,* ed. Martin Broszat (Munich, 1958), p. 140 n. 1.

85. Wrobel, "Liquidation," pp. 8–10.

86. Rudolf Hoess, *Commandant of Auschwitz: The Autobiography of Rudolf Höss* (London, 1961), p. 169.

87. Wrobel, "Liquidation," pp. 12, 16–29, 32.

88. Evelyn le Chêne, *Mauthausen: The History of a Death Camp* (London, 1971), pp. 21f., 36, 199–256; Hans Marsalek, *Die Geschichte des Konzentrationslagers Mauthausen: Dokumentation* (Vienna, 1980), passim; Benjamin Eckstein, *Mauthausen: Concentration and Annihilation Camp* (Jerusalem, 1984), pp. 37–41, 97 (Hebrew).

89. Le Chêne, *Mauthausen: Death Camp*, pp. 84f.; Marsalek, *Mauthausen*, pp. 157–64; Eckstein, *Mauthausen: Concentration and Annihilation Camp*, pp. 43–86, 202–11. On "euthanasia," see chap. 12, "The Final Solution: Overall Planning."

90. On February 2, 1941, Himmler and Heydrich issued a secret directive that defined the four categories of concentration camps and German inmates: 1. Incorrigible prisoners (Dachau, Sachsenhausen, Auschwitz); 1a. Older political prisoners unfit for hard labor (Dachau); 2. Political prisoners convicted of more serious crimes but still capable of being influenced (Buchenwald, Flossenbürg, Neuengamme, Auschwitz II); 3. Prisoners posing a danger to the state, those under sentence of death, and gypsies (Mauthausen). later on these categories were not strictly adhered to. NO-745; PS-1063-A.

91. Marsalek, *Mauthausen*, pp. 119, 128, 173, 226–54, 283.

92. Falk Pingel, *Häftlinge unter SS-Herrschaft: Widerstand, Selbstbehauptung, und Vernichtung im Konzentrationslager* (Hamburg, 1978), p. 140; Marsalek, *Mauthausen*, pp. 87, 180, and p. 227 n. 10; p. 228 n. 16; p. 255 n. 40.

93. Marsalek, *Mauthausen*, p. 100 (on p. 102 the total number of Jews is given as approximately 13,636). According to the table on p. 107, there were 72,392 prisoners in the Mauthausen camp complex on December 31, 1944. For a detailed description of the fate of the Jews in the camp, see Eckstein, *Mauthausen: Concentration and Annihilation Camp*, chap. 10. His figures as well as those of le Chñe, *Mauthansen: Death Camps*, are slightly different.

94. According to Marsalek, *Mauthausen*, p. 51, the tent camp was set up in the fall; according to le Chêne, *Mauthausen: Death Camp*, p. 144, Eichmann visited Mauthausen again in may 1944 and work began on the tent camp in June. Also see Eckstein, *Mauthausen Concentration and Annihilation Camp*, pp. 252–55.

95. Marsalek, *Mauthausen*, pp. 115–19, 139.

96. Le Chêne, *Mauthausen: Death Camp*, pp. 106f., 151. As there was not enough time to burn all the bodies in the crematoria, they were buried in a vast mass grave where some ten thousand of them were discovered after the war. Eckstein, *Mauthausen: Concentration and Annihilation Camp*, pp. 267f.

97. In Mauthansen there were 14,220 Jews registered as having died, but it is estimated that an additional 23,900 perished whose deaths were not recorded; in all approximately 38,120. On the number in all see Eckstein, *Mauthausen: Concentration and Annihilation Camp*, pp. 317–35. There were 199,000 prisoners passed through and 119,000 died. Also see n. 128 below.

98. Le Chêne, *Mauthausen: Death Camp*, pp. 103, 170–74.

99. Josef Katz, *One Who Came Back: The Diary of a Jewish Survivor* (New York, 1973), pp. 200–208. The quote is on pp. 201f.

100. This description follows a research paper based on testimonies taken at Yad Vashem: Olga M. Pickholz-Bernitsch, "The Evaluation of Stutthof Concentration Camp," *Yad Vashem Bulletin*, 17 (1965), 34–49. Various sources equate the number of prisoners with that of the evacuees; in my opinion, however, the number given—110,000—is more correct.

101. Ibid., pp. 45–47. Rudi Goguel, *"Cap Arcona": Report über den Untergang der Flüchtlingsflotte in der Lübecker Bucht am 4. Mai 1945* (Frankfurt on the Main, 1972), passim.

102. The main sources on the history of Buchenwald are Walter Bartel et al., eds., *Buchenwald, Mahnung und Verpflichtung: Dokumente und Berichte (vierte völlig bearbeitete Auflage)* (Berlin, DDR, 1983). This edition is substantially different from that published in Frankfurt on the Main in 1960, which I utilized for the Hebrew version of this work. I shall, therefore, continue to have recourse to the 1960 edition wherever necessary; Kogon, *Der SS-Staat,* passim.

103. Leni Yahil, "Jews in the Concentration Camps in Germany Prior to World War II," in *The Nazi Concentration Camps: Structure and Aims, the Image of the Prisoner, the Jews in the Camps: Proceedings of the Fourth Yad Vashem International Historical Conference,* ed. Yisrael Gutman and Avital Saf. (Jerusalem, 1984), pp. 69–100.

104. Pingel, *Häftlinge unter SS-Herrschaft,* pp. 182–86.

105. Complete annual statistics in *Buchenwald* (1960), pp. 76f., 83–87 (where there is a printing error in the total: instead of 238,380, it should read 238,980); see also Kogon, *Der SS-Staat,* p. 154. According to the table in Bartel et al., *Buchenwald* (1983), p. 708, the profit from prisoners hired out between June 1943 and February 1945 varied between RM 1,003,538 and RM 7,516,755 for men, RM 1,021,236 and RM 2,345,960 for women each month.

106. *Buchenwald* (1960), pp. 273f.; Bartel et al., *Buchenwald* (1983), pp. 276f.

107. The testimony is in CZA, S25/9703; the witness's name was May.

108. Kogon, *Der SS-Staat,* p. 146; *Buchenwald* (1960), pp. 158–81.

109. Close to 32,000 prisoners in satellite camps east of Buchenwald were never brought back; apparently, it is not known if or how they were evacuated or liberated.

110. Kogon, *Der SS-Staat,* p. 87. According to the table on p. 138, 30 percent died.

111. For the complete text of Hitler's will, see Werner Maser ed., *Hitler's Letters and Notes* (New York, 1976), pp. 341–61, Bantam Books. Also see *DOH,* p. 162.

112. Günther Kimmel, "Das Konzentrationslager Dachau," in *Bayern in der NS-Zeit,* ed. Martin Broszat et al. (Munich, 1979), vol. 2, pp. 410f.

113. Kimmel, ibid., pp. 372, 347, 385, and fn. 167. From September 1938 until April 1939, there were 562 prisoners in the camp who died, many of them Jews who had been arrested on Kristallnacht. Also see Paul Berben, *Dachau: The Official History, 1933–1945* (London, 1975), app. 13, pp. 275f.; app. 24, pp. 228f.; and pp. 256–61.

114. Kimmel, "Das Konzentrationslager Dachau," pp. 385, 388. According to Berben, *Dachau: The Official History, app. 19, p. 240, there were 3,016 people sent to Schloss Hartheim in 1942 and another 150 in 1944—3,166 in all; he gives a total of 5,127 victims of the "euthanasia" program.*

115. Kimmel, "Das Konzentrationslager Dachau," p. 391.

116. Alexander Mitscherlich and Fred Mielke, *Medizin ohne Menschlichkeit: Dokumente des Nürnberger Ärztprozesses* (Frankfurt on the Main, 1960), pp. 176f.; No-352, 590, 880; Hilberg, *The Destruction of the European Jews* 1961), pp. 608f.

117. Mitscherlich and Mielke, *Medizin ohne Menschlichkeit,* pp. 170f.

118. Kimmel, "Das Konzentrationslager Dachau," pp. 392–404, 407; Mitscherlich and Mielke, *Medizin ohne Menschlichkeit,* passim; see in particular pp. 68–71.

119. Mitscherlich and Mielke, *Medizin ohne Menschlichkeit,* p. 132.

120. The quotation of Heinrich Müller's order is from the German quoted in Hans A. Jacobsen, "Kommissarbefehl und Massenexekutionen sowjetischer Kriegsgefangener," in *Anatomie des SS-Staats,* ed. Helmut Krausnick et al. (Olten, Switz., 1965), vol. 2, p. 288.

For a description of such an execution see Kimmel, "Das Konzentrationslager Dachau," pp 405f.; Berben, *Dachau: The Official History,* app. 28; p. 269 contains a list of names of the Russian POW officers. It is also related that the international committee of the prisoners' underground gave orders not to work on the day of the execution, but some of the Russian officers persuaded the prisoners to the contrary and a strike was, in fact, called off as there were fears of a massacre by the SS.

121. According to Berben, *Dachau: The Official History,* app. 29, p. 271, Sireni was executed on November 20, 1944. According to Ruth Bondy, *The Emissary, A Life of Enzo Sireni* (Boston, 1977), p. 241, it was recorded in Dachau that he had "died on November 18, 1944"). Clara Urquhart and Peter L. Brent, *Enzo Sireni: A Hero of Our Time* (London, 1967).

122. Kimmel, "Das Konzentrationslager Dachau," pp. 408–11. See also Yehuda Bauer, "The Death Marches January–May 1945," in *Yahadut Zemanenu (Contemporary Jewry: A Research Annual),* (1983), 199–221 (Hebrew with English summary); Shmuel Krakowski, "The Death Marches During the Evacuation of the Camps," in *The Nazi Concentration Camps,* pp. 475–89.

123. Reska Weiss, *Journey Through Hell: A Woman's Account of Her Experiences at the Hands of the Nazis* (London, 1961).

124. Ibid., The quotations are taken from pp. 83, 121, 176, 211, and the preface.

125. Kogon, *Der SS-Staat,* the Table on p. 158, states that 273,150 prisoners died during the liquidation of the camps in 1945, either at the hands of the SS or during the death marches. Kogon does not explain how he arrives at this figure, which refers to all the concentration camps, and he himself remarks that it seems too low.

126. Reimund Schnabel, *Macht ohne Moral: Eine Dokumentation über die SS* (Frankfurt on the Main, 1957), p. 179.

127. Höss, *Kommandant in Auschwitz,* pp. 144, 181. The translation is from the original German text. The English version (see n. 86) is on pp. 172, 212.

128. It has not been possible, in the framework of this study, to detail the history of all the camps, and I have, therefore, used a few major, characteristic examples. The table herewith appears in the "Calendar of Events," *Hefte von Auschwitz* 8 (1964), 107, January 25, 1945, but an estimate can also be reached by means of the numbers I have given. The figures should not be regarded as final in view of the following reservations: many prisoners moved from camp to camp and were consequently counted at least twice, as in the case of the Dutch Jews in Buchenwald and Mauthausen; the numbers of dead in some camps include those prisoners who were executed on orders from above, like the Russian POWs; this is likewise the case with prisoners who perished during death marches, in satellite camps, or who were sent elsewhere for extermination, for example, to Auschwitz. Thus, these figures constitute no more than a guide and an estimate; they are rounded off to the nearest thousand.

Name of Camp	Prisoners Who Passed Through	Prisoners Who Died	Percentage of Dead
Mauthausen	200,000	120,000	60.0
Stutthof	110,000	32,000	29.0
Buchenwald	240,000	70,000	29.2
Dachau	200,000	33,000	16.5
Total	750,000	255,000	

Chapter 19

1. W. A. Visser 't Hooft, *Memoirs* (London, 1973), pp. 165f.

2. This view is supported particularly by Helen Fein, *Accounting for Genocide: National Responses and Jewish Victimization During the Holocaust* (New York, 1979), passim.

3. See Yisrael Gutman, *The Jews of Warsaw 1939–1943: Ghetto, Underground, Revolt* (Bloomington, Ind., 1982), pp. 4f. 120f.

4. See chap. 12, "The Fluctuation in the Composition of the Councils," in Isaiah Trunk, *Judenrat: The Jewish Councils in Eastern Europe Under Nazi Occupation* (New York, 1972). Of 720 known chairmen of the Judenräte, 86 (or 11.9 percent) survived (see Table 9, p. 327).

5. A similar categorization is found in Lucy S. Dawidowicz, *The War Against the Jews 1933–1945* (New York, 1975), chap. 11–13. On the activities of the Polish underground during that period, see chap. 17, "The Armed Struggle of Jews in Nazi-Occupied Countries."

6. Yisrael Gutman and Shmuel Krakowski, *Unequal Victims: Poles and Jews During World War Two* (New York, 1986), pp. 106f.

7. *EJ,* vol. 8, col. 878.

8. Rabbi Shimon Huberband, *Kiddush Hashem* (Tel Aviv, 1969), pp. 184f. The description that follows is largely based on this source. The Nazis did not single out the men alone, they also forbade women to wear wigs in public, see p. 97. Rabbi Huberband perished in Treblinka at the age of thirty-eight. See the obituary on him dated November 15, 1942, in Joseph Kermish, ed., *To Live with Honor and Die with Honor: Selected Documents from the Warsaw Ghetto Underground Archives "O.S." (Oneg Shabbath)* (Jerusalem, 1986), pp. 54–57, 82.

9. Mordekhai Eliav, ed., *Ani Maamin: Eduyot al Ḥayehem u-Motam shel Anshei Emunah bi'imei ha-Shoah* (Jerusalem, 1965), p. 23.

10. Menashe Unger, *Admorim she-nispu ba-Shoah* (Jerusalem, 1969), pp 102–4; the testimony of Rabbi Israel Shapira was recorded after the war by Rabbi Isaac Herzog during a visit to a DP camp in Germany, see pp. 192–97.

11. Of the postwar literature on this subject, we cite in particular Irving J. Rosenbaum, *Holocaust and Halacha* (New York, 1976). The bibliography includes the responsa literature published in Israel, the United States, and London; in particular see Rabbi Ephraim Oshry (of Kovno), *Sefer She'elot u-Tshuvot, mi-Ma-amakim,* 4 vols. (New York, 1959–1970).

12. Rabbi H. J. Zimmels, *The Echo of the Nazi Holocaust in Rabbinic Literature* (London, 1977), p. 99; see also Trunk, *Judenrat,* pp. 187–96.

13. Rosenbaum, *Holocaust and Halacha,* p. 50; Oshry, *Sefer She'elot u-Tshuvot, mi-Ma-amakim,* p. 33 n. 19; see also Joseph Walk, "The Religious Leadership During the Holocaust," in *Patterns of Jewish Leadership in Nazi Europe 1933–1945: Proceedings of the Third Yad Vashem International Historical Conference,* ed. Yisrael Gutman and Cynthia J. Haft (Jerusalem, 1979). pp. 377–91.

14. *Sefer Esh Kodesh: Sermons of Kalonymus K. Shapira* (1979), p. 78. The sources: *Terumot,* chap 7: mishnah 12; Maimonides, *Mishneh Torah: The Book of Knowledge,* trans. Moses Hyamson (Jerusalem, 1965), chap 5; Precepts, p. 40b; Bet Yosef citing Rashi, quoted by Huberband, *Kiddush Hashem,* pp. 32f.

15. The quote is from Dawidowicz, *The War Against the Jews,* p. 285; the talmudic discussion is detailed in Rosenbaum, *Holocaust and Halacha,* pp 18–22, 28–33.

16. Marc Dworzecki, "The Day-to-Day Stand of the Jews," in *The Castrophe of Euro-*

pean Jewry: Antecedents–History—Reflections, Selected Papers, ed. Yisrael Gutman and Livia Rothkirchen (Yad Vashem, Jerusalem, 1976), pp. 377ff.; Peter Schindler, "The Holocaust and *Kiddush Hashem* in Hassidic Thought," *Tradition: A Journal of Orthodox Jewish Thought,* 13, no. 4 (1972/1973); 14, no. 5 (1974/1975).

17. See Shaul Esh, "The Dignity of the Destroyed: Towards a Definition of the Period of the Holocaust," in Gutman and Rothkirchen, *The Castrophe of European Jewry.*

18. Emmanuel Ringelblum, *Ksovim fon Getto,* vol. 2, *1942–1943* (Warsaw, 1963), p. 53.

19. The story was related by Moshe Prager in *Jewish Resistance During the Holocaust. Preceedings of the Conference on Manifestations of Resistance,* April 7–11, 1968 (Yad Vashem, Jerusalem, 1971), p. 188 (Hebrew; the story was omitted in the English edition).

20. Photo archive, Yad Vashem.

21. Nachman Blumenthal and Josef Kermisz, *Resistance and Revolt in the Warsaw Ghetto: A Documentary History* (Jerusalem, 1965), pp. 219f.; see also quote from the letter in *DOH,* pp. 315f.

22. Eugen Kogon, *Der SS-Staat: Das System der Deutschen Konzentrationslager* (Frankfurt on the Main, 1965), p. 72.

23. Victor E. Frankl, "Group Psychotherapeutic Experiences in a Concentration Camp," in *Psychotherapy and Existentialism, Selected Papers on Logotherapy* (New York, 1968), p. 96.

24. Thus Heinrich Himmler; cited by Falk Pingel, *Häftlinge unter SS-Herrschaft: Widerstand, Selbstbehauptung, und Vernichtung im Kozentrationslager* (Hamburg, 1978), p. 41.

25. Leni Yahil, "Jews in the Concentration Camps in Germany Prior to World War II," in *The Nazi Concentration Camps: Structure and Aims, the Image of the Prisoner, the Jews in the Camps: Proceedings of the Fourth Yad Vashem International Historical Conference,* ed. Yisrael Gutman and Avital Saf (Jerusalem, 1984), pp. 69–100.

26. See Victor E. Frankl, *Man's Search for Meaning: An Introduction to Logotherapy* (New York, 1968); Elie A. Cohen, *Human Behavior in the Concentration Camp* (New York, 1953); Hermann Langbein, *Menschen in Auschwitz* (Vienna, 1972); Anna Pawelczyńska, *Values and Violence in Auschwitz: A Sociological Analysis* (Berkeley, Calif., 1979); Terrence des Pres, *The Survivor* (New York, 1978).

27. Primo Levi, *If This Is a Man* (New York, 1959), pp. 164f.

28. Pawelczyńska, *Values and Violence,* p. 67.

29. See Pingel, *Häftlinge unter SS-Herrschaft,* pp. 171–81. E. Cohen, *Human Behavior,* p. 145; Frankl, *Man's Search for Meaning,* pp. 56f.

30. E. Cohen, *Human Behavior,* p. 139.

31. According to Pingel, *Häftlinge unter SS-Herrschaft,* 61 prisoners in protective custody died in Dachau between 1933 and 1936; 69 died in 1937, pp. 50 and 81, respectively.

32. Yahil, "Jews in the Concentration Camps," passim.

33. Martin Broszat, "The Concentration Camps, 1933–45," in *Anatomy of the SS-State,* ed. Helmut Krausnick et al. (London, 1968), pp. 455f.

34. Hugo Burkhard, *Tanz mal Jude: Von Dachau bis Shanghai* (Nürnberg, 1965), pp. 30f.; Leni Yahil, *The Rescue of Danish Jewry: Test of a Democracy* (Philadelphia, pbbk. ed. 1983), pp. 291–96. On the dispatch of parcels to the Generalgouvernement by the JDC, see Gutman, *The Jews of Warsaw,* p. 104.

35. Fredka Mazia, *Comrades in The Storm: The Struggle of Zionist Youth Against the Nazis* (Jerusalem, 1964), pp. 51f. (Hebrew).

36. *DOH,* p. 231; Pawelczyńska, *Values and Violence,* p. 63.

37. Eliahu Yones, *On the Brink of the Death-Pit* (Jerusalem, 1960), p. 84 (Hebrew).

38. A typical case of escape from Poland to Slovakia is described in a report (dated November 19, 1943) from the head of the Jewish Center in Slovakia to Minister of Interior Mach. Fifty-six Jews who had crossed the border illegally in the summer of 1943 were captured, some of them were Polish citizen; others bore Argentinian, Hungarian, and Rumanian passports. Foreign currency, gold, and precious stones were confiscated from them, but they were sent on to Hungary. See Livia Rothkirchen, *The Destruction of Slovak Jewry: A Documentary History* (Jerusalem, 1961), doc. 52, pp. 127–29 (Hebrew).

39. Pingel, *Häftlinge unter SS-Herrschaft,* p. 204.

40. Gutman, *The Jews of Warsaw,* p. 166. On the accounts of Treblinka that reached Warsaw, see pp. 219–23. Yisrael Milgrom, "I Fled from Treblinka," *Yediot Beit Lohamei ha-Getaot,* 21 (1959), 115–19 (Hebrew). Also see *They Fought Back: The Story of the Jewish Resistance in Nazi Europe,* ed. Yuri Suhl (New York, 1975), pp. 146f.

41. Erich Kulka, "Five Escapes from Auschwitz," in Suhl *They Fought Back: The Story of the Jewish Resistance in Nazi Europe,* pp. 196–218; Betsalel Mordowicz, "Twice in Auschwitz," *Yalkut Moreshet,* Periodical 9 (1968), 7–20 (Hebrew).

42. Pingel, *Häftlinge unter SS-Herrschaft,* pp. 205, 307.

43. Ibid., pp. 215–18.

44. E. Cohen, *Human Behavior,* pp. 156f., 169.

45. P. Levi, *If This Is a Man,* p. 31; Kogon discusses the positive aspects of this apathy and the protective element in "emotional death" in *Der SS-Staat,* pp. 368f.

46. Frankl, *Man's Search for Meaning,* p. 93.

47. Ibid., pp. 126f.; see also Pingel, *Häftlinge unter SS-Herrschaft,* pp. 177f.

48. Pawelczyńska, *Values and Violence,* pp. 141, 144.

49. Ibid., pp. 127–130f. The importance of friendship and humor are also stressed by E. Cohen, *Human Behavior,* pp. 181f.; Frankl, *Man's Search for Meaning,* p. 24; Kogon, *Der SS-Staat,* p. 373.

50. P. Levi, *If This Is a Man,* p. 142.

51. Of those who claim that emulation was unavoidable, see in particular Bruno Bettelheim, *The Informed Heart* (London, 1961), and to a more limited extent E. Cohen, *Human Behavior.* The opposite view is held, for example, by Frankl, Pawelczyńska, and Terrence des Pres.

52. Frankl, *Man's Search for Meaning,* vol. 2, p. 11; E. Cohen, *Human Behavior,* p. 140.

53. Frankl, *Man's Search for Meaning,* vol. 2, pp. 28, 33–35.

54. E. Cohen, *Human Behavior,* pp. 167f.

55. Ibid., pp. 159, 162.

56. The following are partial figures: in January–February 1938 150 men and women committed suicide in Vienna, 9 of them Jews (6%); in March–April, there were 357 suicides, 141 of them Jews (39.5%). In other words, the total number of suicides multipled by 2.4, and the number of Jewish suicides by 15.7. In May–June 1938, there were 287 persons who committed suicide, but no mention is made of the number of Jews included in that number. We also have no figures for Kristallnacht in November 1938. The above numbers are statistical data issued by the Vienna municipality and are probably incomplete. Herbert Rosenkranz, *Verfolgung und Selbstbehauptung: Die Juden in Österreich, 1938–1945* (Vienna 1978), pp. 40, 87.

57. Ibid., pp. 301–4. In October 1941, there were 84 suicides and 87 attempted suicides by Jews registered.

58. Gutman, *The Jews of Warsaw,* p. 218

59. E. Cohen, *Human Behavior,* pp. 160.

Chapter 20

1. See Leni Yahil, *The Rescue of Danish Jewry: Test of a Democracy* (Philadelphia, ppbk. ed., 1983); idem, "The Uniqueness of the Rescue of Danish Jewry," in *Rescue Attempts During the Holocaust. Proceedings of the Second Yad Vashem International Historical Conference,* ed. Yisrael Gutman, and Efraim Zuroff (Jerusalem, 1977), pp. 617–25.

2. See chap. 16. In all, approximately fifty-two hundred Jews returned to Holland from the camps in the East, Theresienstadt, and Bergen-Belsen. For statistics on Denmark, see Yahil, *The Rescue of Danish Jewry,* pp. 264, 318f.

3. Ibid., pp. 160–63. This is one of the rare documentary proofs of Hitler's direct orders to implement the final solution.

4. Ulf Torell, *Hjälp till Danmark: Militara og politiska förbindelser, 1943–1945* (Stockholm, 1973, English summary).

5. Joergen Haestrup, *Passage to Palestine: Young Jews in Denmark 1932–1945* (New York, 1983), passim.

6. The description is based mainly on Hannu Rautkallio, *Finland and the Holocaust: The Rescue of Finland's Jews* (New York, 1987).

7. Kersten gives differing versions of this episode when he describes his experiences and conversations with Himmler, see Felix Kersten, *Samtal med Himmler* (Stockholm, 1947); idem, *The Kersten Memoirs, 1940–1945* (London, 1956), introduction by H. R. Trevor-Roper.

8. Marshall L. Miller, *Bulgaria During the Second World War* (Stanford, Calif., 1975), passim.

9. Nissan Oren, *Bulgarian Communism: The Road to Power, 1934–1944* (New York, 1971), passim.

10. Johan M. Snoek, *The Grey Book* (London, 1979), pp. 181f.; Vicki Tamir, *Bulgaria and Her Jews: The History of a Dubious Symbiosis* (New York, 1979), pp. 167–70.

11. See Nissan Oren, "The Bulgarian Exception: A Reassessment of the Salvation of the Jewish Community," *YVS Studies,* 8 (1968), pp. 83–106, quote is on p. 93. See also Tamir, *Bulgaria and Her Jews,* p. 169. On exceptional cases see M. L. Miller, *Bulgaria During the Second World War,* pp. 95f.; Raul Hilberg, *The Destruction of the European Jews* (Chicago, 1961), p. 476.

12. Benjamin Arditi, *Yehudei Bulgaria bi-Shnot ha-Mishtar ha Natzi 1940–1944* (Holon, Isr., 1962), pp. 72, 79–93.

13. M. L. Miller, *Bulgaria During the Second World War,* p. 97. A Bulgarian professor who supported Nazi Germany described the vacillations of the government and the czar in a lengthy memorandum, *Documents of the German Foreign Office on Bulgaria and Bulgarian Jews, 1941–1944,* nos. 486241–48 (photostat in the library of Yad Vashem).

14. On the Jewish cooperative movement, see Eli Baruch, "The Development of the Cooperative Movement," *Entziklopediyah shel Galuyot, Yahadut Bulgaria,* ed. Romano et al. (Jerusalem, 1968), col. 727–54 (Hebrew). The Bulgarian cooperative movement, like its counterparts in Poland and Rumania, developed after World War I. The twelve Jewish cooperative banks financed to a large extent the cultural activities of the Zionist movement. By March 31, 1943, they were 272 out of 438 cooperatives that had ben closed down. Arditi, *Yehudei Bulgaria,* p. 89.

15. *Documents . . . on Bulgaria,* nos. 486237, 486261–62.

16. Chaim Kishales, *Korot Yehudei Bulgaria* (Tel Aviv, 1970), vol. 3., p. 124; according to Oren, "The Bulgarian Exception." p. 89, the ministerial council already agreed to the plan on February 12, 1943.

17. Aleksander Matkovski, "The Destruction of Macedonian Jewry in 1943," *YVS Studies,* 3 (1959), ppl 203–58.

18. Frederick B. Chary, *The Bulgarian Jews and the Final Solution* (Pittsburgh, 1972), pp. 84f.

19. Matkovski, "Destruction of Macedonian Jewry," p. 228.

20. Nadeja Slavi Vasileva, "On the Catastrophe of the Thracian Jews: Recollection," *YVS Studies,* 3 (1959), pp. 295–302.

21. Arditi, *Yehudei Bulgaria;* German reports on three transports, pp. 174–78.

22. For the torments suffered by these Jews, see Chary, *Bulgarian Jews,* pp. 101–28; Oren, "The Bulgarian Exception," pp. 83–106; Matkovski, "Destruction of Macedonian Jewry," p. 228; Arditi, *Yehudei Bulgaria,* pp. 137–56, 191.

23. Matkovski, "Destruction of Macedonian Jewry," p. 252.

24. Chary, *Bulgarian Jews,* pp. 86f.; Arditi, *Yehudei Bulgaria,* pp. 125, 283–85 (on p. 299, Chary states that 8,637 Jews were liable for deportation).

25. On Liliana Fanitsa, See Arditi, *Yehudei Bulgaria,* pp. 336f. The vice-chairman of the Consistoire at the time, Buko Levi, testified at a trial of war criminals held in the spring of 1945 that he had met with Fanitsa from time to time and emphasized that she had not requested any payment for divulging information. Thus Chary, *Bulgarian Jews,* pp. 90f.

26. According to the memoirs of Chaim R. Bakhar, quoted in Kishales, *Korot Yehudei Bulgaria,* vol. 3, pp. 92f. The rescue episode is cited through the literature on Bulgaria, based on testimonies and memoirs that differ in detail but coincide in essentials. Arditi, *Yehudei Bulgaria,* pp. 283–300; Chary, *Bulgarian Jews,* pp. 90–96.

27. Chary, *Bulgarian Jews,* pp. 94.

28. Arditi, *Yehudei Bulgaria,* in particular, defends the czar, passim.

29. Kishales, *Korot Yehudei Bulgaria,* vol. 3, p. 154.

30. Ibid., pp. 97, 158: Patriarch Koril of Plovdiv, Bulgaria's second largest city, informed the authorities in March that he had withdrawn his allegiance to the government and would act according to the dictates of his conscience. He even threatened to lie down on the railroad tracks. On the same day, he sent a telegram to the czar.

31. Chary, *Bulgarian Jews,* pp. 98f.

32. Ribbentrop telegraphed a report to Adolf Beckerle on his meeting with the czar on April 4, 1943, NG-08.

33. Arditi, *Yehudei Bulgaria,* p. 297.

34. On the internal situation in Bulgaria see M. L. Miller, *Bulgaria During the Second World War,* pp. 117–21.

35. Arditi, *Yehudei Bulgaria,* p. 200f.

36. Gabrowski's announcement of May 15, 1943; *Documents . . . on Bulgaria,* nos. 486644–45.

37. Chary, *Bulgarian Jews,* pp. 144–52..

38. NG-2357, NG-096.

39. The most detailed description of the czar's death is in M. L. Miller, *Bulgaria During the Second World War,* pp. 135–48; on the rise of the Communists, see Oren *Bulgarian Communism,* passim.

40. Chary, *Bulgarian Jews,* pp. 203–7.

41. Figures in this discussion are according to various sources; Chary, *Bulgarian Jews,* pp. 62–64, 114, 126–28.

42. Such a study on a sociohistorical basis has been attempted by Helen Fein, *Accounting for Genocide: National Responses and Jewish Victimization During the Holocaust* (New York, 1979).

43. Sara Neshamit, "Rescue in Lithuania During the Nazi Occupation," in Gutman and Zuroff, *Rescue Attempts During the Holocaust,* pp. 289–331.

44. Dov Levin, "The Attitude of the Soviet Union to the Rescue of Jews," in Gutman and Zuroff, *Rescue Attempts During the Holocaust,* pp. 225–36.

45. See Yisrael Gutman and Shmuel Krakowski, *Unequal Victims: Poles and Jews During World War II* (New York, 1986). Thousands of Poles have been honored by Yad Vashem as "Righteous Gentiles" because they hid and helped Jews, thereby risking their own and their family's lives.

46. The situation aud subsequent developments within Western Jewish communities mentioned hereafter have been discussed in chap. 6, 8, 14, 15, and 16.

47. Dan Michman, "German-Jewish Refugees in Holland, 1933–1940 (Ph.D. diss., The Hebrew University, Jerusalem, 1978) (Hebrew). B. A. Sijes, "Several Observations Concerning the Position of the Jews in Occupied Holland During World War II," in Gutman and Zuroff, *Rescue Attempts During the Holocaust,* pp. 527–53.

48. See Leni Yahil, "The Jewish Leadership in France," in *Patterns of Jewish Leadership in Nazi Europe 1933–1945. Proceedings of the Third Yad Vashem International Historical Conference,* ed Yisrael Gutman and Cynthia Haft (Jerusalem, 1979), pp. 317–33. Michael R. Marrus and Robert O. Paxton, *Vichy et les Juifs* (Paris, 1981); also see a different approach in Cynthia Haft, *The Bargain and the Bridle: The General Union of the Israelites of France, 1941–1944* (Chicago, 1983).

49. Béla Vago, too, points out substantial differences in the satellite countries' measure of dependence on Nazi Germany during the various stages of the war; see "The Ambiguity of Collaborationism: The Center of the Jews in Romania," in Gutman and Zuroff, *Rescue Attempts During the Holocaust,* pp. 287.

50. See chap. 8 and 14.

51. Sijes, "Several Observations," p. 551. Various examples of rescue activities by individuals have been described by Moshe Bejski, "The 'Righteous Among the Nations' and Their Part in the Rescue of Jews," in Gutman and Zuroff, *Rescue Attempts During the Holocaust,* pp. 627–56.

52. See Yehuda Bauer's remarks in Gutman and Haft, *Patterns of Jewish Leadership,* pp. 230f.

53. See Chaim Avni, "The Zionist Underground in Holland and France and the Escape to Spain," in Gutman and Zuroff, *Rescue Attempts During the Holocaust,* pp. 555–90; Joseph Ariel, "Jewish Self-defense and Resistance in France During World War II," *YVS Studies,* 6 (1967), pp. 221–50; Renée Poznanski, "A Methodical Approach to the Study of Jewish Resistance in France," *YVS Studies,* 18 (1987), pp. 1–39; Livia Rothkirchen, "The Dual Role of the 'Jewish Center' in Slovakia," in Gutman and Haft, *Patterns of Jewish Leadership,* pp. 219–27.

54. See chap. 8 and 14; also see Vago, "The Ambiguity of Collaborationism," pp. 288f.

55. Theodor Lavi et al., eds, *Pinkas Hakehillot: Encyclopaedia of Jewish Communities, Rumania,* vol. 1 (Jerusalem, 1970), p. 365 (Hebrew).

56. Ibid.,pp. 374f. The shipments were organized primarily by the Committee of Assistance headed by Filderman. The money and supplies were collected in Bucharest and the provinces. Up to the end of 1943 supplies to the value of U.S. $2.7 million had been dispatched. These were augmented by privately organized shipments worth some U.S. $800,000. The campaign continued until 1944 with the support of the JDC.

57. Ibid., pp. 381–83.

58. A detailed description of the economic role of Sweden during the war is found in Klaus Wittman, *Schwedens Wirtschaftsbeziehungen zum Dritten Reich, 1933–1945* (Munich, 1978). At the end of 1939, the head of the Government Trade Committee, Banker

Jacob Wallenberg (an uncle of Raoul Wallenberg), signed a War Trade Agreement *(Kriegshandelsabkommen)* with the Germans. Among other things, Germany supplied Sweden with coal that the latter could no longer obtain from England. Despite mounting reluctance on the part of the Swedish government in 1943, Wallenberg endeavored to improve the conditions of the contract and the agreement was only annulled in April 1945. See especially pp. 65, 163–66, 177, 349, 353, 390. On Allied opposition to the agreement see pp. 367f. and Leni Yahil, "Raoul Wallenberg: His Mission and His Activities in Hungary," *YVS Studies, 15 (1983), pp. 10–14.*

59. Carl Ludwig, *Die Flüchtlingspolitik der Schweiz in den Jahren 1933–1955* (Bern, 1957).

60. The total number of registered aliens was 295,381, ibid., p. 318. On the refugee problem in Switzerland see, in particular, Yehuda Bauer, *American Jewry and the Holocaust: The American Jewish Joint Distribution Committee 1939–1945* (Detroit, Mich., 1981), chap 9.

61. Edgar Bonjour, *Geschichte der Schweizerischen Neutralität* (Basel; French ed., Geneva, 1970), vol. 6, p. 37.

62. Ibid., vol. 7, pp. 140–44; Ludwig, *Die Flüchtlingspolitik der Schweiz,* pp. 170–77, 178–81, 183f., 205, 216f., 222f. For the controversy in parliament and among the general public, see Bonjour, *Geschicte der Schweitzerischen Neutralität,* vol. 6, pp. 21–27; a definition of political refugee is on p. 27 n. 21 .

63. Ludwig, *Die Flüchtlingspolitik der Schweiz,* pp 228–32.

64. Ibid., pp.268 n. 1; 270f.; *Ein Jahrzehnt Schweizerische Jüdische Flüchtlingshilfe* (Zurich, 1944), p. 56.

65. Bonjour, *Geschichte der Schweizerischen Neutralität,* vol. 6, p. 33; among the refugees who were taken in were eighty Jews from Holland who had illegally crossed the French border; Ludwig, *Die Flüchtlingspolitik der Schweiz,* pp. 293, 306, 309.

66. Eberhard Kolb, *Bergen-Belsen* (Hannover, W. Ger., 1962), p. 93.

67. Ludwig, *Die Flüchtlingspolitik der Schweiz,* p. 300; H. G. Adler, *Theresienstadt, 1941–1945: Das Antlitz einer Zwangsgemeinschaft* (Tüblingen, 1960), p. 199.

68. Ludwig, *Die Flüchtlingspolitik der Schweiz,* p. 314; There were 1,365 war criminals turned back at the border, pp. 314f.

69. *Ein Jahrzehnt Schweizerische Jüdische Flüchtlingshilfe,* p. 14; Ludwig, *Die Flüchtlingspolitik der Schweiz,* p. 164.

70. *Ein Jahrzehnt Schweizerische Jüdische Flüchtlingshilfe,* p. 19.

71. Ibid., pp. 50, 60. The Swiss government paid out some SF 350,000 for the refugees up to the outbreak of war, and approximately SF 48 million between 1939 and 1944 (SF 24. million in 1944 alone). Ludwig, *Die Flüchtlingspolitik der Schweiz,* p. 366. Also see Bauer, *American Jewry and the Holocaust,* pp. 230f.

72. *Ein Jahrzehnt Schweizerische Jüdische Flüchtlingshilfe,* pp. 16, 57–59.

73. Quoted in Bonjour, *Geschichte der Schweizerischen Neutralität,* vol. 6, p. 28.

74. Ludwig, *Die Flüchtlingspolitik der Schweiz,* pp. 203, 237f., 299f. fnn. Report of July 30, 1942, by a member of Rothmund's department in Bonjour, *Geschichte der Schweizerischen Neutralität,* vol. 7, pp. 149f.

75. Bonjour, *Geschichte der Schweizerischen Neutralität,* vol. 6, pp. 38–41.

76. On the JDC campaign to raise money for the French underground, see Avni, "The Zionist Underground in Holland and France"; Ariel, Jewish Self-defense and Resistance in France, p. 208; Bauer, *American Jewry and the Holocaust,* pp. 243f., passim.

77. Chaim Avni, *Sfarad ve-ha-Yehudim Bi-Mei ha-Shoah ve-ha-Emantzipatziyah* (Jerusalem, 1975), p. 57. These figures do not appear in the English version (see n. 78).

78. Idem, *Spain, the Jews, and Franco* (Philadelphia, 1982), pp. 90ff.

79. Ibid., pp. 108ff. On the problems of refugees in the Iberian Peninsula, see Bauer, *American Jewry and the Holocaust,* pp. 199, 206–10. His figures, based on documents of the JDC, are slightly different.

80. Hanns G. Reissner, "The Histories of Kaufhaus N. Israel and Wilfrid Israel," *YLB,* 3 (1958), pp. 227–56; Naomi Shepherd, *Wilfrid Israel: German Jewry's Secret Ambassador* (London, 1984).

81. Perez Leshem, "Rescue Effort in the Iberian Peninsula," *YLB,* 14 (1969), pp. 231–56. There were 754 passengers who sailed from Lisbon and Cadiz, Spain, on the first ship, *Nyassa.*

82. Avni, "The Zionist Underground in Holland and France." On the Jewish Agency's activities in Spain and Portugal see Dina Porat, *An Entangled Leadership: The Yishuv and the Holocaust, 1942–1945* (Tel Aviv, 1986), pp. 202–9 (Hebrew).

83. Avni, *Spain, the Jews and Franco,* pp. 124–27. According to a HICEM Report, between 1940 and the fall of 1942 there were 10,500 Jews who were assisted in sailing from Portuguese ports. Only a small number left from Spanish ports during that period.

84. The whole episode of the flight of these Dutch pioneering youths has been summarized in Avni, "The Zionist Underground in Holland and France."

85. Bengt Rundblad, "Invandrar Problem," in *Forskare om befolkningsfraagor* (Stockholm, 1975), pp. 261–68. Hans Lindberg, *Svensk flyktingspolitik under internationellt tryck, 1936–1941* (Stockholm, 1973), pp. 67–74, 105. Between April and August 1938, according to Rundblad, 841 visa applications were approved, 300 were rejected, and several hundred remained pending. Of those who received a visa, apparently only some 150 were immigrants (i.e., Jews,) see "Invandrar Problem," pp. 132–34. Also see Leni Yahil, "Raoul Wallenberg," pp. 14–22.

86. Lindberg, *Svensk flyktingspolitik,* pp. 81–85, 136–51.

87. Ibid., pp. 128, 174–76. higher figures are given in Hugo Valentin, *Judarna i Sverige* (Stockholm, 1964), pp. 168f. According to a report by the Stockholm Jewish community for the period from 1933 to 1945 (YVSA, 048/30), a quota of 150 adult immigrants was approved.

88. Rundblad, "Invandrar Problem," p. 264. I did not find overall figures for transmigrants.

89. Lindberg, *Svensk flyktingspolitik,* pp. 271–77; Walter Laqueur, *The Terrible Secret; An Investigation into the Suppression of Information About Hitler's "Final Solution"* (London, 1980), pp. 48–50, 87.

90. Shalom Adler-Rudel, "A Chronical of Rescue Efforts," *YLB,* 11 (1966), p. 225.

91. Runblad, "Invandrar Problem, p. 269, he mentions twenty thousand textile workers; in all probability, a large number of these were Danish Jews who previously constituted 29 percent of Denmark's textile workers. Yahil, *The Rescue of Danish Jewry,* p. 361.

92. A letter from the secretary of the Stockholm Jewish community's Assistance Committee, dated April 19, 1944; YVSA, 13/29–6.

93. Up to the end of 1939, a sum of Skr 945,000 (approximately U.S.$225,000) had been collected. Close to Skr 810,000 had been spent—a third of that sum in 1939. Report by the Stockholm community's Assistance Committee, December 4, 1939; YVSA, 048/30–2/14.

94. Yahil, *The Rescue of Danish Jewry,* passim; idem, "Raoul Wallenberg."

95. Leni Yahil, "Scandinavian Countries to the Rescue of Concentration Camp Prisoners," *YVS Studies,* 6 (1967), p. 210.

96. The statement was made in the wake of a petition by Agudat Yisrael, which was forwarded by the Colonial Office to the Foreign Office on December 22, 1942 (No. 75338/

92). It was sent from Palestine and contained three proposals: to release funds to provide food parcels for Jews in occupied areas, to facilitate the entry of Jews to countries belonging to the British Empire, and to establish an official worldwide Jewish representation. All three proposals were rejected. The head of the depart, A. W. G. Randall, added in his remarks that the Jews themselves would not accept the concept of an overall representation in view of internal conflicts (e.g., between the Zionists and Agudat Yisrael). *PRO*, F.O. 371/36648–49/49/48.

97. Henry L. Feingold, *The Politics of Rescue: The Roosevelt Administration and the Holocaust, 1938–1945* (New Brunswick, N.J. 1970), p. 289. The Germans were aware of this and an SS officer wrote, "What is Katyn against that? Imagine only that these occurrences become known by the other side and exploited by them! Most likely such propaganda would have no effect only because people who hear and read about it would not be ready to believe it." Report June 13, 1943, *NCA*, vol. 1, p. 1001.

98. Deliberations on the establishment of a worldwide Jewish unbrella organization began in 1932 (see chap. 4). The quote according to *EJ*, 16, col. 637. See Elisabeth Eppler, "Rescue Work of the World Jewish Congress during the Nazi Period," in Gutman and Zuroff, *Rescue Attempts During the Holocaust*, pp. 47–69.

99. Walter Laqueur and Richard Breitman, *Breaking the Silence* (New York, 1986), passim.

100. Arthur D. Morse, *While Six Million Died* (London, 1968), pp. 8–10; also see Monty N. Penkower, *The Jews Were Expendable: Free World Diplomacy and the Holocaust* (Urbana, Ill., 1983), passim; and Laqueur and Breitman, *Breaking the Silence.*

101. For the most comprehensive description of the news that the West received concerning the mass killings, see David S. Wyman, *The Abandonment of the Jews: America and the Holocaust, 1941–1945* (New York, 1984); pt. 2, "A Plan to Exterminate All Jews." See also Laqueur, *The Terrible Secret,* passim.

102. See the answer given in Eden's name to the Jewish Agency, quoted by Adler-Rudel, "A Chronicle of Rescue Efforts," p. 216. The memoranda submitted to the Bermuda Conference by the WJC and the Jewish Agency in Palestine were totally disregarded. The congress memorandum is quoted in Arieh Tartakower and Kurt R. Grossmann, *The Jewish Refugee* (New York, 1944), app., pp. 580–89.

103. For the wording of the declaration, see Moscow Conference October 18 to November 1, 1943, *Foreign Relations of the U.S.A.,* 1943 vol. 1, Annex 10, p. 768. Wyman, *The Abandonment of the Jews,* p. 154.

104. The chain of events is described in Morse, *While Six Million Died,* pp. 71–91; Wyman's report in *The Abandonment of the Jews* is the most extensive. He especially emphasizes the impact of the Bergsonites, passim.

105. Quoted in Wyman, *The Abandonment of the Jews,* p. 209.

106. Telegram of March 7, 1944, that is two weeks before the German invasion of Hungary; *Foreign Relations of the U.S.A.,* 1944, vol. 1, pp. 1001f.

107. See Penkower, *The Jews Were Expendable.*

108. Miriam Kubovy ed., *Ultimate Rescue Efforts: Collection of Documents from the World Jewish Congress in New York,* 2 vols. 1979, p. 5 (from the legacy of Aryeh Kubovy, Yad Vashem library).

109. For a complete assessment see Yehuda Bauer, *My Brother's Keeper. A History of the American Jewish Joint Distribution Committee, 1929–1939* (Philadelphia, 1974); idem, *American Jewry and the Holocaust.*

110. Oscar Handlin, *A Continuing Task: The American Jewish Joint Distribution Committee, 1914–1964* (New York, 1964), pp. 78f.

111. Based on Bauer, *My Brother's Keeper,* pp. 127, 190, 212, 258, 273, 306.

112. According to Handlin, *A Continuing Task,* p. 82, in 1941 the JDC in Poland assisted six hundred thousand persons in 408 locations.

113. Naomi W. Cohen, *Not Free to Desist: A History of the American Jewish Committee, 1960–1966* (Philadelphia, 1972), p. 227.

114. Yehuda Bauer, "The Holocaust in Historical Perspective," in *Ha-Shoah, Hebetim Historiim* (Tel Aviv, 1982), pp. 127–29 (Hebrew).

115. Michael D. Weismandel, *Min ha-Metzar* (New York, 1960), pp. 55–65; also see Gisi Fleischmann's letters in Appendix; Livia Rothkirchen, *The Destruction of Slovak Jewry: A Documentary History* (Jerusalem, 1961), p. 25 (Hebrew). For details of the negotiations with the Slovakians, see Oscar J. Neumann, *Im Schatten des Todes* (Tel Aviv, 1956), pp. 142, 160–65; Bauer, *American Jewry and the Holocaust.* pp. 360–70.

116. Weismandel, *Min ha-Metzar,* pp. 55, 74; the report was written at the end of December 1942. See also a description of how the information was received in Neumann, *Im Schatten des Totes,* p. 145. The manufacture of soap from human fat, which is mentioned there, has not been proved.

117. Letter of August 27, 1942; Rothkirchen, *The Destruction of Slovak Jewry,* p. 227.

118. Weismandel, M*in ha-Metzar,* p. 63.

119. On the Europa Plan, see Nora Levin, *The Holocaust: The Destruction of European Jewry, 1933–1945* (New York, 1973), pp. 535–40. Also see Bauer, *American Jewry and the Holocaust,* pp. 370–79. For details see Weismandel, *Min ha-Metzar,* pp. 63–66, 154–81; Neumann, *Im Schatten des Todes,* pp. 174–76; Rothkirchen, *The Destruction of Slovak Jewry,* pp. 30f., 231–42; Porat, *An Entangled Leadership,* pp. 328–46.

120. On Shanghai, see David Kranzler, *Japanese, Nazis and Jews: The Jewish Refugee Community of, Shanghai 1938–1945* (New York, 1976), pp. 39–67. See Bert V. A. Röling and C. F. Rüter eds., *The Tokyo Judgement: International Military Tribunal for the Far East,* vol. 7 (Amsterdam, 1977), particularly pp. 86–89, 93, 97, 105–16, 131f.

121. Kranzler, *Japanese, Nazis and Jews,* pp. 90, 151, 268.

122. Ibid., pp. 151–61, and notes.

123. Ibid., pp. 236, 267–76. The sum was fixed in U.S. dollars. The Shanghai dollar was worth far less than the U.S. dollar. One of the last refugees to reach Shanghai was an inmate of Buchenwald who was released in March 1940. Hugo Burkhard, *Tanz mal Jude: Von Dachau bis Shanghai* (Nürngerg, 1965), passim. The book also describes the life of the refugees in the city.

124. Kranzler, *Japanese, Nazis and Jews,* pp. 310f.

125. Ibid., pp. 171.

126. Ibid., the Japanese attitude to the Jews is described passim; the quote is on p. 232.

127. Ibid., pp. 315–18.

128. See Yehuda Bauer, "Rescue Operations Through Vilna," *YVS Studies,* 9 (1973), pp. 215–23. The eposide as a whole is described in Zorach Wahrhaftig, *Refugee and Survivor: Rescue Efforts During the Holocaust* (Jerusalem, 1988), passim.

129. Kotsuji converted to Judaism in 1959 and took the name Abraham. He died in Jaffa and was buried in Jerusalem; Abraham Kotsuji, *From Tokyo to Jerusalem* (New York, 1964). Among those saved were some three hundred students of the well-known Mir Yeshiva, who were smuggled across the Polish frontier to Vilna and moved from there to Kovno. They were among the first to use the route discovered by one of their number, Nathan Gutwirth.

130. Yehuda Bauer, *American Jewry and the Holocaust,* pp. 119–28.

131. Ibid. On July 17, 1945, the radio station in Hongkew was bombed and 250 people were killed, including 31 refugees. The Jews played a major role in the aid and rescue activ-

ities. Kranzler, *Japanese, Nazis and Jews*, pp. 553–55. Burkhard, *Tanz mal Jude*, pp. 151–78.

132. Mary Berg, *Warsaw Ghetto* (New York, 1945), passim. Reports and reviews of the situation in Abraham Shulman, *The Case of Hotel Polski: An Account of One of the Most Enigmatic Eposides of World War II* (New York, 1982).

133. Nathan Eck, "The Rescue of Jews with the Aid of Passports and Citizenship Papers of Latin American States," *YVS Studies*, 1 (1957), pp. 125–52.

134. *Foreign Relations of the United States*, 1944, 1 (1966), pp. 1000f. nn. 65, 66; 1029f.

135. Eck, "The Rescue of Jews," pp. 102f.; Kolb, *Bergen-Belsen*, pp. 45f.; Shulman, The Case of Hotel Polski, passim.

136. Nathan Eck, "Jews in Exchange for Germans," *Dapim le-Ḥeker ha-Shoah ve-ha-Mered* (Bet Loḥamei Hagetaot, second series, vol. 2, 1973), pp. 23–25; Jacob Kurz, *Sefer ha-Edut* (Tel Aviv, 1944), p. 363, tells of his journey from Piotrków to Palestine. Of the sixty-nine members of the group, only nine were men; Chaim Barlas, *Hatzalah bi-'imei ha-Shoah* (Hakibbutz Hameuḥad, 1974), pp. 151f.; Kolb, *Bergen-Belsen*, p. 90. Almost double the number of Germans were released. Ruth Zariz, "Officially Approved Emigration from Germany After 1941: A Case Study," *YVS Studies*, 18 (1987), pp. 282–87.

137. For correspondence on the affair, see *Foreign Relations of the United States*, 1944, pp. 1021–27, 1029–31; also see A. L. Kobovy, *Unity in Dispersion: A History of the WJC* (New York, 1948), p. 193.

138. Eck, "The Rescue of Jews," pp. 106f.; Berg, *Warsaw Ghetto*, pp. 231–34.

139. Kolb, *Bergen-Belsen*, pp. 49–52, 100f.

140. Shulman, *The Case of Hotel Polski*, p. 39; Eck, "The Rescue of Jews," p. 133.

141. Barlas, *Hatzalah bi-'imei ha-Shoah*, p. 154, states that there were forty-five hundred "distinguished" Jews from Holland. On the holding up of the five hundred passports see Kolb, *Bergen-Belsen*, p. 51; on Jews from Holland, pp. 55–61. For details of the events in Holland, see Zariz, "The Rescue of Dutch Jews by Means of Certificates," *Yalkut Moreshet*, 23 (1977), 135–62 (Hebrew).

142. Berg, *Warsaw Ghetto*, pp. 249–53.

143. This account is based mainly on Kolb, *Bergen-Belsen*, passim.

144. Ibid., pp. 63f. Jaques Albala first worked as a translator for the Jewish community in Salonika, but he was later promoted to commander of the Jewish police force and finally replaced Rabbi Zvi Koretz as chairman. After the war he was sentenced to fifteen years' imprisonment for collaborating with the Germans. Michael Molho and Joseph Neḥama, *The Destruction of Greek Jewry, 1941–1944* (Jerusalem, 1965), passim (Hebrew). Also see chap. 16, "*Erntefest* (The Harvest Festival)."

145. Ibid., pp. 104f.

146. Ibid., pp. 121f.

147. Ibid., pp.170, 308–16.

148. Barlas, *Hatzalah bi-'imei ha-Shoah*, pp. 18–21, lists 960 from Berlin, 540 from Vienna, 1,150 from Prague, 250 from Bratislava (Pressburg) in all 2,900 certificate holders with their families; Martin Gilbert, "British Government Policy Towards Jewish Refugees (November 1937–September 1939)." *YVS Studies*, 13 (1979), pp. 162–64.

149. Rabbi Y. Goldman, "Rabbi Herzog's First Rescue Journey," *Niv Hamidrashah* (Winter 1964), pp. 5–11. Maisky's telegram to Rabbi Herzog of August 28, 1940, pp. 8f.; Barlas, *Hatzalah bi-imei ha-Shoah*, p. 93. The same route was followed by some five hundred youngsters from Sweden, including members of Youth Aliyah from Denmark, see Chaim Barlas, "Rescue Activities in Istanbul, 1940–1945," *Diyunim be-Vet Loḥamei ha-Getaot*, 1969, pp. 23–26. (Hebrew).

150. Barlas, *Hatzalah bi-'imei ha-Shoah,* pp. 24f.; Porat, *An Entangled Leadership,* passim.

151. Barlas, *Hatzalah bi-'imei ha-Shoah,* pp. 151ff.; Porat, *An Entangled Leadership,* pp. 277–84.

152. On this, see Eliahu Dobkin, member of the Jewish Agency's Executive Committee, *Ha-Aliya ve-ha-Hatzalah bi-Shnot ha-Shoah* (Jerusalem, 1946), p. 52.

153. Ibid., pp. 34f. *Making of Policy: The Diaries of Moshe Sharett,* ed. Ahuvia Malkin and Amnon Sela (Tel Aviv, 1974), vol. 4, pp. 480f. (Hebrew). On the conversation with the British Colonial Minister, Ramsay MacDonald, see pp. 480f.; Dalia Ofer, *Illegal Immigration During the Holocaust,* (Jerusalem, 1988), chap. 6 (Hebrew).

154. Dobkin, *Ha-Aliyah ve-ha-Hatzalah,* p. 47. The number of immigrants is given in *Jewish Agency Report to the Twenty-Second Zionist Congress,* 1947, p. 124a. On British policy regarding Palestine and the white paper, see Bernard Wasserstein, *Britain and the Jews of Europe, 1939–1945* (London, 1979), passim; Yoav Gelber, "Zionist Policy and the Fate of European Jewry, 1943–1945," *Studies in Zionism, of Tel Aviv,* 7 (1983), 133–53.

155. *Jewish Agency Report,* 1947, p. 124a. Nathaniel Katzburg, "British Policy on Immigration to Palestine During World War II," in Gutman and Zuroff, *Rescue Attempts During the Holocaust,* pp. 184–86.

156. For a complete list of members of the Jewish Agency delegation in Geneva, see Barlas, *Hatzalah bi-'imei ha-Shoah,* pp. 18 n. 5; 102. On Istanbul, see Dalia Ofer, "The Activities of the Jewish Agency Delegation in Istanbul in 1943," in Gutman and Zuroff, *Rescue Attempts During the Holocaust,* pp. 435–50.

157. Barlas, *Hatzalah bi-'imei ha-Shoah,* pp. 153f. His claim, "in fact almost all the candidates who received such certificates were saved," has no basis in fact. Barlas, "Rescue Activities in Istanbul," pp. 25, 28. The verified number of 900 exchange candidates is based on a report by Dobkin dated January 18, 1943 to the Zionist Executive Committee, CZA, S25/1295. There are various and conflicting considerations regarding the number of immigrants—both legal and illegal—during the war, and I cannot voice any opinion in this respect. Dobkin, *Ha-Aliyah ve-ha-Hatzalah,* pp. 32, 47–49, and the table in the Appendix. According to the *Jewish Agency Report,* close to 50,000 immigrants arrived in Palestine, 12,000 of them illegally.

158. See Barlas, Hatzalah bi-'imei ha-Shoah; Documents . . . on Bulgaria, pp. 308–10; *Eichmann Trial,* T–1004–1007; on Bulgaria, T–946–952 and T–949 (March 9, 1943) deal with emigration from Rumania and Hungary to Palestine. Reasons for the opposition were:

1. Germany does not permit Jews to emigrate from Axis countries.
2. Rumania might subsequently undertake separate negotiations in other matters as well.
3. Jewish emigration provides the enemy with material for propaganda.
4. Military information might be passed on.
5. Immigration to Palestine violates Reich policy vis-à-vis the Arabs.

According to Porat, *An Entangled Leadership,* pp. 285–308, the original plan provided for the emigration of 29,000 children from Transnistria.

159. Barlas, *Hatzalah bi-'imei ha-Shoah,* p. 191. The *Jewish Agency Report,* pp. 134–35, lists the number of Jews who emigrated officially via Turkey in 1943/1944 as follows: from Bulgaria, 1,681; Hungary, 319; Rumania, 4,488; Greece, 969; Poland, 282; Turkey, 3,234—total: 10,973. In 1945, from Bulgaria and Rumania, 2,086; Turkey, 227—total: 2,313. Grand total: 13,286.

160. See Ofer, *Illegal Immigration,* Introduction and Appendix, pp. 474f.

161. Leni Yahil, "Select British Documents on the Illegal Immigration to Palestine (1939–1940), "*YVS Studies,* 10 (1974), pp. 241–76. Additional details in Wasserstein, *Britain and the Jews of Europe,* passim.

162. See Also Erich G. Steiner, *The Story of the Patria* (New York, 1982).

163. For details, see Ofer, *Illegal Immigration,* passim.

164. Ibid.; on the tragedy of *Struma.*

165. Yehuda Slutsky in *History of the Hagana,* ed. Ben-Zion Dinur et al. (Tel Aviv, 1972), vol. 3, no. 1, pp. 159–61 (Hebrew); Wasserstein, *Britain and the Jews of Europe,* pp. 143–53; Jürgen Rohwer, *Die Versenkung der jüdischen Flüchtlingstransporter: Struma und Mefkure im Schwarzen Meer (Februar 1942–August 1944)* (Stuttgart, 1964).

166. Slutsky, *History of the Hagana,* vol. 3, no. 1, pp. 161–63.

167. *Jewish Agency Report,* pp. 137ff.; Ephraim Dekel, *Seridei Ḥerev: Hatzalat Yeladim be-Shnot Shoah ule-aḥaarea* (Ministry of Defense, 1963),

168. On the political background, see Katzburg, "British Policy on Immigration to Palestine," in Gutman and Zuroff, *Rescue Attempts During the Holocaust,* pp. 151f., 154–56 and fn. 7; Wasserstein, *Britain and the Jews of Europe,* pp. 154–63; Nathaniel Katzburg, *Mediniyut be-Mavoch: Mediniyut Britania be-Eretz Yisrael, 1940–1945* (Jerusalem, 1976), passim.

Chapter 21

1. The income of the JDC in 1944 was over U.S. \$5.5 million. Yehuda Bauer, "The Negotiations Between Saly Mayer and the Representatives of the SS in 1944–1945," in *Rescue Attempts During the Holocaust. Proceedings of the Second Yad Vashem International Historical Converence,* ed. Yisrael Gutman and Ephraim Zuroff (Jerusalem, 1977), p. 16.

2. Béla Vago, "The Intelligence Aspect of the Joel Brand Mission," *YVS Studies,* 10 (1974), p. 111.

3. Yehuda Bauer, "The Mission of Joel Brand," in *The Holocaust in Historical Perspective* (Seattle, 1978), pp. 94–155; Bernard Wasserstein, *Britain and the Jews of Europe, 1939–1945* (London, 1979), pp. 249–63.

4. For details about Bandi Grosz, see Vago, "The Intelligence Aspect of the Joel Brand Mission," pp. 113–28.

5. Chaim Weizmann learned of the deportations from Hungary and Brand's mission from Foreign Minister Anthony Eden's second-in-command, G. R. Hall, on June 2, 1944. It was only four days later, on June 6, that—as he claimed—he recovered sufficiently from the shock to write to Eden, requesting an interview; Eden met with him the following day, June 7. Wasserstein, *Britain and the Jews of Europe,* p. 254.

6. Ibid., pp. 259f.; see the Wasserstein index for Churchill's overall reaction to the Holocaust. Also see Yoav Gelber, "Zionist Policy and the Fate of European Jewry, 1943–1944," *Studies in Zionism* (Tel Aviv), 7 (1983), pp. 153–65; the deliberations of the Committee for Refugee Affairs on Meeting 11, May 30, 1944, PRO/CAB/95/15/JR (44).

7. Randolph L. Braham, *The Politics of Genocide: The Holocaust in Hungary* (New York, 1981), pp. 1106f. Most of the data on the protocols of the British government's Refugee Affairs can also be found in Braham. Also see Yehuda Bauer, *American Jewry and the Holocaust: The American Jewish Joint Distribution Committee, 1939–1945* (Detroit, 1981), pp. 394–98.

8. Braham, *The Politics of Genocide,* pp. 649–52. According to Braham, the Jews numbered 20,787. A directive on the subject was sent by Kaltenbrunner to the mayor of Vienna

on June 30, 1944. It contained detailed instructions concerning the guarding and accomodation of the Jews and stated that they were all liable to be deported if the occasion arose. Randolph L. Braham, *The Destruction of Hungarian Jews: A Documentary Account,* 2 vols. (New York, 1953), no. 184, p. 415. Ernest Landau, ed., *Der Kastner-Bericht über Eichmanns Menschenhandel in Ungarn* (Munich, 1961), pp. 42–45.

9. *Der Kastner-Bericht,* pp. 118–22, 276.

10. Braham, *The Politics of Genocide,* pp. 971f., 936–38.

11. Ibid., pp. 968–76.

12. *Der Kastner-Bericht,* pp. 122–34.

13. See the testimony of Rabbi Philip Freudiger, *Eichmann Trial,* Session 52, May 25, 1961.

14. As one such "proof," Weismandel claimed, for example, that Freudiger had hundreds of trucks at his disposal that he could deliver to the Germans in exchange for the release of Hungarian Jews. On being questioned by Wisliceny, Freudiger immediately confirmed Weismandel's claim although, in actual fact, the latter did not have access to a single truck. See Freudiger's testimony, ibid.

15. Bauer, "The Negotiations Between Saly Mayer and the Representatives of the SS," passim. See also Andreas Biss, *A Million Jews to Save: Check for the Final Solution* (London, 1975).

16. Bauer, "Negotiations Between Saly Mayer and the Representatives of the SS," pp. 24f.

17. David S. Wyman, *The Abandonment of the Jews: America and the Holocaust, 1941–1945* (New York, 1984), pp. 248–50.

18. This has been discussed by Erich Kulka, "Five Escapes from Auschwitz," *Yalkut Moreshet* (1965), 23–38 (Hebrew). The English version of the reports, together with a report by a Polish major who also escaped, are in YVSA, P-12/1116. The two reports by Jews comprise forty typed pages. See also Filip Müller, *Auschwitz Inferno: The Testimony of a Sonderkommando* (London, 1979), pp. 120–24.

19. Oskar Kransznyansky, who recorded the testimonies, testified in 1968 how the report had been circulated. YVSA, 03/3366. Braham discusses the problem in detail in *The Politics of Genocide,* pp. 708–16. Michael D. Weismandel, *Min ha-Metzar* (New York, 1960), pp. 182–89. Martin Gilbert, *Auschwitz and the Allies,* (New York, 1981), pp. 234–36.

20. Gilbert, *Auschwitz and the Allies,* pp. 251f.; Braham, *The Politics of Genocide,* p. 754. Braham, *The Destruction of Hungarian Jews,* vol. 2, no. 187, p. 427; no. 342, pp. 734f.

21. Gilbert, *Auschwitz and the Allies,* pp. 219f.

22. Quoted in Wyman, *The Abandonment of the Jews,* p. 291.

23. Gilbert, *Auschwitz and the Allies,* chap. 28; quote on p. 270.

24. See Wyman, *The Abandonment of the Jews,* chap. 15; quote on p. 307.

25. Braham, *The Politics of Genocide,* pp. 746f., 752f., 1111f; Wyman, *The Abandonment of the Jews,* p. 237.

26. Details in Leni Yahil, "Raoul Wallenberg: His Mission and His Activities in Hungary," *YVS Studies,* 15 (1983), pp. 24–26.

27. Braham, *The Politics of Genocide,* p. 765; the reasons behind the halt in deportations is described in detail in a telegram sent by Veesenmeyer. See Braham, *The Destruction of Hungarian Jews,* no. 187, pp. 425–29. Among other things, Sztójay informed Veesenmeyer about Lichtheim's telegram, which had been intercepted by the Germans. See above and note 20.

28. Braham, *The Destruction of Hungarian Jews,* no. 238, pp. 523f.; nos. 324 and 325, pp. 695–699.

29. Ibid., no. 326, pp. 760f.

30. Braham, *The Politics of Genocide,* p. 766.

31. *PRO,* Premier 4-52/5/H.N., 08197. Braham, *The Politics of Genocide,* pp. 1113–18; O. B. Vago, "The Horthy Offer: A Missed Opportunity for Rescuing Jews in 1944," in *Contemporary Views on the Holocaust,* ed. Randolph L. Braham (Boston, 1983), pp. 23–45.

32. Cabinet meeting of the British government, August 16, 1944; Vago, "The Horthy Offer"; Wasserstein, *Britain and the Jews of Europe,* pp. 262–67. For German reports from Budapest, see Braham, *The Destruction of Hungarian Jews,* no. 327, pp. 702–4; no. 331, pp. 711–13; no. 367, p. 768; no. 378, p. 784.

33. Braham, *The Destruction of Hungarian Jews,* no. 328, p. 705; no. 371, p. 774. This was the reaction to a Swiss request to allow 2,195 Jews to travel to Rumania en route for Palestine. Opposition to emigration in no. 329, pp. 706f.; no. 330, pp. 708–710 (reprint on pp. 936f.); also see Braham, *The Politics of Genocide,* pp. 1077f.

34. Braham, *The Destruction of Hungarian Jews,* no. 331, p. 712.

35. Jenö Lévai, ed., *Eichmann in Hungary,* (Budapest, 1961), pp. 154f. Braham, *The Politics of Genocide,* pp. 847, gives the figure with Salvador; also see *EJ,* 8, col. 1104.

36. Lutz served as Swiss counsul in Palestine in 1939–1941. Raoul Wallenberg worked for six months in a bank in Haifa in 1936. See Yahil, "Raoul Wallenberg," pp 22–24.

37. On the activities of the Swiss legation in 1944, see Braham, *The Politics of Genocide,* pp. 1077–83.

38. On Krausz's activities see Braham, ibid., pp. 977–82.

39. For sources on the events and developments, see Rafi Benshalom, *We Struggled for Life,* (Tel Aviv, 1978), passim (Hebrew); Asher Cohen, *The Halutz Resistance in Hungary, 1942–1944* (Hakibbutz Hameuhad, Israel, 1984. (Hebrew, English summary.).

40. Benshalom, *We Struggled for Life,* p. 81; Yosef Shefer, "The Leadership of the Halutz Underground in Hungary," in *Hanhagat Yehudei Hungaria be-Mivhan ha-Shaoh,* ed. Yisrael Gutman, Bela Vago, and Livia Rothkirchen (Jerusalem, 1976), pp. 141, 148.

41. Benshalom, *We Struggled for Life,* p. 58; for testimony of David Gur, see pp. 179–205; on contacts with the Hungarian underground, see pp. 118–27.

42. Ibid., pp. 49–73; Cohen, *The Halutz Resistence,* says the number of escapees to Rumania was "apparently more than 7,000 (p. 276), and discusses "bunkers" on pp. 230–38.

43. The Glass House was opened on July 24, 1944. See also photographs in Braham, *The Politics of Genocide,* pp. 980f.

44. Benshalom, *We Struggled for Life,* p. 116.

45. Lévai, *Eichmann in Hungary,* pp. 168f.

46. Braham, *The Politics of Genocide,* pp. 1074f.; Lévai, *Eichmann in Hungary,* pp. 153–58.

47. Lévai, *Eichmann in Hungary,* pp. 169–73; on the establishment of the ghetto and conditions therein, see Braham, *The Politics of Genocide,* pp. 850–67.

48. *EJ,* vol. 2, col. 1454; vol. 8, col. 1104.

49. Braham, *The Politics of Genocide,* pp. 854f., 984f; and on Komoly's activities see the index of names; Benshalom, *We Struggled for Life,* pp. 114f., 142f.; Shefer, "The leadership of the Halutz Underground," p. 145.

50. Benshalom, *We Struggled for Life,* p. 132. On the parachutists, see Ben-Zion Dinur et al., eds., *History of the Haganah,* vol. 3, no. 1 (Tel Aviv, 1972), pp. 637–45; Braham, *The Politics of Genocide,* pp. 993–96.

51. Archives of the Swedish Foreign Office, HP 21, Judefraagan allmant, 1939–1945; YVSA, JM/1912, (1–2); see also Leni Yahil, "Scandinavian Countries to the Rescue of Concentration Camp Prisoners," *YVS Studies,* 6 (1967), pp. 181–220.

52. See Shalom Adler-Rudel, "A Chronical of Rescue Efforts," *YLB*, 11 (1966), pp. 220–35; Yahil, "Raoul Wallenberg," passim.

53. Yahil, "Raoul Wallenberg." The description that follows is based on the article, for which documents of the Swedish Foreign Office were utilized: YVSA, 048/30 (1 4).

54. Examples of the temporary passport and save-conduct pass are in Braham, *The Politics of Genocide*, pp. 1006–09.

55. Rudolph Philipp, *Raul Wallenberg: Fighter for Humanity* (Stockholm, 1949), p. 9. According to Philipp, the employees numbered six hundred. As in all the ghettos, this was a way of protecting the inmates.

56. Wallenberg's disappearance on January 17 was made public after the members of the legation had arrived in Rumania. The unsolved riddle of Wallenberg's fate and—presumably—death in a Soviet jail is beyond the framework of this study.

57. Yahil, "Scandinavian Countries to the Rescue," p. 170. If no other source is indicated, the description that follows is based on this article.

58. A telegram from Kubovitzki (Kubovy) to the representative of the WJC in Lisbon, January 1, 1944; Miriam Kubovy, ed. *Ultimate Rescue Efforts: Collection of Documents from WJC Archives in New York,* vol. 1 (1979), in the Yad Vashem Library. Individual packages also arrived in Theresienstadt.

59. Telegrams sent by Leland Harrison, U.S. minister in Bern, on March 24, 1945; April 11, 1945; April 17, 1945; April 25, 1945, ibid.

60. Roosevelt Library Archives, WRB, Container 72: statement of General Eisenhower. Also see Leni Yahil, "Rescue During the Holocaust: Opportunities and Obstacles," in *Proceedings of the Eighth World Congress of Jewish Studies,* Division B (Jerusalem, 1982), pp. 161–66.

61. Kubovy, *Ultimate Rescue Efforts,* pp. 204, 205, 207.

62. Norbert Masur described the episode in a booklet published in Sweden, *En Jude Talar med Himmler* (Stockholm, 1945).

63. This last rescue operation was described by the SS officer in charge, Franz Göring, "Auszug aus meinem Tagebuch über die Befreiung von Menschen aus den deutschen Konzentrationslagern," YVSA, B/29-4, pp. 11–19. Affidavit, *TWC,* 11, no. 40 (Schellenberg Trial). According to Göring, 13,500 women were released from Ravensbrück, of whom 3,000 were Jewish; from other camps 2,350 women were released, 960 of them Jews. The same number of Jewish women also appears in Felix Kersten, *Totenkopf und Treue: Heinrich Himmler ohne die Uniform* (Hamburg, 1952), pp. 330f.

64. From "My Political Testament," printed in *Hitler's Letters and Notes,* ed. Werner Maser (New York, 1976), pp. 341–61, Bantam Books. This translation from *DOH,* p. 162.

Epilogue

1. *NCA,* 2, p. 3.

2. Alexander Bein, "The Jewish Parasite: Notes on the Semantics of the Jewish Problem . . .," *YLB,* vol. 9 (1964), p. 27; quoted in George L. Mosse, *Nazi Culture, Intellectual, Cultural and Social Life in the Third Reich* (New York, 1966), pp. 336f.

3. Hannah Arendt, "Social Sciences and the Concentration Camp," *Jewish Social Sciences,* 12 (1950), pp. 51–61. "The unreality which surrounds the hellish experiment, which is so strongly felt by the inmates themselves and makes the guards, but also the prisoners, forget that murder is being committed when somebody or many are killed, is as strong a handicap for a scientific approach as the non-utilitarian character of the institution."

4. Theodor Heuss, *Hitlers Weg: Eine historisch-politische Studie über den National-sozialismus* (Stuttgart, 1932), p. 103; printed in new edition, ed. Eberhard Jäckel, Theodor Heuss Archiv (Tübingen, 1968).

5. Uriel Tal, "Political Faith of Nazism Prior to the Holocaust," *Annual Lecture of the Jacob M. and Shoshana Schreiber Chair of Contemporary Jewish History,* (Tel Aviv, 1978), p. 14.

6. Bein, "The Jewish Parasite," p. 28.

7. Deuteronomy, 30:19.

8. The source is Tractate Sanhedrin, chap. 4, para. 5, which deals with the warning given to witnesses in capital cases. The full quote runs, "Therefore Adam was created single to teach you that whoever destroys one soul from mankind is considered as if he had destroyed an entire world; and whoever saves one soul from mankind is considered as if he had saved an entire world."

9. On this process, see Isaiah Trunk, *Judenrat: The Jewish Councils in Eastern Europe Under Nazi Occupation* (New York, 1972), chap. 2.

10. See "Interim Summary" at the end of chap. 16.

11. Yisrael Gutman, *The Jews of Warsaw 1939–1943: Ghetto, Underground, Revolt* (Bloomington, Ind., 1982), p. 38; see also chap. 7, "The Jews Struggle for Survival (September 1939 to Spring 1941)."

12. Primo Levi, *The Reawakening* (Toronto, 1965), p. 12.

13. Quoted from Chaim Yahil, "Activities of the Eretz Yisrael Delegation to Sh'erit ha-Pletah 1945–1949," *Yalkut Moreshet,* 30 (1980), 14 (Hebrew).

Abbreviations

AA	Auswärtiges Amt ([German] Foreign Office)
Abwehr	Defense (Military Intelligence)
AJB	Association of Jews in Belgium
AJC	American Jewish Congress
AK	Armia Krajowa (Home Army)
AL	Armia Ludowa (People's Army)
CAR	Comité d'Assistance aux Réfugiés (Aid Committee for Refugees)
Centos	Centrala Opieki nad Sierotani (National Society for the Care of Orphans)
CV	Centralverein deutscher Staatsbürger jüdischer Glaubens (Union of German Citizens of the Jewish Faith)
DAF	Deutsche Arbeitsfront (German Labor Front)
DAP	Deutsche Arbeiterpartei (German Workers' Party)
DAW	Deutsche Ausrüstungswerke (German Equipment Plants)
Degesh	Deutsche Gesellschaft für Schädlingsbekämpfung (German Vermin-Combatting Corporation)
Delasem	Delagazione assistenza emigrant ebrei (Aid Commission for Hebrew Emigrants)
DEST	Deutsche Erd- und Steinwerke (German Soil and Stone Plants)
DNB	Deutsches Nachrichtenbüro (German Information Bureau)
DP	Displaced person
Dulag	Durchgangslager (transit camp)
EIF	Éclaireurs Israélites de France (Jewish Scouts in France)
Ezra	Aid
FPO	Fareinikte Partizaner Organizatzie (United Partisans' Organization)

FTP	Franc-tireurs Partisans (French Marksmen Partisans)
Gestapo	Geheime Staatspolizei (Secret State Police)
GPU	Russian Secret Police
HIAS	Hebrew Sheltering and Immigrant Aid Society
HICEM	HIAS-ICA-Emigdirect (the latter a former Jewish emigrant aid body)
HSSPF	Höherer SS- und Polizeiführer (Higher SS and Police Leader)
HTO	Haupttreuhandstelle Ost (Main Trustee Office East)
ICA	Jewish Colonization Association
IDF	Israel Defense Force
JDC	American Jewish Joint Distribution Committee
Julag	Judenlager (Jewish camp)
Kripo	Kriminalpolizei (Criminal Police)
KZ	Konzentrationslager (concentration camp)
NEZAH	Noar Ziyoni Halutzi (Zionist Pioneer Youth)
NSDAP	Nationalsozialistische Deutsche Arbeiterpartei (National Socialist German Workers' Party)
NSZ	Narodowe Siły Zbrojne (National Armed Forces)
OKH	Oberkommando des Heeres
OKW	Oberkommando der Wehrmacht
Orpo	Ordnungspolizei (Order Police)
ORT	Organization for Rehabilitation Through Training
OS	Oneg Shabbath
OSE	Oeuvres Secours aux Enfants (Aid Operations for Children)
OSTI	Ostindustrie
POW	Prisoner of war
PPR	Polska Partia Robotnicza (Polish Workers' Party)
PPS	Polska Partia Socjalistyczna (Polish Socialist Party)
Relico	Relief Committee for Jewish War Victims
RFSS	Reichsführer SS
RG	Radu Główna Opiekuńcza (Central Council for Social Care)
RSHA	Reichssicherheitshauptamt (Reich Security Main Office)
RUSHA	Rasse- und Siedlungshauptamt (Race and Settlement Main Office)
SA	Sturmabteilung (Storm troopers)
SB	Sonderbehandlung (special treatment)
SD	Sicherheitsdienst (Security Service)
Sipo	Sicherheitspolizei (Security Police)
SS	Schutzstaffel (Guard Corps)
TOZ	Towarzystwo Ochrony Zdrowia (Society for the Preservation of Health)
UGIF	Union Générale des Israélites en France
ÚHÚ	Ústredný Hospodárský Urad (Central Office for the Economy)
UNRRA	United Nations Relief and Rehabilitation Authority
ÚŽ	Ústredna Židov (Center of Jews)

VB	Völkisher Beobachter
WIZO	Women's International Zionist Organization
WJC	World Jewish Congress
WRB	War Refugee Board
WVHA	Wirtschafts- und Verwaltungshauptamt (Economy and Administration Main Office)
Yishuv	The Jewish Population in the Land of Israel
ŻOB	Żydowska Organizacja Bojowa (Jewish Fighting Organization)
ŻSS	Żydowska Samopomoc Spoleczna (Jewish Self-help)
ZVfD	Zionistische Vereinigung für Deutschland (Zionist Organization in Germany)
ŻZW	Żydowski Związek Wojskowy (Jewish Military Union)

Bibliography

This bibliography is comprised of primary sources and various other publications written in a variety of languages. It is divided into the following seven sections: Archives; Reference Books; Trials; Collections of Documents (published); Primary Sources (memoirs, diaries, memorial tributes, contemporary literature); Secondary Sources (monographs, biographies, conference proceedings, essay collections, and Additional Secondary Sources); Newspapers, Periodicals, and Yearbooks.

Sources not available in English are cited in the original language; otherwise an English translation has been used. When an English title refers to a source published in Hebrew, an (H) follows the reference. No unified and generally accepted systems exist for transliteration from the Hebrew (e.g., rules for transliteration differ in English and German). According to English conventions, the two Hebrew gutturals are transliterated as follows: ḥet (ח) by ḥ and kaf (כ) by kh. However, for proper names the more usual German transliteration is preferred (e.g., Chaim Weizmann, Nachman Blumenthal), which is generally in conformity with the cited source.

The literature on the Holocaust is immense, and despite my attempt to provide a representative and multifaceted selection, the informed reader will probably detect some lacunae in the present compilation.

Abbreviations

AA	*Auswärtiges Amt*
BL	*Bulletin des Leo Baeck Instituts*
BZIH	*Biuletyn Żydowskiego Instytutu Historycznego*
CVZtg	*Central Verein Zeitung*
CZA	*Central Zionist Archives*
DGFP	*Documents of German Foreign Policy*

DOH	*Documents on the Holocaust*
EJ	*Encyclopaedia Judaica*
GG	*Das Recht des Generalgouvernements*
IMT	*International Military Tribunal*
JR	*Jüdische Rundschau*
NCA	*Nazi Conspiracy and Aggression*
PRO	*Public Record Office (London)*
RGBL	*Reichsgesetzblatt*
TWC	*Trials of War Criminals*
URO	*United Restitution Organization*
VB	*Völkischer Beobachter*
VJHZ	*Vierteljahrshefte für Zeitgeschichte*
WJC	*World Jewish Congress*
YLB	*Yearbook of the Leo Baeck Institute*
YVSA	*Yad Vashem Archives*

Archives

Auswärtiges Amt, Bonn
Bundesarchiv, Koblenz
Central Archives for the History of the Jewish People, Jerusalem
Central Zionist Archives, Jerusalem
Centre de Documentation Juive Contemporaine, Paris
Foreign Office Archives, Stockholm
Ghetto Fighters' House Archives
Israel State Archives, Jerusalem
Public Record Office, London
Rigsarkivet, Stockholm
Riksarkiv, Copenhagen
Roosevelt Library Archives, Hyde Park, N.Y.
Yad Vashem Archives, Jerusalem

Reference Books

Encyclopedia Hebraica. Jerusalem. (H)
Encyclopedia Judaica. Jerusalem.
Guide to Unpublished Materials of the Holocaust (in Israel). Vols. 1–6, Ed. J. Robinson et al. Jerusalem, 1970–81.
Index of Articles on Jewish Studies. Jerusalem, 1960–88.
Marrus, M. R. *The Holocaust in History.* Hanover, N.H., and London, 1987.
Piekarz, M. *The Holocaust and Its Afermath: Hebrew Books Published in the Years 1933–1972.* Vols. 1–2. Jerusalem, 1974. (H)

————. *The Holocaust and Its Aftermath as Seen Through Hebrew Periodicals. A Bibliography.* Jerusalem, 1978. (H)

Pinkas Hakehillot: Encyclopaedia of Jewish Communities, Germany: Bavaria. Ed. B. Z. Ophir. Jerusalem, 1972. (H)

Pinkas Hakehillot: Encyclopaedia of Jewish Communities, Hungary. Jerusalem, 1976. (H)

Pinkas Hakehillot: Encyclopaedia of Jewish Communities, Poland, vol. 1, *The Communities of Lodz and Its Region.* Ed. D. Dabrowska and A. Wein. Jerusalem, 1976. (H)

Pinkas Hakehillot: Encyclopaedia of Jewish Communities, Poland, vol. 2, *Eastern Galicia.* Ed. D. Dabrowska, A. Wein, and A. Weiss. Jerusalem, 1980. (H)

Pinkas Hakehillot: Encyclopaedia of Jewish Communities, Poland, vol. 3, *Western Galicia and Silesia.* Ed. A. Wein and A. Weiss. Jerusalem, 1984. (H)

Pinkas Hakehillot: Encyclopaedia of Jewish Communities, Rumania. Vol. 1. Ed. T. Lavi et al. Jerusalem, 1969. (H)

Pinkas Hakehillot: Encyclopaedia of Jewish Communities, Rumania. Vol. 2. Ed. J. Ancel and T. Lavi. Jerusalem, 1980. (H)

Pinkas Hakehillot: Encyclopaedia of Jewish Communities, The Netherlands. Ed. J. Michman et al. Jerusalem, 1985. (H)

Robinson, J. *The Holocaust and After: Sources and Literature in English.* Yad Vashem and Yivo Institute. Bibliographical Series no. 12. Jerusalem, 1973.

Robinson, J., and Sachs, H. *The Holocaust: The Nuremberg Evidence.* Jerusalem, 1976.

Schluss-Ausführungen in der Strafsache gegen Adolf Eichmann, vorgelegt von Dr. R. Servatius, Rechtsanwalt. Cologne, 1961.

Schmelz, O. *Jewish Demography and Statistics: Bibliography for 1920–1960.* Jerusalem, 1961.

The Holocaust in Historiography: Proceedings of the Fifth International Historical Conference. Jerusalem, forthcoming.

Wistrich, R. *Who Is Who in Nazi Germany.* London, 1982.

Trials

Eichmann Trial

Ha-Yoetz ha-Mishpati shel ha-Memshala neged Adolf Eichmann (General Attorney Against Adolf Eichmann): Neum ha-Pticha (Opening Address); Neum ha-Sikum (Final Address); Psak ha-Din (The Verdict). Jerusalem, 1961.

Long, J. von. *Das Eichmann Protokoll: Tonbandaufzeichnungen der Israelitischen Verhöre.* Frankfurt on the Main, 1985.

Mishteret Israel, ha-Mateh ha-Artzi, Lishkat 06: Tadpis Haklatat ha-Ḥakirot. Vols. 1–6 (Israeli Police, Headquarters, Bureau 06. Vols. 1–6). Cited as Police Interrogations. (G)

Mismaḥei ha-Hagana (Defence Documents, sign N).

Mismaḥei ha-Tviah she-hugshu le-Beit ha-Mishpat (Prosecution Documents Submitted to the Court, sign T).

Mismaḥim shelo hugshu le-Beit ha-Mishpat (Documents Not Submitted to the Court, sign 06).

Nellessen, B. *Der Prozess von Jerusalem. Ein Dokument.* Düsseldorf, 1964.

Rishum bilti mevukar shel Yeshivot Beit ha-Mishpat ha-Meḥozi (Recorded Proceedings of the Sessions of the District Court. [H or G])

Testimonies. Vols. 1–2. Jerusalem, 1963. (H)

Anklageschrift gegen Karl Wolff. Landgericht München (April 19, 1963). *YVSA,* TR-10/
475 and Urteil (September 30, 1964). *YVSA,* TR-10/639.
Anklageschrift and Urteil, Chelmno. *YVSA,* TR-10/174.
Rückerl, A. *NS-Prozesse.* Karlsruhe, W. Ger., 1971.
————. *NS-Verbrechen vor Gericht.* Heidelberg, 1982.
————. *NS-Vernichtungslager im Spiegel Deutscher Strafprozesse.* London, 1977.
————. *The Investigation of Nazi Crimes: A Documentation.* Heidelberg, 1979.

The Nuremberg Trials

International Military Tribunal (Blue Series, *IMT*)
Nazi Conspiracy and Aggression (Red Series, *NCA*)
Trials of War Criminals (Green Series, *TWC*)
  1. Proceedings
  2. Documents: a. published; b. unpublished. Signatures are: NG, NO, NOKW, NI, D,
     EC, F, L, PS, R. (When unpublished the signatures are cited without additional
     classification.)
The Tokyo Judgement: The International Military Tribunal for the Far East. Ed. B.V.A.
  Roling, and C. F. Ruter. Amsterdam, 1977.

Collections of Documents

Adler, H. G. *Die Verheimlichte Wahrheit: Theresienstädter Dokumente.* Tübingen, 1958.
Ancel, J., ed. *Documents Concerning the Fate of Romanian Jewry During the Holocaust.*
  Vols. 1–12. The Beate Klarsfeld Foundation, Jerusalem, 1986.
Baynes, N. H., ed. *The Speeches of Adolf Hitler, April 1922–August 1939.* Vols. 1–2. Lon-
  don, 1942.
Blumenthal, N., ed. *Documents from the Bialystok Ghetto: Conduct and Actions of a Juden-
  rat.* Jerusalem, 1962. (H, with English translation)
————, ed. *Documents from Lublin Ghetto: Judenrat Without Direction.* Jerusalem, 1967.
  (H and Polish)
Blumenthal, N., and Kermisz, J., eds. *Resistance and Revolt in the Warsaw Ghetto: A Doc-
  umentary History.* Jerusalem, 1965. (H)
Boelke, W. A., ed. *Wollt Ihr den totalen Krieg? Die geheimen Goebbels Konferenzen, 1939–
  1943.* Stuttgart, 1967.
Braham, R. L. *The Destruction of Hungarian Jewry: A Documentary Account.* Vols. 1–2.
  New York, 1963.
Buchenwald: Mahnung und Verpflichtung: Dokumente und Berichte. Berlin, 1960; 4th rev.
  ed., 1983.
Caban, I., and Mankowski, Z., eds. *Zwiazek Walki Zbrojnej: Armia Krajowa w Okregu
  Lubelskim, 1939–1944.* Dokumenty. Vols. 1–2. Warsaw, 1971.
Das Diensttagebuch des deutschen Generalgouverneurs in Polen, 1939–1945. Ed. W. Präg
  and W. Jacobmeyer. Stuttgart, 1975.
Das Recht des Generalgouvernements. Cracow, 1941.
Das Schwarzbuch: Tatsachen und Dokumente. Ed. Comité des Délégations Juives. Paris,
  1934.
De SS en Nederland: Documenten uit SS-Archieven, 1935–1945. Vols. 1–2. Ed. N.C.K.A.
  In't Veld. The Hague, 1976.

Documenten van de Joden vervolging in Nederland, 1940–1945. Ed. Joods Historische Museum. Amsterdam, 1965.

Documents on German Foreign Policy, 1918–1945, Series D. London, 1953–1964.

Documents on the Holocaust, Selected Sources on the Destruction of the Jews of Germany and Austria, Poland, and the Soviet Union. Ed. Y. Arad, Y. Gutman, and A. Margaliot. Jerusalem, 1981.

Domarus, M., ed. *Hitler: Reden und Proklamationen, 1932–1945,* Vols. 1–2. Neustadt an der Aisch, W. Ger., 1962/1963.

Eisenbach, A. *Dokumenty i Materialy do dziejow okupacji niemieckiej w Polsce.* Lodz, 1946.

Eisenbach et al., eds., *Eksterminacja Żydow na Ziemiach Polskich w Okresie okupacji hitlerowskiej: zbior dokumentow.* Warsaw, 1957.

Faschismus—Ghetto—Massenmord. Ed. Jüdisches historisches Institut Warschau. Berlin, 1961.

Foreign Relations of the U.S.A., 1941–1945.

Friedländer, S. *Pius XII and the Third Reich: Documentation.* New York, 1966.

Friedmann, T. *Die Kristallnacht: Dokumentarische Sammlung.* Haifa, 1972.

—————, ed. *Dokumenten-Sammlung über die Deportierung der Juden aus Norwegen nach Auschwitz.* Ramat Gan, Isr., 1963.

"Ha-Pitaron ha-Sofi": Teudot al Hashmadat Yehudei Europa bi'idei Germania ha-Natzit. Ed. T. Shner. Hakibutz Hameuhad, 1961. ("The Final Solution": Documents on the Extermination of the Jews of Europe by Nazi Germany.)

Heiber, H., ed. *Reichsführer! Briefe an und von Himmler.* Stuttgart, 1968.

Hilberg, R., ed. *Documents of Destruction: Germany and Jewry, 1933–1945.* Chicago, 1971.

Hoffer, W. *Der Nationalsozialismus: Dokumente.* Frankfurt on the Main, 1957.

Jacobsen, H. A. *1939–1945, Der Zweite Weltkrieg in Chronik und Dokumenten.* Darmstadt, W. Ger., 1961.

Jacobsen, H. A., and Jochmann, W., eds. *Ausgewählte Dokumente zur Geschichte des Nationalsozialismus, 1933–1935.* Bielefeld, W. Ger., 1966.

Judenverfolgung in Italien, den italienischen besetzten Gebieten und Nordafrika. URO, 1962.

Kempner, R.M.W. *Eichmann und Komplizen.* Zurich, 1961.

Klarsfeld, S., ed. *Die Endlösung der Judenfrage in Frankreich, Deutsche Dokumente,* Paris, 1977.

Klarsfeld, S., and Steinberg, M., eds. *Die Endlösing der Judenfrage in Belgien: Dokumente.* New York, 1980.

Klee, E., ed. *Dokumente zur "Euthanasia."* Frankfurt on the Main, 1985.

Kotze, H. von, et al., eds. *Es spricht der Führer.* Gütersloh, W. Ger., 1966.

Kubovy, M., ed. *Ultimate Rescue Efforts: Collection of Documents from the WJC Archives in New York.* Vols. 1–2, 1979. (Photocopy of typescript in YVS Library.)

Kulka, O. D. *Megamot be-Pitron ha-Baaya ha-Yehudit ba-Reich ha-shlishi: Mivḥar Mekorot.* Akademon, Jerusalem, 1969.

Lemkin, R. *Axis Rule in Occupied Europe.* New York, 1973.

Margaliot, A. *Ha-Irgunim ha-Yehudiim be-Merkaz Europa ve-Yaḥaseihem im ha-Shilton ha-Natzi (1933–1939).* Akademon, Jerusalem, 1971.

Mitscherlich, A., and Mielke F. *Medizin ohne Menschlichkeit: Dokumente des Nürnberger Ärzteprozesses.* Frankfurt on the Main, 1960. (*Doctors of Infamy: The Story of the Nazi Medical Crimes.* New York, 1969).

Monneray, H. *La Persécution des Juifs dans les pays de l'Est.* Paris, 1949.

—————. *La Persécution des Juifs en France et dans les pays de l'Ouest.* Paris, 1949.

Nazi Dokumente Sprechen. Ed. Rat der Jüdischen Gemeinden in den Böhmischen Ländern. Prague, n.d.

Okupacja i Ruch Oporu w dzienniku Hansa Franka, 1939–1945. Vols. 1–2. Warsaw, 1979.

Parliamentary Debates, House of Lords, 128, London.

Pätzold, K., ed. *Verfolgung, Vertreibung, Vernichtung: Dokumente des faschistischen Antisemitismus, 1933 bis 1942.* Leipzig, 1973; Frankfurt on the Main, 1984.

Poliakov, L., and Wulf, J., eds. *Das Dritte Reich und die Juden: Dokumente und Aufsätze.* Berlin, 1955.

Reichsgesetzblatt. Vol. 1, 1933; Vol. 1, 1935; Vol. 1, 1938; Vol. 1, 1939; Vol. 1, 1940; Vol. 1, 1941.

Report of the International Committee of the Red Cross on Its Activities During the Second World War. Vol. 1. Geneva, 1948.

Rothkirchen, L. *The Destruction of Slovak Jewry: A Documentary History.* Jerusalem, 1961. (H, with English introduction).

Smith, F., and Petersen, A. F., eds. *Himmler: Geheimreden 1933–1945 und andere Ansprachen.* Frankfurt on the Main, 1974.

The Chronicle of the Lodz Ghetto. Vols. 1–4. Unabridged edition, translated and annotated by A. Ben-Menachem and J. Rab. Jerusalem 1986–1989. (H)

The Einsatzgruppen Reports: Selections from the Dispatches of the Nazi Death Squads' Campaign Against the Jews, July 1941–January 1943. Ed. Y. Arad, Sh. Krakowski, and Sh. Spector. New York, forthcoming.

To Live with Honor and Die with Honor: Selected Documents from the Warsaw Ghetto Underground Archives "O.S." ("Oneg Shabbath"). Ed. J. Kermish. Jerusalem, 1986.

Walk, J. *Das Sonderrecht für die Juden im NS-Staat: Eine Sammlung der gesetzlichen Massnahmen und Richtlinien, Inhalt und Bedeutung.* Heidelberg, 1981.

Primary Sources

Adler, S. *In the Warsaw Ghetto, 1940–1943: An Account of a Witness.* Jerusalem, 1982.

Auschwitz: Zeugnisse und Berichte. Ed. H. G. Adler, H. Langbein, and E. Lingens-Reiner. Cologne, 1979.

Baeck, L. "In Memory of Two of Our Dead." *YLB.* Vol. 1, 1956, pp. 51–56.

Behrend, E. R. *Verfemt und Verfolgt.* Zurich, 1945.

Ben-Gurion, D. *Zikhronot.* Vol. 2. Tel Aviv, 1972.

Benshalom, R. *We Struggled for Life.* Tel Aviv, 1978. (H)

Berg, M. *Warsaw Ghetto.* New York, 1945.

Binding, K., and Hoche, A. E. *Die Freigabe der Vernichtung lebensunwerten Lebens: Ihr Mass und ihre Form.* Leipzig, 1922.

Blumenfeld, K. *Erlebte Judenfrage: Ein Vierteljahrhundert deutscher Zionismus.* Stuttgart, 1962.

Borinski, A-O. *Erinnerungen.* Kwutzat-Maayan Zwi, 1970.

Burckhardt, C. J. *Meine Danziger Mission, 1937–1939. Gesammelte Werke.* Vol. 3. Bern, 1960.

Burkhard, H. *Tanz mal Jude: Von Dachau bis Shanghai.* Nürnberg, 1965.

Buzikowski, T. *Bein Kirot Noflim.* Hakibbutz Hameuhad, 1964.

Calic, E. *Unmasked: Two Confidential Interviews with Hitler in 1931.* London, 1971.

Chamberlain, H. St. *Demokratie und Freiheit.* Munich, 1917.

―――――. *Deutschlands Kampfziel: Hammer oder Ambos.* Munich, 1916.

―――――. *Rasse und Nation.* Munich, 1918.

————. *The Foundations of the Nineteenth Century.* Vols. 1–2. London, 1914.

Dapei Eduth (Testimonies of Survival: 96 Personal Interviews from Members of Kibbutz Lohamei ha-Getaot.) Vols. 1–4. Ed. Z. Dror. Hakibbutz Hameuhad, 1984.

Datner, T. *"Advanture." Yalkut Moreshet,* Periodical, 9 (1968): 44–57. (H)

Davidson, Gusta. *Yomana shel Justina.* Tel Aviv, 1953.

Dawidowicz, L. S., ed. *A Holocaust Reader.* New York, 1976.

Deisz, R. *Das Recht der Rasse: Kommentar zur Rassengesetzgebung.* Munich, 1938.

Der C.V. Manuskript. Berlin, 1929.

Die Stellung der Nationalsozialistischen Deutschen Arbeiterpartei zur Judenfrage. C.V. Berlin, 1932.

Dinur, B. *Bi'imei Milhama u-Mahapeha: Zikhronot u-Reshimot mi-Derekh Hayim, 1914–1921.* Jerusalem, 1960.

Dobkin, E., *Ha-Aliyah ve-ha-Hatzala bi-Shnot ha-Shoah.* Jerusalem, 1946.

Donat, A., ed. *The Death Camp Treblinka: A Documentary.* New York, 1979.

Dos Buch Fon Lublin, Ed. M. Lerman and M. Litvin. Paris, 1943.

Dubno: A Memorial to the Jewish Community of Dubno, Wolyn. Ed. Y. Adini. Tel Aviv, 1966. (H)

du Prel, M., Freiherr von, ed. *Das Deutsche Generalgouvernement Polen.* Cracow, 1940.

————. *Das Generalgouvernement.* Würzburg, 1942.

Dworzecki, M. *Jerushalaim Delita be-Meri uba-Shoah.* Tel Aviv, 1975.

Eck, N. *Wandering on the Roads of Death: Life and Thoughts in the Days of Destruction.* Jerusalem, 1960. (H)

Ein Jahrzehnt Schweizerische Jüdische Flüchtlingshilfe. Zurich, 1944.

Eliav, M., ed. *Ani Maamin: Eduyot al Hayehem u-Motam shel Anshei Emunah Bi'imei ha-Shoah.* Jerusalem, 1965.

Encyclopedia of the Jewish Diaspora: Bulgaria. Ed. A. Romano and J. Ben. Jerusalem, 1967. (H)

Encyclopedia of the Jewish Diaspora: Lublin. Ed. N. Blumenthal and M. Korzen. Jerusalem, 1957. (H)

Encyclopedia of the Jewish Diaspora: Lwów. Ed. N. M. Gelber. Jerusalem, 1956. (H)

Freier, R. *Let the Children Come: The Early History of the Youth Aliya.* London, 1961.

Friedman, Ph., ed., *Martyrs and Fighters.* New York, 1954.

Führer der Zentralen Fürsorgeabteilung in Ost-Oberschlesien. *YVSA,* 06/16.

Führer durch die jüdische Gemeindeverwaltung und Wohlfahrtspflege in 1932–1933. Zentralwohlfahrtsstelle der deutschen Juden. Berlin, 1933.

Garfunkel, L. *Kovna ha-Yehudit be-Hurbana.* Jerusalem, 1959.

Gobineau, J. A., Comte de. *Essai sur l'inégalité des races humaines.* Paris, 1853–1855.

Goebbels, J. *Vom Kaiserhof zur Reichskanzlei: Eine historische Darstellung in Tagebuchblättern* (vom 1. Januar 1932 bis zum 7. Mar 1933) Munich, 1943.

————. *Tagebücher aus den Jahren 1942–1943.* Ed. L. P. Lochner. Zurich, 1948. New edition: *Die Tagebücher von Josef Goebbels: Sämtliche Fragmente.* Ed. E. Fröhlich. Vols. 1–4. Munich, 1987. (vols. 5–9 forthcoming)

————. Unpublished Diary Fragments, 1941.

Göring, Franz. "Auszug aus meinem Tagebuch über die Befreiung von Menschen aus den deutschen Konzentrationslagern." *YVSA,* B/29–4.

Grossman, Ch. *The Underground Army-Fighters of the Bialystok Ghetto.* New York, 1981.

Grossmann, K. R. *Menschen in Deutschland in dunklen Tagen.* Berlin, 1937.

Habas, B. *His Inner Light: The Life and Death of Joop Westervel.* Hakibbutz Hameuhad, 1964. (H)

Halder, F. *Kriegstagebuch.* Ed. Hans A. Jacobsen. Vol. 2. Stuttgart, 1963.

Henschel, H. "Gemeindearbeit und Evakuierung von Berlin (16. Oktober 1941–16. Juni 1943)." *Zeitschrift für die Geschichte der Juden* (Tel Aviv), 9, nos. 1/2 (1972): 33–52.

Heuss, Th. *Die Machtergreifung und das Ermächtigungsgesetz: Zwei Nachgelassene Kapitel der "Erinnnerungen 1905–1933.* Tübingen, 1967.

————. *Erinnerungen 1905–1933.* Ed. E. Jäckel. Tübingen, 1963.

————. *Hitlers Weg: Eine historisch-politische Studie über den Nationalsozialismus.* Stuttgart, 1932. New Edition: Ed. E. Jackel. Theodor Heuss Archiv, 1968.

Heydrich, H. "Wandlungen unsres Kampfes." *Das Schwarze Korps,* 1, no. 11 (May 15, 1935), pp. 1–11.

Hirsch, Rabbi Z. Sh. *Kiddush Hashem.* Tel Aviv, 1969.

Hitler, A. *Mein Kampf.* New York, 1939.

————. *Monologe im Führerhauptquartier, 1941–1944: Die Aufzeichnungen Heinrich Heims.* Ed. W. Jochmann. Hamburg, 1980.

————. *Rede zum 9. Jahrestag der Machtübernahme. (30. 1. 1942).* Berlin, 1942.

————. *Sämtliche Aufzeichnungen, 1905–1924.* Ed. E. Jäckel and A. Kahn. Stuttgart, 1980.

————. "Der völkische Gedanke und die Partei: Denkschrift Hitlers." In *Ausgewähite Dokumente zur Geschichte des Nationalsozialismus.* Ed. H. A. Jacobsen and W. Jochmann. Bielefeld, W. Ger., 1966. Vol. 1 (1933–1935). Pp. 1–3.

Hitlers Briefe und Notizen. Ed. W. Maser. Düsseldorf, 1973. (*Hitler's Letters and Notes.* Ed. W. Maser. New York, 1974. Bantam Books.)

Hitlers Tischgespräche im Führerhauptquartier, 1941–1942. Ed. H. Picker. Düsseldorf, 1951.

Hitlers zweites Buch. Ed. L. Weinberg. Stuttgart, 1961. (*Hitler's Secret Book,* trans. S. Attanasio. New York, 1961.)

Horodetzki, Sh. A. *Zikhronot.* Tel Aviv, 1957.

Höss, R. *Kommandant in Auschwitz: Autobiographische Aufzeichnungon.* Ed. M. Broszat. Stuttgart, 1958. (*Commandant of Auschwitz: The Autobiography of Rudolf Hoss.* London, 1961.)

Huberband, Rabbi Sh. *Kiddush Hashem.* Tel Aviv, 1969.

"In mitten des grauenvollen Verbrechens: Handschriften von Mitgliedern des Sonderkommandos." *Hefte von Auschwitz,* Sonderheft 1 (1972).

Jacoby, G. *Racial State: The German Nationalities Policy in the Protectorate of Bohemia-Moravia.* New York, 1944.

Jaensch, E. R. *Der Gegentypus.* Leipzig, 1938.

Kapel, S. R. *Le Combat juif en France occupée dans les camps d'internement et dans le sein de l'Organisation de Combat, 1940–1944.* Jerusalem, 1981. (H)

Kaplan, Ch. A. *Scroll of Agony: Hebrew Diary of Ch. A. Kaplan,* September 1, 1939–August 4, 1944 Tel Aviv, 1966. (H)

Karski-Kozielewski, J. *Story of a Secret State.* Boston, 1944.

Katz, J. *One Who Came Back: The Diary of a Jewish Survivor.* New York, 1973.

Katzenelson, Y. *Dos Lid fun Oysgehargetn Yiddishn Folk (Song of the Murdered Jewish People).* New York, 1963.

Kaufman, M. *Churbn Lettland: Die Vernichtung der Juden Lettlands.* Munich, 1947.

Kermish, J. *The Warsaw Ghetto Revolt As Seen by the Enemy: General Jürgen Stroop's Reports.* Jerusalem, 1966. (H). (Stroop, J. *The Stroop Report of "Warsaw Is No More."* Ed. S. Milton. New York, 1979.)

Kersten, F. *Samtal med Himmler.* Stockholm, 1947.

————. *The Kersten Memoirs, 1940–1945*. London, 1956. Introduction by H. R. Trevor-Roper.

————. *Totenkopf und Treue: Heinrich Himmler ohne die Uniform*. Hamburg, 1952.

Kollenscher, M. *Active und Passive Judenpolitik*. Berlin, 1932.

————. *Zionismus und Staatsbürgertum*. Berlin, 1929.

Korchak, R. (Ruźka). *Flames in Ash*. Tel Aviv, 1961; new augmented ed., Merḥavia, 1988. (H)

Korchak-Marle, Ruźka. *The Personality and Philosophy of the Life of a Fighter*. Ed. Yehuda Tubin et al. Tel Aviv, 1988. (H)

Kovner, A. "Ha-Nes be-Ḥidalon": Dvarim be-Kinus be-Modiin. *Sefer Hashomer Hatzair*. Vol. 1. Merḥavia, 1956. Pp. 643–54.

Krausnnick, H. "Denkschrift Himmlers über die Behandlung der Fremdvölkischen im Osten (1940)." *VJHZ*, 5, no. 2 (1957): 194–98.

Kulka, E. "Ḥamesh Briḥot me-Auschwitz." *Yalkut Moreshet,* Periodical, 3 (1965): 23–38.

Kurz, J. *Sefer Edut*. Tel Aviv, 1944.

Lambert, R. R. *Carnet d'un témoin, 1940–1943*. Ed. R. Cohen. Paris, 1985.

Landau, E., ed. *Der Kastner-Bericht über Eichmanns Menschenhandel in Ungarn*. Munich, 1961.

Lebraucher, F. *Incredible Mission*. New York, 1969.

Levi, P. *If This Is a Man*. New York, 1959.

Lior, D. *Ir ha-Metim*. Tel Aviv, 1946.

Liste des israélites domiciliés en Belgique en mai 1940: Déportés, évadés, liberés et décedés. Brussels, 1977. Belgian government publication.

Making of Policy: The Diaries of Moshe Sharet. Ed. A. Malkin and A. Sela. Tel Aviv, 1974. (H)

Mark, B. *The Scroll of Auschwitz*. Tel Aviv, 1977. (Y)

Marr, W. *Der Sieg des Judenthums über das Germanenthum*. Bern, 1879.

Masur, N. *En Jude Talar med Himmler*. Stockholm, 1945.

Mazia, F. *Comrades in the Storm: The Struggle of Zionist Youth Against the Nazis*. Jerusalem 1964. (H)

Mechanicus, Ph. *Waiting for Death: A Diary*. London, 1968.

Menasche, A. *Birkenau (Auschwitz II)*. New York, 1947.

Mendelsohn, M. "Die Pflicht der Selbstvertheidigung": *Jahresbericht des Vorsitzenden in der ersten ordentlichen Generalversammlung des C.V.* Berlin, 1894.

Milgrum, B. "Barachti mi-Treblinka." *Yediot Beith Lohamei ha-Getaot* 21 (1959): 115–19.

Milḥamot ha-Getaot, ed. Y. Zuckerman and M. Basok. Hakibbutz Hameuhad, 1956.

Mintz, B., and Y. Klausner, eds. *Sefer ha-Zvaot*. Jerusalem, 1945.

Mordowicz, B. "Twice in Auschwitz." *Yalkut Moreshet,* Periodical, 9 (1968): 7–20. (H)

Müller, F. *Auschwitz Inferno: The Testimony of a Sonderkommando*. London, 1979.

Neumannn, O. J. *Im Schatten des Todes*. Tel Aviv, 1956.

Novitch, M. *Sobibor: Martyrdom and Revolt*. New York, 1980.

Oshry, E. *Responsa: Sheilos Utshuvos from the Holocaust: Mimaamakim*. New York, 1983.

Pechorsky, A. "Mered be-Sobibor." In *Milḥamot ha-Getaot,* ed. Y. Zuckerman and M. Basok. Hakibbutz Ha-meuḥad, 1956.

Pinkas Bendin: A Memorial to the Jewish Community of Bendin (Poland). Ed. Avraham Stern. Tel Aviv, 1959. (H)

Piotrkow-Trybunalski ve-ha-Svivah: Sefer Zikharon. Ed. J. Maletz and N. Lau. Tel Aviv, 1965.

Prager, M. "Lapidei Kiddush ha-SHem be-Yameinu." *Maḥanayim,* 41 (1948): 137–42.

Radlitzki, T. "Notes from the Period of the German Occupation of Lvov," *Yalkut Moreshet,* Periodical, 21 (1976): 7–34. (H)

Rauschning, H. *Hitler Speaks.* London, 1939.

Reuter, Dr. F. and Waetzold, Dr. *Aufartung durch Ausmerzung.* Berlin, 1936.

Ringelblum, E. *Ksovim fon getto.* Vols. 1–2. Warsaw, 1963.

————. *Polish-Jewish Relations During the Second World War.* Ed. J. Kermish and S. Krakowski. Jerusalem, 1974.

Ron, S. "Kitei Zikhronot." *Yalkut Moreshet,* Periodical, 16 (1973): 43–74.

Rosenberg, A. *Das Parteiprogramm.* Munich, 1922.

————. *Das politische Tagebuch 1934/5, 1939/40.* Ed. H. G. Seraphim. Göttingen, 1964.

————. *Die Protokolle der Weisen von Zion und die jüdische Weltpolitik.* Munich, 1933.

————. *His Selected Writings.* Ed. R. Poi. London, 1970.

————. *Protokole Zions: Das Programm der Internationalen Geheimregierung.* Munich, 1936.

Rosenfeld, E., and Luckner, G., eds. *Lebenszeichen aus Piaski: Briefe Deportierter aus dem Distrikt Lublin.* Munich, 1968.

Rowno: A Memorial to the Jewish Community of Rowno, Wolyn. Ed. A. Avatihi. Tel Aviv, 1956. (H)

Sandberg, M. *My Longest Year: In the Hungarian Labour Service and in the Nazi Camps.* Jerusalem, 1968.

Schoenbaum, D., *The Reawakening: A Liberated Prisoner's Long March Home Through Europe.* Boston, 1965.

"SD-Hauptamt." *Lageberichte* der Zentralabteilung II. Bundesarchiv Koblenz.

Sefer Czestochov. (Encyclopedia shel Galuyot). Vols. 1–2. Ed. M. Shutzman. Jerusalem, 1967.

Sefer Kolo. Ed. M. Halter. Tel Aviv, 1958.

Seidman, H. *Yoman Getto Varsha.* New York, 1947.

Simon, Y. *Mihtavim mi'imei ha-Shoah ve-ha-Mahteret.* Tel Aviv, 1963.

Speer, A. *Erinnerungen.* Frankfurt on the Main, 1969. (*Inside the Third Reich, Memoirs* [London, 1970].)

Stern, S. "Zikhronotav shel Shtern." Ed. T. Erez. *Yalkut Moreshet,* Periodical, 16 (1973): 157–78; 17 (1974): 153–80.

Stuckart, A., and Schiedemair, R. *Rassen-und Erbpflege in der Gesetzgebung des Dritten Reiches.* Leipzig, 1938.

Szende, St. *Der letzte Jude aus Polen.* Zurich, 1945.

Tamir, B. "Pal Kovacs' Diary in the Neuengamme Concentration Camp." *Dapim, Studies on the Holocaust Period* (Haifa) 1 (1978): 229–52. (H)

Tenenbojm-Becker, N., ed. *Ha-Adam ha-Lohem.* Jerusalem, 1974.

Tennenbojm-Tamaroff, M. *Dapim min ha-Dleka: Pirkei Yoman, Mihtavim ve-Reshimot.* Hakibbutz Hameuhad, 1948.

The Diary of Hans Frank, Governor of the General Government. *IMT,* 29, PS-233, pp. 356–725.

"The Extermination of Two Ukrainian Jewish Communities: Testimony of a German Army Officer." *YVS Studies,* Vol. 3. 1959, pp. 283–88.

The Korets Book (Volyn). Ed. E. Leoni. Tel Aviv, 1959. (H)

The Jewish Underground Press in Warsaw, May 1940–October 1941. Vols. 1–4. Ed. J. Kermish. Jerusalem 1980–1989. (H)

The Seventh Day: Soldiers Talk About the Six-Day War. Ed. A. Shapira. New York, 1970.

The Warsaw Diary of Adam Czerniakow: Prelude to Doom Ed. R. Hilberg, S. Sharon, J. Kermisz. New York, 1979.

The Warsaw Diary of Chaim A. Kaplan. Ed. A. I. Katsh. New York, 1965.

They Fought Back: The Story of the Jewish Resistance in Nazi Europe. Ed. Y. Suhl. New York, 1975.

Treue, W. "Hitlers Denkschrift zum Vierjahresplan 1936." *VJHZ,* 3, no. 2 (1955): 184–210.

————. "Rede Hitlers vor der deutschen Presse." *VJHZ,* 6, no. 1 (1958): 175–91.

Trevor-Roper, H. R. "The Mind of Hitler." In *Hitler's Table Talk, 1941–1944,* London, 1973; Oxford, 1988.

Unger, M. *Admorim she-nispu ba-Shoah.* Jerusalem, 1969.

Vasileva, N. S. "On the Catastrophe of the Thracian Jews, Recollection." *YVS Studies,* Vol. 3, 1959, pp. 295–302.

Verniak-Schlesinger, H. "A Testimony." *Yalkut Moreshet,* Periodical 1 (1963): 73–8.

Visser't Hooft, W. A. *Memoirs.* London, 1973.

Vogelsang, Th. "Neue Dokumente zur Geschichte der Reichswehr, 1930–1933." *VJHZ* 2, no. 4 (1954): 394–456.

Walk, J., ed. *Als Jude in Breslau, 1941.* Rarnat Gan, Isr., 1975.

Warhaftig, Z. *Refugee and Survivor: Rescue Efforts During the Holocaust.* Jerusalem, 1988.

Wassermann, J. *Mein Weg als Deutscher und Jude,* Berlin, 1921. *(My Life as German and Jew.* New York, 1933.)

Weismandel, M. B. *Min ha-Metzar.* New York, 1960.

Weiss, Reska. *Journey Through Hell: A Woman's Account of Her Experiences at the Hands of the Nazis.* London, 1961.

Weizmann, Ch. *The Jewish People and Palestine: Statement Made Before the Palestine Royal Commission in Jerusalem, November 25, 1936.* London, 1973.

Wright, M. *Norwegian Diary.* London, 1974.

Yahil, L. *Readings on the History of the Holocaust.* Akademon, Jerusalem, 1971.

Yehezkieli, M. *Hatzalat ha-Rabi mi-Belz mi-Gai ha-Hariga be-Polin.* Jerusalem, 1948.

Yerushalmi, E., *Pinkas Shavli: A Diary from a Lithuanian Ghetto (1941–1944).* Jerusalem, 1958. (H)

Yones, E. *On the Brink of the Death-Pit.* Jerusalem 1960. (H)

Zaderecki, T. *Bimeshol Tslav ha-Keres be-Lvov: Hurban ha-Kehilla ha-Yehudit be-Einei Meḥaber Polani* (Gdy swastyka Lwowem wladala.) Jerusalem, 1982.

Zolli, E. *Before the Dawn.* New York, 1954.

Secondary Sources

(a) Monographs, Biographies, Conference Proceedings, and Essay Collections

Ackermann, J. *Heinrich Himmler als Ideologe.* Göttingen, 1970.

Adam, U. D. *Judenpolitik im Dritten Reich.* Düsseldorf, 1972.

Adler, H. G. *Der verwaltete Mensch; Studien zur Deportation der Juden aus Deutschland.* Tübingen, 1974.

————. *Theresienstadt, 1941–1945: Das Antlitz einer Zwangsgemeinschaft.* Tübingen, 1960.

Anatomy of the SS-State. Ed. H. Krausnick et al. See esp. H. Krausnick, "The Persecution of the Jews," vol. 2, pp. 17–139; M. Broszat, "The Concentrationn Camps, 1933–1945," vol. 2, pp. 141–256. London, 1968–70. (Translated from: *Anatomie des SS-Staates.* Vols. 1–2. Olten, Switz., 1965.)

Arad, Y., *Belzec, Sobibor, Treblinka: The Operation Reinhard Death Camps.* Bloomington, Ind., 1987.

————. *Ghetto in Flames: The Struggle and Destruction of the Jews in Vilna in the Holocaust.* New York, 1982.

————. *Treblinka—Hell and Revolt.* Tel Aviv, 1983. (H)

Aronson, S. *Reinhard Heydrich und die Frühgeschichte von Gestapo und SD.* Stuttgart, 1971.

Avni, Ch. *Spain, the Jews, and Franco.* Philadelphia, 1982.

Bauer, Y. *American Jewry and the Holocaust: The American Jewish Joint Distribution Committee, 1939–1945.* Detroit, Mich., 1981.

————. *My Brother's Keeper: A History of the American Jewish Joint Distribution Committee, 1929–1939.* Philadelphia, 1974.

Berben, P. *Dachau: The Official History, 1933–1945.* London, 1975.

Binion, R. *Hitler Among the Germans: Psychohistory.* New York, 1976.

Birnbaum, M. P. *Staat und Synagoge, 1918–1938.* Tübingen, 1981.

Bondy, R. *Elder of the Jews: Jacob Edelstein of Theresienstadt.* New York, 1989.

Bonjour, E. *Geschichte der Schweizerischen Neutralität.* Vols. 1–9. Basel, 1970–76.

Botz, G. *Wohnungsplitik und Judendeportation.* Salzburg, 1975.

Bracher, K. D., et al. *Die Nationalsozialistische Machtergreifung: Studien zur Errichtung des totalitären Herrschaftssystem in Deutschland, 1933/34.* Frankfurt on the Main, 1960. New edition: Vols. 1–3, Cologne, 1974.

————. *The German Dictatorship: The Origins, Structure, and Effects of National Socialism.* London, 1971.

Braham, R. L. *The Politics of Genocide: The Holocaust in Hungary.* Vols. 1–2. New York, 1981.

Broszat, M. *German National Socialism, 1919–1945.* Santa Barbara, Calif., 1966.

————. *Nationalsozialistische Polenpolitik, 1939–1945.* Stuttgart, 1965.

————. *The Hitler State,* London, 1981.

————. "The Concentration Camps, 1933–1945." In *Anatomy of the SS-State.* Ed. H. Krausnick et al. London, paperback 1970. Pp. 141–256.

Broszat, M., et al., eds. *Bayern in der NS-Zeit.* Vols. 1–6. Munich, 1977–83.

Brown, Z. A., and D. Levin. *The Story of an Underground: The Resistance of the Jews of Kovno (Lithuania) in the Second World War.* Jerusalem, 1962. (H with English introduction)

Buchheim, H. "The SS: Instrument of Domination." In *Anatomy of the SS-State.* Ed. H. Krausnick et al. London, 1968. Vol. 1, pp. 127–301.

Bullock, Allan. *Hitler: A Study in Tyranny.* Completely rev. ed. New York, 1964.

Chary, F. B. *The Bulgarian Jews and the "Final Solution."* Pittsburg, Pa., 1972.

Czech, D. "Kalendarium der Ereignisse im Konzentrationslager Auschwitz-Birkenau." *Hefte von Auschwitz,* nos. 1–8 (1959–64).

Dawidowicz, L. *The War Against the Jews, 1933–1945.* New York, 1975.

De Jong, L. *Het Koningkrijk der Nederlanden in de Twede Wereldoorlog.* Vols. 1–13. The Hague, 1969–1988.

Dekel, A. *Sridei Herev: Hatzalat Yeladim be-Shnot Shoah ule-aharea.* Vols. 1–2. Misrad ha-Bitahon, 1963.

Der Mord an den Juden im Zweiten Weltkrieg: Entschlussbildung und Verwirklichung. Ed. E. Jäckel and J. Rower. Stuttgart, 1985.

Deutsches Judentum in Krieg und Revolution, 1916–1923. Ed. W. E. Mosse. Tübingen, 1971.

Die Juden im Nationalsozialistischen Deutschland: The Jews in Nazi Germany, 1933–1945. Ed. A. Pauker et al. Tübingen, 1986.

Diehl-Thiele, P. *Partei und Staat im Dritten Reich: Untersuchungen zum Verhältnis von NSDAP und allgemeiner innerer Staatsverwaltung.* Munich, 1969.

Eck, N. *The Holocaust of the Jewish People in Europe.* Hakibbutz Hameuḥad, 1975. (H)

Eckstein, B. *Mauthausen: Concentration and Annihilation Camp.* Jerusalem, 1984. (H)

Eisenbach, A. "Nazi Foreign Policy on the Eve of World War II and the Jewish Question." *Acta Polonica Historica* (Warsaw), 5 (1962): 107–39.

Entscheidungsjahr 1932: Zur Judenfrage in der Endphase der Weimarer Republik. Ed. W. E. Mosse and A. Paucker. Tübingen, 1966.

Eschenburg, Th., et al. *The Path to Dictatorship, 1918–1933: Ten Essays.* New York, 1966.

Esh, Sh. *Studies in the Holocaust and Contemporary Jewry.* Ed. J. Walk. Jerusalem, 1973. (H)

Ettinger, Sh. *Modern Anti-Semitism: Studies and Essays.* Tel Aviv, 1978. (H)

Eyck, E. *A History of the Weimar Republic.* Vols. 1–2. New York, 1970.

Feilchenfeld, W., et al. *Haavara-Transfer nach Palästina und Einwanderung deutscher Juden, 1933–1939.* Tübingen, 1972.

Fein, H. *Accounting for Genocide: National Responses and Jewish Victimization During the Holocaust.* New York, 1979.

Feingold, H. L. *The Politics of Rescue: The Roosevelt Administration and the Holocaust, 1938–1945.* New Brunswick, N.J., 1970. 2d ed. New York, forthcoming.

Fest, J. C. *Hitler.* London, 1974.

———. *The Face of the Third Reich.* London, 1970.

Field, G. G. *Evangelist of Race: The Germanic Vision of Houston Stuart Chamberlain.* New York, 1981.

Friedman, Ph. *Roads to Extinction: Essays on the Holocaust.* Ed. A. J. Friedman. Philadelphia, 1980.

From the Emancipation to the Holocaust: Essays on Jewish Literature and History in Central Europe. Ed. K. Kwiet. Kensington, Austr., 1987.

Genschel, H. *Die Verdrängung der Juden aus der Wirtschaft im Dritten Reich.* Göttingen, 1966.

Gutachten des Instituts für Zeitgeschichte. Vol. 1: Munich, 1958; Vol. 2: Stuttgart, 1966.

Gutman, Y. *The Jews of Warsaw 1939–1943: Ghetto, Underground, Revolt.* Bloomington, Ind., 1982.

Hayes, P. M. *The Career and Political Ideas of Vidkun Quisling, 1887–1945.* Newton Abbott, Eng., 1971.

Hilberg, R. *The Destruction of European Jews.* Chicago, 1961. Rev. ed. Vols. 1–3. New York, 1985.

Homze, E. L. *Foreign Labor in Nazi Germany.* Princeton, N.J., 1967.

Hungarian Jewish Studies. Ed. R. L. Braham. Vols. 1–3. New York, 1966, 1969, 1973.

Jacobsen, H. A. *"Deutsche Kriegsführung, 1939–1945: Ein Überblick."* In *Schriftenreihe der Niedersächsischen Landeszentrale für politische Bildung Zeitgeschichte.* Hannover, W. Ger., 1961.

———. "The Kommissarbefehl and Mass Executions of Soviet Russian Prisoners of War." In *Anatomy of the SS-State.* Ed. H. Krausnick et al. London, 1968. Pp. 505–35.

Jäckel, E. *Hitler in History.* Hanover, N.H., and London, 1984.

———. *Hitlers Herrschaft: Vollzug einer Weltanschauung.* Stuttgart, 1986.

————. *Hitlers Weltanschauung: Entwurf einer Herrschaft.* Stuttgart, 1969; enl. ed., 1986 (*Hitler's Weltanschauung: A Blueprint for Power.* Middletown, Conn., 1972.)

Jetzinger, F. *Hitlers Jugend, Phantasien, Lügen—und die Wahrheit.* Munich, 1956.

Jewish Resistance During the Holocaust. Proceedings of the Conference on Manifestations of Jewish Resistance. Jerusalem, 1968; 1972.

Judaism and Christianity Under the Impact of National Socialism. Ed. O. D. Kulka and P. R. Mendes-Flohr. Jerusalem, 1987.

Jüdische Jugend im Übergang: Ludwig Tietz, 1897–1933. Sein Leben und Seine Zeit. Ed. G. Horn. Tel Aviv, 1980.

Katzburg, N., ed. *Pedut, Rescue in the Holocaust: Texts and Studies.* Ramat Gan, Isr., 1984.

Kershaw, J. *Der Hitler-Mythos, Volksmeinung und Propaganda im Dritten Reich.* Stuttgart, 1980.

Kishales, H. *Korot Yehudei Bulgaria.* Vols. 1–4. Tel Aviv, 1970.

Klee, E. *"Euthanasia" im NS-Staat: Die Vernichtung lebensunwerten Lebens.* Frankfurt on the Main, 1983.

Koblik, St. *The Stones Cry Out: Sweden's Response to the Persecution of the Jews, 1933–1945.* New York, 1988.

Kogon, E. *Der SS-Staat: Das System der deutschen Konzentrationslager.* Frankfurt on the Main, 1946, 1965.

————, ed. *Nationalsozialistische Massentötung durch Giftgas.* Frankfurt on the Main, 1983.

Kolb, E. *Bergen-Belsen.* Hannover, W. Ger., 1962.

Krakowski, Sh. *The War of the Doomed: Jewish Armed Resistance in Poland, 1942–1944.* New York, 1984.

Kranzler, D. *Japanese, Nazis and Jews: The Jewish Refugee Community of Shanghai, 1938–1945.* New York, 1976.

Kraus, O., and Kulka, E., eds. *The Death Factory: Documents on Auschwitz.* Oxford, 1959.

Krausnick, H. "The Persecution of the Jews." In *Anatomy of the SS-State.* Ed. H. Krausnick et al. London, paperback 1970. Pp. 17–139.

Krausnick, H., and H. H. Wilhelm. *Die Truppe des Weltanschauungskrieges: Die Einsatzgruppen der Sicherheitspolizei und des SD, 1938–1942.* Stuttgart, 1981.

Lederer, Z. *Ghetto Theresienstadt.* Assen, The Neth., 1953.

Levin, N. *The Holocaust: The Destruction of European Jewry, 1933–1945.* New York, 1973.

Lewy, G. *The Catholic Church and Nazi Germany.* New York, 1964.

Lifton, R. J. *The Nazi Doctors: Medical Killing and the Psychology of Genocide.* New York, 1986.

Lindberg, H. *Svensk flyktingspolitik under internationellt tryck, 1936–1941.* Stockholm, 1973.

Living with Antisemitism: Modern Jewish Responses. Ed. J. Reinharz. Hanover, N.H., 1987.

Ludwig, C. *Die Flüchtlingspolitik der Schweiz in den Jahren 1933–1955.* Bern, 1957.

Madajczyk, C. *Polityka III Rzeszy Okupowanej Polsce.* Vols. 1–2. Warsaw, 1970. *(The Politics of the Third Reich in Occupied Poland)*

Maršálek, H. *Die Geschichte des Konzentrationslagers Mauthausen: Dokumentation.* Vienna, 1980.

Marrus, M. R., and R. O. Paxton. *Vichy France and the Jews.* New York, 1981.

Me-Antishemiut Modernit la-"Pitaron ha-Sofi": *Leket Maamarim.* Ed. O. D. Kulka and Y. Gutman. Jerusalem, 1984.

Michaelis, M. *Mussolini and the Jews. German-Italian Relations and the Jewish Question in Italy.* Oxford, 1978.

Morley, J. F. *Vatican Diplomacy and the Jews During the Holocaust, 1939–1943.* New York, 1980.

Morse, A. D. *While Six Million Died.* London, 1968.

Neustat, M. *Churban ve-Mered shel Yehudei Varsha.* Tel Aviv, 1947.

Patterns of Jewish Leadership in Nazi Europe, 1933–1945: Proceedings of the Third Yad Vashem International Historical Conference. Ed. Y. Gutman and C. Y. Haft. Jerusalem, 1979.

Philipp, R. *Raul Wallenberg: Fighter for Humanity.* Stockholm, 1949.

Pingel, F. *Häftlinge unter SS-Herrschaft: Widerstand, Selbstbehauptung und Vernichtung im Konzentrationslager.* Hamburg, 1978.

Poliakov, L. *Harvest of Hate.* Syracuse, N.Y., 1959. 2nd ed., New York, forthcoming.

Presser, J. *The Destruction of the Dutch Jews.* New York, 1969.

Proudfoot, M. Y. *European Refugees: A Study in Forced Population Movement.* London, 1957.

Rautkallio, H. *Finland and the Holocaust: The Rescue of Finland's Jews.* New York, 1987.

Reitlinger, G. *The Final Solution: The Attempt to Exterminate the Jews of Europe, 1939–1945,* 2d rev. ed. London, 1968.

––––––. *The SS, Alibi of a Nation, 1922–1945.* London, 1956.

Rescue Attempts During the Holocaust: Proceedings of the Second Yad Vashem International Historical Conference. Ed. Y. Gutman and E. Zuroff. Jerusalem, 1977.

Rundblad, B. "Invandrar Problem." In *Forskare om befolkningsfraago.* Ed. T. Hägerstrand and A. Karlquist. Stockholm, 1975. Pp. 257–318.

Scheffler, W. *Judenverfolgung im Dritten Reich 1933 bis 1945.* Frankfurt on the Main, 1961.

Sefer ha-Partizanim ha-Yehudim. Vols. 1–2. Merḥavia, Isr., 1959.

Sereny, G. *Into That Darkness: From Mercy Killing to Mass Murder.* London, 1974.

Shelaḥ, M. "The Murder of Croatian Jewry by the Germans and Their Collaborators During World War II." Ph.D. diss., The Hebrew University, Jerusalem, 1980. (H)

Sherman, A. J. *Island Refuge: Britain and Refugees from the Third Reich, 1933–1939.* London, 1973.

Shirer, W. L. *The Rise and Fall of the Third Reich: A History of Nazi Germany.* New York, 1960.

Slutzky, Y. *History of the Hagana.* Vol. 3, 1. Ed. Benzion Dinur et al. Tel Aviv, 1972.

Tartakover, A., and Grossman, K. R. *The Jewish Refugee.* New York, 1944.

The Catastrophe of European Jewry: Antecedents, History, Reflections. Ed. Y. Gutman and L. Rothkirchen. Jerusalem, 1976.

Tenenbaum, J. *Race and Reich: The Story of an Epoch.* New York, 1956.

The Jews of Czechoslovakia: Historical Studies and Surveys. Vols. 1–3. Philadelphia, 1971–1984.

The Nazi Concentration Camps: Structure and Aims, the Image of the Prisoner, the Jews in the Camps. Proceedings of the Fourth Yad Vashem International Historical Conference. Ed. Y. Gutman and R. Manbar. Jerusalem, 1984.

Towards the Holocaust: The Social and Economic Collapse of the Weimer Republic. Ed. M. M. Dolkowski and I. Wallman. Westport, Conn., 1983.

Trunk, I. *Judenrat: The Jewish Councils in Eastern Europe Under Nazi Occupation.* New York, 1972.

Turner, H. A., Jr. *German Big Business and the Rise of Hitler.* New York, 1985.

Valentin, H. *Judarna i Sverige.* Stockholm, 1964.

Wheeler-Bennet, J. W. *The Nemesis of Power: The German Army in Politics, 1918–1945.* New York, 1967.

Wischnitzer, M. *To Dwell in Safety.* Philadelphia, 1948.

Wittman, K. *Schwedens Wirtschaftsbeziehungen zum Dritten Reich, 1933–1945.* Munich, 1978.

Writing and the Holocaust. Ed. B. Lang. New York, 1988.

Wulf, J. *Heinrich Himmler: Eine biographische Studie.* Berlin, 1960.

Wyman, D. B. *Paper Walls: America and the Refugee Crisis, 1938–1941.* Amherst, Mass., 1968.

————. The Abandonment of the Jews: America and the Holocaust, 1941–1945. New York, 1984.

Yahil, L. *The Rescue of Danish Jewry: Test of a Democracy.* Philadelphia, 1969; paperbook ed., 1983.

Zimmermann, M. *Wilhelm Marr: The Patriarch of Anti-Semitism.* New York, 1986.

(b) Additional Secondary Sources

Adler, J. *The Jews of Paris and the Final Solution: Communal Response and Internal Conflicts, 1940–1944.* New York, 1987.

Adler-Rudel, S. "A Chronicle of Rescue Efforts." *YLB.* Vol. 11, 1966, pp. 213–41.

————. *Jüdische Selbsthilfe unter dem Naziregime, 1933–1939.* Tübingen, 1974.

————. *Ostjuden in Deutschland, 1880–1940.* Tübingen, 1959.

Aleff, E., ed. *Das Dritte Reich.* Hannover, W. Ger., 1970.

Arad, Y. "Jewish Family Camps in the Forests: An Original Means of Rescue." In *Rescue Attempts During the Holocaust. Proceedings of the Second Yad Vashem International Historical Conference.* Ed. Y. Gutman and E. Zuroff. Jerusalem 1977. Pp. 333–53.

————. "The 'Final Solution' in Lithuania in the Light of German Documentation." *YVS Studies.* Vol. 11, 1976, pp. 234–72.

Arditi, B. *Yehudei Bulgaria be-Shnot ha-Mishtar ha-Natzi, 1940–1944.* Holon, Isr., 1962.

Ariel, J. "Jewish Self-defense and Resistance in France During World War II." *YVS Studies.* Vol. 6, 1967, pp. 221–50.

————. "Mismaḥ bilti yadua al ha-Praot be-Konstantin." *Yalkut Moreshet,* Periodical, 3 (1965): 139–51.

Arendt, H. "Social Sciences and the Concentration Camp." *Jewish Social Studies,* 12 (1950): 51–61.

Arndt, I., and Scheffler, W. "Organisierter Massenmord an Juden in nationalsozialistichen Vernichtungslagern." *VJHZ,* 24, no. 2 (1976): 105–35.

Aschheim, St. E. *Brothers and Strangers: The East European Jew in German and German Jewish Consciousness, 1800–1923.* Madison, Wis. 1982.

Avni, Ch. "Spanish Nationals in Greece and Their Fate During the Holocaust." *YVS Studies.* Vol. 8, 1970, pp. 29–63.

————. "The Zionist Underground in Holland and France and the Escape to Spain." In *Rescue Attempts During the Holocaust. Proceedings of the Second Yad Vashem International Historical Conference.* Ed. Y. Gutman and E. Zuroff. Jerusalem, 1977. Pp. 555–90.

Ball-Kaduri, K. J. "Berlin Is Purged of Its Jews: The Jews in Berlin in the Year 1943." *YVS Studies.* Vol. 5, 1963, pp. 271–316.

————. *Das Leben der Juden in Deutschland im Jahre 1933: Ein Zeitbericht.* Frankfurt on the Main, 1963.

————. "The Central Jewish Organizations in Berlin During the Pogrom of November 1938." *YVS Studies.* Vol. 3, 1959, pp. 261–81.

————. "The Illegal Aliya from Germany." *Yalkut Moreshet,* Periodical, 8 (1968): 127–42. (H)

————. *Vor der Katastrophe: Juden in Deutschland, 1934–1939.* Tel Aviv, 1964.

Barlas, Ch. *Hatzala Bi'imei Shoah.* Hakibbutz Hameuḥad, 1975.

Bauer, Y. "Rescue Operations Through Vilna." *YVS Studies.* Vol. 9, 1973, pp. 215–23.

————. "Shlichuto shel Yoel Brand." *Yalkut Moreshet,* Periodical, 26 (1979): 23–60.

————. "The Death Marches, January–May 1945." *Yahadut Zemanenu,* 1 (1983): 199–221. (H with English summary)

————. "The Negotiations Between Saly Mayer and the Representatives of the SS in 1944–1945." In *Rescue Attempts During the Holocaust. Proceedings of the Second Yad Vashem International Historical Conference.* Ed. Y. Gutman and E. Zuroff. Jerusalem, 1977, pp. 5–45.

————. "When Did They Know?" *Midstream,* 14, no. 4 (April 1966): 51–58.

Baum. R. C. *The Holocaust and the German Elite: Genocide and National Suicide in Germany, 1871–1945.* London, 1981.

Bein, A. "The Jewish Parasite: Notes on the Semantics of the Jewish Problem, with Special Reference for Germany." *YLB.* Vol. 9, 1964, pp. 3–40.

Bejski, M. "The 'Righteous Among the Nations' and Their Part in the Rescue of Jews." In *Rescue Attempts During the Holocaust: Proceedings of the Second Yad Vashem International Historical Conference.* Ed. Y. Gutman and E. Zuroff. Jerusalem, 1977, pp. 627–47.

Ben-Elissar, E. *La Diplomatie du IIIe Reich et les juifs, 1933–1939.* Geneva, 1969.

Bennathan, E. "Die demographische und wirtschaftliche Struktur der Juden." In *Entscheidungsjahr 1932: Zur Judenfrage in der Endphase der Weimarer Republik.* Ed. W. E. Mosse. Tübingen, 1965. Pp. 87–131.

Benz, W., and Gral, H., eds. *Sommer 1939: Die Grossmächte und der Europäische Krieg.* Stuttgart, 1979.

Berman, A. A. *The Jewish Resistance.* Tel Aviv, 1971. (H)

Bernett, H. *Der jüdische Sport im nationalsozialistischen Deutschland, 1933–1938.* Schorndorf, W. Ger., 1978.

Besgen, A. *Der Stille Befehl: Medizinalrat Kersten, Himmler und das Dritte Reich.* Munich, 1960.

Bettelheim, B. *The Informed Heart.* London, 1961.

Billig, J. *Le Commissariat général aux questions juives.* Paris, 1955.

Biss, A. *A Million Jews to Save: Check for The Final Solution.* London, 1975.

Bor-Komorowski, T. *The Secret Army.* New York, 1951.

Braham, R. L. *Eichmann and the Destruction of Hungarian Jewry.* New York, 1961.

————. "The Holocaust in Hungary: An Historical Interpretation of the Role of the Hungarian Radical Right." *Societas: A Review of Social History,* 2, no. 3 (1972): 195–220.

————. *The Hungarian Labor Service System, 1939–1945.* New York, 1977.

————. "The Kamenets Podolsk and Délvidék Massacres: Prelude to the Holocaust in Hungary." *YVS Studies.* Vol. 9, 1973, pp. 133–56.

Brandes, D. *Die Tschechen unter deutschem Protektorat.* Vols. 1–2. Munich, 1969, 1975.

Bräutigam, O. *Überblick über die besetzten Ostgebiete während des 2. Weltkrieges.* Tübingen, 1954.

Brol, F., G. Wloch, and J. Pilecki. "Das Bunkerbuch." *Hefte von Auschwitz*, 1 (1959): 7–44.

Browning, Ch. *Fateful Months: Essays on the Emergence of the Final Solution, 1941–1942.* New York, 1985.

―――――. *The Final Solution and the German Foreign Office: A Study of Referat D III of Abteilung Deutschland, 1940–43.* New York, 1978.

―――――. "Unterstaatssekretär Martin Luther and the Ribbentrop Foreign Office." *Journal of Contemporary History* (London), 22 (1977): 313–44.

Canter, Dr. A. "Die Euthanasiamorde." *Frankfurter Allgemeine Zeitung* (June 6, 1963): 8.

Carpi, D. "Notes on the History of the Jews in Greece During the Holocaust Period: The Attitude of the Italians (1941–1943)." *Festschrift in Honor of Dr. George S. Wise.* Tel Aviv, 1981, pp. 25–62.

―――――. "Prisons and Concentration Camps in Italy During the Holocaust Period," in *Dapim le-Ḥeker ha-Shoah ve-ha-Mered.* 2d ed., vol. 1. Pp. 178–204.

―――――. "The Origins and Development of Fascist Anti-Semitism in Italy (1922–1945)." In *The Catastrophe of European Jewry: Antecedents, History, Reflections, Selected Papers.* Ed. Y. Gutman and L. Rothkirchen. Yad Vashem, Jerusalem, 1976. Pp. 283–98.

Cecil, R. *The Myth of the Master Race: Alfred Rosenberg and Nazi Theology.* New York, 1972.

Cholawski, Sh. *Beleaguered in Town and Forest.* Tel Aviv, 1973. (H).

―――――. "Events at Tuczin." *Yalkut Moreshet,* Periodical, 2 (1964): 81–95. (H).

―――――. *In the Eye of the Hurricane: The Jews in Eastern Belorussia During World War II.* Jerusalem, 1988. (H)

―――――. "Minsk: Its Struggle and Destruction." *Yalkut Moreshet,* Periodical, 18 (1974): 101–12. (H)

―――――. *The Jews in Belorussia (White Russia) During World War II.* Jerusalem, 1982. (H)

Clark, A. *Barbarossa: The Russian-German Conflict.* New York, 1965.

Cohen, A. *The Halutz Resistance in Hungary, 1942–1944.* Hakibbutz Hameuhad, Isr., 1984. (H, English summary)

―――――. "The Influence of the Refugees on the Creation of the Chalutz Resistance Movement in Hungary." *Dapim, Studies on the Holocaust Period* (Haifa), 2 (1981): 121–44. (H)

Cohen, E. A. *Human Behavior in the Concentration Camp.* New York, 1953.

Cohen, G. *Churchill and Palestine, 1939–1942.* Jerusalem, 1976.

Cohen, N. W. *Not Free to Desist: A History of the American Jewish Committee, 1906–1966.* Philadelphia, 1972.

Cohen, R. I. *The Burden of Conscience: French Jewish Leadership During the Holocaust.* Bloomington, Ind., 1987.

Cohn, N. *Warrant for Genocide: The Myth of the Jewish World Conspiracy and the "Protocols of the Elders of Zion."* London, 1967.

Colodner, S. *Jewish Education in Germany Under the Nazis.* New York, 1964.

Dallin, A., *German Rule in Russia, 1941–1945: A Study of Occupation Policies,* London, 1981.

De Jong, L. "Zwischen Kollaboration und Resistance." In *Bericht über die Tagung des Instituts für Zeitgesschichte in Tutzig (May 1956).* Munich, 1957, pp. 133–52.

Deak, A. *Razia in Novisad und andere Geschehnisse während des zweiten Weltkrieges in Ungarn und Yugoslavien.* Zurich, 1967.

des Pres, T. *The Survivor.* New York, 1978.

Deuerlein, E. "Hitlers Eintritt in die Politik und die Reichswehr." *VJHZ* 7, no. 2 (1959): 177–227.

Dinur, B. "Kiddush ha-Shem ve-Ḥilul ha-Shem." *Maḥanayim,* 41 (1948): 23–32.

―――. *Remember! Addresses on the Holocaust and Its Moral.* Jerusalem, 1958. (H)

Dörner, K. "Nationalsozialismus und Lebensvernichtung." *VJHZ,* 15, no. 2 (1967): 121–52.

Dworzecki, M. "The Day-to-Day Stand of the Jews." In *The Catastrophe of European Jewry: Antecendents—History—Reflections. Selected papers.* Ed. Y. Gutman and L. Rothkirchen. Jerusalem 1976. Pp. 367–99.

Eck, N. "The March of Death from Serbia to Hungary (September, 1944) and the Slaughter of Cservenka." *YVS Studies.* Vol. 2, 1958, pp. 255–94.

―――. "The Rescue of Jews with the Aid of Passports and Citizenship Papers of Latin American States." *YVS Studies.* Vol. 1, 1957, pp. 125–52.

―――. "Yehudim Tmurat Germanim." *Dapim le-Ḥeker ha-Shoah ve-ha-Mered,* Sidra Shnia, Measef 2 (1973): 23–49.

Edelheim-Mühsam, M. T. "The Jewish Press in Germany." *YLB.* Vol. 1, 1956, pp. 172–88.

Eppler, E. "The Rescue Work of the World Jewish Congress During the Nazi Period." In *Rescue Attempts During the Holocaust. Proceedings of the Second Yad Vashem International Historical Conference.* Ed. Y. Gutman and E. Zuroff, Jerusalem, 1977. Pp. 47–69.

Eschwege, H. "Resistance of German Jews Against the Nazi Regime." *YLB.* Vol. 15, 1970, pp. 143–80.

Esh, Sh. "Between Discrimination and Extermination (The Fateful Year 1938)." *YVS Studies.* Vol. 2 (1958). Pp. 79–93.

―――. "The Dignity of the Destroyed: Towards a Definition of the Period of the Holocaust." In *The Catastrophe of European Jewry: Antecedents—History—Reflections. Selected Papers.* Ed. Y. Gutman and L. Rothkirchen. Jerusalem 1976. Pp. 346–66.

―――. "The Establishment of the 'Reichsvereinigung der Juden in Deutschland' and Its Main Activities." *YVS Studies.* Vol. 7 (1968), Pp. 19–38.

Ettinger, Sh. "Yiḥuda shel ha-Antishemiut be-Yameinu." *Yalkut Moreshet,* Periodical, 18 (1977): 7–22.

Fackenheim, E. L. *The Jewish Return into History: Reflections in the Age of Auschwitz and a New Jerusalem.* New York, 1978.

Falconi, L. *The Silence of Pius XII.* London, 1970.

Feinberg, N. "Jewish Political Activities Against the Nazi Regime in the Years 1933–1939." In *Jewish Resistance During the Holocaust: Proceedings of the Conference on Manifestations of Jewish Resistance.* Jerusalem, 1971. Pp. 74–94.

Fejkiel, W. "Der Hunger in Auschwitz." *Hefte von Auschwitz,* 8 (1964): 3–14.

Fenyö, M. D. *Hitler, Horthy and Hungary: German-Hungarian Relations, 1941–1944.* New Haven, Conn., 1972.

Frankl, V. E. "Group Psychotherapeutic Experiences in a Concentration Camp." In *Psychotherapy and Existentialism, Selected Papers on Logotherapy.* New York, 1968. Pp. 95–105.

Frankl, V. E. *Man's Search for Meaning: An Introduction to Logotherapy.* 2 vols. New York, 1968.

Freeden, H. "Eine gespenstige Theater-Aufführung." *BL,* no. 1 (1957): 19–23.

Friedländer, S. *Counterfeit Nazi: The Ambiguity of Good,* London, 1969.

Friedman, Ph. "Problems of Research on the European Jewish Catastrophe." In *The Catastrophe of European Jewry. Selected Papers.* Ed. Y. Gutman and L. Rothkirchen. Jerusalem, 1970. Pp. 633–60.

————. "Pseudo-saviours in the Polish Ghettos: Mordechai Chaim Rumkowski of Lodz" and "The Messianic Complex of a Nazi Collaborator in a Ghetto: Moses Merin of Sosnowiec." In *Roads to Extinction: Essays on the Holocaust.* Ed. A. J. Friedman. New York, 1980. Pp. 333–51 and 353–64.

————. *Their Brothers' Keepers.* New York, 1978.

————. "The Jewish Ghetto in the Nazi Era." *Jewish Social Studies,* 16, no. 1 (1954): 61–87.

————. "The Lublin Reservation and the Madagascar Plan: Two Aspects of Nazi Jewish Policy During the Second World War." *YIVO Annual of Jewish Social Science.* Vol. 8, 1953, pp. 151–177.

Friedman, S. S. *No Haven for the Oppressed.* Detroit, Mich., 1973.

Gaertner, H. "Problems in Jewish Schools in Germany During the Hitler Regime." *YLB.* Vol. 1, 1956, pp. 123–41.

Garfinkels, B. *Les Belges facent à la persécution raciale, 1940–1944.* Brussels, 1965.

Garlinski, J. *Fighting Auschwitz.* London, 1975.

Gelber, Y. "Zionist Policy and the Fate of European Jewry, 1943–1945." *Studies in Zionism* (Tel Aviv), 7 (1983): 133–53.

Gerlach, W. "Zwischen Kreuz und Davidsstern." Ph.D. diss., University of Hamburg, 1970.

Gilbert, M. *Auschwitz and the Allies.* New York, 1981.

————. "British Government Policy Towards Jewish Refugees (November 1937–September 1939)." *YVS Studies.* Vol. 13, 1979, pp. 127–67.

Goguel, R. *"Cap Arcona": Report über den Untergang der Flüchtlingsflotte in der Lübecker Bucht am 4. Mai. 1945.* Frankfurt on the Main, 1972.

Goshen, Z. "Eichmann und die Nisko-Aktion im Oktober 1939: Eine Fallstudie zur NS-Judenpolitik in der letzten Etappe vor der 'Endlösung'." *VJHZ* 29, no. 1 (1981): 74–96.

Graml, H. *Der 9. November 1938: "Reichskristallnacht."* Bonn, 1955.

————. *Reichskristallnacht: Antisemitismus und Judenverfolgung im Dritten Reich.* Munich, 1988.

Green, W. P. "The Nazi Racial Policy Towards the Karaites." MA thesis, University of Wisconsin.

Grodner, D. "In Soviet Poland Lithuania." In *Contemporary Jewish Record.* Vol. 4, 1941. Pp. 136–41.

Grosser, L., ed. *Sachsenhausen.* Berlin, 1974.

Gruchmann, L. "Euthanasia und Justiz im Dritten Reich." *VJHZ,* 20, no. 3 (1972): 235–79.

Gruenewald, M. "The Beginning of the Reichsvertretung." *YLB.* Vol. 1, 1956, pp. 57–67.

Gutman, Y. "Adam Czerniakow: The Man and His Diary." *Yalkut Moreshet,* Periodical, 10 (1969): 122–43. (H)

————. "Forced Labour in Occupied Countries During the Second World War." *Zion,* 44, no. 1–2 (1978): 119–58. (H)

————. "Jews in General Anders' Army in the Soviet Union." *YVS Studies.* Vol. 12, 1977, pp. 231–96.

————. "Kiddush ha-Shem ve-Kiddush ha-Ḥaim." *Yalkut Moreshet,* Periodical, 24 (1978): 7–22.

—————. "Le-Ofiam shel Maḥanot Rikuz Natziim." *Yalkut Moreshet,* Periodical, 29 (1980): 29–52.

—————. "Youth Movements in the Underground and the Ghetto Revolts." In *Jewish Resistance During the Holocaust. Proceedings of the Conference on Manifestations of Jewish Resistance.* Jerusalem 1968. Pp. 260–84.

Gutman, Y., and Krakowski, Sh. *Unequal Victims: Poles and Jews During World War II.* New York, 1986.

Haestrup, J. *Passage to Palestine: Young Jews in Denmark 1932–1945.* New York, 1983.

Haft, C. *The Bargain and the Bridle: The General Union of the Israelies of France, 1941–1944.* Chicago, 1983.

Hamburger, E. "One Hundred Years of Emancipation." *YLB.* Vol. 14, 1969, pp. 1–66.

Handlin, O. *A Continuing Task: The American Jewish Joint Distribution Committee, 1914–1964.* New York, 1964.

Hanhagat Yehudei Hungaria be-Mivḥan ha-Shoah. Ed. Y. Gutman, B. Vago, and L. Rothkirchen, Jerusalem 1976.

Heschel, A. J. "The Eastern European Era in Jewish History." *YIVO Annual of Jewish Social Science.* Vol. 1, 1946, pp. 86–106.

Heyl, J. D. "Hitler's Economic Thought: A Reappraisal." *Central European History Quarterly,* 6, no. 1 (March 1973): 83–96.

Hilberg, R. "German Railroads, Jewish Souls." *Societas: A Review of Social History,* (November–December, 1976): 60–74.

Hildesheimer, E. "The Central Organization of the German Jews in the Years 1933–1943: Its Legal and Political Status and Its Position in the Jewish Community." Ph.D. diss., The Hebrew University, Jerusalem, 1982. (H)

Hillgruber, A. "Die Endlösung und das deutsche Ostimperium als Kernstück des rassenideologischen Programms des Nationalsozialismus." *VJHZ,* 20, no. 2 (1972): 133–53.

—————. "Kontinuität und Diskontinuität in der deutschen Aussenpolitik von Bismarck bis Hitler." In *Grossmachtpolitik und Militarismus im 20, Jahrhundert.* Düsseldorf, 1974. Pp. 11–36.

Höhne, H. *The Order of the Death's Head: The Story of Hitler's SS.* London, 1969; New York 1970.

Hory, L., and Broszat, M. *Der Kroatische Ustascha-Staat, 1941–1945.* Stuttgart, 1964.

Hubatsch, W. *Hindenburg und der Staat.* Göttingen, 1966.

Huttenbach, H. R. *Destruction of the Jewish Community of Worms, 1933–1935: A Study of Holocaust Experience in Germany.* New York, 1981.

Jelinek, Y. "Hashmadat Serbim, Yehudim ve-Tzoanim be-Medinat Croatia ha-atzmait." *Yalkut Moreshet,* Periodical, 16 (1978): 61–70.

—————. "Loḥamim Yehudim be-Maḥane Novaky." *Yalkut Moreshet,* Periodical, 1, (1963): 47–67.

—————. *The Parish Republic: Hlinka's Slovak People's Party, 1939–1945.* New York, 1976.

Kahanowicz, M. *Milḥemet ha-Partizanim ha-Yehudim be-Mizraḥ Europa.* Tel-Aviv, 1954.

Katz, J. *Jews and Freemasons in Europe, 1723–1939.* Cambridge, Mass., 1970.

—————. *The Darker Side of Genius: Richard Wagner's Anti-Semitism.* Hanover, N.H., 1986.

Katz, R. *Black Sabbath: A Journey Through a Crime Against Humanity.* London, 1969.

Katzburg, N. "British Policy on Immigration to Palestine During World War II." In *Rescue Attempts During the Holocaust. Proceedings of the Second Yad Vashem Interna-*

tional Historical Conference. Ed. Y. Gutman and E. Zuroff. Jerusalem, 1977. Pp. 183–203.

―――. *From Partitition to White Paper: British Policy in Palestine, 1936–1940.* Jerusalem, 1974. (H)

―――. *History of Jews in Hungary.* Jerusalem, 1975. (H)

―――. "Hungarian Jewry in Modern Times: Political and Social Aspects." In *Hungarian Jewish Studies,* Vol. 1. Ed. R. L. Braham. New York, 1966. Pp. 137–70.

―――. "Redifot ha-Yehudim be-Hungaria 1919–1922." *Shnaton Bar-Ilan* (1965), pp. 225–41.

―――. *The Palestine Problem in British Policy, 1940–1945.* Jerusalem 1977. (H)

Kempner, R.M.W. "Der Mord an 35,000 Berliner Juden:" Der Judenmord prozess in Berlin schreibt Geschichte. In *Gegenwart im Rückblick.* Ed. H. A. Strauss and K. R. Grossmann. Heidelberg, 1970. Pp. 180–207.

Kimmel, G. "Das Konzentrationslager Dachau: Eine Studie zu den nationalsozialistischen Gewaltverbrechen." In *Bayern in der NS-Zeit,* Vol. 2. Ed. M. Broszat et al. Munich, 1979. Pp. 349–413.

Kochan, L. *Pogrom: 10 November 1938.* London, 1957.

Kochava, A., and Klinov, R. *Ha-Mahteret ha-Halutzit be-Holand ha-kvusha.* Tel Aviv, 1969.

Kren, G. N., and Rappaport, L. *The Holocaust and the Crisis of Human Behavior.* New York, 1980.

Kubovy, A. L., ed. *Unity in Dispersion: A History of the WJC.* New York, 1948.

Kulka, O. D. "The 'Jewish Question' in the Third Reich as a Factor in National Socialist Ideology and Policy and the Determination of the Status and Activities of the Jews." 2 vols. Ph.D. diss., The Hebrew University, Jerusalem, 1975. (H)

Kurzmann, D. *The Race for Rome.* New York, 1975.

Kuszei, H. "Strafen, die von der SS an Häftlingen des Konzentrationslagers Auschwitz vollzogen wurden." *Hefte von Auschwitz,* 3 (1960): 3–32.

Kwiet, K., and Eschwege, H. *Selbstbehauptung und Widerstand: Deutsche Juden im Kampf um Existenz und Menschenwürde, 1933–1945.* Hamburg, 1984.

Lambert, G. *Operation Hazalah (Budapest 1944).* Indianapolis, Ind., 1974.

Lamm, H. "Über die innere und äussere Entwicklung des deutschen Judentums." Ph.D. diss., University of Erlangen, W. Ger., 1951.

Langbein, H. *Menschen in Auschwitz.* Vienna, 1972.

Laqueur, W. *The Terrible Secret: An Investigation into the Suppression of Information About Hitler's "Final Solution."* London, 1980.

Laqueur, W., and Breitman, R. *Breaking the Silence.* New York, 1986.

Lavi, H. *Yahadut Rumania be-Maavak al Hatzalata.* Jerusalem, 1965.

Le Chêne, E. *Mauthausen: The History of a Death Camp.* London, 1971.

Leshem, P. "Rescue Effort in the Iberian Peninsula." *YLB.* Vol. 14, 1969, pp. 231–56.

Lestchinsky, Y. *Gorala ha-khalkhali shel Yahadut Germania: Aliyata, Tmuroteha, Mashbera, Shkiata.* Hakibbutz Hameuhad, Merhavia, 1963.

―――. "Yidn In Di Gresere Shtet Fun Poiln 1921–1931." *YIVO Bleter,* 21 (1943): 20–46.

Lévai, J. *Black Book on the Martyrdom of Hungarian Jewry.* Zurich, 1948.

―――. *Eichmann in Hungary: Documents.* Budapest, 1961.

―――. *Hungarian Jewry and the Papacy.* London, 1967.

Levin, D. *Fighting Back: Lithuanian Jewish Armed Resistance to the Nazis, 1941–1945.* New York, 1985.

―――. "Yehudei Latvia Bein Histayegut le-vein Histaglut la-Mishtar ha-Sovieti (1940–

1941)." *Behinot Studies: Jews in the USSR and Eastern Europe* (Tel Aviv) 5 (1974): 70–96. (H)

Lévy, C., and Tillard, P. *Betrayal at the Val d'Hiver.* New York, 1967.

Lösener, B. "Das Reichsministerium des Innern und die Judengesetzgebung." *VJHZ,* 9, no. 3 (1961): 262–313.

Lotan, G. "The Zentralwohlfahrtstelle." *YLB.* Vol. 6, 1959, pp. 185–207.

Mahler, R. *Yehudei Polin bein shtei Milhamot ha-Olam.* Tel Aviv, 1968.

Maoz, E. "An Underground Group of German Jewish Communists." *Yalkut Moreshet,* Periodical, 3 (1964): 79–88. (H)

Marcus, E. "The German Foreign Office and the Palestine Question in the Period 1933–1939." *YVS Studies.* Vol. 2, 1958, pp. 179–204.

Margaliot, A. "The Dispute over the Leadership of German Jewry (1933–1938)." *YVS Studies.* Vol. 10, 1974, pp. 129–48.

————. "The Political Reaction of the Jewish Institutions and Organizations in Germany to the Anti-Jewish Policy of the National Socialists in the Years 1932–1935." Vols. 1–2. Ph.D. diss. The Hebrew University, Jerusalem, 1971. (H)

————. "The Struggle for Survival of the Jewish Communities in Germany in the Face of Oppression." In *Jewish Resistance During the Holocaust. Proceedings of the Conference on Manifestations of Jewish Resistance,* Jerusalem, 1972. Pp. 100–111.

Mark, B. "Ha-Kvutza shel Herbert Baum: Kvutzat ha-Hitnagdut ha-Yehudit ba-Shanim, 1937–1942." *Bleter Far Geshichte,* 14 (1961): 27–64.

Marrus, M. R. *The Unwanted: European Refugees in the Twentieth Century.* New York, 1985.

Matkovski, A. "The Destruction of Macedonian Jewry in 1943." *YVS Studies.* Vol. 3, 1959, pp. 187–236. (H)

Meier-Cronemeyer, H. "Jüdische Jugendbewegung." *Germania Judaica,* 8, nos. 1–4 (1969): 1–122.

Michaelis, M. "On the Jewish Question in Fascist Italy: The Attitude of the Fascist Regime to the Jews in Italy." *YVS Studies.* Vol. 4, 1960, pp. 7–41.

Michman, D. "The Jewish Refugees from Germany in the Netherlands, 1933–1940." Vols. 1–2. Ph.D. diss., The Hebrew University, Jerusalem, 1978. (H)

Michman, J. "The Controversial Stand of the Joodse Raad in the Netherlands: Lodewijk E. Visser's Struggle." *YVS Studies.* Vol. 10, 1974, pp. 9–68.

Miller, M. L. *Bulgaria During Second World War.* Stanford, Calif., 1975.

Molho, M., and Nehama, J. *The Destruction of Greek Jewry, 1941–1944.* Jerusalem, 1965. (H)

Mommsen, H. "Aufgabenkreis und Verantwortlichkeit des Staatsekretärs der Reichskanzlei, Dr. W. Kritzinger." In *Gutachten des Instituts für Zeitgeschichte.* Stuttgart, 1966. Vol. 2, pp. 369–98.

————. "Der Reichstagsbrand und seine politischen Folgen." *VJHZ,* 12, no. 4 (1964): 351–415.

Mosse, G. L. *Germans and Jews: The Right, the Left, and the Search for a "Third Force" in Pre-Nazi Germany.* New York, 1970; London 1971.

————. *The Crisis of German Ideology: Intellectual Origins of the Third Reich.* New York, 1971.

————. *The Nationalization of the Masses: Political Symbolism and Mass Movements in Germany from the Napoleonic Wars Through the Third Reich.* New York, 1975.

————. *Towards the Final Solution: A History of European Racism.* New York, 1978.

Müller-Claudius, M. *Der Antisemitismus und das deutsche Vehängnis.* Frankfurt on the Main, 1948.

Müller-Hill, B. *Murderous Science: Elimination by Scientific Selection of Jews, Gypsies, and Others. Germany, 1933–1945*. Oxford, 1988.

Mushkat, M. "The Concept 'Crime Against the Jewish People' in the Light of International Law." *YVS Studies*. Vol. 5, 1963, pp. 237–53.

————, ed. *Lohamim Yehudim ba-Milhama Neged ha-Natzim*. Tel Aviv, 1971.

Neshamit, S. "Rescue in Lithuania During the Nazi Occupation." In *Rescue Attempts During the Holocaust. Proceedings of the Second Yad Vashem International Historical Conference*. Ed. Y. Gutman and E. Zuroff. Jerusalem, 1977. Pp. 289–331.

Nicosia, F. R. "Revisionist Zionism in Germany (I)." *YLB*. Vol. 31, 1986, pp. 209–40.

————. "Revisionist Zionism in Germany (II)." *YLB*. Vol. 32, 1987, pp. 231–68.

————. *The Third Reich and the Palestinian Question*. London, 1985.

Niewyk, D. L. "The Economic and Cultural Role of the Jews in the Weimar Republic." *YLB*. Vol. 16, 1971, pp. 163–73.

————. *The Jews in Weimar Germany*. Baton Rouge, La. 1980.

Nirenberg, Y. *Di Geschichte Fun Lodsher Geto In Di Yorn Fun Yidishn Churbn*. New York, 1948.

Novitch, M. "Gerush Yehudei Saloniki." *Dapim le-Heker ha-Shoah ve-ha-Mered,* Sidra Shnia. Measef 2 (1973): 195–99.

————. *Le Passage des barbares*. Nice, 1973.

Ofer, D. *Illegal Immigration During the Holocaust*. Jerusalem, 1988. (H) (English edition forthcoming.)

Orbach, W. "The Destruction of the Jews in the Nazi-Occupied Territories of the USSR." *Soviet Jewish Affairs* 6, no. 2 (1976): 216–31.

Oren, B. "From Vilna, Across Japan, to the Free World." *Yalkut Moreshet,* Periodical, 11 (1969): 34–54. (H).

Oren, N. *Bulgarian Communism: The Road to Power, 1934–1944*. New York, 1971.

————. "The Bulgarian Exception: A Reassessment on the Salvation of the Jewish Community." *YVS Studies*. Vol. 7, 1968, pp. 83–106.

Paris, E. *Genocide in Sattelite Croatia, 1941–1945: A Record of Racial and Religious Persecutions and Massacres*. Chicago, 1959.

Paucker, A. *Der Jüdische Abwehrkampf*. Hamburg, 1969.

————. "Some Notes on Resistance." *YLB*. Vol. 6, 1971, pp. 239–48.

Pawelczynska, A. *Values and Violence in Auschwitz: A Sociological Analysis*. Berkeley, Calif., 1979.

Paxton, R. O. *Vichy France: Old Guard and New Order, 1940–1944*. New York, 1972.

Pierson, R. L. *German-Jewish Identity in the Weimar Republic*. Ph.D. diss. Yale University, 1970.

Pikarski, M. "Über die führende Rolle der Parteiorganization der KPD in der antifaschistischen Widerstandsgruppe Herbert Baum." *Beitrage zur Geschichte der deutschen Arbeitsbewegung* no. 8 (1966): 867–82.

Pikoholf-Barnitsh, A. M. "Pinuyo shel Mahane ha-Rikuz Stutthof." *Yediot Yad Vashem,* 16 (1966): 26–39.

Poliakov, L., and Sabile, J. *Jews Under the Italian Occupation*. Paris, 1955.

————. "Yiddisher Vidershtaner in Frankraich." *YIVO Bleter,* 37 (1953): 185–97.

Porat, D. *An Entangled Leadership: The Yishuv and the Holocaust, 1942–1945*. Tel Aviv, 1986. (H, English edition forthcoming)

Proctor, R. W. *Racial Hygiene: Medicine Under the Nazis*. Cambridge, Mass., 1988.

Pudah, F. "Thoughts on the Jewish Underground in Lodz Ghetto." *Yalkut Moreshet,* Periodical, 11 (1969): 54–67.

Rawski, T., Stapor, Z., and Zamojski, J. *Wojna Wyzwolencza Narodu Polskiego w latach, 1939–1945: Wezlowe Problemy.* Vols. 1–2. Warsaw, 1963.

Reichmann, E. G. "Diskussionen über die Judenfrage, 1930–1932." In *Entscheidungsjahr 1932.* Ed. W. E. Mosse. Tübingen. Pp. 503–31.

Reinharz, J. "Hashomer Hatzair in Germany (I): 1928–1933." *YLB.* Vol. 31, 1986, pp. 173–208.

————. "Hashomer Hatzair in Germany (II): Under the Shadow of the Swastika, 1933–1938." *YLB.* Vol. 32, 1987, pp. 183–229.

————. "The Zionist Response to Antisemitism in the Weimar Republic." In *The Jewish Response to German Culture: From the Enlightenment to the Second World War.* Ed. J. Reinharz and W. Schatzberg. Hanover, N.H., 1985. Pp. 166–93.

Reissner, H. G. "The Histories of Kaufhaus N. Israel and Wilfred Israel." *YLB.* Vol. 3, 1958, pp. 227–56.

Reitlinger, G. *The House Built on Sand: The Conflicts of German Policy in Russia, 1939–1945.* London, 1960.

Reuter, L. E. *Katholische Kirche als Fluchthelfer im dritten Reich.* Recklinghausen, W. Ger., 1971.

Richardi, H. G. *Schule der Gewalt: Das Konzentrationslager Dachau, 1933–1944.* Munich, 1983.

Rings, W. *Raubgold aus Deutschland: Die "Golddrehscheibe," Schweiz im Zweiten Weltkrieg.* Zurich, 1985.

Robertson, E. M., ed. *The Origins of the Second World War: Historical Interpretations.* London, 1971.

Robinson, J. *And the Crooked Shall Be Made Straight: The Eichmann Trial, the Jewish Catastrophe, and Hannah Arendt's Narrative.* New York, 1965.

Rohwer, J. *Die Versenkung der jüdischen Flüchtlingstransporter: Struma und Mefkure im Schwarzen Meer (Februar 1942–August 1944).* Stuttgart, 1964.

Rosenbaum, E. "M. M. Warburg and Co., Merchant Bankers of Hamburg." *YLB.* Vol. 7, 1962, pp. 121–49.

Rosenkranz, H., *"Reichskristallnacht": 9. November 1938 in Österreich.* Vienna, 1968.

————. "The Anschluss and the Tragedy of Austrian Jewry, 1933–1945." In *The Jews of Austria: Essays on Their Life, History, and Destruction.* Ed. J. Fraenkel. London, 1967. Pp. 479–546.

————. *Verfolgung und Selbstbehauptung: Die Juden in Österreich, 1938–1945.* Vienna, 1978.

Rothkirchen, L. "The Dual Role of the 'Jewish Center' in Slovakia." *Patterns of Jewish Leadership in Nazi Europe 1933–1945. Proceedings of the Third Yad Vashem International Historical Conference.* Ed. Y. Gutman and C. Y. Haft. Jerusalem, 1979. Pp. 219–27.

————. "The Zionist Character of the 'Selfgovernment' of Terezin (Theresienstadt): A Study in Historiography." *YVS Studies.* Vol. 11, 1976, pp. 56–90.

————. "Vatican Policy and the 'Jewish Problem' in 'Independent' Slovakia (1939–1945)." *YVS Studies.* Vol. 6, 1967, pp. 27–53.

Rürup, R. "Das Ende der Emanzipation: Die antijüdische Politik in Deutschland von der 'Machtergeifung' bis zum zweiten Weltkrieg." In *The Jews in Nazi Germany.* Tübingen, 1986. Pp. 97–114.

————. *Emancipation und Antisemitismus: Studien zur "Judenfrage" des Antisemitismus.* Göttingen, 1975.

Schatzker, Ch. The Jewish Youth Movement in Germany in the Holocaust Period (I): Youth in Confrontation with a New Reality." *YLB.* Vol. 32, 1987, pp. 157–81.

————. "The Jewish Youth Movement in Germany in the Holocaust Period (II): The Relations Between the Youth Movement and Hechaluz." *YLB*. Vol. 33, 1988, pp. 301–25.

Shaul, E. "Gviat Eidut mi-Kavran Kfia Yaakov Grojanowski: Izbice–Kolo–Chelmno." *Yalkut Moreshet,* Periodical, 35 (1983): 101–22.

Shefer, Y. "Hanhagat ha-Maḥteret ha-Ḥalutzit be-Hungaria." In *Hanhagat Yehudei Hungaria ba-Shoah,* Ed. Y. Gutman, B. Vago, and L. Rothkirchen. Jerusalem, 1976. Pp. 134–49.

Shelaḥ, M. *Blood Account: The Rescue of Croatian Jews by the Italians, 1941–1943.* Tel Aviv, 1986. (H, English summary)

Shteiner, Y. *Ha-Ḥakika neged ha-Yehudim ve-Nishulam min ha-Khalkhala be-Medinat Slovakia.* Tel Aviv, 1975.

Shulman, A. *The Case of Hotel Polski: An Account of One of the Most Enigmatic Episodes of World War II.* New York, 1982.

Shwersentz, Y. *Maḥteret Ḥalutzim be-Germania ha-Natzit.* Tel Aviv, 1964.

Sijes, B. A. *Studies over Jodenvervolging.* Assen, Neth., 1974.

Simon, E. *Aufbau im Untergang: Jüdische Erwachsenenbildung im nationalsozialistischen Deutschland als geistiger Widerstand.* Tübingen, 1959.

Simonow, C. *The Lublin Extermination Camp.* Moscow, 1944.

Snoek, J. M., *The Grey Book.* London, 1979.

Snyder, L. L. *The War: A Concise History, 1939–1945.* New York, 1961.

Spector, Sh. *The Holocaust of Volhynian Jews, 1941–1944.* Jerusalem, 1986. (H)

————. "The Jews of Volhynia and Their Reaction to Extermination." *YVS Studies.* Vol. 15, 1983, pp. 159–86.

Steinberg, L. *Le Comité de défense des juifs en Belgique, 1942–1944.* Brussels, 1973.

————. *The Part of the Jews in the General Underground in France.* Paris, 1968.

Steinberg, M. *L'Étoile et le fusil.* Vols. 1–3. Brussels, 1983–87.

————. "The Trap of Legality: The Association of the Jews of Belgium." In *Patterns of Leadership in Nazi Europe 1933–1945. Proceedings of the Third Yad Vashem International Historical Conference.* Ed. Y. Gutman and C. Y. Haft. Jerusalem, 1977. Pp. 353–76.

Strauss, H. A. "Jewish Emigration from Germany: Nazi Policies and Jewish Responses." *YLB.* Vol. 25, 1980, pp. 313–61; vol. 26, 1981, pp. 343–409.

Streim, A. "Zum Beispiel: Die Verbrechen der Einsatzgruppen in der Sowjet Union." In *NS-Prozesse.* Ed. A. Rückerl. Karlsruhe, 1971. Pp. 65–116.

Szeintuch, Y. "Introduction to a Research of the Yiddish and Hebrew Literature Under Nazi Occupation in Poland and Lithuania." *Dapim, Studies on the Holocaust Period,* 2 (1981): 27–69. (H)

Tal, U. "Aspects of Consecration of Politics in the Nazi Era." In *Judaism and Christianity Under the Impact of National Socialism.* Ed. O. D. Kulka and P. R. Mendes-Flohr. Jerusalem, 1987. Pp. 63–95.

————. *Christians and Jews in Germany: Religion, Politics, and Ideology in the Second Reich, 1870–1914,* Ithaca, N.Y., 1975.

————. "Ha-Intelektualim ve-ha-Reich ha-shlishi." *Yalkut Moreshet,* Periodical, 19 (1975): 175–84.

————. "Political Faith of Nazism Prior to the Holocaust." *Annual Lecture of the Jacob M. and Shoshana Schreiber Chair of Contemporary Jewish History.* Tel Aviv, 1978.

————. *Religious and Anti-religious Roots of Modern Anti-Semitism. Leo Baeck Memorial Lecture,* 14. New York, 1971.

Talmon, J. L. *The Age of Violence.* Tel Aviv 1975. (H)

————. *The Origins of Totalitarian Democracy.* London, 1961.

Tamir, V. *Bulgaria and Her Jews: The History of a Dubious Symbiosis.* New Haven, Conn., 1979.

Theilhaber, F. *Der Untergang der deutschen Juden.* Munich, 1911.

Tenenbaum, J. "The Crucial Year 1938." *YVS.* Vol. 2, 1958, pp. 49–78.

The Jews in Europe: Their Martyrdom and Their Future. Ed. Board of Deputies. London, 1945.

Thiess, J. *Architekt der Weltherrschaft: Die "Endziele" Hitlers.* Düsseldorf, 1976.

Thomas, G., and Morganwitts, M. *The Voyage of the Damned.* London, 1974.

Tobias, F. *Der Reichstagsbrand: Legende und Wirklichkeit.* Rastatt, W. Ger., 1962.

Tokayer, M., and Swartz, M. *The Fugu Plan: The Untold Story of the Japanese and the Jews During World War 2.* New York, 1979.

Torell, U. *Hjälp till Danmark: Militara og politiska förbindelser, 1943–1945.* Stockholm, 1973. (English summary.)

Touri, J. "From Forced Emigration to Expulsion: The Jewish Exodus over Non-Slavic Borders of the Reich as a Prelude to the 'Final Solution.'" *YVS Studies.* Vol. 17 (1986). Pp. 51–91.

————. "Ha-Mitan ha-Politi ba-Antishemiut: ha-Kayam ve-ha-Mishtane be-Doreinu." In *Study Circle on Diaspora Jewry under the Auspices of the President of Israel.* Ed. Sh. Etinger. Sidra Shniah: Kuntres 3–4. Jerusalem, 1968. Pp. 26–34.

————. "The Anarcho-Totalitarian Chain of Command: Or Who Was Responsible for the Deportation to Camp de Gurs (October 22/23, 1940)?" *Yalkut Moreshet,* Periodical, 40 (1985): 41–66. (English summary)

Treue, W. "Zur Frage der wirtschaftlichen Motive im deutschen Antisemitismus." In *Deutsches Judentum in Krieg und Revolution, 1916–1923.* Ed. W. E. Mosse. Tübingen, 1971. Pp. 387–408.

Trunk, Y. "Ha-Polihierarchia ha-Natzit u-Matzav ha-Yehudim ba-Shtahim ha-kvushim." *Dapim le-Heker ha-Shoah ve-ha-Mered,* Sidra Shniah, Measef 2, 1973, pp. 7–22.

————. "Sikumav shel Mish'al al Havrei ha-Judenratim." *Dapim le-Heker ha-Shoah ve-ha-Mered,* Sidra Shnia, Measef 1, 1970, pp. 119–35.

————. "The Typology of the Judenräte in Eastern Europe." In *Rescue Attempts During the Holocaust. Proceedings of the Second Yad Vashem International Historical Conference.* Ed. Y. Gutman and E. Zuroff. Jerusalem, 1977. Pp. 17–30.

Tubin, Y. "Lebensborn" (The Source of Life)." *Yalkut Moreshet,* Periodical, 20 (1975): 191–94. (H)

Turkov, Y. *Hayo Hayita Varsha Yehudit.* Tel Aviv, 1969.

Tushnet, L. *The Pavement of Hell.* New York, 1972.

Ulstein, R. *Svensketrafikken: Flyktinger till Sverge, 1940–1943.* Oslo, 1974.

Ussoskin, M. *Struggle for Survival: A History of Jewish Credit Cooperatives.* Jerusalem, 1975.

Vago, B. "Germany and the Jewish Policy of the Kállay Government." In *Hungarian Jewish Studies.* Ed. R. L. Braham. New York, 1973. Vol. 2, pp. 183–210.

————. "The Ambiguity of Collaborationism: the Center of the Jews in Rumania (1942–1944)." In *Patterns of Jewish Leadership in Nazi Europe, 1933–1945. Proceedings of the Third Yad Vashem International Historical Conference.* Ed. Y. Gutman and C. Y. Haft. Jerusalem, 1979. Pp. 287–309.

————. "The Intelligence Aspects of the Joel Brand Mission," *YVS Studies.* Vol. 10, 1974, pp. 111–28.

————. "The Jewish Policy of the Monarchist Dictatorship in Rumania 1938–1940." *Zion,* 29, nos. 1–2 (1964): 133–51. (H)

————. *The Shadow of the Swastika: The Rise of Fascism and Anti-Semitism in the Danubian Basin, 1936–1938.* London, 1975.

————. "Tmurot be-Hanhagat Yehudei Hungaria bi'imei Milḥemet ha-Olam ha-Shnia." In *Hanhagat Yehudei Hungaria be-Mivḥan ha-Shoah.* Ed. Y. Gutman, B. Vago, and L. Rothkirchen. Jerusalem, 1976. Pp. 61–76.

Valentin, H. *Antisemitism.* Stockholm, 1962.

Veghazi, I. "The Role of Jewry in the Economic Life of Hungary." In *Hungarian Jewish Studies.* Ed. R. L. Brahman. New York, 1973. Vol. 2, pp. 35–84.

Wallach, J. L. "Feldmarschall Erich von Manstein und die deutsche Judenausrottung in Russland." In *Jahrbuch des Instituts für deutsche Geschichte.* Tel Aviv, 1975. Vol. 4, pp. 457–72.

Warlimont, W. *Im Hauptquartier der deutschen Wehrmacht, 1939–1945.* Frankfurt on the Main, 1962.

Wasserstein, B. *Britain and the Jews of Europe, 1939–1945.* London, 1979.

Weichart, M. *Yidishe Aleinhilf, 1939–1945.* Tel Aviv, 1962.

Weinberg, D. H. *Les Juifs à Paris de 1933 à 1939.* Paris, 1974.

Weingarten, R. *Die Hilfeleistung der westlichen Welt bei der Endlösung der deutschen Judenfrage: Das Intergovernmental Committee on Political Refugees, 1938–1939.* Bern, 1983.

Weinstein, F. *The Dynamics of Nazism: Leadership, Ideology, and the Holocaust.* New York 1980.

Weiss, A. "Le-Darkham shel ha-Judenratim be-Drom Mizraḥ Polin." *Yalkut Moreshet,* Periodical, 15 (1972): 53–122.

————, *The Jewish Police in the Generalgouvernement and East Upper Silesia During the Holocaust.* Ph.D. diss., The Hebrew University, Jerusalem, 1973. (H).

Wellers, G. *L'Etoile jaune à l'heure de Vichy: De Drancy à Auschwitz.* Paris, 1973.

Wertheimer, J. *Unwelcome Strangers.* New York, 1987.

Westphalen, Lüdeger Graf von. *Geschichte des Antisemitismus im 19. und 20. Jahrhundert.* Stuttgart, 1964.

Wheaton, E. B. *The Nazi Revolution, 1933–1935: Prelude to Calamity.* New York, 1969.

Wielek, H. *De Oorlog die Hitler won.* Amsterdam, 1947.

Wiesenthal, S. *The Murderers Among Us.* London, 1967.

Wischnitzer, M. *Visas to Freedom.* Cleveland, 1956.

Wrobel, H. "Die Liquidation des Konzentrationslagers Auschwitz-Birknau." *Hefte von Auschwitz,* 6 (1962): 3–35.

Wulf, J. "Juden in Finland." In *Aus Politik und Zeitgeschichte: Beilage zur Wochenzeitung "Das Parlament."* (April 15, 1959): 161–68.

Wyman, D. B. "Why Auschwitz Was Not Bombed." *Commentary,* 65, no. 5 (1978): 37–46.

Yahil, L. "Euthanasia Contra Racial Extermination: The Moral Aspect." In *Remembering for the Future: The Impact of the Holocaust and Genocide upon Jews and Christians.* Oxford, 1989. Vol. 3, pp. 495–504.

————. "Historians of the Holocaust: A Plea for a New Approach." *The Wiener Library Bulletin,* 22, no. 1 (Winter 1967/1968): 2–5.

————. "Hitler's Rise to Power, Jews and the Holocaust: The Power of Ideology and the Limits of Psychohistory," *Gesher: Journal of Jewish Affairs,* 30, no. 2/111 (Fall 1984): 71–87. (H)

————. "Jewish Assimilation Vis-à-vis German Nationalism in the Weimar Republik." In *Jewish Assimilation in Modern Times.* Ed. B. Vago. Boulder, Colo., 1981. Pp. 41–48.

————. "Jews in Concentration Camps in Germany Prior to World War II." In *The Nazi Concentration Camps: Structure and Aims, the Image of the Prisoner, the Jews in the Camps. Proceedings of the Fourth Yad Vashem International Historical Conference.* Ed. Y. Gutman and A. Saf. Jerusalem 1984. Pp. 69–100.

————. "Madagascar: Phantom of a Solution for the Jewish Question." In *Jews and Non-Jews in Eastern Europe, 1918–1945.* Ed. B. Vago and G. L. Mosse. New York, 1974. Pp. 315–34.

————. "'Memoirs' of Adolf Eichman." *YVS Studies.* Vol. 18, 1987. Pp. 133–62.

————. "Methods of Persecution: A Comparison of the 'Final Solution' in Holland and Denmark." *Scripta Hierosolomytana (Jerusalem),* 23 (1972): 279–300.

————. "Nedudei ha-Yehudim mi-Germania, Austria ve-Czechoslovakia be-Shanim, 1933–1939: Baayot Yesod ve-Kavim khlalliim." *Hartzaot be-Knasei ha-Iyun be-Historia.* The Historical Society of Israel, Jerusalem, 1973, pp. 103–23.

————. "Raoul Wallenberg: His Mission and His Activities in Hungary." *YVS Studies.* Vol. 15, 1983, pp. 7–53.

————. "Rescue During the Holocaust: Opportunities and Obstacles." In *Proceedings of the Eighth World Congress of Jewish Studies, Division B.* Jerusalem, 1982. Pp. 161–66.

————. "Scandinavian Countries to the Rescue of Concentration Camp Prisoners." *YVS Studies.* Vol. 6, 1967, pp. 181–220.

————. "Select British Documents on the Illegal Immigration to Palestine (1939–1940)." *YVS Studies.* Vol. 10, 1974, pp. 241–76.

————. "The Holocaust in Jewish Historiography." In *The Catastrophe of European Jewry: Antecedents, History, Reflections.* Ed. Y. Gutman and L. Rothkirchen. Jerusalem, 1976. Pp. 651–69.

————. "The Uniqueness of the Rescue of Danish Jewry." In *Rescue Attempts During the Holocaust. Proceedings of the Second Yad Vashem International Historical Conference.* Ed. Y. Gutman and E. Zuroff. Jerusalem, 1977, pp. 617–25.

————. "The Warsaw Underground Press: A Case Study in the Reaction to Antisemitism." In *Living with Antisemitism: Modern Jewish Responses.* Ed. J. Reinharz. Hanover, N.H., 1987. Pp. 413–42.

Yisraeli, D. "The Third Reich and the Transfer Agreement." *Journal of Contemporary History,* 6, no. 2 (1971): 129–48.

Zariz, R. "Hatzalat Yehudim mi-Holand be-Emtzaut Ishurei Zertifikatim," *Yalkut Moreshet,* Periodical, 23 (1977): 135–62.

Zimmels, H. J. *The Echo of the Nazi Holocaust in Rabbinic Literature.* London, 1977.

Zwergbaum, A. "From Internment in Bratislava and Detention in Mauritius to Freedom." In *The Jews of Czechoslovakia.* Philadelphia, 1971. Vol. 2, pp. 599–658.

Newspapers, Periodicals, and Yearbooks

Acta Poloniac Historica

Aufbau

Behinot, Studies: Jews in the USSR and Eastern Europe. (Tel Aviv). *(H).*

Biuletyn Głównej Komisji Badania Zbrodni Hitlerowskich w Polsce (Vol. 6–   ).

Biuletyn Głównej Komisji Badania Zbrodni Niemieckich w Polsce (Vols. 1–5).

Bleter far Geshichte

Bulletin des Leo Baeck Instituts

Central European History Quarterly

Central-Verein Zeitung: Blätter für Deutschtum und Judentum

Central-Verein Zeitung: Allgemeine Zeitung des Judentums (since 1935)

Commentary

Contemporary Jewish Record (1935–1945)

Dapim, Studies on the Holocaust Period (Haifa)

Das Scharze Korps

Der Angriff

Foreign Policy Reports

Frankfurter Allgemeine Zeitung

Gazeta Żydowska

Germania Judaica

Gesher: Journal of Jewish Affairs (Jerusalem)

Hefte von Auschwitz

Jahrbuch des Instituts für deutsche Geschichte (University of Tel Aviv)

Jewish Daily Forward

Jewish Social Studies

Journal of Contemporary History (London)

Jüdische Rundschau

Life

Mahanayim

Midstream

News of Norway

Niv Hamidrashal

Publications of the American Jewish Historical Society

Shnaton Bar-Ilan

Scripta Hierosolomytana (The Hebrew University, Jerusalem)

Societas, A Review of Social History

Soviet Jewish Affairs

Soviet War News (London)

Studies in Zionism: An International Journal of Social, Political, and Intellectual History (Tel Aviv)

The Wiener Library Bulletin

Tradition: A Journal of Orthodox Jewish Thought

Verordnungsblatt des Generalgouvernement

Vierteljahrshefte für Zeitgeschichte

Völkischer Beobachter

Weltkampf: die Judenfrage in Geschichte und Gegenwart

Wochenzeitung "Das Parlament" (Bonn)

Yad Vashem Studies

Yahadut Zemanenu (Contemporary Jewry: A Research Annual) (The Hebrew University, Jerusalem) (H, English summary).

Yalkut Moreshet, Periodical

Yearbook of the Leo Baeck Institute of Jews from Germany

Yediot Beit Loḥamei ha-Getaot

Yediot Yad Vashem

YIVO Annual of Jewish Social Science

YIVO Bleter

Zeitschrift für die Geschichte der Juden (University of Tel Aviv)

Zion: A Quarterly for Research in Jewish History (Jerusalem) (H)

Index

Abetz, Otto, 339
Adam, Uwe D., 115
Adler-Rudel, Shalom, 603
Aegean Islands, 408
Agudat Israel, 74, 188–89, 192, 199, 210, 213
Ahasuerus, 36
Aid to Jewish Youth Society. *See* Youth Aliyah
Aktion, 163, 208, 265–70, 272, 274, 278, 282–83, 285–86, 302, 326, 328–29, 333, 341, 367, 379, 382, 384–85, 389–90, 393, 431, 437, 439, 443, 446–48, 453–54, 462, 466–70, 479, 481–82, 520–22, 545, 552, 557, 581–82, 591, 618, 620
Albala, Jacques, 621
Albania, 142–43, 581–82
Albrecht, Emil, 417
Alderney. *See* Aurigny
Aleppo, 633
Algeria, 173, 175, 343, 432, 496
Aliyah Bet. See Palestine: illegal immigration
Alkosh, 555
Almansi, Dante, 423–26
Alps, 487
Alsace-Lorraine, 141, 172, 177–78, 185, 229, 537
Alten, Mark, 199, 200, 205, 329
Altenburg, Günther, 418
Alter, Rabbi Nehemiah, 555
American Jewish Committee, 95, 96
American Jewish Congress, 95–97

American Jewish Joint Distribution Committee (JDC), 98, 119, 177, 181, 190–92, 198, 204, 205, 218, 224, 229–32, 238, 272, 294, 346, 350, 402, 417, 540, 596, 598–602, 604, 606, 611–18, 628, 630, 632, 637, 646, 648, 651
Amsterdam, 29, 175, 181, 235, 238, 392, 437–39, 455
Anders, Wladyslaw, 224
Anglo-Palestine Bank, 101
Angriff, Der, 31
Anielewicz, Mordekhai, 472, 480–82, 559
Ankara, 610
Anthony, Arno, 577
Anthropology, 35
Anti-Semitic League, 36
Anti-Semitism: Algeria, 175; Austria, 46; Baltic States, 275, 588; Bulgaria, 579, 584–85; Christian churches, 39; CV, 15, 26, 27, 29, 31; Denmark, 225; England, 606; Finland, 576–77; France, 230, 590; Germany, 18, 20, 23, 26, 27, 30, 31, 34, 35, 43, 48, 68, 79, 80, 82, 317; Greece, 409; Italy, 590; Jew as an antitype *(der Gegentypus),* 34, 35, 548; Jews' control of world politics, 121, 547; killing of Jews, 306; Nuremberg Laws *(see* Jews: Nuremberg Laws); Poland, 120, 163, 188–89, 194, 545, 656; racism, 4, 34–38; rescue of Jews, 545–46; Rumania, 38, 120, 181–82, 231–32, 345–47, 590, 656; spiritual